NAG HAMMADI STUDIES

VOLUME IX

NAG HAMMADI STUDIES

EDITED BY

MARTIN KRAUSE - JAMES M. ROBINSON
FREDERIK WISSE

IN CONJUNCTION WITH

ALEXANDER BÖHLIG - JEAN DORESSE - SØREN GIVERSEN
HANS JONAS - RODOLPHE KASSER - PAHOR LABIB
GEORGE W. MACRAE - JACQUES-É. MÉNARD - TORGNY SÄVE-SÖDERBERGH
WILLEM CORNELIS VAN UNNIK - R. McL. WILSON
JAN ZANDEE

IX

VOLUME EDITOR

R. McL. WILSON

LEIDEN
E. J. BRILL
1978

THE COPTIC GNOSTIC LIBRARY

EDITED WITH ENGLISH TRANSLATION, INTRODUCTION AND NOTES

published under the auspices of

THE INSTITUTE FOR ANTIQUITY AND CHRISTIANITY

PISTIS SOPHIA

TEXT EDITED BY

CARL SCHMIDT

TRANSLATION AND NOTES BY

VIOLET MACDERMOT

LEIDEN

E. J. BRILL

1978

CONTENTS

THE TEXT AND TRANSLATION

FOREWORD

The Pistis Sophia text which forms the contents of the Askew
Codex was made available to scholars over a century ago. However
a modern English translation of this Coptic gnostic document has
been lacking for some years, and it is advantageous that previously
known gnostic writings should now be included in the Nag Hammadi Studies Series. The admirable edition and German translation by C. Schmidt, re-edited by W. Till (Bibl. 46 and 44) would
be hard to supersede; for this reason a new edition of the Coptic
text is considered unnecessary. The present English translation
is therefore based on the Coptic text as edited and emended by
Schmidt (Bibl. 46), and the Coptic text is reproduced from this
edition unaltered except for minor corrections. For purposes of
study and comparison with the German, the general format of
Bibl. 44 has been retained in the English translation.

For easy reference to previous translations, all the indexes are
based on the page numbers of Schmidt's edition of the Coptic
text (Bibl. 46) which are retained in the present volume, both
for the text and the translation. In the German translation of the
Pistis Sophia (Bibl. 44), these page numbers appear in the right-
hand margin. Division of the text into paragraphs and numbered
chapters corresponds to that in Bibl. 44. The verses of psalms
are likewise numbered.

Any new translation has to be made in the light of those already
in existence, and this one owes much to the work of Schmidt
and Till. An important earlier edition and translation was that
of Schwartze and Petermann (Bibl. 51), to which there are frequent
references in Schmidt's textual notes. In the past there have been
a number of occasions where opinions among scholars have
differed on the correct rendering of various passages in this text.
Although in the main the present translation closely follows that
of Schmidt and Till, there are some minor differences. In such
cases, the alternative readings or versions are given as footnotes.
Till's notes on Schmidt's translation, which appear in the Appendix to Bibl. 44, are also incorporated into the present footnotes.

Schmidt's footnotes to the Coptic text have been checked with the manuscript, and are given here in English translation. His references to Schwartze's readings have been omitted.

The use of modern English poses certain problems in translating the Pistis Sophia. The text contains numerous quotations from and allusions to the Old and New Testaments which, to English-speaking readers, are probably familiar in the language of the Revised Version. It seemed best to adopt a somewhat formal English prose style, and this, it is hoped, will be both suitable and not unduly archaic. It will be seen that words of Greek origin are italicised. The alternative of giving the Greek words in brackets after the English words would have been very repetitive and would have added considerably to the cost of publication. A key to these words of Greek derivation is given on page 776. Certain Greek words, some of which are gnostic technical terms, have been left untranslated. Following Schmidt and Till, it was thought preferable to give words of uncertain meaning in transliteration, rather than to attempt a translation which might be misleading. It has been possible in some cases to indicate in the footnotes a comparable use of such words in the Nag Hammadi texts and elsewhere.

The Bibliography represents a selection from what is now a considerable accumulation of literature. Early writings of historic interest or likely to be of relevance today are included. For others not mentioned here, the bibliographies in G. R. S. Mead (Bibl. 34), J. Moffatt (Bibl. 35) and W. Till (Bibl. 44) should be consulted. Review articles on modern writers are listed in D. M. Scholer: *Nag Hammadi Bibliography*.

My acknowledgements are due to Gyldendal Publishers for permission to reproduce the Coptic text of Pistis Sophia; also to the Trustees of the British Museum and their successors in the British Library for facilities to study the manuscript in the Department of Oriental Manuscripts and Printed Books. I am grateful to Mr. T. A. Edridge, Assistant Manager of E. J. Brill, for his care and attention in the preparation of this volume. My thanks are also due to the Editorial Board of the Nag Hammadi Studies for the opportunity to contribute to their series; in particular to my volume editor, Professor R. McL. Wilson, who has read through the translation and made many helpful suggestions. Any remaining errors are my responsibility. To Professor Martin Krause, for his kind encouragement over many years, I would also like to express my gratitude.

Department of Egyptology,   VIOLET MACDERMOT
University College, London.

INTRODUCTION

History of the Askew Codex

The Askew Codex, a volume of unknown provenance containing the texts of the Pistis Sophia treatises, was named after its first owner, A. Askew, a London doctor. Askew was a collector of old manuscripts, and he bought the codex from a bookseller (probably in London) in 1772.[1] After the death of Askew the manuscript was bought by the British Museum. A copy in the British Museum of the sale catalogue (1785) of Askew's manuscripts contains the entry : "Coptic MS., £10. 0. 0." This reference was presumed by Crum to apply to the present document which appears in his catalogue as AD 5114.[2]

C. G. Woide, to whom Askew gave the task of studying the manuscript, first brought it to the attention of theological readers,[3] introducing it under the title "Pistis Sophia" which it has since retained. Woide also quoted the New Testament citations in his *Appendix ad editionem Novi Testamenti graeci e codice Ms. Alexandrino...* (Oxford 1799). A copy of the whole text was made by Woide, but never published. The first parts to appear were the five "Odes of Solomon" which were published by the Danish bishop, F. Münter[4] in 1812. A further copy of the whole codex was made by E. Dularier between 1838 and 1840, again with the intention that it should be published. However the manuscript of Dularier never appeared in print and is now in the Bibliothèque Nationale in Paris (Bibl. 16).

The next attempt to prepare an edition of the text was made in 1848 by M. G. Schwartze who was sent to England for this

---

[1] J. G. Buhle : *Literarische Briefwechsel von Johann David Michaelis.* Leipzig 1794-1796. Vol. III, p. 69.

[2] W. E. Crum : *Catalogue of the Coptic Manuscripts in the British Museum.* London 1905. p. 173.

[3] J. A. Cramer : *Beyträge zur Beförderung theologischer und anderer wichtiger Kenntnisse.* Kiel und Hamburg 1778. Vol. III, pp. 55 f. and 154 f.

[4] F. Münter : *Odae gnosticae Salomoni tributae thebaice et latine, ...* Copenhagen 1812.

purpose by the Königliche Preussische Akademie der Wissenschaften. Schwartze died before its publication, and the manuscript which he left was published postumously by J. H. Petermann (Bibl. 51). This edition, containing a transcription of the text and a Latin translation, is an outstanding achievement, even by modern standards.

A French translation by E. Amélineau in 1895 was the first to appear in a modern language (Bibl. 2). A year later G. R. S. Mead brought out an English translation, based on the Latin version by Schwartze (Bibl. 34); a second edition appeared in 1921 and reprints in 1947, 1955 and 1963. The only other English translation of the whole text was that of G. Horner which appeared in 1924 (Bibl. 22). This set out to be a literal translation, even keeping to the Coptic word order.

The translation of the text which has stood the test of time was published in Germany by C. Schmidt in 1905 (Bibl. 43). He was given the task of editing and translating the then known Coptic gnostic texts by the Kirchenväter-Kommission (now the Kommission für spätantike Religionsgeschichte) of the Berlin Akademie der Wissenschaften. The volume contained a translation of the Pistis Sophia, followed by translations of the Coptic gnostic texts contained in the Bruce Codex. These translations were fully annotated and preceded by an introductory discussion. A second edition of Schmidt's translation of the Pistis Sophia (Bibl. 47) and his annotated edition of the Coptic text (Bibl. 46) appeared in 1925. Since this date there have been no further editions of the text. In 1954 W. Till published a new edition of Schmidt's (1905 and 1925) translations (Bibl. 44). He followed Schmidt's versions closely, giving his own alternative renderings of certain passages in an appendix. A third edition, revised by Till, appeared in 1959, and a reprint of the third edition in 1962.

Description of the Manuscript

The Askew Codex is described in W. E. Crum's *Catalogue of Coptic Manuscripts in the British Museum* under the heading of Sahidic Manuscripts.

The manuscript, which now consists of 174 leaves in a modern binding, originally comprised 178 leaves of parchment. The leaves measure 21×16.5 cms. The text is written in two columns on both sides of the leaves (354 sides), and is the work of two scribes. The first scribe numbered the pages on the rectos only, the second on rectos and versos. The book consists of 23 quires, the first of which consists of 6 leaves, the last of 4 leaves, and the remainder each of 8 leaves. Four leaves from the inside of one quire are missing, so that there is a lacuna between pages 336 and 345. The first two blank and unnumbered pages and the last four are also missing. The state of preservation of most of the text is very good. On parts of some pages the ink has faded, and in these places the script is only just legible.

The text consists of four "books". Book One ends with the first column on p. 114 (Schmidt 125) and has no title, either at the beginning or end. The second column of p. 114, which was left blank, was later filled with text by another hand.

Book Two begins on p. 115. A title at the head of this page: *The Second Book of the Pistis Sophia* is a later addition. The whole text is now known as the *Pistis Sophia* on the basis of this insertion. A title of the second book occurs on p. 233 (Schmidt 253.17) at the foot of the first column: *A Part of the Books of the Saviour*. The text continues in the second column, and ends in the second column of p. 234 (Schmidt 255.16). The last sentence of p. 234 suggests that this is the end of the book, rather than p. 233. It is suggested by Schmidt and Till that because the contents of the first and second columns of p. 233 appear to follow one another, the title properly belongs at the end of the text on p. 234.

Book Three thus begins on p. 235 (Schmidt 256), and ends on p. 318 (Schmidt 352). A title similar to that of Book Two stands below the last line of the first column on p. 318.

Book Four begins in the second column of p. 318 (Schmidt 353) and ends in the second column of p. 354 (Schmidt 384). A paragraph in a later hand stands at the head of the first column of p. 354 (Schmidt 385).

The end of the Pistis Sophia account proper occurs in Book Two (Schmidt p. 184.6; Chapter 82). Thereafter the text consists of teachings given to the disciples in the form of answers to their questions. It may be noted here that there is a considerable lack of homogeneity in composition. Even within the individual books the narrative appears to rely upon a number of documents placed in approximate sequence. As the various "documents" contain different portions of the account, this gives rise, on the one hand, to repetitions — some episodes are described more than once — and on the other, to anomalies in the names of the speakers. Thus the central figure in Book One is named as Jesus; in Book Two, as the First Mystery, then as Jesus and at the end, as the Saviour; in Book III, as Jesus and the Saviour alternately; and in Book IV, as Jesus. Mary Magdalene appears as Maria and Mariam (Mariham) in different parts of the text. These inconsistencies support the view that the text is a compilation. Its authorship, date, provenance and purpose cannot be discussed here. A guide to the layout of the four books is given below, followed by a brief summary of the contents.

Book I, pp. 1-125, (Chapters 1-62). Untitled, but the title presumed to be *The First Book of the Pistis Sophia.*

Book II, pp. 127-255, (Chapters 63-101). Initial title (in a late hand) *The Second Book of the Pistis Sophia*; final title (original) *A part of the Books of the Saviour.*

Book III, pp. 256-352, (Chapters 102-135). Final title (original) as in Book II.

Book IV, pp. 353-384, (Chapters 136-148). Untitled.

Summary of Contents

Book I

Chapter

1-6 Survey of the post-resurrection teaching of Jesus; description of the coming down of a light-power upon him on the Mount of Olives in the presence of his disciples; his ascension and descent.

7-10 Discourse by Jesus on his garments of light, his incarnation; the incarnation of John the Baptist and the disciples.

11-16 Account by Jesus of his ascension wearing the garment

of light; the rebellion of the aeons against the light, and the removal of power from those that rebelled.

on this mystery as the source of all knowledge; despair of the disciples and answer by Jesus that this mystery is easy to those who renounce the world; another discourse on the knowledge of this mystery; the unimpeded ascent to the height of the souls of those who have received this mystery, and their fellow-rulership with Jesus.

Heimarmene; on the spirit counterpart and destiny; on release by means of the mysteries; on the souls of the patriarchs and prophets.

ABBREVIATIONS

AGSJU   Arbeiten zur Geschichte des späteren Judentums und des Urchristentums.
CH   Corpus Hermeticum (A. D. Nock and A. J. Festugière. Paris, 1960).
Crum   A Coptic Dictionary (W. E. Crum. Oxford, 1962).
DDAU   Doctoral Dissertations accepted by American Universities.
DTT   Dansk Teologisk Tidsskrift.
HRE   Hastings Encyclopaedia of Religion and Ethics.
IMG-E   Les Intailles Magiques Gréco-Égyptiennes (A. Delatte et Ph. Derchain.
           Paris : Bibliothèque Nationale, 1964).
JThS   The Journal of Theological Studies.
NTA   New Testament Abstracts.
NTT   Norsk Teologisk Tidsskrift.
RGG(3)   Die Religion in Geschichte und Gegenwart, 3 Auflage.
RQ   Revue de Qumran.
RV   Revised Version of the New Testament.
SPCK   Society for Promoting Christian Knowledge.
TU   Texte und Untersuchungen zur Geschichte der altchristlichen Literatur.
ZÄS   Zeitschrift für Ägyptische Sprache und Altertumskunde.
ZNW   Zeitschrift für die neutestamentliche Wissenschaft.

Berlin Codex

GMary   BG 8502 1   The Gospel of Mary.
ApJn   2   The Apocryphon of John.
SJC   3   The Sophia of Jesus Christ.

Bruce Codex

J   The Books of Jeu.
U   The Untitled Text.

Nag Hammadi Codices

ApJn II   II, 1   The Apocryphon of John.
GTh   II, 2   The Gospel of Thomas.
GPh   II, 3   The Gospel of Philip.
HypArch   II, 4   The Hypostasis of the Archons.
OnOrgWld   II, 5   On the Origin of the World.
GEgypt   III, 2; IV, 2 The Gospel of the Egyptians.
Eug   V, 1   Eugnostos the blessed.
ApAd   V, 5   The Apocalypse of Adam.
ParaShem   VII, 1   The Paraphrase of Shem.
Zost   VIII, 1   Zostrianus.

Manichaean Literature

Keph   Manichäische Handschriften der Staatlichen Museen, Berlin, Band I :
           Kephalaia. Hrsg. J. Polotsky und A. Böhlig, Stuttgart, 1940.

XIX

SIGLA

( )   Round brackets in the translation indicate material which
is useful to the English version, but not explicitly present
in the Coptic.

⟨ ⟩   Pointed brackets in the text and translation indicate conjec-
tural emendments. The actual readings of the manuscript
and literal translations of the text are given as notes to the
text and translation respectively.

[ ]   Square brackets in the text and translation indicate dittography or other material erroneously interpolated by the
scribe which should be omitted in the translation.

NOTE

The page numbers of the text and translation correspond, but
the line numbers apply to the text only. At the beginning of each
note on the translation, line references to the corresponding page
of the text are given. Other references to the texts and translation
are usually given in brackets at the end of a note. Where the notes
refer to alternative renderings of the translation, Schmidt =
Schmidt's translation, edited by Till (Bibl. 44, pp. 1-254); Till =
Appendix by Till (ibid., pp. 369-82).

The pages of the text and translation carry the page numbers
of Schmidt's edition of the Coptic text (Bibl. 46) in the upper
left and right hand margins respectively. It is to these numbers
that references are made throughout, and all indexes are based
on these numbers.

PISTIS SOPHIA
THE TEXT AND TRANSLATION

ⲀⲤⲰⲰⲠⲈ ⲆⲈ ⲘⲚⲚⲤⲀ ⲦⲢⲈ ⲓ̅ⲥ̅ ⲦⲰⲞⲨⲚ ⲈⲂⲞⲖ ϨⲚ ⲗ̅
ⲚⲈⲦⲘⲞⲞⲨⲦ ⲀⲨⲰ ⲀϤⲢ̅-ⲘⲚⲦⲞⲨⲈ Ⲛ̅ⲢⲞⲘⲠⲈ ⲈϤϢⲀϪⲈ
ⲘⲚ ⲚⲈϤⲘⲀⲐⲎⲦⲎⲤ ⲀⲨⲰ ⲈϤϯⲤⲂⲰ ⲚⲀⲨ ϢⲀ Ⲛ̅ⲦⲞⲠⲞⲤ
ⲘⲘⲀⲦⲈ ⲘⲠϢⲞⲢⲠ-ⲦⲰϢ· ⲀⲨⲰ ϢⲀ Ⲛ̅ⲦⲞⲠⲞⲤ ⲘⲠϢⲞⲢⲠ
5 ⲘⲘⲨⲤⲦⲎⲢⲒⲞⲚ ⲠⲀⲒ ⲈⲦⲠϨⲞⲨⲚ ⲘⲠⲔⲀⲦⲀⲠⲈⲦⲀⲤⲘⲀ ⲈⲦ-
ⲘⲠϨⲞⲨⲚ ⲘⲠϢⲞⲢⲠ ⲚⲦⲰϢ ⲈⲦⲈ ⲚⲦⲞϤ ⲠⲈ ⲠⲘⲈϨϪⲞⲨⲦ-
ⲀϤⲦⲈ ⲘⲘⲨⲤⲦⲎⲢⲒⲞⲚ ⲈⲂⲞⲖ· ⲀⲨⲰ ⲈⲠⲈⲤⲎⲦ ⲚⲀⲒ ⲈⲦ-
ϢⲞⲞⲠ ϨⲘ ⲠⲘⲈϨⲤⲚⲀⲨ Ⲛ̅ⲬⲰⲢⲎⲘⲀ Ⲛ̅ⲦⲈ ⲠⲒϢⲞⲢⲠ ⲘⲘⲨ-
ⲤⲦⲎⲢⲒⲞⲚ ⲈⲦϨⲀⲦⲈϨⲎ ⲘⲘⲨⲤⲦⲎⲢⲒⲞⲚ ⲚⲒⲘ· ⲠⲒⲰⲦ ⲘⲠⲒⲚⲈ
10 Ⲛ̅ϬⲢⲞⲞⲘⲠⲈ· ⲈⲢⲈ ⲓ̅ⲥ̅ ϪⲰ ⲘⲘⲞⲤ ⲚⲚⲈϤⲘⲀⲐⲎⲦⲎⲤ ϪⲈ
Ⲛ̅ⲦⲀⲒⲈⲒ ⲈⲂⲞⲖ ϨⲘ ⲠϢⲞⲢⲠ ⲘⲘⲨⲤⲦⲎⲢⲒⲞⲚ ⲈⲦⲘⲘⲀⲨ ⲈⲦⲈ
ⲚⲦⲞϤ ⲠⲈ* ⲠϨⲀⲈ ⲘⲘⲨⲤⲦⲎⲢⲒⲞⲚ ⲈⲦⲈ ⲠⲘⲈϨϪⲞⲨⲦⲀϤⲦⲈ ⲗ̅ b
ⲠⲈ ⲀⲨⲰ ⲈⲦⲈ ⲘⲠⲈ ⲘⲘⲀⲐⲎⲦⲎⲤ ⲈⲒⲘⲈ ⲀⲨⲰ ⲘⲠⲞⲨⲚⲞⲒ
ϪⲈ ⲞⲨⲚ-ⲖⲖⲀⲨ Ⲙ̅ⲪⲞⲨⲚ ⲘⲠⲘⲨⲤⲦⲎⲢⲒⲞⲚ ⲈⲦⲘⲘⲀⲨ· ⲀⲖⲖⲀ
15 ⲚⲈⲨⲘⲈⲈⲨⲈ ⲠⲈ ⲈⲠⲘⲨⲤⲦⲎⲢⲒⲞⲚ ⲈⲦⲘⲘⲀⲨ ϪⲈ ⲚⲦⲞϤ ⲠⲈ
ⲦⲔⲈⲪⲀⲖⲎ ⲘⲠⲦⲎⲢϤ ⲀⲨⲰ ⲦⲀⲠⲈ Ⲛ̅ⲚⲈⲦϢⲞⲞⲠ ⲦⲎⲢⲞⲨ·

---

1 the first hand runs to 23.15; the second hand continues until 212.18; the first
hand begins again there and completes the main text to 384.23; 385.1-8 is in
a later hand.

5 MS ⲈⲦⲠϨⲞⲨⲚ; perhaps better ⲈⲦⲘ̅ⲠϨⲞⲨⲚ.

7 cryptogram ⲛ̄ⲣ̄ used very frequently for ⲘⲨⲤⲦⲎⲢⲒⲞⲚ.

2

(BOOK I)

1. *But* it happened that after Jesus had risen from the dead he spent eleven years speaking with his *disciples*[1]. And he taught them only as far as the *places* of the first ordinance[2] and as far as the *places* of the First *Mystery* which is within the *veil*[3] which is within the first ordinance, which is the 24th *mystery* outside and below[4], these which are in the second *space* of the First *Mystery* which is before all *mysteries* — the Father in the form of a dove*. And Jesus said to his *disciples*: "I have come forth from that First *Mystery* which is the last *mystery*, namely the 24th". And the *disciples* did not know and *understand* that there was anything within that *mystery*. But they thought that that *mystery* was the *head* of the All[5], and the head of all the things that exist □. | And they thought that it was the com-

---

* cf. Mt. 3.16
□ cf. Jn. 1.3, 4

---

[1] (1-3) see Resch (Bibl. 41), Apocryphon 51, p. 426.
[2] (4) first ordinance; see Bousset (Bibl. 10), p. 166, n. 1; J 122.
[3] (5) veil; see U 237.
[4] (7) outside and below; Till: towards the outer and lower.
[5] (16) the All; the Greek, τὸ πᾶν; see also U 226.

ⲁⲩⲱ ⲛⲉⲩⲙⲉⲉⲩⲉ ⲡⲉ ϫⲉ ⲛ̄ⲧⲟϥ ⲡⲉ ⲡϫⲱⲕ ⲛ̄ⲛ̄ϫⲱⲕ
ⲧⲏⲣⲟⲩ· ⲉⲃⲟⲗ ϫⲉ ⲛⲉⲣⲉ ⲓ̅ⲥ̅ ϫⲱ ⲙ̄ⲙⲟⲥ ⲛⲁⲩ ⲡⲉ ⲉⲧⲃⲉ
ⲡⲙⲩⲥⲧⲏⲣⲓⲟⲛ ⲉⲧⲙ̄ⲙⲁⲩ ϫⲉ ⲛ̄ⲧⲟϥ ⲡⲉⲧⲕⲱⲧⲉ ⲉⲡϣⲟⲣⲡ̄
ⲛ̄ⲧⲱϣ ⲙⲛ̄ ⲡϯⲟⲩ ⲛ̄ⲭⲁⲣⲁⲅⲙⲏ ⲁⲩⲱ ⲙⲛ̄ ⲡⲛⲟϭ ⲛ̄ⲟⲩ-
ⲟⲉⲓⲛ | ⲁⲩⲱ ⲙⲛ̄ ⲡϯⲟⲩ ⲙ̄ⲡⲁⲣⲁⲥⲧⲁⲧⲏⲥ ⲁⲩⲱ ⲙⲛ̄ ⲡⲉⲑⲏ-
ⲥⲁⲩⲣⲟⲥ ⲧⲏⲣϥ̄ ⲙ̄ⲡⲟⲩⲟⲉⲓⲛ· ⲁⲩⲱ ⲟⲛ ⲉⲛⲉⲙ̄ⲡⲉ ⲓ̅ⲥ̅ ϫⲱ
ⲉⲛⲉϥⲙⲁⲑⲏⲧⲏⲥ ⲙ̄ⲡⲥⲱⲣ ⲉⲃⲟⲗ** ⲧⲏⲣϥ̄ ⲛ̄ⲛ̄ⲧⲟⲡⲟⲥ ⲧⲏⲣⲟⲩ [ⲃ̅]
ⲙ̄ⲡⲛⲟϭ ⲛ̄ⲁϩⲟⲣⲁⲧⲟⲥ ⲙⲛ̄ ⲡϣⲟⲙⲛ̄ⲧ ⲛ̄ⲧⲣⲓⲇⲩⲛⲁⲙⲓⲥ
ⲙⲛ̄ ⲡϫⲟⲩⲧⲁϥⲧⲉ ⲛ̄ⲁϩⲟⲣⲁⲧⲟⲥ ⲙⲛ̄ ⲛⲉⲩⲧⲟⲡⲟⲥ ⲧⲏⲣⲟⲩ
ⲙⲛ̄ ⲛⲉⲩⲁⲓⲱⲛ ⲙⲛ̄ ⲛⲉⲩⲧⲁⲝⲓⲥ ⲧⲏⲣⲟⲩ ⲛ̄ⲑⲉ ⲉⲧⲟⲩⲥⲏⲣ
ⲉⲃⲟⲗ ⲙ̄ⲙⲟⲥ ⲛⲁï ⲉⲧⲉ ⲛ̄ⲧⲟⲟⲩ ⲛⲉ ⲛⲉⲡⲣⲟⲃⲟⲗⲟⲟⲩⲉ
ⲙ̄ⲡⲛⲟϭ ⲛ̄ⲁϩⲟⲣⲁⲧⲟⲥ ⲁⲩⲱ ⲙⲛ̄ ⲛⲉⲩⲁⲅⲉⲛⲛⲏⲧⲟⲥ ⲁⲩⲱ
ⲙⲛ̄ ⲛⲉⲩⲁⲩⲧⲟⲅⲉⲛⲏⲥ ⲁⲩⲱ ⲙⲛ̄ ⲛⲉⲩⲅⲉⲛⲛⲏⲧⲟⲥ ⲁⲩⲱ ⲙⲛ̄
ⲛⲉⲩⲫⲱⲥⲧⲏⲣ ⲁⲩⲱ ⲙⲛ̄ ⲛⲉⲩⲭⲱⲣⲓⲥⲥⲩⲛⲍⲩⲅⲟⲥ· ⲁⲩⲱ
ⲙⲛ̄ ⲛⲉⲩⲁⲣⲭⲱⲛ ⲙⲛ̄ ⲛⲉⲩⲉⲝⲟⲩⲥⲓⲁ· ⲙⲛ̄ ⲛⲉⲩϫⲟⲉⲓⲥ ⲙⲛ̄
ⲛⲉⲩⲁⲣⲭⲁⲅⲅⲉⲗⲟⲥ· ⲙⲛ̄ ⲛⲉⲩⲁⲅⲅⲉⲗⲟⲥ· ⲙⲛ̄ ⲛⲉⲩⲇⲉⲕⲁ-
ⲛⲟⲥ· ⲙⲛ̄ ⲛⲉⲩⲗⲓⲧⲟⲩⲣⲅⲟⲥ· ⲙⲛ̄ ⲛ̄ⲟⲓⲕⲟⲥ ⲧⲏⲣⲟⲩ ⲛ̄ⲧⲉ
ⲛⲉⲩⲥⲫⲁⲓⲣⲁ· ⲁⲩⲱ ⲙⲛ̄ ⲛ̄ⲧⲁⲝⲓⲥ ⲧⲏⲣⲟⲩ ⲙ̄ⲡⲟⲩⲁ ⲡⲟⲩⲁ [ⲃ̅b]
ⲙ̄ⲙⲟⲟⲩ· ⲁⲩⲱ ⲉⲛⲉⲙ̄ⲡⲉ ⲓ̅ⲥ̅ ϫⲱ ⲉⲛⲉϥⲙⲁⲑⲏⲧⲏⲥ ⲙ̄ⲡⲥⲱⲣ
ⲉⲃⲟⲗ ⲧⲏⲣϥ̄ ⲛ̄ⲛⲉⲡⲣⲟⲃⲟⲗⲟⲟⲩⲉ ⲙ̄ⲡⲉⲑⲏⲥⲁⲩⲣⲟⲥ ⲟⲩⲇⲉ
ⲛⲉⲩⲧⲁⲝⲓⲥ ⲛ̄ⲑⲉ ⲉⲧⲟⲩⲥⲏⲣ ⲉⲃⲟⲗ ⲙ̄ⲙⲟⲥ ⲟⲩⲇⲉ ⲛⲉ-
ⲙ̄ⲡϥϫⲱ ⲉⲣⲟⲟⲩ ⲡⲉ ⲛ̄ⲛⲉⲩⲥⲱⲧⲏⲣ ⲕⲁⲧⲁ ⲧⲁⲝⲓⲥ ⲙ̄-
ⲡⲟⲩⲁ ⲡⲟⲩⲁ ⲛ̄ⲑⲉ ⲉⲧⲟⲩⲟ ⲙ̄ⲙⲟⲥ· ⲟⲩⲇⲉ ⲛⲉⲙ̄ⲡϥ-

---

8 ⲡⲛⲟϭ written over erasure, 2 letters following ϭ expunged (here and elsewhere letters are expunged by supralinear points); ⲙⲛ̄ⲧ written over erasure; ⲛ̄ in margin before ⲧⲣⲓⲇⲩⲛⲁⲙⲓⲥ.

12 MS ⲛⲉⲩⲁⲅⲅⲉⲛⲛⲏⲧⲟⲥ; the first ⲅ expunged.

23 MS ⲙ̄ⲡⲟⲩⲁ; ⲁⲡⲟⲩⲁ on next line.

pletion of all completions, because Jesus had said to them concerning that *mystery*, that it surrounded the first ordinance and the five *incisions*[1] and the great light and the five *helpers* (*parastatai*) and the whole *Treasury* of Light[2]. And moreover Jesus had not spoken to his *disciples* of the whole extent of all the *places* of the great *invisible one* and the three *triple powers* and the 24 *invisible ones* and all their *places* and their *aeons* and all their *ranks*, how they extend[3] — these which are the *emanations*[4] of the great *invisible one* — and their *unbegotten ones* and their *self-begotten ones* and their *begotten ones* and their *luminaries*[5] and their *unpaired ones* and their *archons* and their *powers* (*exousiai*) and their lords and their *archangels* and their *angels* and their *decans* and their *ministers*[6] and all the *houses* of their *spheres* and all the *ranks* of each one of them. And Jesus had not told his *disciples* of the whole extent of the *emanations* of the *treasury, nor* their *ranks* how they extend, *nor* had he told them of their *saviours, according to* the *rank* of each one, how they are. *Nor* had he | told them which *watcher* is

---

[1] (4) five incisions; see Bousset (Bibl. 10), p. 348-49; J 121.
[2] (5, 6) Treasury of Light; see J 99 etc.
[3] (10) extend; Till: are distributed (also 3.10; see 16.21).
[4] (11) emanations; see J 47 etc.
[5] (14) luminaries; see U 255.
[6] (16, 17) decans and ministers; see CH *Exc. Stob.* VI, Introduction, pp. xxxviii-lxi; J 79.

ⲬⲞⲞⲤ ⲈⲢⲞⲞⲨ ⲠⲈ ⲬⲈ ⲚⲒⲘ Ⲙ̄ⲪⲨⲖⲀⲜ ⲠⲈⲦⲌⲒⲢⲚ̄ ⲦⲞⲨⲈⲒ

ⲦⲞⲨⲈⲒ ⟨Ⲙ̄ⲠⲨⲖⲎ⟩ Ⲙ̄ⲠⲈⲐⲎⲤⲀⲨⲢⲞⲤ Ⲙ̄ⲠⲞⲨⲞⲈⲒⲚ · ⲞⲨⲆⲈ

ⲚⲈⲘ̄Ⲡ̄ϤⲬⲰ ⲈⲢⲞⲞⲨ ⲠⲈ Ⲙ̄ⲠⲦⲞⲠⲞⲤ Ⲛ̄ⲤⲰⲦⲎⲢ Ⲛ̄ⲀⲦⲢⲈ-

ⲈⲨ · ⲈⲦⲈ Ⲛ̄ⲦⲞϤ ⲠⲈ ⲠⲀⲖⲞⲨ Ⲙ̄ⲠⲀⲖⲞⲨ · ⲀⲨⲰ ⲚⲈⲘ̄Ⲡ̄Ϥ-

5 ⲬⲰ ⲈⲢⲞⲞⲨ ⲠⲈ Ⲙ̄ⲠⲦⲞⲠⲞⲤ Ⲙ̄ⲠϢⲞⲘⲚ̄Ⲧ Ⲛ̄ⲀⲘⲎⲚ ⲬⲈ

ⲈⲨⲤⲎⲢ ⲈⲂⲞⲖ’ Ⲍ̄Ⲛ ⲀϢ Ⲛ̄ⲦⲞⲠⲞⲤ · ⲀⲨⲰ ⲚⲈⲘ̄Ⲡ̄ϤⲬⲰ ⲅ̄

ⲈⲢⲞⲞⲨ ⲠⲈ ⲬⲈ ⲈⲢⲈ Ⲡ-ϯⲞⲨ Ⲛ̄ϢⲎⲚ ⲤⲎⲢ ⲈⲂⲞⲖ Ⲍ̄Ⲛ ⲀϢ

Ⲛ̄ⲦⲞⲠⲞⲤ · ⲞⲨⲆⲈ ⲠⲔⲈⲤⲀϢϤ Ⲛ̄ⲀⲘⲎⲚ ⲈⲦⲈ Ⲛ̄ⲦⲞⲞⲨ ⲚⲈ

ⲦⲤⲀϢϤⲈ Ⲛ̄ⲪⲰⲚⲎ ⲬⲈ ⲀϢ ⲠⲈ ⲠⲈⲨⲦⲞⲠⲞⲤ ⲔⲀⲦⲀ ⲐⲈ

10 ⲈⲦⲞⲨⲤⲎⲢ ⲈⲂⲞⲖ Ⲙ̄ⲘⲞⲤ ⲀⲨⲰ ⲈⲚⲈⲘⲠⲈ Ⲓ̄Ⲥ̄ ⲬⲰ ⲈⲚⲈϤ-

ⲘⲀⲐⲎⲦⲎⲤ ⲬⲈ ⲈⲢⲈ Ⲡ-ϯⲞⲨ Ⲙ̄ⲠⲀⲢⲀⲤⲦⲀⲦⲎⲤ Ⲟ’ Ⲛ̄ⲀϢ Ⲛ̄ⲦⲨ-

ⲠⲞⲤ Ⲏ̄ Ⲛ̄ⲦⲀⲨⲚ̄ⲦⲞⲨ Ⲍ̄Ⲛ ⲀϢ Ⲛ̄ⲦⲞⲠⲞⲤ · ⲞⲨⲆⲈ ⲚⲈⲘ̄Ⲡ̄ϤⲬⲰ

ⲈⲢⲞⲞⲨ ⲠⲈ ⲬⲈ Ⲛ̄ⲦⲀ ⲠⲚⲞϬ Ⲛ̄ⲞⲨⲞⲈⲒⲚ ⲤⲰⲢ ⲈⲂⲞⲖ Ⲛ̄ⲀϢ

Ⲛ̄ⲌⲈ · Ⲏ̄ ⲬⲈ Ⲛ̄ⲦⲀⲨⲚ̄Ⲧ̄Ϥ Ⲍ̄Ⲛ ⲀϢ Ⲛ̄ⲦⲞⲠⲞⲤ · ⲞⲨⲆⲈ ⲚⲈ-

15 Ⲙ̄Ⲡ̄ϤⲬⲰ ⲈⲢⲞⲞⲨ ⲠⲈ Ⲙ̄Ⲡ-ϯⲞⲨ Ⲛ̄ⲬⲀⲢⲀⲄⲘⲎ · ⲞⲨⲆⲈ ⲈⲦⲂⲈ

ⲠϢⲞⲢⲠ̄ Ⲛ̄ⲦⲰϢ ⲬⲈ Ⲛ̄ⲦⲀⲨⲚ̄ⲦⲞⲨ Ⲍ̄Ⲛ ⲀϢ Ⲛ̄ⲦⲞⲠⲞⲤ · ⲀⲖ-

ⲖⲀ ⲌⲀⲠⲖⲰⲤ ⲚⲈϤϢⲀⲬⲈ Ⲛ̄ⲘⲘⲀⲨ Ⲙ̄ⲘⲀⲦⲈ ⲠⲈ ⲈϤ-ϯⲤⲂⲰ ⲅ̄ᵇ

ⲚⲀⲨ ⲬⲈ ⲤⲈϢⲞⲞⲠ · ⲀⲖⲖⲀ ⲠⲈⲨⲤⲰⲢ ⲈⲂⲞⲖ Ⲙ̄Ⲛ ⲦⲦⲀⲜⲒⲤ

Ⲛ̄ⲦⲈ ⲚⲈⲨⲦⲞⲠⲞⲤ ⲚⲈⲘ̄Ⲡ̄ϤⲬⲞⲞⲤ ⲈⲢⲞⲞⲨ ⲠⲈ ⲔⲀⲦⲀ ⲐⲈ

20 ⲈⲦⲞⲨϢⲞⲞⲠ Ⲙ̄ⲘⲞⲤ · ⲈⲦⲂⲈ ⲠⲀⲒ̈ ⲢⲰ Ⲙ̄ⲠⲞⲨⲈⲒⲘⲈ ⲬⲈ

ⲞⲨⲚ̄-ⲔⲈⲦⲞⲠⲞⲤ ϢⲞⲞⲠ ⲪⲞⲨⲚ Ⲙ̄ⲠⲘⲨⲤⲦⲎⲢⲒⲞⲚ ⲈⲦⲘ̄ⲘⲀⲨ ·

ⲀⲨⲰ ⲈⲚⲈⲘ̄Ⲡ̄ϤⲬⲞⲞⲤ ⲈⲚⲈϤⲘⲀⲐⲎⲦⲎⲤ ⲬⲈ Ⲛ̄ⲦⲀⲒ̈ⲈⲒ’ ⲈⲂⲞⲖ

Ⲍ̄Ⲛ ⲀϢ Ⲛ̄ⲦⲞⲠⲞⲤ ϢⲀⲚ-ϯⲈⲒ’ ⲈⲌⲞⲨⲚ ⲈⲠⲘⲨⲤⲦⲎⲢⲒⲞⲚ ⲈⲦ-

Ⲙ̄ⲘⲀⲨ · ϢⲀⲚ-ϯⲠⲢⲞⲈⲖⲐⲈ ⲈⲂⲞⲖ Ⲛ̄Ⲍ̄ⲎⲦϤ · ⲀⲖⲖⲀ ⲈϢⲀϤ-

---

1 MS ⲦⲞⲨⲈⲒ, thrice; the third expunged.
2 supply ⲘⲠⲨⲖⲎ.
7 MS originally Ⲡ̄ⲀϢ; Ⲍ inserted above.

over each of the ⟨doors⟩ of the *Treasury* of Light. *Nor* had he told them of the *place* of the twin *saviour* [1] who is the child of the child [2]. Nor had he told them of the *place* of the three *amens* [3], in which *places* they extend, and he had not told them in which *places* the five trees [4] are spread, *nor* of the seven other *amens*, namely the seven *voices* [5], which their *place* is and *how* they extend. And Jesus had not told his *disciples* of what *type* are the five *helpers* [6] (*parastatai*). *Or* into which *places* they are brought. *Nor* had he told them in what manner the great light extends, *or* into which *places* it is brought. *Nor* had he told them of the five *incisions*, *nor* concerning the first ordinance, into which *places* they are brought. *But* he had only spoken to them *in general*, teaching them that they existed. *But* he had not told them their extent and the *rank* of their *places according to* how they exist. Because of this they also did not know that other *places* existed within that *mystery*. And he had not said to his *disciples*: "I came forth from such and such *places* [7] until I entered that *mystery*, until I *came forth* from it". *But* he had | said to them as he taught them: "I came

---

[1] (3) twin saviour: see Diod. Sic. IV, 43; J 119; ATh 11, 31, 39.
[2] (4) child of the child; see J 103, 119; GEgypt III.50; IV.62; Keph XIX p. 61.
[3] (5, 8) three amens, seven amens; see Hippol. VI, 43; J 99, 119.
[4] (7) five trees: see J 100; GTh 84; Keph VI p. 30 etc.
[5] (9) seven voices; see J 100; GEgypt III, 43; IV, 52; on seven vowels, see Hippol. VI, 47; Kropp (Bibl. 26) III, p. 28; Dieterich (Bibl. 15) p. 22 ff.; (see 273.5).
[6] (11) five helpers; see J 107, 121; U 230; GEgypt III.64.
[7] (24) such and such places; Till: such and such a place.

ⲭⲟⲟⲥ ⲛⲁⲩ ⲉϥϯⲥⲃⲱ ⲛⲁⲩ ⲭⲉ ⲛ̄ⲧⲁⲓ̈ⲉⲓ ⲉⲃⲟⲗ ϩ̄ⲙ ⲡⲙⲩⲥⲧⲏⲣⲓⲟⲛ ⲉⲧⲙ̄ⲙⲁⲩ · ⲉⲧⲃⲉ ⲡⲁⲓ̈ ϭⲉ ⲛⲉⲩⲙⲉⲉⲩⲉ ⲉⲡⲙⲩⲥⲧⲏⲣⲓⲟⲛ ⲉⲧⲙ̄ⲙⲁⲩ ⲭⲉ ⲛ̄ⲧⲟϥ ⲡⲉ ⲡⲭⲱⲕ ⲛ̄ⲛⲭⲱⲕ ⲧⲏⲣⲟⲩ · ⲁⲩⲱ ⲭⲉ ⲛ̄ⲧⲟϥ ⲡⲉ ⲧⲕⲉⲫⲁⲗⲏ ⲙ̄ⲡⲧⲏⲣϥ̄ · ⲁⲩⲱ
5 ⲭⲉ ⲛ̄ⲧⲟϥ ⲡⲉ (ⲡⲉ)ⲡⲗⲏⲣⲱⲙⲁ ⲧⲏⲣϥ̄ · ⲉⲡⲓⲇⲏ ⲉϣⲁⲣⲉ [ⲁ̄]
ⲓ̄ⲥ̄ ⲭⲟⲟⲥ ⲉⲛⲉϥⲙⲁⲑⲏⲧⲏⲥ ⲭⲉ ⲡⲙⲩⲥⲧⲏⲣⲓⲟⲛ ⲉⲧⲙ̄ⲙⲁⲩ
ⲛ̄ⲧⲟϥ ⲡⲉⲧⲕⲱⲧⲉ ⲉⲛⲓⲡⲧⲏⲣϥ̄ · ⲛⲉⲛⲧⲁⲓ̈ⲭⲟⲟⲩ ⲉⲣⲱⲧⲛ̄
ⲧⲏⲣⲟⲩ ⲭⲓⲛ ⲙ̄ⲡⲉϩⲟⲟⲩ ⲉⲛⲧⲁⲓ̈ⲁⲡⲁⲛⲧⲁ ⲉⲣⲱⲧⲛ ϩⲉⲱⲥ
ϣⲁϩⲟⲩⲛ ⲉⲡⲟⲟⲩ ⲛ̄ϩⲟⲟⲩ · ⲉⲧⲃⲉ ⲡⲁⲓ̈ ϭⲉ ⲛⲉⲣⲉ ⲙ̄ⲙⲁ-
10 ⲑⲏⲧⲏⲥ ⲙⲉⲉⲩⲉ ⲡⲉ ⲭⲉ ⲙ̄ⲛ-ⲗⲁⲁⲩ ϣⲟⲟⲡ ⲙ̄ⲫⲟⲩⲛ ⲙ̄-
ⲡⲙⲩⲥⲧⲏⲣⲓⲟⲛ ⲉⲧⲙ̄ⲙⲁⲩ :

ⲍ̄ ⲁⲥϣⲱⲡⲉ ϭⲉ ⲉⲣⲉ ⲙ̄ⲙⲁⲑⲏⲧⲏⲥ ϩⲙⲟⲟⲥ ⲙ̄ⲛ-ⲛⲉⲩⲉⲣⲏⲩ
ϩⲓⲭ̄ⲙ ⲡⲧⲟⲟⲩ ⲛ̄ⲛⲭⲟⲉⲓⲧ ⲉⲩⲭⲱ ⲛ̄ⲛⲉⲓ̈ϣⲁⲭⲉ ⲁⲩⲱ ⲉⲩⲣⲁϣⲉ ϩⲛ ⲟⲩⲛⲟϭ ⲛ̄ⲣⲁϣⲉ ⲁⲩⲱ ⲉⲩⲧⲉⲗⲏⲗ ⲉⲙⲁϣⲟ ·
15 ⲁⲩⲱ ⲉⲩⲭⲱ ⲙ̄ⲙⲟⲥ ⲛ̄ⲛⲉⲩⲉⲣⲏⲩ ⲭⲉ ⲁⲛⲟⲛ ϩⲉⲛⲙⲁⲕⲁⲣⲓⲟⲥ ⲁⲛⲟⲛ ⲡⲁⲣⲁ ⲛ̄ⲣⲱⲙⲉ ⲧⲏⲣⲟⲩ ⲉⲧϩⲓⲭ̄ⲙ ⲡⲕⲁϩ ⲭⲉ ⲁ
ⲡⲥⲱⲧⲏⲣ ϭⲁⲡ-ⲛⲁⲓ̈ ⲛⲁⲛ ⲉⲃⲟⲗ · ⲁⲩⲱ ⲁⲛⲭⲓ ⲙ̄ⲡⲉⲡⲗⲏ- [ⲁ̄.ᵇ]
ⲣⲱⲙⲁ ⲙ̄ⲛ ⲡⲭⲱⲕ ⲧⲏⲣϥ̄ · ⲛⲁⲓ̈ ⲉⲩⲭⲱ ⲙ̄ⲙⲟⲟⲩ ⲉⲛⲉⲩⲉⲣⲏⲩ
ⲡⲉ ⲉⲣⲉ ⲓ̄ⲥ̄ ϩⲙⲟⲟⲥ ⲉϥⲟⲩⲏⲩ ⲉⲃⲟⲗ ⲙ̄ⲙⲟⲟⲩ ⲛ̄ⲟⲩϣⲏⲙ ·
20 ⲁⲥϣⲱⲡⲉ ⲇⲉ ϩⲙ ⲡⲙⲛ̄ⲧⲏ ⲙ̄ⲡⲟⲟϩ ⲙ̄ⲡⲉⲃⲟⲧ ⲛ̄ⲧⲱⲃⲉ ⲉⲧⲉ
ⲛ̄ⲧⲟϥ ⲡⲉ ⲡⲉϩⲟⲟⲩ ⲉϣⲁⲣⲉ ⲡⲟⲟϩ ⲭⲱⲕ ⲛ̄ϩⲏⲧϥ̄ · ⲙ̄ⲡⲉ-
ϩⲟⲟⲩ ϭⲉ ⲉⲧⲙ̄ⲙⲁⲩ ⲛ̄ⲧⲉⲣⲉ ⲡⲣⲏ ⲉⲓ ⲉⲃⲟⲗ ϩⲛ ⲧⲉϥⲃⲁⲥⲓⲥ ·
ⲁⲥⲉⲓ ⲉⲃⲟⲗ ⲙ̄ⲛ̄ⲛⲥⲱϥ ⲛ̄ϭⲓ ⲟⲩⲛⲟϭ ⲛ̄ⲇⲩⲛⲁⲙⲓⲥ ⲛ̄ⲟⲩⲟⲉⲓⲛ
ⲉⲥⲣ̄-ⲟⲩⲟⲉⲓⲛ ⲉⲙⲁϣⲟ ⲉⲙⲁϣⲟ · ⲉⲙⲛ̄-ϣⲓ ⲉⲡⲟⲩⲟⲉⲓⲛ
25 ⲉⲧⲥⲟ ⲙ̄ⲙⲟϥ · ⲛ̄ⲧⲁⲥⲉⲓ ⲅⲁⲣ ⲉⲃⲟⲗ ϩⲙ ⲡⲟⲩⲟⲉⲓⲛ ⲛ̄ⲧⲉ

---

1 MS originally ⲙ̄ⲡⲙⲩⲥⲧⲏⲣⲓⲟⲛ; 2 inserted above.
5 ⲡⲉ following the copula ⲡⲉ omitted; ⲉ at the end of line precedes ϣⲁⲣⲉ.

forth from that *mystery*". Because of this they thought now
of that *mystery* that it was the completion of all completions,
and that it was the *head* of the All, and that it was ⟨the⟩
whole *pleroma, since* Jesus had said to his *disciples*: "That
mystery surrounds the totalities of which I have told you all
from the day on which I *met* you until today". Because of
this the *disciples* thought now that there was nothing existing
within that *mystery*.

2. It happened as the *disciples* were sitting with one
another upon the Mount of Olives, as they spoke these
words they rejoiced with great joy, and they were very
jubilant, and they said to one another: "We are *blessed
beyond*[1] all men who are on earth because the *Saviour* has
revealed these things to us, and we have received the *pleroma*
and the whole completion". As they were saying these things
to one another, Jesus was sitting at a short distance from
them.

It happened, *however,* on the 15th of the moon in the
month of Tôbe[2], which is the day on which the moon
becomes full, now on that day when the sun had risen on its
path[3], there came forth after it a great *power* of light, giving
a very great light, and there was no measure to its accom-
panying light[4], *for* it came forth from the Light | of Lights,

---

[1] (16) blessed beyond; Till: more blessed than; Schmidt: blessed before.
[2] (20) Tôbe; fifth month of the Coptic year.
[3] (22) path; lit. basis; perhaps βᾶρις, bark (of the sun); (see 354.21).
[4] (25) to its accompanying light; lit. to the light in which it (the power) is.

ⲚⲞⲨⲞⲈⲒⲚ · ⲀⲨⲰ ⲚⲦⲀⲤⲈⲒ' ⲈⲂⲞⲖ ⲌⲘ ⲪⲀⲈ ⲘⲘⲨⲤⲦⲎⲢⲒⲞⲚ ·
ⲈⲦⲈ ⲚⲦⲞϤ ⲠⲈ ⲠⲘⲈⲌϪⲞⲨⲦⲀϤⲦⲈ ⲘⲘⲨⲤⲦⲎⲢⲒⲞⲚ ϪⲒⲚ
ⲚⲌⲞⲨⲚ ϢⲀⲂⲞⲖ · ⲚⲀⲒ ⲈⲦϢⲞⲞⲠ ⲌⲚ ⲚⲦⲀⲌⲒⲤ ⲚⲦⲈ ⲉ̄
ⲠⲘⲈⲌⲤⲚⲀⲨ ⲚⲬⲰⲢⲎⲘⲀ ⲚⲦⲈ ⲠⲒϢⲞⲢⲠ ⲘⲘⲨⲤⲦⲎⲢⲒⲞⲚ ·
5 ⲚⲦⲞⲤ ⲆⲈ ⲦϬⲞⲘ ⲈⲦⲘⲘⲀⲨ ⲚⲞⲨⲞⲈⲒⲚ ⲀⲤⲈⲒ' ⲈⲌⲢⲀⲒ ⲈϪⲚ
ⲒⲤ ⲀⲨⲰ ⲀⲤⲔⲰⲦⲈ ⲈⲢⲞϤ ⲦⲎⲢϤ · ⲈϤⲘⲞⲞⲤ ⲈϤⲞⲨⲎⲨ ⲈⲂⲞⲖ
ⲚⲚⲈϤⲘⲀⲐⲎⲦⲎⲤ ⲀⲨⲰ ⲚⲈⲀϤⲢ-ⲞⲨⲞⲈⲒⲚ ⲠⲈ ⲈⲘⲀϢⲞ ⲈⲘⲀ-
ϢⲞ · ⲈⲘⲚ-ϢⲒ ⲈⲠⲞⲨⲞⲈⲒⲚ ⲈⲚⲈϤϢⲞⲞⲠ ⲘⲘⲞϤ · ⲀⲨⲰ
ⲈⲚⲈⲘⲠⲈ ⲘⲘⲀⲐⲎⲦⲎⲤ ⲚⲀⲨ Ⲉ̄Ⲥ ⲈⲂⲞⲖ ⲘⲠⲚⲞϬ ⲚⲞⲨⲞⲈⲒⲚ
10 ⲈⲚⲈϤϢⲞⲞⲠ ⲚⲌⲎⲦϤ Ⲏ ⲈⲚⲈϤϢⲞⲞⲠ ⲘⲘⲞϤ · ⲚⲈⲀ ⲚⲈⲨⲂⲀⲖ
ⲄⲀⲢ ⲌⲦⲞⲘⲦⲘ ⲠⲈ ⲈⲂⲞⲖ ⲘⲠⲚⲞϬ ⲚⲞⲨⲞⲈⲒⲚ ⲈⲚⲈϤϢⲞⲞⲠ
ⲚⲌⲎⲦϤ · ⲀⲖⲖⲀ ⲚⲈⲨⲚⲀⲨ ⲘⲘⲀⲦⲈ ⲠⲈ ⲈⲠⲞⲨⲞⲈⲒⲚ · ⲈϤ-
ⲚⲞⲨϪⲈ ⲈⲂⲞⲖ ⲚⲌⲈⲚⲀⲔⲦⲒⲚ ⲚⲞⲨⲞⲈⲒⲚ ⲈⲚⲀϢⲰⲞⲨ · ⲀⲨⲰ
ⲚⲈⲨϢⲎϢ ⲀⲚ ⲠⲈ ⲘⲚ-ⲚⲈⲨⲈⲢⲎⲨ ⲚϬⲒ ⲚⲀⲔⲦⲒⲚ ⲚⲞⲨⲞⲈⲒⲚ · ⲉ̄ᵇ
15 ⲀⲨⲰ ⲚⲈⲢⲈ ⲠⲞⲨⲞⲈⲒⲚ ⲚⲈϤⲞ ⲘⲘⲒⲚⲈ ⲘⲒⲚⲈ ⲠⲈ · ⲀⲨⲰ
ⲚⲈϤⲞ' ⲚⲦⲨⲠⲞⲤ ⲦⲨⲠⲞⲤ ⲠⲈ ϪⲒⲚ ⲘⲠⲈⲤⲎⲦ ⲈⲦⲠⲈ · ⲈⲢⲈ
ⲞⲨⲀ ⲤⲞⲦⲠ ⲈⲞⲨⲀ ⲦⲘⲠⲤⲞⲠ ⲌⲚ ⲞⲨⲚⲞϬ ⲚⲈⲞⲞⲨ
ⲚⲞⲨⲞⲈⲒⲚ ⲚⲀⲦϮϢⲒ ⲈⲢⲞϤ · ⲚⲈϤϪⲒ ϪⲒⲚ ⲠⲈⲤⲎⲦ ⲘⲠⲔⲀⲌ
ϢⲀⲌⲢⲀⲒ ⲈⲘⲠⲎⲨⲈ ·
20 ⲍ ⲀⲨⲰ ⲚⲦⲈⲢⲈ ⲘⲘⲀⲐⲎⲦⲎⲤ ⲚⲀⲨ ⲈⲠⲞⲨⲞⲈⲒⲚ ⲈⲦ-
ⲘⲘⲀⲨ · ⲀⲨϢⲰⲠⲈ ⲌⲚ ⲞⲨⲚⲞϬ ⲚⲌⲞⲦⲈ ⲀⲨⲰ ⲌⲚ ⲞⲨ-
ⲚⲞϬ ⲚϢⲦⲞⲢⲦⲢ ·

ⲍ ⲀⲤϢⲰⲠⲈ ϬⲈ ⲚⲦⲈⲢⲈ ⲦϬⲞⲘ ⲚⲞⲨⲞⲈⲒⲚ ⲈⲦⲘⲘⲀⲨ ⲈⲒ'
ⲈⲌⲢⲀⲒ ⲈϪⲚ ⲒⲤ ⲀⲤⲔⲰⲦⲈ ⲈⲢⲞϤ ⲦⲎⲢϤ ϢⲎⲘ ϢⲎⲘ · ⲦⲞⲦⲈ

---

17 MS originally ⲤⲞⲦⲠϤ; ϥ expunged. MS originally ⲚⲞⲞⲨ'; ⲉ inserted above.
18 MS originally ⲚⲞⲨⲈⲒⲚ.

and it came forth from the last *mystery*, which is the 24th *mystery* from within outwards, these which are in the *ranks* of the second *space* of the First *Mystery*. That light-power, *however*, came down upon Jesus and it surrounded him completely as he was sitting at a distance from his *disciples*, and he gave light exceedingly, there being no measure to the light which was his. And the *disciples* did not see Jesus because of the great light in which he was, *or* which was his, *for* their eyes were darkened because of the great light in which he was. *But* they only saw the light which cast forth many *rays* of light. And the *rays* of light were not equal to one another. And the light was of many kinds, and it was of different *types* from below upwards, so that one (ray) was many times more excellent than another in a great glory of light to which there was no measure. It reached from the earth below [1] upwards to the heavens.

And when the *disciples* saw that light they were in great fear, and in great agitation.

3. Now it happened when the light-power had come down upon Jesus, it gradually surrounded him completely. *Then* | Jesus rose *or* ascended to the height, giving light

---

[1] (18) from the earth below; lit from the bottom of the earth.

Ⲁ Ⲓ̄C̄ ⲦⲞⲒⲖⲈ Ⲛ̄ ⲀϤϬⲰⲖ˙ ⲈⲠϪⲒⳞⲈ ⲈⲀϤⲢ̄-ⲞⲨⲞⲈⲒⲚ ⲈⲘⲀϢⲞ
ⲈⲘⲀϢⲞ ⲌⲚ̄ ⟨ⲞⲨ⟩ⲞⲨⲞⲈⲒⲚ ⲈⲘⲚ̄-ϢⲒ ⲈⲢⲞϤ˙ ⲀⲨⲰ ⲚⲈⲢⲈ
Ⲙ̄ⲘⲀⲐⲎⲦⲎⲤ ϬⲰϢⲦ̄ Ⲛ̄ⲤⲰϤ ⲠⲈ** ⲈⲘⲚ̄-ⲞⲨⲞⲚ Ⲙ̄ⲘⲞⲞⲨ [Ⲉ̄]
ϢⲀϪⲈ˙ ϢⲀⲚⲦϤⲂⲰⲔ ⲈⲌⲢⲀⲒ̈ ⲈⲦⲠⲈ˙ ⲀⲖⲖⲀ ⲚⲈⲨϢⲞⲞⲠ ⲦⲎ-
5 ⲢⲞⲨ ⲌⲚ ⲞⲨⲚⲞϬ Ⲛ̄ⲤⲒⲅⲎ˙ ⲚⲀⲒ̈ ϬⲈ Ⲛ̄ⲦⲀⲨϢⲰⲠⲈ Ⲙ̄ⲠⲘⲚ̄ⲦⲎ
Ⲙ̄ⲠⲞⲞⲌ˙ ⲠⲈϪⲞⲞⲨ ⲈϢⲀϤϪⲰⲔ Ⲛ̄ⲌⲎⲦϤ̄ Ⲙ̄ⲠⲈⲂⲞⲦ Ⲛ̄ⲦⲰⲂⲈ:

    Ⳅ ⲀⲤϢⲰⲠⲈ ϬⲈ Ⲛ̄ⲦⲈⲢⲈ ⲒⲤ ⲂⲰⲔ ⲈⲌⲢⲀⲒ̈ ⲈⲦⲠⲈ ⲘⲚ̄ⲚⲤⲀ
ϢⲞⲘⲦⲈ Ⲛ̄ⲞⲨⲚⲞⲨ˙ ⲀⲨⲰⲦⲞⲢⲦⲢ̄ Ⲛ̄ϬⲒ Ⲛ̄ϬⲞⲘ ⲦⲎⲢⲞⲨ
Ⲛ̄Ⲙ̄ⲠⲎⲨⲈ ⲀⲨⲰ ⲀⲨⲚⲞⲈⲒⲚ ⲦⲎⲢⲞⲨ ⳨Ⲓ ⲚⲈⲨⲈⲢⲎⲨ˙ Ⲛ̄ⲦⲞⲞⲨ
10 ⲘⲚ ⲚⲈⲨⲀⲒⲰⲚ ⲦⲎⲢⲞⲨ ⲘⲚ̄ ⲚⲈⲨⲦⲞⲠⲞⳤ ⲦⲎⲢⲞⲨ˙ ⲀⲨⲰ
ⲘⲚ̄ ⲚⲈⲨⲦⲀⳠⲒⳤ ⲦⲎⲢⲞⲨ ⲀⲨⲰ Ⲁ ⲠⲔⲀⲌ ⲦⲎⲢϤ̄ ⲔⲒⲘ ⲘⲚ̄
ⲚⲈⲦⲞⲨⲎⲌ ⳘⲒϪⲰϤ ⲦⲎⲢⲞⲨ˙ ⲀⲨⲰ ⲀⲨϢⲦⲞⲢⲦⲢ̄ Ⲛ̄ϬⲒ Ⲛ̄-
ⲢⲰⲘⲈ ⲦⲎⲢⲞⲨ ⲈⲦⳘⲘ̄ ⲠⲔⲞⳤⲘⲞⳤ ⲘⲚ̄ Ⲛ̄ⲔⲈⲘⲀⲐⲎⲦⲎⳤ˙
ⲀⲨⲰ ⲚⲈⲨⲘⲈⲈⲨⲈ ⲦⲎⲢⲞⲨ ⲠⲈ ϪⲈ ⲘⲈϢⲀⲔ ⲈⲨⲚⲀϬⲀ- [Ⲉ̄ᵇ]
15 ⲠⲔⲞⳤⲘⲞⳤ˙ ⲀⲨⲰ ⲚⲈⲘⲠⲞⲨⲔⲀ-ⲦⲞⲞⲦⲞⲨ ⲈⲂⲞⲖ ⲠⲈ Ⲛ̄ϬⲒ
Ⲛ̄ϬⲞⲘ ⲦⲎⲢⲞⲨ ⲈⲦⳘⲚ̄ Ⲙ̄ⲠⲎⲨⲈ ⲈⲨϢⲦⲢ̄ⲦⲰⲢ' Ⲛ̄ⲦⲞⲞⲨ ⲘⲚ̄
ⲠⲔⲞⳤⲘⲞⳤ ⲦⲎⲢϤ̄ ⲀⲨⲰ ⲚⲈⲨⲔⲒⲘ ⲦⲎⲢⲞⲨ ⲠⲈ ⲈϪⲚ̄ ⲚⲈⲨ-
ⲈⲢⲎⲨ ϪⲒⲚ Ⳟ̄ⲠϢⲞⲘⲦⲈ Ⲙ̄ⲠⲘⲚ̄ⲦⲎ Ⲙ̄ⲠⲞⲞⲌ ⟨Ⲙ̄ⲠⲈⲂⲞⲦ⟩
Ⲛ̄ⲦⲰⲂⲈ ϢⲀⲌⲢⲀⲒ̈ ⲈⳞⲠ̄Ⲯ̄ⲒⲦⲈ Ⲙ̄ⲠⲈϤⲢⲀⳤⲦⲈ˙ ⲀⲨⲰ ⲚⲈⲢⲈ
20 Ⲛ̄ⲀⲅⲅⲈⲖⲞⳤ ⲦⲎⲢⲞⲨ ⲘⲚ̄ ⲚⲈⲨⲀⲢⲬⲀⲅⲅⲈⲖⲞⳤ ⲀⲨⲰ ⲘⲚ̄
Ⲛ̄ϬⲞⲘ ⲦⲎⲢⲞⲨ Ⲙ̄ⲠϪⳞⲒⳤⲈ ⲚⲈⲨⲌⲨⲘⲚⲈⲨⲈ ⲦⲎⲢⲞⲨ ⲠⲈ ⲈⲠⳤⲀ-
Ⲛ̄ⲌⲞⲨⲚ Ⲛ̄ⲦⲈ ⲚⲒⳤⲀⲚⲌⲞⲨⲚ˙ ⲌⲰⳤⲦⲈ ⲚⲈⲢⲈ ⲠⲔⲞⳤⲘⲞⳤ
ⲦⲎⲢϤ̄ ⲤⲰⲦⳘ̄ ⲈⲠⲈⲨⲌⲢⲞⲞⲨ ⲈⲘⲠⲞⲨⲔⲀ-ⲦⲞⲞⲦⲞⲨ ⲈⲂⲞⲖ
ϢⲀ Ⳟ̄ⲠⲮ̄ⲒⲦⲈ Ⲙ̄ⲠⲈϤⲢⲀⳤⲦⲈ˙ Ⲙ̄ⲘⲀⲐⲎⲦⲎⳤ ⲆⲈ ⲚⲈⲨⲌⲘⲞⲞⳤ
25 ⲠⲈ ⳨Ⲓ ⲚⲈⲨⲈⲢⲎⲨ ⲈⲨⲞ' Ⲛ̄ⲌⲞⲦⲈ˙ ⲀⲨⲰ ⲚⲈⲀⲨϢⲦⲞⲢⲦⲢ̄ ⲠⲈ

---

2   MS Ⲍ̄Ⲛ ⲞⲨⲞⲈⲒⲚ.
18   supply Ⲙ̄ⲠⲈⲂⲞⲦ.

exceedingly, with ⟨a⟩ light to which there was no measure. And the *disciples* gazed after him, and not one of them spoke until he had reached heaven, *but* they all kept a great *silence*. Now these things happened on the 15th of the moon, on the day on which it is full in the month of Tôbe.

Now it happened when Jesus went up to heaven, after three hours all the powers of the heavens were disturbed, and they all shook against one another[1], they and all their *aeons*, and all their *places* and all their *ranks* and the whole earth moved with all who dwelt upon it. And all the men in the *world* were agitated, and also the *disciples*. And they all thought: "Perhaps the *world* will be rolled up". And all the powers which are in the heavens did not cease from their agitation, they and the whole *world*, and they all moved against one another[2] from the third hour of the 15th of the moon in ⟨the month of⟩ Tôbe until the ninth hour of the following day. And all the *angels* and their *archangels* and all the powers of the height all *sang praises* to the innermost of the inner[3], *so that* the whole *world* heard their voices, and they did not cease until the ninth hour of the following day.

4. The *disciples*, *however*, sat with one another in fear, and were greatly agitated. | They were afraid, *however*, on

---

[1] (9) shook against one another; Till: trembled together.
[2] (17) moved against one another; Till: moved upon one another.
[3] (21, 22) innermost of the inner; see J 99.

ЄΜΑϢΟ ЄΜΑϢΟ · ΝЄΥⳞ²ΟΤЄ ΔЄ ΠЄ ЄΤΒЄ ΠΝΟϬ Ν̄- Ζ̄
Κ̄ΜΤΟ ЄΤϢΟΟΠ ΑΥⲰ ΝЄΥΡΙΜЄ ΠЄ Μ̄Ν-ΝЄΥЄΡΗΥ
ЄΥΧⲰ Μ̄ΜΟⳞ ΧЄ ΟΥ ΑΡΑ ΠЄΤΝΑϢⲰΠЄ · ΜЄϢΑΚ ЄΡЄ
ΠϹⲰΤΗΡ ΝΑΒⲰΛ ЄΒΟΛ Ν̄ΝΤΟΠΟϹ ΤΗΡΟΥ :

5 Ζ̄ ΝΑΪ ϬЄ ЄΥΧⲰ Μ̄ΜΟΟΥ ЄΥΡΙΜЄ ЄϨΟΥΝ ЄΝЄΥЄΡΗΥ ·
Μ̄ΠΝΑΥ Ν̄ΧΠ̄ΨΙΤЄ Μ̄ΠЄⳞΡΑϹΤЄ Α Μ̄ΠΗΥЄ ΟΥⲰΝ ΑΥⲰ
ΑΥΝΑΥ ЄΙϹ ЄⳞΝΗΥ ЄΠЄϹΗΤˑ ЄⳞⲢ̄-ΟΥΟЄΙΝ ЄΜΑϢΟ
ЄΜΑϢΟ · ЄΜΝ̄-ϢΙ ЄΠЄⳞΟΥΟЇΝ ЄΤϢΟΟΠ Ν̄ϨΗΤⳞ · ΝЄⳞⲢ̄-
ΟΥΟЄΙΝ ΓΑΡ Ν̄ϨΟΥΟ ЄΠΝΑΥ ЄΝΤΑⳞΒⲰΚ ЄϨΡΑΪ ЄΜ-
10 ΠΗΥЄ · ϨⲰϹΤЄ ΝЄΜΝ̄ϬΟΜ Ν̄ΡΜ̄ΝΚΟϹΜΟϹ ЄϢΑΧЄ
ЄΠΟΥΟЄΙΝ ЄΝЄⳞϢΟΟΠ Μ̄ΜΟⳞ · ΑΥⲰ ΝЄⳞΝЄΧ-ΑΚΤΙΝ
Ν̄ΟΥΟЄΙΝ ЄΒΟΛ ΠЄ ЄΜΑΤЄ ЄΜΑΤЄ ЄΜΝ̄-ϢΙ ЄΝЄⳞ- Ζ̄ᵇ
ΑΚΤΙΝ · ΑΥⲰ ΝЄΡЄ ΠЄⳞΟΥΟЄΙΝ ΝЄⳞϢΗϢ ΑΝ ΠЄ Μ̄Ν-
ΝЄⳞЄΡΗΥ · ΑΛΛΑ ΝЄⳞΟˑ Μ̄ΜΙΝЄ ΜΙΝЄ ΠЄ ΑΥⲰ ΝЄⳞΟˑ
15 Ν̄ΤΥΠΟϹ ΤΥΠΟϹ ΠЄ ЄΡЄ ϨΟЇΝЄ ΟΥΟΤΒ̄ ЄΝЄΥЄΡΗΥ
ΤΜ̄ΠϹΟΠ · ΑΥⲰ ΝЄΡЄ ΠΟΥΟЄΙΝ ΤΗΡⳞ ϨΙ ΝЄⳞЄΡΗΥ ΠЄ ·
ΝЄⳞΟˑ Ν̄ϢΟΜΤЄ Ν̄ϨЄ ΠЄ ΑΥⲰ ΝЄΡЄ ΟΥЄΙ ΟΥΟΤΒ̄
ЄΟΥЄΙ ΠЄ ΤΜ̄ΠϹΟΠ · ΤΜЄϨϹΝ̄ΤЄ ЄΤϨΝ̄ ΤΜΗΤЄ ΝЄϹΟΥ-
ΟΤΒ̄ ΠЄ ЄΤЄϨΟΥЄΙΤЄ ЄΤΜ̄ΠЄϹΗΤ · ΑΥⲰ ΤΜЄϨϢΟΜΤЄ
20 ЄΤϨΙΤΠЄ Μ̄ΜΟΟΥ ΤΗΡΟΥ ΝЄϹΟΥΟΤΒ̄ ΠЄ ЄΤϨΝ̄ΤЄ ЄΤ-
[Ϩ]Μ̄ΠЄϹΗΤ · ΑΥⲰ ΤϢΟΡΠ̄ Ν̄ϹΙΤЄ ΚΗ ЄΤΜ̄ΠЄϹΗΤ
Μ̄ΜΟΟΥ ΤΗΡΟΥ · ЄϹΟ Μ̄ΠΙΝЄ Μ̄ΠΟΥΟЄΙΝ ΠЄΝΤΑⳞϬЄΪˑ [Π̄]
ЄΧΝ̄ ΙϹ ЄΜΠΑΤⳞΒⲰΚ ЄϨΡΑΪ ЄΜΠΗΥЄ ΑΥⲰ ЄⳞϢΗϢ
ΟΥΒΗⳞ Μ̄ΜΑΤЄ Ϩ̄Μ ΠЄⳞΟΥΟЄΙΝ · ΑΥⲰ ΤϢΟΜΤЄ Ν̄ϨЄ
25 Ν̄ΟΥΟЄΙΝ ΝЄΥΟ Μ̄ΜΙΝЄ ΜΙΝЄ Ν̄ΟΥΟЄΙΝ ΠЄ ΑΥⲰ ΝЄΥΟˑ

21 MS ЄΤϨΜ̄Π|ЄϹΗΤ; read ΤΗ ЄΤΜ̄ΠЄϹΗΤ, or ЄΤΚΗ Μ̄ΠЄϹΗΤ.

account of the great earthquake which happened, and they wept together, saying: "What will happen *now*? Perhaps the *Saviour* will destroy all the *places*".

As they were saying these things and were weeping to one another, on the ninth hour of the following day the heavens opened, and they saw Jesus coming down, giving light exceedingly, and there was no measure to the light in which he was. *For* he gave more light than in the hour that he went up to heaven, *so that* the men in the *world* were not able to speak of the light which was his, and it cast forth very many *rays* of light, and there was no measure to its *rays*. And his light was not equal throughout, *but* it was of different kinds, and it was of different *types*, so that some were many times superior to others, and the whole light together was in three forms, and the one was many times superior to the other; the second which was in the middle was superior to the first which was below; and the third which was above them all was superior to the second which was below. And the first ray which was below them all was similar to the light which had come down upon Jesus before he went up to heaven, and it was quite equal to it in its light. And the three light-forms were of different kinds of light and they were | of different *types*. And some were many times superior to others.

ⲚⲦⲨⲠⲞⲤ ⲦⲨⲠⲞⲤ ⲠⲈ· ⲈⲢⲈ ⲍⲞⲒⲚⲈ ⲞⲨⲞⲦⲂ̄ ⲈⲌⲞⲒⲚⲈ ⲦⲘ-
ⲠⲤⲞⲠ·

ⲍ ⲀⲤϢⲰⲠⲈ ⲆⲈ Ⲛ̄ⲦⲈⲢⲈ Ⲙ̄ⲘⲀⲐⲎⲦⲎⲤ ⲚⲀⲨ ⲈⲚⲀⲒ ⲀⲨⲢ̄-
ⲌⲞⲦⲈ ⲈⲘⲀⲦⲈ ⲀⲨⲰ ⲀⲨϢⲦⲞⲢⲦⲢ̄· Ⲓ̄Ⲥ̄ ϬⲈ ⲠⲚⲀⲎⲦ' ⲀⲨⲰ
5 ⲠⲒⲀⲗϬⲎⲦ' Ⲛ̄ⲦⲈⲢⲈϤⲚⲀⲨ ⲈⲚⲈϤⲘⲀⲐⲎⲦⲎⲤ ϪⲈ ⲀⲨϢⲦⲞⲢⲦⲢ̄
Ⲍ̄Ⲛ ⲞⲨⲚⲞϬ Ⲛ̄ϢⲦⲞⲢⲦⲢ̄· ⲀϤϢⲀϪⲈ ⲚⲘⲘⲀⲨ ⲈϤϪⲰ Ⲙ̄ⲘⲞⲤ
ϪⲈ ⲦⲰⲔ Ⲛ̄Ⲍ̄ⲎⲦ' ⲀⲚⲞⲔ ⲠⲈ Ⲙ̄ⲠⲢ̄Ⲣ̄ⲌⲞⲦⲈ·

ⲍ ⲀⲤϢⲰⲠⲈ ϬⲈ Ⲛ̄ⲦⲈⲢⲈ Ⲙ̄ⲘⲀⲐⲎⲦⲎⲤ ⲤⲰⲦⲘ̄ ⲈⲠⲈⲒϢⲀϪⲈ
ⲠⲈϪⲀⲨ ϪⲈ ⲠϪⲞⲈⲒⲤ ⲈϢϪⲈ Ⲛ̄ⲦⲞⲔ ⲠⲈ ⲤⲰⲔ ⲈⲢⲞⲔ Ⲙ̄-
10 ⲠⲈⲔⲞⲨⲞⲈⲒⲚ Ⲛ̄ⲈⲞⲞⲨ ⲦⲀⲢ̄ⲚⲈϢ-ⲀⲌⲈⲢⲀⲦⲚ̄· ⲈⲘⲘⲞⲚ Ⲁ [Ⲡ̄ᵇ]
ⲚⲈⲚⲂⲀⲗ Ⲍ̄ⲦⲞⲘⲦⲘ̄ ⲀⲨⲰ ⲀⲚϢⲦⲞⲢⲦⲢ̄ ⲀⲨⲰ ⲞⲚ ⲀϤ-
ϢⲦⲞⲢⲦⲢ̄ Ⲛ̄ϬⲒ ⲠⲔⲞⲤⲘⲞⲤ ⲦⲎⲢϤ̄ ⲈⲂⲞⲗ Ⲙ̄ⲠⲚⲞϬ Ⲛ̄ⲞⲨⲞⲈⲒⲚ
ⲈⲦϢⲞⲞⲠ Ⲙ̄ⲘⲞⲔ:

ⲍ ⲦⲞⲦⲈ Ⲓ̄Ⲥ̄ ⲀϤⲤⲰⲔ ⲈⲢⲞϤ Ⲙ̄ⲠⲈⲞⲞⲨ Ⲙ̄ⲠⲈϤⲞⲨⲞⲈⲒⲚ·
15 ⲀⲨⲰ Ⲛ̄ⲦⲈⲢⲈ ⲠⲀⲒ ϢⲰⲠⲈ ⲀⲨⲦⲰⲔ Ⲛ̄Ⲍ̄ⲎⲦ' Ⲛ̄ϬⲒ Ⲙ̄ⲘⲀⲐⲎ-
ⲦⲎⲤ ⲦⲎⲢⲞⲨ ⲀⲨⲈⲒ' ⲈⲢⲀⲦϤ̄ Ⲛ̄Ⲓ̄Ⲥ̄ ⲀⲨⲠⲀⲌⲦⲞⲨ ⲦⲎⲢⲞⲨ ⲌⲒ
ⲞⲨⲤⲞⲠ ⲀⲨⲞⲨⲰϢⲦ ⲚⲀϤ ⲈⲨⲢⲀϢⲈ Ⲍ̄Ⲛ ⲞⲨⲚⲞϬ Ⲛ̄ⲢⲀϢⲈ·
ⲠⲈϪⲀⲨ ⲚⲀϤ ϪⲈ Ⲍ̄ⲢⲀⲂⲂⲈⲒ Ⲛ̄ⲦⲀⲔⲂⲰⲔ ⲈⲦⲰⲚ· Ⲏ̄ ⲞⲨ ⲦⲈ
ⲦⲈⲔⲆⲒⲀⲔⲞⲚⲒⲀ Ⲛ̄ⲦⲀⲔⲂⲰⲔ Ⲙ̄ⲘⲞⲤ Ⲏ̄ Ⲍ̄Ⲛ ⲞⲨ Ⲛ̄ⲦⲞϤ ⲚⲈ
20 ⲚⲈⲒϢⲦⲞⲢⲦⲢ̄ ⲦⲎⲢⲞⲨ Ⲙ̄Ⲛ ⲚⲈⲒⲔⲘⲦⲞ ⲦⲎⲢⲞⲨ ⲈⲚⲦⲀⲨ-
ϢⲰⲠⲈ· ⲦⲞⲦⲈ ⲠⲈϪⲀϤ ⲚⲀⲨ Ⲛ̄ϬⲒ Ⲓ̄Ⲥ̄ ⲠⲚⲀⲎⲦ ϪⲈ ⲢⲀϢⲈ
Ⲛ̄ⲦⲈⲦⲚ̄ⲦⲈⲗⲎⲗ ϪⲒⲚ Ⲙ̄ⲠⲈⲒⲚⲀⲨ ϪⲈ ⲀⲒⲂⲰⲔ ϢⲀ Ⲛ̄ⲦⲞ- ⲟ̄
ⲠⲞⲤ ⲈⲚⲦⲀⲒⲈⲒ' ⲈⲂⲞⲗ Ⲛ̄Ⲍ̄ⲎⲦⲞⲨ· ϪⲒⲚ ⲠⲞⲞⲨ ϬⲈ ⲈⲂⲞⲗ
†ⲚⲀϢⲀϪⲈ Ⲛ̄ⲘⲘⲎⲦⲚ̄ Ⲍ̄Ⲛ ⲞⲨⲠⲀⲢⲢⲎⲤⲒⲀ ϪⲒⲚ ⲦⲀⲢⲬⲎ

16

5. It happened, *however*, when the *disciples* saw these they were greatly afraid and agitated. Now Jesus, the com-compassionate and tender-hearted, when he saw that his *disciples* were in great agitation, he spoke to them saying : "Be courageous. It is I, do not fear" *.

6. Now it happened when the *disciples* heard these words, they said : "Lord, if it be thou, draw thy light-glory to thyself so that we can stand, otherwise our eyes are darkened and we are agitated, and also the whole *world* is agitated [1], because of the great light which is thine".

Then Jesus drew to himself the glory of his light. And when this had happened all the *disciples* took courage, they came before Jesus, they all prostrated themselves at the same time, they worshipped him, rejoicing with great joy. They said to him : "Rabbi, where didst thou go, *or* what was thy *service* in which thou didst go, *or* for what reason were all these disturbances and all these earthquakes which happened?" [2]

Then Jesus, the compassionate, said to them : "Rejoice and be glad □ from this hour because I have been to the *places* from whence I came forth. From today onwards now I will speak with you *openly* from the *beginning* | of the

---

*   cf. Mt. 14.27; Mk. 6.50
□   cf. Mt. 5.12

---

[1]   (11, 12) are darkened ... are agitated ... is agitated; lit. have been darkened ... have been agitated ... has been agitated.
[2]   (19) was thy service ... for what reason were; lit. is thy service ... for what reason are; on service, see U 239.

ⲚⲦⲀⲖⲎⲐⲈⲒⲀ ϢⲀ ⲠⲈⲤϪⲰⲔ · ⲀⲨⲰ ⳨ⲚⲀϢⲀϪⲈ ⲚⲘⲘⲎⲦⲚ
Ⲛ2Ⲟ 21 2Ⲟ ⲀⲬⲚ ⲠⲀⲢⲀⲂⲞⲖⲎ · Ⲛ⳨ⲚⲀ2ⲈⲠ-ⲖⲀⲀⲨ ⲈⲢⲰⲦⲚ
ⲀⲚ ϪⲒⲚ ⲠⲈⲒⲚⲀⲨ ⲚⲦⲈ ⲚⲀⲠϪⲒⲤⲈ ⲀⲨⲰ ⲚⲀⲠⲦⲞⲠⲞⲤ ⲚⲦⲀ-
ⲖⲎⲐⲈⲒⲀ · ⲀⲨ⳨-Ⲉ2ⲞⲨⲤⲒⲀ ⲄⲀⲢ ⲚⲀⲒ 21ⲦⲘ ⲠⲒⲀⲦϢⲀϪⲈ
5 ⲈⲢⲞϤ ⲀⲨⲰ 21ⲦⲘ ⲠⲒϢⲞⲢⲠ ⲘⲘⲨⲤⲦⲎⲢⲒⲞⲚ ⲚⲦⲈ ⲘⲘⲨⲤⲦⲎ-
ⲢⲒⲞⲚ ⲦⲎⲢⲞⲨ · ⲈⲦⲢⲀϢⲀϪⲈ ⲚⲘⲘⲎⲦⲚ ϪⲒⲚ ⲦⲀⲢⲬⲎ ϢⲀ
ⲠⲈⲠⲖⲎⲢⲰⲘⲀ · ⲀⲨⲰ ϪⲒⲚ2ⲞⲨⲚ ϢⲀⲂⲞⲖ ⲀⲨⲰ ϪⲒⲚⲂⲞⲖ
ϢⲀ2ⲞⲨⲚ · ⲤⲰⲦⲘ 6Ⲉ ⲦⲀϪⲰ ⲈⲢⲰⲦⲚ Ⲛ2ⲰⲂ ⲚⲒⲘ · ⲀⲤ-
ϢⲰⲠⲈ ⲈⲒ2ⲘⲞⲞⲤ ⲈⲒⲞⲨⲎⲨ ⲈⲂⲞⲖ ⲘⲘⲰⲦⲚ ⲚⲞⲨⲔⲞⲨⲒ ꙳
10 21ϪⲘ ⲠⲦⲞⲞⲨ ⲚⲚϪⲞⲈⲒⲦ ⲈⲒⲘⲈⲈⲨⲈ ⲈⲚⲦⲀ2ⲒⲤ ⲚⲦⲀⲒⲀ-
ⲔⲞⲚⲒⲀ ⲈⲚⲦⲀⲨⲦⲀⲨⲞⲈⲒ ⲈⲦⲂⲎⲎⲦⲤ ϪⲈ ⲀⲤϪⲰⲔ ⲈⲂⲞⲖ ·
ⲀⲨⲰ ⲘⲠⲀⲦϤⲦⲚⲚⲞⲞⲨ ⲚⲀⲒ ⲘⲠⲀⲈⲚⲀⲨⲘⲀ Ⲛ6Ⲓ ⲪⲀⲈ
ⲘⲘⲨⲤⲦⲎⲢⲒⲞⲚ · ⲈⲦⲈ ⲚⲦⲞϤ ⲠⲈ ⲠⲘⲈ2ϪⲞⲨⲦⲀϤⲦⲈ ⲘⲘⲨⲤ-
ⲦⲎⲢⲒⲞⲚ ϪⲒⲚ Ⲛ2ⲞⲨⲚ ϢⲀⲂⲞⲖ · ⲚⲀⲒ ⲈⲦϢⲞⲞⲠ 2Ⲙ ⲠⲘⲈ2-
15 ⲤⲚⲀⲨ ⲚⲬⲰⲢⲎⲘⲀ ⲚⲦⲈ ⲠⲒϢⲞⲢⲠ ⲘⲘⲨⲤⲦⲎⲢⲒⲞⲚ 2Ⲛ ⲦⲦⲀ-
2ⲒⲤ ⲚⲦⲈ ⲠⲈⲬⲰⲢⲎⲘⲀ ⲈⲦⲘⲘⲀⲨ · ⲀⲤϢⲰⲠⲈ 6Ⲉ ⲚⲦⲈⲢⲈⲒ-
ⲈⲒⲘⲈ ϪⲈ ⲀⲤϪⲰⲔ ⲈⲂⲞⲖ Ⲛ6Ⲓ ⲦⲦⲀ2ⲒⲤ ⲚⲦⲀⲒⲀⲔⲞⲚⲒⲀ ⲈⲚⲦ-
ⲀⲒⲈⲒ ⲈⲦⲂⲎⲎⲦⲤ · ⲀⲨⲰ ⲈⲘⲠⲀⲦⲈ ⲠⲘⲨⲤⲦⲎⲢⲒⲞⲚ ⲈⲦⲘⲘⲀⲨ
ⲦⲚⲞⲞⲨ ⲚⲀⲒ ⲘⲠⲀⲈⲚⲀⲨⲘⲀ ⲠⲀⲒ ⲈⲚⲦⲀⲒⲔⲀⲀϤ Ⲛ2ⲎⲦϤ ·
20 ϢⲀⲚⲦϤϪⲰⲔ ⲈⲂⲞⲖ Ⲛ6Ⲓ ⲠⲈϤⲞⲨⲞⲈⲒϢ · ⲚⲀⲒ 6Ⲉ ⲈⲒⲘⲈⲈⲨⲈ
ⲈⲢⲞⲞⲨ ⲈⲒ2ⲘⲞⲞⲤ 21ϪⲘ ⲠⲦⲞⲞⲨ ⲚⲚϪⲞⲈⲒⲦ ⲈⲒⲞⲨⲎⲨ [ⲧ]
ⲘⲘⲰⲦⲚ ⲚⲞⲨϢⲎⲘ · ⲀⲤϢⲰⲠⲈ ⲈⲢⲈ ⲠⲢⲎ ⲚⲎⲨ Ⲉ2ⲢⲀⲒ 2Ⲛ
ⲘⲘⲀⲚϢⲀ · ⲘⲚⲚⲤⲰⲤ 6Ⲉ ⲈⲂⲞⲖ 21ⲦⲞⲞⲦϤ ⲘⲠⲒϢⲞⲢⲠ Ⲙ-
ⲘⲨⲤⲦⲎⲢⲒⲞⲚ · ⲠⲀⲒ ⲈⲚⲈϤϢⲞⲞⲠ ϪⲒⲚ ⲚϢⲞⲢⲠ ⲠⲀⲒ ⲈⲚⲦⲀ

---

10 MS ⲈⲚⲦⲀ2ⲒⲤ; read ⲈⲦⲦⲀ2ⲒⲤ, compare 17.
19 the forms ⲦⲚⲞⲞⲨ and ⲦⲚⲚⲞⲞⲨ both occur; see 17.18, 21.

truth until its completion. And I will speak with you face to face, without *parable**. I will not conceal from you, from this hour onwards, anything of the things of the height and of the *place* of the *truth* [1]. *For* I have been given *authority* [□], through the Ineffable [2] and through the First *Mystery* of all the *mysteries*, that I should speak with you from the *beginning* until the *pleroma*, and from within outwards, and from without inwards. Hear now, so that I tell you all things.

It happened as I was sitting at a short distance from you upon the Mount of Olives, I was thinking of the *rank* [3] of the *service* for which I was sent, that it should be completed, and that my *garment* [4] was not yet sent to me by the First *Mystery*, which is the 24th *mystery* from within outwards. These (24 mysteries) are in the second *space* of the First *Mystery* in the *rank* of that *space*. It happened now when I knew that the *rank* of the *service* for which I had been sent was completed, and that that *mystery* had not yet sent me the *garment*, which I had left behind within it until the time was completed — as I thought of these things, I was sitting upon the Mount of Olives at a short distance from you.

7. It happened when the sun rose in the East now afterwards, through the First *Mystery* which had existed from the beginning, because of which | the All existed, from

---

*   cf. Joh. 16.25
□   cf. Mt. 28.18

---

[1]   (3) place of the truth; see note on 122.10.
[2]   (4) the Ineffable; see U 226.
[3]   (10) the rank; lit. the ranks.
[4]   (12) garment; see ATh 108-113; ParaShem 8 etc.; J 43; U 256.

ΠΤΗΡϤ ϢѠΠЄ ЄΤΒΗΗΤϤ · ΠΑЇ ЄΝΤΑЇЄΙ' ϪѠ ЄΒΟΛ
Ν̄ϨΗΤϤ ΤЄΝΟΥ · Μ̄ΠΙΟΥΟЄΙϢ ΑΝ ЄΜΠΑΤΟΥΣΤΑΥΡΟΥ
Μ̄ΜΟЇ ΑΛΛΑ ΤЄΝΟΥ · ΑΣϢѠΠЄ ϨΙΤ̄Ν ΤΚЄΛЄΥΣΙΣ Μ̄Π-
ΜΥΣΤΗΡΙΟΝ ЄΤΜ̄ΜΑΥ ΑϤΤ̄ΝΝΟΟΥ ΝΑЇ Ν̄ΠΑЄΝΔΥΜΑ
5 Ν̄ΟΥΟЄΙΝ ΠΑЇ ЄΝΤΑϤΤΑΑϤ ΝΑЇ ϪΙΝ ϢΟΡΠ̄ ΠΑЇ ЄΝΤ-
ΑЇΚΑΑϤ Ϩ̄Μ ⲫΑЄ Μ̄ΜΥΣΤΗΡΙΟΝ ЄΤЄ Ν̄ΤΟϤ ΠЄ ΠΜЄϨ-
ϪΟΥΤΑϤΤЄ Μ̄ΜΥΣΤΗΡΙΟΝ ϪΙΝ Ν̄ϨΟΥΝ ЄΒΟΛ ΝΑЇ ЄΤ-
ϢΟΟΠ Ϩ̄Ν Ν̄ΤΑϪΙΣ Ν̄ΤЄ ΠΜЄϨΣΝΑΥ Ν̄ΧѠΡΗΜΑ Ν̄ΤЄ
ΠΙϢΟΡΠ̄ Μ̄ΜΥΣΤΗΡΙΟΝ · ΠЄΝΔΥΜΑ ⟨Ν̄ΟΥ⟩ΟЇΝ ϬЄ [Ι̅ᵇ]
10 ЄΤΜ̄ΜΑΥ ΑΝΟΚ ΠЄΝΤΑЇΚΑΑϤ Ϩ̄Μ ⲫΑЄ Μ̄ΜΥΣΤΗΡΙΟΝ
ϢΑΝΤϤϪѠΚ ЄΒΟΛ Ν̄ϬΙ ΠЄΟΥΟЄΙϢ ЄΤΡΑΤΑΑϤ ϨΙѠѠΤ ·
ΑΥѠ Ν̄ΤΑΑΡΧЄΣΘΑΙ ЄΤΡΑϢΑϪЄ Μ̄Ν ΠΓЄΝΟΣ Ν̄ΤΜ̄Ν̄Τ-
ΡѠΜЄ ΑΥѠ Ν̄ΤΑϬΟΛΠΟΥ ΝΑΥ ЄΒΟΛ ΤΗΡΟΥ ϪΙΝ ΤΑΡ-
ΧΗ Ν̄ΤΑΛΗΘΙΑ ϨЄѠΣ ϢΑ ΠЄΣϪѠΚ ΑΥѠ Ν̄ΤΑϢΑϪЄ
15 ΝΜΜΑΥ ϪΙΝ ΠΣΑΝϨΟΥΝ Ν̄ΤЄ ΝΙΣΑΝϨΟΥΝ ϨЄѠΣ ϢΑ
ΠΣΑΝΒΟΛ Ν̄ΤЄ ΝΙΣΑΝΒΟΛ · ΑΥѠ ϪΙΝ ΠΣΑΝΒΟΛ Ν̄ΤЄ
ΝΙΣΑΝΒΟΛ · ϨЄѠΣ ϢΑ ΠΣΑΝϨΟΥΝ Ν̄ΤЄ ΝΙΣΑΝϨΟΥΝ ·
ΡΑϢЄ ϬЄ Ν̄⟨ΤЄΤΝ̄⟩ΤЄΛΗΛ · ΑΥѠ Ν̄ΤЄΤΝ̄Ρ̄ΟΥЄ-ΡΑϢЄ ·
ϪЄ Ν̄ΤѠΤ̄Ν ΝЄΝΤΑΥΤΑΑΣ ΝΗΤ̄Ν ЄΤΡΑϢΑϪЄ Ν̄ΜΜΗΤ̄Ν
20 Ν̄ϢΟΡΠ̄ ϪΙΝ ΤΑΡΧΗ Ν̄ΤΑΛΗΘΙΑ · ** ϨЄѠΣ ϢΑ ΠЄΣϪѠΚ · Ι̅Α̅
ЄΤΒЄ ΠΑЇ ΡѠ ΑЇΣЄΠΤΗΥΤ̄Ν ϪΙΝ Ν̄ϢΟΡΠ̄ ЄΒΟΛ ϨΙ-

---

1 MS ЄΝΤΑЇ; ЄΙ' inserted above.
2 ΣΤΑΥΡΟΥ written in the form Σ⳨ΟΥ.
4 MS originally Ν̄ϬΙ ΠΑЄΝΔΥΜΑ ; ϬΙ expunged; read Μ̄ΠΑЄΝΔΥΜΑ.
5 MS ϪΙΝ ϢΟΡΠ̄ ; better ϪΙΝ Ν̄ϢΟΡΠ̄.
9 MS ΟЇΝ in margin before ϬЄ ; read Ν̄ΟΥΟЇΝ.
18 MS Ν̄ΤЄΛΗΛ.

which I myself have come just now — not *prior to* my *crucifixion* [1], *but* now — it happened through the *command* of that *mystery*, it sent me my *garment* of light, which it had given to me from the beginning, which I had left behind in the last *mystery* which is the 24th *mystery* from within outwards, these (24 mysteries) which are in the ranks of the second *space* of the First *Mystery*. That *garment* ⟨of light⟩ now I had left behind in the last *mystery* until the time was completed that I should put it on me, and that I should *begin* to speak with the *race* of mankind, and reveal to them all things from the beginning of the *truth* until its completion, and speak to them from the innermost of the inner *to* the outermost of the outer, and from the outermost of the outer *to* the innermost of the inner. Rejoice and be glad *, and rejoice still more, that it is given to you that I should speak with you first from the *beginning* of the *truth* until its completion. Because of this indeed I have chosen you from the beginning | through the First *Mystery*. Rejoice now and

---

*   cf. Mt. 5.12

---

[1]   (2) not prior to my crucifixion; lit. when they had not yet crucified me.

ⲧⲟⲟⲧϥ̄ ⲙ̄ⲡϣⲟⲣⲡ̄ ⲙ̄ⲙⲩⲥⲧⲏⲣⲓⲟⲛ· ⲣⲁϣⲉ ϭⲉ ⲛ̄ⲧⲉⲧⲛ̄ⲧⲉ-
ⲗⲏⲗ ϫⲉ ⲛ̄ⲧⲉⲣⲓⲉⲓ ⲉⲓ̈ⲛⲏⲩ ⲉⲃⲟⲗ ⲉⲡⲕⲟⲥⲙⲟⲥ ϫⲓⲛ ⲛ̄-
ϣⲟⲣⲡ̄ ⲁⲓⲉⲓⲛⲉ ⲙ̄ⲙⲛ̄ⲧⲥⲛⲟⲟⲩⲥ ⲛ̄ϭⲟⲙ ⲛ̄ⲙⲙⲁⲓ̈ ⲕⲁⲧⲁ ⲑⲉ
ⲉⲛⲧⲁⲓ̈ϫⲟⲟⲥ ⲉⲣⲱⲧⲛ̄ ϫⲓⲛ ⲛ̄ϣⲟⲣⲡ̄· ⲉⲛⲧⲁⲓ̈ϫⲓⲧⲟⲩ ⲛ̄ⲧⲟ-
5 ⲟⲧⲟⲩ ⲙ̄ⲙⲛ̄ⲧⲥⲛⲟⲟⲩⲥ ⲛ̄ⲥⲱⲧⲏⲣ ⲛ̄ⲧⲉ ⲡⲉⲑⲏⲥⲁⲩⲣⲟⲥ
ⲛ̄ⲟⲩⲟⲉⲓⲛ ⲕⲁⲧⲁ ⲧⲕⲉⲗⲉⲩⲥⲓⲥ ⲙ̄ⲡϣⲟⲣⲡ̄ ⲙ̄ⲙⲩⲥⲧⲏⲣⲓⲟⲛ·
ⲛⲁⲓ̈ ϭⲉ ⲁⲓ̈ⲛⲟⲭⲟⲩ ⲉⲧⲕⲁⲗⲗⲁⲍⲏ ⲛ̄ⲧⲉⲧⲛ̄ⲙⲁⲁⲩ ϫⲓⲛ ⲉⲓ̈ⲛⲏⲩ
ⲉⲡⲕⲟⲥⲙⲟⲥ ⲉⲧⲉ ⲛⲁⲓ̈ ⲛⲉⲧⲛ̄ ⲡⲉⲧⲛ̄ⲥⲱⲙⲁ ⲙ̄ⲡⲟⲟⲩ· ⲛ̄-
ⲧⲁⲩϯ ⲅⲁⲣ ⲛ̄ⲛⲉⲓ̈ϭⲟⲙ ⲉⲣⲱⲧⲛ̄ ⲡⲁⲣⲁ ⲡⲕⲟⲥⲙⲟⲥ ⲧⲏⲣϥ̄· ϫⲉ
10 ⲛ̄ⲧⲱⲧⲛ̄ ⲛⲉⲧⲛⲁⲛⲟⲩϩⲙ̄ ⲙ̄ⲡⲕⲟⲥⲙⲟⲥ ⲧⲏⲣϥ̄ ⲁⲩⲱ ϫⲉⲕⲁⲥ
ⲉⲧⲉⲧⲛⲉϣϭⲙ̄ϭⲟⲙ ⲛ̄ⲧⲱⲟⲩⲛ ϩⲁ ⲧⲁⲡⲓⲗⲏ ⲛ̄ⲛⲁⲣⲭⲱⲛ ⲙ̄- ⲓ̅ⲁ̅ᵇ
ⲡⲕⲟⲥⲙⲟⲥ· ⲁⲩⲱ ⲙⲛ̄ ⲛ̄ϩⲓⲥⲉ ⲙ̄ⲡⲕⲟⲥⲙⲟⲥ ⲁⲩⲱ ⲙⲛ̄ ⲛⲉⲩ-
ⲕⲓⲛⲇⲩⲛⲟⲥ ⲁⲩⲱ ⲙⲛ̄ ⲛⲉⲩⲇⲓⲱⲅⲙⲟⲥ ⲧⲏⲣⲟⲩ ⲉⲧⲟⲩⲛⲁ-
ⲛ̄ⲧⲟⲩ ⲉϫⲱⲧⲛ̄ ⲛ̄ϭⲓ ⲛ̄ⲁⲣⲭⲱⲛ ⲙ̄ⲡϫⲓⲥⲉ· ⲁⲓ̈ϫⲟⲟⲥ ⲅⲁⲣ
15 ⲛⲏⲧⲛ̄ ⲛ̄ⲟⲩⲙⲏⲏϣⲉ ⲛ̄ⲥⲟⲡ ϫⲉ ⲧϭⲟⲙ ⲉⲧϣⲟⲟⲡ ⲛ̄ϩⲏⲧ-
ⲧⲏⲩⲧⲛ̄· ⲛ̄ⲧⲁⲓ̈ⲛ̄ⲧⲥ ⲉⲃⲟⲗ ϩⲙ̄ ⲡⲙⲛ̄ⲧⲥⲛⲟⲟⲩⲥ ⲛ̄ⲥⲱⲧⲏⲣ·
ⲛⲁⲓ̈ ⲉⲧϣⲟⲟⲡ ϩⲙ̄ ⲡⲉⲑⲏⲥⲁⲩⲣⲟⲥ ⲙ̄ⲡⲟⲩⲟⲉⲓⲛ· ⲉⲧⲃⲉ ⲡⲁⲓ̈
ⲣⲱ ⲁⲓ̈ϫⲟⲟⲥ ⲛⲏⲧⲛ̄ ϫⲓⲛ ⲛ̄ϣⲟⲣⲡ̄ ϫⲉ ⲛ̄ⲧⲱⲧⲛ̄ ⲛ̄ⲧⲉⲧⲛ̄
ϩⲉⲛⲉⲃⲟⲗ ⲁⲛ ϩⲙ̄ ⲡⲕⲟⲥⲙⲟⲥ· ⲡⲁⲓ̈ ϩⲱ ⲁⲛⲟⲕ ⲁⲛⲅ̄ ⲟⲩ-
20 ⲉⲃⲟⲗ ⲁⲛ ⲛ̄ϩⲏⲧϥ̄· ⲣⲱⲙⲉ ⲅⲁⲣ ⲛⲓⲙ ⲉⲧⲙ̄ ⲡⲕⲟⲥⲙⲟⲥ· ⲛ̄-
ⲧⲁⲩϫⲓ-ⲯⲩⲭⲏ ⲉⲃⲟⲗ ϩⲛ̄ ⲧϭⲟⲙ ⲛ̄ⲛⲁⲣⲭⲱⲛ ⲛ̄ⲛⲁⲓⲱⲛ·
ⲧϭⲟⲙ ⲇⲉ ⲉⲧϣⲟⲟⲡ ϩⲛ̄ⲧⲏⲩⲧⲛ̄ ⲟⲩⲉⲃⲟⲗ ⲙ̄ⲙⲟⲓ̈ ⲧⲉ· [ⲓ̅ⲃ̅]
ⲛ̄ⲧⲱⲧⲛ̄ ⲇⲉ ⲉⲣⲉ ⲧⲉⲧⲛ̄ⲯⲩⲭⲏ ⲏⲡ ⲉⲡϫⲓⲥⲉ· ⲛ̄ⲧⲁⲓ̈ⲛ̄-
ⲙⲛ̄ⲧⲥⲛⲟⲟⲩⲥ ⲛ̄ϭⲟⲙ ⲛ̄ⲧⲉ ⲓ̅ⲃ̅ ⲛ̄ⲥⲱⲧⲏⲣ ⲙ̄ⲡⲉⲑⲏⲥⲁⲩⲣⲟⲥ

---

11 MS ⲉⲧⲉⲧⲛⲉϣϭⲛ̄ϭⲟⲙ; ⲉ before ϣϭⲙ̄ϭⲟⲙ expunged.
19 MS ⲁⲛⲅ̄.
21 ⲧϭⲟⲙ written over erasure.
24 ϭⲟⲙ ⲛ̄ⲧⲉ ⲓ̅ⲃ̅ ⲛ̄ added in the same hand in margins.

be glad *, because when I entered the *world* I brought the twelve powers with me, *as* I told you from the beginning, which I took from the twelve *saviours* of the *Treasury* of Light, *according to* the *command* of the First *Mystery*. These now I cast into the wombs of your mothers when I came [1] into the *world*, and it is these which are in your *bodies* today. *For* these powers have been given to you *above* the whole *world*, for you are those who are able to save the whole *world*, so that you should be able to withstand the *threat* of the *archons* of the *world*, and the sufferings of the *world* and their *dangers*, and all their *persecutions* which the *archons* of the height will bring upon you. *For* I have said to you many times that the power which is within you I have brought from the twelve *saviours*, which are in the *Treasury* of Light. For this reason I have indeed said to you from the beginning that you are not from the *world*; I also am not from it □. *For* all men who are in the *world* have received *souls* from ⟨the power⟩ of the *archons* of the *aeons*. The power, *however*, which is in you, is from me but your *souls* belong to the height. I have brought twelve powers of the twelve *saviours* of the Treasury | of

---

*   cf. Mt. 5.12
□   cf. Joh. 15.19; 17.14, 16

---

[1]   (7) when I came; lit. since I came.

ⲘⲠⲞⲨⲞⲈⲒⲚ ⲈⲀⲒ̈ⲬⲒⲧⲞⲨ ⲈⲂⲞⲗ ⲌⲘ ⲠⲘⲈⲢⲞⲤ ⲠⲦⲀ6ⲞⲘ
ⲦⲈⲚⲦⲀⲨⲬⲒⲦⲤ Ⲛ̄ⲰⲞⲢⲠ · ⲀⲨⲰ Ⲛ̄ⲦⲈⲢⲒⲈⲒ̈ ⲈⲒ̈ⲚⲎⲨ ⲈⲒ-
ⲔⲞⲤⲘⲞⲤ ⲀⲒ̈ⲈⲒ ⲈⲦⲘⲎⲦⲈ Ⲛ̄ⲚⲀⲢⲬⲰⲚ Ⲛ̄ⲦⲈⲤⲫⲀⲒⲢⲀ · ⲀⲒ̈Ⲣ-ⲠⲒⲚⲈ
Ⲛ̄ⲅⲀⲂⲢⲒⲎⲗ ⲠⲀⲅⲅⲈⲗⲞⲤ Ⲛ̄ⲦⲈ ⲚⲀⲒⲰⲚ ⲀⲨⲰ Ⲙ̄ⲠⲞⲨⲤⲞⲨⲰⲚⲦ
5 Ⲛ̄6Ⲓ Ⲛ̄ⲀⲢⲬⲰⲚ Ⲛ̄ⲚⲀⲒⲰⲚ · ⲀⲗⲗⲀ ⲚⲈⲨⲘⲈⲈⲨⲈ ⲠⲈ ⲬⲈ ⲀⲚⲞⲔ
ⲠⲈ ⲅⲀⲂⲢⲒⲎⲗ ⲠⲀⲅⲅⲈⲗⲞⲤ · ⲀⲤⲰⲰⲠⲈ 6Ⲉ Ⲛ̄ⲦⲈⲢⲒⲈⲒ ⲈⲦⲘⲎⲦⲈ
Ⲛ̄ⲚⲀⲢⲬⲰⲚ Ⲛ̄ⲚⲀⲒⲰⲚ · ⲀⲒ̈6ⲰⲰⲦ ⲈⲠⲈⲤⲎⲦ ⲈⲠⲔⲞⲤⲘⲞⲤ
Ⲛ̄ⲦⲈ ⲦⲘⲚ̄ⲦⲢⲰⲘⲈ · ⲌⲒⲦⲚ̄ ⲦⲔⲈⲗⲈⲨⲤⲒⲤ Ⲙ̄ⲠⲰⲞⲢⲠ̄ Ⲙ̄ⲘⲨⲤⲦⲎ-
ⲢⲒⲞⲚ · ⲀⲒ̈6ⲒⲚⲈ Ⲛ̄ⲈⲗⲒⲤⲀⲂⲈⲦ ⲦⲘⲀⲀⲨ Ⲛ̄Ⲓ̈ⲰⲌⲀⲚⲚⲎⲤ ⲠⲂⲀⲠ- [Ⲓ̄Ⲃ ᵇ]
10 ⲦⲒⲤⲦⲎⲤ ⲌⲀⲐⲎ ⲈⲘⲠⲀⲦ̄Ⲥ̄Ⲱ̄ Ⲙ̄ⲘⲞ4 ⲀⲒ̈ⲤⲒⲦⲈ Ⲛ̄ⲞⲨ6ⲞⲘ
ⲈⲌⲞⲨⲚ ⲈⲢⲞⲤ ⲦⲀⲒ̈ ⲈⲚⲦⲀⲒ̈ⲬⲒⲦⲤ Ⲛ̄ⲦⲞⲞⲦ4 Ⲙ̄ⲠⲔⲞⲨⲒ̈ Ⲛ̄ⲒⲀⲰ
ⲠⲀⲅⲀⲐⲞⲤ ⲠⲈⲦⲌ̄Ⲛ ⲦⲘⲈⲤⲞⲤ ⲬⲈ Ⲉ4ⲈⲰ6Ⲙ̄6ⲞⲘ Ⲛ̄ⲦⲀⲰⲈ-
ⲞⲈⲒⲰ ⲌⲀⲦⲚ̄ⲈⲌⲎ · ⲀⲨⲰ Ⲛ̄4ⲤⲞⲂⲦⲈ Ⲛ̄ⲦⲀⲌⲒⲎ · ⲀⲨⲰ Ⲛ̄4ⲂⲀⲠ-
ⲦⲒⲌⲈ ⲌⲚ ⲞⲨⲘⲞⲞⲨ Ⲛ̄ⲔⲀⲚⲞⲂⲈ ⲈⲂⲞⲗ · Ⲧ6ⲞⲘ 6Ⲉ ⲈⲦⲘ̄ⲘⲀⲨ
15 Ⲛ̄ⲦⲞⲤ ⲠⲈⲦⲰⲞⲞⲠ ⲌⲚ ⲠⲤⲰⲘⲀ Ⲛ̄Ⲓ̈ⲰⲌⲀⲚⲚⲎⲤ · ⲀⲨⲰ ⲞⲚ
ⲈⲠⲘⲀ Ⲛ̄ⲦⲈⲮⲨⲬⲎ Ⲛ̄ⲚⲀⲢⲬⲰⲚ Ⲉ4ⲎⲠ ⲈⲬⲒⲦⲤ · ⲀⲒ̈6ⲒⲚⲈ
Ⲛ̄ⲦⲈⲮⲨⲬⲎ Ⲛ̄ⲌⲎⲗⲒⲀⲤ ⲠⲈⲠⲢⲞⲫⲎⲦⲎⲤ ⲌⲚ̄ ⲚⲀⲒⲰⲚ Ⲛ̄ⲦⲈ-
ⲤⲫⲀⲒⲢⲀ ⲀⲨⲰ ⲀⲒ̈ⲬⲒⲦ4 ⲈⲌⲞⲨⲚ ⲀⲨⲰ ⲀⲒ̈ⲬⲒ-ⲦⲈ4Ⲯ̄ⲨⲬⲎ ⲞⲚ
ⲀⲒ̈Ⲛ̄ⲦⲤ Ⲛ̄ⲦⲠⲀⲢⲐⲈⲚⲞⲤ Ⲙ̄ⲠⲞⲨⲞⲈⲒⲚ ⲀⲨⲰ ⲀⲤⲦⲀⲀⲤ Ⲛ̄ⲚⲈⲤ-
20 ⲠⲀⲢⲀⲗⲎⲘⲠⲦⲰⲢ ⲀⲨⲚ̄ⲦⲤ ⲈⲦⲈⲤⲫⲀⲒⲢⲀ Ⲛ̄ⲚⲀⲢⲬⲰⲚ ⲀⲨⲰ Ⲓ̄Ⲃ̄
ⲀⲨⲚⲞ̄Ⲭ̄Ⲥ̄ ⲈⲌⲞⲨⲚ ⲈⲦⲔⲀⲗⲀⲌⲎ Ⲛ̄ⲈⲗⲒⲤⲀⲂⲈⲦ · Ⲧ6ⲞⲘ ⲆⲈ
Ⲙ̄ⲠⲔⲞⲨⲒ̈ Ⲛ̄ⲒⲀⲰ ⲠⲀⲦⲘⲈⲤⲞⲤ ⲀⲨⲰ ⲦⲈ4Ⲯ̄ⲨⲬⲎ Ⲛ̄ⲌⲎⲗⲒⲀⲤ ⲠⲈ-

---

2 MS ⲦⲈⲚⲦⲀⲨⲬⲒⲦⲤ; read ⲦⲈⲚⲦⲀⲒ̈ⲬⲒⲦⲤ.
15 MS ⲠⲈⲦⲰⲞⲞⲠ; read ⲦⲈⲦⲰⲞⲞⲠ. MS ⲌⲚ̄; read ⲌⲘ̄.
20 Ⲃ̄ in upper left-hand margin at beginning of quire.

the Light, taking them from the *part* of my power which I received at first. And when I entered the *world* I came to the midst of the *archons* of the *sphere*, and I took the likeness of Gabriel, the *Angel* of the *aeons*, and the *archons* of the *aeons* did not recognise me *[1]. *But* they thought that I was the *Angel* Gabriel. Now it happened that when I came into the midst of the *archons* of the *aeons*, I looked down at the *world* of mankind, at the *command* of the First *Mystery*. I found Elisabeth, the mother of John the *Baptist*◻, before she had conceived him and I cast into her a power which I had received from the Little Jao [2], the *Good*, who is in the *Midst*, so that he should be able to preach before me, and prepare my way and *baptise* with water of forgiveness°. Now that power was in the *body* of John. And again, in place of the *soul* of the *archons* which he was due to receive, I found the *soul* of the *prophet* Elias [3] in the *aeons* of the *sphere*; and I took it in and I took his *soul* again; I brought it to the *Virgin* of the Light [4], and she gave it to her *paralemptors* [5]. They brought it to the *sphere* of the *archons*, and they cast it into the womb of Elisabeth. *But* the power of the Little Jao, he of the *Midst*, and the *soul* of the |

---

* cf. 1 Cor. 2.8
◻ cf. Lk. 1
° cf. Mt. 3.11; 11.10; Mk. 1.2-4; Lk. 7.27

---

[1] (4) did not recognise me; cf. *Ascension of Isaiah* XI.24-28; (see also 21.5ff.).
[2] (11) Jao, the Little; see Odeberg (Bibl. 37); on the Midst, see Iren. I.5.3; 6.4; 7.1; Hippol. VI.32.8.
[3] (17) Elias (Elijah); see Hippol. VIII.10.2.
[4] (19) Virgin of the Light; see J 110.
[5] (20) paralemptor, -es; lit. receiver; see ApJn 66; GEgypt III 64, 66; J 101; U 241.

ⲡⲣⲟⲫⲏⲧⲏⲥ ⲛ̄ⲧⲟⲟⲩ ⲛⲉⲧⲙⲏⲣ ϩⲙ̄ ⲡⲥⲱⲙⲁ ⲛ̄ⲓ̈ⲱϩⲁⲛⲛⲏⲥ
ⲡⲃⲁⲡⲧⲓⲥⲧⲏⲥ · ⲉⲧⲃⲉ ⲡⲁⲓ̈ ϭⲉ ⲁⲧⲉⲧⲛ̄ⲣ̄-ϩⲏⲧⲥⲛⲁⲩ ⲙ̄ⲡⲓⲟⲩ-
ⲟⲉⲓϣ ⲛ̄ⲧⲉⲣⲓⲭⲟⲟⲥ ⲛⲏⲧⲛ̄ ϫⲉ ⲁϥϫⲟⲟⲥ ⲛ̄ϭⲓ ⲓ̈ⲱϩⲁⲛⲛⲏⲥ
ϫⲉ ⲁⲛⲟⲕ ⲁⲛ ⲡⲉ ⲡⲉⲭ̄ⲥ̄ · ⲁⲩⲱ ⲁⲧⲉⲧⲛ̄ϫⲟⲟⲥ ⲛⲁⲓ̈ ϫⲉ
5 ⲉϥⲥⲏϩ ϩⲛ̄ ⲧⲉⲅⲣⲁⲫⲏ ϫⲉ ⲉⲣϣⲁⲛ ⲡⲉⲭ̄ⲥ̄ ⲉⲓ̇ ⲉϥⲛⲏⲩ · ϥⲛⲏⲩ
ⲛ̄ϭⲓ ϩⲏⲗⲓⲁⲥ ϩⲁⲧⲉϥϩⲏ · ⲁⲩⲱ ⲛϥ̄ⲥⲟⲃⲧⲉ ⲛ̄ⲧⲉϥϩⲓⲏ · ⲁⲛⲟⲕ
ⲇⲉ ⲛ̄ⲧⲉⲣⲉⲧⲉⲛ̄ϫⲉ-ⲛⲁⲓ̈ ⲛⲁⲓ̈ ⲁⲓ̈ⲭⲟⲟⲥ ⲛⲏⲧⲛ̄ ϫⲉ ⲁϥⲉⲓ
ⲙⲉⲛ ⲛ̄ϭⲓ ϩⲏⲗⲓⲁⲥ · ⲁⲩⲱ ⲁϥⲥⲟⲃⲧⲉ ⲛ̄ϩⲱⲃ ⲛⲓⲙ ⲕⲁⲧⲁ
ⲑⲉ ⲉⲧⲥⲏϩ · ⲁⲩⲱ ⲁⲩⲉⲓⲣⲉ ⲛⲁϥ ⲛ̄ⲑⲉ ⲉⲧⲉϩⲛⲁⲩ · ⲁⲩⲱ
10 ⲛ̄ⲧⲉⲣⲉⲓⲉⲓⲙⲉ ϫⲉ ⲙ̄ⲡⲉⲧⲛ̄ⲛⲟⲓ̈ ϫⲉ ⲛ̄ⲧⲁⲓ̈ⲭⲟⲟⲥ ⲛⲏⲧⲛ̄
ⲉⲧⲃⲉ ⲧⲉⲯⲩⲭⲏ ⲛ̄ϩⲏⲗⲓⲁⲥ ⲉⲧⲙⲏⲣ ϩⲛ̄ ⲓ̈ⲱϩⲁⲛⲛⲏⲥ ⲡⲃⲁⲡ- ⲓ̅ⲅ̅ᵇ
ⲧⲓⲥⲧⲏⲥ · ⲁⲓ̈ⲟⲩⲱⲱ̄ⲃ ⲛⲏⲧⲛ̄ ϩⲛ̄ ⲡϣⲁϫⲉ ϩⲛ̄ ⲟⲩⲡⲁⲣⲣⲏⲥⲓⲁ ⲛ̄ϩⲟ ⲙⲛ̄ ϩⲟ ϫⲉ ⲉϣϫⲉ ⲉϩⲛⲏⲧⲛ̄ ⲉϫⲓ-ⲓ̈ⲱϩⲁⲛⲛⲏⲥ
ⲡⲃⲁⲡⲧⲓⲥⲧⲏⲥ · ⲛ̄ⲧⲟϥ ⲡⲉ ϩⲏⲗⲓⲁⲥ ⲡⲉⲛⲧⲁⲓ̈ⲭⲟⲟϥ ϫⲉ ϥⲛⲏⲩ ·
15 ⲍ̄ ⲁϥⲟⲩⲱϩ ⲟⲛ ⲉⲧⲟⲟⲧϥ̄ ⲛ̄ϭⲓ ⲓ̅ⲥ̅ ϩⲙ̄ ⲡϣⲁϫⲉ ⲡⲉϫⲁϥ ϫⲉ ⲁⲥϣⲱⲡⲉ ϭⲉ ⲙⲛ̄ⲛⲥⲁ ⲛⲁⲓ̈ ϩⲓⲧⲛ̄ ⲧⲕⲉⲗⲉⲩⲥⲓⲥ
ⲙ̄ⲡϣⲟⲣⲡ̄ ⲙ̄ⲙⲩⲥⲧⲏⲣⲓⲟⲛ · ⲁⲓ̈ϭⲱϣ̄ⲧ ⲟⲛ ⲉⲡⲉⲥⲏⲧ ⲉϫⲙ̄
ⲡⲕⲟⲥⲙⲟⲥ ⲛ̄ⲧⲙⲛ̄ⲧⲣⲱⲙⲉ · ⲁⲓ̈ϭⲓⲛⲉ ⲙ̄ⲙⲁⲣⲓⲁ ⲧⲁⲓ̈ ⲉϣⲁⲩⲙⲟⲩⲧⲉ ⲉⲣⲟⲥ ϫⲉ ⲧⲁⲙⲁⲁⲩ ⲕⲁⲧⲁ ⲡⲥⲱⲙⲁ ⲛ̄ⲑⲩⲗⲏ · ⲁⲓ̈-
20 ϣⲁϫⲉ ⲟⲛ ⲛ̄ⲙⲙⲁⲥ ⲕⲁⲧⲁ ⲡⲧⲩⲡⲟⲥ ⲛ̄ⲅⲁⲃⲣⲓⲏⲗ · ⲁⲩⲱ
ⲛ̄ⲧⲉⲣⲉⲥⲕⲟⲧⲥ̄ ⲉⲡϫⲓⲥⲉ ⲉⲣⲟⲓ̈ ⲁⲓ̈ⲛⲟⲩϫⲉ ⲉϩⲟⲩⲛ ⲉⲣⲟⲥ
ⲛ̄ⲧϣⲟⲣⲡ̄ ⲛ̄ϭⲟⲙ ⲧⲉⲛⲧⲁⲓ̈ϫⲓⲧⲥ̄ ⲛ̄ⲧⲟⲟⲧⲥ̄ ⲛ̄ⲧⲃⲁⲣⲃⲏⲗⲱ
ⲉⲧⲉ** ⲛ̄ⲧⲟϥ ⲡⲉ ⲡⲥⲱⲙⲁ ⲉⲛⲧⲁⲓ̈ⲫⲟⲣⲓ ⲙ̄ⲙⲟϥ ϩⲙ̄ ⲡϫⲓⲥⲉ · [ⲓ̅ⲇ̅]
ⲁⲩⲱ ⲉⲡⲙⲁ ⲛ̄ⲧⲉⲯⲩⲭⲏ · ⲁⲓ̈ⲛⲟⲩϫⲉ ⲉϩⲟⲩⲛ ⲉⲣⲟⲥ ⲛ̄ⲧϭⲟⲙ

---

8   ⲛ of ⲙⲉⲛ inserted above.
12   MS ϩⲛ̄ ⲡϣⲁϫⲉ; read ϩⲙ̄ ⲡϣⲁϫⲉ.

prophet Elias were bound in the *body* of John the *Baptist*. You doubted now at the time when I spoke to you *because* John said : 'I am not the Christ' * and you said to me : 'It is written in the *scripture* : when the Christ shall come, there will come Elias before him and he will prepare his way' □. *But* when you said this to me, I said to you : 'Elias has *indeed* come and he has prepared all things, *as* it is written : And they did to him as they pleased' °. And when I knew that you did not *understand* what I said to you concerning the *soul* of Elias, which was bound in John the *Baptist*, I answered you *openly* in speech, face to face, saying : 'If it pleases you to accept John the *Baptist*, he is Elias of whom I have said that he will come' ▵".

8. Jesus continued again speaking and said : "Now it happened after this, through the *command* of the First *Mystery*, I looked down again upon the *world* of mankind, I found Mary, who is called my mother *according to* the *material body*. I spoke to her in the *type* of Gabriel ♦, and when she turned to the height towards me, I cast into her the first power which I had received from the Barbelo [1], which is the *body* which I *wore* in the height. And in place of the *soul*, I cast into her the power | which I received

---

* cf. Joh. 1.20
□ cf. Mt. 17.10
° cf. Mt. 17.11, 12
▵ cf. Mt. 11.14
♦ cf. Lk. 2

---

[1] (22) Barbelo; see Iren. I.29.1; Epiph. 25.2 ff.; 26.1.9; ApJn 27-32; GEgypt III 42; IV 52 etc.; J 133.

ΤΕΝΤΑΪΧΙΤС Ν̄ΤΟΟΤϤ Μ̄ΠΝΟϬ Ν̄СΑΒΑШΘ ΠΑΓΑΘΟС·
ΠΑΪ ΕΤϢΟΟΠ Ζ̄Μ ΠΤΟΠΟС Ν̄ΤΟΥΝΑΜ· ΑΥШ ΤΜΝ̄Τ-
СΝΟΟΥС Ν̄ϬΟΜ Ν̄ΤΕ ΠΜΝ̄ΤСΝΟΟΥС Ν̄СШΤΗΡ Μ̄ΠΕΘΗ-
САΥΡΟС Μ̄ΠΟΥΟΕΙΝ· ΝΕΝΤΑΪΧΙΤΟΥ Ν̄ΤΟΟΤΟΥ Μ̄Π-
5 ΜΝ̄ΤСΝΟΟΥС Ν̄ΔΙΑΚΟΝΟС ΕΤΖ̄Ν ΤΜΕСΟС· ΑΪΝΟΧΟΥ
ΕΤΕСϤΕΡΑ Ν̄Ν̄ΑΡΧШΝ· ΑΥШ Ν̄ΔΕΚΑΝΟС Ν̄Ν̄ΑΡΧШΝ ΜΝ̄
ΝΕΥΛΙΤΟΥΡΓΟС· ΝΕΥΜΕΕΥΕ ΠΕ ΧΕ ΖΕΝΨΥΧΟΟΥ⟨Ε⟩
ΝΕ Ν̄ΤΕ Ν̄ΑΡΧШΝ ΑΥШ ΑΥΝ̄ΤΟΥ Ν̄ϬΙ Ν̄ΛΙΤΟΥΡΓΟС·
ΑΪΜΟΡΟΥ Ζ̄Μ ΠСШΜΑ Ν̄ΤΕΤΝ̄ΜΑΛΥ· ΑΥШ Ν̄ΤΕΡΕ ΠΕ-
10 ΤΝΟΥΟΕΙϢ ΧШΚ ΕΒΟΛ ΑΥΧΠΕ-ΤΗΥΤΝ̄ Ζ̄Μ ΠΚΟС- [ΙΛ̄ᵇ]
ΜΟС ΕΜΝ̄-ΨΥΧΗ Ν̄ΤΕ Ν̄ΑΡΧШΝ Ζ̄ΝΤΗΥΤΝ̄· ΑΥШ ΑΤΕ-
ΤΝ̄ΧΙ Μ̄ΠΕΤΝ̄ΜΕΡΟС ΕΒΟΛ Ζ̄Ν ΤϬΟΜ ΤΑΪ ΕΝΤΑϤϤΝΙϤΕ
Μ̄ΜΟС ΕΖΟΥΝ ΕΠΚΕΡΑСΜΟС Ν̄ϬΙ ϤΑΕ Μ̄ΠΑΡΑСΤΑΤΗС
ΤΑΪ ΕΤΜΟΧϬ Μ̄Ν Ν̄ΑΖΟΡΑΤΟС ΤΗΡΟΥ ΜΝ̄ Ν̄ΑΡΧШΝ
15 ΤΗΡΟΥ· ΜΝ̄ Ν̄ΑΙШΝ ΤΗΡΟΥ ΖΑΠΑΧ ΖΑΠΛШС ΕСΜΟΧϬ
Ζ̄Μ ΠΚΟСΜΟС Ν̄ΤΕ ΠΤΑΚΟ ΕΤΕ ΠΚΕΡΑСΜΟС ΠΕ ΤΑΪ
ΕΝΤΑΪΝ̄ΤС ΕΒΟΛ Μ̄ΜΟΪ ΧΙΝ Ν̄ϢΟΡΠ̄ ΑΪΝΟΧС ΕΖΟΥΝ
ΕΠϢΟΡΠ̄ Ν̄ΤШϢ ΑΥШ Α ΠϢΟΡΠ̄ Ν̄ΤШϢ ΑϤΝΟΥΧΕ
Ν̄ΟΥΜΕΡΟС Ν̄ΖΗΤС ΕΖΟΥΝ ΕΠΝΟϬ Ν̄ΟΥΟΕΙΝ· ΑΥШ
20 ΠΝΟϬ Ν̄ΟΥΟΕΙΝ ΑϤΝΟΥΧΕ Ν̄ΟΥΜΕΡΟС Ζ̄Μ ΠΕΝΤΑϤ-
ΧΙΤϤ ΕΖΟΥΝ ΕΠϮΟΥ Μ̄ΠΑΡΑСΤΑΤΗС· ΑΥШ ϤΑΕ Μ̄ΠΑ-
ΡΑСΤΑΤΗС ΑϤΧΙ Ν̄ΟΥΜΕΡΟС Ζ̄Μ ΠΕΝΤΑϤΧΙΤϤ· ΑϤ-
ΝΟΧϤ ΕΖΟΥΝ ΕΠΚΕΡΑСΜΟС· ΑΥШ ΑϤϢШΠΕ Ζ̄Ν ΝΕΤ- ΙС̄

---

5 MS ΑΪΝΟΥΧΟΥ; Υ expunged and crossed out.
7 MS ΖΕΝΨΥΧΟΟΥ.
9 MS ΑΪΜΟΡΟΥ; read ΑΥΜΟΡΟΥ.
15 Μ̄Ν Ν̄ΑΙШΝ ΤΗΡΟΥ written in lower margin; omission in MS indicated
   by signs ·/. and ϯ.

from the great Sabaoth, the *Good*[1], who is in the *place*
of the right. And the twelve powers of the twelve *saviours*
of the *Treasury* of the Light, which I received from the twelve
servers which are in the *Midst*, I cast into the *sphere* of the
archons. And the *decans* of the *archons* and their *ministers*
thought that they were *souls* of the *archons*, and the *ministers*
brought them, they bound them in the *bodies* of your
mothers. And when your times were completed, they bore
you into the *world* without there being *souls* of the *archons*
in you. And you have received your *parts* from the power
which the last *helper* (*parastates*) had breathed into the
mixture, this (power) which is mixed with all the *invisible*
ones and all the *archons* and all the *aeons*. *In a word*, it is
mixed with the *world* of destruction, namely the *mixture*.
This (power) which, from the beginning, I brought out of
myself, I cast into the first ordinance. And the first ordinance
cast a *part* of it into the great light. And the great light cast
a *part* of what it received into the five *helpers* (*parastatai*),
and the last *helper* (*parastates*) took a *part* from what it
received and cast it into the *mixture*. And (the part) has
come to be | in all who are in the *mixture*, *as* I have just
said to you."

---

[1]   (1) Sabaoth, the Good; see Iren. I.30.5; Origen c. *Cels.* VI.31; ApJn 40-43;
      GEgypt III 58; HypArch 143; OnOrgWld 151; J 119.

ϢΟΟΠ ΤΗΡΟΥ 2Μ ΠΚΕΡΑϹΜΟϹ ΚΑΤΑ ΘΕ ΕΝΤΑΪΟΥϢ
ΕΪΧϢ ΜΜΟϹ ΝΗΤΝ :

ϫ ΝΑΪ ϬΕ ΝΕΡΕ ΙϹ ΧϢ ΜΜΟΟΥ ΠΕ ΝΝΕϤΜΑΘΗΤΗϹ
2ΙΧΜ ΠΤΟΟΥ ΝΝΧΟΕΙΤ · ΑϤΟΥϢ2 ϬΕ ΟΝ ΕΤΟΟΤϤ ΝϬΙ
5 ΙϹ 2Μ ΠϢΑΧΕ ΜΝ ΝΕϤΜΑΘΗΤΗϹ ΧΕ ΡΑϢΕ ΑΥϢ ΝΤΕ-
ΤΝΤΕΛΗΛ ΑΥϢ ΝΤΕΤΝΟΥΕ2-ΡΑϢΕ ΕΧΜ ΠΕΤΝΡΑϢΕ
ΧΕ ΑΥΧϢΚ ΕΒΟΛ ΝϬΙ ΝΕΥΟΕΙϢ ΕΤΡΑϮ 2ΙϢϢΤ ΜΠΑ-
ΕΝΔΥΜΑ ΠΑΪ ΕΝΕϤϹΒΤϢΤ ΝΑΪ ΧΙΝ ΝϢΟΡΠ · ΠΑΪ ΕΝ-
ΤΑΪΚΑΛϤ 2Μ ΦΑΕ ΜΜΥϹΤΗΡΙΟΝ ϢΑ ΠΕΟΥΟΕΙϢ ΜΠΕϤ-
10 ΧϢΚ ΕΒΟΛ · ΠΕΥΟΕΙϢ ΔΕ ΜΠΕϤΧϢΚ ΕΒΟΛ ΠΕ ΠΕ-
ΟΥΟΕΙϢ ΕΤΟΥΝΑΚΕΛΕΥΕ 2ΙΤΜ ΠϢΟΡΠ ΜΜΥϹΤΗ-
ΡΙΟΝ ΕΤΡΑϢΑΧΕ ΝΜΜΗΤΝ ΧΙΝ ΤΑΡΧΗ ΝΤΑΛΗΘΙΑ ϢΑ
ΠΕϹΧϢΚ · ΑΥϢ ΧΙΝ ΠϹΑΝ2ΟΥΝ * ΝΤΕ ΝΙϹΑΝ2ΟΥΝ · ΙΕ^b
(2ΕϢϹ ϢΑ ΠϹΑΝΒΟΛ ΝΤΕ ΝΙϹΑΝΒΟΛ) ΕΒΟΛ ΧΕ ΕΡΕ
15 ΠΚΟϹΜΟϹ ΝΑΝΟΥ2Μ 2ΙΤΝ-ΤΗΥΤΝ · ΡΑϢΕ ϬΕ ΝΤΕΤΝ-
ΤΕΛΗΛ ΧΕ ΝΤΕΤΝ 2ΕΝΜΑΚΑΡΙΟϹ ΠΑΡΑ ΝΡϢΜΕ ΤΗΡΟΥ
ΕΤ2ΙΧΜ ΠΚΑ2 · ΧΕ ΝΤϢΤΝ ΝΕΤΝΑΝΟΥ2Μ ΜΠΚΟϹΜΟϹ
ΤΗΡϤ :

ϫ ΑϹϢϢΠΕ ϬΕ ΝΤΕΡΕ ΙϹ ΟΥϢ ΕϤΧϢ ΝΝΕΪϢΑΧΕ
20 ΕΝΕϤΜΑΘΗΤΗϹ · ΑϤΟΥϢ2 ΟΝ ΕΤΟΟΤϤ 2Μ ΠϢΑΧΕ ΠΕ-
ΧΑϤ ΝΑΥ · ΧΕ ΕΙϹ2ΗΗΤΕ ϬΕ ΑΪΦΟΡΙ ΜΠΑΕΝΔΥΜΑ ·
ΑΥϢ ΑΥϮ ΝΑΪ ΝΕ2ΟΥϹΙΑ ΝΙΜ 2ΙΤΜ ΠϢΟΡΠ ΜΜΥϹ-
ΤΗΡΙΟΝ · ΕΤΙ ΚΕΚΟΥΪ ΝΟΥΟΕΙϢ ΠΕ ΑΥϢ ϮΝΑΧϢ

---

11 MS ΚΕΥΛΕΥΕ; Υ expunged and crossed out.
14 2ΕϢϹ .... ΝΙϹΑΝΒΟΛ omitted in MS.

Now Jesus was saying these things to his *disciples* upon the Mount of Olives. Jesus now continued again in the discourse with his *disciples*: "Rejoice and be glad*, and add joy to your joy, because the times are completed that I should put on my *garment* which was prepared for me from the beginning, which I left behind in the last *mystery* until the time of its completion. *But* the time of its completion is the time when I am *commanded* by the First *Mystery* to speak to you from the *beginning* of the *truth* to its fulfilment, and from the innermost of the inner ⟨to the outermost of the outer⟩, because the *world* will be saved by you. Rejoice and be glad □ because you are *blessed beyond* all men upon earth, because it is you who will save the whole *world*."

9. It happened now when Jesus finished saying these words to his *disciples*, he continued again with the discourse, and he said to them: "Behold, I have *put on* my *garment* and all *authority* is given to me ° through the First Mystery. *Yet* a little time, and I will tell you | the *mystery* of the

---

* cf. Mt. 5.12

□ cf. Mt. 5.12

° cf. Mt. 28.18

ЄРШΤΝ ΜΠΜΥϹΤΗΡΙΟΝ ΜΠΤΗΡϤ· ΜΝ ΠЄΠΛΗΡШΜΑ Μ-
ΠΤΗΡϤ· ΑΥШ ϮΝΑϨЄΠ-ΛΑΑΥ ЄΡШΤΝ ΑΝ ΧΙΝ ΜΠЄΪ-
ΝΑΥ· ΑΛΛΑ ϨΝ ΟΥ·ΧШΚ ϮΝΑΧЄΚ-ΤΗΥΤΝ ЄΒΟΛ ϨΜ
ΠΛΗΡШΜΑ ΝΙΜ· ΑΥШ ϨΝ ΧШΚ ΝΙΜ ΑΥШ ϨΜ ΜΥϹΤΗ-
5 ΡΙΟΝ ΝΙΜ ЄΤЄ ΝΤΟΟΥ ΝЄ ΠΧШΚ ΝΝΧШΚ ΤΗΡΟΥ·
ΑΥШ ΠЄΠΛΗΡШΜΑ ΝΝЄΠΛΗΡШΜΑ ΤΗΡΟΥ· ΑΥШ ΤЄ- [ΙϚ̄|
ΓΝШϹΙϹ ΝΝЄΓΝШϹΙϹ ΤΗΡΟΥ· ΝΑΪ ЄΤШΟΟΠ ϨΜ ΠΑЄΝ-
ΑΥΜΑ· ϮΝΑΧШ ЄΡШΤΝ ΝΜΜΥϹΤΗΡΙΟΝ ΤΗΡΟΥ ΧΙΝ
ΠϹΑΝΒΟΛ ΝΤЄ ΝΙϹΑΝΒΟΛ ШΑ ΠϹΑΝϨΟΥΝ ΝΤЄ ΝΙϹΑΝ-
10 ϨΟΥΝ :

ϫ ΠΛΗΝ ϹШΤΜ ΤΑΧШ ЄΡШΤΝ ΝϨШΒ ΝΙΜ ЄΝΤΑΥ-
ШШΠЄ ΜΜΟΪ : ΑϹШШΠЄ ϬЄ ΝΤЄΡЄ ΠΡΗ ЄΙ' ЄϨΡΑΪ ϨΝ
ΜΜΑΝШΑ ΑϹЄΙ' ЄΠЄϹΗΤ' ΝϬΙ ΟΥΝΟϬ ΝΔΥΝΑΜΙϹ ΝΟΥ-
ΟЄΙΝ ЄΡЄ ΠΑЄΝΑΥΜΑ ϨΡΑΪ ΝϨΗΤϹ· ΠΑΪ ЄΝΤΑΪΚΑΑϤ ϨΜ
15 ΠΜЄϨΧΟΥΤΑϤΤЄ ΜΜΥϹΤΗΡΙΟΝ ΚΑΤΑ ΘЄ ЄΝΤΑΪΟΥШ
ЄΪΧШ ΜΜΟϹ ΝΗΤΝ ΤЄΝΟΥ· ΑΥШ ΑΪϬΙΝЄ ΝΟΥΜΥϹ-
ΤΗΡΙΟΝ ϨΜ ΠΑЄΝΑΥΜΑ· ЄϤϹΗϨ ϨΝ ϮΗΠ ϹϨΑΪ ΝΤЄ
ΝΑΠΧΙϹЄ· ΖΑΜΑΖΑ ΜΑШΖ ΖΑΡΑΧΑ ΜΑШ ΖΑΪ· ЄΤЄ ΠΑΪ
ΠЄ ΠЄϤΒШΛ· ΧЄ ΠΜΥϹΤΗΡΙΟΝ ЄΤΝΒΟΛ ϨΜ ΠΚΟϹΜΟϹ·
20 ΠΑΪ ЄΝΤΑ ΠΤΗΡϤ ШШΠЄ ЄΤΒΗΗΤϤ· ΠΑΪ ΠЄ ΠЄΙ [ΙϚ̄ᵇ|
ЄΒΟΛ ΤΗΡϤ ΜΝ ΠШΛ' ЄϨΡΑΪ ΤΗΡϤ ΠΑΪ ЄΝΤΑϤϹШΡ ЄΒΟΛ
ΝΝϹШΡ ЄΒΟΛ ΤΗΡΟΥ ΜΝ ΝЄΤΝϨΗΤΟΥ ΤΗΡΟΥ· ΑΥШ
ΠΑΪ ЄΝΤΑ ΜΥϹΤΗΡΙΟΝ ΝΙΜ ШШΠЄ ЄΤΒΗΗΤϤ ΑΥШ ΜΝ
ΝЄΥΤΟΠΟϹ ΤΗΡΟΥ· ΑΜΟΥ ЄϨΡΑΪ ШΑΡΟΝ ΧЄ ΑΝΟΝ
25 ΝЄΚШΒΗΡ-ΜЄΛΟϹ· ΑΝΟΝ ΔЄ ΤΗΡΝ ΝΜΜΑΚ ϨШШΚ ΟΝ·

---

3 MS originally ΟΥΧШΜ; Μ crossed out, and Κ written above.
20 ΠЄΙ inserted above in the same hand.

All and the *pleroma* of the All, and I will not hide anything
from you from this hour, *but* in completion I will complete
you in every *pleroma* and in every completion and in every
mystery; these are the completion of all completions and the
pleroma of all *pleromas* and the *gnosis* of all *gnoses*, these
which are in my *garment*. I will tell you all the *mysteries*
from the outermost of the outer to the innermost of the
inner. Hear, *nevertheless*, and I will tell you everything
which has happened to me.

10.   It happened now when the sun rose in the East,
a great *power* of light came down, in which was my *garment*
which I had left in the 24th *mystery*, *as* I have just been
telling you. And I found a *mystery* in my *garment*, written
in the manner of writing of those of the height[1] : ζαμα
ζαμα ωζζα ραχαμα ωζαι,[2] whose interpretation is : 'O *Mystery* which art outside the *world*[3], because of which the All
exists — this is the whole coming forth and the whole ascent
which has emanated all emanations[4] and all that is within
them, and because of which all *mysteries* and all their *places*
exist — come forth to us because we are thy fellow-*members*.
But we all with thee alone, | we and thou are one and the

---

[1]   (17) in the manner of writing of those of the height; Schmidt : in five words
    of those of the height.
[2]   (18) division of Greek into five words is uncertain.
[3]   (19) outside the world; Schmidt : outside in the world.
[4]   (21) emanated all emanations; lit. distributed all distributions (see 2.10).

ⲁⲛⲟⲛ ⲟⲩⲁ ⲛ̄ⲟⲩⲱⲧ ⲁⲩⲱ ⲛ̄ⲧⲟⲕ ⲡⲉ ⲟⲩⲁ ⲛ̄ⲟⲩⲱⲧ· ⲛ̄ⲧⲟⲕ ⲡⲉ ⲡϣⲟⲣⲡ̄ ⲙ̄ⲙⲩⲥⲧⲏⲣⲓⲟⲛ ⲉⲛⲧⲁϥϣⲱⲡⲉ ϫⲓⲛ ⲛ̄ϣⲟⲣⲡ̄ ϩⲣⲁⲓ̈ ϩⲙ̄ ⲡⲓⲁⲧϣⲁϫⲉ ⲉⲣⲟϥ ϩⲁⲑⲏ ⲉⲙⲡⲁⲧ̄ϥ̄ⲡⲣⲟⲉⲗⲑⲉ ⲉⲃⲟⲗ· ⲁⲩⲱ ⲡⲣⲁⲛ ⲙ̄ⲡⲉⲧⲙ̄ⲙⲁⲩ ⲁⲛⲟⲛ ⲧⲏⲣⲛ̄ ⲡⲉ· ⲧⲉⲛⲟⲩ ϭⲉ ⲁⲛⲟⲛ ⲧⲏⲣⲛ̄ ϩⲓ ⲟⲩⲥⲟⲡ ⲧ̄ⲛⲁϩⲉ ⲉⲣⲟⲕ ϩⲁⲧⲙ̄ ⲫⲁⲉ ⲛ̄ϩⲟⲣⲓⲟⲛ· ⲉⲧⲉ ⲛ̄ⲧⲟϥ ⲡⲉ ⲫⲁⲉ ⲙ̄ⲙⲩⲥⲧⲏⲣⲓⲟⲛ ϫⲓⲛ ⲛ̄ϩⲟⲩⲛ· ⲛ̄ⲧⲟϥ ϩⲱⲱϥ ⲟⲩⲙⲉⲣⲟⲥ ⲡⲉ ⲉⲃⲟⲗ ⲙ̄ⲙⲟⲛ· ⲧⲉⲛⲟⲩ ϭⲉ ⲁⲛⲧⲛ̄ⲛⲟⲟⲩ ⲛⲁⲕ ⲙ̄ⲡⲉⲕⲉⲛⲇⲩ**ⲙⲁ ⲉⲧⲉ ⲡⲱⲕ ⲓⲍ
ⲣⲱⲱ ⲡⲉ ϫⲓⲛ ⲛ̄ϣⲟⲣⲡ̄ ⲡⲁⲓ̈ ⲉⲛⲧⲁⲕⲕⲁⲁϥ ϩⲙ̄ ⲫⲁⲉ ⲛ̄ϩⲟⲣⲟⲥ ⲉⲧⲉ ⲛ̄ⲧⲟϥ ⲡⲉ ⲡϩⲁⲉ ⲙ̄ⲙⲩⲥⲧⲏⲣⲓⲟⲛ ϫⲓⲛϩⲟⲩⲛ· ϣⲁⲛⲧⲉ ⲡⲉϥⲟⲩⲟⲉⲓϣ ϫⲱⲕ ⲉⲃⲟⲗ ⲕⲁⲧⲁ ⲧⲕⲉⲗⲉⲩⲥⲓⲥ ⲙ̄ⲡϣⲟⲣⲡ̄ ⲙ̄ⲙⲩⲥⲧⲏⲣⲓⲟⲛ· ⲉⲓⲥϩⲏⲏⲧⲉ ⲁϥϫⲱⲕ ⲉⲃⲟⲗ ⲛ̄ϭⲓ ⲡⲉϥⲟⲩⲟⲓ̈ϣ ⲧⲁⲁϥ ϩⲓⲱⲱⲕ· ⲁⲙⲟⲩ ϣⲁⲣⲟⲛ ϫⲉ ⲧ̄ⲛⲁϩⲉⲣⲁⲧⲛ̄ ⲉⲣⲟⲕ ⲧⲏⲣⲛ̄ ⲉⲧⲣⲉⲛϯ ϩⲓⲱⲱⲕ ⲙ̄ⲡϣⲟⲣⲡ̄ ⲙ̄ⲙⲩⲥⲧⲏⲣⲓⲟⲛ ⲙⲛ̄ ⲡⲉϥⲉⲟⲟⲩ ⲧⲏⲣϥ̄ ⲉⲃⲟⲗ ϩⲓⲧⲛ̄ ⲧⲉϥⲕⲉⲗⲉⲩⲥⲓⲥ ⲙ̄ⲙⲓⲛ ⲙ̄ⲙⲟϥ ⲉⲁϥⲧⲁⲁϥ ⲛⲁⲛ ⲛ̄ϭⲓ ⲡϣⲟⲣⲡ̄ ⲙ̄ⲙⲩⲥⲧⲏⲣⲓⲟⲛ ⲉϥⲟ ⲛ̄ⲉⲛⲇⲩⲙⲁ ⲥⲛⲁⲩ ⲉⲧⲣⲉⲛⲧⲁⲁϥ ϩⲓⲱⲱⲕ· ⲭⲱⲣⲓⲥ ⲡⲁⲓ̈ ⲉⲛⲧⲁⲛⲧⲛⲟⲟⲩϥ ⲛⲁⲕ ϫⲉ ⲕⲙ̄ⲡϣⲁ ⲙ̄ⲙⲟⲟⲩ· ⲉⲡⲓⲇⲏ ⲛ̄ⲧⲟⲕ ⲡⲉⲧⲟ ⲛ̄ϣⲟⲣⲡ̄ ⲉⲣⲟⲛ ⲁⲩⲱ ⲕϣⲟⲟⲡ ϩⲁⲧⲉⲛⲉϩⲏ· ⲉⲧⲃⲉ ⲡⲁⲓ̈ ϭⲉ ⲁ ⲡϣⲟⲣⲡ̄ ⲙ̄ⲙⲩⲥⲧⲏⲣⲓⲟⲛ ⲁϥⲧⲛⲟⲟⲩ ⲛⲁⲕ ⲉⲃⲟⲗ ϩⲓⲧⲟⲟⲧⲛ̄ ⲙ̄ⲡⲙⲩⲥⲧⲏⲣⲓⲟⲛ ⲙ̄ⲡⲉϥⲉⲟⲟⲩ ⲧⲏⲣϥ̄ ⲉϥⲟ ⲛ̄ⲉⲛⲇⲩⲙⲁ ⲥⲛⲁⲩ· ϣⲟⲣⲡ̄ ⲙⲉⲛ

1 read ⲁⲩⲱ ⲡⲓⲟⲩⲁ ⲛ̄ⲟⲩⲱⲧ ⲛ̄ⲧⲟϥ ⲡⲉ.
9 MS ⲣⲱⲱ; read ⲣⲱ.
15 MS ⲧⲉⲕⲉⲗⲉⲩⲥⲓⲥ; ⲉϥ inserted above in the same hand.
18, 21 see note on 9.19.
22 MS ϣⲟⲣⲡ̄; better ⲡϣⲟⲣⲡ̄.

same. Thou art the First *Mystery* which has existed from the beginning in the Ineffable One, before he *went forth*, and the name of that one is all of us. Now all together we will approach [1] thee at the last *boundary*, which is the last *mystery* from within, itself a *part* of us. Now we have sent thee thy *garment* which has belonged to thee from the beginning, which thou didst leave in the last *boundary*, which is the last *mystery* from within, until its time was completed *according to* the *command* of the First *Mystery*. Behold, the time is completed. Put it on, come to us, that we all approach [1] thee to put on thee the First *Mystery* with all his glory, through his own *command*; as the First *Mystery*, having two *garments* [2], has given it to us that we should put it on thee, *apart from* this which we have sent thee because thou art worthy, *since* thou art first among us and thou didst exist before us *. Because of this the First *Mystery* has sent to thee through us the *mystery* of his whole glory, having two *garments*. *That is*, | in the first is

---

*   Col. 1.17

---

[1]   (5, 14) approach; Till: await (also 19.20).
[2]   (17, 22) having two garments; Schmidt: consisting of two garments.

ⲉϥⲛ̄ϩⲏⲧϥ̄ ⲛ̄ϭⲓ ⲡⲉⲟⲟⲩ ⲧⲏⲣϥ̄ ⲛ̄ⲛⲣⲁⲛ ⲧⲏⲣⲟⲩ ⲛ̄ⲧⲉ ⲙ̄- ⲓⲍ ᵇ
ⲙⲩⲥⲧⲏⲣⲓⲟⲛ ⲧⲏⲣⲟⲩ ⲙ̄ⲛ ⲛⲉⲡⲣⲟⲃⲟⲗⲟⲟⲩⲉ ⲧⲏⲣⲟⲩ ⲛ̄ⲛ-
ⲧⲁⲝⲓⲥ ⲛ̄ⲛⲉⲭⲱⲣⲏⲙⲁ ⲙ̄ⲡⲁⲧⲱϣⲁϫⲉ ⲉⲣⲟϥ · ⲁⲩⲱ ⲡⲙⲉϩⲥⲛⲁⲩ ⲛ̄ⲉⲛⲇⲩⲙⲁ ⲉϥⲛ̄ϩⲏⲧϥ̄ ⲛ̄ϭⲓ ⲡⲉⲟⲟⲩ ⲧⲏⲣϥ̄ ⲙ̄ⲡⲣⲁⲛ
5 ⲛ̄ⲙⲙⲩⲥⲧⲏⲣⲓⲟⲛ ⲧⲏⲣⲟⲩ ⲙ̄ⲛ ⲛⲉⲡⲣⲟⲃⲟⲗⲟⲟⲩⲉ ⲧⲏⲣⲟⲩ ⲛⲁⲓ̈
ⲉⲧϣⲟⲟⲡ ϩⲛ̄ ⲛ̄ⲧⲁⲝⲓⲥ ⲙ̄ⲡⲉⲭⲱⲣⲏⲙⲁ ⲥⲛⲁⲩ ⲛ̄ⲧⲉ ⲡⲓϣⲟⲣⲡ̄
ⲙ̄ⲙⲩⲥⲧⲏⲣⲓⲟⲛ ⲁⲩⲱ ⲡⲉⲓ̈ⲉⲛⲇⲩⲙⲁ ⲉⲛⲧⲁⲛⲧ̄ⲛⲛⲟⲟⲩϥ ⲛⲁⲕ
ⲧⲉⲛⲟⲩ ⲉϥⲛ̄ϩⲏⲧϥ̄ ⲛ̄ϭⲓ ⲡⲉⲟⲟⲩ ⲙ̄ⲡⲣⲁⲛ ⲙ̄ⲡⲙⲩⲥⲧⲏ-
ⲣⲓⲟⲛ ⲙ̄ⲡⲙⲏⲛⲉⲩⲧⲏⲥ ⲉⲧⲉ ⲛ̄ⲧⲟϥ ⲡⲉ ⲡϣⲟⲣⲡ̄ ⲛ̄ⲧⲱϣ ·
10 ⲁⲩⲱ ⲡⲙⲩⲥⲧⲏⲣⲓⲟⲛ ⲙ̄ⲡ⳨ⲟⲩ ⲛ̄ⲭⲁⲣⲁⲅⲙⲏ ⲁⲩⲱ ⲡⲙⲩⲥⲧⲏⲣⲓⲟⲛ ⲙ̄ⲡⲛⲟϭ ⲙ̄ⲡⲣⲉⲥⲃⲉⲩⲧⲏⲥ ⲛ̄ⲧⲉ ⲡⲓⲁⲧϣⲁϫⲉ ⲉⲣⲟϥ
ⲉⲧⲉ ⲛ̄ⲧⲟϥ ⲡⲉ ⲡⲓⲛⲟϭ ⲛ̄ⲟⲩⲟⲉⲓⲛ ⲁⲩⲱ ⲙ̄ⲛ ⲡⲙⲩⲥⲧⲏⲣⲓⲟⲛ ⲙ̄ⲡ⳨ⲟⲩ ⲙ̄ⲡⲣⲟϩⲅⲟⲩⲙⲉⲛⲟⲥ ⲛⲁⲓ̈ ⲉⲧⲉ ⲛ̄ⲧⲟⲟⲩ ⲛⲉ
ⲡ⳨ⲟⲩ ⲙ̄ⲡⲁⲣⲁⲥⲧⲁⲧⲏⲥ ⲁⲩⲱ ⲟⲛ ϥϣⲟⲟⲡ ϩⲙ̄ ⲡⲉⲛⲇⲩⲙⲁ
15 ⲉⲧⲙ̄ⲙⲁⲩ ⲛ̄ϭⲓ ⲡⲉⲟⲟⲩ ⲙ̄ⲡⲣⲁⲛ ⲙ̄ⲡⲙⲩⲥⲧⲏⲣⲓⲟⲛ ⲛ̄ⲛⲧⲁⲝⲓⲥ [ⲓ̄ⲏ̄]
ⲧⲏⲣⲟⲩ ⲛ̄ⲧⲉ ⲛⲉⲡⲣⲟⲃⲟⲗⲟⲟⲩⲉ ⲙ̄ⲡⲉⲑⲏⲥⲁⲩⲣⲟⲥ ⲙ̄ⲡⲟⲩ-
ⲟⲓ̈ⲛ · ⲁⲩⲱ ⲙ̄ⲛ ⲛⲉⲩⲥⲱⲧⲏⲣ · ⲁⲩⲱ ⲙ̄ⲛ ⲛ̄ⲧⲁⲝⲓⲥ ⲛ̄ⲛⲧⲁⲝⲓⲥ
ⲉⲧⲉ ⲛ̄ⲧⲟⲟⲩ ⲛⲉ ⲡⲥⲁϣ̄ϥ ⲛ̄ϩⲁⲙⲏⲛ ⲁⲩⲱ ⲉⲧⲉ ⲛ̄ⲧⲟⲟⲩ
ⲛⲉ ⲡⲥⲁϣ̄ϥ ⲛ̄ⲫⲱⲛⲏ ⲁⲩⲱ ⲙ̄ⲛ ⲡ⳨ⲟⲩ ⲛ̄ϣⲏⲛ · ⲁⲩⲱ
20 ⲙ̄ⲛ ⲡϣⲟⲙⲛ̄ⲧ ⲛ̄ϩⲁⲙⲏⲛ ⲁⲩⲱ ⲙ̄ⲛ ⲡⲥⲱⲧⲏⲣ ⲛ̄ϩⲁⲧⲣⲉⲉⲩ
ⲉⲧⲉ ⲛ̄ⲧⲟⲟⲩ ⲛⲉ ⲡⲁⲗⲟⲩ ⲙ̄ⲡⲁⲗⲟⲩ · ⲁⲩⲱ ⲙ̄ⲛ ⲡⲙⲩⲥⲧⲏⲣⲓⲟⲛ ⲙ̄ⲡⲉⲯⲓⲧ ⲙ̄ⲫⲩⲗⲁⲝ ⲛ̄ⲧϣⲟⲙⲧⲉ ⲙ̄ⲡⲩⲗⲏ ⲙ̄ⲡⲉⲑ-
ⲥⲁⲩⲣⲟⲥ ⲙ̄ⲡⲟⲩⲟⲉⲓⲛ · ⲁⲩⲱ ⲟⲛ ⲉϥⲛ̄ϩⲏⲧϥ̄ ⲛ̄ϭⲓ ⲡⲉⲟⲟⲩ
ⲧⲏⲣϥ̄ ⲙ̄ⲡⲣⲁⲛ ⲉⲧϩⲛ̄ ⲧⲟⲩⲛⲁⲙ ⲙ̄ⲛ ⲛⲉⲧϣⲟⲟⲡ ⲧⲏⲣⲟⲩ

19　MS originally ⲧⲥⲁϣϥⲉ; ⲫⲱⲛⲏ written over erasure.
24　MS ⲉⲧϩⲛ̄; read ⲛ̄ⲡⲉⲧϣⲟⲟⲡ ⲧⲏⲣⲟⲩ ϩⲛ̄ ⲧⲟⲩⲛⲁⲙ.

all the glory of all the names of all the *mysteries* and all
the *emanations* and the *ranks* of the *spaces* of the Ineffable
One. And in the second *garment* is the whole glory of the
name of all the *mysteries* and all the *emanations* which are
in the *ranks* of the two *spaces* of the First *Mystery*. And
in this *garment* which we have now sent thee is the glory
of the name of the *mystery* of the *informer*, which is the
first ordinance, and the *mystery* of the five *incisions*, and
the *mystery* of the great *messenger* of the Ineffable, who is
the great light, and the *mystery* of the five *leaders* who are
the five *helpers* (*parastatai*). And furthermore, there is in
that *garment* the glory of the name of the *mystery* of all the
ranks of the *emanations* of the *Treasury* of the Light, and
their *saviours*, and (the *mystery* of) the *ranks* of the *ranks*,
which are the seven *amens* and the seven *voices* and the
five trees and the three *amens* and the twin *saviour*, namely
the child of the child, and the *mystery* of the nine *watchers*
of the three *gates* of the *Treasury* of the Light [1]. And furthermore there is in it the whole glory of the name ⟨of all
those⟩ who are on the right, and all those who are | in the

---

[1] (22) gates of the Treasury of the Light; see J 123.

2Ν ΤΜΕϹΟϹ · ΑΥШ ΟΝ ΕϤΝ2ΗΤϤ Ν6Ι ΠΕΟΟΥ ΤΗΡϤ
ΜΠΡΑΝ ΜΠΝΟ6 ΝΑ2ΟΡΑΤΟϹ · ΕΤΕ ΝΤΟϤ ΠΕ ΠΝΟ6 Μ-
ΠΡΟΠΑΤШΡ ΑΥШ ΜΝ ⟨Π⟩ΜΥϹΤΗΡΙΟΝ ΜΠϢΟΜΝΤ ΝΤΡΙ-
ΑΥΝΑΜΙϹ · ΑΥШ ΜΝ ΠΜΥϹΤΗΡΙΟΝ ΜΠΕΥΤΟΠΟϹ
⁵ΤΗΡϤ · ΑΥШ ΜΝ ΠΜΥϹΤΗΡΙΟΝ ΝΝΕΥΑ2ΟΡΑΤΟϹ ΤΗ- [ι̅η̅ᵇ]
ΡΟΥ · ΜΝ ΝΕΤϢΟΟΠ ΤΗΡΟΥ 2Μ ΠΜΕ2ΜΝ⟨Τ⟩ϢΟΜΤΕ
ΝΝΑΙШΝ · ΑΥШ ΜΝ ΠΡΑΝ ΜΠΜΝΤϹΝΟΟΥϹ ΝΑΙШΝ · ΑΥШ
ΜΝ ΝΕΥΑΡΧШΝ ΤΗΡΟΥ ΑΥШ ΜΝ ΝΕΥΑΡΧΑΓΓΕΛΟϹ ΤΗ-
ΡΟΥ ΑΥШ ΜΝ ΝΕΥΑΓΓΕΛΟϹ ΤΗΡΟΥ ΑΥШ ΜΝ ΝΕΤ-
¹⁰ϢΟΟΠ ΤΗΡΟΥ 2Μ ΠΜΝΤϹΝΟΟΥϹ ΝΝΑΙШΝ · ΑΥШ
ΠΜΥϹΤΗΡΙΟΝ ΤΗΡϤ ΜΠΡΑΝ ΝΝΕΤϢΟΟΠ ΤΗΡΟΥ 2Ν ΘΙ-
ΜΑΡΜΕΝΗ ΜΝ ΜΠΗΥΕ ΤΗΡΟΥ · ΑΥШ ΠΜΥϹΤΗΡΙΟΝ
ΤΗΡϤ ΜΠΡΑΝ ΝΝΕΤϢΟΟΠ ΤΗΡΟΥ 2Ν ΤΕϹФΕΡΑ ΑΥШ
ΜΝ ΝΕΥϹΤΕΡΕШΜΑ ΜΝ ΝΕΤΝ2ΗΤΟΥ ΤΗΡΟΥ ΑΥШ ΜΝ
¹⁵ΝΕΥΤΟΠΟϹ ΤΗΡΟΥ · ΕΙϹ2ΗΗΤΕ 6Ε ΑΝΤΝΝΟΟΥ ΝΑΚ
ΜΠΕΙΕΝΑΥΜΑ ΕΤΜΜΑΥ ΕΜΠΕ ΛΑΑΥ ΕΙΜΕ ΧΙΝ ΜΠ-
ϢΟΡΠ ΝΤШϢ ΕΠΕϹΗΤ · ΕΒΟΛ ΧΕ ΝΕΡΕ ΠΕΟΟΥ ΜΠΕϤ-
ΟΥΟΕΙΝ 2ΗΠ Ν2ΗΤϤ · ΑΥШ ΝΕϹФΑΙΡΑ ΜΝ ΝΤΟΠΟϹ ι̅ω̅
ΤΗΡΟΥ ΧΙΝ ΜΠϢΟΡΠ ΝΤШϢ ΕΠΕϹΗΤ · 6ΕΠΗ 6Ε †-
²⁰ΠΕΙΕΝΑΥΜΑ 2ΙШШΚ ΑΜΟΥ ϢΑΡΟΝ ΧΕ ΤΝΑ2Ε ΕΡΟΚ
ΕΤΡΕΝ† 2ΙШШΚ ΜΠΕΚΕΝΑΥΜΑ ϹΝΑΥ 2ΙΤΝ ΤΚΕΛΕΥϹΙϹ
ΜΠϢΟΡΠ ΜΜΥϹΤΗΡΙΟΝ ΝΑΙ ΕΥϢΟ⟨Ο⟩Π ΝΑΚ ΧΙΝ ΝϢΟΡΠ
2Α2ΤΕ ΠϢΟΡΠ ΜΜΥϹΤΗΡΙΟΝ ϢΑΝΤΕ ΠΕΟΥΟΕΙϢ

3 MS Π omitted.
4 MS ΜΠΕΥΤΟΠΟϹ; ΠΟ inserted above.
6 MS ΜΝϢΟΜΤΕ.
19 read ΜΠϢΡΠ-ΤШϢ or ΜΠϢΟΡΠ ΝΤШϢ.
22 MS ΕΥϢΟΠ: read ΕΥϢΟΟΠ.
23 ΝΑΙ ... ΜΜΥϹΤΗΡΙΟΝ added in upper margin.

Midst. And furthermore there is in it the whole glory of the
name of the great *invisible one*, who is the great *forefather* [1],
and the *mystery* of the *triple power*, and the *mystery* of their
whole *place*, and the *mystery* of all their *invisible ones* and
of all those who are in the thirteenth *aeon* [2], and the name
of the twelve *aeons* and of all their *archons* and all their
archangels and all their *angels*, and of all those which are
in the twelve *aeons*, and the whole *mystery* of the names of
all those which are in the *Heimarmene* [3] and all the heavens.
And the whole *mystery* of the name of all those in the *sphere*,
and their *firmaments* and all those which are in them, and
all their *places*. Behold now, we have sent thee that *garment*
which no one knew, from the first ordinance downwards,
because the glory of its light was hidden within it. And the
spheres and all the *places* from the first ordinance downwards ⟨did not know it⟩. Behold now, put on this *garment*
quickly. Come to us that we approach thee to put on thee
thy two *garments*, through the *command* of the First *Mystery*,
they having been for thee with the First *Mystery* since the
beginning until the time | appointed by the Ineffable One

---

[1] (3) forefather; see U 228.
[2] (6, 7) thirteenth aeon; see J 134.
[3] (11) Heimarmene; see Jonas (Bibl. 23) p. 156-210; J 117; ApJn 72; OnOrgWld
     155 etc.; CH 1.9.

ⲭⲱⲕ ⲉⲃⲟⲗ ⲡⲁⲓ̈ ⲉⲧⲧⲏϣ ϩⲓⲧⲛ̄ ⲡⲓⲁⲧϣⲁϫⲉ ⲉⲣⲟϥ· ⲉⲓⲥϩⲏⲏⲧⲉ ϭⲉ ⲁϥⲭⲱⲕ ⲉⲃⲟⲗ ⲛ̄ϭⲓ ⲡⲉⲟⲩⲟⲉⲓϣ)· ⲁⲙⲟⲩ ϭⲉ
ϣⲁⲣⲟⲛ ϩⲛ̄ ⲟⲩϭⲉⲡⲏ ⲧⲁⲣⲛ̄ⲧⲁⲁⲩ ϩⲓⲱⲱⲕ ϣⲁⲛⲧⲕ̄ⲭⲱⲕ
ⲉⲃⲟⲗ ⲛ̄ⲧⲇⲓⲁⲕⲟⲛⲓⲁ ⲧⲏⲣⲥ̄ ⲙ̄ⲡⲭⲱⲕ ⲉⲃⲟⲗ ⲙ̄ⲡⲓϣⲟⲣⲡ̄
5 ⲙ̄ⲙⲩⲥⲧⲏⲣⲓⲟⲛ ⲧⲁⲓ̈ ⲉⲧⲧⲏϣ ϩⲓⲧⲛ̄ ⲡⲓⲁⲧϣⲁϫⲉ ⲉⲣⲟϥ·
ⲁⲙⲟⲩ ϭⲉ ϣⲁⲣⲟⲛ ϩⲛ̄ ⲟⲩϭⲉⲡⲏ ⲧⲁⲣⲛ̄ⲧⲁⲁⲩ ϩⲓⲱⲱⲕ
ⲕⲁⲧⲁ ⲧⲕⲉⲗⲉⲩⲥⲓⲥ ⲙ̄ⲡⲓϣⲟⲣⲡ̄ ⲙ̄ⲙⲩⲥⲧⲏⲣⲓⲟⲛ ⲉⲧⲓ ⲅⲁⲣ ⲕⲉ-
ⲕⲟⲩⲓ̈ ⲛ̄ⲟⲩ⟨ⲟ⟩ⲉⲓϣ ⲡⲉ ⲛ̄ⲉⲗⲁⲭⲓⲥⲧⲟⲛ· ⲕⲛⲏⲩ ⲉⲣⲁⲧⲛ̄·
ⲁⲩⲱ ⲕⲛⲁⲗⲟ ϩⲙ̄ ⲡⲕⲟⲥⲙⲟⲥ· *ⲁⲙⲟⲩ ϭⲉ· ϩⲛ̄ ⲟⲩϭⲉⲡⲏ ⲓ̄ⲑ ᵇ
10 ⲧⲁⲣⲉⲕϫⲓ ⲙ̄ⲡⲉⲕⲉⲟⲟⲩ ⲧⲏⲣϥ̄ ⲉⲧⲉ ⲡⲉⲟⲟⲩ ⲡⲉ ⲙ̄ⲡϣⲟⲣⲡ̄
ⲙ̄ⲙⲩⲥⲧⲏⲣⲓⲟⲛ :

ⲍ ⲁⲥϣⲱⲡⲉ ϭⲉ ⲁⲛⲟⲕ ⲛ̄ⲧⲉⲣⲓⲛⲁⲩ ⲉⲡⲙⲩⲥⲧⲏⲣⲓⲟⲛ ⲛ̄ⲛⲉⲓ̈-
ϣⲁϫⲉ ⲧⲏⲣⲟⲩ ϩⲣⲁⲓ̈ ϩⲙ̄ ⲡⲉⲛⲇⲩⲙⲁ ⲉⲛⲧⲁϥⲧⲛ̄ⲛⲟⲟⲩϥ
ⲛⲁⲓ̈· ⲁⲓ̈ⲧⲁⲁϥ ϩⲓⲱⲱⲧ ϩⲛ̄ ⲧⲉⲩⲛⲟⲩ ⲉⲧⲙ̄ⲙⲁⲩ· ⲁⲩⲱ ⲁⲓ̈ⲣ̄-
15 ⲟⲩⲟⲉⲓⲛ ⲉⲙⲁϣⲟ ⲉⲙⲁϣⲟ ⲁⲩⲱ ⲁⲓ̈ϩⲱⲗ ⲉⲡϫⲓⲥⲉ· ⲁⲩⲱ
ⲁⲓ̈ⲉⲓ’ ⲉⲣⲛ̄-ⲧⲡⲩⲗⲏ ⲙ̄ⲡⲉⲥⲧⲉⲣⲉⲱⲙⲁ ⲉⲓⲟ ⲛ̄ⲟⲩⲟⲉⲓⲛ ⲉⲙⲁϣⲟ
ⲉⲙⲁϣⲟ ⲉⲙⲛ̄-ϣⲓ ⲉⲡⲟⲩⲟⲉⲓⲛ ⲉⲛⲉⲓ̈ϣⲟⲟⲡ ⲙ̄ⲙⲟϥ· ⲁⲩⲱ
ⲁⲩϣⲧⲟⲣⲧⲣ̄ ⲉϫⲛ̄ ⲛⲉⲩⲉⲣⲏⲩ ⲛ̄ϭⲓ ⲙ̄ⲡⲩⲗⲏ ⲙ̄ⲡⲉⲥⲧⲉⲣⲉ-
ⲱⲙⲁ ⲁⲩⲟⲩⲱⲛ ⲧⲏⲣⲟⲩ ϩⲓ ⲟⲩⲥⲟⲡ· ⲁⲩⲱ ⲁ ⲛ̄ⲁⲣⲭⲱⲛ
20 ⲧⲏⲣⲟⲩ ⲙⲛ̄ ⲛⲉϩⲟⲩⲥⲓⲁ ⲧⲏⲣⲟⲩ· ⲙⲛ̄ ⲛⲁⲅⲅⲉⲗⲟⲥ ⲧⲏⲣⲟⲩ
ⲉⲧⲛ̄ϩⲏⲧϥ̄ ⲁⲩϣⲧⲟⲣⲧⲣ̄ ⲧⲏⲣⲟⲩ ϩⲓ ⲟⲩⲥⲟⲡ ⲉⲧⲃⲉ ⲡⲛⲟϭ
ⲛ̄ⲟⲩⲟⲉⲓⲛ ⲉⲧϣⲟⲟⲡ ⲙ̄ⲙⲟⲓ̈· ⲁⲩⲱ ⲁⲩϭⲱϣⲧ̄ ⲉⲡⲉⲛ-
ⲇⲩⲙⲁ ⲛ̄ⲟⲩⲟⲉⲓⲛ ⲉⲧϩⲓⲱⲱⲧ’ ⲉⲧⲟ ⁑ ⲛ̄ⲟⲩⲟⲉⲓⲛ ⲁⲩⲛⲁⲩ [ⲕ̄]

---

6   MS after ⲁⲙⲟⲩ, dittography ϭⲉ ϣⲁⲣⲟⲛ ϩⲙⲟⲩ is expunged.
8   MS ⲛ̄ⲟⲩⲉⲓϣ.
17   MS ⲉⲛⲉϣⲟⲟⲡ; ϥ crossed out, and ⲓ̈ inserted above in the same hand;
     read ⲉⲛⲉϥϣⲟⲟⲡ ⲙ̄ⲙⲟⲓ̈; compare 23.23.

is completed. Behold the time is completed. Come now quickly to us that we put them on thee, until thou hast completed the whole *service* of the completion of the First *Mystery*, which is appointed by the Ineffable One. Come now quickly to us that we put them on thee, *according to* the *command* of the First *Mystery*. *For yet* a little time, an *insignificant* one, and thou wilt come to us and leave the world*. Come now quickly, and thou shalt receive the whole glory which is the glory of the First *Mystery* ᵒ'

11. It happened now, when I saw the *mystery* of all these words in the *garment* which was sent to me, I put it on in that hour, and I gave light exceedingly, and I flew to the height, and I came before the *gate* of the *firmament*, shining exceedingly, there being no measure to the light which I had. And the gates of the firmament were agitated against one another, and they all opened at the same time. And all the *archons* and all the *powers* (*exousiai*) and all the *angels* therein were all agitated at the same time because of the great light which I had. And they looked upon the shining *garment* of light which I wore, they saw | the *mystery*

---

*   cf. Joh. 16.16, 28
ᵒ   cf. Joh. 17.5

ЄΠΜΥСΤΗΡΙΟΝ ЄΤЄΡЄ ΠЄΥΡΑΝ ΖΙШШЧ ΑΥΡΖΟΤЄ ЄΜΑΤЄ

ЄΜΑΤЄ ΑΥШ ΑΥΒШΛ ЄΒΟΛ Ν̄6Ι ΝЄΥΜ̄ΡΡЄ ΤΗΡΟΥ

ΝΑЇ ЄΤΟΥΜΗΡ Ν̄ΖΗΤΟΥ ΑΥШ Α ΠΟΥΑ ΠΟΥΑ ΛΟ Ζ̄Ν

ΤЄЧΤΑΞΙС · ΑΥШ ΑΥΠΑΖΤΟΥ ΤΗΡΟΥ Μ̄ΠΑΜΤΟ ЄΒΟΛ

5 ΑΥΟΥШϢ̄Τ ЄΥΧШ Μ̄ΜΟС ΧЄ Ν̄ΑϢ Ν̄ΖЄ ΑЧΟΥΟΤΒ̄Ν

ЄΒΟΛ Ν̄6Ι ΠΧΟЄΙС Μ̄ΠΤΗΡЧ ЄΜΠΝ̄ЄΙΜЄ · ΑΥШ ΑΥΖΥΜ-

ΝЄΥЄ ΤΗΡΟΥ ΖΙ ΟΥСΟΠ ЄΠСΑΝΖΟΥΝ Ν̄ΤЄ ΝΙСΑΝΖΟΥΝ ·

ΑΝΟΚ ΔЄ ΝЄΥΝΑΥ ЄΡΟЇ ΑΝ ΠЄ · ΑΛΛΑ ΝЄΥΝΑΥ

ЄΠΟΥΟЄΙΝ Μ̄ΜΑΤЄ ΑΥШ ΝЄΥϢΟΟΠ ΠЄ Ζ̄Ν ΟΥΝΟ6

10 Ν̄ΖΟΤЄ · ΑΥШ ΝЄΥϢ̄ΡΤШΡ ΠЄ ЄΜΑΤЄ · ΑΥШ ΑΥ-

ΖΥΜΝЄΥЄ ЄΠСΑΝΖΟΥΝ Ν̄ΤЄ ΝΙСΑΝΖΟΥΝ · ΑЇΚΑ-ΠΜΑ

ΔЄ ЄΤΜ̄ΜΑΥ Ν̄СШЇ ΑЇЄΙ' ЄΖΡΑЇ ЄΤϢΟΡΠ̄ Ν̄СΦΑΙΡΑ ЄΙΟ

Ν̄ΟΥΟЄΙΝ ЄΜΑϢΟ ЄΜΑϢΟ Ν̄ΖΟΥΟ ЄΘЄ ЄΝΤΑЇΡ-ΟΥ-

ΟЄΙΝ Ν̄ΖΗΤ̄С Ζ̄Μ ΠЄСΤЄΡЄШΜΑ Ν̄ΖΜЄΨΙΤ' Ν̄ΚШΒ Ν̄СΟΠ · [Κ̄ᵇ]

15 ΑСϢШΠЄ 6Є Ν̄ΤЄΡΙΠШΖ ЄΤΠΥΛΗ Ν̄ΤϢΟΡΠ̄ Ν̄СΦΑΙΡΑ

ΑΥϢΤΟΡΤΡ̄ Ν̄6Ι ΝЄСΠΥΛΗ ΑΥШ ΑΥΟΥШΝ ΜΑΥΑΑΥ

ΖΙ ΟΥСΟΠ · ΑЇЄΙ' ЄΖΟΥΝ ЄΝΟΙΚΟС Ν̄ΤЄСΦΑΙΡΑ ЄΙΟ

Ν̄ΟΥΟЄΙΝ ЄΜΑϢΟ ЄΜΑϢΟ ЄΜΝ-ϢΙ ЄΠΟΥΟЄΙΝ ЄΤ-

ϢΟΟΠ Μ̄ΜΟЇ ΑΥШ ΑΥϢΤΟΡΤΡ̄ ЄΧ̄Ν ΝЄΥЄΡΗΥ Ν̄6Ι

20 Ν̄ΑΡΧШΝ ΤΗΡΟΥ Μ̄Ν ΝЄΤϢΟΟΠ ΤΗΡΟΥ Ζ̄Ν ΤЄСΦΑΙΡΑ

ЄΤΜ̄ΜΑΥ ΑΥШ ΑΥΝΑΥ ЄΠΝΟ6 Ν̄ΟΥΟЄΙΝ ЄΤϢΟΟΠ

Μ̄ΜΟЇ · ΑΥШ ΑΥ6ШϢ̄Τ ЄΠΛЄΝΑΥΜΑ ΑΥΝΑΥ ЄΠΜΥС-

ΤΗΡΙΟΝ Μ̄ΠЄΥΡΑΝ Ν̄ΖΗΤЧ ΑΥШ ΑΥΡΖΟΥЄ-ϢΤΟΡΤΡ̄ ·

ΑΥШ ΑΥϢШΠЄ Ζ̄Ν ΟΥΝΟ6 Ν̄ΖΟΤЄ ЄΥΧШ Μ̄ΜΟС

25 ΧЄ ΠШС Α ΠΧΟЄΙС Μ̄ΠΤΗΡЧ ΟΥΟΤΒ̄Ν ЄΒΟΛ ЄΜΠΝ̄-

ЄΙΜЄ · ΑΥШ ΑΥΒШΛ ЄΒΟΛ Ν̄6Ι ΝЄΥΜ̄ΡΡЄ ΤΗΡΟΥ ΑΥШ

---

1 MS ЄΠΠΜΥСΤΗΡΙΟΝ.

which contained their name. They were exceedingly afraid
and all their bonds in which they were bound were loosened,
and each one abandoned his *rank*. And they all prostrated
themselves in my presence, they worshipped, saying : 'How
has the Lord of the All passed through us without our
knowing?' And they all *sang praises* at once to the innermost of the inner. *However* they did not see me, *but* they
saw the light alone and they were in great fear*. And they
were greatly agitated, and they *sang praises* to the innermost
of the inner.

12.   *Nevertheless* I left that place behind me, I came up
to the first *sphere* shining exceedingly, 49 times more than
when I gave light within the *firmament*. Now it happened
when I reached the *gate* of the first *sphere*, its *gates* were
agitated and they opened of themselves at the same time.
I came into the *houses* of the *spheres* shining exceedingly,
there being no measure to the light which I had. And all
the *archons* and all those who were in that *sphere* were
agitated together. And they saw the great light which I had.
And they looked upon my *garment*, they saw the *mystery*
of their name within it. And they were increasingly agitated,
and they were in great fear, saying : '*How* has the Lord
of the All passed through us without our knowing?' And
all their bonds were loosened, | and their *places* and their

---

*   cf. Acts 22.9

ⲘⲚ ⲚⲈⲨⲦⲞⲠⲞⲤ ⲘⲚ ⲚⲈⲨⲦⲀⲌⲒⲤ · ⲀⲨⲰ Ⲁ ⲠⲞⲨⲀ ⲠⲞⲨⲀ ⲔⲀ

ⲖⲞ ⲌⲚ ⲦⲈⲨⲦⲀⲌⲒⲤ ⲀⲨⲠⲀⲌⲦⲞⲨ ⲦⲎⲢⲞⲨ ⳡⲒ ⲞⲨⲤⲞⲠ ⲀⲨ-

ⲞⲨⲰϢⲦ ⲘⲠⲀⲘⲦⲞ ⲈⲂⲞⲖ ⲏ̈ ⲘⲠⲈⲘⲦⲞ ⲈⲂⲞⲖ ⲘⲠⲀⲈⲚ-

ⲆⲨⲘⲀ · ⲀⲨⲰ ⲀⲨⳡⲨⲘⲚⲈⲨⲈ ⲦⲎⲢⲞⲨ ⳡⲒ ⲞⲨⲤⲞⲠ ⲈⲠⲤⲀⲚ-

5 ⳡⲞⲨⲚ ⲚⲦⲈ ⲚⲒⲤⲀⲚⳡⲞⲨⲚ · ⲈⲨϢⲞⲞⲠ ⲌⲚ ⲞⲨⲚⲞϬ ⲚⳡⲞⲦⲈ

ⲘⲚ ⲞⲨⲚⲞϬ Ⲛ̄ϢⲦⲞⲢⲦⲢ̄ · ⲀⲨⲰ ⲀⲒ̈ⲔⲰ ⲚⲤⲰⲒ̈ ⲘⲠⲘⲀ ⲈⲦ-

ⲘⲘⲀⲨ ⲀⲒ̈ⲈⲒ̈ ϢⲀ ⲦⲠⲨⲖⲎ Ⲛ̄ⲦⲘⲈⳡⲤⲚⲦⲈ ⲚⲤⲫⲀⲒⲢⲀ ⲦⲀⲒ̈ ⲈⲦⲈ

ⲚⲦⲞⲤ ⲦⲈ ⲐⲒⲘⲀⲢⲘⲈⲚⲎ · ⲀⲨϢⲦⲞⲢⲦⲢ̄ ⲆⲈ Ⲛ̄ϬⲒ ⲚⲈⲤⲠⲨⲖⲎ

ⲦⲎⲢⲞⲨ ⲀⲨⲰ ⲀⲨⲞⲨⲰⲚ ⳡⲒ ⲚⲈⲨⲈⲢⲎⲨ · ⲀⲨⲰ ⲀⲒ̈ⲂⲰⲔ

10 ⲈⳡⲞⲨⲚ ⲈⲚⲞⲒⲔⲞⲤ Ⲛ̄ⲐⲒⲘⲀⲢⲘⲈⲚⲎ ⲈⲒ̈Ⲟ Ⲛ̄ⲞⲨⲞⲈⲒⲚ ⲈⲘⲀϢⲞ

ⲈⲘⲀϢⲞ ⲈⲘⲚ̄-ϢⲒ ⲈⲠⲞⲨⲞⲒ̈Ⲛ ⲈⲦϢⲞⲞⲠ ⲘⲘⲞⲒ̈ · ⲚⲈⲒ̈Ⲟ ⲅⲀⲢ

Ⲛ̄ⲞⲨⲞⲈⲒⲚ ⲠⲈ ⳡⲚ ⲐⲒⲘⲀⲢⲘⲈⲚⲎ Ⲛ̄ⳡⲞⲨⲞ ⲈⲦⲈⲤⲫⲀⲒⲢⲀ Ⲛ̄ⳡⲘⲈ-

ⲯⲒⲦ Ⲛ̄ⲔⲰⲂ Ⲛ̄ⲤⲞⲠ · ⲀⲨⲰ ⲀⲨϢⲦⲞⲢⲦⲢ̄ Ⲛ̄ϬⲒ Ⲛ̄ⲀⲢⲬⲰⲚ

ⲦⲎⲢⲞⲨ ⲘⲚ ⲚⲈⲦϢⲞⲞⲠ ⲦⲎⲢⲞⲨ ⳡⲚ ⲐⲒⲘⲀⲢⲘⲈⲚⲎ ⲀⲨⲰ ⲔⲀ b

15 ⲀⲨⳡⲈ ⲈⳠⲚ ⲚⲈⲨⲈⲢⲎⲨ ⲀⲨϢⲰⲠⲈ ⳡⲚ ⲞⲨⲚⲞϬ ⲚⳡⲞⲦⲈ

ⲈⲘⲀⲦⲈ ⲈⲨⲚⲀⲨ ⲈⲠⲚⲞϬ Ⲛ̄ⲞⲨⲞⲈⲒⲚ ⲈϤϢⲞⲞⲠ ⲘⲘⲞⲒ̈ ·

ⲀⲨⲰ ⲀⲨϬⲰϢⲦ ⲈⲠⲀⲈⲚⲆⲨⲘⲀ Ⲛ̄ⲞⲨⲞⲈⲒⲚ ⲀⲨⲚⲀⲨ ⲈⲠ-

ⲘⲨⲤⲦⲎⲢⲒⲞⲚ ⲘⲠⲈⲨⲢⲀⲚ ⳡⲢⲀⲒ̈ ⳡⲘ ⲠⲀⲈⲚⲆⲨⲘⲀ ⲀⲨⲰ ⲀⲨⲢ-

ⳡⲞⲨⲈ-ϢⲦⲞⲢⲦⲢ̄ ⲀⲨϢⲰⲠⲈ ⳡⲚ ⲞⲨⲚⲞϬ ⲚⳡⲞⲦⲈ ⲈⲨⲬⲰ

20 ⲘⲘⲞⲤ ⲬⲈ Ⲛ̄ⲀϢ Ⲛ̄ⳡⲈ Ⲁ ⲠⲬⲞⲒ̈Ⲥ ⲘⲠⲦⲎⲢϤ ⲞⲨⲞⲦⲂⲚ̄ ⲈⲂⲞⲖ

ⲈⲘⲠⲚ̄ⲄⲈⲒⲘⲈ · ⲀⲨⲰ ⲀⲨⲂⲰⲖ ⲈⲂⲞⲖ Ⲛ̄ϬⲒ ⲘⲘⲢ̄ⲢⲈ ⲦⲎⲢⲞⲨ

Ⲛ̄ⲚⲈⲨⲦⲞⲠⲞⲤ ⲘⲚ ⲚⲈⲨⲦⲀⳠⲒⲤ ⲘⲚ ⲚⲈⲨⲞⲒⲔⲞⲤ. ⲀⲨⲈⲒ̈ ⲦⲎ-

ⲢⲞⲨ ⳡⲒ ⲞⲨⲤⲞⲠ ⲀⲨⲠⲀⳡⲦⲞⲨ ⲀⲨⲞⲨⲰϢⲦ ⲘⲠⲀⲘⲦⲞ

ⲈⲂⲞⲖ · ⲀⲨⲰ ⲀⲨⳡⲨⲘⲚⲈⲨ⟨Ⲉ⟩ ⲦⲎⲢⲞⲨ ⳡⲒ ⲞⲨⲤⲞⲠ ⲈⲠⲤⲀ-

25 ⲚⳡⲞⲨⲚ ⲚⲦⲈ ⲚⲒⲤⲀⲚⳡⲞⲨⲚ · ⲈⲨϢⲞⲞⲠ ⳡⲚ ⲞⲨⲚⲞϬ ⲚⳡⲞⲦⲈ

---

23   MS ⲀⲨⲠⲀⳡⲦⲞⲨ; ⲧ inserted above.

24   MS ⲀⲨⳡⲨⲘⲚⲈⲨ.

ranks. And each one abandoned his *rank*. And they all prostrated themselves at the same time, they all worshipped in my presence *or* in the presence of my *garment*. And they all *sang praises* at the same time to the innermost of the inner, being in great fear and great agitation.

13. And I left that place behind me, I came to the *gate* of the second *sphere*, which is the *Heimarmene*. *But* all its *gates* were agitated and they opened of themselves [1]. And I entered into the *houses* of the *Heimarmene*, shining exceedingly, there being no measure to the light which I had, *for* I was shining in the *Heimarmene* 49 times more than in the *sphere*. And all the *archons* and all those who are in the *Heimarmene* were agitated and they fell upon one another, and were in very great fear as they saw the great light which I had. And they looked at my *garment* of light, they saw the *mystery* of their name in my *garment*, and they were increasingly agitated. They were in great fear, saying : 'How has the Lord of the All passed through us without our knowing?' And all the bonds of their *places* and their *ranks* and their *houses* were loosened. They all came at the same time, they prostrated themselves, they worshipped in my presence. And they all *sang praises* at the same time to the innermost of the inner, being in great fear | and great agitation.

---

[1] (9) of themselves; Till : one by one.

ⲘⲚ ⲞⲨⲚⲞϬ Ⲛ̄ϢⲦⲞⲢⲦⲢ̄ · ⲀⲨⲰ Ⲁⲓ̈ⲔⲀ-ⲠⲘⲀ ⲈⲦⲘ̄ⲘⲀⲨ̈ Ⲛ̄ⲤⲰⲓ̈
Ⲁⲓ̈Ⲉⲓ̈ ̔ ⲈϨⲢⲀⲓ̈ ⲈⲚⲚⲞϬ Ⲛ̄Ⲛ̄ⲀⲒⲰⲚ Ⲛ̄ⲦⲈ Ⲛ̄ⲀⲢⲬⲰⲚ Ⲁⲓ̈Ⲉⲓ̈ ̔ ⲈⲢⲚ̄- [ⲕⲃ]
ⲚⲈⲨⲔⲀⲦⲀⲠⲈⲦⲀⲤⲘⲀ · ⲀⲨⲰ ⲘⲚ̄ ⲚⲈⲨⲠⲨⲖⲎ ⲈⲒ̈Ⲟ Ⲛ̄ⲞⲨⲞⲈⲒⲚ
ⲈⲘⲀϢⲞ ⲈⲘⲀϢⲞ ⲀⲨⲰ ⲈⲘⲚ̄-ϢⲒ ⲈⲠⲞⲨⲞⲈⲒⲚ ⲈⲦϢⲞⲞⲠ
5 Ⲙ̄ⲘⲞⲓ̈ ·

ⲀⲤϢⲰⲠⲈ ϬⲈ Ⲛ̄ⲦⲈⲢⲒⲠⲰϨ ⲈⲠⲘⲚ̄ⲦⲤⲚⲞⲞⲨⲤ Ⲛ̄Ⲛ̄ⲀⲒⲰⲚ
ⲀⲨϢⲦⲞⲢⲦⲢ̄ ⲈϪⲚ̄ ⲚⲈⲨⲈⲢⲎⲨ Ⲛ̄ϬⲒ ⲚⲈⲨⲔⲀⲦⲀⲠⲈⲦⲀⲤⲘⲀ
ⲀⲨⲰ ⲘⲚ̄ ⲚⲈⲨⲠⲨⲖⲎ ⲀⲨⲤⲰⲔ ⲘⲀⲨⲀⲀⲨ Ⲛ̄ϬⲒ Ⲛ̄ⲔⲀⲦⲀⲠⲈ-
ⲦⲀⲤⲘⲀ · ⲀⲨⲰ Ⲁ ⲚⲈⲨⲠⲨⲖⲎ ⲞⲨⲰⲚ ⲈϪⲚ̄ ⲚⲈⲨⲈⲢⲎⲨ ·
10 ⲀⲨⲰ Ⲁⲓ̈ⲂⲰⲔ ⲈϨⲞⲨⲚ ⲈⲚⲈⲨⲀⲒⲰⲚ ⲈⲒ̈Ⲟ ̔ Ⲛ̄ⲞⲨⲞⲈⲒⲚ ⲈⲘⲀ-
ϢⲞ ⲈⲘⲀϢⲞ ⲈⲘⲚ̄-ϢⲒ ⲈⲠⲞⲨⲞⲈⲒⲚ ⲈⲦϢⲞⲞⲠ Ⲙ̄ⲘⲞⲓ̈ Ⲛ̄ϨⲞⲨⲞ
ⲈⲠⲞⲨⲞⲈⲒⲚ ⲈⲚⲦⲀⲒ̈Ⲣ̄-ⲞⲨⲞⲈⲒⲚ Ⲛ̄ϨⲎⲦϤ̄ ϨⲚ̄ Ⲛ̄ⲞⲒⲔⲞⲤ Ⲛ̄ⲐⲒ-
ⲘⲀⲢⲘⲈⲚⲎ Ⲛ̄ϨⲘⲈⲨⲮⲒⲦ Ⲛ̄ⲔⲰⲂ Ⲡ̄ⲤⲞⲠ · ⲀⲨⲰ Ⲁ Ⲛ̄ⲀⲄⲄⲈⲖⲞⲤ
ⲦⲎⲢⲞⲨ Ⲛ̄Ⲛ̄ⲀⲒⲰⲚ ⲘⲚ̄ ⲚⲈⲨⲀⲢⲬⲀⲄⲄⲈⲖⲞⲤ ⲘⲚ̄ ⲚⲈⲨⲀⲢ-
15 ⲬⲰⲚ · [ⲘⲚ̄] ⲘⲚ̄ ⲚⲈⲨⲚⲞⲨⲦⲈ · ⲘⲚ̄ ⲚⲈⲨϪⲞⲈⲒⲤ · ⲘⲚ̄
ⲚⲈⲨⲈⳅⲞⲨⲤⲒⲀ · ⲀⲨⲰ ⲘⲚ̄ ⲚⲈⲨⲦⲨⲢⲀⲚⲚⲞⲤ · ⲘⲚ̄ ⲚⲈⲨ- [ⲕⲃᵇ]
ϬⲞⲘ · ⲘⲚ̄ ⲚⲈⲨⲤⲠⲒⲚⲐⲎⲢ ⲘⲚ̄ ⲚⲈⲨⲪⲰⲤⲦⲎⲢ · ⲘⲚ̄ ⲚⲈⲨⲬⲰ-
ⲢⲒⲤⲤⲨⲚⳅⲨⲄⲞⲤ · ⲘⲚ̄ ⲚⲈⲨⲀϨⲞⲢⲀⲦⲞⲤ · ⲀⲨⲰ ⲘⲚ̄ ⲚⲈⲨⲠⲢⲞ-
ⲠⲀⲦⲰⲢ · ⲘⲚ̄ ⲚⲈⲨⲦⲢⲒⲀⳄⲨⲚⲀⲘⲞⲤ ⲀⲨⲚⲀⲨ ⲈⲢⲞⲓ̈ ⲈⲒ̈Ⲟ Ⲛ̄ⲞⲨ-
20 ⲞⲈⲒⲚ ⲈⲘⲀϢⲞ ⲈⲘⲀϢⲞ · ⲈⲘⲚ̄-ϢⲒ ⲈⲠⲞⲨⲞⲈⲒⲚ ⲈⲦϢⲞⲞⲠ
Ⲙ̄ⲘⲞⲓ̈ · ⲀⲨⲰ ⲀⲨϢⲦⲞⲢⲦⲢ̄ ⲈϪⲚ̄ ⲚⲈⲨⲈⲢⲎⲨ · ⲀⲨⲰ ⲀⲨ-
ⲚⲞϬ Ⲛ̄ϨⲞⲦⲈ ϨⲈ ⲈϨⲢⲀⲓ̈ ⲤϪⲰⲞⲨ · ⲈⲨⲚⲀⲨ ⲈⲠⲚⲞϬ Ⲛ̄ⲞⲨ-
ⲞⲈⲒⲚ ⲈⲚⲈϤϢⲞⲞⲠ Ⲙ̄ⲘⲞⲓ̈ · ⲀⲨⲰ ⲠⲈⲨⲚⲞϬ Ⲛ̄ϢⲦⲞⲢⲦⲢ̄ ⲘⲚ̄
ⲦⲈⲨⲚⲞϬ Ⲛ̄ϨⲞⲦⲈ · ⲀⲨⲠⲰϨ ϢⲀ ⲠⲦⲞⲠⲞⲤ Ⲙ̄ⲠⲚⲞϬ Ⲙ̄ⲠⲢⲞ-

---

15 the hand of the second scribe begins with ⲘⲚ̄ which appears for the second
time on the new line.

14.   And I left that place behind me, I came upwards to
the great *aeons* of the *archons*, I came before their *veils* [1] and
their *gates* shining exceedingly, and there was no measure
to the light which I had. Now it happened when I reached
the twelve *aeons* [2], their veils and their *gates* were agitated
against one another. The *veils* drew themselves aside and
the *gates* opened of themselves [3], and I entered into their
aeons shining exceedingly, there being no measure to the
light which I had, 49 times greater than the light with which
I was shining in the *houses* of the *Heimarmene*. And all the
angels of the *aeons* and their *archangels* and their *archons*
and their gods and their lords and their *powers* (*exousiai*)
and their *tyrants* and their powers and their *light-sparks* [4]
and their *luminaries* and their *unpaired ones* and their *invisible
ones* and their *forefathers* and their *triple-powered ones*, they
saw me shining exceedingly, there being no measure to the
light which I had. And they were agitated against one
another, and great fear came upon them as they saw the
great light which I had. And their great agitation and their
great fear reached to the *place* of the great | *invisible fore-*

---

[1]   (3) veils; see J 83.
[2]   (6) twelve aeons; see J 101.
[3]   (9) of themselves; lit. against one another.
[4]   (17) light-sparks; see U 242.

ⲠⲀⲦⲰⲢ ⲚⲀⲌⲞⲢⲀⲦⲞⳠ · ⲀⲨⲰ ⲘⲚ ⲠϢⲞⲘⲚⲦ ⲚⲚⲞϬ ⲚⲦⲢⲒ-
ⲀⲨⲚⲀⲘⲞⳠ · ⲈⲂⲞⲖ ⲆⲈ ⳜⲦⲚ ⲦⲚⲞϬ ⲚⳜⲞⲦⲈ ⲚⲦⲈ ⲠⲈⲨ-
ϢⲦⲞⲢⲦⲢ̄ · ⲀϤϬⲰ ⲈϤⲠⲎⲦ ⲈⲠⲒⳠⲀ ⲘⲚ ⲠⲀⳠ ⳜⲘ ⲠⲈϤⲦⲞⲠⲞⳠ
ⲚϬⲒ ⲠⲚⲞϬ Ⲙ̄ⲠⲢⲞⲠⲀⲦⲰⲢ ⲚⲦⲞϤ ** ⲘⲚ ⲠϢⲞⲘⲚⲦ ⲚⲦⲢⲒ- ⲔⲄ̄
5 ⲀⲨⲚⲀⲘⲞⳠ · ⲀⲨⲰ Ⲙ̄ⲠⲞⲨⲈϢϢⲦⲀⲘ Ⲛ̄ⲚⲈⲨⲦⲞⲠⲞⳠ ⲦⲎ-
ⲢⲞⲨ ⲈⲦⲂⲈ ⲦⲚⲞϬ ⲚⳜⲞⲦⲈ ⲈⲚⲈⲨϢⲞⲞⲠ ⳜⲢⲀⳠ ⲚⳜⲎⲦⳠ ⲀⲨⲰ
ⲀⲨⲔⲒⲘ ⲈⲚⲈⲨⲀⲒⲰⲚ ⲦⲎⲢⲞⲨ ⳜⲒ ⲞⲨⳠⲞⲠ · ⲘⲚ ⲚⲈⲨⳠⲪⲈⲢⲀ
ⲦⲎⲢⲞⲨ ⲘⲚ ⲚⲈⲨⲔⲞⳠⲘⲎⳠⲒⳠ ⲦⲎⲢⲞⲨ · ⲈⲨⲢ̄ⳜⲞⲦⲈ ⲀⲨⲰ
ⲈⲨϢⲦⲢ̄ⲦⲰⲢ ⲈⲘⲀⲦⲈ ⲈⲦⲂⲈ ⲠⲚⲞϬ ⲚⲞⲨⲞⲒⲚ ⲈⲚⲈϤϢⲞⲞⲠ
10 Ⲙ̄ⲘⲞⲒ ⲚⲐⲈ ⲀⲚ Ⲙ̄ⲠⲈⲞⲨⲞⳆϢ ⲈⲚⲈϤϢⲞⲞⲠ Ⲙ̄ⲘⲞⲒ · ⲈⲒϢⲞⲞⲠ
ⳜⲒⲬ̄Ⲙ ⲠⲔⲀⳜ ⲚⲦⲈ ⲦⲘⲚ̄ⲦⲢⲰⲘⲈ Ⲛ̄ⲦⲈⲢⲈϤⲈⲒ ⲈⳜⲢⲀⳆ ⲈⲬⲰⲒ
ⲚϬⲒ ⲠⲈⲚⲆⲨⲘⲀ ⲚⲞⲨⲞⲈⲒⲚ · ⲚⲈⲘⲚ̄Ϣ̄ϬⲞⲘ ⲄⲀⲢ Ⲙ̄ⲠⲔⲞⳠ-
ⲘⲞⳠ ⲈⲦϢⲞⲨⲚ ⳜⲀ ⲠⲞⲨⲞⲈⲒⲚ ⲚⲐⲈ ⲈⲦϤⲞ Ⲙ̄ⲘⲞⳠ ⳜⲚ ⲦⲈϤ-
ⲀⲖⲎⲐⲈⲒⲀ · ⲈⲘⲘⲞⲚ ⲠⲔⲞⳠⲘⲞⳠ ⲚⲀⲂⲰⲖ ⲈⲂⲞⲖ ⲘⲚ ⲚⲈⲦ-
15 ⳜⲒⲬⲰϤ ⲦⲎⲢⲞⲨ ⳜⲒ ⲞⲨⳠⲞⲠ · ⲀⲖⲖⲀ ⲠⲞⲨⲞⲈⲒⲚ ⲈⲚⲈϤϢⲞⲞⲠ
Ⲙ̄ⲘⲞⲒ ⳜⲘ ⲠⲘⲚ̄ⲦⳠⲚⲞⲞⲨⳠ Ⲛ̄ⲚⲀⲒⲰⲚ *ⲚⲀⲀϤ ⲈⲠⲈⲚⲦⲀϤ- ⲔⲄ̄ ᵇ
ϢⲰⲠⲈ Ⲙ̄ⲘⲞⲒ ⳜⲘ ⲠⲔⲞⳠⲘⲞⳠ ⳜⲀⲦⲚ̄ⲦⲎⲨⲦⲚ̄ ⲚϢⲘⲞⲨⲚ
Ⲛϣⲟ · ⲘⲚ ⳠⲀϢϤ ⲚϢⲈ ⲚⲦⲂⲀ ⲚⲔⲰⲂ ⲚⳠⲞⲠ ·

Ⲍ̄ ⲀⳠϢⲰⲠⲈ ϬⲈ ⲚⲦⲈⲢⲈ ⲚⲈⲦϢⲞⲞⲠ ⲦⲎⲢⲞⲨ ⳜⲘ ⲠⲘⲚ̄Ⲧ-
20 ⳠⲚⲞⲞⲨⳠ Ⲛ̄ⲀⲒⲰⲚ · Ⲛ̄ⲦⲈⲢⲞⲨⲚⲀⲨ ⲈⲠⲚⲞϬ ⲚⲞⲨⲞⲈⲒⲚ ⲈⲚⲈϤ-
ϢⲞⲞⲠ Ⲙ̄ⲘⲞⲒ · ⲀⲨϢⲦⲞⲢⲦⲢ̄ ⲦⲎⲢⲞⲨ ⲈⲬ̄Ⲛ ⲚⲈⲨⲈⲢⲎⲨ ⲀⲨⲰ
ⲀⲨⲠⲰⲦ ⲈⲠⲒⳠⲀ ⲘⲚ ⲠⲀⳆ ⳜⲢⲀⳆ ⳜⲚ ⲚⲀⲒⲰⲚ · ⲀⲨⲰ ⲀⲨⲔⲒⲘ
ⲈⲬ̄Ⲛ ⲚⲈⲨⲈⲢⲎⲨ ⲚϬⲒ ⲚⲀⲒⲰⲚ ⲦⲎⲢⲞⲨ ⲘⲚ Ⲙ̄ⲠⲎⲨⲈ ⲦⲎⲢⲞⲨ
ⲘⲚ ⲦⲈⲨⲔⲞⳠⲘⲎⳠⲒⳠ ⲦⲎⲢ̄Ⳡ ⲈⲦⲂⲈ ⲦⲚⲞϬ ⲚⳜⲞⲦⲈ ⲈⲚⲦⲀⳠ-
25 ϢⲰⲠⲈ Ⲙ̄ⲘⲞⲞⲨ ⲈⲂⲞⲖ ⲬⲈ Ⲙ̄ⲠⲞⲨⲈⲒⲘⲈ ⲈⲠⲘⲨⳠⲦⲎⲢⲒⲞⲚ

---

18   after ⲚϢⲈ are further erased letters, perhaps originally ⲀⲨⲰ Ⲙ̄Ⲛ.

father and the three great *triple-powered ones*. *However*, because of the great fear from their agitation, the great *forefather* continued to run from side to side in his *place*, he and the three *triple-powered ones*, and they could not close all their *places* because of the great fear in which they were. And they moved all their *aeons* at the same time, and all their *spheres*, and all their *orders*, fearing and greatly agitated because of the great light which I had. Not as at the time when I had it, in which I was upon the earth of mankind, when the *garment* of light came down upon me, for the *world* would not be able to bear the light as it is in its *reality*, else the *world* and all that is upon it [1] would be dissolved at the same time. But the light which I had in the twelve *aeons* was 8700 myriad [2] times greater than that which I had with you in the *world*.

15.   Now it happened when all those that were in the twelve *aeons* saw the great light which I had, they were all agitated against one another, and they ran from side to side in the *aeons*. And all the *aeons* and all the heavens and their whole *order* moved against one another, because of the great fear which they had because they did not know the *mystery* | which had happened. And Adamas,

---

[1]   (14) all that is upon it; Till: all those that are upon it.
[2]   (18) 8700 myriad; Till: 87 million.

ЄΝΤΑϤϢϢΠЄ ΑΥϢ ΠΑΔΑΜΑϹ ΠΝΟϬ Ν̄ΤΥΡΑΝΝΟϹ ΜΝ̄

Ν̄ΤΥΡΑΝΝΟΥ ΤΗΡΟΥ ЄΤϢΟΟΠ Ζ̄Ν̄ Ν̄ΑΙϢΝ ΤΗΡΟΥ ΑΥΖΙ-

ΤΟΟΤΟΥ ЄΠΟΛЄΜΙ ЄΠΧΙΝΧΗ ΖΡΑΪ Ζ̄Μ ΠΟΥΟЄΙΝ · ΑΥϢ

Μ̄ΠΟΥЄΙΜЄ ΧЄ ⁎⁎ϬΥΠΟΛЄΜЄΙ ΜΝ̄ ΝΙΜ · ЄΒΟΛ ΧЄ ΝЄΥ- Κ̄Δ̄

5 ΝΑΥ ΑΝ ЄΛΛΑΥ Ν̄ϹΑ ΠΟΥΟΪΝ ЄΤΟΥΟΤΒ̄ ЄΜΑϢΟ · ΑϹ-

ϢϢΠЄ ϬЄ Ν̄ΤЄΡΟΥΠΟΛЄΜΙ Ζ̄Μ ΠΟΥΟΪΝ ΑΥϹϢϢΜ

ΤΗΡΟΥ ΖΙ ΝЄΥЄΡΗΥ ΑΥϢ ΑΥΖЄ ЄΠЄϹΗΤ ΖΡΑΪ Ζ̄Ν̄

Ν̄ΑΙϢΝ · ΑΥϢϢΠЄ Ν̄ΘЄ Ν̄ΝΙΡΜ̄Ν̄ΚΑΖ ЄΤΜΟΟΥΤ · ЄΜΝ̄-

ΝΙϤЄ Ν̄ΖΗΤΟΥ · ΑΥϢ ΑΪϤΙ Ν̄ΟΥΟΥϢΝ Ν̄ϢΟΜΝ̄Τ Ζ̄Ν̄

10 ΤЄΥϬΟΜ ΤΗΡΟΥ ΧЄΚΑϹ Ν̄ΝЄΥЄΝЄΡΓΙ Ζ̄Ν̄ ΝЄΥΠΡΑΞΙϹ

ЄΘΟΟΥ · ΑΥϢ ΧЄΚΑϹ ЄΡϢΑΝ Ν̄ΡϢΜЄ ЄΤΖ̄Μ ΠΚΟϹ-

ΜΟϹ ЄΥϢΑΝЄΠΙΚΑΛЄΙ Μ̄ΜΟΟΥ Ζ̄Ν̄ ΝЄΥΜΥϹΤΗΡΙΟΝ · ΝΑΪ

ЄΝΤΑΥΝ̄ΤΟΥ ЄΠЄϹΗΤ Ν̄ϬΙ Ν̄ΑΓΓЄΛΟϹ ЄΝΤΑΥΠΑΡΑΒΑ

ΝΑΪ ЄΤЄ ΝЄΥΜΑΓΙΑ ΝЄ · ΧЄΚΑϹ ϬЄ ЄΥϢΑΝЄΠΙΚΑΛЄΙ

15 Μ̄ΜΟΟΥ Ζ̄Ν̄ ΝЄΥΠΡΑΞΙϹ ЄΘΟΟΥ · Ν̄ΝЄΥЄϢΧΟΚΟΥ

ЄΒΟΛ · ΑΥϢ ΘΙΜΑΡΜЄΝΗ ΜΝ̄ ΤЄϹФΑΙΡΑ ЄΤΟΥΟ' Ν̄-

ΧΟЄΙϹ ЄΡΟΟΥ · ΑΪΠΟΟΝΟΥ ΑΥϢ ΑΪΤΡЄΥΡ̄-ϹΟΟΥ Κ̄Δ̄ᵇ

Ν̄ЄΒΟΤ ЄΥΚΗΤ ЄΖΒΟΥΡ · ΑΥϢ ΑΥΧϢΚ ЄΒΟΛ Ν̄ΝЄΥ-

ΑΠΟΤЄΛЄϹΜΑ · ΑΥϢ ϹΟΟΥ Ν̄ЄΒΟΤ · ЄΥϬϢϢ̄Τ ЄΟΥ-

20 ΝΑΜ ЄΥΧϢΚ ЄΒΟΛ Ν̄ΝЄΥΑΠΟΤЄΛЄϹΜΑ · ЄΒΟΛ ΔЄ

ΖΙΤΝ̄ ΤΚЄΛЄΥϹΙϹ Μ̄ΠϢΟΡΠ̄ Ν̄ΤϢϢ · ΑΥϢ ЄΒΟΛ ΖΙΤΝ̄

ΤΚЄΛЄΥϹΙϹ Μ̄ΠϢΟΡΠ̄ Μ̄ΜΥϹΤΗΡΙΟΝ · ΝЄΝΤΑϤΚΑΑΥ

ΠЄ ЄΥϬϢϢ̄Τ ЄЗΒΟΥΡ Ν̄ΝΑΥ ΝΙΜ Ν̄ϬΙ ΙЄΟΥ ΠЄΠΙϹ-

ΚΟΠΟϹ Μ̄ΠΟΥΟЄΙΝ ЄΥΧϢΚ ЄΒΟΛ Ν̄ΝЄΥΑΠΟΤЄΛЄϹΜΑ ·

---

7   originally ΖΝ ΝЄΥЄΡΗΥ ; Ν erased to give ι.

15 MS ΝЄΥΝЄΥΠΡΑΞΙϹ ; the second ΝЄΥ is expunged.

17 MS originally ΑΥΠΟΟΝΟΥ; Υ is crossed out and ϊ inserted.

18 MS ΑΥΧϢΚ; read ЄΥΧϢΚ.

23 Π altered to ΠЄ after erasure.

the great *tyrant*[1], and all the *tyrants* which are in all the *aeons* began to *wage war* in vain against the light. And they did not know against whom they *waged war*, because they saw nothing except the greatly surpassing light.

Now it happened when they *waged war* against the light, they were all exhausted together, and they were cast down into the *aeons*, and they became like the earth-dwellers who are dead and have no breath in them. And I took a third part of all their power so that they should not *work* their wicked *actions*, and in order that when men who are in the *world call upon* them in their *mysteries* — those which the *transgressing angels** brought down, namely their *magic* — that when now they *call upon* them in their wicked *actions*, they are not able to complete them. And (as for) the *Heimarmene* and the *sphere* over which they rule, I turned them and caused them to spend six months turned to the left, as they complete their (periods of) *influence*, and to look to the right for six months, as they complete their (periods of) *influence*. *However*, through the *command* of the first ordinance and through the *command* of the First *Mystery*, Jeu[2] the *Overseer* of the Light had placed them so that they were looking to the left at all times, as they completed their (periods of) *influence* | and their *actions*.

---

*   cf. Jud. 6

---

[1]   (1) Adamas, the great tyrant; cf. Augustine *c. Faust*. VI 8; as Sabaoth, see Origen *c. Cels* VI 31; J 100; (also 355.17 ff.).

[2]   (23) Jeu; see J 47 ff.; Bousset (Bibl. 10), pp. 165-66.

ⲀⲨⲰ ⲘⲚ ⲚⲈⲨⲠⲢⲀⲜⲒⲤ · ⲀⲤϢⲰⲠⲈ ⲆⲈ ⲚⲦⲈⲢⲒⲈⲒ' ⲈⲠⲈⲨⲦⲞ-
ⲠⲞⲤ ⲀⲨⲀⲦⲀⲔⲦⲒ ⲀⲨⲰ ⲀⲨⲠⲞⲖⲈⲘⲈⲒ ⲈⲀ2ⲎⲦϤ ⲘⲠⲞⲨⲞⲒⲚ
ⲀⲒϤⲒ ⲚⲞⲨⲞⲨⲰⲚ ⲚϢⲞⲘⲚⲦ ⲚⲦⲈ ⲦⲈⲨϬⲞⲘ · ϪⲈ ⲚⲚⲈⲨ-
ⲈϢϬⲘϬⲞⲘ Ⲉ2Ⲱ2Ⲕ ⲈⲂⲞⲖ ⲚⲚⲈⲨⲠⲢⲀⲜⲒⲤ ⲈⲐⲞⲞⲨ · ⲀⲨⲰ
5 ⲐⲒⲘⲀⲢⲘⲈⲚⲎ ⲘⲚ ⲦⲈⲤⲪⲀⲒⲢⲀ · ⲈⲦⲞⲨⲞ' ⲚϪⲞⲈⲒⲤ ⲈⲢⲞⲞⲨ · ⲔⲈ
ⲀⲒⲠⲞⲞⲚⲞⲨ · ⲀⲨⲰ ⲀⲒⲔⲀⲀⲨ ⲈⲨϬⲰϢⲦ Ⲉ2ⲂⲞⲨⲢ ⲚⲤⲞⲞⲨ
ⲚⲈⲂⲞⲦ · ⲈⲨϪⲰⲔ ⲈⲂⲞⲖ ⲚⲚⲈⲨⲀⲠⲞⲦⲈⲖⲈⲤⲘⲀ ⲀⲨⲰ ⲀⲒ-
ⲔⲀⲀⲨ ⲚⲔⲈⲤⲞⲞⲨ ⲚⲈⲂⲞⲦ · ⲈⲨⲔⲎⲦ ⲈⲞⲨⲚⲀⲘ · ⲈⲨϪⲰⲔ
ⲈⲂⲞⲖ ⲚⲚⲈⲨⲀⲠⲞⲦⲈⲖⲈⲤⲘⲀ :

10 ⲚⲀⲒ ϬⲈ ⲚⲦⲈⲢⲈϤϪⲞⲞⲨ ⲈⲚⲈϤⲘⲀⲐⲎⲦⲎⲤ · ⲠⲈϪⲀϤ ⲚⲀⲨ ·
ϪⲈ ⲠⲈⲦⲈ ⲞⲨⲚ-ⲘⲀⲀϪⲈ ⲘⲘⲞϤ ⲈⲤⲰⲦⲘ ⲘⲀⲢⲈϤⲤⲰⲦⲘ ·
ⲀⲤϢⲰⲠⲈ ϬⲈ ⲚⲦⲈⲢⲈ ⲘⲀⲢⲒ2ⲀⲘ ⲤⲰⲦⲘ ⲈⲚⲈⲒϢⲀϪⲈ ⲈϤϪⲰ
ⲘⲘⲞⲞⲨ ⲚϬⲒ ⲠⲤⲰⲦⲎⲢ · ⲀⲤⲒⲰⲢⲘ ⲈⲂⲞⲖ 2Ⲙ ⲠⲀⲎⲢ · Ⲙ-
ⲠⲚⲀⲨ ⲚⲞⲨⲞⲨⲚⲞⲨ · ⲠⲈϪⲀⲤ ϪⲈ ⲠⲀϪⲞⲈⲒⲤ ⲔⲈⲖⲈⲨⲈ ⲚⲀⲒ
15 ⲚⲦⲀϢⲀϪⲈ 2Ⲛ ⲞⲨⲠⲀⲢ2ⲎⲤⲒⲀ ·

Ⳍ ⲀϤⲞⲨⲰϢⲂ ⲚϬⲒ ⲒⲤ ⲠⲚⲀ2Ⲧ · ⲠⲈϪⲀϤ ⲘⲘⲀⲢⲒ2ⲀⲘ · ϪⲈ
ⲘⲀⲢⲒ2ⲀⲘ ⲦⲘⲀⲔⲀⲢⲒⲀ · ⲦⲀⲒ ⲈⲒⲚⲀϪⲞⲔⲤ ⲈⲂⲞⲖ 2Ⲛ ⲘⲘⲨⲤ-
ⲦⲎⲢⲒⲞⲚ ⲦⲎⲢⲞⲨ ⲚⲦⲈ * ⲚⲀⲠϪⲒⲤⲈ · ϢⲀϪⲈ 2Ⲛ ⲞⲨⲠⲀⲢ- ⲔⲈᵇ
2ⲎⲤⲒⲀ ϪⲈ ⲚⲦⲞ ⲦⲈⲦⲈⲢⲈ ⲠⲈⲤ2ⲎⲦ ⲤⲞⲨⲦⲰⲚ Ⲉ2ⲞⲨⲚ
20 ⲈⲦⲘⲚⲦⲈⲢⲞ ⲚⲘⲠⲎⲨⲈ · Ⲛ2ⲞⲨⲞ ⲈⲚⲞⲨⲤⲚⲎⲨ ⲦⲎⲢⲞⲨ ·

Ⳍ ⲦⲞⲦⲈ ⲠⲈϪⲀⲤ ⲚϬⲒ ⲘⲀⲢⲒ2ⲀⲘ ⲘⲠⲤⲰⲦⲎⲢ ϪⲈ ⲠⲀ-
ϪⲞⲈⲒⲤ · ⲠϢⲀϪⲈ ⲈⲚⲦⲀⲔϪⲞⲞϤ ⲚⲀⲚ ϪⲈ ⲠⲈⲦⲈ ⲞⲨⲚ-
ⲘⲀⲀϪⲈ ⲘⲘⲞϤ ⲈⲤⲰⲦⲘ ⲘⲀⲢⲈϤⲤⲰⲦⲘ · ⲈⲔϪⲰ ⲘⲘⲞⲤ ϪⲈ
ⲈⲚⲈⲚⲞⲒ ⲘⲠϢⲀϪⲈ ⲈⲚⲦⲀⲔϪⲞⲞϤ · ⲤⲰⲦⲘ ϬⲈ ⲠⲀϪⲞⲈⲒⲤ ·

16.   Now it happened when I came to their *place*, they *rebelled* and *waged war* against the light. And I took a third part of their power, so that they should not be able to complete their wicked *actions*. And (as for) the *Heimarmene* and the *sphere* over which they rule, I turned them, I placed them looking to the left for six months, as they complete their (periods of) *influence*, and I placed them for another six months turning to the right, as they complete their (periods of) *influence*."

17.   Now when he had said these things to his *disciples*, he said to them : "He who has ears to hear, let him hear" *.

Now it happened when Mariam [1] heard these words as the *Saviour* was saying them, she stared for one hour into the *air* and said : "My Lord, *command* me that I speak *openly*".

Jesus, the compassionate, answered and said to Mariam : "Mariam, thou *blessed one*, whom I will complete in all the *mysteries* of the height, speak *openly*, thou art she whose heart is more directed to the Kingdom of Heaven than all thy brothers".

18.   *Then* Mariam said to the *Saviour* : "My Lord, the word which thou hast spoken to us : 'Who has ears to hear, let him hear' ▫, thou sayest so that we may *understand* the word which thou hast spoken. Hear now, my Lord, | for

---

*   cf. Mk. 4.9
▫   cf. Mk. 4.9

---

[1]   (12) Mariam; see Origen *c. Cels.* V. 62; Hippol. V.7.1; SophJC 90; GTh 84; GPh 59, 63; GMar 9 etc.

ⲧⲁϫⲟⲟⲥ ϨⲚ ⲞⲨⲠⲀⲢϨⲎⲤⲒⲀ· ⲠϢⲀϪⲈ ⲈⲚⲦⲀⲔϪⲞⲞϤ ϪⲈ
ⲀⲒϤⲒ ⲚⲞⲨⲞⲨⲰⲚ ⲚϢⲞⲘⲚⲦ' ϨⲚ ⲦϬⲞⲘ ⲚⲚⲀⲢⲬⲰⲚ ⲚⲚ-
ⲀⲒⲰⲚ ⲦⲎⲢⲞⲨ· ⲀⲨⲰ ϪⲈ ⲀⲒⲠⲰⲰⲚⲈ ⲚⲦⲈⲨϨⲒⲘⲀⲢⲘⲈⲚⲎ·
ⲘⲚ ⲦⲈⲨⲤⲪⲀⲒⲢⲀ ⲚⲀⲒ ⲈⲦⲞⲨⲞ ⲚϪⲞⲈⲒⲤ ⲈϪⲰⲞⲨ· ϪⲈⲔⲀⲤ
5 ⲈⲨϢⲀⲚⲈⲠⲒⲔⲀⲖⲈⲒ ⲘⲘⲞⲞⲨ ⲚϬⲒ ⲠⲄⲈⲚⲞⲤ ⲚⲚⲢⲰⲘⲈ ϨⲚ
ⲚⲈⲨⲘⲨⲤⲦⲎⲢⲒⲞⲚ ⲚⲀⲒ ⲚⲦⲀⲨⲦⲤⲀⲂⲞⲞⲨ ⲈⲢⲞⲞⲨ ⲚϬⲒ ⲚⲀⲄ-
ⲄⲈⲖⲞⲤ ⲈⲚⲦⲀⲨⲠⲀⲢⲀⲂⲀ ⲈⲠⲈⲨϪⲰⲔ ⲈⲂⲞⲖ ⲚⲚⲈⲨϨⲂⲎⲨⲈ
ⲈⲐⲞⲞⲨ· ⲀⲨⲰ ⲚⲀⲚⲞⲘⲞⲚ ϨⲘ ⲠⲘⲨⲤⲦⲎⲢⲒⲞⲚ ⲚⲦⲈⲨ- ⲔⲈ
ⲘⲀⲄⲒⲀ· ϪⲈⲔⲀⲀⲤ ⲈⲚⲚⲈⲨⲈϢϬⲘϬⲞⲘ ϬⲈ ϪⲒⲚ ⲘⲠⲈⲒ̈ⲚⲀⲨ
10 ⲈϪⲰⲔ ⲈⲂⲞⲖ ⲚⲚⲈⲨϨⲂⲎⲨⲈ ⲚⲀⲚⲞⲘⲞⲚ ⲈⲂⲞⲖ ϪⲈ ⲀⲔϤⲒ
ⲚⲦⲈⲨϬⲞⲘ ⲚϨⲎⲦⲞⲨ ⲘⲚ ⲚⲈⲨⲢⲈϤⲔⲀ-ⲞⲨⲚⲞⲨ ⲘⲚ ⲚⲈⲨⲢⲈϤ-
ϢⲒⲚⲈ ⲘⲚ ⲚⲈⲦⲈϢⲀⲨⲦⲀⲘⲈ-ⲚⲢⲰⲘⲈ ⲈⲦϨⲘ ⲠⲔⲞⲤⲘⲞⲤ
ⲈϨⲰⲂ ⲚⲒⲘ ⲈⲦⲚⲀϢⲰⲠⲈ ϪⲈ ⲚⲚⲈⲨⲚⲞⲈⲒ ϪⲒⲚ ⲘⲠⲈⲒ̈ⲚⲀⲨ
ⲈⲦⲀⲘⲞⲞⲨ ⲈⲖⲀⲀⲨ ⲚϨⲰⲂ· ⲈϤⲚⲀϢⲰⲠⲈ ϪⲈ ⲀⲔⲠⲰⲰⲚⲈ
15 ⲚⲚⲈⲨⲤⲪⲀⲒⲢⲀ· ⲀⲨⲰ ⲀⲔⲦⲢⲈⲨⲢ-ⲤⲞⲞⲨ ⲚⲈⲂⲞⲦ· ⲈⲨⲔⲎⲦ
ⲈϨⲂⲞⲨⲢ ⲈⲨϪⲰⲔ ⲈⲂⲞⲖ ⲚⲚⲈⲨⲀⲠⲞⲦⲈⲖⲈⲤⲘⲀ· ⲀⲨⲰ ⲔⲈ-
ⲤⲞⲞⲨ ⲚⲈⲂⲞⲦ ⲈⲨϬⲰϢⲦ ⲈⲞⲨⲚⲀⲘ· ⲈⲨϪⲰⲔ ⲈⲂⲞⲖ
ⲚⲚⲈⲨⲀⲠⲞⲦⲈⲖⲈⲤⲘⲀ· ⲈⲦⲂⲈ ⲠⲈⲒ̈ϢⲀϪⲈ ϬⲈ ⲠⲀϪⲞⲒ̈Ⲥ ⲈⲚⲦ-
ⲀⲤϪⲞⲞϤ ⲚⲦⲈⲒ̈ϨⲈ ⲚϬⲒ ⲦϬⲞⲘ ⲈⲦϨⲚ ⲎⲤⲀⲒ̈ⲀⲤ ⲠⲈⲠⲢⲞⲪⲎ-
20 ⲦⲎⲤ ⲀⲨⲰ ⲚⲦⲀⲤⲦⲀⲨⲞϤ ϨⲚ ⲞⲨⲠⲀⲢⲀⲂⲞⲖⲎ ⲘⲠⲚⲒⲦⲒⲔⲎ ⲔⲈᵇ
ⲘⲠⲒⲞⲨⲞⲈⲒϢ ⲈϤϢⲀϪⲈ ⲈⲦⲂⲈ ⲐⲞⲢⲀⲤⲒⲤ ⲚⲔⲎⲘⲈ· ϪⲈ ⲈⲨ-
ⲦⲰⲚ ϬⲈ ⲔⲎⲘⲈ ⲈⲨⲦⲰⲚ ⲚⲈⲔⲢⲈϤϢⲒⲚⲈ ⲘⲚ ⲚⲈⲔⲢⲈϤⲔⲀ-
ⲞⲨⲚⲞⲨ ⲘⲚ ⲚⲈⲦⲈϢⲀⲨⲘⲞⲨⲦⲈ ⲈⲂⲞⲖ ϨⲘ ⲠⲔⲀϨ ⲘⲚ ⲚⲈⲦ-
ⲈϢⲀⲨⲘⲞⲨⲦⲈ ⲈⲂⲞⲖ ⲚϨⲎⲦⲞⲨ· ⲘⲀⲢⲞⲨⲦⲀⲘⲞⲔ ϬⲈ ϪⲒⲚ

---

13 MS ⲚⲚⲈⲨⲚⲞⲈⲒ.
20 MS ⲘⲠⲚⲒⲦⲒⲔⲎ; read ⲘⲠⲚⲀⲦⲒⲔⲎ.

I will speak *openly*. The word which thou hast spoken :
'I have taken a third part of the power of the *archons* of
all the *aeons*, and I have turned their *Heimarmene* and their
sphere over which they rule, so that when the *race* of
mankind *call upon* them in their *mysteries* — these which
the *transgressing angels* have taught them for the completion
of their evil and *iniquitous* deeds in the *mystery* of their
magic — from this hour now they should not be able to
complete their *iniquitous* deeds, because thou hast taken
their power from them and from their astrologers and from
their soothsayers and from those who tell men who are in
the *world* all things which will happen, so that from this
hour they will not *understand* anything which will happen
so as to tell it. For thou hast turned their *sphere*, and thou
hast made them spend six months turned to the left, completing their (periods of) *influence*, and six months looking
to the right, completing their (periods of) *influence*.' Now
concerning this word, my Lord, the power within the *prophet*
Isaiah has spoken thus and has related once in a *spiritual*
parable, speaking about the *vision* of Egypt : 'Where now
Egypt, where are thy soothsayers and thy astrologers, and
those who call from the earth, and those who call from
their bellies? Let them now tell thee, from | this hour, the

ⲘⲠⲉ·ⲛⲁⲩ ⲉⲛ2ⲂⲎⲩⲉ ⲉⲧ̄ϥⲛⲁⲁⲁⲩ ⲛ̄ϭⲓ ⲠⲬⲟⲉⲓⲥ ⲤⲀⲂⲀⲰⲐ·

ⲚⲦⲀⲤⲠⲢⲟⲫⲎⲦⲉⲩⲉ ϭⲉ 2ⲀⲐⲎ Ⲙ̄ⲠⲀⲦ̄Ⲕⲉⲓ' ⲛ̄ϭⲓ ⲦϭⲟⲘ ⲉⲧ2̄Ⲛ

ⲚⲤⲀ·ⲀⲤ ⲠⲉⲠⲢⲟⲫⲎⲦⲎⲤ ⲚⲦⲀⲤⲠⲢⲟⲫⲎⲦⲉⲩⲉ 2ⲀⲢⲟⲔ Ⲭⲉ

ⲔⲚⲀϥⲓ Ⲛ̄ⲦϭⲟⲘ Ⲛ̄Ⲛ̄ⲀⲢⲬⲰⲚ Ⲛ̄Ⲛ̄ⲀⲓⲰⲚ· ⲀⲨⲰ Ⲛ̄ⲅⲠⲰⲰⲚⲉ

5 Ⲛ̄ⲦⲉⲨⲤⲫⲀⲓⲢⲀ· Ⲙ̄Ⲛ̄ ⲦⲉⲨ2ⲒⲘⲀⲢⲘⲈⲚⲎ Ⲭⲉ Ⲛ̄ⲚⲉⲩⲉⲓⲘⲈ

ⲈⲀⲀⲀⲨ Ⲭⲓⲛ Ⲙ̄Ⲡⲉ·ⲛⲁⲩ· ⲈⲦⲂⲈ ⲠⲀ·ⲓ ⲢⲰ ⲀⲤⲬⲟⲟⲥ Ⲭⲉ

Ⲛ̄ⲦⲈⲦⲚⲀⲈⲒⲘⲈ ⲀⲚ ϭⲉ Ⲭⲉ ⲟⲨ ⲠⲈⲦⲈⲢⲈ ⲠⲬⲟⲉⲓⲥ ⲤⲀ-

ⲂⲀⲰⲐ ⲚⲀⲀⲀϥ· ⲈⲦⲈ ⲠⲀ·ⲓ ⲠⲈ** Ⲭⲉ Ⲙ̄Ⲛ̄-ⲀⲀⲀⲨ 2Ⲛ̄ Ⲛ̄ⲀⲢ- Ⲕ̄ⲅ

ⲬⲰⲚ ⲚⲀⲈⲒⲘⲈ ⲈⲚⲈⲦ̄ⲔⲚⲀⲀⲀⲨ Ⲭⲓⲛ Ⲙ̄Ⲡⲉ·ⲛⲁⲩ ⲈⲦⲈ Ⲛ̄ⲦⲟⲟⲨ

10 ⲠⲈ ⲔⲎⲘⲈ· ⲈⲂⲟⲀ Ⲭⲉ Ⲛ̄ⲦⲟⲟⲨ ⲚⲈ Ⲧ2ⲨⲀⲎ Ⲛ̄ⲦⲀ ⲦϭⲟⲘ

ϭⲉ ⲈⲦ2̄Ⲛ̄ ⲚⲤⲀ·ⲀⲤ· ⲚⲦⲀⲤⲠⲢⲟⲫⲎⲦⲉⲩⲉ 2ⲀⲢⲟⲔ Ⲙ̄ⲠⲒⲟⲨ-

ⲟⲈⲒⲱ ⲈⲤⲬⲰ Ⲙ̄Ⲙⲟⲥ Ⲭⲉ· Ⲛ̄ⲦⲈⲦⲚⲀⲈⲒⲘⲈ ⲀⲚ ϭⲉ Ⲭⲓⲛ

Ⲙ̄Ⲡⲉ·ⲛⲁⲩ ⲈⲚⲈⲦ̄ϥⲚⲀⲀⲀⲨ Ⲛ̄ϭⲓ ⲠⲬⲟⲉⲓⲥ ⲤⲀⲂⲀⲰⲐ· ⲈⲦⲂⲈ

ⲦϭⲟⲘ Ⲛ̄ⲟⲨⲟⲈⲒⲚ ⲈⲚⲦⲀⲔⲬⲒⲦ̄Ⲥ Ⲛ̄Ⲧⲟⲟⲧ̄ϥ Ⲛ̄ⲤⲀⲂⲀⲰⲐ ⲠⲀ-

15 ⲅⲀⲐⲟⲥ ⲠⲀ·ⲓ ⲈⲦⲱⲟⲟⲠ 2̄Ⲙ ⲠⲦⲟⲠⲟⲥ Ⲛ̄ⲦⲟⲨⲚⲀⲘ ⲦⲀ·ⲓ ⲈⲦ-

ⲱⲟⲟⲠ 2̄Ⲙ ⲠⲈⲔⲤⲰⲘⲀ Ⲛ̄2ⲨⲀⲒⲔⲟⲚ Ⲙ̄ⲠⲟⲟⲨ· ⲈⲦⲂⲈ ⲠⲀ·ⲓ

ϭⲉ ⲀⲔⲬⲟⲟⲥ ⲚⲀⲚ ⲠⲀⲬⲟⲉⲓⲥ Ⲓ̄Ⲥ Ⲭⲉ ⲠⲈⲦⲈ ⲟⲨⲛ̄-ⲘⲀⲀⲬⲈ

Ⲙ̄Ⲙⲟϥ ⲈⲤⲰⲦ̄Ⲙ ⲘⲀⲢⲈϥⲤⲰⲦ̄Ⲙ Ⲭⲉ ⲈⲔⲈⲈⲒⲘⲈ Ⲭⲉ ⲚⲒⲘ ⲠⲈⲦ-

ⲈⲢⲈ ⲠⲈϥ2ⲎⲦ ⲬⲟⲔ̄Ⲣ Ⲉ2ⲟⲨⲚ ⲈⲦⲘ̄Ⲛ̄Ⲧⲉ̄Ⲣⲟ Ⲛ̄Ⲙ̄ⲠⲎⲨⲈ·   Ⲕ̄ⲅ ᵇ

20 ⲍ ⲀⲤⲱⲟⲠⲉ ϭⲉ Ⲛ̄ⲦⲈⲢⲈ ⲘⲀⲢⲒⲀ ⲟⲨⲱ ⲈⲤⲬⲰ Ⲛ̄Ⲛⲉ·ⲓ-

ⲱⲀⲬⲈ· ⲠⲈⲬⲀϥ Ⲭⲉ ⲈⲨⲅⲈ ⲘⲀⲢⲒⲀ· Ⲭⲉ Ⲛ̄ⲦⲈ ⲟⲨⲘⲀⲔⲀ-

ⲢⲒⲟⲥ Ⲛ̄Ⲧⲟ ⲠⲀⲢⲀ Ⲥ2ⲒⲘⲈ ⲚⲒⲘ ⲈⲦ2Ⲓ·Ⲭ̄Ⲙ ⲠⲔⲀ2· Ⲭⲉ Ⲛ̄Ⲧⲟ

ⲦⲈⲦⲚⲀⲱⲟⲠⲉ Ⲙ̄ⲠⲀⲎⲢⲰⲘⲀ Ⲛ̄ⲦⲈ ⲚⲒⲠⲀⲎⲢⲰⲘⲀ ⲦⲎⲢⲟⲨ·

ⲀⲨⲰ Ⲛ̄ⲬⲱⲔ Ⲛ̄ⲦⲈ ⲚⲒⲬⲰⲔ ⲦⲎⲢⲟⲨ·

---

10 MS ⲠⲈ; read ⲚⲈ.
14 2 letters erased before ⲦϭⲟⲘ.

things which the Lord Sabaoth will do.' * Now before thou
didst come, the power within Isaiah, the *prophet, prophesied*
concerning thee, that thou wouldst take away the power
of the *archons* of the *aeons,* and that thou wouldst turn their
sphere and their *Heimarmene,* so that from this hour they
would know nothing. Concerning this also it has said : 'You
will not know what the Lord Sabaoth will do' □. That is,
none of the *archons* will know what things thou wilt do
from this hour. They (the *archons*) are Egypt, because they
are *matter.* The power within Isaiah has once *prophesied*
about thee saying : 'You will not know from this hour what
the Lord Sabaoth will do' □. Concerning the power of light
which thou hast taken from Sabaoth the *Good,* who is in
the *place* of the right, and which today is in thy *material
body,* concerning this now, thou hast said to us, my Lord
Jesus : 'He who has ears to hear, let him hear' ∆, so that
thou shouldst know whose heart is directed towards the
Kingdom of Heaven."

19.   Now it happened when Maria finished saying these
words, he said : "*Excellent,* Maria. Thou art *blessed beyond*
all women upon earth, because thou shalt be the *pleroma*
of all *pleromas* and the completion of all completions." |

---

*   cf. Is. 19.3, 12
□   cf. Is. 19.12
∆   Mk. 4.9

ⲋ ⲚⲦⲈⲢⲈ ⲘⲀⲢⲒⲀ ⲆⲈ ⲤⲰⲦⲘ ⲈⲠⲤⲰⲦⲎⲢ ⲈϤϪⲰ ⲚⲚⲈⲒ-
ϢⲀϪⲈ · ⲀⲤⲦⲈⲖⲎⲖ ⲘⲘⲞⲤ ⲈⲘⲀϢⲞ ⲀⲨⲰ ⲀⲤⲈⲒ· ⲈⲐⲎ ⲚⲒⲤ
ⲀⲤⲠⲀⲌⲦⲤ ⲘⲠⲈϤⲘⲦⲞ ⲈⲂⲞⲖ · ⲀⲤⲞⲨⲰϢⲦ ⲚⲚⲈϤⲞⲨⲈⲢⲎⲦⲈ ·
ⲠⲈϪⲀⲤ ⲚⲀϤ ϪⲈ ⲠⲀϪⲞⲈⲒⲤ · ⲤⲰⲦⲘ ⲈⲢⲞⲒ ⲦⲀϪⲚⲞⲨⲔ
5 ⲈⲠⲈⲒϢⲀϪⲈ · ⲈⲘⲠⲀⲦⲔϢⲀϪⲈ ⲚⲘⲘⲀⲚ ⲈⲚⲦⲞⲠⲞⲤ ⲈⲚⲦ-
ⲀⲔⲂⲰⲔ ⲈⲢⲞⲞⲨ ·

ⲋ ⲀϤⲞⲨⲰϢⲂ ⲚϬⲒ ⲒⲤ ⲠⲈϪⲀϤ ⲘⲘⲀⲢⲒⲌⲀⲘ ϪⲈ ϢⲀϪⲈ
ⲌⲚ ⲞⲨⲠⲀⲢⲌⲎⲤⲒⲀ · ⲀⲨⲰ ⲘⲠⲢⲢⲌⲞⲦⲈ · ⲌⲰⲂ ⲚⲒⲘ ⲈⲢⲈϢⲒⲚⲈ ⲔⲎ
ⲚⲤⲰⲞⲨ · ϮⲚⲀϬⲞⲖⲠⲞⲨ ⲚⲈ ⲈⲂⲞⲖ ·

10 ⲋ ⲠⲈϪⲀⲤ ϪⲈ ⲠⲀϪⲞⲈⲒⲤ · ⲢⲰⲘⲈ ⲚⲒⲘ ⲈⲦⲤⲞⲞⲨⲚ Ⲙ-
ⲠⲘⲨⲤⲦⲎⲢⲒⲞⲚ ⲚⲦⲘⲀⲄⲒⲀ ⲚⲚⲀⲢⲬⲰⲚ ⲦⲎⲢⲞⲨ ⲚⲚⲀⲒⲰⲚ ⲦⲎ-
ⲢⲞⲨ · ⲘⲚ ⲦⲘⲀⲄⲒⲀ ⲚⲚⲀⲢⲬⲰⲚ ⲚⲐⲒⲘⲀⲢⲘⲈⲚⲎ ⲘⲚ ⲚⲀⲦⲈ-
ⲤⲪⲀⲒⲢⲀ ⲔⲀⲦⲀ ⲐⲈ ⲈⲚⲦⲀⲨⲦⲤⲀⲂⲞⲞⲨ ⲈⲢⲞⲞⲨ ⲚϬⲒ ⲚⲀⲄ-
ⲄⲈⲖⲞⲤ ⲈⲚⲦⲀⲨⲠⲀⲢⲀⲂⲀ ⲀⲨⲰ ⲈⲨϢⲀⲚⲈⲠⲒⲔⲀⲖⲈⲒ ⲘⲘⲞⲞⲨ
15 ⲌⲚ ⲚⲈⲨⲘⲨⲤⲦⲎⲢⲒⲞⲚ · ⲈⲦⲈ ⲚⲈⲨⲘⲀⲄⲒⲀ ⲚⲈ ⲈⲐⲞⲞⲨ ·
ⲈⲤϢⲰⲦ ⲈⲚⲈⲌⲂⲎⲨⲈ ⲈⲦⲚⲀⲚⲞⲨⲞⲨ · ⲤⲈⲚⲀϪⲞⲔⲞⲨ ⲈⲂⲞⲖ
ⲘⲠⲈⲒⲚⲀⲨ · ϪⲚ ⲘⲘⲞⲚ ·

ⲋ ⲀϤⲞⲨⲰϢⲂ ⲆⲈ ⲚϬⲒ ⲒⲤ ⲠⲈϪⲀϤ ⲘⲘⲀⲢⲒⲀ · ϪⲈ ⲚⲤⲈ-
ⲚⲀϪⲞⲔⲞⲨ ⲀⲚ ⲈⲂⲞⲖ · ⲚⲐⲈ ⲈⲚⲈⲨϪⲰⲔ ⲘⲘⲞⲞⲨ ⲈⲂⲞⲖ
20 ϪⲒⲚ ⲚϢⲞⲢⲠ · ϪⲈ ⲀⲒϤⲒ ⲚⲞⲨⲞⲨⲰⲚ ⲚϢⲞⲘⲚⲦ ⲌⲚ ⲦⲈⲨ-
ϬⲞⲘ · ⲀⲖⲖⲀ ⲤⲈⲚⲀⲈⲒⲢⲈ ⲚⲞⲨⲖⲞⲈⲒϬⲈ ⲌⲚ ⲚⲈⲦⲤⲞⲞⲨⲚ ⲔⲎ ᵇ
ⲚⲘⲘⲨⲤⲦⲎⲢⲒⲞⲚ ⲚⲦⲘⲀⲄⲒⲀ ⲘⲠⲘⲈⲌⲘⲚⲦϢⲞⲘⲦⲈ ⲚⲀⲒⲰⲚ ·
ⲀⲨⲰ ⲈⲨϢⲀⲚⲈⲠⲒⲔⲀⲖⲒ ⲚⲘⲘⲨⲤⲦⲎⲢⲒⲞⲚ ⲚⲦⲘⲀⲄⲒⲀ ⲚⲚⲈⲦ-
ϢⲞⲞⲠ ⲌⲘ ⲠⲘⲈⲌⲘⲚⲦϢⲞⲘⲦⲈ ⲚⲚⲀⲒⲰⲚ · ⲤⲈⲚⲀϪⲞⲔⲞⲨ
25 ⲈⲂⲞⲖ ⲔⲀⲖⲰⲤ ⲌⲚ ⲞⲨⲰⲢϪ ⲈⲂⲞⲖ ϪⲈ ⲘⲠⲒϤⲒ-ϬⲞⲘ ⲌⲘ

---

8   Ⲃ in upper right-hand margin at end of quire.

But when Maria heard the *Saviour* saying these words, she rejoiced greatly and she came before Jesus, she prostrated herself in his presence, she worshipped at his feet, she said to him : "My Lord, hear me that I question thee on this word before thou speakest with us of the *places* to which thou hast gone".

Jesus answered and said to Mariam : "Speak *openly* and do not fear. I will reveal all things which thou seekest".

20. She said : "My Lord, all men who know the *mystery* of the *magic* of all the *archons* of all the *aeons*, and the *magic* of the *archons* of the *Heimarmene* and those of the *sphere*, *as* the *transgressing angels* have taught them, when they *call upon* them in their *mysteries*, that is their evil *magic* to prevent good things : will they, from this hour, fulfil them or not?"

Then Jesus answered and said to Maria : "They will not fulfil them in the manner in which they fulfilled them from the beginning, because I have taken a third part of their power. *But* they will borrow from those who know the *mysteries* of the *magic* of the third *aeon*. And when they *call upon* the *mysteries* of the *magic* of those who are in the third *aeon*, they will fulfil them *well* and certainly because I have not taken power from | that *place, according to* the *command* of the First *Mystery*".

ΠΤΟΠΟС ЄΤⲘⲘΑΥ ΚΑΤΑ ΤΚЄΛЄΥСΙС ⲘΠϢΟΡⲠ ⲘⲘΥС-
ΤΗΡΙΟΝ ·

   Ⳅ ΑСϢΩΠЄ ΔЄ ⲚΤЄΡЄ ⲒС ΟΥΩ ЄϤΧΩ ⲚΝЄⲒϢΑΧЄ ·
ΑСΟΥΩⳌ ΟΝ ЄΤΟΟΤⲤ ⲚϬΙ·ΜΑΡΙΑ ΠЄΧΑС ΧЄ ΠΑΧΟЄΙС
5 ЄⲒЄ ⲚΡЄϤΚΑ-ΟΥΝΟΥ ⲘⲚ ⲚΡЄϤϢΙΝЄ · ЄⲒЄ ⲚСЄΝΑΤΑΜЄ-
ⲚΡΩΜЄ ΑΝ ЄΠЄΤΝΑϢΩΠЄ ⲘΜΟΟΥ ΧΙΝ ⲘΠЄⲒΝΑΥ ·
ΑϤΟΥΩϢⲂ ΔЄ ⲚϬΙ ⲒС ΠЄΧΑϤ ⲘΜΑΡΙΑ ΧЄ ЄΡЄϢΑΝ
ⲚΡЄϤΚΑ-ΟΥΝΟΥ ЄΥϢΑΝⳌЄ ЄΘΙΜΑΡΜЄΝΗ ⲘⲚ ΤЄСⲪΑΙΡΑ
ЄΥΚΗΤ^{**} ЄⳌⲂΟΥΡ ΚΑΤΑ ΠЄΥϢΟΡⲠ ⲚСΩΡ ЄⲂΟΛ · ϢΑΡЄ Κ̄Θ̄
10 ΝЄΥϢΑΧЄ ΑΠΑΝΤΑ · ΑΥΩ СЄΝΑΧΩ ⲘΠЄΤЄϢϢЄ Є-
ϢΩΠЄ · ЄΥϢΑΝΑΠΑΝΤΑ ΔЄ ЄΘΙΜΑΡΜЄΝΗ Η̇ ЄΤЄ-
СⳘΑΙΡΑ ЄΥΚΗΤ ЄΟΥΝΑΜ · ΜЄΥΧΙ-ⲭΛΑΥ ⲚⳌΩⲂ ⲘΜЄ
ЄⲂΟΛ ΧЄ ΑⲒΚΤΟ ⲚΝЄΥΑΠΟΤЄΛЄСΜΑ · ⲘⲚ ΝЄΥϤΤΟΟΥ
ⲚΚΟΟⳌ · ⲘⲚ ΝЄΥϢΟⲘⲚΤ ⲚΚΟΟⳌ · ⲘⲚ ΠЄΥϢΜΟΥΝ
15 ⲚСΜΟΤ · ЄΠЄΙΔΗ ΝЄΥΜΗΝ ЄⲂΟΛ ΠЄ ⲚϬΙ ΝЄΥΑΠΟΤЄ-
ΛЄСΜΑ ΧΙΝ ⲚϢΟΡⲠ ЄΥΚΗΤ ЄⳌⲂΟΥΡ · ⲘⲚ ΝЄΥϤΤΟΟΥ
ⲚΚΟΟⳌ · ⲘⲚ ΝЄΥϢΟⲘⲚΤ ⲚΚΟΟⳌ · ⲘⲚ ΠЄΥϢΜΟΥΝ
ⲚСΜΟΤ · ΤЄΝΟΥ ΔЄ ΑⲒΤΡЄΥⲢ-СΟΟΥ ⲚЄⲂΟΤ ЄΥΚΗΤ
ЄⳌⲂΟΥΡ · ΑΥΩ СΟΟΥ ⲚЄⲂΟΤ ЄΥΚΗΤ ЄΟΥΝΑΜ · ΠЄΤ-
20 ΝΑϬΙΝЄ ϬЄ ⲘΠЄΥΩΠ ΧΙΝ ⲘΠЄΟΥΟЄΙϢ ЄΝΤΑⲒΠΟ-
ΟΝΟΥ · ЄΑⲒΚΛΑΥ ЄΤΡЄΥⲢ-СΟΟΥ ⲚЄⲂΟΤ ЄΥϬΩϢΤ Κ̄Θ̄^b
ЄΝЄΥΜЄΡΟС ⲚⳌⲂΟΥΡ · ΑΥΩ СΟΟΥ ⲚЄⲂΟΤ ЄΥϬΩϢΤ
ЄΝЄΥϬΙΝΜΟΟϢЄ ⲚΟΥΝΑΜ · ΠЄΤΝΑϯⳌΤΗϤ ϬЄ ΝΑΥ
ⲚΤЄⲒⳌЄ ϤΝΑЄΙΜЄ ЄΝЄΥΑΠΟΤЄΛЄСΜΑ ⳌΝ ΟΥΩΡⲭ̄
25 ΑΥΩ ϤΝΑΤΑΥЄ-ⳌΩⲂ ΝΙΜ ЄΤΟΥΝΑΛΑΥ · ⳌΟΜΟΙΩС ΟΝ
ⲚΡЄϤϢΙΝЄ ЄΥϢΑΝЄΠΙΚΑΛΙ ⲘΠΡΑΝ ⲚΝΑΡΧΩΝ · ΝСЄ-

---

9 Ⲅ̄ in upper left-hand margin at beginning of quire.

21. It happened, *however*, when Jesus finished speaking these words, Maria answered again and said: "My Lord, will the astrologers and the soothsayers not tell men, from this hour, what will happen?"

Jesus answered, *however*, and said to Maria: "When the astrologers find the *Heimarmene* and the *sphere* turned to the left, *according to* their first distribution, then their words *concur* and they will say what is due to happen. *But* when they *meet* the *Heimarmene or* the *sphere* turned to the right, they do not speak anything of the truth, because I have turned their (periods of) *influence* and their quadrangles and their triangles and their figures of eight [1], *since* their (periods of) *influence* remained turned to the left from the beginning, together with their quadrangles and their triangles and their figures of eight. *However*, I have now caused them to spend six months turned to the left, and six months turned to the right. He who now will find their reckoning from the time when I turned them, placing them to spend six months looking to their left hand *parts*, and six months looking to their right hand paths, and who will now consult them in this way, will know their (periods of) *influence* with certainty, and he will predict all things that they will do. *Likewise* also the soothsayers, when they *call upon* the name of the *archons*, and they | *meet* them looking to the left,

---

[1] (13, 16) figures of eight; lit. eight(fold) figures (also 31.19).

ⲀⲠⲀⲚⲦⲀ ⲈⲢⲞⲞⲨ ⲈⲨ⳪Ⲱ⳯Ⲧ ⲈⲌⲂⲞⲨⲢ · ⳨ⲰⲂ ⲚⲒⲘ ⲈⲦⲞⲨ-
ⲚⲀϢⲒⲚⲈ ⲚⲚⲈⲨⲆⲈⲔⲀⲚⲞⲤ ⲈⲦⲂⲎⲎⲦⲞⲨ · ⲤⲈⲚⲀϪⲞⲞⲨ Ⲉ-
ⲢⲞⲞⲨ Ⲍ̄Ⲛ ⲞⲨⲰⲢⲬ̄ · ⲈϢⲰⲠⲈ Ⲛ̄ⲦⲞϤ ⲈⲢϢⲀⲚ ⲚⲈⲨⲢⲈϤ-
ϢⲒⲚⲈ ⲈⲨϢⲀⲚⲈⲠⲒⲔⲀⲖⲒ Ⲛ̄ⲚⲈⲨⲢⲀⲚ ⲈⲨ⳪Ⲱ⳯Ⲧ ⲈⲞⲨⲚⲀⲘ ·
5 Ⲛ̄ⲤⲈⲚⲀⲤⲰⲦⲘ̄ ⲈⲢⲞⲞⲨ ⲀⲚ ⲈⲂⲞⲖ Ϫ Ⲉ ⲈⲨ⳪ⲰⲦ Ⲛ̄ⲔⲈ-
ⲤⲘⲞⲦ · ⲠⲀⲢⲀ ⲠⲈⲨϢⲞⲢⲠ̄ Ⲛ̄ⲦⲰϢ · ⲈⲚⲦⲀϤⲤⲘⲚ̄ⲦⲞⲨ Ⲛ̄-
Ⳅ̄ⲎⲦϤ Ⲛ̄ϬⲒ ⲒⲈⲞⲨ · ⲈⲠⲈⲒⲆⲎ ⲞⲨⲈⲦ ⲚⲈⲨⲢⲀⲚ** ⲈⲨⲔⲎⲦ Ⲗ̄
ⲈⳄⲂⲞⲨⲢ · ⲀⲨⲰ ⲞⲨⲈⲦ ⲚⲈⲨⲢⲀⲚ ⲈⲨⲔⲎⲦ ⲈⲞⲨⲚⲀⲘ · ⲀⲨⲰ
ⲈⲨϢⲀⲚⲈⲠⲒⲔⲀⲖⲈⲒ Ⲙ̄ⲘⲞⲞⲨ ⲈⲨⲔⲎⲦ ⲈⲞⲨⲚⲀⲘ · Ⲛ̄ⲤⲈⲚⲀϪⲒ-
10 ⲦⲘⲈ ⲈⲢⲞⲞⲨ ⲀⲚ · ⲀⲖⲖⲀ Ⳅ̄Ⲛ ⲞⲨⳄⲂⲀ ⲤⲈⲚⲀⲢⳄ̄ⲂⲀ Ⲙ̄ⲘⲞⲞⲨ ·
ⲀⲨⲰ Ⳅ̄Ⲛ ⲞⲨⲀⲠⲈⲒⲖⲎ ⲤⲈⲚⲀⲀⲠⲈⲒⲖⲒ ⲈⲢⲞⲞⲨ · ⲚⲈⲦⲤⲞⲞⲨⲚ
ϬⲈ ⲀⲚ Ⲛ̄ⲦⲈⲨϬⲒⲚⲘⲞⲞϢⲈ ⲈⲨⲔⲎⲦ ⲈⲞⲨⲚⲀⲘ · ⲀⲨⲰ Ⲙ̄Ⲛ
ⲚⲈⲨϢⲞⲘⲚ̄Ⲧ Ⲛ̄ⲔⲞⲞ⳨ · ⲀⲨⲰ Ⲙ̄Ⲛ ⲚⲈⲨϤⲦⲞⲞⲨ Ⲛ̄ⲔⲞⲞ⳨ ·
Ⲙ̄Ⲛ ⲚⲈⲨⲤⲘⲞⲦ ⲦⲎⲢⲞⲨ · ⲤⲈⲚⲀϬⲚ̄-ⲖⲀⲀⲨ ⲀⲚ Ⲙ̄ⲘⲈ · ⲀⲖⲖⲀ
15 ⲤⲈⲚⲀⲢⳄ̄ⲂⲀ Ⳅ̄Ⲛ ⲞⲨⲚⲞϬ Ⲛ̄ⳄⲂⲀ · ⲀⲨⲰ ⲤⲈⲚⲀϢⲰⲠⲈ Ⳅ̄Ⲛ ⲞⲨ-
ⲚⲞϬ Ⲙ̄ⲠⲖⲀⲚⲎ · ⲀⲨⲰ ⲤⲈⲚⲀⲤⲰⲢⲘ̄ Ⳅ̄Ⲛ ⲞⲨⲚⲞϬ Ⲛ̄ⲤⲰⲢⲘ̄
ⲈⲂⲞⲖ Ϫ Ⲉ ⲚⲈⳄⲂⲎⲨⲈ ⲈϢⲀⲨⲖⲀⲀⲨ Ⲙ̄ⲠⲒⲞⲨⲞⲈⲒϢ Ⳅ̄Ⲛ ⲚⲈⲨ-
ϤⲦⲞⲞⲨ Ⲛ̄ⲔⲞⲞ⳨ ⲈⲨⲔⲎⲦ ⲈⳄⲂⲞⲨⲢ · ⲀⲨⲰ Ⳅ̄Ⲛ ⲚⲈⲨϢⲞⲘⲚ̄Ⲧ
Ⲛ̄ⲔⲞⲞ⳨ · ⲀⲨⲰ Ⳅ̄Ⲙ ⲠⲈⲨϢⲘⲞⲨⲚ Ⲛ̄ⲤⲘⲞⲦ · ⲚⲀⲒ ⲈⲚⲈⲨⲘⲎⲚ
20 ⲈⲂⲞⲖ Ⲛ̄Ⳅ̄ⲎⲦⲞⲨ* ⲈⲨⲈⲒⲢⲈ Ⲙ̄ⲘⲞⲞⲨ ⲈⲨⲔⲎⲦ Ⲛ̄ⳄⲂⲞⲨⲢ · Ⲗ̄ᵇ
Ⲁ̈ⲒⲠⲞⲞⲚⲞⲨ ⲦⲈⲚⲞⲨ · ⲀⲨⲰ Ⲁ̈ⲒⲦⲢⲈⲨⲢ̄-ⲤⲞⲞⲨ Ⲛ̄ⲈⲂⲞⲦ · ⲈⲨ-
ⲈⲒⲢⲈ Ⲛ̄ⲚⲈⲨⲤⲬⲎⲘⲀ ⲦⲎⲢⲞⲨ ⲈⲨⲔⲎⲦ ⲈⲞⲨⲚⲀⲘ · ϪⲈⲔⲀⲤ
ⲈⲨⲚⲀⲢⳄ̄ⲂⲀ Ⳅ̄Ⲛ ⲞⲨⳄⲂⲀ Ⳅ̄Ⲛ ⲦⲈⲨϬⲒⲚⲘⲞⲨⳅ ⲈⲂⲞⲖ ⲦⲎⲢⲤ̄ ·
ⲀⲨⲰ ⲞⲚ Ⲁ̈ⲒⲦⲢⲈⲨⲢ̄-ⲤⲞⲞⲨ Ⲛ̄ⲈⲂⲞⲦ ⲈⲨⲔⲎⲦ ⲈⳄⲂⲞⲨⲢ ⲈⲨ-
25 ⲈⲒⲢⲈ Ⲛ̄ⲚⲈⳄⲂⲎⲨⲈ Ⲛ̄ⲚⲈⲨⲀⲠⲞⲦⲈⲖⲈⲤⲘⲀ Ⲙ̄Ⲛ ⲚⲈⲨⲤⲬⲎⲘⲀ
ⲦⲎⲢⲞⲨ · ϪⲈⲔⲀⲤ Ⳅ̄Ⲛ ⲞⲨⳄⲂⲀ ⲈⲨⲈⲢ̄ⳄⲂⲀ · ⲀⲨⲰ Ⳅ̄Ⲛ ⲞⲨ-

---

20   Ⲛ̄ⳄⲂⲞⲨⲢ ; read ⲈⳄⲂⲞⲨⲢ.

everything concerning which they will seek of their *decans*, they will tell them with certainty. However, when their soothsayers *call upon* their names as they are looking to the right, they will not hear them, because they look in another form *than* their first ordinance in which Jeu established them, *since* their names are other when they are turned to the left than when they are turned to the right. And when they *call upon* them as they are turned to the right, they will not speak the truth to them, *but* in confusion they will confuse them, and with *threats* they will *threaten* them. Those now who do not know their paths as they are turned to the right, with their triangles and their quadrangles and all their figures, they will find nothing of truth, *but* they will be confused in great confusion, and they will be in great *error*, and they will be deluded in great delusion, because the works which they did in in the time when they were turned to the left in their quadrangles, in their triangles and in their figures of eight, these in which they continued as they were turned to the left, I have now turned. And I have caused them to spend six months making all their *patterns* [1] turned to the right, so that they should be confused in confusion in their whole circuit. And furthermore I have caused them to spend six months turned to the left, doing the works of their (periods of) *influence* and all their *patterns*, so that | the *archons* which are in the *aeons* and in their

---

[1]   (22, 25) on σχῆμα, see CH *Exc. Stob.* VIII.2-4; U 237.

ⲡⲗⲁⲛⲏ ⲉⲩⲉⲡⲗⲁⲛⲁ ⲛ̅ϭⲓ ⲛ̅ⲁⲣⲭⲱⲛ ⲉⲧϣⲟⲟⲡ ϩ̅ⲛ̅ ⲛ̅ⲁⲓⲱⲛ
ⲁⲩⲱ ϩ̅ⲛ̅ ⲛⲉⲩⲥⲫⲁⲓⲣⲁ ⲁⲩⲱ ϩ̅ⲛ̅ ⲛⲉⲩⲙ̅ⲡⲏⲩⲉ· ⲁⲩⲱ ϩ̅ⲛ̅
ⲛⲉⲩⲧⲟⲡⲟⲥ ⲧⲏⲣⲟⲩ· ϫⲉⲕⲁⲥ ⲛ̅ⲛⲉⲩⲛⲟⲓ̈ ⲛ̅ⲧⲉⲩϭⲓⲛⲙⲟ-
ⲟϣⲉ ⲙ̅ⲙⲓⲛ ⲙ̅ⲙⲟⲟⲩ:

ȝ ⲁⲥϣⲱⲡⲉ ϭⲉ ⲛ̅ⲧⲉⲣⲉ ⲓ̅ⲥ̅ ⲟⲩⲱ ⲉϥϫⲱ ⲛ̅ⲛⲉⲓ̈ϣⲁϫⲉ
ⲉⲣⲉ ⲫⲓⲗⲓⲡⲡⲟⲥ ϩⲙⲟⲟⲥ ⲉϥⲥϩⲁⲓ̈ ⲛ̅ϣⲁϫⲉ ⲛⲓⲙ ⲉⲧⲉⲣⲉ ⲓ̅ⲥ̅
ϫⲱ** ⲙ̅ⲙⲟⲟⲩ: ⲁⲥϣⲱⲡⲉ ϭⲉ ⲙ̅ⲛ̅ⲛ̅ⲥⲁ ⲛⲁⲓ̈· ⲁ ⲫⲓⲗⲓⲡⲡⲟⲥ ⲗ̅ⲁ̅
ⲉⲓ' ⲉⲑⲏ ⲁϥⲡⲁϩⲧ̅ϥ̅ ⲁϥⲟⲩⲱϣ̅ⲧ̅ ⲉⲛⲟⲩⲉⲣⲏⲧⲉ ⲛ̅ⲓ̅ⲥ̅ ⲉϥϫⲱ
ⲙ̅ⲙⲟⲥ ϫⲉ ⲡⲁϫⲟⲉⲓⲥ ⲡⲥⲱⲧⲏⲣ· ϯ-ⲧⲉⲝⲟⲩⲥⲓⲁ ⲛⲁⲓ̈ ⲉⲧⲣⲁϣⲁϫⲉ ⲙ̅ⲡⲉⲕⲙ̅ⲧⲟ ⲉⲃⲟⲗ ⲁⲩⲱ ⲛ̅ⲧⲁϫⲛⲟⲩⲕ ⲉⲡⲉⲓ̈-
ϣⲁϫⲉ· ⲉⲙⲡⲁⲧ̅ⲕ̅ϣⲁϫⲉ ⲛ̅ⲙ̅ⲙⲁⲛ ⲉⲛⲧⲟⲡⲟⲥ ⲉⲛⲧⲁⲕⲃⲱⲕ
ⲉⲣⲟⲟⲩ ⲉⲧⲃⲉ ⲧⲉⲕⲇⲓⲁⲕⲟⲛⲓⲁ· ⲁϥⲟⲩⲱϣ̅ⲃ̅ ⲛ̅ϭⲓ ⲡⲥⲱⲧⲏⲣ
ⲛ̅ⲛⲁⲏⲧ· ⲡⲉϫⲁϥ ⲙ̅ⲫⲓⲗⲓⲡⲡⲟⲥ ϫⲉ ⲧⲉⲝⲟⲩⲥⲓⲁ ⲧⲟ ⲛⲁⲕ
ⲉⲧⲁⲩⲉ-ⲡϣⲁϫⲉ ⲉⲧⲉϩⲛⲁⲕ· ⲁϥⲟⲩⲱϣ̅ⲃ̅ ⲇⲉ ⲛ̅ϭⲓ ⲫⲓⲗⲓⲡⲡⲟⲥ ⲡⲉϫⲁϥ ⲛ̅ⲓ̅ⲥ̅ ϫⲉ ⲡⲁϫⲟⲉⲓⲥ· ⲉⲧⲃⲉ ⲁϣ ⲙ̅ⲙⲩⲥⲧⲏ-
ⲣⲓⲟⲛ ⲁⲕⲡⲱⲱⲛⲉ ⲛ̅ⲧϭⲓⲛⲙⲟⲩⲣ ⲛ̅ⲛ̅ⲁⲣⲭⲱⲛ ⲙ̅ⲛ̅ ⲛⲉⲩⲁⲓⲱⲛ
ⲙ̅ⲛ̅ ⲧⲉⲩϩⲓⲙⲁⲣⲙⲉⲛⲏ· ⲙ̅ⲛ̅ ⲧⲉⲩⲥⲫⲁⲓⲣⲁ· ⲙ̅ⲛ̅ ⲛⲉⲩⲧⲟⲡⲟⲥ
ⲧⲏⲣⲟⲩ· ⲁⲩⲱ ϩ̅ⲛ̅ ⲟⲩϩⲃⲁ ⲁⲕⲧⲣⲉⲩⲣ̅ϩⲃⲁ* ϩ̅ⲛ̅ ⲧⲉⲩϭⲓⲛ- ⲗ̅ⲁ̅ b
ⲙⲟⲟϣⲉ ⲁⲩⲱ ⲁⲩⲡⲗⲁⲛⲁ ϩ̅ⲙ̅ ⲡⲉⲩⲇⲣⲟⲙⲟⲥ· ⲛ̅ⲧⲁⲕⲣ̅-ⲡⲁⲓ̈
ϭⲉ ⲛⲁⲩ ⲉⲧⲃⲉ ⲡⲟⲩϫⲁⲓ̈ ⲙ̅ⲡⲕⲟⲥⲙⲟⲥ· ϫ̅ⲛ̅ ⲙ̅ⲙⲟⲛ·

ȝ ⲁϥⲟⲩⲱϣ̅ⲃ̅ ⲇⲉ ⲛ̅ϭⲓ ⲓ̅ⲥ̅ ⲡⲉϫⲁϥ ⲙ̅ⲫⲓⲗⲓⲡⲡⲟⲥ ⲙ̅ⲛ̅ ⲙ̅-
ⲙⲁⲑⲏⲧⲏⲥ ⲧⲏⲣⲟⲩ ϩⲓ ⲛⲉⲩⲉⲣⲏⲩ· ϫⲉ ⲛ̅ⲧⲁⲓ̈ⲡⲱⲱⲛⲉ
ⲛ̅ⲧⲉⲩϭⲓⲛⲙⲟⲟϣⲉ ⲉⲩⲟⲩϫⲁⲓ̈ ⲛ̅ⲛⲉⲯⲩⲭⲟⲟⲩⲉ ⲧⲏⲣⲟⲩ·
ϩⲁⲙⲏⲛ ϩⲁⲙⲏⲛ ϯϫⲱ ⲙ̅ⲙⲟⲥ ⲛⲏⲧ̅ⲛ̅ ϫⲉ ⲛ̅ⲥⲁⲃⲏⲗ ϫⲉ
ⲁⲓ̈ⲡⲱⲱⲙⲉ ⲛ̅ⲧⲉⲩϭⲓⲛⲙⲟⲟϣⲉ ⲛ̅ⲛⲉⲩⲛⲁⲧⲁⲕⲟ ⲡⲉ ⲛ̅ⲟⲩ-

---

25 second ⲟ in ⲙⲟⲟϣⲉ inserted above; MS ⲛ̅ⲛⲉⲩⲛⲁⲧⲁⲕⲟ; read ⲛⲉⲩⲛⲁⲧⲁⲕⲟ.

spheres and in their heavens and in all their *places* should be confused in confusion, and should *wander* in *error*, so that they should not *understand* their own paths".

22. It happened when Jesus finished saying these words, Philip sat writing every word as Jesus said them. Now after this it happened that Philip came forward, he prostrated himself and worshipped at the feet of Jesus, saying: "My Lord, *Saviour*, give me *authority* that I speak in thy presence and that I question thee on this discourse before thou speakest with us of the *places* to which thou hast gone for the sake of thy *service*".

The compassionate *Saviour* answered, he said to Philip: "The *authority* is given to thee to deliver the discourse which thou dost wish".

Then Philip answered and spoke to Jesus: "My Lord, for the sake of what *mystery* hast thou turned the bondage of the *archons* and their *aeons* and their *Heimarmene* and their *sphere* and all their *places*, and in confusion hast thou caused them to be confused in their paths, and to *wander* in their *course*? Hast thou now done this for the sake of the salvation of the *world* or not?"

23. Jesus answered, *however*, and said to Philip and all the *disciples* together: "I have turned their paths for the salvation of all *souls*. *Truly, truly*, I say to you: unless I had turned their paths a multitude of *souls* would have been destroyed. | And they would have spent a long *period* if the

ⲘⲎⲎϢⲈ Ⲙ̄ⲮⲨⲬⲎ · ⲀⲨⲰ ⲚⲈⲨⲚⲀⲢ-ⲞⲨⲚⲞϬ Ⲛ̄ⲬⲢⲞⲚⲞⲤ ⲠⲈ
ⲈⲘⲠⲞⲨⲂⲰⲖ ⲈⲂⲞⲖ Ⲛ̄ϬⲒ Ⲛ̄ⲀⲢⲬⲰⲚ Ⲛ̄Ⲛ̄ⲀⲒⲰⲚ · ⲀⲨⲰ Ⲛ̄ⲀⲢ-
ⲬⲰⲚ Ⲛ̄ⲐⲒⲘⲀⲢⲘⲈⲚⲎ · Ⲙ̄Ⲛ ⲦⲈⲤⲪⲀⲒⲢⲀ · ⲀⲨⲰ Ⲙ̄Ⲛ ⲚⲈⲨⲦⲞ-
ⲠⲞⲤ ⲦⲎⲢⲞⲨ Ⲙ̄Ⲛ ⲚⲈⲨⲘ̄ⲠⲎⲨⲈ ⲦⲎⲢⲞⲨ · Ⲙ̄Ⲛ ⲚⲈⲨⲀⲒⲰⲚ
5 ⲦⲎⲢⲞⲨ · ⲀⲨⲰ ⲚⲈⲢⲈ ⲚⲈⲮⲨⲬⲞⲞⲨⲈ ⲚⲀⲢ-ⲞⲨⲚⲞϬ Ⲙ̄ⲘⲎⲎ-
ϢⲈ Ⲛ̄ⲞⲨⲞⲈⲒϢ Ⲛ̄ⲂⲞⲖ ⲦⲀⲒ̈ · ⲀⲨⲰ ⲚⲈϤⲚⲀⲰⲤⲔ̄ ⲠⲈ ⲈⲬⲰⲔ ⲖⲂ̄
Ⲛ̄ϬⲒ ⲠⲀⲢⲒⲐⲘⲞⲤ Ⲛ̄ⲚⲈⲮⲨⲬⲞⲞⲨⲈ Ⲛ̄ⲦⲈⲖⲈⲒⲞⲚ · ⲚⲀⲒ̈ ⲈⲦ-
ⲚⲀϢⲠ ⲈϨⲞⲨⲚ ⲈⲦⲈⲔⲖⲎⲢⲞⲚⲞⲘⲒⲀ Ⲙ̄ⲠⲬⲒⲤⲈ ϨⲒⲦⲚ̄ Ⲙ̄ⲘⲨⲤ-
ⲦⲎⲢⲒⲞⲚ ⲀⲨⲰ Ⲛ̄ⲤⲈϢⲰⲠⲈ Ϩ̄Ⲙ ⲠⲈⲐⲎⲤⲀⲨⲢⲞⲤ Ⲙ̄ⲠⲞⲨⲞⲈⲒⲚ ·
10 ⲈⲦⲂⲈ ⲠⲀⲒ̈ ϬⲈ ⲀⲖ̄ⲠⲰⲰⲚⲈ Ⲛ̄ⲦⲈⲨϬⲒⲚⲘⲞⲞϢⲈ ⲬⲈ ⲈⲨⲈⲢ̄Ϩ̄ⲂⲀ ·
ⲀⲨⲰ Ⲛ̄ⲤⲈϢⲦⲞⲢⲦ̄Ⲣ Ⲛ̄ⲤⲈⲔⲰ ⲈⲂⲞⲖ Ⲛ̄ⲦϬⲞⲘ · ⲦⲀⲒ̈ ⲈⲦ-
ϢⲞⲞⲠ Ϩ̄Ⲛ ⲐⲨⲖⲎ Ⲙ̄ⲠⲈⲨⲔⲞⲤⲘⲞⲤ ⲦⲀⲒ̈ ⲈϢⲀⲨⲖⲀⲤ Ⲙ̄ⲮⲨ-
ⲬⲎ · ⲬⲈ ⲈⲨⲈⲤⲞⲦⲂⲞⲨ Ϩ̄Ⲛ ⲞⲨϬⲈⲠⲎ ⲀⲨⲰ Ⲛ̄ⲤⲈⲰⲖ ⲈϨⲢⲀⲒ̈
Ⲛ̄ⲚⲈⲦⲚⲀⲞⲨⲬⲀⲒ̈ · Ⲛ̄ⲦⲞⲞⲨ Ⲙ̄Ⲛ ⲦϬⲞⲘ ⲦⲎⲢⲤ̄ · ⲀⲨⲰ Ⲛ̄ⲤⲈ-
15 ⲂⲰⲖ ⲈⲂⲞⲖ Ϩ̄Ⲛ ⲞⲨϬⲈⲠⲎ Ⲛ̄ϬⲒ ⲚⲈⲦⲚⲀⲞⲨⲬⲀⲒ̈ ⲀⲚ ·

Ⳍ ⲀⲤϢⲰⲠⲈ ϬⲈ Ⲛ̄ⲦⲈⲢⲈ Ⲓ̄Ⲥ̄ ⲞⲨⲰ ⲈϤⲬⲰ Ⲛ̄ⲚⲈⲒ̈ϢⲀⲬⲈ
ⲈⲚⲈϤⲘⲀⲐⲎⲦⲎⲤ ⲀⲤⲈⲒ' ⲈⲐⲎ Ⲛ̄ϬⲒ ⲘⲀⲢⲒⲀ ⲦⲈⲦⲚⲈⲤⲰⲤ Ϩ̄Ⲛ
ⲦⲈⲤϬⲒⲚϢⲀⲬⲈ · ⲀⲨⲰ ⲦⲘⲀⲔⲀⲢⲒⲀ ⲀⲤⲠⲀϨ̄ⲦⲤ̄ ⲈⲬⲚ̄ Ⲛ̄ⲞⲨⲈ-
ⲢⲎⲦⲈ Ⲛ̄Ⲓ̄Ⲥ̄ · ⲠⲈⲬⲀⲤ ⲬⲈ ⲠⲀⲬⲞⲈⲒⲤ ⲀⲚⲈⲬⲈ Ⲙ̄ⲘⲞⲒ̈ Ⲛ̄ⲦⲀ- ⲖⲂ̄ᵇ
20 ϢⲀⲬⲈ Ⲙ̄ⲠⲈⲔⲘⲦⲞ ⲈⲂⲞⲖ · ⲀⲨⲰ Ⲙ̄ⲠⲢ̄ϬⲰⲚⲦ ⲈⲢⲞⲒ̈ ⲬⲈ
ϯⲞⲨⲈϨ-ϨⲒⲤⲈ ⲈⲢⲞⲔ Ⲛ̄ⲞⲨⲘⲎⲚϢⲈ Ⲛ̄ⲤⲞⲠ ⲈⲒ̈ϢⲒⲚⲈ Ⲙ̄ⲘⲞⲔ ·
ⲀϤⲞⲨⲰϢ̄Ⲃ Ⲛ̄ϬⲒ ⲠⲤⲰⲦⲎⲢ Ϩ̄Ⲛ ⲞⲨⲘⲚ̄ⲦϢⲀⲚϨ̄ⲦⲎϤ ⲠⲈⲬⲀϤ
Ⲙ̄ⲘⲀⲢⲒⲀ ⲬⲈ ⲀⲬⲒ-ⲠϢⲀⲬⲈ ⲈⲦⲈϨⲚⲈ · ⲀⲨⲰ ⲀⲚⲞⲔ ϯⲚⲀ-
ϬⲞⲖⲠ̄Ϥ ⲚⲈ ⲈⲂⲞⲖ Ϩ̄Ⲛ ⲞⲨⲠⲀⲢⲢⲎⲤⲒⲀ :

25 ⲀⲤⲞⲨⲰϢ̄Ⲃ ⲆⲈ Ⲛ̄ϬⲒ ⲘⲀⲢⲒⲀ ⲠⲈⲬⲀⲤ Ⲛ̄Ⲓ̄Ⲥ̄ ⲬⲈ ⲠⲀ-
ⲬⲞⲈⲒⲤ · Ⲛ̄ⲀϢ Ⲛ̄Ϩ̄Ⲉ ⲚⲈⲢⲈ ⲚⲈⲮⲨⲬⲞⲞⲨⲈ ⲚⲀⲰⲤⲔ̄ ⲂⲂⲞⲖ
ⲦⲀⲒ̈ · Ⲏ̄ ⲈⲨⲚⲀⲤⲞⲦϤⲞⲨ Ⲛ̄ⲦⲞϤ Ϩ̄Ⲛ ⲞⲨϬⲈⲠⲎ Ⲛ̄ⲀϢ Ⲛ̄-

---

14 MS Ⲡ̄ⲚⲈⲦⲚⲀⲞⲨⲬⲀⲒ̈; read Ⲛ̄ϬⲒ ⲚⲈⲦⲚⲀⲞⲨⲬⲀⲒ̈.

archons of the *aeons* and the archons of the *Heimarmene* and the *sphere* and all their *places* and all their heavens and all their *aeons* were not dissolved. And the *souls* would have spent a great (period of) time outside. And there would have been delay in the completion of the *number* of *perfect souls*, which will be accounted among the *inheritance* of the height, through the *mysteries*, and will be in the Treasury of Light. Because of this, I have turned their paths so that they are confused and agitated, and give up the power which is in the *matter* of their *world*, which they make into *souls*, so that those that will be saved with all the power are purified quickly and ascend, and those who will not be saved are quickly dissolved".

24.   It happened now when Jesus finished speaking these words to his *disciples*, Maria, the beautiful in her speech, came forward. The *blessed* one prostrated herself at the feet of Jesus and said : "My Lord, *suffer* me that I speak in thy presence, and be not angry with me because I trouble thee many times, questioning thee". The *Saviour* answered compassionately, he said to Maria : "Speak the discourse which thou dost wish, and I will reveal it to thee *openly*".

Maria answered and said to Jesus : "My Lord, in what manner would the *souls* be delayed outside *or* in what form will they be quickly purified ?" |

67

СΜΟΤ· ΑϤΟΥШϢΒ ΔΕ Ν̄ϬΙ Ι̅С̅ ΠΕΧΑϤ Μ̄ΜΑΡΙΑ ΧΕ ΕΥΓΕ
ΜΑΡΙΑ· ΤΕϢΙΝΕ ΚΑΛШС Ζ̅Ν̅ ΤϬΙΝϢΙΝΕ ΕΤΝΑΝΟΥС·
ΑΥШ ΤΕϯ-ΟΥΟΕΙ Ν̄СΑ Ζ̄ШΒ ΝΙΜ Ζ̄Ν̅ ΟΥШΡΧ̅· ΑΥШ Ζ̄Ν̅
ΟΥΜ̄Ν̅ΤΑΚΡΙΒΗС· ΤΕΝΟΥ ϬΕ Ν̄ϯΝΑΖΕΠ-ΑΛΑΥ ΕΡШΤ̅Ν̅
5 ΑΝ ΧΙΝ Μ̄ΠΕΪΝΑΥ· ΑΛΛΑ ϯΝΑϬΑΠ-Ζ̄ШΒ ΝΙΜ ΝΗΤ̅Ν̅ ΕΒΟΛ ΑΓ
Ζ̄Ν̅ ΟΥШΡΧ̅· ΑΥШ Ζ̄Ν̅ ΟΥΠΑΡΖΗСΙΑ· СШΤΜ̅ ϬΕ ΜΑΡΙΑ·
ΑΥШ ΧΙСΜΗ Ν̄ΤШΤ̅Ν̅ Μ̄ΜΑΘΗΤΗС ΤΗΡΟΥ· ΧΕ ΖΑΘΗ
ΕΜΠΑϯΤΑϢΕΟΕΙϢ Ν̄Ν̅ΑΡΧШΝ ΤΗΡΟΥ Ν̄ΝΑΙШΝ· ΑΥШ
Μ̄Ν̅ Ν̄ΑΡΧШΝ ΤΗΡΟΥ Ν̄ΘΙΜΑΡΜΕΝΗ Μ̄Ν̅ ΤΕСΦΑΙΡΑ·
10 ΝΕΥΜΗΡ ΤΗΡΟΥ ΠΕ Ζ̄Ν̅ ΝΕΥΜ̅ΡΡΕ· ΑΥШ Ζ̄Ν̅ ΝΕΥ-
СΦΑΙΡΑ· ΑΥШ Ζ̄Ν̅ ΝΕΥСΦΡΑΓΙС· ΚΑΤΑ ΘΕ ΕΝΤΑϤ-
ΜΟΡΟΥ Μ̄ΜΟС ΧΙΝ Ν̄ϢΟΡΠ̅ Ν̄ϬΙ Ι̅ΕΟΥ ΠΕΠΙСΚΟΠΟС
Μ̄ΠΟΥΟΕΙΝ· ΑΥШ ΝΕΡΕ ΠΟΥΑ ΠΟΥΑ Μ̄ΜΟΟΥ ΝΕΥ-
ϬΕΕΤ ΠΕ ΖΡΑΪ Ζ̄Ν̅ ΤΕΥΤΑΖΙС ΑΥШ ΝΕΡΕ ΠΟΥΑ ΠΟΥΑ
15 ΜΟΟϢΕ ΠΕ ΚΑΤΑ ΠΕϤΔΡΟΜΟС· ΚΑΤΑ ΘΕ Ν̄ΤΑϤΚΑΑΥ
Μ̄ΜΟС Ν̄ϬΙ Ι̅ΕΟΥ ΠΕΠΙСΚΟΠΟС Μ̄ΠΟΥΟΕΙΝ· ΑΥШ ΕϤ-
ϢΑΝΕΙ' Ν̄ϬΙ ΠΕΟΥΟΕΙϢ Μ̄ΠΑΡΙΘΜΟС Μ̄ΜΕΛΧΙСΕΔΕΚ·
ΠΝΟϬ Μ̄ΠΑΡΑΛΗΜΠΤШΡ Ν̄ΟΥΟΕΙΝ ΝΕϢΑϤΕΙ' ΠΕ ΕΤ- Α̅Γ̅·ᵇ
ΜΗΤΕ Ν̄Ν̅ΑΙШΝ Μ̄Ν̅ Ν̄ΑΡΧШΝ ΤΗΡΟΥ ΕΤΜΗΡ Ζ̄Ν̅ ΤΕ-
20 СΦΑΙΡΑ· ΑΥШ Ζ̄Ν̅ ΘΙΜΑΡΜΕΝΗ· ΑΥШ ϢΑϤϤΙ-ΠСШΤϤ
Μ̄ΠΟΥΟΕΙΝ Ν̄ΤΟΟΤΟΥ Ν̄Ν̅ΑΡΧШΝ ΤΗΡΟΥ Ν̄ΝΑΙШΝ·
ΑΥШ Ν̄ΤΟΟΤΟΥ Ν̄Ν̅ΑΡΧШΝ ΤΗΡΟΥ Ν̄ΘΙΜΑΡΜΕΝΗ· Μ̄Ν̅
ΝΑΤΕСΦΑΙΡΑ· ΝΕϢΑϤϤΙ ΓΑΡ Μ̄ΜΑΥ ΠΕ Μ̄ΠΕΤϢΤΟΡΤ̅Ρ̅
Μ̄ΜΟΟΥ· ΑΥШ ϢΑϤΚΙΜ ΕΠΙСΠΟΥΔΑСΤΗС ΕΤΖΙΧШΟΥ
25 Ν̄ϤΤΡΕΥΚШΤΕ Ν̄ΝΕΥΚΥΚΛΟС Ζ̄Ν̅ ΟΥϬΕΠΗ ΑΥШ ϢΑϤϤΙ-
ΤΕΥϬΟΜ ΕΤΝ̄ΖΗΤΟΥ· Μ̄Ν̅ ΠΝΙϤΕ Ν̄ΤΕΥΤΑΠΡΟ· ΑΥШ
Μ̄Ν̅ Μ̄ΜΟΥΕΙΟΟΥΕ Ν̄ΝΕΥΒΑΛ· ΑΥШ Μ̄Ν̅ Ν̄ϤϢΤΕ Ν̄ΝΕΥ-

---

27 MS ΜΟΥΕΙΟΥΕ; ο inserted above.

25. *However* Jesus answered and said to Maria : "*Excellent*, Maria. Thou dost ask *well* with an excellent question and thou dost seek everything with certainty and with *accuracy*. Now indeed I will not conceal anything from you from this hour, *but* I will reveal everything to you with certainty and *openly*. Hear now, Maria, and give ear, all you *disciples*. Before I preached to all the *archons* of the *aeons*, and all the *archons* of the *Heimarmene* and the *sphere*, they were all bound with their bonds, in their *spheres* and their *seals*, *according to* the manner in which Jeu, the *Overseer* of the Light, had bound them from the beginning. And each one of them was continuing in his *rank* and each one was proceeding *according to* his *course*, *according to* the manner in which Jeu, the *Overseer* of the Light, had settled it. And when the time came [1] of the *number* of Melchizedek [2], the great *Paralemptor* of Light, he came to the midst of the *aeons*, and to all the *archons* which were bound in the *sphere* and in the *Heimarmene*, and he took away what is purified of the light from all the *archons* of the *aeons*, and from all the *archons* of the *Heimarmene*, and from those of the *sphere*, *for* he took away that which agitated them. And he moved the *hastener* that is over them and made their *cycles* turn quickly, and he (Melchizedek) took away their power which was in them, and the breath of their mouths, and the tears of their eyes, and the sweat of their |

---

[1] (16-35.24) verbs in present tense of habitude; (also 36.8-37.5).

[2] (17) Melchisedek; see Epiph. 55.1 ff.; Hippol. VII.36.1; J 110; (also 360 ff.).

ⲥⲱⲙⲁ· ⲁⲩⲱ ⲙⲉⲗⲭⲓⲥⲉⲇⲉⲕ ⲡⲡⲁⲣⲁⲗⲏⲙⲡⲧⲱⲣ ⲙ̄ⲡⲟⲩⲟⲉⲓⲛ· ϣⲁϥⲥⲱⲧ̄ϥ̄ ⲛ̄ⲛ̄ϭⲟⲙ ⲉⲧⲙ̄ⲙⲁⲩ· ⲛ̄ϥϥⲓ-ⲡⲉⲩⲟⲩⲟⲉⲓⲛ ⲉⲡⲉⲑⲏⲥⲁⲩⲣⲟⲥ ⲙ̄ⲡⲟⲩⲟⲉⲓⲛ ⲁⲩⲱ ⲧⲉⲩϩⲩⲗⲏ ⲧⲏⲣⲟⲩ ϩⲓ ⲛⲉⲩⲉⲣⲏⲩ ϣⲁⲩⲥⲟⲟⲩϩⲟⲩ ⲉϩⲟⲩⲛ ⲛ̄ϭⲓ ⲛ̄ⲗⲉⲓⲧⲟⲩⲣⲅⲟⲥ ⲛ̄ⲛ̄ⲁⲣⲭⲱⲛ ** ⲧⲏⲣⲟⲩ· ⲁⲩⲱ ϣⲁⲩϫⲓⲧⲟⲩ ⲛ̄ϭⲓ ⲛ̄ⲗⲉⲓⲧⲟⲩⲣ- ⲗ̄ⲗ̄ ⲅⲟⲥ ⲛ̄ⲛ̄ⲁⲣⲭⲱⲛ ⲧⲏⲣⲟⲩ ⲛ̄ⲑⲓⲙⲁⲣⲙⲉⲛⲏ· ⲙⲛ̄ ⲛ̄ⲗⲉⲓⲧⲟⲩⲣⲅⲟⲥ ⲛ̄ⲧⲉⲥⲫⲁⲓⲣⲁ· ⲛⲁⲓ̈ ⲉⲧⲙ̄ⲡⲉⲥⲏⲧ ⲛ̄ⲁⲓⲱⲛ·. ⲛ̄ⲥⲉⲁⲁⲩ ⲙ̄ⲯⲩⲭⲏ ⲛ̄ⲣⲱⲙⲉ ⲁⲩⲱ ⲛ̄ⲧ̄ⲃ̄ⲛⲏ ⲁⲩⲱ ⲛ̄ϫⲁⲧⲃⲉ· ϩⲓ ⲑⲏⲣⲓⲟⲛ· ϩⲓ ϩⲁⲗⲏⲧ· ⲁⲩⲱ ⲛ̄ⲥⲉϫⲟⲟⲩⲥⲟⲩ ⲉⲡⲉⲉⲓⲕⲟⲥⲙⲟⲥ ⲛ̄ⲧⲉ ⲧⲙ̄ⲛ̄ⲧ̄ⲣⲱⲙⲉ· ⲁⲩⲱ ⲟⲛ ⲙ̄ⲡⲁⲣⲁⲗⲏⲙⲡⲧⲱⲣ ⲙ̄ⲡⲣⲏ ⲙ̄ⲛ̄ ⲙ̄ⲡⲁⲣⲁⲗⲏⲙⲡⲧⲱⲣ ⲙ̄ⲡⲟⲟϩ ⲉⲩϣⲁⲛϭⲱϣ̄ⲧ̄ ⲉⲧⲡⲉ ⲛ̄ⲥⲉⲛⲁⲩ ⲉⲛⲉⲥⲭⲏⲙⲁ ⲛ̄ⲛ̄ϭⲓⲛⲙⲟⲟϣⲉ ⲛ̄ⲛ̄ⲁⲓⲱⲛ· ⲙ̄ⲛ̄ ⲛⲉⲥⲭⲏⲙⲁ ⲛ̄ⲑⲓⲙⲁⲣⲙⲉⲛⲏ· ⲙ̄ⲛ̄ ⲛⲁⲧⲉⲥⲫⲁⲓⲣⲁ· ⲁⲩⲱ ϣⲁϥϥⲓⲧϭⲟⲙ ⲙ̄ⲡⲟⲩⲟⲉⲓⲛ ⲛ̄ⲧⲟⲟⲧⲟⲩ ⲁⲩⲱ ϣⲁⲩⲥⲟⲃⲧⲉ ⲛ̄ϭⲓ ⲙ̄ⲡⲁⲣⲁⲗⲏⲙⲡⲧⲱⲣ ⲙ̄ⲡⲣⲏ ⲛ̄ⲥⲉⲕⲁⲁϥ ϣⲁⲛⲧⲟⲩⲧⲁⲁϥ ⲛ̄ⲙ̄ⲡⲁⲣⲁⲗⲏⲙⲡⲧⲱⲣ ⲙ̄ⲙⲉⲗⲭⲓⲥⲉⲇⲉⲕ· ⲡⲣⲉϥⲥⲱⲧ̄ⲃ̄ ⲛ̄ⲟⲩⲟⲉⲓⲛ· ⲁⲩⲱ ⲡⲉⲩϩⲩⲗⲓⲕⲟⲛ ⲛ̄ⲥⲟⲣⲙ̄· ϣⲁⲩϫⲓⲧ̄ϥ̄ ⲉⲧⲉⲥⲫⲁⲓⲣⲁ. ⲉⲧⲙ̄ⲡⲉⲥⲏⲧ ⲛ̄ⲛ̄ⲁ*ⲓⲱⲛ ⲛ̄ⲥⲉⲁⲁϥ ⲙ̄ⲯⲩⲭⲏ ⲛ̄ⲣⲱⲙⲉ· ⲁⲩⲱ ⲗ̄ⲗ̄ b ⲟⲛ ϣⲁⲩⲁⲁϥ ⲛ̄ϫⲁⲧϥⲉ· ϩⲓ ⲧ̄ⲃ̄ⲛⲏ· ϩⲓ ⲑⲏⲣⲓⲟⲛ· ϩⲓ ϩⲁⲗⲏⲧ· ⲕⲁⲧⲁ ⲡⲕⲩⲕⲗⲟⲥ ⲛ̄ⲛ̄ⲁⲣⲭⲱⲛ ⲛ̄ⲧⲉⲥⲫⲁⲓⲣⲁ ⲉⲧⲙ̄ⲙⲁⲩ· ⲁⲩⲱ ⲕⲁⲧⲁ ⲛⲉⲥⲭⲏⲙⲁ ⲧⲏⲣⲟⲩ ⲛ̄ⲧⲉⲥϭⲓⲛⲕⲱⲧⲉ· ⲁⲩⲱ ⲛ̄ⲥⲉⲛⲟϫⲟⲩ ⲉⲡⲉⲓ̈ⲕⲟⲥⲙⲟⲥ ⲛ̄ⲧⲉ ⲧⲙ̄ⲛ̄ⲧ̄ⲣⲱⲙⲉ· ⲁⲩⲱ ⲛ̄ⲥⲉϣⲱⲡⲉ ⲙ̄ⲯⲩⲭⲏ ϩ̄ⲙ̄ ⲡⲧⲟⲡⲟⲥ ⲉⲧⲙ̄ⲙⲁⲩ ⲕⲁⲧⲁ ⲑⲉ ⲉⲛⲧⲁⲓ̈ⲟⲩⲱ ⲉⲓ̈ϫⲱ ⲙ̄ⲙⲟⲥ ⲛⲏⲧ̄ⲛ̄· ⲛⲁⲓ̈ ϭⲉ ⲛⲉⲩϫⲱⲕ ⲉⲃⲟⲗ ⲙ̄ⲙⲟⲟⲩ ⲡⲉ ⲉⲩⲙⲏⲛ: ϩⲁⲑⲏ ⲉⲙⲡⲁⲧⲉ ⲧⲉⲩϭⲟⲙ

3 MS ⲧⲉⲩϩⲩⲗⲏ; read ⲡⲉⲩϩⲩⲗⲏ.
7 MS ⲡ̄ⲁⲓⲱⲛ ; read ⲛ̄ⲡ̄ⲁⲓⲱⲛ.
13 MS ϣⲁϥϥⲓ ; read ϣⲁⲩϥⲓ.
25 MS ⲉⲩⲙⲏⲛ ; elsewhere ⲉⲩⲙⲏⲛ ⲉⲃⲟⲗ.

bodies. And Melchizedek, the *Paralemptor* of the Light, purified those powers, he carried their light to the *Treasury* of
the Light. And all their *matter* was gathered together by the
ministers of all the *archons* [1]. And the *ministers* of all the
archons of the *Heimarmene* and the *ministers* of the *sphere*
which are below the *aeons* took them (the matter) and made
them into *souls* of men and cattle and reptiles and *beasts*
and birds. And they sent them to this *world* of mankind.
And furthermore the *paralemptors* of the sun and the
paralemptors of the moon when they looked up and they
saw the *patterns* of the paths of the *aeons*, and the *patterns*
of the *Heimarmene* and those of the *sphere*, they took the
lightpower from them. And the *paralemptors* of the sun
prepared to lay it down until they gave it to the *paralemptor*
of Melchizedek, the purifier of the light. And their *material*
dregs they brought to the *sphere* which is below the *aeons*,
and they made it into the *souls* of men and they also made
it into ⟨*souls* of⟩ reptiles and cattle and *beasts* and birds,
according to the *cycle* of the *archons* of that *sphere*, and
according to all the *patterns* of its revolution. And they cast
them into this *world* of mankind, and they became *souls* in
that *place*, *according to* what I have just told you.

26.   These things were now fully completed before their
power | diminished within them, and they declined and they

---

[1]   (5) archons; Till : archons of the aeons.

СВОК 2РΛΪ Ñ2ΗΤΟΥ· ΛΥω ÑCΕϬωჯΒ· ΛΥω Ñ CΕ-
ΛΤΟΝΙ· Ĥ ÑCΕP-ΛΤϬΟΜ· ΛCϢωΠΕ ϬΕ ÑΤΕΡΟΥP-
ΛΤϬΟΜ ΛΥω Λ ΤΕΥϬΟΜ ΛΡჯΙ ÑωჯÑ 2ΡΛΪ Ñ2ΗΤΟΥ
ΛΥω ÑCΕΡϬωΒ 2Ñ ΤΕΥϬΟΜ· ΛΥω ÑႷωჯÑ Ñϭι ΠΕΥ-
5 ΟΥΟΕΙΝ ΕΤϢΟΟΠ 2Μ̄ ΠΕΥΤΟΠΟC· ΛΥω Ñ̄ΤΕ ΤΕΥ-
Μ̄ΝΤΕΡΟ ΒωΛ ΕΒΟΛ· ΛΥω Ñ̄ΤΕ ΠΤΗΡῪ̄ ωΛ**Ε2ΡΛΪ 2Ñ ΛΕ
ΟΥϬΕΠΗ· ΛCϢωΠΕ ϬΕ Ñ̄ΤΕΡΟΥΕΙΜΕ ΕΝΛΪ 2ΡΛΪ 2Μ̄
ΠΕΟΥΟΕΙϢ· ΛΥω ΕႷϢΛΝϢωΠΕ Ñ̄ϭι ΠΛΡΙΘΜΟC Ñ̄ΤΕ-
ΨΗϤΟC Μ̄ΜΕΛჯΙCΕΛΕΚ· ΠΠΛΡΛΛΗΜΠΤωΡ ⟨Μ̄ΠΟΥΟΕΙΝ⟩·
10 ΝΕϢΛႷΕΙˀ ΟΝ ΕΒΟΛ ΠΕ· Ñ̄ႷΒωΚ Ε2ΟΥΝ ΕΤΜΗΤΕ Ñ̄ΝΛΡ-
ჯωΝ Ñ̄ΝΛΙωΝ ΤΗΡΟΥ· ΛΥω ΕΤΜΗΤΕ Ñ̄ΝΛΡჯωΝ ΤΗΡΟΥ
Ñ̄ΘΙΜΛΡΜΕΝΗ· Μ̄Ñ ΝΛΤΕCϤΛΙΡΛ· ΛΥω ϢΛϤϢΤ̄ΡΤω-
ΡΟΥ· Ñ̄ϤΤΡΕΥΚω ΕΒΟΛ Ñ̄ϭι ΝΕΥΚΥΚΛΟC 2Ñ ΟΥ-
ϬΕΠΗ· ΛΥω Ñ̄ΤΕΥΝΟΥ ϢΛΥΘΛΙΒΕ Ñ̄CΕCΙΤΕ Ñ̄ΤϬΟΜ
15 Ñ̄CΛΒΟΛ Μ̄ΜΟΟΥ· ΕΒΟΛ 2Μ̄ ΠΝΙႷΕ Ñ̄ΤΕΥΤΛΠΡΟ· ΛΥω
ΕΒΟΛ 2Ñ Μ̄ΜΟΥΕΙΟΟΥΕ Ñ̄ΝΕΥΒΛΛ· ΛΥω ΕΒΟΛ 2Ñ
Ñ̄ϤωΤΕ Ñ̄ΝΕΥCωΜΛ· ΛΥω ϢΛϤCΟΤϤΟΥ Ñ̄ϭι ΜΕΛ-
ჯΙCΕΛΕΚ ΠΠΛΡΛΛΗΜΠΤωΡ Μ̄ΠΟΥΟΕΙΝ ΚΛΤΛ ΘΕ ΕϢΛϤ-
ΛΛC ΕϤΜΗΝ ΕΒΟΛ· ΛΥω Ñ̄ϤჯΙ-ΠΕΥΟΥΟΕΙΝ ΕΠΕΘΗ- ΛΕ ᵇ
20 CΛΥΡΟC Μ̄ΠΟΥΟΕΙΝ· ΛΥω ΘΥΛΗ Μ̄ΠΕΥCΟΡΜ̄· ϢΛΡΕ
ΝΛΡჯωΝ ΤΗΡΟΥ Ñ̄ΛΙωΝ· ΛΥω Ñ̄ΛΡჯωΝ Ñ̄ΘΙΜΛΡΜΕΝΗ
Μ̄Ñ ΝΛΤΕCϤΛΙΡΛ ϢΛΥΚωΤΕ ΕΡΟC Ñ̄CΕωΜ̄Κ Μ̄ΜΟC·
ΛΥω ΜΕΥΚΛΛΥ ΕΕΙˀ ΕP-ΨΥჯΗ 2Μ̄ ΠΚΟCΜΟC· ϢΛΥ-
ωΜ̄Κ ϬΕ Ñ̄ΤΕΥ2ΥΛΗ· ჯΕ Ñ̄ΝΕΥP-ΛΤϬΟΜ· Ñ̄CΕΛΤΟΝΙ·

9　Μ̄ΠΟΥΟΕΙΝ omitted in MS.
21　MS Ñ̄ΛΙωΠ; read Ñ̄ΝΛΙωΝ.

weakened or they became powerless. It happened when they
became weak, their power *began* to cease within them, and
they became weak in their power. And their light, which
was in their *place*, ceased. And their kingdom dissolved.
And the All was quickly carried up.

It happened now when these things in their time were
known, and when the *number* of the *cipher* of Melchizedek,
the *Paralemptor* ⟨of the Light⟩, occurred, he came forth,
and he went into the midst of the *archons* of all the *aeons*,
and to the midst of all the *archons* of the *Heimarmene* and
those of the *sphere*. And he agitated them, and he caused
them quickly to abandon their *cycles*, and immediately they
were *afflicted*, and they cast the power out of themselves,
out of the breath of their mouths, and out of the tears of
their eyes, and out of the sweat of their *bodies*. And Melchizedek, the *Paralemptor* of the Light purified them, *according
to* the manner in which he did so continually. And he took
their light to the *Treasury* of the Light. And the *matter* of
their dregs was surrounded and swallowed by all the *archons*
of the *aeons* and the *archons* of the *Heimarmene* and those
of the *sphere*, and they did not allow them to go and become
souls in the *world*. They now swallowed their *matter*, that
they might not become powerless and *weak*, | that their

73

ⲀⲨⲰ ⲚⲦⲈ ⲦⲈⲨϬⲞⲘ ⲰⲬⲚ̄ ⲈϨⲢⲀⲒ̈ Ⲛ̄ϨⲎⲦⲞⲨ · ⲀⲨⲰ Ⲛ̄ⲦⲈ
ⲦⲈⲨⲘⲚ̄ⲦⲈⲢⲞ ⲂⲰⲖ ⲈⲂⲞⲖ · ⲀⲖⲖⲀ ϢⲀⲨⲞⲘⲔⲤ̄ ⲬⲈ Ⲛ̄ⲚⲈⲨ-
ⲂⲰⲖ ⲈⲂⲞⲖ ⲀⲖⲖⲀ ⲬⲈ ⲈⲨⲈⲰⲤⲔ̄ Ⲛ̄ⲤⲈⲢ̄-ⲞⲨⲚⲞϬ Ⲛ̄ⲞⲨⲞ-
ⲈⲒϢ ⲈⲘⲠⲈⲒⲬⲰⲔ Ⲙ̄ⲠⲀⲢⲒⲐⲘⲞⲤ Ⲛ̄ⲚⲈⲮⲨⲬⲞⲞⲨⲈ Ⲛ̄ⲦⲈⲖⲒⲞⲚ ·
5 ⲚⲀⲒ̈ ⲈⲦⲚⲀϢⲰⲠⲈ ϨⲘ̄ ⲠⲈⲐⲎⲤⲀⲨⲢⲞⲤ Ⲙ̄ⲠⲞⲨⲞⲈⲒⲚ · ⲀⲤ-
ϢⲰⲠⲈ ϬⲈ ⲈⲢⲈ Ⲛ̄ⲀⲢⲬⲰⲚ Ⲛ̄Ⲛ̄ⲀⲒⲰⲚ ⲘⲚ̄ ⲚⲀⲐⲒⲘⲀⲢⲘⲈⲚⲎ
ⲘⲚ̄ ⲚⲀⲦⲈⲤⲪⲀⲒⲢⲀ · ⲈⲨⲘⲎⲚ ⲈⲂⲞⲖ · ⲈⲨⲈⲒⲢⲈ Ⲙ̄ⲠⲈⲒ̈ⲦⲨⲠⲞⲤ
ⲈⲨⲔⲦⲞ Ⲙ̄ⲘⲞⲞⲨ ⲈⲨⲞⲨⲰⲘ Ⲙ̄ⲠⲤⲞⲢⲘ̄ Ⲛ̄ⲦⲈⲨϨⲨⲬⲎ ⲈⲘ- ⲗ̄ⲉ̈
ⲠⲞⲨⲔⲀⲀⲨ ⲈⲢ̄-ⲮⲨⲬⲎ ϨⲘ̄ ⲠⲔⲞⲤⲘⲞⲤ Ⲛ̄ⲦⲘ̄Ⲛ̄ⲦⲢⲰⲘⲈ ⲬⲈ
10 ⲈⲨⲈⲰⲤⲔ̄ ⲈⲨⲞ Ⲛ̄Ⲣ̄ⲢⲞ · ⲀⲨⲰ Ⲛ̄ⲤⲈⲢ̄-ⲞⲨⲚⲞϬ Ⲛ̄ⲞⲨⲞⲈⲒϢ
Ⲛ̄ⲂⲞⲖ ⲦⲀⲒ̈ Ⲛ̄ϬⲒ Ⲛ̄ϬⲞⲘ · ⲚⲀⲒ̈ ⲈⲦⲞ Ⲛ̄ϬⲞⲘ Ⲛ̄ϨⲎⲦⲞⲨ ⲈⲦⲈ
Ⲛ̄ⲦⲞⲞⲨ ⲚⲈ ⲚⲈⲮⲨⲬⲞⲞⲨⲈ · ⲚⲀⲒ̈ ϬⲈ ⲀⲨϬⲰ ⲈⲨⲈⲒⲢⲈ
Ⲙ̄ⲘⲞⲞⲨ Ⲛ̄ⲔⲨⲔⲖⲞⲤ ⲤⲚⲀⲨ ⲈⲨⲘⲎⲚ ⲈⲂⲞⲖ :

ⲀⲤϢⲰⲠⲈ ϬⲈ Ⲛ̄ⲦⲈⲢⲒⲈⲒ̈ ⲈⲒ̈ⲚⲀⲂⲰⲔ ⲈϨⲢⲀⲒ̈ ⲈⲦⲆⲒⲀⲔⲞⲚⲒⲀ
15 ⲈⲚⲦⲀⲨⲦⲀϨⲘⲈⲦ ⲈⲦⲂⲎⲎⲦⲤ̄ · ϨⲒⲦⲚ̄ ⲦⲔⲈⲖⲈⲨⲤⲒⲤ Ⲙ̄ⲠϢⲞⲢⲠ̄
Ⲙ̄ⲘⲨⲤⲦⲎⲢⲒⲞⲚ · ⲀⲒ̈ⲈⲒ̈ ⲈϨⲢⲀⲒ̈ ⲈⲦⲘⲎⲦⲈ Ⲛ̄Ⲛ̄ⲦⲨⲢⲀⲚⲚⲞⲤ Ⲛ̄Ⲛ̄-
ⲀⲢⲬⲰⲚ Ⲙ̄ⲠⲘ̄Ⲛ̄ⲦⲤⲚⲞⲞⲨⲤ Ⲛ̄ⲀⲒⲰⲚ · ⲈⲢⲈ ⲠⲀⲈⲚⲆⲨⲘⲀ
Ⲛ̄ⲞⲨⲞⲈⲒⲚ ϨⲒⲰⲰⲦ · ⲈⲒ̈Ⲟ Ⲛ̄ⲞⲨⲞⲈⲒⲚ ⲈⲘⲀϢⲞ ⲈⲘⲀϢⲞ ·
ⲈⲘⲚ̄-ϢⲒ ⲈⲠⲞⲨⲞⲈⲒⲚ ⲈⲚⲈϤϢⲞⲞⲠ Ⲙ̄ⲘⲞⲒ̈ · ⲀⲤϢⲰⲠⲈ ϬⲈ
20 Ⲛ̄ⲦⲈⲢⲞⲨⲚⲀⲨ ⲈⲠⲚⲞϬ Ⲛ̄ⲞⲨⲞⲈⲒⲚ ⲈⲦϢⲞⲞⲠ Ⲙ̄ⲘⲞⲒ̈ Ⲛ̄ϬⲒ
ⲚⲒⲦⲨⲢⲀⲚⲚⲞⲤ ⲈⲦⲘ̄ⲘⲀⲨ · Ⲁ ⲠⲚⲞϬ Ⲛ̄ⲀⲆⲀⲘⲀⲤ ⲠⲦⲨⲢⲀⲚ- ⲗ̄ⲉ̄ b
ⲚⲞⲤ ⲘⲚ̄ Ⲛ̄ⲦⲨⲢⲀⲚⲚⲞⲤ ⲦⲎⲢⲞⲨ Ⲙ̄ⲠⲘ̄Ⲛ̄ⲦⲤⲚⲞⲞⲨⲤ Ⲛ̄ⲀⲒⲰⲚ
ⲀⲨⲀⲢⲬⲈⲤⲐⲀⲒ ⲦⲎⲢⲞⲨ Ⲙ̄ⲠⲞⲖⲈⲘⲈⲒ ⲘⲚ̄ ⲠⲞⲨⲞⲈⲒⲚ Ⲙ̄ⲠⲀⲈⲚ-
ⲆⲨⲘⲀ ⲈⲨⲞⲨⲈϢⲔⲀⲦⲈⲬⲈ Ⲙ̄ⲘⲞϤ ϨⲀⲦⲎⲨ · ⲬⲈ ⲈⲨⲈⲰⲤⲔ̄
25 ⲞⲚ ϨⲚ̄ ⲦⲈⲨⲘⲚ̄ⲦⲈⲢⲞ · ⲚⲀⲒ̈ ϬⲈ ⲚⲈⲨⲈⲒⲢⲈ Ⲙ̄ⲘⲞⲞⲨ ⲠⲈ

---

4 MS ⲈⲘⲠⲈⲒⲬⲰⲔ; read ϢⲀⲠⲬⲰⲔ.
11 MS Ⲛ̄ⲦϬⲞⲘ; Ⲧ expunged.
20 MS ⲈⲠⲚϬ; Ⲟ inserted above.

power might not cease within them and their rulership (kingdom) dissolve. *And* they swallowed them so that they should not dissolve, *but* that they should be retarded, and should spend a great time until the completion of the *number* of *perfect souls* which would be in the *Treasury* of the Light.

27. It happened now as the *archons* of the *aeons* and those of the *Heimarmene* and those of the *sphere* continued acting after this *type*; as they turned themselves they ate the dregs of their *matter*, they did not allow them to become *souls* in the *world* of mankind, so that they might be retarded as rulers. And the powers, namely the powers within them which were *souls*, spent a great time outside this. Now these remained making two *cycles* continually.

It happened now when I came to go forth for the *service* for the sake of which I was appointed, through the *command* of the First *Mystery*, I came forth to the midst of the *tyrants* of the *archons* of the twelve *aeons*. And my *garment* of light was upon me, and I was shining exceedingly, there being no measure to the light which I had.

Now it happened, when those *tyrants* saw the great light which I had, the great Adamas, the *Tyrant*, and all the *tyrants* of the twelve *aeons* all *began* to *wage war* with the light of my *garment*, wishing to *restrain* it for themselves, so that they might still be retarded in their rulership (kingdom). These now acted thus, | not knowing with whom

ⲈⲚⲤⲈⲤⲞⲞⲨⲚ ⲀⲚ ⲬⲈ ⲈⲨⲠⲞⲖⲈⲘⲒ ⲘⲚ ⲚⲒⲘ · ⲠⲦⲈⲢⲞⲨ-
ⲀⲦⲀⲔⲦⲒ ⲄⲈ ⲈⲀⲨⲠⲞⲖⲈⲘⲒ ⲘⲚ ⲠⲞⲨⲞⲈⲒⲚ · ⲦⲞⲦⲈ ⲀⲚⲞⲔ
ⲔⲀⲦⲀ ⲦⲔⲈⲖⲈⲨⲤⲒⲤ ⲘⲠⲱⲞⲢⲠ ⲘⲘⲨⲤⲦⲏⲢⲒⲞⲚ · ⲀⲒⲠⲱⲞⲚⲈ
ⲚⲚⲄⲒⲚⲘⲞⲞⲱⲈ ⲘⲚ ⲚⲀⲢⲞⲘⲞⲤ ⲚⲚⲈⲨⲀⲒⲰⲚ · ⲘⲚ ⲚⳘⲒⲚ-
5 ⲘⲞⲞⲱⲈ ⲚⲦⲈⲨⲌⲒⲘⲀⲢⲘⲈⲚⲎ · ⲘⲚ ⲦⲈⲨⲤⲪⲀⲒⲢⲀ · ⲀⲨⲱ
ⲀⲒⲦⲢⲈⲨⲢ-ⲤⲞⲞⲨ ⲚⲈⲂⲞⲦ ⲈⲨⳠⲱⳘⲦ ⲈⲱⲞⲘⲦ ⲚⲔⲞⲞⳠ
ⲚⳈⲂⲞⲨⲢ · ⲀⲨⲱ ⲈⲚⲈⲨⲦⲞⲞⲨ ⲚⲔⲞⲞⳠ · ⲀⲨⲱ ⲈⲚⲈⲦⲘⲠⲈⲨ-
ⳈⲞⲦ ⲈⲂⲞⲖ · ⲀⲨⲱ ⲈⲠⲈⲨⲱⲘⲞⲨⲚ ⲚⲤⲬⲎⲘⲀ ⲔⲀⲦⲀ ⲐⲈ ⲢⲰ
ⲈⲚⲈⲨⲞ ⲘⲘⲞⲤ ⲚⳘⲟⲢⲠ · ⲦⲈⲨⳘⲒⲚⲔⲰⲦⲈ ⲆⲈ ⲏ̈ ⲦⲈⲨⳘⲒⲚ- ⲗ̄ⲍ
10 ⳠⲱⳘⲦ ⲀⲒⲠⲞⲞⲚⲈⲤ ⲈⲔⲈⲦⲀⳘⲒⲤ · ⲀⲨⲱ ⲀⲒⲦⲢⲈⲨⲢ-ⲔⲈⲤⲞⲞⲨ
ⲚⲈⲂⲞⲦ ⲈⲨⳠⲱⳘⲦ ⲈⲚⲈⳈⲂⲎⲨⲈ ⲚⲚⲈⲨⲀⲠⲞⲦⲈⲖⲈⲤⲘⲀ ⳈⲚ
ⲚⲈⲨⲦⲞⲞⲨ ⲚⲔⲞⲞⳠ ⲚⲞⲨⲚⲀⳘ · ⲀⲨⲱ ⳈⲚ ⲚⲈⲨⲱⲞⲘⲦ
ⲚⲔⲞⲞⳠ · ⲀⲨⲱ ⳈⲚ ⲚⲈⲦⲘⲠⲈⲨⳈⲞⲦ ⲈⲂⲞⲖ · ⲀⲨⲱ ⳈⲘ ⲠⲈⲨ-
ⲱⲘⲞⲨⲚ ⲚⲤⲬⲎⲘⲀ · ⲀⲨⲱ ⲀⲒⲦⲢⲈⲨⲢ-ⳈⲂⲀ ⳈⲚ ⲞⲨⲚⲞⳘ
15 ⲚⳈⲂⲀ · ⲀⲨⲱ ⲀⲒⲦⲢⲈⲨⲠⲖⲀⲚⲀ ⳈⲚ ⲞⲨⲠⲖⲀⲚⲎ ⲚⳘⲒ ⲚⲀⲢⲬⲰⲚ
ⲚⲀⲒⲰⲚ · ⲀⲨⲱ ⲚⲀⲢⲬⲰⲚ ⲦⲎⲢⲞⲨ ⲚⲐⲒⲘⲀⲢⲘⲈⲚⲎ ⲘⲚ ⲚⲀ-
ⲦⲈⲤⲪⲀⲒⲢⲀ · ⲀⲨⲱ ⲀⲒⲱⲦⲢⲦⲰⲢⲞⲨ ⲈⲘⲀⲦⲈ · ⲀⲨⲱ ⲘⲠⲞⲨ-
ⲈⲱⳘⳘⲞⲘ ⳠⲈ ⳘⲒⲚ ⲘⲠⲈⲒⲚⲀⲨ ⲈⲔⲞⲦⲞⲨ ⲈⲠⲤⲞⲢⳘ ⲚⲦⲈⲨ-
ⳈⲨⲖⲎ · ⲈⲦⲢⲈⲨⲞⲘⲈⲔϤ · ⳘⲈ ⲈⲢⲈ ⲚⲈⲨⲦⲞⲠⲞⲤ ⲱⲤⲔ ⲈⲨ-
20 ⲘⲎⲚ ⲈⲂⲞⲖ · ⲀⲨⲱ ⳘⲈ ⲈⲨⲈⲢ-ⲞⲨⲚⲟⳘ ⲚⲞⲨⲞⲈⲒⲱ ⲈⲨⲞ
ⲚⲢⲢⲞ · ⲀⲖⲖⲀ ⲚⲦⲈⲢⲒϤⲒ ⲚⲞⲨⲞⲨⲰⲚ ⲚⳘⲞⲘⲦ ⲚⲦⲈ ⲚⲈⲨ-
ⳘⲞⲘ · ⲀⲒⲠⲱⲞⲚⲈ ⲚⲚⲈⲨⲤⲪⲀⲒⲢⲀ ⲈⲦⲢⲈⲨⲢ-ⲞⲨⲞⲨⲞⲒⲱ ⲈⲨ- ⲗ̄ⲍᵇ
ⳠⲱⳘⲦ ⲈⳈⲂⲞⲨⲢ · ⲀⲨⲱ ⲚⲤⲈⲢ-ⲔⲈⲞⲨⲞⲒⲱ ⲈⲨⳠⲱⳘⲦ ⲈⲞⲨ-
ⲚⲀⳘ · ⲀⲒⲠⲱⲞⲚⲈ ⲚⲦⲈⲨⳘⲒⲚⲘⲞⲞⲱⲈ ⲦⲎⲢⳠ ⲘⲚ ⲠⲈⲨ-
25 ⲀⲢⲞⲘⲞⲤ ⲦⲎⲢϤ · ⲀⲨⲱ ⲀⲒⲦⲢⲈⲤⳘⲈⲠⲎ ⲚⳘⲒ ⲦⳘⲒⲚⲘⲞⲞⲱⲈ
ⲘⲠⲈⲨⲀⲢⲞⲘⲞⲤ ⳘⲈ ⲈⲨⲈⲤⲰⲦϤ ⳈⲚ ⲞⲨⳘⲈⲠⲎ · ⲀⲨⲱ

---

16 MS ⲚⲀⲒⲰⲚ ; read ⲚⲚⲀⲒⲰⲚ.

they *waged war*. When they now *rebelled* and *waged war* with the light, I *then* turned the paths and the *courses* of their *aeons*, and the paths of their *Heimarmene* and their *sphere*, according to the *command* of the First *Mystery*, and I caused them to spend six months looking to the triangles of the left, and to the quadrangles, and to those in their aspect [1], and to their *pattern* of eight, *according to* the manner in which they were at first. *But* I turned their rotation *or* their aspect to another *rank*. And I caused them to spend another six months looking to the works of their (periods of) *influence* in the quadrangles of the right, and in their triangles, and in those which are in their aspect, and in their *pattern* of eight. And I caused the *archons* of the *aeons* to be confused with much confusion, and I caused them to *wander* in *error*, together with all the *archons* of the *Heimarmene* and those of the *sphere*. And I agitated them greatly. And they were now, from this time, not able to turn themselves to the dregs of their *matter* in order to swallow it, so that their *places* might be continually retarded, and so that they might spend a great time as rulers. *But* when I had taken a third part of their power, I turned their *sphere* to cause them to spend (a period of) time looking to the left and to spend another (period of) time looking to the right. I turned their whole path and their whole *course*, and I caused the path of their *course* to be accelerated, so that they might be purified quickly, | and they might go

---

[1] (8, 13) in their aspect; Till: opposite them (also 41.20).

ⲡⲥⲉⲱⲗ ⲉϩⲣⲁⲓ ϩⲛ ⲟⲩϭⲉⲡⲏ · ⲁⲩⲱ ⲁⲓⲧⲥⲃⲕⲟ ⲛⲛⲉⲩⲕⲩ-
ⲕⲗⲟⲥ · ⲁⲩⲱ ⲁⲓⲧⲣⲉⲥⲁⲥⲁⲓ ⲛϭⲓ ⲧⲉⲩϭⲓⲛⲙⲟⲟϣⲉ · ⲁⲩⲱ
ⲁⲥϭⲉⲡⲏ ⲉⲙⲁϣⲟ · ⲁⲩⲱ ⲁⲩⲣ̄ϩⲃⲁ ϩⲛ ⲧⲉⲩϭⲓⲛⲙⲟⲟϣⲉ
ⲁⲩⲱ ⲙ̄ⲡⲟⲩϣ̄ϭⲙϭⲟⲙ ϫⲓⲛ ⲙ̄ⲡⲉⲓⲛⲁⲩ ⲉⲱⲙ̄ⲕ ⲛ̄ⲟⲩⲗⲏ

5 ⲙ̄ⲛⲥⲟⲣ̄ⲙ ⲙ̄ⲛⲥⲱⲧϥ ⲙ̄ⲛⲉⲩⲟⲩⲟⲓⲛ ⲁⲩⲱ ⲟⲛ ⲁⲓⲧⲥⲃⲕⲟ
ⲛ̄ⲛⲉⲩⲟⲩⲟⲉⲓϣ ⲙⲛ ⲛⲉⲩⲭⲣⲟⲛⲟⲥ · ϫⲉ ⲉϥⲉϫⲱⲕ ⲉⲃⲟⲗ
ϩⲛ ⲟⲩϭⲉⲡⲏ ⲛϭⲓ ⲡⲁⲣⲓⲑⲙⲟⲥ ⲛ̄ⲧⲉⲗⲓⲟⲛ ⲛ̄ⲧⲉ ⲛⲉⲯⲩⲭⲟⲟⲩⲉ ⲉⲧⲛⲁϫⲓ-ⲙⲩⲥⲧⲏⲣⲓⲟⲛ · ⲛⲁⲓ ⲉⲧⲛⲁϣⲱⲡⲉ ϩⲙ ⲡⲉⲟⲏⲥⲁⲩⲣⲟⲥ ⲙ̄ⲡⲟⲩⲟⲉⲓⲛ · ⲛ̄ⲥⲁⲃⲏⲗ ϭⲉ ϫⲉ ⲁⲓⲡⲱⲱⲛⲉ

10 ⲛ̄ⲛⲉⲩⲁⲣⲟⲙⲟⲥ · ⲁⲩⲱ ⲛ̄ⲥⲁⲃⲏⲗ ϫⲉ ⲁⲓⲧⲥⲃⲕⲟ ⲛ̄ⲛⲉⲩ-
ⲭⲣⲟⲛⲟⲥ ⲛⲉⲩⲛⲁⲕⲁ-ⲗⲁⲁⲩ ⲁⲛ ⲡⲉ ⲙ̄ⲯⲩⲭⲏ ⲉⲉⲓ̄ ⲉⲡⲕⲟⲥⲙⲟⲥ ⲉⲧⲃⲉ ⲟⲩⲗⲏ ⲙ̄ⲡⲉⲩⲥⲟⲣ̄ⲙ ⲉⲧⲟⲩⲱⲙ̄ⲕ ⲙ̄ⲙⲟϥ ⲁⲩⲱ
ⲛⲉⲩⲛⲁⲧⲁⲕⲉ-ⲟⲩⲙⲏⲏϣⲉ ⲙ̄ⲯⲩⲭⲏ ⲡⲉ · ⲉⲧⲃⲉ ⲡⲁⲓ ϭⲉ
ⲁⲓϫⲟⲟⲥ ⲛⲏⲧ̄ⲛ ⲙ̄ⲡⲟⲩⲟⲉⲓϣ ϫⲉ ⲁⲓⲧⲥⲃⲕⲉ-ⲛⲉⲟⲩⲟⲉⲓϣ

15 ⲉⲧⲃⲉ ⲛⲁⲥⲱⲧⲡ̄ ⲉⲙⲙⲟⲛ ⲛⲉ ⲙ̄ⲛⲗⲁⲁⲩ ⲙ̄ⲯⲩⲭⲏ ⲉϣⲟⲩ-
ϫⲁⲓ ⲡⲉ ⲛ̄ⲧⲁⲓⲧⲥⲃⲕⲉ-ⲛⲉⲟⲩⲟⲉⲓϣ ⲇⲉ ⲙⲛ ⲛⲉⲭⲣⲟⲛⲟⲥ ⲉⲧⲃⲉ
ⲡⲁⲣⲓⲑⲙⲟⲥ ⲛ̄ⲧⲉⲗⲉⲓⲟⲛ ⲛ̄ⲛⲉⲯⲩⲭⲟⲟⲩⲉ ⲉⲧⲛⲁϫⲓ-ⲙⲩⲥⲧⲏⲣⲓⲟⲛ ⲉⲧⲉ ⲛ̄ⲧⲟⲟⲩ ⲛⲉ ⲛ̄ⲥⲱⲧⲡ̄ ⲁⲩⲱ ⲉⲛⲉ ⲙ̄ⲡⲓⲧⲥⲃⲕⲉ-
ⲛⲉⲩⲭⲣⲟⲛⲟⲥ · ⲛⲉ ⲙ̄ⲛⲗⲁⲁⲩ ⲙ̄ⲯⲩⲭⲏ ⲛ̄ϩⲩⲗⲓⲕⲏ ⲛⲁⲟⲩ-

20 ϫⲁⲓ · ⲁⲗⲗⲁ ⲛⲉⲩⲛⲁⲁⲛϩⲁⲗⲓⲥⲕⲉ ⲡⲉ ϩⲙ ⲡⲕⲱ̄ⲧ · ⲡⲁⲓ ⲉⲧϣⲟⲟⲡ ϩⲛ ⲧⲥⲁⲣⲝ ⲛ̄ⲛⲁⲣⲭⲱⲛ · ⲡⲁⲓ ϭⲉ ⲡⲉ ⲡϣⲁϫⲉ
ⲉⲧⲉⲣⲉϣⲓⲛⲉ ⲙ̄ⲙⲟⲓ ⲉⲣⲟϥ ϩⲛ ⲟⲩⲙⲛ̄ⲧⲁⲕⲣⲓⲃⲏⲥ ·

ⲍ̄ ⲁⲥϣⲱⲡⲉ ⲇⲉ ⲛ̄ⲧⲉⲣⲉ ⲓ̄ⲥ̄ ⲟⲩⲱ ⲉϥϫⲱ ⲛ̄ⲛⲉⲓϣⲁϫⲉ ⲁ̄ⲏᵇ
ⲉⲛⲉϥⲙⲁⲑⲏⲧⲏⲥ · ⲁⲩⲡⲁϩⲧⲟⲩ ⲧⲏⲣⲟⲩ ϩⲓ ⲟⲩⲥⲟⲡ · ⲁⲩ-

---

3   MS ⲁⲩϭⲉⲡⲏ; ⲩ crossed out, and ⲥ inserted above.
12   MS ⲩ in ⲉⲧⲟϣⲙ̄ⲕ inserted above.
15   MS ϣ in ⲥⲟⲩϫⲁⲓ inserted above.

upwards quickly. And I lessened their *cycles*, and I made their path easier, and it was greatly accelerated, and they were confused in their path, and from this time they were not able to swallow the *matter* of the dregs of what is purified of their light. And further I lessened their times and their *periods*, so that the *perfect number* of *souls* which will receive *mysteries* and which will be in the *Treasury* of the Light should be completed quickly. And unless I had turned their *courses* and unless I had lessened their *periods*, they would not have allowed any *souls* to come to the *world*, on account of the *matter* of their dregs which they swallowed, and they would have destroyed a multitude of *souls*. On account of this now, I have said to you at this time : 'I have lessened the times for the sake of my chosen ones, otherwise none of the *souls* could have been saved'. *But* I have lessened the times and the *periods* for the sake of the *perfect number* of the *souls* which will receive *mysteries*, which are the chosen ones. And had I not lessened their *periods*, none of the *material souls* would have been saved, *but* they would have been *consumed* in the fire which is in the *flesh* of the *archons*. This now is the discourse on which you have questioned me with *accuracy*".

It happened, *however*, when Jesus finished saying these words to his *disciples*, they all prostrated themselves at once, |

ΟΥⲰϢⲦ ⲚⲀϤ · ⲀΥⲰ ⲠⲈⲬⲀΥ ⲚⲀϤ ϪⲈ ⲀⲚⲞⲚ ⲆⲈⲚⲘⲀ-
ⲔⲀⲢⲒⲞⲤ ⲠⲀⲢⲀ ⲢⲰⲘⲈ ⲚⲒⲘ · ⲈⲀⲔϬⲰⲖⲠ ⲚⲀⲚ ⲈⲂⲞⲖ ⲚⲚⲈⲒ̈-
ⲚⲞϬ Ⲙ̄ⲘⲚⲦⲚⲞϬ ·

ⲍ̄ ⲀϤⲞΥⲰϨ ⲞⲚ ⲈⲦⲞⲞⲦ̄ϥ Ⲛ̄ϬⲒ Ⲓ̄Ⲥ̄ Ⲋ̄Ⲙ̄ ⲠϢⲀϪⲈ ⲠⲈⲬⲀϤ
5 Ⲛ̄ⲚⲈϤⲘⲀⲐⲎⲦⲎⲤ ϪⲈ ⲤⲰⲦ̄Ⲙ̄ [ⲤⲰⲦ̄Ⲙ̄] ⲈⲦⲂⲈ Ⲛ̄ϢⲀϪⲈ ⲈⲚⲦ-
ⲀΥϢⲰⲠⲈ Ⲙ̄ⲘⲞⲒ̈ Ϩ̄Ⲛ̄ Ⲛ̄ⲀⲢⲬⲰⲚ Ⲙ̄ⲠⲘⲚⲦⲤⲚⲞⲞΥⲤ Ⲛ̄ⲀⲒⲰⲚ ·
Ⲙ̄Ⲛ̄ ⲚⲈΥⲀⲢⲬⲰⲚ ⲦⲎⲢⲞΥ Ⲙ̄Ⲛ̄ ⲚⲈΥϪⲞⲒ̈Ⲥ Ⲙ̄Ⲛ̄ ⲚⲈΥⲈⲜⲞΥ-
ⲤⲒⲀ · Ⲙ̄Ⲛ̄ ⲚⲈΥⲀⲄⲄⲈⲖⲞⲤ · Ⲙ̄Ⲛ̄ ⲚⲈΥⲀⲢⲬⲀⲄⲄⲈⲖⲞⲤ · Ⲛ̄ⲦⲈ-
ⲢⲞΥⲚⲀΥ ϬⲈ ⲈⲠⲈⲚⲆΥⲘⲀ Ⲛ̄ⲞΥⲞⲈⲒⲚ ⲈⲦϨⲒϪⲰⲦ̄ · Ⲛ̄ⲦⲞⲞΥ
10 Ⲙ̄Ⲛ̄ ⲚⲈΥⲬⲰⲢⲒⲤⲤΥⲚⲌΥⲄⲞⲤ Ⲁ ⲠⲞΥⲀ ⲠⲞΥⲀ Ⲙ̄ⲘⲞⲞΥ ⲀΥ-
ⲚⲀΥ ⲈⲠⲘΥⲤⲦⲎⲢⲒⲞⲚ Ⲙ̄ⲠⲈΥⲢⲀⲚ · ⲈϤϢⲞⲞⲠ Ϩ̄Ⲙ̄ ⲠⲀⲈⲚ-
ⲆΥⲘⲀ Ⲛ̄ⲞΥⲞⲈⲒⲚ ⲠⲀⲒ̈ ⲈⲦϨⲒϪⲰⲦ̄ · ⲀΥⲠⲀϨⲦⲞΥ ⲦⲎⲢⲞΥ Ⲗ̄ⲅ̄
Ϩ̄Ⲓ ⲚⲈΥⲈⲢⲎΥ · ⲀΥⲞΥⲰϢⲦ̄ Ⲙ̄ⲠⲈⲚⲆΥⲘⲀ Ⲛ̄ⲞΥⲞⲈⲒⲚ ⲈⲦ-
ϨⲒϪⲰⲦ̄ · ⲀΥⲰ ⲀΥϢ ⲈⲂⲞⲖ ⲦⲎⲢⲞΥ Ϩ̄Ⲓ ⲞΥⲤⲞⲠ · ⲈΥϪⲰ
15 Ⲙ̄ⲘⲞⲤ · ϪⲈ ⲠⲰⲤ Ⲁ ⲠϪⲞⲈⲒⲤ Ⲙ̄ⲠⲦⲎⲢϤ ⲞΥⲞⲦ̄Ⲃ̄Ⲛ̄ ⲈⲂⲞⲖ
ⲈⲘ̄Ⲡ̄ⲚⲈⲒⲘⲈ · ⲀΥⲰ ⲀΥϨΥⲘⲚⲈΥⲈ ⲦⲎⲢⲞΥ Ϩ̄Ⲓ ⲞΥⲤⲞⲠ ⲈⲠⲤⲀⲚ-
ϨⲞΥⲚ Ⲛ̄ⲦⲈ ⲚⲒⲤⲀⲚϨⲞΥⲚ · ⲀΥⲰ ⲚⲈΥⲦⲢⲒⲆΥⲚⲀⲘⲞⲤ ⲦⲎ-
ⲢⲞΥ Ⲙ̄Ⲛ̄ ⲚⲈΥⲚⲞϬ Ⲙ̄ⲠⲢⲞⲠⲀⲦⲰⲢ · ⲀΥⲰ ⲚⲈΥⲀⲄⲈⲚⲎⲦⲞⲤ
Ⲙ̄Ⲛ̄ ⲚⲈΥⲀΥⲦⲞⲄⲈⲚⲎⲤ · Ⲙ̄Ⲛ̄ ⲚⲈΥⲄⲈⲚⲚⲎⲦⲞⲤ Ⲙ̄Ⲛ̄ ⲚⲈΥ-
20 ⲚⲞΥⲦⲈ · Ⲙ̄Ⲛ̄ ⲚⲈΥⲤⲠⲒⲚⲐⲎⲢ · Ⲙ̄Ⲛ̄ ⲚⲈΥⲪⲰⲤⲦⲎⲢ · ϨⲀⲠⲀⲜ
ϨⲀⲠⲖⲰⲤ Ⲙ̄Ⲛ̄ ⲚⲈΥⲚⲞϬ ⲦⲎⲢⲞΥ · ⲀΥⲚⲀΥ ⲈⲚ̄ⲦΥⲢⲀⲚⲚⲞⲤ
Ⲙ̄ⲠⲈΥⲦⲞⲠⲞⲤ ⲈⲀ[Υ] ⲦⲈΥϬⲞⲘ ⲤⲂⲞⲔ ϨⲢⲀⲒ̈ Ⲛ̄ϨⲎⲦⲞΥ ·
ⲀΥⲰ ⲀΥϢⲰⲠⲈ Ϩ̄Ⲛ̄ ⲞΥⲘⲚ̄ⲦϬⲰⲂ · ⲀΥⲰ ⲀΥϢⲰⲠⲈ ϨⲰⲞΥ
Ϩ̄Ⲛ̄ ⲞΥⲚⲞϬ Ⲛ̄ϨⲞⲦⲈ ⲈⲘⲚ̄-ϢⲒ ⲈⲢⲞⲤ · ⲀΥⲰ ⲚⲈΥⲐⲈⲰⲢⲒ Ⲗ̄ⲅ̄ᵇ

---

5   ⲤⲰⲦ̄Ⲙ̄ : dittography.
20   MS ⲚⲈΥⲤⲪⲰⲤⲦⲎⲢ.
22   MS ⲈⲀΥ; read ⲈⲀ.

they worshipped him and they said to him: "We are *blessed beyond* all men, for thou hast revealed to us these great events".

28.   Jesus continued again with the discourse, he said to his *disciples*: "Hear [hear] concerning the things which happened to me among the *archons* of the twelve *aeons*, and all their *archons* and their lords and their *powers* (*exousiai*) and their *angels* and their *archangels*. Now when they saw the *garment* of light which was upon me, they and their *unpaired ones*, each one of them saw the *mystery* of his name which was in the *garment* of light which was upon me. They all prostrated themselves together, they worshipped the *garment* of light which was upon me. And they all cried out at once, saying: '*How* has the Lord of All passed through us without our knowing?' And they all *sang praises* at once to the innermost of the inner. And all their *triple-powered ones* and their great *forefathers* and their *unbegotten ones* and their *self-begotten ones* and their *begotten ones* and their gods and their *light-sparks* and their *luminaries, in a word,* all their great ones saw the *tyrants* of their *place*, that their power was diminished within them, and that they were in a state of weakness. And they were in great fear, to which there was no measure. And they *contemplated* | the *mystery*

ПЄ ⲘⲠⲘⲨⲤⲦⲎⲢⲒⲞⲚ ⲘⲠⲈⲨⲢⲀⲚ ⳠⲘ ПⲀⲈⲚⲀⲨⲘⲀ ⲀⲨⲰ
ⲚⲈⲀⲨ·ⲦⲞⲞⲦⲞⲨ ПЄ ⲈⲈⲒ· ⲚⲤⲈⲞⲨⲰⲰⲦ ⲘⲠⲘⲨⲤⲦⲎⲢⲒⲞⲚ
ⲘⲠⲈⲨⲢⲀⲚ ⲈⲦⳠⲘ ПⲀⲈⲚⲀⲨⲘⲀ · ⲀⲨⲰ ⲘⲠⲞⲨⲈⲰⳬⲘⳬⲞⲘ ·
ⲈⲦⲂⲈ ПⲒⲚⲞⳬ ⲚⲞⲨⲞⲒⲚ ⲈⲦⲰⲞⲞП ⲚⲘⲘⲀⲒ · ⲀⲖⲖⲀ ⲚⲦ-
5 ⲀⲨⲞⲨⲰⲰⲦ ⲈⲨⲞⲨⲎ Ⲩ ⲘⲘⲞⲒ ПⲞⲨⲰϨⲘ · ⲚⲦⲀⲨⲞⲨ-
ⲰⲰⲦ ⲀⲈ ⲘⲠⲞⲨⲞⲈⲒⲚ ⲘПⲀⲈⲚⲀⲨⲘⲀ · ⲀⲨⲰ ⲀⲨⲰⲰ
ⲈⲂⲞⲖ ⲦⲎⲢⲞⲨ ϨⲒ ⲞⲨⲤⲞП ⲈⲨϨⲨⲘⲚⲈⲨⲈ ⲈПⲤⲀⲚϨⲞⲨⲚ
ⲚⲦⲈ ⲚⲒⲤⲀⲚϨⲞⲨⲚ ·

ⲀⲤⲰⲰПⲈ ⳬⲈ ⲚⲦⲈⲢⲈ ⲚⲀⲒ ⲰⲰПⲈ ⲚⲚⲦⲨⲢⲀⲚⲚⲞⲤ ⲈⲦ-
10 ⲰⲞⲞП ϨⲚ ⲚⲀⲢⲬⲰⲚ ⲀⲨⲤⲰⲰⲘ ⲦⲎⲢⲞⲨ ⲀⲨϨⲈ ⲈПⲈⲤⲎⲦ
ϨⲚ ⲚⲈⲨⲀⲒⲰⲚ ⲀⲨⲰ ⲀⲨⲰⲰПⲈ ⲚⲐⲈ ⲚⲚⲒⲢⲘ-Ⲛ̄ⲔⲞⲤⲘⲞⲤ
ⲈⲦⲘⲞⲞⲨⲦ · ⲈⲘⲚ-ⲚⲒϤⲈ ⲚϨⲎⲦⲞⲨ ⲚⲞⳬ ⲞⲚ ⲈⲚⲦⲀⲨⲀⲀⲤ
ⲘПⲚⲀⲨ ⲚⲦⲀⲒϤⲒ ⲚⲦⲈⲨⳬⲞⲘ ⲚϨⲎⲦⲞⲨ · ⲀⲤⲰⲰПⲈ ⳬⲈ
ⲘⲚⲚⲤⲀ ⲚⲀⲒ · ⲚⲦⲈⲢⲒⲈⲒ· ⲈⲂⲞⲖ ϨⲚ ⲚⲀⲒⲰⲚ ⲈⲦⲘⲘⲀⲨ ·
15 Ⲁ ПⲞⲨⲀ ПⲞⲨⲀ** ⲚⲚⲈⲦⲰⲞⲞП ⲦⲎⲢⲞⲨ ϨⲘ ПⲘⲚⲦⲤⲚⲞⲞⲨⲤ Ⲙ̄
ⲚⲀⲒⲰⲚ · ⲀⲨⲘⲞⲨⲢ ⲦⲎⲢⲞⲨ ⲈϨⲞⲨⲚ ⲈⲚⲈⲨⲦⲀⳉⲒⲤ · ⲀⲨⲰ
ⲀⲨⳉⲰⲔ ⲈⲂⲞⲖ ⲚⲚⲈⲨϨⲂⲎⲨⲈ ⲔⲀⲦⲀ ⲐⲈ ⲈⲚⲦⲀⲒⲔⲀⲀⲨ
ⲘⲘⲞⲤ · ⲈⲦⲢⲈⲨⲢ-ⲤⲞⲞⲨ ⲚⲈⲂⲞⲦ ⲈⲨⲔⲒⲦ ⲈϨⲂⲞⲨⲢ ⲈⲨⲈⲒⲢⲈ
ⲚⲚⲈⲨϨⲂⲎⲨⲈ ϨⲚ ⲚⲈⲨϤⲦⲞⲞⲨ ⲚⲔⲞⲞϨ · ⲘⲚ ⲚⲈⲨⲰⲞⲘⲚⲦ
20 ⲚⲔⲞⲞϨ · ⲘⲚ ⲚⲈⲦⲘПⲈⲨϨⲞⲦ ⲈⲂⲞⲖ · ⲀⲨⲰ ⲞⲚ ⲚⲤⲈⲢ-
ⲔⲈⲤⲞⲞⲨ ⲚⲈⲂⲞⲦ ⲈⲨⳬⲰⲰⲦ ⲈⲞⲨⲚⲀⲘ · ⲀⲨⲰ ⲈⲚⲈⲨ-
ⲰⲞⲘⲚⲦ ⲚⲔⲞⲞϨ · ⲘⲚ ⲚⲈⲨϤⲦⲞⲞⲨ ⲚⲔⲞⲞϨ · ⲘⲚ ⲚⲈⲦ-
ⲘПⲈⲨϨⲞⲦ ⲈⲂⲞⲖ · ⲦⲀⲒ ⲞⲚ ⲦⲈ ⲐⲈ ⲈⲦⲞⲨⲚⲀⲘⲞⲞⲰⲈ
ⲘⲘⲞⲤ ⲚⳬⲒ ⲚⲈⲦⲰⲞⲞП ϨⲚ ⲞⲒⲘⲀⲢⲘⲈⲚⲎ ⲘⲚ ⲦⲈⲤⲪⲀⲒⲢⲀ ·
25 ⲍ ⲀⲤⲰⲰПⲈ ⳬⲈ ⲘⲚⲚⲤⲀ ⲚⲀⲒ ⲀⲒⲈⲒ· ⲈПⳳⲒⲤⲈ ⲰⲀ ⲚⲔⲀ-
ⲦⲀПⲈⲦⲀⲤⲘⲀ ⲘПⲘⲈϨⲘⲚⲦⲰⲞⲘⲦⲈ ⲚⲚⲀⲒⲰⲚ · ⲀⲤⲰⲰПⲈ
ⳬ Ⲉ ⲚⲦⲈⲢⲒⲈⲒ· ⲈⳉⲚ ⲚⲈⲨⲔⲀⲦⲀПⲈⲦⲀⲤⲘⲀ · ⲀⲨⲤⲰⲔ ⲘⲀⲨ-

of their name in my *garment* and they tried to come to worship the *mystery* of their name in my *garment*, and they were not able, on account of the great light which I had. *But* they worshipped at a little distance from me. *However*, they worshipped the light of my *garment*, and they all cried out at once as they *sang praises* to the innermost of the inner.

It happened moreover, when these things happened to the *tyrants* which are among the *archons*, they were all enfeebled, they fell down in their *aeons*, and they became like men of this *world* who are dead, having no breath within them, as they did moreover at the time when I took away their power from them.

It happened now after this, when I came forth from those *aeons*, each one of all those who are in the twelve *aeons* were all bound within their *ranks*, and they completed their works *according to* the manner in which I had disposed it, that they should spend six months turned to the left, doing their works in their quadrangles, and their triangles and those in their aspects; and furthermore that they should spend another six months looking to the right, and to their triangles and their quadrangles and those in their aspects. Furthermore, this is the manner in which those who are in the *Heimarmene* and the *sphere* will proceed.

29.   Now it happened after these things I came to the height to the *veils* of the thirteenth *aeon*. Now it happened that when I reached their *veils*, they drew themselves | and

ⲗⲁⲩ ⲁⲩⲟⲩⲱⲛ ⲛⲁⲓ · ⲁⲓⲉⲓ ⲉ2ⲟⲩⲛ ⲉⲡⲙⲉ2ⲙⲛ̄ⲧⲱⲟⲙⲧⲉ ⲙ̄ᵇ
ⲛ̄ⲛⲁⲓⲱⲛ · ⲁⲓ2ⲉ ⲉⲧⲡⲓⲥⲧⲓⲥ ⲥⲟⲫⲓⲁ ⲉⲥ2ⲙ̄ⲡⲉⲥⲏⲧ ⲙ̄ⲡⲙⲉ2-
ⲙⲛⲧⲱⲟⲙⲧⲉ ⲛ̄ⲁⲓⲱⲛ ⲛ̄ⲧⲟⲥ ⲙⲁⲩⲁⲁⲥ ⲉⲙⲛ̄-ⲟⲩⲟⲛ
ⲙ̄ⲙⲟⲩ 2ⲁⲧⲏⲥ · ⲛⲉⲥ2ⲙⲟⲟⲥ ⲇⲉ ⲡⲉ ⲙ̄ⲡⲙⲁ ⲉⲧⲙ̄ⲙⲁⲩ
5 ⲉⲥⲁⲩⲡⲉⲓ ⲁⲩⲱ ⲉⲥⲣ̄2ⲏⲃⲉ · ϫⲉ ⲙ̄ⲡⲟⲩϫⲓⲧⲉ̄ ⲉⲡⲙⲉ2ⲙⲛ̄ⲧ-
ⲱⲟⲙⲧⲉ ⲛ̄ⲁⲓⲱⲛ ⲡⲉⲥⲧⲟⲡⲟⲥ ⲉⲧⲙ̄ⲡϫⲓⲥⲉ · ⲁⲩⲱ ⲟⲛ ⲛⲉⲥ-
ⲗⲩⲡⲓ ⲡⲉ ⲉⲧⲃⲉ ⲛ̄2ⲓⲥⲉ ⲉⲛⲧⲁϥⲁⲁⲩ ⲛⲁⲥ ⲛ̄ϭⲓ ⲡⲁⲩⲟⲁ-
ⲁⲏⲥ · ⲡⲁⲓ ⲉⲧⲉ ⲟⲩⲁ ⲡⲉ 2ⲙ̄ ⲡϣⲟⲙⲛ̄ⲧ ⲛ̄ⲧⲣⲓⲇⲩⲛⲁⲙⲟⲥ ·
ⲛⲁⲓ ⲇⲉ ⲉⲓϣⲁⲛϣⲁϫⲉ ⲛ̄ⲙⲙⲏⲧⲛ̄ ⲉⲧⲃⲉ ⲡⲉⲩⲥⲱⲣ ⲉⲃⲟⲗ ·
10 ϯⲛⲁϫⲱ ⲉⲣⲱⲧⲛ̄ ⲙ̄ⲡⲙⲩⲥⲧⲏⲣⲓⲟⲛ ϫⲉ ⲡⲱⲥ ⲁ ⲛⲁⲓ ϣⲱⲡⲉ ⲙ̄ⲙⲟⲥ · ⲁⲥϣⲱⲡⲉ ϭⲉ ⲛ̄ⲧⲉⲣⲉⲥⲛⲁⲩ ⲉⲣⲟⲓ ⲛ̄ϭⲓ ⲧⲡⲓⲥⲧⲓⲥ ⲥⲟⲫⲓⲁ ⲉⲓⲟ ⲛ̄ⲟⲩⲟⲉⲓⲛ ⲉⲙⲁϣⲟ ⲉⲙⲁϣⲟ · ⲉⲙⲛ̄-ϣⲓ
ⲉⲡⲟⲩⲟⲉⲓⲛ ⲉⲛⲉϥϣⲟⲟⲡ ⲙ̄ⲙⲟⲓ · ⲁⲥϣⲱⲡⲉ 2ⲛ̄ ⲟⲩⲛⲟϭ
ⲛ̄ϣⲧⲟⲣⲧⲣ̄ ** ⲁⲩⲱ ⲁ(ⲥ)ϭⲱϣⲧ̄ ⲉⲃⲟⲗ 2ⲙ̄ ⲡⲟⲩⲟⲉⲓⲛ ⲙ̄ⲡⲁ- ⲛⲁ
15 ⲉⲛⲇⲩⲙⲁ · ⲁⲥⲛⲁⲩ ⲉⲡⲙⲩⲥⲧⲏⲣⲓⲟⲛ ⲙ̄ⲡⲉⲥⲣⲁⲛ 2ⲙ̄ ⲡⲁⲉⲛⲇⲩⲙⲁ · ⲁⲩⲱ ⲙⲛ̄ ⲡⲉⲟⲟⲩ ⲧⲏⲣϥ ⲙ̄ⲡⲉϥⲙⲩⲥⲧⲏⲣⲓⲟⲛ
ϫⲉ ⲛⲉⲥϣⲟⲟⲡ ⲛ̄ϣⲟⲣⲡ̄ ⲡⲉ 2ⲙ̄ ⲡⲧⲟⲡⲟⲥ ⲙ̄ⲡϫⲓⲥⲉ ·
2ⲙ̄ ⲡⲙⲉ2ⲙⲛⲧϣⲟⲙⲧⲉ ⲛ̄ⲁⲓⲱⲛ · ⲁⲗⲗⲁ ⲛⲉϣⲁⲥ2ⲩⲙⲛⲉⲩⲉ
ⲡⲉ ⲉⲡⲟⲩⲟⲉⲓⲛ ⲉⲧⲙ̄ⲡϫⲓⲥⲉ · ⲡⲁⲓ ⲉⲛⲧⲁⲥⲛⲁⲩ ⲉⲣⲟϥ
20 2ⲙ̄ ⲡⲕⲁⲧⲁⲡⲉⲧⲁⲥⲙⲁ ⲙ̄ⲡⲉⲑⲏⲥⲁⲩⲣⲟⲥ ⲙ̄ⲡⲟⲩⲟⲉⲓⲛ · ⲁⲥϣⲱⲡⲉ ϭⲉ ⲛ̄ⲧⲉⲣⲉⲥϭⲱ ⲉⲥ2ⲩⲙⲛⲉⲩⲉ ⲉⲡⲟⲩⲟⲓ̈ⲛ ⲉⲧⲙ̄-
ⲡϫⲓⲥⲉ · ⲁ ⲛ̄ⲁⲣⲭⲱⲛ ⲧⲏⲣⲟⲩ ϭⲱϣⲧ̄ ⲉⲧ2ⲁⲧⲙ̄ ⲡⲛⲟϭ
ⲥⲛⲁⲩ ⲛ̄ⲧⲣⲓⲇⲩⲛⲁⲙⲟⲥ ⲁⲩⲱ ⲙⲛ̄ ⲡⲉⲥ2ⲟⲣⲁⲧⲟⲥ ⲉⲧ2ⲟⲧⲣ̄

2 MS ⲉⲥ2ⲙ̄ⲡⲉⲥⲏⲧ; 2 crossed out, and ⲙ̄ expunged; read ⲉⲥⲙ̄ⲡⲉⲥⲏⲧ.
14 MS originally ⲁⲩϭⲱϣⲧ̄; ⲩ erased and not replaced.
15 MS ⲙ̄ⲙⲡⲉⲥⲣⲁⲛ.
18 MS ⲛⲉϣⲁⲥⲩⲙⲛⲉⲩⲉ; 2 inserted above.

they opened to me. I entered into the thirteenth *aeon*,
I found the Pistis Sophia [1] below the thirteenth *aeon* alone,
none of them being with her. *But* she dwelt in that place,
sorrowful and grieving because she had not been taken to the
thirteenth *aeon*, her *place* in the height. And furthermore
she was sorrowful on account of the torments which the
Authades [2] inflicted on her, he being one of the three *triple-
powered ones*. *But* when I tell you about their extent, I will
tell you the *mystery* of *how* these things happened.

Now it happened, when the Pistis Sophia saw me shining
exceedingly, there being no measure to the light which
I had, she was in great agitation and she looked at the
light of my *garment*. She saw the *mystery* of her name in
my *garment* and the whole glory of its *mystery* because she
was previously in the *place* of the height in the thirteenth
aeon. *But* she was wont to *sing praises* to the light in the
height which she saw in the *veil* of the *Treasury* of the Light.
It happened now when she continued to *sing praises* to the
light in the height, all the *archons*, which are with the two
great *triple-powered ones*, looked on, and also her *invisible
one* which is paired with her, | and the other 22 *invisible*

---

[1] (2) Pistis Sophia; see U 264.
[2] (7) Authades; as epithet of Jaldabaoth, see ApJn 46.

ЄΡΟС · ΑΥѠ ΠΚΕΧΟΥΤСΝΟΟΥС ⲘΠΡΟΒΟΛΗ Ⲛ̄ΑȤΟΡΑ-
ΤΟС ЄΠЄΙΔΗ ΤΠΙСΤΙС СΟΦΙΑ Ⲙ̄Ν ΠЄССΥΝȤΥΓΟС ·
Ⲛ̄ΤΟΟΥ Ⲙ̄Ν ΠΚΕΧΟΥΤСΝΟΟΥС ⲘΠΡΟΒΟΛΗ ѠΑῩΡ-
ΧΟΥΤΑϤΤЄ ⲘΠΡΟΒΟΛΗ ΝΑΪ ЄΝΤΑϤΠΡΟΒΑΛЄ ⲘⲘΟΟΥ Ⲙ̄Α ᵇ
5 ЄΒΟΛ Ⲛ̄ϬΙ ΠΝΟϬ ⲘΠΡΟΠΑΤѠΡ Ⲛ̄ΑȤΟΡΑΤΟС · Ⲛ̄ΤΟϤ Ⲙ̄Ν
ΠΝΟϬ СΝΑΥ Ⲛ̄ΤΡΙΔΥΝΑΜΟС ·

Ȥ ΑСѠΠЄ ϬЄ ЄΡЄ ῙС̄ ΧѠ Ⲛ̄ΝΑΪ ЄΝЄϤⲘΑΘΗΤΗС ·
ΑСЄΙ' ЄΘΗ Ⲛ̄ϬΙ ΜΑΡΙȤΑΜ ΠЄΧΑС ΧЄ ΠΑΧΟЄΙС · ΑΪСѠΤⲘ
ЄΡΟΚ ⲘΠΙΟΥΟЄΙѠ ЄΚΧѠ Ⲙ̄ΜΟС · ΧЄ ΤΠΙСΤΙС СΟΦΙΑ
10 ΟΥЄΒΟΛ ȤѠѠС ΤЄ Ȥ̄Μ ΠΧΟΥΤΑϤΤЄ ⲘΠΡΟΒΟΛΗ · ΑΥѠ
ΠѠС Ⲛ̄СѠΟΠ ΑΝ Ȥ̄Μ ΠЄΥΤΟΠΟС · ΑΛΛΑ ΑΚΧΟΟС
ΧЄ ΑΪϬΝΤС ЄСⲘΠЄСΝΤ ⲘΠΜЄȤⲘΝΤѠΟΜΤЄ Ⲛ̄ΑΙѠΝ ·

Ȥ ΑϤΟΥѠ͠Β Ⲛ̄ϬΙ ῙС̄ ΠЄΧΑϤ Ⲛ̄ΝЄϤⲘΑΘΗΤΗС · ΧЄ
ΑСѠΠЄ ЄΡЄ ΤΠΙСΤΙС СΟΦΙΑ Ȥ̄Μ ΠΜЄȤⲘΝΤѠΟΜΤЄ
15 Ⲛ̄ΝΑΙѠΝ Ȥ̄Μ ΠΤΟΠΟС Ⲛ̄ΝЄССΝΗΥ ΤΗΡΟΥ ΝΙΑȤΟΡΑΤΟС
ЄΤЄ Ⲛ̄ΤΟΟΥ ΝЄ ΤΧΟΥΤΑϤΤЄ ⲘΠΡΟΒΟΛΗ Ⲛ̄ΤЄ ΠΝΟϬ
Ⲛ̄ΑȤΟΡΑΤΟС · ΑСѠΠЄ** ϬЄ ȤΙΤⲘ̄ ΠΤѠѠ ⲘΠѠΟΡΠ Ⲙ̄Β
Ⲙ̄ΜΥСΤΗΡΙΟΝ · ΑСϬѠ͠ΩΤ ЄΠΧΙСЄ Ⲛ̄ϬΙ ΤΠΙСΤΙС СΟΦΙΑ
ΑСΝΑΥ ЄΠΟΥΟЄΙΝ ⲘΠΚΑΤΑΠЄΤΑСΜΑ ⲘΠЄΘΗСΑΥΡΟС
20 ⲘΠΟΥΟЄΙΝ · ΑΥѠ ΑСЄΠΙΘΥΜΙ ЄΒѠΚ ЄΠΤΟΠΟС ЄΤ-
Ⲙ̄ΜΑΥ · ΑΥѠ Ⲙ̄ΠСϬⲘϬΟΜ ЄΒѠΚ ЄΠΤΟΠΟС ЄΤⲘ̄ΜΑΥ ·
ΑСΛΟ ΔЄ ЄСЄΙΡЄ ⲘΠΜΥСΤΗΡΙΟΝ ⲘΠΜЄȤⲘΝΤѠΟΜΤЄ
Ⲛ̄ΑΙѠΝ · ΑΛΛΑ ΝЄСȤΥΜΝЄΥЄ ΠЄ ЄΠΟΥΟЄΙΝ Ⲙ̄ΠΧΙСЄ
ΠЄΝΤΑСΝΑΥ ЄΡΟϤ Ȥ̄Μ ΠΟΥΟЄΙΝ ⲘΠΚΑΤΑΠЄΤΑСΜΑ
25 ⲘΠЄΘΗСΑΥΡΟС ⲘΠΟΥΟЄΙΝ · ΑСѠΠЄ ϬЄ ЄСȤΥΜΝЄΥЄ
ЄΠΤΟΠΟС ⲘΠΧΙСЄ · Α Ⲛ̄ΑΡΧѠΝ ΤΗΡΟΥ ЄΤѠΟΟΠ Ȥ̄Μ

---

10 MS ΠΧΟΥΤΑϤΤЄ; read ΤΧΟΥΤΑϤΤЄ.

emanations — *since* the Pistis Sophia with her *partner*, with
the other 22 *emanations* make up the 24 *emanations* [1], which
the great *invisible forefather* with the two great *triple-powered
ones* has *emanated*."

30. It happened now when Jesus said these things to
his *disciples*, Mariam came forward and said: "My Lord,
I heard thee at the time when thou didst say that the Pistis
Sophia herself is one of the 24 *emanations*. *How* is she not
in their *place*? *Moreover* thou hast said: 'I found her below
the thirteenth *aeon*'."

Jesus answered and said to his *disciples*: "It happened as
the Pistis Sophia was in the thirteenth *aeon* in the *place*
of all her brethren, the *invisible ones* who are the 24 *emanations* of the great *invisible one* — it happened now,
through the ordinance of the First *Mystery*, the Pistis Sophia
looked to the height, she saw the light of the *veil* of the
Treasury of the *Light*, and she *desired* to go to that *place*.
And she was not able to go to that *place*. *Moreover* she
ceased performing the *mystery* of the thirteenth *aeon*, *but*
she *sang praises* to the light of the height which she saw in
the light of the *veil* of the *Treasury* of the Light.

Now it happened, as she *sang praises* to the *place* of the
height, all the *archons* which are in | the twelve *aeons*

---

[1]   (4) 24 emanations; see J 134.

ΠΜΝ̅ΤСΝΟΟΥС Ν̅ΑΙШΝ ΑΥΜΕСΤШС ΠΑΪ ΕΤΜ̅ΠΕСΗΤ·

ΕΒΟΛ ΧΕ ΑСΛΟ ϨΝ̅ ΝΕΥΜΥСΤΗΡΙΟΝ· ΑΥШ ΕΒΟΛ ΧΕ

ΑСΟΥΕϢΒШΚ ΕΠΧΙСΕ Ν̅С̅Ρ̅-ϨΙΧШΟΥ ΤΗΡΟΥ· ΕΤΒΕ ΠΑΪ

6Ε ΑΥ6ШΝ̅Τ ΕΡΟС ΑΥШ ΑΥΜΕСΤШС· ΑΥШ ΠΝΟ6 ̅ΜΒ̅ᵇ

5 Ν̅ΤΡΙΔΥΝΑΜΟС Ν̅ΑΥΘΑΛΗС ΕΤΕ ΠΜΕϨϢΟΜΝ̅Τ ΠΕ Ν̅-

ΤΡΙΔΥΝΑΜΟС ΠΑΪ ΕΤϢΟΟΠ ϨΜ ΠΜΕϨΜΝ̅ΤϢΟΜΤΕ

Ν̅ΑΙШΝ ΠΑΪ ΕΝΤΑϤΡ̅-ΑΤСШΤΜ ΕΜΠϤΠΡΟΒΑΛΕ ΕΒΟΛ

ΜΠСШΤϤ ΤΗΡϤ Ν̅ΤΕϤ6ΟΜ ΕΤΝ̅ϨΗΤϤ· ΟΥΔΕ ΜΠϤ-|-

ΠСШΤϤ Μ̅ΠΕϤΟΥΟΕΙΝ Μ̅ΠΕΟΥΟΕΙϢ ΕΝΤΑ Ν̅ΑΡΧШΝ -|-

10 ΠΕΥСШΤϤ Ν̅ϨΗΤϤ ΕϤΟΥΕϢ-Ρ̅ΧΟΕΙС ΕϨΡΑΪ ΕΧΜ ΠΜΕϨ-

ΜΤϢΟΜΤΕ Ν̅ΑΙШΝ ΤΗΡϤ ΜΝ ΝΕΤϢΟΟΠ ΕΠΕϤΕСΗΤ·

ΑСϢШΠΕ 6Ε Ν̅ΤΕΡΕ Ν̅ΑΡΧШΝ Μ̅ΠΜΝ̅ΤСΝΟΟΥС Ν̅ΑΙШΝ

Ν̅ΤΕΡΟΥ6ШΝ̅Τ ΕΤΠΙСΤΙС СΟΦΙΑ· ΤΑΪ ΕΤΜ̅ΠΕΥΕΠΠΕ·

ΑΥΜΕСΤШС ΕΜΑΤΕ· ΑΥШ ΠΝΟ6 Ν̅ΤΡΙΔΥΝΑΜΟС Ν̅ΑΥ-

15 ΘΑΛΗС ΠΑΪ ΕΝΤΑΪΟΥШ ΕΪΧШ Μ̅ΜΟС ΝΗΤ̅Ν ΤΕΝΟΥ

ΕΤΒΗΗΤϤ· ΑϤΟΥШϨ** ϨШШϤ Ν̅СΑ Ν̅ΑΡΧШΝ Μ̅ΠΜΝ̅Τ- ̅ΜΓ̅

СΝΟΟΥС Ν̅ΑΙШΝ· ΑΥШ ΑϤ6ШΝ̅Τ ϨШШϤ ΕΤΠΙСΤΙС СΟ-

ΦΙΑ· ΑΥШ ΑϤΜΕСΤШС ΕΜΑΤΕ· ΧΕ ΑСΜΕΕΥΕ ΕΒШΚ

ΕΠΟΥΟΕΙΝ ΠΑΪ ΕΤΧΟСΕ ΕΡΟϤ· ΑΥШ ΑϤΠΡΟΒΑΛΕ ΕΒΟΛ

20 Ν̅ϨΗΤϤ Ν̅ΟΥΝΟ6 Ν̅6ΟΜ Ν̅ϨΟ Μ̅ΜΟΥΪ· ΑΥШ ΕΒΟΛ ϨΝ̅

ΤΕϤϨΥΛΗ ΕΤΝ̅ϨΗΤϤ· ΑϤΠΡΟΒΑΛΕ ΕΒΟΛ Ν̅ΚΕΜΗΗϢΕ

Μ̅ΠΡΟΒΟΛΗ Ν̅ϨΥΛΙΚΗ ΕΥΝΑϢΤ ΕΜΑΤΕ· ΑΥШ ΑϤΧΟ-

ΟΥСΟΥ ΕΝΤΟΠΟС Μ̅ΠΕСΗΤ· ΕΜΜΕΡΟС Μ̅ΠΕΧΛΟС· ΧΕ

ΕΥΕ6ШΡ6̅ ΕΤΠΙСΤΙС СΟΦΙΑ Μ̅ΜΑΥ· ΑΥШ Ν̅СΕϤΙ-ΤΕС-

25 6ΟΜ Ν̅ϨΗΤС· ΕΒΟΛ ΧΕ ΑСΜΕΕΥΕ ΕΒШΚ ΕΠΧΙСΕ· ΠΑΪ

beneath hated her because she ceased from their *mystery*, and because she wished to go to the height and to make herself above them all. Now on account of these things they were angry with her, and they hated her. And the great *triple-powered Authades* — the third *triple-powered one* who is in the thirteenth *aeon*, who had been disobedient — had not *emanated* all that was purified of his inner power, *nor* had he given what was purified of his light at the time when the *archons* had given their purification, and he had wished to be lord over the whole thirteenth *aeon* and those beneath it. Now it happened when the *archons* of the thirteenth *aeon* were angry at the Pistis Sophia, who was above them, they hated her greatly. And the great *triple-powered* Authades, about whom I have just been speaking to you now, was also included among the *archons* of the twelve *aeons*, and he also was angry at the Pistis Sophia, and he hated her greatly, because she thought to go to the light which was above him. And he *emanated* from within himself a great lion-faced power. And from out of the *matter* within him, he *emanated* forth a further multitude of *material emanations* which were very powerful. And he sent them to the *places* below, to the *parts* of the *Chaos*, so that they should pursue the Pistis Sophia there and take her power from her, because she thought to go to the height which |

ⲈⲦϨⲓⲬⲰⲞⲨ ⲦⲎⲢⲞⲨ· ⲀⲨⲰ ⲬⲈ ⲀⳞⲖⲞ ⲞⲚ ⲈⳞⲈⲒⲢⲈ ⲘⲠⲈⲨ-
ⲘⲨⳠⲦⲎⲢⲒⲞⲚ· ⲀⲖⲖⲀ ⲀⳞϬⲰ ⲈⳞⲢϨⲎⲂⲈ ⲈⳞⳎⲒⲚⲈ ⲚⳠⲀ ⲠⲞⲨ-
ⲞⲈⲒⲚ ⲈⲚⲦⲀⳞⲚⲀⲨ ⲈⲢⲞϤ· ⲀⲨⲰ ⲀⲨⲘⲈⳞⲦⲰⳞ ⲚϬⲒ ⲚⲀⲢ-
ⲬⲰⲚ ⲈⲦⲀϨⲈ Ⲏ̄ ⲈⲦϬⲈⲈⲦ ⲈⲠⲘⲨⳞⲦⲎⲢⲒⲞⲚ ⲈⲨⲈⲒⲢⲈ Ⲙ̄ⲘⲞϤ· Ⲙ̄Ⲅ̄ᵇ
5 ⲀⲨⲰ ⲞⲚ Ⲁ⟨Ⲩ⟩ⲘⲈⳞⲦⲰⳞ ⲚϬⲒ ⲚⲈⲪⲨⲖⲀⲝ ⲦⲎⲢⲞⲨ· ⲈⲦϨⲒⲢⲚ̄
Ⲙ̄ⲠⲨⲖⲎ Ⲛ̄ⲚⲀⲒⲰⲚ· ⲀⳞⳎⲰⲠⲈ ϬⲈ Ⲙ̄Ⲛ̄Ⳡⲁ ⲚⲀⲒ ⲈⲂⲞⲖ ϨⲒⲦⲘ̄
ⲠⲦⲰⳎ Ⲙ̄ⲠⳎⲞⲢⲠ̄ Ⲛ̄ⲦⲰⳎ· Ⲁ ⲠⲒⲚⲞϬ Ⲛ̄ⲀⲨⲐⲀⲖⲎⳞ Ⲛ̄ⲦⲢⲒ-
ⲀⲨⲚⲀⲘⲞⳞ ⲈⲞⲨⲀ ⲠⲈ Ϩ̄Ⲙ ⲠⳎⲞⲘⲚⲦ̄ Ⲛ̄ⲦⲢⲒⲀⲨⲚⲀⲘⲞⳞ·
ⲀϤⲀⲒⲰⲔⲈ Ⲛ̄ⲦⲤⲞⲪⲒⲀ ϨⲢⲀⲒ̈ Ϩ̄Ⲙ ⲠⲘⲈϨⲘ̄Ⲛ̄ⲦⳎⲞⲘⲦⲈ Ⲛ̄ⲀⲒⲰⲚ
10 ⲈⲦⲢⲈⳞϬⲰϢⲦ̄ ⲈⲘⲘⲈⲢⲞⳞ Ⲙ̄ⲠⲈⳞⲎⲦ· ⲬⲈ ⲈⳞⲈⲚⲀⲨ ⲈⲦⲈϤ-
ⲀⲨⲚⲀⲘⲒⳞ Ⲛ̄ⲞⲨⲞⲈⲒⲚ Ⲙ̄ⲠⲘⲀ ⲈⲦⲘ̄ⲘⲀⲨ· ⲦⲀⲒ̈ ⲈⲦⲞ Ⲛ̄ϨⲞ
Ⲙ̄ⲘⲞⲨⲒ̈· ⲀⲨⲰ Ⲛ̄ⳞⲈⲠⲒⲐⲨⲘⲒ ⲈⲢⲞⳞ· Ⲛ̄ⳞⲈⲒ' ⲈⲠⲦⲞⲠⲞⳞ ⲈⲦ-
Ⲙ̄ⲘⲀⲨ Ⲛ̄ⳞⲈϤⲒ Ⲙ̄ⲠⲈⳞⲞⲨⲞⲈⲒⲚ Ⲛ̄ϨⲎⲦⳞ:

ⲀⳞⳎⲰⲠⲈ ϬⲈ Ⲙ̄Ⲛ̄Ⳡⲁ ⲚⲀⲒ̈· ⲀⳞϬⲰϢⲦ̄ ⲈⲠⲈⳞⲎⲦ· ⲀⳞ-
15 ⲚⲀⲨ ⲈⲦⲈϤϬⲞⲘ Ⲛ̄ⲞⲨⲞⲈⲒⲚ Ϩ̄Ⲛ Ⲙ̄ⲘⲈⲢⲞⳞ Ⲙ̄ⲠⲈⳞⲎⲦ· ⲀⲨⲰ
ⲚⲈ⟨Ⲙ̄⟩Ⲡ̄ⳞⲈⲒⲘⲈ ⲠⲈ ⲬⲈ ⲦⲀⲠⲒⲦⲢⲒⲀⲨⲚⲀⲘⲞⳞ Ⲛ̄ⲀⲨⲐⲀⲖⲎⳞ
ⲦⲈ· ⲀⲖⲖⲀ ⲚⲈⳞⲘⲈⲈⲨⲈ ⲈⲢⲞⳞ ⲬⲈ ⲞⲨⲈⲂⲞⲖ Ϩ̄Ⲙ ⲠⲞⲨⲞⲈⲒⲚ Ⲙ̄Ⲁ̄
ⲦⲈ· ⲠⲈⲚⲦⲀⳞⲚⲀⲨ ⲈⲢⲞϤ ⲬⲒⲚ Ⲛ̄ⳎⲞⲢⲠ̄ Ϩ̄Ⲙ ⲠⲬⲒⳞⲈ· ⲠⲀⲒ̈
ⲈⲨⲈⲂⲞⲖ ⲠⲈ Ϩ̄Ⲙ ⲠⲔⲀⲦⲀⲠⲈⲦⲀⳞⲘⲀ Ⲙ̄ⲠⲈⲐⲎⳞⲀⲨⲢⲞⳞ Ⲙ̄-
20 ⲞⲨⲞⲈⲒⲚ· ⲀⲨⲰ ⲀⳞⲘⲈⲈⲨⲈ Ⲛ̄ϨⲎⲦⳞ̄ ⲬⲈ ⲈⲒⲚⲀⲂⲰⲔ ⲈⲠⲦⲞ-
ⲠⲞⳞ ⲈⲦⲘ̄ⲘⲀⲨ ⲬⲰⲢⲒⳞ ⲠⲀⳞⲨⲚⲌⲨⲄⲞⳞ Ⲛ̄ⲦⲀϤⲒ Ⲙ̄ⲠⲞⲨⲞⲈⲒⲚ
Ⲛ̄ⲦⲀⲦⲀⲘⲒⲞϤ ⲚⲀⲒ̈ Ⲛ̄ϨⲈⲚⲀⲒⲰⲚ Ⲛ̄ⲞⲨⲞⲈⲒⲚ ⲬⲈ ⲈⲒ̈ⲈⳎϬⲘ̄ϬⲞⲘ

---

4 MS ⲈⲦϬⲈⲈⲦ ⲈⲠⲚ̄Ⲣ̄Ⲓ.
5 MS ⲀⲘⲈⳞⲦⲰⳞ; read ⲀⲨⲘⲈⳞⲦⲰⳞ.
16 MS ⲠⲈⲠ̄ⳞⲈⲒⲘⲈ; read ⲚⲈⲘ̄Ⲡ̄ⳞⲈⲒⲘⲈ.
17 Ⲅ̄ in upper right-hand margin at end of quire.

is above them all, and because she ceased to perform their *mystery*, *but* she remained sorrowing, seeking the light which she saw. And the *archons* which continued *or* persisted in performing the *mystery* hated her. And all the *watchers* which were at the *gates* of the *aeons* also hated her.

It happened now after this, through the ordinance of the first ordinance, the great *triple-powered* Authades, who is one of the three *triple-powered ones*, *persecuted* the Sophia in the thirteenth *aeon*, so that she should look at the *parts* below, so that she should see in that place his light *power*, which has a lion-face, and she should *desire* it, and come to that *place*, and her light would be taken from her.

31. It happened now after this she looked down. She saw his power of light in the *parts* below, and she did not know that it was that of the *triple-powered* Authades. *But* she thought that it was from the light which she had seen from the beginning in the height, which was from the *veil* of the *Treasury* of the Light. And she thought to herself : "I will go to that *place without* my *partner*, and take the light, and create of it for myself *aeons* of light, so that I shall be able | to go to the Light of Lights which is in the highest

ⲚⲂⲰⲔ ⲈⲠⲞⲨⲞⲈⲒⲚ ⲚⲦⲈ ⲚⲒⲞⲨⲞⲈⲒⲚ ⲠⲀⲒ ⲈⲦⲌⲘ ⲠⲬⲒⲤⲈ

ⲚⲚⲬⲒⲤⲈ· ⲚⲀⲒ ϬⲈ ⲈⲤⲘⲈⲈⲨⲈ ⲈⲢⲞⲞⲨ ⲀⲤⲈⲒ· ⲈⲂⲞⲖ ⲌⲘ

ⲠⲈⲤⲦⲞⲠⲞⲤ ⲘⲘⲈⲌⲘⲚⲦⲰⲞⲘⲦⲈ ⲚⲀⲒⲰⲚ· ⲀⲨⲰ ⲀⲤⲈⲒ·

ⲈⲌⲢⲀⲒ ⲈⲠⲘⲈⲌⲘⲚⲦⲤⲚⲞⲞⲨⲤ ⲚⲀⲒⲰⲚ· ⲀⲨⲆⲒⲰⲔⲈ ⲘⲘⲞⳞ

5 ⲚϬⲒ ⲚⲀⲢⲬⲰⲚ ⲚⲚⲀⲒⲰⲚ· ⲀⲨⲰ ⲀⲨϬⲰⲚⲦ ⲈⲢⲞⲤ ⲬⲈ ⲀⲤ-

ⲘⲈⲈⲨⲈ ⲈⲌⲈⲨⲘⲚⲦⲚⲞϬ· ⲀⲤⲈⲒ· ⲆⲈ ⲞⲚ ⲈⲂⲞⲖ ⲌⲘ ⲠⲘⲈⲌ-

ⲘⲚⲦⲤⲚⲞⲞⲨⲤ ⲚⲀⲒⲰⲚ· ⲀⲤⲈⲒ· ⲈⲚⲦⲞⲠⲞⲤ ⲘⲠⲈⲬⲀⲞⲤ·

ⲀⲨⲰ ⲀⲤ†ⲠⲈⲤⲞⲨⲞⲈⲒ Ⲉ†ϬⲞⲘ ⲚⲞⲨⲞⲈⲒⲚ ⲚⲌⲞ ⲘⲘⲞⲨⲒ· ⲘⲀ ᵇ

ⲬⲈ ⲈⲤⲈⲞⲘⲈⲔⳞ· ⲀⲨⲔⲰⲦⲈ ⲆⲈ ⲈⲢⲞⲤ ⲚϬⲒ ⲚⲈⲠⲢⲞⲂⲞ-

10 ⲖⲞⲞⲨⲈ ⲦⲎⲢⲞⲨ ⲚⳞⲨⲖⲒⲔⲞⲚ ⲘⲠⲀⲨⲐⲀⲦⲎⲤ· ⲀⲨⲰ †ⲚⲞϬ

ⲚϬⲞⲘ ⲚⲞⲨⲞⲈⲒⲚ ⲚⲌⲞ ⲘⲘⲞⲨⲒ· ⲀⲤⲰⲘⲔ ⲚⲚⲀⲨⲚⲀⲘⲒⲤ

ⲚⲞⲨⲞⲈⲒⲚ ⲌⲚ ⲦⲤⲞⲪⲒⲀ· ⲀⲨⲰ ⲀⲤⲤⲰⲦⳞ ⲘⲠⲈⲤⲞⲨⲞⲈⲒⲚ

ⲀⲤⲞⲘⲈⲔⳞ· ⲀⲨⲰ ⲦⲈⲤⲌⲨⲖⲎ· ⲀⲨⲚⲞⲬⳞ ⲈⲂⲞⲖ ⲈⲠⲈⲬⲀⲞⲤ·

ⲀⲤⲰⲰⲠⲈ ⲚⲞⲨⲀⲢⲬⲰⲚ ⲚⲌⲞ ⲘⲘⲞⲨⲒ ⲌⲘ ⲠⲈⲬⲀⲞⲤ· ⲈⲢⲈ

15 ⲦⲈⳞⲠⲀⲰⲈ Ⲟ· ⲚⲔⲰⲌⲦ· ⲀⲨⲰ ⲈⲢⲈ ⲦⲈⳞⲔⲈⲠⲀⲰⲈ Ⲟ· ⲚⲔⲀ-

ⲔⲈ· ⲈⲦⲈ ⲚⲦⲞⳞ ⲠⲈ ⲒⲀⲖⲆⲀⲂⲀⲰⲐ· ⲠⲀⲒ ⲈⲚⲦⲀⲒⲬⲞⲞⳞ

ⲈⲢⲰⲦⲚ ⲚⲞⲨⲘⲎⲎⲰⲈ ⲚⲤⲞⲠ· ⲚⲀⲒ ϬⲈ ⲚⲦⲈⲢⲞⲨⲰⲰⲠⲈ

ⲀⲤⲢϬⲰⲂ ⲚϬⲒ ⲦⲤⲞⲪⲒⲀ ⲈⲘⲀⲰⲞ ⲈⲘⲀⲰⲞ ⲀⲨⲰ ⲞⲚ ⲀⲤⲒ-

ⲦⲞⲞⲦⳞ ⲚϬⲒ †ϬⲞⲘ ⲚⲞⲨⲞⲈⲒⲚ ⲚⲌⲞ ⲘⲘⲞⲨⲒ ⲈⲦⲘⲘⲀⲨ

20 ⲈⲦⲢⲈⲤⳞⲒ ⲚⲚϬⲞⲘ ⲦⲎⲢⲞⲨ ⲚⲞⲨⲞⲈⲒⲚ ⲌⲚ ⲦⲤⲞⲪⲒⲀ· ⲀⲨⲰ

ⲚϬⲞⲘ** ⲦⲎⲢⲞⲨ ⲚⳞⲨⲖⲒⲔⲞⲚ ⲚⲦⲈ ⲠⲀⲨⲐⲀⲆⲎⲤ ⲀⲨⲔⲰⲦⲈ ⲘⲈ

ⲈⲦⲤⲞⲪⲒⲀ ⲌⲒ ⲞⲨⲤⲞⲠ ⲀⲨⲌⲰⲬ· ⲘⲘⲞⳞ· ⲀⲤⲰⲰ ⲈⲂⲞⲖ

ⲈⲘⲀⲰⲞ ⲈⲘⲀⲰⲞ ⲚϬⲒ ⲦⲠⲒⲤⲦⲒⲤ ⲤⲞⲪⲒⲀ· ⲀⲤⲰⲰ ⲈⲌⲢⲀⲒ

ⲈⲠⲞⲨⲞⲒⲚ ⲚⲦⲈ ⲚⲒⲞⲨⲞⲈⲒⲚ· ⲠⲀⲒ ⲈⲚⲦⲀⲤⲚⲀⲨ ⲈⲢⲞⳞ ⲬⲒⲚ

3　MS ⲘⲘⲈⲌⲘⲚⲦⲰⲞⲘⲦⲈ; read ⲘⲠⲘⲈⲌⲘⲚⲦⲰⲞⲘⲦⲈ.

6　MS ⲈⲌⲈⲨⲘⲚⲦⲚⲞϬ; ⲌⲈ apparently erased; Schmidt: read ⲈⲨⲘⲚⲦⲚⲞϬ
　　instead of ⲈⲌⲈ ⲈⲨⲘⲚⲦⲚⲞϬ.

21　Ⲁ in upper left-hand margin at beginning of quire.

height." Now as she was thinking these things, she came
forth from her place in the thirteenth *aeon*, and she came
out to the twelve *aeons*[1]. The *archons* of the *aeons persecuted* her, and they were angry with her, because she had
thought to have greatness[2]. *However*, she came forth from
the twelve *aeons*, she came to the *places* of the *Chaos*. And
she made her way to the light-power with a lion-face in
order to swallow it. *But* all the *material emanations* of the
Authades surrounded her. And the great light-power with
a lion-face swallowed the light-*powers* in the Sophia. And
it purified her light and swallowed it, and her *matter* was
cast forth to the *Chaos*. There existed an *archon* with a lion-
face in the *Chaos*, whose one half was fire and whose other
half was darkness, namely Jaldabaoth[3], of whom I have
spoken to you many times. Now when these things had
happened, the Sophia became very greatly weakened. And
again that light-power with a lion-face began to take away
all the light-powers from the Sophia. And all the *material*
powers of the Authades surrounded the Sophia at the same
time, they oppressed her.

32.   The Pistis Sophia cried out very much. She cried
out to the Light of Lights which she had seen from the

---

[1]   (4-7) to the twelve aeons ... from the twelve aeons; MS : to the twelfth aeon ...
from the twelfth aeon.

[2]   (6) thought to have greatness; Schmidt : thought of glory.

[3]   (16) Jaldabaoth; see Iren.I.30.5-14; Epiph. 25.2.2; Hippol. V.7.30; Origen
c. Cels. VI.30-32; J 128; ApJn 38 etc.; HypArch 143; OnOrgWld 148.

ⲛ̄ϣⲟⲣⲡ̄ ⲉⲁⲥⲡⲓⲥⲧⲉⲩⲉ ⲉⲣⲟϥ· ⲁⲩⲱ ⲁⲥϫⲱ ⲛ̄ⲧⲉⲓ̈ⲙⲉⲧⲁⲛⲟⲓⲁ ⲉⲥϫⲱ ⲙ̄ⲙⲟⲥ ⲛ̄ⲧⲉⲓ̈ϩⲉ· ϫⲉ

1. ⲡⲟⲩⲟⲉⲓⲛ ⲛ̄ⲧⲉ ⲛⲓⲟⲩⲟⲉⲓⲛ ⲡⲁⲓ̈ ⲉⲛⲧⲁⲓ̈ⲡⲓⲥⲧⲉⲩⲉ ⲉⲣⲟϥ ϫⲓⲛ ⲛ̄ϣⲟⲣⲡ̄· ⲥⲱⲧⲙ̄ ϭⲉ ⲧⲉⲛⲟⲩ ⲡⲟⲩⲟⲉⲓⲛ ⲉⲧⲁⲙⲉⲧⲁⲛⲟⲓⲁ· ⲛⲁϩⲙⲉⲧ ⲡⲟⲩⲟⲉⲓⲛ ϫⲉ ⲁ ϩⲉⲛⲙⲉⲉⲩⲉ ⲉⲩϩⲟⲟⲩ ⲉⲓ' ⲉϩⲟⲩⲛ ⲉⲣⲟⲓ̈·

2. ⲁⲓ̈ϭⲱϣⲧ̄ ⲱ' ⲡⲟⲩⲟⲉⲓⲛ ⲉⲛⲙⲉⲣⲟⲥ ⲉⲧⲙ̄ⲡⲉⲥⲏⲧ· ⲁⲓ̈ⲛⲁⲩ ⲉⲩⲟⲩⲟⲉⲓⲛ ⲙ̄ⲡⲙⲁ ⲉⲧⲙ̄ⲙⲁⲩ ⲉⲓ̈ⲙⲉⲉⲩⲉ ϫⲉ ⲉⲓ̈ⲛⲁⲃⲱⲕ ⲉⲡⲧⲟⲡⲟⲥ ⲉⲧⲙ̄ⲙⲁⲩ ⲛ̄ⲧⲁϥⲓ-ⲡⲟⲩⲟⲉⲓⲛ ⲉⲧⲙ̄ⲙⲁⲩ· ⲁⲩⲱ ⲁⲓ̈ⲃⲱⲕ ⲁⲓ̈ϣⲱⲡⲉ ϩⲙ̄ ⲡⲕⲁⲕⲉ· ⲉⲧϩⲙ̄ ⲡⲉⲭⲁⲟⲥ ⲙ̄ⲡⲉⲥⲏⲧ· ⲁⲩⲱ ⲙ̄ⲡⲓⲉϣϭⲙ̄ϭⲟⲙ ⲉϩⲱⲗ ⲉⲃⲟⲗ· ⲉⲃⲱⲕ ⲉⲡⲁⲧⲟⲡⲟⲥ ⲉⲃⲟⲗ ϫⲉ ⲁⲓ̈ϩⲱϫ ϩⲛ̄ ⲛⲉⲡⲣⲟⲃⲟⲗⲟⲟⲩⲉ ⲧⲏⲣⲟⲩ ⲙ̄ⲉ̄ b
ⲙ̄ⲡⲁⲩⲑⲁⲇⲏⲥ· ⲁⲩⲱ ϯϭⲟⲙ ⲛ̄ϩⲟ ⲙ̄ⲙⲟⲓ̈ ⲁⲥϥⲓ-ⲡⲁⲟⲩⲟⲉⲓⲛ ⲉⲧⲛ̄ϩⲏⲧ·

3. ⲁⲩⲱ ⲁⲓ̈ⲱϣ ⲉⲃⲟⲗ ⲉⲩⲃⲟⲏⲑⲓⲁ· ⲁⲩⲱ ⲙ̄ⲡⲉ ⲡⲁϩⲣⲟⲟⲩ ⲉⲓ' ⲉϩⲣⲁⲓ̈ ϩⲙ̄ ⲡⲕⲁⲕⲉ· ⲁⲩⲱ ⲁⲓ̈ϭⲱϣⲧ̄ ⲉⲡϫⲓⲥⲉ· ϫⲉ ⲉϥⲉⲃⲟⲏⲑⲓ ⲉⲣⲟⲓ̈ ⲛ̄ϭⲓ ⲡⲟⲩⲟⲉⲓⲛ ⲉⲛⲧⲁⲓ̈ⲛⲁϩⲧⲉ ⲉⲣⲟϥ·

4. ⲁⲩⲱ ⲛ̄ⲧⲉⲣⲓϭⲱϣⲧ̄ ⲉⲡϫⲓⲥⲉ ⲁⲓ̈ⲛⲁⲩ ⲉⲛⲁⲣⲭⲱⲛ ⲧⲏⲣⲟⲩ ⲛ̄ⲛ̄ⲁⲓⲱⲛ ⲉⲛⲁϣⲱⲟⲩ· ⲁⲩⲱ ⲉⲩϭⲱϣⲧ̄ ⲉϩⲣⲁⲓ̈ ⲉϫⲱⲓ̈ ⲉⲩⲣⲁϣⲉ ⲙ̄ⲙⲟⲓ̈ ⲉⲙ̄ⲡⲓⲣ̄-ⲗⲁⲁⲩ ⲛⲁⲩ ⲉⲡⲉⲑⲟⲟⲩ· ⲁⲗⲗⲁ ⲛⲉⲩⲙⲟⲥⲧⲉ ⲙ̄ⲙⲟⲓ̈ ⲡⲉ ⲉⲡϫⲓⲛϫⲏ· ⲁⲩⲱ ⲛ̄ⲧⲉⲣⲟⲩⲛⲁⲩ ⲉⲛⲁⲣⲭⲱⲛ ⲛ̄ⲛ̄ⲁⲓⲱⲛ ⲉⲩⲣⲁϣⲉ ⲙ̄ⲙⲟⲓ̈ ⲛ̄ϭⲓ ⲛⲉⲡⲣⲟⲃⲟⲗⲟⲟⲩⲉ ⲙ̄ⲡⲁⲩⲑⲁⲇⲏⲥ· ⲁⲩⲉⲓⲙⲉ ϫⲉ ⲛ̄ⲥⲉⲛⲁⲃⲟⲏⲑⲓ ⲉⲣⲟⲓ̈ ⲁⲛ ⲛ̄ϭⲓ ⲛ̄ⲁⲣⲭⲱⲛ ⲛ̄ⲁⲓⲱⲛ ⲁⲩⲱ ⲁⲩⲧⲱⲕ ⲛ̄ϩⲏⲧ ⲛ̄ϭⲓ ⲛⲉⲡⲣⲟⲃⲟⲗⲟⲟⲩⲉ ⲉⲧⲙ̄ⲙⲁⲩ· ⲛⲁⲓ̈ ⲉⲛⲉⲩϩⲱϫ ⲙ̄ⲙⲟⲓ̈ ϩⲛ̄ ⲟⲩϫⲓⲛϭⲟⲛⲥ̄· ⲁⲩⲱ ⲡⲟⲩⲟⲉⲓⲛ ⲉⲧⲉ ⲙ̄ⲡⲓϥⲓⲧϥ̄ ⲁⲛⲟⲕ ⲛ̄ⲧⲟⲟⲧⲟⲩ· ⲁⲩϥⲓⲧϥ̄ ⲛ̄ⲧⲟⲟⲧ·

---

7 MS ⲉⲡⲙⲉⲣⲟⲥ; read ⲉⲛⲙⲉⲣⲟⲥ.
20 MS ⲉⲡⲉⲑⲟⲟⲩ; read ⲙ̄ⲡⲉⲑⲟⲟⲩ.

beginning, | in which she had *believed*, and she said this *repentance*, speaking thus :

1. 'O Light of Lights, in whom I have believed from the beginning, hear my *repentance* now at this time, O Light; save me, O Light, for wicked thoughts have entered into me.

2. I looked, *O* Light, to the *parts* below. I saw a light in that *place*, and I thought : I will go to that *place* to receive that light. And I went, and I came to be in the darkness which is in the *Chaos* below. And I was not able to proceed out to go to my *place*, because I was oppressed among all the *emanations* of the Authades. And the lion-faced power took away my inner light.

3. And I cried out for *help*, and my voice did not penetrate the darkness. And I looked to the height, so that the Light in which I had believed might *help* me.

4. And when I looked to the height, I saw all the *archons* of the *aeons*[1], that they were numerous and they looked down upon me, rejoicing over me, although I had done nothing evil to them, *but* they had hated me without cause. And when the *emanations* of the Authades saw the *archons* of the *aeons* rejoicing over me, they knew that the *archons* of the *aeons* would not *help* me. And those *emanations* which oppressed me without cause were encouraged. And they took from me the light which I did not take from them. |

---

[1]   (19) archons of the aeons, that they were numerous and they; Till : archons of the numerous aeons, that they.

5. ⲦⲉⲚⲞⲨ Ϭⲉ ⲠⲞⲨⲞⲈⲓⲚ ⲚⲦⲀⲖⲎⲞⲒⲀ ⲔⲤⲞⲞⲨⲚ ϪⲈ ⲚⲦ· ⲙ̅ⲉ̅
Ⲁⲓ̅ⲢⲚⲀⲒ ⲌⲚ̅ ⲦⲀⲘⲚⲦⲂⲀⲖⲌⲎⲦ · Ⲉⲓ̅ⲘⲈⲈⲨⲈ ϪⲈ ⲈϤⲎⲠ ⲈⲢⲞⲔ
Ⲛ̅ϬⲒ ⲠⲞⲨⲞⲈⲓⲚ Ⲛ̅ⲌⲞ Ⲙ̅ⲘⲞⲨⲒ̈ · ⲀⲨⲱ ⲠⲚⲞⲂⲈ ⲈⲚⲦⲀⲒ̈ⲀⲀϤ
ϤⲞⲨⲞⲚⲌ̅ Ⲙ̅ⲠⲈⲔⲘ̅ⲦⲞ ⲈⲂⲞⲖ ·

5 6. Ⲙ̅Ⲡ̅ⲢⲦⲢⲀϢⲰⲦ Ϭⲉ ⲠϪⲞⲈⲒⲤ · ϪⲈ Ⲛ̅ⲦⲀⲒ̈ⲚⲀⲌⲦⲈ ⲈⲠⲈⲔ-
ⲞⲨⲞⲈⲒⲚ ϪⲒⲚ Ⲛ̅ϢⲞⲢⲠ̅ · ⲠϪⲞⲈⲒⲤ ⲠⲞⲨⲞⲈⲒⲚ Ⲛ̅ⲦⲈ Ⲛ̅ϬⲞⲘ ·
Ⲙ̅Ⲡ̅ⲢⲦⲢⲀϢⲰⲦ Ϭⲉ Ⲙ̅ⲠⲀⲞⲨⲞⲈⲒⲚ ·

7. ϪⲈ ⲈⲦⲂⲈ ⲦⲈⲔⲀⲪⲞⲢⲘⲎ ⲘⲚ ⲠⲈⲔⲞⲨⲞⲈⲒⲚ Ⲛ̅ⲦⲀⲒ̈ϢⲰⲠⲈ
Ⲍ̅Ⲙ ⲠⲈⲒ̈ⲌⲰϪ · ⲀⲨⲱ ⲀⲨϢⲠⲈ ⲌⲰⲂ̅Ⲥ ⲈⲂⲞⲖ ⲈϪⲰⲒ̈ ·

10 8. ⲀⲨⲱ ⲈⲦⲂⲈ ⲦⲖⲞⲈⲒϬⲈ Ⲙ̅ⲠⲈⲔⲞⲨⲞⲈⲒⲚ · ⲀⲒ̅Ⲣ̅ϢⲘⲘⲞ
ⲈⲚⲀⲤⲚⲎⲨ ⲚⲒⲀⲌⲞⲢⲀⲦⲞⲤ · ⲀⲨⲱ ⲘⲚ̅ ⲚⲈⲠⲢⲞⲂⲞⲖⲞⲞⲨⲈ
⟨Ⲛ̅⟩ⲚⲞϬ Ⲛ̅ⲦⲈ ⲦⲂⲀⲢⲂⲎⲖⲰ ·

9. Ⲛ̅ⲦⲀ ⲚⲀⲒ̈ ϢⲰⲠⲈ Ⲙ̅ⲘⲞⲒ̈ Ⲱ̓ ⲠⲞⲨⲞⲈⲒⲚ ϪⲈ ⲀⲒ̈ⲔⲰⲌ
ⲈⲠⲈⲔⲘⲀⲚ̅ϢⲰⲠⲈ · ⲀⲨⲱ ⲀϤⲈⲒ̓ ⲈⲌⲢⲀⲒ̈ ⲈϪⲰⲒ̈ Ⲛ̅ϬⲒ ⲠϬⲰⲚ̅Ⲧ̅
15 Ⲙ̅ⲠⲀⲨⲐⲀⲆⲎⲤ ⲠⲀⲒ̈ ⲈⲦⲈ Ⲙ̅Ⲡ̅ϤⲤⲰⲦⲘ̅ Ⲛ̅ⲤⲀ ⲦⲈⲔⲔⲈⲖⲈⲨⲤⲒⲤ
ⲈⲦⲢⲈϤⲠⲢⲞⲂⲀⲖⲈ ⲈⲂⲞⲖ Ⲍ̅Ⲛ ⲦⲈⲠⲢⲞⲂⲞⲖⲎ Ⲛ̅ⲦⲈϤϬⲞⲘ ⲈⲂⲞⲖ ⲙ̅ⲉ̅ ᵇ
ϪⲈ ⲀⲒ̈ϢⲰⲠⲈ Ⲍ̅Ⲙ ⲠⲈϤⲀⲒⲰⲚ ⲈⲚ†ⲈⲒⲢⲈ ⲀⲚ Ⲙ̅ⲠⲈϤⲘⲨⲤⲦⲎ-
ⲢⲒⲞⲚ ·

10. ⲀⲨⲱ ⲚⲈⲨⲔⲰⲘϢ̅ Ⲙ̅ⲘⲞⲒ̈ ⲠⲈ Ⲛ̅ϬⲒ Ⲛ̅ⲀⲢⲬⲰⲚ ⲦⲎⲢⲞⲨ
20 Ⲛ̅ⲀⲒⲰⲚ ·

11. ⲀⲨⲱ ⲀⲒ̈ϢⲰⲠⲈ Ⲍ̅Ⲙ ⲠⲦⲞⲠⲞⲤ ⲈⲦⲘ̅ⲘⲀⲨ ⲈⲒ̅Ⲣ̅ⲌⲎⲂⲈ ⲈⲒ̈-
ϢⲒⲚⲈ Ⲛ̅ⲤⲀ ⲠⲞⲨⲞⲈⲒⲚ ⲈⲚⲦⲀⲒ̈ⲚⲀⲨ ⲈⲢⲞϤ Ⲍ̅Ⲙ ⲠϪⲒⲤⲈ ·

12. ⲀⲨⲱ ⲚⲈⲨϢⲒⲚⲈ Ⲛ̅ⲤⲰⲒ̈ ⲠⲈ Ⲛ̅ϬⲒ ⲚⲈⲪⲨⲖⲀⲝ Ⲛ̅Ⲙ̅ⲠⲨⲖⲎ
Ⲛ̅Ⲛ̅ⲀⲒⲰⲚ ⲀⲨⲱ ⲚⲈⲨⲤⲔⲰⲠⲦⲈ Ⲙ̅ⲘⲞⲒ̈ ⲦⲎⲢⲞⲨ ⲠⲈ Ⲛ̅ϬⲒ
25 ⲚⲈⲦ[Ⲧ]ⲀⲌⲈ Ⲍ̅Ⲙ ⲠⲈⲨⲘⲨⲤⲦⲎⲢⲒⲞⲚ ·

---

12 MS ⲚⲞϬ; read ⲛ̅ⲚⲞϬ.
25 MS ⲛⲈⲦⲦⲀⲌⲈ; read ⲛⲈⲦⲀⲌⲈ.

5. Now at this time, O *true* Light, thou knowest that I have done these things in my simplicity, thinking that the lion-faced light belonged to thee, and the sin which I have committed is manifest in thy presence.

6. Do not now let me be lacking, O Lord, for I have believed in thy light from the beginning, O Lord, Light of the powers, do not let me now lack my light.

7. For *on account* of thee and thy light I have come to be in this oppression, and shame has covered me.

8. And because of the delusion of thy light, I have become a stranger to my brothers, the *invisible ones*, and also to the great *emanations* of the Barbelo.

9. These things happened to me, *O* Light, because I was eager for thy dwelling-place. And the anger of the Authades came down upon me — this one who did not obey thy *command* to *emanate* from the *emanation* of his power — because I was in his *aeon* and not performing his *mystery*.

10. And all the *archons* of the *aeons* mocked me.

11. And I was in that *place*, sorrowing and seeking the light which I had seen in the height.

12. And the *watchers* of the *gates* of the *aeons* were seeking me, and all those who continued in their *mystery mocked* me. |

13. ΑΝΟΚ ΔΕ ΝΕΪϬΩϢΤ ΕϨΡΑΪ ΕΠΧΙСΕ · ΕϨΡΑΪ ΕΡΟΚ
ΠΟΥΟΪΝ · ΑΥΩ ΑΪΝΑϨΤΕ ΕΡΟΚ · ΤΕΝΟΥ ϬΕ ΠΟΥΟΪΝ
ΝΤΕ ΝΙΟΥΟΕΙΝ ϯϨΗΧ ϨΡΑΪ ϨΜ ΠΚΑΚΕ ΝΤΕ ΝΕΧΛΟС ·
ΕϢΧΕ ΚΟΥΩϢ ϬΕ ΕΕΙ' ΕΝΑϨΜΕΤ · ΟΥΝΟϬ ΠΕ ΠΕΚΝΑ'
5 СΩΤΜ ΕΡΟΪ ϨΝ ΟΥΜΕ · ΑΥΩ ΝΓΝΟΥϨΜ ΜΜΟΪ ·

14. ΝΑϨΜΕΤ ΕΒΟΛ ϨΝ ΘΥΛΗ ΜΠΕΪΚΑΚΕ ΧΕ ΝΝΑϢΜС
ΝϨΗΤϤ ΧΕΚΑС ΕΪΕΝΟΥϨΜ ΕΝΕΠΡΟΒΟΛΟΟΥΕ ΜΠΑΥΘΑ-
ΛΗС ΝΝΟΥΤΕ · ΝΑΪ ΕΤϨΩΧ ΜΜΟΪ · ΑΥΩ ΕΒΟΛ ϨΝ ‾ΜϨ̅
ΝΕΥΠΕΘΟΟΥ ·

10 15. ΜΠΡΤΡΕ ΠΕΪΚΑΚΕ ΟΜΕСΤ · ΑΥΩ ΤΕΪϬΟΜ ΝϨΑ
ΜΜΟΥΪ · ΜΠΡΤΡΕСΩΜΚ ΝΤΑϬΟΜ ΤΗΡС ϢΑΒΟΛ · ΑΥΩ
ΜΠΡΤΡΕ ΠΕΪΧΛΟС ϨΩΒС ΕΒΟΛ ΕΧΝ ΤΑϬΟΜ ·

16. СΩΤΜ ΕΡΟΪ ΠΟΥΟΕΙΝ ΧΕ ΝΑΝΟΥ ΠΕΚΝΑ' ΑΥΩ
ϬΩϢΤ ΕϨΡΑΪ ΕΧΩΪ ΚΑΤΑ ΠΑϢΑΪ ΝΜΝΤΝΑΗΤ ΜΠΕΚΟΥ-
15 ΟΪΝ ·

17. ΜΠΡΚΩΤΕ ΜΠΕΚϨΟ ΝСΑΒΟΛ ΜΜΟΪ ΧΕ ϯϨΗϢ
ΕΜΑΤΕ ·

18. ϬΕΠΗ СΩΤΜ ΕΡΟΪ · ΑΥΩ ΝΓΝΟΥϨΜ ΝΤΑϬΟΜ ·

19. ΝΑϨΜΕΤ ΕΤΒΕ ΝΑΡΧΩΝ ΕΤΜΟСΤΕ ΜΜΟΪ · ΧΕ
20 ΝΤΟΚ ΠΕΤСΟΟΥΝ ΜΠΑϨΩΧ · ΜΝ ΠΑϨΩϢ ΜΝ ΦΩϢ
ΝΤΑϬΟΜ · ΕΝΤΑΥϤΙΤС ΝΤΟΟΤ · СΕϢΟΟΠ ΜΠΕΚΜΤΟ
ΕΒΟΛ · ΝϬΙ ΝΕΝΤΑΥΧΟΪ ϨΝ ΝΕΪΠΕΘΟΟΥ ΤΗΡΟΥ · ΧΡΩ
ΝΑΥ ΚΑΤΑ ΠΕΤΕϨΝΑΚ ·

20. Α ΤΑϬΟΜ ϬΩϢΤ ΕΒΟΛ ϨΝ ΤΜΗΤΕ ΝΝΕΧΛΟС ·
25 ΑΥΩ ϨΝ ΤΜΗΤΕ ΝΝΚΑΚΕ · ΑΪϬΩϢΤ ΕΒΟΛ ϨΗΤϤ ΜΠΑ- ‾ΜϨ̅ b
СΥΝϨΥΓΟС · ΧΕ ΕϤΝΗΥ ΝϤΜΙϢΕ ΕΧΩΪ · ΑΥΩ ΜΠϤΕΙ' ·

---

14 MS ‾ΠΜΤ̅ΠΤΠΛΗΤ; read ‾ΝΤΜΤ̅ΠΤΠΛΗΤ.

13. *But* I looked up to the height to thee, O Light. And I believed in thee. Now at this time, O Light of Lights, I am oppressed in the darkness of the *Chaos*. If now thou dost wish to come to save me — great is thy compassion — hear me truly and save me.

14. Save me out of the *matter* of this darkness, so that I shall not be immersed in it, and that I shall be saved from the *emanations* of the deity, Authades, which oppress me, and from their evils.

15. Do not allow this darkness to immerse me, and do not allow this lion-faced power to swallow up all my power completely. And do not allow this *Chaos* to cover over my power.

16. Hear me, O Light, for thy mercy is precious, and look down upon me, *according to* the great compassion of thy light.

17. Do not turn away thy face from me, for I am greatly afflicted.

18. Hear me quickly and save my power.

19. Save me, on account of the *archons* which hate me, for thou knowest my affliction and my torment, and the torment of my power which they have taken from me. Those who have put me into all these evils are in thy presence. *Deal with* them *according to* thy will.

20. My power looked forth from the midst of the *Chaos*, and from the midst of the darkness. I looked for my *partner*, that he should come and fight for me, and he did not come. |

ⲀⲨⲰ ⲚⲈⲀⲒⳠⲰⳠⲦ ⲠⲈ ⲬⲈ ⲈϤⲚⲎⲨ Ⲛ̄ϤϮ-ϬⲞⲘ ⲚⲀⲒ · ⲀⲨⲰ
Ⲙ̄ⲠⲒ2Ⲉ ⲈⲢⲞϤ · ⲀⲨⲰ Ⲛ̄ⲦⲈⲢⲒⳘ)ⲒⲚⲈ Ⲛ̄ⳠⲀ ⲠⲞⲨⲞⲈⲒⲚ · ⲀⲨϮ
ⲚⲀⲒ Ⲛ̄ⲞⲨⲔⲀⲔⲈ ·

21. ⲀⲨⲰ Ⲛ̄ⲦⲈⲢⲒⳘ)ⲒⲚⲈ Ⲛ̄ⳠⲀ ⲦⲀϬⲞⲘ · ⲀⲨϮ ⲚⲀⲒ Ⲛ̄ⲞⲨ-
5 2ⲨⲖⲎ ·

22. ⲦⲈⲚⲞⲨ ϬⲈ ⲠⲞⲨⲞⲈⲒⲚ Ⲛ̄ⲦⲈ ⲚⲒⲞⲨⲞ̈ⲒⲚ · ⲠⲔⲀⲔⲈ · ⲘⲚ̄
ⲐⲨⲖⲎ · ⲈⲚⲦⲀⲨⲚ̄ⲦⲞⲨ ⲈⲬⲰⲒ Ⲛ̄ϬⲒ ⲚⲈⲠⲢⲞⲂⲞⲖⲞⲞⲨⲈ Ⲙ̄-
ⲠⲀⲨⲐⲀⲖⲎⳠ · ⲘⲀⲢⲞⲨⳘ)ⲰⲠⲈ ⲚⲀⲨ ⲈⲨϬⲞⲢⳠ̄Ⳡ ⲀⲨⲰ ⲘⲀ-
ⲢⲞⲨϬⲖⲞⲘⲖ̄Ⲙ Ⲉ2ⲞⲨⲚ ⲈⲢⲞⲞⲨ ⲀⲨⲰ Ⲛ̄ⲄⲦⲞⲨⲈⲒⲞ ⲚⲀⲨ
10 ⲀⲨⲰ Ⲛ̄ⳠⲈⳠⲔⲀⲚⲆⲀⲖⲒⲌⲈ Ⲛ̄ⳠⲈⲦⲘⲂⲰⲔ ⲈⲠⲦⲞⲠⲞⳠ Ⲙ̄ⲠⲈⲨ-
ⲀⲨⲐⲀⲖⲎⳠ ·

23. ⲘⲀⲢⲞⲨϬⲰ 2Ⲙ̄ ⲠⲔⲀⲔⲈ Ⲛ̄ⳠⲈⲦⲘ̄ⲚⲀⲨ ⲈⲂⲞⲖ ⲈⲠⲞⲨ-
ⲞⲈⲒⲚ · ⲘⲀⲢⲞⲨϬⲰⳠⲦ ⲈⲠⲈⲬⲖⲞⳠ Ⲛ̄ⲚⲀⲨ ⲚⲒⲘ · ⲀⲨⲰ Ⲙ̄ⲠⲢ̄-
ⲦⲢⲈⲨϬⲰⳠⲦ ⲈⲠⲬⲒⳠⲈ ·

15 24. ⲀⲚⲒⲚⲈ Ⲉ2ⲢⲀⲒ ⲈⲬⲰⲞⲨ Ⲙ̄ⲠⲈⲨⲬⲒⲔⲂⲀ · ⲀⲨⲰ ⲘⲀⲢⲈϤ-
ⲦⲀ2ⲞⲞⲨ Ⲛ̄ϬⲒ ⲠⲈⲔ2ⲀⲠ ·   ⲘⲎ̄

25. Ⲙ̄ⲠⲢ̄ⲦⲢⲈⲨⲂⲰⲔ ⲈⲠⲈⲨⲦⲞⲠⲞⳠ ⲬⲒⲚ Ⲙ̄ⲠⲈⲒ̈ⲚⲀⲨ · 2ⲀⲦⲘ̄
ⲠⲈⲨⲀⲨⲐⲀⲖⲎⳠ Ⲛ̄ⲚⲞⲨⲦⲈ · ⲀⲨⲰ Ⲙ̄ⲠⲢ̄ⲦⲢⲈ ⲚⲈϤⲠⲢⲞⲂⲞ-
ⲖⲞⲞⲨⲈ ⲂⲰⲔ ⲈⲚⲈⲨⲦⲞⲠⲞⳠ ⲬⲒⲚ Ⲙ̄ⲠⲈⲒ̈ⲚⲀⲨ · ⲬⲈ ⲞⲨ-
20 ⲀⳠⲈⲂⲎⳠ ⲠⲈ · ⲀⲨⲰ ⲞⲨⲀⲨⲐⲀⲖⲎⳠ ⲠⲈ ⲠⲈⲨⲚⲞⲨⲦⲈ ⲀⲨⲰ
ⲚⲈϤⲘⲈⲈⲨⲈ ⲠⲈ ⲬⲈ Ⲛ̄ⲦⲀϤⲢ̄-ⲚⲈⲒⲠⲈⲐⲞⲞⲨ ⲈⲂⲞⲖ 2ⲒⲦⲞⲞⲦϤ
ⲈⲚϤⳠⲞⲞⲨⲚ ⲢⲰ ⲀⲚ ⲬⲈ Ⲛ̄ⳠⲀⲂⲎⲖ ⲬⲈ ⲀⲨⲐ̄ⲂⲂⲒⲞⲒ̈ ⲔⲀⲦⲀ
ⲠⲈⲔⲦⲰⳘ) Ⲛ̄ⲚⲈϤⲚⲀⳘ)ϬⲘ̄ϬⲞⲘ ⲈⲢⲞⲒ̈ ⲀⲚ ⲠⲈ ·

26. ⲀⲖⲖⲀ Ⲛ̄ⲦⲈⲢⲈⲔⲐ̄ⲂⲂⲒⲞⲒ̈ 2ⲒⲦⲘ̄ ⲠⲈⲔⲦⲰⳘ) · ⲀⲨⲆⲒⲰⲔⲈ
25 Ⲙ̄ⲘⲞⲒ̈ Ⲛ̄2ⲞⲨⲞ · ⲀⲨⲰ Ⲁ ⲚⲈⲨⲠⲢⲞⲂⲞⲖⲞⲞⲨⲈ ⲞⲨⲈ2-2ⲒⳠⲈ
ⲈⲬⲘ̄ ⲠⲀⲐ̄ⲂⲂⲒⲞ ·

And I looked that he should come and give power to me, and I did not find him.

21. And when I sought for light, I was given darkness. And when I sought for my power, I was given *matter* [1].

22. Now at this time, O Light of Lights, let the darkness and the *matter* which the *emanations* of the Authades have brought upon me become a snare for them, and let them be ensnared therein. And do thou repay them and *bring disgrace* upon them, so that they do not come to the *place* of their Authades.

23. Let them remain in darkness and not see the light. Let them look at the *Chaos* at all times, and do not let them look at the height.

24. Bring down upon them their vengeance, and let thy judgment seize them.

25. Do not let them go to their *place* from this time, to their deity, Authades. And do not let his *emanations* go to their *places* from this time. Because their god is *impious* and *insolent*, because he thought that he had done these wicked things of himself, not knowing that, unless I was humbled *according to* thy ordinance, he would have had no power over me.

26. *But* when thou didst humble me, *according to* thy ordinance, I was *persecuted* the more. And their *emanations* inflicted torments upon my humiliation. |

---

[1]   (2-5) Till emends Schmidt's division of verses 20, 21.

27. ⲀⲨⲰ ⲀⲨϤⲒ ⲚⲞⲨϬⲞⲘ ⲚⲞⲨⲞⲈⲒⲚ Ⲛ̄ϨⲎⲦ · ⲀⲨⲰ ⲞⲚ
ⲀⲨϨⲒ-ⲦⲞⲞⲦⲞⲨ Ⲛ̄ⲞⲨⲰϨⲘ̄ · ⲀⲨϨⲰϪ Ⲙ̄ⲘⲞⲒ̈ ⲈⲘⲀϢⲞ ⲈⲦⲢⲈⲨ-
ϤⲒ Ⲙ̄ⲠⲞⲨⲞⲈⲒⲚ ⲦⲎⲢϤ̄ ⲈⲦⲚ̄ϨⲎⲦ · ⲈⲦⲂⲈ ⲚⲈⲚⲦⲀⲨϪⲞⲒ̈ Ⲛ̄ϨⲎ-
ⲦⲞⲨ · Ⲙ̄Ⲡ̄ⲢⲦⲢⲈⲨ̇ⲂⲰⲔ ⲈϨⲢⲀⲒ̈ ⲈⲠⲘⲈϨⲘⲚ̄ⲦϢⲞⲘⲦⲈ Ⲛ̄ⲀⲒⲰⲚ ⲘⲎ ᵇ
5 ⲠⲦⲞⲠⲞⲤ Ⲛ̄ⲦⲀⲒⲔⲀⲒⲞⲤⲨⲚⲎ ·

28. ⲀⲨⲰ Ⲙ̄Ⲡ̄ⲢⲦⲢⲈⲨⲰⲠ ⲈϨⲞⲨⲚ ⲈⲠⲈⲔⲖⲎⲢⲞⲤ Ⲛ̄ⲚⲈⲦⲞⲨ-
ⲤⲰⲦϤ̄ Ⲙ̄ⲘⲞⲞⲨ · Ⲙ̄Ⲛ ⲠⲈⲨⲞⲨⲞⲒ̈Ⲛ · ⲀⲨⲰ Ⲙ̄Ⲡ̄ⲢⲦⲢⲈⲨⲰⲠ
ⲈϨⲞⲨⲚ ⲈⲚⲈⲦⲚⲀⲘⲈⲦⲀⲚⲞⲒ̈ Ϩ̄Ⲛ ⲞⲨϬⲈⲠⲎ · ⲈⲦⲢⲈⲨϪⲒ-ⲘⲨⲤ-
ⲦⲎⲢⲒⲞⲚ Ϩ̄Ⲛ ⲞⲨϬⲠⲎ Ϩ̄Ⲙ ⲠⲞⲨⲞⲈⲒⲚ ·

10 29. ⲈⲂⲞⲖ ϪⲈ ⲀⲨϤⲒ-ⲠⲀⲞⲨⲞⲈⲒⲚ ⲀⲚⲞⲔ Ⲛ̄ϨⲎⲦ · ⲀⲨⲰ Ⲁ
ⲦⲀϬⲞⲘ ⲀⲢϪⲈⲒ Ⲛ̄ⲰⲬⲚ ϨⲢⲀⲒ̈ Ⲛ̄ϨⲎⲦ · ⲀⲨⲰ ⲀⲒ̈ϢⲰϢⲦ Ⲙ̄-
ⲠⲀⲞⲨⲞⲈⲒⲚ ·

30. ⲦⲈⲚⲞⲨ ϬⲈ ⲠⲞⲨⲞⲈⲒⲚ ⲈⲦⲚ̄ϨⲎⲦⲔ̄ ⲠⲈⲦϢⲞⲞⲠ Ⲛ̄ⲘⲘⲀⲒ̈
†ϨⲨⲘⲚⲈⲨⲈ ⲈⲠⲈⲔⲢⲀⲚ ⲠⲞⲨⲞⲒ̈Ⲛ Ϩ̄Ⲛ ⲞⲨⲈⲞⲞⲨ ·

15 31. ⲀⲨⲰ ⲠⲀϨⲨⲘⲚⲞⲤ ⲠⲞⲨⲞⲈⲒⲚ ⲘⲀⲢⲈϤⲢ̄ⲀⲚⲀⲔ Ⲛ̄ⲐⲈ
Ⲛ̄ⲞⲨⲘⲨⲤⲦⲎⲢⲒⲞⲚ ⲈϤⲞⲨⲞⲦⲂ̄ · ⲠⲀⲒ̈ ⲈⲦϪⲒ ⲈϨⲞⲨⲚ ⲈⲘⲠⲨⲖⲎ
Ⲙ̄ⲠⲞⲨⲞⲈⲒⲚ ⲠⲀⲒ̈ ⲈⲦⲞⲨⲚⲀϪⲞⲞϤ Ⲛ̄ϬⲒ ⲚⲈⲦⲚⲀⲘⲈⲦⲀⲚⲞⲈⲒ ·
ⲀⲨⲰ Ⲛ̄ⲤⲈⲤⲰⲦϤ̄ Ⲙ̄ⲠⲈϤⲞⲨⲞⲈⲒⲚ ·   ⲘⲐ

32. ⲦⲈⲚⲞⲨ ϬⲈ ⲘⲀⲢⲈ Ⲛ̄ϨⲨⲖⲎ ⲦⲎⲢⲞⲨ ⲢⲀϢⲈ · ϢⲒⲚⲈ
20 ⲦⲎⲢⲦⲚ̄ Ⲛ̄ⲤⲀ ⲠⲞⲨⲞⲒ̈Ⲛ ⲦⲀⲢⲈⲤⲰⲚϨ̄ Ⲛ̄ϬⲒ ⲦϬⲞⲘ Ⲛ̄ⲦⲈⲦⲘ̄-
ⲮⲨⲬⲎ ⲈⲦϨ̄Ⲛ̄ⲦⲎⲨⲦⲚ̄ ·

33. ϪⲈ Ⲁ ⲠⲞⲨⲞⲈⲒⲚ ⲤⲰⲦⲘ̄ ⲈⲚϨⲨⲖⲎ · ⲀⲨⲰ Ⲛ̄ϤⲚⲀⲔⲀ-
ⲖⲀⲀⲨ ⲀⲚ Ⲛ̄ϨⲨⲖⲎ ⲈⲘⲠϤ̄ⲤⲞⲦϤⲞⲨ ·

34. ⲘⲀⲢⲈ ⲚⲈⲮⲨⲬⲞⲞⲨⲈ Ⲙ̄Ⲛ Ⲛ̄ϨⲨⲖⲎ · ⲤⲘⲞⲨ ⲈⲠϪⲞⲈⲒⲤ
25 Ⲛ̄ⲀⲒⲰⲚ ⲦⲎⲢⲞⲨ · Ⲙ̄Ⲛ Ⲛ̄ϨⲨⲖⲎ · Ⲙ̄Ⲛ ⲚⲈⲦⲚ̄ϨⲎⲦⲞⲨ ⲦⲎ-
ⲢⲞⲨ ·

---

21 MS ⲈⲦⲚ̄ϨⲚ̄ ; first ⲛ crossed out.

27. And they took a light-power from me. And further-more they began to torment me greatly [1], in order to take away all the light that was in me. On account of these things into which I was put, do not let them go up to the thirteenth *aeon*, the *place* of *righteousness*.

28. And do not let them be numbered within the *por-tion* of those who purify themselves and their light. And do not let them be numbered among those who will *repent* quickly, so that they will quickly receive *mysteries* in the light.

29. For they have taken my light from me. And my power has *begun* to decrease within me. And I lack my light.

30. Now at this time, O Light which art in thee and with me, I *sing praises* to thy name, O Light, in glory.

31. And may my *song of praise*, O Light, please thee, like an excellent *mystery* which is received into the *gates* of light, which those who will *repent*, will recite, and whose light they will purify.

32. Now at this time, let all *material things* rejoice; seek the light, all of you, so that the power of your *souls*, which is within you, may live.

33. Because the Light has heard the *material things*, and it will not leave any *material things* which it has not purified.

34. Let the *souls* and the *material things* bless the Lord of all the *aeons* [2]; the *material things* and all things in them. |

---

[1] (2) furthermore they began to torment me greatly; Till: they repeated it again and tormented me greatly.

[2] (24, 25) all the aeons; the material things etc.; Till: (or) all the aeons and the material things etc.

35. ϫⲉ ⲡⲛⲟⲩⲧⲉ ⲛⲁⲛⲟⲩⲙ̄ ⲛ̄ⲧⲉⲩⲯⲩⲭⲏ ⲉⲃⲟⲗ ⲍ̄ⲛ
ⲍⲩⲗⲏ ⲛⲓⲙ · ⲁⲩⲱ ⲥⲉⲛⲁⲥⲟⲃⲧⲉ ⲛ̄ⲟⲩⲡⲟⲗⲓⲥ ⲍⲣⲁⲓ̈ ⲍ̄ⲙ ⲡⲟⲩⲟⲉⲓⲛ · ⲁⲩⲱ ⲛⲉⲯⲩⲭⲟⲟⲩⲉ ⲧⲏⲣⲟⲩ ⲉⲧⲛⲁⲛⲟⲩⲍ̄ⲙ · ⲥⲉ-
ⲛⲁⲟⲩⲱⲍ ⲍ̄ⲛ ⲧⲡⲟⲗⲓⲥ ⲉⲧⲙ̄ⲙⲁⲩ · ⲛ̄ⲥⲉⲕⲗⲏⲣⲟⲛⲟⲙⲓ ⲙ̄ⲙⲟⲥ ·

5 36. ⲁⲩⲱ ⲧⲉⲯⲩⲭⲏ ⲛ̄ⲛⲉⲧⲛⲁϫⲓ-ⲙⲩⲥⲧⲏⲣⲓⲟⲛ ⲥⲛⲁϣⲱⲡⲉ
ⲍ̄ⲙ ⲡⲧⲟⲡⲟⲥ ⲉⲧⲙ̄ⲙⲁⲩ · ⲁⲩⲱ *ⲛⲉⲛⲧⲁⲩϫⲓ-ⲙⲩⲥⲧⲏⲣⲓⲟⲛ ⲙ̄ⲑ ᵇ
ⲍ̄ⲙ ⲡⲉϥⲣⲁⲛ ⲥⲉⲛⲁϣⲱⲡⲉ ⲛ̄ⲍⲏⲧⲥ̄ :

ⲍ̄ ⲁⲥϣⲱⲡⲉ ϭⲉ ⲉⲣⲉ ⲓ̄ⲥ ϫⲱ ⲛ̄ⲛⲉⲓ̈ϣⲁϫⲉ ⲉⲛⲉϥⲙⲁⲑⲏⲧⲏⲥ · ⲡⲉϫⲁϥ ⲛⲁⲩ ϫⲉ ⲡⲁⲓ̈ ⲡⲉ ⲫⲩⲙⲛⲟⲥ ⲉⲛⲧⲁⲥ-
10 ϫⲟⲟⲩ ⲛ̄ϭⲓ ⲧⲡⲓⲥⲧⲓⲥ ⲥⲟⲫⲓⲁ · ⲍ̄ⲛ ⲧⲉⲥϣⲟⲣⲡ̄ ⲙ̄ⲙⲉⲧⲁⲛⲟⲓⲁ ·
ⲉⲥⲙⲉⲧⲁⲛⲟⲓ̈ ⲉⲧⲃⲉ ⲡⲉⲥⲛⲟⲃⲉ · ⲁⲩⲱ ⲉⲥϫⲱ ⲛ̄ⲍⲱⲃ ⲛⲓⲙ
ⲉⲛⲧⲁⲩϣⲱⲡⲉ ⲙ̄ⲙⲟⲥ · ⲧⲉⲛⲟⲩ ϭⲉ ⲡⲉⲧⲉ ⲟⲩⲛ̄-ⲙⲁⲁϫⲉ
ⲙ̄ⲙⲟϥ ⲉⲥⲱⲧⲙ̄ ⲙⲁⲣⲉϥⲥⲱⲧⲙ̄ :

ⲍ̄ ⲁⲥⲉⲓ̓ ⲟⲛ ⲉⲑⲏ ⲛ̄ϭⲓ ⲙⲁⲣⲓⲁ ⲡⲉϫⲁⲥ ϫⲉ ⲡⲁϫⲟⲉⲓⲥ
15 ⲟⲩⲛ̄-ⲙⲁⲁϫⲉ ⲙ̄ⲡⲁⲣⲙ̄ⲛ̄ⲟⲩⲟⲓ̈ⲛ · ⲁⲩⲱ †ⲥⲱⲧⲙ̄ ⲍ̄ⲛ ⲧⲁϭⲟⲙ
ⲛ̄ⲟⲩⲟⲓ̈ⲛ · ⲁⲩⲱ ⲁϥⲛⲏϥⲉ ⲙ̄ⲙⲟⲓ̈ ⲛ̄ϭⲓ ⲡⲉⲕⲡ̄ⲛ̄ⲁ ⲉⲧⲛ̄ⲙⲙⲁⲓ̈
ⲥⲱⲧⲙ̄ ϭⲉ ⲧⲁϣⲁϫⲉ ⲉⲧⲃⲉ ⲧⲙⲉⲧⲁⲛⲟⲓⲁ ⲉⲛⲧⲁⲥϫⲟⲟⲥ
ⲛ̄ϭⲓ ⲧⲡⲓⲥⲧⲓⲥ ⲥⲟⲫⲓⲁ ⲉⲥϫⲱ ⲙ̄ⲡⲉⲥⲛⲟⲃⲉ ⲙⲛ̄ ⲛⲉⲛⲧⲁⲩ-
ϣⲱⲡⲉ ⲙ̄ⲙⲟⲥ ⲧⲏⲣⲟⲩ ⲛ̄ⲧⲁ ⲧⲉⲕϭⲟⲙ**ⲛ̄ⲟⲩⲟⲉⲓⲛ ⲡⲣⲟ- ⲡ̄
20 ⲫⲏⲧⲉⲩⲉ ⲍⲁⲣⲟⲥ ⲙ̄ⲡⲓⲟⲩⲟⲉⲓϣ ⲍⲓⲧⲛ̄ ⲇⲁⲩⲉⲓⲇ ⲡⲉⲡⲣⲟⲫⲏⲧⲏⲥ ⲍ̄ⲙ ⲡⲙⲉⲍⲥⲉϣⲙⲏⲛ ⲙ̄ⲯⲁⲗⲙⲟⲥ · ϫⲉ

1. ⲡⲛⲟⲩⲧⲉ ⲙⲁⲧⲟⲩϫⲟⲓ̈ ϫⲉ ⲁ ⲍⲉⲛⲙⲟⲟⲩ ⲉⲓ̓ ⲉⲍⲟⲩⲛ
ϣⲁ ⲧⲁⲯⲩⲭⲏ ·

---

17 MS ⲁⲥϫⲟⲟϥ; ϥ crossed out and ⲥ inserted above.

35. For God will save their *souls* out of all *matter*, and a *city* will be prepared in the light; and all *souls* which will be saved will dwell in that *city*, and they will *inherit* it.

36. And the *soul* of those who will receive *mysteries* will be in that *place*, and they who have received *mysteries* in his name will be within it'."

33. Now it happened, as Jesus said these words to his *disciples*, he said to them : "This is the *song of praise* which the Pistis Sophia spoke in the first *repentance*, as she *repented* for her sin. And she spoke of all the things which had happened to her. Now at this time, he who has ears to hear, let him hear *."

Maria came forward again and said : "My Lord, there are ears to my man of light [1], and I hear in my light-power, and thy *Spirit*, which is with me, has made me *sober*. Hear now, that I may speak concerning the *repentance* which the Pistis Sophia said, as she spoke of her sin, and all the things which had happened to her. Thy light-power once *prophesied* about it through David, the *prophet*, in the 68th *Psalm* :

1. 'Save me, O God, for the waters have come in to my *soul*. |

---

* cf. Mk. 4.9

---

[1] (15) man of light; Schmidt : light-dweller.

2. ⲁⲓⲧⲱⲁⲥ ⲏ̄ ⲁⲓⲱⲙⲥ̄ ⲉⲧⲁⲟⲓ̈ⲍⲉ ⲙ̄ⲡⲛⲟⲩⲛ ⲁⲩⲱ ⲛⲉⲙⲛ̄-
ⲱϭⲟⲙ ⲡⲉ· ⲁⲓ̈ⲉⲓ' ⲉⲛⲉⲭ̄ⲏⲕ ⲛ̄ⲑⲁⲗⲁⲥⲥⲁ· ⲟⲩⲍ̄ⲁⲧⲏⲩ ⲧⲉ
ⲛ̄ⲧⲁⲥⲟⲙⲉⲥⲧ̄·

3. ⲁⲓ̈ⲍⲓⲥⲉ ⲉⲓ̈ⲭⲓ̈ϣⲕⲁⲕ ⲉⲃⲟⲗ· ⲧⲁϣⲟⲩⲱⲃⲉ ⲧⲉ ⲉⲛⲧ-
ⲁⲥⲍ̄ⲱⲗ· ⲁ ⲛⲁⲃⲁⲗ ⲱⲭ̄ⲛ ⲉⲓ̈ⲕⲱ ⲛ̄ⲍⲧⲏⲓ̈ ⲉⲡⲛⲟⲩⲧⲉ·

4. ⲁⲩⲁϣⲁⲓ̈ ⲉⲍⲟⲩⲉ-ⲛ̄ϥⲱ ⲛ̄ⲧⲁⲁⲡⲉ ⲛ̄ϭⲓ ⲛⲉⲧⲙⲟⲥⲧⲉ ⲙ̄-
ⲙⲟⲓ̈ ⲉⲡϫⲓⲛϫⲏ· ⲁⲩϭⲙϭⲟⲙ ⲛ̄ϭⲓ ⲛⲁⲭⲁⲭⲉ· ⲛⲉⲧⲁⲓⲱⲕⲉ
ⲙ̄ⲙⲟⲓ̈ ⲍ̄ⲛ ⲟⲩϫⲓⲛϭⲟⲛⲥ̄· ⲛⲉⲧⲉ ⲙ̄ⲡⲓⲧⲟⲣⲡⲟⲩ· ⲁⲩϣⲁⲧ̄ⲧ
ⲙ̄ⲙⲟⲟⲩ·

5. ⲡⲛⲟⲩⲧⲉ ⲛ̄ⲧⲟⲕ ⲉⲛⲧⲁⲕⲉⲓⲙⲉ ⲉⲧⲁⲙ̄ⲛ̄ⲧⲁⲑⲏⲧ· ⲁⲩⲱ
ⲛⲁⲛⲟⲃⲉ ⲙ̄ⲡⲟⲩⲍⲱⲡ ⲉⲣⲟⲕ·

ⲛ̄ᵇ

6. ⲙ̄ⲡ̄ⲣ̄ⲧⲣⲉⲩⲭⲓ̈ϣⲓⲡⲉ ⲉⲧⲃⲏⲏⲧ ⲛ̄ϭⲓ ⲛⲉⲧⲍⲩⲡⲟⲙⲓⲛⲉ ⲉⲣⲟⲕ
ⲡϫⲟⲉⲓⲥ· ⲡϫⲟⲉⲓⲥ ⲛ̄ⲛ̄ϭⲟⲙ ⲙ̄ⲡ̄ⲣ̄ⲧⲣⲉⲩⲟⲩⲱⲁⲥ̄ ⲉⲧⲃⲏⲏⲧ
ⲛ̄ϭⲓ ⲛⲉⲧϣⲓⲛⲉ ⲛ̄ⲥⲱⲕ ⲡϫⲟⲓ̈ⲥ ⲡⲛⲟⲩⲧⲉ ⲙ̄ⲡⲓ̄ⲏ̄ⲗ· ⲡⲛⲟⲩⲧⲉ
ⲛ̄ⲛ̄ϭⲟⲙ·

7. ϫⲉ ⲉⲧⲃⲏⲏⲧ̄ⲕ ⲁⲓ̈ϥⲓ ⲉⲣⲟⲓ̈ ⲛ̄ⲟⲩⲛⲟϭⲛⲉϭ· ⲁ ⲡϣⲓⲡⲉ
ⲍⲱⲃⲥ̄ ⲉⲭ̄ⲙ ⲡⲁⲍⲟ·

8. ⲁⲓ̈ⲣ̄ϣⲙⲙⲟ ⲉⲛⲁⲥⲛⲏⲩ ϣ̄ⲙⲙⲟ ⲉⲛϣⲏⲣⲉ ⲛ̄ⲧⲁⲙⲁⲁⲩ·

9. ϫⲉ ⲡⲕⲱⲍ ⲙ̄ⲡⲉⲕⲏⲓ̈ ⲡⲉ ⲛ̄ⲧⲁϥⲟⲩⲟⲙⲧ̄· ⲛ̄ⲛⲟϭⲛⲉϭ
ⲛ̄ⲛⲉⲧⲛⲟϭⲛⲉϭ ⲙ̄ⲙⲟⲓ̈· ⲁⲩⲍⲉ ⲉⲍⲣⲁⲓ̈ ⲉϫⲱⲓ̈·

10. ⲁⲓ̈ⲕⲱⲗⲭ̄ ⲛ̄ⲧⲁⲯⲩⲭⲏ ⲍ̄ⲛ ⲟⲩⲛⲏⲥⲧⲓⲁ· ⲁⲥϣⲱⲡⲉ ⲛⲁⲓ̈
ⲉⲩⲛⲟϭⲛⲉϭ·

11. ⲁⲓ̈ϯ ⲛ̄ⲟⲩϭⲟⲟⲩⲛⲉ ⲍⲓⲱⲱⲧ ⲁⲓ̈ϣⲱⲡⲉ ⲛⲁⲩ ⲙ̄ⲡⲁ-
ⲣⲁⲃⲟⲗⲏ·

---

2 MS ⲉⲛⲉⲭⲏⲕ; read ⲉⲛⲉⲧϣⲏⲕ.
5 MS ⲍⲱⲗ·ⲗ·; second ⲗ crossed out.
20 MS originally ⲙ̄ⲙⲟⲕ.

2. I have sunk *or* been immersed by the mire of the abyss, and there was no power. I came to the depths of the *sea*; a storm wind overwhelmed me.

3. I have suffered as I cried out. My throat has gone. My eyes have failed as I waited upon God.

4. Those who hate me without cause have become more numerous than the hairs of my head. My enemies that *persecute* me with violence have become strong. They deprived me of those things which I did not steal.

5. O God, thou knowest my foolishness; and my sins are not hidden from thee.

6. Let not them that *wait on* thee be ashamed on my account, O Lord, Lord of the powers. Let not those that seek thee be put to shame on my account, O Lord, God of Israel, God of the powers.

7. For I have borne disgrace on thy account; shame has covered my face.

8. I have become a stranger to my brothers, a stranger to the sons of my mother.

9. For the zeal of thy house has eaten me up. The reproaches of those who reproach thee have fallen upon me.

10. I bowed down my *soul* with *fasting*; it became a reproach to me.

11. I put sackcloth upon myself; I became a *proverb* to them. |

12. ⲚⲈⲨϪⲒ ⲚⲈⲢⲀⲨ ⲈⲒⲰⲰⲦ ⲠⲈ ⲚϬⲒ ⲚⲈⲦⲈⲘⲞⲞⲤ [**] ⲈⲚ Ⲙ̄- ⲚⲀ
ⲠⲨⲖⲎ · ⲀⲨⲰ ⲚⲈⲨⲮⲀⲖⲖⲈ ⲈⲢⲞÏ ⲠⲈ ⲚϬⲒ ⲚⲈⲦⲤⲰ Ⲙ̄ⲠⲎⲢ̄Ⲡ̄ ·

13. ⲀⲚⲞⲔ ⲆⲈ ⲚⲈⲈⲒϢⲖⲎⲖ ⲠⲈ Ⲉ̄Ⲛ ⲦⲀⲮⲨⲬⲎ ⲈⲈⲢⲀÏ ⲈⲢⲞⲔ
ⲠϪⲞⲈⲒⲤ · ⲠⲈⲞⲨⲞⲈⲒϢ Ⲙ̄ⲠⲈⲦⲈⲈⲚⲀⲔ ⲠⲈ ⲠⲚⲞⲨⲦⲈ · Ⲉ̄Ⲙ
5 ⲠⲀϢⲀÏ Ⲙ̄ⲠⲈⲔⲚⲀ· ⲤⲰⲦ̄Ⲙ̄ ⲈⲠⲀⲞⲨϪⲀÏ Ⲉ̄Ⲛ ⲞⲨⲘⲈ ·

14. ⲘⲀⲦⲞⲨϪⲞÏ ⲈⲦⲈ̈ⲒⲞⲘⲈ · ϪⲈ Ⲛ̄ⲚⲀⲦⲰⲘⲤ̄ Ⲛ̄ⲈⲎⲦⲤ̄ ·
Ⲉ̈ⲒⲈⲞⲨϪⲀÏ ⲈⲂⲞⲖ Ⲉ̄Ⲛ ⲚⲈⲦⲘⲞⲤⲦⲈ Ⲙ̄ⲘⲞÏ · ⲀⲨⲰ ⲈⲂⲞⲖ Ⲉ̄Ⲙ
ⲠϢⲒⲔ Ⲛ̄Ⲙ̄ⲘⲞⲞⲨ ·

15. Ⲙ̄Ⲡ̄Ⲡ̄ⲦⲢⲈ ⲞⲨⲂⲈⲢⲰ Ⲙ̄ⲘⲞⲞⲨ ⲞⲘⲈⲤ̄Ⲧ̄ · Ⲙ̄Ⲡ̄Ⲡ̄ⲦⲢⲈ ⲠⲚⲞⲨⲚ
10 ⲞⲘⲈⲔ̄Ⲧ̄ · Ⲙ̄Ⲡ̄Ⲡ̄ⲦⲢⲈ ⲞⲨϢⲰⲦⲈ ⲀⲘⲀ̄ⲈⲦⲈ Ⲛ̄ⲢⲰⲤ ⲈϪⲰÏ ·

16. ⲤⲰⲦ̄Ⲙ̄ ⲈⲢⲞÏ ⲠϪⲞⲈⲒⲤ ϪⲈ ⲞⲨⲬⲢⲎⲤⲦⲞⲤ ⲠⲈ ⲠⲈⲔⲚⲀ·
ⲔⲀⲦⲀ ⲠⲀϢⲀÏ Ⲛ̄ⲦⲈⲔⲘ̄Ⲛ̄ⲦϢⲀⲚⲈ̄ⲦⲎϤ ϬⲰⲰ̄Ⲧ̄ ⲈⲈⲢⲀÏ ⲈϪⲰÏ ·

17. Ⲙ̄Ⲡ̄Ⲣ̄ⲔⲦⲈ-ⲠⲈⲔⲈⲞ Ⲛ̄ⲤⲀⲂⲞⲖ Ⲙ̄ⲠⲈⲔⲈⲘⲈⲀⲖ ϪⲈ ϯⲐⲖⲒⲂⲈ ·

18.* ⲤⲰⲦ̄Ⲙ̄ ⲈⲢⲞÏ Ⲉ̄Ⲛ ⲞⲨϬⲈⲠⲎ · ϯⲈⲦⲎⲔ ⲈⲦⲀⲮⲨⲬⲎ Ⲛ̄Ⲅ̄- ⲚⲀᵇ
15 ⲤⲞⲦ̄Ⲥ̄ ·

19. ⲚⲀⲈⲘⲈⲦ ⲈⲦⲂⲈ ⲚⲀϪⲀϪⲈ · Ⲛ̄ⲦⲞⲔ ⲄⲀⲢ ⲈⲦⲈⲒⲘⲈ ⲈⲠⲀ-
ⲚⲞϬⲚⲈϬ Ⲙ̄Ⲛ̄ ⲠⲀϢⲒⲠⲈ · ⲀⲨⲰ ⲠⲀⲞⲨⲰⲘⲤ̄ · ⲚⲈⲦⲐⲖⲒⲂⲈ
Ⲙ̄ⲘⲞÏ ⲦⲎⲢⲞⲨ Ⲙ̄ⲠⲈⲔⲘ̄ⲦⲞ ⲈⲂⲞⲖ ·

20. Ⲁ ⲠⲀⲈⲎⲦ ϬⲰⲰ̄Ⲧ̄ ⲈⲂⲞⲖ Ⲉ̄Ⲛ̄Ⲧ̄ϥ Ⲛ̄ⲞⲨⲚⲞϬⲚⲈϬ Ⲙ̄Ⲛ̄
20 ⲞⲨⲦⲀⲖⲀⲒⲠⲰⲢⲒⲀ · Ⲁ̈ⲒϬⲰⲰ̄Ⲧ̄ ⲈⲂⲞⲖ Ⲉ̄Ⲛ̄Ⲧ̄ϥ Ⲙ̄ⲠⲈⲦⲚⲀⲖⲨⲠⲒ
Ⲛ̄Ⲙ̄ⲘⲀÏ Ⲙ̄ⲠⲒϬⲚ̄Ⲧ̄ϥ ⲀⲨⲰ ⲠⲈⲦⲚⲀⲤ̄ⲤⲰⲦ Ⲙ̄ⲠⲒⲈⲈ ⲈⲢⲞϤ ·

21. ⲀⲨϯ Ⲛ̄ⲞⲨⲤⲒϢⲈ ⲈⲦⲀⲈⲢⲈ · ⲀⲨⲦⲤⲈⲒ̈-ⲞⲨⲈⲘⲬ̄ Ⲉ̄Ⲙ ⲠⲀ-
ⲈⲒⲂⲈ ·

22. ⲘⲀⲢⲈ ⲦⲈⲨⲦⲢⲀⲠⲈⲌⲀ ϢⲰⲠⲈ Ⲙ̄ⲠⲈⲨⲘ̄ⲦⲞ ⲈⲂⲞⲖ ⲈⲨ-
25 ϬⲞⲢϬ̄Ⲥ̄ · Ⲙ̄Ⲛ̄ ⲞⲨⲠⲀϢ · ⲀⲨⲰ ⲞⲨⲦⲰϢⲂⲈ · Ⲙ̄Ⲛ̄ ⲞⲨⲤⲔⲀⲚ-
ⲆⲀⲖⲞⲚ ·

12. They that sat in the *gates* talked against me; and they that drink wine *sang* against me.

13. *But* I was praying in my *soul* to thee, O Lord; it is the time of thy pleasure, O God; in the magnitude of thy mercy, hear truly for my salvation.

14. Save me from this mire, that I do not sink in it. Let me be saved from those that hate me and from the depths of the waters.

15. Let not the water flood immerse me. Let not the abyss swallow me up; let not a pit close its mouth over me.

16. Hear me, O Lord, for *beneficent* is thy mercy; *according to* the magnitude of thy compassion look down upon me.

17. Turn not away thy face from thy servant, for I am *afflicted.*

18. Hear me quickly; give heed to my *soul* and save it.

19. Save me on account of my enemies; *for* thou knowest my reproach and my shame and my infamy. All that *afflict* me are before thee.

20. My heart has looked for reproach and *wretchedness*; I have looked for one to be *sorrowful* with me, I did not find him; and for one to comfort me, I did not meet him.

21. They gave me gall for my food; they made me drink vinegar for my thirst.

22. Let their *table* become a snare in their presence; and a stumbling block and a retribution and a *disgrace.* |

23. N̄ΓΚΑΧ-ΤΕΥΧΙСΕ N̄СΗΥ ΝΙΜ ·

24. ΠΩ2Τ Ε2ΡΑΪ ΕΧΩΟΥ N̄ΤΕΚΟΡΓΗ · ΑΥΩ ΠϬΩΝΤ
N̄ΤΕΚΟΡΓΗ ΜΑΡΕϤΤΑ2ΟΟΥ ·

25. ΜΑΡΕ ΠΕΥΜΑN̄ϢΩΠΕ Ρ̄ΧΑΪΕ · N̄ϤΤΜϢΩΠΕ N̄Ϭι
5 ΠΕΤΟΥΗ2 2N̄ ΝΕΥΜΑN̄ϢΩΠΕ ·

26. ΧΕ ΠΕΝΤΑΚΠΑΤΑССΕ M̄ΜΟϤ · ΑΥΔΙΩΚΕ N̄СΩϤ ·
ΑΥΟΥΩ2 Ε2ΡΑΪ ΕΧM̄ ΠΕM̄ΚΑ2 M̄ΠΕΥСΑϢ ·

27. ΑΥΟΥΕ2-ΑΝΟΜΙΑ · ΕΧN̄ ΝΕΥΑΝΟΜΙΑ · ΑΥΩ M̄ΠΡ-
ΤΡΕΥΕΙ' Ε2ΟΥΝ 2N̄ ΤΕΚΔΙΚΑΙΟСΥΝΗ ·

10 28. ΜΑΡΟΥϤΟΤΟΥ · ΕΒΟΛ 2M̄ ΠΧΩΩΜΕ N̄ΝΕΤΟΝ2 ·
ΑΥΩ M̄ΠΡΤΡΕΥС2ΑΪСΟΥ ΜN̄ N̄ΔΙΚΑΙΟС ·

29. ΑΝΓ̄ ΟΥ⟨2⟩ΗΚΕ ΕϤΡ-ΠΚΕΜΟΚ2 ΠΟΥΧΑΪ M̄ΠΕΚ2Ο
ΠΝΟΥΤΕ ΠΕ N̄ΤΑϤϢΟΠΤ ΕΡΟϤ ·

30. ϯΝΑСΜΟΥ ΕΠΡΑΝ ΕΠΝΟΥΤΕ 2N̄ ΟΥ2ΩΔΗ · ΑΥΩ
15 ϯΝΑΧΙСΕ M̄ΜΟϤ 2N̄ ΟΥСΜΟΥ ·

31. ϤΝΑΡΑΝΑϤ M̄ΠΝΟΥΤΕ Ε2ΟΥΕ-ΟΥΜΑСΕ N̄Β̄ΡΡΕ · ΕϤ-
ΝΕΧ-ΤΑΠ ΕΒΟΛ 2Ι ΪΕΙΒ ·

32. ΜΑΡΕ N̄2ΗΚΕ ΝΑΥ N̄СΕΕΥϕΡΑΝΕ · ϢΙΝΕ N̄СΑ
ΠΝΟΥΤΕ ΤΑΡΕ ΝΕΤM̄ΨΥΧΟΟΥΕ ΩN̄2 ·

20 33. ΧΕ Α ΠΧΟΕΙС СΩΤM̄ ΕΝ2ΗΚΕ · ΑΥΩ M̄ΠϤСΕϢϤ-
ΝΕΤΤΟ M̄ΠΙΝΕ N̄2ΟΜΤ ·

34. ΜΑΡΕ M̄ΠΗΥΕ ΜN̄ ΠΚΑ2 СΜΟΥ ΕΠΧΟΪС ΘΑΛΑССΑ
ΜN̄ ΝΕΤN̄2ΗΤС ΤΗΡΟΥ ·

---

8 MS ΑΥΟΥΕ2; perhaps read ΟΥΕ2 (Greek πρόσθες).
12 MS ΟΥΗΚΕ.
14 MS ΕΠΝΟΥΤΕ; read M̄ΠΝΟΥΤΕ.

23. Do thou bend their backs at all times.

24. Pour out upon them thy *wrath*, and let the fury of thy *wrath* take hold of them.

25. Let their dwelling-place be made desolate and let there be no inhabitant in their dwelling-places.

26. For they have *persecuted* him whom thou hast *smitten*; they have added to the pain of their blow [1].

27. They have added *iniquity* to their *iniquities*; let them not come into thy *righteousness*.

28. Let them be effaced from the book of the living, and let them not be written with the *righteous*.

29. I am a poor man and also a sorrowful one; the salvation of thy face, O God, is that which has accepted me.

30. I will bless the name of God in *song*, and raise him up in blessing.

31. It will please God more than a young bull which carries horns and hoofs.

32. Let the poor see and *rejoice*; seek God that your *souls* may live.

33. For the Lord has heard the poor and he has not despised those in fetters [2].

34. Let the heavens and the earth bless the Lord, the *sea* and all that are within it. |

---

[1]   (7) their blow; Schmidt: their wound.
[2]   (21) in fetters; lit. in copper chains.

35. ϫⲉ ⲡⲛⲟⲩⲧⲉ ⲛⲁⲛⲟⲩ︤ⲍⲙ︥ ⲛ̄ⲥⲓⲱⲛ · ⲁⲩⲱ ⲥⲉⲛⲁⲕⲱⲧ
ⲛ̄ⲙⲡⲟⲗⲉⲓⲥ ⲛ̄ϯⲟⲩⲇⲁⲓⲁ ⲛ̄ⲥⲉⲟⲩⲱϩ ⲙ̄ⲙⲁⲩ ⲛ̄ⲥⲉⲕⲗⲏⲣⲟ-
ⲛⲟⲙⲓ ⲙ̄ⲙⲟⲥ ·

36. ⲡⲉⲥⲡⲉⲣⲙⲁ ⲛ̄ⲛⲉϥϩⲙ̄ϩⲁⲗ ⲛⲁⲁⲙⲁϩⲧⲉ ⲙ̄ⲙⲟⲥ · ⲁⲩⲱ
5 ⲛⲉⲧⲙⲉ ⲙ̄ⲡⲉϥⲣⲁⲛ ⲛⲁⲟⲩⲱϩ ⲛ̄ϩⲏⲧ︤ⲥ︥ ·

ⲅ̄ ⲁⲥϣⲱⲡⲉ ϭⲉ ⲛ̄ⲧⲉⲣⲉ ⲙⲁⲣⲓϩⲁⲙ ⲟⲩⲱ ⲉⲥϫⲱ ⲛ̄ⲛⲉⲓ̈-
ϣⲁϫⲉ ⲉⲓⲥ ϩ̄ⲛ ⲧⲙⲏⲧⲉ ⲛ̄ⲙⲙⲁⲑⲏⲧⲏⲥ · ⲡⲉϫⲁⲥ ⲛⲁϥ ϫⲉ
ⲡⲁϫⲟⲉⲓⲥ · ⲡⲁⲓ̈ ⲡⲉ ⲡⲃⲱⲗ ⟨ⲙ̄ⲡ⟩ⲙⲩⲥⲧⲏⲣⲓⲟⲛ ⲛ̄ⲧⲙⲉⲧⲁⲛⲟⲓⲁ
ⲛ̄ⲧⲡⲓⲥⲧⲓⲥ ⲥⲟⲫⲓⲁ ·

10 ⲅ̄ ⲁⲥϣⲱⲡⲉ ϭⲉ ⲛ̄ⲧⲉⲣⲉ ⲓ̄ⲥ ⲥⲱⲧ︤ⲙ︥ ⲉⲙⲁⲣⲓϩⲁⲙ ⲉⲥϫⲱ ⲛ̄ⲅ
ⲛ̄ⲛⲉⲓ̈ϣⲁϫⲉ · ⲡⲉϫⲁϥ ⲛⲁⲥ ϫⲉ ⲉⲩⲅⲉ ⲙⲁⲣⲓϩⲁⲙ ⲧⲙⲁⲕⲁⲣⲓⲁ · ⲧⲉⲡⲗⲏⲣⲱⲙⲁ ⲏ̀ ⲧⲡⲁⲛⲙⲁⲕⲁⲣⲓⲟⲥ ⲙ̄ⲡⲗⲏⲣⲱⲙⲁ · ⲧⲁⲓ̈
ⲉⲧⲟⲩⲛⲁⲙⲁⲕⲁⲣⲓⲍⲉ ⲙ̄ⲙⲟⲥ ϩ̄ⲛ ⲅⲉⲛⲉⲁ ⲛⲓⲙ ·

ⲅ̄ ⲁϥⲟⲩⲱϩ ⲟⲛ ⲉⲧⲟⲟⲧ︤ϥ︥ ⲛ̄ϭⲓ ⲓ̄ⲥ ϩ̄ⲙ ⲡϣⲁϫⲉ · ⲡⲉϫⲁϥ ·
15 ϫⲉ ⲁⲥⲟⲩⲱϩ ⲟⲛ ⲉⲧⲟⲟⲧ︤ⲥ︥ ⲛ̄ϭⲓ ⲧⲡⲓⲥⲧⲓⲥ ⲥⲟⲫⲓⲁ · ⲁⲥϩⲩⲙⲛⲉⲩⲉ ⲛ̄ⲕⲉⲙⲉϩⲥ︤ⲛ︥ⲧⲉ ⲙ̄ⲙⲉⲧⲁⲛⲟⲓⲁ ⲉⲥϫⲱ ⲙ̄ⲙⲟⲥ
ⲛ̄ⲧⲉⲓ̈ϩⲉ ϫⲉ

1. ⲡⲟⲩⲟⲉⲓⲛ ⲛ̄ⲛⲟⲩⲟⲓ̈ⲛ ⲛ̄ⲧⲁⲓ̈ⲡⲓⲥⲧⲉⲩⲉ ⲉⲣⲟⲕ · ⲙ̄ⲡⲣ̄-
ⲕⲁⲁⲧ ϩ̄ⲙ ⲡⲕⲁⲕⲉ ϣⲁ ⲡϫⲱⲕ ⲙ̄ⲡⲁⲟⲩⲟⲉⲓϣ ·

20 2. ⲃⲟⲏⲑⲓ ⲉⲣⲟⲓ̈ ⲁⲩⲱ ⲛ̄ⲅⲛⲁϩⲙⲉⲧ ϩ̄ⲛ ⲛⲉⲕⲙⲩⲥⲧⲏⲣⲓⲟⲛ ·
ⲣⲓⲕⲉ ⲙ̄ⲡⲉⲕⲙⲁⲁϫⲉ ⲉⲣⲟⲓ̈ ⲁⲩⲱ ⲛ̄ⲅⲛⲟⲩϩ︤ⲙ︥ ⲙ̄ⲙⲟⲓ̈ ·

3. ⲙⲁⲣⲉ ⲧϭⲟⲙ ⲙ̄ⲡⲉⲕⲟⲩⲟⲉⲓⲛ ⲛⲁϩⲙⲉⲧ · ⲁⲩⲱ ⲛ̄ⲅϥⲓⲧ ·
ⲉⲛⲁⲓⲱⲛ ⲉⲧϫⲟⲥⲉ · ϫⲉ ⲛ̄ⲧⲟⲕ ⲡⲉⲧⲛⲁⲛⲁϩⲙⲉⲧ ⲁⲩⲱ
ⲛ̄ⲅϫⲓⲧ ⲉⲡϫⲓⲥⲉ* ⲛ̄ⲧⲉ ⲛⲉⲕⲁⲓⲱⲛ ·   ⲛ̄ⲅ ᵇ

---

1 MS originally ϩ̄ⲛⲥⲓⲱⲛ; ϩ crossed out.
8 MS ⲙ̄ⲡ written small in right-hand margin; ⲛ̄ⲫⲓ in left-hand margin.

35. For God will save Zion; and the *cities* of Judaea will
be built, and (men) will dwell there and *inherit* it.

36. The *seed* of his servants will take possession of it,
and they that love his name will dwell in it'." *

34.   Now it happened when Mariam finished saying these
words to Jesus in the midst of the *disciples*, she said to him;
"My Lord, this is the interpretation of the *mystery* of the
repentance of the Pistis Sophia".

It happened now when Jesus heard Mariam saying these
words, he said to her : "*Excellent*, Mariam, thou *blessed one*,
thou *pleroma or* thou *all-blessed pleroma*, who will be *blessed*
among all *generations*" □.

35.   Jesus continued again with the discourse. He said :
"The Pistis Sophia continued again, she also *sang* a second
repentance, in which she spoke thus :

1. 'O Light of Lights, I have *believed* in thee. Do not
leave me in the darkness until the completion of my time.

2. *Help* me and save me in thy *mysteries*. Incline thy ear
to me and save me.

3. Let the power of thy light save me and carry me to the
aeons on high, for it is thou who savest me and takest me to
the height of thy *aeons*. |

---

*   cf. Ps. 68.1-36
□   cf. Lk. 1.48

4. ⲚⲀⲌⲘⲈⲦ ⲠⲞⲨⲞⲈⲒⲚ ⲚⲦⲞⲞⲦⲤ ⲚⲦⲈⲒϬⲞⲘ ⲚⲌⲞ ⲘⲘⲞⲨⲒ
ⲀⲨⲰ ⲚⲦⲞⲞⲦⲞⲨ ⲚⲚⲈⲠⲢⲞⲂⲞⲖⲞⲞⲨⲈ ⲘⲠⲀⲨⲐⲀⲆⲎⲤ [Ⲛ]Ⲛ-
ⲚⲞⲨⲦⲈ ·

5. ⲬⲈ ⲚⲦⲞⲔ ⲠⲞⲨⲞⲈⲒⲚ ⲠⲈ ⲚⲦⲀⲒⲠⲒⲤⲦⲈⲨⲈ ⲈⲠⲈⲔⲞⲨⲞⲒⲚ

5 6. ⲀⲨⲰ ⲚⲦⲀⲒⲚⲀⲌⲦⲈ ⲢⲰ ⲈⲠⲈⲔⲞⲨⲞⲒⲚ ⲬⲒⲚ ⲚϢⲞⲢⲠ ·
ⲀⲨⲰ ⲀⲒⲠⲒⲤⲦⲈⲨⲈ ⲈⲢⲞϤ ⲬⲒⲚ ⲦⲈⲨⲚⲞⲨ ⲈⲚⲦⲀϤⲠⲢⲞⲂⲀⲖⲈ
ⲘⲘⲞⲒ ⲈⲂⲞⲖ · ⲀⲨⲰ ⲚⲦⲞⲔ ⲢⲰ ⲠⲈ ⲚⲦⲀⲔⲦⲢⲈⲨⲠⲢⲞⲂⲀⲖⲈ
ⲘⲘⲞⲒ ⲈⲂⲞⲖ · ⲀⲨⲰ ⲀⲚⲞⲔ ⲌⲰ ⲀⲒⲠⲒⲤⲦⲈⲨⲈ ⲈⲠⲈⲔⲞⲨⲞⲒⲚ
ⲬⲒⲚ ⲚϢⲞⲢⲠ ·

10 7. ⲀⲨⲰ ⲚⲦⲈⲢⲒⲠⲒⲤⲦⲈⲨⲈ ⲈⲢⲞⲔ · ⲚⲚⲈⲨⲤⲰⲂⲈ ⲘⲘⲞⲒ ⲠⲈ
ⲚϬⲒ ⲚⲀⲢⲬⲰⲚ ⲚⲚⲀⲒⲰⲚ · ⲈⲨⲬⲰ ⲘⲘⲞⲤ ⲬⲈ ⲀⲤⲖⲞ ⲌⲘ
ⲠⲈⲤⲘⲨⲤⲦⲎⲢⲒⲞⲚ · ⲚⲦⲞⲔ ⲠⲈⲦⲚⲀⲚⲀⲌⲘⲈⲦ · ⲀⲨⲰ ⲚⲦⲞⲔ
ⲠⲈ ⲠⲀⲤⲰⲦⲎⲢ · ⲀⲨⲰ ⲚⲦⲞⲔ ⲠⲈ ⲠⲀⲘⲨⲤⲦⲎⲢⲒⲞⲚ ⲠⲞⲨ-
ⲞⲈⲒⲚ ·

15 8. Ⲁ ⲢⲰⲒ ⲘⲞⲨⲌ ⲚⲈⲞⲞⲨ · ⲬⲈⲔⲀⲤ ⲈⲒⲈⲬⲰ ⲘⲠⲘⲨⲤⲦⲎ-
ⲢⲒⲞⲚ ⲚⲦⲈⲔⲘⲚⲦⲚⲞϬ ⲚⲞⲨⲞⲒϢ ⲚⲒⲘ ·   ⲚⲀ

9. ⲦⲈⲚⲞⲨ ϬⲈ ⲠⲞⲨⲞⲈⲒⲚ ⲘⲠⲢⲔⲀⲀⲦ ⲌⲘ ⲠⲈⲬⲀⲞⲤ Ⲙ-
ⲠⲬⲰⲔ ⲈⲂⲞⲖ ⲘⲠⲀⲞⲨⲞⲈⲒϢ ⲦⲎⲢϤ · ⲘⲠⲢⲔⲀⲀⲦ ⲚⲤⲰⲔ
ⲠⲞⲨⲞⲈⲒⲚ ·

20 10. ⲬⲈ ⲀⲨϤⲒ-ⲦⲀϬⲞⲘ ⲦⲎⲢⲤ ⲚⲞⲨⲞⲈⲒⲚ ⲚⲌⲎⲦ · ⲀⲨⲰ
ⲀⲨⲔⲰⲦⲈ ⲈⲢⲞⲒ ⲚϬⲒ ⲚⲈⲠⲢⲞⲂⲞⲖⲞⲞⲨⲈ ⲦⲎⲢⲞⲨ ⲘⲠⲀⲨ-
ⲐⲀⲆⲎⲤ · ⲀⲨⲞⲨⲈϢϤⲒ-ⲠⲀⲞⲨⲞⲒⲚ ⲦⲎⲢϤ ⲌⲢⲀⲒ ⲚⲌⲎⲦ ϢⲀⲂⲞⲖ ·
ⲀⲨⲰ ⲀⲨⲢⲞⲒⲤ ⲈⲦⲀϬⲞⲘ ·

11. ⲈⲨⲬⲰ ⲘⲘⲞⲤ ⲚⲚⲈⲨⲈⲢⲎⲨ 21 ⲞⲨⲤⲞⲠ ⲬⲈ Ⲁ ⲠⲞⲨ-
25 ⲞⲈⲒⲚ ⲔⲀⲀⲦ ⲚⲤⲰϤ · ⲀⲘⲀⲌⲦⲈ ⲘⲘⲞⲤ ⲚⲦⲚϤⲒ-ⲠⲞⲨⲞⲈⲒⲚ
ⲦⲎⲢϤ ⲈⲦⲚ̄ⲌⲎⲦⲤ ·

---

2 MS Ⲡ̄Ⲛ̄ⲚⲞⲨⲦⲈ ; read Ⲡ̄ⲚⲞⲨⲦⲈ.
10 MS ⲠⲚⲈⲨⲤⲰⲂⲈ ; read ⲚⲈⲨⲤⲰⲂⲈ.
25 MS ⲔⲀⲀⲦ; read ⲔⲀⲀⲤ.

4. Save me, O Light, from the hand of this lion-faced power, and from the hands of the *emanations* of the deity, Authades.

5. For thou, O Light, art the one in whose light I have *believed* and in whose light I have trusted from the beginning.

6. And I have believed in it from the hour that it *emanated* me forth. And thou indeed art he who caused me to be *emanated* forth. And I have indeed *believed* in thy light from the beginning.

7. And when I *believed* in thee, the *archons* of the *aeons* mocked me, saying : she has ceased in her *mystery*. It is thou who wilt save me. And thou art my *Saviour*. And thou art my *mystery*, O Light.

8. My mouth has been filled with glory, so that I might tell the *mystery* of thy greatness at all times.

9. Now, O Light, do not leave me in the *Chaos* during the completion of my whole time. Do not abandon me, O Light.

10. For my whole light-power has been taken away from me. And all the *emanations* of the Authades have surrounded me. They wanted to take all my light from me completely, and they watched for my power.

11. They were saying at the same time to one another : the light has left her [1]; let us seize her and take away all the light within her. |

---

[1] (25) the light has left her; MS the light has left me.

12. ⲈⲦⲂⲈ ⲠⲀⲒ̈ ⲄⲈ ⲠⲞⲨⲞⲈⲒⲚ ⲘⲠⲢⲀⲞ ⲄⲀⲢⲞⲒ̈ · ⲔⲞⲦⲔ ⲠⲞⲨ-
ⲞⲈⲒⲚ ⲚⲄⲚⲀⲀⲘⲈⲦ ⲚⲦⲞⲞⲦⲞⲨ ⲚⲚⲒⲀⲦⲚⲀ’ ·

13. ⲘⲀⲢⲞⲨⲀⲈ · ⲀⲨⲰ ⲚⲤⲈⲢⲀⲦⲄⲞⲘ ⲚⲄⲒ ⲚⲀⲒ̈ ⲈⲦⲞⲨⲈⲱ-
ⳡⲒ-ⲦⲀⲄⲞⲘ · ⲘⲀⲢⲞⲨⲄⲞⲞⲖⲞⲨ ⲀⲘ ⲠⲔⲀⲔⲈ ⲀⲨⲰ ⲚⲤⲈⲰⲰⲠⲈ
5 ⲀⲚ ⲞⲨⲘⲚⲦⲀⲄⲞⲘ ⲚⲄⲒ ⲚⲀⲒ̈ ⲈⲦⲞⲨⲈⲰ ⳡⲒ-ⲦⲀⲄⲞⲘ ⲚⲞⲨⲞⲒ̈Ⲛ ⲠⲀ
ⲚⲀⲎⲦ ·

ⲦⲀⲒ̈ ⲄⲈ ⲦⲈ ⲦⲘⲈⲀⲤⲚⲦⲈ ⲘⲘⲈⲦⲀⲚⲞⲒⲀ ⲈⲚⲦⲀⲤⲬⲞⲞⲤ
ⲚⲄⲒ ⲦⲠⲒⲤⲦⲒⲤ ⲤⲞⳅⲒⲀ ⲈⲤⲀⲨⲘⲚⲈⲨⲈ ⲈⲀⲢⲀⲒ̈ ⲈⲠⲞⲨⲞⲈⲒⲚ ·

Ⲁ ⲀⲤⲰⲰⲠⲈ ⲄⲈ ⲚⲦⲈⲢⲈ Ⲓ̅Ⲥ̅ ⲞⲨⲰ ⲈⳡⲬⲰ ⲚⲚⲈⲒ̈ⲀⲀⳆⲈ
10 ⲈⲚⲈⳡⲘⲀⲐⲎⲦⲎⲤ · ⲠⲈⳅⲀ̄ϥ · ⳆⲈ ⲦⲈⲦⲚ̅ⲚⲞⲈⲒ ⳆⲈ ⲈⲒ̈ⲀⲀⳆⲈ
ⲚⲘⲘⲎⲦⲚ̅ ⲚⲀⲀ ⲚⲀⲈ · ⲀϥϥⲞⲄϥ ⲈⲂⲞⲖ ⲚⲄⲒ ⲠⲈⲦⲢⲞⲤ ⲠⲈⳆⲀϥ
ⲚⲒ̅Ⲥ̅ ⳆⲈ ⲠⲀⳆⲞⲈⲒⲤ · ⲦⲚ̅ⲚⲀⲀ-ⲀⲚⲈⳆⲈ ⲀⲚ ⲚⲦⲈⲒ̈ⲤⲀⲒ̈ⲘⲈ ·
ⲈⲤⳆⲒ ⲘⲠⲘⲀ ⲚⲦⲞⲞⲦⲚ̅ · ⲀⲨⲰ ⲘⲠⲤⲔⲀ-ⲞⲨⲞⲚ ⲘⲘⲞⲚ
ⲈⲀⲀⳆⲈ · ⲀⲖⲖⲀ ⲈⲤⲀⲀⳆⲈ ⲚⲀⲀⲀ ⲚⲤⲞⲠ ·

15 ⲀϥⲞⲨⲰⲀⲂ ⲚⲄⲒ Ⲓ̅Ⲥ̅ ⲠⲈⳆⲀϥ ⲚⲚⲈϥⲘⲀⲐⲎⲦⲎⲤ ⳆⲈ ⲠⲈⲦ-
ⲈⲢⲈ ⲦⲄⲞⲘ ⲘⲠⲈϥⲠ̅Ⲛ̅Ⲁ̅ ⲚⲀⲂⲢⲂⲢ ⲀⲢⲀⲒ̈ ⲚⲀⲎⲦϥ · ⲈⲦⲢⲈϥⲚⲞⲈⲒ
ⲘⲠⲈⲦⳡⲬⲰ ⲘⲘⲞϥ · ⲘⲀⲢⲈϥⲈⲒ’ ⲈⲐⲎ · ⲚϥⲀⲀⳆⲈ · ⲠⲖⲎⲚ ⲄⲈ
ⲚⲦⲞⲔ ⲠⲈⲦⲢⲞⲤ ⳝⲚⲀⲨ ⲈⲦⲈⲔⲄⲞⲘ ⲀⲢⲀⲒ̈ ⲚⲀⲎⲦⲔ ⲈⲤⲚⲞⲒ
ⲘⲠⲂⲰⲖ ⲘⲠⲘⲨⲤⲦⲎⲢⲒⲞⲚ ⲚⲦⲘⲈⲦⲀⲚⲞⲒⲀ ⲈⲚⲦⲀⲤⲬⲞⲞⲤ ⲚⲄⲒ
20 ⲦⲠⲒⲤⲦⲒⲤ ⲤⲞⳅⲒⲀ · ⲦⲈⲚⲞⲨ ⲄⲈ ⲚⲦⲞⲔ ⲠⲈⲦⲢⲞⲤ ⳆⲰ Ⲙ-
ⲠⲚⲞⲎⲘⲀ ⲚⲦⲈⲤⲘⲈⲦⲀⲚⲞⲒⲀ ⲚⲦⲘⲎⲦⲈ ⲚⲚⲈⲔⲤⲚⲎⲨ · ⲀϥⲞⲨ-
ⲰⲀⲂ ⲀⲈ ⲚⲄⲒ ⲠⲈⲦⲢⲞⲤ ⲠⲈⳆⲀϥ ⲚⲒ̅Ⲥ̅ ⳆⲈ ⲠⳆⲞⲈⲒⲤ · ⲤⲰⲦⲘ
ⲦⲀⳆⲰ ⲘⲠⲚⲞⲎⲘⲀ ⲚⲦⲈⲤⲘⲈⲦⲀⲚⲞⲒⲀ ⲚⲦⲀⲤⲠⲢⲞⳅⲎⲦⲈⲨⲈ
ⲀⲀⲢⲞⲤ ⲚⲄⲒ ⲦⲈⲔⲄⲞⲘ ⲘⲠⲒⲞⲨⲞⲈⲒ ⲀⲒ̈ⲦⲚ̅ ⲀⲀⲨⲈⲒⲀ ⲠⲈⲠⲢⲞ-
25 ⳅⲎⲦⲎⲤ ⲈⲤⳆⲰ ⲚⲦⲈⲤⲘⲈⲦⲀⲚⲞⲒⲀ · ⲀⲘ ⲠⲘⲈⲀⲀⲀϥⲈ ⲘⳇⲀⲖ-
ⲘⲞⲤ · ⳆⲈ

12. On account of this, O Light, do not cease towards me. Turn thyself, O Light, and save me from the hands of the merciless.

13. May those who want to take away my power fall and become powerless. May those who want to take away my light-power from me be wrapped in darkness and exist in powerlessness.'

This is the second *repentance* which the Pistis Sophia said, *singing praises* to the light."

36. It happened now, when Jesus finished saying these words to his *disciples*, he said : "Do you understand in what manner I am speaking with you?"

Peter leapt forward, he said to Jesus : "My Lord, we are not able to *suffer* this woman who takes the opportunity from us, and does not allow anyone of us to speak, *but* she speaks many times."

Jesus answered, he said to his *disciples* : "Let him in whom the power of his *Spirit* has welled up so that he *understands* what I say, come forward and speak. *Nevertheless*, thou Peter, I see thy power within thee *understands* the interpretation of the *mystery* of the *repentance* which the Pistis Sophia spoke. Now at this time do thou, Peter, speak the *thought* of her *repentance* in the midst of thy brethren."

Peter answered, *however*, he said to Jesus : "Lord, hear, so that I say the *thought* of her *repentance*, about which thy power once *prophesied* through David the *prophet*, saying her *repentance* in the 70th *Psalm* : |

1. ⲠⲚⲞⲨⲦⲈ ⲠⲀⲚⲞⲨⲦⲈ ⲀⲒ̈ⲚⲀ2ⲦⲈ ⲈⲢⲞⲔ · Ⲙ̄Ⲡ̄ⲢⲦⲢⲀⲬⲒ-
ⲰⲒⲠⲈ Ⲛ̄Ⲱ̅ⲀⲈⲚⲈ2 ·

2. ⲘⲀⲦⲞⲨⲬⲞⲒ̈ 2Ⲛ̅ ⲦⲈⲔⲆⲒⲔⲀⲒⲞⲤⲨⲚⲎ · ⲀⲨⲰ Ⲛ̄ⲄⲚⲀ2ⲘⲈⲦ ·
ⲢⲒⲔⲈ Ⲙ̄ⲠⲈⲔⲘⲀⲀⲬⲈ ⲈⲢⲞⲒ̈ Ⲛ̄ⲄⲦⲞⲨ*ⲬⲞⲒ̈ · ⲠⲈ ᵇ

5   3. ⲰⲰⲠⲈ ⲚⲀⲒ̈ ⲈⲨⲚⲞⲨⲦⲈ Ⲛ̄ⲚⲀⲰⲦⲈ · ⲀⲨⲰ ⲈⲨⲘⲀ ⲈϤ-
ⲦⲀⲬⲢⲎⲨ ⲈⲦⲞⲨⲬⲞⲒ̈ · ⲬⲈ Ⲛ̄ⲦⲞⲔ ⲠⲈ ⲠⲀⲦⲀⲬⲢⲞ · ⲀⲨⲰ
ⲠⲀⲘⲀⲚ̄ⲠⲰⲦ ·

4. ⲠⲀⲚⲞⲨⲦⲈ ⲘⲀⲦⲞⲨⲬⲞⲒ̈ ⲈⲦϬⲒⲬ Ⲙ̄ⲠⲢⲈϤⲢ̄ⲚⲞⲂⲈ · ⲀⲨⲰ
ⲈⲂⲞⲖ 2Ⲛ̅ ⲦϬⲒⲬ Ⲙ̄ⲠⲠⲀⲢⲀⲚⲞⲘⲞⲤ ⲘⲚ̅ ⲠⲀⲤⲈⲂⲎⲤ ·

10 5. ⲬⲈ Ⲛ̄ⲦⲞⲔ ⲠⲬⲞⲈⲒⲤ ⲠⲈ ⲦⲀ2ⲨⲠⲞⲘⲞⲚⲎ · ⲠⲬⲞⲈⲒⲤ
Ⲛ̄ⲦⲔ̄ ⲦⲀ2ⲈⲖⲠⲒⲤ ⲬⲒⲚ ⲦⲀⲘⲚ̄ⲦⲔⲞⲨⲒ̈ ·

6. ⲀⲒ̈ⲦⲀⲬⲢⲞⲒ̈ ⲈⲬⲰⲔ ⲬⲒⲚ Ⲛ̄ⲐⲎ Ⲛ̄ⲦⲞⲔ ⲀⲔⲚ̄Ⲧ ⲈⲂⲞⲖ Ⲛ̄-
2ⲎⲦⲤ̄ Ⲛ̄ⲦⲀⲘⲀⲀⲨ · ⲈⲢⲈ ⲠⲀⲢ̄ⲠⲘⲈⲈⲨⲈ Ⲛ̄2ⲎⲦⲔ̄ Ⲛ̄ⲞⲨⲞⲈⲒⲰ ⲚⲒⲘ ·

7. ⲀⲒ̈ⲰⲰⲠⲈ Ⲛ̄ⲐⲈ Ⲛ̄ⲚⲒⲤⲞϬ Ⲛ̄ⲞⲨⲘⲎⲎⲰⲈ · Ⲛ̄ⲦⲔ̄ ⲠⲀⲂⲞ-
15 ⲎⲐⲞⲤ · ⲀⲨⲰ ⲠⲀⲦⲀⲬⲢⲞ · Ⲛ̄ⲦⲔ̄ ⲠⲀⲤⲰⲦⲎⲢ ⲠⲬⲞⲈⲒⲤ ·

8. Ⲁ ⲦⲀⲦⲀⲠⲢⲞ ⲘⲞⲨ2 Ⲛ̄ⲤⲘⲞⲨ ⲬⲈⲔⲀⲤ ⲈⲒ̈ⲈⲤⲘⲞⲨ Ⲉ-
ⲠⲈⲞⲞⲨ Ⲛ̄ⲦⲈⲔⲘⲚ̄ⲦⲚⲞϬ Ⲙ̄ⲠⲈ2ⲞⲞⲨ ⲦⲎⲢϤ̄ ·

9. Ⲙ̄Ⲡ̄ⲢⲚⲞⲬ̄Ⲧ ⲈⲂⲞⲖ ⲈⲨⲞⲨⲞⲒ̈Ⲱ Ⲙ̄ⲘⲚ̄Ⲧ2ⲀⲖⲞ · 2Ⲙ̄ ⲠⲦⲢⲈ
ⲦⲀⲮⲨⲬⲎ ⲰⲬⲚ̄** Ⲙ̄Ⲡ̄ⲢⲔⲀⲀⲦ Ⲛ̄ⲤⲰⲔ · ⲚⲈ̅

20 10. ⲬⲈ Ⲁ ⲚⲀⲬⲒⲬⲈⲈⲨ ⲬⲈ-ⲠⲈⲐⲞⲞⲨ ⲈⲢⲞⲒ̈ · ⲀⲨⲰ ⲚⲈⲦ-
2ⲀⲢⲈ2 ⲈⲦⲀⲮⲨⲬⲎ · ⲀⲨⲬⲒⲰⲞⲬⲚⲈ ⲈⲦⲀⲮⲨⲬⲎ ·

11. ⲈⲨⲬⲰ Ⲙ̄ⲘⲞⲤ 2Ⲓ ⲞⲨⲤⲞⲠ · ⲬⲈ Ⲁ ⲠⲚⲞⲨⲦⲈ ⲔⲀⲀϤ
Ⲛ̄ⲤⲰϤ · ⲠⲰⲦ Ⲛ̄ⲦⲈⲦⲚ̄ⲦⲀ2ⲞϤ ⲬⲈ ⲘⲚ̄-ⲠⲈⲦⲚⲀⲚⲀ2ⲘⲈϤ ·

12. ⲠⲚⲞⲨⲦⲈ †2ⲦⲎⲔ ⲈⲦⲀⲂⲞⲎⲐⲒⲀ ·

25 13. ⲘⲀⲢⲞⲨⲬⲒⲰⲒⲠⲈ Ⲛ̄ⲤⲈⲰⲬⲚ̄ Ⲛ̄ϬⲒ ⲚⲈⲦⲆⲒⲀⲂⲀⲖⲈ Ⲛ̄ⲦⲀ-

---

7   MS ⲠⲀⲘⲀⲚ̄ⲠⲰⲦ; better ⲠⲀⲘⲀⲘ̄ⲠⲰⲦ.

1. 'O God, my God, I have trusted in thee; let me never be put to shame.

2. Save me in thy *righteousness* and deliver me. Incline thy ear to me and save me.

3. Be to me a strong God and a fortified place to save me; for thou art my strength and my place of refuge.

4. My God, save me from the hand of the sinner, and from the hand of the *lawless* and the *impious*.

5. For thou, O Lord, art my *endurance*; O Lord, thou art my *hope* from my youth.

6. I have relied upon thee from the womb; thou hast brought me forth from my mother's womb; my memory is of thee at all times.

7. I have become for many like the crazy; thou art my *help* and my strength, thou art my *Saviour*, O Lord.

8. My mouth has been filled with blessings, so that I might bless the glory of thy greatness all the day.

9. Cast me not out in the time of my old age; when my *soul* diminishes, do not forsake me.

10. For my enemies have spoken evil against me; and they who lie in wait for my *soul* have taken counsel against my *soul*.

11. Saying at the same time : God has forsaken him; run and seize him, for there is none to save him.

12. O God, give heed to my *help*.

13. Let those that *slander* my *soul* be brought to shame

ⲮⲨⲬⲏ· ⲘⲀⲢⲞⲨⳠⲞⲞⲖⲞⲨ ⲚⲞⲨϢⲒⲡⲉ ⲘⲚ ⲞⲨⲞⲨⲱⳠ ⲚϬⲒ
ⲚⲈⲦϢⲒⲚⲈ ⲚⳠⲀ ⳠⲈⲚⲡⲉⲞⲞⲞⲨ ⲈⲢⲞⲓ·

ⲡⲀⲓ Ϭⲉ ⲡⲉ ⲡⲂⲱⲖ ⲚⲦⲘⲉⳠⳠⲚⲦⲉ ⲘⲘⲉⲦⲀⲚⲞⲒⲀ ⲈⲚⲦ-
ⲀⳠⲬⲞⲞⳠ ⲚϬⲒ ⲦⲡⲒⳠⲦⲒⳠ ⳠⲟⲫⲒⲀ :

5   ⲀϤⲞⲨⲱϣⲂ ⲚϬⲒ ⲡⳠⲱⲦⲏⲢ ⲡⲉⲬⲀϤ ⲘⲡⲉⲦⲢⲞⳠ· Ⲭⲉ ⲔⲀ-
ⲖⲱⳠ ⲡⲉⲦⲢⲞⳠ ⲡⲀⲓ ⲡⲉ ⲡⲂⲱⲖ ⲚⲦⲉⳠⲘⲉⲦⲀⲚⲞⲒⲀ· ⲚⲦⲉⲦⲚ
ⳠⲉⲚⲘⲀⲔⲀⲢⲒⲞⳠ ⲚⲦⲱⲦⲚ ⲡⲀⲢⲀ ⲢⲱⲘⲉ ⲚⲒⲘ· ⲈⲦⳠⲒⲬⲘ ⲡⲔⲀⳠ·
Ⲭⲉ ⲀⲓⳠⲱⲖⲡ ⲈⲢⲱⲦⲚ ⲚⲚⲉⲓⲘⲨⳠⲦⲏⲢⲒⲞⲚ· ⳠⲀⲘⲎⲚ ⳠⲀⲘⲎⲚ ⲡⲉ ᵇ
ϯⲬⲱ ⲘⲘⲞⳠ ⲚⲎⲦⲚ Ⲭⲉ ϯⲚⲀⲬⲉⲔ-ⲦⲎⲨⲦⲚ ⲈⲂⲞⲖ ⲘⲡⲖⲏ-
10   ⲢⲱⲘⲀ ⲚⲒⲘ ⲬⲒⲚ ⲘⲘⲨⳠⲦⲏⲢⲒⲞⲚ ⲘⲡⳠⲀⳠⲞⲨⲚ ⳠⲉⲱⳠ ϣⲀ
ⲘⲘⲨⳠⲦⲏⲢⲒⲞⲚ ⲘⲡⳠⲀⲂⲂⲞⲖ· ⲀⲨⲱ ϯⲚⲀⲘⲉⳠⲦⲎⲨⲦⲚ ⲈⲂⲞⲖ
ⳠⲘ ⲡⲉⲡⲚⲀ· Ⲭⲉ ⲈⲨⲈⲘⲞⲨⲦⲉ ⲈⲢⲱⲦⲚ Ⲭⲉ ⲚⲉⲡⲚⲀⲦⲒⲔⲞⳠ
ⲈⲦⲬⲏⲔ ⲈⲂⲞⲖ ⲘⲡⲖⲏⲢⲱⲘⲀ ⲚⲒⲘ· ⲀⲨⲱ ⳠⲀⲘⲎⲚ ⳠⲀⲘⲎⲚ
ϯⲬⲱ ⲘⲘⲞⳠ ⲚⲎⲦⲚ Ⲭⲉ ϯⲚⲀϯ ⲚⲎⲦⲚ ⲚⲘⲘⲨⳠⲦⲏⲢⲒⲞⲚ
15   ⲦⲎⲢⲞⲨ ⲚⲦⲉ ⲚⲦⲞⲡⲞⳠ ⲦⲎⲢⲞⲨ ⲘⲡⲀⲉⲓⲱⲦ· ⲀⲨⲱ ⲚⲦⲉ
ⲚⲦⲞⲡⲞⳠ ⲦⲎⲢⲞⲨ ⲘⲡϣⲞⲢⲡ ⲘⲘⲨⳠⲦⲏⲢⲒⲞⲚ· ⲬⲉⲔⲀⳠ ⲡⲉ-
ⲦⲉⲦⲚⲀⲬⲒⲦϤ ⲈⳠⲞⲨⲚ ⳠⲒⲬⲘ ⲡⲔⲀⳠ ⲈⲨⲈⲬⲒⲦϤ ⲈⳠⲞⲨⲚ
ⲈⲡⲞⲨⲞⲉⲓⲚ ⲘⲡⲬⲒⳠⲉ· ⲀⲨⲱ ⲡⲉⲦⲉⲦⲚⲀⲚⲞⲬϤ ⲈⲂⲞⲖ ⳠⲒⲬⲘ
ⲡⲔⲀⳠ· ⳠⲉⲚⲀⲚⲟⲬϤ ⲈⲂⲞⲖ ⳠⲚ ⲦⲘⲚⲦⲉⲢⲟ ⲘⲡⲀⲓⲱⲦ ⲈⲦⳠⲚ
20   ⲘⲡⲏⲨⲉ· ⲡⲖⲎⲚ Ϭⲉ ⳠⲱⲦⲘ ⲀⲨⲱ ⲚⲦⲉⲦⲚⲬⲒⳠⲘⲎ ** ⲈⲚⲘⲉ- ⲡⳌ
ⲦⲀⲚⲞⲒⲀ ⲦⲎⲢⲞⲨ· ⲚⲀⲓ ⲈⲚⲦⲀⳠⲬⲞⲟⲨ ⲚϬⲒ ⲦⲡⲒⳠⲦⲒⳠ ⳠⲟⲫⲒⲀ·

⳧ ⲀⳠⲞⲨⲱⳠ ⲞⲚ ⲈⲦⲞⲟⲦⳠ ⲀⳠⲬⲱ ⲚⲦⲘⲉⳠϣⲞⲘⲦⲉ ⲘⲘⲉ-
ⲦⲀⲚⲞⲒⲀ ⲈⳠⲬⲱ ⲘⲘⲞⳠ Ⲭⲉ

ⲓ. ⲡⲞⲨⲞⲉⲓⲚ ⲚⲚϬⲞⲘ ϯⳠⲦⲏⲔ ⲀⲨⲱ ⲚⲅⲚⲞⲨⳠⲘ ⲘⲘⲞⲓ·
25   2. ⲘⲀⲢⲞⲨϣⲱⲱⲦ ⲀⲨⲱ ⲚⳠⲉϣⲱⲡⲉ ⳠⲘ ⲡⲔⲀⲔⲉ ⲚϬⲒ
ⲚⲀⲓ ⲈⲦⲞⲨⲉϣϤⲒ ⲘⲡⲀⲟⲨⲟⲉⲓⲚ ⲚⳠⲏⲦ· ⲘⲀⲢⲞⲨⲔⲞⲦⲞⲨ

---

7 MS ⲡⲀⲢⲀⲢⲀ.

and diminished; | let those who seek evil against me be clothed with shame and disgrace.' *

This now is the interpretation of the second *repentance* which the Pistis Sophia said."

37. The *Saviour* answered and said to Peter : "*Well done*, Peter, this is the interpretation of her *repentance*. You are *blessed byond* all men upon earth, for I have revealed to you these *mysteries*. *Truly, truly*, I say to you : I will fulfill you in every *pleroma*, from the *mysteries* of the inner *to* the *mysteries* of the *outer*. And I will fill you with *Spirit* so that you are called *Pneumatics*, fulfilled in every *pleroma*. And *truly, truly*, I say to you that I will give you all the *mysteries* of all the *places* of my Father, and all the *places* of the First *Mystery*, so that he whom you receive on earth will be received into the light of the height. And he whom you cast out upon earth will be cast out of the Kingdom of my Father which is in heaven □. *Nevertheless* now hear and give ear to all the *repentances* which the Pistis Sophia said. She continued again and spoke the third *repentance*, saying :

1. 'O Light of the powers, give heed and save me.

2. May those that want to take away my light from me fail and be in darkness. Let them return | to the *Chaos*,

---

*   cf. Ps. 70.1-13
□   cf. Mt. 16.19; 18.18

ЄΠЄΧΛΟϹ · ΛΥШ ⲚϹЄΧΙϢΠЄ Ⲛ6Ι ΝЄΤΟΥЄϢϤΙ Ⲛ̄ΤΛ-
6ΟΜ ·

3. ΜΛΡΟΥΚΟΤΟΥ ЄΠΚΛΚЄ Ⲍ̄Ν ΟΥ6ЄΠΗ Ⲛ̄6Ι ΝΛΪ ЄΤ-
ⲌШΧ Ⲙ̄ΜΟΪ ЄΤΧШ Ⲙ̄ΜΟϹ ΧЄ ΛΝⲢ̄ΧΟЄΙϹ Є2ΡΛΪ ЄΧШϹ ·

4. ΜΛΡΟΥΡΛϢЄ Ⲛ̄ΤΟϤ · ΛΥШ ⲚϹЄΟΥΡΟΤ Ⲛ̄6Ι ΟΥΟΝ
ΝΙΜ ЄΤϢΙΝЄ Ⲛ̄ϹΛ ΠΟΥΟЄΙΝ · ΛΥШ ΜΛΡΟΥΧΟΟϹ Ⲛ̄ΟΥ-
ΟЄΙϢ ΝΙΜ · ΧЄ ΜΛΡЄϤΧΙϹЄ Ⲛ̄6Ι ΠΜΥϹΤΗΡΙΟΝ Ⲛ̄6Ι ΝЄΤ-
ΟΥЄϢ-ΠЄΚΜΥϹΤΗΡΙΟΝ ·

5. ΛΝΟΚ 6Є ΤЄΝΟΥ ΠΟΥΟΪΝ ΝΟΥⲌ̄Μ Ⲙ̄ΜΟΪ · ΧЄ
ΛΪϢШϢΤ Ⲙ̄ΠΛΟΥΟЄΙΝ Ⲛ̄ΤΛΥϤΙΤϤ · ΛΥШ †Ρ̄*ΧΡΙΛ Ⲛ̄ΤΛ-
6ΟΜ ЄΝΤΛΥϤΙΤ̄Ϲ Ⲛ̄ΤΟΟΤ · Ⲛ̄ΤΟΚ 6Є ΠΟΥΟЄΙΝ Ⲛ̄ΤΟΚ
ΠЄ ΠΛϹШΤΗΡ ΛΥШ Ⲛ̄ΤΟΚ ΠЄ ΠΛΡЄϤΝΟΥⲌ̄Μ ΠΟΥΟΪΝ ·
6ЄΠΗ Ⲛ̄ΓΝΛⲌΜЄΤ ЄΒΟΛ Ⲍ̄Μ ΠЄΪΧΛΟϹ ·

Ⲍ ΛϹϢШΠЄ ΔЄ Ⲛ̄ΤЄΡЄ ῙϹ ΟΥШ ЄϤΧШ Ⲛ̄ΝЄΪϢΛΧЄ
ЄΝЄϤΜΛΘΗΤΗϹ ЄϤΧШ Ⲙ̄ΜΟϹ ΧЄ ΤΛΪ ΤЄ ΤΜЄ2ϢΟΜΤЄ
Ⲙ̄ΜЄΤΛΝΟΙΛ ЄΝΤΛϹΧΟΟϹ Ⲛ̄6Ι ΤΠΙϹΤΙϹ ϹΟΦΙΛ · ΠЄΧΛϤ
ΝΛΥ ΧЄ ΠЄΝΤΛϤΧΙϹЄ Ⲛ̄2ΗΤϤ Ⲛ̄6Ι ΠЄΠⲚ̄Λ Ⲛ̄ΛΙϹΘΗ-
ΤΙΚΟΝ · ΜΛΡЄϤЄΙ' ЄΘΗ Ⲛ̄ϤΧШ Ⲙ̄ΠΝΟΗΜΛ Ⲛ̄ΤΜЄΤΛΝΟΙΛ
ЄΝΤΛϹΧΟΟϤ Ⲛ̄6Ι ΤΠΙϹΤΙϹ ϹΟΦΙΛ ·

Ⲍ ΛϹϢШΠЄ 6Є ЄΜΠΛΤϤΟΥШ ЄϤϢΛΧЄ Ⲛ̄6Ι ῙϹ · ΛϹЄΙ'
ЄΘΗ Ⲛ̄6Ι ΜΛΡΘΛ ΛϹΠΛⲌΤ̄Ϲ ЄΧ̄Ν ΝЄϤΟΥЄΡΗΤЄ ΛϹ†ΠΙ
ЄΡΟΟΥ · ΛϹШϢ ЄΒΟΛ ΛϹΡΙΜЄ Ⲍ̄Ν ΟΥΛϢΚΛΚ · ΛΥШ Ⲍ̄Ν
ΟΥⲐ̄ΒΒΙΟ · ЄϹΧШ Ⲙ̄ΜΟϹ ΧЄ ΠΛΧΟΪϹ ΝΛ' ΝΛΪ · ΛΥШ
Ⲛ̄ΓϢⲚ2ΤΗΚ 2ΛΡΟΪ · ΛΥШ Ⲛ̄ΓΚΛΛΤ ΤΛΧШ Ⲙ̄ΠΒШΛ Ⲛ̄ΤΜЄ-
ΤΛΝΟΙΛ ЄΝΤΛϹΧΟΟϹ Ⲛ̄6Ι ΤΠΙϹΤΙϹ ϹΟΦΙΛ :

and may those who want to take away my power be put to shame.

3. May those that persecute me and say : we have become lords over her, return quickly to the darkness.

4. May all those who seek after the light rejoice and flourish; and may they who want thy *mystery* say at all times : let the *mystery* be raised up.

5. Do thou now at this time save me, O Light, for I am lacking in my light, which has been taken away. And I *need* my power which has been taken from me. Thou, O Light, thou art my *Saviour*, and thou art my rescuer, O Light. Save me quickly out of this *Chaos*'."

38. It happened, *however*, when Jesus finished saying these words to his *disciples*, saying : "This is the third *repentance* which the Pistis Sophia said", he said to them : "Let him in whom the *Spirit* of *perception* has arisen, come forward and speak with *understanding* of the *repentance* which the Pistis Sophia said".

It happened now, before Jesus had finished speaking, Martha [1] came forward, she prostrated herself at his feet, she kissed them. She cried out, she wept aloud in humility, saying : "My Lord, have mercy on me, and be compassionate towards me, and allow me to say the interpretation of the *repentance* which the Pistis Sophia said". |

---

[1]   (21) Martha; see Origen *c.Cels.* V.62.

ⳅ ⲀⲨⲰ Ⲁ ⲓ̅ⲥ̅ ⲦⲦⲞⲞⲦⲤ̅ ⲘⲘⲀⲢⲐⲀ ⲠⲈⲬⲀⳋ ⲚⲀⲤ· ⲬⲈ
ⲞⲨⲘⲀⲔⲀⲢⲒⲞⲤ ⲠⲈ ⲢⲰⲘⲈ ⲚⲒⲘ ⲈϢⲀⳋⲐⲂⲂⲒⲞⳋ· ⲬⲈ Ⲛ̅ⲦⲞⳋ
ⲠⲈ ⲈⲦⲞⲨⲚⲀⲚⲀ' ⲚⲀⳋ· ⲦⲈⲚⲞⲨ ϬⲈ ⲘⲀⲢⲐⲀ Ⲛ̅ⲦⲈ ⲞⲨⲘⲀ-
ⲔⲀⲢⲒⲞⲤ· ⲠⲖⲎⲚ ϬⲈ ⲦⲀⲨⲈ-ⲠⲂⲰⲖ Ⲙ̅ⲠⲚⲞⲎⲘⲀ Ⲛ̅ⲦⲘⲈⲦⲀ-
5 ⲚⲞⲒⲀ Ⲛ̅ⲦⲠⲒⲤⲦⲒⲤ ⲤⲞⲪⲒⲀ· ⲀⲤⲞⲨⲰϢⲂ̅ ⲆⲈ Ⲛ̅ϬⲒ ⲘⲀⲢⲐⲀ
ⲠⲈⲬⲀⲤ Ⲛ̅ⲒⲤ̅ Ⲥ̅Ⲛ̅ ⲦⲘⲎⲦⲈ Ⲛ̅ⲘⲘⲀⲐⲎⲦⲎⲤ ⲬⲈ ⲈⲦⲂⲈ ⲦⲘⲈ-
ⲦⲀⲚⲞⲒⲀ ⲈⲚⲦⲀⲤⲬⲞⲞⲤ Ⲱ' ⲠⲀⲬⲞⲈⲒⲤ ⲒⲤ̅ Ⲛ̅ϬⲒ ⲦⲠⲒⲤⲦⲒⲤ
ⲤⲞⲪⲒⲀ· Ⲛ̅ⲦⲀⲤⲠⲢⲞⲪⲎⲦⲈⲨⲈ Ⲥ̅ⲀⲢⲞⲤ Ⲙ̅ⲠⲒⲞⲨⲞⲈⲒϢ Ⲛ̅ϬⲒ
ⲦⲈⲔϬⲞⲘ Ⲛ̅ⲞⲨⲞⲈⲒⲚ ⲈⲦⲤ̅Ⲛ̅ ⲆⲀⲨⲒ̈Ⲁ Ⲥ̅Ⲙ̅ ⲠⲘⲈⲤⲤⲈⲮⲒⲤ Ⲛ̅-
10 ⲮⲀⲖⲘⲞⲤ· ⲈⳋⲬⲰ Ⲙ̅ⲘⲞⲤ ⲬⲈ

1. ⲠⲬⲞⲈⲒⲤ ⲠⲚⲞⲨⲦⲈ ⲦⲤ̅ⲦⲎⲔ ⲈⲦⲀⲂⲞⲎⲐⲒⲀ·

2. ⲘⲀⲢⲞⲨⳋⲬⲒϢⲒⲠⲈ Ⲛ̅ⲤⲈⲞⲨⲰⲤ̅ Ⲛ̅ϬⲒ ⲚⲈⲦϢⲒⲚⲈ Ⲛ̅ⲤⲀ ⲧⲏⲓ
ⲦⲀⲮⲨⲬⲎ·

3. ⲘⲀⲢⲞⲨⲔⲞⲦⲞⲨ Ⲛ̅ⲦⲈⲨⲚⲞⲨ Ⲛ̅ⲤⲈⲬⲒϢⲒⲠⲈ Ⲛ̅ϬⲒ ⲚⲈⲦ-
15 ⲬⲰ Ⲙ̅ⲘⲞⲤ ⲚⲀⲒ̈ ⲬⲈ ⲈⲨⲄⲈ ⲈⲨⲄⲈ·

4. ⲘⲀⲢⲞⲨⲦⲈⲖⲎⲖ Ⲛ̅ⲤⲈⲞⲨⲚⲞⳋ ⲈⲬⲰⲔ Ⲛ̅ϬⲒ ⲞⲨⲞⲚ ⲚⲒⲘ
ⲈⲦϢⲒⲚⲈ Ⲛ̅ⲤⲰⲔ· Ⲛ̅ⲤⲈⲬⲞⲞⲤ Ⲛ̅ⲞⲨⲞⲈⲒϢ ⲚⲒⲘ ⲬⲈ ⲘⲀⲢⲈ
ⲠⲚⲞⲨⲦⲈ ⲬⲒⲤⲈ Ⲛ̅ϬⲒ ⲚⲈⲦⲘⲈ Ⲙ̅ⲠⲈⲔⲞⲨⲬⲀⲒ̈·

5. ⲀⲚⲞⲔ ⲆⲈ ⲀⲚⲄ̅ ⲞⲨⲤ̅ⲎⲔⲈ ⲀⲚⲄ̅ ⲞⲨⲈⲂⲒⲎⲚ ⲠⲬⲞⲈⲒⲤ
20 ⲂⲞⲎⲐⲒ ⲈⲢⲞⲒ̈· Ⲛ̅ⲦⲔ̅ ⲠⲀⲂⲞⲎⲐⲞⲤ· ⲀⲨⲰ ⲦⲀⲚⲀϢⲦⲈ ⲠⲬⲞⲒ̈Ⲥ
Ⲙ̅Ⲡ̅Ⲣ̅ⲰⲤⲔ̅·

ⲠⲀⲒ̈ ϬⲈ ⲠⲈ ⲠⲂⲰⲖ Ⲛ̅ⲦⲘⲈⲤ̅ϢⲞⲘⲦⲈ Ⲙ̅ⲘⲈⲦⲀⲚⲞⲒⲀ ⲈⲚⲦ-
ⲀⲤⲬⲞⲞⲤ Ⲛ̅ϬⲒ ⲦⲠⲒⲤⲦⲒⲤ ⲤⲞⲪⲒⲀ ⲈⲤⲤ̅ⲨⲘⲚⲈⲨⲈ ⲈⲠⲬⲒⲤⲈ·

ⳅ ⲀⲤϢⲰⲠⲈ ϬⲈ Ⲛ̅ⲦⲈⲢⲈ ⲒⲤ̅ ⲤⲰⲦ̅Ⲙ̅ ⲈⲘⲀⲢⲐⲀ ⲈⲤⲬⲰ
25 Ⲛ̅ⲚⲈⲒ̈ϢⲀⲬⲈ· ⲠⲈⲬⲀⳋ ⲬⲈ ⲈⲨⲄⲈ ⲘⲀⲢⲐⲀ· ⲀⲨⲰ ⲔⲀⲖⲰⲤ·
ⲀⳋⲞⲨⲰⲤ̅ ⲞⲚ ⲈⲦⲞⲞⲦ̅ⳋ Ⲛ̅ϬⲒ ⲒⲤ̅ Ⲥ̅Ⲙ̅ ⲠϢⲀⲬⲈ ⲠⲈⲬⲀⳋ Ⲛ̅ⲚⲈⳋ- ⲡ̅Ⲅ̅

124

And Jesus gave Martha his hand [1], he said to her : "*Blessed is every man who humbles himself, for to him will mercy be given* *. Now at this time, Martha, thou art *blessed. Nevertheless* give now the interpretation of the *thought* of the *repentance* of the Pistis Sophia".

Martha, *however*, answered and said to Jesus in the midst of the *disciples* : "Concerning the *repentance* which the Pistis Sophia said, *O* my Lord Jesus, thy light-power which was in David once *prophesied* in the 69th *Psalm*, saying :

1. 'O Lord God, give heed to my *help*.

2. Let those that seek after my *soul* be put to shame and disgraced.

3. May those that say to me : *excellent, excellent*, be turned back immediately and put to shame.

4. May all those that seek after thee be glad and rejoice over thee; and may those that love thy salvation say at all times : let God be exalted.

5. *But* I am poor and I am needy. O Lord, *help* me; thou art my *help* and my defence. O Lord, do not delay.' □

This now is the interpretation of the third *repentance* which the Pistis Sophia said, *singing praises* to the height."

39. It happened now when Jesus heard Martha saying these words, he said : "*Excellent*, Martha, and *well done*."

Jesus continued again with the discourse. He said to his |

---

*   cf. Mt. 5.3-7
□   cf. Ps. 69.1-5

---

[1]   (1) gave Martha his hand; Till : helped Martha.

ΜΑΘΗΤΗС · ΧΕ ΑСΟΥШ2 ΟΝ ΕΤΟΟΤС Ν̄ϬΙ ΤΠΙСΤΙС
СΟΦΙΑ 2Ν̄ ΤΜΕ2ϤΤΟ Μ̄ΜΕΤΑΝΟΙΑ ΕСΧШ Μ̄ΜΟС ΕΜ-
ΠΑΤΟΥΘΛΙΒΕ Μ̄ΜΟС Μ̄ΠΜΕ2СΟΠ СΝΑΥ ΕΤΡΕΥϤΙ Μ̄ΠΕС-
ΚΕΟΥΟΕΙΝ ΤΗΡϤ ΕΤΝ̄2ΗΤС Ν̄ϬΙ ϯϬΟΜ Ν̄2Ο Μ̄ΜΟΥΪ ΜΝ̄
5 ΝΕΠΡΟΒΟΛΟΟΥΕ ΤΗΡΟΥ Ν̄2ΥΛΙΚΟΝ ΕΤΝΜ̄ΜΑС · ΝΑΪ
ΕΝΤΑ ΠΑΥΘΑΔΗС ΧΟΟΥСΟΥ ΕΠΕΧΛΟС · ΑСΧШ ϬΕ
Ν̄ΤΕΪΜΕΤΑΝΟΙΑ Ν̄ΤΕΪ2Ε · ΧΕ

1. ΠΟΥΟΕΙΝ ΕΝΤΑΪΝΑ2ΤΕ ΕΡΟϤ СШΤΜ̄ ΕΤΑΜΕΤΑ-
ΝΟΙΑ · ΑΥШ ΜΑΡΕ ΠΑ2ΡΟΟΥ ΕΙ' Ε2ΟΥΝ ΕΠΕΚΜΑΝ̄-
10 ШΠΕ ·

2. Μ̄ΠΡ̄ΚШΤΕ Ν̄ΤΕΚ2ΙΚШΝ Ν̄ΟΥΟΪΝ Ν̄САΒΟΛ Μ̄ΜΟΪ ·
ΑΛΛΑ ϯ2ΤΗΚ ΕΡΟΪ · ΕΥШΑΝ2ШΧ Μ̄ΜΟΪ · ϬΕΠΗ ΝΑ2ΜΕΤ ·
Μ̄ΠΕΟΥΟΕΙШ ΕϯΝΑШШ Ε2ΡΑΪ ΟΥΝΚ ·

3. ΧΕ Α ΠΑΟΥΟΕΙШ ШΧΝ̄ ΝΘΕ Ν̄ΟΥΝΙϤ · ΑΥШ ΑΪ- n̄o ᵇ
15 ШΠΕ Ν̄2ΥΛΗ ·

4. ΑΥϤΙ-ΠΑΟΥΟΕΙΝ Ν̄2ΗΤ · ΑΥШ Α ΤΑϬΟΜ ШΟΟΥΕ
ΑΪΡ̄-ΠШΒШ Μ̄ΠΑΜΥСΤΗΡΙΟΝ ΠΑΪ ΕΝΕШΑΪΛΑϤ Ν̄ШΟΡΠ̄ ·

5. ΕΒΟΛ Μ̄ΠΕ2ΡΟΟΥ Ν̄2ΟΤΕ ΜΝ̄ ΤϬΟΜ Μ̄ΠΑΥΘΑΔΗС
Α ΤΑϬΟΜ ШΧΝ̄ 2ΡΑΪ Ν̄2ΗΤ ·

20 6. ΑΪШШΠΕ Ν̄ΘΕ Ν̄ΟΥ2ΙΔΙΟС Ν̄ΔΑΙΜШΝ ΕϤΟΥΗ2 2Ν̄
ΟΥ2ΥΛΗ ΕΜΝ̄-ΟΥΟΪΝ Ν̄2ΗΤϤ · ΑΥШ ΑΪШШΠΕ Ν̄ΘΕ Ν̄ΟΥ-
ΑΝΤΙΜΙΜΟΝ Μ̄ΠΝ̄Α ΕϤ2Ν̄ ΟΥСШΜΑ Ν̄2ΥΛΙΚΟΝ ΕΜΝ̄-ϬΟΜ
Ν̄ΟΥΟΕΙΝ Ν̄2ΗΤϤ ·

7. ΑΥШ ΑΪШШΠΕ ΝΘΕ Ν̄ΟΥΔΕΚΑΝΟС ΕϤ2ΙΧΜ̄ ΠΑΗΡ
25 ΜΑΥΑΑϤ ·

---

13   MS ΟΥΗΚ; archaic form of ΟΥΒΗΚ.

disciples: "The Pistis Sophia continued again with the fourth *repentance*, saying it when the lion-faced power and all the *material emanations* with it, which the Authades had sent to the *Chaos*, had not yet *afflicted* her for the second time, to take away all the remaining light which was in her. She now said this *repentance* thus:

1. 'O Light whom I have trusted, hear my *repentance*; and let my voice come into thy dwelling-place.

2. Do not turn thy *image* of light away from me, *but* give heed to me. If they oppress me, save me quickly at the time when I cry to thee.

3. For my time [1] has vanished like a breath, and I have become *matter*.

4. My light has been taken from me, and my power has dried up. I have forgotten my *mystery* which I performed at first.

5. Through the voice of fear and the power of the Authades, my power has diminished within me.

6. I have become like a *peculiar demon*, which dwells in *matter*, in whom is no light. And I have become like a *spirit counterpart* [2] which is in a *material body*, in which there is no light-power.

7. And I have become like a *decan*, which is upon the *air* alone. |

---

[1] (14) my time; Till: (probably) my light.

[2] (22) spirit counterpart; perhaps counterfeit spirit; see ApJn 71.2-75.10; Böhlig (Bibl. 8), pp. 162-74; Bousset (Bibl. 10), p. 366 ff.; on Coptic translation of ἀντίμιμον, see ApJn(II) 21.9; 26.27 etc. (cf. 281.24).

8. ⲀⲨⲐⲖⲒⲂⲈ ⲘⲘⲞⲒ ⲈⲘⲀⲦⲈ ⲚϬⲒ ⲚⲈⲠⲢⲞⲂⲞⲖⲞⲞⲨⲈ Ⲙ-
ⲠⲀⲨⲐⲀⲆⲎⲤ · ⲀⲨⲰ ⲚⲈⲀϤϪⲞⲞⲤ ⲠⲈ ϨⲢⲀⲒ ⲚϨⲎⲦϤ ⲚϬⲒ
ⲠⲀⲤⲨⲚⲌⲨⲅⲞⲤ ·

9. ϪⲈ ⲈⲠⲘⲀ ⲘⲠⲞⲨⲞⲈⲒⲚ ⲈⲦⲚϨⲎⲦⲤ · ⲀⲨⲘⲀϨⲤ ⲚⲬⲖⲞⲤ
5 ⲀⲒⲰⲘⲔ ⲚⲦϤⲰⲦⲈ ⲚⲦⲀϨⲨⲖⲎ ⲘⲘⲒⲚ ⲘⲘⲞⲒ ⲀⲨⲰ ⲘⲚ ⲪⲰϢ ⳨
ⲚⲘⲘⲞⲨⲈⲒⲞⲞⲨⲈ ⲚⲐⲨⲖⲎ ⲚⲚⲀⲂⲀⲖ · ϪⲈ ⲚⲚⲈⲨϤⲒ-ⲚⲈⲒⲔⲞ-
ⲞⲨⲈ ⲚϬⲒ ⲚⲈⲦϨⲰϪ ⲘⲘⲞⲒ ·

10. ⲚⲀⲒ ⲦⲎⲢⲞⲨ ⲠⲞⲨⲞⲒⲚ ⲚⲦⲀⲨϢⲰⲠⲈ ⲘⲘⲞⲒ ⲈⲂⲞⲖ
ϨⲒⲦⲘ ⲠⲈⲔⲦⲰϢ · ⲀⲨⲰ ⲘⲚ ⲠⲈⲔⲞⲨⲈϨⲤⲀϨⲚⲈ · ⲀⲨⲰ ⲠⲈⲔ-
10 ⲦⲰϢ ⲠⲈ ⲈⲦⲢⲀϢⲰⲠⲈ ϨⲚ ⲚⲀⲒ ·

11. Ⲁ ⲠⲈⲔⲦⲰϢ ⲚⲦ ⲈⲠⲈⲤⲎⲦ · ⲀⲨⲰ ⲀⲒⲈⲒ ⲈⲠⲈⲤⲎⲦ ·
ⲚⲐⲈ ⲚⲞⲨϬⲞⲘ ⲚⲦⲈ ⲠⲈⲬⲖⲞⲤ · ⲀⲨⲰ Ⲁ ⲦⲀϬⲞⲘ ⲰϬⲢ ϨⲢⲀⲒ
ⲚϨⲎⲦ ·

12. ⲚⲦⲞⲔ ⲆⲈ ⲠϪⲞⲈⲒⲤ ⲚⲦⲔ ⲞⲨⲞⲈⲒⲚ ⲚϢⲀⲈⲚⲈϨ · ⲀⲨⲰ
15 ϢⲀⲔϬⲘ-ⲠϢⲒⲚⲈ ⲚⲚⲈⲦϨⲎϪ ⲚⲞⲨⲞⲒϢ ⲚⲒⲘ ·

13. ⲦⲈⲚⲞⲨ ϬⲈ ⲠⲞⲨⲞⲒⲚ ⲦⲰⲞⲨⲚ ⲚⲄϢⲒⲚⲈ ⲚⲤⲀ ⲦⲀ-
ϬⲞⲘ ⲘⲚ ⲦⲈⲮⲨⲬⲎ ⲈⲦⲚϨⲎⲦ · ⲀϤϪⲰⲔ ⲈⲂⲞⲖ ⲚϬⲒ ⲠⲈⲔ-
ⲦⲰϢ ⲈⲚⲦⲀⲔⲦⲞϢϤ ⲈⲢⲞⲒ ϨⲚ ⲚⲀⲐⲖⲒⲮⲒⲤ · Ⲁ ⲠⲀⲞⲨⲞⲈⲒϢ
ϢⲰⲠⲈ ⲈⲦⲢⲈⲔϢⲒⲚⲈ ⲚⲤⲀ ⲦⲀϬⲞⲘ ⲘⲚ ⲦⲀⲮⲨⲬⲎ ⲀⲨⲰ
20 ⲠⲀⲒ ⲠⲈ ⲠⲈⲞⲨⲞⲈⲒϢ ⲈⲚⲦⲀⲔⲦⲞϢϤ ⲈϢⲒⲚⲈ ⲚⲤⲰⲒ · ⳨ ᵇ

14. ϪⲈ Ⲁ ⲚⲈⲔⲢⲈϤⲤⲰⲦⲈ ϢⲒⲚⲈ ⲚⲤⲀ ⲦϬⲞⲘ ⲈⲦϨⲚ ⲦⲀ-
ⲮⲨⲬⲎ ϪⲈ ⲀϤϪⲰⲔ ⲈⲂⲞⲖ ⲚϬⲒ ⲠⲀⲢⲒⲐⲘⲞⲤ ⲀⲨⲰ ⲈⲦⲢⲈⲨ-
ⲚⲞⲨϨⲘ ⲚⲦⲈⲤⲔⲈϨⲨⲖⲎ ·

15. ⲀⲨⲰ ⲦⲞⲦⲈ ⲘⲠⲈⲞⲨⲞⲈⲒϢ ⲈⲦⲘⲘⲀⲨ ⲚⲀⲢⲬⲰⲚ ⲦⲎ-
25 ⲢⲞⲨ ⲚⲚⲀⲒⲰⲚ ⲚϨⲨⲖⲒⲔⲞⲚ · ⲤⲈⲚⲀⲢϨⲞⲦⲈ ϨⲎⲦϤ ⲘⲠⲈⲔⲞⲨ-

---

5 Ⲭ almost erased in upper right-hand margin at end of quire.

8. The *emanations* of the Authades have *afflicted* me greatly; and my *partner* has spoken of it thus :[1] in place of the light within her, they have filled her with *Chaos*[2].

9. I have swallowed the sweat of my *matter* myself and the anguish of the tears of the *matter* of my eyes, lest those that oppress me take away these things also.

10. All these things have happened to me, O Light, through thy ordinance and with thy command. And it is thy ordinance that I should be among these things.

11. Thy ordinance has brought me down, and I have come down like a power of the *Chaos*; and my power has congealed within me.

12. *But* thou, O Lord, art eternal light; and at all times thou dost seek those who are oppressed.

13. Now at this time, O Light, arise and seek after my power and my *soul* within me. Thy ordinance is completed, which thou hast ordained for me in my *affliction*. My time has come, that thou shouldst seek after my power and my *soul*, and this is the time which thou hast ordained to seek me;

14. For thy saviours have sought after the power which is in my *soul*, because the *number* is completed, and that they should save its *matter* also.

15. And *then* in that time all the *archons* of the *material aeons* will fear before thy light; | and all the *emanations*

---

[1] (2) thus; lit. within himself.
[2] (3, 4) Till emends Schmidt's division of verses 8, 9.

ΟΕΙΝ · ΑΥⲰ ΝΕΠΡΟΒΟⲖΟΟΥΕ ΤΗΡΟΥ Ⲙ̄ΠΜΕϨⲘⲚⲦ-
ϢΟⲘⲦΕ Ⲛ̄Ⲛ̄ΑΙⲰΝ Ⲛ̄ϨΥⲖΙΚΟΝ ⲤΕΝΑⲢ̄ϨΟΤΕ ϨΗⲦϤ̄ Ⲙ̄Π-
ⲘΥⲤΤΗΡΙΟΝ Ⲛ̄ΤΕ ΠΕΚΟΥΟΕΙΝ ΕΤΡΕ Ⲛ̄ΚΟΟΥΕ ✝ ϨΙϢΟΥ
Ⲙ̄ΠⲤⲰⲦϤ̄ Ⲙ̄ΠΕΥΟΥΟΕΙΝ ·

5   16. ϪΕ ΠϪΟΕΙⲤ ΝΑϢΙΝΕ Ⲛ̄ⲤΑ ⲦϬΟⲘ Ⲛ̄ΤΕⲦⲘ̄ΨΥⲬΗ ·
ΑϤΟΥⲰⲚϨ ΕΒΟⲖ Ⲙ̄ΠΕϤⲘΥⲤΤΗΡΙΟΝ ·

     17. ϪΕ ΕϤΝΑϬⲰϢⲦ ΕⲦⲘΕΤΑΝΟΙΑ Ⲛ̄ΤΕ ΝΕΤϢΟΟΠ
ϨⲚ̄ Ⲛ̄ΤΟΠΟⲤ Ⲙ̄ΠΕⲤΗⲦ · ΑΥⲰ Ⲙ̄ΠⲔ̄ⲔⲰ Ⲛ̄ⲤⲰϤ Ⲛ̄ΤΕΥⲘΕ-
ΤΑΝΟΙΑ ·

10   18. ΠΑⲒ̈ ϬΕ ΠΕ ΠⲘΥⲤΤΗΡΙΟΝ ΕⲦⲘ̄ⲘΑΥ ⁺⁺ΠΑⲒ̈ ΕΝΤΑϤ- $\overline{\underset{\underline{3\overline{\Lambda}}}{}}$
ϢⲰΠΕ Ⲛ̄ΤΥΠΟⲤ ΕⲦΒΕ ΠΓΕΝΟⲤ ΕΤΟΥΝΑϪΠΟϤ · ΑΥⲰ
ΠΓΕΝΟⲤ ΕΤΟΥΝΑϪΠΟϤ ΝΑϨΥⲘΝΕΥΕ ΕΠϪΙⲤΕ ·

     19. ϪΕ Α ΠΟΥΟΕΙΝ ϬⲰϢⲦ ΕΒΟⲖ ϨⲘ̄ ΠϪΙⲤΕ Ⲙ̄ΠΕϤ-
ΟΥΟΕΙΝ · ϤΝΑϬⲰϢⲦ ΕϨΡΑⲒ̈ ΕϪⲚ̄ ΘΥⲖΗ ΤΗΡⲤ̄ ·

15   20. ΕⲤⲰⲦⲘ̄ ΕΠΑϢϨⲞⲘ Ⲛ̄ΝΕⲦⲘΗΡ · ΕΒⲰⲖ ΕΒΟⲖ Ⲛ̄-
ⲦϬΟⲘ Ⲛ̄ΝΕΨΥⲬΟΟΥΕ ΝΕΝΤΑΥⲘΟΥΡ Ⲛ̄ΤΕΥϬΟⲘ ·

     21. ΕΤΡΕϤⲔⲰ Ⲙ̄ΠΕϤΡΑΝ ϨⲚ̄ ΤΕΨΥⲬΗ · ΑΥⲰ ΠΕϤⲘΥⲤ-
ΤΗΡΙΟΝ ϨΡΑⲒ̈ ϨⲚ̄ ⲦϬΟⲘ ·

     ς ΑⲤϢⲰΠΕ ΔΕ ΕΡΕ Ⲓ̄Ⲥ̄ ϪⲰ Ⲛ̄ΝΕΕΙϢΑϪΕ ΕΝΕϤⲘΑ-
20 ΘΗΤΗⲤ ΕϤϪⲰ Ⲙ̄ⲘΟⲤ ΝΑΥ ϪΕ ΤΑⲒ̈ ΤΕ ΤⲘΕϨⲦΟ Ⲙ̄ⲘΕ-
ΤΑΝΟΙΑ · ΕΝΤΑⲤϪΟΟⲤ Ⲛ̄ϬΙ ΤΠΙⲤΤΙⲤ ⲤΟΦΙΑ · ⲦΕΝΟΥ
ϬΕ ΠΕΤΝΟⲒ̈ · ⲘΑΡΕϤΝΟⲒ̈ · ΑⲤϢⲰΠΕ ϬΕ Ⲛ̄ΤΕΡΕ Ⲓ̄Ⲥ̄ ϪⲰ
Ⲛ̄ΝΕⲒ̈ϢΑϪΕ · ΑϤΕⲒ' ΕΘΗ Ⲛ̄ϬΙ Ⲓ̈ⲰϨΑΝΝΗⲤ ΑϤΟΥⲰϢⲦ
ΕⲦⲘΕⲤⲦⲚ̄ϨΗⲦ Ⲛ̄Ⲓ̄Ⲥ̄ ΠΕϪΑϤ ϪΕ ΠΑϪΟΕΙⲤ · ⲔΕⲖΕΥΕ ΝΑⲒ̈
25 ϨⲰ ΑΥⲰ ⲤΥΓⲬⲰΡΕΙ ΝΑⲒ̈ ΕΤΡΑϪⲰ Ⲙ̄ΠΒⲰⲖ Ⲛ̄ΤⲘΕϨⲦΟ

---

10   Ⲉ̄ in upper left-hand margin at beginning of quire.
16   MS ΝΕΝΤΑΥⲘΟΥΡ; better Ⲡ̄ΝΕΝΤΑΥⲘΟΥΡ.
23   first Ⲛ in Ⲓ̈ⲰϨΑΝΝΗⲤ inserted above.

of the thirteenth *material aeon* will fear before the *mystery* of thy light, that the others may put on themselves what is purified of their light.

16. For the Lord will seek after the power of your *souls*; he has revealed his *mystery*.

17. For he will look at the *repentance* of those who are in the places below; and he has not overlooked their *repentance*.

18. This is that *mystery* which has become a *type* for the *race* which will be born; and the *race* which will be born will sing praises to the *height*.

19. For the light has looked forth from the height of his light. He will look down upon all *matter*;

20. To hear the groaning of those that are bound; to release the power of the *souls* whose power is bound.

21. To place his name in the *soul*, and his *mystery* in the power'."

40. It happened, *however*, while Jesus was speaking these words to his *disciples*, saying to them: "This is the fourth *repentance* which the Pistis Sophia said; now at this time let him who *understands understand*'* — now it happened when Jesus said these words, John came forward. He kissed (lit. worshipped) the breast of Jesus, he said: "My Lord, *command* me also and *allow* me that I speak the interpretation of the fourth | *repentance* which the Pistis Sophia

---

* cf. Mt. 19.12; 24.15

ⲘⲘⲈⲦⲀⲚⲞⲒⲀ · ⲦⲀⲒ ⲈⲚⲦⲀⲤⲬⲞⲞⲤ ⲚϬⲒ ⲦⲠⲒⲤⲦⲒⲤ ⲤⲞⲪⲒⲀ · ⲝⲁᵇ
ⲠⲈⲬⲈ Ⲓ̅Ⲥ̅ Ⲛ̅Ⲓ̈ⲰⲊⲀⲚⲚⲎⲤ ⲬⲈ ϯⲔⲈⲖⲈⲨⲈ ⲚⲀⲔ · ⲀⲨⲰ ϯⲤⲨⲄ-
ⲬⲰⲢⲒ ⲚⲀⲔ ⲈⲦⲢⲈⲔⲬⲰ Ⲙ̅ⲠⲂⲰⲖ Ⲛ̅ⲦⲘⲈⲦⲀⲚⲞⲒⲀ ⲈⲚⲦⲀⲤ-
ⲬⲞⲞⲤ Ⲛ̅ϬⲒ ⲦⲠⲒⲤⲦⲒⲤ ⲤⲞⲪⲒⲀ ·

5　　Ⲍ ⲀϤⲞⲨⲰⲊⲂ Ⲛ̅ϬⲒ Ⲓ̈ⲰⲊⲀⲚⲚⲎⲤ ⲠⲈⲬⲀϤ ⲬⲈ ⲠⲀⲬⲞⲒ̈Ⲥ
ⲠⲤⲰⲦⲎⲢ ⲈⲦⲂⲈ ⲦⲈⲒ̈ⲘⲈⲦⲀⲚⲞⲒⲀ ⲈⲚⲦⲀⲤⲬⲞⲞⲤ Ⲛ̅ϬⲒ ⲦⲠⲒⲤ-
ⲦⲒⲤ ⲤⲞⲪⲒⲀ · ⲀⲤⲠⲢⲞⲪⲎⲦⲈⲨⲈ Ⲙ̅ⲠⲒⲞⲨⲞⲈⲒ(Ⲱ) ⲈⲦⲂⲎⲎⲦⲤ̅
Ⲛ̅ϬⲒ ⲦⲈⲔϬⲞⲘ Ⲛ̅ⲞⲨⲞⲈⲒⲚ ⲈⲦⲊ̅Ⲛ̅ ⲀⲨⲈⲒⲀ · Ⲋ̅Ⲙ̅ ⲠⲘⲈⲊ(Ⲱ)Ⲉ-
ⲞⲨⲀ' Ⲙ̅ⲮⲀⲖⲘⲞⲤ ⲬⲈ

10　　1. ⲠⲬⲞⲈⲒⲤ ⲤⲰⲦ̅Ⲙ̅ ⲈⲠⲀ(Ⲱ)ⲖⲎⲖ · ⲀⲨⲰ ⲘⲀⲢⲈ ⲠⲀⲊⲢⲞⲞⲨ
ⲈⲒ' (Ⲱ)ⲀⲢⲞⲔ ·

2. Ⲙ̅ⲠⲢ̅ⲔⲦⲈ-ⲠⲈⲔⲊⲞ Ⲛ̅ⲤⲀⲂⲞⲖ ⲘⲘⲞⲒ̈ · ⲢⲈⲔⲦ-ⲠⲈⲔⲘⲀⲀⲬⲈ
ⲈⲢⲞⲒ̈ Ⲙ̅ⲠⲈⲊⲞⲞⲨ ⲈϯⲚⲀⲐⲖⲒⲂⲈ · ϬⲈⲠⲎ ⲤⲰⲦ̅Ⲙ̅ ⲈⲢⲞⲒ̈ Ⲋ̅Ⲙ̅ ⲠⲈ-
ⲊⲞⲞⲨ ⲈϯⲚⲀ(Ⲱ)(Ⲱ) ⲈⲊⲢⲀⲒ̈ ⲈⲢⲞⲔ ·

15　　3. ⲬⲈ Ⲁ ⲚⲀⲊⲞⲞⲨ Ⲱ̅Ⲭ̅Ⲛ̅ Ⲛ̅ⲐⲈ Ⲛ̅ⲞⲨⲔⲀⲠⲚⲞⲤ · ⲀⲨⲰ Ⲁ
ⲚⲀⲔⲈⲈⲤ ϬⲰϬ Ⲛ̅ⲐⲈ Ⲛ̅ⲞⲨⲰⲚⲈ ·

4. ⲀⲈⲒ(Ⲱ)ⲰϬⲈ Ⲛ̅ⲐⲈ Ⲛ̅ⲞⲨⲬⲞⲢⲦⲞⲤ · ⲀⲨⲰ Ⲁ ⲠⲀⲊⲎⲦ
(Ⲱ)ⲞⲞⲨⲈ · ⲬⲈ ⲀⲒ̅Ⲣ̅-ⲠⲰⲂ(Ⲱ) Ⲉ̈ⲞⲨⲰⲘ Ⲙ̅ⲠⲀⲞⲈⲒⲔ ·　　ⲝⲃ̅

5. ⲈⲂⲞⲖ Ⲋ̅Ⲙ̅ ⲠⲈⲊⲢⲞⲞⲨ Ⲙ̅ⲠⲀⲀ(Ⲱ)ⲀⲊⲞⲘ · Ⲁ ⲠⲀⲔⲀⲤ ⲦⲰϬⲈ
20　ⲈⲦⲀⲤⲀⲢⲝ̅ ·

6. ⲀⲒ̅Ⲣ̅-ⲐⲈ Ⲛ̅ⲞⲨⲊⲢⲒⲘ Ⲋ̅Ⲓ ⲠⲬⲀⲒ̈Ⲉ · ⲀⲒ̈(Ⲱ)ⲰⲠⲈ Ⲛ̅ⲞⲈ Ⲛ̅ⲞⲨⲂⲀⲒ̈
Ⲋ̅Ⲛ̅ ⲞⲨⲎⲒ̈ ·

7. ⲀⲒ̅Ⲣ̅-ⲞⲨ(Ⲱ)Ⲏ Ⲛ̅ⲢⲞⲈⲒⲤ · ⲀⲒ̅Ⲣ̅-ⲐⲈ Ⲛ̅ⲞⲨⲬⲀⲬ · Ⲋ̅Ⲓ ⲞⲨⲬⲈ-
ⲚⲈⲠⲰⲢ ⲘⲀⲨⲀⲀϤ ·

25　　8. Ⲁ ⲚⲀⲬⲒⲬⲈⲈⲨ ⲚⲈϬⲚⲞⲨϬ̅Ⲧ̅ Ⲙ̅ⲠⲈⲊⲞⲞⲨ ⲦⲎⲢ̅ϥ̅ · ⲀⲨⲰ
ⲚⲈⲦⲦⲀⲒⲞ ⲘⲘⲞⲒ̈ ⲚⲈⲨ(Ⲱ)Ⲣ̅Ⲕ̅ ⲘⲘⲞⲒ̈ ⲠⲈ ·

spoke". Jesus said to John : "I *command* thee and I *allow* thee to give (lit. say) the interpretation of the *repentance* which the Pistis Sophia spoke."

John answered, he said : "My Lord *Saviour*, concerning this *repentance* which the Pistis Sophia spoke, thy light-power, which was in David, once *prophesied* about it in the 101st *Psalm* :

1. 'Lord, hear my prayer and let my voice come to thee.

2. Turn not thy face away from me; incline thy ear to me in the day of my *affliction*; hear me quickly in the day when I shall cry to thee.

3. For my days have vanished like *smoke*, and my bones are parched like a stone.

4. I am scorched like *grass* and my heart is dried up; for I have forgotten to eat my bread.

5. From the voice of my groaning my bone has cleaved to my *flesh*.

6. I have become like a pelican in the wilderness. I have become like an owl in a house.

7. I have spent nights of vigil; I have become like a sparrow alone upon a roof.

8. My enemies have reproached me all day long; and those that honour me have sworn against me. |

9. ϫⲉ ⲁⲓ̈ⲟⲩⲱⲙ ⲛ̅ⲟⲩⲕⲣⲙⲉⲥ ⲉⲡⲙⲁ ⲙ̅ⲡⲗⲟⲉⲓⲕ · ⲁⲓ̈ⲕⲉⲣⲁ ⲙ̅ⲡⲉⲧ̅ⲛⲁⲥⲟⲟϥ Ϩⲓ ⲣ̅ⲙⲉⲓⲏ ·

10. ⲙ̅ⲡⲉⲙⲧⲟ ⲉⲃⲟⲗ ⲛ̅ⲧⲉⲕⲟⲣⲅⲏ · ⲙⲛ̅ ⲡⲉⲕϭⲱⲛⲧ̅ ϫⲉ ⲁⲕϥⲓⲧ · ⲁⲕⲧⲁⲅⲟⲓ̈ ⲉϨⲣⲁⲓ̈ ·

11. ⲁ ⲛⲁϨⲟⲟⲩ ⲣⲓⲕⲉ ⲛ̅ⲑⲉ ⲛ̅ⲟⲩϨⲁⲓ̈ⲃⲉⲥ · ⲁⲩⲱ ⲁⲓ̈ϣⲟⲟⲩⲉ ⲛ̅ⲑⲉ ⲛ̅ⲟⲩⲭⲟⲣⲧⲟⲥ ·

12. ⲛ̅ⲧⲟⲕ ⲇⲉ ⲡϫⲟⲉⲓⲥ ⲕϣⲟⲟⲡ ϣⲁⲉⲛⲉϨ · ⲁⲩⲱ ⲡⲉⲕ-ⲣ̅ⲡⲙⲉⲉⲩⲉ ϣⲁ ⲟⲩⲭⲱⲙ ⲛ̅ⲧⲉ ⲟⲩⲭⲱⲙ ·

13. ⲧⲱⲟⲩⲛ ⲛ̅ⲧⲟⲕ ⲛ̅ⲅϣ̅ⲛ̅Ϩⲧⲏⲕ Ϩⲁ ⲥⲓⲱⲛ · ϫⲉ ⲁ ⲡⲉⲟⲩⲟⲓ̈ϣ ϣⲱⲡⲉ ⲛ̅ϣ̅ⲛ̅Ϩⲧⲏⲕ Ϩⲁⲣⲟⲥ ϫⲉ ⲁ ⲡⲕⲁⲓⲣⲟⲥ ⲉⲓ' ·

14. ⲁ ⲛⲉⲕϨⲙ̅Ϩⲁⲗ ⲟⲩⲉϣ-ⲛⲉⲥⲱⲛⲉ · ⲁⲩⲱ *ⲥⲉⲛⲁϣ̅ⲛ̅- ⲝⲃ ᵇ Ϩⲧⲏⲩ Ϩⲁ ⲡⲉⲥⲕⲁϨ ·

15. ⲛ̅ⲧⲉ ⲛ̅Ϩⲉⲑⲛⲟⲥ ⲣ̅Ϩⲟⲧⲉ Ϩⲏⲧϥ̅ ⲙ̅ⲡⲣⲁⲛ ⲙ̅ⲡϫⲟⲉⲓⲥ · ⲁⲩⲱ ⲛ̅ⲣ̅ⲣⲱⲟⲩ ⲙ̅ⲡⲕⲁϨ ⲥⲉⲛⲁⲣ̅Ϩⲟⲧⲉ Ϩⲏⲧϥ̅ ⲙ̅ⲡⲉⲕⲉⲟⲟⲩ ·

16. ϫⲉ ⲡϫⲟⲉⲓⲥ ⲛⲁⲕⲉⲧ-ⲥⲓⲱⲛ ⲛ̅ϥⲟⲩⲱⲛϨ ⲉⲃⲟⲗ Ϩⲙ̅ ⲡⲉϥⲉⲟⲟⲩ ·

17. ⲁϥϭⲱϣ̅ⲧ ⲉϫⲙ̅ ⲡⲉϣⲗⲏⲗ ⲛ̅ⲛⲉⲧⲑⲃⲃⲓⲏⲩ · ⲁⲩⲱ ⲙ̅ⲡϥ̅ⲥⲉϣ̅ϥ-ⲡⲉⲩⲥⲟⲡⲥ̅

18. ⲙⲁⲣⲟⲩⲥⲉϨ-ⲡⲁⲓ̈ ⲉⲕⲉϫⲱⲙ · ⲁⲩⲱ ⲡⲗⲁⲟⲥ ⲉⲧⲟⲩⲛⲁ-ⲥⲟⲛⲧ̅ϥ ϥⲛⲁⲥⲙⲟⲩ ⲉⲡϫⲟⲉⲓⲥ ·

19. ϫⲉ ⲁϥϭⲱϣ̅ⲧ ⲉⲃⲟⲗ ⲉϫⲙ̅ ⲡⲉϥϫⲓⲥⲉ ⲉⲧⲟⲩⲁⲁⲃ · ⲁ ⲡϫⲟⲉⲓⲥ ϭⲱϣ̅ⲧ ⲉⲃⲟⲗ Ϩⲛ̅ ⲧⲡⲉ ⲉϫⲙ̅ ⲡⲕⲁϨ ·

20. ⲉⲥⲱⲧⲙ̅ ⲉⲡⲁϣϨⲁϨⲟⲙ ⲛ̅ⲛⲉⲧⲙⲏⲣ · ⲉⲃⲱⲗ ⲉⲃⲟⲗ ⲛ̅ⲛ-ϣⲏⲣⲉ ⲛ̅ⲛⲉⲛⲧⲁⲩⲙⲟⲟⲩⲧⲟⲩ ·

21. ⲉϫⲱ ⲙ̅ⲡⲣⲁⲛ ⲙ̅ⲡϫⲟⲉⲓⲥ Ϩⲛ̅ ⲥⲓⲱⲛ ⲁⲩⲱ ⲡⲉϥⲥⲙⲟⲩ Ϩⲛ̅ ⲑⲓⲗⲏⲙ ·

---

20 ⲛ in ⲥⲟⲛⲧ̅ϥ inserted above.

9. For I have eaten ashes in place of my bread; I have *mixed* my drink [1] with tears;

10. In the presence of thy *wrath* and thy anger; for thou hast lifted me up, thou hast cast me down.

11. My days have declined like a shadow, and I am dried up like *grass*.

12. *But* thou, O Lord, dost exist for ever; and thy memory from generation to generation [2].

13. Do thou arise and be compassionate to Zion; for it is (lit. has happened) time for compassion to her; for the *appointed time* has come.

14. Thy servants have desired her stones; and they will show pity on her land.

15. The *peoples* will fear the name of the Lord and the kings of the earth will fear thy glory.

16. For the Lord will build Zion and be manifest in his glory.

17. He has looked upon the prayer of the humble, and he has not despised their petition.

18. Let this be written for another generation; and the *people* which will be created will bless the Lord.

19. Because he has looked forth upon his holy height; the Lord has looked forth from heaven upon the earth;

20. To hear the groaning of those that are bound, to release the sons of those who have been killed;

21. To speak the name of the Lord in Zion, and his blessing in Jerusalem.' * |

---

* Ps. 101.1-21

---

[1]   (2) my drink; lit. what I will drink.
[2]   (8) from generation to generation; lit. to a generation of a generation.

ⲡⲁⲓ̈ ⲡⲉ ⲡⲁⲭⲟⲉⲓⲥ ⲡⲉ ⲡⲃⲱⲗ ⲙ̄ⲡⲙⲩⲥⲧⲏⲣⲓⲟⲛ ⲛ̄ⲧⲙⲉ-
ⲧⲁⲛⲟⲓⲁ ⲉⲛⲧⲁⲥϫⲟⲟⲥ ⲛ̄ϭⲓ ⲧⲡⲓⲥⲧⲓⲥ ⲥⲟⲫⲓⲁ ·

ⲍ ⲁⲥϣⲱⲡⲉ ϭⲉ ⲛ̄ⲧⲉⲣⲉ ⲓ̈ⲱⲁⲛⲛⲏⲥ ⲟⲩⲱ ⲉϥϫⲱ ⲛ̄ⲛⲉⲓ̈-
ϣⲁϫⲉ ⲉⲓ̅ⲥ̅ · ϩⲛ̄ ⲧⲙⲏⲧⲉ** ⲛ̄ⲛⲉϥⲙⲁⲑⲏⲧⲏⲥ · ⲡⲉϫⲁϥ ⲛⲁϥ ⲝ̅ⲅ̅
₅ ϫⲉ ⲉⲩⲅⲉ ⲓ̈ⲱϩⲁⲛⲛⲏⲥ ⲡ̄ⲡⲁⲣⲑⲉⲛⲟⲥ ⲡⲁⲓ̈ ⲉⲧⲛⲁⲁⲣⲭⲉⲓ ϩⲣⲁⲓ̈
ϩⲛ̄ ⲧⲙⲛ̄ⲧⲉⲣⲟ ⲙ̄ⲡⲟⲩⲟⲉⲓⲛ ·

ⲍ ⲁϥⲟⲩⲱϩ ⲇⲉ ⲟⲛ ⲉⲧⲟⲟⲧϥ̄ ⲛ̄ϭⲓ ⲓ̅ⲥ̅ ϩⲙ̄ ⲡϣⲁϫⲉ ⲡⲉϫⲁϥ ⲛ̄ⲛⲉϥⲙⲁⲑⲏⲧⲏⲥ ϫⲉ ⲁⲥϣⲱⲡⲉ ⲟⲛ ⲛ̄ⲧⲉⲉⲓϩⲉ ⲁ ⲛⲉⲡⲣⲟⲃⲟⲗⲟⲟⲩⲉ ⲙ̄ⲡⲁⲩⲑⲁⲇⲏⲥ ⲁⲩϩⲱϫ ⲟⲛ ⲛ̄ⲧⲡⲓⲥⲧⲓⲥ ⲥⲟ-
₁₀ ⲫⲓⲁ ϩⲛ̄ ⲛⲉⲭⲗⲟⲥ · ⲁⲩⲟⲩⲉϣϥ̄-ⲡⲉⲥⲟⲩⲟⲓ̈ⲛ ⲧⲏⲣϥ̄ ⲁⲩⲱ
ⲛⲉⲙ̄ⲡⲁⲧϥ̄ϫⲱⲕ ⲉⲃⲟⲗ ⲡⲉ ⲛ̄ϭⲓ ⲡⲉⲥⲧⲱϣ ⲉⲛ̄ⲧⲥ ⲉϩⲣⲁⲓ̈ ϩⲙ̄
ⲡⲉⲭⲗⲟⲥ · ⲁⲩⲱ ⲛⲉⲙ̄ⲡⲁⲧⲉ ⲧⲕⲉⲗⲉⲩⲥⲓⲥ ⲉⲓ' ⲛⲁⲓ̈ ⲡⲉ ϩⲓⲧⲙ̄
ⲡϣⲟⲣⲡ̄ ⲙ̄ⲙⲩⲥⲧⲏⲣⲓⲟⲛ ⲉⲧⲣⲁⲛⲁϩⲙⲉⲥ ϩⲙ̄ ⲡⲉⲭⲗⲟⲥ · ⲁⲥϣⲱⲡⲉ ϭⲉ ⲛ̄ⲧⲉⲣⲟⲩϩⲱϫ ⲙ̄ⲙⲟⲥ ⲛ̄ϭⲓ ⲛⲉⲡⲣⲟⲃⲟⲗⲟⲟⲩⲉ
₁₅ ⲧⲏⲣⲟⲩ ⲛ̄ϩⲩⲗⲓⲕⲟⲛ ⲛ̄ⲧⲉ ⲡⲁⲩⲑⲁⲇⲏⲥ · ⲁⲥⲱϣ ⲉⲃⲟⲗ
ⲉⲥϫⲱ ⲛ̄ⲧⲙⲉϩ† ⲙ̄ⲙⲉⲧⲁⲛⲟⲓⲁ ⲉⲥϫⲱ ⲙ̄ⲙⲟⲥ ϫⲉ

1. ⲡⲟⲩⲟⲓ̈ⲛ ⲙ̄ⲡⲁⲟⲩϫⲁⲓ̈ · †ϩⲩⲙⲛⲉⲩⲉ ⲉⲣⲟⲕ ϩⲣⲁⲓ̈ ϩⲙ̄
ⲡⲧⲟⲡⲟⲥ ⲙ̄ⲡϫⲓⲥⲉ · ⲁⲩⲱ ⲟⲛ *ϩⲙ̄ ⲡⲉⲭⲗⲟⲥ ·　　　　　　ⲝ̅ⲅ̅ ᵇ

2. †ⲛⲁϩⲩⲙⲛⲉⲩⲉ ⲉⲣⲟⲕ ϩⲙ̄ ⲡⲁϩⲩⲙⲛⲟⲥ · ⲛ̄ⲧⲁⲓ̈ϩⲩⲙⲛⲉⲩⲉ
₂₀ ⲉⲣⲟⲕ ϩⲙ̄ ⲡϫⲓⲥⲉ · ⲁⲩⲱ ⲡⲉⲛⲧⲁⲓ̈ϩⲩⲙⲛⲉⲩⲉ ⲙ̄ⲙⲟϥ ⲉⲣⲟⲕ
ⲉⲓ̈ϩⲙ̄ ⲡⲉⲭⲗⲟⲥ · ⲙⲁⲣⲉϥⲉⲓ' ⲛ̄ⲛⲁϩⲣⲁⲕ · ⲁⲩⲱ †ϩⲧⲏⲕ ⲡⲟⲩⲟⲉⲓⲛ ⲉⲧⲁⲙⲉⲧⲁⲛⲟⲓⲁ ·

3. ϫⲉ ⲁ ⲧⲁϭⲟⲙ ⲙⲟⲩϩ ⲛ̄ⲕⲁⲕⲉ · ⲁⲩⲱ ⲁ ⲡⲗⲟⲩⲟⲓ̈ⲛ ⲉⲓ'
ⲉϩⲣⲁⲓ̈ ⲉⲡⲉⲭⲗⲟⲥ ·

1　first ⲡⲉ superfluous.
2　MS originally ⲡⲃⲱⲗ ⲛ̄ⲧⲙⲉⲧⲁⲛⲟⲓⲁ; ⲙ̄ⲡⲙ̄ⲣ̄ⲓ inserted in right-hand margin;
　　ⲛ in left-hand margin.
24　MS originally ϩⲙ̄ ⲡⲉⲭⲗⲟⲥ; ϩⲙ̄ crossed out and ⲉ inserted above.

This, my Lord, is the interpretation of the *mystery* of the *repentance* which the Pistis Sophia spoke."

41.   Now it happened when John finished saying these words to Jesus in the midst of his disciples, he said to him : "*Excellent*, John, thou *virgin* who wilt *rule* in the Kingdom of the Light."

Jesus, *however*, continued again with the discourse, he said to his *disciples* : "It happened again thus : the *emanations* of the Authades oppressed the Pistis Sophia in the *Chaos(es)*. They wanted to take away all her light, and the ordinance was not yet completed to bring her forth from the *Chaos*, and the *command* had not yet come to me through the First *Mystery* to save her from the *Chaos*. Now it happened, when all the *material emanations* of the Authades oppressed her, she cried out and spoke the fifth *repentance*, saying :

1. 'O Light of my salvation, I *sing praise* to thee in the *place* of the height, and again in the *Chaos*.

2. I will *sing praise* to thee in my *song*, with which I have *praised* thee in the height, and with which I have *praised* thee when I was in the *Chaos*; may it reach thee. And give heed, O Light, to my *repentance*.

3. My power has been filled with darkness; and my light has come down to the *Chaos*. |

137

4. ⲀⲒϢⲰⲠⲈ ϨⲰ ⲚⲞⲈ ⲚⲚⲀⲢⲬⲰⲚ ⲘⲠⲈⲬⲀⲞⲤ ⲚⲀⲒ ⲈⲦⲂⲎⲔ
ⲈⲚⲔⲀⲔⲈ ⲘⲠⲈⲤⲎⲦ· ⲀⲒϢⲰⲠⲈ ⲚⲐⲈ ⲚⲞⲨⲤⲰⲘⲀ ⲚϨⲨⲖⲒⲔⲞⲚ
ⲈⲘⲚⲦⲀϤ ⲘⲘⲀⲨ ⲘⲠⲈⲦⲚⲀⲚⲀϨⲘⲈϤ ϨⲘ ⲠⲬⲒⲤⲈ·

5. ⲀⲒϢⲰⲠⲈ ⲞⲚ ⲚⲐⲈ ⲚϨⲈⲚϨⲨⲖⲎ ⲈⲀⲨϤⲒ-ⲦⲈⲨϬⲞⲘ ⲚϨⲎ-
5 ⲦⲞⲨ ⲈⲨⲚⲎⲬ ϨⲘ ⲠⲈⲬⲀⲞⲤ ⲚⲀⲒ ⲈⲦⲈ ⲘⲠⲔⲚⲀϨⲘⲞⲨ· ⲀⲨⲰ
ⲀⲨⲦⲀⲔⲞ ϨⲘ ⲠⲈⲔⲦⲰϢ·

6. ⲦⲈⲚⲞⲨ ϬⲈ ⲀⲨⲔⲀⲀⲦ ϨⲘ ⲠⲔⲀⲔⲈ ⲘⲠⲈⲤⲎⲦ· ϨⲚ ϨⲈⲚ-
ⲔⲀⲔⲈ ⲀⲨⲰ ϨⲚ ϨⲈⲚϨⲨⲖⲎ ⲈⲨⲘⲞⲞⲨⲦ· ⲀⲨⲰ ⲈⲘⲚϬⲞⲘ
ⲚϨⲎⲦⲞⲨ·

10 7. ⲀⲔⲈⲒⲚⲈ ⲘⲠⲈⲔⲦⲰϢ ⲈϨⲢⲀⲒ ⲈⲬⲰⲒ· ⲀⲨⲰ ⲘⲚ ϨⲰⲂ
ⲚⲒⲘ ⲈⲚⲦⲀⲔⲦⲞϢⲞⲨ·   ⲝⲀ

8. ⲀⲨⲰ Ⲁ ⲠⲈⲔⲠⲚⲀ ⲠⲰⲦ ⲀϤⲔⲀⲀⲦ· ⲀⲨⲰ ⲞⲚ ϨⲒⲦⲘ
ⲠⲈⲔⲦⲰϢ ⲘⲠⲞⲨⲂⲞⲎⲐⲒ ⲈⲢⲞⲒ ⲚϬⲒ ⲚⲈⲠⲢⲞⲂⲞⲖⲞⲞⲨⲈ Ⲙ-
ⲠⲀⲖⲒⲰⲚ· ⲀⲨⲰ ⲀⲨⲘⲈⲤⲦⲰⲒ ⲀⲨⲰ ⲀⲨⲖⲞ ϨⲀⲢⲞⲒ· ⲀⲨⲰ
15 ⲞⲚ ⲘⲠⲒⲦⲀⲔⲞ ϢⲀⲂⲞⲖ·

9. ⲀⲨⲰ Ⲁ ⲠⲀⲞⲨⲞⲈⲒⲚ ⲤⲂⲞⲔ ϨⲢⲀⲒ ⲚϨⲎⲦ· ⲀⲨⲰ ⲀⲒϢⲰ
ⲈϨⲢⲀⲒ ⲈⲠⲞⲨⲞⲈⲒⲚ ϨⲘ ⲠⲞⲨⲞⲒⲚ ⲦⲎⲢϤ ⲈⲦⲚϨⲎⲦ· ⲀⲨⲰ
ⲀⲒⲠⲰⲢϢ ⲚⲚⲀϬⲒⲬ ⲈϨⲢⲀⲒ ⲈⲢⲞⲔ·

10. ⲦⲈⲚⲞⲨ ϬⲈ ⲠⲞⲨⲞⲈⲒⲚ ⲘⲎ ⲈⲔⲚⲀⲬⲰⲔ ⲈⲂⲞⲖ ⲘⲠⲈⲔ-
20 ⲦⲰϢ ϨⲘ ⲠⲈⲬⲀⲞⲤ· ⲀⲨⲰ ⲚⲢⲈϤⲚⲞⲨϨⲘ ⲚⲀⲒ ⲈⲦⲚⲎⲨ
ⲔⲀⲦⲀ ⲠⲈⲔⲦⲰϢ· ⲘⲎ ⲈⲨⲚⲀⲦⲰⲞⲨⲚ ϨⲘ ⲠⲔⲀⲔⲈ ⲚⲤⲈⲈⲒ'
ⲚⲤⲈⲘⲀⲐⲎⲦⲈⲨⲈ ⲚⲀⲔ·

11. ⲘⲎ ⲈⲨⲚⲀⲬⲰ ⲘⲠⲘⲨⲤⲦⲎⲢⲒⲞⲚ ⲘⲠⲈⲔⲢⲀⲚ ϨⲘ ⲠⲈ-
ⲬⲀⲞⲤ·

---

7 MS originally ϨⲘⲠⲤⲎⲦ; ⲔⲀⲔⲈ inserted in margin after ϨⲘⲛ, and ⲘⲠⲈ in
left-hand margin.
17 ϨⲘ ⲠⲞⲨⲞⲒⲚ; dittography, the first expunged.

4. I have become like the *archons* of the *Chaos* which have gone to the darkness below; I have become like a *material body*, which has no one in the height who will save it.

5. I have become like *material things* whose power has been taken from them as they were cast into the *Chaos*, which thou hast not saved; and they have been destroyed by thy ordinance.

6. Now at this time I have been placed in the darkness below, in dark things and in *material things* which are dead; and there is no power within them.

7. Thou hast brought thy ordinance upon me; with all things which thou hast ordained.

8. And the *Spirit* has departed and left me; and again, through thy ordinance, the *emanations* of my *aeon* have not *helped* me; and they have hated me and they have ceased towards me, and yet I am not completely destroyed.

9. And my light has diminished within me, and I have cried out to the light with all the light that is in me; and I have stretched out my hands to thee.

10. Now at this time, O Light, wilt thou *perhaps* fulfil thy ordinance in the *Chaos*? And will the saviours, *perhaps*, who came *according to* thy ordinance, arise in the darkness and come and *be disciples* to thee?

11. Will they, *perhaps*, say the *mystery* of thy name in the *Chaos*? |

12. Ĥ ⲘⲘⲞⲚ ⲚⲦⲞϤ ⲈⲨⲚⲀⲬⲰ ⲘⲠⲈⲔⲢⲀⲚ ⲌⲚ ⲞⲨⲌⲨⲖⲎ
ⲚⲬⲀⲞⲤ · ⲠⲀⲒ ⲈⲦⲈ ⲚⲄⲚⲀⲤⲰⲦϤ̄ ⲀⲚ Ⲛ̄ⲌⲎⲦϤ̄ ·

13. ⲀⲚⲞⲔ ⲆⲈ ⲀⲒ̇ⲌⲨⲘⲚⲈⲨⲈ ⲈⲌⲢⲀⲒ ⲈⲢⲞⲔ ⲠⲞⲨⲞⲈⲒⲚ ⲀⲨⲰ Ⲍⲗ̄ᵇ
ⲦⲀⲘⲈⲦⲀⲚⲞⲒⲀ ⲚⲀⲦⲀⲌⲞⲔ ⲈⲌⲢⲀⲒ ⲈⲠⲬⲒⲤⲈ ·

5   14. ⲘⲀⲢⲈ ⲠⲈⲔⲞⲨⲞⲒ̈Ⲛ ⲈⲒ· ⲈⲌⲢⲀⲒ ⲈⲬⲰⲒ̈ ·

15. ⲬⲈ ⲀⲨϤⲒ-ⲠⲀⲞⲨⲞⲒ̈Ⲛ ⲌⲢⲀⲒ Ⲛ̄ⲌⲎⲦ · ⲀⲨⲰ ⳁϢⲞⲞⲠ ⲌⲚ
ⲌⲈⲚⲌⲒⲤⲈ ⲈⲦⲂⲈ ⲠⲞⲨⲞⲒ̈Ⲛ · ⲬⲒⲚ Ⲙ̄ⲠⲈⲞⲨⲞⲈⲒϢ ⲈⲚⲦⲀⲨⲠⲢⲞ-
ⲂⲀⲖⲈ ⲘⲘⲞⲒ̈ ⲈⲂⲞⲖ · ⲀⲨⲰ Ⲛ̄ⲦⲈⲢⲒϬⲰϢⲦ ⲈⲠⲬⲒⲤⲈ ⲈⲠⲞⲨ-
ⲞⲒ̈Ⲛ ⲀⲨⲰ ⲀⲒ̈ϬⲰϢⲦ ⲈⲠⲈⲤⲎⲦ ⲈⳁϬⲞⲘ Ⲛ̄ⲞⲨⲞⲒ̈Ⲛ ⲈⲦⲌⲘ̄
10 ⲠⲈⲬⲀⲞⲤ · ⲀⲒ̈ⲦϢⲞⲨⲚ̄ ⲀⲒ̈ⲈⲒ· ⲈⲠⲈⲤⲎⲦ ·

16. Ⲁ ⲠⲈⲔⲦⲰϢ ⲈⲒ· ⲈⲌⲢⲀⲒ ⲈⲬⲰⲒ̈ ⲀⲨⲰ Ⲛ̄ⲌⲞⲦⲈ ⲈⲚⲦ-
ⲀⲔⲦⲞϢⲞⲨ ⲈⲢⲞⲒ̈ ⲀⲨϢⲦⲢ̄ⲦⲰⲢⲦ̄ ·

17. ⲀⲨⲰ ⲀⲨⲔⲰⲦⲈ ⲈⲢⲞⲒ̈ ⲈⲨⲞϢ Ⲛ̄ⲐⲈ Ⲛ̄ⲞⲨⲘⲞⲞⲨ ⲀⲨ-
ⲀⲘⲀⲌⲦⲈ ⲘⲘⲞⲒ̈ ⲌⲒ ⲞⲨⲤⲞⲠ Ⲙ̄ⲠⲀⲞⲨⲞⲒ̈Ϣ ⲦⲎⲢϤ̄ ·

15 18. ⲀⲨⲰ ⲌⲒⲦⲘ̄ ⲠⲈⲔⲦⲰϢ Ⲙ̄ⲠⲔⲔⲀ-ⲚⲀϢⲂⲢ̄ⲠⲢⲞⲂⲞⲖⲎ Ⲉ-
ⲂⲞⲎⲐⲒ ⲈⲢⲞⲒ̈ · ⲀⲨⲰ Ⲙ̄ⲠⲔⲔⲀ-ⲠⲀⲤⲨⲚⳎⲨⲄⲞⲤ ⲈⲚⲀⲌⲘⲈⲦ
ⲈⲂⲞⲖ ⲌⲚ̄ ⲚⲀⲐⲖⲒⲮⲒⲤ ·

ⲦⲀⲒ̈˙˙ϬⲈ ⲦⲈ ⲦⲘⲈⲌⳁ Ⲙ̄ⲘⲈⲦⲀⲚⲞⲒⲀ ⲈⲚⲦⲀⲤⲬⲞⲞⲤ Ⲛ̄ϬⲒ ⳎⲈ
ⲦⲠⲒⲤⲦⲒⲤ ⲤⲞⲫⲒⲀ ⲌⲢⲀⲒ Ⲍ̄Ⲙ ⲠⲈⲬⲀⲞⲤ Ⲛ̄ⲦⲈⲢⲞⲨⲞⲨⲰⲌ ⲈⲦⲞⲞ-
20 ⲦⲞⲨ ⲀⲨⲐⲖⲒⲂⲈ ⲘⲘⲞⲤ Ⲛ̄ϬⲒ ⲚⲈⲠⲢⲞⲂⲞⲖⲞⲞⲨⲈ ⲦⲎⲢⲞⲨ
Ⲛ̄ⲌⲨⲖⲒⲔⲞⲚ Ⲛ̄ⲦⲈ ⲠⲀⲨⲐⲀⲆⲎⲤ :

ⳅ ⲚⲀⲒ̈ ϬⲈ ⲈⲢⲈ Ⲓ̄Ⲥ̄ ⲬⲰ Ⲙ̄ⲘⲞⲞⲨ ⲈⲚⲈϤⲘⲀⲐⲎⲦⲎⲤ · ⲠⲈ-
ⲬⲀϤ ⲚⲀⲨ ⲬⲈ ⲠⲈⲦⲈ ⲞⲨⲚ̄-ⲘⲀⲀⲬⲈ ⲘⲘⲞϤ ⲈⲤⲰⲦⲘ̄ · ⲘⲀ-

---

12 MS ⲈⲈⲢⲞⲒ̈; the second ⲉ expunged. ⲀⲨ in ⲀⲨϢⲦⲢ̄ⲦⲰⲢⲦ̄ written over
erasure.

12. *Or* will they not rather say thy name in *matter* of the *Chaos*, this in which thou wilt not purify?

13. *But* I have *sung praises* to thee, O Light, and my *repentance* will reach thee in the height.

14. May thy light come down upon me.

15. My light has been taken from me and I am in distress on account of the light, from the time when I was *emanated* forth. And when I looked to the height to the light, I looked down to the light-power which is in the *Chaos*; I rose, I came down.

16. Thy ordinance came down upon me, and the fears which thou didst ordain for me, agitated me.

17. And they surrounded me roaring[1] like water, they seized me at once for all my time.

18. And through thy ordinance, thou didst not allow my fellow-*emanations* to *help* me; and thou didst not allow my *partner* to save me from my *afflictions*.'

This now is the fifth *repentance* which the Pistis Sophia said in the *Chaos*, when all the *material emanations* of the Authades continued to *afflict* her."

42. Now when Jesus said these things to his *disciples*, he said to them: "He who has ears to hear, let him |

---

[1]   (13) roaring; Schmidt: numerous.

ⲣⲉϥⲥⲱⲧⲙ̄ · ⲁⲩⲱ ⲡⲉⲧⲉⲣⲉ ⲡⲉϥⲡⲛ̄ⲁ̄ ⲃ̄ⲣ̄ⲃ̄ⲣ̄ ⲛ̄ϩⲏⲧϥ̄ · ⲙⲁⲣⲉϥⲉⲓ' ⲉⲑⲏ ⲛ̄ϥ̄ⲭⲱ ⲙ̄ⲡⲃⲱⲗ ⲙ̄ⲡⲛⲟⲏⲙⲁ ⲛ̄ⲧⲙⲉϩϯ ⲙ̄ⲙⲉ-
ⲧⲁⲛⲟⲓⲁ ⲛ̄ⲧⲡⲓⲥⲧⲓⲥ ⲥⲟⲫⲓⲁ ꞉ ⲁⲩⲱ ⲛ̄ⲧⲉⲣⲉ ⲓ̄ⲥ̄ ⲟⲩⲱ ⲉϥⲭⲱ
ⲛ̄ⲛⲉⲓ̈ϣⲁϫⲉ · ⲁϥϥⲟⲃ̄ϥ̄ ⲉϩⲣⲁⲓ̈ ⲛ̄ϭⲓ ⲫⲓⲗⲓⲡⲡⲟⲥ ⲁϥⲁϩⲉⲣⲁⲧϥ̄ ·
5 ⲁϥⲕⲁ-ⲡϫⲱⲱⲙⲉ ⲉⲧⲛ̄ⲧⲟⲟⲧϥ̄ ⲉⲡⲉⲥⲏⲧ · ⲛ̄ⲧⲟϥ ⲅⲁⲣ ⲡⲉ
ⲉⲧⲥϩⲁⲓ̈ ⲛ̄ϣⲁϫⲉ ⲛⲓⲙ ⲉⲛⲉⲣⲉ ⲓ̄ⲥ̄ ϫⲱ ⲙ̄ⲙⲟⲟⲩ · ⲁⲩⲱ ⲙⲛ̄
ⲛⲉⲧϥⲉⲓⲣⲉ ⲙ̄ⲙⲟⲟⲩ ⲧⲏⲣⲟⲩ · ⲁϥⲉⲓ' ϭⲉ ⲉⲑⲏ ⲛ̄ϭⲓ ⲫⲓⲗⲓⲡ- ⲝ̄ⲉ̄ b
ⲡⲟⲥ ⲡⲉϫⲁϥ ⲛⲁϥ ϫⲉ ⲡⲁϫⲟⲉⲓⲥ · ⲙⲏⲧⲓ ⲁⲛⲟⲕ ⲙⲁⲩⲁⲁⲧ
ⲡⲉ ⲉⲛⲧⲁⲕⲧⲁⲁⲥ ⲛⲁⲓ̈ ⲉⲧⲣⲁϥⲓ-ⲡⲣⲟⲟⲩϣ ⲙ̄ⲡⲓⲕⲟⲥⲙⲟⲥ
10 ⲛ̄ⲧⲁⲥϩⲁⲓ̈ ⲛ̄ϣⲁϫⲉ ⲛⲓⲙ ⲉⲧⲛⲁϫⲟⲟⲩ · ⲁⲩⲱ ⲙⲛ̄ ⲛⲉⲧⲛ-
ⲛⲁⲁⲁⲩ · ⲁⲩⲱ ⲙ̄ⲡⲕ̄ⲕⲁⲁⲧ ⲉⲉⲓ' ⲉⲑⲏ ⲛ̄ⲧⲁϫⲓ-ⲡⲃⲱⲗ ⲛ̄ⲙ̄-
ⲙⲩⲥⲧⲏⲣⲓⲟⲛ ⲛ̄ⲧⲙⲉⲧⲁⲛⲟⲓⲁ ⲛ̄ⲧⲡⲓⲥⲧⲓⲥ ⲥⲟⲫⲓⲁ · ⲁ ⲡⲁⲡⲛ̄ⲁ̄
ⲅⲁⲣ ⲃ̄ⲣ̄ⲃ̄ⲣ̄ ⲛ̄ϩⲏⲧ · ⲛⲟⲩⲙⲏⲏϣⲉ ⲛ̄ⲥⲟⲡ · ⲁⲩⲱ ⲁϥⲃⲱⲗ
ⲉⲃⲟⲗ · ⲁⲩⲱ ⲁϥⲁⲛⲁⲅⲕⲁⲍⲉ ⲙ̄ⲙⲟⲓ̈ ⲉⲙⲁⲧⲉ ⲉⲧⲣⲁⲉⲓ' ⲉⲑⲏ ·
15 ⲛ̄ⲧⲁϫⲉ-ⲡⲃⲱⲗ ⲛ̄ⲧⲙⲉⲧⲁⲛⲟⲓⲁ ⲛ̄ⲧⲡⲓⲥⲧⲓⲥ ⲥⲟⲫⲓⲁ · ⲁⲩⲱ
ⲙ̄ⲡⲓϣⲉⲓ' ⲉⲑⲏ · ⲉⲃⲟⲗ ϫⲉ ⲁⲛⲟⲕ ⲡⲉ ⲉⲧⲥϩⲁⲓ̈ ⲛ̄ϣⲁϫⲉ
ⲛⲓⲙ ·

ϛ ⲁⲥϣⲱⲡⲉ ϭⲉ ⲛ̄ⲧⲉⲣⲉ ⲓ̄ⲥ̄ ⲥⲱⲧⲙ̄ ⲉⲫⲓⲗⲓⲡⲡⲟⲥ ⲡⲉϫⲁϥ
ⲛⲁϥ ϫⲉ ⲥⲱⲧⲙ̄ ⲫⲓⲗⲓⲡⲡⲉ ⲡⲙⲁⲕⲁⲣⲓⲟⲥ ⲛ̄ⲧⲁϣⲁϫⲉ ⲛ̄ⲙ-
20 ⲙⲁⲕ ϫⲉ ⲛ̄ⲧⲟⲕ ⲙⲛ̄ ⲑⲱⲙⲁⲥ ⲙⲛ̄ ⲙⲁⲑⲑⲁⲓⲟⲥ ⲛⲉⲛⲧⲁⲩ-
ⲧⲁⲁⲥ ⲛⲏⲧⲛ̄ ϩⲙ̄ ⲡϣⲟⲣⲡ̄ ⲙ̄ⲙⲩⲥⲧⲏⲣⲓⲟⲛ ⲉⲥⲉϩ-ϣⲁϫⲉ ⲛⲓⲙ
ⲉϯⲛⲁϫⲟⲟⲩ ·** ⲙⲛ̄ ⲛⲉϯⲛⲁⲁⲁⲩ · ⲁⲩⲱ ⲙⲛ̄ ϩⲱⲃ ⲛⲓⲙ ⲝ̄ⲉ̄
ⲉⲧⲉⲧⲛⲁⲛⲁⲩ ⲉⲣⲟⲟⲩ · ⲛ̄ⲧⲟⲕ ⲇⲉ ⲙ̄ⲡⲁⲧϥ̄ϫⲱⲕ ⲉⲃⲟⲗ
ϣⲁ ⲧⲉⲛⲟⲩ ⲛ̄ϭⲓ ⲡⲁⲣⲓⲑⲙⲟⲥ ⲛ̄ⲛ̄ϣⲁϫⲉ ⲉⲧⲕ̄ⲛⲁⲥϩⲁⲓ̈ⲥⲟⲩ ·
25 ⲉϥϣⲁⲛϫⲱⲕ ϭⲉ ⲉⲃⲟⲗ · ⲕⲛⲁⲉⲓ' ⲉⲑⲏ ⲛ̄ⲅ̄ⲧⲁⲩⲉ-ⲡⲉⲧⲉ-
ϩⲛⲁⲕ · ⲧⲉⲛⲟⲩ ϭⲉ ⲛ̄ⲧⲱⲧⲛ̄ ⲙ̄ⲡϣⲟⲙⲧ̄ ⲛⲉⲧⲛⲁⲥϩⲁⲓ̈ ⲛ̄-

---

10 MS ⲉⲧⲛⲁϫⲟⲟⲩ; read ⲉⲧⲛ̄ⲛⲁϫⲟⲟⲩ.

hear*. And he whose *Spirit* wells up within him, let him come forward and say the interpretation of the *thought* of the fifth *repentance* of the Pistis Sophia."

And when Jesus finished saying these words, Philip sprang up, he took his stand, he laid down the book which was in his hand — *for* he is the scribe of all the words which Jesus said, and of all the things which he did — Philip now came forward, he said to him : "My Lord, *indeed* am I alone he to whom thou hast given to take care for the *world*, and to write down all the words which thou wilt say, and all things which thou wilt do? And thou hast not allowed me to come forward to say the interpretation of the *mystery* of the *repentance* of the Pistis Sophia. *For* my *Spirit* has welled up in me many times, and it was released and it *compelled* me strongly to come forward and say the interpretation of the *repentance* of the Pistis Sophia. And I could not come forward because it is I who write all the words."

It happened now, when Jesus heard Philip, he said to him : "Hear, Philip, thou *blessed* one, with whom I spoke; for thou and Thomas and Matthew are those to whom was given, through the First *Mystery*, to write all the words which I will say, and those things which I will do, and everything which you will see. But as for thee, up till now the *number* of the words which thou shalt write is not yet completed. Now when it is completed thou shalt come forward and say what thou dost please. Now at this time it is you three who will write | every word which I will say, and

---

*   Mk. 4.9

ϢⲀϪⲈ ⲚⲒⲘ ⲈϮⲚⲀϪⲞⲞⲨ · ⲘⲚ ⲚⲈϮⲚⲀⲀⲀⲨ · ⲘⲚ ⲚⲈϮ-
ⲚⲀⲚⲀⲨ ⲈⲢⲞⲞⲨ · ⲀⲨⲰ Ⲛ̄ⲦⲀⲢⲘ̄ⲚⲦⲢⲈ Ⲛ̄ϨⲰⲂ ⲚⲒⲘ Ⲛ̄ⲦⲈ
ⲦⲘⲚⲦⲈⲢⲞ Ⲛ̄Ⲙ̄ⲠⲎⲨⲈ · ⲚⲀⲒ ϬⲈ Ⲛ̄ⲦⲈⲢⲈϤϪⲞⲞⲨ Ⲛ̄ϬⲒ Ⲓ̄Ⲥ̄ ·
ⲠⲈϪⲀϤ Ⲛ̄ⲚⲈϤⲘⲀⲐⲎⲦⲎⲤ ϪⲈ ⲠⲈⲦⲈ ⲞⲨⲚ̄-ⲘⲀⲀϪⲈ Ⲙ̄ⲘⲞϤ
5 ⲈⲤⲰⲦ̄Ⲙ · ⲘⲀⲢⲈϤⲤⲰⲦ̄Ⲙ · ⲀⲤϬⲞϬⲤ̄ ⲞⲚ ⲈⲐⲎ Ⲛ̄ϬⲒ ⲘⲀⲢⲒϨⲀⲘ ·
ⲀⲤⲈⲒ' ⲈⲦⲘⲎⲦⲈ ⲀⲤⲀϨⲈⲢⲀⲦ̄Ⲥ̄ ϨⲀⲦⲘ̄ ⲪⲒⲖⲒⲠⲠⲞⲤ ⲠⲈϪⲀⲤ
Ⲛ̄Ⲓ̄Ⲥ̄ ϪⲈ ⲠⲀⲬⲞⲈⲒⲤ · ⲞⲨⲚ̄-ⲘⲀⲀϪⲈ Ⲙ̄ⲠⲀⲢⲘ̄ⲚⲞⲨⲞⲒⲚ ⲀⲨⲰ
ϮⳘⲂⲦⲰⲦ ⲈⲤⲰⲦ̄Ⲙ ⲈⲂⲞⲖ ϨⲚ ⲦⲀϬⲞⲘ · ⲀⲨⲰ ⲀⲒ̈ⲚⲞⲒ̈ Ⲙ̄-
ⲠϢⲀϪⲈ *ⲈⲚⲦⲀⲔϪⲞⲞϤ · ⲦⲈⲚⲞⲨ ϬⲈ ⲠⲀⲬⲞⲈⲒⲤ ⲤⲰⲦ̄Ⲙ Ⲝ̄Ⲉ̄ ᵇ
10 ⲦⲀϪⲞⲞⲤ ϨⲚ ⲞⲨⲠⲀⲢϨⲎⲤⲒⲀ · Ⲛ̄ⲦⲀⲔϪⲞⲞⲤ ⲈⲢⲞⲚ ϪⲈ ⲠⲈ-
ⲦⲈ ⲞⲨⲚ̄-ⲘⲀⲀϪⲈ Ⲙ̄ⲘⲞϤ ⲈⲤⲰⲦ̄Ⲙ ⲘⲀⲢⲈϤⲤⲰⲦ̄Ⲙ · ⲈⲦⲂⲈ
ⲠϢⲀϪⲈ Ⲛ̄ⲦⲀⲔϪⲞⲞϤ ⲈⲪⲒⲖⲒⲠⲠⲞⲤ ϪⲈ Ⲛ̄ⲦⲞⲔ ⲘⲚ ⲐⲰ-
ⲘⲀⲤ ⲘⲚ ⲘⲀⲐⲐⲀⲒⲞⲤ ⲚⲈ Ⲛ̄ⲦⲀⲨⲦⲀⲀⲤ ⲚⲎⲦⲚ̄ Ⲙ̄ⲠϢⲞⲘⲦ
ϨⲒⲦ̄Ⲙ ⲠϢⲞⲢⲠ̄ Ⲙ̄ⲘⲨⲤⲦⲎⲢⲒⲞⲚ ⲈⲤϨⲀⲒ̈ Ⲛ̄ϢⲀϪⲈ ⲚⲒⲘ Ⲛ̄ⲦⲈ
15 ⲦⲘⲚⲦⲈⲢⲞ Ⲙ̄ⲠⲞⲨⲞⲒ̈Ⲛ · ⲀⲨⲰ Ⲛ̄ⲦⲈⲦⲚ̄ⲢⲘ̄ⲚⲦⲢⲈ ϨⲀⲢⲞⲞⲨ ·
ⲤⲰⲦ̄Ⲙ ϬⲈ ⲦⲀⲦⲀⲨⲈ-ⲠⲂⲰⲖ Ⲙ̄ⲠⲈⲒ̈ϢⲀϪⲈ ⲠⲀⲒ̈ ⲠⲈ Ⲛ̄ⲦⲀ
ⲦⲈⲔϬⲞⲘ Ⲛ̄ⲞⲨⲞⲈⲒⲚ ⲠⲢⲞⲪⲎⲦⲈⲨⲈ Ⲙ̄ⲘⲞϤ Ⲙ̄ⲠⲒⲞⲨⲞⲈⲒϢ
ϨⲒⲦ̄Ⲙ ⲘⲰ̈ⲨⲤⲎⲤ · ϪⲈ ϨⲒⲦⲚ̄ ⲘⲚⲦⲢⲈ ⲤⲚⲀⲨ ⲀⲨⲰ ϢⲞⲘⲦ̄ ·
ⲈⲢⲈ ϨⲰⲂ ⲚⲒⲘ ⲚⲀⲀϨⲈⲢⲀⲦϤ̄ · ⲠϢⲞⲘⲦ̄ Ⲙ̄ⲘⲚ̄ⲦⲢⲈ ⲠⲈ ⲪⲒ-
20 ⲖⲒⲠⲠⲞⲤ ⲘⲚ ⲐⲰⲘⲀⲤ ⲘⲚ ⲘⲀⲐⲐⲀⲒⲞⲤ :

ⲀⲤϢⲰⲠⲈ ϬⲈ Ⲛ̄ⲦⲈⲢⲈ Ⲓ̄Ⲥ̄ ⲈⲰⲦ̄Ⲙ ⲈⲠⲈⲒ̈ϢⲀϪⲈ · ⲠⲈϪⲀϤ
ϪⲈ ⲈⲨⲄⲈ ⲘⲀⲢⲒⲀ · ⲠⲀⲒ̈ ⲠⲈ ⲠⲂⲰⲖ** Ⲙ̄ⲠϢⲀϪⲈ · ⲦⲈⲚⲞⲨ Ⲝ̄Ⲋ̄

---

1 MS ⲚⲈϮⲚⲀⲚⲀⲨ ; read ⲚⲈⲦⲈⲦⲚ̄ⲚⲀⲚⲀⲨ.
2 Ⲛ̄ⲦⲀⲢⲘ̄ⲚⲦⲢⲈ; read Ⲛ̄ⲦⲈⲦⲚ̄ⲢⲘ̄ⲚⲦⲢⲈ ; ⲦⲈ in Ⲛ̄ⲦⲈ inserted above.

the things which I will do, and the things which you will see. And you will bear witness to all things of the Kingdom of Heaven."

43. Now when Jesus said these things he said to his *disciples*: "He who has ears to hear, let him hear." *

Mariam sprang up again, she came to the midst, she stood beside Philip, she said to Jesus: "My Lord, my man of light has ears, and I am prepared to hear by means of my power. And I have *understood* the word which thou hast spoken. Now at this time, my Lord, hear, so that I speak *openly*, for thou hast said to us: 'He who has ears to hear, let him hear.' *

Concerning the word which thou didst say to Philip: 'Thou and Thomas and Matthew are the three to whom it has been given, through the First *Mystery*, to write every word of the Kingdom of the Light, and to bear witness to them'; hear now that I give the interpretation of these words. It is this which thy light-power once *prophesied* through Moses: 'Through two and three witnesses everything will be established' □. The three witnesses are Philip and Thomas and Matthew".

Now it happened when Jesus heard these words, he said: "*Excellent*, Maria, this is the interpretation of the word. Now at this time, | do thou, Philip, come forward and give

---

* Mk. 4.9
□ cf. Deut. 19.15; Mt. 18.16

ϭⲉ ⲛ̄ⲧⲟⲕ ⲫⲓⲗⲓⲡⲡⲟⲥ ⲁⲙⲟⲩ ⲉⲑⲏ ⲛ̄ⲅⲧⲁⲩⲉ-ⲡⲃⲱⲗ ⲙ̄ⲡⲙⲩⲥ-
ⲧⲏⲣⲓⲟⲛ ⲛ̄ⲧⲙⲉϩϯ ⲙ̄ⲙⲉⲧⲁⲛⲟⲓⲁ ⲛ̄ⲧⲡⲓⲥⲧⲓⲥ ⲥⲟⲫⲓⲁ· ⲁⲩⲱ
ⲙⲛ̄ⲛ̄ⲥⲱⲥ ϩⲙⲟⲟⲥ ⲉϩⲣⲁⲓ̈ ⲛ̄ⲅⲥϩⲁⲓ̈ ⲛ̄ϣⲁϫⲉ ⲛⲓⲙ ⲉϯⲛⲁϫⲟⲟⲩ ϣⲁⲛⲧϥϫⲱⲕ ⲉⲃⲟⲗ ⲛ̄ϭⲓ ⲡⲁⲣⲓⲑⲙⲟⲥ ⲙ̄ⲡⲉⲕⲙⲉⲣⲟⲥ
5 ⲉⲧⲕ̄ⲛⲁⲥϩⲁⲓ̈ϥ ϩⲛ̄ ⲛ̄ϣⲁϫⲉ ⲛ̄ⲧⲙⲛ̄ⲧⲉⲣⲟ ⲙ̄ⲡⲟⲩⲟⲉⲓⲛ ⲙⲛ̄-
ⲛ̄ⲥⲁ ⲛⲁⲓ̈ ⲉⲕⲉⲉⲓ· ⲉⲑⲏ ⲛ̄ⲅⲭⲱ ⲙ̄ⲡⲉⲧⲉⲣⲉ ⲡⲉⲕⲡ̄ⲛ̄ⲁ ⲛⲁⲛⲟⲓ̈
ⲙ̄ⲙⲟϥ· ⲡⲗⲏⲛ ϭⲉ ⲧⲉⲛⲟⲩ ⲧⲁⲩⲉ-ⲡⲃⲱⲗ ⲙ̄ⲡⲙⲩⲥⲧⲏⲣⲓⲟⲛ
ⲛ̄ⲧⲙⲉϩϯ ⲙ̄ⲙⲉⲧⲁⲛⲟⲓⲁ ⲛ̄ⲧⲡⲓⲥⲧⲓⲥ ⲥⲟⲫⲓⲁ· ⲁϥⲟⲩⲱϣⲃ̄
ⲇⲉ ⲛ̄ϭⲓ ⲫⲓⲗⲓⲡⲡⲟⲥ ⲡⲉϫⲁϥ ⲛ̄ⲓⲥ̄· ϫⲉ ⲡⲁϫⲟⲉⲓⲥ· ⲥⲱⲧⲙ̄
10 ⲧⲁⲭⲱ ⲙ̄ⲡⲃⲱⲗ ⲛ̄ⲧⲉⲥⲙⲉⲧⲁⲛⲟⲓⲁ· ⲁ ⲧⲉⲕϭⲟⲙ ⲅⲁⲣ ⲡⲣⲟⲫⲏⲧⲉⲩⲉ ⲉⲧⲃⲏⲏⲧⲥ̄ ϩⲓⲧⲛ̄ ⲇⲁⲩⲉⲓⲇ ⲙ̄ⲡⲓⲟⲩⲟⲉⲓϣ ⲉⲥϫⲱ
ⲙ̄ⲙⲟⲥ ϩⲙ̄ ⲡⲙⲉϩϩⲙⲉⲛⲉⲥⲁϣϥⲉ ⲙ̄ⲯⲁⲗⲙⲟⲥ· ϫⲉ   ⲝ̄ⲍ b

1. ⲡϫⲟⲓ̈ⲥ ⲡⲛⲟⲩⲧⲉ ⲙ̄ⲡⲁⲟⲩϫⲁⲓ̈ ⲁⲓ̈ⲱϣ ⲉϩⲣⲁⲓ̈ ⲉⲣⲟⲕ
ⲙ̄ⲡⲉϩⲟⲟⲩ ⲙⲛ̄ ⲧⲉⲩϣⲏ·

15 2. ⲙⲁⲣⲉ ⲡⲁϣⲗⲏⲗ ⲉⲓ̈ ⲉϩⲟⲩⲛ ⲙ̄ⲡⲉⲕⲙ̄ⲧⲟ ⲉⲃⲟⲗ· ⲣⲓⲕⲉ
ⲙ̄ⲡⲉⲕⲙⲁⲁϫⲉ ⲡϫⲟⲉⲓⲥ ⲉⲡⲁⲥⲟⲡⲥ̄·

3. ϫⲉ ⲁ ⲧⲁⲯⲩⲭⲏ ⲙⲟⲩϩ ⲙ̄ⲡⲉⲑⲟⲟⲩ· ⲁ ⲡⲁⲱⲛ̄ϩ ϩⲱⲛ
ⲉϩⲟⲩⲛ ⲉⲁⲙⲛ̄ⲧⲉ·

4. ⲁⲩⲟⲡⲧ̄ ⲙⲛ̄ ⲛⲉⲧⲃⲏⲕ ⲉⲡⲉⲥⲏⲧ ⲉⲡϣⲏⲓ̈· ⲁⲓ̈ⲣⲑⲉ ⲛ̄ⲟⲩ-
20 ⲣⲱⲙⲉ ⲉⲙⲛ̄ⲧϥⲃⲟⲏⲑⲟⲥ·

5. ⲛ̄ⲉⲗⲉⲩⲑⲉⲣⲟⲥ ϩⲛ̄ ⲛⲉⲧⲙⲟⲟⲩⲧ· ⲛ̄ⲑⲉ ⲛ̄ϩⲉⲛϩⲁⲧⲃⲉⲥ
ⲉⲩⲛⲏϫ· ⲉⲩⲛ̄ⲕⲟⲧⲕ̄ ϩⲛ̄ ϩⲉⲛⲧⲁⲫⲟⲥ· ⲛⲁⲓ̈ ⲉⲧⲉ ⲙ̄ⲡⲕⲣ̄ⲡⲉⲩ-
ⲙⲉⲉⲩⲉ ϭⲉ· ⲁⲩⲱ ⲛ̄ⲧⲟⲟⲩ ⲁⲩⲧⲁⲕⲟ ⲉⲃⲟⲗ ϩⲛ̄ ⲛⲉⲕϭⲓϫ·

6. ⲁⲩⲕⲁⲁⲧ ϩⲛ̄ ⲟⲩϣⲏⲓ̈ ⲙ̄ⲡⲉⲥⲏⲧ· ϩⲛ̄ ϩⲉⲛⲕⲁⲕⲉ· ⲙⲛ̄
25 ⲑⲁⲓ̈ⲃⲉⲥ ⲙ̄ⲡⲙⲟⲩ·

---

22   ⲍⲉ in ϩⲉⲛⲧⲁⲫⲟⲥ   inserted above.

the interpretation of the *mystery* of the fifth *repentance* of the Pistis Sophia. And afterwards sit and write every word which I shall speak until the completion of the *number* of thy *part* in the words of the Kingdom of the Light, which thou wilt write. After this thou shalt come forward and speak whatever thy *Spirit* shall *understand. Nevertheless* now, at this time give the explanation of the *mystery* of the fifth *repentance* of the Pistis Sophia.

But Philip answered and said to Jesus: "My Lord, hear that I say the interpretation of her *repentance. For* thy power once *prophesied* about it through David in the 87th *Psalm*, saying:

1. 'O Lord God of my salvation, I have cried to thee by day and night.

2. Let my prayer come before thy presence. Incline thy ear, O Lord, to my petition.

3. For my soul is filled with evil; my life has approached Amente[1].

4. I am numbered with those who have gone down to the pit, I have become like a man without a *helper.*

5. The *free* among the dead are like the slain who are cast out and sleep in *graves*, whom now thou dost not remember; and they are destroyed through thy hands.

6. I have been laid in a pit below in darknesses and the shadow of death. |

---

[1] (18) Amente; lit. the western place; Hades; see ApJn 41.

7. ⲁ ⲡⲉⲕϭⲱⲛ̄ⲧ ⲧⲁϫⲣⲟ ⲉϩⲣⲁï ⲉϫⲱï· ⲁⲩⲱ ⲁ ⲛⲉⲕⲣⲟⲟⲩϣ ⲧⲏⲣⲟⲩ ⲁⲩⲉⲓ' ⲉϩⲣⲁï ⲉϫⲱï· ⲇⲓⲁⲯⲁⲗⲙⲁ·

8. ⲁⲕⲧⲣⲉ ⲛⲉⲧⲥⲟⲟⲩⲛ ⲙ̄ⲙⲟï· ⲟⲩⲉ ⲙ̄ⲙⲟï· ⲁⲩⲕⲁⲁⲧ
ⲛⲁⲩ ⲛ̄ⲃⲟⲧⲉ· **ⲁⲩⲕⲁⲁⲧ· ⲁⲩⲱ ⲙ̄ⲡⲓⲃⲱⲕ· ⲝ̄ⲏ̄

9. ⲁ ⲡⲁⲃⲁⲗ ϭ̄ⲃ̄ⲃⲉ ⲉⲃⲟⲗ ϩ̄ⲛ̄ ⲧⲁⲙ̄ⲛ̄ⲧϩⲏⲕⲉ· ⲁïϫⲓϣⲕⲁⲕ ⲉϩⲣⲁⲉⲓ ⲉⲣⲟⲕ ⲡϫⲟⲉⲓⲥ ⲙ̄ⲡⲉϩⲟⲟⲩ ⲧⲏⲣ̄ϥ ⲁïⲡⲱⲣ̄ϣ ⲛ̄ⲛⲁϭⲓϫ ⲉϩⲣⲁï ⲉⲣⲟⲕ·

10. ⲙⲏ ⲉⲕⲛⲁⲣ̄-ⲛⲉⲕϣⲡⲏⲣⲉ ϩ̄ⲛ̄ ⲛⲉⲧⲙⲟⲟⲩⲧ· ⲙⲏ ⲛ̄ⲥⲁïⲛ ⲛⲉⲧⲛⲁⲧⲱⲟⲩⲛ̄ ⲛ̄ⲥⲉϩⲟⲙⲟⲗⲟⲅⲓ ⲛⲁⲕ·

11. ⲙⲏ ⲉⲩⲛⲁϫⲱ ⲙ̄ⲡⲉⲕⲣⲁⲛ ϩ̄ⲛ̄ ⲛ̄ⲧⲁⲫⲟⲥ·

12. ⲁⲩⲱ ⲧⲉⲕⲇⲓⲕⲁⲓⲟⲥⲩⲛⲏ ϩ̄ⲛ̄ ⲟⲩⲕⲁϩ ⲉⲁⲕⲣ̄ⲡⲉϥⲱⲃ̄ϣ·

13. ⲁⲛⲟⲕ ⲇⲉ ⲁïϫⲓϣⲕⲁⲕ ⲉϩⲣⲁï ⲉⲣⲟⲕ ⲡϫⲟⲉⲓⲥ ⲁⲩⲱ ⲡⲁϣⲗⲏⲗ ⲛⲁⲧⲁϩⲟⲕ ⲙ̄ⲡⲛⲟⲩ ⲛ̄ϣⲱⲣⲡ·

14. ⲙ̄ⲡⲣ̄ⲕⲱⲧⲉ ⲙ̄ⲡⲉⲕϩⲟ ⲛ̄ⲥⲁⲃⲟⲗ ⲙ̄ⲙⲟï·

15. ϫⲉ ⲁⲛ̄ⲅ ⲟⲩϩⲏⲕⲉ ⲁⲛⲟⲕ· ⲉïϩ̄ⲛ̄ ϩⲉⲛϩⲓⲥⲉ ϫⲓⲛ ⲧⲁⲙ̄ⲛ̄ⲧⲕⲟⲩï· ⲛ̄ⲧⲉⲣⲓϫⲓⲥⲉ ⲇⲉ ⲁïⲑⲃ̄ⲃⲓⲟï· ⲁⲩⲱ ⲁïⲧⲱⲟⲩⲛ̄·

16. ⲁ ⲛⲉⲕⲟⲣⲅⲏ ⲉⲓ' ⲉϩⲣⲁï ⲉϫⲱï· ⲁⲩⲱ ⲁ ⲛⲉⲕϩⲟⲧⲉ ϣⲧ̄ⲣ̄ⲧⲱⲣ̄ⲧ·

17. ⲁⲩⲕⲱⲧⲉ ⲉⲣⲟï ⲛ̄ⲑⲉ ⲛ̄ⲟⲩⲙⲟⲟⲩ ⲁⲩⲁⲙⲁϩⲧⲉ ⲙ̄ⲙⲟï ⲙ̄ⲡⲉϩⲟⲟⲩ ⲧⲏⲣ̄ϥ·

18. ⲁⲕⲧⲣⲉ ⲛⲁϣⲃⲉⲉⲣ ⲟⲩⲉ ⲙ̄ⲙⲟï· ⲁⲩⲱ ⲛⲉ*ⲧⲥⲟⲟⲩⲛ̄ ⲝ̄ⲏ̄ b
ⲙ̄ⲙⲟï ⲉⲃⲟⲗ ϩ̄ⲛ̄ ⲧⲁⲧⲁⲗⲁⲓⲡⲱⲣⲓⲁ·

ⲡⲁï ϭⲉ ⲡⲉ ⲡⲃⲱⲗ ⲙ̄ⲡⲙⲩⲥⲧⲏⲣⲓⲟⲛ ⲛ̄ⲧⲙⲉϩϯ ⲙ̄ⲙⲉⲧⲁⲛⲟⲓⲁ ⲛ̄ⲧⲁⲥϫⲟⲟⲥ ⲛ̄ϭⲓ ⲧⲡⲓⲥⲧⲓⲥ ⲥⲟⲫⲓⲁ· ⲛ̄ⲧⲉⲣⲟⲩⲑⲗⲓⲃⲉ ⲙ̄ⲙⲟⲥ ϩ̄ⲙ̄ ⲡⲉⲭⲁⲟⲥ·

---

4 MS ⲁⲩⲕⲁⲁⲧ; perhaps better ⲁⲩⲧⲁⲁⲧ.

13 MS ⲙ̄ⲡⲛⲟⲩ; read ⲙ̄ⲡⲛⲁⲩ.

7. Thy anger has pressed down upon me; and all thy cares have come down upon me. *Pause.*

8. Thou hast caused those that know me to be distant from me; they have set me as an abomination to themselves; they have set me and I did not go.

9. My eye(s) became weak through my poverty; I cried to thee, O Lord, all the day; I spread out my hands to thee.

10. Wilt thou *perhaps* do thy wonders among the dead? Will shades [1] rise that they *confess* thee?

11. Will thy name *perhaps* be spoken in the *graves*?

12. And thy *righteousness* in a land which thou hast forgotten?

13. *But* I have cried to thee, O Lord, and my prayer will reach thee at the hour of daybreak.

14. Turn not thy face away from me.

15. For I am poor; I have been in distress since my youth; *but* when I was exalted I humbled myself, and I arose.

16. Thy *rages* have come down upon me, and thy fears have agitated me.

17. They have surrounded me like water; they have seized me all day.

18. Thou hast caused my companions to be distant from me; and those that know me on account of my *wretchedness' *.

This now is the interpretation of the fifth *repentance* which the Pistis Sophia said when she was *afflicted* in the *Chaos.* |

---

*   Ps. 87.1-18

---

[1]   (8) shades; Schmidt : physicians (Coptic mistranslation of Hebrew rephaim).

ⲍ ⲁⲥϣⲱⲡⲉ ϭⲉ ⲛ̄ⲧⲉⲣⲉ ⲓ̅ⲥ̅ ⲥⲱⲧ̅ⲙ̅ ⲉⲛⲉⲓ̈ϣⲁϫⲉ ⲉϥϫⲱ
ⲙ̄ⲙⲟⲟⲩ ⲛ̄ϭⲓ ⲫⲓⲗⲓⲡⲡⲟⲥ · ⲡⲉϫⲁϥ ϫⲉ ⲉⲩⲅⲉ ⲫⲓⲗⲓⲡⲡⲟⲥ
ⲡⲙⲉⲣⲓⲧ· ⲧⲉⲛⲟⲩ ϭⲉ ⲁⲙⲟⲩ ϩⲙⲟⲟⲥ ⲛ̄ⲅⲥϩⲁⲓ̈ ⲙ̄ⲡⲉⲕⲙⲉⲣⲟⲥ
ⲛ̄ϣⲁϫⲉ ⲛⲓⲙ ⲉⲧ⳿ⲛⲁϫⲟⲟⲩ · ⲁⲩⲱ ⲙ̅ⲛ̅ ⲛⲉ†ⲛⲁⲁⲁⲩ · ⲙ̅ⲛ̅
5 ϩⲱⲃ ⲛⲓⲙ ⲉⲧⲕ̄ⲛⲁⲛⲁⲩ ⲉⲣⲟⲟⲩ · ⲁⲩⲱ ⲛ̄ⲧⲉⲩⲛⲟⲩ ⲉⲧⲙ̅-
ⲙⲁⲩ ⲁϥϩⲙⲟⲟⲥ ⲉϩⲣⲁⲓ̈ ⲛ̄ϭⲓ ⲫⲓⲗⲓⲡⲡⲟⲥ ⲁϥⲥϩⲁⲓ̈ ·

ⲍ ⲁⲥϣⲱⲡⲉ ⲟⲛ ⲙⲛ̅ⲛ̅ⲥⲁ ⲛⲁⲓ̈ ⲁ ⲓ̅ⲥ̅ ⲟⲩⲱϩ ⲟⲛ ⲉⲧⲟⲟⲧ̅ϥ̅
ϩⲙ ⲡϣⲁϫⲉ ⲡⲉϫⲁϥ ⲛ̄ⲛⲉϥⲙⲁⲑⲏⲧⲏⲥ · ϫⲉ ⲧⲟⲧⲉ ⲁⲥⲱϣ
ⲉϩⲣⲁⲓ̈ ⲉⲡⲟⲩⲟⲉⲓⲛ ⲛ̄ϭⲓ ⲧⲡⲓⲥⲧⲓⲥ ⲥⲟⲫⲓⲁ · ⲁϥⲕⲱ ⲉⲃⲟⲗ
10 ⲙ̄ⲡⲉⲥⲛⲟⲃⲉ ϫⲉ ⲁⲥⲕⲁ-ⲡⲉⲥⲧⲟⲡⲟⲥ ⲛ̄ⲥⲱⲥ ⲁⲥⲉⲓ̈ ⲉϩⲣⲁⲓ̈
ⲉⲡⲕⲁⲕⲉ ⲁⲥϫⲱ ⲛ̄ⲧⲙⲉϩ**ⲥⲟ ⲙ̄ⲙⲉⲧⲁⲛⲟⲓⲁ ⲉⲥϫⲱ ⲙ̄ⲙⲟⲥ ⲍ̅ⲟ̅
ⲛ̄ⲧⲉⲓ̈ϩⲉ ϫⲉ

1. ⲁⲓ̈ϩⲩⲙⲛⲉⲩⲉ ⲉϩⲣⲁⲓ̈ ⲉⲣⲟⲕ ⲡⲟⲩⲟⲓ̈ⲛ ϩ̄ⲙ ⲡⲕⲁⲕⲉ ⲙ̄-
ⲡⲉⲥⲏⲧ ·

15 2. ⲥⲱⲧ̅ⲙ̅ ⲉⲧⲁⲙⲉⲧⲁⲛⲟⲓⲁ ⲁⲩⲱ ⲙⲁⲣⲉ ⲡⲉⲕⲟⲩⲟⲉⲓⲛ †-
ϩⲧⲏϥ ⲉⲡⲉϩⲣⲟⲟⲩ ⲙ̄ⲡⲁⲧⲱⲃⲁϩ ·

3. ⲡⲟⲩⲟⲉⲓⲛ ⲉⲕϣⲁⲛⲣ̄ⲡⲙⲉⲉⲩⲉ ⲙ̄ⲡⲁⲛⲟⲃⲉ · ⲛ̄†ⲛⲁϣⲉⲓ̈
ⲁⲛ ⲛ̄ⲛⲁϩⲣⲁⲕ ⲁⲩⲱ ⲕⲛⲁⲕⲁⲁⲧ ⲛ̄ⲥⲱⲕ ·

4. ϫⲉ ⲛ̄ⲧⲟⲕ ⲡⲟⲩⲟⲉⲓⲛ ⲡⲉ ⲡⲁⲛⲟⲩϩ̄ⲙ ⲉⲧⲃⲉ ⲡⲟⲩⲟⲉⲓⲛ
20 ⲙ̄ⲡⲉⲕⲣⲁⲛ· ⲛ̄ⲧⲁⲓ̈ⲡⲓⲥⲧⲉⲩⲉ ⲉⲣⲟⲕ ⲡⲟⲩⲟⲉⲓⲛ ·

5. ⲁⲩⲱ ⲁ ⲧⲁϭⲟⲙ ⲡⲓⲥⲧⲉⲩⲉ ⲉⲡⲉⲕⲙⲩⲥⲧⲏⲣⲓⲟⲛ ⲁⲩⲱ
ⲟⲛ ⲁ ⲧⲁϭⲟⲙ ⲛⲁϩⲧⲉ ⲉⲡⲟⲩⲟⲉⲓⲛ ⲉϥϣⲟⲟⲡ ϩ̄ⲛ ⲛⲁⲡϫⲓⲥⲉ
ⲁⲩⲱ ⲁⲥⲛⲁϩⲧⲉ ⲉⲣⲟϥ ⲉⲥϩ̄ⲙ ⲡⲉⲭⲁⲟⲥ ⲙ̄ⲡⲉⲥⲏⲧ ·

6. ⲙⲁⲣⲉ ϭⲟⲙ ⲛⲓⲙ ⲉⲧⲛ̄ϩⲏⲧ ⲛⲁϩⲧⲉ ⲉⲡⲟⲩⲟⲉⲓⲛ ⲉⲓ̈ϩ̄ⲙ
25 ⲡⲕⲁⲕⲉ ⲙ̄ⲡⲉⲥⲏⲧ· ⲁⲩⲱ ⲟⲛ ⲙⲁⲣⲟⲩⲛⲁϩⲧⲉ ⲉⲣⲟϥ ⲉⲩϣⲁⲛ-
ⲉⲓ̈ ⲉⲡⲧⲟⲡⲟⲥ ⲙ̄ⲡϫⲓⲥⲉ ·

---

22 MS ⲉϥϣⲟⲟⲡ ; read ⲉⲥϣⲟⲟⲡ.

44. It happened now when Jesus heard these words which Philip said [1], he said to him : "*Excellent*, Philip, thou beloved one. Come now at this time, sit and write thy *part* of every word which I shall say, and what I shall do, and everything which thou shalt see". And immediately Philip sat down and wrote.

It happened furthermore after this Jesus continued again with the discourse. He said to his *disciples* : "*Then* the Pistis Sophia cried out to the Light. He forgave her sin, that she had forsaken her *place*, she had come down to the darkness. She spoke the sixth *repentance* in this way, saying :

1. I have *sung praises* to thee, O Light, in the darkness below.

2. Hear my *repentance*, and may thy light give heed to the voice of my entreaty.

3. O Light, if thou dost remember my sins I shall not be able to come before thee, and thou wilt forsake me.

4. For thou, O Light, art my Saviour on account of the light of thy name. I have *believed* in thee, O Light.

5. And my power *believed* in thy *mystery*. And furthermore, my power trusted in the light, when it was in those of the height, and it (my power) trusted it (the light) when it (my power) was in the *Chaos* below.

6. May all the powers within me trust the light, when I am in the darkness below, and may they trust it when they come to the *place* of the height. |

---

[1]   (1, 2) when Jesus heard these words which Philip said; see 117, n. 2.

7. ϪⲈ ⲚⲦⲞϤ ⲠⲈⲦⲚⲀ ⲚⲀⲨ ⲀⲨⲰ ⲚϤⲤⲞⲦⲚ · ⲀⲨⲰ ⲞⲨⲚ-
ⲞⲨⲚⲞϬ ⲘⲘⲨⲤⲦⲎⲢⲒⲞⲚ ⲚⲚⲞⲨϨⲘ ⲚϨⲎⲦϤ ·   ⲍⲟ ᵇ

8. ⲀⲨⲰ ⲚⲦⲞϤ ⲠⲈ ⲈⲦⲚⲀⲚⲞⲨϨⲘ ⲚⲚϬⲞⲘ ⲦⲎⲢⲞⲨ ⲈⲂⲞⲗ
ϨⲘ ⲠⲈϪⲀⲞⲤ ⲈⲦⲂⲈ ⲦⲀⲠⲀⲢⲀⲂⲀⲤⲒⲤ ϪⲈ ⲀⲒⲔⲰ ⲚⲤⲰⲒ ⲘⲠⲀ-
5 ⲦⲞⲠⲞⲤ ⲀⲒⲈⲒ ' ⲈϨⲢⲀⲒ ⲈⲠⲈϪⲀⲞⲤ ·

ⲦⲈⲚⲞⲨ ϬⲈ ⲠⲈⲦⲈⲢⲈ ⲠⲈϤⲚⲞⲨⲤ ϪⲞⲤⲈ ⲘⲀⲢⲈϤⲚⲞⲒ ·

Ⲍ ⲀⲤϢⲰⲠⲈ ϬⲈ ⲚⲦⲈⲢⲈ ⲒⲤ ⲞⲨⲰ ⲈϤϪⲰ ⲚⲚⲈⲒϢⲀϪⲈ
ⲈⲚⲈϤⲘⲀⲐⲎⲦⲎⲤ · ⲠⲈϪⲀϤ ⲚⲀⲨ ϪⲈ ⲦⲈⲦⲚⲚⲞⲒ ϪⲈ ⲈⲒ-
ϢⲀϪⲈ ⲚⲘⲘⲎⲦⲚ ⲚⲀϢ ⲚϨⲈ · ⲀϤⲈⲒ ' ⲈⲐⲎ ⲚϬⲒ ⲀⲚⲆⲢⲈⲀⲤ
10 ⲠⲈϪⲀϤ ϪⲈ ⲠⲀϪⲞⲈⲒⲤ · ⲈⲦⲂⲈ ⲠⲂⲰⲗ ⲚⲦⲘⲈϨⲤⲞ ⲘⲘⲈⲦⲀ-
ⲚⲞⲒⲀ ⲚⲦⲠⲒⲤⲦⲒⲤ ⲤⲞⲫⲒⲀ · Ⲁ ⲦⲈⲔϬⲞⲘ ⲚⲞⲨⲞⲈⲒⲚ ⲠⲢⲞ-
ⲫⲎⲦⲈⲨⲈ ⲘⲠⲒⲞⲨⲞⲒϢ ϨⲒⲦⲚ ⲆⲀⲨⲈⲒⲆ · ϨⲘ ⲠⲘⲈϨϢⲈϪⲞⲨⲦ-
ⲮⲒⲤ ⲚⲮⲀⲗⲘⲞⲤ ⲈⲤϪⲰ ⲘⲘⲞⲤ · ϪⲈ

1. ⲀⲒⲰϢ ⲈϨⲢⲀⲒ ⲈⲢⲞⲔ ⲠϪⲞⲈⲒⲤ ϨⲚ ⲚⲈⲦϢⲎⲔ ·

15 2. ⲤⲰⲦⲘ ⲈⲠⲀϨⲢⲞⲞⲨ · ⲘⲀⲢⲈ ⲚⲈⲔⲘⲀⲀϪⲈ ϮϨⲦⲎⲨ
ⲈⲠⲈϨⲢⲞⲞⲨ ⲘⲠⲀⲤⲞⲠⲤ ·

3. ⲠϪⲞⲈⲒⲤ ⲈⲔϢⲀⲚϮϨⲦⲎⲔ ⲈⲚⲀⲚⲞⲘⲒⲀ ⲚⲒⲘ ⲠⲈⲦⲚⲀ- ⲟ̄
ϢⲀϨⲈⲢⲀⲦϤ ·

4. ϪⲈ ⲈⲢⲈ ⲠⲔⲰ ⲈⲂⲞⲗ ⲚⲦⲞⲞⲦⲔ · ⲈⲦⲂⲈ ⲠⲈⲔⲢⲀⲚ ⲀⲒϨⲨ-
20 ⲠⲞⲘⲒⲚⲈ ⲈⲢⲞⲔ ⲠϪⲞⲈⲒⲤ ·

5. Ⲁ ⲦⲀⲮⲨⲬⲎ ϨⲨⲠⲞⲘⲒⲚⲈ ⲈⲠⲈⲔϢⲀϪⲈ ·

6. Ⲁ ⲦⲀⲮⲨⲬⲎ ϨⲈⲗⲠⲒⲌⲈ ⲈⲠϪⲞⲈⲒⲤ · ϪⲒⲚ ϨⲦⲞⲞⲨⲈ ϢⲀ
ⲢⲞⲨϨⲈ · ⲘⲀⲢⲈ ⲠⲒⲎⲗ ϨⲈⲗⲠⲒⲌⲈ ⲈⲠϪⲞⲈⲒⲤ ϪⲒⲚ ϨⲦⲞⲞⲨ ϢⲀ
ⲢⲞⲨϨⲈ ·

---

1 MS ⲠⲈⲦⲚⲀⲚⲀⲨ; read ⲠⲈⲦⲚⲀ ⲚⲀⲚ; ⲀⲨⲰ inserted above.
13 MS ⲚⲮⲀⲗⲘⲞⲤ; read ⲘⲮⲀⲗⲘⲞⲤ.
23 MS ϨⲦⲞⲞⲨ; better ϨⲦⲞⲞⲨⲈ.

7. For it (the light) is merciful to us [1] and saves us, and there is a great *mystery* of salvation within it.

8. And it will save all the powers from the *Chaos* on account of my *transgression*, because I have forsaken my *place*, I have come down to the *Chaos*.'

At this time now, he whose *understanding* (*mind*) is uplifted [2], let him *understand*."

45. Now it happened when Jesus finished saying these words to his *disciples*, he said to them : "Do you *understand* in what manner I am speaking with you?" Andrew came forward, he said : "My Lord, concerning the interpretation of the sixth *repentance* of the Pistis Sophia, thy light-power *prophesied* once, through David, in the 129th *Psalm*, saying :

1. 'Out of the depths I have cried to thee, O Lord.

2. Hear my voice; let thine ears be inclined to the voice of my supplication.

3. O Lord, if thou givest heed to my *iniquities* who will be able to stand?

4. For forgiveness is with thee; I have *waited for* thee, O Lord, for thy name's sake.

5. My *soul* has *waited on* thy word.

6. My *soul* has *hoped* in the Lord from morning until evening; may Israel *hope* in the Lord from morning until evening. |

---

[1] (1) is merciful to us; Till : will be merciful to us (MS : them), or : will see.
[2] (6) uplifted; Till : up to the mark i.e. efficient (also 114.5).

7. ⲭⲉ ⲉⲣⲉ ⲡⲛⲁ' ⲛⲧⲟⲟⲧϥ ⲙⲡⲭⲟⲉⲓⲥ· ⲁⲩⲱ ⲟⲩⲛ-
ⲟⲩⲛⲟϭ ⲛⲥⲱⲧⲉ ⲍⲁⲍⲧⲏϥ·

8. ⲁⲩⲱ ⲛⲧⲟϥ ⲡⲉⲧⲛⲁⲥⲱⲧⲉ ⲙⲡⲓⲥⲗ ⲉⲃⲟⲗ ⲍⲛ ⲛⲉϥⲁ-
ⲛⲟⲙⲓⲁ ⲧⲏⲣⲟⲩ·

5 ⲡⲉⲭⲁϥ ⲛⲁϥ ⲛϭⲓ ⲓⲥ ⲭⲉ ⲉⲩⲅⲉ ⲁⲛⲇⲣⲉⲁⲥ ⲡⲙⲁⲕⲁⲣⲓⲟⲥ
ⲡⲁⲓ ⲡⲉ ⲡⲃⲱⲗ ⲛⲧⲉⲥⲙⲉⲧⲁⲛⲟⲓⲁ· ⲍⲁⲙⲏⲛ ⲍⲁⲙⲏⲛ ϯⲭⲱ
ⲙⲙⲟⲥ ⲛⲏⲧⲛ ⲭⲉ ϯⲛⲁⲭⲉⲕ-ⲧⲏⲩⲧⲛ ⲉⲃⲟⲗ ⲙⲙⲩⲥⲧⲏⲣⲓⲟⲛ
ⲛⲓⲙ ⲛⲧⲉ ⲡⲟⲩⲟⲉⲓⲛ· ⲁⲩⲱ ⲙⲛ ⲅⲛⲱⲥⲓⲥ ⲛⲓⲙ ⲭⲓⲛ ⲙⲡⲥⲁ-
ⲛⲍⲟⲩⲛ ⲛⲛⲥⲁⲛⲍⲟⲩⲛ· ⲱⲁ ⲡⲥⲁⲛⲃⲟⲗ ⲛⲛⲥⲁⲛⲃⲟⲗ· ⲭⲓⲛ
10 ⲡⲓⲁⲧⲱⲁⲭⲉ ⲉⲣⲟϥ ⲱⲁ ⲡⲕⲁⲕⲉ ⲛⲛⲕⲁⲕⲉ· *ⲁⲩⲱ ⲭⲓⲛ ⲡⲟⲩ- ⲟ̄ᵇ
ⲟⲓⲛ ⲛⲛⲟⲩⲟⲓⲛ: ⲱⲁ ⲫⲁⲗⲃ ⲛⲑⲩⲗⲏ· ⲭⲓⲛ ⲛⲛⲟⲩⲧⲉ ⲧⲏ-
ⲣⲟⲩ· ⲱⲁ ⲛⲁⲗⲁⲓⲙⲟⲛⲓⲟⲛ· ⲭⲓⲛ ⲛⲭⲟⲉⲓⲥ ⲧⲏⲣⲟⲩ· ⲱⲁ
ⲛⲁⲉⲕⲁⲛⲟⲥ· ⲭⲓⲛ ⲛⲉⲝⲟⲩⲥⲓⲁ ⲧⲏⲣⲟⲩ· ⲱⲁ ⲛⲗⲓⲧⲟⲩⲣ-
ⲅⲟⲥ· ⲭⲓⲛ ⲡⲧⲁⲙⲓⲟ ⲛⲣⲣⲱⲙⲉ· ⲱⲁ ⲛⲉⲑⲏⲣⲓⲟⲛ· ⲙⲛ ⲛⲧⲃ-
15 ⲛⲟⲟⲩⲉ· ⲙⲛ ⲛⲭⲁⲧϥⲉ· ⲭⲉ ⲉⲩⲉⲙⲟⲩⲧⲉ ⲉⲣⲱⲧⲛ ⲭⲉ
ⲛⲧⲉⲗⲉⲓⲟⲥ· ⲉⲧⲭⲏⲕ ⲉⲃⲟⲗ ⲍⲙ ⲡⲗⲏⲣⲱⲙⲁ ⲛⲓⲙ· ⲍⲁⲙⲏⲛ
ⲍⲁⲙⲏⲛ ϯⲭⲱ ⲙⲙⲟⲥ ⲛⲏⲧⲛ ⲭⲉ ⲡⲧⲟⲡⲟⲥ ⲉϯⲛⲁⲱⲱⲡⲉ
ⲛⲍⲏⲧϥ ⲍⲛ ⲧⲙⲛⲧⲉⲣⲟ ⲙⲡⲁⲉⲓⲱⲧ· ⲧⲉⲧⲛⲁⲱⲱⲡⲉ ⲍⲱⲧ-
ⲧⲏⲩⲧⲛ ⲙⲙⲁⲩ ⲛⲙⲙⲁⲓ· ⲁⲩⲱ ⲉϥⲱⲁⲛⲭⲱⲕ ⲛϭⲓ ⲡⲁⲣⲓⲑ-
20 ⲙⲟⲥ ⲛⲧⲉⲗⲉⲓⲟⲥ ⲉⲧⲣⲉϥⲃⲱⲗ ⲉⲃⲟⲗ ⲛϭⲓ ⲡⲕⲉⲣⲁⲥⲙⲟⲥ·
ϯⲛⲁⲕⲉⲗⲉⲩⲉ ⲛⲥⲉⲉⲓⲛⲉ ⲛⲛⲟⲩⲧⲉ ⲧⲏⲣⲟⲩ ⲛⲧⲩⲣⲁⲛⲛⲟⲥ
ⲛⲁⲓ ⲉⲧⲉ ⲙⲡⲟⲩϯ-ⲡⲥⲱⲧϥ ⲙⲡⲉⲩⲟⲩⲟⲓⲛ· ⲁⲩⲱ ϯⲛⲁⲕⲉⲗⲉⲩⲉ ⲙⲡⲓⲕⲱⲍⲧ ⲛⲥⲁⲃⲉ· **ⲡⲁⲓ ⲉⲱⲁⲣⲉ ⲛⲧⲉⲗⲓⲟⲥ ⲭⲓ- ⲟ̄ⲗ
ⲟⲟⲣ ⲙⲙⲟϥ· ⲉⲧⲣⲉϥⲟⲩⲱⲙ ⲉⲍⲟⲩⲛ ⲛⲥⲁ ⲛⲧⲩⲣⲁⲛⲛⲟⲥ
25 ⲉⲧⲙⲙⲁⲩ ⲱⲁⲛⲧⲟⲩϯ-ⲡⲍⲁⲉ ⲛⲥⲱⲧϥ ⲛⲧⲉ ⲡⲉⲩⲟⲩⲟⲉⲓⲛ·

---

22 MS ϯⲓⲡ|ⲁⲕⲉⲗⲉⲩⲅ; ⲓ expunged.

7. For mercy is in the hand of the Lord, and with him is a great salvation.

8. And he will save Israel out of all his *iniquities'* * ".

Jesus said to him : "*Excellent*, Andrew, thou *blessed one*. This is the interpretation of her *repentance. Truly, truly,* I say to you, I will fulfil you in all the *mysteries* of the light, and every *gnosis*, from the innermost of the inner to the outermost of the outer; from the Ineffable to the darkness of darknesses; and from the Light of Lights to the (? matter) [1] of *matter*; from all the gods to the *demons*; from all the lords to the *decans*; from all the *powers* (*exousiai*) to the *ministers*; from the creation of men to (that of) *beasts* and cattle and reptiles, in order that you be called *perfect*, fulfilled in every *pleroma. Truly, truly,* I say to you that, in the *place* in which I shall be in the Kingdom of my Father, you will also be there with me ⸆. And when the *perfect number* is completed so that the *mixture* is dissolved, I will *command* that all the *tyrant* gods who did not give (up) what is purified of their light be brought. I will *command* the fire of wisdom, which the *perfect ones* transmit, to consume those *tyrants* until they give (up) the last of what is purified of their light." |

---

*   Ps. 129.1-8
⸆   cf. Mt. 26.29; Lk. 22.30

---

[1]   (11) (? matter); Till : bottom (? dregs).

ⳅ ⲀⲤϢⲰⲠⲈ ⳓⲈ ⲚⲦⲈⲢⲈ ⲒⲤ ⲞⲨⲰ ⲈϤϪⲰ ⲚⲚⲈⲒϢⲀϪⲈ
ⲈⲚⲈϤⲘⲀⲐⲎⲦⲎⲤ · ⲠⲈϪⲀϤ ⲚⲀⲨ ϪⲈ ⲦⲈⲦⲚ̅ⲚⲞⲒ ϪⲈ ⲈⲒ̈-
ϢⲀϪⲈ ⲚⲘⲘⲎⲦⲚ̅ ⲚⲀϢ Ⲛ̅Ⲁ̅ⲀⲨⲘⲘⲎⲦⲚ̅ ⲚⲀϢ Ⲛ̅Ⲁ̅Ⲉ · ⲠⲈϪⲈ ⲘⲀⲢⲒⲀ ϪⲈ ⲤⲈ ⲠϪⲞ-
ⲈⲒⲤ ⲀⲒ̈ⲚⲞⲒ̈ Ⲙ̅ⲠϢⲀϪⲈ ⲈⲦⲕ̅ϪⲰ Ⲙ̅ⲘⲞϤ · ⲈⲦⲂⲈ ⲠϢⲀϪⲈ ⳓⲈ

5 ⲈⲚⲦⲀⲕϪⲞⲞϤ ϪⲈ ⲌⲢⲀⲒ̈ Ⲋ̅Ⲙ̅ ⲠⲂⲰⲖ ⲈⲂⲞⲖ Ⲙ̅ⲠⲕⲈⲢⲀⲤⲘⲞⲤ
ⲦⲎⲢϤ̅ · ⲔⲚⲀⳘⲘⲞⲞⲤ ⲌⲒϪⲚ̅ ⲞⲨⳓⲞⲘ Ⲛ̅ⲞⲨⲞⲈⲒⲚ · ⲀⲨⲰ Ⲛ̅ⲦⲈ
ⲚⲈⲔⲘⲀⲐⲎⲦⲎⲤ ⲈⲦⲈ ⲀⲚⲞⲚ ⲠⲈ Ⲛ̅ⲦⲚ̅ⳘⲘⲞⲞⲤ ⳘⲒ ⲞⲨⲚⲀⳘ
Ⲙ̅ⲘⲞⲔ · Ⲛ̅Ⲅ̅†ⳌⲀⲠ ⲈⲚⲚⲞⲨⲦⲈ Ⲛ̅ⲦⲨⲢⲀⲚⲚⲞⲤ · ⲚⲀⲒ̈ ⲈⲦⲈ
Ⲙ̅ⲠⲞⲨ†-ⲠⲤⲰⲦϤ̅ Ⲙ̅ⲠⲈⲨⲞⲨⲞⲈⲒⲚ · ⲀⲨⲰ ⲠⲔⲰⳌⲦ̅ Ⲛ̅ⲤⲀⲂⲈ

10 ⲚⲀⲞⲨⲰⲘ Ⲛ̅ⲤⲰⲞⲨ ϢⲀⲚⲦⲞⲨ†-ⲠⳌⲀⳘⲈ Ⲛ̅ⲞⲨⲞⲈⲒⲚ ⲈⲦⲚ̅-
ⳌⲎⲦⲞⲨ · *ⲈⲦⲂⲈ ⲠⲈⲒ̈ϢⲀϪⲈ ⳓⲈ Ⲁ ⲦⲈⲔⳓⲞⲘ Ⲛ̅ⲞⲨⲞ̈Ⲓ̈Ⲛ ⲠⲢⲞ- Ⲟ̅Ⲗ̅ᵇ
ⲫⲎⲦⲈⲨⲈ Ⲙ̅ⲠⲒⲞⲨⲞⲈⲒϢ ⳌⲒⲦⲚ̅ ⲀⲀⲨⲒ̈Ⲁ ⲈⲤϪⲰ Ⲙ̅ⲘⲞⲤ Ⲋ̅Ⲙ̅
ⲠⲘⲈⳌϤⲦⲞⲨⲬⲞⲨⲰⲦ ⲘⲚ̅ ⲞⲨⲀ᾽ Ⲙ̅ⲮⲀⲖⲘⲞⲤ · ϪⲈ

   1. ⲠⲚⲞⲨⲦⲈ ⲚⲀⳌⲘⲞⲞⲤ Ⲋ̅Ⲛ̅ ⲦⲤⲨⲚⲀⲅⲰⲄⲎ Ⲛ̅ⲚⲚⲞⲨⲦⲈ

15 Ⲛ̅Ϥ†ⳌⲀⲠ ⲈⲚⲚⲞⲨⲦⲈ ·

   ⲠⲈϪⲀϤ ⲚⲀⲤ Ⲛ̅ⳓⲒ ⲒⲤ ϪⲈ ⲈⲨⲄⲈ᾽ ⲘⲀⲢⲒⲀ ·

ⳅ ⲀϤⲞⲨⲰⳌ ⲞⲚ ⲈⲦⲞⲞⲦϤ̅ Ⲛ̅ⳓⲒ ⲒⲤ Ⲋ̅Ⲙ̅ ⲠϢⲀϪⲈ ⲠⲈϪⲀϤ
Ⲛ̅ⲚⲈϤⲘⲀⲐⲎⲦⲎⲤ ϪⲈ ⲀⲤϢⲰⲠⲈ Ⲛ̅ⲦⲈⲢⲈ ⲦⲠⲒⲤⲦⲒⲤ ⲤⲞⲪⲒⲀ
ⲞⲨⲰ ⲈⲤϪⲰ Ⲛ̅ⲦⲘⲈⳌⲤⲞ Ⲙ̅ⲘⲈⲦⲀⲚⲞⲒⲀ · ⲈⲦⲂⲈ ⲠⲔⲰ ⲈⲂⲞⲖ

20 Ⲛ̅ⲦⲈⲤⲠⲀⲢⲀⲂⲀⲤⲒⲤ · ⲀⲤⲔⲞⲦⲤ̅ ⲞⲚ ⲈⲠϪⲒⲤⲈ ⲈⲚⲀⲨ ϪⲈ ⲀⲨⲔⲰ
ⲚⲀⲤ ⲈⲂⲞⲖ Ⲛ̅ⲚⲈⲤⲚⲞⲂⲈ ⲀⲨⲰ, ⲈⲚⲀⲨ ϪⲈ ⲈⲚⲈⲤⲈⲚⲀⲚ̅ⲦⲤ̅
ⲈⳌⲢⲀⲒ̈ Ⲋ̅Ⲙ̅ ⲠⲈⲬⲀⲞⲤ · ⲀⲨⲰ ⲚⲈⲘⲠⲀⲦⲞⲨⲤⲰⲦⲘ̅ ⲈⲢⲞⲤ ⲠⲈ
ⳌⲒⲦⲚ̅ ⲦⲔⲈⲖⲈⲨⲤⲒⲤ Ⲙ̅ⲠϢⲞⲢⲠ̅ Ⲙ̅ⲘⲨⲤⲦⲎⲢⲒⲞⲚ ⲈⲦⲢⲈⲨⲔⲰ
ⲈⲂⲞⲖ Ⲙ̅ⲠⲈⲤⲚⲞⲂⲈ · ⲀⲨⲰ Ⲛ̅ⲤⲈⲚ̅ⲦⲤ̅ ⲈⳌⲢⲀⲒ̈ Ⲋ̅Ⲙ̅ ⲠⲈⲬⲀⲞⲤ ·

It happened, when Jesus finished saying these words to his *disciples*, he said to them : "Do you *understand* in what manner I have spoken to you?"

Maria said : "Yes, O Lord, I have *understood* the discourse which thou hast spoken. Concerning the word now which thou didst say : 'At the dissolving of the whole *mixture* thou wilt sit upon a light-power, and thy *disciples*, that is we, we will sit to the right of thee*. And thou wilt judge the *tyrant* gods which did not give (up) what is purified of their light. And the fire of wisdom will consume them until they give (up) the last of the light which is in them.' Now concerning this word, thy light-power once *prophesied*, through David, in the 81st *Psalm*, saying : 'God will sit in the *assembly* of gods and will judge the gods' ▫".

Jesus said to her : "*Excellent*, Maria."

46.   Jesus continued again with the discourse, he said to his *disciples* : "It happened when the Pistis Sophia finished saying the sixth *repentance* concerning the forgiveness of her *transgression*, she turned again to the height to see whether her sins were forgiven her, and to see whether she would be brought up from the *Chaos*. And she was not yet heard, through the *command* of the First *Mystery*, that her sin would be forgiven, and that she would be brought out of the *Chaos*. | When she turned to the height to see whether

---

*   cf. Lk. 22.30
▫   Ps. 81.1

ⲚⲦⲈⲢⲈⲤⲔⲞⲦⲤ ϬⲈ ⲈⲠⲬⲒⲤⲈ ⲈⲚⲀⲨ ⲬⲈ ⲀⲨⲬⲒ-ⲦⲈⲤⲘⲈⲦⲀ- ⁻ⲟⲃ

ⲚⲞⲒⲀ ⲚⲦⲞⲞⲦⲤ · ⲀⲤⲚⲀⲨ ⲈⲚⲀⲢⲬⲰⲚ ⲦⲎⲢⲞⲨ ⲘⲠⲘ̄ⲦⲤⲚⲞ-

ⲞⲨⲤ ⲚⲀⲒⲰⲚ ⲈⲨⲤⲰⲂⲈ ⲚⲤⲰⲤ · ⲀⲨⲰ ⲈⲨⲢⲀϢⲈ Ⲙ̄ⲘⲞⲤ ·

ⲈⲂⲞⲖ ⲬⲈ Ⲙ̄ⲠⲞⲨⲬⲒ-ⲦⲈⲤⲘⲈⲦⲀⲚⲞⲒⲀ ⲚⲦⲞⲞⲦⲤ̄ · ⲚⲦⲈⲢⲈⲤ-

⁵ ⲚⲀⲨ ϬⲈ ⲈⲢⲞⲞⲨ ⲈⲨⲤⲰⲂⲈ ⲚⲤⲰⲤ · ⲀⲤⲖⲨⲠⲒ ⲈⲘⲀⲦⲈ ⲀⲤϤⲒ-

ϨⲢⲀⲤ ⲈϨⲢⲀⲒ̈ ⲈⲠⲬⲒⲤⲈ ⲈⲤⲬⲰ Ⲙ̄ⲘⲞⲤ ϨⲚ̄ ⲦⲘⲈϨⲤⲀϢϤⲈ

Ⲙ̄ⲘⲈⲦⲀⲚⲞⲒⲀ ⲬⲈ

1. ⲠⲞⲨⲞⲈⲒⲚ ⲀⲒ̈ϤⲒ ⲚⲦⲀϬⲞⲘ ⲈϨⲢⲀⲒ̈ ⲈⲢⲞⲔ ⲠⲀⲞⲨⲞⲈⲒⲚ ·

2. ⲀⲒ̈ⲠⲒⲤⲦⲈⲨⲈ ⲈⲢⲞⲔ Ⲙ̄ⲠⲢⲦⲢⲀⲬⲒⲤⲰϢ · ⲀⲨⲰ Ⲙ̄ⲠⲢⲦⲢⲈⲨ-

¹⁰ ⲢⲀϢⲈ Ⲙ̄ⲘⲞⲒ̈ Ⲛ̄ϬⲒ Ⲛ̄ⲀⲢⲬⲰⲚ Ⲙ̄ⲠⲘ̄ⲚⲦⲤⲚⲞⲞⲨⲤ ⲚⲀⲒⲰⲚ ⲚⲀⲒ̈

ⲈⲦⲘⲞⲤⲦⲈ Ⲙ̄ⲘⲞⲒ̈ ·

3. ⲞⲨⲞⲚ ⲄⲀⲢ ⲚⲒⲘ ⲈⲦⲠⲒⲤⲦⲈⲨⲈ ⲈⲢⲞⲔ Ⲛ̄ⲤⲈⲚⲀⲬⲒϢⲒⲠⲈ

ⲀⲚ · ⲈⲨⲈϬⲰ ϨⲚ̄ ⲞⲨⲔⲀⲔⲈ Ⲛ̄ϬⲒ ⲚⲈⲚⲦⲀⲨϤⲒ ⲚⲦⲀϬⲞⲘ Ⲛ̄ⲤⲈ-

ⲚⲀϮϨⲎⲨ Ⲙ̄ⲘⲞⲤ ⲀⲚ ⲀⲖⲖⲀ ⲤⲈⲚⲀϤⲒⲦⲤ̄ ⲚⲦⲞⲞⲦⲞⲨ ·

¹⁵ 4. ⲠⲞⲨⲞⲈⲒⲚ ⲘⲀⲦⲀⲘⲞⲒ̈ ⲈⲚⲈⲔϨⲒⲞⲞⲨⲈ ⲀⲨⲰ ϮⲚⲀⲚⲞⲨϨⲘ̄

Ⲛ̄ϨⲎⲦⲞⲨ · ⲀⲨⲰ ⲘⲀⲦⲀⲘⲞⲒ̈ ⲈⲚⲈⲔⲘⲀⲘ̄ⲘⲞⲞϢⲈ ⲬⲈ ⲈⲒ̈Ⲉ- ⁻ⲟⲃᵇ

ⲚⲞⲨϨⲘ̄ ϨⲘ̄ ⲠⲈⲬⲖⲞⲤ ·

5. ⲀⲨⲰ ⲬⲒⲘⲞⲈⲒⲦ ϨⲎⲦ ϨⲘ̄ ⲠⲈⲔⲞⲨⲞⲒ̈Ⲛ · ⲀⲨⲰ ⲘⲀⲢⲒ-

ⲈⲒⲘⲈ Ⲱ’ ⲠⲞⲨⲞⲈⲒⲚ ⲬⲈ Ⲛ̄ⲦⲞⲔ ⲠⲈ ⲠⲀⲢⲈϤⲚⲞⲨϨⲘ̄ · ϮⲚⲀ-

²⁰ ⲚⲀϨⲦⲈ ⲈⲢⲞⲔ Ⲙ̄ⲠⲀⲞⲨⲞⲈⲒϢ ⲦⲎⲢϤ ·

6. ϮϨⲦⲎⲔ ⲈⲦⲢⲈⲔⲚⲞⲨϨⲘ̄ Ⲙ̄ⲘⲞⲒ̈ ⲠⲞⲨⲞⲒ̈Ⲛ ⲬⲈ ⲦⲈⲔⲘ̄ⲚⲦ-

ⲚⲀⲎⲦ ϢⲞⲞⲠ Ⲛ̄ϢⲀⲈⲚⲈϨ ·

7. ⲈⲦⲂⲈ ⲦⲀⲠⲀⲢⲀⲂⲀⲤⲒⲤ ⲈⲚⲦⲀⲒ̈ⲀⲀⲤ ⲬⲒⲚ Ⲛ̄ϢⲞⲢⲠ̄ ϨⲚ̄ ⲦⲀ-

Ⲙ̄Ⲙ̄ⲚⲦⲀⲦⲤⲞⲞⲨⲚ̄ · Ⲙ̄ⲠⲢⲞⲠⲤ̄ ⲈⲢⲞⲒ̈ ⲠⲞⲨⲞⲒ̈Ⲛ · ⲀⲖⲖⲀ ⲚⲀϨⲘⲈⲦ

²⁵ Ⲛ̄ⲦⲞϤ · ϨⲘ̄ ⲠⲈⲔⲚⲞϬ Ⲙ̄ⲘⲨⲤⲦⲎⲢⲒⲞⲚ Ⲛ̄ⲢⲈϤⲔⲀⲚⲞⲂⲈ ⲈⲂⲞⲖ ·

ⲈⲦⲂⲈ ⲦⲈⲔⲘ̄ⲚⲦⲀⲄⲀⲐⲞⲤ ⲠⲞⲨⲞⲒ̈Ⲛ ·

her *repentance* was accepted, she saw all the *archons* of the twelve *aeons* mocking her and rejoicing over her, because her *repentance* was not yet accepted. When she now saw them mocking her, she was very *sorrowful*, she lifted up her voice to the height, saying in the seventh *repentance* :

1. 'O Light, I have raised up my power to thee, my Light.

2. I have *believed* in thee; do not make me to be despised. Do not make the *archons* of the twelve *aeons*, which hate me, rejoice over me.

3. *For* all those that *believe* in thee will not be brought to shame. May those who have taken away my power remain in darkness, and have no profit from it, *but* have it taken away from them.

4. O Light, show me thy ways, and I will be saved by them; and show me thy paths, so that I be saved in the *Chaos*.

5. And lead me in thy light, and may I know, O Light, that thou art my Saviour; I will trust thee in my whole time.

6. Give heed, so that thou savest me, O Light, because thy compassion exists for ever.

7. Concerning my *transgression* which I have committed from the beginning in my ignorance, do not count it against me, O Light, *but* rather save me through thy great *mystery* of forgiveness of sins, for the sake of thy *goodness*, O Light. |

8. ϪⲈ ⲞⲨⲀⲄⲀⲐⲞⲤ ⲀⲨⲰ ⲈϤⲤⲞⲨⲦⲰⲚ ⲠⲈ ⲠⲞⲨⲞⲈⲒⲚ·
ⲈⲦⲂⲈ ⲠⲀⲒ ϤⲚⲀ†-ⲦⲀϨⲒⲎ ⲚⲀⲒ ⲈⲦⲢⲀⲚⲞⲨϨⲘ̄ ϨⲚ̄ ⲦⲀⲠⲀⲢⲀ-
ⲂⲀⲤⲒⲤ·

9. ⲀⲨⲰ ⲚⲀ6ⲞⲘ ⲈⲚⲦⲀⲨⲤⲂⲞⲔ ϨⲒⲦⲚ̄ ⲐⲞⲦⲈ Ⲛ̄ⲚⲈⲠⲢⲞⲂⲞ-
ⲗⲞⲞⲨⲈ Ⲛ̄ϨⲨⲗⲒⲔⲞⲚ** Ⲙ̄ⲠⲀⲨⲐⲀⲀⲎⲤ ϤⲚⲀⲤⲰⲔ ϨⲎⲦⲞⲨ ϨⲘ̄ Ⲟⲅ·
ⲠⲈϤⲦⲰϢ· ⲀⲨⲰ ⲚⲀ6ⲞⲘ ⲈⲚⲦⲀⲨⲤⲂⲞⲔ ϨⲒⲦⲚ̄ ⲚⲒⲀⲦⲚⲀ'
ϤⲚⲀⲦⲤⲀⲂⲞⲞⲨ ⲈⲠⲈϤⲤⲞⲞⲨⲚ·

10. ϪⲈ Ⲛ̄ⲤⲞⲞⲨⲚ̄ ⲦⲎⲢⲞⲨ Ⲙ̄ⲠⲞⲨⲞⲒⲚ ϨⲈⲚⲚⲞⲨϨⲘ ⲚⲈ·
ⲀⲨⲰ ϨⲈⲚⲘⲨⲤⲦⲎⲢⲒⲞⲚ ⲚⲈ Ⲛ̄ⲞⲨⲞⲚ ⲚⲒⲘ ⲈⲦϢⲒⲚⲈ Ⲛ̄ⲤⲀ
Ⲛ̄ⲦⲞⲠⲞⲤ Ⲛ̄ⲦⲈϤⲔⲗⲎⲢⲞⲚⲞⲘⲒⲀ ⲘⲚ̄ ⲚⲈϤⲘⲨⲤⲦⲎⲢⲒⲞⲚ·

11. ⲈⲦⲂⲈ ⲠⲘⲨⲤⲦⲎⲢⲒⲞⲚ Ⲙ̄ⲠⲈⲔⲢⲀⲚ ⲠⲞⲨⲞⲈⲒⲚ ⲔⲰ ⲈⲂⲞⲗ
Ⲛ̄ⲦⲀⲠⲀⲢⲀⲂⲀⲤⲒⲤ ϪⲈ ⲞⲨⲚⲞ6 ⲦⲈ·

12. ⲞⲨⲞⲚ ⲚⲒⲘ ⲈⲦⲚⲀϨⲦⲈ ⲈⲠⲞⲨⲞⲈⲒⲚ· ϤⲚⲀ-† ⲚⲀϤ
Ⲙ̄ⲠⲘⲨⲤⲦⲎⲢⲒⲞⲚ ⲈⲦⲈϨⲚⲀϤ·

13. ⲀⲨⲰ ⲦⲈϤⲮⲨⲬⲎ ⲚⲀϢⲰⲠⲈ ϨⲚ̄ Ⲛ̄ⲦⲞⲠⲞⲤ Ⲙ̄ⲠⲞⲨⲞⲈⲒⲚ·
ⲀⲨⲰ ⲦⲈϤ6ⲞⲘ ⲚⲀⲔⲗⲎⲢⲞⲚⲞⲘⲒ Ⲙ̄ⲠⲈⲐⲎⲤⲀⲨⲢⲞⲤ Ⲙ̄ⲠⲞⲨ-
ⲞⲈⲒⲚ·

14. ⲠⲞⲨⲞⲈⲒⲚ ⲠⲈ ⲈⲦ-†-6ⲞⲘ Ⲛ̄ⲚⲈⲦⲠⲒⲤⲦⲈⲨⲈ ⲈⲢⲞϤ·
ⲀⲨⲰ ⲠⲢⲀⲚ Ⲙ̄ⲠⲈϤⲘⲨⲤⲦⲎⲢⲒⲞⲚ ⲠⲀⲚⲈⲦⲚⲀϨⲦⲈ ⲈⲢⲞϤ ⲠⲈ·
ⲀⲨⲰ ϤⲚⲀⲦⲀⲘⲞⲞⲨ ⲈⲠⲦⲞⲠⲞⲤ Ⲛ̄ⲦⲈⲔⲗⲎⲢⲞⲚⲞⲘⲒⲀ ⲈⲦϨⲘ̄
ⲠⲈⲐⲎⲤⲀⲨⲢⲞⲤ Ⲙ̄ⲠⲞⲨⲞⲈⲒⲚ·

15. ⲀⲚⲞⲔ ⲆⲈ ⲀⲒⲠⲒⲤⲦⲈⲨⲈ ⲈⲠⲞⲨⲞⲈⲒⲚ Ⲛ̄ⲞⲨⲞⲈⲒϢ ⲚⲒⲘ
ϪⲈ Ⲛ̄ⲦⲞϤ ⲠⲈ ⲈⲦⲚⲀⲚⲞⲨϨⲘ̄ Ⲛ̄ⲚⲀⲞⲨⲈⲢⲎⲦⲈ ⲈⲂⲞⲗ ϨⲚ̄
Ⲙ̄Ⲙ̄ⲢⲢⲈ Ⲙ̄ⲠⲔⲀⲔⲈ·

16. †ϨⲦⲎⲔ ⲈⲢⲞⲒ ⲠⲞⲨⲞⲒⲚ ⲀⲨⲰ Ⲛ̄ⲄⲚⲞⲨϨⲘ̄ Ⲙ̄ⲘⲞⲒ· ϪⲈ
ⲀⲚⲞⲔ ⲄⲀⲢ ⲀⲨϤⲒ-ⲠⲀⲢⲀⲚ Ⲛ̄ϨⲎⲦ ϨⲘ̄ ⲠⲈⲬⲀⲞⲤ·

8. For the Light is *good* and upright. Because of this he (the Light) will allow me (lit. give me my way) to be saved from my *transgression*.

9. And my powers, which are diminished through fear of the *material emanations* of the Authades, he will draw out [1] thence by his ordinance. And to my powers, which are diminished through lack of mercy, he will teach his knowledge.

10. For all knowledges of the light are salvations and are *mysteries* to everyone who seeks the *places* of his *inheritance* and his *mysteries*.

11. For the sake of the *mystery* of thy name, O Light, forgive my *transgression*, for it is great.

12. To everyone who trusts the light, he will give the *mystery* which pleases him.

13. And his *soul* will exist in the *places* of the light; and his power will *inherit* the *Treasury* of the Light.

14. It is the light which gives power to those that *believe* in it. And the name of its *mystery* is for those that trust it. And it will show them the *place* of the *inheritance* which is in the *Treasury* of the Light.

15. *Moreover* I have *believed* in the light at all times, that it is this which will save my feet from the bonds of the darkness.

16. Give heed to me, O Light, and save me, *for* my name has been taken from me in the *Chaos*. |

---

[1] (5) draw out; Till: lead, guide.

17. ΠΑΡΑ ΝΕΠΡΟΒΟΛΟΟΥΕ ΤΗΡΟΥ · ΑΥΑϢΑΪ ΕΜΑΤΕ
Ν̄ϬΙ ΝΑΘΛΙΨΙϹ Μ̄Ν ΠΑϨΩΧ · ΝΑϨΜΕΤ ΕΒΟΛ ϨΝ̄ ΤΑΠΑ-
ΡΑΒΑϹΙϹ · ΑΥΩ Μ̄Ν ΠΕΪΚΑΚΕ ·

18. ΑΥΩ ΑΝΑΥ ΕⲪΙϹΕ Μ̄ΠΑϨΩΧ · Ν̄ΓΚΩ ΕΒΟΛ Ν̄ΤΑ-
5 ΠΑΡΑΒΑϹΙϹ ·

19. ϮϨΤΗΚ ΕΝΑΡΧΩΝ Μ̄ΠΜ̄Ν̄ΤϹΝΟΟΥϹ Ν̄ΑΙΩΝ · ΝΑΪ
ΕΝΤΑΥΜΕϹΤΩΪ ϨΝ̄ ΟΥΚΩϨ ·

20. ΡΟΪϹ ΕΤΑϬΟΜ ΑΥΩ Ν̄ΓΝΟΥϨΜ̄ Μ̄ΜΟΪ · ΑΥΩ Μ̄ΠΡ-
ΤΡΑϬΩ ϨΜ̄ ΠΕΪΚΑΚΕ · ΧΕ ΑΪΠΙϹΤΕΥΕ ΕΡΟΚ ·

10 21. ΑΥΩ ΑΥΛΑΤ Ν̄ϹΟϬ ΕΜΑΤΕ ΧΕ ΑΪΠΙϹΤΕΥΕ ΕΡΟΚ Οⲗ
ΠΟΥΟΕΙΝ ·

22. ΤΕΝΟΥ ϬΕ ΠΟΥΟΪΝ ΝΟΥϨΜ̄ Ν̄ΝΑϬΟΜ ϨΡΑΪ ϨΝ̄ ΝΕ-
ΠΡΟΒΟΛΟΟΥΕ Μ̄ΠΑΥΘΑΛΗϹ ΝΑΪ ΕϮϨΧ Ν̄ϨΗΤΟΥ ·

ΤΕΝΟΥ ϬΕ ΠΕΤΝΗⲪΕ ΜΑΡΕϤΝΗⲪΕ · ΝΑΪ ϬΕ Ν̄ΤΕΡΕ
15 ῙϹ ΧΟΟΥ ΕΝΕϤΜΑΘΗΤΗϹ · ΑϤΕΙ ΕΘΗ Ν̄ϬΙ ΘΩΜΑϹ ΠΕ-
ΧΑϤ ΧΕ ΠΑΧΟΕΙϹ · ϮΝΗⲪΕ ϮΡϨΟΥΕ-ΝΗⲪΕ ΑΥΩ ΠΑ-
Π̄Ν̄Α ΡΟΟΥΤ ϨΡΑΪ Ν̄ϨΗΤ · ΑΥΩ ϮΤΕΛΗΛ ΕΜΑϢΟ ΧΕ
ΑΚϬΩⲗΠ̄ ΝΑΝ ΕΒΟΛ Ν̄ΝΕΪϢΑΧΕ · ΠΛΗΝ ϬΕ ΕΪΑΝΕΧΕ
Ν̄ΝΑϹΝΗΥ ϢΑ ΤΕΝΟΥ ΧΕ Ν̄ΝΑϮϬΩΝ̄Τ ΝΑΥ · ΑΛΛΑ
20 ϮΑΝΕΧΕ Μ̄ΠΟΥΑ ΠΟΥΑ Μ̄ΜΟΟΥ ΕϤΝΗΥ ΕΘΗ Μ̄ΜΟΚ ·
ΕΥΧΩ Μ̄ΠΒΩΛ Ν̄ΤΜΕΤΑΝΟΙΑ Ν̄ΤΠΙϹΤΙϹ ϹΟⲪΙΑ · ΤΕ-
ΝΟΥ ϬΕ ΠΑΧΟΕΙϹ ΕΤΒΕ ΠΒΩΛ Ν̄ΤΜΕϨϹΑϢϤΕ Μ̄ΜΕ-
ΤΑΝΟΙΑ Ν̄ΤΠΙϹΤΙϹ ϹΟⲪΙΑ Α ΤΕΚϬΟΜ ΝΟΥΟΪΝ ΠΡΟ- Οⲗ ᵇ
ⲪΗΤΕΥΕ ϨΑΡΟϹ ϨΙΤΝ̄ ΛΑΥΕΙΛ · ΠΕΠΡΟⲪΗΤΗϹ ΕϹΧΩ
25 Μ̄ΜΟϹ Ν̄ΤΕΕΙϨΕ ϨΜ̄ ΠΜΕϨΧΟΥΤΑϤΤΕ Μ̄ΨΑΛΜΟϹ ΧΕ

17. *Beyond* all the *emanations*, my *afflictions* and my oppressions are very numerous; save me from my *transgression* and this darkness.

18. And look upon the distress of my oppression and forgive my *transgression*.

19. Give heed to the *archons* of the twelve *aeons* which hate me with envy.

20. Watch over my power and save me; and let me not remain in this darkness, for I have *believed* in thee.

21. And they have committed a great folly for I have *believed* in thee, O Light.

22. Now at this time, O Light, save my powers from the *emanations* of the Authades, by which I am oppressed.'

Now at this time, he who is *sober*, let him be *sober*."

Now when Jesus had said these things to his *disciples*, Thomas came forward, he said: "My Lord, I am *sober*, I have become more *sober*, and my *Spirit* is ready within me. And I rejoice greatly because thou hast revealed to us these words. *Nevertheless* I have *suffered* my brothers up till now lest I cause anger in them. *But* I *suffer* each one of them to come before thee to say the interpretation of the *repentance* of the Pistis Sophia. Now at this time, O Lord, concerning the interpretation of the seventh *repentance* of the Pistis Sophia, thy light-power *prophesied* about it, through David the *prophet*, saying it thus in the 24th *Psalm* : |

1. ⲠⲬⲞⲈⲒⲤ ⲀⲒϤⲒ ⲚⲦⲀⲮⲨⲬⲎ ⲈϨⲢⲀⲒ ⲈⲢⲞⲔ ⲠⲀⲚⲞⲨⲦⲈ ·

2. ⲀⲒⲔⲀϨⲦⲎⲒ ⲈⲢⲞⲔ · ⲘⲠⲢⲦⲢⲀⲬⲒⲱⲒⲠⲈ · ⲞⲨⲆⲈ ⲘⲠⲢⲦⲢⲈ
ⲚⲀⲬⲀⲬⲈ ⲤⲰⲂⲈ ⲚⲤⲰⲒ ·

3. ⲔⲀⲒⲄⲀⲢ ⲞⲨⲞⲚ ⲚⲒⲘ ⲈⲦϨⲨⲠⲞⲘⲒⲚⲈ ⲈⲢⲞⲔ ⲚⲤⲈⲚⲀⲬⲒ-
5 ⲱⲒⲠⲈ ⲀⲚ · ⲈⲨⲈⲬⲒⲱⲒⲠⲈ ⲚϬⲒ ⲚⲈⲦⲀⲚⲞⲘⲒ ⲈⲠⲬⲒⲚⲬⲎ ·

4. ⲠⲬⲞⲈⲒⲤ ⲘⲀⲦⲀⲘⲞⲒ ⲈⲚⲈⲔϨⲒⲞⲞⲨⲈ ⲀⲨⲱ ⲦⲤⲀⲂⲞⲒ
ⲈⲚⲈⲔⲘⲀⲘⲘⲞⲟⲱⲈ ·

5. ⲬⲒⲘⲞⲈⲒⲦ ϨⲎⲦ · ϨⲒ ⲦⲈϨⲒⲎ ⲚⲦⲈⲔⲘⲈ · ⲀⲨⲱ ⲚⲄⲦⲤⲀⲂⲞⲒ
ⲬⲈ ⲚⲦⲞⲔ ⲠⲀⲚⲞⲨⲦⲈ ⲠⲀⲤⲰⲦⲎⲢ · ϯⲚⲀϨⲨⲠⲞⲘⲒⲚⲈ ⲈⲢⲞⲔ
10 ⲘⲠⲈϨⲞⲞⲨ ⲦⲎⲢϤ :

6. ⲀⲢⲒⲠⲘⲈⲈⲨⲈ ⲚⲚⲈⲔⲘⲚⲦϢⲀⲚϨⲦⲎϤ ⲠⲬⲞⲈⲒⲤ · ⲀⲨⲱ
ⲚⲈⲔⲚⲀ' ⲬⲈ ⲤⲈϢⲞⲞⲠ ⲬⲒⲚ ⲈⲚⲈϨ ·   ⲞⲤ

7. ⲚⲚⲞⲂⲈ ⲚⲦⲀⲘⲚⲦⲔⲞⲨⲒ ⲘⲚ ⲚⲀⲦⲀⲘⲚⲦⲀⲦⲤⲞⲞⲨⲚ
ⲘⲠⲢⲢⲠⲈⲨⲘⲈⲈⲨⲈ · ⲀⲢⲒⲠⲀⲘⲈⲈⲨⲈ ⲚⲦⲞϤ ⲔⲀⲦⲀ ⲠⲀϢⲀⲒ
15 ⲘⲠⲈⲔⲚⲀ' · ⲈⲦⲂⲈ ⲦⲈⲔⲘⲚⲦⲬⲢⲤ ⲠⲬⲞⲈⲒⲤ ·

8. ⲞⲨⲬⲢⲤ ⲀⲨⲱ ⲈϤⲤⲞⲨⲦⲰⲚ ⲠⲈ ⲠⲬⲞⲈⲒⲤ · ⲈⲦⲂⲈ ⲠⲀⲒ
ϤⲚⲀϯⲤⲂⲰ ⲚⲚⲈⲦⲢⲚⲞⲂⲈ ϨⲒ ⲦⲈϨⲒⲎ ·

9. ϤⲚⲀⲬⲒⲘⲞⲈⲒⲦ ϨⲎⲦⲞⲨ ⲚⲚⲢⲘⲢⲀϢ ϨⲚ ⲞⲨϨⲀⲠ · ϤⲚⲀⲦ-
ⲤⲀⲂⲈ-ⲚⲢⲘⲢⲀϢ ⲈⲚⲈϤϨⲒⲞⲞⲨⲈ ·

20 10. ⲚⲈϨⲒⲞⲞⲨⲈ ⲦⲎⲢⲞⲨ ⲘⲠⲬⲞⲈⲒⲤ ϨⲈⲚⲚⲀ' ⲚⲈ ϨⲒ ⲘⲈ ·
ⲚⲈⲦϢⲒⲚⲈ ⲚⲤⲀ ⲦⲈϤⲆⲒⲔⲀⲒⲞⲤⲨⲚⲎ ⲀⲨⲱ ⲚⲈϤⲘⲚⲦⲘⲚⲦⲢⲈ ·

11. ⲈⲦⲂⲈ ⲠⲈⲔⲢⲀⲚ ⲠⲬⲞⲈⲒⲤ ⲔⲀ-ⲠⲀⲚⲞⲂⲈ ⲚⲀⲒ ⲈⲂⲞⲗ
⟨ⲬⲈ⟩ ⲈϤⲞϢ ⲈⲘⲀⲦⲈ ·

12. ⲚⲒⲘ ⲠⲈ ⲠⲢⲱⲘⲈ ⲈⲦⲢϨⲞⲦⲈ ϨⲎⲦϤ ⲘⲠⲬⲞⲈⲒⲤ · ϤⲚⲀ-
25 ⲤⲘⲚ-ⲚⲞⲘⲞⲤ ⲚⲀϤ ϨⲒ ⲦⲈϨⲒⲎ ⲈⲚⲦⲀϤⲞⲨⲀϢⲤ ·

13. ⲦⲈϤⲮⲨⲬⲎ ⲚⲀϢⲰⲠⲈ ϨⲚ ϨⲈⲚⲀⲄⲀⲐⲞⲚ · ⲀⲨⲱ ⲠⲈϤ- ⲞⲤ ᵇ
ⲤⲠⲈⲢⲘⲀ ⲚⲀⲔⲗⲎⲢⲞⲚⲞⲘⲒ ⲘⲠⲔⲀϨ ·

---

23 erasure in MS.

1. O Lord, I have lifted up my *soul* to thee, my God.

2. I have relied on thee; let me not be put to shame, *nor* let my enemies mock at me.

3. *Because* everyone that *waits upon* thee will not be put to shame. Let those that *commit iniquity* without cause be ashamed.

4. O Lord, show me thy ways, and teach me thy paths.

5. Lead me in the way of thy truth, and teach me for thou art my God, my *Saviour*. I will *wait on* thee the whole day.

6. Remember thy compassion, O Lord, and thy mercies, for they are from eternity.

7. Remember not the sins of my youth and those of my ignorance. Remember me rather *according to* the greatness of thy mercy, for the sake of thy *benificence*, O Lord.

8. *Beneficent* and upright is the Lord; because of this, he will teach the sinners on the way.

9. He will guide the compassionate in judgment; he will teach the compassionate his ways.

10. All the ways of the Lord are mercy and truth for those that seek his *righteousness* and his witness.

11. For thy name's sake, O Lord, forgive me my sin, (for) it is very great.

12. Who is the man who fears the Lord? He will appoint (the) *law*[1] for him in the way which he has chosen.

13. His *soul* will be in *good things*; and his *seed* will *inherit* the earth. |

---

[1] (25) appoint (the) law for, i.e. instruct; Schmidt : appoint laws for.

14. ПХОЄІС ПЄ ПТАϪΡΟ N̄NЄT̄P̄ϨΟΤЄ ϨΗΤ̄Ϥ ΑΥѠ
ПРАN M̄ПХΟΪС ПΑΝЄΤ̄P̄ϨΟΤЄ ϨΗΤ̄Ϥ ПЄ· ЄΤΑΜΟΟΥ
ЄΤЄϤΔΙΑΘΗΚΗ·

15. ЄРЄ ΝΑΒΑΛ ЄΙΟР̄Μ ЄПХОЄІС N̄ΟΥΟЄΙѠ NIM ХЄ
5 N̄ΤΟϤ ПЄΤΝΑΤЄΚΜ-ΝΑΟΥЄΡΗΤЄ ЄΒΟΛ ϨΜ П̄ПΑѠ·

16. ϬѠϢ̄Τ ЄϨΡΑΪ ЄХѠΪ N̄ΓΝΑ΄ ΝΑΪ· ХЄ ΑΝΓ̄ ΟΥϢΗΡЄ
N̄ΟΥѠΤ· ΑΝΓ̄ ΟΥϨΗΚЄ ΑΝΟΚ·

17. Α ΝЄΘΛΙΨΙС M̄ПΑϨΗΤ ΟΥѠϢ̄C ЄΒΟΛ· ΑΝΙΤ ЄΒΟΛ
ϨΝ ΝΑΑΝΑΓΚΗ·

10 18. ΑΝΑΥ ЄПΛΑΘΒΒΙΟ M̄N ПΑϨΙСЄ· N̄ΓΚѠ ЄΒΟΛ N̄ΝΑ-
ΝΟΒЄ ΤΗΡΟΥ·

19. ΑΝΑΥ ЄΝΑХΑХЄ ХЄ ΑΥΟΥѠϢ̄C ЄΒΟΛ· ΑΥѠ
ΑΥΜЄСΤѠΪ ϨΝ̄ ΟΥΜΟСΤЄ N̄ХΙΝϬΟΝϹ·

20. ϨΑΡЄϨ ЄΤΑΨΥХΗ N̄ΓΤΟΥХΟΪ· M̄П̄ΡΤΡΑХΙϢΠЄ ХЄ   ο̄ε̄
15 ΑΪϨЄΛПΙZЄ ЄΡΟΚ·

21. Β̄ΒΑΛϨΗΤ M̄N ΝЄΤСΟΥΤѠN ΑΥΤΟϬΟΥ ЄΡΟΪ· ХЄ
ΑΪϨΥПΟΜΙΝЄ ЄΡΟΚ ПХОЄІС·

22. ПΝΟΥΤЄ СѠΤ M̄ПῙС̄Λ ЄΒΟΛ ϨΝ ΝЄϤΘΛΙΨΙС ΤΗ-
ΡΟΥ·

20 Ӡ N̄ΤЄΡЄ ῙС̄ ΔЄ СѠΤ̄Μ ЄΝϢΑХЄ N̄ΘѠΜΑС· ПЄХΑϤ
ΝΑϤ ХЄ ЄΥΓЄ ΘѠΜΑС· ΑΥѠ ΚΑΛѠС· ПΑΪ ПЄ ПΒѠΛ
N̄ΤΜЄϨСΑϢϤЄ M̄ΜЄΤΑΝΟΙΑ N̄ΤПΙСΤΙС СΟΦΙΑ· ϨΑΜΗΝ
ϨΑΜΗΝ ϮХѠ M̄ΜΟС ΝΗΤN ХЄ СЄΝΑΜΑΚΑΡΙZЄ M̄ΜѠΤN
ϨΙΧ̄Μ ПΚΑϨ N̄ϬΙ N̄ΓЄΝЄΑ ΤΗΡΟΥ M̄ПΚΟСΜΟС ХЄ ΑΪϬΑП-

---

14 ε̄ in upper right-hand margin at end of quire.
18 MS сѠτ; better сѠτЄ.
22 MS Π̄τПΙСΙСΤΙС.

14. The Lord is the strength of those that fear him; and the name of the Lord, to those that fear him, is that which tells them of his *covenant*.

15. My eyes are directed to the Lord at all times; for it is he who will draw my feet out of the snare.

16. Look down upon me and have mercy on me; for I am an only son [1], I am poor.

17. The *afflictions* of my heart have multiplied; lead me forth from my *necessities*.

18. Look upon my humbleness and my distress, and forgive all my sins.

19. Look upon my enemies, for they have multiplied and they have hated me with an unjust hatred.

20. Guard my *soul* and save me; let me not be put to shame for I have *hoped* in thee.

21. The harmless and the upright have joined themselves to me; for I have *waited upon* thee, O Lord.

22. O God, save Israel from all his *afflictions'* *".

When *however* Jesus heard the words of Thomas, he said to him : "*Excellent*, Thomas, and *well done*. This is the interpretation of the seventh *repentance* of the Pistis Sophia. *Truly, truly*, I say to you that all the *generations* of the *world* will *bless* you upon the earth, because I have revealed |

---

* Ps. 24.1-22

---

[1]   (7) an only son; Schmidt : solitary.

ⲚⲀⲒ ⲚⲎⲦⲚ ⲈⲂⲞⲗ · ⲀⲨⲰ ⲀⲦⲈⲦⲚϫⲒ ⲈⲂⲞⲗ ⲌⲘ ⲠⲀⲠⲚⲀ ·
ⲀⲨⲰ ⲀⲦⲈⲦⲚ̄ϣⲰⲠⲈ Ⲛ̄ⲚⲞⲈⲢⲞⲥ ⲀⲨⲰ Ⲙ̄ⲠⲚ̄ⲀⲦⲒⲕⲞⲥ ⲈⲦⲈ-
ⲦⲚⲚⲞⲒ̈ ⲈⲚⲈ†ϫⲰ Ⲙ̄ⲘⲞⲞⲨ · ⲀⲨⲰ Ⲙ̄Ⲛ̄Ⲛ̄ⲤⲀ ⲚⲀⲒ̈ †ⲚⲀⲘⲈⲌ- ⲟ̄ⲉ̄ b
ⲦⲎⲨⲦⲚ̄ ⲈⲂⲞⲗ ⲌⲘ ⲠⲞⲨⲞⲈⲒⲚ ⲦⲎⲢϥ ⲀⲨⲰ Ⲙ̄Ⲛ ⲦϭⲞⲘ ⲦⲎⲢⲤ̄
5 Ⲛ̄ⲦⲈ ⲠⲈⲠⲚⲀ · ϫⲈⲕⲀⲥ ⲈⲦⲈⲦⲚⲚⲞⲒ̈ ϫⲒⲚ Ⲙ̄ⲠⲈⲒ̈ⲚⲀⲨ Ⲛ̄ⲚⲈⲦ-
ⲞⲨⲚⲀϫⲞⲞⲨ ⲈⲢⲰⲦⲚ̄ ⲦⲎⲢⲞⲨ ⲀⲨⲰ Ⲙ̄Ⲛ ⲚⲈⲦⲚⲀⲚⲀⲨ
ⲈⲢⲞⲞⲨ · ⲈⲦⲒ ⲕⲈⲕⲞⲨⲒ̈ Ⲛ̄ⲞⲨⲞⲈⲒϣ ⲠⲈ · †ⲚⲀϣⲀϫⲈ Ⲛ̄Ⲙ̄-
ⲘⲎⲦⲚ̄ ⲈⲚⲀⲠϫⲒⲤⲈ ⲦⲎⲢⲞⲨ ϫⲒⲚ Ⲛ̄ⲂⲞⲗ ϣⲀⲌⲞⲨⲚ · ⲀⲨⲰ
ϫⲒⲚ Ⲛ̄ⲌⲞⲨⲚ ϣⲀⲂⲞⲗ ·
10 ⳅ ⲀϥⲞⲨⲰⲌ ⲞⲚ ⲈⲦⲞⲞⲦϥ Ⲛ̄ϭⲒ Ⲓ̄Ⲥ̄ ⲌⲘ ⲠϣⲀϫⲈ ⲠⲈϫⲀϥ
Ⲛ̄Ⲙ̄ⲘⲀⲐⲎⲦⲎⲤ · ϫⲈ ⲀⲤϣⲰⲠⲈ ϭⲈ Ⲛ̄ⲦⲈⲢⲈⲤϫⲰ Ⲛ̄ⲦⲈⲤⲘⲈⲌ-
ⲤⲀϣϥⲈ Ⲙ̄ⲘⲈⲦⲀⲚⲞⲒⲀ ⲌⲘ ⲠⲈϫⲗⲞⲤ Ⲛ̄ϭⲒ ⲦⲠⲒⲤⲦⲒⲤ ⲤⲞⲫⲒⲀ ·
ⲀⲨⲰ ⲚⲈⲘⲠⲀⲦⲈ ⲦⲕⲈⲗⲈⲨⲤⲒⲤ ⲈⲒ' ⲚⲀⲒ̈ ⲈⲂⲞⲗ ⲠⲈ ⲌⲒⲦⲘ
Ⲡϣ̄ⲞⲢⲠ̄ Ⲙ̄ⲘⲨⲤⲦⲎⲢⲒⲞⲚ ⲈⲦⲢⲀⲚⲞⲨⲌⲘ Ⲙ̄ⲘⲞⲤ · Ⲛ̄ⲦⲀⲚ̄Ⲧ̄Ⲥ̄
15 ⲈⲌⲢⲀⲒ̈ ⲌⲘ ⲠⲈϫⲗⲞⲤ · ⲀⲗⲗⲀ ⲀⲚⲞⲕ ⲈⲂⲞⲗ ⲌⲒⲦⲞⲞⲦ Ⲙ̄ⲘⲒⲚ
Ⲙ̄ⲘⲞⲒ̈ Ⲍ̄Ⲛ ⲞⲨⲘⲚ̄ⲦⲚⲀⲎⲦ ⲀϫⲚ̄ ** ⲕⲈⲗⲈⲨⲤⲒⲤ ⲀⲒ̈Ⲛ̄Ⲧ̄Ⲥ̄ ⲈⲨⲦⲞ- ⲟ̄ⲍ̄
ⲠⲞⲤ ⲈϥⲞⲨⲞϣⲤ̄ ⲈⲂⲞⲗ Ⲛ̄ⲞⲨϣⲎⲘ ⲌⲘ ⲠⲈϫⲗⲞⲤ · ⲀⲨⲰ
Ⲛ̄ⲦⲈⲢⲞⲨⲈⲒⲘⲈ Ⲛ̄ϭⲒ ⲚⲈⲠⲢⲞⲂⲞⲗⲞⲞⲨⲈ Ⲛ̄ⲌⲨⲗⲒⲕⲞⲚ Ⲛ̄ⲦⲈ
ⲠⲀⲨⲐⲀⲗⲎⲤ · ϫⲈ ⲀⲨⲚ̄Ⲧ̄Ⲥ̄ ⲈⲨⲦⲞⲠⲞⲤ ⲈϥⲞⲨⲞϣⲤ̄ ⲈⲂⲞⲗ
20 Ⲛ̄ⲞⲨϣⲎⲘ ⲌⲘ ⲠⲈϫⲗⲞⲤ · ⲀⲨⲗⲞ ⲈⲨⲌⲰϫ Ⲙ̄ⲘⲞⲤ Ⲛ̄ⲞⲨ-
ϣⲕⲘ · ⲈⲨⲘⲈⲈⲨⲈ ϫⲈ ⲈⲨⲚⲀⲚ̄Ⲧ̄Ⲥ̄ ⲈⲌⲢⲀⲒ̈ ⲌⲘ ⲠⲈϫⲗⲞⲤ
ⲈⲠⲦⲎⲢϥ̄ · ⲚⲀⲒ̈ ϭⲈ Ⲛ̄ⲦⲈⲢⲞⲨϣⲰⲠⲈ ⲚⲈⲤⲤⲞⲞⲨⲚ ⲀⲚ ⲠⲈ
Ⲛ̄ϭⲒ ⲦⲠⲒⲤⲦⲒⲤ ⲤⲞⲫⲒⲀ · ϫⲈ ⲀⲚⲞⲕ ⲠⲈ ⲈⲦⲂⲞⲎⲐⲒ ⲈⲢⲞⲤ ·
ⲞⲨⲆⲈ ⲚⲈⲤⲤⲞⲞⲨⲚ Ⲙ̄ⲘⲞⲒ̈ ⲀⲚ ⲈⲠⲦⲎⲢϥ̄ · ⲀⲗⲗⲀ ⲚⲈϣⲀⲤϭⲰ
25 ⲈⲤⲌⲨⲘⲚⲈⲨⲈ ⲈⲠⲞⲨⲞⲈⲒⲚ Ⲙ̄ⲠⲈⲐⲎⲤⲀⲨⲢⲞⲤ ⲠⲀⲒ̈ ⲈⲚⲦⲀⲤ-

---

6   MS ⲚⲈⲦⲚⲀⲚⲀⲨ; read ⲚⲈⲦⲈⲦⲚⲀⲚⲀⲨ.
8   MS ⲀⲨϣϫⲒⲚ.
16   ⳅ in upper left-hand margin at beginning of quire.

this to you, and you have received of my *Spirit*, and you have become *understanding* and *Pneumatic*, since you have *understood* what I have said. And after this I will fill you with all the light and all the power of the *Spirit*, so that from this time you will *understand* all those things which will be said to you, and those things which you will see. *Yet* a little time and I will speak with you of all the things of the height, from the outer to the inner, and from the inner to the outer."

47. Jesus continued again with the discourse, he said to the *disciples*: "Now it happened when the Pistis Sophia said her seventh *repentance* in the *Chaos*, the *command*, through the First *Mystery*, that I should save her and bring her up from the *Chaos*, had not yet come forth to me. *But* I of myself, out of compassion, without *command*, I brought her to a *place* in the *Chaos* which was a little wider. And when the *material emanations* of the Authades knew she had been brought to a *place* in the *Chaos* which was a little wider, they ceased a little from oppressing her, thinking she would be brought up from the *Chaos* completely. Now when these things happened, the Pistis Sophia did not know that it was I who *helped* her, *nor* did she know me at all. *But* she continued *singing praises* to the light of the *Treasury* |

ΝΑΥ ΕΡΟϤ ⲘⲠΟΥΟΕΙϢ· ΑΥⲰ ⲠΑΪ ΕΝΤΑ⳯ΠΙ⳿Ⲥⲧⲉⲩⲉ
ΕΡΟϤ ΑΥⲰ ΝⲈⳅⲘⲈⲈⲨⲈ ϪⲈ ⲚⲦΟϤ ΟΝ ⲠⲈ ⲈⲦⲂΟⲎⲐⲈⲒ
ⲈⲢΟⲤ· ΑΥⲰ ⲚⲦΟϤ ⲠⲈ ⲈⲚⲈⳅⳅⲨⲘⲚⲈⲨⲈ ⲈⲢΟϤ· ⲈⳅⲘⲈⲈⲨⲈ
ϪⲈ ⲚⲦΟϤ ⲠⲈ ⲠΟⲨΟⲈⲒⲚ ⲚⲦⲀⲖⲎⲐⲒⲀ· ⲀⲖⲖⲀ ⲈⲠⲈⲒⲆⲎ Ⲁⳅ- ⲟⲍ̄^h

5 ⲠⲒⲤⲦⲈⲨⲈ ⲈⲠΟⲨΟⲈⲒⲚ ⲠⲀⲒ̈ ⲈⲦⲎⲠ ⲈⲦⲀⲖⲎⲐⲒⲀ ⲘⲠⲈⲐⲎ-
ⲤⲀⲨⲢΟⳅ· ⲈⲦⲂⲈ ⲠⲀⲒ̈ ⳅⲈⲚⲀ̄ⲚⲦⳅ ⲈⳅⲢⲀⲒ̈ ⳅⲘ̄ ⲠⲈⳓⲖⲀΟⳅ ⲀⲨⲰ
ⲚⳅⲈϪⲒ-ⲦⲈⳅⲘⲈⲦⲀⲚΟⲒⲀ ⲚⲦΟΟⲦⳅ̄· ⲀⲖⲖⲀ ⲈⲦⲈ ⲘⲠⲀⲦϤ-
ϪⲰⲔ ⲈⲂΟⲖ ⲚⳓⲒ ⲠⲦⲰϢ ⲘⲠϢΟⲢⲠ ⲘⲘⲨⳅⲦⲎⲢⲒΟⲚ ⲈⲦⲢⲈⲨ-
ϪⲒ ⲚⲦⲈⳅⲘⲈⲦⲀⲚΟⲒⲀ ⲚⲦΟΟⲦⳅ̄· ⲠⲖⲎⲚ ⳓⲈ ⲤⲰⲦⲘ̄ ⲦⲀϪⲰ

10 ⲈⲢⲰⲦⲚ̄ ⲚⲚϢⲀϪⲈ ⲦⲎⲢΟⲨ ⲈⲚⲦⲀⲨϢⲰⲠⲈ ⲚⲦⲠⲒⳅⲦⲒⳅ ⲤΟ-
ⲫⲒⲀ· ⲀⳅϢⲰⲠⲈ ⲚⲦⲈⲢⲒ̄ⲚⲦⳅ ⲈⲨⲦΟⲠΟⳅ ⲈϤΟϢ̄ⳅ ⲈⲂΟⲖ
ⲚΟⲨϢⲎⲘ ⳅⲘ̄ ⲠⲈⳓⲖⲀΟⳅ· ⲀⲨⲖΟ ⲈⲨⳅⲰϪ ⲘⲘΟⳅ ⲦΟⲚⲰ
ⲚⳓⲒ ⲚⲈⲠⲢΟⲂΟⲖΟΟⲨⲈ ⲘⲠⲀⲨⲐⲀⲆⲎⳅ ⲈⲨⲘⲈⲈⲨⲈ ϪⲈ ⲈⲨ-
ⲚⲀ̄ⲚⲦⳅ ⲈⳅⲢⲀⲒ̈ ⳅⲘ̄ ⲠⲈⳓⲖⲀΟⳅ ⲈⲠⲦⲎⲢϤ· ⲀⳅϢⲰⲠⲈ ⳓⲈ ⲚⲦⲈ-

15 ⲢΟⲨⲈⲒⲘⲈ ⲚⳓⲒ ⲚⲈⲠⲢΟⲂΟⲖΟΟⲨⲈ ⲘⲠⲀⲨⲐⲀⲆⲎⳅ· ϪⲈ Ⲙ̄-
ⲠΟⲨⲚ̄-ⲦⲠⲒⳅⲦⲒⳅ ⲤΟⲫⲒⲀ ⳅⲢⲀⲒ̈ ⳅⲘ̄ ⲠⲈⳓⲖⲀΟⳅ· ⲀⲨⲔΟⲦΟⲨ ΟⲚ
ⳄⲒ ΟⲨⲤΟⲠ ⲈⲨⳅⲰϪ ⲘⲘΟⳅ ⲈⲘⲀϢΟ· ⲈⲦⲂⲈ ⲠⲀⲒ̈ ⳓⲈ Ⲁⳅ- ⲟⲏ̄
ϪⲰ ⲚⲦⲘⲈⳅϢⲘΟⲨⲚⲈ ⲘⲘⲈⲦⲀⲚΟⲒⲀ· ϪⲈ ⲚⲈⲀⲨⲖΟ ⲈⲨ-
ⳅⲰϪ ⲘⲘΟⳅ ⲠⲈ ⲀⲨⲰ ΟⲚ ⲀⲨⲔΟⲦΟⲨ ⲀⲨⳅⲰϪ ⲘⲘΟⳅ

20 ⲈϤⲀⲈ· ⲀⳅϪⲰ ⲚⲦⲈⲒ̈ⲘⲈⲦⲀⲚΟⲒⲀ ⲈⳅϪⲰ ⲘⲘΟⳅ ⲚⲦⲈⲒ̈ⳅⲈ ϪⲈ

   1. ⲀⲒ̈ⲔⲀ-ⳅⲦⲎⲒ̈ ⲈⲢΟⲔ ⲠΟⲨΟⲈⲒⲚ ⲘⲠⲢⲔⲀⲀⲦ ⳅⲘ̄ ⲠⲈⳓⲖⲀΟⳅ
ⲤⲰⲦⲈ ⲘⲘΟⲒ̈ ⲀⲨⲰ ⲚⲄⲚⲀⳅⲘⲈⲦ ⳅⲘ̄ ⲠⲈⲔⲤΟΟⲨⲚ̄·

   2. ϯⳅⲦⲎⲔ ⲈⲢΟⲒ̈ ⲀⲨⲰ ⲚⲄⲚⲀⳅⲘⲈⲦ ϢⲰⲠⲈ ⲚⲀⲒ̈ ⲚⲢⲈϤ-
ⲚΟⲨⳅⲘ̄ Ⲱ ⲠΟⲨΟⲒ̈Ⲛ ⲀⲨⲰ ⲚⲄⲚⲀⳅⲘⲈⲦ ⲚⲄⲚⲦ ⲈⲢⲀⲦϤ

25 ⲘⲠⲈⲔΟⲨΟⲈⲒⲚ·

   3. ϪⲈ ⲚⲦΟⲔ ⲠⲈ ⲠⲀⲤⲰⲦⲎⲢ ⲀⲨⲰ ⲔⲚⲀ̄ⲚⲦ ⲈⲢⲀⲦⲔ̄·
ⲀⲨⲰ ⲈⲦⲂⲈ ⲠⲘⲨⲤⲦⲎⲢΟⲚ ⲘⲠⲈⲔⲢⲀⲚ ϪⲒⲘΟⲈⲒⲦ ⳅⲎⲦ·
ⲀⲨⲰ ⲚⲄϯ ⲚⲀⲒ̈ ⲘⲠⲈⲔⲘⲨⳅⲦⲎⲢΟⲚ·

---

11   MS ⲈϤΟⲰ̄Ⲥ; read ⲈϤΟⲨΟⲰ̄Ⲥ.

which she had once seen, and in which she *believed*. And she thought, furthermore, that it was he who *helped* her. And it was he to whom she *sang praises*, thinking that he was the *true* light. *But since* she *believed* in the light which belongs to the *true Treasury*, for this reason she will be brought up from the *Chaos* and her *repentance* will be received. *But* the ordinance of the First *Mystery* that her *repentance* should be received was not yet completed. *Therefore* hear now, and I will tell you all the things (lit. words) which happened to the Pistis Sophia.

It happened when I brought her to a *place* in the Chaos, which was a little wider, the *emanations* of the Authades ceased from oppressing her greatly [1], thinking she would be brought up from the *Chaos* completely. Now it happened when the *emanations* of the Authades knew that the Pistis Sophia was not brought up from the *Chaos*, they turned again at the same time to oppress her greatly. Because of this she now said the eighth *repentance*, because they had ceased [2] from oppressing her, and they had turned again to oppress her to the last. She spoke this *repentance*, saying it thus :

1. 'I have hoped in thee, O Light. Leave me not in the *Chaos*; save me and deliver me with thy knowledge.

2. Give heed to me and save me. Be to me a Saviour, O Light, and save me and bring me into the presence of thy light.

3. For thou art my *Saviour* and thou wilt bring me to thy presence. And for the sake of the *mystery* of thy name, lead me and give me thy *mystery*. |

---

[1]   (12) ceased from oppressing her greatly; Schmidt : ceased completely from oppressing her.

[2]   (18, 19) they had ceased; Schmidt : they had not ceased.

171

4. ⲁⲩⲱ ⲕⲛⲁⲛⲁϩⲙⲉⲧ ⲉⲧⲉϊϭⲟⲙ ⲛ̄ϩⲟ ⲙ̄ⲙⲟⲩϊ ⲉⲛⲧⲁⲩ-
ϭⲟⲣϭ̄ⲥ̄ ⲉⲣⲟϊ ϫⲉ ⲛ̄ⲧⲟⲕ ⲡⲉ ⲡⲁⲥⲱⲧⲏⲣ·

5. ⲁⲩⲱ ϯⲛⲁϯ-ⲡⲥⲱⲧ̄ϥ̄ ⲙ̄ⲡⲗⲟⲩⲟⲉⲓⲛ ⲉⲛⲉⲕϭⲓϫ· ⲁⲕ-
*ⲛⲁϩⲙⲉⲧ ⲡⲟⲩⲟϊⲛ ϩ̄ⲙ̄ ⲡⲉⲕⲥⲟⲟⲩⲛ· ⲟ̄ⲏ̄ b

6. ⲁⲕϭⲱⲛ̄ⲧ̄ ⲉⲛⲉⲧⲣⲟϊⲥ ⲉⲣⲟϊ ⲛⲁϊ ⲉⲧⲉ ⲛ̄ⲥⲉⲛⲁϣⲁⲙⲁϩⲧⲉ ⲙ̄ⲙⲟϊ ⲁⲛ ϣⲁⲃⲟⲗ· ⲁⲛⲟⲕ ⲇⲉ ⲁϊⲛⲁϩⲧⲉ ⲉⲡⲟⲩⲟϊⲛ·

7. ϯⲛⲁⲣⲁϣⲉ ⲧⲁϩⲩⲙⲛⲉⲩⲉ ϫⲉ ⲁⲕϣ̄ⲛ̄ϩⲧⲏⲕ ϩⲁⲣⲟϊ· ⲁⲩⲱ ⲁⲕϯϩⲧⲏⲕ ⲉⲫⲱϣ ⲉϯϣⲟⲟⲡ ⲛ̄ϩⲏⲧ̄ϥ̄· ⲁⲩⲱ ⲁⲕⲛⲁϩⲙⲉⲧ· ⲁⲩⲱ ⲟⲛ ⲕⲛⲁⲧⲟⲩϫⲉ-ⲧⲁϭⲟⲙ ⲉⲃⲟⲗ ϩ̄ⲙ̄ ⲡⲉⲭⲁⲟⲥ·

8. ⲁⲩⲱ ⲙ̄ⲡ̄ⲕⲕⲁⲁⲧ ⲛ̄ⲧⲟⲟⲧ̄ⲥ̄ ⲛ̄ⲧϭⲟⲙ ⲛ̄ϩⲁ ⲙ̄ⲙⲟⲩϊ· ⲁⲗⲗⲁ ⲁⲕⲛ̄ⲧ̄ ⲉⲩⲧⲟⲡⲟⲥ ⲉⲛ̄ϥ̄ϩⲏϫ ⲁⲛ·

ʒ ⲛⲁϊ ϭⲉ ⲛ̄ⲧⲉⲣⲉ ⲓ̄ⲥ̄ ϫⲟⲟⲩ ⲉⲛⲉϥⲙⲁⲑⲏⲧⲏⲥ ⲁϥⲟⲩ-
ⲱϣ̄ⲃ̄ ⲟⲛ ⲡⲉϫⲁϥ ⲛⲁⲩ ϫⲉ ⲁⲥϣⲱⲡⲉ ϭⲉ ⲛ̄ⲧⲉⲣⲉⲥⲉⲓⲙⲉ
ⲛ̄ϭⲓ ϯϭⲟⲙ ⲛ̄ϩⲟ ⲙ̄ⲙⲟⲩϊ ϫⲉ ⲙ̄ⲡⲟⲩⲛ̄-ⲧⲡⲓⲥⲧⲓⲥ ⲥⲟⲫⲓⲁ
ⲉϩⲣⲁϊ ϩ̄ⲙ̄ ⲡⲉⲭⲁⲟⲥ ⲉⲡⲧⲏⲣ̄ϥ̄· ⲁⲥⲉⲓʾ ⲟⲛ ⲙ̄ⲛ̄ ⲛ̄ⲕⲉⲡⲣⲟⲃⲟ-
ⲗⲟⲟⲩⲉ ⲧⲏⲣⲟⲩ ⲛ̄ϩⲩⲗⲓⲕⲟⲛ ⲙ̄ⲡⲁⲩⲑⲁⲇⲏⲥ ** ⲁⲩϩⲱϫ ⲟⲛ ⲟ̄ⲑ̄
ⲛ̄ⲧⲡⲓⲥⲧⲓⲥ ⲥⲟⲫⲓⲁ· ⲁⲥϣⲱⲡⲉ ϭⲉ ⲛ̄ⲧⲉⲣⲟⲩϩⲱϫ ⲙ̄ⲙⲟⲥ·
ⲁⲥⲱϣ ⲉⲃⲟⲗ ϩ̄ⲛ̄ ⲧⲉϊⲙⲉⲧⲁⲛⲟⲓⲁ ⲛ̄ⲟⲩⲱⲧ· ⲉⲥϫⲱ ⲙ̄-
ⲙⲟⲥ ϫⲉ·

9. ϣⲛ̄ϩⲧⲏⲕ ϩⲁⲣⲟϊ ⲡⲟⲩⲟϊⲛ ϫⲉ ⲁⲩϩⲱϫ ⲟⲛ ⲙ̄ⲙⲟϊ· ⲁϥϣⲧⲟⲣⲧ̄ⲣ̄ ⲉⲧⲃⲉ ⲡⲉⲕⲧⲱϣ ⲛ̄ϭⲓ ⲡⲟⲩⲟϊⲛ ⲉⲧⲛ̄ϩⲏⲧ· ⲁⲩⲱ ⲙ̄ⲛ̄ ⲧⲁϭⲟⲙ· ⲙ̄ⲛ̄ ⲡⲁⲛⲟⲩⲥ.·

10. ⲁ ⲧⲁϭⲟⲙ ⲁⲣⲭⲓ ⲛ̄ⲱϫ̄ⲛ̄ ⲉϊϣⲟⲟⲡ ϩ̄ⲛ̄ ⲛⲉϊϩⲱϫ· ⲁⲩⲱ ⲧⲏⲡⲉ ⲙ̄ⲡⲗⲟⲩⲟⲉⲓϣ ⲉⲥϣⲟⲟⲡ ϩ̄ⲙ̄ ⲡⲉⲭⲁⲟⲥ· ⲁ

25 MS ⲉⲥϣⲟⲟⲡ; read ⲉϊϣⲟⲟⲡ.

4. And thou wilt save me as I am ensnared by[1] this lion-faced power; for thou art my *Saviour*.

5. And I will give what is purified of my light into thy hands; thou hast saved me, O Light, with thy knowledge.

6. Thou hast been angry with those who watch for me, who will not be able to seize me at all. *But* I have *believed* in the light.

7. I will rejoice and *sing praises*, for thou hast had compassion on me; and thou hast given heed to the oppression in which I am. And thou hast saved me. And also thou wilt deliver my power from the *Chaos*.

8. And thou didst not leave me to be in the hands of the lion-faced power, *but* thou hast brought me to a *place* which is not oppressed'."

48. When Jesus had said these things to his *disciples*, he answered again and said to them: "It happened now when the lion-faced power knew that the Pistis Sophia was not brought up from the *Chaos* at all, it came again with all the rest of the *material emanations* of the Authades. They oppressed the Pistis Sophia again. Now it happened when they oppressed her, she cried out in this same *repentance*, in which she spoke thus:

9. Have compassion on me, O Light, for they have oppressed me again. The light within me has been agitated on account of thy ordinance; and my power and my *understanding* (*mind*).

10. My power has *begun* to decrease while I am in these oppressions; and the reckoning of my time while I am in the Chaos. | My light has diminished, for they have

---

[1] (1, 2) as I am ensnared by; Schmidt: which they have set as a snare for me.

173

ⲠⲖⲞⲨⲞⲈⲒⲚ ⲤⲂⲞⲔ ⲬⲈ ⲀⲨϤⲒ-ⲦⲀϬⲞⲘ Ⲛ̄ⲀⲞ̄Ⲧ · ⲀⲨⲰ ⲀⲨⲤⲀ-
ⲖⲈⲨⲈ Ⲛ̄ϬⲒ Ⲛ̄ϬⲞⲘ ⲦⲎⲢⲞⲨ ⲈⲦⲚ̄ϨⲎⲦ ·

11. ⲀⲒ̈Ⲣ̄-ⲀⲦϬⲞⲘ ⲠⲀⲢⲀ Ⲛ̄ⲀⲢⲬⲰⲚ ⲦⲎⲢⲞⲨ Ⲛ̄ⲚⲀⲒⲰⲚ · ⲚⲀⲒ̈
ⲈⲦⲘⲞⲤⲦⲈ Ⲙ̄ⲘⲞⲒ̈ · ⲀⲨⲰ ⲠⲀⲢⲀ ⲦⲬⲞⲨⲦⲀϤⲦⲈ Ⲙ̄ⲠⲢⲞⲂⲞⲖⲎ ·
ⲚⲀⲒ̈ ⲈⲚⲈⲒ̈ϢⲞⲞⲠ Ϩ̄Ⲙ ⲠⲈⲨⲦⲞⲠⲞⲤ · ⲀⲨⲰ ⲀϤⲢ̄ϨⲞⲦⲈ ⲈⲂⲞ-
ⲎⲒ ⲈⲢⲞⲒ̈ Ⲛ̄ϬⲒ ⲠⲀⲤⲞⲚ · ⲠⲀⲤⲨⲚⲌⲨⲄⲞⲤ ⲈⲦⲂⲈ *ⲚⲈⲚⲦⲀⲨ- ⲟ̄ⲟ̄ᵇ
ⲬⲞⲒ̈ Ⲛ̄ϨⲎⲦⲞⲨ ·

12. ⲀⲨⲰ Ⲛ̄ⲀⲢⲬⲰⲚ ⲦⲎⲢⲞⲨ Ⲙ̄ⲠⲬⲒⲤⲈ · ⲀⲨⲞⲠⲦ̄ ⲈⲦⲞⲞ-
ⲦⲞⲨ Ⲛ̄ⲐⲈ Ⲛ̄ⲞⲨϨⲨⲖⲎ ⲈⲘⲚ̄-ⲞⲨⲞⲈⲒⲚ Ⲛ̄ϨⲎⲦⲤ̄ · ⲀⲒ̈ϢⲰⲠⲈ
Ⲛ̄ⲐⲈ Ⲛ̄ⲞⲨϬⲞⲘ Ⲛ̄ϨⲨⲖⲒⲔⲞⲚ · ⲈⲀⲤϨⲈ ⲈⲂⲞⲖ Ϩ̄Ⲛ Ⲛ̄ⲀⲢⲬⲰⲚ ·

13. ⲀⲨⲰ ⲀⲨⲬⲞⲞⲤ Ⲛ̄ϬⲒ ⲚⲈⲦϢⲞⲞⲠ ⲦⲎⲢⲞⲨ Ϩ̄Ⲛ Ⲛ̄ⲀⲒⲰⲚ
ⲬⲈ ⲀⲤⲢ̄-ⲬⲀⲞⲤ · ⲀⲨⲰ Ⲙ̄Ⲛ̄Ⲛ̄ⲤⲀ ⲚⲀⲒ̈ ⲀⲨⲔⲰⲦⲈ ⲈⲢⲞⲒ̈ ϨⲒ
ⲞⲨⲤⲞⲠ Ⲛ̄ϬⲒ Ⲛ̄ϬⲞⲘ Ⲛ̄ⲀⲦⲚⲀ' · ⲀⲨⲰ ⲀⲨⲬⲞⲞⲤ ⲈϤⲒ-ⲠⲖⲞⲨ-
ⲞⲈⲒⲚ ⲦⲎⲢ̄Ϥ ⲈⲦⲚ̄ϨⲎⲦ ·

14. ⲀⲚⲞⲔ ⲆⲈ ⲀⲒ̈ⲚⲀϨⲦⲈ ⲈⲢⲞⲔ ⲠⲞⲨⲞⲒ̈Ⲛ · ⲀⲨⲰ ⲀⲒ̈ⲬⲞⲞⲤ
ⲬⲈ Ⲛ̄ⲦⲞⲔ ⲠⲈ ⲠⲀⲤⲰⲦⲎⲢ ·

15. ⲀⲨⲰ ⲈⲢⲈ ⲠⲀⲦⲰϢ ⲈⲚⲦⲀⲔⲦⲞϢ̄Ϥ ⲈⲢⲞⲒ̈ ⲈϤϢⲞⲞⲠ
Ϩ̄Ⲛ ⲚⲈⲔϬⲒⲬ · ⲚⲀϨⲘⲈⲦ ⲈⲦⲞⲞⲦⲞⲨ Ⲛ̄ⲚⲈⲠⲢⲞⲂⲞⲖⲞⲞⲨⲈ
Ⲙ̄ⲠⲀⲨⲐⲀⲆⲎⲤ ⲚⲀⲒ̈ ⲈⲦϨⲰⲬ Ⲙ̄ⲘⲞⲒ̈ ⲀⲨⲰ ⲈⲦⲠⲎⲦ Ⲛ̄ⲤⲰⲒ̈ ·

16. ⲦⲀⲨⲈ-ⲠⲈⲔⲞⲨⲞⲈⲒⲚ ⲈϨⲢⲀⲒ̈ ⲈⲬⲰⲒ̈ ⲬⲈ ⲀⲚⲄ̄ ⲞⲨⲖⲀⲀⲨ
Ⲛ̄ⲚⲀϨⲢⲀⲔ · ⲀⲨⲰ ⲚⲀϨⲘⲈⲦ Ϩ̄Ⲛ ⲦⲈⲔⲘⲚ̄ⲦϢⲀⲚϨⲦⲎϤ · ⲡ̄

17. Ⲙ̄ⲠⲢ̄ⲦⲢⲀⲬⲒⲤⲰϢ ⲬⲈ Ⲛ̄ⲦⲞⲔ ⲠⲈ Ⲛ̄ⲦⲀⲒ̈ϨⲨⲘⲚⲈⲨⲈ
ⲈⲢⲞⲔ ⲠⲞⲨⲞⲈⲒⲚ ⲈⲢⲈ ⲠⲈⲬⲖⲞⲤ ϨⲰⲂⲤ̄ ⲈⲂⲞⲖ ⲈⲬⲚ̄ ⲚⲈⲠⲢⲞ-
ⲂⲞⲖⲞⲞⲨⲈ Ⲙ̄ⲠⲀⲨⲐⲀⲆⲎⲤ ⲀⲨⲰ Ⲛ̄ⲤⲈⲬⲒⲦⲞⲨ ⲈⲠⲈⲤⲎⲦ
ⲈⲠⲔⲀⲔⲈ ·

taken away my power from me, and all the powers within me have been *shaken*.

11. I have become powerless *before* [1] all the archons of the *aeons* which hate me, and *before* the 24 *emanations* in whose *places* I was. And my brother, my *partner*, feared to *help* me, on account of those among whom I was held.

12. And all the *archons* of the height have reckoned me to be *matter* without light in it. I have become like a *material* power which has fallen out of the *archons*.

13. And all those who were in the *aeons* said: she has become *Chaos*. And after this the merciless powers surrounded me at the same time, and spoke to take away all my light that was in me.

14. *But* I trusted thee, O Light, and I said: thou art my *Saviour*.

15. And my ordinance which thou hast ordained for me is in thy hands; save me from the hands of the *emanations* of the Authades which oppress me and pursue after me.

16. Send down thy light upon me, for I am nothing before thee; and save me in thy compassion.

17. Let me not be despised, for thou art he to whom I have *sung praises*, O Light. May the *Chaos* cover over the *emanations* of the Authades, and may they be cast down to the darkness. |

---

[1]　(3, 4) powerless before; or: more powerless than.

18. ⲘⲀⲢⲈϢⲰⲦⲀⲘ ⲚϬⲒ ⲦⲦⲀⲠⲢⲞ ⲚⲚⲈⲦⲞⲨⲈϢⲞⲘⲔⲦ ϨⲚ
ⲞⲨⲔⲢⲞϤ· ⲚⲀⲒ ⲈⲦϪⲰ ⲘⲘⲞⳊ ϪⲈ ⲘⲀⲢⲈⲚϤ-ⲠⲞⲨⲞⲒⲚ
ⲦⲎⲢϤ ⲈⲦⲚϨⲎⲦϤ ⲈⲘⲠⲒⲢ-ⲀⲀⲀⲨ ⲚⲀⲨ ⲘⲠⲈⲐⲞⲞⲨ·

ⲚⲀⲒ ⲆⲈ ⲚⲦⲈⲢⲈϤϪⲞⲞⲨ ⲚϬⲒ ⲒⲤ· ⲀϤⲈⲒ ⲈⲐⲎ ⲚϬⲒ ⲘⲀ-
5 ⲐⲀⲒⲞⲤ ⲠⲈϪⲀϤ ϪⲈ ⲠⲀϪⲞⲈⲒⲤ· Ⲁ ⲠⲈⲔⲠⲚⲀ ⲔⲒⲘ ⲈⲢⲞⲒ·
ⲀⲨⲰ ϤⲚⲎϤⲈ ⲘⲘⲞⲒ ⲚϬⲒ ⲠⲈⲔⲞⲨⲞⲈⲒⲚ· ⲈⲦⲢⲀⲦⲀⲨⲈ-ⲦⲘⲈϨ-
ϢⲘⲞⲨⲚⲈ ⲘⲘⲈⲦⲀⲚⲞⲒⲀ ⲚⲦⲠⲒⲤⲦⲒⲤ ⲤⲞⳘⲒⲀ· Ⲁ ⲦⲈⲔϬⲞⲘ
ⲄⲀⲢ ⲠⲢⲞⳘⲎⲦⲈⲨⲈ ϨⲀⲢⲞⲤ ⲘⲠⲒⲞⲨⲞⲈⲒϢ ϨⲒⲦⲚ ⲀⲀⲨⲈⲒⲀ
ϨⲘ ⲠⲘⲈϨⲘⲀⲀⲂ ⲘⳘⲀⲀⲘⲞⲤ ⲈⲤϪⲰ ⲘⲘⲞⲤ· ϪⲈ

10 1. ⲀⲒⲔⲀ-ϨⲦⲎⲒ ⲈⲢⲞⲔ ⲠϪⲞⲈⲒⲤ· ⲘⲠⲢⲦⲢⲀϪⲒϢⲒⲠⲈ ⲚϢⲀ- ⲡ ᵇ
ⲈⲚⲈϨ· ⲘⲀⲦⲞⲨϪⲞⲒ ϨⲚ ⲦⲈⲔⲆⲒⲔⲀⲒⲞⲤⲨⲚⲎ·

2. ⲢⲒⲔⲈ ⲘⲠⲈⲔⲘⲀⲀϪⲈ ⲈⲢⲞⲒ· ϬⲈⲠⲎ ⲚⲄⲦⲞⲨϪⲞⲒ· ϢⲰ-
ⲠⲈ ⲚⲀⲒ ⲈⲨⲚⲞⲨⲦⲈ ⲚⲚⲀϢⲦⲈ· ⲀⲨⲰ ⲞⲨⲎⲒ ⲘⲘⲀⲘⲠⲰⲦ
ⲈⲦⲞⲨϪⲞⲒ·

15 3. ϪⲈ ⲚⲦⲞⲔ ⲠⲈ ⲠⲀⲦⲀⳘⲢⲞ· ⲀⲨⲰ ⲠⲀⲘⲀⲘⲠⲰⲦ· ⲈⲦⲂⲈ
ⲠⲈⲔⲢⲀⲚ ⲔⲚⲀϪⲒⲘⲞⲈⲒⲦ ϨⲎⲦ·

4. ⲀⲨⲰ ⲚⲄⲤⲀⲚⲞⲨϢⲦ ⲀⲨⲰ ⲔⲚⲀⲚⲦ ⲈⲂⲞⲀ ϨⲘ ⲠⲈⲒ-
ⲠⲀϢ· ⲠⲀⲒ ⲈⲚⲦⲀⲨϨⲞⲠϤ ⲈⲢⲞⲒ· ϪⲈ ⲚⲦⲞⲔ ⲠⲈ ⲦⲀⲚⲀϢⲦⲈ·

5. ϯⲚⲀϬⲞⲒⲀⲈ ⲈⲠⲀⲠⲚⲀ ⲈⲚⲈⲔϬⲒϪ· ⲀⲔⲤⲞⲦⲦ ⲠϪⲞⲈⲒⲤ
20 ⲠⲚⲞⲨⲦⲈ ⲚⲦⲘⲈ·

6. ⲀⲔⲘⲈⲤⲦⲈ-ⲚⲈⲦϨⲀⲢⲈϨ ⲈⲘⲠⲈⲦϢⲞⲨⲒⲦ ⲈⲠϪⲒⲚϪⲎ·
ⲀⲚⲞⲔ ⲆⲈ ⲀⲒⲚⲀϨⲦⲈ· ⲀⲨⲰ ϯⲚⲀⲦⲈⲀⲎⲀ ⲈϪⲘ ⲠϪⲞⲈⲒⲤ·

7. ⲀⲨⲰ ϯⲚⲀⲈⲨⳘⲢⲀⲚⲈ ⲈϪⲘ ⲠⲈⲔⲚⲀ· ϪⲈ ⲀⲔϬⲰϢⲦ
ⲈϪⲘ ⲠⲀⲐⲂⲂⲒⲞ ⲀⲨⲰ ⲀⲔⲦⲞⲨϪⲈ-ⲦⲀⳘⲨⲭⲎ ⲈⲂⲞⲀ ϨⲚ ⲚⲀ-
25 ⲀⲚⲀⲄⲔⲎ·

---

19 MS ⲈⲠⲀⲠⲚⲀ; read ⲘⲠⲀⲠⲚⲀ.
21 ⲞⲨ in ϢⲞⲨⲒⲦ inserted above.

18. May the mouth be shut of those who, with cunning, want to swallow me; who say : let us take away all the light within her, although I have done nothing wicked to them'."

49.   When, *however*, Jesus had said these things, Matthew came forward and said : "My Lord, thy *Spirit* has moved me, and thy light has made me *sober*, so that I should tell the eighth *repentance* of the Pistis Sophia. *For* thy power once *prophesied* about it through David, in the 30th *Psalm*, saying :

1. 'I have hoped in thee, O Lord. Let me not be put to shame for ever; save me in thy *righteousness.*

2. Incline thine ear to me; save me quickly, be to me a protecting God and a house of refuge to save me.

3. For thou art my support and my refuge; for the sake of thy name thou wilt guide me and nourish me.

4. And thou wilt bring me forth from this snare which they have hidden for me, for thou art my protector.

5. I will give up my *spirit* into thy hands. Thou hast saved me, O Lord, God of truth.

6. Thou hast hated those who idly keep to what is vain. *But* I have trusted;

7. And I will rejoice over the Lord [1], and I will be *glad* over thy mercy; for thou hast looked upon my humbleness, and thou hast saved my *soul* out of my *necessities.* |

---

[1]   (22, 23) Till emends Schmidt's division of verses 6, 7.

8. ⲀⲨⲰ Ⲙ̄ⲠⲔⲰⲦⲀⲘ ⲈⲢⲰⲒ Ⲍ̄Ⲛ Ⲛ̄ⲊⲒⲬ Ⲙ̄ⲠⲒⲬⲀⲬⲈ· ⲀⲔ-
ⲦⲀⲌⲈ-ⲚⲀⲞⲨⲈⲢⲎⲦⲈ ⲈⲢⲀⲦⲞⲨ Ⲍ̄Ⲛ ⲞⲨⲞⲨⲞ̈ⲤⲦⲚ̄·   ⲠⲀ

9. ⲚⲀ' ⲚⲀⲒ̈ ⲠⲬⲞⲈⲒⲤ ⲬⲈ ϮⲐⲖⲒⲂⲈ· Ⲁ ⲠⲀⲂⲀⲖ ⲰⲦⲞⲢⲦⲢ̄
Ⲍ̄Ⲙ ⲠⲊⲰ̄ⲚⲦ· ⲀⲨⲰ ⲦⲀⲮⲨⲬⲎ ⲘⲚ̄ ⲌⲎⲦ·

10. ⲬⲈ Ⲁ ⲚⲀⲢ̄ⲘⲠⲞⲞⲨⲈ ⲰⲬ̄Ⲛ Ⲍ̄Ⲛ ⲞⲨⲘ̄ⲔⲀⲌ Ⲛ̄ⲌⲎⲦ· ⲀⲨⲰ
Ⲁ ⲠⲀⲰ̄ⲚⲌ ⲰⲬ̄Ⲛ Ⲍ̄Ⲛ ⲌⲈⲚⲀⲰⲀⲌⲞⲘ· Ⲁ ⲦⲀⲊⲞⲘ Ⲋ̄ⲂⲂⲈ Ⲍ̄Ⲛ
ⲞⲨⲘ̄Ⲛ̄ⲦⲌⲎⲔⲈ· ⲀⲨⲰ ⲀⲨⲰⲦⲞⲢⲦⲢ̄ Ⲛ̄ⲊⲒ ⲚⲀⲔⲈⲈⲤ·

11. ⲀⲒ̈ⲰⲰⲠⲈ Ⲛ̄ⲚⲞⲊⲚⲈⲊ Ⲛ̄ⲚⲀⲬⲀⲬⲈ ⲦⲎⲢⲞⲨ· ⲀⲨⲰ
Ⲛ̄ⲚⲈⲦⲌⲎⲚ ⲈⲢⲞⲒ̈· ⲀⲒ̈ⲰⲰⲠⲈ Ⲛ̄ⲌⲞⲦⲈ Ⲛ̄ⲚⲈⲦⲤⲞⲞⲨⲚ Ⲙ̄ⲘⲞⲒ̈·
ⲀⲨⲰ ⲚⲈⲦⲚⲀⲨ ⲈⲢⲞⲒ̈ ⲀⲨⲠⲰⲦ Ⲛ̄ⲤⲀⲂⲞⲖ Ⲙ̄ⲘⲞⲒ̈·

12. ⲀⲨⲢ̄-ⲠⲀⲰⲂⲰ̄ Ⲛ̄ⲐⲈ Ⲛ̄ⲞⲨⲔⲰⲰⲤ Ⲍ̄Ⲙ ⲠⲈⲨⲌⲎⲦ· ⲀⲨⲰ
ⲀⲒ̈Ⲣ̄-ⲐⲈ Ⲛ̄ⲞⲨⲤⲔⲈⲨⲞⲤ ⲈⲀⲊⲤⲰⲢⲘ̄·

13. ⲬⲈ ⲀⲒ̈ⲤⲰⲦⲘ̄ ⲈⲠⲤⲰⲰ Ⲛ̄ⲌⲈⲚⲘⲎⲎⲰⲈ ⲈⲨⲔⲰⲦⲈ ⲈⲢⲞⲒ̈
Ⲙ̄ⲠⲀⲔⲰⲦⲈ· Ⲍ̄Ⲙ ⲠⲦⲢⲈⲨⲤⲰⲞⲨⲌ ⲈⲌⲢⲀⲒ̈ ⲈⲬⲰⲒ̈ ⲌⲒ ⲞⲨⲤⲞⲠ·
ⲀⲨⲰⲞⲬⲚⲈ ⲈⲊⲒ-ⲦⲀⲮⲨⲬⲎ Ⲛ̄ⲦⲞⲞⲦ·

14. ⲀⲚⲞⲔ ⲀⲈ ⲀⲒ̈ⲚⲀⲌⲦⲈ ⲈⲢⲞⲔ ⲠⲬⲞⲈⲒⲤ· ⲀⲒ̈ⲬⲞⲞⲤ ⲬⲈ
Ⲛ̄ⲦⲞⲔ ⲠⲈ ⲠⲀⲚⲞⲨⲦⲈ·

15. Ⲉ̈ⲢⲈ ⲚⲀⲔⲖⲎⲢⲞⲤ Ⲍ̄Ⲛ ⲚⲈⲔⲊⲒⲬ· ⲚⲀⲌⲘⲈⲦ ⲈⲦⲊⲒⲬ Ⲛ̄ⲚⲀ-   ⲠⲀ ᵇ
ⲬⲀⲬⲈ· ⲀⲨⲰ ⲦⲞⲨⲬⲞⲒ̈ ⲈⲚⲈⲦⲠⲎⲦ Ⲛ̄ⲤⲰⲒ̈·

16. ⲞⲨⲰⲚⲌ ⲠⲈⲔⲌⲞ ⲈⲌⲢⲀⲒ̈ ⲈⲬⲘ ⲠⲈⲔⲌⲘ̄ⲌⲀⲖ· ⲀⲨⲰ ⲦⲞⲨ-
ⲬⲞⲒ̈ Ⲍ̄Ⲙ ⲠⲈⲔⲚⲀ' ⲠⲬⲞⲒ̈Ⲥ·

17. Ⲙ̄ⲠⲢ̄ⲦⲢⲀⲬⲒⲰⲒⲠⲈ ⲬⲈ ⲀⲒ̈ⲰⲰ ⲈⲌⲢⲀⲒ̈ ⲈⲢⲞⲔ· ⲘⲀⲢⲞⲨ-
ⲬⲒⲰⲒⲠⲈ Ⲛ̄ⲊⲒ Ⲛ̄ⲀⲤⲈⲂⲎⲤ· ⲀⲨⲰ Ⲛ̄ⲤⲈⲔⲞⲦⲞⲨ ⲈⲀⲘ̄ⲚⲦⲈ·

18. ⲘⲀⲢⲞⲨⲢ̄ⲘⲠⲞ Ⲛ̄ⲊⲒ ⲚⲈⲤⲠⲞⲦⲞⲨ Ⲛ̄ⲔⲢⲞϤ· ⲚⲈⲦⲦⲀⲨⲞ
Ⲛ̄ⲞⲨⲀⲚⲞⲘⲒⲀ Ⲛ̄ⲤⲀ ⲠⲀⲒⲔⲀⲒⲞⲤ Ⲍ̄Ⲛ ⲞⲨⲘ̄Ⲛ̄ⲦⲬⲀⲤⲒⲌⲎⲦ· ⲘⲚ̄
ⲞⲨⲤⲰⲰϤ·

3. Ⲛ̄ⲦⲈⲢⲈ ⲒⲤ̄ ⲀⲈ ⲤⲰⲦⲘ̄ ⲈⲚⲈⲒ̈ⲰⲀⲬⲈ· ⲠⲈⲬⲀϤ ⲬⲈ ⲔⲀ-

---

20 MS ⲞⲨⲰⲠⲌ ⲠⲈⲔⲌⲞ; better ⲞⲨⲈⲚⲌ ⲠⲈⲔⲌⲞ.

8. Thou hast not shut me in the hands of the enemy; thou hast set my feet in a wide place.

9. Have mercy on me, O Lord, for I am *afflicted*; my eye is [1] troubled with anger; and my *soul* and my belly.

10. For my years have been spent in distress and my life has been spent in groanings; my power has become weak in poverty, and my bones are troubled.

11. I have become a reproach to all my enemies and my neighbours. I have become a fear to those that know me, and those that saw me ran away from me.

12. I have been forgotten like a corpse in their hearts; and I have become like a broken *vessel*.

13. I have heard contempt from many at my side who surrounded me; when they gathered together against me, they took counsel to take away my *soul* from me.

14. *But* I have trusted thee, O Lord, I have said: thou art my God.

15. My *lots* are in thy hands; save me from the hand of my enemies, and deliver me from those that persecute me.

16. Reveal thy face over thy servant, and save me in thy mercy, O Lord.

17. Let me not be put to shame, for I have cried to thee; let the *impious* be put to shame and turned to Amente.

18. Let the cunning lips be dumb, who speak *iniquity* against the *righteous* with pride and contempt'.*"

50. When *however* Jesus heard these words, he said: "*Well done*, | Matthew. Now at this time *truly* I say to

---

* Ps. 30.1-18

---

[1] (3) my eye is; lit. my eye has been.

ⲗⲱⲥ ⲙⲁⲑⲁⲓⲟⲥ· ⲧⲉⲛⲟⲩ ϭⲉ ϩⲁⲙⲏⲛ ϯϫⲱ (ⲙ̄)ⲙⲟⲥ ⲛⲏⲧ̄ⲛ̄
ϫⲉ ⲉϥϣⲁⲛϫⲱⲕ ⲉⲃⲟⲗ ⲛ̄ϭⲓ ⲡⲁⲣⲓⲑⲙⲟⲥ ⲛ̄ⲧⲉⲗⲉⲓⲟⲥ· ⲁⲩⲱ
ⲛ̄ⲧⲉ ⲡⲧⲏⲣ̄ϥ ⲱ ⲉϩⲣⲁⲓ̈ ϯⲛⲁϩⲙⲟⲟⲥ ϩ̄ⲙ ⲡⲉⲑⲏⲥⲁⲩⲣⲟⲥ
ⲙ̄ⲡⲟⲩⲟⲓ̈ⲛ ⲁⲩⲱ ⲛ̄ⲧⲱⲧ̄ⲛ ϩⲱⲧⲧⲏⲩⲧ̄ⲛ ⲧⲉⲧⲛⲁϩⲙⲟⲟⲥ
5 ϩⲓϫⲛ̄ ⲙ̄ⲛⲧⲥⲛⲟⲟⲩⲥ ⲛ̄ϭⲟⲙ ⲛ̄ⲟⲩⲟⲉⲓⲛ ϣⲁⲛⲧⲛ̄ⲁⲡⲟⲕⲁ-　ⲡⲃ
ⲑⲓⲥⲧⲁ ⲛ̄ⲛ̄ⲧⲁⲝⲓⲥ ⲧⲏⲣⲟⲩ ⲙ̄ⲡⲙ̄ⲛⲧⲥⲛⲟⲟⲩⲥ ⲛ̄ⲥⲱⲧⲏⲣ ⲉⲡⲧⲟⲡⲟⲥ ⲛ̄ⲛⲉⲕⲗⲏⲣⲟⲛⲟⲙⲓⲁ ⲙ̄ⲡⲟⲩⲁ ⲡⲟⲩⲁ ⲙ̄ⲙⲟⲟⲩ :

ⲍ ⲛⲁⲓ̈ ⲇⲉ ⲛ̄ⲧⲉⲣⲉϥϫⲟⲟⲩ· ⲡⲉϫⲁϥ ϫⲉ ⲧⲉⲧⲛ̄ⲛⲟⲓ ϫⲉ
ⲉⲓ̈ϫⲱ ⲙ̄ⲙⲟⲥ ϫⲉ ⲟⲩ· ⲁⲥⲉⲓ̈ ⲉⲑⲏ ⲛ̄ϭⲓ ⲙⲁⲣⲓⲁ ⲡⲉϫⲁⲥ
10 ϫⲉ ⲡϫⲟⲉⲓⲥ· ⲉⲧⲃⲉ ⲡⲁⲓ̈ ⲣⲱ ⲁⲕϫⲟⲟⲥ ⲉⲣⲟⲛ ⲙ̄ⲡⲓⲟⲩ-
ⲟⲉⲓϣ ϩ̄ⲛ ⲟⲩⲡⲁⲣⲁⲃⲟⲗⲏ· ϫⲉ ⲛ̄ⲧⲱⲧ̄ⲛ ⲁⲧⲉⲧ̄ⲛ̄ϩⲩⲡⲟⲙⲓⲛⲉ
ⲛ̄ⲙⲙⲁⲓ̈ ϩ̄ⲛ ⲙ̄ⲡⲓⲣⲁⲥⲙⲟⲥ· ϯⲛⲁⲥⲙⲓⲛⲉ ⲛ̄ⲙⲙⲏⲧ̄ⲛ ⲛ̄ⲟⲩⲙ̄ⲛⲧ-
ⲉⲣⲟ ⲕⲁⲧⲁ ⲑⲉ ⲉⲛⲧⲁ ⲡⲁⲓ̈ⲱⲧ ⲥ̄ⲙⲛⲧⲥ ⲛ̄ⲙⲙⲁⲓ̈· ϫⲉ ⲉⲧⲉ-
ⲧⲛ̄ⲉⲟⲩⲱⲙ· ⲛ̄ⲧⲉⲧ̄ⲛ̄ⲥⲱ ϩⲓϫ̄ⲛ ⲧⲁⲧⲣⲁⲡⲉⲍⲁ ϩ̄ⲛ ⲧⲁⲙ̄ⲛⲧ-
15 ⲉⲣⲟ· ⲁⲩⲱ ⲛ̄ⲧⲱⲧ̄ⲛ ⲧⲉⲧⲛⲁϩⲙⲟⲟⲥ ϩⲓϫ̄ⲛ ⲙ̄ⲛⲧⲥⲛⲟⲟⲩⲥ
ⲛ̄ⲑⲣⲟⲛⲟⲥ ⲛ̄ⲧⲉⲧ̄ⲛ̄ⲕⲣⲓⲛⲉ ⲛ̄ⲧⲙ̄ⲛⲧⲥⲛⲟⲟⲩⲥ ⲙ̄ⲫⲩⲗⲏ ⲙ̄ⲡⲓⲗ·

ⲍ ⲡⲉϫⲁϥ ⲛⲁⲥ ϫⲉ ⲉⲩⲅⲉ ⲙⲁⲣⲓⲁ· ⲁϥⲟⲩⲱϩ ⲟⲛ ⲉⲧⲟ-
ⲟⲧ̄ϥ ⲛ̄ϭⲓ ⲓ̄ⲥ ⲡⲉϫⲁϥ ⲛ̄ⲛⲉϥⲙⲁⲑⲏⲧⲏⲥ ϫⲉ ⲁⲥϣⲱⲡⲉ ϭⲉ　ⲡⲃ ᵇ
ⲟⲛ ⲙ̄ⲛⲛ̄ⲥⲁ ⲛⲁⲓ̈ ⲛ̄ⲧⲉⲣⲟⲩϩⲱϫ ⲛ̄ⲧⲡⲓⲥⲧⲓⲥ ⲥⲟⲫⲓⲁ ϩ̄ⲙ ⲡⲉ-
20 ⲭⲁⲟⲥ ⲛ̄ϭⲓ ⲛⲉⲡⲣⲟⲃⲟⲗⲟⲟⲩⲉ ⲙ̄ⲡⲁⲩⲑⲁⲇⲏⲥ· ⲁⲥϫⲱ ⲛ̄-
ⲧⲙⲉϩϣⲓⲧⲉ ⲙ̄ⲙⲉⲧⲁⲛⲟⲓⲁ ⲉⲥϫⲱ ⲙ̄ⲙⲟⲥ· ϫⲉ

1. ⲱ᾽ ⲡⲟⲩⲟⲉⲓⲛ ⲡⲁⲧⲁⲥⲥⲉ ⲛ̄ⲛⲉⲛⲧⲁⲩϥⲓ-ⲧⲁϭⲟⲙ ⲛ̄-
ⲧⲟⲟⲧ· ⲁⲩⲱ ⲛ̄ⲅϥⲓ-ⲧϭⲟⲙ ⲛ̄ⲛⲉⲛⲧⲁⲩϥⲓ-ⲧⲱⲓ̈ ⲛ̄ϩⲏⲧ·

2. ϫⲉ ⲁⲛⲟⲕ ⲡⲉ ⲧⲉⲕϭⲟⲙ· ⲙ̄ⲛ ⲡⲉⲕⲟⲩⲟⲉⲓⲛ ⲁⲙⲟⲩ
25 ⲛ̄ⲅⲛⲁϩⲙⲉⲧ·

1　MS ⲙⲟⲥ.
16　MS ⲙ̄ⲡⲓⲗ for ⲙ̄ⲡⲓⲥⲁ or ⲙ̄ⲡⲓⲏⲗ.

you, when the *perfect number* is completed and the All is raised up, I will sit in the *Treasury* of the Light, and you yourselves will sit on twelve light-powers, until we have *set up* again all the *ranks* of the twelve *saviours* at the *place* of the *inheritance* of each one of them."

But when he had said these things, he said: "Do you *understand* what I say?"

Maria came forward and said: "O Lord, concerning this, thou didst once say to us in a *parable*: 'You have *endured* with me in *temptations*. I will establish a kingdom for you *in the way in which* my Father established it for me [1], so that you may eat and drink at my *table* in my kingdom. And you will sit upon twelve *thrones* and *judge* the twelve *tribes* of Israel'.*"

He said to her: "*Excellent*, Maria."

Jesus continued again and said to his *disciples*: "Now it happened after these things, when the *emanations* of the Authades oppressed the Pistis Sophia in the *Chaos*, she spoke the *ninth repentance*, saying:

1. '*O* Light, *smite down* those who have taken my power away from me; and take the power from those who have taken mine from me.

2. For I am thy power and thy light; come and save me. |

---

*   cf. Lk. 22.28-30

---

[1]   (12) I will establish a kingdom for you ... for me; Till: I will establish a kingdom with you ... with me.

3. ⲘⲀⲢⲈ ⲞⲨⲚⲞϭ Ⲛ̄ⲔⲀⲔⲈ ϨⲰⲂⲤ̄ ⲈⲂⲞⲖ ⲈϪ̄Ⲛ ⲚⲈⲦϨⲰϪ
Ⲙ̄ⲘⲞⲒ̈ · ⲀϪⲒⲤ Ⲛ̄ⲦⲀϭⲞⲘ ϪⲈ ⲀⲚⲞⲔ ⲠⲈⲦⲚⲀⲚⲀϨⲘⲈ ·

4. ⲘⲀⲢⲞⲨϢⲰϢⲦ Ⲛ̄ⲦⲈⲨϭⲞⲘ Ⲛ̄ϭⲒ ⲚⲀⲒ ⲦⲎⲢⲞⲨ ⲈⲦⲞⲨ-
ⲈϢϤⲒ·ⲠⲖⲞⲨⲞⲒ̈Ⲛ Ⲛ̄ϨⲎⲦ ⲈⲠⲦⲎⲢϤ̄ · ⲘⲀⲢⲞⲨⲔⲞⲦⲞⲨ ⲈⲠⲈ-
5 ϪⲀⲞⲤ · ⲀⲨⲰ Ⲛ̄ⲤⲈⲢ̄-ⲀⲦϭⲞⲘ Ⲛ̄ϭⲒ ⲚⲈⲦⲞⲨⲈϢϤⲒ Ⲙ̄ⲠⲖⲞⲨⲞⲒ̈Ⲛ
Ⲛ̄ϨⲎⲦ ⲈⲠⲦⲎⲢϤ̄ ·

5. ⲘⲀⲢⲈ ⲦⲈⲨϭⲞⲘ ϢⲰⲠⲈ Ⲛ̄ⲞⲈ Ⲛ̄ⲞⲨϢⲞⲒ̈Ϣ · ⲀⲨⲰ ⲘⲀ-
ⲢⲈϤⲠⲀⲦⲀⲤⲤⲈ Ⲙ̄ⲘⲞⲞⲨ Ⲛ̄ϭⲒ Ⲓ̅Ⲉ̅Ⲟ̅Ⲩ̅ ⲠⲈⲔⲀⲄⲄⲈⲖⲞⲤ ·   ⲡ̅ⲅ̅

6. ⲀⲨⲰ ⲈⲨϢⲀⲚⲈⲒ' ⲈⲨⲚⲎⲨ ⲈⲠϪⲒⲤⲈ · ⲘⲀⲢⲈ ⲞⲨⲔⲀⲔⲈ
10 ⲦⲀϨⲞⲞⲨ · ⲀⲨⲰ Ⲛ̄ⲤⲈⲤⲖⲀⲀⲦⲈ Ⲛ̄ⲤⲈⲔⲞⲦⲞⲨ ⲈⲠⲈϪⲀⲞⲤ ·
ⲀⲨⲰ ⲘⲀⲢⲈϤⲠⲰⲦ Ⲛ̄ⲤⲰⲞⲨ Ⲛ̄ϭⲒ Ⲓ̅Ⲉ̅Ⲟ̅Ⲩ̅ ⲠⲈⲔⲀⲄⲄⲈⲖⲞⲤ Ⲛ̄Ϥ-
ϪⲚⲀⲨ ⲈⲠⲔⲀⲔⲈ Ⲙ̄ⲠⲈⲤⲎⲦ ·

7. ϪⲈ ⲀⲨϭⲰⲢϭ̄ ⲈⲢⲞⲒ̈ Ⲛ̄ⲞⲨϭⲞⲘ Ⲛ̄ϨⲞ Ⲙ̄ⲘⲞⲨⲒ̈ ⲈⲘⲠⲒⲢ-ⲠⲈ-
ⲞⲞⲨ ⲚⲀⲨ ⲦⲀⲒ̈ ⲈⲦⲞⲨⲚⲀϤⲒ Ⲙ̄ⲠⲈⲨⲞⲨⲞⲈⲒⲚ ϨⲢⲀⲒ̈ Ⲛ̄ϨⲎⲦⲤ̄
15 ⲀⲨϨⲰϪ Ⲛ̄ⲦϭⲞⲘ ⲈⲦⲚ̄ϨⲎⲦ · ⲦⲀⲒ̈ ⲈⲦⲈ Ⲛ̄ⲤⲈⲚⲀϢϤⲒⲦⲤ̄ ⲀⲚ ·

8. ⲦⲈⲚⲞⲨ ϭⲈ ⲠⲞⲨⲞⲈⲒⲚ ϤⲒ-ⲠⲤⲰⲦϤ̄ Ⲛ̄ⲦϭⲞⲘ Ⲛ̄ϨⲞ Ⲙ̄-
ⲘⲞⲨⲒ̈ ⲈⲘⲠⲤⲈⲒⲘⲈ · ⲀⲨⲰ ⲠⲘⲈⲈⲨⲈ ⲈⲚⲦⲀϤⲘⲈⲈⲨⲈ ⲈⲢⲞϤ
Ⲛ̄ϭⲒ ⲠⲀⲨⲐⲀⲖⲎⲤ ⲈϤⲒ-ⲠⲖⲞⲨⲞⲈⲒⲚ · ϤⲒ-ⲠⲰϤ ϨⲰⲰϤ · ⲀⲨⲰ
ⲘⲀⲢⲞⲨϤⲒ-ⲠⲞⲨⲞⲒ̈Ⲛ Ⲛ̄ⲦϭⲞⲘ Ⲛ̄ϨⲞ Ⲙ̄ⲘⲞⲨⲒ̈ ⲦⲀⲒ̈ ⲈⲦϭⲰⲢϭ̄
20 ⲈⲢⲞⲒ̈ ·

9. ⲦⲀϭⲞⲘ Ⲛ̄ⲦⲞⲤ ⲚⲀⲞⲨⲢⲞⲦ ϨⲘ̄ ⲠⲞⲨⲞⲈⲒⲚ · ⲀⲨⲰ ⲤⲚⲀ-
ⲢⲀϢⲈ · ϪⲈ ϤⲚⲀⲚⲀϨⲘⲈⲤ ·

10. ⲀⲨⲰ ⲤⲈⲚⲀϪⲞⲞⲤ Ⲛ̄ϭⲒ Ⲙ̄ⲘⲈⲢⲞⲤ ⲦⲎⲢⲞⲨ Ⲛ̄ⲦⲀϭⲞⲘ
ϪⲈ Ⲙ̄Ⲛ ϭⲈ ⲢⲈϤⲚⲞⲨϨⲘ̄ Ⲛ̄ⲤⲀⲂⲖⲖⲀⲔ · ϪⲈ Ⲛ̄ⲦⲞⲔ* ⲠⲈⲦⲚⲀ- ⲡ̅ⲅ̅ ᵇ
25 ⲚⲀϨⲘⲈⲦ Ⲛ̄ⲦⲞⲞⲦⲤ̄ Ⲛ̄ϯϭⲞⲘ Ⲛ̄ϨⲞ Ⲙ̄ⲘⲞⲨⲒ̈ ⲦⲀⲒ̈ ⲈⲚⲦⲀⲤϤⲒ-

3. May a great darkness cover over those that oppress me; say to my power : it is I who will save thee.

4. All those who want to take my light from me completely : may their power fail; those who want to take my light from me completely : may they turn to the *Chaos* and become powerless.

5. May their power become like dust; and may Jeu, thine *angel, smite* them *down.*

6. And if they come to go to the height, may a darkness seize them, so that they stumble and turn to the *Chaos*; and may thine *angel*, Jeu, pursue them and send them to the darkness below.

7. For without my having done evil to them, they have ensnared me with a lion-faced power from which their light will be taken; they have oppressed the power within me, which they will not able to take away.

8. Now at this time, O Light, take away what is purified from the lion-faced power, without his knowing; and the thought which the Authades had (lit. thought), to take away my light : take his own away; and let the light of the lion-faced power, which ensnared me, be taken away.

9. My power will flourish in the light and will rejoice because it will save it.

10. And all the *parts* of my power will say : there is now no saviour except thee; for it is thou who wilt save me from the hands of the lion-faced power which has taken |

ΤΑϬΟΜ Ν̄ϨΗΤ · ΑΥⲱ Ν̄ΤΟΚ ΠΕΤΝΟΥϨⲘ ⲘⲘΟΪ ΕΒΟΛ ϨΙ-
ΤΟΟΤΟΥ Ν̄ΝΕΝΤΑΥϤΙ-ΤΑϬΟΜ Ν̄ϨΗΤ ⲘΝ̄ ΠΛΟΥΟΪΝ ·

11. ϪΕ ΑΥϨϨΕΡΑΤΟΥ ΕΡΟΪ ΕΥϪΙϬΟΛ ΕΡΟΪ · ΑΥⲱ
ΕΥϪⲱ ⲘⲘΟⳞ ϪΕ ⳁϹΟΟΥΝ̄ ΕΠΜΥϹΤΗΡΙΟΝ ⲘΠΟΥΟΪΝ
5 ΕΤϨⲘ ΠϪΙϹΕ ΠΑΪ ΕΝΤΑΪΠΙϹΤΕΥΕ ΕΡΟϤ · ΑΥⲱ ΑΥΑΝΑΓ-
ΚΑΖΕ ⲘⲘΟΪ ϪΕ Ϫⲱ ΕΡΟΝ ⲘΠΜΥϹΤΗΡΙΟΝ ⲘΠΟΥΟΕΙΝ
ΕΤϨⲘ ΠϪΙϹΕ · ΠΑΪ ΑΝΟΚ ΕΤΕ Ν̄ⳁϹΟΟΥΝ̄ ⲘⲘΟϤ ΑΝ ·

12. ΑΥⲱ ΑΥΤⲱⲱΒΕ ΝΑΪ Ν̄ΝΕΪΠΕΘΟΟΥ ΤΗΡΟΥ ΕΒΟΛ
ϪΕ ΑΪΠΙϹΤΕΥΕ ΕΠΟΥΟΕΙΝ ⲘΠϪΙϹΕ · ΑΥⲱ ΑΥϤ̄-ΤΑϬΟΜ
10 Ν̄ΑΤΟΥΟΕΙΝ ·

13. ΑΝΟΚ ΔΕ Ν̄ΤΕΡΟΥΑΝΑΓΚΑΖΕ ⲘⲘΟΪ · ΑΪϨΜΟΟϹ
ΕϨΡΑΪ ϨⲘ ΠΚΑΚΕ · ΕΡΕ ΤΑΨΥΧΗ ⲐΒΒΙΗΥ ϨΝ̄ ΟΥϨΗΒΕ ·

14. ΑΥⲱ ΠΟΥΟΪΝ ΕⳁϨΥΜΝΕΥΕ ΕΡΟΚ ΕΤΒΗΗΤϤ [ϪΕ]
ΝΟΥϨⲘ ⲘⲘΟΪ · ⳁϹΟΟΥΝ̄ ϪΕ ΚΝΑΝΑϨΜΕΤ ΕΒΟΛ ϪΕ
15 ΝΕΪΕΙΡΕ ΠΕ ⲘΠΕΚΟΥⲱϢ ϪΙΝ ΕΪϢΟΟΠ ΠΕ ϨⲘ ΠΛΑΙⲱΝ · π̄λ
ΝΕΪΕΙΡΕ ΠΕ ⲘΠΕΚΟΥⲱϢ Ν̄ΘΕ Ν̄ΝΙΑϨΟΡΑΤΟϹ ΕΤϢΟΟΠ
ϨⲘ ΠΑΤΟΠΟϹ · ΑΥⲱ Ν̄ΘΕ ⲘΠΑϹΥΝϨΥΓΟϹ · ΑΥⲱ ΝΕΪϤ̄-
ϨΗΒΕ ΠΕ ΕΪΪΟΡⲘ ΕΪϢΙΝΕ Ν̄ϹΑ ΠΕΚΟΥΟΪΝ ·

15. ΤΕΝΟΥ ϬΕ ΑΥΚⲱΤΕ ΕΡΟΪ Ν̄ϬΙ ΝΕΠΡΟΒΟΛΟΟΥΕ
20 ΤΗΡΟΥ ⲘΠΑΥΘΑΔΗϹ · ΑΥⲱ ΑΥΡΑϢΕ ΕϨΡΑΪ ΕϪⲱΪ ·
ΑΥⲱ ΑΥϨⲱϪ ⲘⲘΟΪ ΕΜΑϢΟ ΕΝⳁϹΟΟΥΝ̄ ⟨ⲘⲘΟΟΥ⟩ ΑΝ ·
ΑΥⲱ ΑΥΠⲱΤ · ΑΥΛΟ ϨΑΡΟΪ · ΑΥⲱ ⲘΠΟΥΝΑ᾽ ΝΑΪ ·

16. ΑΥΚΟΤΟΥ ΟΝ ΑΥΠΙΡΑΖΕ ⲘⲘΟΪ · ΑΥⲱ ΑΥϨⲱϪ

---

6 MS ⲘⲘ̄ⲘΥϹΤΗΡΙΟΝ.
13 omit ϪΕ.
18 first ϊ in ΕΪΪΟΡⲘ inserted above.
21 supply ⲘⲘΟΥ.

my power from me. And it is thou who savest me from the hands of those who have taken my power and my light from me.

11. For they stood up against me and told lies about me. And they say : I know the *mystery* of the light which is in the height, in which I have *believed*. And they have *compelled* me, saying : Tell us the *mystery* of the light which is in the height, this one which I do not know.

12. And they have repaid me with all these wicked things, because I have *believed* in the light of the height; and they have made my power to be without light.

13. *But* when I was *compelled*, I sat in the darkness, while my *soul* was humble in sorrow.

14. And, O Light, concerning whom I *sing praises* to thee, save me; I know that thou wilt save me, because I have done thy will since I was in my *aeon*. I have done thy will like the *invisible ones* who are in my *place*, and like my *partner*; and I became sorrowful as I looked, seeking for thy light.

15. Now at this time all the *emanations* of the Authades have surrounded me; and have rejoiced over me, and they have oppressed me greatly, without my knowing; and they have run away, they have left me, and they have not been merciful to me.

16. They turned again and *tempted* me, and they oppressed | me with great oppression; they gnashed their

ⲘⲘⲞⲒ ⲌⲘ ⲠⲚⲞϬ Ⲛ̄ⲌⲰⲬ· ⲀⲨⲌⲢⲞⲬⲢⲈⲬ Ⲛ̄ⲚⲈⲨⲞⲂⲌⲈ ⲈⲌⲞⲨⲚ
ⲈⲢⲞⲒ ⲈⲨⲞⲨⲈϢϤⲒ-ⲠⲀⲞⲨⲞⲒ̈Ⲛ Ⲛ̄ⲌⲎⲦ ⲈⲠⲦⲎⲢϤ·

17. ϢⲀ ⲦⲚⲀⲨ ϬⲈ ⲠⲞⲨⲞⲈⲒⲚ ⲈⲔⲀⲚⲈⲬⲈ Ⲙ̄ⲘⲞⲞⲨ ⲈⲨ-
ⲌⲰⲬ Ⲙ̄ⲘⲞⲒ· ⲚⲞⲨⲌⲘ Ⲛ̄ⲦⲀϬⲞⲘ ⲈⲂⲞⲀ ⲌⲚ ⲚⲈⲨⲘⲈⲈⲨⲈ
5 ⲈⲐⲞⲞⲨ ⲀⲨⲰ Ⲛ̄ⲄⲚⲀⲌⲘⲈⲦ Ⲛ̄ⲦⲞⲞⲦⲤ̄ Ⲛ̄ϯϬⲞⲘ Ⲛ̄ⲌⲞ Ⲙ̄-
ⲘⲞⲨⲒ̈· ⲬⲈ ⲀⲚⲞⲔ ⲘⲀⲨⲀⲀⲦ ⲌⲚ Ⲛ̄ⲀⲌⲞⲢⲀⲦⲞⲤ ⲠⲈⲦϢⲞⲞⲠ
ⲌⲘ ⲠⲈⲒ̈ⲦⲞⲠⲞⲤ·   Ⲡⲗ̄ ᵇ

18. ϯⲚⲀⲌⲨⲘⲚⲈⲨⲈ ⲈⲢⲞⲔ ⲠⲞⲨⲞⲒ̈Ⲛ ⲈⲒ̈Ⲍ̄Ⲛ ⲦⲘⲎⲦⲈ Ⲛ̄ⲚⲈⲦ-
ⲤⲞⲞⲨⲌ ⲦⲎⲢⲞⲨ ⲈⲢⲞⲒ· ⲀⲨⲰ ϯⲚⲀϢⲰϢ ⲈⲌⲢⲀⲒ̈ ⲞⲨⲎⲔ ⲌⲚ
10 ⲦⲘⲎⲦⲈ Ⲛ̄ⲚⲈⲦⲌⲰⲬ Ⲙ̄ⲘⲞⲒ̈ ⲦⲎⲢⲞⲨ·

19. ⲦⲈⲚⲞⲨ ϬⲈ ⲠⲞⲨⲞⲒ̈Ⲛ Ⲙ̄ⲠⲢⲦⲢⲈⲨⲢⲀϢⲈ Ⲙ̄ⲘⲞⲒ̈ Ⲛ̄ϬⲒ
ⲚⲈⲦⲘⲞⲤⲦⲈ Ⲙ̄ⲘⲞⲒ̈· ⲀⲨⲰ ⲈⲨⲞⲨⲈϢϤⲒ-ⲦⲀϬⲞⲘ Ⲛ̄ⲌⲎⲦ· ⲚⲀⲒ̈
ⲈⲦⲘⲞⲤⲦⲈ Ⲙ̄ⲘⲞⲒ̈ ⲈⲦⲔⲒⲘ Ⲛ̄ⲚⲈⲨⲂⲀⲀ ⲈⲌⲞⲨⲚ ⲈⲢⲞⲒ̈· ⲈⲘⲠⲒⲢ̄-
ⲀⲀⲀⲨ ⲚⲀⲨ·

15 20. ⲬⲈ ⲚⲈⲨⲔⲰⲢ̄Ϣ ⲘⲈⲚ ⲈⲢⲞⲒ̈ ⲠⲈ ⲌⲚ ⲌⲈⲚϢⲀⲬⲈ ⲈⲨ-
ⲚⲞⲦ̄Ⲙ ⲈⲨϢⲒⲚⲈ Ⲙ̄ⲘⲞⲒ̈ ⲈⲘ̄ⲘⲨⲤⲦⲎⲢⲒⲞⲚ Ⲙ̄ⲠⲞⲨⲞⲒ̈Ⲛ ⲚⲀⲒ̈
ⲈⲦⲈ Ⲛ̄ϯⲤⲞⲞⲨⲚ̄ Ⲙ̄ⲘⲞⲞⲨ ⲀⲚ· ⲈⲨⲬⲰ Ⲙ̄ⲘⲞⲤ ⲈⲢⲞⲒ̈ ⲈⲨⲞ
Ⲛ̄ⲔⲢⲞϤ ⲈⲢⲞⲒ̈· ⲀⲨⲰ ⲈⲨϬⲞⲚⲦ̄ ⲈⲢⲞⲒ̈ ⲬⲈ ⲀⲒ̈ⲠⲒⲤⲦⲈⲨⲈ
ⲈⲠⲞⲨⲞⲈⲒⲚ ⲈⲦⲌⲘ̄ ⲠⲬⲒⲤⲈ·

20 21. ⲀⲨⲞⲨⲰⲚ Ⲛ̄ⲢⲰⲞⲨ ⲈⲌⲞⲨⲚ ⲈⲢⲞⲒ̈· ⲠⲈⲬⲀⲨ ⲬⲈ ⲤⲈ
ⲦⲚ̄ⲚⲀϤⲒ-ⲠⲈⲤⲞⲨⲞⲒ̈Ⲛ·

22. ⲦⲈⲚⲞⲨ ϬⲈ ⲠⲞⲨⲞⲈⲒⲚ ⲀⲔⲈⲒⲘⲈ ⲈⲠⲈⲨⲔⲢⲞϤ Ⲙ̄ⲠⲢ̄-
ⲀⲚⲈⲬⲈ Ⲙ̄ⲘⲞⲞⲨ· ⲀⲨⲰ Ⲙ̄ⲠⲢ̄ⲦⲢⲈ ⲦⲈⲔⲂⲞⲎⲐⲒⲀ ⲞⲨⲈ Ⲛ̄ⲤⲀ-
ⲂⲞⲀ Ⲙ̄ⲘⲞⲒ̈·   Ⲡⲉ̄

25 23. ϬⲈⲠⲎ ⲠⲞⲨⲞⲈⲒⲚ· ⲀⲢⲒ-ⲠⲀⲌⲀⲠ· Ⲙ̄Ⲛ ⲠⲀⲔⲂⲀ·

---

9 ⲞⲨⲏⲕ; archaic form of ⲞⲨⲃⲏⲕ.

teeth at me, wanting to take away my light from me completely.

17. How long now, O Light, dost thou *suffer* them, that they oppress me? Save my power from their wicked thoughts, and save me from the lion-faced power, for I alone among the *invisible ones* am in this *place*.

18. I will *sing praise* to thee, O Light, while I am in the midst of all those gathered against me. And I will cry out to thee in the midst of all those that oppress me.

19. Now at this time, O Light, let not those that hate me and want to take away my power from me, rejoice over me; these who hate me, as they move their eyes against me, without my having done anything to them.

20. For *indeed* they flatter me with sweet words while they seek from me the *mysteries* of the light which I do not know; speaking to me with cunning against me, and raging against me, because I have *believed* in the light which is in the height.

21. They have opened their mouths against me; they have said: Yes. We will take away her light.

22. Now at this time, O Light, thou hast known their cunning; *suffer* them not, and let not thy *help* be far from me.

23. Make haste, O Light, judge me and avenge me. |

24. ⲀⲨⲰ ⲦϨⲀⲠ ⲈⲢⲞⲒ̈ ϨⲚ ⲦⲈⲔⲘⲚⲦⲀⲄⲀⲐⲞⲤ · ⲦⲈⲚⲞⲨ ϬⲈ
ⲠⲞⲨⲞⲒ̈Ⲛ ⲚⲚⲞⲨⲞⲒ̈Ⲛ ⲘⲠⲢⲦⲢⲈⲨϤⲒ-ⲠⲀⲞⲨⲞⲈⲒⲚ ⲚⲦⲞⲞⲦ ·

25. ⲀⲨⲰ ⲘⲠⲢⲦⲢⲈⲨ̅ⲬⲞⲞⲤ ϨⲢⲀⲒ̈ Ⲛ̅ϨⲎⲦⲞⲨ · ⲬⲈ Ⲁ ⲦⲈⲚ-
ϬⲞⲘ ⲤⲈⲒ̈ ⲘⲠⲈⲤⲞⲨⲞⲒ̈Ⲛ ⲀⲨⲰ ⲘⲠⲢⲦⲢⲈⲨⲬⲞⲞⲤ ⲬⲈ ⲀⲚⲰ-
5 ⲘⲔ ⲚⲦⲈⲤϬⲞⲘ ·

26. ⲀⲖⲖⲀ ⲘⲀⲢⲈ ⲞⲨⲔⲀⲔⲈ ⲚⲦⲞϤ ⲈⲒ̈ ⲈϨⲢⲀⲒ̈ ⲈⲬⲰⲞⲨ ·
ⲀⲨⲰ ⲘⲀⲢⲞⲨⲢ̅-ⲀⲦϬⲞⲘ Ⲛ̅ϬⲒ ⲚⲈⲦⲞⲨⲈϢϤⲒ-ⲠⲀⲞⲨⲞⲒ̈Ⲛ Ⲛ̅-
ⲦⲞⲞⲦ · ⲀⲨⲰ ⲘⲀⲢⲞⲨⲦ ϨⲒⲰⲞⲨ ⲚⲞⲨⲬⲀⲞⲤ ⲘⲚ ⲞⲨⲔⲀⲔⲈ ·
Ⲛ̅ϬⲒ ⲚⲈⲦⲬⲰ ⲘⲘⲞⲤ ⲬⲈ ⲦⲚⲚⲀϤⲒ ⲘⲠⲈⲤⲞⲨⲞⲈⲒⲚ ⲘⲚ
10 ⲦⲈⲤϬⲞⲘ ·

27. ⲦⲈⲚⲞⲨ ϬⲈ ⲚⲀϨⲘⲈⲦ ⲦⲀⲢⲒⲢⲀϢⲈ ⲬⲈ ⲦⲞⲨⲈϢ-ⲠⲘⲈϨ-
ⲘⲚⲦϢⲞⲘⲦⲈ Ⲛ̅ⲀⲒⲰⲚ ⲠⲦⲞⲠⲞⲤ Ⲛ̅ⲦⲀⲒⲔⲀⲒⲞⲤⲨⲚⲎ · ⲀⲨⲰ
ⲦⲚⲀⲬⲞⲞⲤ ⲚⲞⲨⲞⲈⲒϢ ⲚⲒⲘ ⲬⲈ ⲈϤⲈⲢϨⲞⲨⲈ-ⲞⲨⲞⲒ̈Ⲛ Ⲛ̅ϬⲒ
ⲠⲞⲨⲞⲒ̈Ⲛ Ⲛ̅ⲒⲈⲞⲨ ⲠⲈⲔⲀⲄⲄⲈⲖⲞⲤ ·

15 28. ⲀⲨⲰ ⲠⲀⲖⲀⲤ ⲚⲀϨⲨⲘⲚⲈⲨⲈ ⲈⲢⲞⲔ ϨⲘ ⲠⲈⲔⲤⲞⲞⲨⲚ ⲠⲈ ᵇ
ⲘⲠⲀⲞⲨⲞⲈⲒϢ ⲦⲎⲢϤ ϨⲘ ⲠⲘⲈϨⲘⲚⲦϢⲞⲘⲦⲈ Ⲛ̅ⲀⲒⲰⲚ :

Ⳝ ⲀⲤϢⲰⲠⲈ ⲚⲦⲈⲢⲈ Ⲓ̅Ⲥ̅ ⲞⲨⲰ ⲈϤⲬⲰ ⲚⲚⲈⲒ̈ϢⲀⲬⲈ ⲈⲚⲈϤ-
ⲘⲀⲐⲎⲦⲎⲤ · ⲠⲈⲬⲀϤ ⲚⲀⲨ ⲬⲈ ⲠⲈⲦⲚⲎϤⲈ ϨⲚⲦⲎⲨⲦⲚ · ⲘⲀ-
ⲢⲈϤⲦⲀⲨⲈ-ⲠⲈⲨⲂⲰⲖ · ⲀϤⲈⲒ̈ ⲈⲐⲎ Ⲛ̅ϬⲒ Ⲓ̈ⲀⲔⲰⲂⲞⲤ · ⲀϤⲦⲠⲒ
20 ⲈⲢⲚ ⲦⲘⲈⲤⲦⲚϨⲎⲦ ⲚⲒ̅Ⲥ̅ ⲠⲈⲬⲀϤ ⲬⲈ ⲠⲀⲬⲞⲈⲒⲤ · ⲀϤⲚⲎϤⲈ
ⲘⲘⲞⲒ̈ Ⲛ̅ϬⲒ ⲠⲈⲔⲠⲚⲀ · ⲀⲨⲰ ⲦⲢⲞⲞⲨⲦ ⲈⲦⲀⲨⲈ-ⲠⲈⲨⲂⲰⲖ ·
ⲈⲦⲂⲈ ⲠⲀⲒ̈ ⲢⲰ Ⲁ ⲦⲈⲔϬⲞⲘ ⲠⲢⲞⲪⲎⲦⲈⲨⲈ ⲘⲠⲒⲞⲨⲞⲒ̈Ϣ ϨⲒⲦⲚ
ⲆⲀⲨⲈⲒⲆ ϨⲘ ⲠⲘⲈϨⲘⲀⲂⲦⲀϤⲦⲈ ⲘⲯⲀⲖⲘⲞⲤ ⲈϤⲬⲰ ⲘⲘⲞⲤ
ⲚⲦⲈⲒ̈ϨⲈ ⲈⲦⲂⲈ ⲦⲘⲈϨⲯⲒⲦⲈ ⲘⲘⲈⲦⲀⲚⲞⲒⲀ Ⲛ̅ⲦⲠⲒⲤⲦⲒⲤ ⲤⲞ-
25 ⲪⲒⲀ · ⲬⲈ

1. ⲦϨⲀⲠ ⲠⲬⲞⲈⲒⲤ ⲈⲚⲈⲦⲬⲒ ⲘⲘⲞⲒ̈ Ⲛ̅ϬⲞⲚⲤ̅ · ⲘⲒϢⲈ ⲘⲚ
ⲚⲈⲦⲘⲒϢⲈ ⲚⲘⲘⲀⲒ̈ ·

24. And give judgment to me in thy *goodness*; now at this time, O Light of Lights, let them not take my light from me.

25. And do not let them say in their hearts [1]: Our power has satisfied itself with her light; and let them not say: We have swallowed her power.

26. *But* rather let darkness come down upon them; and let those that want to take away my light from me become powerless; and those that say: We will take away her light and her power, let them be covered with *Chaos* and darkness.

27. Now at this time, save me, that I may rejoice, because I want [2] the thirteenth *aeon*, the *place* of *righteousness*. And I will say at all times: May the light of Jeu, thy *angel*, give more light.

28. And my tongue will *sing praises* to thee in thy knowledge, all my time in the thirteenth *aeon*'."

51. It happened when Jesus finished saying these words to his *disciples*, he said to them: "He who is *sober* among you, let him give their interpretation."

James came forward, he kissed the breast of Jesus and said: "My Lord, thy *Spirit* has made me *sober* [3], and I am willing to give their interpretation. Concerning this, indeed, thy power *prophesied* once, through David, in the 34th *Psalm*, speaking thus about the ninth *repentance* of the Pistis Sophia:

1. 'Judge, O Lord, those who do injustice to me; fight with those who fight with me. |

---

[1]   (3) in their hearts; Till: within themselves, i.e. to themselves.

[2]   (11) I want; Till: I love.

[3]   (20, 21) thy Spirit has made me sober; Till: thy Spirit has become sober (awake) in me.

2. ⲀⲘⲀ̅ⲊⲦⲈ Ⲛ̅ⲞⲨϨⲞⲠⲖⲞⲚ ⲘⲚ̅ ⲞⲨⲐⲨⲢⲰⲚ Ⲛ̅ⲅⲦⲰⲞⲨⲚ
ⲈⲂⲞⲎⲐⲒ ⲈⲢⲞⲒ̈ ·

3. ⲠⲰϨ̅Ⲧ ⲈⲂⲞⲖ Ⲛ̅ⲞⲨⲤⲎϤⲈ · ⲀⲨⲰ⁎⁎Ⲛ̅ⲅϨⲞⲬⲠⲤ̅ ⲘⲠⲈⲘⲦⲞ ⲠⲈ̅
ⲈⲂⲞⲖ Ⲛ̅ⲚⲈⲦⲐⲖⲒⲂⲈ Ⲙ̅ⲘⲞⲒ̈ · ⲀⲬⲒⲤ Ⲛ̅ⲦⲀⲮⲨⲬⲎ ⲬⲈ ⲀⲚⲞⲔ
5 ⲠⲈ ⲠⲞⲨⲞⲨⲬⲀⲒ̈ ·

4. ⲘⲀⲢⲞⲨⲬⲒϢⲒⲠⲈ Ⲛ̅ⲤⲈⲞⲨⲰⲖ̅Ⲥ Ⲛ̅ϬⲒ ⲚⲈⲦϢⲒⲚⲈ Ⲛ̅ⲤⲀ
ⲦⲀⲮⲨⲬⲎ · ⲘⲀⲢⲞⲨⲔⲞⲦⲞⲨ ⲈⲠⲀϨⲞⲨ Ⲛ̅ⲤⲈⲬⲒϢⲒⲠⲈ Ⲛ̅ϬⲒ
ⲚⲈⲦⲘⲈⲈⲨⲈ ⲈⲢⲞⲒ̈ ⲈϨⲈⲚⲠⲈⲐⲞⲞⲨ ·

5. ⲘⲀⲢⲞⲨⲢ̅ⲐⲈ Ⲛ̅ⲞⲨϢⲞⲈⲒϢ ⲘⲠⲈⲘⲦⲞ ⲈⲂⲞⲖ Ⲛ̅ⲞⲨⲦⲎⲨ ·
10 ⲀⲨⲰ ⲈⲢⲈ ⲠⲀⲄⲄⲈⲖⲞⲤ ⲘⲠⲬⲞⲈⲒⲤ ⲠⲎⲦ Ⲛ̅ⲤⲰⲞⲨ ·

6. ⲘⲀⲢⲈ ⲦⲈⲨϨⲒⲎ Ϣ(Ⲱ)ⲠⲈ Ⲛ̅ⲔⲀⲔⲈ · ⲀⲨⲰ Ⲛ̅ⲤⲤⲖⲀⲀⲦⲈ ·
ⲀⲨⲰ ⲈⲢⲈ ⲠⲀⲄⲄⲈⲖⲞⲤ ⲘⲠⲬⲞⲈⲒⲤ ⲐⲖⲒⲂⲈ Ⲙ̅ⲘⲞⲞⲨ ·

7. ⲬⲈ ⲀⲨϨⲰⲠ ⲈⲢⲞⲒ̈ Ⲛ̅ⲞⲨⲠⲀϢ ⲘⲠⲬⲒⲚⲬⲎ · ⲈⲠⲈⲨⲦⲀⲔⲞ
ⲘⲀⲨⲀⲀⲨ · ⲀⲨⲰ ⲀⲨⲚⲈϬⲚⲈϬ-ⲦⲀⲮⲨⲬⲎ ⲈⲠⲠⲈⲦϢⲞⲨⲈⲒⲦ ·

15 8. ⲘⲀⲢⲈϤⲈⲒ̓ ⲚⲀⲨ Ⲛ̅ϬⲒ Ⲡ̅ⲠⲀϢ ⲈⲦⲈ Ⲛ̅ⲤⲈⲤⲞⲞⲨⲚ Ⲙ̅ⲘⲞϤ
ⲀⲚ · ⲀⲨⲰ ⲘⲀⲢⲈⲤϬⲞⲠⲞⲨ Ⲛ̅ϬⲒ ⲦϬⲞⲢⲤ̅ ⲈⲚⲦⲀⲨϨⲞⲠⲤ̅ ⲈⲢⲞⲒ̈ ·
ⲀⲨⲰ ⲤⲈⲚⲀϨⲈ ⲈϨⲢⲀⲒ̈ ⲈⲠⲈⲒ̈ⲠⲀϢ ·

9. ⲦⲀⲮⲨⲬⲎ ⲆⲈ ⲚⲀⲦⲈⲖⲎⲖ ⲈⲬ̅Ⲙ ⲠⲬⲞⲈⲒⲤ · ⁎ ⲀⲨⲰ ⲤⲚⲀ-　ⲠⲈ̅ᵇ
ⲞⲨⲢⲞⲦ ⲈⲬ̅Ⲙ ⲠⲈⲤⲞⲨⲬⲀⲒ̈ ·

20 10. ⲚⲀⲔⲈⲈⲤ ⲦⲎⲢⲞⲨ ⲚⲀⲬⲞⲞⲤ ⲬⲈ ⲠⲬⲞⲈⲒⲤ ⲚⲒⲘ ⲠⲈ
ⲈⲦⲚⲀϢⲈⲒⲚⲈ Ⲙ̅ⲘⲞⲔ · ⲈⲔⲦⲞⲨⲬⲞ Ⲙ̅ⲫⲎⲔⲈ ⲈⲦϬⲒⲬ Ⲙ̅ⲠⲈⲦ-
ⲬⲞⲞⲢ ⲈⲢⲞϤ · ⲀⲨⲰ ⲈⲔⲚⲞⲨϨ̅Ⲙ Ⲛ̅ⲞⲨϨⲎⲔⲈ ⲘⲚ̅ ⲞⲨⲈⲂⲒⲎⲚ
Ⲛ̅ⲦⲞⲞⲦⲞⲨ Ⲛ̅ⲚⲈⲦⲦⲰⲢⲠ̅ Ⲙ̅ⲘⲞϤ ·

11. ⲀⲨⲦⲰⲞⲨⲚ̅ Ⲛ̅ϬⲒ ϨⲈⲚⲘⲚ̅ⲦⲢⲈ Ⲛ̅ⲬⲒⲚϬⲞⲚⲤ · ⲀⲨϢⲚⲦ
25 ⲈⲚⲈⲦⲈ Ⲛ̅Ⲧ̵ⲤⲞⲞⲨⲚ Ⲙ̅ⲘⲞⲞⲨ ⲀⲚ ·

9　MS Ⲙ̅ⲠⲈⲘ̅ⲦⲞ.
11　MS ϢϢⲠⲤ.
16　MS ⲦϬⲞⲢⲤ; read ⲦϬⲞⲢⲤ̅.

2. Take hold of a *weapon* and *shield*, and rise to *help* me.

3. Draw forth a sword and unsheath it in the presence of those that *afflict* me; say to my *soul*: I am thy[1] salvation.

4. May they be put to shame and disgrace that seek my *soul*; may those that think wicked things about me be turned back and be put to shame.

5. May they become like dust[2] before the wind; and may the *angel* of the Lord pursue them.

6. May their paths become dark and slippery; and may the *angel* of the Lord *afflict* them.

7. For, without cause, they have hidden for me a snare to their own destruction; and in vain they have slandered my *soul*.

8. May the snare which they do not know come to them; and may the net, which they have hidden for me, catch them, and may they fall into this snare.

9. *But* my *soul* will rejoice over the Lord, and be glad over its salvation.

10. All my bones will say: O Lord, who can resemble thee? Thou dost save the poor out of the hand of those that are stronger than he; and thou dost save a poor man and a needy from the hands of those that rob him.

11. Unjust witnesses have arisen; they have questioned me about things which I do not know. |

---

[1] (5) thy; lit. their.
[2] (9) dust; Schmidt : chaff.

12. ⲁⲩⲧⲱϣⲃⲉ ⲛⲁⲓ̈ ⲛ̄ϩⲉⲛⲡⲉⲑⲟⲟⲩ· ⲉⲡⲙⲁ ⲛ̄ϩⲉⲛⲡⲉⲧⲛⲁⲛⲟⲩⲟⲩ· ⲁⲩⲱ ⲟⲩⲙ̄ⲛ̄ⲧⲁⲧϣⲏⲣⲉ ⲛ̄ⲧⲁⲯⲩⲭⲏ·

13. ⲁⲛⲟⲕ ⲇⲉ ⲛ̄ⲧⲉⲣⲟⲩⲉⲛⲱⲭⲗⲓ ⲛⲁⲓ̈· ⲁⲓ̈ϯ ϩⲓⲱⲱⲧ ⲛ̄ⲟⲩϭⲟⲟⲩⲛⲉ· ⲁⲩⲱ ⲁⲓ̈ⲑ̄ⲃ̄ⲃⲓⲉ-ⲧⲁⲯⲩⲭⲏ ϩ̄ⲛ̄ ⲟⲩⲛⲏⲥⲧⲓⲁ· ⲉⲣⲉ ⲡⲁϣⲗⲏⲗ ⲛⲁⲕⲟⲧ̄ϥ̄ ⲉϩⲣⲁⲓ̈ ⲉⲕⲟⲩⲟⲩⲛ̄ⲧ̄·

14. ⲁⲓ̈ⲣ̄ⲁⲛⲁⲕ ⲛ̄ⲑⲉ ⲙ̄ⲡⲉⲧϩⲓⲧⲟⲩⲱⲓ̈· ⲁⲩⲱ ⲛ̄ⲑⲉ ⲙ̄ⲡⲁⲥⲟⲛ· ⲁⲩⲱ ⲁⲓ̈ⲑ̄ⲃ̄ⲃⲓⲟⲓ̈ ⲛ̄ⲑⲉ ⲙ̄ⲡⲉⲧⲣ̄ϩⲏⲃⲉ· ⲁⲩⲱ ⲛ̄ⲑⲉ ⲙ̄ⲡⲉⲧⲟⲕ̄ⲙ̄·

15. ⲁⲩⲉⲩⲫⲣⲁⲛⲉ ⲉ**ϩⲣⲁⲓ̈ ⲉϫⲱⲓ̈· ⲁⲩⲱ ⲁⲩϫⲓϣⲓⲡⲉ· ⲁ ⲡⲍ
ϩⲉⲛⲙⲁⲥⲧⲓⲅ̄ⲝ̄ ⲥⲱⲟⲩϩ ⲉϩⲣⲁⲓ̈ ⲉϫⲱⲓ̈· ⲁⲩⲱ ⲙ̄ⲡⲓⲉⲓⲙⲉ ⲁⲩⲡⲱⲣ̄ϫ̄ ⲁⲩⲱ ⲙ̄ⲡⲟⲩⲙ̄ⲕⲁϩ ⲛ̄ϩⲏⲧ·

16. ⲁⲩⲡⲓⲣⲁⲍⲉ ⲙ̄ⲙⲟⲓ̈· ⲁⲩⲱ ⲁⲩⲕⲱⲙ̄ϣ̄ ⲛ̄ⲥⲱⲓ̈ ϩ̄ⲛ̄ ⲟⲩⲕⲱⲙ̄ϣ̄· ⲁⲩϩⲣⲟϫⲣⲉϫ ⲛ̄ⲛⲉⲩⲟⲃϩⲉ ⲉϩⲣⲁⲓ̈ ⲉϫⲱⲓ̈·

17. ⲡϫⲟⲉⲓⲥ ⲉⲕⲛⲁϭⲱϣ̄ⲧ̄ ⲉϩⲣⲁⲓ̈ ⲉϫⲱⲓ̈ ⲧⲛⲁⲩ· ⲧⲁϩⲉⲧⲁⲯⲩⲭⲏ ⲉⲣⲁⲧ̄ⲥ̄ ⲉⲃⲟⲗ ϩ̄ⲛ̄ ⲛⲉⲩϩⲃⲏⲩⲉ ⲉⲑⲟⲟⲩ· ⲁⲩⲱ ⲛⲁϩⲙ̄-ⲧⲁⲙ̄ⲛ̄ⲧϣⲏⲣⲉ ⟨ⲛ̄⟩ⲟⲩⲱⲧ· ⲉⲧⲟⲟⲧⲟⲩ ⲛ̄ⲙ̄ⲙⲟⲩⲓ̈·

18. ϯⲛⲁⲟⲩⲱⲛ̄ϩ̄ ⲛⲁⲕ ⲉⲃⲟⲗ ⲡϫⲟⲉⲓⲥ ϩ̄ⲛ̄ ⲟⲩⲉⲕⲕⲗⲏⲥⲓⲁ ⲉⲛⲁϣⲱⲥ· ⲁⲩⲱ ϯⲛⲁⲥⲙⲟⲩ ⲉⲣⲟⲕ ϩ̄ⲛ̄ ⲟⲩⲗⲁⲟⲥ ⲉⲙ̄ⲛ̄ⲧϥ̄ⲏⲡⲉ ⲙ̄ⲙⲁⲩ·

19. ⲙ̄ⲡⲣ̄ⲧⲣⲉⲩⲣⲁϣⲉ ⲙ̄ⲙⲟⲓ̈ ⲛ̄ϭⲓ ⲛⲉⲧⲟ ⲛ̄ϫⲁϫⲉ ⲉⲣⲟⲓ̈ ϩ̄ⲛ̄ ⲟⲩϫⲓⲛϭⲟⲛ̄ⲥ̄· ⲛⲉⲧⲙⲟⲥⲧⲉ ⲙ̄ⲙⲟⲓ̈ ⲉϫⲓⲛϫⲏ· ⲁⲩⲱ ⲉⲩϫⲱⲣ̄ⲙ̄ ⲛ̄ⲛⲉⲩⲃⲁⲗ·

20. ϫⲉ ⲁⲛⲟⲕ ⲙⲉⲛ ϣⲁⲩϣⲁϫⲉ ⲛ̄ⲙ̄ⲙⲁⲓ̈ ϩ̄ⲛ̄ ϩⲉⲛϣⲁϫⲉ ⲛ̄ⲉⲓⲣⲏⲛⲓⲕⲟⲛ· ⲁⲩⲱ ϣⲁⲩ*ⲙⲟⲕⲙⲉⲕ ⲉⲩⲟⲣⲅⲏ ϩ̄ⲛ̄ ϩⲉⲛ- ⲡⲍ b
ⲕⲣⲟϥ·

---

10 MS ⲙⲁⲥⲥⲧⲓⲅ̄ⲝ̄.
16 MS ⲟⲩⲱⲧ.

12. They repaid me evil things for good, and childlessness to my *soul*.

13. *But* I, when they *troubled* me, I put on sackcloth, and I humbled my *soul* with *fasting*; and my prayer will return again to my bosom.

14. I was agreeable as if to my neighbour, and as if to my brother; and I humbled myself like a mourner and a sorrowful one.

15. They have *rejoiced* over me and have been put to shame. *Scourges* were gathered against me and I did not know; they were separated and they were not distressed.

16. They *tempted* me, and they sneered at me contemptuously; they gnashed their teeth against me.

17. O Lord, when wilt thou look down upon me? Establish my *soul* away from their wicked deeds; and save my only-begotten one [1] from the lions.

18. I will confess thee, O Lord, in a great *congregation*, and I will bless thee among countless *people*.

19. Let not those who are enemies to me unjustly, who hate me without cause and wink with their eyes, rejoice over me.

20. For *indeed* they speak to me with *peaceful* words; and they imagine *wrath* with cunning. |

---

[1]   (16) only-begotten one; lit. only-son-ship.

21. ⲁⲩⲟⲩⲱϣ̄⟨ⲥ⟩ ⲉⲃⲟⲗ ⲛ̄ⲧⲉⲩⲧⲁⲡⲣⲟ ⲉϩⲣⲁï ⲉϫⲱï· ⲁⲩⲱ ⲁⲩϫⲟⲟⲥ ϫⲉ ⲉⲩⲅⲉ ⲁ ⲛⲉⲛⲃⲁⲗ ⲙⲉϩⲉⲓⲁⲧⲛ̄ ⲙ̄ⲙⲟϥ·

22. ⲁⲕⲛⲁⲩ ⲡϫⲟⲉⲓⲥ ⲙ̄ⲡⲣ̄ⲕⲁⲣⲱⲕ ⲡϫⲟⲉⲓⲥ ⲙ̄ⲡⲣ̄ⲥⲁϩⲱⲕ ⲥⲁⲃⲟⲗ ⲙ̄ⲙⲟï·

23. ⲧⲱⲟⲩⲛ̄ ⲡϫⲟⲉⲓⲥ ⲛ̄ⲅ̄ⲧ̄ϩⲧⲏⲕ ⲉⲡⲁϩⲁⲡ· ⲧ̄ϩⲧⲏⲕ ⲉⲡⲁϫⲓⲕⲃⲁ ⲡⲁⲛⲟⲩⲧⲉ ⲁⲩⲱ ⲡⲁϫⲟⲉⲓⲥ·

24. ⲕⲣⲓⲛⲉ ⲙ̄ⲙⲟï ⲡϫⲟⲉⲓⲥ ⲕⲁⲧⲁ ⲧⲁⲇⲓⲕⲁⲓⲟⲥⲩⲛⲏ· ⲙ̄ⲡⲣ̄ⲧⲣⲉⲩⲣⲁϣⲉ ⲙ̄ⲙⲟï ⲡⲁⲛⲟⲩⲧⲉ·

25. ⲟⲩⲇⲉ ⲙ̄ⲡⲣ̄ⲧⲣⲉⲩϫⲟⲟⲥ ϫⲉ ⲉⲩⲅⲉ ⲧⲉⲛⲯⲩⲭⲏ· ⲙ̄ⲡⲣ̄ⲧⲣⲉⲩϫⲟⲟⲥ ϫⲉ ⲁⲛⲟⲙⲕ̄ϥ·

26. ⲙⲁⲣⲟⲩϫⲓϣⲓⲡⲉ ⲛ̄ⲥⲉⲟⲩⲱϫ̄ⲥ ϩⲓ ⲟⲩⲥⲟⲡ· ⲛ̄ϭⲓ ⲛⲉⲧⲣⲁϣⲉ ⲉϫ̄ⲛ ⲛⲁⲡⲉⲑⲟⲟⲩ· ⲙⲁⲣⲟⲩⲧ̄ ϩⲓⲱⲟⲩ ⲛ̄ⲟⲩϣⲓⲡⲉ ⲙⲛ̄ ⲟⲩⲟⲩⲱϫ̄ⲥ ⲛ̄ϭⲓ ⲛⲉⲧϫⲉ-ⲛⲟϭ ⲛ̄ϣⲁϫⲉ ⲉϩⲣⲁï ⲉϫⲱï·

27. ⲙⲁⲣⲟⲩⲧⲉⲗⲏⲗ· ⲛ̄ⲥⲉⲟⲩⲛⲟϥ ⲛ̄ϭⲓ ⲛⲉⲧⲟⲩⲉϣ-ⲧⲁⲇⲓⲕⲁⲓⲟⲥⲩⲛⲏ·** ⲁⲩⲱ ⲙⲁⲣⲟⲩϫⲟⲟⲥ ϫⲉ ⲙⲁⲣⲉ ⲡϫⲟⲉⲓⲥ ⲣ̄- ⲡⲏ
ⲛⲟϭ ⲛ̄ϥϫⲓⲥⲉ ⲛ̄ϭⲓ ⲛⲉⲧⲟⲩⲉϣ-ⲧ̄ⲣⲏⲛⲏ ⲙ̄ⲡⲉϥϩⲙ̄ϩⲁⲗ·

28. ⲡⲁⲗⲁⲥ ⲛⲁⲧⲉⲗⲏⲗ ⲛ̄ⲧⲉⲕⲇⲓⲕⲁⲓⲟⲥⲩⲛⲏ ⲙⲛ̄ ⲡⲉⲕⲧⲁïⲟ ⲙ̄ⲡⲉϩⲟⲟⲩ ⲧⲏⲣϥ̄·

ⲍ ⲛⲁï ϭⲉ ⲛ̄ⲧⲉⲣⲉϥϫⲟⲟⲩ ⲛ̄ϭⲓ ïⲁⲕⲕⲱⲃⲟⲥ ⲡⲉϫⲁϥ ⲛ̄ϭⲓ ⲓ̄ⲥ̄ ϫⲉ ⲉⲩⲅⲉ ⲕⲁⲗⲱⲥ ïⲁⲕⲕⲱⲃⲟⲥ ⲡⲁï ⲡⲉ ⲡⲃⲱⲗ ⲛ̄ⲧⲙⲉϩⲯⲓⲧⲉ ⲙ̄ⲙⲉⲧⲁⲛⲟⲓⲁ ⲛ̄ⲧⲡⲓⲥⲧⲓⲥ ⲥⲟⲫⲓⲁ· ϩⲁⲙⲏⲛ ϩⲁⲙⲏⲛ ⲧ̄ϫⲱ ⲙ̄ⲙⲟⲥ ⲛⲏⲧⲛ̄ ϫⲉ ⲧⲉⲧⲛⲁⲣ̄ϣⲟⲣⲡ̄ ⲉϩⲟⲩⲛ ⲉⲧⲙⲛ̄ⲧⲉⲣⲟ ⲛ̄ⲙ̄ⲡⲏⲩⲉ ϩⲁⲑⲏ ⲛ̄ⲛ̄ⲁϩⲟⲣⲁⲧⲟⲥ ⲧⲏⲣⲟⲩ ⲙⲛ̄ ⲛ̄ⲛⲟⲩⲧⲉ ⲧⲏⲣⲟⲩ· ⲙⲛ̄ ⲛ̄ⲁⲣⲭⲱⲛ ⲧⲏⲣⲟⲩ· ⲛⲁï ⲉⲧϣⲟⲟⲡ ϩⲙ̄ ⲡⲙⲉϩⲙⲛ̄ⲧϣⲟⲙⲧⲉ ⲛ̄ⲁⲓⲱⲛ· ⲁⲩⲱ ϩⲙ̄ ⲡⲙⲉϩⲙ̄ⲛ̄ⲧⲥⲛⲟⲟⲩⲥ ⲛ̄ⲁⲓⲱⲛ· ⲛ̄ⲧⲱⲧⲛ̄ ⲇⲉ ⲁⲛ ⲙⲁⲩⲁⲧⲧⲏⲩ*ⲧⲛ̄· ⲁⲗⲗⲁ ⲟⲩⲟⲛ ⲡⲏ b

---

1 MS ⲁⲩⲟⲩⲱϣ.
7 MS ⲧⲁⲇⲓⲕⲁⲓⲟⲥⲩⲛⲏ; read ⲧⲉⲕⲇⲓⲕ.
23 MS ⲙⲛ̄ ⲛ̄ⲛⲟⲩⲧⲉ ⲧⲏⲣⲟⲩ; dittography, the second expunged.

21. They opened wide their mouths against me and they said: *Excellent*, our eyes have had a full view of him.

22. Thou hast seen, O Lord, be not silent, O Lord; draw not back from me.

23. Arise, O Lord, give heed to my judgment; give heed to my revenge, my God and my Lord.

24. *Judge* me, O Lord, *according to* my *righteousness*; let them not rejoice over me, my God.

25. *Neither* let them say: *Excellent*, our *soul*; let them not say: We have swallowed him.

26. Let those that rejoice over my misfortunes be put to shame, and disgraced at the same time; let those that speak great words against me be covered with shame and disgrace.

27. Let those that wish my *righteousness* be glad and rejoice; and may those that wish the *peace* of his servant say: let the Lord be magnified and lifted up.

28. My tongue will rejoice at thy *righteousness* and thy glory all the day'*."

52. When James had said these things, Jesus said: *Excellent, well done*, James. This is the interpretation of the ninth *repentance* of the Pistis Sophia. *Truly, truly*, I say to you that you will become first in the Kingdom of Heaven, before all the *invisible ones*, and all the gods, and all the *archons*, which are in the thirteenth *aeon*, and in the twelfth *aeon*. *But* not only you, | *but* also everyone who will perform my *mysteries*."

---

* Ps. 34.1-28

ⲚⲒⲘ ⲞⲚ ⲈⲦⲚⲀⲢ̄-ⲚⲀⲘⲨⲤⲦⲎⲢⲒⲞⲚ : ⲚⲀⲒ ⲆⲈ Ⲛ̄ⲦⲈⲢⲈϤϪⲞⲞⲨ
ⲠⲈϪⲀϤ ⲚⲀⲨ ϪⲈ ⲦⲈⲦⲚ̄ⲚⲞⲈⲒ ϪⲈ ⲈⲒϢⲀϪⲈ Ⲛ̄ⲘⲘⲎⲦⲚ̄
ⲚⲀϢ Ⲛ̄ⲎⲈ : ⲀⲤϬⲞϬⲤ̄ ⲞⲚ ⲈⲂⲞⲗ Ⲛ̄ϬⲒ ⲘⲀⲢⲒ2ⲀⲘ · ⲠⲈϪⲀⲤ
ϪⲈ ⲤⲈ ⲠϪⲞⲈⲒⲤ · ⲠⲀⲒ ⲠⲈ ⲈⲚⲦⲀⲔϪⲞⲞϤ ⲚⲀⲚ Ⲙ̄ⲠⲒⲞⲨⲞⲒϢ
5 ϪⲈ Ⲛ̄2ⲀⲈⲈⲨ ⲚⲀⲢ̄ϢⲞⲢⲠ̄ · ⲀⲨⲱ Ⲛ̄ⲦⲈ Ⲛ̄ϢⲞⲢⲠ̄ Ⲣ̄2ⲀⲈ · Ⲛ̄-
ϢⲞⲢⲠ̄ ϬⲈ ⲈⲚⲦⲀⲨⲦⲀⲘⲒⲞⲞⲨ 2ⲀⲦⲚ̄2Ⲏ ⲚⲈ Ⲛ̄Ⲁ2ⲞⲢⲀⲦⲞⲤ ·
ⲈⲠⲈⲒⲆⲎ Ⲛ̄ⲦⲞⲞⲨ ⲠⲈ ⲈⲚⲦⲀⲨϢⲱⲠⲈ 2ⲀⲐⲎ Ⲛ̄ⲦⲘⲚ̄ⲦⲢⲱⲘⲈ
Ⲛ̄ⲦⲞⲞⲨ ⲘⲚ̄ Ⲛ̄ⲚⲞⲨⲦⲈ ⲘⲚ̄ Ⲛ̄ⲀⲢⲭⲰⲚ ⲀⲨⲱ Ⲛ̄ⲢⲰⲘⲈ ⲈⲦ-
ⲚⲀϪⲒ-ⲘⲨⲤⲦⲎⲢⲒⲞⲚ ⲤⲈⲚⲀⲢ̄ϢⲞⲢⲠ̄ ⲈⲢⲞⲞⲨ Ⲉ2ⲞⲨⲚ ⲈⲦⲘⲚ̄Ⲧ-
10 ⲈⲢⲞ Ⲛ̄ⲘⲠⲎⲨⲈ · ⲠⲈϪⲀϤ ⲚⲀⲤ Ⲛ̄ϬⲒ Ⲓ̄Ⲥ̄ ϪⲈ ⲈⲨⲄⲈ ⲘⲀⲢⲒ2ⲀⲘ ·
ⲀϤⲞⲨⲰ2 ⲞⲚ ⲈⲦⲞⲞⲦϤ̄ Ⲛ̄ϬⲒ Ⲓ̄Ⲥ̄ ⲠⲈϪⲀϤ Ⲛ̄ⲚⲈϤⲘⲀⲐⲎⲦⲎⲤ ·
ϪⲈ ⲀⲤϢⲰⲠⲈ ϬⲈ Ⲛ̄ⲦⲈⲢⲈⲤⲦⲀⲨⲈ**-ⲦⲘⲈ2ϤⲒⲦⲈ Ⲙ̄ⲘⲈⲦⲀⲚⲞⲒⲀ Ⲡ̄Ⲟ̄
Ⲛ̄ϬⲒ ⲦⲠⲒⲤⲦⲒⲤ ⲤⲞⲫⲒⲀ · ⲀⲤ2ⲰϪ ⲞⲚ Ⲙ̄ⲘⲞⲤ Ⲛ̄ϬⲒ †ϬⲞⲘ
Ⲛ̄2Ⲟ Ⲙ̄ⲘⲞⲨⲒ̈ · ⲈⲤⲞⲨⲈϢϤⲒ-ϬⲞⲘ ⲚⲒⲘ Ⲛ̄2ⲎⲦⲤ̄ · ⲀⲤⲰϢ ⲞⲚ
15 Ⲉ2ⲢⲀⲒ̈ ⲈⲠⲞⲨⲞⲈⲒⲚ ⲈⲤϪⲰ Ⲙ̄ⲘⲞⲤ ϪⲈ ⲠⲞⲨⲞⲒ̈Ⲛ ⲈⲚⲦⲀⲒ̈-
ⲠⲒⲤⲦⲈⲨⲈ ⲈⲢⲞϤ ϪⲒⲚ Ⲛ̄ϢⲞⲢⲠ̄ ⲈⲚⲦⲀⲒ̈ϢⲈⲠ-ⲚⲈⲒ̈ⲚⲞϬ Ⲛ̄2ⲒⲤⲈ
ⲈⲦⲂⲎⲎⲦⲔ̄ ⲂⲞⲎⲐⲒ ⲈⲢⲞⲒ̈ · ⲀⲨⲱ ⲀⲨϪⲒ Ⲛ̄ⲦⲞⲞⲦⲤ̄ Ⲛ̄ⲦⲈⲤ-
ⲘⲈⲦⲀⲚⲞⲒⲀ Ⲛ̄ⲦⲈⲨⲚⲞⲨ ⲈⲦⲘ̄ⲘⲀⲨ · ⲀϤⲤⲰⲦⲘ̄ ⲈⲢⲞⲤ Ⲛ̄ϬⲒ
ⲠⲒϢⲞⲢⲠ̄ Ⲙ̄ⲘⲨⲤⲦⲎⲢⲒⲞⲚ · ⲀⲨⲱ ⲀⲨⲦⲚ̄ⲚⲞⲞⲨⲦ 2ⲒⲦⲚ̄ ⲦⲈϤ-
20 ⲔⲈⲖⲈⲨⲤⲒⲤ ⲀⲒ̈ⲈⲒ' ⲈⲂⲞⲎⲐⲒ ⲈⲢⲞⲤ · ⲀⲒ̈Ⲛ̄ⲦⲤ Ⲉ2ⲢⲀⲒ̈ 2Ⲙ̄ ⲠⲈϤ-
ⲬⲀⲞⲤ · ϪⲈ ⲀⲤⲘⲈⲦⲀⲚⲞⲒ̈ · ⲀⲨⲱ ⲞⲚ ⲈⲂⲞⲖ ϪⲈ ⲀⲤⲠⲒⲤ-
ⲦⲈⲨⲈ ⲈⲠⲞⲨⲞⲈⲒⲚ · ⲀⲤϢⲈⲠ-ⲚⲈⲒ̈ⲚⲞϬ Ⲛ̄2ⲒⲤⲈ · ⲘⲚ̄ ⲚⲈⲒ̈ⲚⲞϬ
Ⲛ̄ϬⲒⲚⲆⲨⲚⲞⲤ · ⲀⲨⲢ̄2ⲀⲖ Ⲙ̄ⲘⲞⲤ 2ⲒⲦⲘ̄ ⲠⲒⲀⲨⲐⲀⲆⲎⲤ Ⲛ̄-
ⲚⲞⲨⲦⲈ · ⲀⲨⲱ Ⲙ̄ⲠⲞⲨⲢ̄2ⲀⲖ Ⲙ̄ⲘⲞⲤ 2ⲒⲦⲚ̄ ⲖⲀⲀⲨ Ⲛ̄2ⲰⲂ* ⲈⲒ- Ⲡ̄Ⲟ̄ᵇ
25 ⲘⲎⲦⲒ 2ⲒⲦⲚ̄ ⲞⲨⲆⲨⲚⲀⲘⲒⲤ Ⲛ̄ⲞⲨⲞⲒ̈Ⲛ ⲈⲦⲂⲈ ⲠⲈⲒⲚⲈ Ⲙ̄ⲠⲞⲨ-

---

7 MS ⲠⲈ; read ⲚⲈ.
25 MS ⲈⲦⲂⲈ; in margin 2ⲒⲦ; read 2ⲒⲦⲚ̄ for ⲈⲦⲂⲈ.

When he had said these things, he said to them : "Do you *understand* in what manner I am speaking with you?"

Mariam sprang up again, she said : "Yes, O Lord. This is what thou didst say to us once : 'The last will become first and the first will become last.' * Now the first, which were created before us, are the *invisible ones, since* they existed before mankind, they and the gods and the *archons*; and the men who will receive *mysteries* will precede them in the Kingdom of Heaven."

Jesus said to her : "*Excellent*, Mariam."

Jesus continued again, he said to his *disciples* : "Now it happened when the Pistis Sophia had said the ninth *repentance*, the lion-faced power oppressed her again, wanting to take away all the power within her. She cried again to the Light, saying :

'O Light, in whom I have *believed* from the beginning, for whose sake I have suffered great afflictions, *help* me.'

And in that hour her *repentance* was accepted. The First *Mystery* heard her. And I was sent at his *command*, I came to *help* her. I brought her up from the *Chaos* because she had *repented*, and also because she had *believed* in the light, and she had suffered these great afflictions and these great *dangers*. She was deceived by the deity Authades. And she was deceived by nothing *except* a light-*power*, because of the likeness of the light | in which she *believed*. Now because

---

* cf. Mt. 19.30; 20.16; Mk. 10.31; Lk. 13.30

ⲞⲈⲒⲚ ⲚⲦⲀⲤⲠⲒⲤⲦⲈⲨⲈ ⲈⲢⲞϤ · ⲈⲦⲂⲈ ⲠⲀⲒ ϬⲈ ⲀⲨⲦⲚⲚⲞ-
ⲞⲨⲦ ϨⲒⲦⲚ ⲦⲔⲈⲖⲈⲨⲤⲒⲤ ⲘⲠⲒϢⲞⲢⲠ ⲘⲘⲨⲤⲦⲎⲢⲒⲞⲚ · Ⲉ-
ⲦⲢⲀⲂⲞⲎⲐⲒ ⲈⲢⲞⲤ ϨⲚ ⲞⲨⲠⲈⲐⲎⲠ · ⲚⲚⲈⲘⲠⲀϮⲈⲒ' ⲀⲈ ⲠⲈ
ⲈⲠⲦⲞⲠⲞⲤ ⲚⲚⲀⲒⲰⲚ ⲈⲠⲦⲎⲢϤ · ⲀⲖⲖⲀ ⲀⲒⲈⲒ' ⲈⲂⲞⲖ ϨⲚ ⲦⲈⲨ-
5 ⲘⲎⲦⲈ ⲦⲎⲢⲞⲨ ⲈⲘⲠⲈ ⲖⲀⲀⲨ ⲚϬⲞⲘ ⲈⲒⲘⲈ · ⲞⲨⲦⲈ ⲚⲀⲠⲤⲀ-
ⲚϨⲞⲨⲚ ⲚⲦⲈ ⲠⲤⲀⲚϨⲞⲨⲚ · ⲞⲨⲦⲈ ⲚⲀⲠⲤⲀⲂⲂⲞⲖ ⲚⲦⲈ ⲠⲤⲀ-
ⲚⲂⲞⲖ · ⲈⲒⲘⲎⲦⲒ ⲈⲠⲒϢⲞⲢⲠ ⲘⲘⲨⲤⲦⲎⲢⲒⲞⲚ ⲘⲘⲀⲦⲈ ·

   Ⳍ ⲀⲤϢⲰⲠⲈ ϬⲈ ⲚⲦⲈⲢⲒⲈⲒ' ⲈⲠⲈⲬⲖⲞⲤ ⲈⲂⲞⲎⲐⲒ ⲈⲢⲞⲤ ·
ⲀⲤⲚⲀⲨ ⲈⲢⲞⲒ ⲈⲒⲞ ⲚⲚⲞⲈⲢⲞⲤ · ⲀⲨⲰ ⲈⲒⲞ ⲚⲞⲨⲞⲈⲒⲚ ⲈⲘⲀ-
10 ϢⲞ · ⲈⲒϢⲞⲞⲠ ϨⲚ ⲞⲨⲘⲚⲦⲚⲀⲎⲦ ⲈϨⲞⲨⲚ ⲈⲢⲞⲤ · ⲚⲈⲒⲞ
ⲄⲀⲢ ⲀⲚ ⲠⲈ ⲚⲀⲨⲐⲀⲆⲎⲤ ⲚⲐⲈ ⲚϮϬⲞⲘ ⲚϨⲞ ⲘⲘⲞⲨⲒ ⲦⲀⲒ
ⲈⲚⲦⲀⲤϤⲒ-ⲦϬⲞⲘ ⲚⲞⲨⲞⲒⲚ ϨⲚ ⲦⲤⲞⲪⲒⲀ · ⲀⲨⲰ ⲞⲚ ⲦⲀⲒ
ⲈⲦϨⲰϪ ⲘⲘⲞⲤ ⲈϤⲒ-ⲠⲞⲨⲞⲈⲒⲚ ⲦⲎⲢϤ ⲈⲦⲚϨⲎⲦⲤ · ⲀⲤⲚⲀⲨ ϥ̄
ϬⲈ ⲈⲢⲞⲒ ⲈⲒⲞ ⲚⲞⲨⲞⲒⲚ ⲚϬⲒ ⲦⲤⲞⲪⲒⲀ ⲚϨⲞⲨⲞ ⲈϮⲀⲨⲚⲀ-
15 ⲘⲒⲤ ⲚϨⲞ ⲘⲘⲞⲨⲒ ⲚⲞⲨⲎⲠⲈ ⲚⲦⲂⲀ ⲚⲔⲰⲂ ⲚⲤⲞⲠ · ⲀⲨⲰ
ⲈⲒϢⲞⲞⲠ ϨⲚ ⲞⲨⲚⲞϬ ⟨Ⲙ⟩ⲘⲚⲦⲚⲀⲎⲦ ⲈϨⲞⲨⲚ ⲈⲢⲞⲤ · ⲀⲨⲰ
ⲀⲤⲈⲒⲘⲈ ϪⲈ ⲀⲚⲄ ⲞⲨⲈⲂⲞⲖ ϨⲘ ⲠⲬⲒⲤⲈ ⲚⲚⲬⲒⲤⲈ · ⲠⲀⲒ
ⲈⲚⲦⲀⲤⲠⲒⲤⲦⲈⲨⲈ ⲈⲠⲈϤⲞⲨⲞⲒⲚ ϪⲒⲚ ⲚϢⲞⲢⲠ · ⲀⲤⲦⲰⲔ ϬⲈ
ⲚϨⲎⲦ ⲚϬⲒ ⲦⲠⲒⲤⲦⲒⲤ ⲤⲞⲪⲒⲀ · ⲀⲨⲰ ⲀⲤⲬⲰ ⲚⲦⲘⲈϨⲘⲎⲦⲈ
20 ⲘⲘⲈⲦⲀⲚⲞⲒⲀ ⲈⲤⲬⲰ ⲘⲘⲞⲤ ϪⲈ

   1. ⲀⲒⲰϢ ⲈϨⲢⲀⲒ ⲈⲢⲞⲔ ⲠⲞⲨⲞⲈⲒⲚ ⲚⲦⲈ ⲚⲒⲞⲨⲞⲈⲒⲚ ϨⲘ
ⲠⲦⲢⲈⲒϨⲰϢ ⲀⲔⲤⲰⲦⲘ ⲈⲢⲞⲒ ·

   2. ⲠⲞⲨⲞⲈⲒⲚ ⲚⲞⲨϨⲘ ⲚⲦⲀϬⲞⲘ ⲈⲂⲞⲖ ϨⲚ ϨⲈⲚⲤⲠⲞⲦⲞⲨ
ⲚϪⲒⲚϬⲞⲚⲤ · ⲀⲨⲰ ⲚⲀⲚⲀⲘⲞⲤ · ⲀⲨⲰ ⲈⲂⲞⲖ ϨⲚ ϨⲈⲚ-
25 ϬⲞⲢϬⲤ ⲚⲔⲢⲞϤ ·

---

7   MS ⲈⲠⲒϢⲞⲢⲠ; read ⲠⲒϢⲞⲢⲠ.
16   MS ϨⲚ ⲞⲨⲘⲚⲦⲚⲀⲎⲦ; ⲚⲞϬ in left-hand margin.
22   MS ϨⲘ ⲠⲦⲢⲈⲒϨⲰϢ; archaic form of ϨⲘ ⲠⲦⲢⲀϨⲰϢ.
24   MS ⲚⲀⲚⲀⲘⲞⲤ; read ⲚⲀⲚⲞⲘⲞⲤ.

of this I was sent, through the *command* of the First *Mystery*, to *help* her secretly. *But* I had not yet come to the *place* of the *aeons* at all. *But* I came forth from the midst of them all without any power knowing; *neither* the innermost ones of the inner, *nor* the outermost ones of the outer, *except for* the First *Mystery* alone.

Now it happened when I came to the *Chaos*, to *help* her, she saw that I was *understanding*, and that I was shining exceedingly and with compassion towards her. *For* I was not *insolent* like the lion-faced power, which had taken away the power of light from the Sophia, and which had also afflicted her, to take away all the light within her. Now the Sophia saw me, that I was shining ten thousand times more than the lion-faced *power*, and that I had great compassion towards her. And she knew that I was from out of the height of heights, in the light of which she had *believed* from the beginning. The Pistis Sophia took courage and she spoke the tenth *repentance*, saying:

1. 'I have cried out to thee, O Light of Lights, in my affliction, and thou hast heard me.

2. O Light, save my power from unjust and *iniquitous* lips, and from cunning snares. |

3. ⲡⲟⲩⲟⲉⲓⲛ ⲉⲧⲟⲩⲛⲁϭⲓⲧϥ̄ ⲛ̄ϩⲏⲧ · ϩ̄ⲛ ⲟⲩϭⲟⲣϭ̄ⲥ ⲛ̄-
ⲕⲣⲟϥ · ⲛⲉⲩⲛⲁⲛⲧϥ̄ ⲛⲁⲕ ⲁⲛ ·

4. ⲛ̄ϭⲟⲣϭ̄ⲥ ⲅⲁⲣ ⲙ̄ⲡⲁⲩⲟⲗⲁⲏⲥ ⲥⲏⲣ ⲉⲃⲟⲗ · ⲁⲩⲱ ⲙ̄ⲛ
ⲛ̄ϩⲁϭⲉ ⲛ̄ⲧⲉ ⲡⲓⲁⲧⲛⲁ̇ ·

5 5. ⲟⲩⲟⲓ̈ * ⲛⲁⲓ̈ ⲁⲛⲟⲕ ϫⲉ ⲁ ⲡⲁⲙⲁⲛϣ̄ϣⲱⲡⲉ ⲟⲩⲉ · ⲁⲩⲱ ϥ̄ᵇ
ⲁⲓ̈ϣⲱⲡⲉ ϩⲛ̄ ⲙ̄ⲙⲁⲛϣ̄ϣⲱⲡⲉ ⲛ̄ⲧⲉ ⲡⲉⲭⲗⲟⲥ ·

6. ⲁ ⲧⲁϭⲟⲙ ϣⲱⲡⲉ ϩ̄ⲛ ϩⲉⲛⲧⲟⲡⲟⲥ ⲉⲛⲛⲟⲩⲓ̈ ⲁⲛ ⲛⲉ ·

7. ⲁⲩⲱ ⲁⲓ̈ⲕⲱⲣϣ̄ ⲉⲛⲓⲁⲧⲛⲁ̇ ⲉⲧⲙ̄ⲙⲁⲩ · ⲁⲩⲱ ⲉⲓ̈ϣⲁⲛ-
ⲕⲱⲣϣ̄ ⲉⲣⲟⲟⲩ · ϣⲁⲩϯⲟⲩⲃⲏⲓ̈ ⲉⲡϫⲓⲛϫⲏ ·

10 ⲛⲁⲓ̈ ϭⲉ ⲛ̄ⲧⲉⲣⲉ ⲓ̄ⲥ̄ ϫⲟⲟⲩ ⲉⲛⲉϥⲙⲁⲑⲏⲧⲏⲥ ⲡⲉϫⲁϥ ⲛⲁⲩ
ϫⲉ ⲧⲉⲛⲟⲩ ϭⲉ ⲡⲉⲧⲉⲣⲉ ⲡⲉϥⲡ̄ⲛ̄ⲁ̄ ⲕⲓⲙ ⲉⲣⲟϥ · ⲙⲁⲣⲉϥⲉⲓ̇
ⲉⲑⲏ · ⲛ̄ϥϫⲱ ⲙ̄ⲡⲃⲱⲗ ⲛ̄ⲧⲙⲉϩⲙⲏⲧⲉ ⲙ̄ⲙⲉⲧⲁⲛⲟⲓⲁ ⲛ̄ⲧⲡⲓⲥ-
ⲧⲓⲥ ⲥⲟⲫⲓⲁ · ⲁϥⲟⲩⲱϣ̄ⲃ ⲛ̄ϭⲓ ⲡⲉⲧⲣⲟⲥ ⲡⲉϫⲁϥ ϫⲉ
ⲡϫⲟⲉⲓⲥ · ⲉⲧⲃⲉ ⲡⲁⲓ̈ ⲟⲛ ⲁ ⲧⲉⲕϭⲟⲙ ⲛ̄ⲟⲩⲟⲉⲓⲛ ⲡⲣⲟⲫⲏ-
15 ⲧⲉⲩⲉ ϩⲓⲧⲛ̄ ⲇⲁⲩⲉⲓⲇ · ⲙ̄ⲡⲓⲟⲩⲟⲓ̈ϣ ⲉⲥϫⲱ ⲙ̄ⲙⲟⲥ ϩ̄ⲙ
ⲡⲙⲉϩϣⲉ ⲙⲛ̄ ⲙⲛ̄ⲧϯⲥ ⲙ̄ⲯⲁⲗⲙⲟⲥ · ϫⲉ

1. ⲁⲓ̈ϣϣ ⲉϩⲣⲁⲓ̈ ⲉⲣⲟⲕ ⲡϫⲟⲉⲓⲥ ϩ̄ⲙ ⲡⲧⲣⲁϩϣⲱϣ · ⲁⲕ-
ⲥⲱⲧⲙ̄ ⲉⲣⲟⲓ̈ ·

2. ⲡϫⲟⲓ̈ⲥ ⲛⲟⲩϩ̄ⲙ ⲛ̄ⲧⲁⲯⲩⲭⲏ** ⲉⲃⲟⲗ ϩ̄ⲛ ϩⲉⲛⲥⲡⲟⲧⲟⲩ ___
20 ⲛ̄ϫⲓⲛϭⲟⲛⲥ · ⲁⲩⲱ ⲉⲃⲟⲗ ϩⲓⲧⲛ̄ ⲟⲩⲗⲁⲥ ⲛ̄ⲕⲣⲟϥ · ϥⲁ

3. ⲉⲩⲛⲁϯ ⲟⲩ ⲛⲁⲕ ⲁⲩⲱ ⲉⲩⲛⲁⲟⲩⲉϩ ⲟⲩ ⲉⲣⲟⲕ · ⲛ̄-
ⲛⲁϩⲣⲛ̄ ⲟⲩⲗⲁⲥ ⲛ̄ⲕⲣⲟϥ ·

4. ⲛ̄ⲥⲟⲧⲉ ⲙ̄ⲡϫⲱⲱⲣ ϣⲟⲗϭ ⲙ̄ⲛ ⲛ̄ⲁⲛⲑⲣⲁⲝ ⲛ̄ⲧⲉ ⲡϫⲁⲓ̈ⲉ ·

5. ⲟⲩⲟⲓ̈ ⲛⲁⲓ̈ ϫⲉ ⲁ ⲡⲁⲙⲁⲛϣ̄ϣⲱⲡⲉ ⲟⲩⲉ ⲉⲃⲟⲗ · ⲁⲓ̈-
25 ⲟⲩⲱϩ ϩ̄ⲛ ⲙ̄ⲙⲁⲛϣ̄ϣⲱⲡⲉ ⲛ̄ⲕⲏⲇⲁⲣ ·

3. The light which was taken away from me with a cunning snare will not be brought to thee.

4. *For* the snares of the Authades are widespread, with the traps of the merciless.

5. Woe to me, for my dwelling was far off and I was in the dwellings of the *Chaos.*

6. My power was in *places* which were not mine.

7. And I flattered those merciless ones, and when I flattered them, they attacked me without cause'."

53. Now when Jesus had said these things to his *disciples*, he said to them: "Now at this time let him whose *spirit* moves him, come forth and say the interpretation of the tenth *repentance* of the Pistis Sophia."

Peter answered and said: "O Lord, concerning this also, thy power *prophesied* once, through David, in the 119th *Psalm*, saying:

1. 'I cried to thee, O Lord, in my affliction and thou didst hear me.

2. O Lord, save my *soul* from unjust lips and from a cunning tongue.

3. What will be given to thee and what will be taken from thee with a cunning tongue?

4. The arrows of the strong are sharpened, together with the *coals* of the desert.

5. Woe on me, for my dwelling was far off. I dwelt in the dwellings of Kedar. |

6. ⲁ ⲦⲀⲮⲨⲬⲎ ⲣ̄-ⲣⲙ̄ⲛ̄ⲅⲟⲉⲓⲗⲉ ⳍ̄ⲛ ⲟⲨⲘⲎⲎϢⲈ ⲙ̄ⲙⲀ ·

7. ⲚⲈⲒⲞ ⲚⲈⲒⲢⲎⲚⲒⲔⲞⲤ ⲠⲈ ⲘⲚ̄ ⲚⲈⲦⲘⲞⲤⲦⲈ ⲚⲦⳋⲢⲎⲚⲎ ·
ⲈⲒϢⲀⲚϢⲀⲬⲈ ⲚⲘⲘⲀⲨ · ϢⲀⲨⲘⲒϢⲈ ⲚⲘⲘⲀⲒ ⲚϪⲒⲚϪⲎ ·
ⲠⲀⲒ ⳊⲈ ⲦⲈⲚⲞⲨ ⲠϪⲞⲈⲒⲤ ⲠⲈ ⲠⲂⲰⲖ ⲚⲦⲘⲈⳍⲘⲎⲦⲈ Ⲙ-
ⲘⲈⲦⲀⲚⲞⲒⲀ ⲚⲦⲠⲒⲤⲦⲒⲤ ⲤⲞⲪⲒⲀ · ⲦⲈⲚⲦⲀⲤϪⲞⲞⲤ ⲈⲨⳍⲰϪ
ⲘⲘⲞⲤ ⲚⳋⲒ ⲚⲈⲠⲢⲞⲂⲞⲖⲞⲞⲨⲈ ⲚⳍⲨⲖⲒⲔⲞⲚ ⲚⲦⲈ ⲠⲀⲨⲐⲀ-
ⲀⲎⲤ · ⲚⲦⲞⲞⲨ ⲘⲚ̄ ⲦⲈϤⳋⲞⲘ ⲚⳍⲞ ⲘⲘⲞⲨⲒ · ⲀⲨⲰ ⲚⲦⲈ-
ⲢⲞⲨⲐⲖⲒⲂⲈ ⲘⲘⲞⲤ ⲈⲘⲀϢⲞ · ⲠⲈϪⲀϤ ⲚⲀϤ ⲚⳋⲒ ⲒⲤ ⲬⲈ ⳌⲀ
ⲈⲨⲄⲈ ⲠⲈⲦⲢⲞⲤ ⲀⲨⲰ ⲔⲀⲖⲰⲤ · ⲠⲀⲒ ⲠⲈ ⲠⲂⲰⲖ ⲚⲦⲘⲈⳍ-
ⲘⲎⲦⲈ ⲘⲘⲈⲦⲀⲚⲞⲒⲀ ⲚⲦⲠⲒⲤⲦⲒⲤ ⲤⲞⲪⲒⲀ ·

ⳍ ⲀϤⲞⲨⲰⳍ ⲞⲚ ⲈⲦⲞⲞⲦϤ̄ ⲚⳋⲒ ⲒⲤ ⳍⲘ ⲠϢⲀϪⲈ ⲠⲈϪⲀϤ
ⲚⲚⲈϤⲘⲀⲐⲎⲦⲎⲤ ϪⲈ ⲀⲤϢⲰⲠⲈ ⳊⲈ ⲚⲦⲈⲢⲈⲤⲚⲀⲨ ⲈⲢⲞⲒ ⲚⳋⲒ
ⳋⳋⲞⲘ ⲚⳍⲞ ⲘⲘⲞⲨⲒ ⲈⲀⲒⳍⲰⲚ ⲈⳍⲞⲨⲚ ⲈⲦⲠⲒⲤⲦⲒⲤ ⲤⲞⲪⲒⲀ
ⲈⲒⲞ ⲚⲞⲨⲞⲒⲚ ⲈⲘⲀϢⲞ ⲈⲘⲀϢⲞ · ⲀⲤϬⲰⲚⲦ ⲈⲠⲈⳍⲞⲨⲞ ·
ⲀⲨⲰ ⲀⲤⲠⲢⲞⲂⲀⲖⲈ ⲈⲂⲞⲖ ⲚⳍⲎⲦⲤ ⲚⲔⲈⲘⲎⲎϢⲈ ⲘⲠⲢⲞⲂⲞⲖⲎ
ⲈⲨⲚⲀϢⲦ ⲈⲘⲀϢⲞ · ⲚⲀⲒ ⳊⲈ ⲚⲦⲈⲢⲞⲨϢⲰⲠⲈ ⲀⲤϪⲰ Ⲛ-
ⲦⲘⲈⳍⲘⲚ̄ⲦⲞⲨⲈ ⲘⲘⲈⲦⲀⲚⲞⲒⲀ ⲚⳋⲒ ⲦⲠⲒⲤⲦⲒⲤ ⲤⲞⲪⲒⲀ ⲈⲤϪⲰ
ⲘⲘⲞⲤ · ϪⲈ ⲀⳍⲢⲞⲤ ⲀⲤϪⲒⲤⲈ ⲘⲘⲞⲤ ⲚⳋⲒ ⳋⳋⲞⲘ ⲚⲬⲰⲰⲢ
ⳍⲢⲀⲒ ⳍⲚ ⳍⲈⲚⲠⲈⲐⲞⲞⲨ · ⲈⲢⲈ ⲠⲈⲤⲘⲈⲈⲨⲈ ϤⲒ ⲘⲠⲞⲨⲞⲒⲚ
ⲚⳍⲎⲦ ⲚⲞⲨⲞⲒϢ ⲚⲒⲘ · ⲀⲨⲰ ⲚⲐⲈ ⲚⲞⲨⲠⲈⲚⲒⲠⲈ ⲈⲨϢⲰⲰⲦ
ⲀⲨϤⲒ ⲚⲞⲨϬⲞⲘ ⲚⳍⲎⲦ ⲀⲒⲘⲈⲢⲈ-ⲈⲒ ⲈⲠⲈⲤⲎⲦ ⲈⲠⲈⲬⲀⲞⲤ · ⳌⲂ
ⲚⳍⲞⲨⲞ ⲈϬⲰ ⳍⲘ ⲠⲘⲞⲨ ⲘⲠⲘⲈⳍⲘⲚ̄ⲦϢⲞⲘⲦⲈ ⲚⲀⲒⲰⲚ ·
ⲠⲦⲞⲠⲞⲤ ⲚⲦⲀⲒⲔⲀⲒⲞⲤⲨⲚⲎ · ⲀⲨⲰ ⲀⲨⲞⲨⲰϢ ⲈⲬⲒⲦ Ⲛ-
ⲔⲢⲞϤ ⲈⲦⲢⲈⲨⲰⲘⲔ ⲘⲠⲀⲞⲨⲞⲈⲒⲚ ⲦⲎⲢϤ · ⲈⲦⲂⲈ ⲠⲀⲒ ⳊⲈ
ⲠⲞⲨⲞⲈⲒⲚ ⲚⲀϤⲒ-ⲠⲈⲨⲞⲨⲞⲈⲒⲚ ⲦⲎⲢϤ · ⲀⲨⲰ ⲚⲤϢⲞⲢϢⲢ

---

20 MS ⲈⲨϢⲰⲰⲦ; read ⲈϤϢⲰⲰⲦ.
21 ⳍ in upper right-hand margin at end of quire.
22 MS ⲠⲘⲞⲨ; read ⲠⲘⲀ.

6. My *soul* has been a sojourner in many places.

7. I was *peaceful* with those who hate *peace*. When I spoke with them they fought me without cause.' *

Now at this time, O Lord, this is the interpretation of the tenth *repentance* of the Pistis Sophia, which she said when the *material emanations* of the Authades oppressed her, they and his lion-faced power, [and when they *afflicted* her greatly]." [1]

Jesus said to him : "*Excellent*, Peter, and *well done*. This is the interpretation of the tenth *repentance* of the Pistis Sophia."

54. Jesus continued again with the discourse, he said to his *disciples* : "Now it happened when the lion-faced power saw me approaching the Pistis Sophia, that I was shining exceedingly, it was more angry, and it *emanated* from itself another multitude of very powerful *emanations*. Now when these things happened, the Pistis Sophia spoke the eleventh *repentance*, saying :

1. 'Why has the strong power risen among the wicked? [2]

2. Its thought took the light away from me at all times. And like sharp iron they took [3] power from me.

3. I preferred to come down to the *Chaos* more than to remain in the place of the thirteenth *aeon*, the *place* of *righteousness*.

4. And they wanted to take me by cunning, that they might swallow all my light.

5. Because of this now, the light will take all their light, |

---

* Ps. 119.1-7

---

[1] (7, 8) [and when ... greatly]; Schmidt : delete as tautology.
[2] (19) among the wicked; lit. in what is wicked; Till : with wicked deeds.
[3] (20) like sharp iron they took; MS : like iron as they cut they took.

 N̄6ι ΤΕΥΚΕ2ΥλΗ ΤΗΡⲤ· λΥω ⳍΝλⳍ Ⲙ̄ΠΕΥΟΥΟΕΙΝ λΥω

Ν̄ⳍΤΜΚλλΥ Εωωπε 2Μ̄ ΠΜΕ2Μ̄Τωοмτε Ν̄λιωΝ ΠΕΥ-

ΜλΝωωΠε· λΥω Ν̄ⳍΤΜΚλ-ΠΕΥΡλΝ 2Μ̄ ΠΤΟΠΟⲤ Ν̄ΝΕΤ-

Νλωⲛ̄2· λΥω ⲤΕΝλΝλΥ ΕΝΕΝΤλΥωωΠε Μ̄ΜΟ ω'

5　Τ6ΟΜ Ν̄2Ο Μ̄ΜΟΥΪ Ν̄6ι †ΧΟΥΤλⳍΤΕ Μ̄ΠΡΟΒΟλΗ· Ν̄-

ⲤΕΡ2ΟΤΕ· λΥω Ν̄ⲤΕΤΜ̄Ρ-λΤⲤωΤΜ̄· λλλλ Ν̄ⲤΕ† Μ̄-

ΠⲤωΤⳍ Μ̄ΠΕΥΟΥΟΪΝ· λΥω ⲤΕΝλΝλΥ ΕΡΟ· Ν̄ⲤΕΡλωε

Ε2Ρλ̈Ι ΕΧω· Ν̄ⲤΕΧΟΟⲤ ΧΕ ΕΙⲤ ΟΥΠΡΟΒΟλΗ ΕΜ̄ΠⲤ†- ⳌΒ ᵇ

ΠⲤωΤⳍ Μ̄ΠΕⲤΟΥΟΪΝ ΧΕ ΕⲤΕΝΟΥ2Μ̄· λλλλ ⲤωΟΥωΟΥ

10　Μ̄ΜΟⲤ 2Μ̄ Πλωλ̈Ι Μ̄ΠΟΥΟΕΙΝ Ν̄ΤΕⲤ6ΟΜ· ΕΒΟλ ΧΕ Μ̄-

ΠⲤΠΡΟΒλλΕ ΕΒΟλ 2Ν̄ Τ6ΟΜ ΕΤΝ̄2ΗΤⲤ̄· λΥω λⲤΧΟΟⲤ

ΧΕ †Νλⳍι-ΠΟΥΟΪΝ Ν̄ΤΠΙⲤΤΙⲤ ⲤΟⲪΙλ· Πλ̈Ι ΕΤΟΥΝλ-

ⳍΙΤⳍ Ν̄ΤΟΟΤⲤ· ΤΕΝΟΥ 6Ε ΠΕΝΤλ ΤΕⳍ6ΟΜ ΧΙⲤΕ

Ν̄2ΗΤⳍ· ΜλΡΕⳍΕΙ' ΕΘΗ Ν̄ⳍΤλΥΕ-ΠΒωλ Ν̄ΤΜΕ2Μ̄Ν̄ΤΟΥΕ

15　Μ̄ΜΕΤλΝΟΙλ Ν̄ΤΠΙⲤΤΙⲤ ⲤΟⲪΙλ· ΤΟΤΕ λⲤΕΙ' ΕΘΗ Ν̄6ι

ⲤλλωΜΗ ΠΕΧλⲤ ΧΕ ΠλΧΟΕΙⲤ· ΕΤΒΕ Πλ̈Ι λ ΤΕΚ6ΟΜ

Ν̄ΟΥΟΕΙΝ ΠΡΟⲪΗΤΕΥΕ Μ̄ΠΙΟΥΟΕΙω 2ΙΤΝ̄ λλΥΕΙλ ΕⲤ-

Χω Μ̄ΜΟⲤ 2Μ̄ ΠΜΕ2ΤλΪΟΥ Μ̄Ν ΟΥλ Μ̄ΨλλΜΟⲤ· ΧΕ

　1. λ2ΡΟⳍ ΠλΥΝλΤΟⲤ ωΟΥωΟΥ Μ̄ΜΟⳍ 2Ν̄ ΤΕⳍΚλ-

20　ΚΙλ·

　2. λ ΠΕΚλλⲤ ΜΕλΕΤλ Μ̄ΠΧΙΝ6ΟΝⲤ̄ Μ̄ΠΕ2ΟΟΥ ΤΗΡⳍ

Ν̄ΘΕ Ν̄ΟΥΤΟΚ Ν̄2ωωΚ** ΕⳍΤΗΜ· λΚΕΙΡΕ Ν̄ΟΥΚΡΟⳍ·　⳽Γ·

　3. λΚΜΕΡΕ-ΤΚλΚΙλ Ν̄2ΟΥΟ ΕΠλΓλΘΟΝ· λΚΜΕΡΕ-ΠΧΙ-

Ν̄6ΟΝⲤ̄ Ε2ΟΥΟ Εωλ ΧΕ ΕΤλΙΚλΙΟⲤΥΝΗ·

22　Ⲍ̄ in upper left-hand margin at beginning of quire.

and also their whole *matter* will be destroyed. And he will take their light, and he will not let them exist in the thirteenth *aeon*, their dwelling place, and he will not let their names be in the *place* of those that will live.

6. And the 24 *emanations* will see what has happened to thee, *O* lion-faced power, and they will fear and they will not be disobedient, *but* they will give what is purified of their light.

7. And they will see thee, and they will rejoice over thee and they will say: Behold an *emanation* which has not given what is purified of its light, that it might be saved, *but* it boasts of the magnitude of the light of its power, because it did not *emanate* the power within it; and it said: I will take away the light of the Pistis Sophia, this which will be taken from her.'

Now at this time, let him in whom his power has arisen come forward and give the interpretation of the eleventh *repentance* of the Pistis Sophia."

Then Salome [1] came forward and said: "My Lord, concerning this, thy light-power once *prophesied*, through David, in the 51st *Psalm*, saying:

1. 'Why does the *mighty* boast of his *evil*?

2. Thy tongue has *devised* injustice all the day; like a sharp cutting knife thou hast practised deceit.

3. Thou hast loved *evil* more than *goodness*; thou hast loved injustice more than to speak *righteousness*. |

---

[1]   (16) Salome; see Origen *c.Cels.* V.62; GTh 90.

4. ΑΚΜΕΡΕ Ⲛ̄ϢⲀϪⲈ ΤΗΡΟΥ Ⲙ̄ⲠⲰⲘⲤ · Ⲙ̄Ⲛ ΟΥΛΑⲤ Ⲛ̄-
ⲔⲢΟϤ ·

5. ⲈⲦⲂⲈ ⲠⲀÏ ⲠⲚΟΥⲦⲈ ⲚⲀ̅ϢⲢϢⲢⲔ̅ ϢⲀⲂΟⲖ ϤⲚⲀⲠΟⲢ-
Ⲕ̅Ⲕ̅ · ⲀΥⲰ Ⲛ̄ϤⲦΟⲔⲘⲈⲔ ⲈⲂΟⲖ Ⲋ̄Ⲙ ⲠⲈⲔⲘⲀⲚ̄ϢⲰⲠⲈ ⲀΥⲰ
5 ϤⲚⲀⲦⲰⲖⲔ̅ Ⲛ̄ⲦⲈⲔⲚΟΥⲚⲈ Ⲛ̄ϤⲚΟⲬ̅Ⲥ̅ ⲤⲀⲂΟⲖ Ⲛ̄ⲚⲈⲦΟⲚ̄Ⲋ̄ ·
ⲆⲒⲀⲮⲀⲖⲘⲀ ·

6. Ⲛ̄ⲆⲒⲔⲀⲒΟⲤ ⲚⲀⲚⲀΥ Ⲛ̄ⲤⲈⲢ̅Ⲋ̄ΟⲦⲈ ⲀΥⲰ ⲤⲈⲚⲀⲤⲰⲂⲈ
Ⲉ�Ⲋ̄ⲢⲀÏ ⲈϪⲰϤ Ⲛ̄ⲤⲈϪΟΟⲤ ·

7. ϪⲈ ⲈⲒⲤ ΟΥⲢⲰⲘⲈ ⲈⲘⲠϤⲔⲀ-ⲠⲚΟΥⲦⲈ ⲚⲀϤ Ⲛ̄ⲂΟⲎ-
10 ⲐΟⲤ · ⲀⲖⲖⲀ ⲀϤⲚⲀⲊⲦⲈ ⲈϪⲚ̄ ⲦⲈϤⲘⲚ̄ⲦⲢⲘ̄ⲘⲀΟ ⲈⲚⲀϢⲰⲤ ·
ⲀΥⲰ ⲀϤϬ̅Ⲙ̄ϬΟⲘ ⲈϪ̅Ⲙ̄ ⲠⲈϤⲠⲈⲦϢΟΥⲈΙⲦ ·

8. ⲀⲚΟⲔ ⲆⲈ ⲈΪΟ Ⲛ̄ⲐⲈ ΟΥⲂⲰ Ⲛ̄ϪΟⲈΙⲦ Ⲛ̄ⲢⲈϤⲦ-ⲔⲀⲢ-
ⲠΟⲤ Ⲋ̄Ⲙ̄ ⲠⲎⲒ Ⲙ̄ⲠⲚΟΥⲦⲈ · ⲀΪⲚⲀⲊⲦⲈ ⲈⲠⲚⲀ̓ Ⲙ̄ⲠⲚΟΥⲦⲈ ϢⲀ
ⲈⲚⲈⲊ Ⲛ̄ⲦⲈ ⲠΙⲈⲚⲈⲊ ·   ϥⲅ̅ᵇ

15 9. ⲀΥⲰ ⳥ⲚⲀΟΥⲰⲚ̄Ⲋ̄ ⲚⲀⲔ ⲈⲂΟⲖ ϪⲈ ⲀⲔⲈΙⲢⲈ Ⲛ̄ⲘⲘⲀΪ ·
ⲀΥⲰ ⳥Ⲋ̄ΥⲠΟⲘⲒⲚⲈ ⲈⲠⲈⲔⲢⲀⲚ ϪⲈ ΟΥⲬⲢⲎⲤⲦΟⲚ ⲠⲈ Ⲙ̄-
ⲠⲈⲘⲦΟ ⲈⲂΟⲖ Ⲛ̄ⲚⲈⲔⲠⲈⲦΟΥⲀⲀⲂ ·

ⲠⲀΪ ϬⲈ ⲦⲈⲚΟΥ ⲠⲀϪΟⲈΙⲤ ⲠⲈ ⲠⲂⲰⲖ Ⲛ̄ⲦⲘⲈⲊⲘⲚ̄ⲦΟΥⲈ
Ⲙ̄ⲘⲈⲦⲀⲚΟΙⲀ Ⲛ̄ⲦⲠΙⲤⲦΙⲤ ⲤΟⲪΙⲀ · ⲈⲀ ⲦⲈⲔϬΟⲘ Ⲛ̄ΟΥΟⲈΙⲚ
20 ⲔΙⲘ ⲈⲢΟΪ ⲀΪϪΟΟϤ ⲔⲀⲦⲀ ⲠⲈⲔΟΥⲰϢ :

ⳡ ⲀⲤϢⲰⲠⲈ ϬⲈ Ⲛ̄ⲦⲈⲢⲈ Ι̅Ⲥ̅ ⲤⲰⲦ̅Ⲙ̄ ⲈⲚⲈΪϢⲀϪⲈ ⲈⲚⲦⲀⲤ-
ϪΟΟΥ Ⲛ̄ϬΙ ⲤⲀⲖⲰⲘⲎ ⲠⲈϪⲀϤ ϪⲈ ⲈΥⲅⲈ ⲤⲀⲖⲰⲘⲎ · Ⲋ̄Ⲁ-
ⲘⲎⲚ Ⲋ̄ⲀⲘⲎⲚ ⳥ϪⲰ Ⲙ̄ⲘΟⲤ ⲚⲎⲦⲚ̄ · ϪⲈ ⳥ⲚⲀϪⲈⲔ-ⲦⲎΥⲦⲚ̄

---

6 MS ⲆⲒⲀⲖⲀⲮⲀⲖⲘⲀ.
15 MS originally ⲀΥⲚⲀΟΥⲰⲚ̄Ⲋ̄; ⲱ⳥ inserted above.
16 MS ⳥Ⲋ̄ΥⲠΟⲘⲒⲚⲈ; read ·ⳡ·ⲚⲀⲊⲢ̄ΥⲠΟⲘⲒⲚⲈ.

4. Thou hast loved all words of subterfuge and a cunning tongue.

5. For this reason God will destroy thee completely. He will uproot thee; and he will draw thee from thy dwelling, and he will pluck out thy root and cast it outside of those that are living. *Pause.*

6. The *righteous* will see and will fear; and they will mock at him and say :

7. Behold a man who did not make God his *helper, but* he trusted in his great wealth and he had power upon his vanity.

8. *But* I am like a *fruit*-bearing olive tree in the House of God; I have trusted in the mercy of God for ever and ever.

9. And I will give thanks to thee, for thou hast dealt with me; and I will *wait upon* thy name, for it is *beneficent* in the presence of thy holy ones.' *

Now at this time, my Lord, this is the interpretation of the eleventh *repentance* of the Pistis Sophia. As thy light-power moved me, I said it *according to* thy will."

Now it happened when Jesus heard these words which Salome said, he said : "Excellent, Salome. *Truly, truly,* I say to you that I will complete you | in all *mysteries* of the Kingdom of the Light."

---

* Ps. 51.1-9

ⲈⲂⲞⲖ ⲌⲘ ⲘⲨⲤⲦⲎⲢⲒⲞⲚ ⲚⲒⲘ ⲚⲦⲈ ⲦⲘⲚⲦⲈⲢⲞ ⲘⲠⲞⲨⲞⲈⲒⲚ·
ⲀϤⲞⲨⲰⲌ ⲀⲈ ⲞⲚ ⲈⲦⲞⲞⲦϤ ⲚϬⲒ ⲒⲤ ⲌⲘ ⲠⲰⲀϪⲈ ⲠⲈϪⲀϤ
ⲚⲚⲈϤⲘⲀⲐⲎⲦⲎⲤ ϪⲈ ⲀⲤϢⲰⲠⲈ ϬⲈ ⲘⲚⲚⲤⲀ ⲚⲀⲒ· ⲀⲒϢⲰⲚ
ⲈϨⲞⲨⲚ ⲈⲠⲈϪⲀⲞⲤ· ⲈⲒⲞ ⲚⲞⲨⲞⲈⲒⲚ ⲈⲘⲀϢⲞ ⲈⲘⲀϢⲞ ϪⲈ
5　ⲈⲒⲈϤⲒ ⲘⲠⲞⲨⲞⲒⲚ ⲚⲦⲈ ⲦϬⲞⲘ ⲚⲌⲞ ⲘⲘⲞⲨⲒ ⲈⲦⲘⲘⲀⲨ· ⲈⲒⲞ
ⲚⲞⲨⲞⲒⲚ ⲈⲘⲀϢⲞ ⲀⲤⲢϨⲞⲦⲈ ⲀⲨⲰ ⲀⲤⲰϢ ⲈϨⲢⲀⲒ ⲈⲠⲈⲤ- ϥⲁ
ⲚⲞⲨⲦⲈ ⲚⲀⲨⲀⲐⲀⲀⲎⲤ ⲈⲦⲢⲈϤⲂⲞⲎⲐⲒ ⲈⲢⲞⲤ ⲀⲨⲰ ⲚⲦⲈⲨ-
ⲚⲞⲨ ⲈⲦⲘⲘⲀⲨ ⲀϤϬⲰϢⲦ ⲈⲂⲞⲖ ⲌⲘ ⲠⲘⲈϨϢⲘⲚⲦϢⲞⲘⲦⲈ
ⲚⲀⲒⲰⲚ ⲚϬⲒ ⲠⲚⲞⲨⲦⲈ ⲚⲀⲨⲐⲀⲀⲎⲤ· ⲀϤϬⲰϢⲦ ⲈⲠⲈⲤⲚⲦ
10　ⲈⲠⲈϪⲀⲞⲤ· ⲈϤϬⲞⲚⲦ ⲈⲘⲀϢⲞ ⲈϤⲞⲨⲈϢⲂⲞⲎⲐⲒ ⲈⲦⲈϤϬⲞⲘ
ⲚⲌⲞ ⲘⲘⲞⲨⲒ ⲀⲨⲰ ⲚⲦⲈⲨⲚⲞⲨ ⲈⲦⲘⲘⲀⲨ ⲀⲤⲔⲰⲦⲈ ⲈⲦⲠⲒⲤ-
ⲦⲒⲤ ⲤⲞⲪⲒⲀ ⲚϬⲒ ⲦϬⲞⲘ ⲚⲌⲞ ⲘⲘⲞⲨⲒ ⲚⲦⲞⲤ ⲘⲚ ⲚⲈⲤ-
ⲠⲢⲞⲂⲞⲖⲞⲞⲨⲈ ⲦⲎⲢⲞⲨ ⲈⲨⲞⲨⲈϢϤⲒ-ⲠⲞⲨⲞⲒⲚ ⲦⲎⲢϤ ⲈⲦϨⲚ
ⲦⲤⲞⲪⲒⲀ· ⲀⲤϢⲰⲠⲈ ϬⲈ ⲚⲦⲈⲢⲞⲨϨⲰϪ ⲚⲦⲤⲞⲪⲒⲀ· ⲀⲤⲰϢ
15　ⲈϨⲢⲀⲒ ⲈⲠϪⲒⲤⲈ ⲈⲤⲰϢ ⲈϨⲢⲀⲒ ⲈⲢⲞⲒ ⲈⲦⲢⲀⲂⲞⲎⲐⲒ ⲈⲢⲞⲤ·
ⲀⲤϢⲰⲠⲈ ϬⲈ ⲚⲦⲈⲢⲈⲤϬⲰϢⲦ ⲈⲠϪⲒⲤⲈ ⲀⲤⲚⲀⲨ ⲈⲠⲀⲨ-
ⲐⲀⲀⲎⲤ ⲈϤϬⲞⲚⲦ ⲈⲘⲀϢⲞ· ⲀⲨⲰ ⲀⲤⲢϨⲞⲦⲈ· ⲀⲤϪⲰ Ⲛ-
ⲦⲘⲈϨⲘⲚⲦⲤⲚⲞⲞⲨⲤ ⲘⲘⲈⲦⲀⲚⲞⲒⲀ ⲈⲦⲂⲈ ⲠⲀⲨⲐⲀⲀⲎⲤ ⲘⲚ ϥⲁ b
ⲚⲈϤⲠⲢⲞⲂⲞⲖⲞⲞⲨⲈ ⲀⲤⲰϢ ⲀⲈ ⲈϨⲢⲀⲒ ⲞⲨⲂⲎⲒ ⲈⲤϪⲰ Ⲙ-
20　ⲘⲞⲤ ⲚⲦⲈⲒϨⲈ ϪⲈ

　　1. ⲘⲠⲢⲞⲂϢⲔ ⲠⲞⲨⲞⲈⲒⲚ ⲈⲠⲀϨⲨⲘⲚⲞⲤ·

　　2. ϪⲈ ⲀⲨⲞⲨⲰⲚ ⲚⲢⲰⲞⲨ ⲈϨⲢⲀⲒ ⲈϪⲰⲒ ⲚϬⲒ ⲠⲀⲨⲐⲀ-
ⲀⲎⲤ ⲘⲚ ⲦⲈϤϬⲞⲘ ⲚⲌⲞ ⲘⲘⲞⲨⲒ ⲀⲨⲢⲔⲢⲞϤ ⲈⲢⲞⲒ·

1　MS originally ⲚⲦⲈⲢⲞ ; ⲦⲘⲚⲦⲈ inserted in margins.
6　ⲀⲨⲰ added in margins.

55. Jesus, *however*, continued again with the discourse. He said to his disciples : "It happened now after these things I entered into the *Chaos*, shining exceedingly, in order that I might take away the light of that lion-faced power. As I was of exceeding light, it was afraid, it cried out to its deity, Authades, to *help* it. And at that hour the deity Authades looked forth from the thirteenth *aeon*, he looked down upon the *Chaos*. He was exceedingly angry, wishing to *help* his lion-faced power. And at that hour the lion-faced power and all its *emanations* turned to the Pistis Sophia, wishing to take away all the light which was in the Sophia. It happened now when they oppressed the Sophia, she cried out to the height, she cried out to me, that I should *help* her. Now it happened when she looked to the height, she saw the Authades who was very angry, and she was afraid. She said the twelfth *repentance* because of the Authades and his *emanations*. *But* she cried out to me, saying thus :

1. 'O Light, forget not my *song of praise*.

2. For the Authades and his lion-faced power opened their mouths against me, they dealt cunningly with me. |

3. ⲀⲨⲰ ⲀⲨⲔⲰⲦⲈ ⲈⲢⲞⲒ̈ ⲈⲨⲞⲨⲈϢϤⲒ ⲚⲦⲀϬⲞⲘ ⲀⲨⲰ
ⲀⲨⲘⲈⲤⲦⲰⲒ̈ ϪⲈ ⲀⲒ̈ⲤⲨⲘⲚⲈⲨⲈ ⲈⲢⲞⲔ·

4. ⲈⲠⲘⲀ ⲚⲤⲈⲘⲈⲢⲒⲦ· ⲀⲨⲆⲒⲀⲂⲀⲖⲈ ⲘⲘⲞⲒ̈· ⲀⲚⲞⲔ ⲆⲈ
ⲚⲈⲒ̈ⲤⲨⲘⲚⲈⲨⲈ ⲠⲈ·

5 5. ⲀⲨϢⲞϪⲚⲈ ⲈⲦⲢⲈⲨϤⲒ ⲚⲦⲀϬⲞⲘ ϪⲈ ⲀⲒ̈ⲤⲨⲘⲚⲈⲨⲈ
ⲈⲢⲞⲔ ⲠⲞⲨⲞⲒ̈Ⲛ· ⲀⲨⲰ ⲀⲨⲘⲈⲤⲦⲰⲒ̈ ϪⲈ ⲀⲒ̈ⲘⲈⲢⲒⲦⲔ·

6. ⲘⲀⲢⲈ ⲠⲔⲀⲔⲈ ⲈⲒ̓ ⲈϨⲢⲀⲒ̈ ⲈϪⲘ ⲠⲀⲨⲐⲀⲆⲎⲤ· ⲀⲨⲰ
ⲘⲀⲢⲈϤϬⲰ ϨⲒ ⲞⲨⲚⲀⲘ ⲘⲘⲞϤ ⲚϬⲒ ⲠⲀⲢⲬⲰⲚ ⲘⲠⲔⲀⲔⲈ ⲈⲦ-
ϨⲒⲂⲞⲖ·

10 7. ⲀⲨⲰ ϨⲘ ⲠⲦⲢⲈⲔ†ϨⲀⲠ ⲈⲢⲞϤ·⁺⁺ϤⲒ ⲚⲦⲈϤϬⲞⲘ ⲚϨⲎⲦϤ· ⳡⲉ
ⲀⲨⲰ ⲪⲰⲂ ⲈⲚⲦⲀϤⲘⲈⲈⲨⲈ ⲈⲢⲞϤ ⲈϤⲒ ⲠⲀⲞⲨⲞⲒ̈Ⲛ ⲚϨⲎⲦ·
ⲈⲔⲈϤⲒ-ⲠⲰϤ ⲚϨⲎⲦϤ·

8. ⲀⲨⲰ ⲘⲀⲢⲞⲨⲰϪⲚ ⲚϬⲒ ⲚⲈϤϬⲞⲘ ⲦⲎⲢⲞⲨ ⲚⲦⲈ ⲚⲈϤ-
ⲞⲨⲞⲒ̈Ⲛ ⲈⲦⲚϨⲎⲦϤ· ⲀⲨⲰ ⲘⲀⲢⲈ ⲔⲈⲞⲨⲀ ϪⲒ ⲚⲦⲈϤⲘⲚⲦ-
15 ⲚⲞϬ ϨⲘ ⲠϢⲞⲘⲦ ⲚⲦⲢⲒⲆⲨⲚⲀⲘⲞⲤ·

9. ⲘⲀⲢⲞⲨⲢ-ⲀⲦⲞⲨⲞⲒ̈Ⲛ ⲚϬⲒ ⲚϬⲞⲘ ⲦⲎⲢⲞⲨ ⲚⲦⲈ ⲚⲈϤ-
ⲠⲢⲞⲂⲞⲖⲞⲞⲨⲈ· ⲀⲨⲰ ⲚⲦⲈ ⲦⲈϤϨⲨⲖⲎ ϢⲰⲠⲈ ⲈⲘⲚ-ⲞⲨⲞⲒ̈Ⲛ
ⲚϨⲎⲦⲤ·

10. ⲘⲀⲢⲈ ⲚⲈϤⲠⲢⲞⲂⲞⲖⲞⲞⲨⲈ ϬⲰ ϨⲘ ⲠⲈⲬⲖⲀⲞⲤ· ⲚⲤⲈ-
20 ⲦⲘⲔⲀⲀⲨ ⲈⲂⲰⲔ ⲈⲠⲈⲨⲦⲞⲠⲞⲤ· ⲘⲀⲢⲈ ⲠⲈⲨⲞⲨⲞⲈⲒⲚ ⲰϪⲚ
ⲈⲦⲚϨⲎⲦⲞⲨ ⲀⲨⲰ ⲘⲠⲢⲦⲢⲈⲨⲔⲀⲀⲨ ⲈⲂⲰⲔ ⲈϨⲢⲀⲒ̈ ⲈⲠⲘⲈϨ-
ⲘⲚⲦϢⲞⲘⲦⲈ ⲚⲀⲒⲰⲚ ⲠⲈⲨⲦⲞⲠⲞⲤ·

11. ⲘⲀⲢⲈϤⲤⲰⲦϤ ⲚⲚⲞⲨⲞⲒ̈Ⲛ ⲦⲎⲢⲞⲨ ⲈⲦϢⲞⲞⲠ ϨⲘ ⲠⲀⲨ-
ⲐⲀⲆⲎⲤ ⲚϬⲒ ⲠⲠⲀⲢⲀⲖⲎⲘⲦⲎⲤ ⲠⲢⲈϤⲤⲰⲦϤ ⲚⲚⲞⲨⲞⲒ̈Ⲛ· ⲀⲨⲰ ⳡⲉ ᵇ
25 ⲘⲀⲢⲈϤϤⲒⲦⲞⲨ ⲚⲦⲞⲞⲦⲞⲨ·

12. ⲘⲀⲢⲞⲨⲀⲘⲀϨⲦⲈ ⲈϪⲚ ⲚⲈϤⲠⲢⲞⲂⲞⲖⲞⲞⲨⲈ ⲚϬⲒ ⲚⲀⲢ-
ⲬⲰⲚ ⲘⲠⲔⲀⲔⲈ ⲘⲠⲈⲤⲎⲦ· ⲀⲨⲰ ⲘⲠⲢⲦⲢⲈ ⲖⲀⲀⲨ ϢⲞⲠϤ

24　MS ⲦⲠⲞⲨⲞⲒ̈Ⲛ; read ⲚⲞⲨⲞⲒ̈Ⲛ.

3. And they surrounded me, wishing to take away my power; and they hated me because I *sang praises* to thee.

4. Instead of loving me, they *slandered* me, *but* I *sang praises*.

5. They planned to take away my power because I *sang praises* to thee, O Light. And they hated me because I loved thee.

6. Let the darkness come over the Authades, and may the *archon* of the outer darkness remain at his right hand.

7. And when thou dost judge him, take his power away from him; and that which he thought — to take away my light from me — do thou take his from him.

8. And may all his powers of his light [1] within him diminish; and may another one take his greatness in the three *triple-powered ones*.

9. May all the powers of his *emanations* become without light; and may his *matter* be without light in it.

10. May his *emanations* remain in the *Chaos*, and may they not be allowed to go to their *place*; may their light which is in them diminish, and let them not be allowed to go up to the thirteenth *aeon*, their *place*.

11. May the *paralemptes*, the purifier of the lights, purify all the lights which are in the Authades; and may he take them from them.

12. May the *archons* of the darkness below rule over his *emanations*, and let not anyone receive him | to himself in

---

[1] (13, 14) all his powers of his light; lit. all his powers of his lights.

ЄΡΟЧ 2Μ ΠЄЧΤΟΠΟС · ΑΥѠ ΜΠΡΤΡЄ ΛΑΑΥ СѠΤΜ
ЄΤ6ΟΜ ΝΝЄЧΠΡΟΒΟΛΟΟΥЄ 2Μ ΠЄΧΛΟС ·

13. ΜΑΡΟΥЧΙ-ΠΟΥΟΪΝ ЄΤ2Ν ΝЄЧΠΡΟΒΟΛΟΟΥЄ ΑΥѠ
ΝСЄΛΑ6Є ЄΠЄΥΡΑΝ 2ΡΑΪ 2Μ ΠΜЄ2ΜΝΤϢΟΜΤЄ ΝΑΙѠΝ ·
5 ΝΤΟЧ 2ѠѠЧ ΝСЄЧΙ-ΠЄЧΡΑΝ ЄΒΟΛ 2Μ ΠΤΟΠΟС ЄΤΜ-
ΜΑΥ ϢΑ ЄΝЄ2 ·

14. ΑΥѠ Τ6ΟΜ Ν2Ο ΜΜΟΥΪ ΜΑΡΟΥЄΙΝЄ Є2ΡΑΪ ЄΧѠС
ΜΠΝΟΒЄ ΜΠЄΝΤΑЧΠΡΟΒΑΛЄ ΜΜΟС ЄΒΟΛ · ΜΠЄΜΤΟ
ЄΒΟΛ ΜΠΟΥΟЄΙΝ · ΝСЄΤΜЧѠΤЄ ЄΒΟΛ ΝΤΑΝΟΜΙΑ Ν-
10 ΘΥΛΗ ЄΝΤΑСΤΑΥΟЧ ЄΒΟΛ ·

15. ᵃ*ΑΥѠ ΠЄΥΝΟΒЄ 2Ι ΟΥСΟΠ ЄЧЄϢѠΠЄ ΜΠЄΜΤΟ 9Є̄
ЄΒΟΛ ΜΠΟΥΟΪΝ ΝϢΑЄΝЄ2 · ΑΥѠ ΝСЄΤΜΚΑΑΥ ЄΝΑΥ
ЄΒΟΛ · ΝСЄЧΙ-ΠЄΥΡΑΝ 2Ν ΤΟΠΟС ΝΙΜ ·

16. ЄΒΟΛ ΧЄ ΜΠΟΥϯСΟ ЄΡΟΪ · ΑΥѠ ΑΥ2ѠΧ ΜΠЄΝΤ-
15 ΑΥЧΙ-ΠЄЧΟΥΟΪΝ · ΜΝ ΤЄЧ6ΟΜ · ΑΥѠ ΟΝ ΜΝΝСΑ ΝЄΝ-
ΤΑΥΧΟΪ Ν2ΗΤΟΥ · ΑΥΟΥЄϢЧΙ-ΠΛΟΥΟΪΝ ΤΗΡЧ Ν2ΗΤ ·

17. ΑΥΜЄΡЄ-ЄΙᵎ ЄΠЄСΗΤ ЄΠЄΧΛΟС · ЄΥЄϢѠΠЄ Ν2Η-
ΤЧ · ΑΥѠ ΝΝЄЧΝΤΟΥ Є2ΡΑΪ ΧΙΝ ΜΠЄΪΝΑΥ ΜΠΟΥЄϢ-
ΠΜΑΝϢѠΠЄ ΜΠΤΟΠΟС ΝΤΑΙΚΑΙΟСΥΝΗ ΑΥѠ ΝΝЄΥ-
20 ΧΙΤΟΥ ЄΡΟЧ ΧΙΝ ΜΠЄΪΝΑΥ ·

18. ΑЧϯ-ΠΚΑΚЄ 2ΙѠѠЧ ΝΘЄ ΝΟΥЄΝΑΥΜΑ ΑΥѠ ΑЧ-
ΒѠΚ Є2ΟΥΝ Є2ΗΤЧ ΝΘЄ ΝΟΥΜΟΟΥ · ΑΥѠ ΑЧΒѠΚ
Є2ΟΥΝ ЄΝЄЧ6ΟΜ ΤΗΡΟΥ ΝΘЄ ΝΟΥΝЄ2 ·

19. *ΜΑΡЄЧ6ΟΟΛЄЧ ΜΠЄΧΛΟС ΝΘЄ ΝΟΥ2ΟΪΤЄ · ΑΥѠ 9Є̄ᵇ
25 ΝЧΜΟΡЄЧ ΜΠΚΑΚЄ ΝΘЄ ΝΟΥΝ2ѠΝΗ ΝϢΑΑΡ ΝΟΥΟЄΙϢ
ΝΙΜ ·

---

18 MS ΝΝЄЧΝΤΟΥ; read ΠΝЄΥΝΤΟΥ. MS ΜΠΟΥЄϢ; read ΜΠΟΥΟΥЄϢ.

his *place*; and let not anyone hear the power of his *emanations* in the *Chaos*.

13. May the light which is in his *emanations* be taken away, and may their name be removed from the thirteenth *aeon*; indeed rather may his name be taken away from that *place* for ever.

14. And upon the lion-faced power, may there be brought the sin of him who *emanated* it in the presence of the light; and may the *iniquity* of the *matter* which brought him (the Authades) forth not be erased.

15. And may their sin immediately be in the presence of the eternal light [1]; and may they not be allowed to see, and may their name be removed from every *place*;

16. Because they did not spare me, and they oppressed the one whose light and power they took away. And afterwards they put me among them, wishing to take [2] away all my light from me.

17. They loved to come down to the *Chaos*; may they be within it, and not be brought forth from this time hence. They did not want the *place* of *righteousness* as dwelling place, and they will not be taken to it from this time forth.

18. He put on the darkness like a garment; and it (the darkness) went into him like water, and it went into all his powers like oil.

19. May he wrap himself in the *Chaos* like a *garment*, and gird himself with the darkness like a leather *girdle* at all times. |

---

[1] (12) in the presence of the eternal light; Schmidt: in the presence of the light eternally.

[2] (15, 16) they put me among them, wishing to take; or: those who put me among them wished to take.

20. ⲈⲢⲈ ⲚⲀⲒ ϢⲰⲠⲈ ⲚⲚⲈⲚⲦⲀⲨⲚ-ⲚⲀⲒ ⲈⲬⲰⲒ ⲈⲦⲂⲈ ⲠⲞⲨ-
ⲞⲒⲚ · ⲀⲨⲰ ⲚⲈⲚⲦⲀⲨⲬⲞⲞⲤ ⲬⲈ ⲘⲀⲢⲚϤⲒ-ⲦⲈⲤϬⲞⲘ ⲦⲎⲢⲤ ·

21. ⲚⲦⲞⲔ ⲆⲈ ⲠⲞⲨⲞⲒⲚ ϢⲚ2ⲦⲎⲔ 2ⲀⲢⲞⲒ ⲈⲦⲂⲈ ⲠⲘⲨⲤ-
ⲦⲎⲢⲒⲞⲚ ⲘⲠⲈⲔⲢⲀⲚ · ⲀⲨⲰ ⲚⲀ2ⲘⲈⲦ 2Ⲛ ⲦⲘⲚⲦⲬⲢⲤ ⲚⲦⲈ
5 ⲠⲈⲔⲚⲀ ·

22. ⲈⲂⲞⲖ ⲬⲈ ⲀⲨϤⲒ-ⲠⲀⲞⲨⲞⲒⲚ ⲘⲚ ⲦⲀϬⲞⲘ · ⲀⲨⲰ Ⲁ
ⲦⲀϬⲞⲘ ⲤⲀⲖⲈⲨⲈ 2Ⲓ2ⲞⲨⲚ ⲘⲘⲞⲒ · ⲀⲨⲰ ⲘⲠⲒϢⲀ2ⲈⲢⲀⲦ 2Ⲛ
ⲦⲈⲨⲘⲎⲦⲈ ·

23. ⲀⲒⲢ̄ⲐⲈ ⲚⲞⲨ2ⲨⲖⲎ ⲈⲀⲤ2Ⲉ · ⲀⲨⲚⲞⲨⲬⲈ ⲘⲘⲞⲒ ⲈⲠⲒⲤⲀ
10 ⲘⲚ ⲠⲀⲒ ⲚⲐⲈ ⲚⲞⲨⲢⲈϤϢⲞⲞⲢ ⲈϤ2Ⲛ ⲠⲀⲎⲢ ·

24. Ⲁ ⲦⲀϬⲞⲘ ⲦⲀⲔⲞ ⲬⲈ ⲘⲚⲦⲀⲒ-ⲘⲨⲤⲦⲎⲢⲒⲞⲚ ⲘⲘⲀⲨ ·
ⲀⲨⲰ Ⲁ ⲦⲀ2ⲨⲖⲎ 2ⲰⲔⲘ ⲈⲦⲂⲈ ⲠⲀⲞⲨⲞⲒⲚ ⲬⲈ ⲀⲨϤⲒⲦϤ ·

25. ⲀⲨⲰ ⲀⲚⲞⲔ ⲚⲈⲨⲤⲔⲰⲠⲦⲈ ⲘⲘⲞⲒ ⲠⲈ · ϢⲀⲨϬⲰϢⲦ ⳗ⳽
ⲈⲢⲞⲒ ⲈⲨⲬⲰⲢⲘ ⲈⲢⲞⲒ ·

15 26. ⲂⲞⲎⲐⲒ ⲈⲢⲞⲒ ⲔⲀⲦⲀ ⲦⲈⲔⲘⲚⲦϢⲀⲚ2ⲦⲎϤ ·

ⲦⲈⲚⲞⲨ ϬⲈ ⲠⲈⲦⲈⲢⲈ ⲠⲈϤ̄Ⲡ̄Ⲛ̄Ⲁ̄ ⲢⲞⲞⲨⲦ · ⲘⲀⲢⲈϤⲈⲒ ' ⲈⲐⲎ
ⲚϤⲬⲈ-ⲠⲂⲰⲖ ⲚⲦⲘⲈ2ⲘⲚⲦⲤⲚⲞⲞⲨⲤ ⲘⲘⲈⲦⲀⲚⲞⲒⲀ ⲚⲦⲠⲒⲤ-
ⲦⲒⲤ ⲤⲞⲪⲒⲀ · ⲀϤⲈⲒ' ⲆⲈ ⲈⲐⲎ ⲚϬⲒ ⲀⲚⲆⲢⲈⲀⲤ ⲠⲈⲬⲀϤ ⲬⲈ
ⲠⲀⲬⲞⲒⲤ ⲠⲤⲰⲦⲎⲢ Ⲁ ⲦⲈⲔϬⲞⲘ ⲚⲞⲨⲞⲒⲚ ⲠⲢⲞⲪⲎⲦⲈⲨⲈ Ⲙ-
20 ⲠⲒⲞⲨⲞⲒϢ 2ⲒⲦⲚ ⲆⲀⲨⲈⲒⲆ · ⲈⲦⲂⲈ ⲦⲈⲒⲘⲈⲦⲀⲚⲞⲒⲀ ⲈⲚⲦⲀⲤ-
ⲬⲞⲞⲤ ⲚϬⲒ ⲦⲠⲒⲤⲦⲒⲤ ⲤⲞⲪⲒⲀ · ⲀⲨⲰ ⲀⲤⲬⲞⲞⲤ 2Ⲙ ⲠⲘⲈ2-
ϢⲈ ⲘⲚ ϢⲘⲞⲨⲚ ⲘⲮⲀⲖⲘⲞⲤ ⲬⲈ

1. ⲠⲚⲞⲨⲦⲈ ⲘⲠⲢⲔⲀⲢⲰⲔ ⲈⲠⲀⲤⲘⲞⲨ ·

2. ⲬⲈ ⲦⲦⲀⲠⲢⲞ ⲘⲠⲢⲈϤⲢⲚⲞⲂⲈ ⲘⲚ ⲠⲈⲔⲢⲞϤ · ⲀⲨⲞⲨⲰⲚ

---

5   MS originally ⲠⲈⲔⲠ̄Ⲛ̄Ⲁ̄; ⲛ crossed out.

20. While these things happen to those who brought these things upon me on account of the light; and they said : let us take away all her power.

21. *But* thou, O Light, have compassion on me, on account of the *mystery* of thy name; and save me in the *beneficence* of thy mercy.

22. Because they have taken away my light and my power, and my power is *shaken* within me, and I have not been able to stand upright in their midst,

23. I have become like *matter* which has fallen; I have been cast on this side and that, like a demon which is in the *air*.

24. My power has been destroyed, for I possess no *mystery*; and my *matter* has faded because of my light, for they took it away.

25. And as for me, they *mocked* me; they looked at me as they winked about me.

26. *Help* me according to thy compassion.'

Now at this time, he whose *spirit* is eager, let him come forward and say the interpretation of the twelfth *repentance* of the Pistis Sophia."

56.   Andrew *however* came forward, he said : "My Lord and *Saviour*, thy light-power *prophesied* once, through David, concerning this *repentance* which the Pistis Sophia said, and spoke in the 108th *Psalm*, saying :

1. 'O God, do not be silent to my praise.

2. For the mouths of the sinner and the cunning, they have opened | against me; they have spoken about me with a cunning tongue.

215

ⲚⲢⲰⲞⲨ ⲈⲈⲢⲀⲒ ⲈⲖⲰⲒ · ⲀⲨⲰϪⲀϪⲈ ⲚⲤⲰⲒ ⲈⲚ ⲞⲨⲖⲀⲤ Ⲛ-
ⲔⲢⲞϤ ·

3. ⲀⲨⲰ ϢⲀⲨⲔⲰⲦⲈ ⲈⲢⲞⲒ ⲈⲚ ⲈⲈⲚϢⲀϪⲈ ⲘⲘⲞⲤⲦⲈ · ϥⲍ ᵇ
ⲀⲨⲰ ⲀⲨⲘⲒϢⲈ ⲚⲘⲘⲀⲒ ⲈⲠϪⲒⲚϪⲎ ·

5 4. ⲈⲠⲘⲀ ⲚⲤⲈⲘⲈⲢⲒⲦ · ⲀⲨⲆⲒⲀⲂⲀⲖⲈ ⲘⲘⲞⲒ · ⲀⲚⲞⲔ ⲆⲈ
ⲚⲈⲒϢⲖⲎⲖ ⲠⲈ ·

5. ⲀⲨⲤⲘⲒⲚⲈ ⲚⲞⲨⲎⲒ ⲚⲈⲈⲚⲠⲈⲐⲞⲞⲨ ⲈⲠⲘⲀ ⲚⲈⲈⲚⲠⲈⲦ-
ⲚⲀⲚⲞⲨⲞⲨ · ⲀⲨⲰ ⲞⲨⲘⲞⲤⲦⲈ ⲈⲠⲘⲀ ⲚⲦⲀⲀⲄⲀⲠⲎ ·

6. ⲔⲀⲐⲒⲤⲦⲀ ⲚⲞⲨⲢⲈϤⲢⲚⲞⲂⲈ ⲈⲈⲢⲀⲒ ⲈⲖⲰϤ · ⲀⲨⲰ ⲘⲀⲢⲈ
10 ⲠⲆⲒⲀⲂⲞⲖⲞⲤ ⲀⲈⲈⲢⲀⲦϤ ⲈⲒ ⲞⲨⲚⲀⲘ ⲘⲘⲞϤ ·

7. ⲈⲨϢⲀⲚⲦⲈⲀⲠ ⲈⲢⲞϤ · ⲘⲀⲢⲈϤ⟨ⲈⲒ⟩ ⲈⲂⲞⲖ ⲈϤⲦⲞⲖⲎⲨ ·
ⲀⲨⲰ ⲘⲀⲢⲈ ⲠⲈϤϢⲖⲎⲖ ϢⲰⲠⲈ ⲈⲨⲚⲞⲂⲈ ·

8. ⲘⲀⲢⲈ ⲚⲈϤⲞⲞⲨ ⲤⲂⲞⲔ ⲀⲨⲰ ⲘⲀⲢⲈ ⲔⲈⲞⲨⲀ ϪⲒ Ⲛ-
ⲦⲈϤⲘⲚⲦⲈⲠⲒⲤⲔⲞⲠⲞⲤ ·

15 9. ⲘⲀⲢⲈ ⲚⲈϤϢⲎⲢⲈ ⲢⲞⲢⲪⲀⲚⲞⲤ · ⲀⲨⲰ ⲘⲀⲢⲈ ⲦⲈϤⲤⲈⲒⲘⲈ
ⲢⲬⲎⲢⲀ ·

10. ⲘⲀⲢⲞⲨⲔⲒⲘ ⲈⲚⲈϤϢⲎⲢⲈ · ⲀⲨⲰ ⲘⲀⲢⲞⲨⲠⲞⲞⲚⲞⲨ
ⲈⲂⲞⲖ ⲚⲤⲈⲦⲰⲂⲈ · ⲘⲀⲢⲞⲨⲚⲞϪⲞⲨ ⲈⲂⲞⲖ ⲈⲚ ⲚⲈⲨⲎⲒ ·

11. ⲘⲀⲢⲈ ⲠⲆⲀⲚⲒⲤⲦⲎⲤ ⲘⲈϢⲦ-ⲚⲈⲦϢⲞⲞⲠ ⲚⲀϤ ⲦⲎⲢⲞⲨ · ϥⲏ ᵇ
20 ⲀⲨⲰ ⲘⲀⲢⲈ ⲈⲈⲚϢⲘⲘⲞ ⲦⲰⲢⲠ ⲚⲚⲈϤⲈⲒⲤⲈ ⲦⲎⲢⲞⲨ ·

12. ⲘⲠⲢⲦⲢⲈϤϢⲰⲠⲈ ⲚϬⲒ ⲠⲈⲦⲚⲀⲦⲦⲞⲞⲦϤ · ⲞⲨⲆⲈ ⲘⲠⲢ-
ⲦⲢⲈ ϢⲀⲚⲈⲦⲎϤ ϢⲰⲠⲈ ⲚⲚⲈϤⲞⲢⲪⲀⲚⲞⲤ ·

13. ⲘⲀⲢⲞⲨϬⲈⲦ-ⲚⲈϤϢⲎⲢⲈ ⲈⲂⲞⲖ ⲀⲨⲰ ⲘⲀⲢⲞⲨϬⲈⲦ-ⲠⲈϤ-
ⲢⲀⲚ ⲈⲂⲞⲖ ⲈⲚ ⲞⲨⲄⲈⲚⲈⲀ ⲚⲞⲨⲰⲦ ·

---

7   MS ⲚⲞⲨⲎⲒ; read ⲞⲨⲎⲒ.
11 MS ⲘⲀⲢⲈϤ; read ⲘⲀⲢⲈϤⲈⲒ.
19 MS ⲚⲈⲦⲚⲈⲦϢⲞⲞⲠ.

3. And they surround me with words of hatred; and they have fought against me without a cause.

4. Instead of loving me, they *slandered* me, *but* I prayed.

5. They established for me evil in the place of good, and hatred in the place of my *love*.

6. *Set* a sinner over him, and let the *devil* stand at his right hand.

7. When he is judged, may he come forth condemned, and may his prayer become sin.

8. May his days be diminished, and may another take his *office*.

9. May his sons become *orphans*, and may his wife become a *widow*.

10. May his sons be moved, and may they be turned out and beg; may they be cast forth from their house.

11. May the *creditor* search all his belongings; and may strangers rob all his efforts.

12. May there not exist for him anyone who gives him a hand, *or* who is compassionate to his *orphans*.

13. May his sons be blotted out; and may his name be blotted out in one *generation*. |

14. ΜΑΡΟΥⲢΠΜⲈⲈΥⲈ ⲘΠΝΟΒⲈ ⲚΝⲈϤⲤΙΟΤⲈ ⲘΠⲈΜΤΟ
ⲈΒΟⲖ ⲘΠΧΟⲈΙⲤ · ⲀΥⲰ ⲘⲠⲢΤΡⲈΥϤⲰΤⲈ ⲈΒΟⲖ ⲚΤⲀΝΟ-
ΜΙⲀ ⲚΤⲈϤΜⲀⲀΥ ·

15. ΜΑΡΟΥϢⲰΠⲈ ⲘΠⲈΜΤΟ ⲈΒΟⲖ ⲘΠΧΟⲈΙⲤ ⲚΟΥΟΪϢ
5 ΝΙΜ · ΜΑΡΟΥΧⲈΡⲈ-ΠⲈϤⲢΠΜⲈⲈΥⲈ ⲈΒΟⲖ ⳨Μ ΠΚⲀⳞ ·

16. ⲈΠΜⲀ ΧⲈ ⲘΠϤⲢΠΜⲈⲈΥⲈ ⲈⲈΙΡⲈ ⲚΟΥΝⲀ' · ⲀΥⲰ
ⲀϤΠⲰΤ ⲚⲤⲀ ΟΥΡⲰΜⲈ ⲚⳞΗΚⲈ · ⲀΥⲰ ⲚⲈΒΙΗΝ · ⲀΥϤ-
ⲀΙⲰΚⲈ ⲚⲤⲀ ΟΥⲀ' ⲈϤΜΟΚⳞ ⲚⳞΗΤ · ⲈΜΟΟΥΤϤ ·   ϤΗ ᵇ

17. ⲀϤΜⲈΡⲈ-ΠⲤⲀⳞΟΥ ⲀΥⲰ ⲈϤⲈⲈΙ' ΝⲀϤ · ⲘΠϤΟΥⲈϢ-
10 ΠⲈⲤΜΟΥ ⲈϤⲈΟΥⲈ ⲈΒΟⲖ ⲘΜΟϤ ·

18. ⲀϤ†-ΠⲤⲀⳞΟΥ ⳞΙⲰⲰϤ ⲚΟⳞ ⲚΟΥϢΤΗΝ · ⲀΥⲰ ⲀϤ-
ΒⲰΚ ⲈΝⲈϤⲤⲀΝⳞΟΥΝ ⲚΟⳞ ⲚΟΥΜΟΟΥ · ⲀϤⲢΟⳞ ⲚΟΥΝⲈⳞ
⳨Ν ΝⲈϤΚⲈⲈⲤ ·

19. ΜΑΡⲈϤϢⲰΠⲈ ΝⲀϤ ⲚΟⳞ ⲚΟΒⲤⲰ ⲈΤϤΝⲀⳞΟΟⲖⲈϤ
15 ⲘΜΟϤ · ⲀΥⲰ ⲚΟⳞ ⲚΟΥⲚⳞⲰΝΗ ⲈϤΝⲀΜΟⲢϤ ⲘΜΟⲤ ⲚΟΥ-
ΟΪϢ ΝΙΜ ·

20. ΠⲀΪ ΠⲈ ϤⲰΒ ⲚΝⲈΤⲀΙⲀΒⲀⲖⲈ ⟨ⲘΜΟΪ⟩ ⳞⲀⲦΜ ΠΧΟΪⲤ
ⲀΥⲰ ΝⲈΤΧⲰ ⲚⳞⲈΝΠⲀΡⲀΝΟΜΟΝ ⲈⳞΟΥΝ ⲈΤⲀΨΥΧΗ ·

21. ⲚΤΟΚ ⲆⲈ ΠΧΟⲈΙⲤ ΠΧΟⲈΙⲤ ⲀΡΙ-ΟΥΝⲀ' ⲚΜΜⲀΪ
20 ⲈΤΒⲈ ΠⲈΚΡⲀΝ · ΜⲀΤΟΥΧΟΪ ·

22. ΧⲈ ⲀⲚⳠ ΟΥⳞΗΚⲈ ⲀΥⲰ ⲀⲚⳠ ΟΥⲈΒΙΗΝ · Ⲁ ΠⲀⳞΗΤ
ϢΤΟⲢⲦⲢ ⲘΠⲀⲤⲀΝⳞΟΥΝ ·

23. ⲀΥϤΙΤ ⲚΤΜΗΤⲈ ⲚΟⳞ Ⲛ[Ν]ΟΥⳞⲀΪΒⲈⲤ ⲈⲀⲤΡΙΚⲈ · ⲀΥ-
ΝΟϢⲚΤ ⲈΒΟⲖ ⲚΟⳞ ⲚⳞⲈΝϢΧⲈ ·

---

15 MS ⲘΜΟϤ; read ⲘΜΟⲤ.
17 supply ⲘΜΟΪ.
23 MS ⲚΝΟΥⳞⲀΪΒⲈⲤ; ΟΥ inserted; read ⲚΟΥⳞⲀΪΒⲈⲤ.
24 MS ΝΟϢⲚΤ; read ΝΟϢⲠΤ; see Crum 236b.

14. May the sin of his fathers be remembered in the presence of the Lord; and let not the *iniquity* of his mother be blotted out.

15. May they be in the presence of the Lord at all times; and may his memory be wiped out from the earth.

16. Because he did not remember to show mercy; and he pursued a poor man and a wretched one, and he *persecuted* one who was afflicted, to kill him.

17. He loved cursing and may it come to him; he did not wish to bless and may it be removed from him.

18. He put on cursing like a garment, and it went to his interior like water; it became like oil in his bones.

19. May it be to him like the garment with which he will wrap himself; and like a *girdle* with which he will gird himself at all times.

20. This is the dealing for those that *slander* me before the Lord, and those that speak *lawless things* into my *soul*.

21. *But* thou, O Lord, Lord show mercy on me, on account of thy name; save me.

22. For I am a poor man and I am a wretched one; my heart is agitated within me.

23. I have been taken into the midst like a shadow which goes down; I am blown forth like locusts. |

24. ⲁ ⲛⲁⲡⲁⲧ ϭ̅ⲃ̅ⲃ̅ⲉ̅ ϩ̅ⲛ̅ ⲧⲛⲏⲥⲧⲓⲁ· ⲁⲩⲱ ⲁ ⲧⲁⲥⲁⲣⲝ̅ ϥ̅ⲑ̅ ϣⲓⲃⲉ ⲉⲧⲃⲉ ⲡⲛⲉϩ·

25. ⲁⲛⲟⲕ ⲇⲉ ⲁⲓ̈ϣⲱⲡⲉ ⲛⲁⲩ ⲛ̅ⲛⲟϭⲛⲉϭ· ⲁⲩⲛⲁⲩ ⲉⲣⲟⲓ̈ ⲁⲩⲱ ⲁⲩⲕⲓⲙ ⲛ̅ⲛⲉⲩⲁⲡⲏⲩⲉ·

26. ⲃⲟⲏⲑⲓ ⲉⲣⲟⲓ̈ ⲡϫⲟⲉⲓⲥ ⲡⲛⲟⲩⲧⲉ ⲁⲩⲱ ⲧⲟⲩϫⲟⲓ̈ ⲕⲁⲧⲁ ⲡⲉⲕⲛⲁ'·

27. ⲙⲁⲣⲟⲩⲉⲓⲙⲉ ϫⲉ ⲧⲁⲓ̈ ⲧⲉ ⲧⲉⲕϭⲓϫ· ⲁⲩⲱ ⲛ̅ⲧⲟⲕ ⲁⲕⲧⲁⲙⲓⲟⲥ ⲡϫⲟⲉⲓⲥ·

ⲡⲁⲓ̈ ϭⲉ ⲡⲉ ⲡⲃⲱⲗ ⲛ̅ⲧⲙⲉϩⲙ̅ⲛ̅ⲧ̅ⲥⲛⲟⲟⲩⲥ ⲙ̅ⲙⲉⲧⲁⲛⲟⲓ̈ⲁ· ⲧⲁⲓ̈ ⲉⲛⲧⲁⲥϫⲟ⟨ⲟ⟩ⲥ ⲛ̅ϭⲓ ⲧⲡⲓⲥⲧⲓⲥ ⲥⲟⲫⲓⲁ ⲉⲥϩ̅ⲙ̅ ⲡⲉⲭⲁⲟⲥ· ⲁϥⲟⲩⲱϩ ⲇⲉ ⲟⲛ ⲉⲧⲟⲟⲧϥ̅ ⲛ̅ϭⲓ ⲓ̅ⲥ̅ ϩ̅ⲙ̅ ⲡϣⲁϫⲉ ⲡⲉϫⲁϥ ⲛ̅ⲛⲉϥⲙⲁⲑⲏⲧⲏⲥ· ϫⲉ ⲁⲥϣⲱⲡⲉ ⲟⲛ ⲙ̅ⲛ̅ⲛ̅ⲥⲁ ⲛⲁⲓ̈ ⲁⲥⲱϣ ⲉϩⲣⲁⲓ̈ ⲟⲩⲏⲓ̈ ⲛ̅ϭⲓ ⲧⲡⲓⲥⲧⲓⲥ ⲥⲟⲫⲓⲁ ⲉⲥϫⲱ̅ ⲙ̅ⲙⲟⲥ ϫⲉ ⲡⲟⲩⲟⲓ̈ⲛ ⲛ̅ⲛ̅ⲟⲩⲟⲓ̈ⲛ ⲛ̅ⲧⲁⲓ̈ⲡⲁⲣⲁⲃⲁ ϩ̅ⲙ̅ ⲡⲙ̅ⲛ̅ⲧ̅*ⲥⲛⲟⲟⲩⲥ ⲛ̅- ϥ̅ⲟ̅ b ⲁⲓⲱⲛ· ⲁⲓ̈ⲉⲓ' ⲉⲡⲉⲥⲏⲧ ⲛ̅ϩⲏⲧⲟⲩ· ⲉⲧⲃⲉ ⲡⲁⲓ̈ ⲁⲓ̈ϫⲱ ⲛ̅ϯⲙ̅ⲛ̅ⲧ̅ⲥⲛⲟⲟⲩⲥ ⲙ̅ⲙⲉⲧⲁⲛⲟⲓⲁ ⲕⲁⲧⲁ ⲡⲟⲩⲁ ⲡⲟⲩⲁ ⲛ̅ⲁⲓⲱⲛ· ⲧⲉⲛⲟⲩ ϭⲉ ⲡⲟⲩⲟⲓ̈ⲛ ⲛ̅ⲛ̅ⲟⲩⲟⲓ̈ⲛ ⲕⲱ ⲛⲁⲓ̈ ⲉⲃⲟⲗ ⲛ̅ⲧⲁⲡⲁⲣⲁⲃⲁⲥⲓⲥ ϫⲉ ⲟⲩⲛⲟϭ ⲉⲙⲁⲧⲉ ⲧⲉ ϫⲉ ⲁⲓ̈ⲕⲱ ⲛ̅ⲥⲱⲓ̈ ⲛ̅ⲛ̅ⲧⲟⲡⲟⲥ ⲙ̅ⲡϫⲓⲥⲉ ⲁⲓ̈ⲉⲓ' ⲁⲓ̈ⲟⲩⲱϩ ϩ̅ⲛ̅ ⲛ̅ⲧⲟⲡⲟⲥ ⲙ̅ⲡⲉⲭⲁⲟⲥ· ⲛⲁⲓ̈ ϭⲉ ⲛ̅ⲧⲉⲣⲉⲥϫⲟⲟⲩ ⲛ̅ϭⲓ ⲧⲡⲓⲥⲧⲓⲥ ⲥⲟⲫⲓⲁ· ⲁⲥⲟⲩⲱϩ ⲟⲛ ⲉⲧⲟⲟⲧⲥ̅ ϩ̅ⲛ̅ ⲧⲙⲉϩⲙ̅ⲛ̅ⲧ̅ϣⲟⲙⲧⲉ ⲙ̅ⲙⲉⲧⲁⲛⲟⲓⲁ ⲉⲥϫⲱ ⲙ̅ⲙⲟⲥ· ϫⲉ ⲥⲱⲧ̅ⲙ̅ ⲉⲣⲟⲓ̈ ⲉⲓ̈ϩⲩⲙⲛⲉⲩⲉ ⲉⲣⲟⲕ ⲡⲟⲩⲟⲓ̈ⲛ ⲛ̅ⲛ̅ⲟⲩⲟⲓ̈ⲛ· ⲥⲱⲧ̅ⲙ̅ ⲉⲣⲟⲓ̈ ⲉⲓ̈ϫⲱ ⲛ̅ⲧⲙⲉⲧⲁⲛⲟⲓⲁ ⲙ̅ⲡⲙⲉϩⲙ̅ⲛ̅ⲧ̅ϣⲟⲙⲧⲉ ⲛ̅ⲁⲓⲱⲛ· ⲡⲧⲟⲡⲟⲥ ⲉⲛⲧⲁⲓ̈ⲉⲓ' ⲉⲡⲉⲥⲏⲧ ⲉⲃⲟⲗ ⲛ̅ϩⲏⲧϥ̅· ϫⲉⲕⲁⲥ ⲉⲥⲉϫⲱⲕ ⲉⲃⲟⲗ ⲛ̅ϭⲓ ⲧⲙⲉϩⲙ̅ⲛ̅ⲧ̅ϣⲟⲙⲧⲉ ⲙ̅ⲙⲉⲧⲁⲛⲟⲓⲁ ⲛ̅ⲧⲉ**ⲡⲙⲉϩⲙ̅ⲛ̅ⲧ̅ϣⲟⲙⲧⲉ ⲛ̅ⲁⲓⲱⲛ· ⲛⲁⲓ̈ | ⲛ̅ⲧⲁⲓ̈- ⲣ̅

10 MS ⲉⲛⲧⲁⲥϫⲟⲥ.

24. My knees are weak with *fasting*; and my *flesh* is changed on account of the (lack of) oil.

25. *But* I have become a mockery to them; they saw me and they shook their heads.

26. *Help* me, O Lord God, and save me, *according to* thy mercy.

27. May they know that this is thy hand, and thou hast created it, O Lord.' *

This is the interpretation of the twelfth *repentance* which the Pistis Sophia said, as she was in the *Chaos*."

57.   Jesus continued again, *however*, with the discourse. He said to his *disciples* : "It happened again after these things, the Pistis Sophia cried out to me, saying : 'O Light of Lights, I have *transgressed* against the twelve *aeons*. I came down from them. For this reason I have said the twelve *repentances*, one *according to* each *aeon*. Now at this time, O Light of Lights, forgive me my *transgression*, for it is very great. Because I left the *places* of the height. I came to dwell in the *places* of the *Chaos*.'

Now when the Pistis Sophia finished saying these things, she continued again with the thirteenth *repentance*, saying :

1. 'Hear me as I *sing praises* to thee, O Light of Lights. Hear me as I say the *repentance* of the thirteenth *aeon*, the *place* from which I came down, so that the thirteenth *repentance* of the thirteenth *aeon* be completed. These (aeons) | against which I have *transgressed*, from them I came down.

---

* Ps. 108.1-27

221

ΠΑΡΑΒΑ ΑΪΕΙˊ ΕΠΕСΗΤ ΕΒΟΛ Ν̄2ΗΤΟΥˑ ΤΕΝΟΥ 6Ε ΠΟΥ-
ΟΕΙΝ Ν̄ΝΟΥΟΪΝ СШΤΜ̄ ΕΡΟΪ ΕΪ2ΥΜΝΕΥΕ ΕΡΟΚ 2Μ̄
ΠΜΕ2ΜΝΤϢΟΜΤΕ Ν̄ΑΙШΝ ΠΑΤΟΠΟС ΕΝΤΑΪΕΙˊ ΕΒΟΛ Ν̄-
2ΗΤϤ ΝΑ2ΜΕΤ ΠΟΥΟΪΝ 2Μ̄ ΠΕΚΝΟ6 Μ̄ΜΥСΤΗΡΙΟΝˑ
5 ΑΥШ ΚШ ΕΒΟΛ Ν̄ΤΑΠΑΡΑΒΑСΙС 2ΡΑΪ 2Ν ΤΕΚΜΝΤΡΕϤΚШ
ΕΒΟΛˑ ΑΥШ ΜΑ ΝΑΪ Μ̄ΠΒΑΠΤΙСΜΑ Ν̄ΓΚШ ΕΒΟΛ Ν̄ΝΑ-
ΝΟΒΕˑ ΑΥШ Ν̄Γ̄ΤΒΒΟΪ ΕΒΟΛ 2Ν̄ ΤΑΠΑΡΑΒΑСΙСˑ ΑΥШ
ΤΑΠΑΡΑΒΑСΙС ΑΝΟΚ ΤΕ †6ΟΜ Ν̄2Ο Μ̄ΜΟΥΪ ΤΑΪ ΕΤΕ
Ν̄ΝΕС2ШΠ ΕΡΟΚ Ν̄ΟΥΟΪϢ ΝΙΜˑ ΧΕ Ν̄ΤΑΪΕΙˊ ΕΠΕСΗΤ
10 ΕΤΒΗΗΤС̄ˑ ΑΥШ ΑΝΟΚ ΑΪΠΑΡΑΒΑ ΜΑΥΑΑΤˑ 2Ν Ν̄Α2Ο-
ΡΑΤΟС Ε†ϢΟΟΠ 2Μ̄ ΠΕΥΤΟΠΟСˑ ΑΪΕΙˊ ΕΠΕСΗΤ ΕΠΕ-
ΧΛΟСˑ * ΑΪΠΑΡΑΒΑ Ν̄ΝΑ2ΡΑΚˑ ΧΕΚΑС ΕΡΕ ΠΕΚΤШϢ ᴾ ᵇ
ΧШΚ ΕΒΟΛˑ ΝΑΪ 6Ε ΑСΧΟΟΥ Ν̄6Ι ΤΠΙСΤΙС СΟΦΙΑˑ
ΤΕΝΟΥ 6Ε ΠΕΤΕΡΕ ΠΕϤΠΝ̄Α ΚΙΜ ΕΡΟϤ ΕΤΡΕϤΝΟΕΙ Ν̄-
15 ΝΕСϢΑΧΕˑ ΜΑΡΕϤΕΙˊ ΕΘΗ Ν̄ϤΤΑΥΕ-ΠΕΥΝΟΗΜΑˑ ΑСΕΙˊ
ΕΘΗ Ν̄6Ι ΜΑΡΘΑ ΠΕΧΑС ΧΕ ΠΑΧΟΕΙСˑ ΠΑΠΝ̄Α ΚΙΜ
ΕΡΟΪ ΕΤΡΑΤΑΥΕ-ΠΒШΛ Ν̄ΝΕΝΤΑСΧΟΟΥ Ν̄6Ι ΤΠΙСΤΙС СΟ-
ΦΙΑˑ Α ΤΕΚ6ΟΜ ΠΡΟΦΗΤΕΥΕ Μ̄ΠΙΟΥ⟨Ο⟩ΪϢ ΕΤΒΗΗΤΟΥ
2ΙΤΝ̄ ΛΑΥΕΙΛˑ 2Μ̄ ΠΜΕ2ΤΑΪΟΥ Μ̄ΨΑΛΜΟС ΕСΧШ Μ̄ΜΟС
20 Ν̄ΤΕΪ2Εˑ ΧΕ

1. ΝΑˊ ΝΑΪ ΠΝΟΥΤΕ ΚΑΤΑ ΠΕΚΝΟ6 Ν̄ΝΑˊ ΚΑΤΑ ΠΑ-
ϢΑΪ Ν̄ΝΕΚΜΝΤϢΑΝ2ΤΗϤˑ

2. ϤШΤΕ ΕΒΟΛ Μ̄ΠΑΝΟΒΕˑ ΕΙΑΛΤ ΕΜΑΤΕ ΕΒΟΛ 2Ν̄ ΤΑ-
ΛΝΟΜΙΑˑ

---

18   MS Μ̄ΠΙΟΥΪϢ.

222

2. Now at this time, O Light of Lights, hear me as I *sing praises* to thee in the thirteenth *aeon*, my *place* from which I came forth.

3. Save me, O Light, in thy great *mystery* and forgive my *transgression* in thy forgiveness.

4. And give me the *baptism* and forgive my sins and purify me from my *transgression*.

5. And this my *transgression* is the lion-faced power, which was not hidden from thee at any time, for on account of it I came down.

6. And I alone among the *invisible ones*, in whose *place* I existed, *transgressed*, and I came down to the *Chaos*. I *transgressed* before thee so that thy ordinance should be fulfilled.'

The Pistis Sophia now said these things. Now at this time let him whose *spirit* moves him to *understand* her words, come forth and give their *thought*."

Martha came forward and said: "My Lord, my *spirit* moves me to give the interpretation of those things which the Pistis Sophia said. Concerning them, thy power once *prophesied* through David in the 50th *Psalm*, speaking thus:

1. 'Have mercy upon me, O God, *according to* thy great pity; *according to* the multitude of thy mercies blot out my sin [1].

2. Wash me thoroughly from my *iniquity*. |

---

[1] (22, 23) Till emends Schmidt's division of verses 1, 2.

3. ⲀⲨⲰ ⲠⲀⲚⲞⲂⲈ ⲘⲠⲀⲘⲦⲞ^{**} ⲈⲂⲞⲖ ⲚⲞⲨⲞⲈⲒⲰ ⲚⲒⲘ ·   ⲢⲀ

4. ⲬⲈⲔⲀⲤ ⲈⲔⲈⲦⲘⲀⲒⲞ ⲤⲚ ⲚⲈⲔⲰⲀⲬⲈ · ⲀⲨⲰ ⲚⲄⲬⲢⲞ
ⲤⲘ ⲠⲦⲢⲈⲔϯⲤⲀⲠ ⲈⲢⲞⲒ ·

ⲠⲀⲒ ⲠⲈ ⲠⲂⲰⲖ ⲚⲚⲰⲀⲬⲈ ⲚⲦⲀⲤⲬⲞⲞⲨ ⲚϬⲒ ⲦⲠⲒⲤⲦⲒⲤ
5 ⲤⲞⲪⲒⲀ · ⲠⲈⲬⲀϤ ⲚⲀⲤ ⲚϬⲒ ⲒⲤ · ⲬⲈ ⲈⲨⲄⲈ ⲔⲀⲖⲰⲤ ⲘⲀⲢⲞⲖ
ⲦⲘⲀⲔⲀⲢⲒⲀ · ⲀϤⲞⲨⲰⲤ ⲆⲈ ⲞⲚ ⲈⲦⲞⲞⲦϤ ⲚϬⲒ ⲒⲤ ⲤⲘ ⲠⲰⲀ-
ⲬⲈ ⲠⲈⲬⲀϤ ⲚⲚⲈϤⲘⲀⲐⲎⲦⲎⲤ ⲬⲈ ⲀⲤⲰⲰⲠⲈ ϬⲈ ⲚⲦⲈⲢⲈ
ⲦⲠⲒⲤⲦⲒⲤ ⲤⲞⲪⲒⲀ ⲬⲰ ⲚⲚⲈⲒⲰⲀⲬⲈ ⲀϤⲬⲰⲔ ⲈⲂⲞⲖ ⲚϬⲒ
ⲠⲈⲞⲨⲞⲒⲰ ⲈⲦⲢⲈⲨⲚⲦⲤ ⲈⲤⲢⲀⲒ ⲤⲘ ⲠⲈⲬⲀⲞⲤ ⲀⲨⲰ ⲈⲂⲞⲖ
10 ⲤⲒⲦⲞⲞⲦ ⲘⲘⲒⲚ ⲘⲘⲞⲒ ⲬⲰⲢⲒⲤ ⲠⲰⲞⲢⲠ ⲘⲘⲨⲤⲦⲎⲢⲒⲞⲚ · ⲀⲒ-
ⲈⲒⲚⲈ ⲚⲞⲨϬⲞⲘ ⲚⲞⲨⲞⲒⲚ ⲈⲂⲞⲖ ⲚⲤⲎⲦ · ⲀⲒⲬⲚⲀⲤ ⲈⲤⲢⲀⲒ
ⲈⲠⲈⲬⲀⲞⲤ · ⲈⲦⲢⲈⲤⲚ-ⲦⲠⲒⲤⲦⲒⲤ ⲤⲞⲪⲒⲀ ⲈⲤⲢⲀⲒ ⲤⲚ ⲚⲦⲞⲠⲞⲤ
ⲈⲦⲰⲎⲔ ⲚⲦⲈ ⲠⲈⲬⲀⲞⲤ · ⲚⲤⲈⲚⲦⲤ ⲈⲠⲒⲦⲞⲠⲞⲤ ⲈⲦⲘⲠⲈⲦⲠⲈ   ⲢⲀ ᵇ
ⲘⲠⲈⲬⲀⲞⲤ · ⲰⲀⲚⲦⲈ ⲦⲔⲈⲖⲈⲨⲤⲒⲤ ⲈⲒ᾽ ⲈⲂⲞⲖ ⲤⲒⲦⲘ ⲠⲰⲞⲢⲠ
15 ⲘⲘⲨⲤⲦⲎⲢⲒⲞⲚ · ⲈⲦⲢⲈⲨⲚⲦⲤ ⲈⲤⲢⲀⲒ ⲤⲘ ⲠⲈⲬⲀⲞⲤ ⲈⲠⲦⲎⲢϤ ·
ⲀⲨⲰ Ⲁ ⲦⲀϬⲞⲘ ⲚⲞⲨⲞⲒⲚ ⲀⲤⲚ-ⲦⲠⲒⲤⲦⲒⲤ ⲤⲞⲪⲒⲀ ⲈⲤⲢⲀⲒ
ⲈⲚⲦⲞⲠⲞⲤ ⲈⲦⲘⲠⲤⲀⲚⲦⲠⲈ ⲘⲠⲈⲬⲀⲞⲤ · ⲀⲤⲰⲰⲠⲈ ϬⲈ
ⲚⲦⲈⲢⲞⲨⲈⲒⲘⲈ ⲚϬⲒ ⲚⲈⲠⲢⲞⲂⲞⲖⲞⲞⲨⲈ ⲘⲠⲀⲨⲐⲀⲆⲎⲤ ⲬⲈ
ⲀⲨⲚ-ⲦⲠⲒⲤⲦⲒⲤ ⲤⲞⲪⲒⲀ ⲈⲤⲢⲀⲒ ⲈⲚⲦⲞⲠⲞⲤ ⲈⲦⲘⲠⲤⲀⲚⲦⲠⲈ
20 ⲘⲠⲈⲬⲀⲞⲤ · ⲀⲨⲠⲰⲦ ⲞⲚ ⲚⲤⲰⲤ ⲈⲠⲬⲒⲤⲈ ⲈⲨⲞⲨⲈⲰⲬⲒⲦⲤ
ⲞⲚ ⲈⲚⲦⲞⲠⲞⲤ ⲈⲦⲘⲠⲈⲬⲀⲞⲤ ⲘⲠⲈⲤⲎⲦ · ⲀⲨⲰ ⲚⲈⲤⲢⲞⲨ-
ⲞⲒⲚ ⲠⲈ ⲈⲘⲀⲦⲈ ⲚϬⲒ ⲦⲀϬⲞⲘ ⲚⲞⲨⲞⲒⲚ ⲦⲀⲒ ⲈⲚⲦⲀⲒⲬⲞⲞⲨⲤ
ⲈⲚ-ⲦⲤⲞⲪⲒⲀ ⲈⲤⲢⲀⲒ ⲤⲘ ⲠⲈⲬⲀⲞⲤ · ⲀⲤⲰⲰⲠⲈ ϬⲈ ⲚⲦⲈⲢⲞⲨ-
ⲠⲰⲦ ⲚⲤⲀ ⲦⲤⲞⲪⲒⲀ ⲚϬⲒ ⲚⲈⲠⲢⲞⲂⲞⲖⲞⲞⲨⲈ ⲘⲠⲀⲨⲐⲀⲆⲎⲤ

---

1 MS ⲤⲈⲂⲞⲖ.
21 MS ⲈⲦⲘⲠⲈⲬⲀⲞⲤ ⲘⲠⲈⲤⲎⲦ; read ⲈⲦⲤⲘ ⲠⲈⲬⲀⲞⲤ ⲘⲠⲈⲤⲎⲦ or ⲈⲦ-
ⲘⲠⲈⲤⲎⲦ ⲘⲠⲈⲬⲀⲞⲤ.

3. And my sin is present to me at all times.

4. That thou shouldst be justified in thy words and victorious when thou judgest me.'*

This is the explanation of the words which the Pistis Sophia said."

Jesus said to her: "*Excellent, well done* Martha, thou *blessed one.*"

58. Jesus *however* continued again with the discourse. He said to his *disciples*: "Now it happened when the Pistis Sophia said these words, the time was fulfilled that she should be brought forth from the *Chaos*. And by myself alone, *without* the First *Mystery*, I brought forth from myself a light-power. I sent it down to the *Chaos* that it should bring the Pistis Sophia up from the deep *places* of the *Chaos* and bring her to the upper *place* of the *Chaos*, until the *command* came forth from the First *Mystery* that she should be brought up from the *Chaos* completely. And my light-power brought the Pistis Sophia up to the upper *places* of the *Chaos*. Now it happened when the *emanations* of the Authades knew that the Pistis Sophia was brought up to the upper *places* of the *Chaos*, they followed her upwards, wanting to take her again to the lower *places* of the *Chaos*. And my light-power, which I had sent to bring the Sophia up from the *Chaos*, gave light exceedingly. Now it happened when the *emanations* of the Authades followed the Sophia | when she was brought to the upper *places* of

---

*   Ps. 50.1-4

225

ⲚⲦⲈⲢⲞⲨⲚⲦⲤ ⲈⲚⲦⲞⲠⲞⲤ ⲈⲦⲘ̅ⲠⲤⲀ Ⲛ̅ⲦⲠⲈ Ⲙ̅ⲠⲈⲬⲖⲞⲤ · ⲀⲤ-
ⲎⲨⲘⲚⲈⲨⲈ ⲞⲚ ⲀⲨⲰ ⲀⲤⲰϢ ⲈⲎⲢⲀⲒ ⲞⲨⲎⲒ̈ ⲈⲤⲬⲰ Ⲙ̅ⲘⲞⲤ
ⲬⲈ

1. ⳦ⲚⲀⲎⲨⲘⲚⲈⲨⲈ ⲈⲎⲢⲀⲒ ⲈⲢⲞⲔ ⲠⲞⲨⲞⲒ̈Ⲛ ⲬⲈ ⲀⲒ̈ⲞⲨⲈϢⲈⲒ'
5 ⲈⲢⲀⲦ̅Ⲕ ⳦ⲚⲀⲎⲨⲠⲚⲈⲨⲈ ⲈⲎⲢⲀⲒ ⲈⲢⲞⲔ ⲠⲞⲨⲞⲒ̈Ⲛ ⲬⲈ Ⲛ̅ⲦⲞⲔ
ⲠⲈ ⲠⲀⲢⲈϤⲚⲞⲨⲎ̅Ⲙ ·

2. Ⲙ̅Ⲡ̅ⲢⲔⲀⲀⲦ Ⲏ̅Ⲙ ⲠⲈⲬⲖⲞⲤ · ⲚⲀⲎⲘⲈⲦ ⲠⲞⲨⲞⲒ̈Ⲛ Ⲛ̅ⲦⲈ
ⲠⲬⲒⲤⲈ ⲬⲈ Ⲛ̅ⲦⲞⲔ ⲠⲈ Ⲛ̅ⲦⲀⲒ̈ⲎⲨⲘⲚⲈⲨⲈ ⲈⲢⲞⲔ ·

3. ⲀⲔⲦ̅ⲚⲚⲞⲞⲨ ⲚⲀⲒ̈ Ⲙ̅ⲠⲈⲔⲞⲨⲞⲈⲒⲚ ⲈⲂⲞⲖ ⲎⲒⲦⲞⲞⲦ̅Ⲕ
10 ⲀⲨⲰ ⲀⲔⲚⲀⲎⲘⲈⲦ · ⲀⲔⲚ̅Ⲧ ⲈⲚⲦⲞⲠⲞⲤ ⲈⲦⲘ̅ⲠⲤⲀ Ⲛ̅ⲦⲠⲈ Ⲙ̅-
ⲠⲈⲬⲖⲞⲤ ·

4. ⲘⲀⲢⲞⲨⲎⲈ ϬⲈ ⲈⲠⲈⲤⲎⲦ ⲈⲚⲦⲞⲠⲞⲤ ⲈⲦⲎⲒⲠⲈⲤⲎⲦ Ⲙ̅ⲠⲈ-
ⲬⲖⲞⲤ Ⲛ̅ϬⲒ ⲚⲈⲠⲢⲞⲂⲞⲖⲞⲞⲨⲈ Ⲙ̅ⲠⲀⲨⲐⲀⲖⲎⲤ ⲚⲀⲒ̈ ⲈⲦⲠⲎⲦ
Ⲛ̅ⲤⲰⲒ̈ · ⲀⲨⲰ Ⲙ̅Ⲡ̅ⲢⲦⲢⲈⲨⲈⲒ' ⲈⲚⲦⲞⲠⲞⲤ ⲈⲦⲘ̅ⲠⲤⲀ Ⲛ̅ⲦⲠⲈ
15 ⲈⲦⲢⲈⲨⲚⲀⲨ. ⲈⲢⲞⲒ̈ ·   Ⲣ̅Ⲃᵇ

5. ⲀⲨⲰ ⲘⲀⲢⲈ ⲞⲨⲚⲞϬ Ⲛ̅ⲔⲀⲔⲈ ⲎⲰⲂ̅Ⲥ ⲈⲂⲞⲖ ⲈⲬⲰⲞⲨ ·
ⲀⲨⲰ ⲘⲀⲢⲈϤⲈⲒ' ⲚⲀⲨ Ⲛ̅ϬⲒ ⲞⲨⲎⲖⲞⲤⲦ̅Ⲛ Ⲛ̅ⲔⲀⲔⲈ · ⲀⲨⲰ Ⲙ̅-
Ⲡ̅ⲢⲦⲢⲈⲨⲚⲀⲨ ⲈⲢⲞⲒ̈ Ⲏ̅Ⲙ ⲠⲞⲨⲞⲒ̈Ⲛ Ⲛ̅ⲦⲈⲔϬⲞⲘ ⲦⲀⲒ̈ ⲈⲚⲦⲀⲔ-
Ⲧ̅ⲚⲚⲞⲞⲨⲤ ⲚⲀⲒ̈ ⲈⲚⲀⲎⲘⲈⲦ · ⲬⲈ Ⲛ̅ⲚⲈⲨⲀⲘⲀⲎⲦⲈ ⲞⲚ ⲈⲎⲢⲀⲒ
20 ⲈⲬⲰⲒ̈ ·

6. ⲀⲨⲰ ⲠⲈⲨϢⲞⲬⲚⲈ ⲈⲚⲦⲀⲨⲘⲈⲈⲨⲈ ⲈⲢⲞϤ ⲈⲦⲢⲈⲨϤⲒ-
ⲦⲀϬⲞⲘ · Ⲙ̅Ⲡ̅ⲢⲦⲢⲈϤϢⲰⲠⲈ ⲚⲀⲨ · ⲀⲨⲰ ⲔⲀⲦⲀ ⲐⲈ ⲈⲚⲦ-
ⲀⲨϢⲀⲬⲈ ⲈⲢⲞⲒ̈ ⲈϤⲒ-ⲠⲖⲞⲨⲞⲒ̈Ⲛ Ⲛ̅ⲎⲎⲦ · ϤⲒ-ⲠϢⲞⲨ ⲎⲰⲞⲨ
ⲈⲠⲘⲀ Ⲙ̅ⲠⲰⲒ̈ ·

25 7. ⲀⲨⲰ ⲀⲨⲬⲞⲞⲤ ⲈϤⲒ-ⲠⲖⲞⲨⲞⲈⲒⲚ ⲦⲎⲢ̅Ϥ · ⲀⲨⲰ ⲚⲈ-
Ⲙ̅ⲠⲞⲨⲈϢϤⲒⲦϤ · ⲬⲈ ⲦⲈⲔϬⲞⲘ Ⲛ̅ⲞⲨⲞⲒ̈Ⲛ ϢⲞⲞⲠ Ⲛ̅ⲦⲞⲔ
Ⲛ̅ⲘⲘⲀⲒ̈ ·

---

5 MS ⳦ⲚⲀⲎⲨⲠⲚⲤⲨⲤ ; read ⳦ⲚⲀⲎⲨⲘⲚⲤⲨⲤ .

the *Chaos*, she *sang praises* again and she cried out to me, saying :

1. 'I will *sing praises* to thee, O Light, for I wanted to come to thee. I will *sing praises* to thee, O Light, for thou art my Saviour.

2. Leave me not in the *Chaos*. Save me, O Light of the height, for thou art he to whom I have *sung praises*.

3. By thyself thou hast sent to me thy light and thou hast saved me. Thou hast brought me to the upper *places* of the *Chaos*.

4. May the *emanations* of the Authades which follow me fall down to the lower *places* of the *Chaos*. And let them not come to the upper *places* so that they see me.

5. And may a great darkness cover them over and may a cloud of darkness come to them. And let them not see me in the light of thy power which thou hast sent to me to save me, lest they gain power over me again.

6. And their plan which they thought of, to take away my power, let it not happen for them. And *according to* how they spoke against me to take away my light from me, take theirs rather instead of mine.

7. And they have spoken to take away all my light. And they were not able to take it, for thy light-power was with me; |

227

8· ЄΒΟⲗ ⲬЄ ⲀⲨϢΟⲬΝЄ ⲀⲬⲘ ⲠЄⲔⲦϢϢ ⲠΟⲨΟⲒⲚ·
ЄⲦΒЄ ⲠⲀⲒ ⲘⲠΟⲨЄϢϤⲒ-ⲠⲗⲀΟⲨΟЄⲒⲚ ЄΒΟⲗ·

9. ⲬЄ ⲚⲦⲀⲒⲠⲒⲤⲦЄⲨЄ ЄⲠΟⲨΟⲒⲚ· ⲚϯⲚⲀⲢϩΟⲦЄ ⲀⲚ ⲀⲨϢ
ⲠΟⲨΟЄⲒⲚ ⲠЄ ⲠⲀⲢЄϤⲚΟⲨϩⲘ· ⲀⲨϢ ⲚϯⲚⲀⲢϩΟⲦЄ ⲀⲚ·

5   ⲦЄⲚΟⲨ ϬЄ ⲠЄⲦЄⲢЄ ⲦЄϤϬΟⲘ ⲬΟⲤЄ· ⲘⲀⲢЄϤⲬϢ Ⲙ-
ⲠΒϢⲗ ⲚⲚϢⲀⲬЄ ⲚⲦⲀⲤⲬΟΟⲨ ⲚϬⲒ ⲦⲠⲒⲤⲦⲒⲤ ⲤΟⲫⲒⲀ· ⲀⲤ-
ϢϢⲠЄ ⲆЄ ⲚⲦЄⲢЄ ⲒⲤ ΟⲨϢ ЄϤⲬϢ ⲚⲚЄЄⲒϢⲀⲬЄ ЄⲚЄϤ-
ⲘⲀΘⲎⲦⲎⲤ· ⲀⲤЄⲒ' ЄΘⲎ ⲚϬⲒ ⲤⲀⲗϢⲘⲎ ⲠЄⲬⲀⲤ ⲬЄ ⲠⲀ-
ⲬΟЄⲒⲤ ⲦⲀϬΟⲘ ⲀⲚⲀⲅⲔⲀⲌЄ ⲘⲘΟⲒ ЄⲦⲢⲀⲬϢ ⲘⲠΒϢⲗ
10   ⲚⲚϢⲀⲬЄ ⲚⲦⲀⲤⲬΟΟⲨ ⲚϬⲒ ⲦⲠⲒⲤⲦⲒⲤ ⲤΟⲫⲒⲀ· Ⲁ ⲦЄⲔϬΟⲘ
ⲠⲢΟⲪⲎⲦЄⲨЄ ⲘⲠⲒΟⲨΟⲒϢ ϩⲒⲦⲚ ⲤΟⲗΟⲘϢⲚ ЄⲤⲬϢ Ⲙ-
ⲘΟⲤ ⲬЄ .

1. ϯⲚⲀΟⲨΟⲚϩⲦ ⲚⲀⲔ ЄΒΟⲗ ⲠⲬΟЄⲒⲤ ⲬЄ ⲚⲦΟⲔ ⲠЄ
ⲠⲀⲚΟⲨⲦЄ·

15   2. ⲘⲠⲢⲔⲀⲀⲦ ⲠⲬΟЄⲒⲤ ⲬЄ ⲚⲦΟⲔ ⲠЄ ⲦⲀϩЄⲗⲠⲒⲤ·

3. ⲀⲔϯ ⲚⲀⲒ ⲘⲠЄⲔϩⲀⲠ ⲚⲬⲒⲚⲬⲎ· ⲀⲨϢ ⲀⲒⲚΟⲨϩⲘ ЄΒΟⲗ
ϩⲒⲦΟΟⲦⲔ·

4. ⲘⲀⲢΟⲨϩЄ ⲚϬⲒ ⲚЄⲦⲠⲎⲦ ⲚⲤϢⲒ ⲀⲨϢ ⲘⲠⲢⲦⲢЄⲨⲚⲀⲨ
ЄⲢΟⲒ·

20   5. ⲘⲀⲢЄ ΟⲨⲔⲗΟΟⲗЄ ⲚⲔⲢⲘⲦⲤ ϩϢΒⲤ ЄΒΟⲗ ЄⲬⲚ ⲚЄⲨ-
ΒⲀⲗ· ⲀⲨϢ ΟⲨⲚⲒϤ ⲚⲀⲎⲢ· ⲘⲀⲢЄϤⲢⲔⲀⲔЄ ЄⲢΟΟⲨ· ⲀⲨϢ
ⲘⲠⲢⲦⲢЄⲨⲚⲀⲨ ЄⲠЄϩΟΟⲨ ⲬЄ ⲚⲚЄⲨⲘⲀⲤⲦЄ ⲘⲘΟⲒ·

6. ⲘⲀⲢЄϤⲢ-ⲀⲦϬΟⲘ ⲚϬⲒ ⲠЄⲨϢΟⲬⲚЄ· ⲀⲨϢ ⲚЄⲚⲦⲀⲨ-
ϢΟⲬⲚЄ ЄⲢΟΟⲨ ⲘⲀⲢΟⲨЄⲒ' Єϩ ⲢⲀⲒ ЄⲬϢΟⲨ·

8. Because they deliberated without thy ordinance, O Light. On account of this they were not able to take away my light.

9. Because I have *believed* in the light, I will not fear; and the light is my saviour, and I will not fear.'

Now at this time let him whose power is elevated say the interpretation of the words which the Pistis Sophia said."

But it happened when Jesus finished saying these words to his *disciples*, Salome came forward. She said : "My Lord, my power *compels* me to say the interpretation of the words which the Pistis Sophia said. Thy power *prophesied* once through Solomon, saying thus :

1. I will give thanks to thee, O Lord, for thou art my God.

2. Leave me not, O Lord, for thou art my *hope*.

3. Thou hast given me thy judgment freely, and I have been saved through thee.

4. May those that persecute me fall and let them not see me.

5. May a cloud of smoke cover their eyes, and may a misty *air* darken them; and let them not see the day, lest they seize me.

6. May their counsels become powerless; and may those things which they have devised come upon them. |

7. ⲀⲨⲘⲈⲔⲘⲞⲨⲔⲞⲨ ⲈⲨϢⲞⳎⲚⲈ · ⲀⲨⲱ ⲘⲡⲩϢⲱⲡⲉ
ⲚⲀⲨ ·

8. ⲀⲨⲱ ⲀⲨⳎⲢⲞ ⲈⲢⲞⲞⲨ ⲈⲨϬⲘϬⲞⲘ · ⲀⲨⲱ ⲚⲈⲚⲦⲀⲨ-
ⲤⲂⲦⲰⲦⲞⲨ ⲔⲀⲔⲰⲤ · ⲀⲨⲚⲈ ⲈⲡⲈⲤⲏⲦ ⲈⲢⲞⲞⲨ ·

5   9. ⲈⲢⲈ ⲦⲀⲚⲈⲗⲡⲓⲤ ⳎⲘ ⲡⳎⲞⲈⲓⲤ · ⲀⲨⲱ ⲚϯⲚⲀⲢⲚⲞⲦⲈ ⲀⲚ
ⳎⲈ ⲚⲦⲞⲔ ⲡⲈ ⲡⲀⲚⲞⲨⲦⲈ ** ⲡⲀⲤⲰⲦⲏⲢ ·   ⲢⲀ

ⲋ ⲀⲤϢⲱⲡⲈ ϬⲈ ⲚⲦⲈⲢⲈ ⲤⲀⲗⲱⲘⲏ ⲞⲨⲱ ⲈⲤⳎⲱ ⲚⲚⲈⲈⲓ-
ϢⲀⳎⲈ · ⲡⲈⳎⲀⲩ ⲚⲀⲤ ⲚϬⲓ ⲓⲤ ⳎⲈ ⲈⲨⲄⲈ ⲤⲀⲗⲱⲘⲏ ⲀⲨⲄⲰ
ⲔⲀⲗⲰⲤ · ⲡⲀⲓ ⲡⲈ ⲡⲂⲱⲗ ⲚⲚϢⲀⳎⲈ ⲈⲚⲦⲀⲤⳎⲞⲞⲨ ⲚϬⲓ
10 ⲦⲡⲓⲤⲦⲓⲤ ⲤⲟⲫⲓⲀ .

ⲋ ⲀⲩⲞⲨⲱⳅ ⲆⲈ ⲞⲚ ⲈⲦⲞⲞⲦⲩ ⲚϬⲓ ⲓⲤ ⳎⲘ ⲡϢⲀⳎⲈ ⲡⲈ-
ⳎⲀⲩ ⲚⲚⲈⲩⲘⲀⲐⲏⲦⲏⲤ · ⳎⲈ ⲀⲤϢⲱⲡⲈ ϬⲈ ⲚⲦⲈⲢⲈ ⲦⲡⲓⲤⲦⲓⲤ
ⲤⲟⲫⲓⲀ ⲞⲨⲱ ⲈⲤⳎⲱ ⲚⲚⲈⲓϢⲀⳎⲈ ⳎⲘ ⲡⲈⳎⲗⲞⲤ · ⲀⲓⲦⲢⲈ
ϯϬⲞⲘ ⲚⲞⲨⲞⲈⲓⲚ ⲈⲚⲦⲀⲓⳎⲞⲞⲨⲤ ⲚⲀⲤ ⲈⲦⲢⲈⲤⲚⲀⳍⲘⲈⲤ
15 ⲀⲓⲦⲢⲈⲤⲢ-ⲞⲨⲔⲗⲞⲘ ⲚⲞⲨⲞⲓⲚ ⲈⲦⲈⲤⲀⲡⲈ · ⳎⲈ ⲚⲚⲈⲩⲈϢ-
ϬⲘϬⲞⲘ ⲈⲢⲞⲤ ⳎⲓⲚ ⲘⲡⲈⲈⲓⲚⲀⲩ ⲚϬⲓ ⲚⲈⲡⲢⲞⲂⲟⲗⲞⲞⲨⲈ
ⲘⲡⲀⲩⲐⲀⲆⲏⲤ ⲀⲨⲱ ⲚⲦⲈⲢⲈⲤⲢ-ⲞⲨⲔⲗⲟⲘ ⲚⲞⲨⲟⲓⲚ ⲈⲦⲈⲤ-
ⲀⲡⲈ · ⲀⲨⲔⲓⲘ ⲈⲚⳍⲨⲗⲏ ⲦⲏⲢⲞⲨ ⲈⲐⲞⲟⲨ ⲈⲦⲚⳍⲏⲦⲤ · ⲀⲨⲱ
ⲀⲨⲤⲱⲦⲩ ⲈⲂⲟⲗ ⲦⲏⲢⲟⲨ ⲚⳍⲏⲦⲤ · *ⲀⲨⲦⲀⲔⲞ ⲀⲨⲱ ⲀⲨ-   ⲢⲀ ᵇ
20 ϢⲱⲡⲈ ⳎⲘ ⲡⲈⳎⲗⲞⲤ ⲈⲨϬⲱϢⲦ ⲈⲢⲞⲟⲩ ⲚϬⲓ ⲚⲈⲡⲢⲟⲂⲟ-
ⲗⲟⲞⲨⲈ ⲘⲡⲀⲩⲐⲀⲆⲏⲤ ⲀⲨⲱ ⲈⲨⲢⲀϢⲈ ⲘⲘⲟⲟⲩ · ⲀⲨⲱ
ⲚⲤⲱⲦⲩ ⲚⲞⲨⲞⲈⲓⲚ ⲚⳍⲓⲗⲓⲔⲢⲓⲚⲈⲤ ⲈⲦⳍⲚ ⲦⲤⲟⲫⲓⲀ · ⲀⲨϯ-
ϬⲞⲘ ⲘⲡⲞⲨⲞⲈⲓⲚ ⲚⲦⲀϬⲞⲘ ⲚⲞⲨⲟⲓⲚ · ⲦⲀⲓ ⲈⲚⲦⲀⲤⲢ-ⲞⲨ-

---

18 MS originally ⲈⲦⲚⳍⲏⲦⲦⲤ with ⲐⲞⲞⲨ ⲈⲦⲚ in the same hand in the margins,
giving ⲈⲦⲚⲐⲞⲞⲨ ⲈⲦⲚⳍⲏⲦⲦⲤ with ⲦⲚ expunged before ⲐⲞⲞⲨ.

7. They have devised a counsel, and it has not happened for them.

8. And they, the powerful, are vanquished; and those things which they prepared with *evil intent* are cast down [1].

9. My *hope* is in the Lord and I will not fear; for thou art my God, my *Saviour'*. *"

Now it happened when Salome finished saying these words, Jesus said to her : "*Excellent*, Salome, and *well done*. This is the interpretation of the words which the Pistis Sophia said."

59. Jesus continued again, *however*, with the discourse. He said to his *disciples* : "Now it happened when the Pistis Sophia finished saying these words in the *Chaos*, I caused the light-power which I had sent to save her, I caused it to become a crown of light on her head, so that from this hour the *emanations* of the Authades would have no power over her. And when it became a crown of light on her head, all the evil *materials* which were in her were moved, and they were all purified within her; they were destroyed and came to be in the *Chaos*, while the *emanations* of the Authades saw them and they rejoiced. And what was purified of the *pure* light within the Sophia gave power to the light of my light-power which had become a | crown

---

* Ps. Sol. 5.1-9

---

[1] (4) are cast down; Schmidt : have fallen down upon them.

ⲕⲗⲟⲙ ⲛ̄ⲧⲉⲥⲁⲡⲉ· ⲁⲥϣⲱⲡⲉ ϭⲉ ⲟⲛ ⲉⲥⲕⲱⲧⲉ ⲉⲡⲟⲩⲟⲉⲓⲛ
ⲛ̄ϩⲓⲗⲓⲕⲣⲓⲛⲉⲥ ⲉⲧⲍ̄ⲛ ⲧⲥⲟⲫⲓⲁ· ⲁⲩⲱ ⲡⲉⲥϩⲓⲗⲓⲕⲣⲓⲛⲉⲥ ⲛ̄ⲟⲩ-
ⲟⲓⲛ ⲙ̄ⲡ̄ϥⲣ̄ⲡⲃⲟⲗ ⲙ̄ⲡⲉⲕⲗⲟⲙ ⲛ̄ϭⲟⲙ ⲙ̄ⲡⲓϣⲁϩ ⲛ̄ⲟⲩⲟⲓⲛ ϫⲉ
ⲛ̄ⲛⲉⲩϭⲱϭⲉ ⲉⲣⲟϥ ⲛ̄ϭⲓ ⲛⲉⲡⲣⲟⲃⲟⲗⲟⲟⲩⲉ ⲙ̄ⲡⲁⲩⲑⲁⲇⲏⲥ·
5 ⲛⲁⲓ̈ ϭⲉ ⲛ̄ⲧⲉⲣⲟⲩϣⲱⲡⲉ ⲙ̄ⲙⲟⲥ· ⲁⲥϩⲓⲧⲟⲟⲧ̄ⲥ̄ ⲁⲥϩⲩⲙⲛⲉⲩⲉ
ⲛ̄ϭⲓ ⲧϭⲟⲙ ⲛ̄ϩⲓⲗⲓⲕⲣⲓⲛⲉⲥ ⲛ̄ⲟⲩⲟⲓⲛ ⲉⲧⲍ̄ⲛ ⲧⲥⲟⲫⲓⲁ· ⲛ̄ⲧ-
ⲁⲥϩⲩⲙⲛⲉⲩⲉ ⲇⲉ ⲉⲧⲁϭⲟⲙ ⲛ̄ⲟⲩⲟⲓⲛ ⲉⲧⲟ ⲛ̄ⲟⲩⲕⲗⲟⲙ
ⲉⲧⲉⲥⲁⲡⲉ· ⲁⲥϩⲩⲙⲛⲉⲩⲉ ⲇⲉ ⲉⲥϫⲱ ⲙ̄ⲙⲟⲥ ϫⲉ   ⲣ̅ⲋ̅

1. ⲡⲟⲩⲟⲉⲓⲛ ⲟ’ ⲛ̄ⲟⲩⲕⲗⲟⲙ ⲉⲧⲁⲁⲡⲉ ⲁⲩⲱ ⲛ̄ϯⲛⲁⲣⲡⲉϥ-
10 ⲃⲟⲗ ⲁⲛ ϫⲉ ⲛ̄ⲛⲉⲩϭⲱϭⲉ ⲉⲣⲟⲓ̈ ⲛ̄ϭⲓ ⲛⲉⲡⲣⲟⲃⲟⲗⲟⲟⲩⲉ ⲙ̄-
ⲡⲁⲩⲑⲁⲇⲏⲥ·

2. ⲁⲩⲱ ⲉⲩϣⲁⲛⲕⲓⲙ ⲛ̄ϭⲓ ⲛ̄ϩⲩⲗⲏ ⲧⲏⲣⲟⲩ· ⲁⲛⲟⲕ ⲇⲉ
ⲛ̄ϯⲛⲁⲕⲓⲙ ⲁⲛ·

3. ⲁⲩⲱ ⲉⲩϣⲁⲛⲧⲁⲕⲟ ⲛ̄ϭⲓ ⲛⲁϩⲩⲗⲏ ⲧⲏⲣⲟⲩ ⲛ̄ⲥⲉϭⲱ
15 ϩ̄ⲙ ⲡⲉⲭⲗⲟⲥ· ⲛⲁⲓ̈ ⲉⲧⲟⲩⲛⲁⲩ ⲉⲣⲟⲟⲩ ⲛ̄ϭⲓ ⲛⲉⲡⲣⲟⲃⲟⲗⲟⲟⲩⲉ ⲙ̄ⲡⲁⲩⲑⲁⲇⲏⲥ· ⲁⲛⲟⲕ ⲇⲉ ⲛ̄ϯⲛⲁⲧⲁⲕⲟ ⲁⲛ·

4. ϫⲉ ⲡⲟⲩⲟⲓ̈ⲛ ϣⲟⲟⲡ ⲛ̄ⲙⲙⲁⲓ̈· ⲁⲩⲱ ⲁⲛⲟⲕ ϩⲱ
ϯϣⲟⲟⲡ ⲙ̄ⲛ ⲡⲟⲩⲟⲓ̈ⲛ·

ⲛⲉⲓ̈ϣⲁϫⲉ ⲇⲉ ⲁⲥϫⲟⲟⲩ ⲛ̄ϭⲓ ⲧⲡⲓⲥⲧⲓⲥ ⲥⲟⲫⲓⲁ· ⲧⲉ-
20 ⲛⲟⲩ ϭⲉ ⲡⲉⲧⲛⲟⲓ̈ ⲙ̄ⲡⲛⲟⲏⲙⲁ ⲛ̄ⲛⲉⲓ̈ϣⲁϫⲉ· ⲙⲁⲣⲉϥⲉⲓ’ ⲉⲑⲏ
ⲛ̄ϥⲧⲁⲩⲉ-ⲡⲉⲩⲃⲱⲗ· ⲁⲥⲉⲓ’ ⲇⲉ ⲉⲑⲏ ⲛ̄ϭⲓ ⲙⲁⲣⲓⲁ ⲧⲙⲁⲁⲩ
ⲛ̄ⲓ̅ⲥ̅ ⲡⲉⲭⲁⲥ ϫⲉ ⲡⲁϣⲏⲣⲉ ⲕⲁⲧⲁ ⲡⲕⲟⲥⲙⲟⲥ ⲡⲁⲛⲟⲩⲧⲉ ⲣ̅ⲋ̅ᵇ
ⲁⲩⲱ ⲡⲁⲥⲱⲧⲏⲣ ⲕⲁⲧⲁ ⲡϫⲓⲥⲉ ⲕⲉⲗⲉⲩⲉ ⲛⲁⲓ̈ ⲧⲁⲧⲁⲩⲉ-
ⲡⲃⲱⲗ ⲛ̄ⲛϣⲁϫⲉ ⲉⲛⲧⲁⲥϫⲟⲟⲩ ⲛ̄ϭⲓ ⲧⲡⲓⲥⲧⲓⲥ ⲥⲟⲫⲓⲁ·
25 ⲁϥⲟⲩⲱϣ̄ⲃ ⲇⲉ ⲛ̄ϭⲓ ⲓ̅ⲥ̅ ⲡⲉⲭⲁϥ ϫⲉ ⲛ̄ⲧⲟ ϩⲱⲱⲧⲉ ⲙⲁ-
ⲣⲓⲁ· ⲧⲁⲓ̈ ⲉⲛⲧⲁⲥϫⲓ-ⲙⲟⲣⲫⲏ ⲉⲧⲍ̄ⲛ ⲧⲃⲁⲣⲃⲏⲗⲱ ⲕⲁⲧⲁ ⲟⲩ-

on her head. Now it happened further, as it surrounded the *pure* light within the Sophia, her *pure* light was not (left) without [1] the crown of the flame of the light-power, so that the *emanations* of the Authades did not steal it.

Now when these things had happened, the *pure* light-power within the Sophia began to *sing praises*; *but* she *sang praises* to my light-power which had become a crown on her head. She *sang praises*, saying thus :

1. 'The light has become a crown on my head and I will not be (left) without it, so that the *emanations* of the Authades do not steal it from me.

2. And even if all the *materials* move, I *however* will not move.

3. And even if all my *materials* are destroyed and remain in the *Chaos* — these which the *emanations* of the Authades see — I *however* will not be destroyed.

4. For the light is with me, and I myself am [2] with the light.'

But the Pistis Sophia said these words. Now at this time let him who *understands* the *thought* of these words come forward and give their interpretation."

Mary, the mother of Jesus, came forward. She said : "My son *according to* the *world*, my God and my *Saviour according to* the height, *command* me that I give the explanation of the words which the Pistis Sophia said."

But Jesus answered and said : "Thou also, Mary, thou hast received *form* [3] which is in the Barbelo *according to* the *matter*, | and thou hast received likeness which is in the

---

[1]   (3) was not (left) without; Till : was not separate from (see 116.10; 117.12).

[2]   (17) I myself am; Till : I also am.

[3]   (26) received form; see Iren. I.4.1, 5; U 226.

ⲗ̅ⲏ̅· ⲁⲩⲱ ⲁⲣⲉⲭⲓ-ⲉⲓⲛⲉ ⲉⲍ̅ⲛ̅ ⲧⲡⲁⲣⲑⲉⲛⲟⲥ ⲙ̅ⲡⲟⲩⲟⲓ̈ⲛ ⲕⲁⲧⲁ
ⲡⲟⲩⲟⲓ̈ⲛ ⲛ̅ⲧⲟ ⲙ̅ⲛ̅ ⲧⲕⲉⲙⲁⲣⲓ̈ⲍⲁⲙ ⲧⲙⲁⲕⲁⲣⲓⲟⲥ· ⲁⲩⲱ ⲛ̅ⲧⲁ
ⲡⲕⲁⲕⲉ ⲱ̅ⲡⲉ ⲉⲧⲃⲏⲏⲧⲉ ⲁⲩⲱ ⲟⲛ ⲛ̅ⲧⲁϥⲉⲓ' ⲉⲃⲟⲗ ⲛ̅ϩⲏⲧⲉ
ⲛ̅ϭⲓ ⲡⲥⲱⲙⲁ ⲛ̅ⲟⲩⲗⲏ ⲉϥⲱⲟⲟⲡ ⲛ̅ϩⲏⲧϥ̅ ⲡⲁⲓ̈ ⲉⲛⲧⲁⲓ̈ⲧⲃⲃⲟϥ·
5 ⲁⲩⲱ ⲁⲓ̈ⲥⲟⲧϥ̅ϥ̅· ⲧⲉⲛⲟⲩ ϭⲉ ϯⲕⲉⲗⲉⲩⲉ ⲛⲉ ⲉⲧⲣⲉⲧⲁⲩⲉ-
ⲡⲃⲱⲗ ⲛ̅ⲛ̅ⲱⲁϫⲉ ⲛⲁⲓ̈ ⲉⲛⲧⲁⲥⲭⲟⲟⲥ ⲛ̅ϭⲓ ⲧⲥⲟⲫⲓⲁ· ⲁⲥⲟⲩ-
ⲱ̅ⲃ ⲇⲉ ⲛ̅ϭⲓ ⲙⲁⲣⲓⲁ ⲧⲙⲁⲁⲩ ⲛ̅ⲓ̅ⲥ̅ ⲡⲉϫⲁⲥ ϫⲉ ⲡⲁⲭⲟⲉⲓⲥ·
ⲁ ⲧⲉⲕϭⲟⲙ ⲛ̅ⲟⲩⲟⲓ̈ⲛ ⲡⲣⲟⲫⲏⲧⲉⲩⲉ ϩⲁ ⲛⲉⲓ̈ⲱⲁϫⲉ ⲙ̅ⲡⲓ- ⲣ̅ⲉ̅
ⲟⲩⲟⲉⲓ̈ⲱ ϩⲓⲧ̅ⲛ̅ ⲥⲟⲗⲟⲙⲱⲛ ϩ̅ⲛ̅ ⲧⲉϥⲙⲉϩⲙⲛ̅ⲧ·ⲯⲓⲧⲉ ⲛ̅ⲱⲇⲏ
10 ⲁⲩⲱ ⲡⲉϫⲁⲥ ϫⲉ

    ⲁ. ⲡϫⲟⲉⲓⲥ ϩⲓⲭ̅ⲛ̅ ⲧⲁⲁⲡⲉ ⲛ̅ⲑⲉ ⲛ̅ⲟⲩⲕⲗⲟⲙ· ⲁⲩⲱ ⲛ̅-
ϯⲛⲁⲣ̅ⲡⲉϥⲃⲟⲗ ⲁⲛ·

    ⲃ. ⲁⲩⲱⲱⲛⲧ ⲛⲁⲓ̈ ⲙ̅ⲡⲉⲕⲗⲟⲙ ⲛ̅ⲧⲁⲗⲏⲑⲓⲁ· ⲁⲩⲱ ⲁϥⲧⲣⲉ
ⲛⲉⲕⲕⲗⲁⲇⲟⲥ ϯⲟⲩⲱ ϩⲣⲁⲓ̈ ⲛ̅ϩⲏⲧ·

15   ⲅ. ϫⲉ ⲉϥⲉⲓⲛⲉ ⲁⲛ ⲛ̅ⲟⲩⲕⲗⲟⲙ ⲉϥⲱⲟⲩⲱⲟⲩ ⲉⲙⲉϥϯ-
ⲟⲩⲱ· ⲁⲗⲗⲁ ⲕⲟⲛ̅ⲥ̅ ϩⲓⲭ̅ⲛ̅ ⲧⲁⲁⲡⲉ· ⲁⲩⲱ ⲁⲕϯⲟⲩⲱ ϩⲣⲁⲓ̈
ϩⲓϫⲱⲓ̈·

    ⲇ. ⲛⲉⲕⲕⲁⲣⲡⲟⲥ ⲥⲉⲙⲉϩ· ⲁⲩⲱ ⲥⲉϫⲏⲕ· ⲉⲩⲙⲉϩ ⲉⲃⲟⲗ
ϩ̅ⲙ̅ ⲡⲉⲕⲟⲩϫⲁⲓ̈·

20 ⲁⲥⲱⲡⲉ ϭⲉ ⲛ̅ⲧⲉⲣⲉ ⲓ̅ⲥ̅ ⲥⲱⲧ̅ⲙ̅ ⲉⲛⲉⲓ̈ⲱⲁϫⲉ ⲉⲥϫⲱ
ⲙ̅ⲙⲟⲟⲩ ⲛ̅ϭⲓ ⲙⲁⲣⲓⲁ ⲧⲉϥⲙⲁⲁⲩ· ⲡⲉϫⲁϥ ⲛⲁⲥ ϫⲉ ⲉⲩⲅⲉ
ⲕⲁⲗⲱⲥ· ϩⲁⲙⲏⲛ ϩⲁⲙⲏⲛ ϯϫⲱ ⲙ̅ⲙⲟⲥ ⲛⲉ ϫⲉ ⲥⲉⲛⲁ-
ⲙⲁⲕⲁⲣⲓⲍⲉ ⲙ̅ⲙⲟ ϫⲓⲛ ⲁⲣⲏⲭ̅ϥ̅ ⲙ̅ⲡⲕⲁϩ ⲱⲁ ⲁⲣⲏⲭ̅ϥ̅· ϫⲉ
ⲁⲥϭⲟⲉⲓⲗⲉ ⲉⲣⲟ ⲛ̅ϭⲓ ⲧⲡⲁⲣⲁⲑⲏⲕⲏ ⲙ̅ⲡⲱⲟⲣⲡ̅ ⲙ̅ⲙⲩⲥⲧⲏ- ⲣ̅ⲉ̅ ᵇ

---

18   MS ⲥⲉⲙⲥϩ and ⲥⲩⲙⲥϩ; better ⲥⲉⲙⲏϩ and ⲥⲩⲙⲏϩ.

Virgin of the Light *according to* the light, thou and the other Mary, the *blessed one*. And for thy sake the darkness exists and furthermore, from thee has come forth the *material body* in which I exist, which I have cleaned and purified. Now at this time I *command* thee to give the interpretation of the words which the Sophia said.

However Mary, the mother of Jesus, answered, she said : "My Lord, thy light-power once *prophesied* about these words through Solomon in the 19th *Ode* and said :

1. 'The Lord is upon my head like a crown and I shall not be without him.

2. They plaited for me the *true* crown [1], and it caused thy *branches* to sprout in me.

3. For it is not like a withered crown which does not sprout; *but* thou livest upon my head and thou dost sprout upon me.

4. Thy *fruits* are full and ripe, filled with thy salvation'. *"

Now it happened when Jesus heard these words which Mary his mother spoke [2], he said to her : "*Excellent, well done. Truly, truly*, I say that they will *bless* thee from end to end of the earth □, for the *pledge* of the First *Mystery* was entrusted to thee. | And by means of that *pledge* all those

---

* Ps. Sol. 19.1-4
□ cf. Lk. 1.48

---

[1] (13) true crown; lit. crown of truth.
[2] (20, 21) when Jesus heard these words which ... spoke; Till: when Jesus had heard ... speaking these words; (cf. 124.11, 12; 125.14, 15 etc.).

ΡΙΟΝ · ΑΥѠ ЄΒΟΛ ϨΙΤΟΟΤϤ ΝΤΠΑΡΑΘΗΚΗ ЄΤΜΜΑΥ
ЄΥΝΑΝΟΥϨΜ ΝϬΙ ΝΑΠΚΑϨ ΤΗΡΟΥ ΜΝ ΝΑΠϪΙϹЄ ΤΗΡΟΥ ·
ΑΥѠ ΤΠΑΡΑΘΗΚΗ ЄΤΜΜΑΥ · ΝΤΟϹ ΤЄ ΤΑΡΧΗ ΑΥѠ
ΠϪѠΚ ·

5　ΑϤΟΥѠϨ ΔЄ ΟΝ ЄΤΟΟΤϤ ΝϬΙ ΙϹ ϨΜ ΠϢΑϪЄ ΠЄ-
ϪΑϤ ΝΝЄϤΜΑΘΗΤΗϹ · ϪЄ ΑϹϢѠΠЄ ΝΤЄΡЄϹϪѠ Ν-
ΤΜЄϨΜΝΤϢΟΜΤЄ ΜΜЄΤΑΝΟΙΑ ΝϬΙ ΤΠΙϹΤΙϹ ϹΟΦΙΑ · Ν-
ΤЄΥΝΟΥ ΔЄ ЄΤΜΜΑΥ ΑϤϪѠΚ ЄΒΟΛ ΝϬΙ ΠΤѠϢ ΝΝЄ-
ΘΛΙΨΙϹ ΤΗΡΟΥ · ΝΑΪ ЄΝΤΑΥΤΟϢΟΥ ЄΠΙϹΤΙϹ ϹΟ-
10　ΦΙΑ · ЄΤΒЄ ΠϪѠΚ ЄΒΟΛ ΜΠϢΟΡΠ ΜΜΥϹΤΗΡΙΟΝ ΠΑΪ
ЄΤϢΟΟΠ ϪΙΝ ΝϢΟΡΠ · ΑΥѠ ΑϤЄΙ' ΝϬΙ ΠЄΟΥΟЄΙϢ
ЄΤΡЄΥΝΑϨΜЄϹ ϨΜ ΠЄΧΛΟϹ** ΑΥѠ ΝϹЄΝΤϹ ЄϨΡΑΪ ϨΝ Ρ Ζ
ΝΚΑΚЄ ΤΗΡΟΥ · ΑΥϪΙ ΓΑΡ ЄΤΟΟΤϹ ΝΤЄϹΜЄΤΑΝΟΙΑ
ϨΙΤΜ ΠΙϢΟΡΠ ΜΜΥϹΤΗΡΙΟΝ · ΑΥѠ ΝΤΟϤ ΠΜΥϹΤΗΡΙΟΝ
15　ЄΤΜΜΑΥ ΑϤΤΝΝΟΟΥ ΝΑΪ ΝΟΥΝΟϬ ΝϬΟΜ ΝΟΥΟΪΝ
ЄΒΟΛ ϨΜ ΠϪΙϹЄ · ЄΤΡΑΒΟΗΘΙ ЄΠΙϹΤΙϹ ϹΟΦΙΑ · ΑΥѠ
ΝΤΑΝΤϹ ЄϨΡΑΪ ЄΠЄΧΛΟϹ · ΑΪϬѠϢΤ ΔЄ ЄΠϪΙϹЄ Ν-
ΛΙѠΝ · ΑΪΝΑΥ ЄΤϬΟΜ ΝΟΥΟЄΙΝ ЄΝΤΑϤΤΝΝΟΟΥϹ ΝΑΪ
ΝϬΙ ΠΙϢΟΡΠ ΜΜΥϹΤΗΡΙΟΝ ϪЄ ЄΪЄΝΟΥϨΜ ΝΤϹΟΦΙΑ ϨΜ
20　ΠЄΧΛΟϹ · ΑϹϢѠΠЄ ϬЄ ΝΤЄΡΙΝΑΥ ЄΡΟϹ ЄϹΝΗΥ ЄΒΟΛ
ϨΝ ΝΛΙѠΝ · ΑΥѠ ЄϹΠΗΤ ЄϨΟΥΝ ЄΡΟΪ · ΑΝΟΚ ΔЄ ΝЄΪ-
ϨΙϪΜ ΠЄΧΛΟϹ ΠЄ · Α ΚЄϬΟΜ ΝϬΟΜ ΝΟΥΟΪΝ ЄΙ' ЄΒΟΛ
ΝϨΗΤ ϨѠ ϪЄ ЄϹЄΒΟΗΘΙ ϨѠѠϹ ЄΠΙϹΤΙϹ ϹΟΦΙΑ · ΑΥѠ
ΤϬΟΜ ΝΟΥΟΪΝ ЄΝΤΑϹЄΙ' ЄΒΟΛ ϨΜ ΠϪΙϹЄ ϨΙΤΜ ΠΙ- Ρ Ζ b
25　ϢΟΡΠ ΜΜΥϹΤΗΡΙΟΝ ΑϹЄΙ' ЄΠЄϹΗΤ ЄϪΝ ΤϬΟΜ ΝΟΥ-

13　MS ЄΤΟΟΤϹ; read ΠΤΟΟΤϹ.
17　MS ЄϨΡΑΪ ЄΠЄϹϪΛΟϹ; Ϲ erased; read ЄϨΡΑΪ ϨΜ ΠЄΧΛΟϹ. MS. ΝΛΙѠΝ;
　　read ΝΝΛΙѠΝ.
22　MS ΚЄϬΟΜ ΝϬΟΜ; omit ΝϬΟΜ.

of the earth and all those of the height will be saved. And that *pledge* is the *beginning* and the end." *

60. Jesus *however* continued with the discourse. He said to his *disciples* : "It happened when the Pistis Sophia said the thirteenth *repentance, moreover* at that hour the ordinance was completed of all the *afflictions* which had been ordained for the Pistis Sophia, because of the completion of the First *Mystery*, which had been since the beginning. And the time came that she should be saved from the *Chaos* and brought forth from all the darknesses. *For* her *repentance* was received by the First *Mystery*. And that *Mystery* sent me a great light-power from the height, so that I should *help* the Pistis Sophia and bring her up from the *Chaos*. *But* I looked to the *aeons* of the height [1], I saw the light-power which the First *Mystery* had sent to me so that I should save the Sophia from the *Chaos*. Now it happened, when I saw it coming forth from the *aeons* and it hastened towards me — *but* I was above the *Chaos* — another light-power also came forth from me, in order to *help* the Pistis Sophia. And the light-power which came forth from the height through the First *Mystery* came down upon the light-power | which came forth from me. And they

---

* cf. Rev. 21.6; 22.13

---

[1] (17, 18) the aeons of the height; lit. the height of the aeons.

ΟΕΙΝ ΕΝΤΑϭΕΙ' ΕΒΟΛ ΜΜΟΪ · ΑΥⲰ ΑΥⲀΠΑΝΤΑ ΕΝΕΥ-
ΕΡΗΥ ΑΥⲢ-ΟΥΝΟϭ ΝⲀΠΟΡΡΟΙⲀ Ν̄ΟΥΟΪΝ ·

Ⲍ ΝΑΪ ϭΕ Ν̄ΤΕΡΕϥϪΟΟΥ Ν̄ϬΙ ΙⲤ Ν̄ΝΕϥΜⲀⲐΗΤΗⲤ · ΠΕ-
ϪⲀϥ ϪΕ ΤΕΤⲚ̄ΝΟΪ ϪΕ ΕΪϢⲀϪΕ Ν̄ΜΜΗΤⲚ̄ Ν̄ⲀϢ Ν̄ⲌΕ ·
5 ΑⲤϬΟϬⲤ ΟΝ ΕΒΟΛ Ν̄ϬΙ ΜⲀΡΙⲌⲀΜ ΠΕϪⲀⲤ ϪΕ ΠⲀϪΟΕΙⲤ
ϮΝΟΪ ϪΕ ΕΚϪΕ-ΟΥ · ΕΤΒΕ ΠΒⲰΛ Μ̄ΠΕΪϢⲀϪΕ Α ΤΕΚ-
ϬΟΜ Ν̄ΟΥΟΪΝ ΠΡΟΦΗΤΕΥΕ Μ̄ΠΙΟΥΟΪϢ ⲀΙΤⲚ̄ ⲀⲀΥΪⲀ
ⲀΜ ΠΜΕⲌⲌΜΕΝΕΤⲀϥΤΕ Μ̄ΨⲀΛΜΟⲤ ΕⲤϪⲰ Μ̄ΜΟⲤ · ϪΕ

10. Α ΠΝⲀ' Μ̄Ν ΤΜΕ ΤⲰΜⲦ ΕΝΕΥΕΡΗΥ · ΑΥⲰ ΤⲀΙ-
10 ΚⲀΙΟⲤΥΝΗ Μ̄Ν ϮΡΗΝΗ ΑΥϮΠΙ ΕΝΕΥΕΡΗΥ .

11. Α ΤΜΕ ϮΟΥⲰ ΕΒΟΛ ⲀΜ ΠΚⲀⲌ · ΑΥⲰ Α ΤⲀΙΚⲀΙ- ҏ̄
ΟⲤΥΝΗ ϬⲰϢⲦ ΕΒΟΛ ⲀΝ ΤΠΕ ·

ΠΝⲀ' ϭΕ ΠΕ ϮϬΟΜ Ν̄ΟΥΟΪΝ ΕΝΤΑϭΕΙ' ΕΒΟΛ ⲀΙΤΜ ΠΙ-
ϢΟΡⲠ̄ Μ̄ΜΥⲤΤΗΡΙΟΝ · ϪΕ ΑϥⲤⲰΤⲘ̄ ΕΠΙⲤΤΙⲤ ⲤΟΦΙⲀ
15 Ν̄ϬΙ ΠΙϢΟΡⲠ̄ Μ̄ΜΥⲤΤΗΡΙΟΝ ΑϥΝⲀ' ΝⲀⲤ ⲀΝ ΝΕⲤⲐΛΙΨΙⲤ
ΤΗΡΟΥ · ΤΜΕ ⲌⲰⲰϥ ΤΕ ϮϬΟΜ ΕΝΤΑϭΕΙ' ΕΒΟΛ Ν̄ⲀΗΤⲔ̄
ΕΒΟΛ ϪΕ ΑΚϪⲰΚ ΕΒΟΛ Ν̄ΤΜΕ ΕΤΡΕΚΝⲀⲀΜΕⲤ ⲀΜ ΠΕ-
ϪⲀΟⲤ · ΑΥⲰ ΟΝ ΤⲀΙΚⲀΙΟⲤΥΝΗ ΤΕ ϮϬΟΜ ΕΝΤΑϭΕΙ'
ΕΒΟΛ ⲀΙΤⲘ̄ ΠΙϢΟΡⲠ̄ Μ̄ΜΥⲤΤΗΡΙΟΝ ΤΑΪ ΕΤΝⲀⲢⲀΜΜΕ
20 Ν̄ΤΠΙⲤΤΙⲤ ⲤΟΦΙⲀ · ΑΥⲰ ΟΝ ϮΡΗΝΗ ΠΕ ϮϬΟΜ Ν̄ΤⲀϭΕΙ'
ΕΒΟΛ Μ̄ΜΟΚ ΕΒΟΛ ϪΕ ΕⲤΝⲀΒⲰΚ ΕⲀΟΥΝ ΕΝΕΠΡΟΒΟ-
ΛΟΟΥΕ Μ̄ΠⲀΥⲐⲀⲀΗⲤ Ν̄ⲤϥΙ Ν̄ⲀΗΤΟΥ Ν̄ΝΟΥΟΪΝ ΕΝΤ-

---

11 Z̄ in upper right-hand margin at end of quire.
20 MS ΠΕ; read ΤΕ.

met one another and became a great *outpouring* of light."

Now when Jesus had said these things to his *disciples* he said : "Do you *understand* the manner in which I am speaking with you?"

Mariam sprang up, she said : "My Lord, I *understand* what thou dost say. Concerning the interpretation of these words, thy light-power once *prophesied* through David in the 84th *Psalm*, saying :

10. 'Mercy and truth have met one another, and *righteousness* and *peace* have kissed one another.

11. Truth has sprouted from the earth and *righteousness* has looked forth from heaven.' *

Now mercy is the light-power which came forth through the First *Mystery*, for the First *Mystery* heard the Pistis Sophia, and had mercy on her in all her *afflictions*. Truth, on the other hand, is the power which came forth from thee, because thou didst fulfil the truth that thou shouldst save her (the Pistis Sophia) from the *Chaos*. And furthermore, *righteousness* is the power which came forth through the First *Mystery*, which will guide the Pistis Sophia. And again *peace* is the power which came forth from thee, because it will go into the *emanations* of the Authades and take away from them the lights | which they took from

---

* Ps. 84.10, 11

ⲗⲩϥⲓⲧⲟⲩ ⲍ̄ⲛ ⲧⲡⲓⲥⲧⲓⲥ ⲥⲟⲫⲓⲁ · ⲉⲧⲉ ⲡⲁⲓ̈ ⲡⲉ ⲛ̄ⲧⲥⲟⲟⲩ-
ⲍⲟⲩ ⲉⲍⲟⲩⲛ ⲉⲧⲥⲟⲫⲓⲁ ⲛ̄ⲅⲁⲁⲩ ⲛ̄ⲉⲓⲣⲏⲛⲏ ⲙⲛ̄ ⲧⲉⲥϭⲟⲙ · ⲣ̄ⲓ̄ᵇ
ⲧⲙⲉ ⲍⲱⲱⲥ ⲧⲉ ⲧϭⲟⲙ ⲉⲛⲧⲁⲥⲉⲓ̓ ⲉⲃⲟⲗ ⲛ̄ⲍⲏⲧⲕ̄ ⲉⲕⲍ̄ⲛ
ⲛ̄ⲧⲟⲡⲟⲥ ⲙ̄ⲡⲉⲥⲏⲧ ⲙ̄ⲡⲉⲭⲗⲁⲟⲥ · ⲉⲧⲃⲉ ⲡⲁⲓ̈ ⲁ ⲧⲉⲕϭⲟⲙ
5 ⲭⲟⲟⲥ ⲍⲓⲧⲛ̄ ⲇⲁⲩⲉⲓⲁ · ⲭⲉ

ⲁ ⲧⲙⲉ ϯⲟⲩⲱ ⲉⲃⲟⲗ ⲍ̄ⲙ ⲡⲕⲁⲍ · ⲉⲃⲟⲗ ⲭⲉ ⲉⲕⲍ̄ⲛ
ⲛ̄ⲧⲟⲡⲟⲥ ⲙ̄ⲡⲉⲥⲏⲧ ⲙ̄ⲡⲉⲭⲗⲁⲟⲥ · ⲧⲁⲓⲕⲁⲓⲟⲥⲩⲛⲏ ⲍⲱⲱⲥ
ⲛ̄ⲧⲁⲥϭⲱϣⲧ ⲉⲃⲟⲗ ⲍ̄ⲛ ⲧⲡⲉ · ⲛ̄ⲧⲟⲥ ⲇⲉ ⲧϭⲟⲙ ⲉⲛⲧⲁⲥⲉⲓ̓
ⲉⲃⲟⲗ ⲍ̄ⲙ ⲡ̄ⲭⲓⲥⲉ ⲍⲓⲧ̄ⲙ ⲡⲓϣⲟⲣ̄ⲡ̄ ⲙ̄ⲙⲩⲥⲧⲏⲣⲓⲟⲛ · ⲧⲁⲓ̈ ⲉⲛⲧ-
10 ⲁⲥⲃⲱⲕ ⲉⲍⲟⲩⲛ ⲉⲧⲥⲟⲫⲓⲁ ·

ⲍ̄ ⲁⲥϣⲱⲡⲉ ϭⲉ ⲛ̄ⲧⲉⲣⲉ ⲓ̄ⲥ̄ ⲥⲱⲧ̄ⲙ ⲉⲛⲉⲓ̈ϣⲁⲭⲉ · ⲡⲉⲭⲁϥ
ⲭⲉ ⲉⲩⲅⲉ ⲙⲁⲣⲓⲍⲁⲙ ⲧⲙⲁⲕⲁⲣⲓⲁ ⲧⲁⲓ̈ ⲉⲧⲛⲁⲕⲗⲏⲣⲟⲛⲟⲙⲓ
ⲛ̄ⲧⲙⲛ̄ⲧⲉⲣⲟ ⲧⲏⲣⲥ̄ ⲙ̄ⲡⲟⲩⲟⲓ̈ⲛ · ⲙⲛ̄ⲛ̄ⲥⲁ ⲛⲁⲓ̈ ⲁⲥⲉⲓ̓ ⲍⲱⲱⲥ
ⲉⲑⲏ ⲛ̄ϭⲓ ⲙⲁⲣⲓⲁ ⲧⲙⲁⲁⲩ ⲛ̄ⲓ̄ⲥ̄ ⲡⲉⲭⲁⲥ ⲭⲉ ⲡⲁⲭⲟⲉⲓⲥ
15 ⲁⲩⲱ ⲡⲁⲥⲱⲧⲏⲣ ⲕⲉⲗⲉⲩⲉ ⲛⲁⲓ̈ ⲍⲱ ⲉⲧⲣⲁⲭⲱ ⲙ̄ⲡⲉⲓ̈ϣⲁⲭⲉ ⲣ̄ⲟ̄
ⲛⲟⲩⲱⲍ̄ⲙ · ⲡⲉⲭⲁϥ ⲛ̄ϭⲓ ⲓ̄ⲥ̄ ⲭⲉ ⲡⲉⲧⲉⲣⲉ ⲡⲉϥⲡ̄ⲛ̄ⲁ ⲛⲁⲣ̄-
ⲛⲟⲉⲣⲟⲥ · ⲛ̄ϯⲛⲁⲕⲱⲗⲩ ⲙ̄ⲙⲟϥ ⲁⲛ ⲁⲗⲗⲁ ϯⲡⲣⲟⲧⲣⲉⲡⲉ
ⲙ̄ⲙⲟϥ ⲛ̄ⲍⲟⲩⲟ ⲉⲧⲣⲉϥⲭⲱ ⲙ̄ⲡⲛⲟⲏⲙⲁ ⲉⲛⲧⲁϥⲕⲓⲙ ⲉⲣⲟϥ ·
ⲧⲉⲛⲟⲩ ϭⲉ ⲙⲁⲣⲓⲁ ⲧⲁⲙⲁⲁⲩ ⲕⲁⲧⲁ ⲑⲩⲗⲏ ⲧⲉⲛⲧⲁⲓ̈ϭⲟⲓⲗⲉ
20 ⲉⲣⲟⲥ ϯⲕⲉⲗⲉⲩⲉ ⲛⲉ ⲉⲧⲣⲉⲭⲱ ⲍⲱⲱⲧⲉ ⲙ̄ⲡⲛⲟⲏⲙⲁ ⲙ̄-
ⲡϣⲁⲭⲉ ꞉ ⲁⲥⲟⲩⲱϣ̄ⲃ ⲇⲉ ⲛ̄ϭⲓ ⲙⲁⲣⲓⲁ ⲡⲉⲭⲁⲥ ⲭⲉ ⲡⲁⲭⲟⲉⲓⲥ ⲉⲧⲃⲉ ⲡϣⲁⲭⲉ ⲉⲛⲧⲁ ⲧⲉⲕϭⲟⲙ ⲡⲣⲟⲫⲏⲧⲉⲩⲉ
ⲙ̄ⲙⲟϥ ⲍⲓⲧⲛ̄ ⲇⲁⲩⲉⲓⲁ · ⲭⲉ

8　MS ⲛ̄ⲧⲟⲥ ⲧⲉ ⲧϭⲟⲙ.
15　ⲡ̄ in upper left-hand margin at beginning of quire.

the Pistis Sophia; that is, thou dost gather them within the Sophia and dost make them to be at *peace* with her power. Truth, on the other hand, is the power which came forth from thee when thou wast in the lower *places* of the *Chaos*. Concerning this, thy power spoke through David thus: 'Truth has sprouted from the earth'*, because thou wast in the lower *places* of the *Chaos*. *Righteousness*, on the other hand, which looked forth from heaven, is the power which came forth from the height, through the First *Mystery*, and which entered into the Sophia."

61. Now it happened when Jesus heard these words, he said: "*Excellent*, Mariam, thou *blessed one* who wilt *inherit* the whole Kingdom of the Light."

After these things Mary, the mother of Jesus, also came forward and said: "My Lord and my *Saviour, command* me also that I answer [1] this discourse."

Jesus said: "I will not *prevent* him whose *spirit* has become *understanding, but* I *urge* him the more to speak the *thought* which has moved him. Now at this time, Mary, my mother *according to* the *matter*, to whom I was entrusted, I *command* thee that thou also sayest the *thought* of the discourse."

Mary answered, however, and said: "My Lord, concerning the word which thy power *prophesied* through David: |

---

*   Ps. 84.11

---

[1]   (15) answer; Till: explain.

10. Ⲁ ⲠⲚⲀ' ⲘⲚ ⲦⲘⲈ ⲦⲰⲘⲦ ⲈⲚⲈⲨⲈⲢⲎⲨ · ⲦⲀⲒⲔⲀⲒ-
ⲟⲥⲨⲚⲎ ⲘⲚ ⳨ⲢⲎⲚⲎ ⲀⲨ⳨ⲠⲒ ⲈⲢⲚ ⲚⲈⲨⲈⲢⲎⲨ ·

11. Ⲁ ⲦⲘⲈ ⳨ⲞⲨⲰ ⲈⲂⲞⲖ ⳨Ⲙ ⲠⲔⲀⳞ · ⲀⲨⲰ Ⲁ ⲦⲀⲒⲔⲀⲒ-
ⲟⲥⲨⲚⲎ ⳘⲰⳘⲦ ⲈⲂⲞⲖ ⳥Ⲛ ⲦⲠⲈ · ⲚⲦⲀ ⲦⲈⲔⳘⲞⲘ ⲠⲢⲞⲪⲎ-
5 ⲦⲈⲨⲈ ⲘⲠⲈⳆⲰⲀⳐⲈ ⲘⲠⲈⳆⲞⲨⲞⳆⳘ ⲈⲦⲂⲎⲎⲦⲔ · ⲈⲔⲞ ⲚⲔⲞⲨⳆ ·
ⲈⲘⲠⲀⲦⲈ ⲠⲈⲠⲚⲀ ⲈⳆ' ⲈⳐⲰⲔ ⲈⲔⳘⲞⲞⲠ ⳥Ⲛ ⲞⲨⲘⲀ ⲚⳇⲖⲞ- ⲣⲟ ᵇ
ⲞⲖⲈ ⲘⲚ ⳆⲰⲤⲎ⳽ · ⲀⳑⲈⳆ' ⲚⳕⲒ ⲠⲈⲠⲚⲀ ⲈⲂⲞⲖ ⳥Ⲙ ⲠⳐⲒⳘⲈ ·
ⲀⳑⲈⳆ' ⲚⲀⳆ ⲈⳞⲞⲨⲚ ⲈⲠⲀⲎⳆ · ⲈⳑⲈⳆⲚⲈ ⲘⲘⲞⲔ · ⲀⲨⲰ ⲈⲚⲈ-
ⲘⲠⲒⲤⲞⲨⲰⲚⳑ ⲠⲈ ⲀⲨⲰ ⲚⲈⳆⲘⲈⲈⲨⲈ ⳐⲈ ⲚⲦⲞⲔ ⲠⲈ · ⲀⲨⲰ
10 ⲠⲈⳐⲀⳑ ⲚⲀⳆ ⲚⳕⲒ ⲠⲈⲠⲚⲀ ⳐⲈ ⲈⳑⲦⲰⲚ ⲒⳘ ⲠⲀⲤⲞⲚ ⲦⲀⳑ-
ⲠⲀⲚⲦⲀ ⲈⲢⲞⳑ · ⲀⲨⲰ ⲚⲦⲈⲢⲈⳑⳐⲈ-ⲠⲀⳆ ⲚⲀⳆ · ⲀⳆⲀⲠⲞⲢⳆ · ⲀⲨⲰ
ⲚⲈⳆⲘⲈⲈⲨⲈ ⲠⲈ ⳐⲈ ⲞⲨⲪⲀⲚⲦⲀⳘⲘⲀ ⲠⲈ ⲈⲠⲒⲢⲀⳞⲈ ⲘⲘⲞⳆ ·
ⲀⳆⳑⲒⲦⳑ ⲆⲈ ⲀⳆⲘⲞⲢⳑ ⲈⳞⲞⲨⲚ ⲈⲦⲞⲨⲈⲢⲎⲦⲈ ⲘⲠⲘⲀ ⲚⲚⲔⲞⲦⲔ
ⲈⲦ⳥Ⲙ ⲠⲀⲎⳆ · ⳘⲀⲚⳘⳆⲈⳆ' ⲚⲎⲦⲚ ⲈⲂⲞⲖ ⲈⲦⲤⲰⳘⲈ · ⲚⲦⲞⲔ
15 ⲘⲚ ⳆⲰⲤⲎ⳽ ⲀⲨⲰ ⲚⲦⲀⳞⲈ ⲈⲢⲰⲦⲚ ⳥Ⲙ ⲠⲘⲀ ⲚⲈⲖⲞⲞⲖⲈ ·
ⲈⲢⲈ ⳆⲰⲤⲎ⳽ ⳨ ⲘⲠⲘⲀ ⲚⲈⲖⲞⲞⲖⲈ ⲈⲠⲔⲀⳘ · ⲀⲤⳘⲰⲠⲈ ⳕⲈ
ⲚⲦⲈⲢⲈⲔⲤⲰⲦⲘ ⲈⲢⲞⳆ ⲈⳆⳐⲰ ⲘⲠⳘⲀⳐⲈ ⲈⳆⲰⲤⲎ⳽ ⲀⲔⲚⲞⳆ
ⲘⲠⳘⲀⳐⲈ ⲀⲔⲢⲀⳘⲈ · ⲀⲨⲰ ⲠⲈⳐⲀⲔ ⳐⲈ ⲈⳑⲦⲰⲚ ⲦⲀⲚⲀⲨ
ⲈⲢⲞⳑ · ⲈⲘⲘⲞⲚ · ⲈⳆⳕⲈⲈⲦ** ⲞⲨⲂⲎⳑ ⳥Ⲙ ⲠⲈⳆⲦⲞⲠⲞⲤ · ⲀⲤ- ⲣⲒ
20 ⳘⲰⲠⲈ ⲆⲈ ⲚⲦⲈⲢⲈ ⳆⲰⲤⲎ⳽ ⲤⲰⲦⲘ ⲈⲢⲞⲔ ⲈⲔⳐⲰ ⲚⲚⲈⳆ-
ⳘⲀⳐⲈ · ⲀⳑⳘⲦⲞⲢⲦⳓ ⲀⲨⲰ ⲀⲚⲈⳆ' ⲈⳞⲢⲀⳆ ⳞⲒ ⲞⲨⲤⲞⲠ ⲀⲚ-
ⲂⲰⲔ ⲈⳞⲞⲨⲚ ⲈⲠⲎⳆ ⲀⲚⳞⲈ ⲈⲠⲈⲠⲚⲀ ⲈⳑⲘⲎⲢ ⲈⳞⲞⲨⲚ ⲈⲠⲘⲀ
ⲚⲚⲔⲞⲦⲔ ⲀⲨⲰ ⲀⲚⳕⲰⳘⲦ ⲈⲢⲞⲔ ⲚⲘⲘⲀⳑ ⲀⲚⳞⲈ ⲈⲢⲞⲔ
ⲈⲔⲈⲒⲚⲈ ⲘⲘⲞⳑ · ⲀⲨⲰ ⲀⳑⲂⲰⲖ ⲈⲂⲞⲖ ⲚⳕⲒ ⲠⲈⲦⲘⲎⲢ ⲈⲠⲈ-

---

12 MS ⲈⲠⲒⲠⲒⲢⲀⳞⲈ; read ⲈⲠⲒⲢⲀⳞⲈ.
19 ⲡⲓ in upper right-hand margin repeated.

10. 'Mercy and truth have met one another; *righteousness* and *peace* have kissed one another.

11. Truth has sprouted from the earth and *righteousness* has looked forth from heaven.' *

Thy power once *prophesied* in these words about thee. When thou wast small, before the *Spirit* came upon thee, while thou wast in a vineyard with Joseph, the Spirit came forth from the height □, he came to me into my house, he resembled thee. And I did not recognise him and I thought that he was thou. And the *Spirit* said to me : 'Where is Jesus, my brother, that I *meet* him?' And when he said these things to me, I was *confused* and I thought that he was a *phantom* to *tempt* me. *But* I took him, I bound him to the leg of the bed in my house, until I came out to you in the field, thou and Joseph, and I found you in the vineyard, as Joseph was hedging the vineyard with reeds. Now it happened, when thou didst hear me speaking the word to Joseph, thou didst *understand* the word and thou didst rejoice. And thou didst say : 'Where is he that I may see him? Or else I await him in this *place*'. *But* it happened when Joseph heard thee saying these words, he was agitated and we came up at the same time, we went into the house. We found the *Spirit* bound to the bed. And we looked at thee with him, we found thee like him. And he that was bound to | the bed

---

*   Ps. 84.10, 11
□   cf. Mt. 3.16

ϬΛΟΛ· ΑϤϪⲰΛϬ ΕΡΟΚ ΑϤϯΠΙ ΕΡⲰΚ· ΑΥⲰ ⲚΤΟΚ ϨⲰⲰΚ
ΑΚϯΠΙ ΕΡⲰϤ ΑΤΕⲦⲚⲢ-ΟΥΑ ⲚΟΥⲰΤ· ΠΑΪ ϬΕ ΠΕ ΠϢΑ-
ϪΕ ⲘⲚ ΠΕϤⲂⲰⲖ· ΠⲚΑ' ⟨ΠΕ⟩ ΠΕⲠⲚⲀ ΕⲚΤΑϤΕΙ' ΕⲂΟⲖ ⲌⲘ
ΠϪΙⲤⲈ ⲌΙⲦⲘ ΠΙϢΟⲢⲠ ⲘⲘΥⲤⲦⲎΡΙΟⲚ ΕⲂΟⲖ ϪΕ ΑϤⲚΑ'
5 ϨΑ ΠΓΕⲚΟⲤ ⲚⲢⲢⲰⲘⲈ ΑϤⲦⲚⲚΟΟΥ ⲘΠΕϤⲠⲚⲀ ΕΤΡΕϤⲔⲰ
ΕⲂΟⲖ ⲚⲚⲚΟⲂⲈ ⲘΠⲔΟⲤⲘΟⲤ ⲦⲎⲢϤ· ΑΥⲰ ⲚⲤⲈϪⲒ-ⲘΥⲤⲦⲎⲢ-
ΡΙΟⲚ· ΑΥⲰ ⲚⲤⲈⲔⲖⲎⲢΟⲚΟⲘⲒ ⲚⲦⲘⲚⲦⲈⲢΟ ⲘⲠΟΥΟⲒⲚ· ⲦⲘⲈ
ϨⲰⲰⲤ ⲦⲈ ⲦϬΟⲘ ΕⲚΤΑⲤϬΟⲖⲈ ΕΡΟⲒ ⲈΑⲤⲈⲒ' *ΕⲂΟⲖ ϨⲚ Ⲣ̅Ⲓ ᵇ
ⲦⲂΑⲢⲂⲎⲖⲰ ΑⲤϢⲰⲠⲈ ⲚΑⲔ ⲚⲤⲰⲘΑ ⲚϨΥⲖⲒⲔΟⲚ· ΑΥⲰ
10 ΑⲤⲔⲎⲢΥⲤⲤⲈ ϨΑ ΠⲦΟΠΟⲤ ⲚⲦΑⲖⲎⲐⲒΑ· ⲦⲀⲒⲔΑⲒΟⲤΥⲚⲎ ΠⲈ
ΠⲈⲔⲠⲚⲀ ΠΑϊ ΕⲚΤΑϤⲈⲒⲚⲈ ⲚⲘⲘΥⲤⲦⲎⲢΙΟⲚ ΕⲂΟⲖ ϨⲘ
ΠϪⲒⲤⲈ ΕΤΡΕϤⲦΑⲀΥ ⲘⲠΓΕⲚΟⲤ ⲚⲦⲈ ⲦⲘⲚⲦⲢⲰⲘⲈ· ϯⲢⲎⲚⲎ
ϨⲰⲰⲤ ⲦⲈ ⲦϬΟⲘ ΕⲚΤΑⲤϬΟⲖⲈ ⲈΠⲈⲔⲤⲰⲘΑ ⲚϨΥⲖⲒⲔΟⲚ
ⲔΑⲦΑ ΠⲔΟⲤⲘΟⲤ ΠΑϊ ⲈⲚΤΑϤⲂΑⲠⲦⲒⲌⲈ ⲘⲠΓⲈⲚΟⲤ ⲚⲦ-
15 ⲘⲚⲦⲢⲰⲘⲈ ϢΑⲚⲦϤⲦΑΑΥ ⲚϢⲘⲘΟ ⲈⲠⲚΟⲂⲈ· ΑΥⲰ ⲚϤⲦΑΑΥ
ⲚⲈΙⲢⲎⲚⲎ ⲘⲚ ΠⲈⲔⲠⲚⲀ· ΑΥⲰ ⲚⲤⲈϢⲰⲠⲈ ⲈΥΟ ⲚⲈΙⲢⲎⲚⲎ
ⲘⲚ ⲚⲈΠⲢΟⲂΟⲖΟΟΥⲈ ⲘⲠΟΥΟⲒⲚ ⲈⲦⲈ ΠⲀⲒ ΠⲈ ϪⲈ ⲦⲀⲒ-
ⲔΑⲒΟⲤΥⲚⲎ ⲘⲚ ϯⲢⲎⲚⲎ ΑΥϯΠΙ ⲈⲚⲈΥⲈⲢⲎΥ· ΑΥⲰ ⲔΑⲦΑ
ⲐⲈ ⲈⲚΤΑϤϪΟΟⲤ ϪⲈ Α ⲦⲘⲈ ϯΟΥⲰ ⲈⲂΟⲖ ϨⲘ ΠⲔΑϨ·
20 ⲦⲘⲈ ⲆⲈ ΠⲈ ΠⲈⲔⲤⲰⲘΑ ⲚϨΥ**ⲖⲒⲔΟⲚ ΠⲀⲒ ⲈⲚΤΑϤϯΟΥⲰ ⲢⲒΑ
ⲈⲂΟⲖ ⲚϨⲎⲦ· ⲔΑⲦΑ ΠⲔΑϨ ⲚⲦⲘⲦⲢⲰⲘⲈ ΠⲀⲒ ⲈⲚΤΑϤⲔⲎ-
ⲢΥⲤⲤⲈ ϨΑ ΠⲦΟΠΟⲤ ⲚⲦⲘⲈ ⲚⲦΑⲖⲎⲐⲒΑ· ΑΥⲰ ΟⲚ ⲔΑⲦΑ
ⲐⲈ ⲈⲚΤΑϤϪΟΟⲤ ϪⲈ Α ⲦⲀⲒⲔΑⲒΟⲤΥⲚⲎ ϯΟΥⲰ ⲈⲂΟⲖ ϨⲚ
ⲦⲠⲈ· ⲦⲀⲒⲔΑⲒΟⲤΥⲚⲎ ⲦⲈ ⲦϬΟⲘ ⲈⲚΤΑⲤϬⲰϢⲦ ⲈⲂΟⲖ ϨⲘ

1　MS ϬΛΟΛ; read ϬΛΟϬ.
3　MS ΠⲚΑ' ΠⲈⲠⲚⲀ; read ΠⲚΑ' ΠⲈ ΠⲈⲠⲚⲀ.
8　MS originally ϨⲒ.
22　omit either ⲚⲦⲘⲈ or ⲚⲦΑⲖⲎⲐⲒΑ; but see 128.5 ⲚⲦⲘⲈ ⲚⲦⲈ ⲦΑⲖⲎⲐⲒΑ.
23　MS ϯⲟⲩⲱ ⲈⲂΟⲖ; read ϬⲰϢⲦ ⲈⲂΟⲖ.

was released, he embraced thee, he kissed thee. And thou also, thou didst kiss him and you became one.

This now is the discourse and its interpretation. Mercy is the *Spirit* which came forth from the height, through the First *Mystery*, because he (the First Mystery) had mercy on the *race* of men. He sent his *Spirit* that it should forgive the sins of the whole *world* so that they (men) should receive *mysteries* and *inherit* the Kingdom of the Light. Truth, on the other hand, is the power which was entrusted to me; when it came forth from the Barbelo, it became for thee a *material body*. And it *preached* about the *place* of the truth [1]. *Righteousness* is thy *Spirit* which has brought the *mysteries* forth from the height, to give them to the *race* of mankind. *Peace*, on the other hand, is the power which was entrusted to thy *material body*, *according to* the *world*, which *baptised* the *race* of mankind until they became strangers to sin. And it made them to be at *peace* with thy *Spirit*, and they came to be at *peace* with the *emanations* of the light. That is, *righteousness* and *peace* have kissed one another. * And *as* it was said: 'Truth has sprouted from the earth': □ truth *however* is thy *material body*, which sprouted from me, *according to* the earth of mankind, and which has *preached* about the *place* of the *truth*. And also *as* it was said: '*Righteousness* ⟨looked forth⟩ [2] from heaven': ° *righteousness* is the power which looked forth from | the height, which will give the mysteries of the light

---

* Ps. 84.10
□ Ps. 84.11
° Ps. 84.11

---

[1] (10, 22) place of the truth; Schmidt: true place; (see 9.3; 123.18; 128.5, 24; 372.14).
[2] (23) ⟨looked forth⟩; MS: sprouted from.

245

ΠΧΙСЄ ΤΑΪ ЄΤΝΑ† N̄ΜΜΥСΤΗΡΙΟΝ Μ̄ΠΟΥΟΪΝ Μ̄ΠΓЄΝΟС

N̄ΤΜΝΤΡШΜЄ · ΑΥШ N̄СЄШΠЄ N̄ΔΙΚΑΙΟС ΑΥШ N̄СЄР̄-

ΑΓΑΘΟС N̄СЄΚΛΗΡΟΝΟΜΙ N̄ΤΜΝΤЄΡΟ Μ̄ΠΟΥΟΪΝ ·

ΑСШΠЄ 6Є N̄ΤЄΡЄ Ι͞С СШΤ͞Μ ЄΝЄΪШΑΧЄ ЄΝΤ-

5 ΑСΧΟΟΥ N̄6Ι ΜΑΡΙΑ ΤЄЧΜΑΑΥ · ΠЄΧΑЧ ΧЄ ЄΥΓЄ ΚΑ-

ΛШС ΜΑΡΙΑ · ΑСЄΪ ЄΘΗ N̄6Ι ΤΚЄΜΑΡΙΑ ΠЄΧΑС ΧЄ ΠΑ-

ΧΟΪС ΑΝЄΧЄ Μ̄ΜΟΪ ΑΥШ Μ̄ΠΡ6ШΝΤ ЄΡΟΪ ЄΜΜΟΝ ΧΙΝ

Μ̄ΠΝΑΥ ЄΡЄ ΤЄΚΜΑΑΥ ШΑΧЄ N̄ΜΜΑΚ ЄΤΒЄ ΠΒШΛ N̄ΝЄΪ- ΡΙΑ b

ШΑΧЄ · Α ΤΑ6ΟΜ ШΤΡΤШΡ͞Τ · ЄΤΡΑЄΪ ЄΘΗ N̄ΤΑΧШ

10 2Ш Μ̄ΠΒШΛ N̄ΝЄΪШΑΧЄ · ΠЄΧΑЧ ΝΑС N̄6Ι Ι͞С ΧЄ †ΚЄ-

ΛЄΥЄ ΝЄ ЄΤΡЄΧШ Μ̄ΠЄΥΒШΛ · ΠЄΧΑС N̄6Ι ΜΑΡΙΑ ΧЄ

ΠΑΧΟЄΙС ΠΝΑ᾽ Μ̄Ν ΤΜЄ ΑΥΤШΜ͞Ν͞Τ ЄΝЄΥЄΡΗΥ · ΠΝΑ᾽

6Є ΠЄ ΠЄΠΝ͞Α ЄΝΤΑЧЄΪ Є2ΡΑΪ ЄΧШΚ N̄ΤЄΡЄΚΧΙ-ΒΑΠ-

ΤΙСΜΑ 2ΙΤ͞Ν ΪШ2ΑΝΝΗС · ΠΝΑ᾽ 6Є ΠЄ ΠЄΠΝ͞Α N̄ΤΜΝΤ-

15 ΝΟΥΤЄ ΠΑΪ ЄΝΤΑЧЄΪ Є2ΡΑΪ ЄΧШΚ ΑЧΝΑ᾽ Μ̄ΠΓЄΝΟС

N̄ΤΜΝΤΡШΜЄ ΑЧЄΪ ЄΠЄСΗΤ ΑЧΑΠΑΝΤΑ ЄΤ6ΟΜ N̄СΑ-

ΒΑШΘ ΠΑΓΑΘΟС ΤΑΪ ЄΤN̄2ΗΤ͞Κ · ΤΑΪ ЄΝΤΑСΚΗΡΥССЄ

2Α N̄ΤΟΠΟС N̄ΤΑΛΗΘΙΑ · ΑЧΧΟΟС ΔЄ ΟΝ ΧЄ ΤΔΙΚΑΙΟ-

СΥΝΗ Μ̄Ν †ΡΗΝΗ ΑΥ†ΠΙ ЄΡN̄ ΝЄΥЄΡΗΥ · ΤΔΙΚΑΙΟСΥΝΗ ΡΙΒ

20 6Є ⟨ΠЄ⟩ ΠЄΠΝ͞Α Μ̄ΠΟΥΟЄΙΝ · ΠΑΪ N̄ΤΑЧЄΪ Є2ΡΑΪ ЄΧШΚ ·

ЄΝΤΑЧN̄-Μ̄ΜΥСΤΗΡΙΟΝ Μ̄ΠΧΙСЄ ЄΤΡЄЧΤΑΑΥ Μ̄ΠΓЄΝΟС

N̄ΤΜΤΡШΜЄ · †ΡΗΝΗ 2ШШС ΤЄ Τ6ΟΜ ЄΤN̄2ΗΤ͞Κ N̄ΤЄ

СΑΒΑШΘ ΠΑΓΑΘΟС · ΠΑΪ ЄΝΤΑЧΒΑΠΤΙΖЄ ΑЧΚШ ЄΒΟΛ

---

19 MS ΝЄΥΝЄΥЄΡΗΥ.

20 MS 6ЄΠЄΠΝ͞Α.

21 MS originally ЄΤΡЄΥ; Ч inserted above.

to the *race* of mankind. And they will become *righteous* and *good* and *inherit* the Kingdom of the Light."

Now it happened when Jesus heard these words which Mary his mother said, he said : "*Excellent, well done*, Mary."

62.   The other Mary came forward and said : "My Lord, *suffer* me and be not angry with me, for since the time that thy mother spoke with thee concerning the interpretation of these words, my power has agitated me that I should come forward and also say the interpretation of these words."

Jesus said to her : "I *command* thee to say their interpretation."

Maria said : "My Lord : 'Mercy and truth have met one another'. * Now mercy is the *Spirit* which came down upon thee when thou didst receive *baptism* from John ᵒ. Now mercy is the *Spirit* of Godhood which came forth upon thee, which had mercy upon the *race* of mankind. It came down, it *met* the power of Sabaoth the *Good* which is within thee and which has *preached* on the *places* of the *truth*. But it is said furthermore : 'Righteousness* and *peace* have kissed one another' ᵒ. Now *righteousness* is the *Spirit* of the light, which came down upon thee, bringing the *mysteries* of the height in order to give them to the *race* of mankind. *Peace*, on the other hand, is the power of Sabaoth the *Good* which is within thee. It is this which *baptised* and forgave | the

---

*   Ps. 84.10
ᵒ   cf. Mt. 3.13
ᵒ   Ps. 84.10

ⲙ̅ⲡⲅⲉⲛⲟⲥ ⲛ̅ⲧⲙ̅ⲛ̅ⲧⲣⲱⲙⲉ ⲁⲩⲱ ⲁⲥⲁⲁⲩ ⲛ̅ⲉⲓⲣⲏⲛⲏ ⲙⲛ̅ ⲛ̅-
ϣⲏⲣⲉ ⲙ̅ⲡⲟⲩⲟⲉⲓⲛ· ⲁⲩⲱ ⲟⲛ ⲕⲁⲧⲁ ⲑⲉ ⲉⲛⲧⲁ ⲧⲉⲕϭⲟⲙ
ϫⲟⲟⲥ ϩⲓⲧⲛ̅ ⲇⲁⲩⲉⲓⲇ· ϫⲉ ⲁ ⲧⲙⲉ ϯⲟⲩⲱ ⲉⲃⲟⲗ ϩ̅ⲙ
ⲡⲕⲁϩ ⲉⲧⲉ ⲛ̅ⲧⲟⲥ ⲧⲉ ⲧϭⲟⲙ ⲛ̅ⲧⲉ ⲥⲁⲃⲁⲱⲑ ⲡⲁⲅⲁⲑⲟⲥ·
5 [ⲛ̅ⲧⲁϥϫⲟⲟⲥ ϫⲉ· ⲁⲥϯⲟⲩⲱ ⲉⲃⲟⲗ ϩ̅ⲙ ⲡⲕⲁϩ·] ⲧⲁⲓ ⲉⲛⲧⲁⲥϯⲟⲩⲱ ⲉⲃⲟⲗ ϩ̅ⲙ ⲙⲁⲣⲓⲁ ⲧⲉⲕⲙⲁⲁⲩ· ϯⲣⲙ̅ⲛ̅ⲕⲁϩ· ⲧⲁⲓ-
ⲕⲁⲓⲕⲁⲓⲛⲏ ϩⲱⲱⲥ ⲉⲛⲧⲁⲥϭⲱ̅ⲧ̅ ⲉⲃⲟⲗ ϩ̅ⲛ ⲧⲡⲉ· ⲛ̅ⲧⲟϥ
ⲡⲉ *ⲡⲉⲡⲛ̅ⲁ̅ ⲉⲧϩ̅ⲙ ⲡϫⲓⲥⲉ· ⲡⲁⲓ ⲉⲛⲧⲁϥⲛ̅-ⲙ̅ⲙⲩⲥⲧⲏⲣⲓⲟⲛ ⲣ̅ⲓ̅ⲃ̅ ᵇ
ⲧⲏⲣⲟⲩ ⲉⲃⲟⲗ ϩ̅ⲙ ⲡϫⲓⲥⲉ· ⲁϥⲧⲁⲁⲩ ⲙ̅ⲡⲅⲉⲛⲟⲥ ⲛ̅ⲧⲙ̅ⲛ̅ⲧ-
10 ⲣⲱⲙⲉ ⲁⲩⲣ̅ⲇⲓⲕⲁⲓⲟⲥ ⲁⲩⲱ ⲁⲩⲣ̅ⲁⲅⲁⲑⲟⲥ· ⲁⲩⲕⲗⲏⲣⲟⲛⲟⲙⲓ
ⲛ̅ⲧⲙ̅ⲛ̅ⲧⲉⲣⲟ ⲙ̅ⲡⲟⲩⲟⲉⲓⲛ· ⲁⲥϣⲱⲡⲉ ⲇⲉ ⲛ̅ⲧⲉⲣⲉ ⲓ̅ⲥ̅ ⲟⲩⲱ
ⲉϥⲥⲱⲧ̅ⲙ̅ ⲉⲛⲉⲓ̈ϣⲁϫⲉ ⲉⲥϫⲱ ⲙ̅ⲙⲟⲟⲩ ⲛ̅ϭⲓ ⲙⲁⲣⲓϩⲁⲙ· ⲡⲉϫⲁϥ ϫⲉ ⲉⲩⲅⲉ ⲙⲁⲣⲓϩⲁⲙ ⲧⲉⲕⲗⲏⲣⲟⲛⲟⲙⲟⲥ ⲙ̅ⲡⲟⲩⲟⲉⲓⲛ·
ⲁⲥⲉⲓ̈ ⲟⲛ ⲉⲑⲏ ⲛ̅ϭⲓ ⲙⲁⲣⲓⲁ ⲧⲙⲁⲁⲩ ⲛ̅ⲓ̅ⲥ̅ ⲁⲥⲡⲁϩⲧ̅ⲥ̅ ⲉϫⲛ̅
15 ⲛⲉϥⲟⲩⲉⲣⲏⲧⲉ· ⲁⲥϯⲡⲓ ⲉⲣⲱⲟⲩ· ⲁⲩⲱ ⲡⲉϫⲁⲥ· ϫⲉ ⲡⲁ-
ϫⲟⲉⲓⲥ· ⲁⲩⲱ ⲡⲁϣⲏⲣⲉ· ⲁⲩⲱ ⲡⲁⲥⲱⲧⲏⲣ· ⲙ̅ⲡⲣ̅ϭⲱ̅ⲛ̅ⲧ̅
ⲉⲣⲟⲓ̈· ⲁⲗⲗⲁ ϯⲥⲟ ⲉⲣⲟⲓ̈· ⲧⲁϫⲱ ⲙ̅ⲡⲃⲱⲗ ⲛ̅ⲛⲉⲓ̈ϣⲁϫⲉ
ⲛ̅ⲕⲉⲥⲟⲡ· ⲁ ⲡⲛ̅ⲁ̅ ⲙⲛ̅ ⲧⲙⲉ ⲧⲱ̅ⲙⲛ̅ⲧ ⲉⲛⲉⲩⲉⲣⲏⲩ· ⲁ̅ⲛⲟⲕ ⲣ̅ⲓ̅ⲅ̅ **
ⲧⲉ ⲙⲁⲣⲓⲁ ⲧⲉⲕⲙⲁⲁⲩ· ⲙⲛ̅ ⲉⲗⲓⲥⲁⲃⲉⲧ· ⲧⲙⲁⲁⲩ ⲛ̅ⲓ̈ⲱϩⲁⲛ-
20 ⲛⲏⲥ ⲛ̅ⲧⲁⲓ̈ⲧⲱⲙⲛ̅ⲧ ⲉⲣⲟⲥ· ⲡⲛ̅ⲁ̅ ϭⲉ ⲡⲉ ⲧϭⲟⲙ ⲉⲧⲛ̅ϩⲏⲧ ⲛ̅ⲧⲉ
ⲥⲁⲃⲁⲱⲑ· ⲧⲁⲉⲓ ⲉⲛⲧⲁⲥⲉⲓ̈ ⲉⲃⲟⲗ ϩ̅ⲛ ⲣⲱⲓ̈ ⲉⲧⲉ ⲛ̅ⲧⲟⲕ ⲡⲉ·
ⲁⲕⲛ̅ⲁ̅ ⲙ̅ⲡⲅⲉⲛⲟⲥ ⲧⲏⲣϥ̅ ⲛ̅ⲧⲙ̅ⲛ̅ⲧⲣⲱⲙⲉ· ⲧⲙⲉ ϩⲱⲱⲥ ⲧⲉ
ⲧϭⲟⲙ ⲉⲧϩ̅ⲛ̅ ⲉⲗⲓⲥⲁⲃⲉⲧ ⲉⲧⲉ ⲓ̈ⲱϩⲁⲛⲛⲏⲥ ⲡⲉ· ⲡⲁⲓ ⲉⲛⲧ-
ⲁϥⲉⲓ̈ ⲁϥⲕⲏⲣⲩⲥⲥⲉ ϩⲁ ⲧⲉϩⲓⲏ ⲛ̅ⲧⲙⲉ· ⲉⲧⲉ ⲛ̅ⲧⲟⲕ ⲡⲉ ⲉⲛⲧ-

---

1 MS ⲁⲥⲁⲥⲁⲁⲩ; second ⲁⲥ expunged.
5 words in brackets better omitted.
6, 7 read ⲧⲇⲓⲕⲁⲓⲟⲥⲩⲛⲏ.

race of mankind and made them to be at *peace* with the
Sons of the Light [1]. And furthermore, *as* thy power has said
through David : 'Truth has sprouted from the earth' * : that
is, the power of Sabaoth the *Good*, [as it said : 'It sprouted
from the earth'] it is this which sprouted from Mary thy
mother, the earth-dweller [2]. On the other hand, *righteousness*
which looked forth from heaven □ is the Spirit which is in
the height, which has brought forth all the *mysteries* from
the height. It gave them to the *race* of mankind, and they
became *righteous* and *good* and they *inherited* the Kingdom of the Light."

It happened *however* when Jesus finished hearing these
words which Mariam spoke, he said; "*Excellent*, Mariam,
thou *inheritor* of the light."

Mary, the mother of Jesus, came forward again. She
prostrated herself at his feet, she kissed them, and she said :
"My Lord and my Son and my *Saviour*, be not angry with
me, *but* forgive me that I say the interpretation of these
words a second time : 'Mercy and truth have met one
another'.° I am Mary thy mother [3], and Elisabeth, the
mother of John whom I met ᐃ. Now mercy is the power in me
of the Sabaoth which came forth from me [4], which is thou.
Thou hast had mercy on the whole *race* of mankind. On
the other hand, truth is the power which was in Elisabeth,
which is John who came and *preached* on the true way,
which is thou, | before whom he *preached*. And further-

---

*   Ps. 84.11
□   Ps. 84.11
°   Ps. 84.10
ᐃ   cf. Lk. 1.39 ff.

---

[1]   (2) Sons of the Light; see J 101; (also 359.7).
[2]   (6) thy mother, the earth dweller; Till: i.e. thy earthly mother.
[3]   (18, 19) I am Mary, thy mother; Till: that am I, Mary thy mother.
[4]   (21) came forth from me; lit. came forth from my mouth.

ⲁϥⲕⲏⲣⲩⲥⲥⲉ ϩⲁⲧⲉⲕϩⲏ · ⲁⲩⲱ ⲟⲛ ⲡⲛⲁ̀ ⲙⲛ̄ ⲧⲙⲉ ⲛ̄ⲧⲁⲩ-
ⲧⲱⲙⲛ̄ⲧ ⲉⲛⲉⲩⲉⲣⲏⲩ · ⲛ̄ⲧⲟⲕ ⲡⲉ ⲡⲁϫⲟⲉⲓⲥ ⲉⲛⲧⲁⲕⲧⲱⲙⲛⲧ̄
ⲉ̈ⲓⲱϩⲁⲛⲛⲏⲥ · ⲙ̄ⲡⲉϩⲟⲟⲩ ⲉⲕⲛⲁϫⲓ-ⲃⲁⲡⲧⲓⲥⲙⲁ · ⲛ̄ⲧⲟⲕ ⲁⲉ
ⲟⲛ ⲙⲛ̄ ⲓ̈ⲱϩⲁⲛⲛⲏⲥ ⲛⲉ ⲧⲁⲓⲕⲁⲓⲟⲥⲩⲛⲏ ⲙⲛ̄ ϯⲣⲏⲛⲏ · ⲛ̄ⲧ- ⲣⲓⲅ ᵇ
5 ⲁⲩϯⲡⲓ ⲉⲣⲛ̄ ⲛⲉⲩⲉⲣⲏⲩ · ⲛ̄ⲧⲁ ⲧⲙⲉ ϯⲟⲩⲱ ⲉⲃⲟⲗ ϩⲙ̄
ⲡⲕⲁϩ · ⲁⲩⲱ ⲛ̄ⲧⲁ ⲧⲁⲓⲕⲁⲓⲟⲥⲩⲛⲏ ϭⲱϣ̄ⲧ ⲉⲃⲟⲗ ϩⲛ̄ ⲧⲡⲉ
ⲉⲧⲉ ⲡⲁⲓ̈ ⲡⲉ ⲡⲉⲟⲩⲟⲉⲓϣ ⲉⲛⲧⲁⲕⲁⲓⲁⲕⲟⲛⲓ ⲛⲁⲕ ⲙ̄ⲙⲓⲛ
ⲙ̄ⲙⲟⲕ · ⲁⲕⲣ̄-ⲡⲧⲩⲡⲟⲥ ⲛ̄ⲅⲁⲃⲣⲓⲏⲗ · ⲁⲕϭⲱϣ̄ⲧ ϩⲣⲁⲓ̈ ⟨ⲉ⟩ϫⲱⲓ̈
ⲉⲃⲟⲗ ϩⲛ̄ ⲧⲡⲉ ⲁⲕϣⲁϫⲉ ⲛ̄ⲙⲙⲁⲓ̈ ⲁⲩⲱ ⲛ̄ⲧⲉⲣⲉⲕϣⲁϫⲉ
10 ⲛ̄ⲙⲙⲁⲓ̈ · ⲁⲕϯⲟⲩⲱ ⲉⲃⲟⲗ ϩⲣⲁⲓ̈ ⲛ̄ϩⲏⲧ · ⲉⲧⲉ ⲧⲙⲉ ⲧⲉ ·
ⲉⲧⲉ ⲛ̄ⲧⲟⲥ ⲧⲉ ⲧϭⲟⲙ ⲛ̄ⲥⲁⲃⲁⲱⲑ ⲡⲁⲅⲁⲑⲟⲥ · ⲧⲁⲓ̈ ⲉⲧϣⲟⲟⲡ
ϩⲙ̄ ⲡⲉⲕⲥⲱⲙⲁ ⲛ̄ϩⲩⲗⲓⲕⲟⲛ · ⲉⲧⲉ ⲧⲁⲓ̈ ⲧⲉ ⲧⲙⲉ ⲉⲛⲧⲁⲥϯⲟⲩⲱ ⲉⲃⲟⲗ ϩⲙ̄ ⲡⲕⲁϩ ·

ⲁⲥϣⲱⲡⲉ ϭⲉ ⲛ̄ⲧⲉⲣⲉ ⲓ̄ⲥ̄ ⲥⲱⲧⲙ̄ ⲉⲛⲉⲓ̈ϣⲁϫⲉ ⲉⲥϫⲱ ⲣⲓⲇ
15 ⲙ̄ⲙⲟⲟⲩ ⲛ̄ϭⲓ ⲙⲁⲣⲓⲁ ⲧⲉϥⲙⲁⲁⲩ ⲡⲉϫⲁϥ ϫⲉ ⲉⲩⲅⲉ ⲁⲩⲱ
ⲕⲁⲗⲱⲥ · ⲡⲁⲓ̈ ⲡⲉ ⲡⲃⲱⲗ ⲛ̄ⲛ̄ϣⲁϫⲉ ⲧⲏⲣⲟⲩ ⲛⲁⲓ̈ ⲉⲛⲧⲁ
ⲧⲁϭⲟⲙ ⲛ̄ⲟⲩⲟⲓ̈ⲛ ⲡⲣⲟⲫⲏⲧⲉⲩⲉ ϩⲁⲣⲟⲟⲩ ⲙ̄ⲡⲓⲟⲩⲟⲉⲓϣ
ϩⲓⲧⲛ̄ ⲇⲁⲩⲉⲓⲇ ⲡⲉⲡⲣⲟⲫⲏⲧⲏⲥ : ⳽   ⳽   ⳽   ⳽   ⳽

⳽   ⳽   ⳽   ⳽   ⳽   ⳽   ⳽   ⳽   ⳽   ⳽   ⳽

---

8 MS originally ⲉⲃⲟⲗ ϫⲱⲓ̈ ⲉⲃⲟⲗ; ⲃⲟⲗ inserted above ϩⲣⲁⲓ̈.
10 MS ⲧⲙⲉ ⲉⲧⲉ.

more : 'Mercy and truth have met one another' * : that is thou, my Lord, who didst meet John on the day when thou didst receive *baptism* ◻. *But* furthermore, thou and John are *righteousness* and *peace*, which kissed one another. 'Truth has sprouted from the earth and *righteousness* has looked forth from heaven' ○ : that is the time when thou didst do *service* to thyself. Thou didst take the *type* of Gabriel, thou didst look down upon me from heaven △, thou didst speak with me; and when thou didst speak with me thou didst sprout from me [1]. That is, the truth which is the power of Sabaoth the *Good* which is in thy *material body* — that is the truth which sprouted from the earth."

Now it happened when Jesus heard these words which Mary, his mother, spoke, he said : "*Excellent* and *well done.* This is the interpretation of all the words about which my light-power once *prophesied* through David the *prophet.*

---

*   Ps. 84.10
◻   Mt. 3.13 ff.
○   Ps. 84.11
△   cf. Lk. 1.26 ff.

---

[1]   (10) sprout from me; lit. sprout within me.

ΝΑΙ ΔΕ ΝΕ Ν̄ΡΑΝ Ε†ΝΑΤΑΑΥ ΧΙΝ ΠΙΑΠΕ-
ΡΑΝΤΟΣ ΣϨΑΪΣΟΥ Ϩ̄Ν ΟΥΜΑΪΝ ΧΕΚΑΣ ΕΡΕ
Ν̄ϢΗΡΕ Μ̄ΠΝΟΥΤΕ ΝΑΟΥϢΝϨ ΕΒΟΛ ΧΙΝ Μ̄ΠΕΪ-
ΜΑ · ΠΑΪ ΠΕ ΠΡΑΝ Μ̄ΠΑΘΑΝΑΤΟΣ ᾹΛ̄Ᾱ Ϣ̄Ϣ̄Ϣ̄
5   ΑΥϢ ΠΑΪ ΠΕ ΠΡΑΝ Ν̄ΤΕΣΜΗ ΤΑΪ ΕΝΤΑ ΠΡϢΜΕ
Ν̄ΤΕΛΙΟΣ ΚΙΜ ΕΤΒΗΤ̄Σ̄ Π̄Π̄ ΝΑΪ ΔΕ ΝΕ Ν̄ϨΕΡ-
ΜΗΝΙΑ [Ν̄Ν̄ΡΑΝ] Ν̄Ν̄ΡΑΝ Ν̄ΝΕΪΜΥΣΤΗΡΙΟΝ
ΠϢΟΡΠ̄ ΕΤΕ ΑΛΑ ΤΕϤϨΕΡΜΗΝΙΑ ΤΕ ϕϕϕ ·
ΠΜΕϨΣΝΑΥ ΕΤΕ ΜΜΜ ΠΕ Η̇ ΕΤΕ ϢϢϢ ΠΕ
10 ΤΕϤϨΕΡΜΗΝΙΑ ΤΕ ΑΛΑ ΠΜΕϨϢΟΜΝ̄Τ ΕΤΕ ѱѱѱ ·
ΤΕϤϨΕΡΜΗΝΙΑ ΠΕ ΟΟΟ ΠΜΕϨϤΤΟΟΥ ΕΤΕ ϕϕϕ
ΠΕ ΤΕϤϨΕΡΜΗΝΙΑ ΠΕ ΝΝΝ ΠΜΕϨ†ΟΥ ΕΤΕ ΛΛΛ
ΤΕϤϨΕΡΜΗΝΙΑ ΠΕ ΑΛΑ ΠΕΤϨΙΧ̄Ν̄ ΠΕΘΡΟΝΟΣ
ΠΕ ΑΛΑ ΤΑΪ ΤΕ ΘΕΡΜΗΝΙΑ Μ̄ΠΜΕϨΣΝΑΥ ΑΛΑΛ
15 ΑΛΑΛ ΑΛΑΛ ΤΑΪ ΤΕ ΘΕΡΜΗΝΙΑ Μ̄ΠΡΑΝ ΤΗΡϤ ϟϟ

ʒ　　ϟ　　ϟ　　ϟ　　ϟ　　ϟ　　ϟ　　ϟ　　ϟ

6　MS ΕΤΒΗΤ̄Σ̄; read ΕΤΒΗΗΤ̄Σ̄.
7　omit Ν̄Ν̄ΡΑΝ.
15　MS ϹΤΕ; the first Ϲ crossed out.

These, *however*, are the names which I will give from the *endless one*. Write them with a sign so that the sons of God will be manifest from here. This is the name of the *immortal one* : ααα ωωω; and this is the name of the voice by which the *perfect man* is moved : ιι. But these are the *interpretations* of the names of these *mysteries* : the first name which is ααα, its *interpretation* is φφφ; the second which is μμμ, its *interpretation* is ωωω; the third which is ψψψ, its *interpretation* is οοο, the fourth which is φφφ, its *interpretation* is ννν, the fifth which is δδδ, its *interpretation* is ααα. That which is on the *throne* is ααα; this is the *interpretation* of the second : αααα, αααα, αααα; this is the *interpretation* of the whole name [1].

---

[1] (4-15) on *ephesia grammata*, see Kropp (Bibl. 26) III, pp. 135-138.

⳧ ⳧ ⳧ ⳧ ⳧ ⳧ ⳧

ⲠⲘⲉⲌⲤⲚⲀⲨ Ⲛ̄ⲦⲞⲘⲞⲤ Ⲛ̄ⲦⲠⲓⲤⲦⲓⲤ ⲤⲞⲫⲓⲀ

⳧ ⳧ ⳧ ⳧ ⳧ ⳧ ⳧

ⳅ ⲀϤⲉⲓ̈ ⲌⲱⲱϤ ⲉⲐⲎ Ⲛ̄Ϭⲓ Ⲓ̈ⲰⲌⲀⲚⲚⲎⲤ ⲠⲉⲬⲀϤ Ⲭⲉ ⲠⲬⲞⲉⲓⲤ·
ⲔⲉⲗⲉⲨⲈ ⲚⲀⲒ̈ Ⲍⲱ ⲉⲦⲢⲀⲬⲱ Ⲙ̄ⲠⲂⲰⲖ Ⲛ̄Ⲛ̄ϢⲀⲬⲈ ⲉⲚⲦⲀ ⲦⲈⲔ-
ϬⲞⲘ Ⲛ̄ⲞⲨⲞⲒ̈Ⲛ ⲠⲢⲞⲫⲎⲦⲈⲨⲈ Ⲙ̄ⲘⲞⲞⲨ Ⲙ̄ⲠⲒⲞⲨⲞⲈⲒϢ ⲌⲒⲦⲚ̄
5 ⲀⲀⲨⲉⲓⲀ· ⲀϤⲞⲨⲱϢ̄Ⲃ ⲀⲈ Ⲛ̄Ϭⲓ Ⲓ̄Ⲥ ⲠⲉⲬⲀϤ Ⲛ̄Ⲓ̈ⲰⲌⲀⲚⲚⲎⲤ
ⲬⲈ Ⲛ̄ⲦⲞⲔ ⲌⲱⲰⲔ Ⲓ̈ⲰⲌⲀⲚⲚⲎⲤ ϯⲔⲉⲖⲈⲨⲈ ⲚⲀⲔ ⲉⲦⲢⲈⲔⲬⲱ
Ⲙ̄ⲠⲂⲰⲖ ⲉⲂⲞⲖ Ⲛ̄Ⲛ̄ϢⲀⲬⲈ ⲚⲀⲒ̈ ⲉⲚⲦⲀ ⲦⲀϬⲞⲘ Ⲛ̄ⲞⲨⲞⲒ̈Ⲛ ⲠⲢⲞ-
ⲫⲎⲦⲈⲨⲈ Ⲙ̄ⲘⲞⲞⲨ ⲌⲒⲦ̄Ⲛ̄ ⲀⲀⲨⲒ̈Ⲁ· ⲬⲈ

10. Ⲁ ⲠⲚⲀ' Ⲙ̄Ⲛ̄ ⲦⲘⲉ ⲦⲱⲘ̄Ⲛ̄Ⲧ ⲉⲚⲈⲨⲈⲢⲎⲨ· ⲀⲨⲱ Ⲁ ⲦⲀⲒ-
10 ⲔⲀⲒⲞⲤⲨⲚⲎ Ⲙ̄Ⲛ̄ ϯⲢⲎⲚⲎ ϯⲠⲒ ⲉⲢ̄Ⲛ̄ ⲚⲈⲨⲈⲢⲎⲨ·

11. Ⲁ ⲦⲘⲉ ϯⲞⲨⲱ ⲉⲂⲞⲖ Ⲍ̄Ⲙ̄ ⲠⲔⲀⲌ· ⲀⲨⲱ Ⲁ ⲦⲀⲒⲔⲀⲒⲞ-
ⲤⲨⲚⲎ ϬⲱϢ̄Ⲧ ⲉⲂⲞⲖ Ⲍ̄Ⲛ̄ ⲦⲠⲉ·

ⲀϤⲞⲨⲱϢ̄Ⲃ ⲀⲈ Ⲛ̄Ϭⲓ Ⲓ̈ⲰⲌⲀⲚⲚⲎⲤ· Ⲡⲉ*ⲬⲀϤ ⲬⲈ ⲠⲀⲒ̈ ⲠⲈ ⲢⲓⲤ ᵇ
ⲠϢⲀⲬⲈ ⲉⲚⲦⲀⲔⲬⲞⲞϤ ⲉⲢⲞⲚ Ⲙ̄ⲠⲒⲞⲨⲞⲒϢ ⲬⲈ ⲀⲒ̈ⲉⲓ ⲉⲂⲞⲖ
15 Ⲍ̄Ⲙ̄ ⲠⲬⲒⲤⲉ ⲀⲒ̈ⲂⲰⲔ ⲉⲌⲞⲨⲚ ⲉⲤⲀⲂⲀⲰⲐ ⲠⲀⲅⲀⲐⲞⲤ· ⲀⲒ̈ⲌⲰⲖϬ
ⲉϯϬⲞⲘ Ⲛ̄ⲞⲨⲞⲈⲒⲚ ⲉⲦⲚ̄ⲌⲎⲦ̄Ϥ· ⲦⲉⲚⲞⲨ ϬⲈ ⲠⲚⲀ' Ⲙ̄Ⲛ̄ ⲦⲘⲉ
ⲉⲚⲦⲀⲨⲦⲱⲘ̄Ⲛ̄Ⲧ ⲉⲚⲈⲨⲈⲢⲎⲨ· Ⲛ̄ⲦⲞⲔ ⲠⲈ ⲠⲚⲀ' Ⲛ̄ⲦⲀⲨⲦ̄Ⲛ̄-
ⲚⲞⲞⲨⲔ ⲉⲂⲞⲖ Ⲍ̄Ⲛ̄ Ⲛ̄ⲦⲞⲠⲞⲤ Ⲙ̄ⲠⲬⲒⲤⲉ ⲌⲒⲦⲘ̄ ⲠⲈⲔⲉⲒⲰⲦ· ⲠⲒ-
ϢⲞⲢ̄Ⲡ Ⲙ̄ⲘⲨⲤⲦⲎⲢⲒⲞⲚ ⲉⲦϬⲱϢ̄Ⲧ ⲉⲌⲞⲨⲚ· ⲉⲀϤⲦ̄ⲚⲚⲞⲞⲨⲔ
20 ⲉⲦⲢⲈⲔⲚⲀ Ⲙ̄ⲠⲔⲞⲤⲘⲞⲤ ⲦⲎⲢϤ· ⲦⲘⲉ ⲌⲱⲱϤ ⲦⲈ ϯϬⲞⲘ

(BOOK II)

THE SECOND *BOOK* OF THE PISTIS SOPHIA

63. John also came forward, he said : "O Lord, *command* me also that I say the interpretation of the words which thy light-power once *prophesied* through David."

But Jesus answered and said to John : "Thou also, John, I *command* thee to say the interpretation of the words which my light-power *prophesied* through David :

10. 'Mercy and truth have met one another, and *righteousness* and *peace* have kissed one another.

11. Truth has sprouted from the earth and *righteousness* has looked forth from heaven'. *"

John answered, *however*, and said : "This is the word which thou hast said to us once : 'I came forth from the height, I entered into Sabaoth the *Good*, I embraced the light-power within him.' Now at this time : 'Mercy and truth have met one another' ▫. Thou art the mercy which was sent forth from the *places* of the height through thy Father, the First *Mystery*, who looks within. He sent thee that thou shouldst have mercy on the whole *world*. Truth, on the other hand, is the power | of Sabaoth the *Good*

---

* Ps. 84.10, 11
▫ Ps. 84.10

255

ⲚⲦⲈ ⲤⲀⲂⲀⲰⲐ ⲠⲀⲄⲀⲐⲞⲤ · ⲦⲀⲒ ⲈⲚⲦⲀⲤⲦⲞⲟ̄Ⲥ ⲈⲢⲞⲔ · ⲦⲀⲒ
ⲈⲚⲦⲀⲔⲚⲞⲭ̄Ⲥ ⲈⲂⲞⲨⲢ · Ⲛ̄ⲦⲞⲔ ⲠⲒϢⲞⲢⲠ̄ Ⲙ̄ⲘⲨⲤⲦⲎⲢⲒⲞⲚ ⲈⲦ-
ϬⲰϢ̄Ⲧ ⲈⲂⲞⲖ · ⲀⲨⲰ ⲀϤⲬⲒⲦⲤ̄ Ⲛ̄ϬⲒ ⲠⲔⲞⲨⲒ Ⲛ̄ⲤⲀⲂⲀⲰⲐ ⲠⲀ-
ⲄⲀⲐⲞⲤ · ⲀϤⲚⲞⲭ̄Ⲥ ⲈⲞⲨⲚ ⲈⲐⲨⲖⲎ Ⲛ̄ⲦⲂⲀⲢⲂⲎⲖⲰ**ⲀⲨⲰ Ⲣ̄Ⲉ̄
5 ⲀϤⲔⲎⲢⲨⲤⲤⲈ ϨⲀ ⲠⲦⲞⲠⲞⲤ Ⲛ̄ⲦⲘⲈ Ⲛ̄ⲦⲈ ⲦⲀⲖⲎⲐⲒⲀ ϨⲢⲀⲒ Ϩ̄Ⲛ
Ⲛ̄ⲦⲞⲠⲞⲤ ⲦⲎⲢⲞⲨ Ⲛ̄ⲦⲈ ⲚⲀϨⲂⲞⲨⲢ · ⲐⲨⲖⲎ ϬⲈ ⲈⲦⲘ̄ⲘⲀⲨ
Ⲛ̄ⲦⲈ ⲦⲂⲀⲢⲂⲎⲖⲰ Ⲛ̄ⲦⲞⲤ ⲦⲈⲦϢⲞⲞⲠ ⲚⲀⲔ Ⲛ̄ⲤⲰⲘⲀ Ⲙ̄ⲠⲞⲞⲨ ·
ⲀⲨⲰ ⲦⲀⲒⲔⲀⲒⲞⲤⲨⲚⲎ Ⲙ̄Ⲛ ϯⲢⲎⲚⲎ ⲈⲚⲦⲀⲨϯⲠⲒ ⲈⲢ̄Ⲛ ⲚⲈⲨ-
ⲈⲢⲎⲨ · ⲦⲀⲒⲔⲀⲒⲞⲤⲨⲚⲎ ⲠⲈ Ⲛ̄ⲦⲞⲔ Ⲛ̄ⲦⲀⲔⲚ̄-Ⲙ̄ⲘⲨⲤⲦⲎⲢⲒⲞⲚ
10 ⲈⲂⲞⲖ ⲦⲎⲢⲞⲨ ϨⲒⲦⲘ̄ ⲠⲈⲔⲈⲒⲰⲦ ⲠⲒϢⲞⲢⲠ̄ Ⲙ̄ⲘⲨⲤⲦⲎⲢⲒⲞⲚ ⲈⲦ-
ϬⲰϢ̄Ⲧ ⲈϨⲞⲨⲚ ⲀⲨⲰ ⲀⲔⲂⲀⲠⲦⲒⲌⲈ Ⲛ̄ϯϬⲞⲘ Ⲛ̄ⲦⲈ ⲤⲀⲂⲀⲰⲐ
ⲠⲀⲄⲀⲐⲞⲤ · ⲀⲨⲰ ⲀⲔⲈⲒ' ⲈⲠⲦⲞⲠⲞⲤ Ⲛ̄ⲚⲀⲢⲬⲰⲚ ⲀⲔϯ ⲚⲀⲨ
Ⲛ̄Ⲙ̄ⲘⲨⲤⲦⲎⲢⲒⲞⲚ Ⲙ̄ⲠⲬⲒⲤⲈ　ⲀⲨⲰ ⲀⲨⲢ̄ⲆⲒⲔⲀⲒⲞⲤ · ⲀⲨⲰ
ⲀⲨⲢ̄ⲀⲄⲀⲐⲞⲤ · ϯⲢⲎⲚⲎ ϨⲰⲰϤ ⲦⲈ ϯϬⲞⲘ Ⲛ̄ⲦⲈ ⲤⲀⲂⲀⲰⲐ ·
15 ⲦⲀⲒ ⲈⲦⲈ Ⲛ̄ⲦⲞⲤ ⲦⲈ ⲦⲈⲔⲯⲨⲬⲎ · ⲦⲀⲒ ⲈⲚⲦⲀⲤⲂⲰⲔ ⲈϨⲞⲨⲚ
ⲈⲐⲨⲖⲎ *Ⲛ̄ⲦⲂⲀⲢⲂⲎⲖⲰ · ⲀⲨⲰ Ⲛ̄ⲀⲢⲬⲰⲚ ⲦⲎⲢⲞⲨ Ⲙ̄ⲠⲤⲞⲞⲨ ⲢⲒⲈ̄ᵇ
Ⲛ̄ⲀⲒⲰⲚ Ⲛ̄ⲦⲈ ⲒⲀⲂⲢⲀⲰⲐ · ⲀⲨⲀⲀⲨ Ⲛ̄ⲈⲒⲢⲎⲚⲎ Ⲙ̄Ⲛ ⲠⲘⲨⲤⲦⲎ-
ⲢⲒⲞⲚ Ⲙ̄ⲠⲞⲨⲞⲒⲚ · ⲀⲨⲰ ⲦⲘⲈ ⲈⲚⲦⲀⲤϯⲞⲨⲰ ⲈⲂⲞⲖ Ϩ̄Ⲙ
ⲠⲔⲀϨ · Ⲛ̄ⲦⲞⲤ ⲦⲈ ϯϬⲞⲘ Ⲛ̄ⲦⲈ ⲤⲀⲂⲀⲰⲐ ⲠⲀⲄⲀⲐⲞⲤ · ⲦⲀⲒ
20 ⲈⲚⲦⲀⲤⲈⲒ' ⲈⲂⲞⲖ Ϩ̄Ⲙ ⲠⲦⲞⲠⲞⲤ Ⲛ̄ⲦⲞⲨⲚⲀⲘ · ⲠⲀⲒ ⲈⲦⲘ̄ⲠⲤⲀ-
ⲚⲂⲞⲖ Ⲙ̄ⲠⲈⲐⲎⲤⲀⲨⲢⲞⲤ Ⲙ̄ⲠⲞⲨⲞⲒⲚ · ⲀⲨⲰ ⲀⲤⲂⲰⲔ ⲈⲠⲦⲞ-
ⲠⲞⲤ Ⲛ̄ⲚⲀϨⲂⲞⲨⲢ · ⲀⲤⲂⲰⲔ ⲈϨⲞⲨⲚ ⲈⲐⲨⲖⲎ Ⲛ̄ⲦⲂⲀⲢⲂⲎⲖⲰ ·
ⲀⲨⲰ ⲀⲤⲔⲎⲢⲨⲤⲤⲈ ⲚⲀⲨ Ⲛ̄Ⲙ̄ⲘⲨⲤⲦⲎⲢⲒⲞⲚ Ⲙ̄ⲠⲦⲞⲠⲞⲤ Ⲛ̄ⲦⲀ-
ⲖⲎⲐⲒⲀ · ⲦⲀⲒⲔⲀⲒⲞⲤⲨⲚⲎ ϨⲰⲰⲤ ⲈⲚⲦⲀⲤϬⲰϢ̄Ⲧ ⲈⲂⲞⲖ Ϩ̄Ⲛ

---

16 MS Ⲙ̄ⲠⲤⲞⲞⲨ Ⲛ̄Ⲛ̄ⲀⲒⲰⲚ; the first ⲛ expunged.

which bound itself to thee, which thou didst cast to the
left, thou, the First *Mystery* which looks forth. The Little
Sabaoth[1] the *Good* received it, he cast it into the *matter*
of the Barbelo, and he *preached* on the true *place* of the
truth in all the *places* of those of the left. Now it is that
matter of the Barbelo which is a *body* to thee today. 'And
righteousness and *peace* have kissed one another'*. *Righteousness* is thou who didst bring all the *mysteries* through
thy Father, the First *Mystery* who looks within, and thou
didst *baptise* the power of Sabaoth the *Good*. And thou didst
come to the *place* of the *archons*, thou didst give to them
the *mysteries* of the height and they became *righteous* and
good. *Peace*, on the other hand, is the power of Sabaoth,
namely thy *soul* which entered into the *matter* of the Barbelo.
And all the *archons* of the six *aeons* of Jabraoth[2] have
made *peace*[3] with the *mystery* of the light. And : 'Truth which
has sprouted from the earth'□. This is the power of Sabaoth
the *Good* which came forth from the *place* of the right, which
is outside the *Treasury* of the light, and which went to the
place of those of the left. It entered into the *matter* of the
Barbelo, and it *preached* to them the *mysteries* of the *place*
of the *truth*. *Righteousness*, on the other hand, which looked
forth from | heaven* is thou, the First *Mystery* which looked

---

*   Ps. 84.10
□   Ps. 84.11

---

[1]   (3) Sabaoth, the Little; as Zeus, see 357.4, 5; 361.18.
[2]   (17) Jabraoth; brother of Adamas Sabaoth; see J 82 (also 355.17, 18).
[3]   (17) made peace; lit. made themselves peaceful.

ⲧⲡⲉ ⲛ̄ⲧⲟⲕ ⲡⲉ ⲡⲓϣⲟⲣⲡ̄ ⲙ̄ⲙⲩⲥⲧⲏⲣⲓⲟⲛ ⲉⲧϭⲱϣ̄ⲧ̄ ⲉⲃⲟⲗ
ⲉⲁⲕⲉⲓʼ ⲉⲃⲟⲗ ϩ̄ⲛ̄ ⲛⲉⲭⲱⲣⲏⲙⲁ ⲙ̄ⲡϫⲓⲥⲉ · ⲙ̄ⲛ̄ ⲙ̄ⲙⲩⲥⲧⲏⲣⲓⲟⲛ
ⲛ̄ⲧⲙⲛ̄ⲧⲉⲣⲟ ⲙ̄ⲡⲟⲩⲟ̈ⲓⲛ · ⲁⲩⲱ ** ⲁⲕⲉⲓʼ ⲉϩⲣⲁ̈ⲓ ⲉϫⲛ̄ ⲡⲉⲛⲇⲩⲙⲁ ⲣ̄ⲓ̄ⲍ̄
ⲙ̄ⲡⲟⲩⲟ̈ⲓⲛ ⲡⲁ̈ⲓ ⲉⲛⲧⲁⲕϫⲓⲧ̄ϥ̄ ⲛ̄ⲧⲟⲟⲧ̄ⲥ̄ ⲛ̄ⲧⲃⲁⲣⲃⲏⲗⲱ ⲉⲧⲉ
ⲓ̄ⲥ̄ ⲡⲉ ⲡⲉⲛⲥⲱⲧⲏⲣ · ⲉⲁⲕⲉⲓʼ ⲉϩⲣⲁ̈ⲓ ⲉϫⲱϥ ⲛ̄ⲑⲉ ⲛ̄ⲟⲩϭⲣⲟ-
ⲟⲙⲡⲉ :

ⲍ ⲁⲥϣⲱⲡⲉ ϭⲉ ⲛ̄ⲧⲉⲣⲉ ⲓ̈ⲱϩⲁⲛⲛⲏⲥ ⲧⲁⲩⲉ-ⲛⲉⲓ̈ϣⲁϫⲉ ·
ⲡⲉϫⲁϥ ⲛⲁϥ ⲛ̄ϭⲓ ⲡⲓϣⲟⲣⲡ̄ ⲙ̄ⲙⲩⲥⲧⲏⲣⲓⲟⲛ ⲉⲧⲥⲱϣ̄ⲧ̄ ⲉⲃⲟⲗ
ϫⲉ ⲉⲩⲅⲉ ⲓ̈ⲱϩⲁⲛⲛⲏⲥ ⲡⲥⲟⲛ ⲙ̄ⲡⲙⲉⲣⲓⲧ · ⲁϥⲟⲩⲱϩ ⲟⲛ
ⲉⲧⲟⲟⲧ̄ϥ̄ ⲛ̄ϭⲓ ⲡⲓϣⲟⲣⲡ̄ ⲙ̄ⲙⲩⲥⲧⲏⲣⲓⲟⲛ ⲉϥϫⲱ ⲙ̄ⲙⲟⲥ · ϫⲉ
ⲁⲥϣⲱⲡⲉ ϭⲉ ⲁ ϯϭⲟⲙ ⲉⲛⲧⲁⲥⲉⲓʼ ⲉⲃⲟⲗ ϩ̄ⲙ̄ ⲡϫⲓⲥⲉ ⲉⲧⲉ
ⲁⲛⲟⲕ ⲡⲉ ⲉⲁ ⲡⲁⲉⲓⲱⲧ ⲧ̄ⲛ̄ⲛⲟⲟⲩⲧ ⲉⲧⲣⲁⲛⲟⲩϩ̄ⲙ̄ ⲛ̄ⲧⲡⲓⲥ-
ⲧⲓⲥ ⲥⲟⲫⲓⲁ ϩ̄ⲙ̄ ⲡⲉⲭⲁⲟⲥ · ⲁⲛⲟⲕ ϭⲉ ⲙ̄ⲛ̄ ⲧⲕⲉϭⲟⲙ ⲉⲛⲧⲁⲥⲉⲓʼ ⲉⲃⲟⲗ ⲙ̄ⲙⲟ̈ⲓ ⲁⲩⲱ ⲧⲉⲯⲩⲭⲏ ⲛ̄ⲧⲁ̈ⲓϫⲓⲧ̄ⲥ̄ ⲛ̄ⲧⲟⲟⲧ̄ϥ̄
ⲛ̄ⲥⲁⲃⲁⲱⲑ ⲡⲁⲅⲁⲑⲟⲥ · ⲁⲩⲉⲓʼ ⲉⲧⲟⲩⲛ̄-ⲛⲉⲩ*ⲉⲣⲏⲩ · ⲁⲩⲣ̄- ⲣ̄ⲓ̄ⲍ̄ b
ⲟⲩⲁⲡⲟⲣⲣⲟⲓⲁ ⲛ̄ⲟⲩⲱⲧ ⲛ̄ⲟⲩⲟⲉⲓⲛ · ⲉⲥⲟ ⲛ̄ⲟⲩⲟ̈ⲓⲛ ⲉⲙⲁϣⲟ
ⲉⲙⲁϣⲟ · ⲁ̈ⲓⲙⲟⲩⲧⲉ ⲉⲅⲁⲃⲣⲓⲏⲗ ⲉⲡⲉⲥⲏⲧ ⲉⲃⲟⲗ ϩ̄ⲛ̄ ⲛ̄ⲁⲓⲱⲛ
ⲁⲩⲱ ⲙ̄ⲛ̄ ⲙⲓⲭⲁⲏⲗ ⲉⲃⲟⲗ ϩⲓⲧ̄ⲛ̄ ⲧⲕⲉⲗⲉⲩⲥⲓⲥ ⲙ̄ⲡⲁ̈ⲓⲱⲧ ⲡⲓ-
ϣⲟⲣⲡ̄ ⲙ̄ⲙⲩⲥⲧⲏⲣⲓⲟⲛ ⲉⲧϭⲱϣ̄ⲧ̄ ⲉϩⲟⲩⲛ ⲁ̈ⲓϯ ⲛⲁⲩ ⲛ̄-
ⲧⲁⲡⲟϩⲣⲟⲓⲁ ⲛ̄ⲟⲩⲟ̈ⲓⲛ ⲁ̈ⲓⲧⲣⲉⲩⲃⲱⲕ ⲉⲡⲉⲥⲏⲧ ⲉⲡⲉⲭⲁⲟⲥ
ⲉⲧⲣⲉⲩⲃⲟⲏⲑⲓ ⲉⲧⲡⲓⲥⲧⲓⲥ ⲥⲟⲫⲓⲁ · ⲁⲩⲱ ⲛ̄ⲥⲉϥⲓ ⲛ̄ⲛ̄ϭⲟⲙ
ⲛ̄ⲟⲩⲟ̈ⲓⲛ ⲛⲁ̈ⲓ ⲛ̄ⲧⲁⲩϥⲓⲧⲟⲩ ⲛ̄ⲧⲟⲟⲧ̄ⲥ̄ ⲛ̄ϭⲓ ⲛⲉⲡⲣⲟⲃⲟⲗⲟⲟⲩⲉ ⲙ̄ⲡⲁⲩⲑⲁⲇⲏⲥ ⲛ̄ⲥⲉϥⲓⲧⲟⲩ ⲛ̄ⲧⲟⲟⲧⲟⲩ · ⲁⲩⲱ ⲛ̄ⲥⲉ-
ⲧⲁⲁⲩ ⲛ̄ⲧⲡⲓⲥⲧⲓⲥ ⲥⲟⲫⲓⲁ · ⲁⲩⲱ ⲛ̄ⲧⲉⲩⲛⲟⲩ ⲛ̄ⲧⲁⲩϫⲓ-

---

9 MS ⲙ̄ⲡⲙⲉⲣⲓⲧ; read ⲙ̄ⲙⲉⲣⲓⲧ.

forth, having come forth from *spaces* of the height with the *mysteries* of the kingdom [1] of the light. And thou didst come down upon the *garment* of light which thou didst receive from the hand of the Barbelo; thou didst come down upon him who is Jesus our *Saviour*, like a dove [2]."

Now it happened when John had spoken these words, the First *Mystery* who looks forth said to him : "*Excellent, John, thou beloved brother.*"

64. The First *Mystery* continued again, saying : "Now it happened, the power which came forth from the height, namely I myself, whom my Father sent to save the Pistis Sophia from the *Chaos* — now I with the other power which came forth from me and the *soul* which I received from Sabaoth the *Good*, they came towards one another, they made one *outpouring* of light which was exceedingly bright. I called Gabriel and Michael down from the *aeons*, by the command of my Father, the First *Mystery* who looks within, and I gave them the *outpouring* of light. I caused them to go down to the *Chaos* to *help* the Pistis Sophia, and to take the light-powers which the *emanations* of the Authades had taken from her, to take them from them and to give them to the Pistis Sophia. And in the hour that they brought | the *outpouring* of light down to the *Chaos*, it gave

---

*   Ps. 84.11
□   cf. Mt. 3.16

---

[1]   (2) with the mysteries; Till : and the mysteries.
[2]   (3-5) thou didst come down ... like a dove; lit. thou didst come down upon the garment of light which thou didst receive from the hand of the Barbelo, who is Jesus our Saviour, thou didst come down upon him like a dove.

ⲧⲁⲡⲟϩⲣⲟⲓⲁ ⲛ̄ⲟⲩⲟⲉⲓⲛ ⲉⲡⲉⲥⲏⲧ ⲉⲡⲉⲭⲁⲟⲥ· ⲁⲥⲣ̄ⲟⲩⲟⲓ̈ⲛ
ⲉⲙⲁϣⲟ ⲉⲙⲁϣⲟ ϩⲙ̄ ⲡⲉⲭⲁⲟⲥ ⲧⲏⲣϥ̄· ⲁⲩⲱ ⲁⲥⲟⲩⲱϣ̄ⲥ̄
ⲉⲃⲟⲗ ϩⲛ̄ ⲛⲉⲩⲧⲟⲡⲟⲥ ⲧⲏⲣⲟⲩ· ⲁⲩⲱ ⲛ̄ⲧⲉⲣⲟⲩⲛⲁⲩ
ⲉⲡⲛⲟϭ **ⲛ̄ⲟⲩⲟⲉⲓⲛ ⲛ̄ⲧⲁⲡⲟϩⲣⲟⲓⲁ ⲉⲧⲙ̄ⲙⲁⲩ ⲛ̄ϭⲓ ⲛⲉⲡⲣⲟ- ⲣ̄ⲓ̈ⲏ
ⲃⲟⲗⲟⲟⲩⲉ ⲙ̄ⲡⲁⲩⲑⲁⲇⲏⲥ ⲁⲩⲣ̄ϩⲟⲧⲉ ⲉϫⲛ̄ ⲛⲉⲩⲉⲣⲏⲩ· ⲁⲩⲱ
ⲧⲁⲡⲟϩⲣⲟⲓⲁ ⲉⲧⲙ̄ⲙⲁⲩ ⲁⲥⲧⲱⲕⲙ̄ ⲉⲃⲟⲗ ⲛ̄ϩⲏⲧⲟⲩ ⲛ̄ϭⲟⲙ
ⲛⲓⲙ ⲛ̄ⲟⲩⲟⲉⲓⲛ ⲛⲁⲓ̈ ⲛ̄ⲧⲁⲩϥⲓⲧⲟⲩ ⲛ̄ⲧⲟⲟⲧⲥ̄ ⲛ̄ⲧⲡⲓⲥⲧⲓⲥ
ⲥⲟⲫⲓⲁ· ⲁⲩⲱ ⲙ̄ⲡⲟⲩϣⲧⲟⲗⲙⲁ ⲛ̄ϭⲓ ⲛⲉⲡⲣⲟⲃⲟⲗⲟⲟⲩⲉ ⲙ̄-
ⲡⲁⲩⲑⲁⲇⲏⲥ ⲉⲁⲙⲁϩⲧⲉ ⲛ̄ⲧⲁⲡⲟϩⲣⲟⲓⲁ ⲛ̄ⲟⲩⲟⲉⲓⲛ ⲉⲧⲙ̄ⲙⲁⲩ
ϩⲙ̄ ⲡⲉⲭⲁⲟⲥ ⲛ̄ⲕⲁⲕⲉ· ⲟⲩⲇⲉ ⲙ̄ⲡⲟⲩϣⲁⲙⲁϩⲧⲉ ⲙ̄ⲙⲟⲥ ϩⲛ̄
ⲧⲧⲉⲭⲛⲏ ⲙ̄ⲡⲁⲩⲑⲁⲇⲏⲥ ⲡⲁⲓ̈ ⲉⲧⲁⲙⲁϩⲧⲉ ⲉϫⲛ̄ ⲛⲉⲡⲣⲟⲃⲟ-
ⲗⲟⲟⲩⲉ· ⲁⲩⲱ ⲅⲁⲃⲣⲓⲏⲗ ⲙⲛ̄ ⲙⲓⲭⲁⲏⲗ· ⲁⲩⲉⲓⲛⲉ ⲛ̄ⲧⲁ-
ⲡⲟϩⲣⲟⲓⲁ ⲛ̄ⲟⲩⲟⲉⲓⲛ ⲉϫⲙ̄ ⲡⲥⲱⲙⲁ ⲛ̄ⲑⲩⲗⲏ ⲛ̄ⲧⲡⲓⲥⲧⲓⲥ ⲥⲟ-
ⲫⲓⲁ· ⲁⲩⲱ ⲁⲩⲛⲟⲩϫⲉ ⲉϩⲟⲩⲛ ⲉⲣⲟⲥ ⲛ̄ⲛⲉⲥⲟⲩⲟⲓ̈ⲛ ⲧⲏⲣⲟⲩ ⲉⲛⲧⲁⲩϥⲓⲧⲟⲩ ⲛ̄ⲧⲟⲟⲧⲥ̄· ⲁⲩⲱ ⲁϥϫⲓ-ⲟⲩⲟⲓ̈ⲛ ⲧⲏⲣϥ̄
ⲛ̄ϭⲓ ⲡⲥⲱⲙⲁ ⲛ̄ⲧⲉⲥϩⲩⲗⲏ· *ⲁⲩⲱ ⲟⲛ ⲁⲩϫⲓ-ⲟⲩⲟⲓ̈ⲛ ⲛ̄ϭⲓ ⲣ̄ⲓ̈ⲏ b
ⲛⲉⲥϭⲟⲙ ⲧⲏⲣⲟⲩ ⲉⲧⲛ̄ϩⲏⲧⲥ̄ ⲛⲁⲓ̈ ⲉⲛⲧⲁⲩϥⲓ-ⲡⲉⲩⲟⲩⲟⲓ̈ⲛ
ⲁⲩⲱ ⲁⲩⲗⲟ ⲉⲩϣⲁⲁⲧ ⲛ̄ⲟⲩⲟⲓ̈ⲛ ϫⲉ ⲁⲩϥⲓ-ⲡⲉⲩⲟⲩⲟⲓ̈ⲛ
ⲉⲛⲧⲁⲩϥⲓⲧϥ̄ ⲛ̄ⲧⲟⲟⲧⲟⲩ· ⲉⲃⲟⲗ ϫⲉ ⲛ̄ⲧⲁⲩϯ-ⲡⲟⲩⲟⲓ̈ⲛ
ⲛⲁⲩ ⲉⲃⲟⲗ ϩⲓⲧⲟⲟⲧ· ⲁⲩⲱ ⲙⲓⲭⲁⲏⲗ· ⲙⲛ̄ ⲅⲁⲃⲣⲓⲏⲗ· ⲛⲁⲓ̈
ⲉⲛⲧⲁⲩⲇⲓⲁⲕⲟⲛⲓ ⲛⲁⲓ̈ ⲉⲛⲧⲁⲩϫⲓ-ⲧⲁⲡⲟϩⲣⲟⲓⲁ ⲛ̄ⲟⲩⲟⲓ̈ⲛ | ⲉⲡⲉ-
ⲭⲁⲟⲥ· ⲥⲉⲛⲁϯ ⲛⲁⲩ ⲛ̄ⲙ̄ⲙⲩⲥⲧⲏⲣⲓⲟⲛ ⲙ̄ⲡⲟⲩⲟⲓ̈ⲛ ⲛ̄ⲧⲟⲟⲩ
ⲛⲉ ⲛ̄ⲧⲁⲩⲧⲁⲛϩⲟⲩⲧⲟⲩ ⲉⲧⲁⲡⲟϩⲣⲟⲓⲁ ⲛ̄ⲟⲩⲟⲓ̈ⲛ· ⲧⲁⲓ̈ ⲉⲛⲧ-

---

11 MS ⲧ inserted before ⲧⲉⲭⲛⲏ.
18 MS ⲁⲩϥⲓ ; read ⲁⲩϫⲓ.

light exceedingly in the whole *Chaos*, and it spread in all their (the emanations') *places*. And when the *emanations* of the Authades saw the great light of that *outpouring*, they were all afraid together. And that *outpouring* drew forth from them all the light-powers which they had taken from the Pistis Sophia. And the *emanations* of the Authades did not *dare* to take hold of that *outpouring* of light in the dark *Chaos*; *nor* were they able to take hold of it by the *artifice* of the Authades who had hold of the *emanations*. And Gabriel and Michael brought the *outpouring* of light over the *body* of *matter* of the Pistis Sophia. And they cast into her all her lights which had been taken from her. And the *body* of her *matter* received light completely. And furthermore, all her powers within her, whose light had been taken away, received light and they ceased to lack light, because they received their light which had been taken from them, because the light was given to them by me. And Michael and Gabriel, who *served* me and brought the *outpouring* of light to the *Chaos*, will give the *mysteries* of the light to them; these are they who were entrusted with the *out-pouring* of light | which I gave to them, I brought it to the ⲁⲓ̈ⲧⲁⲁⲥ ⲛⲁⲩ ⲁⲓ̈ϫⲓⲧⲥ̄ ⲉⲡⲉⲭⲁⲟⲥ· ⲁⲩⲱ ⲙⲓⲭⲁⲏⲗ ⟨ⲙⲛ̄⟩ ⲅⲁⲃⲣⲓⲏⲗ· ⲙ̄ⲡⲟⲩϥⲓ-ⲗⲁⲁⲩ ⲛ̄ⲟⲩⲟⲓ̈ⲛ ⲛⲁⲩ ϩⲛ̄ ⲛ̄ⲟⲩⲟⲓ̈ⲛ ⲛ̄ⲧⲡⲓⲥⲧⲓⲥ ⲥⲟⲫⲓⲁ· ⲛⲁⲓ̈ ⲉⲛⲧⲁⲩϥⲓⲧⲟⲩ ⲛ̄ⲧⲟⲟⲧⲟⲩ ⲛ̄ⲛⲉⲡⲣⲟⲃⲟⲗⲟⲟⲩⲉ ⲙ̄ⲡⲁⲩⲑⲁⲇⲏⲥ· ⲁⲥϣⲱⲡⲉ ϭⲉ ⲛ̄ⲧⲉⲣⲉ ⲧⲁⲡⲟϩⲣⲟⲓⲁ ⲛ̄ⲟⲩⲟⲓ̈ⲛ ** ⲛ̄ⲧⲉⲣⲉⲥⲛⲟⲩϫⲉ ⲉϩⲟⲩⲛ ⲉⲧⲡⲓⲥⲧⲓⲥ (ⲣⲓⲑ) ⲥⲟⲫⲓⲁ ⲛ̄ⲛⲉⲥϭⲟⲙ ⲧⲏⲣⲟⲩ ⲛ̄ⲟⲩⲟⲓ̈ⲛ· ⲛⲁⲓ̈ ⲛ̄ⲧⲁⲥϥⲓⲧⲟⲩ ⲛ̄ⲧⲟⲟⲧⲟⲩ ⲛ̄ⲛⲉⲡⲣⲟⲃⲟⲗⲟⲟⲩⲉ ⲙ̄ⲡⲁⲩⲑⲁⲇⲏⲥ· ⲁⲥⲣ̄ⲟⲩⲟⲓ̈ⲛ ⲧⲏⲣⲥ̄· ⲁⲩⲱ ⲛ̄ⲕⲉϭⲟⲙ ⲛ̄ⲟⲩⲟⲓ̈ⲛ ⲛⲁⲓ̈ ⲉⲧϣⲟⲟⲡ ϩⲛ̄ ⲧⲡⲓⲥⲧⲓⲥ ⲥⲟⲫⲓⲁ· ⲛⲁⲓ̈ ⲉⲧⲉ ⲙ̄ⲡⲟⲩϥⲓⲧⲟⲩ ⲛ̄ϭⲓ ⲛⲉⲡⲣⲟⲃⲟⲗⲟⲟⲩⲉ ⲙ̄ⲡⲁⲩⲑⲁⲇⲏⲥ ⲁⲩⲟⲩⲣⲟⲧ ⲟⲛ· ⲁⲩⲱ ⲁⲩⲙⲟⲩϩ ⲛ̄ⲟⲩⲟⲓ̈ⲛ· ⲁⲩⲱ ⲛ̄ⲟⲩⲟⲓ̈ⲛ ⲉⲛⲧⲁⲩⲛⲟϫⲟⲩ ⲉϩⲟⲩⲛ ⲉⲧⲡⲓⲥⲧⲓⲥ ⲥⲟⲫⲓⲁ· ⲁⲩⲧⲁⲛϩⲉ-ⲡⲥⲱⲙⲁ ⲛ̄ⲧⲉⲥϩⲩⲗⲏ· ⲧⲁⲓ̈ ⲉⲧⲉ ⲙⲛ̄-ⲟⲩⲟⲓ̈ⲛ ⲛ̄ϩⲏⲧⲥ̄· ⲧⲁⲓ̈ ⲉⲛⲉⲥⲛⲁⲧⲁⲕⲟ ⲡⲉ· ⲏ ⲧⲁⲓ̈ ⲉϣⲁⲥⲧⲁⲕⲟ· ⲁⲩⲱ ⲁⲩⲧⲁϩⲟ ⲉⲣⲁⲧⲟⲩ ⲛ̄ⲛⲉⲥϭⲟⲙ ⲧⲏⲣⲟⲩ ⲛⲁⲓ̈ ⲉⲛⲉⲩⲛⲁⲃⲱⲗ ⲉⲃⲟⲗ· ⲁⲩⲱ ⲁⲩϫⲓ ⲛⲁⲩ ⲛ̄ⲟⲩϭⲟⲙ ⲛ̄ⲟⲩⲟⲓ̈ⲛ· ⲁⲩⲣ̄ⲑⲉ ⲟⲛ ⲉⲛⲉⲩⲟ ⲙ̄ⲙⲟⲥ ⲛ̄ϣⲟⲣⲡ̄· * ⲁⲩⲱ ⲟⲛ ⲁⲩϫⲓⲥⲉ (ⲣⲓⲑ b) ϩⲛ̄ ⲧⲁⲓⲥⲑⲏⲥⲓⲥ ⲛ̄ⲟⲩⲟⲓ̈ⲛ· ⲁⲩⲱ ⲛ̄ϭⲟⲙ ⲧⲏⲣⲟⲩ ⲛ̄ⲟⲩⲟⲓ̈ⲛ ⲛ̄ⲧⲉ ⲧⲥⲟⲫⲓⲁ· ⲁⲩⲥⲟⲩⲛ̄-ⲛⲉⲩⲉⲣⲏⲩ ⲉⲃⲟⲗ ϩⲓⲧⲛ̄ ⲧⲁⲁⲡⲟϩⲣⲟⲓⲁ ⲛ̄ⲟⲩⲟⲓ̈ⲛ· ⲁⲩⲱ ⲁⲩⲛⲟⲩϩⲙ̄ ϩⲓⲧⲙ̄ ⲡⲟⲩⲟⲉⲓⲛ ⲛ̄ⲧⲁⲡⲟϩⲣⲟⲓⲁ ⲉⲧⲙ̄ⲙⲁⲩ· ⲁⲩⲱ ⲧⲁⲁⲡⲟϩⲣⲟⲓⲁ ⲛ̄ⲟⲩⲟⲉⲓⲛ ⲛ̄ⲧⲉⲣⲉⲥϥⲓ ⲛ̄ⲛⲟⲩⲟⲉⲓⲛ ⲛ̄ⲧⲟⲟⲧⲟⲩ ⲛ̄ⲛⲉⲡⲣⲟⲃⲟⲗⲟⲟⲩⲉ ⲙ̄ⲡⲁⲩⲑⲁⲇⲏⲥ ⲛⲁⲓ̈ ⲉⲛⲧⲁⲩϥⲓⲧⲟⲩ ⲛ̄ⲧⲟⲟⲧⲥ̄ ⲛ̄ⲧⲡⲓⲥⲧⲓⲥ ⲥⲟⲫⲓⲁ· ⲁⲥⲛⲟϫⲟⲩ ⲉϩⲟⲩⲛ ⲉⲧⲡⲓⲥⲧⲓⲥ ⲥⲟⲫⲓⲁ· ⲁⲩⲱ ⲁⲥⲕⲟⲧⲥ̄ ⲁⲥⲉⲓ ⲉϩⲣⲁⲓ̈ ϩⲙ̄ ⲡⲉⲭⲁⲟⲥ: ⲛⲁⲓ̈ ϭⲉ ⲉⲣⲉ ⲡⲓϣⲟⲣⲡ̄

1 MS ⲙⲓⲭⲁⲏⲗ inserted in margins; ⲙⲛ̄ before ⲅⲁⲃⲣⲓⲏⲗ omitted.

Chaos. And Michael ⟨and⟩ Gabriel did not take any light for themselves from the lights of the Pistis Sophia, which they took away from the *emanations* of the Authades.

Now it happened when my *outpouring* of light cast into the Pistis Sophia all her light-powers which it took away from the *emanations* of the Authades, she became completely lighted. And also the light-powers which were in the Pistis Sophia, which the *emanations* of the Authades did not take away, rejoiced again and they were filled with light. And the lights which were cast into the Pistis Sophia gave life to the *body* of her matter which had no light in it, which was about to be destroyed *or* was being destroyed, and they set up all its powers which were about to be dissolved. And they received light-power for themselves, they became as they were at first and they increased in *perception* of the light. And all the light-powers of the Sophia recognised one another through my *outpouring* of light. And they were saved through the light of that *outpouring*. And my *outpouring* of light, when it took the lights from the *emanations* of the Authades, which had taken them from the Pistis Sophia, it cast them into the Pistis Sophia. And it turned itself and came up out of the Chaos."

Now when the First | Mystery said to the *disciples* that

ⲙ̄ⲙⲩⲥⲧⲏⲣⲓⲟⲛ ⲭⲱ ⲙ̄ⲙⲟⲟⲩ ⲉⲙ̄ⲙⲁⲑⲏⲧⲏⲥ ⲭⲉ ⲁⲩⲱⲱⲡⲉ
ⲛ̄ⲧⲡⲓⲥⲧⲓⲥ ⲥⲟⲫⲓⲁ ϩ̄ⲙ ⲡⲉⲭⲗⲟⲥ · ⲁϥⲟⲩⲱ̄ϣ̄ⲃ ⲡⲉⲭⲁϥ ⲛⲁⲩ
ⲭⲉ ⲧⲉⲧⲛ̄ⲛⲟⲓ̈ ⲭⲉ ⲉⲓ̈ϣⲁⲭⲉ ⲛ̄ⲙⲙⲏⲧⲛ̄ ⲛ̄ⲁϣ ⲛ̄ϩⲉ :

ⲋ ⲁϥⲉⲓ' ⲉⲑⲏ ⲛ̄ϭⲓ ** ⲡⲉⲧⲣⲟⲥ ⲡⲉⲭⲁϥ ⲭⲉ ⲡⲁⲭⲟⲉⲓⲥ · ⲉⲧ- ⲣ̄ⲕ

5 ⲃⲉ ⲡⲃⲱⲗ ⲛ̄ⲛ̄ϣⲁⲭⲉ ⲉⲛⲧⲁⲕⲭⲟⲟⲩ · ⲁ ⲧⲉⲕϭⲟⲙ ⲛ̄ⲟⲩⲟⲓ̈ⲛ
ⲡⲣⲟⲫⲏⲧⲉⲩⲉ ϩⲁⲣⲟⲟⲩ ⲙ̄ⲡⲓⲟⲩⲟⲉⲓϣ ϩⲓⲧⲛ̄ ⲥⲟⲗⲟⲙⲱⲛ ϩⲛ̄
ⲛⲉϥϣⲁⲗⲏ · ⲭⲉ

7. ⲁⲥⲉⲓ' ⲉⲃⲟⲗ ⲛ̄ϭⲓ ⲟⲩⲁⲡⲟϩⲣⲟⲓⲁ ⲁⲥⲣ̄-ⲟⲩⲛⲟϭ ⲛ̄ⲓ̈ⲉⲣⲟ
ⲉϥⲟⲩⲟ̄ϣ̄ⲥ ·

10   8. ⲁⲥⲥⲟⲕⲟⲩ ⲧⲏⲣⲟⲩ · ⲁⲩⲱ ⲁⲥⲕⲟⲧⲥ̄ ⲉϫ̄ⲙ ⲡⲉⲣⲡⲉ ·

9. ⲙ̄ⲡⲟⲩϣⲁⲙⲁϩⲧⲉ ⲙ̄ⲙⲟⲥ · ϩⲛ̄ ϩⲉⲛⲱⲣϫ̄ · ⲙⲛ̄ ϩⲉⲛⲙⲁ
ⲉⲩⲕⲏⲧ · ⲟⲩⲁⲉ ⲙ̄ⲡⲟⲩϣⲁⲙⲁϩⲧⲉ ⲙ̄ⲙⲟⲥ ⲛ̄ϭⲓ ⲛ̄ⲧⲉⲭⲛⲏ
ⲛ̄ⲛⲉⲧⲁⲙⲁϩⲧⲉ ⲙ̄ⲙⲟⲟⲩ ·

10. ⲁⲩⲛ̄ⲧⲥ̄ ⲉϫ̄ⲙ ⲡⲕⲁϩ ⲧⲏⲣϥ̄ · ⲁⲩⲱ ⲁⲥⲁⲙⲁϩⲧⲉ ⲙ̄ⲙⲟⲟⲩ
15 ⲧⲏⲣⲟⲩ ·

11. ⲁⲩⲥⲱ ⲛ̄ϭⲓ ⲛⲉⲧϣⲟⲟⲡ ϩⲓϫ̄ⲙ ⲡϣⲱ ⲉⲧϣⲟⲩⲟⲩ ·
ⲁ ⲡⲉⲩⲉⲓⲃⲉ ⲃⲱⲗ ⲉⲃⲟⲗ ⲁⲩⲱ ⲁϥⲱ̄ϣ̄ⲙ ⲛ̄ⲧⲉⲣⲟⲩ† ⲛⲁⲩ
ⲙ̄ⲡⲥⲱ ⲛ̄ⲧⲟⲟⲧϥ̄ ⲙ̄ⲡⲉⲧϫⲟⲥⲉ ·

12. ϩⲉⲛⲙⲁⲕⲁⲣⲓⲟⲥ ⲛⲉ ⲛ̄ⲁⲓⲁⲕⲱⲛ ⲙ̄ⲡⲥⲱ ⲉⲧⲙ̄ⲙⲁⲩ ⲛⲏ ⲣ̄ⲕ ᵇ
20 ⲉⲛⲧⲁⲩⲧⲁⲛϩⲟⲩⲧⲟⲩ ⲉⲡⲙⲟⲟⲩ ⲙ̄ⲡϫⲟⲉⲓⲥ ·

13. ⲁⲩⲕⲧⲟ ⲛ̄ϩⲉⲛⲥⲡⲟⲧⲟⲩ ⲉⲁⲩϣⲟⲟⲩⲉ · ⲁⲩϫⲓ ⲛ̄ⲟⲩ-
ⲟⲩⲣⲟⲧ ⲛ̄ϩⲏⲧ ⲛ̄ϭⲓ ⲛⲏ ⲉⲧⲃⲏⲗ ⲉⲃⲟⲗ ⲁⲩⲁⲙⲁϩⲧⲉ ⲛ̄ϩⲉⲛ-
ⲯⲩⲭⲏ ⲉⲩⲛⲟⲩϫⲉ ⲙ̄ⲡⲧⲏⲩ ⲭⲉ ⲛ̄ⲛⲉⲩⲙⲟⲩ ·

14. ⲁⲩⲧⲁϩⲟ ⲛ̄ϩⲉⲛⲙⲉⲗⲟⲥ ⲉⲣⲁⲧⲟⲩ ⲉⲁⲩϩⲉ · ⲁⲩ†-ϭⲟⲙ
25 ⲛ̄ⲧⲉⲩⲡⲁⲣϩⲏⲥⲓⲁ · ⲁⲩⲱ ⲁⲩ†-ⲟⲩⲟⲓ̈ⲛ ⲛ̄ⲛⲉⲩⲃⲁⲗ ·

---

22   MS ⲁⲩⲁⲙⲁϩⲧⲥ; read ⲁⲩⲧⲁϩⲟ; see 135.6.

those things had happened to the Pistis Sophia in the *Chaos*, he answered and said to them : "Do you *understand* in what manner I am speaking with you?"

65.   Peter came forward and said : "My Lord, concerning the interpretation of the words which thou hast spoken, thy light-power once *prophesied* through Solomon in his *Ode* :

7. 'There went forth an *outpouring*; it became a great broad river.

8. It gathered all things; it turned towards the Temple.

9. It could not be restrained with restrainers and buildings, *nor* could the *artifices* of those who restrain water restrain it.

10. It was brought over the whole earth and it took hold of all things.

11. Those who were on the dry sand were given to drink, their thirst was relieved and quenched when they were given to drink by the hand of the Most High.

12. *Blessed* are the *servers* of that drink to whom the water of the Lord is entrusted.

13. They have changed dry lips; those that were fainting received joy of heart. Souls were ⟨given life⟩ [1], and breath was cast in so that they did not die.

14. They have set upright *limbs* that had fallen; they have given power to their *feebleness* [2] and light to their eyes. |

---

[1]   (22) souls were ⟨given life⟩; MS : souls were held fast (see 135.6).
[2]   (25) feebleness (πάρεσις); MS : openness; see Harris (Bibl. 21) note.

15. ϫⲉ ⲚⲦⲞⲞⲨ ⲦⲎⲢⲞⲨ ⲀⲨⲤⲞⲨⲰⲚⲞⲨ ϨⲘ ⲠϪⲞⲈⲒⲤ·
ⲀⲨⲰ ⲀⲨⲚⲞⲨϨⲘ ϨⲒⲦⲚ ⲞⲨⲘⲞⲞⲨ ⲚⲰⲚϨ ⲚϢⲀⲈⲚⲈϨ:

ⲤⲰⲦⲘ ϬⲈ ⲠⲀⲬⲞⲈⲒⲤ ⲦⲀⲦⲀⲨⲈ-ⲠϢⲀϪⲈ ϨⲚ ⲞⲨⲠⲀⲢ-
ϨⲎⲤⲒⲀ· ⲔⲀⲦⲀ ⲐⲈ ⲚⲦⲀ ⲦⲈⲔϬⲞⲘ ⲠⲢⲞⲪⲎⲦⲈⲨⲈ ϨⲒⲦⲚ ⲤⲞ-
5 ⲗⲞⲘⲰⲚ· ϫⲉ ⲞⲨⲀⲠⲞϨⲢⲞⲒⲀ ⲀⲤⲈⲒ ⲈⲂⲞⲗ ⲀⲤⲢ-ⲞⲨⲚⲞϬ
ⲚⲒⲈⲢⲞ ⲈϤⲞⲨⲞϢⲤ· ⲈⲦⲈ ⲠⲀⲒ ⲠⲈ ϫⲉ Ⲁ ϯⲀⲠⲞϨⲢⲞⲒⲀ ⲚⲞⲨ-
ⲞⲒ̈Ⲛ ⲞⲨⲰϢⲤ ⲈⲂⲟⲗ ϨⲘ ⲠⲈⲬⲀⲟⲤ· ϨⲚ ⲚⲦⲞⲠⲞⲤ ⲦⲎⲢⲞⲨ ⲢⲔⲀ
ⲚⲚⲈⲠⲢⲞⲂⲞⲗⲞⲞⲨⲈ ⲘⲠⲀⲨⲐⲀⲆⲎⲤ· ⲀⲨⲰ ⲠϢⲀϪⲈ ⲞⲚ
ⲈⲚⲦⲀ ⲦⲈⲔϬⲞⲘ ϪⲞⲞϤ ϨⲒⲦⲚ ⲤⲞⲗⲞⲘⲰⲚ· ϫⲉ ⲀⲤⲤⲞⲔⲞⲨ
10 ⲦⲎⲢⲞⲨ· ⲀⲤⲚⲦⲞⲨ ⲈϪⲘ ⲠⲈⲢⲠⲈ ⲈⲦⲈ ⲠⲀⲒ ⲠⲈ ϫⲉ ⲀⲤⲤⲰⲔ
ⲚⲚϬⲞⲘ ⲦⲎⲢⲞⲨ ⲚⲞⲨⲞⲈⲒⲚ ⲈⲂⲞⲗ ϨⲚ ⲚⲈⲠⲢⲞⲂⲞⲗⲞⲞⲨⲈ
ⲘⲠⲀⲨⲐⲀⲆⲎⲤ ⲚⲀⲒ̈ ⲈⲚⲦⲀⲨϬⲒⲦⲞⲨ ϨⲚ ⲦⲠⲒⲤⲦⲒⲤ ⲤⲞⲪⲒⲀ·
ⲀⲨⲰ ⲀⲤⲚⲞⲬⲞⲨ ⲈϨⲞⲨⲚ ⲈⲦⲠⲒⲤⲦⲒⲤ ⲤⲞⲪⲒⲀ ⲚⲔⲈⲤⲞⲠ·
ⲀⲨⲰ ⲠϢⲀϪⲈ ⲞⲚ ⲈⲚⲦⲀ ⲦⲈⲔϬⲞⲘ ϪⲞⲞϤ ϫⲉ ⲘⲠⲞⲨ-
15 ϢⲀⲘⲀϨⲦⲈ ⲘⲘⲞⲤ ⲚϬⲒ ϨⲈⲚⲰⲢϪ· ⲘⲚ ϨⲈⲚⲘⲀ ⲈⲨⲔⲎⲦ· ⲈⲦⲈ
ⲠⲀⲒ̈ ⲠⲈ ϫⲉ ⲘⲠⲈ ⲚⲈⲠⲢⲞⲂⲞⲗⲞⲞⲨⲈ ⲘⲠⲀⲨⲐⲀⲆⲎⲤ ⲘⲠⲞⲨ-
ϢⲀⲘⲀϨⲦⲈ ⲚϯⲀⲠⲞϨⲢⲞⲒⲀ ⲚⲞⲨⲞⲈⲒⲚ ϨⲢⲀⲒ̈ ϨⲚ ⲚⲤⲞⲂⲦ Ⲙ-
ⲠⲔⲀⲔⲈ ⲚⲦⲈ ⲠⲈⲬⲀⲟⲥ· ⲀⲨⲰ ⲠϢⲀϪⲈ ⲞⲚ ⲈⲚⲦⲀⲤϪⲞⲞϤ ⲢⲔⲀ ᵇ
ϫⲉ ⲚⲦⲀⲨⲚⲦⲤ ⲈϪⲘ ⲠⲔⲀϨ ⲦⲎⲢϤ· ⲀⲨⲰ ⲀⲤⲘⲈϨ-ⲚⲔⲀ ⲚⲒⲘ·
20 ⲈⲦⲈ ⲠⲀⲒ̈ ⲠⲈ ϫⲉ ⲚⲦⲈⲢⲈ ⲄⲀⲂⲢⲒⲎⲗ ⲘⲚ ⲘⲒⲬⲀⲎⲗ· ⲚⲦⲈ-
ⲢⲞⲨⲚⲦⲤ ⲈϪⲘ ⲠⲤⲰⲘⲀ ⲚⲦⲠⲒⲤⲦⲒⲤ ⲤⲞⲪⲒⲀ ⲀⲤⲚⲞⲨϪⲈ
ⲈϨⲞⲨⲚ ⲈⲢⲞⲤ ⲚⲚⲞⲨⲞⲈⲒⲚ ⲦⲎⲢⲞⲨ ⲚⲀⲒ̈ ⲈⲚⲦⲀⲨϬⲒⲦⲞⲨ
ⲚϨⲎⲦⲤ ⲚϬⲒ ⲚⲈⲠⲢⲞⲂⲞⲗⲞⲞⲨⲈ ⲘⲠⲀⲨⲐⲀⲆⲎⲤ ⲀⲨⲰ ⲀϤⲢ-
ⲞⲨⲞⲈⲒⲚ ⲚϬⲒ ⲠⲤⲰⲘⲀ ⲚⲦⲈⲤϨⲨⲗⲎ· ⲀⲨⲰ ⲠϢⲀϪⲈ ⲈⲚⲦ-

---

21 MS ⲀⲤⲚⲞⲨϪⲈ; read ⲀⲨⲚⲞⲨϪⲈ.

15. For they have all known themselves in the Lord; and they have been saved through a water of eternal life' *.

Hear now, my Lord, and I will give the discourse *openly* [1]. *As* thy power *prophesied* through Solomon: 'There went forth an *outpouring*, it became a great, broad river': that is, the *outpouring* of light was spread out in the *Chaos* in all the *places* of the *emanations* of the Authades. And again, the word which thy power spoke through Solomon: 'It gathered all things, it brought them over the Temple': that is, it gathered out of the *emanations* of the Authades all the light-powers which they had taken from the Pistis Sophia, and it cast them into the Pistis Sophia again. And the word which thy power spoke: 'It could not be restrained with restrainers and buildings': that is, the *emanations* of the Authades were not able to restrain the *outpouring* of light in the walls of the darkness of the *Chaos*. And the word which it spoke: 'It was brought over the whole earth and filled all things': that is, when Gabriel and Michael had brought it (the outpouring of light) over the *body* of the Pistis Sophia, they cast into her [2] all the lights which the *emanations* of the Authades had taken away from her, and the *body* of her *matter* gave light. And the word which |

---

*   Ode Sol. 6.7-15

---

[1]   (4) openly. As thy power; Till: (perhaps) openly, as thy power.
[2]   (21) they cast into her; MS: it cast into her.

ⲁⲥϫⲟⲟϥ ϫⲉ ⲁⲩⲥⲱ ⲛ̄ϭⲓ ⲛⲉⲧϣⲟⲟⲡ ϩⲓϫ̄ⲙ̄ ⲡϣⲱ ⲉⲧϣⲟⲩⲱⲟⲩ· ⲉⲧⲉ ⲡⲁ̈ⲓ ⲡⲉ ϫⲉ ⲁⲩϫⲓ-ⲟⲩⲟ̈ⲓⲛ ⲛ̄ϭⲓ ⲛⲉⲧϣⲟⲟⲡ ⲧⲏⲣⲟⲩ ϩ̄ⲛ̄ ⲧⲡⲓⲥⲧⲓⲥ ⲥⲟⲫⲓⲁ· ⲛⲁ̈ⲓ ⲉⲛⲧⲁⲩϥⲓ-ⲡⲉⲩⲟⲩⲟ̈ⲓⲛ ⲛ̄ϣⲟⲣ̄ⲡ̄· ⲁⲩⲱ ⲡϣⲁϫⲉ ⲉⲛⲧⲁⲥϫⲟⲟϥ ϫⲉ ⲁ ⲡⲉⲩⲉⲓⲃⲉ ⲃⲱⲗ ⲉⲃⲟⲗ ⲁⲩⲱ ⲁϥⲱϣ̄ⲙ̄· ⲉⲧⲉ ⲡⲁ̈ⲓ ⲡⲉ ϫⲉ ⲁ ⲛⲉⲥϭⲟⲙ ⲗⲟ ⲉⲩϣⲁⲁⲧ ⲛ̄ⲟⲩⲟ̈ⲓⲛ ⲁⲩⲱ ⲁⲩⲥⲉⲓ ⲛ̄ⲟⲩⲟ̈ⲓⲛ ϫⲉ ⲁⲩϯ ⲛⲁⲩ ⲙ̄ⲡⲉⲩⲟⲩⲟ̈ⲓⲛ ** ⲉⲛⲧⲁⲩϥⲓⲧ̄ϥ̄ ⲛ̄ⲧⲟⲟⲧⲟⲩ· ⲣ̄ⲕ̄ⲃ̄ ⲁⲩⲱ ⲟⲛ ⲕⲁⲧⲁ ⲑⲉ ⲟⲛ ⲉⲛⲧⲁⲥϫⲟⲟⲥ ⲛ̄ϭⲓ ⲧⲉⲕϭⲟⲙ· ϫⲉ ⲛ̄ⲧⲁⲩϯ ⲛⲁⲩ ⲙ̄ⲡⲥⲱ ⲉⲃⲟⲗ ϩⲓⲧⲟⲟⲧ̄ϥ̄ ⲙ̄ⲡⲉⲧϫⲟⲥⲉ· ⲉⲧⲉ ⲡⲁ̈ⲓ ⲡⲉ ϫⲉ ⲛ̄ⲧⲁⲩϯ-ⲡⲟⲩⲟⲉⲓⲛ ⲛⲁⲩ ⲉⲃⲟⲗ ϩⲓⲧⲟⲟⲧ̄ⲥ̄ ⲛ̄ϯ-ⲁⲡⲟϩⲣⲟⲓⲁ ⲛ̄ⲟⲩⲟ̈ⲓⲛ· ⲧⲁ̈ⲓ ⲉⲛⲧⲁⲥⲉⲓ' ⲉⲃⲟⲗ ⲛ̄ϩⲏⲧ ⲁⲛⲟⲕ ⲡⲓϣⲟⲣ̄ⲡ̄ ⲙ̄ⲙⲩⲥⲧⲏⲣⲓⲟⲛ· ⲁⲩⲱ ⲕⲁⲧⲁ ⲑⲉ ⲉⲛⲧⲁⲥϫⲟⲟⲥ ⲛ̄ϭⲓ ⲧⲉⲕϭⲟⲙ ϫⲉ ϩⲉⲛⲙⲁⲕⲁⲣⲓⲟⲥ ⲛⲉ ⲛ̄ⲇⲓⲁⲕⲱ⟨ⲛ⟩ ⲙ̄ⲡⲥⲱ ⲉⲧⲙ̄ⲙⲁⲩ· ⲉⲧⲉ ⲡⲁ̈ⲓ ⲡⲉ ⲡϣⲁϫⲉ ⲉⲛⲧⲁⲕϫⲟⲟϥ ϫⲉ ⲙⲓⲭⲁⲏⲗ· ⲙ̄ⲛ̄ ⲅⲁⲃⲣⲓⲏⲗ· ⲛⲁ̈ⲓ ⲛ̄ⲧⲁⲩⲇⲓⲁⲕⲟⲛⲓ· ⲁⲩϫⲓ-ⲧⲁⲡⲟϩⲣⲟⲓⲁ ⲛ̄ⲟⲩⲟⲉⲓⲛ ⲉⲡⲉⲭⲁⲟⲥ· ⲁⲩⲱ ⲟⲛ ⲁⲩⲛ̄ⲧ̄ⲥ̄ ⲉϩⲣⲁ̈ⲓ· ⲥⲉⲛⲁϯ ⲛⲁⲩ ⲛ̄ⲙ̄ⲙⲩⲥⲧⲏⲣⲓⲟⲛ ⲙ̄ⲡⲟⲩⲟⲉⲓⲛ ⲙ̄ⲡϫⲓⲥⲉ· ⲛⲁ̈ⲓ ⲛ̄ⲧⲁⲩⲧⲁⲛϩⲟⲩⲧⲟⲩ ⲉⲧⲁⲡⲟϩⲣⲟⲓⲁ ⲙ̄ⲡⲟⲩⲟⲉⲓⲛ· ⲁⲩⲱ ⲟⲛ ⲕⲁⲧⲁ ⲑⲉ ⲉⲛⲧⲁⲥϫⲟⲟⲥ ⲛ̄ϭⲓ ⲧⲉⲕϭⲟⲙ ϫⲉ ⲁⲩⲕⲧⲟ * ⲛ̄ϩⲉⲛ- ⲣ̄ⲕ̄ⲃ̄ b ⲥⲡⲟⲧⲟⲩ ⲉⲁⲩϣⲟⲟⲩⲉ· ⲉⲧⲉ ⲡⲁ̈ⲓ ⲡⲉ ⲅⲁⲃⲣⲓⲏⲗ· ⲙ̄ⲛ̄ ⲙⲓⲭⲁⲏⲗ· ⲙ̄ⲡⲟⲩϥⲓ ⲛⲁⲩ ⲉⲃⲟⲗ ϩ̄ⲛ̄ ⲛ̄ⲟⲩⲟⲉⲓⲛ ⲛ̄ⲧⲡⲓⲥⲧⲓⲥ ⲥⲟⲫⲓⲁ· ⲛⲁ̈ⲓ ⲛ̄ⲧⲁⲩⲧⲟⲣⲡⲟⲩ ⲛ̄ⲧⲟⲟⲧⲟⲩ ⲛ̄ⲛⲉⲡⲣⲟⲃⲟⲗⲟⲟⲩⲉ ⲙ̄ⲡⲁⲩⲑⲁⲇⲏⲥ· ⲁⲗⲗⲁ ⲁⲩⲛⲟϫⲟⲩ ⲉϩⲟⲩⲛ ⲉⲧⲡⲓⲥⲧⲓⲥ ⲥⲟⲫⲓⲁ· ⲁⲩⲱ ⲟⲛ ⲡϣⲁϫⲉ ⲛ̄ⲧⲁⲥϫⲟⲟϥ ϫⲉ ⲁⲩϫⲓ ⲛ̄ⲟⲩ-

13 MS ⲛ̄ⲇⲓⲁⲕⲱ.
20 ⲉ' in ⲉⲁⲩϣⲟⲟⲩⲉ inserted above.

it spoke: 'Those who were on dry sand were given to drink': that is, all those received light who were in the Pistis Sophia, those whose light was taken away at first. And the word which it spoke: 'And their thirst was relieved and quenched': that is, her powers ceased to lack light and they were satisfied with light, because they were given their light which had been taken from them. And again, *as* thy power spoke: 'They were given to drink by the hand of the Most High': that is, they were given light by (the hand of) the *outpouring* of light which came forth from me [1], the First *Mystery*. And *as* thy power spoke: '*Blessed* are the *servers* of that drink': that is, the word which thou didst say: Michael and Gabriel who have *served* brought the outflowing of light to the *Chaos* and furthermore they brought her up. They will give to them the *mysteries* of the light of the height, these to whom the *outpouring* of light was entrusted. And furthermore *as* thy power spoke: 'They have changed dry lips': that is, Gabriel and Michael have not taken for themselves from the lights of the Pistis Sophia, which they seized from the *emanations* of the Authades, *but* they cast them into the Pistis Sophia. And again the word which it spoke: | 'Those that were fainting

---

[1]   (11) from me (i.e. Jesus, not Peter).

ΟΥΡΟΤ Ν̄ϩΗΤ Ν̄ϬΙ ΝΗ ΕΤΒΗΛ ΕΒΟΛ· ΕΤΕ ΠΑΪ ΠΕ ϪΕ
Ν̄ΚΕϬΟΜ ΤΗΡΟΥ Ν̄ΤΠΙСΤΙС СΟΦΪΑ· ΝΑΪ ΕΤΕ Μ̄ΠΟΥ-
ϤΙΤΟΥ Ν̄ϬΙ ΝΕΠΡΟΒΟΛΟΟΥΕ Μ̄ΠΑΥΘΑΛΗС ΑΥΟΥΡΟΤ
ΤΟΝΩ· ΑΥΩ ΑΥΜΟΥϩ Ν̄ΟΥΟΕΙΝ ΕΒΟΛ ϨΜ̄ ΠΕΥϢΒ̄Ρ-
5 ΟΥΟΪΝ· ϪΕ ΑΥΝΟϪΟΥ ΕϨΟΥΝ ΕΡΟΟΥ· ΑΥΩ ΠϢΑϪΕ
ΕΝΤΑ ΤΕΚϬΟΜ ϪΟΟϤ ϪΕ ΑΥΤΑΝϨΟ Ν̄ϨΕΝΨΥΧΗ ΕΥ-
ΝΟΥϪΕ Μ̄ΠΤΗΥ· ϪΕ Ν̄ΝΕΥΜΟΥ·** ΕΤΕ ΠΑΪ ΠΕ ϪΕ Ν̄ΤΕ- ΡΚΓ
ΡΟΥΝΟΥϪΕ Ν̄ΝΟΥΟΕΙΝ ΕϨΟΥΝ ΕΤΠΙСΤΙС СΟΦΪΑ· ΑΥ-
ΤΑΝϨΟ Μ̄ΠСΩΜΑ Ν̄ΤΕСϨΥΛΗ· ΠΑΪ ΕΝΤΑΥϤΙ-ΝΕϤΟΥΟΕΙΝ
10 Ν̄ϨΗΤ̄Ϥ Ν̄ϢΟΡΠ̄· ΠΑΪ ΕΝΕϤΝΑΤΑΚΟ ΠΕ: ΑΥΩ ΟΝ ΠϢΑϪΕ
ΕΝΤΑ ΤΕΚϬΟΜ ϪΟΟϤ ϪΕ ΑΥΤΑϨΟ Ν̄ϨΕΝΜΕΛΟС ΕΡΑ-
ΤΟΥ ΕΛΥϨΕ· Η̇ ϪΕ Ν̄ΝΕΥϨΕ· ΕΤΕ ΠΑΪ ΠΕ ϪΕ Ν̄ΤΕ-
ΡΟΥΝΟΥϪΕ ΕϨΟΥΝ ΕΡΟС Ν̄ΝΕСΟΥΟΕΙΝ ΑΥΤΑϨΟ ΕΡΑ-
ΤΟΥ Ν̄ΝΕСϬΟΜ ΤΗΡΟΥ· ΝΑΪ ΕΝΕΥΝΑΒΩΛ ΕΒΟΛ· ΑΥΩ
15 ΟΝ ΚΑΤΑ ΘΕ ΕΝΤΑ ΤΕΚϬΟΜ Ν̄ΟΥΟΪΝ ϪΟΟС ϪΕ ΑΥϮ
Ν̄ΟΥϬΟΜ Ν̄ΤΕΥΠΑΡϨΗСΙΑ· ΕΤΕ ΠΑΪ ΠΕ ϪΕ ΑΥϪΙ ΟΝ
Μ̄ΠΕΥΟΥΟΪΝ· ΑΥΩ ΑΥΡ̄ΘΕ ΕΝΕΥΟ Μ̄ΜΟС Ν̄ϢΟΡΠ̄·
ΑΥΩ ΟΝ ΠϢΑϪΕ ΕΝΤΑСϪΟΟϤ ϪΕ ΑΥϮ-ΟΥΟΥΟΕΙΝ ΡΚΓ^b
ΕΝΕΥΒΑΛ ΕΤΕ ΠΑΪ ΠΕ ϪΕ ΑΥϪΙ-ΑΙСΘΗСΙС ϨΜ̄ ΠΟΥΟΪΝ
20 ΑΥΩ ΑΥСΟΥΝ̄-ΤΑΠΟϨΡΟΙΑ Ν̄ΟΥΟΪΝ ϪΕ ΕСΗΠ ΕΠϪΙСΕ·
ΑΥΩ ΟΝ ΠϢΑϪΕ ΕΝΤΑСϪΟΟϤ· ϪΕ Ν̄ΤΟΟΥ ΤΗΡΟΥ
ΑΥСΟΥΩΝΟΥ ϨΜ̄ ΠϪΟΕΙС· ΕΤΕ ΠΑΪ ΠΕ ϪΕ Α Ν̄ϬΟΜ
ΤΗΡΟΥ Ν̄ΤΠΙСΤΙС СΟΦΙΑ· ΑΥСΟΥΝ̄-ΝΕΥΕΡΗΥ ϨΙΤΝ̄
ϮΑΠΟϨΡΟΙΑ Ν̄ΟΥΟΪΝ· ΑΥΩ ΟΝ ΠϢΑϪΕ ΕΝΤΑСϪΟΟϤ

---

14   С in ΝΕСϬΟΜ inserted above.
22   MS letter before ϬΟΜ is Τ or Π; read Α Ν̄ϬΟΜ.
23   MS Ν̄ΤΠΙСΤΙСΤΙС.

received joy of heart': that is, all the other powers of the Pistis Sophia, those that were not taken away by the *emanations* of the Authades, rejoiced greatly and they were filled with light through their fellow light(s), because they were cast into them. And the word which thy power spoke: '*Souls* were given life, breath was cast in so that they did not die': that is, when they cast the lights into the Pistis Sophia, they gave life to the *body* of her *matter*, from which its light had been taken at first and which was about to perish. And again the word which thy power spoke: 'They have set upright *limbs* that have fallen, *or* lest they fall': that is, when they cast her lights into her, they set upright all her powers which were about to collapse. And furthermore *as* thy light-power spoke: 'They have given power to their *feebleness*': that is, they have received their light again and they have become as they were at first. And again the word which it said: 'They have given light to their eyes': that is, they have received *perception* in the light, and they have known the *outpouring* of light, that it belongs to the height. And again the word which it spoke: 'They have all known themselves in the Lord': that is, all the powers of the Pistis Sophia have known one another through the *outpouring* of light. And again the word which it spoke: | 'They have been

ϪЄ ΑΥΝΟΥϨⲘ ϨΙΤⲚ ΟΥΜΟΟΥ Ⲛ̄ⲰⲚϨ Ⲛ̄ϢⲀⲈⲚⲈϨ· ⲈⲦⲈ

ⲠⲀⲒ ⲠⲈ ϪⲈ ⲀΥΝΟΥϨⲘ ϨΙⲦⲚ̄ ϮⲀⲠⲞϨⲢΟⲒⲀ Ⲛ̄ΟΥΟⲒⲚ ⲦⲎⲢⲤ̄·

ⲀΥⲰ ⲠϢⲀϪⲈ ⲈⲚⲦⲀⲤϪⲞΟϤ ϪⲈ ⲀⲤⲤΟⲔⲞΥ ⲦⲎⲢΟΥ Ⲛ̄ϬⲒ

ϮⲀⲠⲞϨⲢΟⲒⲀ Ⲛ̄ΟΥΟⲒⲚ ⲀΥⲰ ⲀⲤⲤΟⲔΟΥ ⲈⲐ̄Ⲙ ⲠⲢ̄ⲠⲈ· ⲈⲦⲈ

5 ⲠⲀⲒ ⲠⲈ ϪⲈ Ⲛ̄ⲦⲈⲢⲈ ⲦⲀⲠⲞϨⲢΟⲒⲀ Ⲛ̄ΟΥΟⲈⲒⲚ Ⲛ̄ⲦⲈⲢⲈⲤϤⲒ ⲢⲔⲀ̄

Ⲛ̄ΝΟΥΟⲈⲒⲚ ⲦⲎⲢΟΥ Ⲛ̄ⲦⲠⲒⲤⲦⲒⲤ ⲤΟⲪⲒⲀ· ⲀΥⲰ Ⲛ̄ⲦⲈⲢⲈⲤ-

ⲦⲞⲢⲠΟΥ Ⲛ̄ⲦΟΟⲦΟΥ Ⲛ̄ΝⲈⲠⲢΟⲂΟⲖΟΟΥⲈ Ⲙ̄ⲠⲀΥⲐⲀⲆⲎⲤ·

ⲀⲤΝΟϪΟΥ ⲈϨΟΥⲚ ⲈⲦⲠⲒⲤⲦⲒⲤ ⲤΟⲪⲒⲀ· ⲀΥⲰ ⲀⲤⲔΟⲦⲤ̄

ⲀⲤⲈⲒ̄ ⲈⲂΟⲖ Ⲉ̄Ⲙ ⲠⲈϪⲖⲞⲤ· ⲀⲤⲈⲒ̄ ⲈϨⲢⲀⲒ̄ ⲈϪⲰⲔ· ⲈⲦⲈ

10 Ⲛ̄ⲦΟⲔ ⲠⲈ ⲠⲈⲢⲠⲈ ⲠⲀⲒ ⲠⲈ ⲠⲂⲰⲖ Ⲛ̄Ⲛ̄ϢⲀϪⲈ ⲦⲎⲢΟΥ ΝⲀⲒ

Ⲛ̄ⲦⲀⲤϪΟΟΥ Ⲛ̄ϬⲒ ⲦⲈⲔϬΟⲘ Ⲛ̄ΟΥΟⲈⲒⲚ ϨⲒⲦⲚ̄ ⲦⲰⲆⲎ Ⲛ̄ⲤΟ-

ⲖΟⲘⲰⲚ :

ⲀⲤϢⲰⲠⲈ ϬⲈ Ⲛ̄ⲦⲈⲢⲈ ⲠⲒϢΟⲢⲠ̄ Ⲙ̄ⲘΥⲤⲦⲎⲢⲒΟⲚ ⲤⲰⲦⲘ̄

ⲈⲚⲈⲒ̈ϢⲀϪⲈ ⲈϤϪⲰ Ⲙ̄ⲘΟΟΥ Ⲛ̄ϬⲒ ⲠⲈⲦⲢΟⲤ ⲠⲈϪⲀϤ ΝⲀϤ·

15 ϪⲈ ⲈΥⲄⲈ ⲠⲘⲀⲔⲀⲢⲒΟⲤ ⲠⲈⲦⲢⲈ ⲠⲀⲒ ⲠⲈ ⲠⲂⲰⲖ Ⲛ̄Ⲛ̄ϢⲀϪⲈ

ⲈⲚⲦⲀΥϪΟΟΥ· ⲀϤΟΥⲰϨ ⲆⲈ ΟⲚ ⲈⲦΟΟⲦϤ̄ Ⲉ̄Ⲙ ⲠϢⲀϪⲈ

Ⲛ̄ϬⲒ ⲠⲒϢΟⲢⲠ̄ Ⲙ̄ⲘΥⲤⲦⲎⲢⲒΟⲚ ⲠⲈϪⲀϤ ϪⲈ ⲀⲤϢⲰⲠⲈ ϬⲈ

ⲈⲘⲠⲀϮⲚ̄-ⲦⲠⲒⲤⲦⲒⲤ ⲤΟⲪⲒⲀ ⲈϨⲢⲀⲒ̄ Ⲉ̄Ⲙ ⲠⲈϪⲖⲞⲤ· ⲈⲂΟⲖ ϪⲈ

Ⲙ̄ⲠⲀⲦΟΥⲔⲈⲖⲈⲨⲈ ΝⲀⲒ ϨⲒⲦⲘ̄ ⲠⲀⲒ̈ⲰⲦ· *ⲠⲒϢΟⲢⲠ̄ Ⲙ̄ⲘΥⲤⲦⲎ- ⲢⲔⲀ̄ᵇ

20 ⲢⲒΟⲚ ⲈⲦϬⲰϢⲦ̄ ⲈϨΟΥⲚ· ⲦΟⲦⲈ ϬⲈ ⲘⲚ̄ⲚⲤⲀ 〈ΝⲀ〉Ⲓ̈ Ⲛ̄ⲦⲈⲢΟΥ-

ⲈⲒⲘⲈ Ⲛ̄ϬⲒ ΝⲈⲠⲢΟⲂΟⲖΟΟΥⲈ Ⲙ̄ⲠⲀΥⲐⲀⲆⲎⲤ ϪⲈ Ⲁ ⲦⲀⲖⲀ-

ⲠΟϨⲢΟⲒⲀ Ⲛ̄ΟΥΟⲈⲒⲚ ϤⲒ-Ⲛ̄ϬΟⲘ Ⲛ̄ΟΥΟⲈⲒⲚ Ⲛ̄ϨⲎⲦΟΥ ΝⲀⲒ

Ⲛ̄ⲦⲀΥϤⲒⲦΟΥ Ⲉ̄Ⲛ ⲦⲠⲒⲤⲦⲒⲤ ⲤΟⲪⲒⲀ· ⲀΥⲰ [ⲀⲤΝΟϪΟΥ

---

3   Υ in ⲀⲤⲤΟⲔΟΥ inserted above.

5   Ⲏ̄ in upper right-hand margin at end of quire.

20   MS Ⲙ̄Ⲛ̄ⲚⲤⲀⲒ̈; read Ⲙ̄Ⲛ̄ⲚⲤⲀ ⲠⲀⲒ̈.

23   words in brackets better omitted.

saved through a water of eternal life' : that is, they have been saved through the whole *outpouring* of light. And the word which it spoke : 'The *outpouring* of light gathered all things and it gathered them over the Temple' : that is, when the *outpouring* of light took all the lights of the Pistis Sophia and seized them from the *emanations* of the Authades, it cast them into the Pistis Sophia, and it turned itself, it came forth from the *Chaos*. It came down upon thee, thou who art the Temple. This is the interpretation of all the words which thy power of light spoke through the *Ode* of Solomon."

Now it happened when the First *Mystery* heard these words which Peter said, he said to him : "*Excellent*, thou *blessed one*, Peter, this is the interpretation of the words which were spoken."

66.   The First *Mystery however* continued again with the discourse. He said : "Now it happened before I brought the Pistis Sophia up from the *Chaos*, because I was not yet *commanded* by my Father, the First *Mystery* who looks within, now *at that time* after this the *emanations* of the Authades knew that my *outpouring* of light had taken away from them the light-powers which they had taken away from the Pistis Sophia, and had cast them | [the *outpouring* of

ⲈⲌⲞⲨⲚ ⲚϬⲒ ϯⲀⲠⲞⲌⲢⲞⲒⲀ ⲚⲞⲨⲞⲒⲚ·] ⲀⲤⲚⲞⲬⲞⲨ ⲈⲌⲞⲨⲚ
ⲈⲦⲠⲒⲤⲦⲒⲤ ⲤⲞⲪⲒⲀ· ⲀⲨⲰ ⲞⲚ ⲀⲨⲚⲀⲨ ⲈⲦⲠⲒⲤⲦⲒⲤ ⲤⲞⲪⲒⲀ
ⲈⲤⲞ ⲚⲞⲨⲞⲒⲚ ⲚⲐⲈ ⲈⲚⲈⲤⲞ ⲘⲘⲞⲤ ⲬⲒⲚ ⲚϢⲞⲢⲠ ⲀⲨ-
ϬⲰⲚⲦ ⲈⲦⲠⲒⲤⲦⲒⲤ ⲤⲞⲪⲒⲀ· ⲀⲨⲰ ⲞⲚ ⲀⲨⲰϢ ⲈⲌⲢⲀⲒ ⲞⲨⲂⲈ
5 ⲠⲈⲨⲀⲨⲐⲀⲆⲎⲤ ⲈⲦⲢⲈϤⲈⲒ ⲚϤⲂⲞⲎⲐⲒ ⲈⲢⲞⲞⲨ ⲚⲤⲈϤⲒ ⲚⲚϬⲞⲘ
ⲈⲦⲌⲚ ⲦⲤⲞⲪⲒⲀ ⲚⲔⲈⲤⲞⲠ· ⲀⲨⲰ Ⲁ ⲠⲀⲨⲐⲀⲆⲎⲤ ⲦⲚⲚⲞⲞⲨ
ⲈⲂⲞⲖ ⲌⲘ ⲠⲬⲒⲤⲈ ⲌⲘ ⲠⲘⲈⲌⲘⲚⲦϢⲞⲘⲦⲈ ⲚⲀⲒⲰⲚ ⲀϤⲦⲚ-
ⲚⲞⲞⲨ ⲚⲔⲈⲚⲞϬ ⲚϬⲞⲘ ⲚⲞⲨⲞⲈⲒⲚ ⲀⲤⲈⲒ ⲈⲠⲈⲤⲎⲦ ⲈⲠⲈ-
ⲬⲖⲞⲤ ⲚⲐⲈ ⲚⲞⲨⲤⲞⲦⲈ ⲈϤⲌⲎⲖ· ⲬⲈ ⲈϤⲈⲂⲞⲎⲐⲈⲒ ⲈⲚⲈϤ-
10 ⲠⲢⲞⲂⲞⲖⲞⲞⲨⲈ ⲚⲤⲈϤⲒ-ⲚⲞⲨⲞⲈⲒⲚ ⲚⲦⲠⲒⲤⲦⲒⲤ ⲤⲞⲪⲒⲀ ⲚⲔⲈ- ⲢⲔⲈ
ⲤⲞⲠ· ⲀⲨⲰ ⲚⲦⲈⲢⲈⲤⲈⲒ ⲈⲠⲈⲤⲎⲦ ⲚϬⲒ ⲦϬⲞⲘ ⲚⲞⲨⲞⲈⲒⲚ
ⲈⲦⲘⲘⲀⲨ· Ⲁ ⲚⲈⲠⲢⲞⲂⲞⲖⲞⲞⲨⲈ ⲘⲠⲀⲨⲐⲀⲆⲎⲤ ⲚⲀⲒ ⲈⲦ-
ϢⲞⲞⲠ ⲌⲘ ⲠⲈⲬⲖⲞⲤ ⲈⲦⲐⲖⲒⲂⲈ ⲚⲦⲠⲒⲤⲦⲒⲤ ⲤⲞⲪⲒⲀ ⲀⲨⲦⲰⲔ
ⲚⲌⲎⲦ ⲈⲘⲀϢⲞ· ⲀⲨⲰ ⲀⲨⲠⲰⲦ ⲞⲚ ⲚⲤⲀ ⲦⲠⲒⲤⲦⲒⲤ ⲤⲞⲪⲒⲀ
15 ⲌⲚ ⲞⲨⲚⲞϬ ⲚⲌⲞⲦⲈ ⲀⲨⲰ ⲌⲚ ⲞⲨⲚⲞϬ ⲚϢⲦⲞⲢⲦⲢ· ⲀⲨⲰ
ⲀⲨⲐⲖⲒⲂⲈ ⲘⲘⲞⲤ ⲚϬⲒ ⲌⲞⲒⲚⲈ ⲌⲚ ⲚⲈⲠⲢⲞⲂⲞⲖⲞⲞⲨⲈ ⲘⲠⲀⲨ-
ⲐⲀⲆⲎⲤ ⲞⲨⲀ ⲘⲈⲚ ⲚⲌⲎⲦⲞⲨ ⲀϤϢ⟨Ⲃ⟩ⲦϤ ⲈⲨⲘⲞⲢⲪⲎ ⲚⲚⲞϬ
ⲚⲌⲞϤ· ⲔⲈⲨⲀ ⲞⲚ ⲀϤϢⲂⲦϤ ⲈⲨⲘⲞⲢⲪⲎ ⲚⲌⲞϤ ⲚⲤⲒⲦ ⲈⲨⲚ-
ⲤⲀϢϤⲈ ⲚⲀⲠⲈ ⲘⲘⲞϤ· ⲔⲈⲞⲨⲀ ⲞⲚ ⲀϤϢⲂⲦϤ ⲈⲨⲘⲞⲢⲪⲎ
20 ⲚⲀⲢⲀⲔⲰⲚ· ⲀⲨⲰ ⲘⲚ ⲦⲔⲈϢⲞⲢⲠ ⲚⲀⲨⲚⲀⲘⲒⲤ ⲚⲦⲈ ⲠⲀⲨ- ⲢⲔⲈ b
ⲐⲀⲆⲎⲤ ⲈⲦⲞ ⲚⲌⲞ ⲘⲘⲞⲨⲒ· ⲀⲨⲰ ⲘⲚ ⲚⲈϤⲔⲈⲠⲢⲞⲂⲞⲖⲞ-

---

9   ⲟ̄ in upper left-hand margin at beginning of quire.
17   MS ⲀϤϢⲦϤ.

light had cast them] into the Pistis Sophia. And furthermore
when they saw the Pistis Sophia lighted as she was from
the beginning, they were angry against the Pistis Sophia.
And they cried again to their Authades, that he should come
and *help* them, so that they should take away the powers
which were in the ⟨Pistis⟩ Sophia once again. And the
Authades sent out of the height, out of the thirteenth aeon,
he sent another great light-power. It came down to the *Chaos*
like a flying arrow, in order that he (the Authades) should
help his *emanations*, so that they should take the lights from
the Pistis Sophia once again. And when that light-power
came down, the *emanations* of the Authades, which were in
the *Chaos* and *afflicted* the Pistis Sophia, were encouraged
greatly. And they again pursued the Pistis Sophia with a great
terror and a great disturbance. And some of the *emanations*
of the Authades *afflicted* her. *For* one of them changed to
the *form* of a great serpent; again another changed to the
form of a basilisk, having seven heads; again another changed
to the *form* of a *dragon*; with the other previous *power*
of the Authades which has a lion-face; and with all his
other very numerous *emanations*. | And they came together,

ΟΥΕ ΤΗΡΟΥ ΕΝΑϢϢΟΥ ΕΜΑΤΕ · ΑΥΩ ΑΥΕΙ' Ε2Ν ΝΕΥ-
ΕΡΗΥ ΑΥ2ΩΧ Ν̄ΤΠΙΣΤΙΣ ΣΟΦΙΑ · ΑΥΩ ΟΝ ΑΥΝ̄ΤΣ ΕΝ-
ΤΟΠΟΣ ΕΤΜ̄ΠΕΣΗΤ Μ̄ΠΕΧΛΑΟΣ · ΑΥΩ ΟΝ ΑΥϢΤ̄ΡΤΩΡΣ̄
ΕΜΑΤΕ · ΑΣϢΩΠΕ 6Ε Ν̄ΤΕΡΟΥϢΤ̄ΡΤΩΡΣ̄ · ΑΣΠΩΤ Ν̄-
5 ΤΟΟΤΟΥ ΑΣΕΙ' ΕΝΤΟΠΟΣ ΕΤΜ̄ΠΣΑ Ν̄ΤΠΕ Μ̄ΠΕΧΛΑΟΣ ·
ΑΥΩ ΑΥΠΩΤ Ν̄ΣΩΣ Ν̄6Ι ΝΕΠΡΟΒΟΛΟΟΥΕ Μ̄ΠΑΥΘΑ-
ΔΗΣ · ΑΥϢΤ̄ΡΤΩΡΣ̄ ΕΜΑΤΕ · ΑΣϢΩΠΕ 6Ε Μ̄ΝΝΣΑ ΝΑΪ
Α46ΩϢΤ ΕΒΟΛ 2Μ ΠΜΝ̄ΤΣΝΟΟΥΣ Ν̄ΑΙΩΝ Ν̄6Ι ΠΑΔΑ-
ΜΑΣ ΠΤΥΡΑΝΝΟΣ ΠΑΪ ΟΝ ΕΝΕ46ΟΝΤ̄ ΕΤΠΙΣΤΙΣ ΣΟΦΙΑ ·
10 ΕΒΟΛ ΧΕ ΝΕΣΟΥΕϢΒΩΚ ΕΠΟΥΟΕΙΝ Ν̄ΤΕ ΝΙΟΥΟΕΙΝ ·
ΠΑΪ ΕΝΕ4Ν̄ΤΠΕ Μ̄ΜΟΟΥ** ΤΗΡΟΥ · ΕΤΒΕ ΠΑΪ ΝΕ46ΟΝΤ̄
ΕΡΟΣ ΠΕ · ΑΣϢΩΠΕ 6Ε Ν̄ΤΕΡΕ ΠΑΔΑΜΑΣ ΠΤΥΡΑΝΝΟΣ
Ν̄ΤΕΡΕ46ΩϢΤ ΕΒΟΛ 2Μ ΠΜΝ̄ΤΣΝΟΟΥΣ Ν̄ΑΙΩΝ · Α4ΝΑΥ
ΕΝΕΠΡΟΒΟΛΟΟΥΕ Μ̄ΠΑΥΘΑΔΗΣ ΕΥ2ΩΧ Ν̄ΤΠΙΣΤΙΣ ΣΟ-
15 ΦΙΑ · ϢΑΝΤΟΥ4Ι-Ν̄ΟΥΟΕΙΝ ΤΗΡΟΥ Ν̄2ΗΤ̄Σ · ΑΣϢΩΠΕ
ΔΕ Ν̄ΤΕΡΕ ΤΔΥΝΑΜΙΣ Μ̄ΠΑΔΑΜΑΣ ΕΙ' ΕΠΕΣΗΤ ΕΠΕ-
ΧΛΑΟΣ ΕΡΑΤΟΥ Ν̄ΝΕΠΡΟΒΟΛΟΟΥΕ ΤΗΡΟΥ Μ̄ΠΑΥΘΑΔΗΣ ·
ΑΣϢΩΠΕ 6Ε Ν̄ΤΕΡΕ ΠΔΑΙΜΟΝΙΟΝ ΕΤΜ̄ΜΑΥ ΕΙ' ΕΠΕΣΗΤ
ΕΠΕΧΛΑΟΣ Α4ΤΑΥΕ-ΤΠΙΣΤΙΣ ΣΟΦΙΑ ΕΠΕΣΗΤ · ΑΥΩ †-
20 6ΟΜ Ν̄2Ο Μ̄ΜΟΥΪ · Μ̄Ν ΠΙ2Α Ν̄2Ο4 · ΑΥΩ Μ̄Ν ΠΙ2Α Ν̄ΣΙΤ
Ν̄2Ο4 · ΑΥΩ Μ̄Ν ΠΙ2Α Ν̄ΔΡΑΚΩΝ · ΑΥΩ Μ̄Ν Ν̄ΚΕΠΡΟ-
ΒΟΛΟΟΥΕ ΤΗΡΟΥ Ν̄ΤΕ ΠΑΥΘΑΔΗΣ ΕΝΑϢϢΟΥ ΕΜΑ-
ΤΕ · ΑΥΚΩΤΕ ΤΗΡΟΥ ΕΤΠΙΣΤΙΣ ΣΟΦΙΑ 2Ι ΟΥΣΟΠ · ΕΥ-
ΟΥΕϢ4Ι-ΝΕΣ6ΟΜ ΕΤΝ̄2ΗΤ̄Σ Ν̄ΚΕΣΟΠ · ΑΥΩ ΑΥ2ΩΧ
25 Ν̄ΤΠΙΣΤΙΣ ΣΟΦΙΑ ΕΜΑϢΟ · ΑΥΩ ΑΥΑΠΙΛΕΙ ΕΡΟΣ · ΑΣ-
ϢΩΠΕ 6Ε Ν̄ΤΕΡΟΥ2ΩΧ Μ̄ΜΟΣ ΑΥΩ Ν̄ΤΕΡΟΥϢΤΡ-
ΤΩΡΣ̄ ΕΜΑΤΕ · ΑΣΩϢ ΟΝ Ε2ΡΑΪ ΟΥΒΕ ΠΟΥΟΪΝ ΑΥΩ

they oppressed the Pistis Sophia. And again they brought
her to the *places* below in the *Chaos*. And again they
agitated her greatly. Now it happened when they agitated
her, she ran from them, she came to the upper *places* of the
Chaos. And the *emanations* of the Authades pursued her,
they agitated her greatly. Now it happened after these
things Adamas, the *Tyrant*, looked forth from the twelve
aeons. He also was angry with the Pistis Sophia, because
she wished to go to the Light of Lights which was above
them all; because of this he was angry with her. Now it
happened when Adamas, the *Tyrant*, looked forth from
the twelve *aeons*, he saw the *emanations* of the Authades
oppressing the Pistis Sophia until they took away all her
light from her. *But* it happened when the *power* of the
Adamas came down to the *Chaos* to the presence of all
the *emanations* of the Authades — now it happened when
that *demon* came down to the *Chaos* — he threw the Pistis
Sophia down. And the lion-faced power and the serpent-face
and the basilisk-face and the *dragon*-face and all the other
emanations of the Authades, which were very numerous,
surrounded the Pistis Sophia at one time, wishing to take
her inner powers once again. And they oppressed the
Pistis Sophia greatly, and they *threatened* her. Now it
happened when they oppressed her and when they agitated
her greatly, she cried again to the light and | she *sang praises*,
saying :

ΑⲤϨⲨⲘⲚⲈⲨⲈ ⲈⲤⲬⲰ ⲘⲘⲞⲤ ϪⲈ ⲠⲞⲨⲞⲈⲒⲚ ⲚⲦⲞⲔ ⲠⲈ
ⲚⲦⲀⲔⲂⲞⲎⲐⲒ ⲈⲢⲞⲒ ⲘⲀⲢⲈ ⲠⲈⲔⲞⲨⲞⲒⲚ ⲈⲒ' ⲈϨⲢⲀⲒ ⲈϪⲰⲒ ϪⲈ
ⲚⲦⲞⲔ ⲠⲈ ⲠⲀⲢⲈϤϢⲞⲠⲦ ⲈⲢⲞⲔ ⲀⲨⲰ ⲈⲒⲚⲎⲨ ⲈⲢⲀⲦⲔ ⲠⲞⲨ-
ⲞⲒⲚ: ⲈⲒⲠⲒⲤⲦⲈⲨⲈ ⲈⲢⲞⲔ ⲠⲞⲨⲞⲈⲒⲚ ϪⲈ ⲚⲦⲞⲔ ⲠⲈ ⲠⲀ-
5 ⲢⲈϤⲚⲞⲨϨⲘ ⲘⲘⲞⲒ ⲈⲚⲈⲠⲢⲞⲂⲞⲖⲞⲞⲨⲈ ⲘⲠⲀⲨⲐⲀⲆⲎⲤ· ⲀⲨⲰ
ⲘⲚ ⲠⲀⲆⲀⲘⲀⲤ ⲠⲦⲨⲠⲀⲚⲚⲞⲤ· ⲀⲨⲰ ⲚⲦⲞⲔ ⲠⲈⲦⲚⲀⲚⲀϨⲘⲈⲦ
ⲈⲚⲈϤⲀⲠⲒⲖⲎ ⲦⲎⲢⲞⲨ ⲈⲦⲚⲀϢⲰⲦ·   ̅Ⲣ̅Ⲕ̅Ⲍ̅

ⲚⲀⲒ ⲆⲈ ⲚⲦⲈⲢⲈⲤϪⲞⲞⲨ ⲚϬⲒ ⲦⲠⲒⲤⲦⲒⲤ ⲤⲞⲪⲒⲀ· ⲦⲞⲦⲈ
ⲞⲚ ϨⲒⲦⲚ ⲦⲔⲈⲖⲈⲨⲤⲒⲤ ⲘⲠⲀⲒⲰⲦ ⲠⲒϢⲞⲢⲠ ⲘⲘⲨⲤⲦⲎⲢⲒⲞⲚ
10 ⲈⲦϬⲰϢⲦ ⲈϨⲞⲨⲚ ⲀⲒϪⲞⲞⲨ ⲞⲚ ⲚⲄⲀⲂⲢⲒⲎⲖ· ⲘⲚ ⲘⲒⲬⲀⲎⲖ
ⲘⲚ ϮⲚⲞϬ ⲚⲚⲀⲠⲞϨⲢⲞⲒⲀ ⲚⲞⲨⲞⲈⲒⲚ ϪⲈ ⲈⲨⲈⲂⲞⲎⲐⲒ ⲈⲦⲠⲒⲤ-
ⲦⲒⲤ ⲤⲞⲪⲒⲀ· ⲀⲨⲰ ⲀⲒϪⲰⲚ ⲈⲦⲞⲞⲦϤ ⲚⲄⲀⲂⲢⲒⲎⲖ ⲘⲚ ⲘⲒ-
ⲬⲀⲎⲖ· ϪⲈ ⲈⲨⲈϤⲒ-ⲦⲠⲒⲤⲦⲒⲤ ⲤⲞⲪⲒⲀ ϨⲒϪⲚ ⲚⲈⲨϬⲒϪ ϪⲈ
ⲚⲚⲈ ⲚⲈⲤⲞⲨⲈⲢⲎⲦⲈ ϪⲒ ⲈⲠⲔⲀⲔⲈ ⲘⲠⲈⲤⲎⲦ· ⲀⲨⲰ ⲞⲚ
15 ⲀⲒϨⲰⲚ ⲈⲦⲞⲞⲦⲞⲨ ⲈⲦⲢⲈⲨⲢϨⲘⲘⲈ ⲘⲘⲞϤ ϨⲚ ⲚⲦⲞⲠⲞⲤ Ⲙ-
ⲠⲈⲬⲀⲞⲤ ⲚⲀⲒ ⲈⲦⲞⲨⲚⲀⲚⲦⲤ ⲈϨⲢⲀⲒ ⲚϨⲎⲦⲞⲨ· ⲀⲤϢⲰⲠⲈ
ϬⲈ ⲚⲦⲈⲢⲈ ⲚⲀⲄⲄⲈⲖⲞⲤ ⲂⲰⲔ ⲈⲠⲈⲤⲎⲦ ⲈⲠⲈⲬⲀⲞⲤ ⲚⲦⲞⲞⲨ
ⲘⲚ ⲦⲀⲠⲞϨⲢⲞⲒⲀ ⲚⲞⲨⲞⲒⲚ· ⲀⲨⲰ ⲞⲚ Ⲁ ⲚⲈⲠⲢⲞⲂⲞⲖⲞⲞⲨⲈ
ⲦⲎⲢⲞⲨ ⲘⲠⲀⲨⲐⲀⲆⲎⲤ ⲘⲚ ⲦⲈⲠⲢⲞⲂⲞⲖⲎ ⲘⲠⲀⲆⲀⲘⲀⲤ· ⲀⲨ- ̅Ⲣ̅Ⲕ̅Ⲍ̅ b
20 ⲚⲀⲨ ⲈⲦⲀⲠⲞϨⲢⲞⲒⲀ ⲚⲞⲨⲞⲈⲒⲚ ⲈⲤⲞ' ⲚⲞⲨⲞⲈⲒⲚ ⲈⲘⲀϢⲞ
ⲈⲘⲀϢⲞ· ⲈⲘⲚ-ϢⲒ ⲈⲠⲞⲨⲞⲈⲒⲚ ⲈⲦϢⲞⲞⲠ ⲘⲘⲞⲤ· ⲀⲨⲢ-
ϨⲞⲦⲈ· ⲀⲨⲰ ⲀⲨⲔⲰ ⲈⲂⲞⲖ ⲚⲦⲠⲒⲤⲦⲒⲤ ⲤⲞⲪⲒⲀ· ⲀⲨⲰ Ⲁ
ⲦⲚⲞϬ ⲚⲀⲠⲞϨⲢⲞⲒⲀ ⲚⲞⲨⲞⲒⲚ ⲀⲤⲔⲰⲦⲈ ⲈⲦⲠⲒⲤⲦⲒⲤ ⲤⲞⲪⲒⲀ·
ϨⲒ ⲤⲀ ⲚⲒⲘ ⲘⲘⲞⲤ· ϨⲒ ϨⲂⲞⲨⲢ ⲘⲘⲞⲤ· ⲀⲨⲰ ϨⲒ ⲞⲨⲚⲀⲘ

---

11 MS originally ⲠⲒ; emended to ϯ and ⲓ expunged. MS Ⲛ̅ⲚⲀⲠⲞϨⲢⲞⲒⲀ;
read Ⲛ̅ⲀⲠⲞϨⲢⲞⲒⲀ.

1. 'O Light, who hast *helped* me, may thy light come down upon me.

2. For thou art my shelter and I come to thee, O Light, *believing* in thee, O Light.

3. For thou art my Saviour from the *emanations* of the Authades and Adamas, the *Tyrant*; and it is thou who wilt save me from all his powerful *threats*.'

However, when the Pistis Sophia had said these things, *then* again through the *command* of my Father, the First Mystery who looks within, I again sent Gabriel and Michael and the great *outpouring* of light, that they should *help* the Pistis Sophia. And I commanded Gabriel and Michael that they should carry the Pistis Sophia upon their hands, lest her feet touch the darkness below. And again I commanded them that they should guide her in the *places* of the *Chaos* from whence they would bring her out. Now it happened when the *angels* went down to the *Chaos*, they and the *outpouring* of light, and all the *emanations* of the Authades and the *emanation* of Adamas saw the *outpouring* of light, that it was exceedingly shining, there being no measure to the light which it had, they were afraid and they released the Pistis Sophia. And the great *outpouring* of light surrounded the Pistis Sophia on every side of her, on her left, and on her right, | and on every side of her, and it made a crown of

ⲙⲙⲟⲥ· ⲁⲩⲱ ϩⲓ ⲥⲁ ⲛⲓⲙ ⲙⲙⲟⲥ ⲁⲩⲱ ⲁⲥⲣ-ⲟⲩⲕⲗⲟⲙ
ⲛⲟⲩⲟⲓⲛ ⲉⲧⲉⲥⲁⲡⲉ· ⲁⲥϣⲱⲡⲉ ϭⲉ ⲛⲧⲉⲣⲉ ⲧⲁⲡⲟϩⲣⲟⲓⲁ
ⲛⲟⲩⲟⲉⲓⲛ ⲕⲱⲧⲉ ⲉⲧⲡⲓⲥⲧⲓⲥ ⲥⲟⲫⲓⲁ· ⲁⲥⲧⲱⲕ ⲛϩⲏⲧ ⲉⲙⲁϣⲟ ⲉⲙⲁϣⲟ· ⲁⲩⲱ ⲙⲡⲥⲗⲟ ⲉⲥⲕⲱⲧⲉ ⲉⲣⲟⲥ ϩⲓ ⲥⲁ ⲛⲓⲙ
5 ⲙⲙⲟⲥ· ⲁⲩⲱ ⲙⲡⲥⲣϩⲟⲧⲉ ϩⲏⲧⲟⲩ ⲛⲛⲉⲡⲣⲟⲃⲟⲗⲟⲟⲩⲉ ⲙ-
ⲡⲁⲩⲑⲁⲇⲏⲥ ⲛⲁⲓ ⲉⲧϣⲟⲟⲡ ϩⲙ ⲡⲉⲭⲁⲟⲥ· ⲁⲩⲇⲉ ⲟⲛ ⲙ-
ⲡⲥⲣϩⲟⲧⲉ ϩⲏⲧⲥ ⲛⲧⲕⲉϭⲟⲙ ⲃⲃⲣⲣⲉ ⲛⲧⲉ ⲡⲁⲩⲑⲁⲇⲏⲥ ⲧⲁⲓ ^{ⲣⲕⲏ}
ⲉⲛⲧⲁϥⲛⲟϫⲥ ⲉⲡⲉⲥⲏⲧ ⲉⲡⲉⲭⲁⲟⲥ· ⲛⲑⲉ ⲛⲟⲩⲥⲟⲧⲉ ⲉϥ-
ϩⲏⲗ· ⲟⲩⲇⲉ ⲟⲛ ⲙⲡⲥⲥⲧⲱⲧ ϩⲏⲧⲥ ⲛⲧϭⲟⲙ ⲛⲇⲁⲓⲙⲟⲛⲓⲟⲛ
10 ⲛⲧⲉ ⲡⲁⲇⲁⲙⲁⲥ ⲧⲁⲓ ⲉⲛⲧⲁⲥⲉⲓ ⲉⲃⲟⲗ ϩⲛ ⲛⲁⲓⲱⲛ· ⲁⲩⲱ
ⲟⲛ ϩⲓⲧⲛ ⲧⲁⲕⲉⲗⲉⲩⲥⲓⲥ ⲁⲛⲟⲕ ⲡⲓϣⲟⲣⲡ ⲙⲙⲩⲥⲧⲏⲣⲓⲟⲛ
ⲉⲧϭⲱϣⲧ ⲉⲃⲟⲗ· ⲁⲥⲣⲟⲩⲟⲉⲓⲛ ⲉⲙⲁϣⲟ ⲉⲙⲁϣⲟ ⲛϭⲓ ⲧⲁⲡⲟϩⲣⲟⲓⲁ ⲛⲟⲩⲟⲉⲓⲛ ⲧⲁⲓ ⲉⲛⲧⲁⲥⲕⲱⲧⲉ ⲉⲧⲡⲓⲥⲧⲓⲥ ⲥⲟⲫⲓⲁ
ϩⲓ ⲥⲁ ⲛⲓⲙ ⲙⲙⲟⲥ· ⲁⲩⲱ ⲁ ⲧⲡⲓⲥⲧⲓⲥ ⲥⲟⲫⲓⲁ ϭⲱ ⲛⲧⲙⲏⲧⲉ
15 ⲙⲡⲟⲩⲟⲉⲓⲛ· ⲉⲣⲉ ⲟⲩⲛⲟϭ ⲛⲟⲩⲟⲉⲓⲛ ϩⲓ ϩⲃⲟⲩⲣ ⲙⲙⲟⲥ
ⲁⲩⲱ ϩⲓ ⲟⲩⲛⲁⲙ ⲙⲙⲟⲥ· ⲁⲩⲱ ϩⲓ ⲥⲁ ⲛⲓⲙ ⲙⲙⲟⲥ· ⲁⲩⲱ
ⲉϥⲟ ⲛⲟⲩⲕⲗⲟⲙ ⲉⲧⲉⲥⲁⲡⲉ· ⲁⲩⲱ ⲛⲉⲡⲣⲟⲃⲟⲗⲟⲟⲩⲉ ⲧⲏⲣⲟⲩ ⲙⲡⲁⲩⲑⲁⲇⲏⲥ ⲙⲡⲟⲩ(ⲉϣ)ϣⲓⲃⲉ ⲟⲛ ⲙⲡⲉⲩϩⲟ ⲟⲩⲇⲉ
ⲙⲡⲟⲩⲉϣⲧⲱⲟⲩⲛ ϩⲁ ⲑⲟⲣⲙⲏ ⲙⲡⲛⲟϭ[*] ⲛⲟⲩⲟⲉⲓⲛ ⲛⲧⲁ- ^{ⲣⲕⲏ b}
20 ⲡⲟϩⲣⲟⲓⲁ· ⲧⲁⲓ ⲉⲧⲟ ⲛⲟⲩⲕⲗⲟⲙ ⲉⲧⲉⲥⲁⲡⲉ· ⲁⲩⲱ ⲛⲉⲡⲣⲟ-
ⲃⲟⲗⲟⲟⲩⲉ ⲧⲏⲣⲟⲩ ⲙⲡⲁⲩⲑⲁⲇⲏⲥ ⲁⲩⲙⲛⲏϣⲉ ⲛϩⲏⲧⲟⲩ
ϩⲉ ϩⲓ ⲟⲩⲛⲁⲙ ⲙⲙⲟⲥ ⲉⲃⲟⲗ ϫⲉ ⲛⲉⲥⲟ ⲛⲟⲩⲟⲉⲓⲛ ⲡⲉ
ⲉⲙⲁϣⲟ ⲉⲙⲁϣⲟ· ⲁⲩⲱ ⲁ ϩⲉⲛⲕⲉⲙⲏⲏϣⲉ ϩⲉ ϩⲓ ϩⲃⲟⲩⲣ
ⲙⲙⲟⲥ· ⲁⲩⲱ ⲛⲉⲙⲡⲟⲩⲉϣϩⲱⲛ ⲉϩⲟⲩⲛ ⲉⲧⲡⲓⲥⲧⲓⲥ ⲥⲟ-

---

10 MS ⲛⲡⲇⲁ ⲡⲁⲇⲁⲙⲁⲥ; read ⲛⲧⲉ ⲡⲁⲇⲁⲙⲁⲥ.
18 MS ⲙⲡⲟⲩϣⲓⲃⲉ.

light for her head. Now it happened when the *outpouring* of light surrounded the Pistis Sophia, she took courage very greatly. And it (the outpouring) did not cease surrounding her on every side. And she was not afraid of the *emanations* of the Authades, which were in the *Chaos. Nor* again was she afraid of the other new power of the Authades which he had cast down into the *Chaos* like a flying arrow. *Nor* did she tremble at the *demonic* power of the Adamas which came forth from the *aeons.* And again through my command, I, the First Mystery who look forth, my *outpouring* of light which surrounded the Pistis Sophia on all sides gave light exceedingly. And the Pistis Sophia remained in the midst of the light, while a great light was on her left and on her right and on all sides, and it was a crown for her head. And all the *emanations* of the Authades were not able to change their faces again, *nor* were they able to bear the *impact* of the great light of my *outpouring* which was a crown of light for her head. And all the *emanations* of the Authades, a multitude of them fell at her right because she was greatly lighted, and another multitude fell at her left; and they were not able to approach the Pistis Sophia | at all because of

ϕⲓⲁ ⲉⲡⲧⲏⲣϥ ⲉⲃⲟⲗ ⲙ̄ⲡⲛⲟϭ ⲛ̄ⲟⲩⲟⲓ̈ⲛ · ⲡⲗⲏⲛ ⲁⲩ︤ⲥ︥ⲉ ⲧⲏⲣⲟⲩ ⲉ︤ⲭ︦ⲛ︥ ⲛⲉⲩⲉⲣⲏⲩ · ⲏ̇ ⲁⲩⲉⲓ̇ ⲧⲏⲣⲟⲩ ⲉⲧⲟⲩ︤ⲛ̄︥-ⲛⲉⲩ-
ⲉⲣⲏⲩ · ⲁⲩⲱ ⟨ⲙ̄⟩ⲡⲟⲩⲱ︤ⲣ̄︥-ⲗⲁⲁⲩ ⲙ̄ⲡⲉⲑⲟⲟⲩ ⲛ̄ⲧⲡⲓⲥⲧⲓⲥ ⲥⲟϕⲓⲁ · ⲉⲃⲟⲗ ⲭⲉ ⲛⲉⲥⲛⲁ︤ⲥ︥ⲧⲉ ⲡⲉ ⲉⲡⲟⲩⲟⲉⲓⲛ · ⲁⲩⲱ ⲉⲃⲟⲗ
5 ︤ⲥ︥ⲓⲧⲛ ⲧⲕⲉⲗⲉⲩⲥⲓⲥ ⲙ̄ⲡⲁⲓ̈ⲱⲧ ⲡⲓϣⲟⲣ︤ⲡ︥ ⲙ̄ⲙⲩⲥⲧⲏⲣⲓⲟⲛ ⲉⲧ-
ϭⲱ︤ϣ︥ⲧ ⲉ︤ⲥ︥ⲟⲩⲛ · ⲁⲛⲟⲕ ︤ⲥ︥ⲱ ⲁⲓ̈ⲉⲓ̇ ⲉⲡⲉⲥⲏⲧ ⲉⲡⲉⲭⲁⲟⲥ ⲉⲓ̈ⲟ
ⲛ̄ⲟⲩⲟⲉⲓⲛ ⲉⲙⲁϣⲟ · ⲉⲙⲁϣⲟ ·· ⲁⲓ̈†-ⲡⲗⲟⲩⲟⲓ̈ ⲉ†ϭⲟⲙ ⲛ̄︤ⲥ︥ⲟ ___
ⲙ̄ⲙⲟⲩⲓ̈ ⲧⲁⲓ̈ ⲉⲛⲉⲥⲟ ⲛ̄ⲟⲩⲟⲉⲓⲛ ⲉⲙⲁϣⲟ ⲁⲩⲱ ⲁⲓ̈ϫⲓ-ⲡⲉⲥ-   ⲣ̄ⲕ̄ⲑ̄
ⲟⲩⲟⲓ̈ⲛ ⲧⲏⲣϥ̄ ⲉⲧ︤ⲛ̄︥ⲥ︤ⲏ̄ⲧ︥ⲥ · ⲁⲩⲱ ⲁⲓ̈ⲕⲁⲧⲉⲭⲉ ⲉⲛⲉⲡⲣⲟⲃⲟ-
10 ⲗⲟⲟⲩⲉ ⲧⲏⲣⲟⲩ ⲙ̄ⲡⲁⲩⲑⲁⲇⲏⲥ ⲉⲧⲙ̄ⲧⲣⲉⲩⲃⲱⲕ ⲉⲡⲉⲩⲧⲟ-
ⲡⲟⲥ ϫⲓⲛ ⲙ̄ⲡⲉⲓ̈ⲛⲁⲩ · ⲉⲧⲉ ⲡⲙⲉ︤ⲥ̄︥ⲙ︤ⲛ̄ⲧ︥ϣⲟⲙⲧⲉ ⲡⲉ ⲛ̄ⲁⲓⲱⲛ ·
[ⲁⲩ]ⲁⲩⲱ ⲁⲓ̈ϥⲓ-ⲧϭⲟⲙ ︤ⲥ̄ⲛ︥ ⲛⲉⲡⲣⲟⲃⲟⲗⲟⲟⲩⲉ ⲧⲏⲣⲟⲩ ⲙ̄ⲡⲁⲩ-
ⲑⲁⲇⲏⲥ · ⲁⲩⲱ ⲁⲩ︤ⲥ︥ⲉ ⲧⲏⲣⲟⲩ ︤ⲥ̄ⲙ︥ ⲡⲉⲭⲁⲟⲥ ⲉⲩⲟ ⲛ̄ⲁⲧ-
ϭⲟⲙ · ⲁⲩⲱ ⲁⲓ̈︤ⲛ̄︥-ⲧⲡⲓⲥⲧⲓⲥ ⲥⲟϕⲓⲁ ⲉⲃⲟⲗ ⲉⲥ︤ⲥ︥ⲓ ⲟⲩⲛⲁⲙ
15 ︤ⲛ̄︥ⲅⲁⲃⲣⲓⲏⲗ · ⲙ̄ⲛ ⲙⲓⲭⲁⲏⲗ · ⲁⲩⲱ †ⲛⲟϭ ⲛ̄ⲁⲡⲟ︤ⲥ︥ⲣⲟⲓⲁ ⲛ̄ⲟⲩ-
ⲟⲓ̈ⲛ ⲁ︤ⲥ︥ⲃⲱⲕ ⲟⲛ ⲉ︤ⲥ︥ⲟⲩⲛ ⲉⲣⲟⲟⲩ · ⲁⲩⲱ ⲁⲥⲙⲉ︤ⲥ︥ⲉⲓⲁ︤ⲧ̄ⲥ︥
ⲛ̄ⲛⲉⲥⲭⲁϫⲉ ︤ⲛ̄︥ϭⲓ ⲧⲡⲓⲥⲧⲓⲥ ⲥⲟϕⲓⲁ ⲭⲉ ⲁⲓ̈ϥⲓ-ⲧⲉⲩϭⲟⲙ ⲛ̄-
ⲟⲩⲟⲓ̈ⲛ ︤ⲛ̄︥︤ⲥ︥ⲏⲧⲟⲩ · ⲁⲩⲱ ⲁⲓ̈︤ⲛ̄︥-ⲧⲡⲓⲥⲧⲓⲥ ⲥⲟϕⲓⲁ ⲉⲃⲟⲗ ︤ⲥ̄ⲙ︥
ⲡⲉⲭⲁⲟⲥ · ⲉⲁⲥ︤ⲥ︥ⲱⲙ ⲉ︤ⲥ︥ⲣⲁⲓ̈ ⲉ︤ⲭ̄ⲛ︥ ⲧⲉⲡⲣⲟⲃⲟⲗⲏ ⲙ̄ⲡⲁⲩⲑⲁ-   ⲣ̄ⲕ̄ⲑ̄ ᵇ
20 ⲇⲏⲥ †︤ⲥ︥ⲟ ⲛ̄︤ⲥ︥ⲟϥ · ⲁⲩⲱ ⲟⲛ ⲛⲉⲥ︤ⲥ︥ⲱⲙ ⲉ︤ⲭ̄ⲛ︥ ⲧⲉⲡⲣⲟⲃⲟⲗⲏ
ⲛ̄︤ⲥ︥ⲟ ︤ⲛ̄︥ⲥⲓⲧ ︤ⲛ̄︥︤ⲥ︥ⲟϥ ⲉⲣⲉ ⲥⲁϣϥⲉ ⲛ̄ⲁⲡⲉ ⲉⲣⲟϥ · ⲁⲩⲱ ⲉⲥ︤ⲥ︥ⲱⲙ
ⲉ︤ⲭ̄ⲛ︥ †ϭⲟⲙ ⲛ̄︤ⲥ︥ⲟ ⲙ̄ⲙⲟⲩⲓ̈ · ⲙ̄ⲛ †︤ⲥ︥ⲟ ⲛ̄ⲁⲣⲁⲕⲱⲛ · ⲁⲓ̈ⲧⲣⲉ

---

3 MS ⲡⲟⲩⲱ︤ⲣ̄︥.
8 MS ⲉⲥⲟ; ⲛⲉⲥ inserted in margin and first ⲥ crossed out.
12 MS ⲁⲩⲁⲩⲱ.
16 MS ⲉⲣⲟⲟⲩ; read ⲉⲣⲟⲥ.
21 20 ⲛ̄ inserted above ︤ⲛ̄ⲥ︥ⲓⲧ.

the great light. *Rather* they all fell upon one another *or*
they all came close to one another. And they were not able
to do any evil to the Pistis Sophia, because she trusted in the
light. And through the *command* of my Father, the First
Mystery who looks within, I also came down to the *Chaos*
shining exceedingly. I made my way to the lion-faced power
which was shining greatly, and I took away all its light
from within it. And I *restrained* all the *emanations* of the
Authades so that from this hour they did not go to their
place, namely the Thirteenth *Aeon*. And I took the power
from all the *emanations* of the Authades, and they all fell
powerless into the *Chaos*. And I brought the Pistis Sophia
forth on the right of Gabriel and Michael. And the great
outpouring of light went again into her. And the Pistis
Sophia saw with her eyes her enemies, that I had taken [1]
their light-power from them. And I brought forth the Pistis
Sophia from the *Chaos*, while she trampled upon the *emanation* of the Authades with a serpent-face; and furthermore
she trampled upon the *emanation* with a basilisk-face with
seven heads; and she trampled upon the power with a lion-
face, and the *dragon*-face. | I caused the Pistis Sophia to

----

[1] (17) that I had taken; Till : because I had taken.

ⲧⲡⲓⲥⲧⲓⲥ ⲥⲟⲫⲓⲁ ϭⲱ ⲉⲥⲁⲍⲉⲣⲁⲧⲥ ⲉϫⲛ ⲧⲉⲡⲣⲟⲃⲟⲗⲏ ⲙ̄-
ⲡⲁⲩⲑⲁⲇⲏⲥ ⲧⲁⲓ ⲉⲧⲟ ⲛ̄ϩⲁ ⲛ̄ⲥⲓⲧ ⲛ̄ϩⲟϥ ⲉⲣⲉ ⲥⲁϣϥⲉ
ⲛ̄ⲁⲡⲉ ⲙ̄ⲙⲟϥ ⲛ̄ⲧⲟⲥ ⲇⲉ ⲛⲉⲥⲭⲟⲟⲣ ⲉⲣⲟⲟⲩ ⲧⲏⲣⲟⲩ ϩⲛ̄
ⲛⲉⲥⲡⲉⲑⲟⲟⲩ · ⲁⲩⲱ ⲁⲛⲟⲕ ⲡⲓϣⲟⲣⲡ̄ ⲙ̄ⲙⲩⲥⲧⲏⲣⲓⲟⲛ ⲁⲓ̈ⲁϩ-
5 ⲉⲣⲁⲧ ϩⲓϫⲱⲥ · ⲁⲩⲱ ⲁⲓ̈ϥⲓ ⲛ̄ϭⲟⲙ ⲧⲏⲣⲟⲩ ⲉⲧⲛ̄ϩⲏⲧⲥ ·
ⲁⲩⲱ ⲁⲓ̈ⲧⲁⲕⲉ-ⲧⲉⲥϩⲩⲗⲏ ⲧⲏⲣⲥ̄ ϫⲉ ⲛ̄ⲛⲉⲥⲡⲉⲣⲙⲁ ⲛ̄ϩⲏⲧⲥ̄
ⲧⲱⲟⲩⲛ ϫⲓⲛ ⲙ̄ⲡⲉⲓ̈ⲛⲁⲩ :

ⲛⲁⲓ̈ ⲇⲉ ⲉⲣⲉ ⲡⲓϣⲟⲣⲡ̄ ⲙ̄ⲙⲩⲥⲧⲏⲣⲓⲟⲛ ϫⲱ ⲙ̄ⲙⲟⲟⲩ ⲉⲙⲙⲁⲑⲏⲧⲏⲥ · ⲁϥⲟⲩⲱϣⲃ̄ ⲉϥϫⲱ ⲙ̄ⲙⲟⲥ ϫⲉ ⲧⲉⲧⲛ̄ⲛⲟⲓ̈ ϫⲉ
10 ⲉⲓ̈ϣⲁϫⲉ**·* ⲛⲙ̄ⲙⲏⲧⲛ̄ ⲛⲁϣ ⲛ̄ϩⲉ · ⲁϥⲉⲓ̇ ⲉⲑⲏ ⲛ̄ϭⲓ ⲓ̈ⲁⲕⲕⲱ- ⲣ̄ⲁ
ⲃⲟⲥ ⲡⲉϫⲁϥ ϫⲉ ⲡⲁϫⲟⲉⲓⲥ ⲉⲧⲃⲉ ⲡⲃⲱⲗ ϭⲉ ⲛ̄ⲛ̄ϣⲁϫⲉ
ⲉⲛⲧⲁⲕϫⲟⲟⲩ · ⲁⲥⲡⲣⲟⲫⲏⲧⲉⲩⲉ ϩⲁⲣⲟⲟⲩ ⲙ̄ⲡⲓⲟⲩⲟⲓ̈ϣ ⲛ̄ϭⲓ
ⲧⲉⲕϭⲟⲙ ⲛ̄ⲟⲩⲟⲓ̈ⲛ ϩⲓⲧⲛ̄ ⲇⲁⲩⲉⲓⲇ · ϩⲙ̄ ⲡⲙⲉϩⲡ̄ⲥⲧⲁⲓ̈ⲟⲩ
ⲙ̄ⲯⲁⲗⲙⲟⲥ ϫⲉ

15 1. ⲡⲉⲧⲟⲩⲏϩ ϩⲁ ⲧⲃⲟⲏⲑⲓⲁ ⲙ̄ⲡⲉⲧϫⲟⲥⲉ ϥⲛⲁϣⲱⲡⲉ ϩⲁ
ⲑⲁⲓ̈ⲃⲉⲥ ⲙ̄ⲡⲛⲟⲩⲧⲉ ⲛ̄ⲧⲡⲉ ·

2. ϥⲛⲁϫⲟⲟⲥ ⲙ̄ⲡϫⲟⲉⲓⲥ ϫⲉ ⲛ̄ⲧⲟⲕ ⲡⲉ ⲡⲁⲣⲉϥϣⲟⲡⲧ̄
ⲉⲣⲟⲕ · ⲁⲩⲱ ⲡⲁⲙⲁⲙⲡⲱⲧ ⲡⲁⲛⲟⲩⲧⲉ ⲉⲓ̈ⲛⲁϩⲧⲉ ⲉⲣⲟϥ ·

3. ϫⲉ ⲛ̄ⲧⲟϥ ⲡⲉⲧⲛⲁⲧⲟⲩϫⲟⲓ̈ ⲉⲧϭⲟⲣϭⲥ̄ ⲛ̄ⲛ̄ϭⲉⲣⲏϭ ·
20 ⲁⲩⲱ ⲉⲩϣⲁϫⲉ ⲉϥⲛⲁϣ̄ⲧ ·

4. ϥⲛⲁⲣ̄-ϩⲁⲓ̈ⲃⲉⲥ ⲉⲣⲟⲕ ϩⲁ ⲧⲉⲕⲙⲉⲥⲧⲛ̄ϩⲏⲧ ⲁⲩⲱ ⲕⲛⲁ-
ⲛⲁϩⲧⲉ ϩⲁ ⲛⲉϥⲧⲛ̄ϩ · ⲧⲉϥⲙⲉ* ⲛⲁⲕⲱⲧⲉ ⲉⲣⲟⲕ ⲛ̄ⲑⲉ ⲛ̄ⲟⲩ- ⲣ̄ⲁᵇ
ϩⲟⲡⲗⲟⲛ ·

5. ⲛ̄ⲅⲛⲁⲣ̄ϩⲟⲧⲉ ⲁⲛ ϩⲏⲧⲥ ⲛ̄ⲟⲩϩⲟⲧⲉ ⲛ̄ϭⲱⲣϩ · ⲁⲩⲱ
25 ϩⲏⲧϥ̄ ⲛ̄ⲟⲩⲥⲟⲧⲉ ⲉϥϩⲏⲗ ⲙ̄ⲡⲉϩⲟⲟⲩ ·

---

21 MS ⲧⲉⲕⲙⲉⲥⲧⲛ̄ϩⲏⲧ; read ⲧⲉϥⲙⲉⲥⲧⲛ̄ϩⲏⲧ.

remain standing upon the *emanation* of the Authades. *But* the one with a basilisk-face and seven heads was stronger than them all in its evil. And I, the First *Mystery*, stood upon it. And I took away all the powers within it, I destroyed all its *matter*, so that from this hour no *seed* from it should arise."

67. When, *however*, the First *Mystery* said these things to the *disciples*, he answered, saying: "Do you *understand* in what manner I speak with you?"

James came forward and said: "My Lord, concerning the interpretation of the words which thou hast spoken, thy light-power once *prophesied* about them, through David, in the 90th *Psalm*:

1. 'He that dwells in the *help* of the Highest will be under the shadow of the God of heaven.

2. He will say to the Lord: Thou art my shelter and my refuge, my God in whom I have trusted.

3. For he will save me from the snare of the hunters and a powerful word.

4. He will overshadow thee with his breast and under his wings thou wilt trust. His truth will surround thee like a *shield*.

5. Thou shalt not fear from terror by night and from an arrow that flies by day. |

6. ϨΗΤϤ ΝΟΥϨⲰΒ · ΕϤΜΟΟϢΕ ϨΜ ΠΚΑΚΕ · ΕΒΟΛ ϨΝ
ΟΥϨΤΟΠ ΝΔΑΙΜΟΝΙΟΝ ΜΠΝΑΥ ΜΜΕΕΡΕ ·

7. ΟΥΝ-ϢΟ ΝΑϨΕ ϨΙ ϨΒΟΥΡ ΜΜΟΚ · ΑΥⲰ ΟΥΤΒΑ ϨΙ
ΟΥΝΑΜ ΜΜΟΚ · ΝϹΕΝΑϨⲰΝ ΔΕ ΕΡΟΚ ΑΝ ·

8. ΠΛΗΝ ΚΝΑΜΕϨΕΙΑΤΚ ΜΜΟΟΥ · ΚΝΑΝΑΥ ΕΠΤⲰⲰΒΕ
ΝΡΡΕϤΡΝΟΒΕ ·

9. ΧΕ ΝΤΟΚ ΠΧΟΕΙϹ ΠΕ ΤΑϨΕΛΠΙϹ · ΑΚΚⲰ ΝΑΚ Μ-
ΠΕΤΧΟϹΕ ΜΜΑΜΠⲰΤ ·

10. ΜΝ ΠΕΘΟΟΥ ΝΑϨⲰΝ ΕΡΟΚ · ΜΝ ΜΑϹΤΙΓⲞ ΝΑϨⲰΝ
ΕϨΟΥΝ ΕΠΕΚΜΑΝϢⲰΠΕ ·

11. ΧΕ ϤΝΑϨⲰΝ ΕΤΟΟΤΟΥ ΝΝΕϤΑΓΓΕΛΟϹ ΕΤΒΗΗΤΚ ⟨ΡΛΔ⟩
ΕΤΡΕΥϨΑΡΕϨ ΕΡΟΚ ϨΝ ΝΕΚϨΙΟΟΥΕ ΤΗΡΟΥ ·

12. ΝϹΕϤΙΤΚ ΕΧΝ ΝΕΥϬΙΧ · ΜΗΠΟΤΕ ΝΓΧⲰΡΠ ΕΥ-
ⲰΝΕ ϨΝ ΤΕΚΟΥΕΡΗΤΕ ·

13. ΚΝΑΤΑΛΕ ΕϨΡΑⲒ ΕΧΝ ΟΥϨΟϤ · ΜΝ ΟΥϹΙΤ · ΝΓϨⲰΜ
ΕΧΝ ΟΥΜΟΥⲒ ΜΝ ΟΥΔΡΑΚⲰΝ ·

14. ΧΕ ΑϤΝΑϨΤΕ ΕΡΟⲒ · ϮΝΑΤΟΥΧΟϤ ϮΝΑΡ-ϨΑⲒΒΕϹ
ΕΡΟϤ ΧΕ ΑϤϹΟΥΝ-ΠΑΡΑΝ ·

15. ϤΝΑⲰϢ ΕϨΡΑⲒ ΕΡΟⲒ ΑΥⲰ ΑΝΟΚ ϮΝΑϹⲰΤΜ ΕΡΟϤ ·
ϮϢΟΟΠ ΝΜΜΑϤ ϨΝ ΤΕϤΘΛΙⲮΙϹ · ΑΥⲰ ϮΝΑΤΟΥΧΟϤ ·
ΤΑϮ-ΕΟΟΥ ΝΑϤ ·

16. ΤΑΤΑϢΟϤ ϨΝ ΟΥΜΗΗϢΕ ΝϨΟΟΥ · ΤΑΤϹΑΒΟϤ
ΕΠΑΟΥΧΑⲒ ·

ΠΑⲒ ΠΕ ΠΑΧΟⲒϹ ΠΒⲰΛ ΝΝϢΑΧΕ ΕΝΤΑΚΧΟΟΥ · ϹⲰ-
ΤΜ ϬΕ ΤΑΧΟΟΥ ϨΝ ΟΥΠΑΡϨΗϹΙΑ · ΠϢΑΧΕ ϬΕ ΕΝΤΑ

---

2   MS ΝΔΑΙΜΟΝΙΟΝ; Schmidt : read ΜΝ ΟΥΔΑΙΜΟΝΙΟΝ.

6. From anything which walks in darkness; from a *demonic* blow [1] at midday.

7. A thousand will fall at thy left and ten thousand at thy right, *but* they will not approach thee.

8. *Rather* thou wilt observe them with thy eyes and see the reward of sinners.

9. For thou, O Lord, art my *hope*; thou hast set the Highest as thy refuge.

10. No evil will approach thee, no *scourge* will enter thy dwelling.

11. For he will command his *angels* concerning thee, that they guard thee in all thy ways.

12. They will bear thee upon their hands *lest* thou strikest a stone with thy foot.

13. Thou wilt tread upon the serpent and basilisk, and thou wilt trample upon the lion and *dragon* [2].

14. Because he has trusted in me I will save him; I will overshadow him because he has known my name.

15. He will cry to me and I will hear him; I will be with him in his *affliction*, and I will save him and honour him.

16. I will increase him with many days, I will teach him my salvation'. *

This, O Lord, is the interpretation of the words which thou didst speak. Hear now that I speak *openly*. Now the word which | thy power spoke through David: 'He that

---

*   Ps. 90.1-16

---

[1]   (2) a demonic blow; lit. a demonic fall; Schmidt: a fall (misfortune) and a demon; RV: destruction that wasteth (see 146.1, 5, 8).

[2]   (15, 16) the serpent and basilisk ... the dragon; lit. a serpent and basilisk ... a dragon (see also 148.21, 22).

*ⲧⲉⲕϭⲟⲙ ϫⲟⲟϥ ϩⲓⲧⲛ̅ ⲇⲁⲩⲉⲓⲇ · ϫⲉ ⲡⲉⲧⲟⲩⲏϩ ϩⲁ ⲧⲃⲟ- ⟨ⲣ̅ⲗ̅ⲁ̅⟩b
ⲏⲑⲓⲁ ⲙ̅ⲡⲉⲧϫⲟⲥⲉ · ϥⲛⲁϣⲱⲡⲉ ϩⲁ ⲑⲗⲓ̈ⲃⲉⲥ ⲙ̅ⲡⲛⲟⲩⲧⲉ
ⲛ̅ⲧⲡⲉ · ⲉⲧⲉ ⲡⲁ̈ⲓ ⲡⲉ ϫⲉ ⲛ̅ⲧⲉⲣⲉ ⲧⲥⲟⲫⲓⲁ ⲛⲁϩⲧⲉ ⲉⲡⲟⲩⲟⲉⲓⲛ · ⲁⲥϣⲱⲡⲉ ϩⲁ ⲡⲟⲩⲟⲉⲓⲛ ⲛ̅ϯⲁⲡⲟϩⲣⲟⲓⲁ ⲛ̅ⲟⲩⲟⲉⲓⲛ ·
ⲧⲁ̈ⲓ ⲉⲛⲧⲁⲥⲉⲓ' ϩ̅ⲙ̅ ⲡϫⲓⲥⲉ ⲉⲃⲟⲗ ϩⲓⲧⲟⲟⲧⲕ̅ · ⲁⲩⲱ ⲡϣⲁϫⲉ
ⲉⲛⲧⲁ ⲧⲉⲕϭⲟⲙ ϫⲟⲟϥ ϩⲓⲧⲛ̅ ⲇⲁⲩⲉⲓⲇ · ϫⲉ ϯⲛⲁϫⲟⲟⲥ
ⲙ̅ⲡϫⲟⲉⲓⲥ ϫⲉ ⲛ̅ⲧⲟⲕ ⲡⲉ ⲡⲁⲣⲉϥϣⲟⲡⲧ̅ ⲉⲣⲟⲕ · ⲁⲩⲱ ⲡⲁ-
ⲙⲁⲙ̅ⲡⲱⲧ ⲡⲁⲛⲟⲩⲧⲉ · ⲁ̈ⲓⲛⲁϩⲧⲉ ⲉⲣⲟϥ · ⲛ̅ⲧⲟϥ ⲡⲉ ⲡϣⲁϫⲉ ⲉⲛⲧⲁⲥϩⲩⲙⲛⲉⲩⲉ ⲙ̅ⲙⲟϥ ⲛ̅ϭⲓ ⲧⲡⲓⲥⲧⲓⲥ ⲥⲟⲫⲓⲁ · ϫⲉ
ⲛ̅ⲧⲟⲕ ⲡⲉ ⲡⲁⲣⲉϥϣⲟⲡⲧ̅ ⲉⲣⲟϥ · ⲁⲩⲱ ⲉ̈ⲓⲛⲏⲩ ⲉⲣⲁⲧⲕ̅ ·
ⲁⲩⲱ ⲟⲛ ⲡϣⲁϫⲉ ⲛ̅ⲧⲁ ⲧⲉⲕϭⲟⲙ ϫⲟⲟϥ ϫⲉ ⲡⲁⲛⲟⲩⲧⲉ
ⲉⲉⲓⲛⲁϩⲧⲉ ⲉⲣⲟⲕ · ⲛ̅ⲧⲟⲕ **ⲡⲉⲧⲛⲁⲧⲟⲩϫⲟⲓ̈ ⲉⲧϭⲟⲣϭ̅ⲥ̅ ⲛ̅ⲛ̅- ⲣ̅ⲗ̅ⲃ̅
ϭⲉⲣⲏϭ ⲁⲩⲱ ⲉⲩϣⲁϫⲉ ⲉϥⲛⲁϣ̅ⲧ̅ · ⲛ̅ⲧⲟϥ ⲡⲉ ⲛ̅ⲧⲁⲥϫⲟⲟϥ
ⲛ̅ϭⲓ ⲧⲡⲓⲥⲧⲓⲥ ⲥⲟⲫⲓⲁ ϫⲉ ⲡⲟⲩⲟ̈ⲓⲛ ⲉ̈ⲓⲡⲓⲥⲧⲉⲩⲉ ⲉⲣⲟⲕ ϫⲉ
ⲛ̅ⲧⲟⲕ ⲡⲉⲧⲛⲁⲛⲁϩⲙⲉⲧ ⲉⲛⲉⲡⲣⲟⲃⲟⲗⲟⲟⲩⲉ ⲙ̅ⲡⲁⲩⲑⲁⲇⲏⲥ ·
ⲁⲩⲱ ⲙ̅ⲛ̅ ⲛⲁⲡⲁⲇⲁⲙⲁⲥ ⲡⲧⲩⲣⲁⲛⲛⲟⲥ · ⲁⲩⲱ ⲛ̅ⲧⲟⲕ ⲟⲛ
ⲡⲉ ⲉⲧⲛⲁⲛⲁϩⲙⲉⲧ ⲉⲛⲉⲩⲁⲡⲓⲗⲏ ⲧⲏⲣⲟⲩ ⲉⲧⲛⲁϣ̅ⲧ̅ · ⲁⲩⲱ
ⲟⲛ ⲡϣⲁϫⲉ ⲉⲛⲧⲁⲥϫⲟⲟϥ ⲛ̅ϭⲓ ⲧⲉⲕϭⲟⲙ ϩⲓⲧⲛ̅ ⲇⲁⲩⲉⲓⲇ ·
ϫⲉ ϥⲛⲁⲣ̅-ϩⲁⲉⲓⲃⲉⲥ ⲉⲣⲟⲕ ϩⲁ ⲧⲉⲕⲙⲉⲥⲧ̅ⲛ̅ϩⲏⲧ · ⲁⲩⲱ ⲕⲛⲁ-
ⲛⲁϩⲧⲉ ϩⲁ ⲛⲉϥⲧⲛ̅ϩ · ⲉⲧⲉ ⲡⲁ̈ⲓ ⲡⲉ ϫⲉ ⲁ ⲧⲡⲓⲥⲧⲓⲥ ⲥⲟⲫⲓⲁ
ⲁⲥϣⲱⲡⲉ ϩ̅ⲙ̅ ⲡⲟⲩⲟⲉⲓⲛ ⲛ̅ϯⲁⲡⲟϩⲣⲟⲓⲁ ⲛ̅ⲟⲩⲟⲉⲓⲛ · ⲧⲁ̈ⲓ ⲉⲛⲧⲁⲥⲉⲓ' ⲉⲃⲟⲗ ⲙ̅ⲙⲟⲕ ⲁⲩⲱ ⲁⲥϭⲱ ⲉⲥⲧⲏⲕ ⲛ̅ϩⲏⲧ ⲙ̅ⲡⲟⲩⲟ̈ⲓⲛ
ⲉⲧϩⲓ ϩⲃⲟⲩⲣ ⲙ̅ⲙⲟⲥ · *ⲙ̅ⲛ̅ ⲡⲉⲧϩⲓ ⲟⲩⲛⲁⲙ ⲙ̅ⲙⲟⲥ · ⲉⲧⲉ ⲣ̅ⲗ̅ⲃ̅b
ⲛ̅ⲧⲟⲟⲩ ⲛⲉ ⲛ̅ⲧⲛ̅ϩ ⲛ̅ⲧⲁⲡⲟϩⲣⲟⲓⲁ ⲛ̅ⲟⲩⲟ̈ⲓⲛ · ⲁⲩⲱ ⲡϣⲁϫⲉ

8 MS ⲁ̈ⲓⲛⲁϩⲧⲉ; read ⲉ̈ⲓⲛⲁϩⲧⲉ.
13 MS originally ⲛ̅ⲧⲁϥϫⲟⲟϥ.
19 MS again ⲧⲉⲕⲙⲉⲥⲧ̅ⲛ̅ϩⲏⲧ; read ⲧⲉϥⲙⲉⲥⲧ̅ⲛ̅ϩⲏⲧ.

dwells in the *help* of the Highest will be under the shadow
of the God of heaven' * : that is, when the Sophia trusted
in the light, she was under the light of the *outpouring* of light
which came from the height through thee. And the word
which thy power spoke through David : 'I will say to the
Lord : Thou art my shelter and my refuge, my God in whom
I have trusted' □ : that is, the word with which the Pistis
Sophia *sang praises* : 'Thou art my shelter and I come to
thee'. And again the word which thy power said : 'My God
in whom I have trusted, thou who wilt save me from the
snare of the hunters and a powerful word' ° : that is, what
the Pistis Sophia said : 'O Light, I *believe* in thee, thou art
my Saviour from the *emanations* of the Authades and
Adamas, the tyrant; and it is thou who wilt save me from
their powerful *threats*'. And furthermore, the word which
thy power spoke through David : 'He will overshadow thee
under his breast, and under his wings thou wilt trust' ᴬ :
that is, the Pistis Sophia was in the light of the *outpouring*
of light which came forth from thee, and she continued to
be encouraged by the light upon her left and upon her right,
which are the wings of the *outpouring* of light. And the word |

*   Ps. 90.1
□   Ps. 90.2
°   Ps. 90.2, 3
ᴬ   Ps. 90.4

ЄΝΤΑ ΤΕΚϬΟΜ Ν̄ΟΥΟΪΝ ΠΡΟΦΗΤΕΥΕ Μ̄ΜΟϤ ϨΙΤΝ̄ ΛΑΥ-
ϹΙΑ· ϪΕ ΤΜΕ ΝΑΚⲰΤΕ ΕΡΟΚ Ν̄ΘΕ Ν̄ΟΥϨΟΠΛΟΝ· Ν̄ΤΟϤ
ΠΕ ΠΟΥΟΕΙΝ Ν̄ΤΑΠΟϨΡΟΙΑ Ν̄ΟΥΟΕΙΝ· ΠΕΝΤΑϤΚⲰΤΕ
ΕΤΠΙϹΤΙϹ ϹΟΦΙΑ ϨΙ ϹΑ ΝΙΜ Μ̄ΜΟϹ Ν̄ΘΕ Ν̄ΟΥϨΟΠΛΟΝ·
5 ΑΥⲰ ΠϢΑϪΕ ΕΝΤΑ ΤΕΚϬΟΜ ϪΟΟϤ ϪΕ Ν̄ϤΝΑΡ̄ϨΟΤΕ
ΑΝ ϨΗΤϹ̄ Ν̄ΟΥϨΟΤΕ Ν̄ϬⲰΡϨ̄ ΕΤΕ ΠΑΪ ΠΕ ϪΕ Μ̄ΠΕ ΤΠΙϹ-
ΤΙϹ ϹΟΦΙΑ Ρ̄ϨΟΤΕ ϨΗΤΟΥ Ν̄Ν̄ϨΟΤΕ Μ̄Ν̄ Ν̄ϢΤΟΡΤ̄Ρ̄ ΝΑΪ
ЄΝΤΑΥϪΟϹ Ν̄ϨΗΤΟΥ ϨΜ̄ ΠΕϪΛΟϹ ΕΤΕ Ν̄ΤΟϤ ΠΕ
⟨Π⟩ϬⲰΡϨ̄· ΑΥⲰ ΠϢ⟨Α⟩ϪΕ ЄΝΤΑ ΤΕΚϬΟΜ ϪΟΟϤ ϪΕ
10 Ν̄ϤΝΑΡ̄ϨΟΤΕ ΑΝ ϨΗΤϤ̄ Ν̄ΟΥϹΟΤΕ ЄϤϨΗΛ ϨΜ̄ ΠΕϨΟΟΥ·
ΕΤΕ ΠΑΪ ΠΕ ϪΕ Μ̄ΠΕ ΤΠΙϹΤΙϹ ϹΟΦΙΑ· Μ̄ΠϹΡ̄ϨΟΤΕ ϨΗΤϹ̄
Ν̄ΤϬΟΜ ΤΑΪ ЄΝΤΑ ΠΑΥΘΑΛΗϹ Τ̄ΝΝΟΟΥϹ ЄΒΟΛ ϨΜ̄
ΠϪΙϹΕ Μ̄ΦΛΕ· ΤΑΪ ЄΝΤΑϹΕΙ̅ ΕΠΕϪΛΟϹ ЄϹΟ Ν̄ΘΕ Ν̄ΟΥ-
ϹΟΤΕ ЄϤϨΗΛ· Ν̄ΤΑ ΤΕΚϬΟΜ ϬΕ Ν̄ΟΥΟΕΙΝ ϪΟΟϹ ϪΕ
15 Ν̄ΓΝΑΡ̄ϨΟΤΕ ΑΝ ϨΗΤϤ̄ Ν̄ΟΥϹΟΤΕ ЄϤϨΗΛ ϨΜ̄ ΠΕϨΟΟΥ·
ЄΒΟΛ ϪΕ Ν̄ΤΑ ΤϬΟΜ ΕΤΜ̄ΜΑΥ ΕΙ̅ ЄΒΟΛ ϨΜ̄ ΠΜΕϨΜΝ̄Τ-
ϢΟΜΤΕ Ν̄ΑΙⲰΝ· ЄΝΤΟϤ ΠΕ ЄΤΟ Ν̄ϪΟΕΙϹ ЄϪΝ̄ ΠΜΕϨ-
ΜΝ̄ΤϹΝΟΟΥϹ Ν̄ΑΙⲰΝ ΑΥⲰ Ν̄ΤΟϤ ΠΕ ЄΤΟ Ν̄ΟΥΟΕΙΝ
ЄΝΑΙⲰΝ ΤΗΡΟΥ· ЄΤΒΕ ΠΑΪ ϬΕ ΑϤϪΟΟϹ ϪΕ ΠΕϨΟΟΥ·
20 ΑΥⲰ ΠϢΑϪΕ ΟΝ ЄΝΤΑ ΤΕΚϬΟΜ ϪΟΟϤ ϪΕ Ν̄ϤΝΑΡ̄-
ϨΟΤΕ ΑΝ ϨΗΤϤ̄ Ν̄ΟΥϨⲰΒ ЄϤΜΟΟϢΕ ϨΜ̄ ΠΚΑΚΕ· ЄΤΕ
ΠΑΪ ΠΕ ϪΕ Μ̄ΠΕ ΤϹΟΦΙΑ Ρ̄ϨΟΤΕ ϨΗΤϹ̄ Ν̄ΤϯΠΡΟΒΟΛΗ Ν̄Λ
Ν̄ϨΟϤ· ΤΑΪ ЄΝΕϹ†ϨΟΤΕ Ν̄ΤΠΙϹΤΙϹ ϹΟΦΙΑ ϨΜ̄ ΠΕϪΛΟϹ
ЄΤΕ Ν̄ΤΟϤ ΠΕ ΠΚΑΚΕ· ΑΥⲰ ΠϢΑϪΕ ЄΝΤΑ ΤΕΚϬΟΜ

---

9   MS ϬⲰΡϨ̄; read ΠϬⲰΡϨ̄. MS ΠϢϪΕ.
11 Μ̄ in Μ̄ΠΕ inserted above.
17 MS ΠΜΕϨΜΝ̄ΤϹΝΟΟΥϹ; perhaps read ΠΜ̄ΠΤϹΝΟΟΥϹ.
22 MS ϯΠϹ; read Μ̄ΠΕ.

which thy light-power *prophesied* through David : 'Truth
will surround thee like a *shield* * : that is the light of the
outpouring of light which surrounded the Pistis Sophia on
all sides like a *shield*. And the word which thy power spoke :
'He shall not fear from terror by night' ⁰ : that is, that the
Pistis Sophia did not fear the terrors and disturbances which
were contained in the *Chaos* which is the night. And the
word which thy power spoke : 'He shall not fear from an
arrow that flies by day' ○ : that is, that the Pistis Sophia did
not fear the power which the Authades finally sent from
the height, which came to the *Chaos* like an arrow which
flies. Now thy light-power said : 'Thou shalt not fear an
arrow that flies by day' △, because that power came forth
from the thirteenth (probably twelfth) *aeon*. He is lord
over the twelfth *aeon* and it is he who lights all the *aeons*;
because of this he has said 'the day'. And the word which
thy power spoke : 'He will not fear anything which walks
in the darkness' ◦ : that is, the Pistis Sophia did not fear the
emanation with a serpent-face, which causes fear to the Pistis
Sophia in the *Chaos* which is the darkness. And the word
which thy power | said : 'He shall not fear a *demonic* blow

---

*   Ps. 90.4
□   Ps. 90.5
○   Ps. 90.5
△   Ps. 90.5
◦   Ps. 90.6

ϪⲞⲞϤ ϪⲈ ⲚϤⲚⲀⲢϨⲞⲦⲈ ⲀⲚ ϨⲎⲦϤ ⲚⲞⲨϨⲦⲞⲠ ⲘⲚ ⲞⲨ-
ⲀⲓⲘⲞⲚⲓⲞⲚ ⲘⲠⲚⲀⲨ ⲘⲘⲈⲈⲢⲈ ⲈⲦⲈ ⲠⲀⲒ ⲠⲈ ϪⲈ ⲘⲠⲈ
ⲦⲠⲒⲤⲦⲒⲤ ⲤⲞⲫⲒⲀ ⲢϨⲞⲦⲈ ϨⲎⲦⲤ Ⲛ†ⲠⲢⲞⲂⲞⲖⲎ ⲚⲀⲓⲘⲞⲚⲓⲞⲚ
ⲚⲦⲈ ⲠⲀⲀⲀⲘⲀⲤ ⲠⲦⲨⲢⲀⲚⲚⲞⲤ · ⲦⲀⲒ ⲈⲚⲦⲀⲤⲦⲀⲨⲈ-ⲦⲠⲒⲤ-
5 ⲦⲒⲤ ⲤⲞⲫⲒⲀ ⲈⲠⲈⲤⲎⲦ ϨⲚ ⲞⲨⲚⲞϬ ⲚϨⲦⲞⲠ · ⲦⲀⲒ ⲈⲚⲦ-
ⲀⲤⲈⲒ' ⲈⲂⲞⲖ ϨⲘ ⲠⲀⲀⲀⲘⲀⲤ ⲈⲂⲞⲖ ϨⲘ ⲠⲘⲈϨⲘⲚⲦⲤⲚⲞⲞⲨ
ⲚⲚⲀⲒⲰⲚ · ⲈⲦⲂⲈ ⲠⲀⲒ ϬⲈ ⲀⲤϪⲞⲞϤ ⲚϬⲒ ⲦⲈⲔϬⲞⲘ · ϪⲈ
ⲚϤⲚⲀⲢϨⲞⲦⲈ ⲀⲚ ϨⲎⲦϤ ⲚⲞⲨϨⲦⲞⲠ ⲚⲀⲀⲒⲘⲞⲚⲓⲞⲚ ⲘⲠⲚⲀⲨ ⲢⲀⲀ
ⲘⲘⲈⲈⲢⲈ · ⲠⲚⲀⲨ ⲘⲘⲈⲈⲢⲈ ⲠⲈ ϪⲈ ⲚⲦⲀⲤⲈⲒ' ⲈⲂⲞⲖ ϨⲘ
10 ⲠⲘⲚⲦⲤⲚⲞⲞⲨⲤ ⲚⲀⲒⲰⲚ · ⲈⲦⲈ ⲚⲦⲞϤ ⲠⲈ ⲠⲚⲀⲨ ⲘⲘⲈⲈⲢⲈ ·
ⲀⲨⲰ ⲞⲚ ⲚⲦⲀⲤⲈⲒ' ⲈⲂⲞⲖ ϨⲘ ⲠⲈϪⲖⲞⲤ · ⲈⲦⲈ ⲚⲦⲞϤ ⲠⲈ
ⲦⲈⲨϢⲎ · ⲀⲨⲰ ϬⲰⲢϨ ⲚⲦⲀⲤⲈⲒ' ⲈⲂⲞⲖ ϨⲘ ⲠⲘⲈϨⲘⲚⲦⲤⲚⲞ-
ⲞⲨⲤ ⲚⲀⲒⲰⲚ · ⲠⲀⲒ ⲈⲦϨⲚ ⲦⲈⲨⲘⲎⲦⲈ ⲘⲠⲈⲤⲚⲀⲨ · ⲈⲦⲂⲈ
ⲠⲀⲒ Ⲁ ⲦⲈⲔϬⲞⲘ ⲚⲞⲨⲞⲈⲒⲚ ϪⲞⲞⲤ ϪⲈ ⲠⲚⲀⲨ ⲘⲘⲈⲈⲢⲈ ·
15 ϪⲈ ⲠⲘⲚⲦⲤⲚⲞⲞⲨⲤ ⲚⲀⲒⲰⲚ · ⲤⲈ ⲚⲦⲘⲎⲦⲈ ⲘⲠⲘⲈϨⲘⲚⲦ-
ϢⲞⲘⲦⲈ ⲚⲀⲒⲰⲚ · ⲀⲨⲰ ⲚⲦⲘⲎⲦⲈ ⲘⲠⲈϪⲖⲞⲤ: ⲀⲨⲰ ⲠϢⲀ-
ϪⲈ ⲞⲚ ⲈⲚⲦⲀ ⲦⲈⲔϬⲞⲘ ⲚⲞⲨⲞⲒⲚ ϪⲞⲞϤ ϨⲒⲦⲚ ⲀⲀⲨⲒⲀ ·
ϪⲈ ⲞⲨⲚ-ϢⲞ ⲚⲀϨⲈ ϨⲒ ϨⲂⲞⲨⲢ ⲘⲘⲞϤ · ⲀⲨⲰ ⲞⲨⲦⲂⲀ ϨⲒ
ⲞⲨⲚⲀⲘ ⲘⲘⲞϤ · ⲀⲨⲰ ⲚⲤⲈⲚⲀϨⲰⲚ ⲈⲢⲞϤ ⲀⲚ · ⲈⲦⲈ ⲠⲀⲒ
20 ⲠⲈ ϪⲈ ⲚⲦⲈⲢⲈ ⲚⲈⲠⲢⲞⲂⲞⲖⲞⲞⲨⲈ ⲘⲠⲀⲨⲐⲀⲀⲎⲤ ⲚⲀⲒ ⲈⲦ- ⲢⲀⲀ ᵇ
ⲞϢ ⲈⲘⲀⲦⲈ · ⲚⲦⲈⲢⲞⲨⲦⲘⲈϢϬⲘϬⲞⲘ ⲈⲦϢⲞⲨⲚ ϨⲀ ⲠⲚⲞϬ
ⲚⲞⲨⲞⲈⲒⲚ Ⲛ†ⲀⲠⲞϨⲢⲞⲒⲀ ⲚⲞⲨⲞⲈⲒⲚ · ⲀⲨⲘⲎⲎϢⲈ ⲚϨⲎⲦⲞⲨ
ϨⲈ ϨⲒ ϨⲂⲞⲨⲢ ⲚⲦⲠⲒⲤⲦⲒⲤ ⲤⲞⲫⲒⲀ · ⲀⲨⲰ ⲀⲨⲘⲎⲎϢⲈ ϨⲈ ϨⲒ

---

1 cf. 143.2.
4 MS ⲠⲠⲦⲨⲢⲀⲚⲚⲞⲤ.
7 MS ⲚⲚⲀⲒⲰⲚ ; read ⲚⲀⲒⲰⲚ.
11,12 text corrupt; read ⲀⲨⲰ ⲞⲚ ⲠϬⲰⲢϨ ϪⲈ ⲚⲦⲀⲤⲈⲒ' ⲈⲂⲞⲖ ϨⲘ ⲠⲈϪⲖⲞⲤ
       ⲈⲦⲈ ⲚⲦⲞϤ ⲠⲈ ⲦⲈⲨϢⲎ ⲀⲨⲰ ϪⲈ ⲚⲦⲀⲤⲈⲒ.
15 MS ⲤⲈ ⲚⲦⲘⲎⲦⲤ ; read ⲤⲈⲞ ⲚⲦⲘⲎⲦⲈ.

at midday' *: that is the Pistis Sophia did not fear the
demonic emanation of Adamas the *Tyrant*, which cast the
Pistis Sophia down with a great blow, which came forth
from Adamas from the twelfth *aeon*. Because of this thy
power said : 'He shall not fear a *demonic* blow at midday' □.
'Midday', because it came from the twelfth (lit. twelve)
aeon, which is the hour of midday. And furthermore ⟨'night'
because⟩ it came forth from the *Chaos*, which is the night,
and it came forth from the twelfth *aeon*, which is the
middle between the two. Because of this thy light-power
said : 'the hour of midday', because the twelve *aeons* are
in the middle between the thirteenth *aeon* and the *Chaos*.
And the word which thy light-power spoke through David :
'A thousand will fall at his left and ten thousand at his
right, and they will not approach him' ○ : that is, when the
emanations of the Authades which were very numerous were
not able to bear the great light of the *outpouring* of light,
a multitude of them fell at the left of the Pistis Sophia,
and a multitude fell | at her right. And they were not able

---

*   Ps. 90.6
□   Ps. 90.6
○   Ps. 90.7

ΟΥΝΑΜ Μ̄ΜΟΣ· ΑΥѠ ΕΝΕ Μ̄ΠΟΥΕѠ2ѠΝ ΕΡΟΣ ΕΠΛΑΤΕ
Μ̄ΜΟΣ· ΑΥѠ ΠѠΑΧΕ ΕΝΤΑ ΤΕΚϬΟΜ Ν̄ΟΥΟΕΙΝ ΧΟΟϤ
2ΙΤΝ̄ ΔΑΥΪΔ· ΧΕ ΠΛΗΝ ΚΝΑΜΕ2ΕΙΑΤΚ̄ Μ̄ΜΟΟΥ· ΑΥѠ
ΚΝΑΝΑΥ ΕΠΤΟΥΪΟ Ν̄Ν̄ΡΕϤΡ̄ΝΟΒΕ· ΧΕ Ν̄ΤΟΚ ΠΧΟΕΙΣ
5 ΠΕ ΤΑ2ΕΛΠΙΣ· ΕΤΕ ΠΑΪ ΠΕ ΠѠΑΧΕ· ΧΕ Ν̄ΤΑ ΤΠΙΣΤΙΣ
ΣΟΦΙΑ ΜΕ2ΕΙΑΤΣ̄ Ν̄ΝΕΣΧΑΧΕ· ΕΤΕ ΝΕΠΡΟΒΟΛΟΟΥΕ
Μ̄ΠΑΥΘΑΔΗΣ ΝΕ ΝΑΪ ΕΝΤΑΥ2Ε ΤΗΡΟΥ ΕΧΝ̄ ΝΕΥΕΡΗΥ
ΟΥΜΟΝΟΝ ΑΣΜΕ2ΕΙΑΤΣ̄ Μ̄ΜΟΟΥ 2Μ ΠΑΪ· ΑΛΛΑ Ν̄ΤΟΚ ΡΛΕ
2ѠѠΚ ΟΝ ΠΑΧΟΕΙΣ ΠΙѠΟΡΠ̄ Μ̄ΜΥΣΤΗΡΙΟΝ ΑΚϤΙ-ΤϬΟΜ
10 Ν̄ΟΥΟΕΙΝ ΕΤѠΟΟΠ 2Ν̄ †ϬΟΜ Ν̄2Ο Μ̄ΜΟΥΪ ΑΥѠ ΟΝ
ΑΚϤΙ-ΤϬΟΜ Ν̄ΝΕΠΡΟΒΟΛΟΟΥΕ ΤΗΡΟΥ Μ̄ΠΑΥΘΑΔΗΣ
ΑΥѠ ΟΝ ΑΚΚΑΤΕΧΕ Μ̄ΜΟΟΥ 2Μ ΠΕΧΛΟΣ ΕΤΜ̄ΜΑΥ
⟨ΕΤΜΤΡΕΥ⟩ΒѠΚ ΕΠΕΥΤΟΠΟΣ ΧΙΝ Μ̄ΠΕΪΝΑΥ· ΕΤΒΕ ΠΑΪ
ϬΕ Α ΤΠΙΣΤΙΣ ΣΟΦΙΑ ΜΕ2ΕΙΑΤΣ̄ Ν̄ΝΕΣΧΑΧΕ· ΕΤΕ ΝΕ-
15 ΠΡΟΒΟΛΟΟΥΕ ΝΕ Μ̄ΠΑΥΘΑΔΗΣ 2Ν̄ 2ѠΒ ΝΙΜ ΕΝΤΑϤ-
ΠΡΟΦΗΤΕΥΕ Μ̄ΜΟΟΥ Ν̄ϬΙ ΔΑΥΕΙΑ 2Α ΤΠΙΣΤΙΣ ΣΟΦΙΑ·
ΕϤΧѠ Μ̄ΜΟΣ ΧΕ ΠΛΗΝ ΚΝΑΜΕ2ΕΙΑΤΚ̄ Μ̄ΜΟΟΥ· ΑΥѠ
ΚΝΑΝΑΥ ΕΠΤѠѠΒΕ Ν̄Ν̄ΡΕϤΡ̄ΝΟΒΕ· ΟΥΜΟΝΟΝ ΧΕ ΑΣΜΕ-
2ΕΙΑΤΣ̄ Μ̄ΜΟΟΥ· ⟨ΧΕ⟩ ΑΥ2Ε ΕΧΝ̄ ΝΕΥΕΡΗΥ 2Μ ΠΕΧΛΟΣ·
20 ΑΛΛΑ ΑΣΝΑΥ ΟΝ ΕΠΕΥΚΕΤΟΥΪΟ· ΠΑΪ ΕΝΤΑΥΤΟΟΒΕϤ ΡΛΕ b
ΝΑΥ· ΚΑΤΑ ΘΕ ΕΝΤΑ ΝΕΠΡΟΒΟΛΟΟΥΕ Μ̄ΠΑΥΘΑΔΗΣ
ΜΕΕΥΕ ΕϤΙ-ΠΟΥΟΪΝ Ν̄ΤΣΟΦΙΑ Ν̄2ΗΤΣ̄· ΑΚΤѠѠΒΕ ΝΑΥ·
ΑΥѠ ΑΚΤΟΥΪΟ ΝΑΥ· ΑΥѠ ΑΚϤΙ-ΤϬΟΜ Ν̄ΟΥΟΕΙΝ ΕΤ-

---

1 Schmidt : ΠΛΑΤΕ = ΠΛΑΤΕΙΝ (?); see 148.9.
13 MS ΒѠΚ.
18 supply ΧΕ before ΑΥ2Ε.

to approach her to ... [1] her. And the word which thy light-power spoke through David : '*Rather* thou wilt observe them with thine eyes and see the reward of sinners, for thou, O Lord, art my *hope*' * : that is [2], the Pistis Sophia observed with her eyes her enemies, namely the *emanations* of the Authades which had all fallen upon one another. *Not only* did she observe them in this with her eyes, *but* thou also, my Lord, the First *Mystery*, thou didst take away the light-power which was in the lion-faced power; and further thou didst take away the power of all the *emanations* of the Authades, and thou didst *restrain* them in that *Chaos*, ⟨that they should not go⟩ to their *place* from that hour. Now because of this, the Pistis Sophia observed with her eyes her enemies, namely the *emanations* of the Authades, in everything which David *prophesied* about the Pistis Sophia, saying : '*Rather* thou wilt observe them with thy eyes and see the reward of sinners' ▫. *Not only* did she observe them with her eyes, that they fell against one another in the *Chaos*, *but* she also saw their reward with which they were rewarded. *As* the *emanations* of the Authades thought to take away the light of the Sophia from her, thou didst reward them and repay them. And thou didst take away the light-power which is | in them, instead

---

*   Ps. 90.8, 9
▫   Ps. 90.8   ·

---

[1]   (1) unknown word; Schmidt: perhaps corruption of πελάζειν or πλάσσειν; perhaps form of πλήσσειν; (also 148.9).
[2]   (5) that is; lit. this is the word.

ⲛ̄ϩⲏⲧⲟⲩ· ⲉⲡⲙⲁ ⲛ̄ⲛⲟⲩⲟⲉⲓⲛ ⲛ̄ⲧⲥⲟⲫⲓⲁ ⲧⲁⲓ̈ ⲉⲛⲧⲁⲥⲡⲓⲥⲧⲉⲩⲉ ⲉⲡⲟⲩⲟⲓ̈ⲛ ⲙ̄ⲡϫⲓⲥⲉ: ⲁⲩⲱ ⲕⲁⲧⲁ ⲑⲉ ⲉⲛⲧⲁ ⲧⲉⲕϭⲟⲙ ⲛ̄ⲟⲩⲟⲉⲓⲛ ϫⲟⲟⲥ ϩⲓⲧⲛ̄ ⲇⲁⲩⲓ̈ⲇ· ϫⲉ ⲁⲕⲕⲁ-ⲡⲉⲧ-
ϫⲟⲥⲉ ⲛⲁⲕ ⲙ̄ⲙⲁ ⲙ̄ⲡⲱⲧ· ⲙ̄ⲛ ⲡⲉⲑⲟⲟⲩ ⲛⲁϣϩⲱⲛ ⲉⲣⲟⲕ·
5 ⲁⲩⲱ ⲙ̄ⲛ ⲙⲁⲥⲧⲓⲅⲝ̄ ⲛⲁϩⲱⲛ ⲉϩⲟⲩⲛ ⲉⲡⲉⲕⲙⲁ ⲛ̄ϣⲱⲡⲉ·
ⲉⲧⲉ ⲡⲁⲓ̈ ⲡⲉ ϫⲉ ⲛ̄ⲧⲉⲣⲉ ⲧⲡⲓⲥⲧⲓⲥ ⲥⲟⲫⲓⲁ ⲡⲓⲥⲧⲉⲩⲉ ⲉⲣⲁⲧϥ̄
ⲙ̄ⲡⲟⲩⲟⲉⲓⲛ· ⲁⲩⲱ ⲛ̄ⲧⲉⲣⲉⲥϩⲱϣ ⲁⲥϩⲩⲙⲛⲉⲩⲉ ⲉϩⲣⲁⲓ̈
ⲉⲣⲟϥ· ⲙ̄ⲡⲟⲩⲱϣⲣ̄-ⲗⲁⲁⲩ ⲙ̄ⲡⲉⲑⲟⲟⲩ ⲛⲁⲥ ⲛ̄ϭⲓ ⲛⲉⲡⲣⲟⲃⲟⲗⲟⲟⲩⲉ ⲙ̄ⲡⲁⲩⲑⲁⲇⲏⲥ** ⲟⲩⲇⲉ ⲙ̄ⲡⲟⲩⲉϣⲡⲗⲁⲧⲉ ⲙ̄ⲙⲟⲥ· ⟨ⲣⲁⲉ⟩
10 ⲁⲩⲱ ⲙ̄ⲡⲟⲩⲉϣϩⲱⲛ ⲉⲣⲟⲥ ⲉⲡⲧⲏⲣϥ̄· ⲁⲩⲱ ⲡϣⲁϫⲉ ⲛ̄ⲧⲁ
ⲧⲉⲕϭⲟⲙ ⲛ̄ⲟⲩⲟⲓ̈ⲛ ϫⲟⲟϥ ϩⲓⲧⲛ̄ ⲇⲁⲩⲉⲓⲇ· ϫⲉ ϥⲛⲁϩⲱⲛ
ⲉⲧⲟⲟⲧⲟⲩ ⲛ̄ⲛⲉϥⲁⲅⲅⲉⲗⲟⲥ ⲉⲧⲃⲏⲏⲧⲕ̄· ϫⲉ ⲉⲩⲉϩⲁⲣⲉϩ
ⲉⲣⲟⲕ ϩⲛ̄ ⲛⲉⲕϩⲓⲟⲟⲩⲉ ⲧⲏⲣⲟⲩ· ⲁⲩⲱ ⲛ̄ⲥⲉϥⲓⲧⲕ̄ ϩⲓϫⲛ̄
ⲛⲉⲩϭⲓϫ· ⲙⲏⲡⲟⲧⲉ ⲛ̄ⲅϫⲱⲣⲡ̄ ⲉⲩⲱⲛⲉ ϩⲛ̄ ⲧⲉⲕⲟⲩⲉⲣⲏⲧⲉ·
15 ⲛ̄ⲧⲟϥ ⲟⲛ ⲡⲉ ⲡϣⲁϫⲉ ϫⲉ ⲁⲕϩⲱⲛ ⲉⲧⲟⲟⲧϥ̄ ⲛ̄ⲅⲁⲃⲣⲓⲏⲗ·
ⲙ̄ⲛ ⲙⲓⲭⲁⲏⲗ· ⲉⲧⲣⲉⲩⲣ̄ϩⲙ̄ⲙⲉ ⲛ̄ⲧⲥⲟⲫⲓⲁ ϩⲛ̄ ⲛ̄ⲧⲟⲡⲟⲥ ⲧⲏⲣⲟⲩ ⲙ̄ⲡⲉⲭⲁⲟⲥ· ϣⲁⲛⲧⲟⲩⲛ̄ⲧⲥ ⲉϩⲣⲁⲓ̈ ⲛ̄ⲥⲉⲧⲱⲟⲩⲛ̄ ⲙ̄ⲙⲟⲥ
ϩⲛ̄ ⲛⲉⲩϭⲓϫ· ϫⲉ ⲛ̄ⲛⲉ ⲛⲉⲥⲟⲩⲉⲣⲏⲧⲉ ϫⲓ ⲉⲡⲕⲁⲕⲉ ⲙ̄ⲡⲉ-
ⲥⲏⲧ· ⲛ̄ⲥⲉⲁⲙⲁϩⲧⲉ ϩⲱⲟⲩ ⲙ̄ⲙⲟⲥ ⲛ̄ϭⲓ ⲛⲁⲡⲕⲁⲕⲉ ⲙ̄ⲡⲉ-
20 ⲥⲏⲧ: ⲁⲩⲱ ⲡϣⲁϫⲉ ⲉⲛⲧⲁ ⲧⲉⲕϭⲟⲙ ⲛ̄ⲟⲩⲟⲉⲓⲛ* ϫⲟⲟϥ ⟨ⲣⲁⲉ⟩
ϩⲓⲧⲛ̄ ⲇⲁⲩⲉⲓⲇ· ϫⲉ ⲕⲛⲁϩⲱⲙ ⲉϫⲛ̄ ⲟⲩϩⲟϥ ⲙ̄ⲛ ⲟⲩⲥⲓⲧ·
ⲁⲩⲱ ⲕⲛⲁϩⲱⲙ ⲉϫⲛ̄ ⲟⲩⲙⲟⲩⲓ̈ ⲙ̄ⲛ ⲟⲩⲇⲣⲁⲕⲱⲛ· ϫⲉ ⲁϥ-
ⲛⲁϩⲧⲉ ⲉⲣⲟⲓ̈ †ⲛⲁⲧⲟⲩϫⲟϥ· ⲁⲩⲱ †ⲛⲁⲣ̄ϩⲁⲓ̈ⲃⲉⲥ ⲉⲣⲟϥ
ϫⲉ ⲁϥⲥⲟⲩⲛ̄-ⲡⲁⲣⲁⲛ· ⲉⲧⲉ ⲡⲁⲓ̈ ⲡⲉ ⲡϣⲁϫⲉ ϫⲉ ⲛ̄ⲧⲉⲣⲉ
25 ⲧⲡⲓⲥⲧⲓⲥ ⲥⲟⲫⲓⲁ ⲉⲓ̈· ⲉⲥⲛⲏⲩ ⲉϩⲣⲁⲓ̈ ϩⲙ̄ ⲡⲉⲭⲁⲟⲥ· ⲁⲥϩⲱⲙ
ⲉϫⲛ̄ ⲛⲉⲡⲣⲟⲃⲟⲗⲟⲟⲩⲉ ⲙ̄ⲡⲁⲩⲑⲁⲇⲏⲥ· ⲁⲥϩⲱⲙ ⲉϫⲛ̄

9　see 147.1.

of the lights of the Sophia who *believed* in the light of the height. And *as* thy light-power said through David : 'Thou hast set the Most High as thy refuge. No evil will be able to approach thee, and no *scourge* will enter thy dwelling' * : that is, when the Pistis Sophia *believed* in the light and was oppressed, she *sang praises* to it, and the *emanations* of the Authades were not able to do any evil to her, *nor* were they able to ... [1] her, and they were not able to approach her at all. And the word which thy power said through David : 'He will command his *angels* concerning thee, that they guard thee in all thy ways; and they will bear thee upon their hands, *lest* thou strike a stone with thy foot' □ : that is furthermore the word : 'Thou didst command Gabriel and Michael that they should guide the Sophia in all the *places* of the *Chaos* until they bring her up, and that they should raise her upon their hands, lest her feet touch the darkness below and those of the darkness below seize her'. And the word which thy light-power spoke through David : 'Thou wilt tread upon the serpent and basilisk, and thou wilt trample upon the lion and *dragon*. Because he has trusted in me, I will save him and I will overshadow him because he has known my name' ° : that is the word : 'When the Pistis Sophia came to emerge from the *Chaos*, she trampled upon the *emanations* of the Authades. She trampled upon |

---

*   Ps. 90.9, 10
□   Ps. 90.11, 12
°   Ps. 90.13, 14

---

[1]   (9) see 147, n. 1.

ΝΕΤΟ Ν̄2Ο Ν̄2ΟΥ· ΑΥШ ΕΧ̄Ν ΝΕΤΟ Ν̄2Ο Ν̄ϹΙΤ Ν̄2ΟΥ·
ΕΡΕ ϹΑШϤΕ Ν̄ΑΠΕ Μ̄ΜΟΟΥ· ΑΥШ ΑϹ2Ш̄Μ ΕΧ̄Ν ϯϬΟΜ
Ν̄2Ο Μ̄ΜΟΥΪ Μ̄Ν ΤΗ ΕΤΟ Ν̄2Ο Ν̄ΑΡΑΚШΝ ΕΒΟΛ ΧΕ ΑϹ-
ΠΙϹΤΕΥΕ ΕΠΟΥΟΪΝ ΑϹΝΟΥ2Μ̄ ΕΒΟΛ 2ΙΤΟΟΤΟΥ ΤΗΡΟΥ·
5 ΠΑΪ ΠΕ ΠΑΧΟΕΙϹ ΠΒШΛ Ν̄ΝШΑΧΕ Ν̄ΤΑΚΧΟΟΥ·

3 ΑϹШΠΕ ϬΕ Ν̄ΤΕΡΕ ΠΙШ̄Ο̈ΡΠ̄ Μ̄ΜΥϹΤΗΡΙΟΝ ϹШΤΜ̄ ⲢⲀⲌ
ΕΝΕΪШΑΧΕ· ΠΕΧΑϤ ΧΕ ΕΥΓΕ ΪΑΚΚШΒΟϹ ΠΜΕΡΙΤ:
ΑϤΟΥШ2 ΔΕ ΟΝ ΕΤΟΟΤϤ̄ 2Μ̄ ΠШΑΧΕ Ν̄ϬΙ ΠΙШΟΡΠ̄ Μ̄-
ΜΥϹΤΗΡΙΟΝ ΠΕΧΑϤ Ν̄ΜΜΑΘΗΤΗϹ· ΧΕ ΑϹШΠΕ Ν̄ΤΕ-
10 ΡΙΝ̄-ΤΠΙϹΤΙϹ ϹΟΦΙΑ Ε2ΡΑΪ 2Μ̄ ΠΕΧΑΟϹ· ΑϹШШ ΟΝ ΕΒΟΛ
ΕϹΧШ Μ̄ΜΟϹ ΧΕ

1. ΑΪΝΟΥ2Μ̄ 2Μ̄ ΠΕΧΑΟϹ· ΑΥШ ΑΪΒШΛ ΕΒΟΛ 2Ν̄ Μ̄-
Μ̄ΡΡΕ Μ̄ΠΚΑΚΕ· ΑΪΕΙ' ΕΡΑΤ̄Κ ΠΟΥΟΕΙΝ·

2. ΧΕ ΑΚШΠΕ Ν̄ΟΥΟΕΙΝ 2Ι ϹΑ ΝΙΜ Μ̄ΜΟΪ ΕΚΝΟΥ2Μ̄
15 Μ̄ΜΟΪ ΑΥШ ΕΚϯ Ν̄ΤΟΟΤ·

3. ΑΥШ ΝΕΠΡΟΒΟΛΟΟΥΕ Μ̄ΠΑΥΘΑΔΗϹ ΝΑΪ ΕΥϯ
Ν̄ΟΥΗΪ· ΑΚΚШΛΥ Μ̄ΜΟΟΥ 2ΙΤΜ̄ ΠΕΚΟΥΟΕΙΝ· ΑΥШ Μ̄-
ΠΟΥΕШ2ШΝ Ε2ΟΥΝ ΕΡΟΪ· ΧΕ ΝΕΡΕ ΠΕΚΟΥΟΪΝ ШΟΟΠ
Ν̄ΜΜΑΪ ΠΕ· ΑΥШ ΕϤΝΟΥ2Μ̄ Μ̄ΜΟΪ 2Ν̄ ΤΕΚΑΠΟ2ΡΟΙΑ
20 Ν̄ΟΥΟΪΝ·

4. ΕΒΟΛ ΓΑΡ ΧΕ Α ΝΕΠΡΟΒΟΛΟΟΥΕ Μ̄ΠΑΥΘΑΔΗϹ ⲢⲀⲌ ᵇ
2ШΧ Μ̄ΜΟΪ· ΑΥϤΙ-ΤΑϬΟΜ Ν̄2ΗΤ· ΑΥΝΟΧ̄Τ ΕΒΟΛ 2Ν̄
ΝΕΧΑΟϹ ΕΜ̄Ν-ΟΥΟΕΙΝ Ν̄2ΗΤ· ΑΪΡϪΕ Ν̄ΟΥ2ΥΛΗ ΕϹ2ΟΡϢ̄
Ν̄ΝΑ2ΡΑΥ·

25 5. ΑΥШ ΜΝ̄ΝϹΑ ΝΑΪ ΑΥϬΟΜ Ν̄ΑΠΟ2ΡΟΙΑ ΕΙ' ΝΑΪ ΕΒΟΛ
2ΙΤΟΟΤ̄Κ ΕϹΝΟΥ2Μ̄ Μ̄ΜΟΪ· ΑϹΡ2ΟΥΟΪΝ 2Ι 2ΒΟΥΡ Μ̄ΜΟΪ·
ΑΥШ 2Ι ΟΥΝΑΜ Μ̄ΜΟΪ· ΑΥШ ΝΕϹΚШΤΕ ΕΡΟΪ ΠΕ· 2Ι

17　MS Ⲛ̄ΟΫΗⲒ̈; read ⲞⲨ̈ΗⲒ̈.

those with serpent-faces and upon those with basilisk-faces having seven heads. And she trampled upon the lion-faced power and that with a *dragon*-face, because she *believed* in the light she was saved from them all'. This, my Lord, is the interpretation of the words which thou hast spoken."

68. It happened when the First *Mystery* heard these words, he said : "*Excellent*, James, thou beloved one."

The First *Mystery* continued again, *however*, with the discourse. He said to the *disciples* : "It happened when I brought the Pistis Sophia forth from the *Chaos*, she cried out again saying :

1. 'I have been saved from the *Chaos* and released from the bonds of darkness. I have come to thee, O Light.

2. For thou hast been light on every side of me as thou didst save and help me.

3. And the *emanations* of the Authades, as they rose against me, thou didst *prevent* them through thy light. And they were not able to approach me, because thy light was with me, and saving me through thy *outpouring* of light.

4. *For* because the *emanations* of the Authades oppressed me, they took away my power from me, they cast me into the *Chaos(es)* there being no light in me. I became like *matter* which was heavy, before them.

5. And after these things an *outpouring* power came to me from thee, saving me; it gave light on my left and on my right, and it surrounded me on | every side of me, so that no *part* of me was without light.

299

ⲥⲁ ⲛⲓⲙ ⲙⲙⲟⲓ̈ ⲡⲉ · ϫⲉⲕⲁⲥ ⲛⲛⲉ ⲗⲁⲁⲩ ⲙⲙⲉⲣⲟⲥ ⲛⲧⲁⲓ̈
ϣⲱⲡⲉ ⲉϥⲟ ⲛ̄ⲁⲧⲟⲩⲟⲓ̈ⲛ ·

6. ⲁⲩⲱ ⲁⲕϩⲱⲃⲥ ⲉⲃⲟⲗ ⲉϫⲱⲓ̈ ⲙ̄ⲡⲟⲩⲟⲓ̈ⲛ ⲛ̄ⲧⲉⲕⲁⲡⲟ-
ϩⲣⲟⲓⲁ · ⲁⲩⲱ ⲁⲕⲥⲱⲧϥ̄ ⲉⲃⲟⲗ ⲛ̄ϩⲏⲧ ⲛ̄ⲛⲁϩⲩⲗⲏ ⲧⲏⲣⲟⲩ
5 ⲉⲑⲟⲟⲩ · ⲁⲩⲱ ⲁⲓ̈ⲣ̄-ⲥⲁⲧⲡⲉ ⲛ̄ⲛⲁϩⲩⲗⲏ ⲧⲏⲣⲟⲩ ⲉⲧⲃⲉ ⲡⲉⲕ-
ⲟⲩⲟⲓ̈ⲛ ·

7. ⲁⲩⲱ ⲧⲉⲕⲁⲡⲟϩⲣⲟⲓⲁ ⲛ̄ⲟⲩⲟⲉⲓⲛ · ⲛ̄ⲧⲟⲥ ⲧⲉ ⲛ̄ⲧⲁⲥ-
ϫⲓⲥⲉ ⲙ̄ⲙⲟⲓ̈ · ⲁⲩⲱ ⲁⲥϥⲓ ⲉⲃⲟⲗ ⲙ̄ⲙⲟⲓ̈ ⲛ̄ⲛⲉⲡⲣⲟⲃⲟⲗⲟⲟⲩⲉ
ⲙ̄ⲡⲁⲩⲑⲁⲇⲏⲥ ⲛⲁⲓ̈ ⲉϣⲁⲩ̈ⲑⲗⲓⲃⲉ ⲙ̄ⲙⲟⲓ̈ ·   ⲣ̄ⲙⲏ

10 8. ⲁⲩⲱ ⲁⲓ̈ϣⲱⲡⲉ ⲉⲓ̈ⲧⲏⲕ ⲛ̄ϩⲏⲧ ϩⲙ̄ ⲡⲉⲕⲟⲩⲟⲉⲓⲛ · ⲁⲩⲱ
⟨ⲉⲓ̈ⲟ⟩ ⲛ̄ⲟⲩⲟⲉⲓⲛ ⲉϥⲥⲟⲧϥ̄ ⲛ̄ⲧⲉ ⲧⲉⲕⲁⲡⲟϩⲣⲟⲓⲁ ·

9. ⲁⲩⲱ ⲁⲩⲟⲩⲉ ⲛ̄ⲥⲁⲃⲟⲗ ⲙ̄ⲙⲟⲓ̈ ⲛ̄ϭⲓ ⲛⲉⲡⲣⲟⲃⲟⲗⲟⲟⲩⲉ
ⲙ̄ⲡⲁⲩⲑⲁⲇⲏⲥ ⲛⲁⲓ̈ ⲉⲛⲉⲩϩⲱϫ ⲙ̄ⲙⲟⲉⲓ · ⲁⲩⲱ ⲁⲓ̈ⲣ̄ⲟⲩⲟⲉⲓⲛ
ϩⲛ̄ ⲧⲉⲕⲛⲟϭ ⲛ̄ϭⲟⲙ · ϫⲉ ⲛ̄ⲧⲟⲕ ϣⲁⲕⲛⲟⲩϩⲙ̄ ⲛ̄ⲟⲩⲟⲉⲓϣ
15 ⲛⲓⲙ ·

ⲧⲁⲓ̈ ⲧⲉ ⲧⲙⲉⲧⲁⲛⲟⲓⲁ ⲉⲛⲧⲁⲥϫⲟⲟⲥ ⲛ̄ϭⲓ ⲧⲡⲓⲥⲧⲓⲥ ⲥⲟⲫⲓⲁ ⲛ̄ⲧⲉⲣⲉⲥⲉⲓ̈ ⲉϩⲣⲁⲓ̈ ϩⲙ̄ ⲡⲉⲭⲁⲟⲥ · ⲁⲩⲱ ⲛ̄ⲧⲉⲣⲉ⟨ⲥ⟩ⲃⲱⲗ
ⲉⲃⲟⲗ ϩⲛ̄ ⲙ̄ⲙⲣ̄ⲣⲉ ⲙ̄ⲡⲉⲭⲁⲟⲥ · ⲧⲉⲛⲟⲩ ϭⲉ ⲡⲉⲧⲉ ⲟⲩⲛ̄-
ⲙⲁⲁϫⲉ ⲙ̄ⲙⲟϥ ⲉⲥⲱⲧⲙ̄ · ⲙⲁⲣⲉϥⲥⲱⲧⲙ̄ :

20 ⲁⲥϣⲱⲡⲉ ϭⲉ ⲛ̄ⲧⲉⲣⲉ ⲡⲓϣⲟⲣⲡ̄ ⲙ̄ⲙⲩⲥⲧⲏⲣⲓⲟⲛ ⲟⲩⲱ ⲉϥϫⲱ ⲛ̄ⲛⲉⲓ̈ϣⲁϫⲉ ⲉⲙⲙⲁⲑⲏⲧⲏⲥ · ⲁϥⲉⲓ̈ ⲉⲑⲏ ⲛ̄ϭⲓ ⲑⲱⲙⲁⲥ
ⲡⲉϫⲁϥ ϫⲉ ⲡⲁϫⲟⲉⲓⲥ · ⲟⲩⲛ̄-ⲙⲁⲁϫⲉ ⲙ̄ⲡⲁⲣⲙ̄ⲛⲟⲩⲟⲉⲓⲛ ·
ⲁⲩⲱ ⲁ ⲡⲁⲛⲟⲩⲥ ⲛⲟⲉⲓ ⲛ̄ⲛ̄ϣⲁϫⲉ ⲉⲛⲧⲁⲕϫⲟⲟⲩ · ⲧⲉ-   ⲣ̄ⲙⲏ ᵇ
ⲛⲟⲩ ϭⲉ ⲕⲉⲗⲉⲩⲉ ⲛⲁⲓ̈ ⲧⲁⲧⲁⲩⲉ-ⲡⲃⲱⲗ ⲛ̄ⲛ̄ϣⲁϫⲉ ⲫⲁ-
25 ⲛⲉⲣⲱⲥ · ⲁϥⲟⲩⲱϣ̄ⲃ ⲇⲉ ⲛ̄ϭⲓ ⲡⲓϣⲟⲣⲡ̄ ⲙ̄ⲙⲩⲥⲧⲏⲣⲓⲟⲛ ⲡⲉ-

---

1 omit ⲡⲉ.
11 supply ⲉⲓ̈ⲟ.
17 MS ⲛ̄ⲧⲉⲣⲉⲃⲱⲗ.

6. And thou hast clothed me with the light of thy *out-pouring*. And thou hast purified from me all my evil *materials*. And I have become raised over all my *materials* because of thy light.

7. And thy *outpouring* of light is that which has raised me, and it has taken away from me the *emanations* of the Authades, which *afflicted* me.

8. And in thy light I became courageous and a pure light of thy *outpouring*.

9. And the *emanations* of the Authades which oppressed me have gone far from me, and I have become lighted in thy great power, for thou dost save me at all times.'

This is the *repentance* which the Pistis Sophia said when she came out of the *Chaos* and was released from the bonds of the *Chaos*. Now at this time, he who has ears to hear, let him hear." *

69. Now it happened when the First *Mystery* finished saying these words to the *disciples*, Thomas came forward and said: "My Lord, my man of light has ears and my *mind* has *understood* the words which thou hast said. Now at this time *command* me that I give the interpretation of the words *clearly*."

But the First *Mystery* answered | and said to Thomas:

---

* Mk. 4.9

ⲬⲀϤ ⲚⲐⲰⲘⲀⲤ ϪⲈ ϮⲔⲈⲖⲈⲨⲈ ⲚⲀⲔ ⲈⲦⲢⲈⲔⲦⲀⲨⲈ-ⲠⲂⲰⲖ
ⲘⲠⲦⲨⲘⲚⲞⲤ · ⲠⲈⲚⲦⲀⲤⲨⲘⲚⲈⲨⲈ ⲘⲘⲞϤ �collⲀⲒ ⲞⲨⲚⲒ̈ ⲚϬⲒ
ⲦⲠⲒⲤⲦⲒⲤ ⲤⲞⲪⲒⲀ · ⲀϤⲞⲨⲰ ⲆⲈ ⲚϬⲒ ⲐⲰⲘⲀⲤ ⲠⲈϪⲀϤ
ϪⲈ ⲠⲀⲬⲞⲈⲒⲤ ⲈⲦⲂⲈ ⲪⲨⲘⲚⲞⲤ ⲈⲚⲦⲀⲤϪⲞⲞϤ ⲚϬⲒ ⲦⲠⲒⲤⲦⲒⲤ
5 ⲤⲞⲪⲒⲀ ϪⲈ ⲀⲤⲚⲞⲨϨⲘ ⲈⲂⲞⲖ ϨⲘ ⲠⲈⲬⲀⲞⲤ · Ⲁ ⲦⲈⲔϬⲞⲘ
ⲚⲞⲨⲞⲈⲒⲚ ⲠⲢⲞⲪⲎⲦⲈⲨⲈ ϨⲀⲢⲞϤ ⲘⲠⲒⲞⲨⲞⲈⲒⲰ · ϨⲒⲦⲚ ⲤⲞ-
ⲖⲞⲘⲰⲚ ⲠⲰϨⲢⲈ ⲚⲆⲀⲨⲈⲒⲆ · ϨⲚ ⲚⲈϤⲰⲆⲎ ϪⲈ

1. ⲀⲒ̈ⲚⲞⲨϨⲘ ⲈⲂⲞⲖ ϨⲚ ⲘⲘⲢⲢⲈ ⲀⲒ̈ⲠⲰⲦ ⲈⲢⲀⲦⲔ ⲠⲬⲞⲈⲒⲤ ·

2. ϪⲈ ⲀⲔⲰⲰⲠⲈ ⲚⲀⲒ̈ ⲚⲞⲨⲚⲀⲘ ·** ⲈⲔⲚⲞⲨϨⲘ ⲘⲘⲞⲒ̈ · ⲢⲖⲐ
10 [ⲀⲨⲰ ⲈⲔⲚⲞⲨϨⲘ ⲘⲘⲞⲒ̈] ⲀⲨⲰ ⲈⲔϮ ⲚⲦⲞⲞⲦ ·

3. ⲀⲔⲔⲰⲖⲨ ⲚⲚⲈⲦϮⲞⲨⲂⲎⲒ̈ · ⲀⲨⲰ ⲘⲠⲞⲨⲞⲨⲰⲚϨ ⲈⲂⲞⲖ ·
ϪⲈ ⲚⲈⲢⲈ ⲠⲈⲔϨⲞ ⲰⲞⲞⲠ ⲚⲘⲘⲀⲒ̈ ⲠⲈ ⲈϤⲚⲞⲨϨⲘ ⲘⲘⲞⲒ̈ ϨⲚ
ⲦⲈⲔⲬⲀⲢⲒⲤ ·

4. ⲀⲒ̈ϪⲒⲤⲰⲰ ⲘⲠⲈⲘⲦⲞ ⲈⲂⲞⲖ ⲚⲞⲨⲘⲎⲎⲰⲈ · ⲀⲨⲰ ⲀⲨ-
15 ⲚⲞϪⲦ ⲈⲂⲞⲖ · ⲀⲒ̈ⲢⲐⲈ ⲚⲞⲨⲦⲀϨⲦ ⲘⲠⲈⲨⲘⲦⲞ ⲈⲂⲞⲖ ·

5. ⲀⲤⲰⲰⲠⲈ ⲚⲀⲒ̈ ⲚϬⲒ ⲞⲨϬⲞⲘ ⲈⲂⲞⲖ ϨⲒⲦⲞⲞⲦⲔ · ⲈⲤϮ
ⲚⲦⲞⲞⲦ · ϪⲈ ⲀⲔⲔⲰ ⲚϨⲈⲚϨⲎⲂⲤ ⲚⲤⲀ ⲞⲨⲚⲀⲘ ⲘⲘⲞⲒ̈ ·
ⲀⲨⲰ ⲚⲤⲀ ϨⲂⲞⲨⲢ ⲘⲘⲞⲒ̈ ϪⲈⲔⲀⲤ ⲚⲚⲈ ⲖⲀⲀⲨ ⲚⲤⲀ ⲘⲘⲞⲒ̈
ⲰⲰⲠⲈ ⲈϤⲞ ⲚⲀⲦⲞⲨⲞⲈⲒⲚ ·

20 6. ⲀⲔⲤⲔⲈⲠⲀⲌⲈ ⲘⲘⲞⲒ̈ ϨⲀ ⲐⲀⲒ̈ⲂⲈⲤ ⲘⲠⲈⲔⲚⲀ' ⲀⲨⲰ ⲀⲒ̈Ⲣ-
ⲠⲈⲦⲠⲈ ⲚⲚⲈϢⲦⲎⲚ ⲚϢⲀⲀⲢ ·

7. ⲦⲈⲔⲞⲨⲚⲀⲘ ⲦⲈ ⲚⲦⲀⲤϪⲒⲤⲈ ⲘⲘⲞⲒ̈ ⲀⲨⲰ ⲀⲔϤⲒ-ⲠⲰϢ-
ⲚⲈ* ⲚⲤⲀⲂⲞⲖ ⲘⲘⲞⲒ̈ ·   ⲢⲖⲐ b

---

2 MS ⲠⲈⲚⲦⲀⲤⲨⲠⲞⲘⲚⲈⲨⲈ; ⲠⲞ erased. MS ϨⲢⲀⲒ̈ ⲚⲞⲨⲚⲒ̈; Ⲛ crossed out;
   read ⲈϨⲢⲀⲒ̈ ⲞⲨⲚⲒ̈.
10 ⲀⲨⲰ ⲈⲔⲚⲞⲨϨⲘ ⲘⲘⲞⲒ̈ : dittography.

"I *command* thee to give the interpretation of the *song of praise* in which the Pistis Sophia *sang praises* to me."

Thomas *however* answered and said: "My Lord, concerning the *song of praise* which the Pistis Sophia spoke because she was saved from the *Chaos*, thy light-power once *prophesied* about it through Solomon, the son of David, in his *Odes*, thus:

1. I have been saved from the bonds; I have fled to thee, O Lord.

2. For thou hast been a right hand to me; saving me [and saving me] and helping me.

3. Thou hast *prevented* those that rise against me; and they have not been revealed because thy face was with me, saving me with thy *grace*.

4. I was despised in the presence of a multitude; and they cast me forth; I became like lead in their presence.

5. There has been for me a power from thee, helping me; for thou hast placed lamps on my right side and on my left side, lest any side of me should be without light.

6. Thou hast *sheltered* me with the shadow of thy mercy, and I became raised above garments of skin.

7. It was thy right hand which raised me and thou hast taken away sickness from me. |

8. ⲀⲒϢⲰⲠⲈ ⲈⲒ6Ⲙ6ⲞⲘ ⲘⲚ ⲦⲈⲔⲘⲚ̄ⲦⲘⲈ ⲈⲒⲦⲂⲂⲎⲨ ⲘⲚ
ⲦⲈⲔⲆⲒⲔⲀⲒⲞⲤⲨⲚⲎ ·

9. ⲀⲨⲞⲨⲈ ⲈⲂⲞⲖ ⲘⲘⲞⲒ̈ ⲚⲆⲒ ⲚⲈⲦⲦⲞⲨⲂⲎⲒ̈ ⲀⲨⲰ ⲀⲒ-
ⲦⲘⲀⲒⲞ ⲘⲚ ⲦⲈⲔⲘⲚ̄ⲦⲬⲢⲎⲤⲦⲞⲤ · ϪⲈ ⲠⲈⲔⲘ̄ⲦⲞⲚ ϢⲞⲞⲠ
5 ϢⲀⲈⲚⲈ2 Ⲛ̄ⲦⲈ ⲠⲒⲈⲚⲈ2 ·

ⲠⲀⲒ̈ 6Ⲉ Ⲱ' ⲠⲀϪⲞⲈⲒⲤ ⲠⲈ ⲠⲂⲰⲖ Ⲛ̄ⲦⲘⲈⲦⲀⲚⲞⲒⲀ ⲈⲚⲦ-
ⲀⲤϪⲞⲞⲤ Ⲛ̄ⲆⲒ ⲦⲠⲒⲤⲦⲒⲤ ⲤⲞⲫⲒⲀ Ⲛ̄ⲦⲈⲢⲈⲤⲚⲞⲨ2Ⲙ 2Ⲙ ⲠⲈ-
ϪⲀⲞⲤ · ⲤⲰⲦⲘ̄ 6Ⲉ ⲦⲀϪⲞⲞⲨ 2Ⲛ ⲞⲨⲠⲀⲢ2ⲎⲤⲒⲀ · ⲠϢⲀϪⲈ
6Ⲉ ⲈⲚⲦⲀ ⲦⲈⲔ6ⲞⲘ Ⲛ̄ⲞⲨⲞⲈⲒⲚ ϪⲞⲞⲨ 2ⲒⲦ̄Ⲛ ⲤⲞⲖⲞⲘⲰⲚ ·
10 ϪⲈ ⲀⲒ̈ⲚⲞⲨ2Ⲙ ⲈⲂⲞⲖ 2Ⲛ Ⲙ̄ⲘⲢⲢⲈ ⲀⲒ̈ⲠⲰⲦ ⲈⲢⲀⲦⲔ ⲠϪⲞⲒⲤ
Ⲛ̄ⲦⲞϤ ⲠⲈ ⲠϢⲀϪⲈ ⲈⲚⲦⲀⲤϪⲞⲞϤ Ⲛ̄ⲆⲒ ⲦⲠⲒⲤⲦⲒⲤ ⲤⲞⲫⲒⲀ ·
ϪⲈ ⲀⲒ̈ⲂⲰⲖ ⲈⲂⲞⲖ 2Ⲛ Ⲙ̄ⲘⲢⲢⲈ Ⲙ̄ⲠⲔⲀⲔⲈ · ⲀⲒ̈ⲈⲒ' ⲈⲢⲀⲦⲔ
ⲠⲞⲨⲞⲒ̈Ⲛ** ⲀⲨⲰ ⲠϢⲀϪⲈ ⲈⲚⲦⲀⲤϪⲞⲞϤ Ⲛ̄ⲆⲒ ⲦⲈⲔ6ⲞⲘ ϪⲈ Ⲣ̄Ⲙ
ⲀⲔϢⲰⲠⲈ ⲚⲀⲒ̈ Ⲛ̄ⲞⲨⲚⲀⲘ ⲈⲔⲚⲞⲨ2Ⲙ Ⲙ̄ⲘⲞⲒ̈ · ⲀⲨⲰ ⲈⲔⲦ
15 Ⲛ̄ⲦⲞⲞⲦ · Ⲛ̄ⲦⲞϤ ⲞⲚ ⲠⲈ ⲠϢⲀϪⲈ ⲈⲚⲦⲀⲤϪⲞⲞϤ Ⲛ̄ⲆⲒ ⲦⲠⲒⲤ-
ⲦⲒⲤ ⲤⲞⲫⲒⲀ ϪⲈ ⲀⲔϢⲰⲠⲈ Ⲛ̄ⲞⲨⲞⲈⲒⲚ 2Ⲓ ⲤⲀ ⲚⲒⲘ Ⲙ̄ⲘⲞⲈⲒ ·
(ⲈⲔⲚⲞⲨ2Ⲙ Ⲙ̄ⲘⲞⲒ̈) ⲀⲨⲰ ⲈⲔⲦ Ⲛ̄ⲦⲞⲞⲦ · ⲀⲨⲰ ⲠϢⲀϪⲈ
ⲈⲚⲦⲀ ⲦⲈⲔ6ⲞⲘ Ⲛ̄ⲞⲨⲞⲈⲒⲚ ϪⲞⲞϤ ϪⲈ ⲀⲔⲔⲰⲖⲨ Ⲛ̄ⲚⲈⲦ-
ⲦⲞⲨⲂⲎⲒ̈ · ⲀⲨⲰ Ⲙ̄ⲠⲞⲨⲞⲨⲰⲚ2 ⲈⲂⲞⲖ · Ⲛ̄ⲦⲞϤ ⲠⲈ ⲠϢⲀϪⲈ
20 ⲈⲚⲦⲀⲤϪⲞⲞϤ Ⲛ̄ⲆⲒ ⲦⲠⲒⲤⲦⲒⲤ ⲤⲞⲫⲒⲀ ϪⲈ ⲀⲨⲰ ⲚⲈⲠⲢⲞⲂⲞ-
ⲖⲞⲞⲨⲈ Ⲙ̄ⲠⲀⲨⲐⲀⲆⲎⲤ ⲚⲀⲒ̈ ⲈⲦⲦⲞⲨⲂⲎⲒ̈ · ⲀⲔⲔⲰⲖⲨ Ⲙ̄ⲘⲞⲞⲨ
2ⲒⲦⲘ ⲠⲈⲔⲞⲨⲞⲈⲒⲚ · ⲀⲨⲰ Ⲙ̄ⲠⲞⲨⲈϢ2ⲰⲚ Ⲉ2ⲞⲨⲚ ⲈⲢⲞⲒ̈ ·
ⲀⲨⲰ ⲠϢⲀϪⲈ ⲈⲚⲦⲀ ⲦⲈⲔ6ⲞⲘ ϪⲞⲞϤ · ϪⲈ ⲚⲈⲢⲈ ⲠⲈⲔ2Ⲟ
ϢⲞⲞⲠ Ⲛ̄ⲘⲘⲀⲒ̈ ⲠⲈ ⲈϤⲚⲞⲨ2Ⲙ Ⲙ̄ⲘⲞⲒ̈ 2Ⲛ ⲦⲈⲔⲬⲀⲢⲒⲤ · Ⲛ̄ⲦⲞϤ

---

13 Ō in upper right-hand margin at end of quire.
17 supply ⲈⲔⲚⲞⲨ2Ⲙ̄ Ⲙ̄ⲘⲞⲒ̈.

8. I have become powerful in thy truth and purified in thy *righteousness*.

9. Those that rose against me have gone far from me; and I have been justified in thy *beneficence*, for thy rest exists for ever and ever'. *

Now, *O* my Lord, this is the interpretation of the *repentance* which the Pistis Sophia spoke when she was saved from the *Chaos*. Hear now and I will say it *openly*.

Now the word which thy light-power spoke through Solomon : 'I have been saved from my bonds; I have fled to thee, O Lord' : that is the word which the Pistis Sophia spoke : 'I have been released from the bonds of darkness; I have come to thee, O Light'. And the word which thy power spoke : 'Thou hast been a right hand to me; saving me and helping me' : that again is the word which the Pistis Sophia said : 'Thou hast been a light on every side of me ⟨saving me⟩ and helping me'. And the word which thy light-power spoke : 'Thou hast *prevented* those that rise against me and they have not been revealed' : that is the word which the Pistis Sophia said : 'And the *emanations* of the Authades, which rose against me, thou didst *prevent* them through thy light; and they were not able to approach me'. And the word which thy power spoke : 'For thy face was with me, saving me with thy *grace*' : that is | the word

---

* Ode Sol. 25.1-11

ΠΕ ΠϢΑϪΕ Ν̄ΤΑСϪΟΟϤ Ν̄ϬΙ ΤΠΙСΤΙС СΟΦΙΑ· ϪΕ ΝΕΡΕ ΡΜ ᵇ

ΠΕΚΟΥΟΕΙΝ ϢΟΟΠ Ν̄ΜΜΑΪ ΠΕ ΕϤΝΟΥⳘΜ̄ ΜΜΟΪ ⳘΝ ΤΕΚ-

ΑΠΟⳘΡΟΙΑ Ν̄ΟΥΟΪΝ· ΑΥⲰ ΠϢΑϪΕ ΕΝΤΑ ΤΕΚϬΟΜ

ϪΟΟϤ ϪΕ ΑΪСⲰϢ Μ̄ΠΕΜΤΟ ΕΒΟΛ Ν̄ΟΥΜΗΗϢΕ ΑΥⲰ

5 ΑΥΝΟϪΤ̄ ΕΒΟΛ· Ν̄ΤΟϤ ΠΕ ΠϢΑϪΕ ΕΝΤΑСϪΟΟϤ Ν̄ϬΙ

ΤΠΙСΤΙС СΟΦΙΑ· ϪΕ ΑΥⳘⲰϪ Μ̄ΜΟΪ Ν̄ϬΙ ΝΕΠΡΟΒΟ-

ΛΟΟΥΕ Μ̄ΠΑΥΘΑΔΗС· [ΑΥⲰ] ΑΥⲰ ΑΥϤΙ-ΤΑϬΟΜ Ν̄ⳘΗΤ·

ΑΥⲰ ΑΪСⲰϢϤ Ν̄ΝΑⳘΡΑΥ· ΑΥⲰ ΑΥΝΟϪΤ ΕΒΟΛ ⳘΜ ΠΕ-

ϪΛΟС ΕΜΝ̄-ΟΥΟΪΝ Ν̄ⳘΗΤ· ΑΥⲰ ΠϢΑϪΕ ΕΝΤΑ ΤΕΚϬΟΜ

10 ϪΟΟϤ ϪΕ ΑΪΡΘΕ Ν̄ΟΥΤΑⳘΤ̄ Μ̄ΠΕΥΜΤΟ ΕΒΟΛ· Ν̄ΤΟϤ

ΠΕ ΠϢΑϪΕ ΕΝΤΑСϪΟΟϤ Ν̄ϬΙ ΤΠΙСΤΙС СΟΦΙΑ· ϪΕ Ν̄-

ΤΕΡΟΥϤΙ-ΝΑΟΥΟΪΝ Ν̄ⳘΗΤ· ΑΪϢⲰΠΕ Ν̄ΘΕ Ν̄ΟΥⳘΥΛΗ

ΕСⳘΟΡⲰϢ Ν̄ΝΑⳘΡΑΥ·*** ΑΥⲰ ΠϢΑϪΕ ΟΝ ΕΝΤΑ ΤΕΚϬΟΜ ΡΜΑ

ϪΟΟϤ ϪΕ ΑΥⲰ ΑСϢⲰΠΕ ΝΑΪ Ν̄ϬΙ ΟΥϬΟΜ ΕΒΟΛ ⳘΙ-

15 ΤΟΟΤ̄Κ ΕСϯ Ν̄ΤΟΟΤ· Ν̄ΤΟϤ ΟΝ ΠΕ ΠϢΑϪΕ ΕΝΤΑС-

ϪΟΟϤ Ν̄ϬΙ ΤΠΙСΤΙС СΟΦΙΑ ϪΕ ΑΥⲰ Μ̄ΝΝ̄СΑ ΝΑΪ ΑΥ-

ϬΟΜ Ν̄ΟΥΟΕΙΝ ΕΙ' ΝΑΪ ΕΒΟΛ ⳘΙΤΟΟΤ̄Κ ΕСΝΟΥⳘΜ̄ Μ̄ΜΟΪ·

ΑΥⲰ ΠϢΑϪΕ ΕΝΤΑ ΤΕΚϬΟΜ ϪΟΟϤ ϪΕ ΑΚΚⲰ Ν̄ⳘΕΝ-

ⳘΗΒ̄С Ν̄СΑ ΟΥΝΑΜ Μ̄ΜΟΪ· ΑΥⲰ СΑ ⳘΒΟΥΡ Μ̄ΜΟΪ ϪΕ-

20 ΚΑС Ν̄ΝΕ ΛΑΑΥ Ν̄СΑ Μ̄ΜΟΪ ϢⲰΠΕ ΕϤΟ Ν̄ΑΤΟΥΟΕΙΝ·

Ν̄ΤΟϤ ΠΕ ΠϢΑϪΕ ΕΝΤΑСϪΟΟϤ Ν̄ϬΙ ΤΠΙСΤΙС СΟΦΙΑ·

ϪΕ Α ΤΕΚϬΟΜ Ρ̄ΟΥΟΕΙΝ ⳘΙ ΟΥΝΑΜ Μ̄ΜΟΪ· ΑΥⲰ ⳘΙ

ⳘΒΟΥΡ Μ̄ΜΟΪ· ΑΥⲰ ΕСΚⲰΤΕ ΕΡΟΪ ⳘΙ СΑ ΝΙΜ Μ̄ΜΟΪ·

ϪΕΚΑС Ν̄ΝΕ ΛΑΑΥ Ν̄СΑ Μ̄ΜΟΪ ϢⲰΠΕ ΕϤΟ Ν̄ΑΤΟΥΟΕΙΝ·

25 ΑΥⲰ ΠϢΑϪΕ ΕΝΤΑ ΤΕΚϬΟΜ ϪΟΟϤ ϪΕ ΑΚСΚΕΠΑⳘΕ

Μ̄ΜΟΪ ⳘΝ ΘΑΪΒΕС Μ̄ΠΕΚΝΑ' Ν̄ΤΟϤ ΟΝ ΠΕ ΠϢΑϪΕ ΕΝΤ- ΡΜΑ ᵇ

2　first M̄ in M̄ΜΟΪ inserted above.

7　ΑΥⲰ: dittography.

13　Ῑ in upper left-hand margin at beginning of quire.

which the Pistis Sophia said : 'Because thy light was with
me, saving me through thy *outpouring* of light'. And the
word which thy power spoke : 'I was despised in the presence
of a multitude and they cast me forth' : that is the word
which the Pistis Sophia said : 'For the *emanations* of the
Authades oppressed me [and] and they took away my power
from me; and I was despised before them and they cast
me into the *Chaos*, there being no light in me'. And the
word which thy power spoke : 'I became like lead in their
presence' : that is the word which the Pistis Sophia said :
'When they took away my lights from me I became like
matter which was heavy, before them'. And the word which
thy power spoke : 'There has been for me a power from
thee, helping me' : that is the word which the Pistis Sophia
said : 'And after these things a light-power came to me
from thee, saving me'. And the word which thy power spoke :
'Thou hast placed lamps on my right side and on my left
side, lest any side of me should be without light' : that is
the word which the Pistis Sophia said : 'Thy power gave
light on my right and on my left, and it surrounded me on
every side of me, so that no part of me was without light'.
And the word which thy power spoke : 'Thou hast *sheltered*
me in the shadow of thy mercy' : that is the word | which

ⲀⲤⲬⲞⲞϤ ⲚϬⲒ ⲦⲠⲒⲤⲦⲒⲤ ⲤⲞⲫⲒⲀ· ⲬⲈ ⲀⲨⲰ ⲀⲔϨⲰⲂⲤ ⲈⲂⲞⲖ
ⲈⲬⲰⲒ ⲘⲠⲞⲨⲞⲈⲒⲚ ⲚⲦⲈⲔⲀⲠⲞϨⲢⲞⲒⲀ· ⲀⲨⲰ ⲠϢⲀⲬⲈ ⲈⲚⲦⲀ
ⲦⲈⲔϬⲞⲘ ⲬⲞⲞϤ ⲬⲈ ⲀⲒⲢ-ⲤⲀⲦⲠⲈ ⲚⲚⲈϢⲦⲎⲚ ⲚϢⲀⲀⲢ·
ⲚⲦⲞϤ ⲞⲚ ⲠⲈ ⲠϢⲀⲬⲈ ⲈⲚⲦⲀⲤⲬⲞⲞϤ ⲚϬⲒ ⲦⲠⲒⲤⲦⲒⲤ ⲤⲞ-
5　ⲫⲒⲀ· ⲬⲈ ⲀⲨⲰ ⲀⲨⲤⲰⲦϤ ⲈⲂⲞⲖ ⲘⲘⲞⲒ ⲚⲚⲀϨⲨⲖⲎ ⲦⲎⲢⲞⲨ
ⲈⲐⲞⲞⲨ· ⲀⲨⲰ ⲀⲒⲬⲒⲤⲈ ⲈⲢⲞⲞⲨ ⲈⲂⲞⲖ ϨⲘ ⲠⲈⲔⲞⲨⲞⲈⲒⲚ·
ⲀⲨⲰ ⲠϢⲀⲬⲈ ⲈⲚⲦⲀ ⲦⲈⲔϬⲞⲘ ⲬⲞⲞϤ ϨⲒⲦⲚ ⲤⲞⲖⲞⲘⲰⲚ·
ⲬⲈ ⲦⲈⲔⲞⲨⲚⲀⲘ ⲦⲈ ⲚⲦⲀⲤⲬⲒⲤⲈ ⲘⲘⲞⲒ· ⲀⲨⲰ ⲀⲤϤⲒ-
ⲠϢⲰⲚⲈ ⲚⲤⲀⲂⲞⲖ ⲘⲘⲞⲒ· ⲚⲦⲞϤ ⲠⲈ ⲠϢⲀⲬⲈ ⲈⲚⲦⲀⲤ-
10　ⲬⲞⲞϤ ⲚϬⲒ ⲦⲠⲒⲤⲦⲒⲤ ⲤⲞⲫⲒⲀ· ⲬⲈ ⲀⲨⲰ ⲦⲈⲔⲀⲠⲞϨⲢⲞⲒⲀ
ⲚⲞⲨⲞⲈⲒⲚ· ⲚⲦⲞⲤ ⲦⲈ ⲚⲦⲀⲤⲬⲒⲤⲈ ⲘⲘⲞⲒ ϨⲘ ⲠⲈⲔⲞⲨⲞⲒⲚ·
ⲀⲨⲰ ⲀⲤϤⲒ ⲚⲤⲀⲂⲞⲖ ⲘⲘⲞⲒ ⲚⲚⲈⲠⲢⲞⲂⲞⲖⲞⲞⲨⲈ ⲘⲠⲀⲨⲐⲀ-　ⲢⲘⲂ
ⲀⲎⲤ ⲚⲀⲒ ⲈⲚⲈⲨⲐⲖⲒⲂⲈ ⲘⲘⲞⲒ : ⲀⲨⲰ ⲠϢⲀⲬⲈ ⲈⲚⲦⲀ ⲦⲈⲔ-
ϬⲞⲘ ⲬⲞⲞϤ ⲬⲈ ⲀⲒϢⲰⲠⲈ ⲈⲒϬⲘϬⲞⲘ ϨⲚ ⲦⲈⲔⲘⲈ ⲀⲨⲰ
15　ⲈⲒⲦⲂⲂⲎⲨ ϨⲚ ⲦⲈⲔⲀⲒⲔⲀⲒⲞⲤⲨⲚⲎ· ⲚⲦⲞϤ ⲠⲈ ⲠϢⲀⲬⲈ ⲈⲚⲦ-
ⲀⲤⲬⲞⲞϤ ⲚϬⲒ ⲦⲠⲒⲤⲦⲒⲤ ⲤⲞⲫⲒⲀ ⲬⲈ ⲀⲒϢⲰⲠⲈ ⲈⲒϬⲘϬⲞⲘ
ϨⲘ ⲠⲈⲔⲞⲨⲞⲈⲒⲚ· ⲀⲨⲰ ⲈⲒⲞ ⲚⲞⲨⲞⲈⲒⲚ ⲈϤⲤⲞⲦϤ ϨⲚ ⲦⲈⲔ-
ⲀⲠⲞϨⲢⲞⲒⲀ· ⲀⲨⲰ ⲠϢⲀⲬⲈ ⲈⲚⲦⲀ ⲦⲈⲔϬⲞⲘ ⲬⲞⲞϤ ⲬⲈ
ⲀⲨⲞⲨⲈ ⲈⲂⲞⲖ ⲘⲘⲞⲒ ⲚϬⲒ ⲚⲈⲦϤ†ⲞⲨⲂⲎⲒ· ⲚⲦⲞϤ ⲠⲈ ⲠϢⲀ-
20　ⲬⲈ ⲈⲚⲦⲀⲤⲬⲞⲞϤ ⲚϬⲒ ⲦⲠⲒⲤⲦⲒⲤ ⲤⲞⲫⲒⲀ· ⲬⲈ ⲀⲨⲞⲨⲈ
ⲈⲂⲞⲖ ⲘⲘⲞⲒ ⲚϬⲒ ⲚⲈⲠⲢⲞⲂⲞⲖⲞⲞⲨⲈ ⲘⲠⲀⲨⲐⲀⲀⲎⲤ ⲚⲀⲒ
ⲈⲚⲈⲨϨⲰⲬ ⲘⲘⲞⲒ· ⲀⲨⲰ ⲠϢⲀⲬⲈ ⲈⲚⲦⲀ ⲦⲈⲔϬⲞⲘ ⲚⲞⲨ-
ⲞⲈⲒⲚ ⲬⲞⲞϤ ϨⲒⲦⲚ ⲤⲞⲖⲞⲘⲰⲚ ⲬⲈ ⲀⲨⲰ ⲀⲒⲦⲘⲀⲒⲞ ϨⲚ ⲦⲈⲔ-
ⲘⲚⲦⲬⲢⲎⲤⲦⲞⲤ ⲬⲈ ⲠⲈⲔⲘⲦⲞⲚ ϢⲞⲞⲠ ϢⲀ ⲈⲚⲈϨ ⲚⲈⲚⲈϨ·　ⲢⲘⲂ ᵇ
25　ⲚⲦⲞϤ ⲠⲈ ⲠϢⲀⲬⲈ ⲈⲚⲦⲀⲤⲬⲞⲞϤ ⲚϬⲒ ⲦⲠⲒⲤⲦⲒⲤ ⲤⲞⲫⲒⲀ

5　MS ⲀⲨⲤⲰⲦϤ; Schmidt : read ⲀⲔⲤⲰⲦϤ.

the Pistis Sophia said : 'And thou hast clothed me with the light of thy *outpouring*'. And the word which thy power spoke : 'I became raised above garments of skin' : that is the word which the Pistis Sophia said : 'I have been purified [1] from all my evil *materials*, and I have become raised over them in thy light'. And the word which thy power spoke through Solomon : 'It was thy right hand which raised me and it took away sickness from me' : that is the word which the Pistis Sophia spoke : 'And thy *outpouring* of light is that which has raised me in thy light, and it has taken away from me the *emanations* of the Authades which *afflicted* me'. And the word which thy power spoke : 'I have become powerful in thy truth and purified in thy *righteousness*' : that is the word which the Pistis Sophia said : 'And in thy light I became powerful and a pure light in thy *outpouring*'. And the word which thy power spoke : 'Those that rose against me have gone far from me' : that is the word which the Pistis Sophia said : 'And the *emanations* of the Authades which oppressed me have gone far from me'. And the word which thy light-power spoke through Solomon : 'And I have been justified in thy *beneficence*, for thy rest exists for ever and ever' : that is the word which the Pistis Sophia said : |

---

[1]　(5) I have been purified; cf. 150, v. 6.

ⲭⲉ ⲁⲓ̈ⲛⲟⲩϩⲙ̄ ϩⲛ̄ ⲧⲉⲕⲙⲛ̄ⲧⲭⲣⲏⲥⲧⲟⲥ· ⲭⲉ ⲛ̄ⲧⲟⲕ ϣⲁⲕ-
ⲛⲟⲩϩⲙ̄ ⲛ̄ⲟⲩⲟⲛ ⲛⲓⲙ·

ⲡⲁⲓ̈ ϭⲉ ⲱ’ ⲡⲁⲭⲟⲉⲓⲥ ⲡⲉ ⲡⲃⲱⲗ ⲧⲏⲣϥ̄ ⲛ̄ⲧⲙⲉⲧⲁⲛⲟⲓⲁ
ⲉⲛⲧⲁⲥⲭⲟⲟⲥ ⲛ̄ϭⲓ ⲧⲡⲓⲥⲧⲓⲥ ⲥⲟⲫⲓⲁ ⲛ̄ⲧⲉⲣⲉⲥⲛⲟⲩϩⲙ̄ ϩⲙ̄
5 ⲡⲉⲭⲁⲟⲥ ⲁⲩⲱ ⲁⲥⲃⲱⲗ ⲉⲃⲟⲗ ϩⲛ̄ ⲙ̄ⲙⲣ̄ⲣⲉ ⲙ̄ⲡⲕⲁⲕⲉ·

ⲁⲥϣⲱⲡⲉ ϭⲉ ⲛ̄ⲧⲉⲣⲉ ⲡϣⲟⲣⲡ̄ ⲙ̄ⲙⲩⲥⲧⲏⲣⲓⲟⲛ ⲥⲱⲧⲙ̄
ⲉⲑⲱⲙⲁⲥ ⲉϥϫⲱ ⲛ̄ⲛⲉⲓ̈ϣⲁϫⲉ· ⲡⲉⲭⲁϥ ⲛⲁϥ ⲭⲉ ⲉⲩⲅⲉ
ⲕⲁⲗⲱⲥ ⲑⲱⲙⲁⲥ ⲡⲙⲁⲕⲁⲣⲓⲟⲥ· ⲡⲁⲓ̈ ⟨ⲡⲉ⟩ ⲡⲃⲱⲗ ⲙ̄ⲫⲩⲙⲛⲟⲥ
ⲉⲛⲧⲁⲥⲭⲟⲟϥ ⲛ̄ϭⲓ ⲧⲡⲓⲥⲧⲓⲥ ⲥⲟⲫⲓⲁ· ⲁϥⲟⲩⲱϩ ⲇⲉ ⲟⲛ
10 ⲉⲧⲟⲟⲧϥ̄ ⲛ̄ϭⲓ ⲡϣⲟⲣⲡ̄ ⲙ̄ⲙⲩⲥⲧⲏⲣⲓⲟⲛ ⲡⲉⲭⲁϥ ⲛ̄ⲙⲙⲁⲑⲏ-
ⲧⲏⲥ· ⲭⲉ ⲁⲥⲟⲩⲱϩ ⲇⲉ ⲟⲛ ⲉⲧⲟⲟⲧⲥ̄ ⲛ̄ϭⲓ ⲧⲡⲓⲥⲧⲓⲥ ⲥⲟ- ⲣⲙ̄ⲅ̄
ⲫⲓⲁ· ⲁⲥϩⲩⲙⲛⲉⲩⲉ ⲉϩⲣⲁⲓ̈ ⲉⲣⲟⲓ̈ ⲉⲥϫⲱ ⲙ̄ⲙⲟⲥ· ⲭⲉ

1. ϯϩⲩⲙⲛⲉⲩⲉ ⲉϩⲣⲁⲓ̈ ⲉⲣⲟⲕ ⲡⲁⲓ̈ ⲉⲃⲟⲗ ϩⲓⲧⲙ̄ ⲡⲉⲕⲧⲱϣ
ⲁⲕⲛ̄ⲧ ⲉⲃⲟⲗ ϩⲓⲧⲙ̄ ⲡⲁⲓⲱⲛ ⲉⲧϫⲟⲥⲉ ⲉⲧⲙ̄ⲡⲥⲁ ⲛ̄ⲧⲡⲉ· ⲁⲩⲱ
15 ⲁⲕⲛ̄ⲧ ⲉϩⲣⲁⲓ̈ ⲉⲛⲧⲟⲡⲟⲥ ⲉⲧⲙ̄ⲡⲉⲥⲏⲧ·

2. ⲁⲩⲱ ⲟⲛ ϩⲓⲧⲙ̄ ⲡⲉⲕⲧⲱϣ ⲁⲕⲛⲁϩⲙⲉⲧ ⲉⲃⲟⲗ ϩⲉⲛ
ⲛ̄ⲧⲟⲡⲟⲥ ⲉⲧⲙ̄ⲡⲉⲥⲏⲧ· ⲁⲩⲱ ⲉⲃⲟⲗ ϩⲓⲧⲟⲟⲧⲕ̄ ⲁⲕϥⲓ-ⲟⲩ-
ⲗⲏ ⲙ̄ⲙⲁⲩ ⲉⲧϣⲟⲟⲡ ϩⲛ̄ ⲛⲁϭⲟⲙ ⲛ̄ⲟⲩⲟⲓ̈ⲛ ⲁⲩⲱ ⲁⲓ̈ⲛⲁⲩ
ⲉⲣⲟⲥ·

20 3. ⲁⲩⲱ ⲛ̄ⲧⲟⲕ ⲡⲉⲧⲭⲱⲱⲣⲉ ⲥⲁⲃⲟⲗ ⲙ̄ⲙⲟⲓ̈ ⲛ̄ⲛⲉⲡⲣⲟⲃⲟ-
ⲗⲟⲟⲩⲉ ⲙ̄ⲡⲁⲩⲑⲁⲇⲏⲥ ⲛⲁⲓ̈ ⲉⲛⲉⲩϩⲱϫ ⲙ̄ⲙⲟⲓ̈· ⲁⲩⲱ ⲉⲩⲟ
ⲛ̄ⲭⲁϫⲉ ⲉⲣⲟⲓ̈· ⲁⲩⲱ ⲁⲕϯ ⲛⲁⲓ̈ ⲛ̄ⲧⲉϩⲟⲩⲥⲓⲁ ⲉⲧⲣⲁⲃⲱⲗ
ⲉⲃⲟⲗ ⲛ̄ⲙⲙⲣ̄ⲣⲉ ⲛ̄ⲛⲉⲡⲣⲟⲃⲟⲗⲟⲟⲩⲉ ⲙ̄ⲡⲁⲇⲁⲙⲁⲥ· ⲣⲙ̄ⲅ̄ b

---

2 in the ode ⲛ̄ⲟⲩⲟⲓ̈ϣ ⲛⲓⲙ; see 150.14, 15.
8 MS ⲡⲁⲓ̈ ⲡⲃⲱⲗ.
14 MS ϩⲓⲧⲙ̄; read ϩⲙ̄.
17 MS originally ⲉⲛ̄ⲧⲟⲡⲟⲥ; emended to ϩⲉⲛ ⲛ̄ⲧⲟⲡⲟⲥ; read ϩⲛ̄ ⲛ̄ⲧⲟⲡⲟⲥ.
20 MS ⲡⲉⲧⲭⲱⲱⲣⲉ; read ⲡⲉⲛⲧⲁⲕⲭⲱⲱⲣⲉ.

'I have been saved in thy *beneficence*, for thou dost save everyone'.[1]

Now *O* my Lord, this is the whole interpretation of the *repentance* which the Pistis Sophia spoke when she was saved from the *Chaos*, and she was released from the bonds of the darkness."

70. Now it happened when the First *Mystery* heard Thomas saying these words, he said to him: "*Excellent, well done* Thomas, thou *blessed one*. This is the interpretation of the *song of praise* which the Pistis Sophia spoke."

The First *Mystery*, however, continued again. He said to the *disciples*: "*But* the Pistis Sophia continued again, she *sang praises* to me, saying:

1. 'I *sing praise* to thee; through thy ordinance thou didst bring me forth from the *aeon* on high, which is above, and thou didst bring me to the *places* below.

2. And again through thy ordinance thou didst save me from the *places* below; and through thyself thou hast there taken the *matter* which is in my light-power, and I saw it.

3. And thou hast dispelled from me the *emanations* of the Authades which oppressed me, and they were hostile to me; and thou didst give to me the *authority* that I should be released from the bonds[2] of the *emanations* of the Adamas. |

---

[1] (2) save everyone; in the ode : save me at all times; (see 150.14, 15).
[2] (22) that I should be released from the bonds; Till: that I should release the bonds.

4. ⲀⲨⲰ ⲀⲔⲠⲀⲦⲀⲤⲤⲈ ⲘⲪⲞϤ ⲚⲤⲒⲦ · ⲠⲀ†ⲤⲀϢϤⲈ ⲚⲀⲠⲈ ·
ⲀⲔⲚⲞⲬ̄Ϥ ⲈⲂⲞⲗ Ⲍ̄Ⲛ ⲚⲀϬⲒⲬ · ⲀⲨⲰ ⲀⲔⲦⲀⲌⲞⲒ̈ ⲈⲢⲀⲦ ⲈⲬ̄Ⲛ
ⲦⲈϤⲌⲨⲗⲎ · ⲀⲔⲦⲀⲔⲞⲤ ⲬⲈⲔⲀⲤ ⲈⲚⲚⲈ ⲠⲈϤⲤⲠⲈⲢⲘⲀ ⲦⲰ-
ⲞⲨⲚ̄ ⲬⲒⲚ Ⲙ̄ⲠⲈⲒ̈ⲚⲀⲨ ·

5   5. ⲀⲨⲰ Ⲛ̄ⲦⲞⲔ ⲠⲈⲦⲈ ⲚⲈⲔϢⲞⲞⲠ Ⲛ̄ⲘⲘⲀⲒ̈ ⲈⲔ†ϬⲞⲘ ⲚⲀⲒ̈
Ⲍ̄Ⲛ ⲚⲀⲒ̈ ⲦⲎⲢⲞⲨ · ⲀⲨⲰ Ⲁ ⲠⲈⲔⲞⲨⲞⲈⲒⲚ ⲔⲰⲦⲈ ⲈⲢⲞⲒ̈ Ⲍ̄Ⲛ
ⲦⲞⲠⲞⲤ ⲚⲒⲘ [ⲦⲎⲢⲞⲨ] ⲀⲨⲰ ⲈⲂⲞⲗ ⲌⲒⲦⲞⲞⲦ̄Ⲕ ⲀⲔⲢ̄-ⲚⲈⲠⲢⲞ-
ⲂⲞⲗⲞⲞⲨⲈ ⲦⲎⲢⲞⲨ Ⲙ̄ⲠⲀⲨⲐⲀⲆⲎⲤ Ⲛ̄ⲀⲦϬⲞⲘ .

6. ⲬⲈ ⲀⲔϤⲒ-ⲦϬⲞⲘ Ⲙ̄ⲠⲈⲨⲞⲨⲞⲒ̈Ⲛ ⲌⲢⲀⲒ̈ Ⲛ̄ⲌⲎⲦⲞⲨ · ⲀⲨⲰ
10 ⲀⲔⲤⲞⲞⲨⲦ̄Ⲛ Ⲛ̄ⲦⲀⲌⲒⲎ ⲈⲚⲦ̄ ⲈⲂⲞⲗ Ⲍ̄Ⲙ ⲠⲈⲬⲀⲞⲤ ·

7. ⲀⲨⲰ ⲀⲔⲠⲞⲞⲚⲈⲦ ⲈⲂⲞⲗ Ⲍ̄Ⲛ ⲚⲒⲔⲀⲔⲈ Ⲛ̄ⲌⲨⲗⲒⲔⲞⲚ ·
ⲀⲨⲰ ⲀⲔϤⲒ-ⲚⲀϬⲞⲘ ⲦⲎⲢⲞⲨ Ⲛ̄ⲦⲞⲞⲦⲞⲨ · ⁑ⲚⲀⲒ̈ ⲈⲚⲦⲀⲨϤⲒ- ͞ⲢⲘⲆ
ⲠⲈⲨⲞⲨⲞⲈⲒⲚ ·

8. ⲀⲔⲚⲞⲨⲬⲈ ⲈⲌⲞⲨⲚ ⲈⲢⲞⲞⲨ Ⲛ̄ⲞⲨⲞⲨⲞⲈⲒⲚ ⲈϤⲤⲞⲦ̄Ϥ ·
15 ⲀⲨⲰ ⲚⲀⲘⲈⲗⲞⲤ ⲦⲎⲢⲞⲨ ⲚⲀⲒ̈ ⲈⲦⲈ Ⲙ̄Ⲛ-ⲞⲨⲞⲈⲒⲚ Ⲛ̄ⲌⲎⲦⲞⲨ ·
ⲀⲔ† ⲚⲀⲨ Ⲛ̄ⲞⲨⲞⲨⲞⲈⲒⲚ ⲈϤⲤⲞⲦ̄Ϥ · ⲈⲂⲞⲗ Ⲍ̄Ⲙ ⲠⲞⲨⲞⲈⲒⲚ
Ⲙ̄ⲠⲬⲒⲤⲈ ·

9. ⲀⲨⲰ ⲀⲔⲤⲞⲨⲦ̄Ⲛ-ⲦⲈⲌⲒⲎ ⲚⲀⲨ · ⲀⲨⲰ ⲠⲞⲨⲞⲈⲒⲚ Ⲙ̄-
ⲠⲈⲔⲌⲞ · ⲀϤϢⲰⲠⲈ ⲚⲀⲒ̈ Ⲛ̄ⲞⲨⲰⲚⲌ Ⲛ̄ⲀⲦⲦⲀⲔⲞ ·

20   10. ⲀⲔⲚ̄Ⲧ ⲈⲌⲢⲀⲒ̈ Ⲙ̄ⲠⲈⲦⲠⲈ Ⲙ̄ⲠⲈⲬⲀⲞⲤ · ⲠⲦⲞⲠⲞⲤ Ⲙ̄ⲠⲈ-
ⲬⲀⲞⲤ Ⲙ̄Ⲛ ⲠⲦⲀⲔⲞ ⲬⲈⲔⲀⲤ ⲈⲨⲈⲂⲰⲗ ⲈⲂⲞⲗ Ⲛ̄ϬⲒ Ⲛ̄ⲌⲨⲗⲎ
ⲦⲎⲢⲞⲨ ⲈⲦⲚ̄ⲌⲎⲦ̄Ϥ ⲚⲀⲒ̈ ⲈⲦϢⲞⲞⲠ Ⲍ̄Ⲙ ⲠⲦⲞⲠⲞⲤ ⲈⲦⲘ̄ⲘⲀⲨ ·
ⲀⲨⲰ Ⲛ̄ⲤⲈⲢ̄Ⲃ̄Ⲣ̄ⲢⲈ Ⲛ̄ϬⲒ ⲚⲀϬⲞⲘ ⲦⲎⲢⲞⲨ Ⲍ̄Ⲙ ⲠⲈⲔⲞⲨⲞⲈⲒⲚ ·
ⲀⲨⲰ Ⲛ̄ⲦⲈ ⲠⲈⲔⲞⲨⲞⲈⲒⲚ ϢⲰⲠⲈ Ⲛ̄ⲌⲎⲦⲞⲨ ⲦⲎⲢⲞⲨ ·

25   11. ⲀⲔⲔⲀ-ⲠⲞⲨⲞⲈⲒⲚ Ⲛ̄ⲦⲈⲔⲀⲠⲞⲌⲢⲞⲒⲀ Ⲛ̄ⲌⲎⲦ · ⲀⲒ̈ϢⲰⲠⲈ
Ⲛ̄ⲞⲨⲞⲈⲒⲚ ⲈϤⲤⲞⲦ̄Ϥ ·

---

3 MS ⲀⲔⲦⲀⲔⲞⲤ ; read ⲀⲔⲦⲀⲔⲞϤ.
7 omit ⲦⲎⲢⲞⲨ after ⲚⲒⲘ.

4. And thou hast *smitten* the basilisk with seven heads, thou hast cast it out with my hands; and thou hast set me up over its *matter*. Thou hast destroyed it, lest its *seed* rise up from this hour.

5. And thou wast with me giving power to me in all these things; and thy light surrounded me in all *places*, and through thyself thou hast made all the *emanations* of the Authades powerless.

6. For thou hast taken away from them the power of their light; and thou hast made straight my way to bring me forth from the *Chaos*.

7. And thou hast removed me out of the *material* darkness(es) and thou hast taken away from them all my powers, the light of which had been taken.

8. Thou hast cast into them (my powers) pure light; and to all my *members*, in which there was no light, thou hast given pure light out of the light of the height.

9. And thou hast made straight the way for them (my members); and the light of thy face has become for me imperishable life.

10. Thou hast brought me above the *Chaos*, the *place* of the *Chaos* and the destruction, so that all the *materials* within it which are in that *place* should be released, so that all my powers should be renewed in thy light and that thy light should be within them all.

11. Thou hast placed the light of thy *outpouring* in me. I have become purified light'. |

ᐧⲠⲀⲒ ⲞⲚ ⲠⲈ ⲠⲘⲈⲨ̅ⲤⲚⲀⲨ Ⲛ̅ⲌⲨⲘⲚⲞⲤ ⲈⲚⲦⲀⲤⲬⲞⲞϤ Ⲛ̅ϬⲒ ⲢⲘⲀ̅ ᵇ

ⲦⲠⲒⲤⲦⲒⲤ ⲤⲞⲪⲒⲀ· ⲠⲈⲦⲚⲞⲈⲒ ϬⲈ Ⲛ̅ⲦⲈⲒ̈ⲘⲈⲦⲀⲚⲞⲒⲀ ⲘⲀⲢⲈϤⲈⲒᐧ

ⲈⲐⲎ Ⲛ̅ϤⲬⲞⲞϤ· ⲀⲤϢⲰⲠⲈ ϬⲈ Ⲛ̅ⲦⲈⲢⲈ ⲠⲒϢⲞⲢⲠ̅ Ⲙ̅ⲘⲨⲤⲦⲎ-

ⲢⲒⲞⲚ ⲞⲨⲰ ⲈϤⲬⲰ Ⲛ̅ⲚⲈⲒ̈ϢⲀⲬⲈ ⲀϤⲈⲒᐧ ⲈⲐⲎ Ⲛ̅ϬⲒ ⲘⲀⲐⲀⲒⲞⲤ

5 ⲠⲈⲬⲀϤ ⲬⲈ ⲀⲒ̈ⲚⲞⲒ Ⲙ̅ⲠⲂⲰⲖ Ⲙ̅ⲠⲌⲨⲘⲚⲞⲤ ⲠⲀⲒ̈ ⲈⲚⲦⲀⲤⲬⲞⲞϤ

Ⲛ̅ϬⲒ ⲦⲠⲒⲤⲦⲒⲤ ⲤⲞⲪⲒⲀ· ⲦⲈⲚⲞⲨ ϬⲈ ⲔⲈⲖⲈⲨⲈ ⲚⲀⲒ̈ ⲦⲀⲬⲞⲞϤ

Ⲥ̅Ⲛ ⲞⲨⲠⲀⲢⲢⲎⲤⲒⲀ· ⲀϤⲞⲨⲰϢ̅Ⲃ ⲆⲈ Ⲛ̅ϬⲒ ⲠⲒϢⲞⲢⲠ̅ Ⲙ̅ⲘⲨⲤⲦⲎ-

ⲢⲒⲞⲚ ⲠⲈⲬⲀϤ ⲬⲈ ϮⲔⲈⲖⲈⲨⲈ ⲚⲀⲔ ⲘⲀⲐⲀⲒⲞⲤ ⲈⲦⲢⲈⲔⲦⲀⲨⲈ-

ⲠⲂⲰⲖ Ⲙ̅ⲠⲌⲨⲘⲚⲞⲤ ⲈⲚⲦⲀⲤⲬⲞⲞϤ Ⲛ̅ϬⲒ ⲦⲠⲒⲤⲦⲒⲤ ⲤⲞⲪⲒⲀ·

10 ⲀϤⲞⲨⲰϢ̅Ⲃ ⲆⲈ Ⲛ̅ϬⲒ ⲘⲀⲐⲀⲒⲞⲤ ⲠⲈⲬⲀϤ ⲬⲈ ⲈⲦⲂⲈ ⲠⲂⲰⲖ

Ⲙ̅ⲪⲨⲘⲚⲞⲤ ⲈⲚⲦⲀⲤⲬⲞⲞϤ Ⲛ̅ϬⲒ ⲦⲠⲒⲤⲦⲒⲤ ⲤⲞⲪⲒⲀ· Ⲁ ⲦⲈⲔ-

ϬⲞⲘ Ⲛ̅ⲞⲨⲞⲈⲒⲚ** ⲠⲢⲞⲪⲎⲦⲈⲨⲈ Ⲥ̅ⲀⲢⲞϤ Ⲙ̅ⲠⲒⲞⲨⲞⲈⲒϢ ϨⲒⲦⲚ̅ ⲢⲘⲈ

ⲦⲰⲆⲎ Ⲛ̅ⲤⲞⲖⲞⲘⲰⲚ ⲬⲈ

1. ⲠⲈⲚⲦⲀϤⲚⲦ ⲈⲠⲈⲤⲎⲦ ⲈⲂⲞⲖ Ⲥ̅Ⲛ Ⲙ̅ⲘⲀ ⲈⲦⲬⲞⲤⲈ ⟨Ⲉ⟩Ⲧ-

15 ⲤⲀⲦⲠⲈ· ⲀⲨⲰ ⲀϤⲚⲦ̅ ⲈϨⲢⲀⲒ̈ Ⲥ̅Ⲛ Ⲙ̅ⲘⲀ ⲈⲦⲘ̅ⲠϬⲞⲚ Ⲙ̅ⲠⲈⲤⲎⲦ·

2. ⲠⲈⲚⲦⲀϤϤⲒ Ⲙ̅ⲘⲀⲨ Ⲛ̅ⲚⲈⲦⲤ̅Ⲛ ⲦⲘⲎⲦⲈ· ⲀⲨⲰ ⲀϤⲦⲤⲀⲂⲞⲞⲨ

ⲈⲢⲞⲞⲨ·

3. ⲠⲈⲚⲦⲀϤⲬⲰⲰⲢⲈ ⲈⲂⲞⲖ Ⲛ̅ⲚⲀⲬⲀⲬⲈ Ⲙ̅Ⲛ ⲚⲀⲀⲚⲦⲒ-

ⲆⲒⲔⲞⲤ· ⲠⲈⲚⲦⲀϤϮ ⲚⲀⲒ̈ Ⲛ̅ⲞⲨⲈⲌⲞⲨⲤⲒⲀ ⲈϨⲢⲀⲒ̈ ⲈⲬⲚ̅ ϨⲈⲚ-

20 Ⲙ̅ⲢⲢⲈ ⲈⲂⲞⲖⲞⲨ ⲈⲂⲞⲖ·

4. ⲠⲈⲚⲦⲀϤⲠⲀⲦⲀⲤⲤⲈ Ⲙ̅ⲪⲞϤ ⲈⲦⲞ Ⲛ̅ⲤⲀϢϤⲈ Ⲛ̅ⲀⲠⲈ Ⲥ̅Ⲛ

ⲚⲀϬⲒⲬ· ⲀϤⲦⲀϨⲞⲒ̈ ⲈⲢⲀⲦ ϨⲒⲬⲚ̅ ⲦⲈϤⲚⲞⲨⲚⲈ ⲬⲈⲔⲀⲤ ⲈⲒ̈Ⲉ-

ϤⲰⲦⲈ ⲈⲂⲞⲖ Ⲙ̅ⲠⲈϤⲤⲠⲈⲢⲘⲀ·

5. ⲀⲨⲰ Ⲛ̅ⲦⲞⲔ ⲚⲈⲔⲚ̅ⲘⲘⲀⲒ̈ ⲠⲈ ⲈⲔϮ Ⲛ̅ⲦⲞⲞⲦ· ϨⲢⲀⲒ̈ Ⲥ̅Ⲙ

25 ⲘⲀ ⲚⲒⲘ· ⲀϤⲔⲰⲦⲈ ⲈⲢⲞⲒ̈ Ⲛ̅ϬⲒ ⲠⲈⲔⲢⲀⲚ·

---

8 MS originally ⲈⲦⲢⲈⲔⲬⲰ Ⲙ̅; ⲬⲰ Ⲙ̅ crossed out, ⲦⲀⲨⲈ inserted.

14 ⲈⲂⲞⲖ in margin. MS ⲈⲦⲬⲞⲤⲈ ⲦⲤⲀⲦⲠⲈ.

This again is the second *song of praise* which the Pistis Sophia spoke. Now let him who *understands* this *repentance* come forth and say it."

71. Now it happened when the First *Mystery* finished saying these words, Matthew came forward and said : "I have *understood* the interpretation of the *song of praise* which the Pistis Sophia spoke. Now at this time *command* me that I say it *openly*.

The First *Mystery*, however, answered and said : "I *command* thee, Matthew, to give the interpretation of the *song of praise* which the Pistis Sophia spoke."

Matthew, *however*, answered and said : "Concerning the interpretation of the *song of praise* which the Pistis Sophia spoke, thy light-power once *prophesied* about it through the *Ode* of Solomon, thus :

1. 'He who brought me down from the high places which are above has brought me up from the places in the depth below.

2. He who there has taken those that are in the midst has taught me [1] of them.

3. He who has dispelled my enemies and my *adversaries* has given me *authority* over bonds, to release them.

4. He who has *smitten* the serpent with seven heads with my hands has set me up over its root, so that I might wipe out its *seed*.

5. And thou wast with me, helping me. In all places thy name surrounded me. |

---

[1] (16) taught me; MS : taught them.

6. ⲁ ⲧⲉⲕⲟⲩⲛⲁⲙ ⲧⲁⲕⲉ-ⲧⲙⲁⲧⲟⲩ ⲙ̅ⲡⲣⲉϥϫⲉ-ⲡⲉ*ⲑⲟⲟⲩ · ⲣ̅ⲙ̅ⲉ̅ b
ⲁ ⲧⲉⲕϭⲓϫ ⲕⲉϩ-ⲧⲉϩⲓⲏ ⲛ̅ⲛⲉⲕⲡⲓⲥⲧⲟⲥ ·

7. ⲁⲕⲥⲟⲧⲟⲩ ⲉⲃⲟⲗ ϩ̅ⲛ̅ ⲛ̅ⲧⲁⲫⲟⲥ ⲁⲩⲱ ⲁⲕⲡⲟⲟⲛⲟⲩ ⲉⲃⲟⲗ ϩ̅ⲛ̅ ⲧⲙⲏⲧⲉ ⲛ̅ⲛ̅ⲕⲱⲱⲥ ·

8. ⲁⲕϫⲓ ⲛ̅ϩⲉⲛⲕⲁⲥ ⲉⲩⲙⲟⲟⲩⲧ · ⲁⲕϯ ϩⲓⲱⲟⲩ ⲛ̅ⲟⲩⲥⲱⲙⲁ · ⲁⲩⲱ ⲛⲉⲧⲉ ⲛ̅ⲥⲉⲕⲓⲙ ⲁⲛ · ⲁⲕϯ ⲛⲁⲩ ⲛ̅ⲟⲩⲉⲛⲉⲣⲅⲓⲁ ⲛ̅ⲱⲛ̅ϩ̅ ·

9. ⲁ ⲧⲉⲕϩⲓⲏ ϣⲱⲡⲉ ⲛ̅ⲟⲩⲙ̅ⲛ̅ⲧ̅ⲁⲧⲧⲁⲕⲟ · ⲁⲩⲱ ⲙ̅ⲛ̅ ⲡⲉⲕϩⲟ ·

10. ⲁⲕⲛ̅-ⲡⲉⲕⲁⲓⲱⲛ ⲉϫ̅ⲙ̅ ⲡⲧⲁⲕⲟ · ϫⲉⲕⲁⲥ ⲉⲩⲉⲃⲱⲗ ⲉⲃⲟⲗ ⲧⲏⲣⲟⲩ · ⲁⲩⲱ ⲛ̅ⲥⲉⲣ̅ⲃ̅ⲣ̅ⲣⲉ · ⲁⲩⲱ ⲛ̅ⲧⲉ ⲡⲉⲕⲟⲩⲟïⲛ ⲣ̅-ⲥ̅ⲛ̅ⲧⲉ ⲛⲁⲩ ⲧⲏⲣⲟⲩ ·

11. ⲁⲕⲕⲉⲧ-ⲧⲉⲕⲙ̅ⲛ̅ⲧ̅ⲣ̅ⲙ̅ⲙⲁⲟ ϩⲓⲱⲟⲩ · ⲁⲩⲱ ⲁⲩⲣ̅-ⲟⲩⲙⲁ-ⲛ̅ϣⲱⲡⲉ ⲉϥⲟⲩⲁⲁⲃ ·

ⲡⲁï ϭⲉ ⲡⲁϫⲟⲉⲓⲥ ⲡⲉ ⲡⲃⲱⲗ ⲙ̅ⲫⲩⲙⲛⲟⲥ ⲉⲛⲧⲁⲥϫⲟⲟϥ ⲛ̅ϭⲓ ⲧⲡⲓⲥⲧⲓⲥ ⲥⲟⲫⲓⲁ · ⲥⲱⲧ̅ⲙ̅ ϭⲉ ⲧⲁϫⲟⲟϥ ϩ̅ⲛ̅ ⲟⲩⲟⲩⲱⲛ̅ϩ̅ ⲉⲃⲟⲗ · ⲡϣⲁϫⲉ ⲉⲛⲧⲁ ⲧⲉⲕϭⲟⲙ ϫⲟⲟϥ ϩⲓⲧ̅ⲛ̅ ⲥⲟⲗⲟⲙⲱⲛ · ϫⲉ **ⲡⲉⲛⲧⲁϥⲛ̅ⲧ̅ ⲉⲡⲉⲥⲏⲧ ⲉⲃⲟⲗ ϩ̅ⲛ̅ ⲙ̅ⲙⲁ ⲉⲧ- ⲣ̅ⲙ̅ⲉ̅
ϫⲟⲥⲉ ⲉⲧϩⲓⲡⲥⲁⲛ̅ⲧ̅ⲡⲉ · ⲁⲩⲱ ⲟⲛ ⲁⲕⲛ̅ⲧ̅ ⲉϩⲣⲁï ϩ̅ⲛ̅ | ⲙ̅ⲙⲁ ⲉⲧϩ̅ⲛ̅ ⲡϭⲟⲛ ⲙ̅ⲡⲉⲥⲏⲧ · ⲛ̅ⲧⲟϥ ⲡⲉ ⲡϣⲁϫⲉ ⲉⲛⲧⲁⲥϫⲟⲟϥ ⲛ̅ϭⲓ ⲧⲡⲓⲥⲧⲓⲥ ⲥⲟⲫⲓⲁ ϫⲉ ⟨ϯ⟩ϩⲩⲙⲛⲉⲩⲉ ⲉϩⲣⲁï ⲉⲣⲟⲕ ⲡⲁï ⲉⲃⲟⲗ ϩⲓⲧ̅ⲙ̅ ⲡⲉⲕⲧⲱϣ ⲁⲕⲛ̅ⲧ̅ ⲉⲃⲟⲗ ϩ̅ⲙ̅ ⲡⲉïⲁⲓⲱⲛ ⲉⲧϫⲟⲥⲉ ⲉⲧⲙ̅ⲡⲥⲁ ⲛ̅ⲧⲡⲉ ⲁⲩⲱ ⲁⲕⲛ̅ⲧ̅ ⲉⲛⲧⲟⲡⲟⲥ ⲙ̅ⲡⲉⲥⲏⲧ · ⲁⲩⲱ ⲟⲛ ⲁⲕⲛⲁϩⲙⲉⲧ ϩⲓⲧ̅ⲛ̅ ⲡⲉⲕⲧⲱϣ ⲁⲕⲛ̅ⲧ̅ ⲉϩⲣⲁï ϩ̅ⲛ̅ ⲛ̅ⲧⲟⲡⲟⲥ ⲉⲧⲙ̅ⲡⲉⲥⲏⲧ · ⲁⲩⲱ ⲡϣⲁϫⲉ ⲉⲛⲧⲁ ⲧⲉⲕϭⲟⲙ ϫⲟⲟϥ ϩⲓⲧ̅ⲛ̅ ⲥⲟⲗⲟⲙⲱⲛ ϫⲉ ⲡⲉⲛⲧⲁϥϥⲓ ⲙ̅ⲙⲁⲩ ⲛ̅ⲛⲉⲧϩ̅ⲛ̅ ⲧⲙⲏⲧⲉ · ⲁⲩⲱ

21 MS ϩⲩⲙⲛⲉⲩⲉ.

6. Thy right hand has destroyed the poison of the slanderer; thy hand has made the way for thy *faithful ones*.

7. Thou hast freed them from the *graves* and hast removed them from the midst of the corpses.

8. Thou hast taken dead bones and thou hast clothed them with a *body*; and to those that do not move thou hast given *energy* of life.

9. Thy way has become indestructible, and thy face.

10. Thou hast brought thy *aeon* to destruction that all things should be dissolved and be made new and that thy light should become a foundation for them all.

11. Thou hast built thy wealth upon them, and they have become a holy dwelling place'. *

This now, my Lord, is the interpretation of the *song of praise* which the Pistis Sophia spoke. Hear now that I say it openly. The word which thy power spoke through Solomon : 'He who brought me down from the high places which are above also brought me forth [1] from the places in the depth below' : that is the word which the Pistis Sophia said : 'I *sing praise* to thee; through thy ordinance thou didst bring me forth from the *aeon* on high which is above, and thou didst bring me to the *places* below. And again through thy ordinance thou didst save me and bring me out of the *places* below'. And the word which thy power spoke through Solomon : 'He who there has taken those that are in the midst | has taught me of them' : that is the word which

---

* Ode Sol. 22.1-12

---

[1] (18, 19) he who ... also brought me forth; MS : he who ... and thou didst also bring me forth.

ⲁϥⲧⲥⲁⲃⲟⲓ ⲉⲣⲟⲟⲩ· ⲛ̄ⲧⲟϥ ⲡⲉ ⲡϣⲁϫⲉ ⲉⲛⲧⲁⲥϫⲟⲟϥ ⲛ̄ϭⲓ
ⲧⲡⲓⲥⲧⲓⲥ ⲥⲟⲫⲓⲁ· ϫⲉ ⲁⲩⲱ ⲟⲛ ⲉⲃⲟⲗ ϩⲓⲧⲟⲟⲧ̄ⲕ̄ ⲁⲕⲧⲣⲉⲥ-
ⲥⲱⲧϥ ⲉⲃⲟⲗ ⲛ̄ϭⲓ ⲑⲩⲗⲏ ⲉⲧϩ̄ⲛ̄ ⲧⲙⲏⲧⲉ ⲛ̄ⲧⲁϭⲟⲙ· ⲁⲩⲱ
ⲁⲓ̈ⲛⲁⲩ* ⲉⲣⲟⲥ· ⲁⲩⲱ ⲟⲛ ⲡϣⲁϫⲉ ⲉⲛⲧⲁ ⲧⲉⲕϭⲟⲙ ϫⲟⲟϥ ⲣ̄ⲙⲉ̄ᵇ
5 ϩⲓⲧ̄ⲛ̄ ⲥⲟⲗⲟⲙⲱⲛ ϫⲉ ⲡⲉⲛⲧⲁϥϫⲱⲱⲣⲉ ⲉⲃⲟⲗ ⲛ̄ⲛⲁϫⲁϫⲉ
ⲙ̄ⲛ ⲛⲁⲁⲛⲧⲓⲇⲓⲕⲟⲥ· ⲛ̄ⲧⲟϥ ⲡⲉ ⲡϣⲁϫⲉ ⲉⲛⲧⲁⲥϫⲟⲟϥ ⲛ̄ϭⲓ
ⲧⲡⲓⲥⲧⲓⲥ ⲥⲟⲫⲓⲁ ϫⲉ ⲁⲩⲱ ⲛ̄ⲧⲟⲕ ⲡⲉ ⲛ̄ⲧⲁⲕϫⲱⲱⲣⲉ ⲛ̄ⲥⲁ-
ⲃⲟⲗ ⲙ̄ⲙⲟⲓ̈ ⲛ̄ⲛⲉⲡⲣⲟⲃⲟⲗⲟⲟⲩⲉ ⲧⲏⲣⲟⲩ ⲙ̄ⲡⲁⲩⲑⲁⲇⲏⲥ ⲛⲁⲓ̈
ⲉⲛⲉⲩϩⲱϫ ⲙ̄ⲙⲟⲓ̈· ⲁⲩⲱ ⲛⲁⲓ̈ ⲉⲛⲉⲩⲟ ⲛ̄ϫⲁϫⲉ ⲉⲣⲟⲓ̈· ⲁⲩⲱ
10 ⲡϣⲁϫⲉ ⲉⲛⲧⲁ ⲧⲉⲕϭⲟⲙ ϫⲟⲟϥ ϫⲉ ⲡⲉⲛⲧⲁϥϯ ⲛⲁⲓ̈ ⲛ̄-
ⲧⲉϥⲥⲟⲫⲓⲁ ⲉϩⲣⲁⲓ̈ ⲉϫ̄ⲛ̄ ϩⲉⲛⲙ̄ⲣ̄ⲣⲉ ⲉⲃⲟⲗⲟⲩ ⲉⲃⲟⲗ· ⲛ̄ⲧⲟϥ
ⲡⲉ ⲡϣⲁϫⲉ ⲉⲛⲧⲁⲥϫⲟⲟϥ ⲛ̄ϭⲓ ⲧⲡⲓⲥⲧⲓⲥ ⲥⲟⲫⲓⲁ ϫⲉ ⲁⲩⲱ
ⲁϥϯ ⲛⲁⲓ̈ ⲛ̄ⲧⲉϥⲥⲟⲫⲓⲁ· ⲉⲧⲣⲁⲃⲱⲗ ⲉⲃⲟⲗ ϩⲛ̄ ⲙ̄ⲙⲣ̄ⲣⲉ ⲛ̄ⲛⲉ-
ⲡⲣⲟⲃⲟⲗⲟⲟⲩⲉ ⲉⲧⲙ̄ⲙⲁⲩ· ⲁⲩⲱ ⲡϣⲁϫⲉ ⲉⲛⲧⲁ ⲧⲉⲕϭⲟⲙ
15 ϫⲟⲟϥ ϫⲉ ⲡⲉⲛⲧⲁϥⲡⲁⲧⲁⲥⲥⲉ ⲙ̄ⲫⲟϥ ⲉⲧⲟ ⲛ̄ⲥⲁϣϥⲉ ⲛ̄ⲁⲡⲉ
ϩⲛ̄ ⲛⲁϭⲓϫ·** ⲁⲩⲱ ⲁϥⲧⲁϩⲟⲓ̈ ⲉⲣⲁⲧ ϩⲓϫ̄ⲛ̄ ⲧⲉϥⲛⲟⲩⲛⲉ ϫⲉ- ⲣ̄ⲙⲍ̄
ⲕⲁⲥ ⲉⲓ̈ⲉϥⲱⲧⲉ ⲉⲃⲟⲗ ⲙ̄ⲡⲉϥⲥⲡⲉⲣⲙⲁ· ⲛ̄ⲧⲟϥ ⲡⲉ ⲡϣⲁϫⲉ
ⲉⲛⲧⲁⲥϫⲟⲟϥ ⲛ̄ϭⲓ ⲧⲡⲓⲥⲧⲓⲥ ⲥⲟⲫⲓⲁ ϫⲉ ⲁⲩⲱ ⲁⲕⲡⲁⲧⲁⲥⲥⲉ
ⲙ̄ⲡϩⲟϥ ⲡⲁϯⲥⲁϣϥⲉ ⲛ̄ⲁⲡⲉ ⲉⲃⲟⲗ ϩⲓⲧⲛ̄ ⲛⲁϭⲓϫ· ⲁⲩⲱ ⲁⲕ-
20 ⲧⲁϩⲟⲓ̈ ⲉⲣⲁⲧ ⲉϩⲣⲁⲓ̈ ⲉϫ̄ⲛ̄ ⲧⲉϥϩⲩⲗⲏ· ⲁⲕⲧⲁⲕⲟϥ ϫⲉⲕⲁⲥ
ⲛ̄ⲛⲉ ⲡⲉϥⲥⲡⲉⲣⲙⲁ ⲧⲱⲟⲩⲛ ϫⲓⲛ ⲙ̄ⲡⲉⲓ̈ⲛⲁⲩ· ⲁⲩⲱ ⲡϣⲁϫⲉ
ⲉⲛⲧⲁ ⲧⲉⲕϭⲟⲙ ϫⲟⲟϥ ϫⲉ ⲁⲩⲱ ⲛ̄ⲧⲟⲕ ⲛⲉⲕⲛ̄ⲙⲙⲁⲓ̈ ⲡⲉ
ⲛⲉⲕϯ ⲛ̄ⲧⲟⲟⲧ· ⲛ̄ⲧⲟϥ ⲡⲉ ⲡϣⲁϫⲉ ⲉⲛⲧⲁⲥϫⲟⲟϥ ⲛ̄ϭⲓ
ⲧⲡⲓⲥⲧⲓⲥ ⲥⲟⲫⲓⲁ ϫⲉ ⲁⲩⲱ ⲛ̄ⲧⲟⲕ ⲛⲉⲕⲛ̄ⲙⲙⲁⲓ̈ ⲡⲉ ⲉⲕϯ-
25 ϭⲟⲙ ⲛⲁⲓ̈ ϩⲛ̄ ⲛⲁⲓ̈ ⲧⲏⲣⲟⲩ· ⲁⲩⲱ ⲡϣⲁϫⲉ ⲉⲛⲧⲁ ⲧⲉⲕϭⲟⲙ
ϫⲟⲟϥ ϫⲉ ⲁⲩⲱ ⲁ ⲡⲉⲕⲣⲁⲛ ⲕⲱⲧⲉ ⲉⲣⲟⲓ̈ ϩⲣⲁⲓ̈ ϩⲙ̄ ⲙⲁ ⲛⲓⲙ·

---

11 MS ⲡ̄ⲧⲉϥⲥⲟⲫⲓⲁ; read ⲡ̄ⲧⲉϥⲉⲝⲟⲩⲥⲓⲁ; see 157.19.
23 MS ⲁⲩⲱ ⲡⲉⲕ·ϯ·; ⲁⲩⲱ crossed out, but not ⲛ; read ⲉⲕ·ϯ·

the Pistis Sophia said : 'And again through thyself thou hast caused the *matter* in the midst of my power to be purified, and I saw it'. And again the word which thy power spoke through Solomon : 'He who has dispelled my enemies and my *adversaries*' : that is the word which the Pistis Sophia said : 'And thou hast dispelled from me the *emanations* of the Authades which oppressed me, and were hostile to me'. And the word which thy power said : 'He who gave to me his *wisdom* [1] over bonds, to release them' : that is the word which the Pistis Sophia said : 'And he gave to me his *wisdom* to release me from the bonds of those *emanations*'. And the word which thy power spoke : 'He who has *smitten* the serpent with seven heads with my hands, has set me up over its root, that I should wipe out its *seed*' : that is the word which the Pistis Sophia said : 'And thou hast *smitten* the serpent with seven heads with my hands; and thou hast set me up over its *matter*. Thou hast destroyed it that its *seed* may not rise up from this hour'. And the word which thy power spoke : 'And thou wast with me helping me' : that is the word which the Pistis Sophia said : 'And thou wast with me giving power to me in all these things'. And the word which thy power spoke : 'In all places thy name surrounded me' : | that is the word which the Pistis

---

[1]   (11) wisdom; compare 157.19 : authority.

ⲚⲦⲞϤ ⲠⲈ ⲠϢⲀⲬⲈ ⲈⲚⲦⲀⲤⲬⲞⲞϤ ⲚϬⲒ ⲦⲠⲒⲤⲦⲒⲤ ⲤⲞⲫⲒⲀ · ⲣⲙⲍ^b

ⲬⲈ ⲀⲨⲰ Ⲁ ⲠⲈⲔⲞⲨⲞⲒ̈Ⲛ ⲔⲰⲦⲈ ⲈⲢⲞⲒ̈ ϨⲢⲀⲒ̈ ϨⲚ ⲚⲈⲨⲦⲞⲠⲞⲤ

ⲦⲎⲢⲞⲨ · ⲀⲨⲰ ⲠϢⲀⲬⲈ ⲈⲚⲦⲀ ⲦⲈⲔϬⲞⲘ ⲬⲞⲞϤ ⲬⲈ ⲀⲨⲰ

Ⲁ ⲦⲈⲔⲞⲨⲚⲀⲘ ⲦⲀⲔⲈ-ⲦⲘⲀⲦⲞⲨ ⲘⲠⲢⲈϤⲬⲈ-ⲠⲈⲐⲞⲞⲨ ·

5 ⲚⲦⲞϤ ⲠⲈ ⲠϢⲀⲬⲈ ⲚⲦⲀⲤⲬⲞⲞϤ ⲚϬⲒ ⲦⲠⲒⲤⲦⲒⲤ ⲤⲞⲫⲒⲀ ·

ⲬⲈ ⲀⲨⲰ ⲈⲂⲞⲖ ϨⲒⲦⲞⲞⲦⲔ ⲀⲨⲢⲀⲦϬⲞⲘ ⲚϬⲒ ⲚⲈⲠⲢⲞⲂⲞ-

ⲖⲞⲞⲨⲈ ⲘⲠⲀⲨⲐⲀⲖⲎⲤ ⲬⲈ ⲀⲔϤⲒ-ⲠⲞⲨⲞⲈⲒⲚ ⲚⲦⲈⲨϬⲞⲘ

ϨⲢⲀⲒ̈ ⲚϨⲎⲦⲞⲨ · ⲀⲨⲰ ⲠϢⲀⲬⲈ ⲈⲚⲦⲀ ⲦⲈⲔϬⲞⲘ ⲬⲞⲞϤ ⲬⲈ

Ⲁ ⲦⲈⲔϬⲒⲬ ⲔⲈϨ-ⲦⲈϨⲒⲎ ⲚⲚⲈⲔⲠⲒⲤⲦⲞⲤ · ⲚⲦⲞϤ ⲠⲈ ⲠϢⲀⲬⲈ

10 ⲈⲚⲦⲀⲤⲬⲞⲞϤ ⲚϬⲒ ⲦⲠⲒⲤⲦⲒⲤ ⲤⲞⲫⲒⲀ ⲬⲈ ⲀⲔⲤⲞⲨⲦⲚ-ⲦⲀϨⲒⲎ

ⲈⲚⲦ ⲈⲂⲞⲖ ϨⲘ ⲠⲈⲬⲀⲞⲤ ⲬⲈ ⲀⲒ̈ⲠⲒⲤⲦⲈⲨⲈ ⲈⲢⲞⲔ : ⲀⲨⲰ

ⲠϢⲀⲬⲈ ⲈⲚⲦⲀ ⲦⲈⲔϬⲞⲘ ⲬⲞⲞϤ · ⲬⲈ ⲀⲔⲤⲞⲦⲞⲨ ⲈⲂⲞⲖ

ϨⲚ ⲚⲦⲀⲫⲞⲤ ⲀⲨⲰ ⲀⲔⲠⲞⲞⲚⲞⲨ ⲈⲂⲞⲖ ϨⲚ ⲦⲘⲎⲦⲈ ⲚⲚ-

ⲔⲰⲰⲤ · ⲚⲦⲞϤ ⲠⲈ ⲠϢⲀⲬⲈ ⲈⲚⲦⲀⲤⲬⲞⲞϤ ⲚϬⲒ ⲦⲠⲒⲤⲦⲒⲤ ⲣⲙⲏ

15 ⲤⲞⲫⲒⲀ · ⲬⲈ ⲀⲨⲰ ⲀⲔⲤⲞⲦⲦ ⲈⲂⲞⲖ ϨⲘ ⲠⲈⲬⲀⲞⲤ · ⲀⲨⲰ

ⲀⲔⲠⲞⲞⲚⲈⲦ ⲈⲂⲞⲖ ϨⲚ ⲚⲔⲀⲔⲈ ⲚϨⲨⲖⲒⲔⲞⲚ · ⲈⲦⲈ ⲚⲦⲞⲞⲨ

ⲚⲈ ⲚⲈⲠⲢⲞⲂⲞⲖⲞⲞⲨⲈ ⲚⲔⲀⲔⲈ ⲈⲦϨⲘ ⲠⲈⲬⲀⲞⲤ · ⲚⲀⲒ̈ ⲈⲚⲦ-

ⲀⲔϤⲒ-ⲠⲈⲨⲞⲨⲞⲈⲒⲚ ϨⲢⲀⲒ̈ ⲚϨⲎⲦⲞⲨ · ⲀⲨⲰ ⲠϢⲀⲬⲈ ⲈⲚⲦⲀ

ⲦⲈⲔϬⲞⲘ ⲬⲞⲞϤ ⲬⲈ ⲀⲔϤⲒ ⲚϨⲈⲚⲔⲀⲤ ⲈⲨⲘⲞⲞⲨⲦ ⲀⲔϯ

20 ϨⲒⲰⲞⲨ ⲚⲞⲨⲤⲰⲘⲀ · ⲀⲨⲰ ⲚⲈⲦⲈ ⲚⲤⲈⲔⲒⲘ ⲀⲚ · ⲀⲔϯ ⲚⲀⲨ

ⲚⲞⲨⲈⲚⲈⲢⲄⲒⲀ ⲚⲰⲚϨ · ⲚⲦⲞϤ ⲠⲈ ⲠϢⲀⲬⲈ ⲈⲚⲦⲀⲤⲬⲞⲞϤ

ⲚϬⲒ ⲦⲠⲒⲤⲦⲒⲤ ⲤⲞⲫⲒⲀ · ⲬⲈ ⲀⲨⲰ ⲀⲔϤⲒ-ⲚⲀϬⲞⲘ ⲦⲎⲢⲞⲨ

ⲚⲀⲒ̈ ⲈⲦⲈ ⲘⲚ-ⲞⲨⲞⲈⲒⲚ ⲚϨⲎⲦⲞⲨ ⲀⲔϯ ⲈϨⲞⲨⲚ ⲈⲢⲞⲞⲨ Ⲛ-

ⲞⲨⲞⲨⲞⲒ̈Ⲛ ⲈϤⲤⲞⲦϤ · ⲀⲨⲰ ⲚⲀⲘⲈⲖⲞⲤ ⲦⲎⲢⲞⲨ ⲚⲀⲒ̈ ⲈⲦⲈ

25 ⲘⲚ-ⲞⲨⲞⲈⲒⲚ ⲔⲒⲘ ⲚϨⲎⲦⲞⲨ ⲀⲔϯ ⲚⲀⲨ ⲚⲞⲨⲞⲨⲞⲒ̈Ⲛ ⲚⲰⲚϨ

ϨⲘ ⲠⲈⲔⲬⲒⲤⲈ · ⲀⲨⲰ ⲠϢⲀⲬⲈ ⲈⲚⲦⲀ ⲦⲈⲔϬⲞⲘ ⲬⲞⲞϤ ⲬⲈ

Sophia said: 'And thy light surrounded me in all their *places*'. And the word which thy power spoke: 'Thy right hand has destroyed the poison of the slanderer': that is the word which the Pistis Sophia said: 'And through thyself the *emanations* of the Authades were made powerless. For thou hast taken away from them the light of their power'. And the word which thy power spoke: 'Thy hand has made the way for thy *faithful ones*': that is the word which the Pistis Sophia spoke: 'Thou hast made straight my way, to bring me forth from the *Chaos* because I have *believed* in thee'. And the word which thy power spoke: 'Thou hast freed them from the *graves* and hast removed them from the midst of the corpses': that is the word which the Pistis Sophia said: 'And thou hast freed me from the *Chaos* and thou hast removed me out of the *material* darknesses which are the dark *emanations* in the Chaos, the light of which thou hast taken away from them'. And the word which thy power spoke: 'Thou hast taken dead bones and thou hast clothed them with a *body*; and to those that do not move thou hast given *energy* of life': that is the word which the Pistis Sophia said: 'Thou hast taken all my powers in which there was no light, thou hast put into them pure light. And to all my *members* in which no light moved, thou hast given living light from thy height'. And the word which thy power spoke: | 'Thy way has become indestructible, and ⲁ ⲧⲉⲕ2ⲓⲏ ϣⲱⲡⲉ ⲛ̄ⲟⲩⲙⲛ̄ⲧⲁⲧⲧⲁⲕⲟ · ⲙⲛ̄ ⲡⲉⲕ2ⲟ · * ⲛ̄ⲧⲟ ϥ ⲣ̄ⲙⲏ b

ⲡⲉ ⲡϣⲁϫⲉ ⲉⲛⲧⲁⲥϫⲟⲟϥ ⲛ̄ϭⲓ ⲧⲡⲓⲥⲧⲓⲥ ⲥⲟⲫⲓⲁ ϫⲉ ⲁⲩⲱ

ⲁⲕⲥⲟⲩⲧⲛ̄-ⲧⲉⲕ2ⲓⲏ ⲛⲁⲓ̈ · ⲙⲛ̄ ⲡⲟⲩⲟⲓ̈ⲛ ⲙ̄ⲡⲉⲕ2ⲟ ⲁⲩϣⲱⲡⲉ

ⲛⲁⲓ̈ ⲛ̄ⲟⲩⲱⲛ2̄ ⲛ̄ⲁⲧⲧⲁⲕⲟ · ⲁⲩⲱ ⲡϣⲁϫⲉ ⲉⲛⲧⲁ ⲧⲉⲕϭⲟⲙ

5 ϫⲟⲟϥ ϫⲉ ⲁⲕⲛ̄-ⲡⲉⲕⲗⲓⲱⲛ ⲉϫ̄ⲙ ⲡⲧⲁⲕⲟ · ϫⲉⲕⲁⲥ ⲉⲩ-

ⲉⲃⲱⲗ ⲉⲃⲟⲗ ⲛ̄ⲥⲉⲣ̄ⲃ̄ⲣ̄ⲣⲉ ⲧⲏⲣⲟⲩ · ⲛ̄ⲧⲟϥ ⲡⲉ ⲡϣⲁϫⲉ ⲉⲛⲧ-

ⲁⲥϫⲟⲟϥ ⲛ̄ϭⲓ ⲧⲡⲓⲥⲧⲓⲥ ⲥⲟⲫⲓⲁ · ϫⲉ ⲁⲕⲛ̄ⲧ̄ ⲁⲛⲟⲕ ⲧⲉⲕ-

ϭⲟⲙ ⲉ2ⲣⲁⲓ̈ ⲉϫ̄ⲙ ⲡⲉⲭⲁⲟⲥ · ⲁⲩⲱ ⲉϫ̄ⲙ ⲡⲧⲁⲕⲟ · ϫⲉⲕⲁⲥ

ⲉⲩⲉⲃⲱⲗ ⲉⲃⲟⲗ ⲛ̄ϭⲓ ⲛ̄2ⲩⲗⲏ ⲧⲏⲣⲟⲩ ⲉⲧϣⲟⲟⲡ 2̄ⲙ ⲡⲧⲟ-

10 ⲡⲟⲥ ⲉⲧⲙ̄ⲙⲁⲩ · ⲁⲩⲱ ⲛ̄ⲥⲉⲣ̄ⲃ̄ⲣ̄ⲣⲉ ⲛ̄ϭⲓ ⲛⲁϭⲟⲙ ⲧⲏⲣⲟⲩ 2̄ⲙ

ⲡⲟⲩⲟⲓ̈ⲛ · ⲁⲩⲱ ⲡϣⲁϫⲉ ⲉⲛⲧⲁ ⲧⲉⲕϭⲟⲙ ϫⲟⲟϥ ϫⲉ

ⲁⲩⲱ ⲡⲉⲕⲟⲩⲟⲉⲓⲛ ⲣ̄-ⲥ̄ⲛⲧⲉ ⲛⲁⲩ ⲧⲏⲣⲟⲩ · ⲛ̄ⲧⲟϥ ⲡⲉ

ⲡϣⲁϫⲉ ⲉⲛⲧⲁⲥϫⲟⲟϥ ⲛ̄ϭⲓ ⲧⲡⲓⲥⲧⲓⲥ ⲥⲟⲫⲓⲁ ϫⲉ ⲁⲩⲱ ⲁ

ⲡⲉⲕⲟⲩⲟⲓ̈ⲛ ϣⲱⲡⲉ ⲛ̄2ⲏⲧⲟⲩ ** ⲧⲏⲣⲟⲩ · ⲁⲩⲱ ⲡϣⲁϫⲉ ⲣ̄ⲙⲑ

15 ⲉⲛⲧⲁ ⲧⲉⲕϭⲟⲙ ⲛ̄ⲟⲩⲟⲉⲓⲛ ϫⲟⲟϥ 2ⲓⲧⲛ̄ ⲥⲟⲗⲟⲙⲱⲛ ϫⲉ

ⲁⲕⲕⲁ-ⲧⲉⲕⲙⲛ̄ⲧ̄ⲣ̄ⲙⲙⲁⲟ 2ⲓϫⲱϥ · ⲁⲩⲱ ⲁϥⲣ̄-ⲟⲩⲙⲁⲛ̄ϣⲱⲡⲉ

ⲉϥⲟⲩⲁⲁⲃ · ⲛ̄ⲧⲟϥ ⲡⲉ ⲡϣⲁϫⲉ ⲛ̄ⲧⲁⲥϫⲟⲟϥ ⲛ̄ϭⲓ ⲧⲡⲓⲥⲧⲓⲥ

ⲥⲟⲫⲓⲁ ϫⲉ ⲁⲕⲧⲁⲭⲣⲉ-ⲡⲟⲩⲟⲉⲓⲛ ⲛ̄ⲧⲉⲕⲁⲡⲟ2ⲣⲟⲓⲁ 2ⲓϫⲱⲓ̈ ·

ⲁⲩⲱ ⲁ̈ⲓϣⲱⲡⲉ ⲛ̄ⲟⲩⲟⲉⲓⲛ ⲉϥⲥⲟⲧϥ · ⲡⲁⲓ̈ ϭⲉ ⲡⲁϫⲟⲉⲓⲥ

20 ⲡⲉ ⲡⲃⲱⲗ ⲙ̄ⲫⲩⲙⲛⲟⲥ ⲉⲛⲧⲁⲥϫⲟⲟϥ ⲛ̄ϭⲓ ⲧⲡⲓⲥⲧⲓⲥ ⲥⲟⲫⲓⲁ ·

ⳅ ⲁⲥϣⲱⲡⲉ ϭⲉ ⲛ̄ⲧⲉⲣⲉ ⲡⲓϣⲟⲣⲡ̄ ⲙ̄ⲙⲩⲥⲧⲏⲣⲓⲟⲛ ⲥⲱⲧⲙ̄

ⲉⲛⲉⲓ̈ϣⲁϫⲉ ⲉϥϫⲱ ⲙ̄ⲙⲟⲟⲩ ⲛ̄ϭⲓ ⲙⲁⲑⲁⲓⲟⲥ ⲡⲉϫⲁϥ ϫⲉ

ⲉⲩⲅⲉ ⲙⲁⲑⲁⲓⲟⲥ · ⲁⲩⲱ ⲕⲁⲗⲱⲥ ⲡⲙⲉⲣⲓⲧ · ⲡⲁⲓ̈ ⲡⲉ ⲡⲃⲱⲗ

ⲙ̄ⲫⲩⲙⲛⲟⲥ ⲉⲛⲧⲁⲥϫⲟⲟϥ ⲛ̄ϭⲓ ⲧⲡⲓⲥⲧⲓⲥ ⲥⲟⲫⲓⲁ · ⲁϥⲟⲩⲱ2

25 ⲇⲉ ⲟⲛ ⲉⲧⲟⲟⲧϥ ⲛ̄ϭⲓ ⲡⲓϣⲟⲣⲡ̄ ⲙ̄ⲙⲩⲥⲧⲏⲣⲓⲟⲛ ⲡⲉϫⲁϥ ϫⲉ

ⲁⲥⲟⲩⲱ2 ⲇⲉ ⲟⲛ ⲉⲧⲟⲟⲧⲥ̄ ⲛ̄ϭⲓ ⲧⲥⲟⲫⲓⲁ 2̄ⲙ ⲡⲉⲓ̈2ⲩⲙⲛⲟⲥ ·

ⲡⲉϫⲁⲥ ϫⲉ

---

3 MS ⲁⲩϣⲱⲡⲉ; read ⲁϥϣⲱⲡⲉ.

thy face' : that is the word which the Pistis Sophia said :
'And thou hast made straight thy way for me, and the light
of thy face has become for me imperishable life'. And the
word which thy power spoke : 'Thou hast brought thy *aeon*
to destruction, that all things should be dissolved and made
new' : that is the word which the Pistis Sophia said : 'Thou
hast brought me, thy power, above the *Chaos* and above
the destruction, so that all the *materials* which are in that
place should be dissolved, and that all my powers should
be renewed in the light'. And the word which thy power
spoke : 'And thy light becomes a foundation for them all' :
that is the word which the Pistis Sophia spoke : 'And thy
light has been in them all'. And the word which thy light-
power spoke through Solomon : 'Thou hast placed thy
wealth upon it, and it has become a holy dwelling place' :
that is the word which the Pistis Sophia said : 'Thou hast
made fast the light of thy *outpouring* upon me, and I have
become purified light'. This now, my Lord, is the interpretation of the *song of praise* which the Pistis Sophia said."

72. Now it happened when the First *Mystery* heard
these words which Matthew spoke, he said : "*Excellent*,
Matthew, and *well done*, thou beloved one. This is the
interpretation of the *song of praise* which the Pistis Sophia
spoke."

The First *Mystery however* continued again, he said : "The
Pistis Sophia, *however*, continued again in this *song of
praise*. She said : |

1. ϯⲛⲁϫⲟⲟⲥ ϫⲉ ⲛⲧⲟⲕ ⲡⲉ ⲡⲟⲩⲟⲉⲓⲛ ⲡⲉⲧϫⲟⲥⲉ ϫⲉ ⲣⲙⲑᵇ
ⲁⲕⲛⲟⲩϩⲙ ⲙⲙⲟⲓ· ⲁⲩⲱ ⲁⲕⲛⲧ ⲉⲣⲁⲧⲕ ⲁⲩⲱ ⲙⲡⲕⲧⲣⲉⲩϭⲓ-
ⲡⲁⲟⲩⲟⲓⲛ ⲛϭⲓ ⲛⲉⲡⲣⲟⲃⲟⲗⲟⲟⲩⲉ ⲙⲡⲁⲩⲑⲁⲇⲏⲥ ⲛⲁⲓ ⲉⲧⲟ
ⲛϫⲁϫⲉ ⲉⲣⲟⲓ·

5   2. ⲡⲟⲩⲟⲓⲛ ⲛⲧⲉ ⲛⲓⲟⲩⲟⲓⲛ· ⲁⲓϩⲩⲙⲛⲉⲩⲉ ⲉϩⲣⲁⲓ ⲟⲩⲃⲏⲕ·

3. ⲁⲕⲛⲁϩⲙⲉⲧ ⲡⲟⲩⲟⲉⲓⲛ ⲁⲕⲛ-ⲧⲁϭⲟⲙ ⲉϩⲣⲁⲓ ϩⲙ ⲡⲉ-
ϫⲁⲟⲥ· ⲁⲕⲛⲁϩⲙⲉⲧ ⲉⲃⲟⲗ ϩⲓⲧⲛ ⲛⲉⲧⲃⲏⲕ ⲉⲡⲉⲥⲏⲧ ⲉⲡⲕⲁⲕⲉ·
ⲛⲉⲓϣⲁϫⲉ ⲟⲛ ⲁⲥϫⲟⲟⲩ ⲛϭⲓ ⲧⲡⲓⲥⲧⲓⲥ ⲥⲟⲫⲓⲁ· ⲧⲉⲛⲟⲩ
ϭⲉ ⲡⲉⲛⲧⲁ ⲡⲉϥⲛⲟⲩⲥ ⲣⲛⲟⲉⲣⲟⲥ ⲉⲁϥⲛⲟⲓ ⲛⲛϣⲁϫⲉ ⲉⲛⲧ-
10 ⲁⲥϫⲟⲟⲩ ⲛϭⲓ ⲧⲡⲓⲥⲧⲓⲥ ⲥⲟⲫⲓⲁ· ⲙⲁⲣⲉϥⲉⲓ· ⲉⲑⲏ ⲛϥⲧⲁⲩⲉ-
ⲡⲉⲩⲃⲱⲗ:

ⲍ ⲁⲥ(ϣ)ⲱⲡⲉ ϭⲉ ⲛⲧⲉⲣⲉ ⲡⲓϣⲟⲣⲡ ⲙⲙⲩⲥⲧⲏⲣⲓⲟⲛ ⲟⲩⲱ
ⲉϥϫⲱ ⲛⲛⲉⲓϣⲁϫⲉ ⲉⲙⲙⲁⲑⲏⲧⲏⲥ· ⲁⲥⲉⲓ· ⲉⲑⲏ ⲛϭⲓ ⲙⲁ-
ⲣⲓⲁ· ⲡⲉϫⲁⲥ ϫⲉ ⲡⲁϫⲟⲉⲓⲥ· ⲡⲁⲛⲟⲩⲥ ⲟⲩⲛⲟⲉⲣⲟⲥ ⲡⲉ
15 ⲛⲟⲩⲟⲉⲓϣ ⲛⲓⲙ ⲉⲧⲣⲁⲉⲓ· ⲉⲑⲏ ⲛⲥⲟⲡ ⲛⲓⲙ· ⲧⲁⲧⲁⲩⲉ-ⲡⲃⲱⲗ
ⲛⲛϣⲁϫⲉ ⲉⲛⲧⲁⲥϫⲟⲟⲩ· ⲁⲗⲗⲁ**ⲉⲓⲣϩⲟⲧⲉ ϩⲏⲧϥ ⲙⲡⲉ-ⲣⲡ
ⲧⲣⲟⲥ ϫⲉ ϣⲁϥⲁⲡⲓⲗⲉⲓ ⲉⲣⲟⲓ· ⲁⲩⲱ ϥⲙⲟⲥⲧⲉ ⲙⲡⲉⲛⲅⲉ-
ⲛⲟⲥ· ⲛⲁⲓ ⲇⲉ ⲛⲧⲉⲣⲉⲥϫⲟⲟⲩ ⲡⲉϫⲁϥ ⲛⲁⲥ ⲛϭⲓ ⲡⲓϣⲟⲣⲡ
ⲙⲙⲩⲥⲧⲏⲣⲓⲟⲛ ϫⲉ ⲟⲩⲟⲛ ⲛⲓⲙ ⲉⲧⲛⲁⲙⲟⲩϩ ⲉⲃⲟⲗ ϩⲙ ⲡⲉ-
20 ⲡⲛⲁ ⲛⲟⲩⲟⲉⲓⲛ ⲉⲧⲣⲉϥⲉⲓ· ⲉⲑⲏ ⲛϥⲧⲁⲩⲉ-ⲡⲃⲱⲗ ⲛⲛⲉϯϫⲱ
ⲙⲙⲟⲟⲩ· ⲙⲛ-ⲗⲁⲁⲩ ⲛⲁϣⲕⲱⲗⲩ ⲙⲙⲟϥ· ⲧⲉⲛⲟⲩ ϭⲉ ⲛⲧⲟ
ⲱ' ⲙⲁⲣⲓⲁ· ⲧⲁⲩⲉ-ⲡⲃⲱⲗ ⲛⲛϣⲁϫⲉ ⲛⲁⲓ ⲛⲧⲁⲥϫⲟⲟⲩ ⲛϭⲓ
ⲧⲡⲓⲥⲧⲓⲥ ⲥⲟⲫⲓⲁ· ⲁⲥⲟⲩⲱϣⲃ ϭⲉ ⲛϭⲓ ⲙⲁⲣⲓⲁ ⲡⲉϫⲁⲥ ⲙⲡⲓ-

---

7   MS ⲉⲃⲟⲗ ϩⲓⲧⲛ; read ⲉⲃⲟⲗ ϩⲛ.
20   MS ⲛⲛϣⲁϫⲉ; read ⲛⲛⲉ·ϯ·ϫⲱ.

1. 'I will say that thou art the light which is on high, for thou didst save me, and thou hast brought me to thyself. And thou didst not allow the *emanations* of the Authades, which are my enemies, to take away my light.

2. O Light of Lights, I have *sung praises* to thee; thou hast saved me [1].

3. O Light, thou hast brought my power up from the *Chaos*; thou hast saved me from among those that go down to the darkness.'

The Pistis Sophia said these words also. Now at this time, he whose *mind* has become *understanding* to *understand* the words which the Pistis Sophia spoke, let him come forward and give their interpretation."

Now it happened when the First Mystery finished saying these words to the *disciples*, Maria came forward. She said: "My Lord, my *mind* is *understanding* at all times that I should come forward at any time and give the interpretation of the words which she spoke, *but* I am afraid of Peter, for he *threatens* me and he hates our *race*."

But when she said these things, the First *Mystery* said to her: "Everyone who will be filled with the *Spirit* of light to come forward and give the interpretation of those things which I say, him will no one be able to *prevent*. Now at this time, thou *O* Maria, give the interpretation of the words which the Pistis Sophia said."

Now Maria answered and said to the | First *Mystery*

---

[1] (5, 6) Verse division differs from Coptic text; cf. 163.7-9, 164.

ϢΟΡⲠ ⲘⲘⲨⲤⲦⲎⲢⲒⲞⲚ ⲚⲦⲘⲎⲦⲈ ⲚⲘⲘⲀⲐⲎⲦⲎⲤ· ϪⲈ ⲠⲀ-
ϪⲞⲒⲤ· ⲈⲦⲂⲈ ⲠⲂⲰⲖ ⲚⲚϢⲀϪⲈ ⲈⲚⲦⲀⲤϪⲞⲞⲨ ⲚϬⲒ ⲦⲠⲒⲤ-
ⲦⲒⲤ ⲤⲞⲪⲒⲀ· Ⲁ ⲦⲈⲔϬⲞⲘ ⲚⲞⲨⲞⲈⲒⲚ ⲠⲢⲞⲪⲎⲦⲈⲨⲈ ⲘⲘⲞⲞⲨ
ⲘⲠⲒⲞⲨⲞⲈⲒϢ ϨⲒⲦⲚ ⲆⲀⲨⲈⲒⲆ· ϪⲈ

5   1. ϮⲚⲀϪⲀⲤⲦⲔ ⲠϪⲞⲈⲒⲤ· ϪⲈ ⲀⲔϢⲞⲠⲦ ⲈⲢⲞⲔ· ⲀⲨⲰ
ⲘⲠⲔⲈⲨⲪⲢⲀⲚⲈ ⲚⲚⲀϪⲀϪⲈ ⲈϨⲢⲀⲒ ⲈϪⲰⲒ·

   2. ⲠϪⲞⲈⲒⲤ ⲠⲀⲚⲞⲨⲦⲈ ⲀⲒϢϢ ⲈϨⲢⲀⲒ ⲈⲢⲞⲔ· ⲀⲨⲰ ⲀⲔ- ‾ⲢⲎ‾ᵇ
ⲦⲀⲖϬⲞⲒ·

   3. ⲠϪⲞⲒⲤ ⲀⲔⲚ-ⲦⲀⲮⲨⲬⲎ ⲈϨⲢⲀⲒ ϨⲚ ⲀⲘⲚⲦⲈ· ⲀⲔⲦⲞⲨ-
10 ϪⲞⲒ ⲈⲚⲈⲦⲂⲎⲔ ⲈⲠⲈⲤⲚⲦ ⲈⲠϢⲎⲒ·

    ⲚⲀⲒ ⲆⲈ ⲚⲦⲈⲢⲈⲤϪⲞⲞⲨ ⲚϬⲒ ⲘⲀⲢⲒⲀ ⲠⲈϪⲀϤ ⲚⲀⲤ ⲚϬⲒ
ⲠⲒϢⲞⲢⲠ ⲘⲘⲨⲤⲦⲎⲢⲒⲞⲚ ϪⲈ ⲈⲨⲄⲈ ⲔⲀⲖⲰⲤ ⲘⲀⲢⲒⲀ ⲦⲘⲀ-
ⲔⲀⲢⲒⲞⲤ· ⲀϤⲞⲨⲰϨ ⲆⲈ ⲞⲚ ⲈⲦⲞⲞⲦϤ ϨⲘ ⲠϢⲀϪⲈ ⲠⲈϪⲀϤ
ⲚⲘⲘⲀⲐⲎⲦⲎⲤ ϪⲈ ⲀⲤⲞⲨⲰϨ ⲞⲚ ⲈⲦⲞⲞⲦⲤ ⲚϬⲒ ⲦⲠⲒⲤⲦⲒⲤ
15 ⲤⲞⲪⲒⲀ ϨⲘ ⲠⲈⲒϨⲨⲘⲚⲞⲤ· ⲠⲈϪⲀⲤ ϪⲈ

   1. Ⲁ ⲠⲞⲨⲞⲈⲒⲚ ϢⲰⲠⲈ ⲚⲀⲒ ⲚⲢⲈϤⲚⲞⲨϨⲘ·

   2. ⲀⲨⲰ ⲀϤⲔⲦⲈ-ⲠⲀⲔⲀⲔⲈ ⲚⲀⲒ ⲈⲨⲞⲨⲞⲈⲒⲚ· ⲀⲨⲰ ⲀϤ-
ⲠⲈϨ-ⲠⲈϪⲖⲞⲤ ⲈⲦⲔⲰⲦⲈ ⲈⲢⲞⲒ· ⲀϤⲘⲞⲢⲦ ⲚⲞⲨⲞⲨⲞⲈⲒⲚ·

    ⲀⲤϢⲰⲠⲈ ϬⲈ ⲚⲦⲈⲢⲈ ⲠⲒϢⲞⲢⲠ ⲘⲘⲨⲤⲦⲎⲢⲒⲞⲚ ⲞⲨⲰ ⲈϤ-
20 ϪⲰ ⲚⲚⲈⲒϢⲀϪⲈ· ⲀⲤⲈⲒ' ⲈⲐⲎ ⲚϬⲒ ⲘⲀⲢⲐⲀ ⲠⲈϪⲀⲤ ϪⲈ
ⲠⲀϪⲞⲈⲒⲤ· ⲚⲦⲀ ⲦⲈⲔϬⲞⲘ ⲠⲢⲞⲪⲎⲦⲈⲨⲈ ⲘⲠⲒ**ⲟⲨⲟⲉⲓϢ ‾ⲢⲘⲀ‾
ϨⲒⲦⲚ ⲆⲀⲨⲒⲆ· ⲈⲦⲂⲈ ⲚⲈⲒϢⲀϪⲈ ϪⲈ

   10. Ⲁ ⲠϪⲞⲈⲒⲤ ϢⲰⲠⲈ ⲚⲀⲒ ⲚⲂⲞⲎⲐⲞⲤ·

   11. ⲀϤⲔⲦⲈ-ⲠⲀⲚⲈϨⲠⲈ ⲚⲀⲒ ⲈⲨⲢⲀϢⲈ· ⲀϤⲠⲈϨ-ⲦⲀϬⲞⲞⲨⲚⲈ
25 ⲀϤⲘⲞⲢⲦ ϨⲚ ⲞⲨⲞⲨⲚⲞϤ·

---

9   MS ϨⲚ.

in the midst of the *disciples* : "My Lord, concerning the interpretation of the words which the Pistis Sophia spoke, thy light-power once *prophesied* through David thus :

1. 'I will exalt thee, O Lord, for thou hast received me and thou hast not given to my enemies *to rejoice* over me.

2. O Lord, my God, I cried to thee and thou didst heal me.

3. O Lord thou hast brought my *soul* up from Amente; thou hast saved me from those who go down to the pit'. *

73.   *However*, when Maria had said these things, the First *Mystery* said to her : "*Excellent, well done*, Maria, thou *blessed one*."

But he (the First Mystery) continued again with the discourse. He said to the *disciples* : "The Pistis Sophia continued again with this *song of praise*, she said :

1. 'The Light has become my Saviour.

2. And it has turned my darkness into light for me. And it has rent the *Chaos* which surrounded me. It has girded me with light'."

Now it happened when the First *Mystery* finished speaking these words, Martha came forward and said : "My Lord, thy power *prophesied* once, through David, concerning these words, saying :

10. 'The Lord has become my *helper*.

11. He has turned my lament into rejoicing for me, he has rent my sackcloth; he has girded me with gladness' ▫." |

---

*   Ps. 29.1-3
▫   Ps. 29.10, 11

ⲁⲥϣⲱⲡⲉ ⲇⲉ ⲛ̄ⲧⲉⲣⲉ ⲡⲓϣⲟⲣⲡ̄ ⲙ̄ⲙⲩⲥⲧⲏⲣⲓⲟⲛ ⲟⲩⲱ
ⲉϥⲥⲱⲧⲙ̄ ⲉⲛⲉⲓ̈ϣⲁϫⲉ ⲉⲥϫⲱ ⲙ̄ⲙⲟⲟⲩ ⲛ̄ϭⲓ ⲙⲁⲣⲟⲁ· ⲡⲉϫⲁϥ ϫⲉ ⲉⲩⲅⲉ ⲁⲩⲱ ⲕⲁⲗⲱⲥ ⲙⲁⲣⲟⲁ· ⲁϥⲟⲩⲱϩ ⲇⲉ ⲟⲛ
ⲉⲧⲟⲟⲧϥ̄ ⲛ̄ϭⲓ ⲡⲓϣⲟⲣⲡ̄ ⲙ̄ⲙⲩⲥⲧⲏⲣⲓⲟⲛ ⲡⲉϫⲁϥ ⲛ̄ⲙⲙⲁⲑⲏ-
5 ⲧⲏⲥ· ϫⲉ ⲁⲥⲟⲩⲱϩ ⲟⲛ ⲉⲧⲟⲟⲧⲥ̄ ϩⲙ̄ ⲫⲩⲙⲛⲟⲥ ⲛ̄ϭⲓ
ⲧⲡⲓⲥⲧⲓⲥ ⲥⲟⲫⲓⲁ ⲁⲩⲱ ⲡⲉϫⲁⲥ ϫⲉ

1. ⲧⲁϭⲟⲙ ϩⲩⲙⲛⲉⲩⲉ ⲉⲡⲟⲩⲟⲓ̈ⲛ ⲁⲩⲱ ⲙ̄ⲡⲣ̄-ⲡⲱⲃϣ̄
ⲛ̄ⲛ̄ϭⲟⲙ ⲧⲏⲣⲟⲩ ⲙ̄ⲡⲟⲩⲟⲉⲓⲛ ⲛⲁⲓ̈ ⲉⲛⲧⲁϥⲧⲁⲁⲩ ⲛⲉ·

2. ⲁⲩⲱ ⲛ̄ϭⲟⲙ ⲧⲏⲣⲟⲩ ⲉⲧⲛ̄ϩⲏⲧ· ϩⲩⲙⲛⲉⲩⲉ ⲉⲡⲣⲁⲛ
10 ⲙ̄ⲡⲉϥⲙⲩⲥⲧⲏⲣⲓⲟⲛ ⲉⲧⲟⲩⲁⲁⲃ·

3. ⲡⲉⲧⲕⲱ ⲉⲃⲟⲗ ⲛ̄ⲧⲟⲩⲡⲁⲣⲁⲃⲁⲥⲓⲥ ⲧⲏⲣⲥ̄· ⲡⲉⲧⲛⲟⲩϩⲙ̄
ⲙ̄ⲙⲟ ⲉⲃⲟⲗ ϩⲛ̄ ⲛⲟⲩϩⲱϫ ⲧⲏⲣⲟⲩ· ⲛⲁⲓ̈ ⲉⲛⲧⲁⲩⲟⲗⲓⲃⲉ ⲣ̄ⲡⲁ
ⲙ̄ⲙⲟ ⲛ̄ϩⲏⲧⲟⲩ ⲛ̄ϭⲓ ⲛⲉⲡⲣⲟⲃⲟⲗⲟⲟⲩⲉ ⲙ̄ⲡⲁⲩⲑⲁⲇⲏⲥ·

4. ⲡⲉⲛⲧⲁϥⲛⲟⲩϩⲙ̄ ⲙ̄ⲡⲟⲩⲟⲩⲟⲉⲓⲛ ⲉⲃⲟⲗ ϩⲛ̄ ⲛⲉⲡⲣⲟⲃⲟ-
15 ⲗⲟⲟⲩⲉ ⲙ̄ⲡⲁⲩⲑⲁⲇⲏⲥ ⲛⲁⲓ̈ ⲉⲧⲏⲡ ⲉⲡⲧⲁⲕⲟ· ⲡⲉⲛⲧⲁϥϯ
ⲛ̄ⲟⲩⲕⲗⲟⲙ ⲛ̄ⲟⲩⲟⲓ̈ⲛ ⲉϫⲱ ϩⲛ̄ ⲧⲉϥⲙⲛ̄ⲧϣⲁⲛϩⲧⲏϥ ϣⲁⲛ-
ⲧϥ̄ⲛⲁϩⲙⲉ·

5. ⲡⲉⲛⲧⲁϥⲙⲁϩⲉ ⲛ̄ⲟⲩⲟⲉⲓⲛ ⲉϥⲥⲟⲧϥ̄· ⲁⲩⲱ ⲧⲟⲩⲁⲣⲭⲏ
ⲛⲁⲣⲃ̄ⲣ̄ⲣⲉ· ⲛ̄ⲑⲉ ⲛ̄ⲟⲩϩⲟⲣⲁⲧⲟⲥ ⲛ̄ⲧⲉ ⲡϫⲓⲥⲉ·

20 ⲛⲉⲓ̈ϣⲁϫⲉ ⲛⲉⲣⲉ ⲧⲡⲓⲥⲧⲓⲥ ⟨ⲥⲟⲫⲓⲁ⟩ ϩⲩⲙⲛⲉⲩⲉ ⲙ̄ⲙⲟⲟⲩ
ⲡⲉ ϫⲉ ⲁⲥⲛⲟⲩϩⲙ̄· ⲁⲩⲱ ⲉⲥⲣ̄ⲡⲙⲉⲉⲩⲉ ⲛ̄ⲛⲉϩⲃⲏⲩⲉ ⲧⲏⲣⲟⲩ ⲉⲛⲧⲁⲓ̈ⲁⲁⲩ ⲛⲁⲥ· ⲁⲥϣⲱⲡⲉ ϭⲉ ⲛ̄ⲧⲉⲣⲉ ⲡⲓϣⲟⲣⲡ̄
ⲙ̄ⲙⲩⲥⲧⲏⲣⲓⲟⲛ ⲟⲩⲱ ⲉϥⲧⲁⲩⲟ ⲛ̄ⲛⲉⲓ̈ϣⲁϫⲉ ⲉⲙⲙⲁⲑⲏⲧⲏⲥ·
ⲡⲉϫⲁϥ ⲛⲁⲩ ϫⲉ ⲡⲉⲛⲧⲁϥⲛⲟⲓ̈ ⲉⲡⲃⲱⲗ ⲛ̄ⲛⲉⲓ̈ϣⲁϫⲉ· ⲙⲁ-
25 ⲣⲉϥⲉⲓ̈ ⲉⲑⲏ· ⲛ̄ϥϫⲟⲟⲩ ϩⲛ̄ ⲟⲩⲡⲁⲣϩⲏⲥⲓⲁ· ⲁⲥⲉⲓ̈ ⲟⲛ ⲉⲑⲏ ⲣ̄ⲡⲃ

It happened, *however*, when the First *Mystery* finished hearing these words which Martha spoke, he said : "*Excellent* and *well done*, Martha."

But the First Mystery continued again, he said to the *disciples* : "The Pistis Sophia continued again with the *song of praise* and she said :

1. 'My power, *sing praise* to the Light and forget not all the powers of the light which he has given to thee.

2. And all the powers within me, *sing praise* to the name of his holy *mystery*.

3. Who forgives all thy *transgressions*, who saves thee from all thy oppressions with which the *emanations* of the Authades have *afflicted* thee.

4. Who has saved thy light from the *emanations* of the Authades which belong to destruction; who has crowned thee with light in his compassion until he saves thee.

5. Who has filled thee with pure light; and thy *beginning* will be renewed like an *invisible one* of the height.'

With these words the Pistis Sophia *sang praises* because she was saved. And she remembered all the things which I had done for her."

74. Now it happened when the First *Mystery* finished saying these words to the *disciples*, he said to them : "He who *understands* the interpretation of these words, let him come forward and speak *openly*." |

ⲛϭⲓ ⲙⲁⲣⲓⲁ ⲡⲉϫⲁⲥ ϫⲉ ⲡⲁϫⲟⲉⲓⲥ· ⲉⲧⲃⲉ ⲛⲉⲉⲓϣⲁϫⲉ
ⲉⲛⲧⲁⲥϨⲩⲙⲛⲉⲩⲉ ⲙ̄ⲙⲟⲟⲩ ⲛ̄ϭⲓ ⲧⲡⲓⲥⲧⲓⲥ ⲥⲟⲫⲓⲁ· ⲁ ⲧⲉⲕϭⲟⲙ ⲛ̄ⲟⲩⲟⲉⲓⲛ ⲡⲣⲟⲫⲏⲧⲉⲩⲉ ⲙ̄ⲙⲟⲟⲩ Ϩⲓⲧⲛ̄ ⲇⲁⲩⲉⲓⲇ·
ϫⲉ

5　1. ⲧⲁⲯⲩⲭⲏ ⲥⲙⲟⲩ ⲉⲡϫⲟⲉⲓⲥ· ⲛⲉⲧⲛ̄ⲡⲁⲥⲁⲛ̄Ϩⲟⲩⲛ ⲧⲏⲣⲟⲩ ⲥⲙⲟⲩ ⲉⲡⲉϥⲣⲁⲛ ⲉⲧⲟⲩⲁⲁⲃ·

　　2. ⲧⲁⲯⲩⲭⲏ ⲥⲙⲟⲩ ⲉⲡϫⲟⲉⲓⲥ· ⲁⲩⲱ ⲙ̄ⲡⲣ̄ⲣ̄-ⲡⲱⲃϣ ⲛ̄-
ⲛⲉϥⲧⲱⲱⲃⲉ ⲧⲏⲣⲟⲩ·

　　3. ⲡⲉⲧⲕⲱ ⲛⲉ ⲉⲃⲟⲗ ⲛ̄ⲛⲟⲩⲁⲛⲟⲙⲓⲁ ⲧⲏⲣⲟⲩ· ⲡⲉⲧⲧⲁⲗ-
10 ϭⲟ ⲛ̄ⲛⲟⲩϣⲱⲛⲉ ⲧⲏⲣⲟⲩ·

　　4. ⲡⲉⲧⲥⲱⲧⲉ ⲙ̄ⲡⲟⲩⲱⲛϨ ⲉⲃⲟⲗ Ϩ̄ⲙ ⲡⲧⲁⲕⲟ· ⲡⲉⲧϯ ⲛ̄ⲟⲩⲕⲗⲟⲙ ⲛ̄ⲛⲁ̍ Ϩⲓϫⲱ Ϩⲓ ⲙ̄ⲛⲧϣⲁⲛϨⲧⲏϥ·

　　5. ⲡⲉⲧⲥⲓⲟ ⲙ̄ⲡⲟⲩⲟⲩⲱϣ ⲛ̄ⲁⲅⲁⲑⲟⲛ· ⲧⲟⲩⲙ̄ⲛ̄ⲧⲕⲟⲩⲓ̈
ⲛⲁⲣ̄ⲃⲣ̄ⲣⲉ ⲛ̄ⲑⲉ ⲛ̄ⲧⲁⲟⲩⲁⲉⲧⲟⲥ·

15　ⲉⲧⲉ ⲡⲁⲓ̈ ⲡⲉ ϫⲉ ⲧⲥⲟⲫⲓⲁ ⲛⲁⲣ̄ⲑⲉ ⲛ̄ⲛⲁϨⲟⲣⲁⲧⲟⲥ ⲉⲧ-
ⲙ̄ⲡϫⲓⲥⲉ*ⲛ̄ⲧⲁϥϫⲟⲟⲥ ϭⲉ ϫⲉ ⲛ̄ⲑⲉ ⲛ̄ⲟⲩⲁⲉⲧⲟⲥ· ⲉⲃⲟⲗ
ϫⲉ ⲉⲣⲉ ⲡⲙⲁⲛ̄ϣⲱⲡⲉ ⲛ̄ⲛⲁⲉⲧⲟⲥ Ϩ̄ⲙ ⲡϫⲓⲥⲉ· ⲁⲩⲱ ⲉⲣⲉ ⲣ̅ⲛ̅ⲃ ᵇ
ⲛ̄ⲁϨⲟⲣⲁⲧⲟⲥ Ϩⲱⲟⲩ Ϩ̄ⲙ ⲡϫⲓⲥⲉ ⲉⲧⲉ ⲡⲁⲓ̈ ⲡⲉ ϫⲉ ⲧⲥⲟⲫⲓⲁ
ⲛⲁⲣ̄ⲟⲩⲟⲉⲓⲛ ⲛ̄ⲑⲉ ⲛ̄ⲛⲁϨⲟⲣⲁⲧⲟⲥ· ⲛ̄ⲑⲉ ⲉⲛⲉⲥⲟ̍ ⲙ̄ⲙⲟⲥ
20 ϫⲓⲛ ⲧⲉⲥⲁⲣⲭⲏ:

　　ⲁⲥϣⲱⲡⲉ ϭⲉ ⲛ̄ⲧⲉⲣⲉ ⲡϣⲟⲣⲡ ⲙ̄ⲙⲩⲥⲧⲏⲣⲓⲟⲛ ⲥⲱⲧⲙ̄
ⲉⲛⲉⲓ̈ϣⲁϫⲉ ⲉⲥϫⲱ ⲙ̄ⲙⲟⲟⲩ ⲛ̄ϭⲓ ⲙⲁⲣⲓⲁ· ⲡⲉϫⲁϥ ϫⲉ
ⲉⲩⲅⲉ ⲱ̍ ⲙⲁⲣⲓⲁ ⲧⲙⲁⲕⲁⲣⲓⲟⲥ· ⲁⲥϣⲱⲡⲉ ϭⲉ ⲙ̄ⲛ̄ⲛⲥⲁ ⲛⲁⲓ̈

12　Ϩⲓϫⲱ should precede ⲛ̄ⲛⲁ.
13　MS ⲡⲉⲧⲥⲓⲟ; read ⲡⲉⲧⲧⲥⲓⲟ.

Maria came forward again and said: "My Lord, concerning these words with which the Pistis Sophia *sang praises*, thy lightpower *prophesied* them through David thus:

1. Bless the Lord, my *soul*, and all that is within me, bless his holy name.

2. Bless the Lord, my *soul*, and forget not all his rewards.

3. Who forgives all thy *iniquities* and who heals all thy sicknesses.

4. Who saves thy life from destruction, who crowns thee with mercy and compassion.

5. Who satisfies thy desire with *good things*; thy youth will be renewed like that of an *eagle*.'*

That is [1], the Sophia will become like the *invisible ones* in the height. He has now said: 'like an *eagle*', because the dwelling place of the *eagles* is in the height, and the *invisible ones* are also in the height; that is, the Sophia will be lighted like the *invisible ones* as she was from her *beginning*."

Now it happened when the First *Mystery* heard these words which Maria spoke, he said: "*Excellent, O* Maria, thou *blessed* one."

Now it happened after these things, | the First *Mystery*

---

* Ps. 102.1-5

---

[1] (15) MS: explanation of the first four verses of the psalm is lacking.

ⲁϥⲟⲩⲱϩ ⲟⲛ ⲉⲧⲟⲟⲧϥ ϩⲙ ⲡϣⲁϫⲉ ⲛϭⲓ ⲡⲓϣⲟⲣⲡ ⲙⲙⲩⲥⲧⲏⲣⲓⲟⲛ ⲡⲉϫⲁϥ ⲛⲙⲙⲁⲑⲏⲧⲏⲥ ϫⲉ ⲁⲓϥⲓ-ⲧⲡⲓⲥⲧⲓⲥ ⲥⲟⲫⲓⲁ
ⲁⲓⲛⲧⲥ ⲉϩⲣⲁⲓ ⲉⲩⲧⲟⲡⲟⲥ ⲉϥⲥⲁⲡⲉⲥⲏⲧ ⲙⲡⲙⲉϩⲙⲛⲧϣⲟⲙⲧⲉ
ⲛⲁⲓⲱⲛ · ⲁⲩⲱ ⲁⲓϯ ⲛⲁⲥ ⲛⲟⲩⲙⲩⲥⲧⲏⲣⲓⲟⲛ ⲛⲃⲣⲣⲉ ⲛⲧⲉ
5 ⲡⲟⲩⲟⲉⲓⲛ ⲉⲙⲡⲁⲡⲉⲥⲁⲓⲱⲛ ⲁⲛ ⲡⲉ ⲡⲧⲟⲡⲟⲥ ⲛⲛⲁϩⲟⲣⲁ-
ⲧⲟⲥ · ⲁⲩⲱ ⲟⲛ ⲁⲓϯ ⲛⲁⲥ ⲛⲟⲩϩⲩⲙⲛⲟⲥ ⲛⲧⲉ ⲡⲟⲩⲟⲉⲓⲛ ⲣⲙⲅ̅
ϫⲉ ⲛⲛⲉⲩⲉϣϭⲙϭⲟⲙ ⲉⲣⲟⲥ ϫⲓⲛ ⲙⲡⲉⲓⲛⲁⲩ ⲛϭⲓ ⲛⲁⲣⲭⲱⲛ ⲛⲁⲓⲱⲛ · ⲁⲩⲱ ⲁⲓⲕⲁⲁⲥ ϩⲙ ⲡⲧⲟⲡⲟⲥ ⲉⲧⲙⲙⲁⲩ ·
ϣⲁⲛϯⲉⲓ ⲛⲥⲱⲥ ⲛⲧⲁϫⲓⲧⲥ ⲉⲡⲉⲥⲧⲟⲡⲟⲥ ⲉⲧⲙⲡϫⲓⲥⲉ ·
10 ⲁⲥϣⲱⲡⲉ ϭⲉ ⲛⲧⲉⲣⲓⲕⲁⲁⲥ ϩⲙ ⲡⲧⲟⲡⲟⲥ ⲉⲧⲙⲙⲁⲩ · ⲁⲥϫⲱ
ⲟⲛ ⲙⲡⲉⲓϩⲩⲙⲛⲟⲥ ⲉⲥϫⲱ ⲙⲙⲟⲥ ⲛⲧⲉⲓϩⲉ ϫⲉ

1. ϩⲛ ⲟⲩⲡⲓⲥⲧⲓⲥ ⲁⲓⲡⲓⲥⲧⲉⲩⲉ ⲉⲡⲟⲩⲟⲉⲓⲛ · ⲁⲩⲱ ⲁϥⲣ-
ⲡⲁⲙⲉⲉⲩⲉ ⲁϥⲥⲱⲧⲙ ⲉⲡⲁϩⲩⲙⲛⲟⲥ ·

2. ⲁϥⲛ-ⲧⲁϭⲟⲙ ⲉϩⲣⲁⲓ ϩⲙ ⲡⲉⲭⲁⲟⲥ · ⲙⲛ ⲡⲕⲁⲕⲉ ⲙⲡⲉ-
15 ⲥⲏⲧ ⲛⲧⲉ ⲑⲩⲗⲏ ⲧⲏⲣⲥ · ⲁⲩⲱ ⲁϥⲛⲧ ⲉϩⲣⲁⲓ ⲁϥⲕⲁⲁⲧ ϩⲛ
ⲟⲩⲁⲓⲱⲛ ⲉϥϫⲟⲥⲉ · ⲁⲩⲱ ⲉϥⲧⲁϫⲣⲏⲩ · ⲁϥⲕⲁⲁⲧ ϩⲓ ⲧⲉϩⲓⲏ ⲉⲧⲃⲏⲕ ⲉⲡⲁⲧⲟⲡⲟⲥ ·

3. ⲁⲩⲱ ⲁϥϯ ⲛⲁⲓ ⲛⲟⲩⲙⲩⲥⲧⲏⲣⲓⲟⲛ ⲛⲃⲣⲣⲉ · ⲉⲙⲡⲁ-
ⲡⲁⲓⲱⲛ ⲁⲛ ⲡⲉ · ⲁⲩⲱ ⲁϥϯ ⲛⲁⲓ ⲛⲟⲩϩⲩⲙⲛⲟⲥ ⲛⲧⲉ ⲣⲙⲅ̅ᵇ
20 ⲡⲟⲩⲟⲉⲓⲛ · ⲧⲉⲛⲟⲩ ϭⲉ ⲡⲟⲩⲟⲓⲛ ⲛⲁⲣⲭⲱⲛ ⲧⲏⲣⲟⲩ ⲛⲁⲛⲁⲩ ⲉⲛⲉⲛⲧⲁⲕⲁⲁⲩ ⲛⲙⲙⲁⲓ · ⲛⲥⲉⲣϩⲟⲧⲉ · ⲁⲩⲱ ⲛⲥⲉⲡⲓⲥⲧⲉⲩⲉ ⲉⲡⲟⲩⲟⲉⲓⲛ ·

ⲡⲉⲓϩⲩⲙⲛⲟⲥ ϭⲉ ⲁⲥϫⲟⲟϥ ⲛϭⲓ ⲧⲡⲓⲥⲧⲓⲥ ⲥⲟⲫⲓⲁ ⲉⲥ-
ⲣⲁϣⲉ ϫⲉ ⲁⲩⲛⲧⲥ ⲉϩⲣⲁⲓ ϩⲙ ⲡⲉⲭⲁⲟⲥ · ⲁⲩⲱ ⲁⲩⲛⲧⲥ

---

8 MS ⲛⲁⲓⲱⲛ; read ⲛ̅ⲛ̅ⲁⲓⲱⲛ.
11 ϫⲉ inserted in margin.
19 ⲁⲓⲱⲛ: dittography, expunged.

continued again with the discourse, he said to the disciples :
"I took the Pistis Sophia, I brought her out to a *place* which
is below the thirteenth *aeon*. And I gave to her a new *mystery*
of the light, which is not that of her *aeon*, the *place* of the
invisible ones. And I gave to her a *song of praise* of the light
so that from this time the *archons* of the *aeons* would not
be able to have power over her. And I set her in that *place*
until I should come for her and take her to her *place* which
is in the height.

Now it happened when I set her in that *place*, she spoke
again this *song of praise*, saying thus :

1. 'In *faith* I have *believed* in the Light; and he remembered
me, he heard my *song of praise*.

2. He brought my power out of the *Chaos* of all the
matter, and the darkness below. And he brought me out,
he placed me in an *aeon* on high which is strong; he has
set me on the way which leads to my *place*.

3. And he gave me a new *mystery* which is not that of my
aeon; and he gave me a *song of praise* of the light. Now at
this time, O Light, all the *archons* of the light will see what
thou hast done for me, and they will be afraid, and they
will *believe* in the light.'

Now the Pistis Sophia spoke this *song of praise*, rejoicing
because she was brought out of the *Chaos*, and she was
brought | to the *places* which are below the thirteenth *aeon*.

ЄΝΤΟΠΟϹ ЄΤ⳯ΠЄϹΗΤ ⳯ΠΜЄⳕ⳯ΝΤϢΟΜΤЄ Ν̄ΑΙϢΝ· ΤЄ-
ΝΟΥ 6Є ΠЄΤЄΡЄ ΠЄ4ΝΟΥϹ ΚΙΜ ЄΡΟ4 ЄΤΡЄ4ΝΟΪ Μ̄-
ΠΒϢⳕ ⳯ΠΠΝΟΗΜⳆ ⳯ΦΥΜΝΟϹ ΠЄΝΤⳆϹⳊΟΟ4 Ν̄61 ΤΠΙϹΤΙϹ
ϹΟΦΙⳆ· ΜⳆΡЄ4ЄΙ' 6ΘΗ Ν̄ⳊΟΟ4· Α4ЄΙ' 6ΘΗ Ν̄61 ⳆΝ-
5 ⳆΡЄⳆϹ ΠЄⳊⳆ4 ⳊЄ ΠⳆⳊΟЄΙϹ· ΠⳆΪ ΠЄ Ν̄ΤⳆ ΤЄΚ6ΟΜ
Ν̄ΟΥΟЄΙΝ ΠΡΟΦΗΤЄΥ6 ⳕⳆΡΟ4 ⳯ΠΙΟΥΟЄΙϢ ⳕΙΤⲚ̄ ⳆⳆΥ-
ЄΙⳆ· ⳊЄ

　　1. ⳕⲚ̄ ΟΥⳕΥΠΟΜΟΝΗ ⳆΪⳕΥΠΟΜΙΝЄ ЄΠⳊΟΪϹ[**] Α4†ⳕΤΗ4 ⟨ΡⲚⳆ⟩
ЄΡΟΪ ⳆΥϢ Α4ϹϢΤⲘ̄ ЄΠⳆϹΟⳕⲤ̄·

10 　　2. Α4Ν̄-ΤⳆⳅΥⳊΗ ЄⳕΡⳆΪ ⳕⲘ̄ ΠϢΗΪ Ν̄ΤΤⳆⳆⳆΙΠϢΡΙⳆ ⲘⲚ̄
ΠΟΜЄ Ν̄ΤⳆⳊΟΪⳕЄ· Α4ΤⳆⳕЄ-ΝⳆΟΥЄΡΗΤЄ ЄΡⳆΤΟΥ ⳕΙⳊⲚ̄
ΟΥΠЄΤΡⳆ· ⳆΥϢ Α4ϹΟΥΤⲚ̄-ΝⳆΤⳆ6ϹЄ·

　　3. Α4ΝΟΥⳊЄ ЄΡϢΪ Ν̄ΟΥⳊϢ Ν̄ΒΡΡЄ ΟΥϹΜΟΥ ⳯ΠЄΝ-
ΝΟΥΤЄ· ΟΥΝ-ⳕⳆⳕ ΝⳆΝⳆΥ Ν̄ϹЄΡⳕΟΤЄ ⳆΥϢ Ν̄ϹЄⳕЄⳆΠΙⳕЄ
15 ЄΠⳊΟЄΙϹ·

　　ⳆϹϢϢΠЄ 6Є Ν̄ΤЄΡЄ ⳆΝⳆΡЄⳆϹ ΤⳆΥ6-ΠΝΟΗΜⳆ Ν̄Τ-
ΠΙϹΤΙϹ ϹΟΦΙⳆ ΠЄⳊⳆ4 ΝⳆ4 Ν̄61 ΠΙϢΟΡⲠ̄ ⳯ΜΥϹΤΗΡΙΟΝ
ⳊЄ ЄΥ6Є ⳆΝⳆΡЄⳆϹ ΠΜⳆΚⳆΡΙΟϹ· Α4ΟΥϢⳕ ⳆЄ ΟΝ
ЄΤΟΟΤ4 ⳕⲘ̄ ΠϢⳆⳊЄ ΠЄⳊⳆ4 Ν̄ⲘⲘⳆΘΗΤΗϹ ⳊЄ ΝⳆΪ ΝЄ
20 Ν̄ϢⳆⳊЄ ΤΗΡΟΥ ЄΝΤⳆΥϢϢΠЄ Ν̄ΤΠΙϹΤΙϹ ϹΟΦΙⳆ· ⳆϹ-
ϢϢΠЄ 6Є Ν̄ΤЄΡⲠ̄Ⲧ̄Ⲥ̄ ЄΠΤΟΠΟϹ ЄΤ⳯ΠЄϹⳕΤ ⳯ΠΜЄⳕ-
ⲘⲚ̄ΤϢΟΜΤЄ Ν̄ΝⳆΙϢΝ· ⳆΪЄΙ' ЄΪΝⳆΒϢΚ ЄΠΟΥΟЄΙΝ Ν̄ΤⳆ-⟨ΡⲚⳆ [b]⟩
ⳆΟ ⳕⳆΡΟϹ· ΠЄⳊⳆϹ ΝⳆΪ ⳊЄ ΠΟΥΟЄΙΝ Ν̄ΝΟΥΟЄΙΝ ЄΚ-

1　MS ⳯ΠΜЄⳕ⳯⳯Ⲛ̄ΤϢΟΜΤЄ.
20　MS Ν̄Π̄ΠΙϹΤΙϹ ; second Ν expunged.
22　MS Ν̄ΠⳆΙϢ⳩Ν; read Ν̄ΑΙϢ⳩.

Now at this time, he whose *mind* moves him to *understand* the interpretation of the *thought* in the *song of praise* which the Pistis Sophia spoke, let him come forward and say it."

Andrew came forward, he said : "My Lord, this is what thy light-power once *prophesied* through David, saying :

1. 'I *waited* with *endurance* for the Lord; he gave heed to me and he heard my supplication.

2. He brought my *soul* up from the pit of *wretchedness* and the miry clay; he has set my feet upon a *rock* and he has directed my steps.

3. He has put a new song into my mouth, a blessing for our God. Many will see and will be afraid, and will *hope* in the Lord' *."

Now it happened when Andrew gave the *thought* of the Pistis Sophia, the First *Mystery* said to him : "*Excellent, Andrew, thou blessed one.*"

75. *However* he (the First Mystery) continued again with the discourse. He said to the *disciples* : "These are all the events which happened to the Pistis Sophia. Now it happened when I brought her to the *place* which is below the thirteenth *aeon*, I was about to go to the light and to abandon her, she said to me : 'O Light of Lights, thou | wilt go to the

---

*   Ps. 39.1-3

ΝΑΒωΚ ΕΠΟΥΟΪΝ Ν̄ΓΛΟ ϨΑΡΟΪ · ΑΥω Ν̄ϤΕΙΜΕ Ν̄6Ι ΠΑ-

ΔΑΜΑC ΠΤΥΡΑΝΝΟC ΧΕ ΑΚΛΟ ϨΑΡΟΪ · ΑΥω Ν̄ϤΕΙΜΕ

ΧΕ Ν̄ϤϢΟΟΠ ΑΝ Ν̄6Ι ΠΕΤΝΑΝΑϨΜΕΤ · ϤΝΗΥ ΟΝ ΕΡΟΪ

ΕΠΕΪΤΟΠΟC Ν̄ΤΟϤ Μ̄Ν ΝΕϤΑΡΧωΝ ΤΗΡΟΥ ΕΤΜΟCΤΕ

5 Μ̄ΜΟΪ ΑΥω ΟΝ ΠΑΥΘΑΔΗC ΝΑϮ-6ΟΜ Ν̄ΤΕϤΠΡΟΒΟΛΗ

Ν̄ϨΟ Μ̄ΜΟΥΪ Ν̄CΕΕΙ' ΤΗΡΟΥ Ν̄CΕϨωΧ Μ̄ΜΟΪ ϨΙ ΟΥCΟΠ ·

ΑΥω Ν̄CΕϤΙ-ΠΑΟΥΟΕΙΝ ΤΗΡϤ ϨΡΑΪ Ν̄ϨΗΤ · ΑΥω Ν̄ΤΑ-

ϢωΠΕ Ν̄ΑΤ6ΟΜ · ΑΥω ΟΝ ΤΑϢωΠΕ Ν̄ΑΤΟΥΟΕΙΝ · ΤΕ-

ΝΟΥ 6Ε ΠΟΥΟΕΙΝ ΑΥω ΠΑΟΥΟΕΙΝ ϤΙ-Τ6ΟΜ Μ̄ΠΕΥΟΥ-⟨ρπ̄6⟩

10 ΟΪΝ Ν̄ϨΗΤΟΥ · ΧΕΚΑΑC Ν̄ΝΕΥΕϢ6Μ6ΟΜ Ν̄ϨωΧ Μ̄ΜΟΪ

ΧΙΝ Μ̄ΠΕΪΝΑΥ · ΑCϢωΠΕ 6Ε Ν̄ΤΕΡΙCωΤΜ̄ ΕΝΕΪϢΑΧΕ

ΕCΧω Μ̄ΜΟΟΥ Ν̄6Ι ΤΠΙCΤΙC CΟΦΙΑ · ΑΪΟΥωϢΒ̄ ΝΑC

ΕΪΧω Μ̄ΜΟC ΧΕ Μ̄ΠΑΤΕ ΠΑΪωΤ ΚΕΛΕΥΕ ΝΑΪ ΠΕΝΤ-

ΑϤΠΡΟΒΑΛΕ Μ̄ΜΟΪ ΕΒΟΛ · ΕΤΡΑϤΙ-ΠΕΥΟΥΟΪΝ Ν̄ϨΗΤΟΥ ·

15 ΑΛΛΑ ϮΝΑCΦΡΑΓΙΖΕ Ν̄Ν̄ΤΟΠΟC Μ̄ΠΑΥΘΑΔΗC Μ̄Ν ΝΕϤ-

ΑΡΧωΝ ΤΗΡΟΥ ΝΑΪ ΕΤΜΟCΤΕ Μ̄ΜΟ · ΧΕ ΑΡΕΠΙCΤΕΥΕ

ΕΠΟΥΟΕΙΝ · ΑΥω ΟΝ ϮΝΑCΦΡΑΓΙΖΕ Ν̄Ν̄ΤΟΠΟC Μ̄ΠΑ-

ΔΑΜΑC Μ̄Ν ΝΕϤΑΡΧωΝ ΧΕ Ν̄ΝΕϢ ΟΥΟΝ Μ̄ΜΟΟΥ 6Μ-

6ΟΜ ΕΠΟΛΕΜΕΙ Ν̄Μ̄ΜΕ · ϢΑΝΤΕ ΠΕΥΟΕΙϢ ΧωΚ ΕΒΟΛ ·

20 ΑΥω ϢΑΝΤϤΕΙ' Ν̄6Ι ΠΚΑΙΡΟC Ν̄ϤΚΕΛΕΥΕ ΝΑΪ Ν̄6Ι ΠΑ-⟨ρπ̄6 ᵇ⟩

ΕΙωΤ · Ν̄ΤΑϤΙ-ΠΕΥΟΥΟΕΙΝ Ν̄ϨΗΤΟΥ · ΜΝΝ̄CωC ΔΕ ΟΝ

ΠΕΧΑΪ ΝΑC · ΧΕ CωΤΜ ΤΑϢΑΧΕ Ν̄Μ̄ΜΕ ΕΠΕΥΟΥΟΕΙϢ

ΕΤΕΡΕ ΝΑΪ ΝΑϢωΠΕ Ν̄ϨΗΤϤ ΕΤΕ ΝΕΝΤΑΪΧΟΟΥ ΝΕ ·

---

13   MS Μ̄ΠΑΤΕΠΑΤΕ ; last four letters crossed out.
24   MS ΝΕΝΕ.

light and abandon me, and Adamas, the *Tyrant*, will know
that thou hast abandoned me, and he will know that there
is no one who will save me. He will come again to me to
this *place*, he and all his *archons* which hate me. And the
Authades will again give power to his lion-faced *emanation*,
that they all come and oppress me at the same time and take
away all my light from me, so that I become powerless, and
I also become without light. Now at this time, O Light and
my Light, take the power of their light from them, so that
they have not the power to oppress me from this time.'

Now it happened when I heard these words which the
Pistis Sophia said, I answered her, saying: 'My Father
who *emanated* me has not yet *commanded* me to take away
their light from them, *but* I will *seal* the *places* of the
Authades and all his *aeons* which hate thee, because thou
hast *believed* in the light. And furthermore I will *seal* the
places of Adamas and his *archons*, so that none of them are
able to *wage war* on thee until their time is completed, and
until the *appointed time* comes when my Father *commands*
me to take away their light from them.'

76. *But* after this I said to her again : 'Hear that I speak
with thee about their time, in which these things will happen
which I have said to thee. | They will happen when the
three times are completed.'

ⲈⲨⲚⲀϢⲰⲠⲈ ⲈⲢⲈϢⲀⲚ ϢⲞⲘⲚⲦ ⲚⲞⲨⲞⲈⲓϢ ϪⲰⲔ ⲈⲂⲞⲖ.
ⲀⲤⲞⲨⲰϢⲂ ⲚϬⲒ ⲦⲠⲒⲤⲦⲒⲤ ⲤⲞⲪⲒⲀ· ⲠⲈϪⲀⲤ ⲚⲀⲒ· ϪⲈ ⲠⲞⲨ-
ⲞⲈⲒⲚ· ⲈⲒⲚⲀⲈⲒⲘⲈ ⲦⲰⲚ ⲈⲨϢⲀⲚϢⲰⲠⲈ ⲚϬⲒ ⲠϢⲞⲘⲚⲦ
ⲚⲞⲨⲞⲈⲒϢ· ϪⲈⲔⲀⲤ ⲈⲒⲈⲞⲨⲚⲞϤ ⲘⲘⲞⲒ· ⲀⲨⲰ ⲚⲦⲀⲢⲀϢⲈ
5 ϪⲈ ⲀϤϨⲰⲚ ⲈϨⲞⲨⲚ ⲚϬⲒ ⲠⲈⲞⲨⲞⲈⲒϢ ⲈⲦⲢⲈⲔϪⲒⲦ ⲈⲠⲀⲦⲞ-
ⲠⲞⲤ· ⲀⲨⲰ ⲞⲚ ⲦⲚⲀⲢⲀϢⲈ ϪⲈ ⲀϤⲈⲒ' ⲚϬⲒ ⲠⲈⲞⲨⲞⲈⲒϢ
ⲈⲔⲚⲀϤⲒ-ⲚϬⲞⲘ ⲚⲞⲨⲞⲈⲒⲚ ϨⲚ ⲚⲎ ⲦⲎⲢⲞⲨ ⲈⲦⲘⲞⲤⲦⲈ ⲘⲘⲞⲒ·
ϪⲈ ⲀⲠⲒⲤⲦⲈⲨⲈ ⲈⲠⲈⲔⲞⲨⲞⲈⲒⲚ· ⲀⲚⲞⲔ ⲆⲈ ⲀⲒⲞⲨⲰϢⲂ ⲢⲚⲈ
ⲠⲈϪⲀⲒ ⲚⲀⲤ ϪⲈ ⲈⲢⲈϢⲀⲚⲚⲀⲨ ⲈⲦⲠⲨⲖⲎ ⲘⲠⲈⲐⲎⲤⲀⲨⲢⲞⲤ
10 ⲘⲠⲚⲞϬ ⲚⲞⲨⲞⲒⲚ ⲦⲀⲒ ⲈⲦⲞⲨⲎⲚ ⲈⲠⲘⲈϨⲘⲚⲦϢⲞⲘⲦⲈ Ⲛ-
ⲀⲒⲰⲚ ⲈⲦⲈ ⲦⲈϨⲂⲞⲨⲢ ⲦⲈ ⲈⲨϢⲀⲚⲞⲨⲰⲚ ⲚⲦⲠⲨⲖⲎ ⲈⲦⲘ-
ⲘⲀⲨ· ⲈⲒⲈ ⲀⲨϪⲰⲔ ⲈⲂⲞⲖ ⲚϬⲒ ⲠϢⲞⲘⲚⲦ ⲚⲞⲨⲞⲈⲒϢ·
ⲀⲤⲞⲨⲰϢⲂ ⲞⲚ ⲚϬⲒ ⲦⲤⲞⲪⲒⲀ ⲠⲈϪⲀⲤ ϪⲈ ⲠⲞⲨⲞⲈⲒⲚ·
ⲈⲒⲚⲀⲈⲒⲘⲈ ⲦⲰⲚ ⲈⲒϨⲘ ⲠⲈⲒⲦⲞⲠⲞⲤ· ϪⲈ ⲀⲨⲞⲨⲰⲚ ⲚⲦⲠⲨ-
15 ⲖⲎ ⲈⲦⲘⲘⲀⲨ· ⲀⲚⲞⲔ ⲆⲈ ⲀⲒⲞⲨⲰϢⲂ ⲠⲈϪⲀⲒ ⲚⲀⲤ ϪⲈ
ⲈⲨϢⲀⲚⲞⲨⲰⲚ ⲚⲦⲠⲨⲖⲎ ⲈⲦⲘⲘⲀⲨ· ⲤⲈⲚⲀⲈⲒⲘⲈ ⲚϬⲒ ⲚⲈⲦ-
ϢⲞⲞⲠ ϨⲚ ⲚⲀⲒⲰⲚ ⲦⲎⲢⲞⲨ ⲈⲦⲂⲈ ⲠⲚⲞϬ ⲚⲞⲨⲞⲒⲚ ⲈⲦⲚⲀ-
ϢⲰⲠⲈ ϨⲚ ⲚⲈⲨⲦⲞⲠⲞⲤ ⲦⲎⲢⲞⲨ· ⲠⲖⲎⲚ ϬⲈ ⲈⲒⲤϨⲎⲎⲦⲈ
ⲀⲒⲔⲀⲀⲤ ϪⲈ ⲚⲚⲈⲨⲦⲞⲖⲘⲀ ⲈⲢⲞ ϨⲚ ⲖⲀⲀⲨ ⲘⲠⲈⲐⲞⲞⲨ·
20 ϢⲀⲚⲦⲞⲨϪⲰⲔ ⲈⲂⲞⲖ ⲚϬⲒ ⲠϢⲞⲘⲚⲦ ⲚⲞⲨⲞⲈⲒϢ· ⲚⲦⲞ ⲢⲚⲈᵇ
ⲆⲈ ⲦⲈⲢⲀϢⲰⲠⲈ ⲈⲨⲚⲦⲈ ⲦⲈϨⲞⲨⲤⲒⲀ ⲘⲘⲀⲨ ⲈⲂⲰⲔ ⲈϨⲢⲀⲒ
ⲈⲠⲈⲨⲘⲚⲦⲤⲚⲞⲞⲨⲤ ⲚⲀⲒⲰⲚ ⲘⲠⲈⲞⲨⲞⲈⲒϢ ⲈⲦⲈϨⲚⲈ· ⲀⲨⲰ
ⲞⲚ ⲚⲦⲈⲔⲞⲦⲈ ⲚⲦⲈⲈⲒ' ⲈⲠⲞⲨⲦⲞⲠⲞⲤ· ⲠⲀⲒ ⲈⲦⲘⲠⲈⲤⲎⲦ
ⲘⲠⲘⲈϨⲘⲚⲦϢⲞⲘⲦⲈ ⲚⲀⲒⲰⲚ· ⲠⲀⲒ ⲈⲢⲈϢⲞⲞⲠ ⲚϨⲎⲦϤ ⲦⲈ-

---

1 MS ϢⲞⲘⲦⲦ; read ⲠϢⲞⲘⲦⲦ.
8 Ⲧ in upper right-hand margin at end of quire.
16 ⲚϬⲒ ⲚⲈⲦϢⲞⲞⲠ in margin.

The Pistis Sophia answered, she said to me : 'O Light, by
what shall I know when the three times will happen, that
I may rejoice and be glad, because the time has arrived that
thou takest me to my *place*? And furthermore I will rejoice
because the time has come that thou wilt take away the
light-power from all those that hate me because I *believed*
in thy light.'

However, I answered and said to her : 'When thou seest
the *gate* of the *Treasury* of the great Light — this which
opens to the thirteenth *aeon*, namely the left — when that
gate is opened the three times are completed.'

The Pistis Sophia answered again, she said : 'O Light,
by what shall I know, when I am in this *place*, that *gate*
has been opened?'

But I answered and said to her : 'When that *gate* is opened,
those who are in all the *aeons* will know, because of the
great light which will happen in all their *places. Nevertheless*
see, I have now established it that they (the archons) will
not *dare* anything evil against thee, until the three times are
completed. *But* thou wilt have the *authority* there to go to
their twelve *aeons* at the time which pleases thee, and to
return again, and to come to thy *place* in which thou art at
this time, which is below the thirteenth *aeon*. | *But* thou

339

ΝΟΥ· ΑΛΛΑ Ν̄ΤΕΡΑϢϢΠΕ ΑΝ ΕΥΝ̄-ΤΕϪΟΥCΙΑ Μ̄ΜΑΥ·
ΕΒϢΚ ΕϨΟΥΝ ΕΤΠΥΛΗ Μ̄ΠϪΙCΕ· ΤΑΪ ΕΤϢΟΟΠ Ϩ̄Μ
ΠΜΕϨΜΝ̄ΤϢΟΜΤΕ Ν̄ΑΙϢΝ· ΕΤΡΕΒϢΚ ΕϨΟΥΝ ΕΠΟΥΤΟ-
ΠΟC ΠΑΪ Ν̄ΤΑΡΕΕΙˊ ΕΒΟΛ Ν̄ϨΗΤϤ· ΠΛΗΝ ϬΕ ΕΥϢΑΝ-
5 ϪϢΚ ΕΒΟΛ Ν̄ϬΙ ΠϢΟΜΝ̄Τ Ν̄ΟΥΟΕΙϢ)· ϤΝΑϨϢϪ Μ̄ΜΟ
ΟΝ Ν̄ϬΙ ΠΑΥΘΑΛΗC ΜΝ̄ ΝΕϤΑΡΧϢΝ ΤΗΡΟΥ ΕΤΡΕΥϤΙ-
ΠΟΥΟΥΟΪΝ Ν̄ϨΗΤΕ·⋆⋆ ΕϤϬΟΝ̄Τ ΕΡΟ· ΕϤΜΕΕΥΕ ϪΕ Ν̄ΤΟ ρπη
ΑΡΕΚΑΤΕΧΕ Ν̄ΤΕϤϬΟΜ Ϩ̄Μ ΠΕΧΛΑΟC· ΑΥϢ ΕϤΜΕΕΥΕ
ϪΕ Ν̄ΤΟ ΑΡΕϤΙ-ΠΕCΟΥΟΕΙΝ Ν̄ϨΗΤC· ϤΝΑΝΟΥϬC ϬΕ
10 ΕΡΟ ΕΤΡΕϤϤΙ-ΠΟΥΟΥΟΕΙΝ Ν̄ϨΗΤΕ ϪΕ ΕϤΕΧΟΟΥϤ ΕΠΕ-
ΧΛΑΟC· Ν̄CΕΤΑΛϤ ΕϨΟΥΝ ΕΤΕϤΠΡΟΒΟΛΗ ΕΤΜ̄ΜΑΥ ϪΕ-
ΚΑC ΕCΕϢϬΜ̄ϬΟΜ Ν̄ΕΙˊ ΕϨΡΑΪ Ϩ̄Μ ΠΕΧΛΑΟC· ΑΥϢ Ν̄CΕΙˊ
ΕΠΕϤΤΟΠΟC· ΝΑΪ ΔΕ ϤΝΑϨΙΤΟΟΤϤ ΕΡΟΟΥ Ν̄ϬΙ ΠΛΑΔ-
ΜΑC· ΑΝΟΚ ΔΕ ϮΝΑϤΙ-ΝΟΥϬΟΜ ΤΗΡΟΥ Ν̄ϨΗΤϤ· ΤΑ-
15 ΤΑΑΥ ΝΕ· ΑΥϢ ϮΝΑΕΙˊ Ν̄ΤΑϤΙΤΟΥ· ΤΕΝΟΥ ϬΕ ΕΥ-
ϢΑΝϨϢϪ Μ̄ΜΟ Μ̄ΠΕΟΥΟΕΙϢ) ΕΤΜ̄ΜΑΥ· ϨΥΜΝΕΥΕ ΕϨΡΑΪ
ΕΠΟΥΟΕΙΝ· ΑΥϢ ΑΝΟΚ Ν̄ϮΝΑϢϢΚ ΑΝ ΕΤΡΑΒΟΗΘΕΙ
ΕΡΟ· ΑΥϢ ϮΝΗΥ ΕΡΑΤΕ Ϩ̄Ν ΟΥϬΕΠΗ· ΕΒΟΛ Ϩ̄Ν Ν̄ΤΟ-
ΠΟC ΕΤΜ̄ΠΟΥΕCΗΤ· ΑΥϢ ϮΝΗΥ ΕϨΡΑΪ ΕΝΕΥΤΟΠΟC· ρπη ᵇ
20 ΤΑϤΙ-ΠΕΥΟΥΟΕΙΝ Ν̄ϨΗΤΟΥ· ΑΥϢ ϮΝΗΥ ΕΠΕΪΤΟΠΟC
ΕΝΤΑΪΚΑΑΤΕ Ν̄ϨΗΤϤ ΠΑΪ ΕΤΝ̄ΠΕCΗΤ Μ̄ΠΜΕϨΜΝ̄ΤϢΟΜΤΕ
Ν̄ΑΙϢΝ· ϢΑΝϮϪΙΤΕ ΕΠΟΥΤΟΠΟC ΠΑΪ Ν̄ΤΑΡΕΕΙˊ ΕΒΟΛ
Ν̄ϨΗΤϤ·

1　MS ΕΥΝ ΤΕϪΟΥCΙΑ; read ΕΥΝ̄ΤΕ ΤΕϪΟΥCΙΑ.
7　ῙᾹ in upper left-hand margin at beginning of quire.
18　MS ΕΒΟΛ Ϩ̄Ν Ν̄ΤΟΠΟC; read ΕΝ̄ΤΟΠΟC.
21　MS ΕΤΝ̄ΠΕCΗΤ; read ΕΤΜ̄ΠΕCΗΤ.

wilt not have *authority* there to go within the *gate* of the
height which is in the thirteenth *aeon*, to go within to thy
place from which thou didst come forth. *Nevertheless*, when
the three times are now completed, the Authades and all
his *archons* will oppress thee again to take away thy light
from thee. He will be angry with thee, thinking that thou
hast *restrained* his power in the *Chaos*, and thinking that
thou hast taken away the light (of his power) from it. He
will now be infuriated against thee to take away thy light
from thee, so that he may send it down to the *Chaos* and put
it into those *emanations* of his, so that they should have
power to come out of the *Chaos*, and to come to his (the
Authades) *place*. *But* Adamas will begin these things. *But*
I will take away all thy powers from him and give them
to thee, and I will come and take them. Now at the moment
when they oppress thee at that time, *sing praises* to the light
and I will not delay to *help* thee. And I will come to thee
in haste to the *places* [1] below thee. And I will come down
to their *places* to take their light from them. And I will come
to this *place* in which I have established thee, which is below
the thirteenth *aeon*, until I take thee to thy *place* from which
thou didst come forth.' |

---

[1] (18) to the places; MS: out of the places.

ⲋ ⲁⲥϣⲱⲡⲉ ϭⲉ ⲛ̄ⲧⲉⲣⲉ ⲧⲡⲓⲥⲧⲓⲥ ⲥⲟⲫⲓⲁ ⲥⲱⲧⲙ̄ ⲉⲛⲉⲓ̈-
ϣⲁϫⲉ ⲉⲓ̈ϫⲱ ⲙ̄ⲙⲟⲟⲩ ⲛⲁⲥ· ⲁⲥⲣⲁϣⲉ ⲍ̄ⲛ ⲟⲩⲛⲟϭ ⲛ̄ⲣⲁ-
ϣⲉ· ⲁⲛⲟⲕ ⲇⲉ ⲁⲓ̈ⲕⲁⲁⲥ ⲍ̄ⲙ ⲡⲧⲟⲡⲟⲥ ⲉⲧⲙ̄ⲡⲉⲥⲏⲧ ⲙ̄ⲡⲙⲉⲍ-
ⲙⲛ̄ⲧϣⲟⲙⲧⲉ ⲛ̄ⲁⲓⲱⲛ· ⲁⲓ̈ⲃⲱⲕ ⲉⲡⲟⲩⲟⲉⲓⲛ· ⲁⲓ̈ⲗⲟ ⲍⲁⲣⲟⲥ·
5 ⲛⲉⲓ̈ϣⲁϫⲉ ⲇⲉ ⲧⲏⲣⲟⲩ ⲛⲉⲣⲉ ⲡⲓϣⲟⲣⲡ̄ ⲙ̄ⲙⲩⲥⲧⲏⲣⲓⲟⲛ ϫⲱ
ⲙ̄ⲙⲟⲟⲩ ⲛ̄ⲙ̄ⲙⲁⲑⲏⲧⲏⲥ ϫⲉ ⲁⲩϣⲱⲡⲉ ⲛ̄ⲧⲡⲓⲥⲧⲓⲥ ⲥⲟⲫⲓⲁ·
ⲁⲩⲱ ⲛⲉϥⲍⲙⲟⲟⲥ ⲡⲉ ⲍⲓϫⲙ̄ ⲡⲧⲟⲟⲩ ⲛ̄ⲛ̄ϫⲟⲉⲓⲧ· ⲉϥϫⲱ
ⲛ̄ⲛⲉⲓ̈ϣⲁϫⲉ ⲧⲏⲣⲟⲩ ⲛ̄ⲧⲙⲏⲧⲉ ⲛ̄ⲙ̄ⲙⲁⲑⲏⲧⲏⲥ·

ⲁϥⲟⲩⲱⲍ ⲇⲉ ⲟⲛ ⲉⲧⲟⲟⲧϥ̄ ⲡⲉϫⲁϥ ⲛⲁⲩ ϫⲉ ⲁⲥϣⲱⲡⲉ
10 ⲇⲉ ⲟⲛ ⲙⲛ̄ⲛ̄ⲥⲁ ⲛⲁⲓ̈ ⲧⲏⲣⲟⲩ ⲉⲓ̈ϣⲟⲟⲡ ⲍ̄ⲙ ⲡⲕⲟⲥⲙⲟⲥ ⲛ̄-ᴾᴺᴴ
ⲧⲙⲛ̄ⲧⲣⲱⲙⲉ· ⲉⲓ̈ⲍⲙⲟⲟⲥ ⲍⲁⲧⲛ̄ ⲧⲉⲍⲓⲏ ⲉⲧⲉ ⲡⲉⲓ̈ⲧⲟⲡⲟⲥ ⲡⲉ
ⲉⲧⲉ ⲡⲧⲟⲟⲩ ⲛ̄ⲛ̄ϫⲟⲓⲧ ⲡⲉ· ⲍⲁⲑⲏ ⲉⲙⲡⲁⲧⲟⲩⲧⲛ̄ⲛⲉⲩ-ⲡⲁ-
ⲉⲛⲇⲩⲙⲁ ⲛⲁⲓ̈· ⲡⲁⲓ̈ ⲉⲛⲧⲁⲓ̈ⲕⲁⲁϥ ⲍ̄ⲙ ⲡⲙⲉⲍϫⲟⲩⲧⲁϥⲧⲉ ⲙ̄-
ⲙⲩⲥⲧⲏⲣⲓⲟⲛ ϫⲛ̄ⲍⲟⲩⲛ· ⲡϣⲟⲣⲡ̄ ⲇⲉ ⲍⲱⲱϥ ⲡⲉ ϫⲓⲛⲃⲟⲗ·
15 ⲡⲁⲓ̈ ⲉⲧⲉ ⲛ̄ⲧⲟϥ ⲡⲉ ⲡⲛⲟϭ ⲛ̄ⲁⲭⲱⲣⲏⲧⲟⲥ· ⲡⲁⲓ̈ ⲉⲛⲧⲁⲓ̈-
ⲃⲟⲩⲃⲟⲩ ⲛ̄ⲍⲏⲧϥ̄· ⲁⲩⲱ ⲍⲁⲑⲏ ⲉⲙⲡⲁ†ⲃⲱⲕ ⲉⲡϫⲓⲥⲉ ⲉϫⲓ-
ⲡⲁⲕⲉⲉⲛⲇⲩⲙⲁ ⲥⲛⲁⲩ· ⲉⲓ̈ⲍⲙⲟⲟⲥ ⲍⲁⲧⲛ̄ⲧⲏⲩⲧⲛ̄ ⲍ̄ⲙ ⲡⲉⲓ̈-
ⲧⲟⲡⲟⲥ ⲉⲧⲉ ⲛ̄ⲧⲟϥ ⲡⲉ ⲡⲧⲟⲟⲩ ⲛ̄ⲛ̄ϫⲟⲉⲓⲧ· ⲁϥϫⲱⲕ ⲛ̄ϭⲓ
ⲡⲉⲟⲩⲟⲉⲓϣ ⲉⲛⲧⲁⲓ̈ϫⲟⲟϥ ⲛ̄ⲧⲡⲓⲥⲧⲓⲥ ⲥⲟⲫⲓⲁ ϫⲉ ϥⲛⲁⲍⲱϫ
20 ⲙ̄ⲙⲟ ⲛ̄ϭⲓ ⲡⲁⲇⲁⲙⲁⲥ ⲙⲛ̄ ⲛⲉϥⲁⲣⲭⲱⲛ ⲧⲏⲣⲟⲩ· ⲁⲥϣⲱⲡⲉ
ϭⲉ ⲛ̄ⲧⲉⲣⲉϥϣⲱⲡⲉ ⲛ̄ϭⲓ ⲡⲉⲟⲩⲟⲉⲓϣ ⲉⲧⲙ̄ⲙⲁⲩ· ⲁⲛⲟⲕ ⲇⲉ ᴾᴺᴴᵇ
ⲛⲉⲓ̈ϣⲟⲟⲡ ⲡⲉ ⲍ̄ⲙ ⲡⲕⲟⲥⲙⲟⲥ ⲛ̄ⲧⲙⲛ̄ⲧⲣⲱⲙⲉ· ⲉⲓ̈ⲍⲙⲟⲟⲥ
ⲍⲁⲧⲛ̄ⲧⲏⲩⲧⲛ̄ ⲍ̄ⲙ ⲡⲉⲓ̈ⲧⲟⲡⲟⲥ ⲉⲧⲉ ⲡⲧⲟⲟⲩ ⲛ̄ⲛ̄ϫⲟⲉⲓⲧ ⲡⲉ·
ⲁϥϭⲱϣⲧ ⲛ̄ϭⲓ ⲡⲁⲇⲁⲙⲁⲥ ⲉⲃⲟⲗ ⲍ̄ⲙ ⲡⲙⲛ̄ⲧⲥⲛⲟⲟⲩⲥ ⲛ̄-
25 ⲁⲓⲱⲛ· ⲁϥϭⲱϣⲧ ⲉⲡⲉⲥⲏⲧ ⲉⲛⲧⲟⲡⲟⲥ ⲙ̄ⲡⲉⲭⲗⲁⲟⲥ ⲁϥⲛⲁⲩ
ⲉⲧⲉϥϭⲟⲙ ⲛ̄ⲇⲁⲓⲙⲟⲛⲓⲟⲛ ⲉⲧⲍ̄ⲙ ⲡⲉⲭⲗⲁⲟⲥ ⲉⲙⲛ̄-ⲟⲩⲟⲓ̈ⲛ ⲛ̄-

---

14 MS originally ⲍ̄ⲡⲍⲟⲩⲛ; ϫ written over erasure of ⲍ, giving ϫ̄ⲡⲍⲟⲩⲛ;
read ϫⲓⲛⲍⲟⲩⲛ.

Now it happened when the Pistis Sophia heard these words which I spoke to her, she rejoiced with great joy. *But* I set her in the *place* which is below the thirteenth *aeon*, I went to the light, I abandoned her."

77. The First *Mystery however* spoke to the *disciples* of all these events, for they happened to the Pistis Sophia. And he was sitting on the Mount of Olives, speaking all these words in the midst of the *disciples*. He continued again *however*, he said to them : "*But* it happened again after all these things, as I was in the *world* of mankind, as I was sitting by the wayside that is this *place*, namely the Mount of Olives, before I had yet been sent my *garment* — which I had left behind in the 24th *mystery* from within, *but* the first from without, which is the great *incomprehensible one* in which I shone — and before I went to the height to receive my second *garment*, as I was sitting before you [1] in this *place* which is the Mount of Olives, the time was completed of which I had spoken to the Pistis Sophia thus : 'Adamas and all his *archons* will oppress thee.'

Now it happened when that time came — I *however* was in the *world* of mankind, sitting before you in this *place* which is the Mount of Olives — Adamas looked forth from the twelve *aeons*. He looked down to the *places* of the *Chaos*, he saw his *demonic* power which was in the *Chaos* with no light | at all in it, for I had taken away its light

---

[1] (17, 23) before you; Till : with you (see 173.4).

ϩⲏⲧⲥ ⲉⲡⲧⲏⲣϥ ϫⲉ ⲛⲉⲁⲓ̈ϥⲓ-ⲡⲉⲥⲟⲩⲟⲓ̈ⲛ ϩⲣⲁⲓ̈ ⲛϩⲏⲧⲥ ⲁⲩⲱ ⲁϥⲛⲁⲩ ⲉⲣⲟⲥ ⲉⲥⲟʾ ⲛⲕⲁⲕⲉ· ⲁⲩⲱ ⲉⲙⲡⲥⲉϣϭⲙϭⲟⲙ ⲉⲉⲓʾ ⲉⲡⲉϥⲧⲟⲡⲟⲥ· ⲉⲧⲉ ⲡⲙⲛⲧⲥⲛⲟⲟⲩⲥ ⲡⲉ ⲛⲁⲓⲱⲛ· ⲁϥⲣⲡⲙⲉⲉⲩⲉ ⲟⲛ ⲛϭⲓ ⲡⲁⲇⲁⲙⲁⲥ ⲛⲧⲡⲓⲥⲧⲓⲥ ⲥⲟⲫⲓⲁ ⲁⲩⲱ ⲁϥϭⲱⲛⲧ ⲉⲣⲟⲥ ⲉⲙⲁϣⲟ ⲉⲙⲁϣⲟ· ⲉϥⲙⲉⲉⲩⲉ ϫⲉ ⲛⲧⲟⲥ ⲧⲉ ⲛⲧⲁⲥⲕⲁⲧⲉⲭⲉ ⲛⲧⲉϥϭⲟⲙ ϩⲣⲁⲓ̈ ϩⲙ ⲡⲉⲭⲁⲟⲥ ** ⲁⲩⲱ ⲉϥ- ⲣⲛⲑ ⲙⲉⲉⲩⲉ ϫⲉ ⲛⲧⲟⲥ ⲧⲉ ⲛⲧⲁⲥϥⲓ-ⲡⲉⲥⲟⲩⲟⲉⲓⲛ ⲛϩⲏⲧⲥ ⲁⲩⲱ ⲁϥⲛⲟⲩϭⲥ ⲉⲙⲁⲧⲉ ⲁⲩⲱ ⲁϥⲟⲩⲉϩ-ϭⲱⲛⲧ ⲉϫⲛ ϭⲱⲛⲧ· ⲁϥⲡⲣⲟⲃⲁⲗⲉ ⲉⲃⲟⲗ ⲛϩⲏⲧϥ ⲛⲟⲩⲡⲣⲟⲃⲟⲗⲏ ⲛⲕⲁⲕⲉ· ⲁⲩⲱ ⲙⲛ ⲕⲉⲟⲩⲓ̈ ⲛⲭⲁⲟⲥ ⲙⲡⲟⲛⲏⲣⲟⲛ ⲉⲥⲛⲁϣⲧ· ϫⲉ ⲉϥⲉϣⲧⲣⲧⲣ-ⲧⲡⲓⲥⲧⲓⲥ ⲥⲟⲫⲓⲁ ϩⲣⲁⲓ̈ ⲛϩⲏⲧⲟⲩ· ⲁⲩⲱ ⲁϥⲧⲁⲙⲓⲟ ⲛⲟⲩⲧⲟⲡⲟⲥ ⲛⲕⲁⲕⲉ ϩⲣⲁⲓ̈ ϩⲙ ⲡⲉϥⲧⲟⲡⲟⲥ· ϫⲉ ⲉϥⲉϩⲱϫ ⲛⲧⲥⲟⲫⲓⲁ ϩⲣⲁⲓ̈ ⲛϩⲏⲧϥ· ⲁⲩⲱ ⲁϥϫⲓ ⲛϩⲉⲛⲙⲏⲏϣⲉ ⲛⲁⲣⲭⲱⲛ ⲛⲧⲁϥ ⲁⲩⲡⲱⲧ ⲛⲥⲁ ⲧⲥⲟⲫⲓⲁ· ⲉⲧⲣⲉⲩⲛⲧⲥ ⲉⲡⲓⲭⲁⲟⲥ ⲛⲕⲁⲕⲉ ⲉⲛⲧⲁϥⲧⲁⲙⲓⲟϥ· ⲁⲩⲱ ⲛⲥⲉϩⲱϫ ⲙⲙⲟⲥ ϩⲙ ⲡⲧⲟⲡⲟⲥ ⲉⲧⲙⲙⲁⲩ· ⲁⲩⲱ ⲛⲥⲉϣⲧⲣⲧⲱⲣⲥ ⲛϭⲓ ϯⲡⲣⲟⲃⲟⲗⲏ ⲥⲛⲧⲉ ⲛⲕⲁⲕⲉ· ⲛⲁⲓ̈ ⲉⲛⲧⲁϥⲡⲣⲟⲃⲁⲗⲉ ⲙⲙⲟⲟⲩ ⲉⲃⲟⲗ ⲛϭⲓ ⲡⲁⲇⲁⲙⲁⲥ * ⲣⲛⲑ b ϣⲁⲛⲧⲟⲩϥⲓ-ⲡⲉⲥⲟⲩⲟⲉⲓⲛ ⲧⲏⲣϥ ⲛϩⲏⲧⲥ ⲁⲩⲱ ⲛⲧⲉ ⲡⲁⲇⲁⲙⲁⲥ ϥⲓ-ⲡⲟⲩⲟⲉⲓⲛ ⲛⲧⲡⲓⲥⲧⲓⲥ ⲥⲟⲫⲓⲁ· ⲛϥⲧⲁⲁϥ ⲛϯⲡⲣⲟⲃⲟⲗⲏ ⲥⲛⲧⲉ ⲛⲕⲁⲕⲉ ⲉⲧⲛⲁϣⲧ· ⲛⲥⲉϫⲓⲧϥ ⲉⲡⲛⲟϭ ⲛⲭⲁⲟⲥ ⲉⲧⲙⲡⲉⲥⲏⲧ ⲡⲁⲓ̈ ⲉⲧⲟ | ⲛⲕⲁⲕⲉ· ⲁⲩⲱ ⲛⲥⲉⲛⲟϫϥ ⲉϩⲟⲩⲛ ⲉⲧⲉϥϭⲟⲙ ⲛⲕⲁⲕⲉ ⲉⲧⲟ ⲛⲭⲁⲟⲥ· ϫⲉ ⲙⲉϣⲁⲕ ⲉⲥⲉϣϭⲙϭⲟⲙ ⲉⲉⲓʾ ⲉⲡⲉϥⲧⲟⲡⲟⲥ· ⲉⲃⲟⲗ ϫⲉ ⲛⲉⲁⲥⲣⲕⲁⲕⲉ ⲡⲉ ⲉⲙⲁⲧⲉ· ϫⲉ ⲁⲓ̈ϥⲓ-ⲧⲉⲥϭⲟⲙ ⲛⲟⲩⲟⲉⲓⲛ ⲛϩⲏⲧⲥ·

ⲁⲥϣⲱⲡⲉ ϭⲉ ⲛⲧⲉⲣⲟⲩⲡⲱⲧ ⲛⲥⲁ ⲧⲡⲓⲥⲧⲓⲥ ⲥⲟⲫⲓⲁ· ⲁⲥⲱϣ ⲟⲛ ⲉⲃⲟⲗ ⲁⲥϩⲩⲙⲛⲉⲩⲉ ⲉϩⲣⲁⲓ̈ ⲉⲡⲟⲩⲟⲉⲓⲛ ⲉⲡⲉⲓⲇⲏ

3 MS ⲡⲉ ⲛⲁⲓⲱⲛ; read ⲛⲁⲓⲱⲛ ⲡⲉ.

from it. And he saw it, that it was dark and not able to come to his *place*, namely the twelve *aeons*. Adamas again remembered the Pistis Sophia and he was exceedingly angry with her, for he thought that it was she who had *restrained* his power in the *Chaos*, and he thought that it was she who had taken away its light from it (the power of Adamas). And he was very wrathful and added anger to anger. He *emanated* forth a dark *emanation* and another *chaotic* and *wicked* one which was powerful, so that through them he should agitate the Pistis Sophia. And he created a dark *place* in his *place*, so that he should oppress the Sophia within it. And he took many of his *archons*, they pursued the Pistis Sophia to bring her to the dark *Chaos* which he had created. And the two dark *emanations* which Adamas had *emanated* oppressed her in that *place*, and they agitated her until they took away all her light from her. And Adamas took the light of the Pistis Sophia, and he gave it to the two dark and powerful *emanations* to take to the great *Chaos* below, which is dark, and to cast it within to his dark power which is *chaotic*, so that perhaps it (the power) would be able to come to his *place*, for it had become very dark because I had taken away its light-power from it.

Now it happened when they pursued the Pistis Sophia, she cried out again, she *sang praises* to the light *since* |

ⲀⲒ̈ⲬⲞⲞ⳯ ⲚⲀⳤ ⲬⲈ ⲈⲨϢⲀⲚⳞⲰⲬ ⲘⲘⲞ ⲚⲦⲈⳞⲨⲘⲚⲈⲨⲈ Ⲉ-
ⳞⲢⲀⲒ̈ ⲈⲢⲞⲒ̈ †ⲚⲎⲨ Ⳟ̄Ⲛ ⲞⲨⳐⲈⲠⲎ · ⲚⲦⲀⲂⲞⲎⲞⲒ ⲈⲢⲞ · ⲀⳐ-
ϢⲰⲠⲈ ⳐⲈ ⲚⲦⲈⲢⲞⲨⳞⲰⲬ ⲘⲘⲞⳐ · ⲀⲚⲞⲔ ⲆⲈ ⲚⲈⲒ̈ⳞⲘⲞⲞⳐ Ⲡⲅ̄
ⲠⲈ ⳞⲀⲦ̄ⲚⲦⲎⲚⲞⲨ Ⳟ̄Ⲙ ⲠⲈⲒ̈ⲦⲞⲠⲞⳐ · ⲈⲦⲈ ⲠⲦⲞⲞⲨ Ⲛ̄ⲚⲬⲞⲒ̈Ⲧ
5 ⲠⲈ ⲀⳐⳞⲨⲘⲚⲈⲨⲈ ⲈⳞⲢⲀⲒ̈ ⲈⲠⲞⲨⲞⲈⲒⲚ ⲈⳐⲬⲰ ⲘⲘⲞⳐ ⲬⲈ

1. ⲠⲞⲨⲞⲈⲒⲚ Ⲛ̄ⲚⲞⲨⲞⲈⲒⲚ ⲀⲒ̈ⲠⲒⳐⲦⲈⲨⲈ ⲈⲢⲞⲔ · ⲚⲀⳞⲘⲈⲦ
ⲈⲚⲈⲒ̈ⲀⲢⲬⲰⲚ ⲦⲎⲢⲞⲨ ⲈⲦⲠⲎⲦ Ⲛ̄ⳐⲰⲒ̈ · ⲀⲨⲰ Ⲛ̄Ⲅ̄ⲂⲞⲎⲞⲒ ⲈⲢⲞⲒ̈ ·

2. ⲘⲎⲠⲞⲦⲈ Ⲛ̄ⳐⲈⳞⲒ-ⲠⲀⲞⲨⲞⲈⲒⲚ Ⲛ̄ⳞⲎⲦ · ⲚⲞⲈ Ⲛ̄†ⳐⲞⲘ
Ⲛ̄ⳞⲀ ⲘⲘⲞⲨⲒ̈ ⲬⲈ ⲠⲈⲔⲞⲨⲞⲒ̈Ⲛ ϢⲞⲞⲠ ⲀⲚ Ⲛ̄ⲘⲘⲀⲒ̈ Ⲙ̄Ⲛ ⲦⲈⲔ-
10 ⲀⲠⲞⳞⲢⲞⲒⲀ Ⲛ̄ⲞⲨⲞⲈⲒⲚ ⲈⲦⲢⲈⳐⲨⲚⲀⳞⲘⲈⲦ · ⲈⲘⲘⲞⲚ · ⲀⳐⳐⲰⲚⲦ
ⲈⲢⲞⲒ̈ Ⲛ̄ⳐⲒ ⲠⲀⲆⲀⲘⲀⳐ ⲈⳐⲬⲰ ⲘⲘⲞⳐ ⲚⲀⲒ̈ ⲬⲈ Ⲛ̄ⲦⲞ ⲀⲢⲈⲔⲀⲦ-
ⲈⲬⲈ Ⲛ̄ⲦⲀⳐⲞⲘ Ⳟ̄Ⲙ ⲠⲈⲬⲀⲞⳐ ·

3. ⲦⲈⲚⲞⲨ ⳐⲈ ⲠⲞⲨⲞⲈⲒⲚ Ⲛ̄ⲚⲞⲨⲞⲈⲒⲚ ⲈϢⲬⲈ ⲀⲚⲞⲔ
ⲀⲒ̄Ⲣ̄-ⲠⲀⲒ̈ · ⲀⲒ̈ⲔⲀⲦⲈⲬⲈ ⲘⲘⲞⳐ · ⲈϢⲬⲈ ⲀⲒ̄Ⲣ̄-ⲀⲀⲀⲨ Ⲛ̄ⲬⲒⲚⳐⲞⲚⳐ̄
15 Ⲛ̄ⲦⳐⲞⲘ ⲈⲦⲘ̄ⲘⲀⲨ ·

4. Ⲏ̇ ⲈϢⲬⲈ ⲀⲒ̈ⳞⲰⲬ ⲘⲘⲞⳐ Ⲛ̄ⲞⲈ Ⲛ̄ⲦⲀⳐⳞⲰⲬ ⲘⲘⲞⲒ̈ ·
ⲈⲨⲈⳐⲒ-ⲠⲀⲞⲨⲞⲈⲒⲚ Ⲛ̄ⳞⲎⲦ · Ⲛ̄ⳐⲒ ⲚⲈⲒ̈ⲀⲢⲬⲰⲚ ⲦⲎⲢⲞⲨ ⲈⲦⲠⲎⲦ Ⲡⲝ̄ᵇ
Ⲛ̄ⳐⲰⲒ̈ · ⲀⲨⲰ ⲈⲨⲈⲔⲀⲀⲦ ⲈⲂⲞⲀ ⲈⲒ̈ϢⲞⲨⲈⲒⲦ ·

5. ⲀⲨⲰ ⲈⲢⲈ ⲠⲬⲀⲬⲈ ⲠⲀⲆⲀⲘⲀⳐ ⲈⳐⲈⲠⲰⲦ Ⲛ̄ⳐⲀ ⲦⲀ-
20 ⳐⲞⲘ Ⲛ̄ⳐⲦⲀⳞⲞⳐ · ⲀⲨⲰ ⲈⳐⲈⳐⲒ-ⲠⲀⲞⲨⲞⲈⲒⲚ Ⲛ̄ⲦⲞⲞⲦ · Ⲛ̄Ⳑ-
ⲚⲞⲬ̄Ⳑ ⲈⳞⲞⲨⲚ ⲈⲦⲈⳐⳐⲞⲘ Ⲛ̄ⲔⲀⲔⲈ ⲦⲀⲒ̈ ⲈⲦⳞ̄Ⲙ ⲠⲈⲬⲀⲞⳐ ·
ⲀⲨⲰ ⲈⳐⲈⲔⲀ-ⲦⲀⳐⲞⲘ Ⳟ̄Ⲙ ⲠⲈⲬⲀⲞⳐ ·

6. ⲦⲈⲚⲞⲨ ⳐⲈ ⲠⲞⲨⲞⲈⲒⲚ ⲦⲀⳐⲞⲒ̈ Ⳟ̄Ⲙ ⲠⲈⲔⳐⲰⲚ̄Ⲧ · ⲀⲨⲰ
ⲬⲒⳐⲈ Ⲛ̄ⲦⲈⲔⳐⲞⲘ ⲈⲬ̄Ⲛ ⲚⲀⲬⲀⲬⲈ · ⲚⲀⲒ̈ ⲈⲚⲦⲀⲨⲦⲰⲞⲨⲚ̄
25 ⲈⲬⲰⲒ̈ Ⲛ̄ⳞⲀⲈ ·

7. ⳐⲈⲠⲎ ⲘⲀⲦⲀⲚⳞⲞⲒ̈ · ⲔⲀⲦⲀ ⲐⲈ ⲈⲚⲦⲀⲔⲬⲞⲞⳐ ⲬⲈ †ⲚⲀ-
ⲂⲞⲎⲞⲒ ⲈⲢⲞ :

I had said to her : 'When thou art oppressed and dost *praise* me, I will come in haste to *help* thee.'

Now it happened when she was oppressed — *but* I sat before you in this *place* which is the Mount of Olives — she *sang praises* to the light, saying :

1. 'O Light of Lights, I have *believed* in thee. Save me from all these *archons* which pursue me, and *help* me.

2. *Lest* they take away my light from me, like the lion-faced power, for thy light and thy *outpouring* of light are not with me to save me. Rather Adamas was angry with me, saying to me : It is thou who hast *restrained* my power in the *Chaos*.

3. Now O Light of Lights, if I have done this — if I have *restrained* it, if I have done anything unjust to that power.

4. If I have oppressed it as it has oppressed me — may all these *archons* which pursue me take away my light from me and leave me empty.

5. And may the enemy Adamas pursue my power and seize it and take away my light from me, and cast it into his dark power which is in the *Chaos*; and may he place my power in the *Chaos*.

6. Now O Light, seize me in thy anger, and raise thy power against my enemies which have risen against me at last.

7. Save me quickly, *according to* what thou hast said : I will *help* thee'." |

ⲍ ⲀⲤϢⲰⲠⲈ ⳓⲈ ⲚⲦⲈⲢⲈ ⲠϢⲞⲢⲠ ⲘⲘⲨⲤⲦⲎⲢⲒⲞⲚ ⲞⲨⲰ
ⲈϤⲬⲰ ⲚⲚⲈⲒϢⲀⲬⲈ ⲈⲘⲘⲀⲐⲎⲦⲎⲤ · ⲠⲈⲬⲀϤ ⲬⲈ ⲠⲈⲚⲦ-
ⲀϤⲚⲞⲒ ⲚⲚⲈⲒϢⲀⲬⲈ ⲈⲚⲦⲀⲒⲬⲞⲞⲨ · ⲘⲀⲢⲈϤⲈⲒ' ⲈⲐⲚ ⲚϤ-
ⲦⲀⲨⲈ-ⲠⲈⲨⲂⲰⲖ · ⲀϤⲈⲒ'⟨Ⲉ⟩ⲐⲚ ⲚⳓⲒ ⲒⲀⲔⲔⲰⲂⲞⲤ ⲠⲈⲬⲀϤ ⲬⲈ
5 ⲠⲀⲬⲞⲈⲒⲤ · ⲈⲦⲂⲈ ⲠⲈⲒⳅⲨⲘⲚⲞⲤ ⲈⲚⲦⲀⲤⳅⲨⲠⲚⲈⲨⲈ ⲚⳍⲎⲦϤ ⲢⳜⲀ
ⲚⳓⲒ ⲦⲠⲒⲤⲦⲒⲤ ⲤⲞⲪⲒⲀ · Ⲁ ⲦⲈⲔⳓⲞⲘ ⲚⲞⲨⲞⲈⲒⲚ ⲠⲢⲞⲪⲎⲦⲈⲨⲈ
ⲘⲘⲞⲞⲨ ⲘⲠⲒⲞⲨⲞⲒϢ ⳅⲒⲦⲚ ⲆⲀⲨⲈⲒⲆ · ⳅⲘ ⲠⲘⲈⳅⲤⲀϢϤ Ⲙ-
ⲯⲀⲖⲘⲞⲤ ⲬⲈ

1. ⲠⲬⲞⲈⲒⲤ ⲠⲀⲚⲞⲨⲦⲈ ⲀⲒⲚⲀⳅⲦⲈ ⲈⲢⲞⲔ · ⲘⲀⲦⲞⲨⲬⲞⲒ
10 ⲈⲚⲈⲦⲠⲎⲦ ⲚⲤⲰⲒ ⲀⲨⲰ ⲚⲄⲚⲀⳅⲘⲈⲦ ·

2. ⲘⲎⲠⲞⲦⲈ ⲚϤⲦⲰⲢⲠ ⲚⲦⲀⲯⲨⲬⲎ ⲚⲐⲈ ⲚⲞⲨⲘⲞⲨⲒ · ⲈⲘⲚ-
ⲠⲈⲦⲤⲰⲦⲈ ⲀⲨⲰ ⲠⲈⲦⲚⲞⲨⳅⲘ ·

3. ⲠⲬⲞⲈⲒⲤ ⲠⲀⲚⲞⲨⲦⲈ ⲈϢⲬⲈ ⲀⲒⲢ-ⲠⲀⲒ · ⲈϢⲬⲈ ⲞⲨⲚ-
ⲬⲒⲚⳓⲞⲚⲤ ⳅⲚ ⲚⲀⳓⲒⳄ ·

15 4. ⲈϢⲬⲈ ⲀⲒⲦⲰⲰⲂⲈ ⲚⲚⲈⲦⲦⲰⲰⲂⲈ ⲚⲀⲒ ⲚⳅⲈⲚⲠⲤⲞⲞⲞⲨ ·
ⲈⲒⲈⳅⲈ ⲈⲂⲞⲖ ⳅⲒⲦⲚ ⲚⲀⲬⲀⲬⲈ ⲈⲒϢⲞⲨⲒⲦ ·

5. ⲚⲦⲈ ⲠⲬⲀⲬⲈ ⲠⲰⲦ ⲚⲤⲀ ⲦⲀⲯⲨⲬⲎ · ⲀⲨⲰ ⲚϤⲦⲀⳅⲞⲤ
ⲚϤⳅⲰⲘ ⲘⲠⲀⲰⲚⳅ ⲈⳅⲢⲀⲒ ⲈⲠⲔⲀⳅ · ⲀⲨⲰ ⲚϤⲦⲢⲈ ⲠⲀⲤⲞⲞⲨ
ϢⲰⲠⲈ ⳅⲘ ⲠⲈⲬⲞⲨⲤ · ⲚⲆⲒⲀⲯⲀⲖⲘⲀ ·

20 6. ⲦⲰⲞⲨⲚ ⲠⲬⲞⲈ⟨Ⲓ⟩Ⲥ ⳅⲚ ⲦⲈⲔⲞⲢⲄⲎ ⲬⲒⲤⲈ ⲚⲐⲀⲎ ⲚⲚⲀ- ⲢⳜⲀ ᵇ
ⲬⲀⲬⲈ ·

ⲦⲰⲞⲨⲚ ⳅⲘ ⲠⲞⲨⲈⳅⲤⲀⳅⲚⲈ ⲚⲦⲀⲔⳅⲰⲚ ⲘⲘⲞϤ ·

---

4   MS ⲀϤⲈⲒ ⲐⲎ.
5   MS ⲈⲚⲦⲀⲤⳅⲨⲠⲚⲈⲨⲈ; read ⲈⲚⲦⲀⲤⳅⲨⲘⲚⲈⲨⲈ.
20 MS ⲠⲬⲞⲈⲤ.

78. Now it happened when the First *Mystery* finished saying these words to the *disciples*, he said : "He who has *understood* these words which I have said, let him come forward and give their explanation." James came forward and said : "My Lord, concerning this *song of praise* which the Pistis Sophia has *sung*, thy light-power once *prophesied* it, through David, in the 7th *Psalm*, thus :

1. 'O Lord my God, I have trusted thee; save me from those that pursue me, and deliver me.

2. Lest he seize my *soul* like a lion; while there is no one who delivers and saves.

3. O Lord my God, if I have done this; if there is injustice at my hands;

4. If I have repaid those who repaid me with evil things, may I fall down empty through my enemies.

5. And may the enemy pursue my *soul* and seize it, and trample my life upon the earth, and make my glory to be in the *dust*. *Pause*.

6. Arise, O Lord, in thy *wrath*, be exalted in the boundary of my enemies. Arise in the commandment which thou hast decreed'*." |

---

* Ps. 7.1-6.

ϩ ⲀⲤϢⲰⲠⲈ ϬⲈ ⲚⲦⲈⲢⲈ ⲠⲒϢⲞⲢⲠ ⲘⲘⲨⲤⲦⲎⲢⲒⲞⲚ ⲤⲰⲦⲘ
ⲈⲚⲈⲒϢⲀϪⲈ ⲈϤϪⲰ ⲘⲘⲞⲞⲨ ⲚϬⲒ ⲒⲀⲔⲔⲰⲂⲞⲤ· ⲠⲈϪⲀϤ ϪⲈ
ⲈⲨⲄⲈ ⲒⲀⲔⲔⲰⲂⲞⲤ ⲠⲘⲈⲢⲒⲦ· ⲀϤⲞⲨⲰϩ ⲆⲈ ⲞⲚ ⲈⲦⲞⲞⲦϤ
ⲚϬⲒ ⲠⲒϢⲞⲢⲠ ⲘⲘⲨⲤⲦⲎⲢⲒⲞⲚ ⲠⲈϪⲀϤ ⲚⲘⲘⲀⲐⲎⲦⲎⲤ· ϪⲈ
5 ⲀⲤϢⲰⲠⲈ ϬⲈ ⲚⲦⲈⲢⲈ ⲦⲠⲒⲤⲦⲒⲤ ⲤⲞⲪⲒⲀ ⲞⲨⲰ ⲈⲤϪⲰ ⲚⲚ-
ϢⲀϪⲈ ⲘⲠⲈⲒϨⲨⲘⲚⲞⲤ· ⲀⲤⲔⲞⲦⲤ ⲈⲠⲀϨⲞⲨ ⲈⲚⲀⲨ ϪⲈ Ⲁ
ⲠⲀⲆⲀⲘⲀⲤ ⲔⲞⲦϤ ⲈⲠⲀϨⲞⲨ ⲘⲚ ⲚⲈϤⲀⲢⲬⲰⲚ ⲈⲦⲢⲈⲨⲂⲰⲔ
ⲈⲠⲈⲨⲀⲒⲰⲚ· ⲀⲨⲰ ⲀⲤⲚⲀⲨ ⲈⲢⲞⲞⲨ ⲈⲨⲠⲎⲦ ⲚⲤⲰⲤ· ⲀⲤ-
ⲔⲞⲦⲤ ⲈⲢⲞⲞⲨ ⲠⲈϪⲀⲤ ⲚⲀⲨ ϪⲈ
10 1. ⲀϨⲢⲰⲦⲚ ⲦⲈⲦⲚⲠⲎⲦ ⲚⲤⲰⲒ ⲈⲦⲈⲦⲚϪⲰ ⲘⲘⲞⲤ ϪⲈ
ⲘⲚⲦⲀⲒ ⲞⲨⲂⲞⲎⲐⲒⲀ ⲘⲘⲀⲨ· ⲈⲦⲢⲈϤⲚⲀϨⲘⲈⲦ ⲚⲦⲈⲦⲎⲨⲦⲚ·
2. ⲦⲈⲚⲞⲨ ϬⲈ ⲞⲨⲢⲈϤϯϨⲀⲠ (ⲘⲘⲈ) ⲠⲈ ⲠⲞⲨⲞⲈⲒⲚ· ⲀⲨⲰ ⲣ̅ϫ̅ⲃ̅
ⲞⲨⲬⲰⲢⲈ ⲠⲈ· ⲀⲖⲖⲀ ϤⲞ ⲚϨⲀⲢϢϨⲎⲦ· ϢⲀ ⲠⲈⲞⲨⲞⲈⲒϢ
ⲈⲚⲦⲀϤϪⲞⲞϤ ⲚⲀⲒ ϪⲈ ϯⲚⲎⲨ ⲦⲀⲂⲞⲎⲐⲒ ⲈⲢⲞ· ⲀⲨⲰ ⲚϤ-
15 ⲚⲀⲈⲒⲚⲈ ⲀⲚ ⲚⲦⲈϤⲞⲢⲄⲎ ⲈϪⲚ ⲦⲎⲨⲦⲚ ⲚⲚⲀⲨ ⲚⲒⲘ· ⲀⲨⲰ
ⲠⲀⲒ ⲠⲈ ⲠⲈⲞⲨⲞⲈⲒϢ ⲈⲚⲦⲀϤϪⲞⲞϤ ⲚⲀⲒ·
3. ⲦⲈⲚⲞⲨ ϬⲈ ⲈⲦⲈⲦⲚⲦⲘⲔⲈⲦⲦⲎⲨⲦⲚ ⲈⲠⲀϨⲞⲨ ⲀⲨⲰ
ⲚⲦⲈⲦⲚⲀⲖⲞ ⲈⲦⲈⲦⲚⲠⲎⲦ ⲚⲤⲰⲒ· ⲠⲞⲨⲞⲈⲒⲚ ⲚⲀⲤⲂⲦⲈ-ⲦⲈϤ-
ϬⲞⲘ· ⲀⲨⲰ ϤⲚⲀⲤⲞⲂⲦⲈ ϨⲚ ⲚⲈϤϬⲞⲘ ⲦⲎⲢⲞⲨ·
20 4. ⲀⲨⲰ ⲀϤⲤⲞⲂⲦⲈ ϨⲚ ⲦⲈϤϬⲞⲘ ⲈⲦⲢⲈϤϤⲒ ⲚⲚⲈⲦⲚⲞⲨ-
ⲞⲈⲒⲚ ⲈⲦⲚϨⲎⲦⲦⲎⲚⲞⲨ ⲀⲨⲰ ⲚⲦⲈⲦⲚϢⲰⲠⲈ ⲚⲔⲀⲔⲈ· ⲀⲨⲰ
ⲚⲈϤϬⲞⲘ ⲀϤⲦⲀⲘⲒⲞⲞⲨ ⲈⲦⲢⲈϤϤⲒ ⲚⲦⲈⲦⲚϬⲞⲘ ⲚϨⲎⲦⲦⲎⲚⲞⲨ
ⲚⲦⲈⲦⲚⲦⲀⲔⲞ :
ⲚⲀⲒ ⲆⲈ ⲚⲦⲈⲢⲈⲤϪⲞⲞⲨ ⲚϬⲒ ⲦⲠⲒⲤⲦⲒⲤ ⲤⲞⲪⲒⲀ· ⲀⲤϬⲰϢⲦ
25 ⲈⲠⲦⲞⲠⲞⲤ ⲘⲠⲀⲆⲀⲘⲀⲤ ⲀⲤⲚⲀⲨ ⲈⲠⲦⲞⲠⲞⲤ ⲚⲔⲀⲔⲈ ⲀⲨⲰ ⲣ̅ϫ̅ⲃ̅ᵇ

4 MS ϪⲈ expunged follows ⲠⲈϪⲀϤ.
8 MS ⲀⲨⲠⲀⲨ; Ⲩ altered to ϥ.
12 ⲘⲘⲈ omitted in MS.
25 MS ⲈⲈⲠⲦⲞⲠⲞⲤ; read ⲈⲠⲦⲞⲠⲞⲤ.

Now it happened when the First *Mystery* heard these words which James spoke, he said : "*Excellent*, James, thou beloved one."

79. *However*, the First *Mystery* continued, he said to the *disciples*: "Now it happened when the Pistis Sophia finished saying the words of this *song of praise*, she turned back to see whether Adamas and his *archons* had turned back to go to their *aeon*. And she saw them as they were pursuing her. She turned to them and said to them :

1. 'Why do you pursue me and say : there is no one to be a *help* to me, to save me from you?

2. Now at this time the light is a (true) judge and a strong one. *But* he is long-suffering until the time of which he has spoken to me thus : I will come and *help* thee; and he will not bring his *wrath* upon you at all times. And this is the time of which he has spoken to me.

3. Now at this time, if you do not turn yourselves back and cease to pursue me, the light will prepare his power, and he will prepare with all his powers.

4. And he has prepared with his power, that he may take away your light which is within you, so that you become dark; and he has created his powers, that he may take away your power from you and you be destroyed.'

But when the Pistis Sophia had said these things, she looked to the *place* of Adamas. She saw the dark and *chaotic place* | which he had created. And she saw further-

ⲚⲬⲀⲞⲤ ⲠⲀⲒ ⲚⲦⲀϤⲦⲀⲘⲒⲞϤ ⲀⲨⲰ ⲞⲚ ⲀⲤⲚⲀⲨ ⲈⲦⲈⲠⲢⲞ-
ⲂⲞⲖⲎ ⲤⲚⲦⲈ ⲚⲔⲀⲔⲈ· ⲈⲦⲚⲀϢⲦ ⲈⲘⲀⲦⲈ ⲚⲀⲒ ⲈⲚⲦⲀϤⲠⲢⲞ-
 ⲂⲀⲖⲈ ⲘⲘⲞⲞⲨ ⲈⲂⲞⲖ ⲚϬⲒ ⲠⲀⲆⲀⲘⲀⲤ· ⲬⲈⲔⲀⲤ ⲈⲨⲈⲀⲘⲀϨⲦⲈ
ⲚⲦⲠⲒⲤⲦⲒⲤ ⲤⲞⲪⲒⲀ· ⲀⲨⲰ ⲚⲤⲈⲚⲞⲬⲤ ⲈⲠⲈⲤⲎⲦ ⲈⲠⲈⲬⲀⲞⲤ
5 ⲈⲚⲦⲀϤⲦⲀⲘⲒⲞϤ· ⲚⲤⲈϨⲰⲬ ⲘⲘⲞⲤ ϨⲘ ⲠⲘⲀ ⲈⲦⲘⲘⲀⲨ· ⲀⲨⲰ
ⲚⲤⲈϢⲦⲢⲦⲰⲢⲤ ϢⲀⲚⲦⲞⲨϤⲒ-ⲠⲈⲤⲞⲨⲞⲈⲒⲚ ⲚϨⲎⲦⲤ· ⲀⲤϢⲰ-
ⲠⲈ ϬⲈ ⲚⲦⲈⲢⲈ ⲦⲠⲒⲤⲦⲒⲤ ⲤⲞⲪⲒⲀ ⲚⲀⲨ ⲈⲦⲈⲠⲢⲞⲂⲞⲖⲎ ⲤⲚⲦⲈ
ⲚⲔⲀⲔⲈ ⲈⲦⲘⲘⲀⲨ· ⲀⲨⲰ ⲘⲠⲦⲞⲠⲞⲤ ⲚⲔⲀⲔⲈ ⲚⲀⲒ ⲈⲚⲦⲀϤ-
ⲦⲀⲘⲒⲞⲞⲨ ⲚϬⲒ ⲠⲀⲆⲀⲘⲀⲤ· ⲀⲤⲢϨⲞⲦⲈ ⲀⲨⲰ ⲀⲤϢ ⲈϨⲢⲀⲒ
10 ⲈⲠⲞⲨⲞⲈⲒⲚ ⲈⲤⲬⲰ ⲘⲘⲞⲤ· ⲬⲈ

1. ⲠⲞⲨⲞⲈⲒⲚ ⲈⲒⲤϨⲎⲎⲦⲈ ⲀϤϬⲰⲚⲦ ⲚϬⲒ ⲠⲀⲆⲀⲘⲀⲤ ⲠⲈϤ-
ⲬⲒⲚϬⲞⲚⲤ ⲀϤⲦⲀⲘⲒⲞ ⲚⲞⲨⲠⲢⲞⲂⲞⲖⲎ ⲚⲔⲀⲔⲈ· ⲀⲨⲰ ⲞⲚ ⲢⲜⲒ
ⲀϤⲠⲢⲞⲂⲀⲖⲈ ⲈⲂⲞⲖ ⲚⲔⲈⲞⲨⲈⲒ ⲚⲬⲀⲞⲤ·

2. ⲀⲨⲰ ⲀϤⲦⲀⲘⲒⲈ-ⲔⲈⲞⲨⲈⲒ ⲚⲔⲀⲔⲈ ⲀⲨⲰ ⲚⲬⲀⲞⲤ· ⲀⲨⲰ
15 ⲀϤⲤⲂⲦⲰⲦϤ·

3. ⲦⲈⲚⲞⲨ ϬⲈ Ⲱ' ⲠⲞⲨⲞⲈⲒⲚ ⲠⲈⲬⲀⲞⲤ ⲚⲦⲀϤⲦⲀⲘⲒⲞϤ Ⲉ-
ⲦⲢⲈϤⲚⲞⲬⲦ ⲈⲢⲞϤ ⲚϤϤⲒ-ⲦⲀϬⲞⲘ ⲚⲞⲨⲞⲈⲒⲚ ⲚϨⲎⲦ· ϤⲒ-ⲦⲰϤ
ⲚϨⲎⲦϤ·

4. ⲀⲨⲰ ⲠⲘⲈⲈⲨⲈ ⲈⲚⲦⲀϤⲘⲈⲈⲨⲈ ⲈⲢⲞϤ ⲈⲦⲢⲈϤϤⲒ-ⲠⲀⲞⲨ-
20 ⲞⲈⲒⲚ· ⲤⲈⲚⲀ⟨ϤⲒ-⟩ⲠⲰϤ ⲚϨⲎⲦϤ· ⲀⲨⲰ ⲠⲬⲒⲚϬⲞⲚⲤ ⲈⲚⲦ-
ⲀϤⲬⲞⲞϤ ⲈⲦⲢⲈϤϤⲒ-ⲚⲀⲞⲨⲞⲈⲒⲚ ⲚϨⲎⲦ· ϤⲒ-ⲚⲞⲨϤ ⲦⲎⲢⲞⲨ·

ⲚⲀⲒ ⲚⲈ ⲚϢⲀⲬⲈ ⲈⲚⲦⲀⲤⲬⲞⲞⲨ ⲚϬⲒ ⲦⲠⲒⲤⲦⲒⲤ ⲤⲞⲪⲒⲀ·
ϨⲢⲀⲒ ϨⲘ ⲠⲈⲤⲨⲘⲚⲞⲤ· ⲦⲈⲚⲞⲨ ϬⲈ ⲠⲈⲦⲚⲎⲪⲈ ϨⲘ ⲠⲈϤⲠⲚⲀ·
ⲘⲀⲢⲈϤⲈⲒ' ⲈⲐⲎ ⲚϤⲦⲀⲨⲈ-ⲠⲂⲰⲖ ⲚⲚϢⲀⲬⲈ ⟨ⲚⲀⲒ ⲈⲚⲦⲀⲤ-
25 ⲬⲞⲞⲨ⟩ ⲚϬⲒ ⲦⲠⲒⲤⲦⲒⲤ ⲤⲞⲪⲒⲀ ϨⲢⲀⲒ ϨⲘ ⲠⲈⲤⲨⲘⲚⲞⲤ ⲀⲤⲈⲒ'
ⲞⲚ ⲈⲐⲎ ⲚϬⲒ ⲘⲀⲢⲐⲀ ⲠⲈⲬⲀⲤ· ⲬⲈ ⲠⲀⲬⲞⲈⲒⲤ· ⳨ⲚⲎⲪⲈ

---

20 ϤⲒ omitted in MS.
24 ⲚⲀⲒ ⲈⲚⲦⲀⲤⲬⲞⲞⲨ omitted in MS.

more the two dark *emanations*, of exceeding strength, which Adamas had *emanated*, so that they should seize the Pistis Sophia and should cast her down to the *Chaos* which he had created, and should oppress her in that place, and should agitate her until they took her light away from her. Now it happened when the Pistis Sophia saw those two dark *emanations* and the dark *place* which Adamas had created, she was afraid and she cried out to the light, saying:

1. 'O Light, behold Adamas the violent is angry. He has created a dark *emanation*, and furthermore he has *emanated* another *chaotic* one.

2. And he has created another dark and *chaotic* one; and he has prepared it.

3. Now at this time O Light, the *Chaos* which he has created so that he should cast me into it and take away my light-power from me — take away his (light) from him.

4. And the thought which he conceived to take away my light, let his be (taken) from him. And the violence which he has spoken, to take away my lights from me — take away all his (lights).'

These are the words which the Pistis Sophia spoke in her *song of praise*. Now at this time he who is *sober* in his *spirit*, let him come forward and give the interpretation of the words ⟨which the Pistis Sophia spoke⟩ in her *song of praise*."

80. Martha came forward again and said: "My Lord, I am *sober* | in my *spirit*, and I *understand* the words which

ϨⲘ ⲠⲀⲠⲚⲀ· ⲀⲨⲰ ϯⲚⲞⲈⲒ ⲚⲚϢⲀϪⲈ ⲈⲦⲔϪⲰ ⲘⲘⲞⲞⲨ· ⲣ̅ϫ̅ⲅ̅ ᵇ
ⲦⲈⲚⲞⲨ ϬⲈ ⲔⲈⲖⲈⲨⲈ ⲚⲀⲒ ⲦⲀⲦⲀⲨⲈ-ⲠⲈⲨⲂⲰⲖ ϨⲚ ⲞⲨⲠⲀⲢ-
ⲢⲎⲤⲒⲀ· ⲀϤⲞⲨⲰϣ̅ⲃ̅ ⲆⲈ ⲚϬⲒ ⲠⲒϢⲞⲢⲠ ⲘⲘⲨⲤⲦⲎⲢⲒⲞⲚ ⲠⲈ-
ϪⲀϤ ⲘⲘⲀⲢⲐⲀ. ϪⲈ ϯⲔⲈⲖⲈⲨⲈ ⲚⲈ ⲘⲀⲢⲐⲀ ⲈⲦⲢⲈⲦⲀⲨⲈ-
5 ⲠⲂⲰⲖ ⲚⲚϢⲀϪⲈ ⲚⲀⲒ ⲈⲚⲦⲀⲤϪⲞⲞⲨ ⲚϬⲒ ⲦⲤⲞⲪⲒⲀ ϨⲘ ⲠⲈⲤ-
ϨⲨⲘⲚⲞⲤ· ⲀⲤⲞⲨⲰϣ̅ⲃ̅ ⲆⲈ ⲚϬⲒ ⲘⲀⲢⲐⲀ ⲠⲈϪⲀⲤ ϪⲈ ⲠⲀ-
ϪⲞⲈⲒⲤ· ⲚⲀⲒ ⲚⲈ ⲚϢⲀϪⲈ ⲚⲦⲀ ⲦⲈⲔϬⲞⲘ ⲚⲞⲨⲞⲈⲒⲚ ⲠⲢⲞ-
ⲪⲎⲦⲈⲨⲈ ⲘⲘⲞⲞⲨ ⲘⲠⲒⲞⲨⲞⲈⲒϢ ϨⲒⲦⲚ ⲆⲀⲨⲈⲒⲀ· ϨⲘ ⲠⲘⲈϨ-
ⲤⲀϣ̅ϥ̅ ⲘⲮⲀⲖⲘⲞⲤ ϪⲈ

10   11. ⲠⲚⲞⲨⲦⲈ ⲞⲨⲔⲢⲒⲦⲎⲤ ⲘⲘⲈ ⲠⲈ ⲚϪⲰⲰⲢⲈ ⲚϨⲀⲢϢ̅-
ϨⲎⲦ· ⲈⲘⲈϤⲈⲒⲚⲈ ⲚⲦⲈϤⲞⲢⲄⲎ ⲘⲘⲎⲚⲈ·

    12. ⲈⲦⲈⲦⲚⲦⲘⲔⲈⲦⲦⲎⲨ⟨ⲦⲚ⟩ ϤⲚⲀϪⲰⲢ ⲚⲦⲈϤⲤⲎϤⲈ· ⲀϤ-
ⲤⲰⲘⲦ ⲚⲦⲈϤⲠⲒⲦⲈ ⲀϤⲤⲂⲦⲰⲦⲤ·

    13. ⲀϤⲤⲞⲂⲦⲈ ⲚϨⲎⲦⲤ ⲚϨⲈⲚⲤⲔⲈⲨⲞⲤ ⲘⲘⲞⲨ· ⲚⲈϤⲤⲞⲦⲈ ⲣ̅ϫ̅ⲇ̅
15 ⲀϤⲦⲀⲘⲒⲞⲞⲨ ⲚⲚⲈⲦⲞⲨⲚⲀⲢⲞⲔϨⲞⲨ·

    14. ⲈⲒⲤϨⲎⲎⲦⲈ Ⲁ ⲠϪⲒⲚϬⲞⲚⲤ ϯⲚⲀⲀⲔⲈ ⲀϤϢⲰ̀Ⲱ̀ ⲘⲠϨⲒⲤⲈ
ⲀϤϪⲠⲈ-ⲦⲀⲚⲞⲘⲒⲀ·

    15. ⲀϤϢⲈⲔⲦ-ⲞⲨϢⲎⲒ̈ ⲀϤϬⲢⲎ ⲘⲘⲞϤ ϤⲚⲀϨⲈ ⲈϨⲢⲀⲒ̈ ⲈⲠⲈ-
ϨⲒⲈⲒⲦ ⲈⲚⲦⲀϤⲦⲀⲘⲒⲞϤ·

20   16. ⲠⲈϤϨⲒⲤⲈ ⲚⲀⲔⲞⲦϤ ⲈϪⲚ ⲦⲈϤⲀⲠⲈ ⲀⲨⲰ ⲠⲈϤϪⲒⲚϬⲞⲚⲤ
ⲚⲎⲨ ⲈϪⲚ ⲦⲘⲎⲦⲈ ⲚϪⲰϤ·

    ⲚⲀⲒ ⲆⲈ ⲚⲦⲈⲢⲈⲤϪⲞⲞⲨ ⲚϬⲒ ⲘⲀⲢⲐⲀ ⲠⲈϪⲀϤ ⲚⲀⲤ ⲚϬⲒ
ⲠⲒϢⲞⲢⲠ ⲘⲘⲨⲤⲦⲎⲢⲒⲞⲚ ⲈⲦϬⲰϣ̅Ⲧ ⲈⲂⲞⲖ ϪⲈ ⲈⲨⲄⲈ ⲔⲀ-
ⲖⲰⲤ ⲘⲀⲢⲐⲀ ⲦⲘⲀⲔⲀⲢⲒⲀ·

---

10   MS ⲈⲠⲈ.
12   MS ⲈⲦⲈⲦⲚⲦⲘⲔⲈⲦⲦⲎⲨ·

thou dost speak. Now at this time *command* me that I give their interpretation *openly*."

The First *Mystery*, *however*, answered and said to Martha : "I *command* thee, Martha, that thou givest the interpretation of the words which the Sophia said in her *song of praise*."

Martha, *however*, answered and said : "My Lord, these are the words which thy light-power once *prophesied* through David in the 7th *Psalm* :

11. 'God is a righteous *judge*, and strong and long-suffering, who does not bring down his *wrath* every day.

12. If you do not turn round he will sharpen his sword; he has bent his bow and made it ready.

13. He has prepared in it *instruments* of death; he has made his arrows for those who will be burnt.

14. Behold, violence has travailed; he has conceived trouble, he has given birth to *iniquity*.

15. He has dug a pit, he has hollowed it; he will fall into the hole which he has made.

16. His trouble will return upon his head and his violence will come down upon the crown of his head' *."

But when Martha had spoken these things, the First *Mystery* which looks forth said to her : "*Excellent, well done* Martha, thou *blessed one*." |

---

*   Ps. 7.11-16

ϩ ⲁⲥϣⲱⲡⲉ ϭⲉ ⲛ̄ⲧⲉⲣⲉ ⲓ̅ⲥ̅ ⲟⲩⲱ ⲉϥϫⲱ ⲉⲛⲉϥⲙⲁⲑⲏⲧⲏⲥ ⲛ̄ⲛⲉϩⲃⲏⲩⲉ ⲧⲏⲣⲟⲩ ⲉⲛⲧⲁⲩϣⲱⲡⲉ ⲛ̄ⲧⲡⲓⲥⲧⲓⲥ ⲥⲟⲫⲓⲁ
ⲉⲥϩⲙ̄ ⲡⲉⲭⲁⲟⲥ · ⲁⲩⲱ ⲙ̄ⲛ ⲑⲉ ⲉⲛⲧⲁⲥϩⲩⲙⲛⲉⲩⲉ ⲉϩⲣⲁⲓ̈
ⲉⲡⲟⲩⲟⲉⲓⲛ ϣⲁⲛⲧⲉϥⲛⲟⲩϩⲙ̄ ⲙ̄ⲙⲟⲥ ⲛ̄ϥⲉⲓⲛⲉ ⲙ̄ⲙⲟⲥ ⲉϩⲣⲁⲓ̈
5 ϩⲙ̄ ⲡⲉⲭⲁⲟⲥ · * ⲛ̄ϥⲉⲓⲛⲉ ⲙ̄ⲙⲟⲥ ⲉϩⲟⲩⲛ ⲉⲡⲙⲉϩⲙ̄ⲛ̄ⲧⲥⲛⲟⲟⲩⲥ ⲣ̅ⲝ̅ⲁ̅ ᵇ
ⲛ̄ⲁⲓⲱⲛ · ⲁⲩⲱ ⲙ̄ⲛ ⲑⲉ ⲉⲛⲧⲁϥⲛⲁϩⲙⲉⲥ ⲉⲃⲟⲗ ϩⲛ̄ ⲛⲉⲥϩⲱϫ
ⲧⲏⲣⲟⲩ ⲛⲁⲓ̈ ⲛ̄ⲧⲁⲩϩⲉϫϩⲱϫⲧ ⲛ̄ϩⲏⲧⲟⲩ ⲛ̄ϭⲓ ⲛ̄ⲁⲣⲭⲱⲛ ⲛ̄ⲧⲉ
ⲛⲉⲭⲁⲟⲥ ⲉⲃⲟⲗ ϫⲉ ⲁⲥⲉⲡⲓⲑⲩⲙⲉⲓ ⲉⲃⲱⲕ ⲉⲣⲁⲧϥ̄ ⲙ̄ⲡⲟⲩ-
ⲟⲓ̈ⲛ ·

10 ϩ ⲁϥⲟⲩⲱϩ ⲟⲛ ⲉⲧⲟⲟⲧϥ̄ ϩⲙ̄ ⲡϣⲁϫⲉ ⲛ̄ϭⲓ ⲓ̅ⲥ̅ ⲡⲉϫⲁϥ
ⲛ̄ⲛⲉϥⲙⲁⲑⲏⲧⲏⲥ ϫⲉ ⲁⲥϣⲱⲡⲉ ϭⲉ ⲙⲛ̄ⲛ̄ⲥⲁ ⲛⲁⲓ̈ ⲧⲏⲣⲟⲩ
ⲁⲓ̈ϥⲓ ⲛ̄ⲧⲡⲓⲥⲧⲓⲥ ⲥⲟⲫⲓⲁ ⲁⲓ̈ⲛ̄ⲧⲥ̄ ⲉϩⲟⲩⲛ ⲉⲡⲙⲉϩⲙ̄ⲛ̄ⲧϣⲟⲙⲧⲉ
ⲛ̄ⲁⲓⲱⲛ ⲉⲓ̈ⲟ ⲛ̄ⲟⲩⲟⲓ̈ⲛ ⲉⲙⲁϣⲟ ⲉⲙⲁϣⲟ · ⲉⲙⲛ̄-ϣⲓ ⲉⲡⲟⲩⲟⲉⲓⲛ ⲉⲛⲉϥϣⲟⲟⲡ ⲙ̄ⲙⲟⲓ̈ ⲁⲓ̈ⲉⲓ' ⲉϩⲟⲩⲛ ⲉⲡⲧⲟⲡⲟⲥ ⲙ̄ⲡⲙⲉϩ-
15 ϫⲟⲩⲧⲁϥⲧⲉ ⲛ̄ⲁϩⲟⲣⲁⲧⲟⲥ ⲉⲓ̈ⲟ ⲛ̄ⲟⲩⲟⲉⲓⲛ ⲉⲙⲁϣⲟ ⲉⲙⲁϣⲟ · ⲁⲩⲱ ⲁⲩϣⲧⲟⲣⲧⲣ̄ ϩⲛ̄ ⲟⲩⲛⲟϭ ⲛ̄ϣⲧⲟⲣⲧⲣ̄ ⲁⲩϭⲱϣⲧ̄
ⲁⲩⲛⲁⲩ ⲉⲧⲥⲟⲫⲓⲁ ⲉⲛⲉⲥⲛ̄ⲙⲙⲁⲓ̈ ⲁⲩⲥⲟⲩⲱⲛⲥ̄ ** ⲁⲛⲟⲕ ⲇⲉ ⲣ̅ⲝ̅ⲥ̅
ⲙ̄ⲡⲟⲩⲥⲟⲩⲱⲛⲧ̄ ϫⲉ ⲁⲛⲟⲕ ⲛⲓⲙ · ⲁⲗⲗⲁ ⲛⲉⲩⲙⲉⲉⲩⲉ ⲉⲣⲟⲓ̈
ⲡⲉ ⲛ̄ⲑⲉ ⲛ̄ⲟⲩⲡⲣⲟⲃⲟⲗⲏ ⲛ̄ⲧⲉ ⲡⲕⲁϩ ⲙ̄ⲡⲟⲩⲟⲉⲓⲛ · ⲁⲥ-
20 ϣⲱⲡⲉ ϭⲉ ⲛ̄ⲧⲉⲣⲉ ⲧⲥⲟⲫⲓⲁ ⲛⲁⲩ ⲉⲛⲉⲥϣⲃⲉⲉⲣ ⲛ̄ⲁϩⲟⲣⲁ-
ⲧⲟⲥ · ⲁⲥⲣⲁϣⲉ ϩⲛ̄ ⲟⲩⲛⲟϭ ⲛ̄ⲣⲁϣⲉ · ⲁⲩⲱ ⲁⲥⲧⲉⲗⲏⲗ
ⲉⲙⲁϣⲟ · ⲁⲥⲟⲩⲱϣ ⲉⲧⲁⲙⲟⲟⲩ ⲉⲛⲉϣⲡⲏⲣⲉ ⲉⲛⲧⲁⲓ̈ⲁⲁⲩ
ⲛ̄ⲙⲙⲁⲥ ⲙ̄ⲡⲉⲥⲏⲧ ϩⲙ̄ ⲡⲕⲁϩ ⲛ̄ⲧⲉ ⲧⲙⲛ̄ⲧⲣⲱⲙⲉ ϩⲉⲱⲥ

---

7 MS ⲛ̄ⲧⲁⲩϩⲉϫϩⲱϫⲧ; final ⲧ inserted above and expunged; read
ⲛ̄ⲧⲁⲩϩⲉϫϩⲱϫ̄ⲥ̄.
23 ⲥ in ϩⲉⲱⲥ inserted above.

81. Now it happened when Jesus finished saying to his *disciples* all the events which had happened to the Pistis Sophia when she was in the *Chaos*, and the manner in which she had *sung praises* to the Light until he saved her and brought her out from the *Chaos*, and brought her into the twelfth *aeon*, and the manner in which he had saved her from all her oppressions with which the *archons* of the *Chaos(es)* had oppressed her, because she *desired* to go to the light, Jesus continued again with the discourse. He said to his *disciples*: "Now it happened after all these things, I took the Pistis Sophia, I brought her into the thirteenth *aeon*. And I was shining exceedingly, there being no measure to the light which I had. I came into the *place* of the 24 *invisible ones* and I was shining exceedingly. And they were agitated with great agitation. They looked and saw the Sophia who was with me. They recognised her, *but* as for me they did not recognise who I was. *But* they thought of me as being like an *emanation* of the Land of the Light.

Now it happened when the Sophia saw her fellow *invisible ones* she rejoiced with great joy and she was very glad. She wished to tell them the wonders which I had done for her on the earth of mankind below, | *until* I saved her. She came

ϢⲀⲚ-ϮⲚⲞⲨ⳿ϨⲘ ⲘⲘⲞⲤ · ⲀⲤⲈⲒ⳿ ⲈϨⲢⲀⲒ ⲈⲦⲘⲎⲦⲈ ⲚⲚⲀϨⲞⲢⲀ-
ⲦⲞⲤ ⲀⲤϨⲨⲘⲚⲈⲨⲈ ⲈⲢⲞⲒ ϨⲚ ⲦⲈⲨⲘⲎⲦⲈ ⲈⲤϪⲰ ⲘⲘⲞⲤ ϪⲈ

1. ϮⲚⲀⲞⲨⲰⲚϨ ⲚⲀⲔ ⲈⲂⲞⲗ ⲠⲞⲨⲞⲈⲒⲚ ϪⲈ ⲚⲦⲔ ⲞⲨⲤⲰ-
ⲦⲎⲢ · ⲀⲨⲰ ⲚⲦⲔ ⲞⲨⲢⲈϤⲤⲰⲦⲈ ⲚⲞⲨⲞⲈⲒϢ ⲚⲒⲘ ·

2. ϮⲚⲀϪⲰ ⲘⲠⲈⲒϨⲨⲘⲚⲞⲤ ⲈⲠⲞⲨⲞⲈⲒⲚ ϪⲈ ⲀϤⲚⲞⲨϨⲘ
ⲘⲘⲞⲒ · ⲀⲨⲰ ⲀϤⲚⲀϨⲘⲈⲦ ⲈⲂⲞⲗ ϨⲚ ⲦϬⲒϪ ⲚⲚⲀⲢⲬⲰⲚ Ⲛ-
ⲚⲀϪⲒϪⲈⲈⲨ ·   ⲢϪ̅Ⲋ̅ ᵇ

3. ⲀⲨⲰ ⲀⲔⲚⲀϨⲘⲈⲦ ϨⲚ ⲚⲦⲞⲠⲞⲤ ⲦⲎⲢⲞⲨ · ⲀⲨⲰ ⲀⲔ-
ⲚⲀϨⲘⲈⲦ ϨⲘ ⲠϪⲒⲤⲈ ⲘⲚ ⲠϨⲂⲂⲈ ⲚⲦⲈ ⲚⲈⲬⲗⲀⲞⲤ · ⲀⲨⲰ ϨⲚ
ⲚⲀⲒⲰⲚ ⲚⲚⲀⲢⲬⲰⲚ ⲚⲦⲈ ⲦⲈⲤⲪⲈⲢⲀ ·

4. ⲀⲨⲰ ⲚⲦⲈⲢⲒⲈⲒ⳿ ⲈⲂⲞⲗ ϨⲘ ⲠϪⲒⲤⲈ ⲀⲒⲤⲰⲢⲘ ϨⲚ ϨⲈⲚ-
ⲦⲞⲠⲞⲤ ⲈⲘⲚ-ⲞⲨⲞⲈⲒⲚ ⲚϨⲎⲦⲞⲨ · ⲘⲠⲒϢⲔⲞⲦⲦ ⲈⲠⲘⲀϨ-
ⲘⲚⲦϢⲞⲘⲦⲈ ⲚⲀⲒⲰⲚ ⲠⲀⲘⲀⲚϢⲰⲠⲈ ·

5. ϪⲈ ⲘⲚ-ⲞⲨⲞⲈⲒⲚ ⲚϨⲎⲦ ⲞⲨⲦⲈ ϬⲞⲘ · Ⲁ ⲦⲀϬⲞⲘ
ⲘⲞⲨⲔ ⲈⲠⲦⲎⲢϤ ·

6. ⲀⲨⲰ Ⲁ ⲠⲞⲨⲞⲈⲒⲚ ⲚⲀϨⲘⲈⲦ ϨⲚ ⲚⲀⲐⲗⲒⲯⲒⲤ ⲦⲎⲢⲞⲨ ·
ⲀⲒϨⲨⲘⲚⲈⲨⲈ ⲈϨⲢⲀⲒ ⲈⲠⲞⲨⲞⲒⲚ · ⲀϤⲤⲰⲦⲘ ⲈⲢⲞⲒ ⲚⲦⲈⲢⲞⲨ-
ⲞⲗⲒⲂⲈ ⲘⲘⲞⲒ ·

7. ⲀϤϪⲒⲘⲞⲈⲒⲦ ϨⲎⲦ ϨⲘ ⲠⲤⲰⲚⲦ ⲚⲦⲈ ⲚⲀⲒⲰⲚ ⲈⲦⲢⲈϤⲚⲦ
ⲈϨⲢⲀⲒ ⲈⲠⲘⲈϨⲘⲚⲦϢⲞⲘⲦⲈ ⲚⲀⲒⲰⲚ ⲠⲀⲘⲀⲚϢⲰⲠⲈ ·

8. ϮⲚⲀⲞⲨⲰⲚϨ ⲚⲀⲔ ⲈⲂⲞⲗ ⲠⲞⲨⲞⲈⲒⲚ ϪⲈ ⲀⲔⲚⲀϨⲘⲈⲦ ·
ⲀⲨⲰ ⲚⲈⲔϢⲠⲎⲢⲈ ϨⲘ ⲠⲄⲈⲚⲞⲤ ⲚⲦⲈ* ⲦⲘⲚⲦⲢⲰⲘⲈ ·   ⲢϪ̅Ⲋ̅

9. ⲚⲦⲈⲢⲒϢⲰⲰⲦ ⲚⲦⲀϬⲞⲘ ⲀⲔ-Ϯ-ϬⲞⲘ ⲚⲀⲒ · ⲀⲨⲰ ⲚⲦⲈ-
ⲢⲒϢⲰⲰⲦ ⲘⲠⲀⲞⲨⲞⲈⲒⲚ ⲀⲔⲘⲀϨⲦ ⲚⲞⲨⲞⲈⲒⲚ ⲈϤⲤⲞⲦϤ ·

10. ⲀⲒϢⲰⲠⲈ ϨⲘ ⲠⲔⲀⲔⲈ ⲘⲚ ⲐⲗⲒⲂⲈⲤ ⲚⲦⲈ ⲠⲈⲬⲗⲀⲞⲤ ·

---

7 MS ⲚⲚⲀϪⲒϪⲈⲈⲨ ; read ⲚⲀϪⲒϪⲈⲈⲨ.
15 MS ⲘⲞⲨⲔ; read ⲘⲞⲨⲔϨ.

to the midst of the *invisible ones*, she *sang praises* to me in
their midst, saying :

1. 'I will give thanks to thee, O Light, for thou art
a *Saviour*, and thou art a deliverer at all times.

2. I will speak this *song of praise* to the light, for he
has saved me and he has delivered me out of the hand of
the *archons*, my enemies.

3. And thou hast saved me from all the *places*. And thou
hast saved me from the height and the depth of the *Chaos*,
and from the *aeons* of the *archons* of the *sphere*.

4. And when I came forth from the height I went astray
in *places* in which there was no light. And I was not able
to return to the thirteenth *aeon*, my dwelling place.

5. For there was no light in me, *nor* power. For my power
had weakened [1] completely.

6. And the light saved me from all my *afflictions*. I *sang
praises* to the light; he heard me when I was *afflicted*.

7. He guided me in the creation of the *aeons* in order to
bring me to the thirteenth *aeon*, my dwelling place.

8. I will give thanks to thee, O Light, for thou hast saved
me, and for thy wonders among the *race* of mankind.

9. When I lacked my power thou didst give power to me;
and when I lacked my light thou didst fill me with purified
light.

10. I have been in the darkness and the shadow of the

---

[1]   (15) weakened; Till : disappeared.

ⲉⲓⲙⲏⲣ ϨⲚ Ⲙ̄Ⲙⲣⲣⲉ ⲉⲩⲚⲀϢ̄Ⲧ Ⲛ̄Ⲧⲉ ⲠⲉⲬⲀⲟⲤ ⲉⲘⲚ-ⲞⲨⲞⲒⲚ
Ⲛ̄ϨⲎⲦ ·

11. Ⲭⲉ Ⲁⲓ̈ϯⲚⲞⲨϬⲤ Ⲙ̄ⲠⲦⲰϢ Ⲙ̄ⲠⲞⲨⲞⲉⲒⲚ Ⲁⲓ̈ⲠⲀⲣⲀⲂⲀ ·
ⲀⲨⲰ Ⲁⲓ̈ϯ-ϬⲰⲚ̄Ⲧ Ⲙ̄ⲠⲦⲰϢ Ⲙ̄ⲠⲞⲨⲞⲉⲒⲚ Ⲭⲉ Ⲁⲓ̈ⲉⲒ ⲈⲂⲞⲖ
5 ϨⲘ̄ ⲠⲀⲦⲞⲠⲞⲤ ·

12. ⲀⲨⲰ Ⲛ̄ⲦⲉⲣⲓⲉⲒ ⲉⲠⲉⲤⲎⲦ · Ⲁⲓ̈ϢⲰϢⲦ Ⲛ̄ⲦⲀϬⲞⲘ · ⲀⲨⲰ
Ⲁⲓ̈Ⲣ̄-ⲀⲦⲞⲨⲞⲉⲒⲚ · ⲀⲨⲰ ⲚⲉⲘⲠⲉ ⲖⲀⲀⲨ ⲂⲞⲎⲞⲒ ⲉⲣⲞⲓ̈ Ⲡⲉ ·

13. ⲀⲨⲰ ϨⲘ̄ ⲠⲦⲣⲉⲨⲞⲖⲒⲂⲉ Ⲙ̄ⲘⲞⲓ̈ · Ⲁⲓ̈ϨⲨⲘⲚⲉⲨⲉ ⲈϨⲣⲀⲓ̈
ⲉⲠⲞⲨⲞⲉⲒⲚ ⲀⲨⲰ ⲀϤⲚⲀϨⲘⲉⲦ ⲈⲂⲞⲖ ϨⲚ ⲚⲀⲐⲖⲒⲯⲒⲤ ⲦⲎⲣⲞⲨ ·

10 14. ⲀⲨⲰ ⲞⲚ ⲀϤⲤⲰⲖ̄Ⲡ Ⲛ̄ⲚⲀⲘⲣⲣⲉ ⲦⲎⲣⲞⲨ · ⲀϤⲚⲦ ⲈϨⲣⲀⲓ̈
ϨⲘ̄ ⲠⲔⲀⲔⲉ ⲘⲚ ⲠϨⲞⲬϨⲬ̄ Ⲛ̄Ⲧⲉ ⲠⲉⲬⲀⲟⲤ ·

15. ϯⲚⲀⲞⲨⲰⲚϨ ⲚⲀⲔ ⲈⲂⲞⲖ ⲠⲞⲨⲞⲉⲒⲚ Ⲭⲉ ⲀⲔⲚⲀϨⲘⲉⲦ Ⲣ̄Ⲝⲉ ᵇ
ⲀⲨⲰ Ⲁ ⲚⲉⲔϢⲠⲏⲣⲉ ϢⲰⲠⲉ ϨⲘ̄ ⲠⲄⲉⲚⲞⲤ Ⲛ̄Ⲧⲉ ⲦⲘⲚⲦⲣⲰⲘⲉ ·

16. ⲀⲨⲰ ⲀⲔⲞⲨⲰϢ̄Ⲡ Ⲛ̄Ⲙ̄ⲠⲨⲖⲎ ⲈⲦⲬⲞⲤⲉ Ⲛ̄Ⲧⲉ ⲠⲔⲀⲔⲉ ·
15 ⲀⲨⲰ Ⲙ̄Ⲛ Ⲙ̄ⲘⲞⲬⲖⲞⲤ ⲈⲦⲚⲀϢ̄Ⲧ Ⲛ̄Ⲧⲉ ⲠⲉⲬⲀⲟⲤ ·

17. ⲀⲨⲰ ⲀⲔⲦⲣⲀⲣⲀⲔ̄Ⲧ ⲈⲂⲞⲖ Ⲙ̄ⲠⲦⲞⲠⲞⲤ ⲉⲚⲦⲀⲓ̈ⲠⲀⲣⲀⲂⲀ
Ⲛ̄ϨⲎⲦ̄Ϥ ⲀⲨⲰ ⲞⲚ Ⲛ̄ⲦⲀⲨϤⲒ Ⲛ̄ⲦⲀϬⲞⲘ Ⲭⲉ Ⲁⲓ̈ⲠⲀⲣⲀⲂⲀ ·

18. ⲀⲨⲰ Ⲁⲓ̈Ⲗⲟ ϨⲚ Ⲙ̄ⲘⲨⲤⲦⲎⲣⲒⲞⲚ · Ⲁⲓ̈ⲉⲒ ⲈϨⲣⲀⲓ̈ ϨⲚ Ⲙ̄ⲠⲨⲖⲎ
Ⲙ̄ⲠⲉⲬⲀⲟⲤ ·

20 19. ⲀⲨⲰ Ⲛ̄ⲦⲉⲣⲞⲨⲐⲖⲒⲂⲉ Ⲙ̄ⲘⲞⲓ̈ · Ⲁⲓ̈ϨⲨⲘⲚⲉⲨⲉ ⲈϨⲣⲀⲓ̈ ⲉ-
ⲠⲞⲨⲞⲉⲒⲚ ⲀϤⲚⲀϨⲘⲉⲦ ⲈⲂⲞⲖ ϨⲚ ⲚⲀⲐⲖⲒⲯⲒⲤ ⲦⲎⲣⲞⲨ ·

20. ⲀⲔⲦⲚ̄ⲚⲞⲞⲨ Ⲛ̄ⲦⲉⲔⲀⲠⲞϨⲣⲞⲒⲀ ⲀⲤϯ-ϬⲞⲘ ⲚⲀⲓ̈ ⲀⲨⲰ
ⲀⲤⲚⲀϨⲘⲉⲦ ⲈⲂⲞⲖ ϨⲚ ⲚⲀϨⲞⲬϨⲬ̄ ⲦⲎⲣⲞⲨ ·

21. ϯⲚⲀⲞⲨⲰⲚϨ ⲚⲀⲔ ⲈⲂⲞⲖ ⲠⲞⲨⲞⲉⲒⲚ Ⲭⲉ ⲀⲔⲚⲀϨⲘⲉⲦ ·
25 ⲀⲨⲰ ⲚⲉⲔϢⲠⲏⲣⲉ ϨⲘ̄ ⲠⲄⲉⲚⲞⲤ Ⲛ̄Ⲧⲉ ⲦⲘⲚⲦⲣⲰⲘⲉ :   Ⲣ̄Ⲝⲍ

---

1   MS ⲉⲩⲚⲀϢ̄Ⲧ ; read ⲉⲦⲚⲀϢ̄Ⲧ.
16   MS ⲈⲂⲞⲖ Ⲙ̄ⲠⲦⲞⲠⲞⲤ; read ⲈⲂⲞⲖ ϨⲘ̄ ⲠⲦⲟⲡⲟⲤ.

Chaos, | bound with the strong bonds of the *Chaos*, and there was no light in me.

11. I have caused wrath to the ordinance of the light, I have *transgressed*; I have caused anger to the ordinance of the light, for I came forth from my *place*.

12. And when I came down I lacked my power, and I was without light; and there was no one to *help* me.

13. And when I was *afflicted* I *sang praises* to the light, and he saved me from all my *afflictions*.

14. And furthermore he broke all my bonds, he brought me out of the darkness and the oppression of the *Chaos*.

15. I will thank thee, O Light, for thou hast saved me; and thy wonders exist among the *race* of mankind.

16. Thou hast broken the high *gates* of the darkness and the strong *bars* of the *Chaos*.

17. And thou didst cause me to turn away from the *place* in which I *transgressed*; and furthermore my power was taken because I *transgressed*.

18. And I desisted from the *mysteries*; I went down to the *gates* of the *Chaos*.

19. And when they *afflicted* me I *sang praises* to the light; he saved me from all my *afflictions*.

20. Thou didst send thy *outpouring* (of light); it gave power to me and it saved me from all my oppressions.

21. I will thank thee, O Light, for thou hast saved me; and thy wonders are among the *race* of mankind.' |

ΠΑΪ ϬΕ ΠΕ ΠϨΥΜΝΟΣ ΕΝΤΑΣΧΟΟϤ ⲚϬΙ ΤΠΙΣΤΙΣ ΣΟ-
ΦΙΑ ΕΣϨⲚ ΤΜΗΤΕ ⲘΠΧΟΥΤΑϤΤΕ ⲚΑϨΟΡΑΤΟΣ ΕΣΟΥШϢ
ΕΤΡΕΥϬΙΜΕ ΤΗΡΟΥ ΕΝΕϢΠΗΡΕ ΤΗΡΟΥ ΕΝΤΑΪΑΑΥ ⲚⲘ-
ΜΑΣ · ΑΥШ ΕΣΟΥϢϢ ΕΤΡΕΥϬΙΜΕ ΧΕ ΑΪΒШΚ ΕΠΚΟΣ-
5 ΜΟΣ ⲚΤΕ ΤⲘΝΤΡШΜΕ ΑΪ† ΝΑΥ ⲚΜΜΥΣΤΗΡΙΟΝ ⲘΠΧΙ-
ΣΕ · ΤΕΝΟΥ ϬΕ ΠΕΤΧΟΣΕ ϨⲘ ΠΕϤΝΟΗΜΑ ΜΑΡΕϤϬΙ' ΕϨΗ
ⲚϤΧШ ⲘΠΒШΛ ΕΒΟΛ ⲘΠϨΥΜΝΟΣ ΕΝΤΑΣΧΟΟϤ ⲚϬΙ ΤΣΟ-
ΦΙΑ ·

ΑΣϢШΠΕ ϬΕ ⲚΤΕΡΕ ⲒⲤ ΟΥШ ΕϤΧШ ⲚΝΕΪϢΑΧΕ ·
10 ΑϤΕΙ' ΕϨΗ ⲚϬΙ ΦΙΛΙΠΠΟΣ ΠΕΧΑϤ ΧΕ ⲒⲤ ΠΑΧΟΕΙΣ ·
ϤΧΟΣΕ ⲚϬΙ ΠΑΝΟΗΜΑ · ΑΥШ ΑΪΝΟΪ ⲘΠΒШΛ ΕΒΟΛ Ⲙ-
ΠϨΥΜΝΟΣ ⲚΤΑΣΧΟΟϤ ⲚϬΙ ΤΣΟΦΙΑ ⲚΤΑϤΠΡΟΦΗΤΕΥΕ
ΟΝ ϨΑΡΟΣ ⲘΠΙΟΥΟΪϢ ⲚϬΙ ΔΑΥΕΙΑ ΠΕΠΡΟΦΗΤΗΣ · ΕϤ- ⲢⲌⲌ ᵇ
ΧШ ⲘΜΟΣ ϨⲘ ΠΜΕϨϢΕΣΟΟΥ ⲘⳲΑΛΜΟΣ · ΧΕ

15 1. ΟΥШⲚϨ ΕΒΟΛ ⲘΠΧΟΕΙΣ ΧΕ ΟΥΧΡΗΣΤΟΣ ΠΕ ΧΕ
ΟΥϢΑΕΝΕϨ ΠΕ ΠΕϤΝΑ' ·

2. ΜΑΡΕ ΝΕΝΤΑ ΠΧΟΕΙΣ ΣΟΤΟΥ ΧΕ-ΠΑΪ [ΠΕ] ΑϤ-
ΣΟΤΟΥ ΕΒΟΛ ϨⲚ ΤϬΙΧ ⲚΝΕΥΧΑΧΕ ·

3. ΑϤΣΟΟϨΟΥ ΕϨΟΥΝ ϨⲚ ΝΕΥΧШΡΑ ΕΒΟΛ ϨⲘ ΠΕΪΒΤ
20 ΜⲚ ΠΕΜⲚΤ ΜⲚ ΠΕΜϨΙΤ · ΜⲚ ΘΑΛΑΣΣΑ ·

---

3 ΤΗΡΟΥ after ϬΙΜΕ expunged. MS originally ϬⲚΤΑ ⲚⲘΜΑΣ; ΪΑΑΥ inserted
above in another hand.
7 MS originally ⲚΝΕ ΠϨΥΜΝΟΣ; Μ written over erasure.
10 ΧΕ erased before ΠΑΧΟΕΙΣ.
17 omit ΠΕ.
20 MS ΠΕΜΜϨΙΤ; ϬΜ inserted in margin and second Μ crossed out.

Now this is the *song of praise* which the Pistis Sophia spoke as she was in the midst of the 24 *invisible ones*, wishing that they should know all the wonders which I had done for her. And she wished that they should know that I went to the *world* of mankind, I gave them the *mysteries* of the height. Now at this time, he who is elevated in his *thought*, let him come forward and say the interpretation of the *song of praise* which the Pistis Sophia spoke."

82. Now it happened when Jesus finished saying these words, Philip came forward. He said : "Jesus, my Lord, my *thought* is elevated and I have *understood* the interpretation of the *song of praise* which the Sophia spoke. David, the *prophet*, once also *prophesied* about it, saying in the 106th *Psalm* :

1. 'Give thanks to the Lord, for he is *beneficent*; for his mercy is eternal.

2. May those whom the Lord has saved say this; he has saved them out of the hands of their enemies.

3. He has gathered them together out of their *countries*; from the east, and from the west, and from the north, and from the *sea*. |

4. ⲀⲨⲠⲖⲀⲚⲀ ϨⲒ ⲠⲬⲀⲒⲈ ⲌⲚ ⲞⲨⲘⲀ ⲈⲘⲚ-ⲘⲞⲞⲨ ⲚϨⲎⲦϤ ·
ⲘⲠⲞⲨϬⲚ-ⲦⲈϨⲒⲎ ⲚⲦⲠⲞⲖⲒⲤ ⲘⲠⲈⲨⲘⲀⲚϢⲰⲠⲈ ·

5. ⲈⲨϨⲔⲀⲈⲒⲦ · ⲈⲨⲞⲂⲈ Ⲁ ⲦⲈⲨⲮⲨⲬⲎ ⲰϪⲚ ⲚϨⲎⲦⲞⲨ ·

6. ⲀϤⲚⲀϨⲘⲞⲨ ⲈⲂⲞⲖ ⲌⲚ ⲚⲈⲨⲀⲚⲀⲄⲔⲎ · ⲀⲨⲬⲒϢⲔⲀⲔ
ⲈϨⲢⲀⲒ ⲈⲠⲬⲞⲈⲒⲤ · ⲀϤⲤⲰⲦⲘ ⲈⲢⲞⲞⲨ ϨⲘ ⲠⲦⲢⲈⲨϨⲰϢ ·

7. ⲀϤⲬⲒⲘⲞⲈⲒⲦ ϨⲎⲦⲞⲨ ⲈⲨϨⲒⲎ ⲈⲤⲤⲞⲨⲦⲰⲚ ⸺ⲈⲦⲢⲈⲨⲂⲰⲔ ‾Ⲣ̄Ⲏ
ⲈϨⲢⲀⲒ ⲈⲠⲦⲞⲠⲞⲤ ⲘⲠⲈⲨⲘⲀⲚϢⲰⲠⲈ ·

8. ⲘⲀⲢⲞⲨⲞⲨⲰⲚϨ ⲈⲂⲞⲖ ⲘⲠⲬⲞⲈⲒⲤ ϨⲚ ⲚⲈϤⲚⲀ᾿ · ⲀⲨⲰ
ⲚⲈϤϢⲠⲎⲢⲈ ϨⲚ Ⲛ̄ϢⲎⲢⲈ Ⲛ̄ⲚⲢⲰⲘⲈ ·

9. ϪⲈ ⲀϤⲦⲤⲒⲞ Ⲛ̄ⲞⲨⲮⲨⲬⲎ ⲈⲤϨⲔⲀⲒⲦ · ⲞⲨⲮⲨⲬⲎ ⲈⲤ-
ϨⲔⲀⲒⲦ ⲀϤⲘⲀϨⲤ Ⲛ̄ⲀⲄⲀⲐⲞⲚ ·

10. ⲚⲈⲦϨⲘⲞⲞⲤ ϨⲘ ⲠⲔⲀⲔⲈ ⲘⲚ ⲐⲀⲒ̈ⲂⲈⲤ ⲘⲠⲘⲞⲨ ⲚⲈⲦ-
ⲘⲎⲢ ϨⲚ ⲞⲨⲘⲚⲦϨⲎⲔⲈ ⲘⲚ ⲠⲠⲈⲚⲒⲠⲈ ·

11. ϪⲈ ⲀϤϮⲚⲞⲨϬⲤ ⲘⲠϢⲀϪⲈ ⲘⲠⲚⲞⲨⲦⲈ ⲀⲨϮϬⲰⲚⲦ
ⲘⲠϢⲞϪⲚⲈ ⲘⲠⲈⲦϪⲞⲤⲈ ·

12. Ⲁ ⲠⲈⲨϨⲎⲦ ⲐⲂⲂⲒⲞ ϨⲚ ⲚⲈⲨϨⲒⲤⲈ · ⲀⲨⲢϬⲰⲂ · ⲀⲨⲰ
ⲘⲚ-ⲠⲈⲦⲂⲞⲎⲐⲒ ⲈⲢⲞⲞⲨ ·

13. ⲀⲨⲬⲒϢⲔⲀⲔ ⲈϨⲢⲀⲒ ⲈⲠⲬⲞⲈⲒⲤ ϨⲘ ⲠⲦⲢⲈⲨϨⲰϢ ⲀϤ-
ⲚⲀϨⲘⲞⲨ ⲈⲂⲞⲖ ϨⲚ ⲚⲈⲨⲀⲚⲀⲄⲔⲎ ·

14. ⲀϤⲚⲦⲞⲨ ⲈⲂⲞⲖ ϨⲘ ⲠⲔⲀⲔⲈ ⲘⲚ ⲐⲀⲒ̈ⲂⲈⲤ ⲘⲠⲘⲞⲨ
ⲀⲨⲰ ⲀϤⲤⲰⲖⲠ Ⲛ̄ⲚⲈⲨⲘⲢ̄ⲢⲈ ·

15. ⲘⲀⲢⲞⲨⲞⲨⲰⲚϨ ⲈⲂⲞⲖ ⲘⲠⲬⲞⲈⲒⲤ ϨⲚ ⲚⲈϤⲚⲀ᾿ · ⲀⲨⲰ
ⲚⲈϤϢⲠⲎⲢⲈ Ⲛ̄Ⲛ̄ϢⲎⲢⲈ ⲚⲢⲢⲰⲘⲈ ·   ‾Ⲣ̄Ⲏ̄ᵇ

16. ϪⲈ ⲀϤⲞⲨⲰϢϤ Ⲛ̄ϨⲈⲚⲠⲨⲖⲎ Ⲛ̄ϨⲞⲘⲚⲦ · ⲀϤϨⲰⲢⲂ Ⲛ̄-
ϨⲈⲚⲘⲞⲬⲖⲞⲤ ⲘⲠⲈⲚⲒⲠⲈ ·

---

6 MS ⲀϤⲀϤⲬⲒ.
14 MS ⲀϤϮ; read ⲀⲨϮ.
23 MS Ⲛ̄Ⲛ̄Ⲛ̄ϢⲎⲢⲈ; the last ⲛ is partly ⲣ.

4. They have *wandered* in the desert in a place without water; they did not find the way to the *city* of their dwelling.

5. Hungry and thirsty, their *soul* fainted in them.

6. He saved them in their *necessity*. They cried to the Lord, he heard them in their distress.

7. He guided them into a straight path, that they might go to the *place* of their dwelling.

8. Let them thank the Lord for his mercies, and his wonders among the sons of men.

9. For he has satisfied a hungry *soul*, he has filled a hungry *soul* with *good things*.

10. They who sit in the darkness and the shadow of death, who are bound in poverty and iron.

11. For they have made wrathful[1] the word of God, they have made angry the counsel of the Most High.

12. Their heart was humbled with their troubles, they became weak and there was no one to *help* them.

13. They cried out to the Lord in their distress, he saved them in their *necessity*.

14. He brought them forth from the darkness and the shadow of death, and broke their bonds.

15. Let them thank the Lord for his mercies and his wonders to the sons of men.

16. For he has shattered the *gates* of brass, he has broken the *bars* of iron. |

---

[1] (14) they have made wrathful; MS : he has made wrathful.

17. ⲀⳞⳡⲞⲠⲞⲨ ⲈⲢⲞⳞ ⲌⲚ ⲦⲈⲌⲒⲎ ⲚⲦⲈⲨⲀⲚⲞⲘⲒⲀ · ⲚⲦⲀⲨ-
ⲞⲂⲂⲒⲞ ⲄⲀⲢ ⲈⲦⲂⲈ ⲚⲈⲨⲀⲚⲞⲘⲒⲀ ·

18. Ⲁ ⲠⲈⲨⲌⲎⲦ ⲂⲈⲦ-ϬⲒⲚⲞⲨⳠⲘ ⲚⲒⳘ · ⲀⲨⲌⳠⲚ ⲈⲌⲞⲨⲚ
ⲈⲘⲠⲨⲀⲎ ⲘⲠⲘⲞⲨ ·

5   19. ⲀⲨⲬⲒⳡⲔⲀⲔ ⲈⲌⲢⲀⲒ ⲈⲠⲬⲞⲈⲒⲤ ⲌⳘ ⲠⲦⲢⲈⲨⲌⳠⳡ ⲀⳞ-
ⲚⲀⲌⲘⲞⲨ ⲈⲂⲞⲀ ⲌⲚ ⲚⲈⲨⲀⲚⲀⲄⲔⲎ ·

20. ⲀⳞⲬⲞⲞⳞ ⲘⲠⲈⳞⳠⲀⲬⲈ ⲀⳞⲦⲀⲀϬⲞⲞⲨ · ⲀⳞⲦⲞⲨⲬⲞⲞⲨ
ⲈⲂⲞⲀ ⲌⲚ ⲚⲈⲨⲌⲒⲤⲈ ·

21. ⲘⲀⲢⲞⲨⲞⲨⳠⲚⲌ ⲈⲂⲞⲀ ⲘⲠⲬⲞⲈⲒⲤ ⲌⲚ ⲚⲈⳞⲚⲀ' · ⲀⲨⳠ
10 ⲚⲈⳞⳠⲠⲎⲢⲈ ⲌⲚ ⲚⳠⲎⲢⲈ ⲚⲢⲢⳠⲘⲈ ·

ⲠⲀⲒ ⲞⲨⲚ ϬⲈ ⲠⲀⲬⲞⲈⲒⲤ ⲠⲈ ⲠⲂⳠⲀ ⲈⲂⲞⲀ ⲘⲠⲌⲨⲘⲚⲞⲤ
ⲚⲦⲀⲤⲬⲞⲞⳞ ⲚϬⲒ ⲦⲤⲞⳘⲒⲀ · ⲤⳠⲦⳘ ⲞⲨⲚ ⲠⲀⲬⲞⲈⲒⲤ · ⲦⲀ-
ⲬⲞⲞⳞ ⳞⲀⲚⲈⲢⳠⲤ · ⲠⳠⲀⲬⲈ ⲘⲈⲚ ⲚⲦⲀⳞⲬⲞⲞⳞ ⲚϬⲒ ⲀⲀⲨ-
ⲈⲒⲀ · ⲬⲈ ⲞⲨⳠⲚⲌ ⲈⲂⲞⲀ**⁻ⲘⲠⲬⲞⲈⲒⲤ ⲬⲈ ⲞⲨⲬⲢⲎⲤⲦⲞⲤ ⲠⲈ ⲢⲞ̄
15 ⲬⲈ ⲞⲨⳠⲀⲈⲚⲈⳌ ⲠⲈ ⲠⲈⳞⲚⲀ' · ⲚⲦⲞⳞ ⲠⲈ ⲠⳠⲀⲬⲈ ⲈⲚⲦ-
ⲀⲤⲬⲞⲞⳞ ⲚϬⲒ ⲦⲤⲞⳘⲒⲀ · ⲬⲈ ϯⲚⲀⲞⲨⳠⲚⲌ ⲚⲀⲔ ⲈⲂⲞⲀ
ⲠⲞⲨⲞⲈⲒⲚ ⲬⲈ ⲚⲦⲔ ⲞⲨⲤⳠⲦⲎⲢ ⲀⲨⳠ ⲚⲦⲔ ⲞⲨⲢⲈⳞⲤⳠⲦⲈ
ⲚⲞⲨⲞⲈⲒⳠ ⲚⲒⳘ · ⲀⲨⳠ ⲠⳠⲀⲬⲈ ⲚⲦⲀⳞⲬⲞⲞⳞ ⲚϬⲒ ⲀⲀⲨ-
ⲈⲒⲀ · ⲬⲈ ⲘⲀⲢⲈ ⲚⲈⲚⲦⲀ ⲠⲬⲞⲈⲒⲤ ⲤⲞⲦⲞⲨ ⲬⲈ-ⲠⲀⲒ · ⲀⳞ-
20 ⲤⲞⲦⲞⲨ ⲈⲂⲞⲀ ⲌⲚ ⲦϬⲒⲬ ⲚⲚⲈⲨⲬⲀⲬⲈ · ⲚⲦⲞⳞ ⲠⲈ ⲠⳠⲀ-
ⲬⲈ ⲈⲚⲦⲀⲤⲬⲞⲞⳞ ⲚϬⲒ ⲦⲤⲞⳘⲒⲀ ⲬⲈ ϯⲚⲀⲬⳠ ⲘⲠⲈⲈⲒ-
ⲌⲨⲘⲚⲞⲤ ⲈⲠⲞⲨⲞⲈⲒⲚ ⲬⲈ ⲀⳞⲚⲞⲨⲌⳘ ⲘⲘⲞⲒ ⲀⲨⳠ ⲀⳞⲚⲀⲌ-
ⲘⲈⲦ ⲈⲂⲞⲀ ⲌⲚ ⲦϬⲒⲬ ⲚⲚⲀⲢⲬⳠⲚ ⲚⲀⲬⲒⲬⲈⲈⲨ · ⲘⲚ ⲠⲔⲈ-
ⲤⲈⲈⲠⲈ ⲘⳠⲀⲀⲘⲞⲤ · ⲠⲀⲒ ⲞⲨⲚ ⲠⲀⲬⲞⲈⲒⲤ ⲠⲈ ⲠⲂⳠⲀ ⲈⲂⲞⲀ
25 ⲘⲠⲌⲨⲘⲚⲞⲤ ⲚⲦⲀⲤⲬⲞⲞⳞ ⲚϬⲒ ⲦⲤⲞⳘⲒⲀ ⲌⲚ ⲦⲘⲎⲦⲈ Ⲙ-
ⲠⲬⲞⲨⲦⲀⳞⲦⲈ ⲚⲀⲌⲞⲢⲀⲦⲞⲤ ⲈⲤⲞⲨⳠⳠ ⲈⲦⲢⲈⲨⲈⲒⲘⲈ ⲈⲚⲈ-

---

21 ⲚϬⲒ ⲦⲤⲞ written over erasure; ⳘⲒⲀ ⲬⲈ inserted in margin.

17. He has taken them from the path of their *iniquity*; for they were humbled on account of their *iniquity*.

18. Their heart abhorred all food; they entered into the *gates* of death.

19. They cried out to the Lord in their distress; he saved them in their *necessity*.

20. He spoke his word, he healed them, he delivered them from their troubles.

21. Let them thank the Lord for his mercies and his wonders among the sons of men' *.

This *now*, my Lord, is the interpretation of the *song of praise* which the Sophia spoke. Hear now, my Lord, that I speak *clearly*. The word, *moreover*, which David spoke: 'Give thanks to the Lord for he is *beneficent*; for his mercy is eternal' □ : that is the word which the Sophia said: 'I will give thanks to thee, O Light, for thou art a *Saviour* and thou art a deliverer at all times'. And the word which David spoke: 'May those whom the Lord has saved say this; he has saved them out of the hands of their enemies' ○ : that is the word which the Sophia said: 'I will speak this *song of praise* to the light, for he has saved me, and he has delivered me out of the hand of the *archons*, my enemies.' And the rest of the *Psalm*.

This *now*, my Lord, is the interpretation of the *song of praise* which the Sophia said in the midst of the 24 *invisible ones*, wishing that they should know | all the wonders

---

*   Ps. 106.1-21
□   Ps. 106.1
○   Ps. 106.2

ϣⲏⲣⲉ ⲧⲏⲣⲟⲩ ⲉⲛⲧⲁⲓ̈ⲁⲁⲩ ⲛ̄ⲙⲙⲁⲥ· ⲁⲩⲱ ⲁⲥⲟⲩⲱϣ ⲣ̄ⲝ̄ ᵇ
ⲉⲧⲣⲉⲩⲉⲓⲙⲉ ϫⲉ ⲁⲕ⳨ ⲛ̄ⲛⲉⲕⲙⲩⲥⲧⲏⲣⲓⲟⲛ ⲙ̄ⲡⲅⲉⲛⲟⲥ ⲛ̄ⲧ-
ⲙⲛ̄ⲧⲣⲱⲙⲉ: ⲁⲥϣⲱⲡⲉ ϭⲉ ⲛ̄ⲧⲉⲣⲉ ⲓ̅ⲥ̅ ⲥⲱⲧ̄ⲙ ⲉⲛⲉⲓ̈ϣⲁϫⲉ·
ⲉϥϫⲱ ⲙ̄ⲙⲟⲟⲩ ⲛ̄ϭⲓ ⲫⲓⲗⲓⲡⲡⲟⲥ ⲡⲉϫⲁϥ ϫⲉ ⲉⲩⲅⲉ ⲡⲙⲁ-
5 ⲕⲁⲣⲓⲟⲥ ⲫⲓⲗⲓⲡⲡⲟⲥ ⲡⲁⲓ̈ ⲡⲉ ⲡⲃⲱⲗ ⲉⲃⲟⲗ ⲙ̄ⲡϩⲩⲙⲛⲟⲥ ⲉⲛⲧⲁⲥϫⲟⲟϥ ⲛ̄ϭⲓ ⲧⲥⲟⲫⲓⲁ·

ⲁⲥϣⲱⲡⲉ ϭⲉ ⲟⲛ ⲙ̄ⲛ̄ⲛⲥⲁ ⲛⲁⲓ̈ ⲧⲏⲣⲟⲩ ⲁⲥⲉⲓ̄ ⲉϩⲟⲩⲛ ⲛ̄ϭⲓ
ⲙⲁⲣⲓϩⲁⲙ ⲁⲥⲟⲩⲱϣⲧ ⲉⲛⲟⲩⲉⲣⲏⲧⲉ ⲛ̄ⲓ̅ⲥ̅ ⲡⲉϫⲁⲥ ϫⲉ ⲡⲁϫⲟⲉⲓⲥ ⲙ̄ⲡⲣ̄ϭⲱⲛ̄ⲧ ⲉⲣⲟⲓ̈ ⲉⲓ̈ϣⲓⲛⲉ ⲙ̄ⲙⲟⲕ· ϫⲉ ⲉⲛϣⲓⲛⲉ
10 ⲛ̄ⲥⲁ ϩⲱⲃ ⲛⲓⲙ ϩⲛ̄ ⲟⲩⲱⲣ̄ϫ̄ ⲙⲛ̄ ⲟⲩⲁⲥⲫⲁⲗⲓⲁ· ⲁⲕϫⲟⲟⲥ
ⲅⲁⲣ ⲉⲣⲟⲛ ⲙ̄ⲡⲓⲟⲩⲟⲉⲓϣ· ϫⲉ ϣⲓⲛⲉ ⲧⲁⲣⲉⲧⲛ̄ϭⲓⲛⲉ ⲁⲩⲱ
ⲧⲱϩ̄ⲙ ⲧⲁⲣⲟⲩⲟⲩⲱⲛ ⲛⲏⲧⲛ̄ ϫⲉ ⲟⲩⲟⲛ ⲅⲁⲣ ⲛⲓⲙ ⲉⲧϣⲓⲛⲉ
ϥⲛⲁϭⲓⲛⲉ· ⲁⲩⲱ ⲟⲩⲟⲛ ⲛⲓⲙ ⲉⲧⲧⲱϩ̄ⲙ ⲉϩⲟⲩⲛ· ⲥⲉⲛⲁ- ⲣ̄ⲟ
ⲟⲩⲱⲛ ⲛⲁϥ· ⲧⲉⲛⲟⲩ ϭⲉ ⲡⲁϫⲟⲉⲓⲥ ⲛⲓⲙ ⲡⲉ⳨ⲛⲁϭⲛ̄ⲧϥ ⲏ̄
15 ⲛⲓⲙ ⲡⲉⲧⲛ̄ⲛⲁⲧⲱϩ̄ⲙ ⲉⲣⲟϥ· ⲏ̄ ⲛⲓⲙ ⲛ̄ⲧⲟϥ ⲡⲉⲧⲉ ⲟⲩⲛ̄-
ϣϭⲟⲙ ⲙ̄ⲙⲟϥ ⲉϫⲱ ⲉⲣⲟⲛ ⲛ̄ⲧⲁⲡⲟⲫⲁⲥⲓⲥ ⲛ̄ⲛ̄ϣⲁϫⲉ ⲉⲧⲛ̄-
ⲛⲁϣ̄ⲛ̄ⲧⲕ ⲉⲣⲟⲟⲩ· ⲏ̄ ⲛⲓⲙ ⲛ̄ⲧⲟϥ ⲡⲉ ⲉⲧⲥⲟⲟⲩⲛ ⲛ̄ⲧϭⲟⲙ
ⲛ̄ⲛ̄ϣⲁϫⲉ ⲉⲧⲛ̄ⲛⲁϣⲓⲛⲉ ⲛ̄ⲥⲱⲟⲩ· ⲉⲃⲟⲗ ϫⲉ ϩⲛ̄ ⲟⲩⲛⲟⲩⲥ
ⲁⲕ⳨ⲛⲟⲩⲥ ⲛⲁⲛ ⲛ̄ⲧⲉ ⲡⲟⲩⲟⲉⲓⲛ· ⲁⲩⲱ ⲁⲕ⳨ ⲛⲁⲛ ⲛ̄ⲟⲩ-
20 ⲁⲓⲥⲑⲏⲥⲓⲥ ⲙⲛ̄ ⲟⲩⲙⲉⲉⲩⲉ ⲉϥϫⲟⲥⲉ ⲉⲙⲁⲧⲉ· ⲉⲧⲃⲉ ⲡⲁⲓ̈
ⲟⲩⲛ ⲙⲛ̄-ⲗⲁⲁⲩ ⲉϥϣⲟⲟⲡ ϩ̄ⲙ ⲡⲕⲟⲥⲙⲟⲥ ⲛ̄ⲧⲉ ⲧⲙⲛ̄ⲧ-
ⲣⲱⲙⲉ· ⲟⲩⲇⲉ ⲉϥϣⲟⲟⲡ ϩ̄ⲙ ⲡϫⲓⲥⲉ ⲛ̄ⲧⲉ ⲛ̄ⲁⲓⲱⲛ ⲉⲩⲛ̄-
ϣϭⲟⲙ ⲙ̄ⲙⲟϥ ⲉϫⲱ ⲉⲣⲟⲛ ⲛ̄ⲧⲁⲡⲟⲫⲁⲥⲓⲥ ⲛ̄ⲛ̄ϣⲁϫⲉ ⲉⲧⲛ̄-

---

1 ⲉⲛⲧⲁⲓ̈ⲁⲁⲩ; read ⲉⲛⲧⲁⲕⲁⲁⲩ. MS ⲁⲥⲟⲩⲱϣ; better ⲉⲥⲟⲩⲱϣ.
8 MS originally ⲁⲥ⳨·ⲟⲩⲱϣⲧ; ⳨ erased.

which thou hast done [1] for her. And she wished that they should know that thou hast given thy *mysteries* to the *race* of mankind."

Now it happened when Jesus heard these words which Philip spoke, he said : "*Excellent*, thou *blessed one*, Philip. This is the interpretation of the *song of praise* which the Sophia spoke."

83.   Now it happened again after all these things Maria came forward. She worshipped at the feet of Jesus and said : "My Lord, be not angry with me, that I question thee [2], for we question all things with assurance and *certainty*. *For* thou hast once said to us : 'Seek and ye shall find, and knock and it shall be opened to you, for everyone that seeks will find, and to everyone that knocks it will be opened to him' *. Now at this time, my Lord, whom will I find, *or* to whom shall we knock, *or* rather who is able to say to us the *answer* to the words on which we question thee, *or* rather who knows the power of the words which we will question? Because with *understanding* (*mind*) thou hast given us *understanding* (*mind*) of the light; and thou hast given us *perception* and greatly elevated thought. For this reason *now* there is no one who exists in the *world* of mankind, *nor* who exists in the height of the *aeons* who is able to say to us the *answer* to the words | which we question, *except* thyself

---

*   Mt. 7.7, 8; Lk. 11.9, 10

---

[1]   (1) thou hast done; MS : I have done.
[2]   (9) question; the Coptic word also means "seek" and is so translated in 184.11, 12; also 250.4, 5; in passages elsewhere it is translated as "question" (e.g. 185.1-7).

ϢΙΝΕ Ν̅ⲤϢⲞⲨ · ΕΙΜΗΤΙ Ν̅ⲦⲞⲔ ⲞⲨⲀⲀⲔ ΠⲀΪ ΕⲦⲤⲞⲞⲨⲚ̅
Μ̅ΠⲦⲎⲢϤ̅ · ⲀⲨϢ ΕⲦΧⲎⲔ ΕⲂⲞⲖ ⲌⲘ̅ ΠⲦⲎⲢϤ̅ · ΕⲂⲞⲖ ΧΕ ⲢⲞ ᵇ
ΝΕΪϢΙΝΕ ⲀⲚ Ν̅ⲤⲀ ⲐΕ ΕⲦⲞⲨϢΙΝΕ Μ̅ΜⲞⲤ Ν̅ϬΙ Ν̅ⲢϢΜΕ
Ν̅ⲦΕ ΠⲔⲞⲤΜⲞⲤ · ⲀⲖⲖⲀ ΕⲚϢΙΝΕ ⲀΝⲞΝ ⲌⲘ̅ ΠⲤⲞⲞⲨⲚ̅ Ν̅ⲦΕ
⁵ ΠΧΙⲤΕ ΠⲀΪ ΕΝⲦⲀⲔⲦⲀⲀϤ ΝⲀΝ ⲀⲨϢ ΕΝϢΙΝΕ ⲞΝ ⲌⲘ̅
ΠⲦⲨΠⲞⲤ Ν̅ϬΙΝϢΙΝΕ ΕⲦⲞⲨⲞⲦⲂ̅ · ⲦⲀΪ Ν̅ⲦⲀⲔⲦⲤⲀⲂⲞΝ
ΕⲢⲞⲤ ΕⲦⲢΕΝϢΙΝΕ Ν̅ⲌⲎⲦⲤ̅ ·

ⳤ ⲦΕΝⲞⲨ ϬΕ ΠⲀΧⲞΕΙⲤ Μ̅ΠⲢ̅ϬϢΝ̅Ⲧ ΕⲢⲞΪ · ⲀⲖⲖⲀ ϬϢⲖⲠ̅
ΝⲀΪ ΕⲂⲞⲖ Μ̅ΠϢⲀΧΕ ΕϮΝⲀϢ̅Ν̅ⲦⲔ ΕⲢⲞϤ · ⲀⲤϢϢΠΕ Ν̅ⲦΕ-
¹⁰ ⲢΕ Ι̅Ⲥ̅ ⲤϢⲦⲘ ΕΝΕΪϢⲀΧΕ ΕⲤΧϢ Μ̅ΜⲞⲞⲨ Ν̅ϬΙ ΜⲀⲢΙⲀ
ⲦΜⲀⲄⲀⲖⲖⲎΝⲎ · ⲀϤⲞⲨϢϢ̅Ⲃ ⲆΕ Ν̅ϬΙ Ι̅Ⲥ̅ ΠΕΧⲀϤ ΝⲀⲤ ΧΕ
ϢΙΝΕ Ν̅ⲤⲀ ΠΕⲦΕⲢΕⲞⲨΕϢϢΙΝΕ Ν̅ⲤϢϤ · ⲀⲨϢ ⲀΝⲞⲔ
ϮΝⲀϬⲞⲖΠϤ̅ ΝΕ ΕⲂⲞⲖ ⲌΝ ⲞⲨϢⲢΧ̅ ΜΝ ⲞⲨⲀⲤⲪⲀⲖΕΙⲀ · ⲌⲀ-
ΜⲎΝ ⲌⲀΜⲎΝ ϮΧϢ Μ̅ΜⲞⲤ ΝⲎⲦΝ̅ ΧΕ ⲢⲀϢΕ ⲌΝ ⲞⲨΝⲞϬ
¹⁵ Ν̅ⲢⲀϢΕ · ⲀⲨϢ Ν̅ⲦΕⲦⲚ̅ⲦΕⲖⲎⲖ ΕΜⲀϢⲞ ΕΜⲀϢⲞ · ΕⲦΕⲦⲚ̅- ⲢⲞⲖ
ϢΙΝΕ Ν̅ⲤⲀ ⲌϢⲂ ΝΙΜ ⲌΝ ⲞⲨϢⲢΧ̅ · ⲀⲨϢ ϮΝⲀⲦΕⲖⲎⲖ
ΕΜⲀϢⲞ ΕΜⲀϢⲞ ΧΕ ⲦΕⲦΝ̅ϢΙΝΕ Ν̅ⲤⲀ ⲌϢⲂ ΝΙΜ ⲌΝ ⲞⲨ-
ϢⲢΧ̅ · ⲀⲨϢ ⲦΕⲦΝ̅ϢΙΝΕ Ν̅ⲤⲀ ⲐΕ ΕⲦϢⲞⲨϢΙΝΕ Μ̅ΜⲞⲤ ·
ⲦΕΝⲞⲨ ϬΕ ϢΙΝΕ Ν̅ⲤⲀ ΠΕⲦΕϢΙΝΕ Ν̅ⲤϢϤ · ⲀⲨϢ ϮΝⲀ-
²⁰ ϬⲞⲖΠϤ̅ ΝΕ ΕⲂⲞⲖ ⲌΝ ⲞⲨⲢⲀϢΕ · ⲀⲤϢϢΠΕ ϬΕ Ν̅ⲦΕⲢΕ
ΜⲀⲢΙⲀ ⲤϢⲦⲘ̅ ΕΝΕΪϢⲀΧΕ ΕϤΧϢ Μ̅ΜⲞⲞⲨ Ν̅ϬΙ ΠⲤϢⲦⲎⲢ ·
ⲀⲤⲢⲀϢΕ ⲌΝ ⲞⲨΝⲞϬ Ν̅ⲢⲀϢΕ · ⲀⲨϢ ⲀⲤⲦΕⲖⲎⲖ Μ̅ΜⲞⲤ
ΕΜⲀϢⲞ ΕΜⲀϢⲞ · ΠΕΧⲀⲤ Ν̅Ι̅Ⲥ̅ ΧΕ ΠⲀΧⲞΕΙⲤ · ⲀⲨϢ ΠⲀ-
ⲤϢⲦⲎⲢ · ΕΪΕ ΕⲢΕ ΠΧⲞⲨⲦⲀϤⲦΕ Ν̅ⲀⲌⲞⲢⲀⲦⲞⲤ Ⲟ’ Ν̅ⲀϢ
²⁵ Μ̅ΜΙΝΕ ⲀⲨϢ ΕⲨⲞ’ Ν̅ⲀϢ Ν̅ⲦⲨΠⲞⲤ Ⲏ̅ Μ̅ΜⲞΝ Ν̅ⲦⲞϤ ΕⲨⲞ’
Ν̅ⲀϢ Ν̅ϬⲞⲦ · Ⲏ̅ ΕΪΕ ΕϤⲞ Ν̅ⲀϢ Ν̅ϬⲞⲦ Ν̅ϬΙ ΠΕⲨⲞⲨⲞΕΙΝ ·

---

3   MS ⲚⲈΪϢΙⲚⲈ; better ⲚⲈⲚϢΙⲚⲈ.

alone who knowest the All, and art complete in the All. Because we do not question[1] in the manner in which men of the *world* question, but we question with the knowledge of the height which thou hast given to us, and we question with the *type* of superior questioning which thou hast taught us, that we should question therewith. Now at this time, my Lord, be not angry with me, but reveal to me the subject on which I will question thee."

It happened when Jesus heard these words which Maria Magdalene spoke, he, Jesus, answered *moreover* and said to her: "Question that which thou dost wish to question, and I will reveal it with assurance and *certainty*. *Truly, truly*, I say to you: rejoice with great joy, and be exceedingly glad. If you question everything with assurance, I will be exceedingly glad because you question everything with assurance, and you ask about the manner in which one should inquire. Now at this time question that which thou dost question, and I will reveal it with joy."

Now it happened when Maria heard these words which the *Saviour* said, she rejoiced with great joy, and she was exceedingly glad. She said to Jesus: "My Lord and my *Saviour*, of what kind are the 24 *invisible ones*, and of what *type*, *or* rather, of what form are they, *or* of what form is their light?" |

---

[1]   (3) we do not question; MS: I do not question.

ⲀϤⲞⲨⲱϨⲘ ⲆⲈ ⲚϬⲒ ⲓ̅ⲥ̅ ⲠⲈⲪⲀϤ ⲘⲘⲀⲢⲒⲀ · ϪⲈ ⲞⲨ ⲠⲈ ⲈⲦ- ⲢⲞⲀ ᵇ
ϨⲘ ⲠⲈⲒⲔⲞⲤⲘⲞⲤ ⲈϤⲈⲒⲚⲈ ⲘⲘⲞⲞⲨ · ⲏ Ⲁⲱ ⲚⲦⲞϤ ⲚⲦⲞⲠⲞⲤ
ⲠⲈ ⲈⲦϨⲘ ⲠⲈⲒⲔⲞⲤⲘⲞⲤ ⲠⲈ ⲈⲦⲦⲚⲦⲞⲚⲦ ⲈⲢⲞⲞⲨ · ⲦⲈⲚⲞⲨ
ϬⲈ ⲈⲈⲒⲚⲀⲦⲚⲦⲱⲚⲞⲨ ⲈⲞⲨ ⲏ ⲞⲨ ⲚⲦⲞϤ ⲠⲈ ⲈϤⲚⲀϪⲞⲞϤ
5 ⲈⲦⲂⲎⲎⲦⲞⲨ · ⲘⲚ-ⲀⲀⲀⲨ ⲄⲀⲢ ϨⲘ ⲠⲈⲒⲔⲞⲤⲘⲞⲤ ⲈⲒⲚⲀⲱⲦⲚ-
ⲦⲱⲚⲞⲨ ⲈⲢⲞϤ · ⲀⲨⲱ ⲘⲚ-ⲀⲀⲀⲨ ⲚⲈⲒⲀⲞⲤ ⲚϨⲎⲦϤ ⲈϤ-
ⲚⲀⲱϨⲞⲘⲞⲒⲱϪⲈ ⲈⲢⲞⲞⲨ · ⲦⲈⲚⲞⲨ ϬⲈ ⲘⲚ-ⲀⲀⲀⲨ ϨⲘ ⲠⲈⲒ-
ⲔⲞⲤⲘⲞⲤ ⲈϤⲞ ⲚⲦϬⲞⲦ ⲚⲦⲠⲈ · ϨⲀⲘⲎⲚ ϯϪⲱ ⲘⲘⲞⲤ ⲚⲎ-
ⲦⲚ ϪⲈ ⲠⲞⲨⲀ ⲠⲞⲨⲀ ⲚⲀϨⲞⲢⲀⲦⲞⲤ ⲚⲀⲀϤ ⲈⲦⲠⲈ ⲘⲚ ⲦⲈ-
10 ⲤⲪⲀⲒⲢⲀ ⲈⲦϨⲒϪⲱⲤ · ⲀⲨⲱ ⲘⲚ ⲠⲘⲚⲦⲤⲚⲞⲞⲨⲤ ⲚⲀⲒⲱⲚ ϨⲒ
ⲞⲨⲤⲞⲠ ⲚϮⲤ ⲚⲔⲱⲂ ⲚⲤⲞⲠ · ⲔⲀⲦⲀ ⲐⲈ ⲈⲚⲦⲀⲒⲞⲨⲱ ⲈⲒϪⲱ
ⲘⲘⲞⲤ ⲚⲎⲦⲚ ⲚⲔⲈⲤⲞⲠ · ⲀⲨⲱ ⲘⲚ-ⲀⲀⲀⲨ ⲚⲞⲨⲞⲈⲒⲚ ϨⲘ
ⲠⲈⲒⲔⲞⲤⲘⲞⲤ · ⲈϤⲞⲨⲞⲦⲂ ⲈⲠⲞⲨⲞⲈⲒⲚ ⲘⲠⲢⲎ · ϨⲀⲘⲎⲚ ϨⲀ- ⲢⲞⲂ
ⲘⲎⲚ ϯϪⲱ ⲘⲘⲞⲤ ⲚⲎⲦⲚ ϪⲈ ⲠϪⲞⲨⲦⲀϤⲦⲈ ⲚⲀϨⲞⲢⲀⲦⲞⲤ
15 ⲤⲈⲞ' ⲚⲞⲨⲞⲒⲚ ϨⲞⲨⲞ ⲠⲞⲨⲞⲈⲒⲚ ⲘⲠⲢⲎ ⲈⲦϨⲘ ⲠⲈⲒⲔⲞⲤ-
ⲘⲞⲤ ⲚⲞⲨⲦⲂⲀ ⲚⲔⲱⲂ ⲚⲤⲞⲠ · ⲔⲀⲦⲀ ⲐⲈ ⲈⲚⲦⲀⲒⲞⲨⲱ ⲈⲒ-
Ϫⲱ ⲘⲘⲞⲤ ⲚⲎⲦⲚ ⲚⲔⲈⲤⲞⲠ ⲈⲂⲞⲀ ϪⲈ ⲠⲞⲨⲞⲈⲒⲚ ⲘⲠⲢⲎ
ϨⲚ ⲦⲈϤⲀⲀⲎⲐⲈⲒⲀ ⲘⲘⲞⲢⲪⲎ ⲚϤϨⲘ ⲠⲈⲒⲦⲞⲠⲞⲤ ⲀⲚ ⲈⲂⲞⲀ
ⲄⲀⲢ ϪⲈ ϤϪⲱⲦⲈ ⲚϬⲒ ⲠⲈϤⲞⲨⲞⲈⲒⲚ ⲚⲞⲨⲘⲎⲎⲱⲈ ⲚⲔⲀⲦⲀ-
20 ⲠⲈⲦⲀⲤⲘⲀ ⲚⲦⲞⲠⲞⲤ · ⲀⲀⲀⲀ ⲠⲞⲨⲞⲈⲒⲚ ⲘⲠⲢⲎ ϨⲚ ⲦⲈϤⲀ-
ⲀⲎⲐⲈⲒⲀ ⲘⲘⲞⲢⲪⲎ ⲠⲀⲒ ⲈⲦⲱⲞⲞⲠ ϨⲘ ⲠⲦⲞⲠⲞⲤ ⲚⲦⲠⲀⲢ-
ⲐⲈⲚⲞⲤ ⲘⲠⲞⲨⲞⲈⲒⲚ · ϤⲞ' ⲚⲞⲨⲞⲈⲒⲚ ⲚϨⲞⲨⲞ ⲈⲠⲬⲞⲨⲦ-
ⲀϤⲦⲈ ⲚⲀϨⲞⲢⲀⲦⲞⲤ · ⲀⲨⲱ ⲘⲚ ⲠⲚⲞϬ ⲘⲠⲢⲞⲠⲀⲦⲱⲢ Ⲛ-
ⲀϨⲞⲢⲀⲦⲞⲤ ⲀⲨⲱ ⲘⲚ ⲠⲔⲈⲚⲞϬ ⲚⲦⲢⲒⲀⲨⲚⲀⲘⲒⲤ ⲚⲚⲞⲨⲦⲈ
25 ⲚⲞⲨⲦⲂⲀ ⲚⲔⲱⲂ ⲚⲤⲞⲠ · ⲔⲀⲦⲀ ⲐⲈ ⲈⲚⲦⲀⲒⲞⲨⲱ ⲈⲒϪⲱ

---

13 ⲒⲀ̅ in upper right-hand margin at end of quire.
15 MS ⲈϨⲞⲨⲞ ⲠⲞⲨⲞⲈⲒⲚ; read ⲈϨⲞⲨⲞ ⲈⲠⲞⲨⲞⲈⲒⲚ.

84. Jesus answered *however* and said to Maria : "What is there in this *world* that resembles them, *or* rather, what *place* is there in this *world* that is comparable to them? Now at this time with what shall I compare them, *or* rather, what shall I say concerning them? *For* there is nothing in this *world* with which I will be able to compare them, and no *kind*[1] exists in it which can *be likened* to them. Now at this time there is nothing in this *world* which is of the form of heaven. *Truly*, I say to you, each one of the *invisible ones* is nine times greater than the heaven and the *sphere* above it, including the twelve *aeons*, *as* I have already said to you at another time. And there is no light in this *world* which is superior to the light of the sun. *Truly, truly*, I say to you, the 24 *invisible ones* are lighted ten thousand times more than the light of the sun which is in this *world*, as I have already said to you at another time. For the light of the sun in its *true form* is not in this *place because* its light passes through a multitude of *veils* and *places*[2]. *But* the light of the sun in its *true form*, which is in the *place* of the *Virgin* of the Light, is lighted ten thousand times more than the 24 *invisible ones* and the great *invisible forefather* and also the great *triple-powered* God, *as* I have already said | to you at another time. Now at this time,

---

[1] (6) kind; Till: thing (see 187.2).
[2] (19, 20) of veils and places; MS: of veils of places.

ⲘⲘⲞⲤ ⲚⲎⲦⲚ ⲚⲔⲈⲤⲞⲠ· ⲦⲈⲚⲞⲨ ⳠⲈ ⲘⲀⲢⲒⲀ ⲘⲚ-ⲀⲗⲀⲨ ⲣⲟⲃ ᵇ
ⲚⲈⲒⲆⲞⲤ ⲒⲘ ⲠⲈⲒⲔⲞⲤⲘⲞⲤ ⲞⲨⲆⲈ ⲘⲚ-ⲞⲨⲞⲈⲒⲚ ⲞⲨⲆⲈ ⲘⲚ-
ⲘⲞⲢⲪⲎ ⲈϤⲦⲚⲦⲞⲚⲦ ⲈⲠⲬⲞⲨⲦⲀϤⲦⲈ ⲚⲀⲌⲞⲢⲀⲦⲞⲤ· ⲬⲈ
ⲈⲒⲈⲦⲚⲦⲰⲚⲞⲨ ⲈⲢⲞⲞⲨ· ⲀⲗⲗⲀ ⲈⲦⲒ ⲔⲈⲔⲞⲨⲒ ⲚⲞⲨⲞⲈⲒϢ
5 ⲚⲦⲞ ⲘⲚ ⲚⲞⲨⲤⲚⲎⲨ ⲚϢⲂⲢ-ⲘⲀⲐⲎⲦⲎⲤ ϯⲚⲀⲬⲒⲦⲎⲨⲦⲚ ⲈⲚ-
ⲦⲞⲠⲞⲤ ⲦⲎⲢⲞⲨ ⲚⲦⲈ ⲠⲬⲒⲤⲈ· ⲀⲨⲰ ϯⲚⲀⲬⲒⲦⲎⲨⲦⲚ Ⲉ-
ⲠϢⲞⲘⲚⲦ ⲚⲬⲰⲢⲎⲘⲀ ⲘⲠⲒϢⲞⲢⲠ ⲘⲘⲨⲤⲦⲎⲢⲒⲞⲚ ϢⲀⲦⲚ
ⲚⲦⲞⲠⲞⲤ ⲘⲘⲀⲦⲈ ⲘⲠⲈⲬⲰⲢⲎⲘⲀ ⲘⲠⲒⲀⲦϢⲀⲬⲈ ⲈⲢⲞϤ· ⲀⲨⲰ
ⲦⲈⲦⲚⲚⲀⲚⲀⲨ ⲈⲚⲈⲨⲘⲞⲢⲪⲎ ⲦⲎⲢⲞⲨ ⲒⲚ ⲞⲨⲀⲗⲎⲐⲒⲀ ⲀⲬⲚ
10 ⲦⲞⲚⲦⲚ· ⲀⲨⲰ ⲈⲒϢⲀⲚⲬⲒⲦⲎⲨⲦⲚ ⲈⲠⲬⲒⲤⲈ· ⲈⲦⲈⲦⲚⲚⲀ-
ⲚⲀⲨ ⲈⲠⲈⲞⲞⲨ ⲚⲚⲀⲠⲬⲒⲤⲈ· ⲀⲨⲰ ⲦⲈⲦⲚⲚⲀϢⲰⲠⲈ ⲒⲚ ⲞⲨ-
ⲚⲞϬ ⲚϢⲠⲎⲢⲈ ⲈⲘⲀϢⲞ ⲈⲘⲀϢⲞ· ⲀⲨⲰ ⲈⲒϢⲀⲚⲬⲒⲦⲎⲨⲦⲚ
ⲈⲠⲦⲞⲠⲞⲤ ⲚⲚⲀⲢⲬⲰⲚ ⲚⲐⲒⲘⲀⲢⲘⲈⲚⲎ ** ⲦⲈⲦⲚⲚⲀⲚⲀⲨ ⲈⲠⲈ- ⲣⲟⲅ
ⲞⲞⲨ ⲈⲦⲞⲨϢⲞⲞⲠ ⲚⲌⲎⲦϤ· ⲀⲨⲰ ⲈⲂⲞⲗ ⲒⲘ ⲠⲈⲨⲚⲞϬ Ⲛ-
15 ϬⲞⲞⲨ ⲈⲦⲞⲨⲞⲦⲂ ⲦⲈⲦⲚⲚⲀⲈⲠ-ⲠⲈⲒⲔⲞⲤⲘⲞⲤ ⲚⲚⲀⲌⲢⲎⲦⲚ
ⲒⲰⲤ ⲔⲀⲔⲈ ⲚⲔⲀⲔⲈ· ⲀⲨⲰ ⲚⲦⲈⲦⲚⲚⲀϬⲰϢⲦ ⲈⲂⲞⲗ ⲈⲬⲘ
ⲠⲔⲞⲤⲘⲞⲤ ⲦⲎⲢϤ ⲚⲦⲈ ⲦⲘⲦⲢⲰⲘⲈ ⲈϤⲚⲀⲢ-ⲦϬⲞⲦ ⲚⲞⲨ-
ⲚⲀⲠⲚⲈ ⲚϢⲞⲒϢ ⲚⲚⲀⲌⲢⲎⲦⲚ ⲈⲂⲞⲗ ⲘⲠⲚⲞϬ ⲚⲞⲨⲈ ⲈⲦϤ-
ⲞⲨⲎⲨ ⲘⲘⲞϤ ⲈⲘⲀϢⲞ ⲈⲘⲀϢⲞ· ⲘⲚ ⲦⲚⲞϬ ⲚϬⲞⲦ· ⲈⲦ-
20 ϤⲚⲀⲀⲀϤ ⲈⲢⲞϤ ⲈⲘⲀϢⲞ· ⲀⲨⲰ ⲈⲒϢⲀⲚⲬⲒⲦⲎⲨⲦⲚ ⲈⲠⲘⲚⲦ-
ⲤⲚⲞⲞⲨⲤ ⲚⲀⲒⲰⲚ ⲦⲈⲦⲚⲚⲀⲚⲀⲨ ⲈⲠⲈⲞⲞⲨ ⲈⲦⲞⲨϢⲞⲞⲠ
ⲚⲌⲎⲦϤ ⲀⲨⲰ ⲈⲂⲞⲗ ⲘⲠⲚⲞϬ ⲚⲈⲞⲞⲨ· ⲠⲦⲞⲠⲞⲤ ⲚⲚⲀⲢ-
ⲬⲰⲚ ⲚⲐⲒⲘⲀⲢⲘⲈⲚⲎ ⲚⲀϢⲠ ⲚⲚⲀⲌⲢⲎⲦⲚ ⲚⲐⲈ ⲘⲠⲔⲀⲔⲈ ⲚⲚ-
ⲔⲀⲔⲈ· ⲀⲨⲰ ϤⲚⲀⲢ-ⲦϬⲞⲦ ⲚⲞⲨⲚⲀⲠⲚⲈ ⲚϢⲞⲒϢ ⲚⲚⲀⲌⲢⲚ-

---

13 ⲒⲂ in upper left-hand margin at beginning of quire.
16 MS ⲚⲦⲈⲦⲚⲚⲀϬⲰϢⲦ; read ⲦⲈⲦⲚⲚⲀϬⲰϢⲦ.
20 MS ⲈⲦϤⲚⲀⲀⲀϤ; read ⲈⲦϤⲚⲀⲀϤ.

Maria, there is no *kind* in this *world*, *nor* light, *nor form*, which compares with the 24 *invisible ones*, with which I can compare them, *but yet* a little while and I will take thee with thy brothers and fellow *disciples* to all the *places* of the height. And I will take you to the three *spaces* of the First *Mystery*, with the exception only of the *places* of the *space* of the Ineffable, and you will see all their *forms* in *truth*, without semblance. And when I take you to the height and you shall see the glory of those of the height, you will be in exceedingly great amazement. And when I take you to the *place* of the *archons* of the *Heimarmene*, you shall see the glory in which they are. And as a result of their exceedingly great glory you will reckon this *world* before you *as* darkness of darknesses [1]. And you will look forth upon the whole *world* of mankind, and it will become the size of a speck of dust before you as a result of the great distance, by which it is exceedingly distant from it, and (as a result of) the large size by which it greatly exceeds it. And when I take you to the twelve *aeons* you will see the great glory in which they are. And as a result of the great glory, the *place* of the *archons* of the *Heimarmene* will count before you as darkness of darknesses. And it will become the size of a speck of dust before | you as a result

---

[1] (16) darkness of darknesses; Till: darkest darkness (see 188.13).

ΤΗΝΟΥ ΕΒΟΛ Μ̄ΠΝΟϬ Ν̄ΟΥΕ ΕΤϤΟΥΗϤ ΕΒΟΛ Μ̄ΜΟϤ
ΕΜΑΤΕ· Μ̄Ν ΤΝΟϬ Ν̄ϬΟΤ· ΕΤϤΝΑΛΑϤ ΕΡΟϤ ΕΜΑϢΟ· _{ΡΟΓ} b
ΚΑΤΑ ΘΕ Ν̄ΤΑΪΟΥϢ ΕΪΧϢ Μ̄ΜΟΣ ΕΡϢΤΝ̄ Ν̄ΚΕΣΟΠ·
ΑΥϢ ΟΝ ΕΪϢΑΝΧΙΤΗΥΤΝ̄ ΕΠΜΕϨΜΝ̄ΤϢΟΜΤΕ Ν̄ΑΙϢΝ·
5 ΑΥϢ ΤΕΤΝ̄ΝΑΝΑΥ ΕΠΕΟΟΥ ΕΤΟΥϢΟΟΠ Ν̄ϨΗΤϤ· ΠΜΝ̄Τ-
ΣΝΟΟΥΣ Ν̄ΑΙϢΝ ΝΑϢΠ Ν̄ΝΑϨΡΗΤΝ̄ Ν̄ΘΕ Μ̄ΠΚΑΚΕ Ν̄Ν-
ΚΑΚΕ· ΑΥϢ ΤΕΤΝ̄ΝΑϬϢϢΤ ΕΧ̄Μ ΠΜΝ̄ΤΣΝΟΟΥΣ Ν̄-
ΑΙϢΝ· ΕϤΝΑΡ̄-ΠΙΝΕ Ν̄ΟΥΝΑΠΝΕ Ν̄ϢΟΪϢ Ν̄ΝΑϨΡΝ̄ΤΗΝΟΥ
ΕΒΟΛ Μ̄ΠΝΟϬ Ν̄ΟΥΕ ΕΤϤΟΥΗϤ ΕΒΟΛ Μ̄ΜΟϤ ΕΜΑΤΕ·
10 Μ̄Ν ΤΝΟϬ Ν̄ϬΟΤ ΕΤϤΝΑΛΑϤ ΕΡΟϤ ΕΜΑϢΟ· ΑΥϢ ΕΪ-
ϢΑΝΧΙΤΗΥΤΝ̄ ΕΠΤΟΠΟΣ Ν̄ΑΤΜΕΣΟΣ· ΤΕΤΝ̄ΝΑΝΑΥ
ΕΠΕΟΟΥ ΕΤΟΥϢΟΟΠ Ν̄ϨΗΤϤ· ΠΜΝ̄ΤϢΟΜΤΕ Ν̄ΑΙϢΝ
ΝΑϢΠ Ν̄ΝΑϨΡΗΤΝ̄ Ν̄ΘΕ Μ̄ΠΚΑΚΕ Ν̄ΝΚΑΚΕ· ΑΥϢ ΟΝ ΤΕ-
ΤΝ̄ΝΑϬϢϢΤ ΕΒΟΛ ΕΧ̄Μ ΠΜΝ̄ΤΣΝΟΟΥΣ Ν̄ΑΙϢΝ· ΑΥϢ
15 Μ̄Ν ΘΙΜΑΡΜΕΝΗ ΤΗΡΣ̄· ΑΥϢ Μ̄Ν ΤΚΟΣΜΗΣΙΣ ΤΗΡΣ̄·
ΑΥϢ Μ̄Ν ΝΕΣΦΑΙΡΑ ΤΗΡΟΥ ^{**} Μ̄Ν ΝΕΥΤΑΞΙΣ ΤΗΡΟΥ ΡΟΛ·
ΕΤΟΥϢΟΟΠ Ν̄ϨΗΤΟΥ ΣΕΝΑΡ̄-ΤϬΟΤ Ν̄ΟΥΝΑΠΝΕ Ν̄ϢΟ-
ΕΙϢ Ν̄ΝΑϨΡΝ̄ΤΗΝΟΥ ΕΒΟΛ Μ̄ΠΝΟϬ Ν̄ΟΥΕ ΕΤϤΟΥΗϤ
Μ̄ΜΟϤ· ΑΥϢ Μ̄Ν ΤΝΟϬ Ν̄ϬΟΤ ΕΤϤΝΑΛΑϤ ΕΡΟϤ ΕΜΑ-
20 ϢΟ· ΑΥϢ ΕΪϢΑΝΧΙΤΗΥΤΝ̄ ΕΠΤΟΠΟΣ Ν̄ΝΑΟΥϬΙΝΑΜ·
ΤΕΤΝ̄ΝΑΝΑΥ ΕΠΕΟΟΥ ΕΤΟΥϢΟΟΠ Ν̄ϨΗΤϤ· ΠΤΟΠΟΣ
Ν̄ΑΤΜΕΣΟΣ ΝΑϢΠ Ν̄ΝΑϨΡΝ̄ΤΗΝΟΥ Ν̄ΟΕ Ν̄ΤΕΥϢΗ ΕΤ-
ϨΜ ΠΚΟΣΜΟΣ Ν̄ΤΕ ΤΜΤΡϢΜΕ· ΑΥϢ ΕΤΕΤΝ̄ϢΑΝϬϢ-
ϢΤ ΕΒΟΛ ΕΧ̄Ν ΤΜΕΣΟΣ· ϤΝΑΡ̄-ΤϬΟΤ Ν̄ΟΥΝΑΠΝΕ Ν̄-

---

11 MS Π̄ΑΤΜΕΣΟϹ; read Π̄ΝΑΤΜΕΣΟϹ.
22 MS Π̄ΑΤΜΕϹΟϹ; read Π̄ΝΑΤΜΕϹΟϹ.

of the great distance by which it is very distant from it, and the large size by which it greatly exceeds it, *as* I have already said to you at another time. And further, when I take you to the thirteenth *aeon*, you will see the glory in which they are. The twelve *aeons* will count before you as darkness of darknesses. And you will look upon the twelve *aeons*, and it (the place of the twelve aeons) will become like a speck of dust before you as a result of the great distance, by which it is very distant from it, and the large size, by which it greatly exceeds it. And when I take you to the *place* of those of the *Midst*, you will see the glory in which they are. The thirteen *aeons* will count before you as darkness of darknesses. And again you will look forth upon the twelve *aeons* and the whole *Heimarmene*, and the whole *order* and all the *spheres* and all their *ranks* in which they are; they will become the size of a speck of dust before you, as a result of the great distance by which it is distant from it, and the large size by which it greatly exceeds it. And when I take you to the *place* of those of the right, you will see the glory in which they are. The *place* of those of the *Midst* will count before you as night in the *world* of mankind. And when you look forth upon the *Midst*, it will become the size of a speck | of dust before you as

ϣⲟⲉⲓϣ ⲛ̄ⲛⲁϩⲣ̄ⲛⲧⲏⲛⲟⲩ ⲉⲃⲟⲗ ⲙ̄ⲡⲛⲟϭ ⲛ̄ⲟⲩⲉ ⲉⲧⲉⲣⲉ
ⲡⲧⲟⲡⲟⲥ ⲛ̄ⲛⲁⲟⲩⲉⲓⲛⲁⲙ ⲟⲩⲏⲩ ⲉⲃⲟⲗ ⲙ̄ⲙⲟϥ ⲉⲙⲁϣⲟ·
ⲁⲩⲱ ⲉⲓϣⲁⲛⲭⲓⲧⲏⲩⲧⲛ̄ ⲉⲡⲕⲁϩ ⲙ̄ⲡⲟⲩⲟⲓⲛ ⲉⲧⲉ ⲛ̄ⲧⲟϥ ⲡⲉ
ⲡⲉⲟⲏⲥⲁⲩⲣⲟⲥ ⲙ̄ⲡⲟⲩⲟⲉⲓⲛ ⲛ̄ⲧⲉⲧⲛ̄ⲛⲁⲩ ⲉⲡⲉⲟⲟⲩ ⲉⲧⲟⲩ-
5 ϣⲟⲟⲡ ⲛ̄ϩⲏⲧϥ· ⲡⲧⲟⲡⲟⲥ ⲛ̄ⲛⲁⲧⲟⲩⲛⲁⲙ ⲛⲁϣⲡ ⲛ̄ⲛⲁϩⲣⲏ- ̄ⲣⲟⲗ [ᵇ]
ⲧⲛ̄ ⲛ̄ⲟⲉ ⲙ̄ⲡⲟⲩⲟⲉⲓⲛ ⲙ̄ⲡⲛⲁⲩ ⲙ̄ⲙⲉⲉⲣⲉ ϩⲙ̄ ⲡⲕⲟⲥⲙⲟⲥ ⲛ̄ⲧⲉ
ⲧⲙⲛ̄ⲧⲣⲱⲙⲉ ⲉⲙⲡⲣⲏ ⲛ̄ⲃⲟⲗ ⲁⲛ ⲁⲩⲱ ⲉⲧⲉⲧⲛ̄ϣⲁⲛϭⲱϣⲧ
ⲉϩⲣⲁⲓ̈ ⲉⲭⲙ̄ ⲡⲧⲟⲡⲟⲥ ⲛ̄ⲛⲁⲟⲩⲉⲓⲛⲁⲙ ϥⲛⲁⲣ-ⲧϭⲟⲧ ⲛ̄ⲟⲩ-
ⲛⲁⲡⲛⲉ ⲛ̄ϣⲟⲉⲓϣ ⲛ̄ⲛⲁϩⲣ̄ⲛⲧⲏⲛⲟⲩ ⲉⲃⲟⲗ ⲙ̄ⲡⲛⲟϭ ⲛ̄ⲟⲩⲉ
10 ⲉⲧϥ̄ⲟⲩⲏⲩ ⲉⲃⲟⲗ ⲙ̄ⲙⲟϥ ⲉⲙⲁⲧⲉ ⲛ̄ϭⲓ ⲡⲉⲟⲏⲥⲁⲩⲣⲟⲥ ⲙ̄-
ⲡⲟⲩⲟⲉⲓⲛ· ⲁⲩⲱ ⲉⲓϣⲁⲛⲭⲓⲧⲏⲩⲧⲛ̄ ⲉⲡⲧⲟⲡⲟⲥ ⲛ̄ⲛⲉⲛⲧ-
ⲁⲩⲭⲓ-ⲛⲉⲕⲗⲏⲣⲟⲛⲟⲙⲓⲁ ⲛ̄ⲛⲉⲛⲧⲁⲩⲭⲓ ⲛ̄ⲙ̄ⲙⲩⲥⲧⲏⲣⲓⲟⲛ ⲙ̄-
ⲡⲟⲩⲟⲉⲓⲛ· ⲛ̄ⲧⲉⲧⲛ̄ⲛⲁⲩ ⲉⲡⲉⲟⲟⲩ ⲙ̄ⲡⲟⲩⲟⲉⲓⲛ ⲉⲧⲟⲩϣⲟⲟⲡ ⲛ̄ϩⲏⲧϥ· ⲡⲕⲁϩ ⲙ̄ⲡⲟⲩⲟⲓⲛ ⲛⲁϣⲡ ⲛ̄ⲛⲁϩⲣ̄ⲛⲧⲏⲛⲟⲩ
15 ⲛ̄ⲟⲉ ⲙ̄ⲡⲟⲩⲟⲉⲓⲛ ⲙ̄ⲡⲣⲏ ⲉⲧϩⲙ̄ ⲡⲕⲟⲥⲙⲟⲥ ⲛ̄ⲧⲉ ⲧⲙⲧ-
ⲣⲱⲙⲉ· ⲁⲩⲱ ⲉⲧⲉⲧⲛ̄ϣⲁⲛϭⲱϣⲧ ⲉϩⲣⲁⲓ̈ ⲉⲭⲙ̄ ⲡⲕⲁϩ ⲙ̄- ̄ⲣⲟⲥ
ⲡⲟⲩⲟⲓⲛ ϥⲛⲁϣⲡ ⲛ̄ⲛⲁϩⲣ̄ⲛⲧⲏⲛⲟⲩ ⲛ̄ⲟⲉ ⲛ̄ⲟⲩⲛⲁⲡⲛⲉ ⲛ̄-
ϣⲟⲉⲓϣ ⲉⲃⲟⲗ ⲙ̄ⲡⲛⲟϭ ⲛ̄ⲟⲩⲉ ⲉⲧϥ̄ⲟⲩⲏⲩ ⲉⲃⲟⲗ ⲙ̄ⲙⲟϥ
ⲛ̄ϭⲓ ⲡⲕⲁϩ ⲙ̄ⲡⲟⲩⲟⲓⲛ ⲁⲩⲱ ⲉⲃⲟⲗ ⲛ̄ⲧⲙⲛ̄ⲧⲛⲟϭ ⲉⲧϥ̄ⲛⲁ-
20 ⲗⲁϥ ⲉⲣⲟϥ ⲉⲙⲁϣⲟ·

ⳅ ⲁⲥϣⲱⲡⲉ ϭⲉ ⲛ̄ⲧⲉⲣⲉ ⲓ̄ⲥ ⲟⲩⲱ ⲉϥϫⲱ ⲛ̄ⲛⲉⲓ̈ϣⲁϫⲉ
ⲉⲛⲉϥⲙⲁⲑⲏⲧⲏⲥ· ⲁⲥϭⲟϭⲥ ⲉⲃⲟⲗ ⲛ̄ϭⲓ ⲙⲁⲣⲓⲁ ⲧⲙⲁⲅⲇⲁⲗⲏⲛⲏ ⲡⲉϫⲁⲥ ϫⲉ ⲡⲁϫⲟⲉⲓⲥ· ⲙ̄ⲡⲣ̄ϭⲱⲛ̄ⲧ ⲉⲣⲟⲓ̈ ⲉⲓϣⲓⲛⲉ
ⲙ̄ⲙⲟⲕ· ⲉⲃⲟⲗ ϫⲉ ⲉⲛϣⲓⲛⲉ ⲛ̄ⲥⲁ ϩⲱⲃ ⲛⲓⲙ ϩⲛ̄ ⲟⲩⲱⲣⲭ·
25 ⲁϥⲟⲩⲱϩⲙ̄ ⲇⲉ ⲛ̄ϭⲓ ⲓ̄ⲥ ⲡⲉϫⲁϥ ⲙ̄ⲙⲁⲣⲓⲁ ϫⲉ ϣⲓⲛⲉ ⲛ̄ⲥⲁ

---

11   MS ⲛ̄ⲛⲉⲛⲧⲁⲩⲭⲓ; ⲛ̄ⲧⲁⲩⲭⲓ crossed out, giving ⲛ̄ⲛⲉⲕⲗⲏⲣⲟⲛⲟⲙⲓⲁ.
13   MS originally ⲉⲡⲉⲩⲥⲟⲟⲩ; ⲩ erased; read ⲉⲡⲥⲟⲟⲩ.

a result of the great distance by which the *place* of those of the right is very distant from it. And when I take you to the Land of the Light, which is the *Treasury* of the Light, and you see the glory in which they are, the *place* of those of the right will count before you like the light at the time of midday in the *world* of mankind, but without the sun. And when you look upon the *place* of those of the right, it will become the size of a speck of dust before you as a result of the great distance by which the *Treasury* of the Light is very distant from it. And when I take you to the *place* of [those who have received] the *inheritances* of those who have received the *mysteries* of the light [1], and you see the glory of the light in which they are, the Land of the Light will count before you like the light of the sun which is in the *world* of mankind. And when you look upon the Land of the Light, it will count before you like a speck of dust as a result of the great distance by which the Land of the Light is distant from it, and on account of the greatness by which it much exceeds it."

85. Now it happened when Jesus finished saying these words to his *disciples*, Maria Magdalene sprang up and said: "My Lord, be not angry with me for questioning thee, because we question all things with assurance."

But Jesus answered and said to Maria: "Ask | what you

---

[1] (11-13) the place of [those who have received] the inheritances of those who have received the mysteries of the light; Schmidt: the place of those who have received the inheritances and have received the mysteries of the light.

ⲡⲉⲧⲉⲟⲩⲉϣϣⲓⲛⲉ ⲛ̄ⲥⲱϥ ⲁⲩⲱ ⲁⲛⲟⲕ ϯⲛⲁϭⲟⲗⲡϥ ⲛⲉ
ⲉⲃⲟⲗ ϩ̄ⲛ ⲟⲩⲡⲁⲣϩⲏⲥⲓⲁ· ⲁϫ̄ⲛ ⲡⲁⲣⲁⲃⲟⲗⲏ· ⲁⲩⲱ ϩⲱⲃ ⲛⲓⲙ
ⲉⲧⲉϣⲓⲛⲉ ⲛ̄ⲥⲱⲟⲩ· ϯⲛⲁϫⲟⲟⲩ ⲛⲉ ϩ̄ⲛ ⲟⲩⲱⲣ̄ϫ̄ ⲙ̄ⲛ ⲟⲩ-
ⲁⲥⲫⲁⲗⲓⲁ· ⲁⲩⲱ ϯⲛⲁϫⲉⲕⲧⲏⲛⲟⲩ ⲉⲃⲟⲗ ϩ̄ⲛ ϭⲟⲙ ⲛⲓⲙ·
5 ⲙ̄ⲛ ⲡⲗⲏⲣⲱⲙⲁ ⲛⲓⲙ· ϫⲓⲛ ⲡⲥⲁ̄ⲛ̄ϩⲟⲩⲛ ⲛ̄ⲧⲉ ⲛⲓⲥⲁ̄ⲛ̄ϩⲟⲩⲛ·　ⲣⲟⲥ ᵇ
ϩⲉⲱⲥ ϣⲁ ⲡⲥⲁ̄ⲛ̄ⲃⲟⲗ ⲛ̄ⲧⲉ ⲛⲓⲥⲁ̄ⲛ̄ⲃⲟⲗ· ϫⲓⲛ ⲡⲓⲁⲧⲱϣⲁϫⲉ
ⲉⲣⲟϥ· ϩⲉⲱⲥ ϣⲁ ⲡⲕⲁⲕⲉ ⲛ̄ⲛ̄ⲕⲁⲕⲉ· ϫⲉ ⲉⲩⲉⲙⲟⲩⲧⲉ
ⲟⲩⲃⲉⲧⲏⲛⲟⲩ ϫⲉ ⲛⲉⲡⲗⲏⲣⲱⲙⲁ ⲉⲧϫⲏⲕ ⲉⲃⲟⲗ ⲛ̄ⲥⲟⲟⲩⲛ
ⲛⲓⲙ· ⲧⲉⲛⲟⲩ ϭⲉ ⲙⲁⲣⲓⲁ ϣⲓⲛⲉ ⲛ̄ⲥⲁ ⲡⲉⲧⲉⲣⲉϣⲓⲛⲉ ⲛ̄ⲥⲱϥ·
10 ⲁⲩⲱ ϯⲛⲁϭⲟⲗⲡϥ ⲛⲉ ⲉⲃⲟⲗ ϩ̄ⲛ ⲟⲩⲛⲟϭ ⲛ̄ⲣⲁϣⲉ ⲙ̄ⲛ ⲟⲩⲛⲟϭ ⲛ̄ⲧⲉⲗⲏⲗ· ⲁⲥϣⲱⲡⲉ ϭⲉ ⲛ̄ⲧⲉⲣⲉ ⲙⲁⲣⲓⲁ ⲥⲱⲧⲙ̄ ⲉⲛⲉⲓϣⲁϫⲉ ⲉϥϫⲱ ⲙ̄ⲙⲟⲟⲩ ⲛ̄ϭⲓ ⲡⲥⲱⲧⲏⲣ ⲁⲥⲣⲁϣⲉ ϩ̄ⲛ ⲟⲩⲛⲟϭ ⲛ̄ⲣⲁϣⲉ ⲉⲙⲁϣⲟ· ⲁⲩⲱ ⲁⲥⲧⲉⲗⲏⲗ ⲡⲉϫⲁⲥ ϫⲉ ⲡⲁ-
ϫⲟⲉⲓⲥ· ⲉⲉⲓⲉ ⲛ̄ⲣⲱⲙⲉ ⲛ̄ⲧⲉ ⲡⲕⲟⲥⲙⲟⲥ ⲛⲁⲓ̈ ⲛ̄ⲧⲁⲩϫⲓ ⲛ̄ⲙ-
15 ⲙⲩⲥⲧⲏⲣⲓⲟⲛ ⲛ̄ⲧⲉ ⲡⲟⲩⲟⲓ̈ⲛ ⲥⲉⲛⲁϣⲱⲡⲉ ⲉⲩⲟⲧⲃ̄ ⲉⲛⲉⲡⲣⲟⲃⲟⲗⲟⲟⲩⲉ ⲙ̄ⲡⲉⲑⲏⲥⲁⲩⲣⲟⲥ ϩⲣⲁⲓ̈ ϩ̄ⲛ ⲧⲉⲕⲙ̄ⲛ̄ⲧⲉⲣⲟ
ⲉⲃⲟⲗ ϫⲉ ⲁⲓ̈ⲥⲱⲧⲙ̄ ⲉⲣⲟⲕ ⲉⲕϫⲱ ⲙ̄ⲙⲟⲥ ϫⲉ ⲉⲉⲓϣⲁⲛϫⲓ-　ⲣⲟⲥ ᶜ
ⲧⲏⲩⲧ̄ⲛ̄ ⲉⲡⲧⲟⲡⲟⲥ ⲙ̄ⲡⲉⲣϫⲓ-ⲙ̄ⲙⲩⲥⲧⲏⲣⲓⲟⲛ ⲡⲧⲟⲡⲟⲥ ⟨ⲛ̄ⲛⲉ-
ⲡⲣⲟⲃⲟⲗⲟⲟⲩⲉ⟩ ⲡⲕⲁϩ ⲙ̄ⲡⲟⲩⲟⲉⲓⲛ ϥⲛⲁϣⲱⲡ ⲛ̄ⲛⲁϩⲣⲏⲧ̄
20 ⲛ̄ⲑⲉ ⲛ̄ⲟⲩⲛⲁⲡⲛⲉ ⲛ̄ϣⲟⲉⲓϣ ⲉⲃⲟⲗ ⲙ̄ⲡⲛⲟϭ ⲛ̄ⲟⲩⲉ ⲉⲧ-
ϥ̄ⲟⲩⲏⲩ ⲉⲃⲟⲗ ⲛ̄ϩⲏⲧ̄ϥ· ⲁⲩⲱ ⲙ̄ⲛ ⲡⲛⲟϭ ⲛ̄ⲉⲟⲟⲩ ⲉⲧϥ̄-
ϣⲟⲟⲡ ⲛ̄ϩⲏⲧϥ̄· ⲉⲧⲉ ⲡⲕⲁϩ ⲙ̄ⲡⲟⲩⲟⲉⲓⲛ ⲡⲉ ⲙ̄ⲡⲉⲑⲏⲥⲁⲩ-
ⲣⲟⲥ ⲡⲧⲟⲡⲟⲥ ⲛ̄ⲛⲉⲡⲣⲟⲃⲟⲗⲟⲟⲩⲉ· ⲉⲉⲓⲉ ⲟⲩⲕⲟⲩⲛ ⲡⲁ-

9　MS ⲡⲉⲧⲉⲣⲉϣⲓⲛⲉ; better ⲡⲉⲧⲉⲟⲩⲉϣϣⲓⲛⲉ.
15　MS ⲉⲩⲟⲧⲃ̄; read ⲉⲩⲟⲩⲟⲧⲃ̄.
18　letters erased before and after ⲛ̄ⲣ̄ⲓ; ⲙ̄ⲡⲟⲩⲟⲉⲓⲛ omitted; after ⲡⲧⲟⲡⲟⲥ
　　supply ⲛ̄ⲛⲉⲡⲣⲟⲃⲟⲗⲟⲟⲩⲉ.
21　MS originally ⲟⲩⲟⲉⲓⲛ; ⲟⲉⲓⲛ crossed out and ⲉⲟ inserted in left-hand margin.
22　MS ⲙ̄ⲡⲉⲟⲏⲥⲁⲩⲣⲟⲥ; read ⲡⲥⲟⲏⲥⲁⲩⲣⲟⲥ.

wish to question and I will reveal it *openly*, without *parable*. And all things which you question I will say with assurance and *certainty*. And I will fulfil you in all powers and all *pleromas* from the innermost of the inner *to* the outermost of the outer; from the Ineffable himself *to* the darkness of the darknesses, so that you may be called the *pleromas*, fulfilled with all knowledge. Now at this time, Maria, ask thy question and I will reveal it with great joy and great gladness."

It happened now when Maria heard these words which the *Saviour* spoke, she rejoiced with very great joy and was glad. She said : "My Lord, will men of the *world* who have received the *mysteries* of the light be superior to the *emanations* of the *Treasury* in thy kingdom? Because I heard thee saying : 'When I take you to the *place* of those who receive the *mysteries* of the light, then the *place* ⟨of the emanations⟩, the Land of the Light, will count to you like a speck of dust, as a result of the great distance by which it is distant from it, and the great glory in which it is; that is, the Land of the Light is the *Treasury*, which is the *place* of the *emanations*. *Therefore* my | Lord, will the men

ⲭⲟⲉⲓⲥ ⲉⲓⲉ ⲛ̄ⲣⲱⲙⲉ ⲉⲣⲭⲓ-ⲙ̄ⲙⲩⲥⲧⲏⲣⲓⲟⲛ ⲥⲉⲛⲁϣⲱⲡⲉ ⲉⲩ-
ⲟⲩⲟⲧⲃ̄ ⲉⲡⲕⲁϩ ⲙ̄ⲡⲟⲩⲟⲉⲓⲛ· ⲁⲩⲱ ⲛ̄ⲥⲉϣⲱⲡⲉ ⲉⲩⲟⲩ-
ⲟⲧⲃ̄ ⲉⲣⲟⲟⲩ ϩⲣⲁⲓ̈ ϩⲛ̄ ⲧⲙⲛⲧⲉⲣⲟ ⲙ̄ⲡⲟⲩⲟⲉⲓⲛ·

ⲁϥⲟⲩⲱϩⲙ̄ ⲇⲉ ⲛ̄ϭⲓ ⲓ̅ⲥ̅ ⲡⲉϫⲁϥ ⲙ̄ⲙⲁⲣⲓⲁ ϫⲉ ⲕⲁⲗⲱⲥ
5 ⲙⲉⲛⲧⲟⲓⲅⲉ ⲧⲉϣⲓⲛⲉ ⲛ̄ⲥⲁ ϩⲱⲃ ⲛⲓⲙ ϩⲛ̄ ⲟⲩⲱⲣⲝ̄ ⲙⲛ ⲟⲩ-
ⲁⲥⲫⲁⲗⲓⲁ· ⲁⲗⲗⲁ ⲥⲱⲧⲙ ⲙⲁⲣⲓⲁ· ⲧⲁϣⲁϫⲉ ⲛ̄ⲙⲙⲉ ⲉϩⲣⲁⲓ̈
ⲉⲧⲥⲩⲛⲧⲉⲗⲉⲓⲁ ⲙ̄ⲡⲁⲓⲱⲛ· ⲙⲛ ⲡⲱⲗ ⲉϩⲣⲁⲓ̈ *ⲙ̄ⲡⲧⲏⲣϥ ⲛ̄ⲛⲉⲥ-   ⲣ̅ⲟ̅ⲉ̅ ᵇ
ⲛⲁϣⲱⲡⲉ ⲁⲛ ϩⲓ ⲛⲁⲓ̈· ⲁⲗⲗⲁ ⲛ̄ⲧⲁⲓ̈ⲭⲟⲟⲥ ⲉⲣⲱⲧⲛ̄ ϫⲉ ⲉⲓ̈-
ϣⲁⲛϫⲓⲧⲏⲩⲧⲛ̄ ⲉⲡⲧⲟⲡⲟⲥ ⲛ̄ⲛⲉⲕⲗⲏⲣⲟⲛⲟⲙⲓⲁ ⲛ̄ⲛⲉⲧⲛⲁϫⲓ
10 ⲙ̄ⲡⲙⲩⲥⲧⲏⲣⲓⲟⲛ ⲙ̄ⲡⲟⲩⲟⲓⲛ ⲙ̄ⲡⲉⲑⲏⲥⲁⲩⲣⲟⲥ ⲙ̄ⲡⲟⲩⲟⲉⲓⲛ
ⲡⲧⲟⲡⲟⲥ ⲛ̄ⲛⲉⲡⲣⲟⲃⲟⲗⲟⲟⲩⲉ ϥⲛⲁϣⲡ ⲛ̄ⲛⲁϩⲣ̄ⲛⲧⲏⲛⲟⲩ
ⲛ̄ⲑⲉ ⲛ̄ⲟⲩⲛⲁⲡⲛⲉ ⲛ̄ϣⲟⲓ̈ϣ ⲁⲩⲱ ⲛ̄ⲑⲉ ⲙ̄ⲡⲟⲩⲟⲓ̈ⲛ ⲙ̄ⲡⲣⲏ
ⲛ̄ⲧⲉ ⲡⲉϩⲟⲟⲩ ⲙ̄ⲙⲁⲧⲉ· ⲛ̄ⲧⲁⲩϫⲟⲟⲥ ⲟⲩⲛ ϫⲉ ⲉⲣⲉ ⲛⲁⲓ̈
ⲛⲁϣⲱⲡⲉ ϩⲙ̄ ⲡⲉⲟⲩⲟⲓ̈ϣ ⲛ̄ⲧⲥⲩⲛⲧⲉⲗⲉⲓⲁ ⲙ̄ⲡⲱⲗ ⲉϩⲣⲁⲓ̈ ⲙ̄-
15 ⲡⲧⲏⲣϥ· ⲡⲙⲛⲧⲥⲛⲟⲟⲩⲥ ⲛ̄ⲥⲱⲧⲏⲣ ⲙ̄ⲡⲉⲑⲏⲥⲁⲩⲣⲟⲥ ⲙⲛ
ⲧⲙⲛⲧⲥⲛⲟⲟⲩⲥ ⲛ̄ⲧⲁⲝⲓⲥ ⲙ̄ⲡⲟⲩⲁ ⲡⲟⲩⲁ ⲙ̄ⲙⲟⲟⲩ ⲉⲧⲉ ⲛ̄-
ⲧⲟⲟⲩ ⲡⲉ ⲛⲉⲡⲣⲟⲃⲟⲗⲟⲟⲩⲉ ⲛ̄ⲧⲥⲁϣϥⲉ ⲙ̄ⲫⲱⲛⲏ ⲙⲛ
ⲡ†ⲟⲩ ⲛ̄ϣⲏⲛ ⲥⲉⲛⲁϣⲱⲡⲉ ⲛ̄ⲙⲙⲁⲓ̈ ϩⲙ̄ ⲡⲧⲟⲡⲟⲥ ⲛ̄ⲛⲉⲕⲗⲏ-
ⲣⲟⲛⲟⲙⲓⲁ ⲙ̄ⲡⲟⲩⲟⲉⲓⲛ· ⲉⲩⲟ ⲛ̄ⲣⲣⲟ ⲛ̄ⲙⲙⲁⲓ̈ ϩⲛ̄ ⲧⲁⲙⲛⲧ-
20 ⲉⲣⲟ· ⲉⲣⲉ ⲡⲟⲩⲁ ⲡⲟⲩⲁ ⲙ̄ⲙⲟⲟⲩ ⲉϥⲟ ⲛ̄ⲣⲣⲟ **ⲉϩⲣⲁⲓ̈ ⲉϫⲛ̄   ⲣ̅ⲟ̅ⲍ̅
ⲛⲉϥⲡⲣⲟⲃⲟⲗⲟⲟⲩⲉ· ⲁⲩⲱ ⲟⲛ ⲉⲣⲉ ⲡⲟⲩⲁ ⲡⲟⲩⲁ ⲙ̄ⲙⲟⲟⲩ
ⲉϥⲟ ⲛ̄ⲣⲣⲟ ⲕⲁⲧⲁ ⲡⲉϥⲉⲟⲟⲩ· ⲡⲛⲟϭ ⲕⲁⲧⲁ ⲧⲉϥⲙⲛⲧⲛⲟϭ
ⲡⲕⲟⲩⲉⲓ ⲕⲁⲧⲁ ⲧⲉϥⲙⲛⲧⲕⲟⲩⲓ̈· ⲁⲩⲱ ⲡⲥⲱⲧⲏⲣ ⲛ̄ⲛⲉⲡⲣⲟ-
ⲃⲟⲗⲟⲟⲩⲉ ⲛ̄ⲧϣⲟⲣⲡ̄ ⲙ̄ⲫⲱⲛⲏ ⲥⲉⲛⲁϣⲱⲡⲉ ϩⲙ̄ ⲡⲧⲟⲡⲟⲥ

---

10 ⲙ̄ⲡⲉ inserted in margins before ⲑⲏⲥⲁⲩⲣⲟⲥ.
13 MS ⲛ̄ⲧⲁⲩⲭⲟⲟⲥ; better ⲛ̄ⲧⲁⲓ̈ⲭⲟⲟⲥ.
14 MS ⲙ̄ⲡⲱⲗ; better ⲙ̄ⲡⲓ ⲡⲱⲗ.
24 MS ⲥⲉⲛⲁϣⲱⲡⲉ; read ϥⲛⲁϣⲱⲡⲉ.

who receive *mysteries* be superior to (the *emanations* of)
the Land of the Light, and be superior to them in the
Kingdom of the Light?''

86.   Jesus *however* answered and said to Maria : *"Well
done, in truth* thou dost question everything with assurance
and *certainty. But* hear, Maria, that I speak with thee upon
the *end* of the *aeon** and the ascent of the All. It will not
happen now, *but* I have said to you : 'When I take you to
the *place* of the *inheritances* of those who receive the *mystery*
of the light of the *Treasury* of the Light, the *place* of the
emanations will count before you as a speck of dust, and
only like the light of the sun by day'. I have *now* said[1] :
'This will happen at the time of the *end* and the ascent of
the All.' The twelve *saviours* of the *Treasury* and the twelve
ranks of each one of them, which are the *emanations* of the
seven *voices* and the five trees, they will be with me in the
place of the *inheritances* of the light, as rulers (kings) with
me in my kingdom. Each one of them will rule (be king)
over his *emanations*, and moreover, each one of them will
rule (be king) *according to* his glory : the great *according to*
his greatness, the small *according to* his smallness. And the
saviour of the *emanations* of the first *voice* will be in the
place | of the *souls* of those who receive[2] the first *mystery*

---

*   cf. Mt. 13.39

---

[1]   (13) I have now said; MS : they have now said.
[2]   (192.1) receive; Till : have received (also 192.7 and parallel passages).

ⲛ̄ⲛⲉⲯⲩⲭⲟⲟⲩⲉ ⲛ̄ⲛⲉⲣⲭⲓ ⲙ̄ⲡϣⲟⲣⲡ̄ ⲙ̄ⲙⲩⲥⲧⲏⲣⲓⲟⲛ ⲛ̄ⲧⲉ
ⲡϣⲟⲣⲡ̄ ⟨ⲙ̄⟩ⲙⲩⲥⲧⲏⲣⲓⲟⲛ ⲥⲛ̄ ⲧⲁⲙⲛ̄ⲧⲉⲣⲟ· ⲁⲩⲱ ⲡⲥⲱⲧⲏⲣ ⲛ̄-
ⲛⲉⲡⲣⲟⲃⲟⲗⲟⲟⲩⲉ ⲛ̄ⲧⲙⲉⲥⲥⲛ̄ⲧⲉ ⲙ̄ⲫⲱⲛⲏ· ϥⲛⲁϣⲱⲡⲉ ⲥⲙ̄
ⲡⲧⲟⲡⲟⲥ ⲛ̄ⲛⲉⲯⲩⲭⲟⲟⲩⲉ ⲛ̄ⲛⲉⲛⲧⲁⲩⲭⲓ ⲙ̄ⲡⲙⲉⲥⲥⲛⲁⲩ ⲙ̄-
5 ⲙⲩⲥⲧⲏⲣⲓⲟⲛ ⲛ̄ⲧⲉ ⲡϣⲟⲣⲡ̄ ⲙ̄ⲙⲩⲥⲧⲏⲣⲓⲟⲛ· ⲥⲟⲙⲟⲓⲱⲥ ⲟⲛ
ⲡⲥⲱⲧⲏⲣ ⲛ̄ⲛⲉⲡⲣⲟⲃⲟⲗⲟⲟⲩⲉ ⲛ̄ⲧⲙⲉⲥϣⲟⲙⲧⲉ ⲙ̄ⲫⲱⲛⲏ·
ϥⲛⲁϣⲱⲡⲉ ⲥⲙ̄ ⲡⲧⲟⲡⲟⲥ ⲛ̄ⲛⲉⲯⲩⲭⲟⲟⲩⲉ ⲛ̄ⲛⲉⲣⲭⲓ ⲙ̄ⲡⲙⲉⲥ-
ϣⲟⲙⲛ̄ⲧ ⲙ̄ⲙⲩⲥⲧⲏⲣⲓⲟⲛ ⲛ̄ⲧⲉ ⲡϣⲟⲣⲡ̄ ⲙ̄ⲙⲩⲥⲧⲏⲣⲓⲟⲛ ⲥⲣⲁⲓ̈
ⲥⲛ̄ ⲧⲉⲕⲗⲏⲣⲟⲛⲟⲙⲓⲁ ⲙ̄ⲡⲟⲩⲟⲉⲓⲛ· ⲁⲩⲱ ⲡⲥⲱⲧⲏⲣ ⲛ̄ⲛⲉ-
10 ⲡⲣⲟⲃⲟⲗⲟⲟⲩⲉ ⲛ̄ⲧⲙⲉⲥϥ̄ⲧⲟ ⲙ̄ⲫⲱⲛⲏ ⲙ̄ⲡⲉⲑⲏⲥⲁⲩⲣⲟⲥ ⲙ̄-   ⲣ̅ⲟⲍ ᵇ
ⲡⲟⲩⲟⲉⲓⲛ· ϥⲛⲁϣⲱⲡⲉ ⲥⲙ̄ ⲡⲧⲟⲡⲟⲥ ⲛ̄ⲛⲉⲯⲩⲭⲟⲟⲩⲉ ⲛ̄-
ⲛⲉⲣⲭⲓ ⲙ̄ⲡⲙⲁⲥϥ̄ⲧⲟⲟⲩ ⲙ̄ⲙⲩⲥⲧⲏⲣⲓⲟⲛ ⲛ̄ⲧⲉ ⲡϣⲟⲣⲡ̄ ⲙ̄-
ⲙⲩⲥⲧⲏⲣⲓⲟⲛ ⲥⲛ̄ ⲛⲉⲕⲗⲏⲣⲟⲛⲟⲙⲓⲁ ⲙ̄ⲡⲟⲩⲟⲓ̈ⲛ· ⲁⲩⲱ ⲡⲙⲁⲥ-
ϯⲟⲩ ⲛ̄ⲥⲱⲧⲏⲣ ⲛ̄ⲧⲙⲁⲥϯ ⲙ̄ⲫⲱⲛⲏ ⲙ̄ⲡⲉⲑⲏⲥⲁⲩⲣⲟⲥ ⲙ̄ⲡⲟⲩ-
15 ⲟⲉⲓⲛ· ϥⲛⲁϣⲱⲡⲉ ⲥⲙ̄ ⲡⲧⲟⲡⲟⲥ ⲛ̄ⲛⲉⲯⲩⲭⲟⲟⲩⲉ ⲛ̄ⲛⲉⲣⲭⲓ
ⲙ̄ⲡⲙⲉⲥϯⲟⲩ ⲙ̄ⲙⲩⲥⲧⲏⲣⲓⲟⲛ ⲛ̄ⲧⲉ ⲡϣⲟⲣⲡ̄ ⲙ̄ⲙⲩⲥⲧⲏⲣⲓⲟⲛ·
ⲥⲣⲁⲓ̈ ⲥⲛ̄ ⲛⲉⲕⲗⲏⲣⲟⲛⲟⲙⲓⲁ ⲙ̄ⲡⲟⲩⲟⲓ̈ⲛ· ⲁⲩⲱ ⲡⲙⲉⲥⲥⲟⲟⲩ
ⲛ̄ⲥⲱⲧⲏⲣ ⲛ̄ⲧⲉ ⲛⲉⲡⲣⲟⲃⲟⲗⲟⲟⲩⲉ ⲛ̄ⲧⲉ ⲧⲙⲉⲥⲥⲟ ⲙ̄ⲫⲱⲛⲏ
ⲙ̄ⲡⲉⲑⲏⲥⲁⲩⲣⲟⲥ ⲙ̄ⲡⲟⲩⲟⲉⲓⲛ· ϥⲛⲁϣⲱⲡⲉ ⲥⲙ̄ ⲡⲧⲟⲡⲟⲥ ⲛ̄-
20 ⲛⲉⲯⲩⲭⲟⲟⲩⲉ ⲛ̄ⲛⲉⲣⲭⲓ ⲙ̄ⲡⲙⲉⲥⲥⲟⲟⲩ ⲙ̄ⲙⲩⲥⲧⲏⲣⲓⲟⲛ ⲛ̄ⲧⲉ
ⲡϣⲟⲣⲡ̄ ⲙ̄ⲙⲩⲥⲧⲏⲣⲓⲟⲛ· ⲁⲩⲱ ⲡⲙⲉⲥⲥⲁϣϥ̄ ⲛ̄ⲥⲱⲧⲏⲣ ⲛ̄-
ⲛⲉⲡⲣⲟⲃⲟⲗⲟⲟⲩⲉ ⲛ̄ⲧⲙⲉⲥⲥⲁϣϥⲉ ⲙ̄ⲫⲱⲛⲏ ⲙ̄ⲡⲉⲑⲏⲥⲁⲩⲣⲟⲥ
ⲙ̄ⲡⲟⲩⲟⲉⲓⲛ· ϥⲛⲁϣⲱⲡⲉ ⲥⲙ̄ ⲡⲧⲟⲡⲟⲥ ⲛ̄ⲛⲉⲯⲩⲭⲟⲟⲩⲉ ⲛ̄-   ⲣ̅ⲟⲏ
ⲛⲉⲣⲭⲓ ⲙ̄ⲡⲙⲉⲥⲥⲁϣϥ̄ ⲙ̄ⲙⲩⲥⲧⲏⲣⲓⲟⲛ ⲛ̄ⲧⲉ ⲡϣⲟⲣⲡ̄ ⲙ̄ⲙⲩⲥ-
25 ⲧⲏⲣⲓⲟⲛ ⲥⲙ̄ ⲡⲉⲑⲏⲥⲁⲩⲣⲟⲥ ⲙ̄ⲡⲟⲩⲟⲉⲓⲛ· ⲁⲩⲱ ⲡⲙⲉⲥ-

---

1   ⲛ̄ⲧⲉ ⲡⲓϣⲟⲣⲡ̄ ⲛ̄ⲣ̄ⲓ in margin; read ⲛ̄ⲧⲉ ⲡⲓϣⲟⲣⲡ̄ ⲙ̄ⲙⲩⲥⲧⲏⲣ.
14   MS ⲧⲙⲁⲥ⳿|·; read ⲧⲙⲁⲥϯⲉ.

of the First *Mystery* in my kingdom. And the *saviour* of the *emanations* of the second *voice* will be in the *place* of the *souls* of those who have received the second *mystery* of the First *Mystery*. *Likewise* also the *saviour* of the *emanations* of the third *voice* will be in the *place* of the *souls* of those who receive the third *mystery* of the First *Mystery* in the *inheritance* of the light. And the *saviour* of the *emanations* of the fourth *voice* of the *Treasury* of the Light will be in the *place* of the *souls* of those who receive the fourth *mystery* of the First *Mystery* in the *inheritances* of the light. And the fifth *saviour* of the fifth *voice* of the *Treasury* of the Light will be in the place of the *souls* of those who receive the fifth *mystery* of the First *Mystery* in the *inheritances* of the light. And the sixth *saviour* of the *emanations* of the sixth *voice* of the *Treasury* of the Light will be in the *place* of the *souls* of those who receive the sixth *mystery* of the First *Mystery*. And the seventh *saviour* of the *emanations* of the seventh *voice* of the *Treasury* of the Light will be in the *place* of the *souls* of those who receive the seventh *mystery* of the First *Mystery* in the *Treasury* of the Light. And | the eighth *saviour* who is the *saviour* of the *emanations*

ϢΜΟΥΝ ⲚⲤⲰⲦⲎⲢ ⲈⲦⲈ ⲚⲦⲞϤ ⲠⲈ ⲠⲤⲰⲦⲎⲢ ⲚⲚⲈⲠⲢⲞⲂⲞ-
ⲖⲞⲞⲨⲈ ⲘⲠϢⲞⲢⲠ ⲚϢⲎⲚ ⲘⲠⲈⲐⲎⲤⲀⲨⲢⲞⲤ ⲘⲠⲞⲨⲞⲈⲒⲚ·
ϤⲚⲀϢⲰⲠⲈ ϨⲘ ⲠⲦⲞⲠⲞⲤ ⲚⲚⲈⲮⲨⲬⲞⲞⲨⲈ ⲚⲈⲢⲬⲒ ⲘⲠⲘⲈϨ-
ϢΜΟΥΝ ⲘⲘΥⲤⲦⲎⲢⲒⲞⲚ ⲚⲦⲈ ⲠⲒϢⲞⲢⲠ ⲘⲘΥⲤⲦⲎⲢⲒⲞⲚ ϨⲢⲀⲒ
5 ϨⲚ ⲚⲈⲔⲖⲎⲢⲞⲚⲞⲘⲒⲀ ⲘⲠⲞⲨⲞⲈⲒⲚ· ⲀΥⲰ ⲠⲘⲀϨⲮⲒⲤ ⲚⲤⲰ-
ⲦⲎⲢ ⲈⲦⲈ ⲚⲦⲞϤ ⲠⲈ ⲠⲤⲰⲦⲎⲢ ⲚⲚⲈⲠⲢⲞⲂⲞⲖⲞⲞⲨⲈ ⲘⲠⲘⲈϨ-
ⲤⲚⲀΥ ⲚϢⲎⲚ ⲘⲠⲈⲐⲎⲤⲀⲨⲢⲞⲤ ⲘⲠⲞⲨⲞⲈⲒⲚ· ϤⲚⲀϢⲰⲠⲈ
ϨⲘ ⲠⲦⲞⲠⲞⲤ ⲚⲚⲈⲮⲨⲬⲞⲞⲨⲈ ⲚⲚⲈⲢⲬⲒ ⲘⲠⲘⲈϨⲮⲒⲤ ⲘⲘΥⲤ-
ⲦⲎⲢⲒⲞⲚ ⲚⲦⲈ ⲠⲒϢⲞⲢⲠ ⲘⲘΥⲤⲦⲎⲢⲒⲞⲚ ϨⲢⲀⲒ ϨⲚ ⲚⲈⲔⲖⲎ-
10 ⲢⲞⲚⲞⲘⲒⲀ ⲘⲠⲞⲨⲞⲈⲒⲚ· ⲀΥⲰ ⲠⲘⲀϨⲘⲎⲦ ⲚⲤⲰⲦⲎⲢ ⲈⲦⲈ
ⲚⲦⲞϤ ⲠⲈ ⲠⲤⲰⲦⲎⲢ ⲚⲚⲈⲠⲢⲞⲂⲞⲖⲞⲞⲨⲈ ⲘⲠⲘⲈϨϢⲞⲘⲦ Ⲛ-
ϢⲎⲚ ⲘⲠⲈⲐⲎⲤⲀⲨⲢⲞⲤ ⲘⲠⲞⲨⲞⲈⲒⲚ· ϤⲚⲀϢⲰⲠⲈ ϨⲘ ⲠⲦⲞ-   ⲢⲞⲎ ᵇ
ⲠⲞⲤ ⟨Ⲛ⟩ⲚⲈⲮⲨⲬⲞⲞⲨⲈ ⲚⲚⲈⲢⲬⲒ ⲘⲠⲘⲈϨⲘⲎⲦ ⲘⲘΥⲤⲦⲎⲢⲒⲞⲚ
ⲚⲦⲈ ⲠⲒϢⲞⲢⲠ ⲘⲘΥⲤⲦⲎⲢⲒⲞⲚ ϨⲢⲀⲒ ϨⲚ ⲚⲈⲔⲖⲎⲢⲞⲚⲞⲘⲒⲀ Ⲙ-
15 ⲠⲞⲨⲞⲈⲒⲚ· ϨⲞⲘⲞⲒⲰⲤ ⲞⲚ ⲠⲘⲀϨⲘⲚⲦⲞⲨⲈ ⲚⲤⲰⲦⲎⲢ ⲈⲦⲈ
ⲚⲦⲞϤ ⲠⲈ ⲠⲤⲰⲦⲎⲢ ⲘⲠⲘⲀϨϤⲦⲞⲞⲨ ⲚϢⲎⲚ ⲚⲦⲈ ⲠⲈⲐⲎ-
ⲤⲀⲨⲢⲞⲤ ⲘⲠⲞⲨⲞⲈⲒⲚ· ϤⲚⲀϢⲰⲠⲈ ϨⲘ ⲠⲦⲞⲠⲞⲤ ⲚⲚⲈⲮⲨ-
ⲬⲞⲞⲨⲈ ⲚⲚⲈⲢⲬⲒ ⲘⲠⲘⲀϨⲘⲚⲦⲞⲨⲈ ⲘⲘΥⲤⲦⲎⲢⲒⲞⲚ ⲚⲦⲈ ⲠⲒ-
ϢⲞⲢⲠ ⲘⲘΥⲤⲦⲎⲢⲒⲞⲚ ϨⲢⲀⲒ ϨⲚ ⲚⲈⲔⲖⲎⲢⲞⲚⲞⲘⲒⲀ ⲘⲠⲞⲨ-
20 ⲞⲈⲒⲚ ⲀΥⲰ ⲠⲘⲀϨⲘⲚⲦⲤⲚⲞⲞⲨⲤ ⲚⲤⲰⲦⲎⲢ ⲈⲦⲈ ⲚⲦⲞϤ ⲠⲈ
ⲠⲤⲰⲦⲎⲢ ⲚⲚⲈⲠⲢⲞⲂⲞⲖⲞⲞⲨⲈ ⲘⲠⲘⲀϨ†ⲞⲨ ⲚϢⲎⲚ ⲘⲠⲈⲐⲎ-
ⲤⲀⲨⲢⲞⲤ ⲘⲠⲞⲨⲞⲈⲒⲚ· ϤⲚⲀϢⲰⲠⲈ ϨⲘ ⲠⲦⲞⲠⲞⲤ ⲚⲚⲈⲮⲨ-
ⲬⲞⲞⲨⲈ ⲚⲚⲈⲚⲦⲀΥⲬⲒ ⲘⲠⲘⲀϨⲘⲚⲦⲤⲚⲞⲞⲨⲤ ⲘⲘΥⲤⲦⲎⲢⲒⲞⲚ
ⲚⲦⲈ ⲠⲒϢⲞⲢⲠ ⲘⲘΥⲤⲦⲎⲢⲒⲞⲚ ϨⲢⲀⲒ ϨⲚ ⲚⲈⲔⲖⲎⲢⲞⲚⲞⲘⲒⲀ Ⲙ-
25 ⲠⲞⲨⲞⲒⲚ· ⲀΥⲰ ⲠⲤⲀϢϤ ⲚϨⲀⲘⲎⲚ ⲘⲚ ⲠⲦⲞⲨ ⲚϢⲎⲚ

---

3 MS ⲚⲈⲢⲬⲒ; read ⲚⲚⲈⲢⲬⲒ.
25 MS originally ⲠⲘⲈϨⲤⲀϢϤ; ⲘⲈϨ erased.

of the first tree of the *Treasury* of the Light, he will be
in the *place* of the *souls* of those who receive the eighth
mystery of the First *Mystery* in the *inheritances* of the light.
And the ninth *saviour* who is the *saviour* of the *emanations*
of the second tree of the *Treasury* of the Light, he will be
in the *place* of the *souls* of those who receive the ninth
mystery of the First *Mystery* in the *inheritances* of the light.
And the tenth *saviour* who is the *saviour* of the *emanations*
of the third tree of the *Treasury* of the Light, he will be in
the *place* of the *souls* of those who receive the tenth *mystery*
of the First *Mystery* in the *inheritances* of the light. *Likewise*
also the eleventh *saviour* who is the *saviour* of the fourth
tree of the *Treasury* of the Light, he will be in the *place*
of the *souls* of those who receive the eleventh *mystery* of
the First *Mystery* in the *inheritances* of the light. And the
twelfth *saviour* who is the *saviour* of the *emanations* of the
fifth tree of the *Treasury* of the Light, he will be in the
place of the *souls* of those who have received the twelfth
mystery of the First *Mystery* in the *inheritances* of the light.
And the seven *amens* and the five trees | and the three

ⲘⲚ ⲠϢⲞⲘⲚ̅ⲧ̅·* Ⲛ̅ⲀⲘⲎⲚ ⲤⲈⲚⲀϢⲰⲠⲈ ϨⲒ ⲞⲨⲚⲀⲘ Ⲙ̅ⲘⲞⲒ̈ ⲣ̅ⲟ̅ⲟ̅

ⲈⲨⲞ Ⲛ̅ⲢⲢⲞ ϨⲢⲀⲒ̈ Ϩ̅Ⲛ̅ ⲚⲈⲔⲖⲎⲢⲞⲚⲞⲘⲒⲀ Ⲙ̅ⲠⲞⲨⲞⲈⲒⲚ · ⲀⲨⲰ

ⲠⲤⲰⲦⲎⲢ Ⲛ̅ϨⲀⲦⲢⲈⲨ ⲈⲦⲈ Ⲛ̅ⲦⲞⲞⲨ ⲠⲈ ⲠⲀⲖⲞⲨ Ⲙ̅ⲠⲀⲖⲞⲨ ·

ⲀⲨⲰ Ⲙ̅Ⲛ̅ ⲠⲈϤⲒⲤ Ⲙ̅ⲫⲨⲖⲀⲝ ⲤⲈⲚⲀϬⲰ Ϩ̅ⲰⲞⲨ ⲞⲚ ϨⲒ ϨⲂⲞⲨⲢ

5 Ⲙ̅ⲘⲞⲒ̈ ⲈⲨⲞ’ Ⲛ̅ⲢⲢⲞ ϨⲢⲀⲒ̈ Ϩ̅Ⲛ̅ ⲚⲈⲔⲖⲎⲢⲞⲚⲞⲘⲒⲀ Ⲙ̅ⲠⲞⲨⲞⲈⲒⲚ

ⲀⲨⲰ ⲠⲞⲨⲀ ⲠⲞⲨⲀ Ⲛ̅Ⲛ̅ⲤⲰⲦⲎⲢ ϤⲚⲀⲢ̅ⲢⲞ ⲈϪ̅Ⲛ̅ Ⲛ̅ⲦⲀⳍⲒⲤ Ⲛ̅-

ⲚⲈϤⲠⲢⲞⲂⲞⲖⲞⲞⲨⲈ ϨⲢⲀⲒ̈ Ϩ̅Ⲛ̅ ⲚⲈⲔⲖⲎⲢⲞⲚⲞⲘⲒⲀ Ⲙ̅ⲠⲞⲨⲞⲈⲒⲚ ·

Ⲛ̅ⲐⲈ ⲞⲚ ⲈⲦⲞⲨⲞ Ⲙ̅ⲘⲞⲤ Ϩ̅Ⲙ̅ ⲠⲈⲐⲎⲤⲀⲨⲢⲞⲤ Ⲙ̅ⲠⲞⲨⲞⲈⲒⲚ ·

ⲀⲨⲰ ⲠⲈϤⲒⲤ Ⲙ̅ⲫⲨⲖⲀⳍ Ⲙ̅ⲠⲈⲐⲎⲤⲀⲨⲢⲞⲤ Ⲙ̅ⲠⲞⲨⲞⲈⲒⲚ · ⲤⲈ-

10 ⲚⲀϢⲰⲠⲈ ⲈⲨⲞⲨⲞⲦⲂ̅ ⲈⲚⲤⲰⲦⲎⲢ ϨⲢⲀⲒ̈ Ϩ̅Ⲛ̅ ⲚⲈⲔⲖⲎⲢⲞⲚⲞⲘⲒⲀ

Ⲙ̅ⲠⲞⲨⲞⲈⲒⲚ · ⲀⲨⲰ Ⲛ̅ϨⲀⲦⲢⲈⲨ Ⲛ̅ⲤⲰⲦⲎⲢ · ⲤⲈⲚⲀϢⲰⲠⲈ

ⲈⲨⲞⲨⲞⲦⲂ̅ ⲈⲠⲈϤⲒⲤ Ⲙ̅ⲫⲨⲖⲀⳍ ϨⲢⲀⲒ̈ Ϩ̅Ⲛ̅ ⲦⲘ̅Ⲛ̅ⲦⲈⲢⲞ · ⲀⲨⲰ

ⲠϢⲞⲘⲚ̅ⲧ̅ Ⲛ̅ⲀⲘⲎⲚ ⲤⲈⲚⲀϢⲰⲠⲈ ⲈⲨⲞⲦⲂ̅ ⲈⲚϨⲀⲦⲢⲈⲨ Ⲛ̅- ⲣ̅ⲟ̅ⲟ̅ᵇ

ⲤⲰⲦⲎⲢ ϨⲢⲀⲒ̈ Ϩ̅Ⲛ̅ ⲦⲘ̅Ⲛ̅ⲦⲈⲢⲞ · ⲀⲨⲰ ⲠϯⲞⲨ Ⲛ̅ϢⲎⲚ ⲤⲈⲚⲀ-

15 ϢⲰⲠⲈ ⲈⲨⲞⲨⲞⲦⲂ̅ ⲈⲠϢⲞⲘⲚ̅ⲧ̅ Ⲛ̅ⲀⲘⲎⲚ ϨⲢⲀⲒ̈ Ϩ̅Ⲛ̅ ⲚⲈⲔⲖⲎ-

ⲢⲞⲚⲞⲘⲒⲀ Ⲙ̅ⲠⲞⲨⲞⲒ̈Ⲛ · ⲀⲨⲰ Ⲓ̅ⲈⲞⲨ Ⲙ̅Ⲛ̅ ⲠⲈϤⲨⲖⲀⳍ Ⲙ̅ⲠⲔⲀ-

ⲦⲀⲠⲈⲦⲀⲤⲘⲀ Ⲙ̅ⲠⲚⲞϬ Ⲛ̅ⲞⲨⲞⲈⲒⲚ · Ⲙ̅Ⲛ̅ Ⲙ̅ⲠⲀⲢⲀⲖⲎⲘⲦⲰⲢ

Ⲛ̅ⲞⲨⲞⲈⲒⲚ · Ⲙ̅Ⲛ̅ ⲠⲚⲞϬ ⲤⲚⲀⲨ Ⲙ̅ⲠⲢⲞϨⲎⲄⲞⲨⲘⲈⲚⲞⲤ · Ⲙ̅Ⲛ̅

ⲠⲚⲞϬ Ⲛ̅ⲤⲀⲂⲀⲰⲐ ⲠⲀⲄⲀⲐⲞⲤ ⲤⲈⲚⲀϢⲰⲠⲈ ⲈⲨⲞ Ⲛ̅ⲢⲢⲞ Ϩ̅Ⲙ̅

20 ⲠϢⲞⲢⲠ̅ Ⲛ̅ⲤⲰⲦⲎⲢ Ⲛ̅ⲦⲈ ⲦϢⲞⲢⲠ̅ Ⲙ̅ⲫⲰⲚⲎ Ⲙ̅ⲠⲈⲐⲎⲤⲀⲨⲢⲞⲤ

Ⲙ̅ⲠⲞⲨⲞⲒ̈Ⲛ ⲠⲀⲒ̈ ⲈⲦⲚⲀϢⲰⲠⲈ Ϩ̅Ⲙ̅ ⲠⲦⲞⲠⲞⲤ Ⲛ̅ⲚⲈⲢⳍⲒ Ⲙ̅-

ⲠϢⲞⲢⲠ̅ Ⲙ̅ⲘⲨⲤⲦⲎⲢⲒⲞⲚ Ⲛ̅ⲦⲈ ⲠⲒϢⲞⲢⲠ̅ Ⲙ̅ⲘⲨⲤⲦⲎⲢⲒⲞⲚ ·

ⲈⲂⲞⲖ ⲄⲀⲢ ϪⲈ Ⲓ̅ⲈⲞⲨ Ⲙ̅Ⲛ̅ ⲠⲈϤⲨⲖⲀⳍ Ⲙ̅ⲠⲦⲞⲠⲞⲤ Ⲛ̅ⲚⲀⲞⲨ-

ⲈⲒⲚⲀⲘ Ⲙ̅Ⲛ̅ ⲘⲈⲖⲬⲒⲤⲈⲆⲈⲔ ⲠⲚⲞϬ Ⲙ̅ⲠⲀⲢⲀⲖⲎⲘⲠⲦⲰⲢ Ⲙ̅ⲠⲞⲨ-

---

5 ï perhaps inserted after ϨⲢⲀ.
6 MS ϤⲚⲀⲢ̅ⲢⲞ ; read ϤⲚⲀⲢ̅ⲢⲢⲞ.
13 MS ⲈⲨⲞⲦⲂ̅ ; read ⲈⲨⲞⲨⲞⲦⲂ̅.
17 MS originally Ⲙ̅ⲠⲀⲢⲀⲂⲞⲖⲎⲘⲦⲰⲢ ; ⲂⲞ erased.

amens will be on my right as rulers (kings) in the *inheritances* of the light. And the twin *saviours*, who are the child of the child, and the nine *watchers*, will remain on my left as rulers (kings) in the *inheritances* of the light. And each one of the *saviours* will rule over the *ranks* of his *emanations* in the *inheritances* of the light, as they also do in the *Treasury* of the Light. And the nine *watchers* of the *Treasury* of the Light will be superior to the *saviours* in the *inheritances* of the light. And the twin *saviours* will be superior to the nine *watchers* in the kingdom. And the three *amens* will be superior to the twin *saviours* in the kingdom. And the five trees will be superior to the three *amens* in the *inheritances* of the light. And Jeu and the *watcher* of the *veil* of the great light, and the *paralemptors* of the light, and the two great *leaders*, and the Great Sabaoth the *Good* will be rulers (kings) in the first *saviour* of the first *voice* of the *Treasury* of the Light, who (the first saviour) will be in the *place* of those who receive the first *mystery* of the First *Mystery*. *For* Jeu and the *watcher* of the *place* of those of the right, and Melchisedek the great *paralemptor* | of the light, and

ΟΕΙΝ· ⲘⲚ ⲠⲚⲞⳔ ⲤⲚⲀⲨ ⲘⲠⲢⲞⲌⲎⲄⲞⲨⲘⲈⲚⲞⳤ ⲚⲦⲀⲨⲠⲢⲞⲗⲈ ⲣⲡ
ⲈⲂⲞⲗ ⲌⲘ ⲠⲞⲨⲞⲈⲒⲚ ⲈⲦⲤⲞⲦⲠ ⲈⲦⲞ ⲚⳞⲒⲗⲒⲔⲢⲒⲚⲈⲤ ⲈⲘⲀϢⲞ
ⲚⲦⲈ ⲠϢⲞⲢⲠ ⲚϢⲎⲚ· ⳞⲈⲰⲤ ϢⲀ ⲠⲘⲀⳞϯⲞⲨ· ⲒⲈⲞⲨ ⲘⲈⲚ
ⲚⲦⲞϤ ⲠⲈ ⲠⲈⲠⲒⲤⲔⲞⲠⲞⳤ ⲘⲠⲞⲨⲞⲈⲒⲚ ⲚⲦⲀϤⲠⲢⲞⲗⲈ ⲈⲂⲞⲗ
5 ⲚϢⲞⲢⲠ ⳞⲢⲀⲒ ⲌⲘ ⲠⳞⲒⲗⲒⲔⲢⲒⲚⲈⲤ ⲚⲞⲨⲞⲈⲒⲚ ⲚⲦⲈ ⲠⲒϢⲞⲢⲠ
ⲚϢⲎⲚ· ⲠⲈϤⲨⲗⲀⳜ ⳞⲰⲰϤ ⲘⲠⲔⲀⲦⲀⲠⲈⲦⲀⲤⲘⲀ ⲚⲚⲀⲞⲨⲈ
ⲈⲒⲚⲀⲘ ⲚⲦⲀϤⲠⲢⲞⲗⲈ ⲈⲂⲞⲗ ⲌⲘ ⲠⲘⲈⳞⲤⲚⲀⲨ ⲚϢⲎⲚ· ⲀⲨⲰ
ⲠⲈⲠⲢⲞⳞⲄⲞⲨⲘⲈⲚⲞⳤ ⲤⲚⲀⲨ ⲚⲦⲀⲨⲠⲢⲞⲗⲈ ⳞⲰⲞⲨ ⲈⲂⲞⲗ
ⲌⲘ ⲠⳞⲒⲗⲒⲔⲢⲒⲚⲈⲤ ⲚⲞⲨⲞⲈⲒⲚ ⲈϤⲤⲞⲦϤ ⲈⲘⲀϢⲞ ⲚⲦⲈ ⲠⲘⲈⳞ
10 ϢⲞⲘⲚⲦ ⲚϢⲎⲚ ⲘⲚ ⲠⲘⲈⳞϤⲦⲞⲞⲨ ⲌⲘ ⲠⲈⲞⲚⳞⲀⲨⲢⲞⳤ Ⲙ
ⲠⲞⲨⲞⲈⲒⲚ· ⲘⲈⲗⳜⲒⲤⲈⲗⲈⲔ ⳞⲰⲰϤ ⲚⲦⲀϤⲠⲢⲞⲗⲈ ⲈⲂⲞⲗ ⲌⲘ
ⲠⲘⲀⳞϯⲞⲨ ⲚϢⲎⲚ· ⲤⲀⲂⲀⲰⲐ ⲠⲚⲞⳔ ⳞⲰⲰϤ ⲚⲀⲅⲀⲐⲞⳤ ⲠⲀⲒ
ⲈⲚⲦⲀⲒⲘⲞⲨⲦⲈ ⲈⲢⲞϤ ϪⲈ ⲠⲀⲈⲒⲰⲦ· ⲚⲦⲀϤⲠⲢⲞⲗⲈ ⲈⲂⲞⲗ ⳞⲚ ⲣⲡᵇ
ⲒⲈⲞⲨ ⲠⲈⲠⲒⲤⲔⲞⲠⲞⳤ ⲘⲠⲞⲨⲞⲈⲒⲚ· ⲠⲈⲒⲤⲞⲞⲨ ⳔⲈ ⳞⲒⲦⲚ
15 ⲦⲔⲈⲗⲈⲨⲤⲒⳤ ⲘⲠⲒϢⲞⲢⲠ ⲘⲘⲨⲤⲦⲎⲢⲒⲞⲚ Ⲁ ϤⲀⳞ ⲘⲠⲀⲢⲀⲤⲦⲀ
ⲦⲎⳤ ⲀϤⲦⲢⲈⲨϢⲰⲠⲈ ⲌⲘ ⲠⲦⲞⲠⲞⳤ ⲚⲚⲀⲞⲨⲈⲒⲚⲀⲘ ⲠⲢⲞⳤ
ⲦⲞⲒⲔⲞⲚⲞⲘⲒⲀ ⲘⲠⲤⲰⲟⳞ ⲈⳞⲞⲨⲚ ⲘⲠⲞⲨⲞⲈⲒⲚ ⲈⲦⲘⲠϪⲒⲤⲈ
ⲚⲚⲀⲒⲰⲚ ⲚⲦⲈ ⲚⲀⲢⳜⲰⲚ· ⲀⲨⲰ ⳞⲚ ⲚⲔⲞⲤⲘⲞⳤ ⲘⲚ ⲄⲈⲚⲞⳤ
ⲚⲒⲘ ⲈⲦⲚⳞⲎⲦⲞⲨ· ⲚⲀⲒ ⲈϯⲚⲀϪⲰ ⲈⲢⲰⲦⲚ ⲘⲠⳞⲰⲂ ⲘⲠⲞⲨⲀ
20 ⲠⲞⲨⲀ ⲚⲦⲀⲨⲔⲀⲀϤ ⳞⲒϪⲰϤ ⲌⲘ ⲠⲤⲰⲢ ⲈⲂⲞⲗ ⲘⲠⲦⲎⲢϤ: ⲈⲦ
ⲂⲈ ⲠϪⲒⲤⲈ ⲞⲨⲚ ⲘⲠⳞⲰⲂ ⲈⲚⲦⲀϤⲔⲀⲀϤ ⲚⳞⲎⲦϤ· ⲤⲈⲚⲀ
ϢⲰⲠⲈ ⲚϢⲂⲢⲢⲢⲞ ⲌⲘ ⲠⲒϢⲞⲢⲠ ⲘⲘⲨⲤⲦⲎⲢⲒⲞⲚ ⲚⲦⲈ ⲦϢⲞ
ⲢⲠ ⲘϤⲰⲚⲎ ⲘⲠⲈⲞⲚⳞⲀⲨⲢⲞⳤ ⲘⲠⲞⲨⲞⲈⲒⲚ ⲠⲀⲒ ⲈⲦⲚⲀϢⲰⲠⲈ

---

1   MS originally ⲚⲦⲀⲨⲠⲢⲞⲂⲀⲗⲈ; ⲂⲀ here and in following lines erased, giving
    ⲠⲢⲞⲗⲈ; read ⲠⲢⲞⲈⲗⲞⳤ.
2   MS ⲈⲦⲤⲞⲦⲠ; read ⲈⲦⲤⲞⲦϤ.
21   MS ⲈⲚⲦⲀϤⲔⲀⲀϤ; Schmidt : read ⲈⲚⲦⲀⲨⲔⲀⲀϤ.
22   MS ⲘⲘⲨⲤⲦⲎⲢⲒⲞⲚ; read ⲠⲤⲰⲦⲎⲢ.

the two great *leaders* have *come forth* from the purified and
very *pure* light of the first tree, *as far as* the fifth tree. Jeu
indeed is the *overseer* of the light, he who *came forth* first
from the *pure* light of the first tree. The *watcher* of the
veil of those of the right also *came forth* from the second
tree. And the two *leaders* also *came forth* from the *pure*
light, which is much purified, of the third and fourth trees
in the *Treasury* of the Light. Melchisedek also *came forth*
from the fifth tree. The Great Sabaoth the *Good*, he whom
I have called my Father, also *came forth* from Jeu, the
overseer of the light. Now, at the *command* of the First
Mystery, the last *helper* (*parastates*) has caused these six to
be in the *place* of those of the right for the *organisation*
of the gathering together of the light of the height, from
the *aeons* of the *archons* and from the *world* and all the
races in them. On the work of each of these, over which he
is placed [1] in the distribution of the All, I will speak to you.
Now concerning the elevation of the work in which they
are placed [2], they will be fellow-rulers (kings) with the first
⟨saviour⟩ [3] of the first *voice* of the *Treasury* of the Light,
which will be | in the *place* of the *souls* of those who receive

---

[1]   (20) he is placed; Schmidt: he was placed; MS: they have placed him.
[2]   (21) they are placed; Schmidt: he was placed; MS: he has placed himself.
[3]   (22) first ⟨saviour⟩; MS: first mystery.

ⲍ̄ⲙ ⲡⲧⲟⲡⲟⲥ ⲛ̄ⲛⲉⲯⲩⲭⲟⲟⲩⲉ ⲛ̄ⲛⲉⲣⲭⲓ-ⲡⲓϣⲟⲣⲡ̄ ⲙ̄ⲙⲩⲥⲧⲏ-
ⲣⲓⲟⲛ ⲛ̄ⲧⲉ ⲡⲓϣⲟⲣⲡ̄ ⲙ̄ⲙⲩⲥⲧⲏⲣⲓⲟⲛ · ⲁⲩⲱ ⲧⲡⲁⲣⲑⲉⲛⲟⲥ
ⲙ̄ⲡⲟⲩⲟⲉⲓⲛ · ⲙ̄ⲛ ⲡⲛⲟϭ**ⲛ̄ⲍⲏⲅⲟⲩⲙⲉⲛⲟⲥ ⲛ̄ⲧⲉ ⲧⲙⲉⲥⲟⲥ ⲣ̄ⲡⲁ
ⲡⲁⲓ̈ ⲉϣⲁⲣⲉ ⲛ̄ⲁⲣⲭⲱⲛ ⲛ̄ⲧⲉ ⲛ̄ⲁⲓⲱⲛ ⲉϣⲁⲩⲙⲟⲩⲧⲉ ⲉⲣⲟϥ
5 ϫⲉ ⲡⲛⲟϭ ⲛ̄ⲓ̈ⲁⲱ ⲕⲁⲧⲁ ⲡⲣⲁⲛ ⲛ̄ⲟⲩⲛⲟϭ ⲛ̄ⲁⲣⲭⲱⲛ ⲉⲧⲍ̄ⲙ
ⲡⲉⲩⲧⲟⲡⲟⲥ · ⲛ̄ⲧⲟϥ ⲙ̄ⲛ ⲧⲡⲁⲣⲑⲉⲛⲟⲥ ⲙ̄ⲡⲟⲩⲟⲉⲓⲛ · ⲙ̄ⲛ
ⲡⲉϥⲙ̄ⲛ̄ⲧⲥⲛⲟⲟⲩⲥ ⲛ̄ⲇⲓⲁⲕⲱⲛ ⲛⲁⲓ̈ ⲛ̄ⲧⲁⲧⲉⲧⲛ̄ϫⲓ-ⲙⲟⲣⲫⲏ
ⲛ̄ⲍⲏⲧⲟⲩ · ⲁⲩⲱ ⲁⲧⲉⲧⲛ̄ϫⲓ ⲛ̄ⲧϭⲟⲙ ⲉⲃⲟⲗ ⲛ̄ⲍⲏⲧⲟⲩ · ⲥⲉⲛⲁϣⲱⲡⲉ ⲍⲱⲟⲩ ⲧⲏⲣⲟⲩ ⲉⲩⲟ ⲛ̄ⲣ̄ⲣⲟ · ⲙ̄ⲛ ⲡϣⲟⲣⲡ̄ ⲛ̄ⲥⲱ-
10 ⲧⲏⲣ ⲛ̄ⲧⲉ ⲧϣⲟⲣⲡ̄ ⲙ̄ⲫⲱⲛⲏ ⲍ̄ⲙ ⲡⲧⲟⲡⲟⲥ ⲛ̄ⲛⲉⲯⲩⲭⲟⲟⲩⲉ
ⲛ̄ⲛⲉⲧⲛⲁϫⲓ ⲙ̄ⲡϣⲟⲣⲡ̄ ⲙ̄ⲙⲩⲥⲧⲏⲣⲓⲟⲛ ⲛ̄ⲧⲉ ⲡⲓϣⲟⲣⲡ̄ ⲙ̄ⲙⲩⲥ-
ⲧⲏⲣⲓⲟⲛ ⲍⲣⲁⲓ̈ ⲍ̄ⲛ ⲛⲉⲕⲗⲏⲣⲟⲛⲟⲙⲓⲁ ⲙ̄ⲡⲟⲩⲟⲓ̈ⲛ ⲁⲩⲱ ⲙ̄ⲛ
ⲡⲙ̄ⲛ̄ⲧⲏ ⲙ̄ⲡⲁⲣⲁⲥⲧⲁⲧⲏⲥ ⲛ̄ⲧⲥⲁϣϥⲉ ⲙ̄ⲡⲁⲣⲑⲉⲛⲟⲥ ⲙ̄ⲡⲟⲩⲟ-
ⲉⲓⲛ ⲛⲁⲓ̈ ⲉⲧϣⲟⲟⲡ ⲍ̄ⲛ ⲧⲙⲉⲥⲟⲥ ⲥⲉⲛⲁⲥⲱⲣ ⲉⲃⲟⲗ ⲍⲣⲁⲓ̈ ⲍ̄ⲛ
15 ⲛ̄ⲧⲟⲡⲟⲥ ⲙ̄ⲡⲙ̄ⲛ̄ⲧⲥⲛⲟⲟⲩⲥ ⲛ̄ⲥⲱⲧⲏⲣ · ⲙ̄ⲛ ⲡⲕⲉⲥⲉⲉⲡⲉ ⲛ̄- ⲣ̄ⲡⲁᵇ
ⲁⲅⲅⲉⲗⲟⲥ ⲛ̄ⲧⲉ ⲧⲙⲉⲥⲟⲥ ⲡⲟⲩⲁ ⲡⲟⲩⲁ ⲕⲁⲧⲁ ⲡⲉϥⲉⲟⲟⲩ
ⲛ̄ⲥⲉⲣ̄ⲣⲣⲟ ⲛⲙ̄ⲙⲁⲓ̈ ⲍⲣⲁⲓ̈ ⲍ̄ⲛ ⲛⲉⲕⲗⲏⲣⲟⲛⲟⲙⲓⲁ ⲙ̄ⲡⲟⲩⲟⲉⲓⲛ ·
ⲁⲩⲱ ⲁⲛⲟⲕ †ⲛⲁⲣ̄ⲣ̄ⲣⲟ ⲍⲣⲁⲓ̈ ⲉϫⲱⲟⲩ ⲧⲏⲣⲟⲩ ⲉⲍⲣⲁⲓ̈ ⲍ̄ⲛ
ⲛⲉⲕⲗⲏⲣⲟⲛⲟⲙⲓⲁ ⲙ̄ⲡⲟⲩⲟⲉⲓⲛ ·

20   ⲍ ⲛⲁⲓ̈ ϭⲉ ⲧⲏⲣⲟⲩ ⲛ̄ⲧⲁⲓ̈ϫⲟⲟⲩ ⲛⲏⲧⲛ̄ ⲛ̄ⲥⲉⲛⲁϣⲱⲡⲉ
ⲁⲛ ⲍ̄ⲙ ⲡⲉⲓ̈ⲟⲩⲟⲉⲓϣ · ⲁⲗⲗⲁ ⲉⲩⲛⲁϣⲱⲡⲉ ⲍ̄ⲛ ⲧⲥⲩⲛⲧⲉ-
ⲗⲉⲓⲁ ⲙ̄ⲡⲁⲓⲱⲛ · ⲉⲧⲉ ⲛ̄ⲧⲟϥ ⲡⲉ ⲡⲃⲱⲗ ⲉⲃⲟⲗ ⲙ̄ⲡⲧⲏⲣϥ ·
ⲁⲩⲱ ⲛ̄ⲧⲟϥ ⲡⲉ ⲡⲱⲍ ⲉⲍⲣⲁⲓ̈ ⲧⲏⲣϥ ⲛ̄ⲧⲁⲣⲓⲑⲙⲏⲥⲓⲥ ⲛ̄ⲛⲉⲯⲩ-
ⲭⲟⲟⲩⲉ ⲛ̄ⲧⲉⲗⲓⲟⲥ ⲛ̄ⲧⲉ ⲛⲉⲕⲗⲏⲣⲟⲛⲟⲙⲓⲁ ⲙ̄ⲡⲟⲩⲟⲉⲓⲛ · ⲍⲁ-
25 ⲑⲏ ϭⲉ ⲟⲩⲛ ⲛ̄ⲧⲥⲩⲛⲧⲉⲗⲉⲓⲁ ⲛⲁⲓ̈ ⲛ̄ⲧⲁⲓ̈ϫⲟⲟⲩ ⲛⲏⲧⲛ̄ ⲛ̄-
ⲥⲉⲛⲁϣⲱⲡⲉ ⲁⲛ · ⲁⲗⲗⲁ ⲉⲣⲉ ⲡⲟⲩⲁ ⲡⲟⲩⲁ ⲛⲁϣⲱⲡⲉ ⲍ̄ⲙ

---

18   MS ⲍⲣⲁⲓ̈ ⲉϫⲱⲟⲩ; read ⲉⲍⲣⲁⲓ̈ ⲉϫ̄. MS ⲉⲍⲣⲁⲓ̈ ⲍ̄ⲛ̄ ; read ⲍⲣⲁⲓ̈ ⲍ̄ⲛ̄.

the first *mystery* of the First *Mystery*. And the *Virgin* of the
Light and the great *hegumen* of the *Midst* — whom the
archons of the *aeons* are wont to call the Great Jao [1],
according to the name of a great *archon* in their *place* —
he and the *Virgin* of the Light and his twelve *servers*, from
whom you have received *form* and from whom you have
received power, they also will all be rulers (kings) with the
first *saviour* of the first *voice* in the *place* of the *souls* of
those who will receive the first *mystery* of the First *Mystery*
in the *inheritances* of the light. And the fifteen *helpers* (*parastatai*) of the seven *virgins* of the light [2], which are in the
Midst, will be distributed in the *places* of the twelve *saviours*,
and the rest of the *angels* of the *Midst*. Each one *according to*
his glory will rule (be king) with me in the *inheritances* of
the light, and I will rule (be king) over them all in the
inheritances of the light.

Now all these things which I have said to you will not
happen at this time, but they will happen at the *end* of
the *aeon*, that is, at the dissolution of the All. And this is the
whole ascent of the *number* of the *perfect souls* [3] of the
inheritances of the light. *Now* before the *end* these things
which I have said to you will not happen, *but* each one
will be in his *place* | in which he was *placed* from the

---

[1]   (5) Jao, the Great; see Iren. I.30.5, 11; Origen *c.Cels.* VI.31; J 119; ApJn 42.
[2]   (13) seven virgins of the light; see J 107.
[3]   (23, 24) the number of the perfect souls; Till: the complete number of souls
       (see 197.2, 3; 197.8, 9); lit. the reckoning of the perfect souls.

ПЕЧТОПОС · ЄΝΤΑΥΚΑΑЧ Ν̄ЗΗΤЧ̄ ХІΝ Ν̄ϢΟΡП̄ · ϢΑΝ-
ΤΟΥΧϢΚ ЄΒΟΛ Ν̄ΤΑΡΙΟΜΗⲤΙⲤ Μ̄ПⲤϢΟΥ2 Є2ΟΥΝ Ν̄ΝЄ-   <u>ρπв</u>
ΨΥΧΟΟΥЄ Ν̄ΤЄΛΙΟⲤ · ΤⲤΑϢЧЄ Μ̄ΦϢΝΗ ΜΝ̄ П†ΟΥ Ν̄-
ϢΗΝ · ΑΥϢ ΜΝ̄ ПϢΟΜΝ̄Τ Ν̄2ΑΜΗΝ · ΑΥϢ ΜΝ̄ ΦΑΤΡЄΕΥ
5 Ν̄ⲤϢΤΗΡ ΜΝ̄ ПЄΨΙⲤ Μ̄ΦΥΛΑΞ · ΑΥϢ ΜΝ̄ ПΜΝ̄ΤⲤΝΟΟΥⲤ
Ν̄ⲤϢΤΗΡ · ΑΥϢ ΜΝ̄ ΝΑПΤΟПΟⲤ Ν̄ΝΑΟΥЄΙΝΑΜ · ΑΥϢ
ΜΝ̄ ΝΑПΤΟПΟⲤ Ν̄ΤΜЄⲤΟⲤ ПΟΥΑ ПΟΥΑ ΝΑϬϢ 2Μ̄ ПΤΟ-
ПΟⲤ ЄΝΤΑΥΚΑΑΥ Ν̄2ΗΤЧ̄ ϢΑΝΤΟΥϢΑ Є2ΡΑΪ ΤΗΡΟΥ
Ν̄ϬΙ ΤΑΡΙΟΜΗⲤΙⲤ Ν̄ΤЄΛЄΙΟⲤ Ν̄ΝЄΨΥΧΟΟΥЄ Ν̄ΝЄΚΛΗΡΟ-
10 ΝΟΜΙΑ Μ̄ПΟΥΟЄΙΝ · ΑΥϢ Ν̄ΚЄΑΡΧϢΝ ΤΗΡΟΥ Ν̄ΤΑΥ-
ΜЄΤΑΝΟΪ · ⲤЄΝΑϬϢ 2ϢΟΥ 2Μ̄ ПΤΟПΟⲤ Ν̄ΤΑΥΚΑΑΥ Ν̄-
2ΗΤЧ̄ ϢΑΝΤΟΥϢΑ Є2ΡΑΪ ΤΗΡΟΥ Ν̄ϬΙ ΤΑΡΙΘΜΗⲤΙⲤ Ν̄ΝЄ-
ΨΥΧΟΟΥЄ Μ̄ПΟΥΟЄΙΝ ⲤЄΝΗΥ ΤΗΡΟΥ ΤΟΥЄΙ ΤΟΥЄΙ
2Μ̄ ПЄΥΟЄΙϢ ЄΤⲤΝΑΧΙ-ΜΥⲤΤΗΡΙΟΝ Ν̄2ΗΤЧ̄ · ΑΥϢ ⲤЄ-
15 ΝΑΟΥϢΤВ̄ Ν̄ΝΑΡΧϢΝ ΤΗΡΟΥ Ν̄ΤΑΥΜЄΤΑΝΟΪ · ΑΥϢ ⲤЄ-   <u>ρπв</u> b
ΝΗΥ ЄПΤΟПΟⲤ Ν̄ΝΑΤΜЄⲤΟⲤ · ΑΥϢ ΝΑΤΜЄⲤΟⲤ ΝΑΒΑП-
ΤΙΖЄ Μ̄ΜΟΟΥ · Ν̄ⲤЄ† ΝΑΥ Μ̄ПΤϢ2Ⲥ Μ̄ПΝЄΥΜΑΤΙΚΟΝ ·
ΑΥϢ Ν̄ⲤЄⲤΦΡΑΓΙΖЄ Μ̄ΜΟΟΥ 2ΡΑΪ 2Ν̄ ΝЄⲤΦΡΑΓΙⲤ Ν̄ΤЄ
ΝЄΥΜΥⲤΤΗΡΙΟΝ · ΑΥϢ ⲤЄΝΑΟΥϢΤВ̄ Є2ΟΥΝ ЄΝΑΝ̄ΤΟ-
20 ПΟⲤ ΤΗΡΟΥ Ν̄ΤΜЄⲤΟⲤ · ΑΥϢ ⲤЄΝΑΟΥϢΤВ̄ Є2ΟΥΝ Μ̄-
ПΤΟПΟⲤ Ν̄ΝΑΟΥЄΙΝΑΜ · ΑΥϢ П2ΟΥΝ Μ̄ПΤΟПΟⲤ Μ̄ПЄ-
ΨΙⲤ Μ̄ΦΥΛΑΞ · ΑΥϢ П2ΟΥΝ Μ̄ПΤΟПΟⲤ Μ̄П2ΑΤΡЄЄΥ
Ν̄ⲤϢΤΗΡ · ΑΥϢ П2ΟΥΝ Μ̄ПΤΟПΟⲤ Μ̄ПϢΟΜΝ̄Τ Ν̄2ΑΜΗΝ ·
ΜΝ̄ ПΜΝ̄ΤⲤΝΟΟΥⲤ Ν̄ⲤϢΤΗΡ · ΑΥϢ П2ΟΥΝ Μ̄П†ΟΥ Ν̄-
25 ϢΗΝ · ΜΝ̄ ΤⲤΑϢЧЄ Μ̄ΦϢΝΗ ЄΡЄ ПΟΥΑ ПΟΥΑ † ΝΑΥ
Ν̄ΝЄΥⲤΦΡΑΓΙⲤ Ν̄ΤЄ ΝЄΥΜΥⲤΤΗΡΙΟΝ · ΑΥϢ Ν̄ⲤЄΡПЄΥ-

beginning until the *number* of the gathering together of the *perfect souls* is completed. The seven voices and the five trees and the three *amens* and the twin *saviours* and the nine *watchers* and the twelve *saviours* and those of the *place* of the right and those of the *place* of the *Midst*, each one will remain in the *place* in which he was set until the *number* of the *perfect souls* of the *inheritances* of the light all ascend. And all the other *archons* which have *repented* will also remain in the *place* in which they were set until the *number* of the *souls* of the light all ascend. They will all come, each one at the time at which he will receive the *mystery*. And all the *archons* which have *repented* will pass through, and they will come to the *place* of those of the *Midst*. And those of the *Midst* will *baptise* them, and they will give them the *spiritual* inunction [1], and they will *seal* them with the *seals* [2] of their *mysteries*. And they will pass within those of all the *places* of the *Midst*. And they will pass within the *place* of those of the right, and within the *place* of the nine *watchers*, and within the *place* of the twin *saviours*, and within the *place* of the three *amens* and the twelve *saviours*, and within the five trees and the seven voices. Each one gives them the *seals* of his *mysteries*, and they enter into them [3] all | and

---

[1]   (17) spiritual inunction; see J 102.

[2]   (18) seal(s); see J 83; U 232.

[3]   (26) they enter into them all; Till: they all enter their interior (see 198.12).

ϨΟΥΝ ΤΗΡΟΥ · Ν̅ΣΕΒⲰΚ ΕΠΤΟΠΟΣ Ν̅ΝΕΚⲖΗΡΟΝΟΜΙⲀ
Μ̅Π̈ΟΥΟΕΙΝ ΠΟΥⲀ ΠΟΥⲀ Ν̅ϤϬⲰ Ϩ̅Μ ΠΤΟΠΟΣ ΕΝΤⲀϤΧΙ- ⲣ̅π̅ⲅ̅ᵃ
ΜΥΣΤΗΡΙΟΝ ϢⲀΡΟϤ Ϩ̅Ν ΝΕΚⲖΗΡΟΝΟΜΙⲀ Μ̅ΠΟΥΟΪΝ ϨⲀ-
ΠⲀϨ ϨⲀΠⲖⲰΣ ΝΕΨΥΧΟΟΥΕ ΤΗΡΟΥ Ν̅ΤΜΝ̅ΤΡⲰΜΕ ΝⲀΪ
5 ΕΤΝⲀΧΙ Ν̅ΜΜΥΣΤΗΡΙΟΝ Μ̅ΠΟΥΟΕΙΝ Ν̅ΣΕΝⲀⲣ̅ϢΟΡⲠ ΕΝ-
ⲀΡΧⲰΝ ΤΗΡΟΥ ΕΝΤⲀΥΜΕΤⲀΝΟΪ · ⲀΥⲰ ΣΕΝⲀⲣ̅ϢΟΡⲠ̅
ΕΝⲀΠΤΟΠΟΣ ΤΗΡΟΥ Ν̅ΝⲀΤΜΕΣΟΣ · Μ̅Ν ΝⲀΠΤΟΠΟΣ
ΤΗⲣ̅Ϥ Ν̅ΝⲀΟΥΕΙΝⲀΜ · ⲀΥⲰ ΣΕΝⲀⲣ̅ϢΟΡⲠ ΕΝⲀΠΤΟΠΟΣ
ΤΗⲣ̅Ϥ Μ̅ΠΕΘΗΣⲀΥΡΟΣ Μ̅ΠΟΥΟΕΙΝ · ϨⲀΠⲀϨ ϨⲀΠⲖⲰΣ ΣΕ-
10 ΝⲀⲣ̅ϢΟΡⲠ ΕΝⲀΠΤΟΠΟΣ ΤΗΡΟΥ · ⟨Μ̅ΠΕΘΗΣⲀΥΡΟΣ⟩ ⲀΥⲰ
ΣΕΝⲀⲣ̅ϢΟΡⲠ ΕΝⲀΠΤΟΠΟΣ ΤΗΡΟΥ Μ̅ΠϢΟΡⲠ Ν̅ΤⲰϢ
ⲀΥⲰ Ν̅ΣΕⲣ̅ΠΕΥϨΟΥΝ ΤΗΡΟΥ Ν̅ΣΕΒⲰΚ ΕΤΕΚⲖΗΡΟΝΟ-
ΜΙⲀ Μ̅ΠΟΥΟΕΙΝ ϢⲀ ΠΤΟΠΟΣ Μ̅ΠΕΥΜΥΣΤΗΡΙΟΝ Ν̅ΤΕ
ΠΟΥⲀ ΠΟΥⲀ ϬⲰ Ϩ̅Μ ΠΤΟΠΟΣ ΕΝΤⲀΥΧΙ-ΜΥΣΤΗΡΙΟΝ
15 ϢⲀΡΟϤ · ⲀΥⲰ ΝⲀΠΤΟΠΟΣ Ν̅ΤΜΕΣΟΣ · Μ̅Ν ΝⲀΟΥΕΙΝⲀΜ · ⲣ̅π̅ⲅ̅ᵇ
ⲀΥⲰ Μ̅Ν ΝⲀΠΤΟΠΟΣ ΤΗⲣ̅Ϥ Μ̅ΠΕΘΗΣⲀΥΡΟΣ ΠΟΥⲀ ΠΟΥⲀ
Ϩ̅Μ ΠΤΟΠΟΣ Ν̅ΤΤⲀϨΙΣ Ν̅ΤⲀΥΚⲀⲀϤ Ν̅ϨΗΤΣ ΧΙΝ Ν̅ϢΟΡⲠ ·
ϨΕⲰΣ ϢⲀΝΤΕ ΠΤΗⲣ̅Ϥ ⲰⲖ ΕϨΡⲀΪ ΕΡΕ ΠΟΥⲀ ΠΟΥⲀ Μ̅-
ΜΟΟΥ ΧⲰΚ ΕΒΟⲖ Ν̅ΤΕϤΟΙΚΟΝΟΜΙⲀ ΕΝΤⲀΥΚⲀⲀϤ Ν̅ϨΗ-
20 ΤΣ · ΕΤΒΕ ΠΣⲰΟΥϨ ΕϨΟΥΝ Ν̅ΝΕΨΥΧΟΟΥΕ ΕΝΤⲀΥΧΙ-
ΜΥΣΤΗΡΙΟΝ ΕΤΒΕ ΤΕΪΟΙΚΟΝΟΜΙⲀ · ΧΕ ΕΥΕΣϤΡⲀΓΙΖΕ
Ν̅ΝΕΨΥΧΟΟΥΕ ΤΗΡΟΥ ΕΤΝⲀΧΙ-ΜΥΣΤΗΡΙΟΝ ΝⲀΪ ΕΤΝⲀ-
ΟΥⲰⲦ̅Β ΕΠΕΥϨΟΥΝ ΕΤΕΚⲖΗΡΟΝΟΜΙⲀ Μ̅ΠΟΥΟΪΝ · ΤΕ-
ΝΟΥ ϬΕ ΜⲀΡΙⲀ ΠⲀΪ ΠΕ ΠϢⲀΧΕ ΕΤΕϢΙΝΕ Μ̅ΜΟΪ ΕΡΟϤ
25 Ϩ̅Ν ΟΥⲰⲣ̅Χ Μ̅Ν ΟΥⲀΣϤⲀⲖΕΙⲀ · ⲖΟΙΠΟΝ ϬΕ ΤΕΝΟΥ ΠΕΤΕ
ΟΥⲚ̅-ΜⲀⲀΧΕ Μ̅ΜΟϤ ΕΣⲰⲦΜ · ΜⲀΡΕϤΣⲰⲦ̅Μ̅ ·

10　MS Μ̅ΠΕΘΗΣⲀΥΡΟΣ omitted.

they go to the *place* of the *inheritances* of the light. Each one remains in the *place* as far as which he has received *mysteries* in the *inheritances* of the light. *In a word*, all the *souls* of mankind who will receive the *mysteries* of the light will precede all the *archons* who have *repented*. And they will precede all those of the *place* of those of the *Midst*, and those of the whole *place* of those of the right[1]. And they will precede those of the whole *place* of the *Treasury* of the Light. *In a word*, they will precede all those of the *place* ⟨of the *Treasury*⟩, and they will precede all those of the *place* of the first ordinance and they will enter within them all and go to the *inheritance* of the light as far as the *place* of their *mystery*. Each one remains in the *place* as far as which he has received *mysteries*. And those of the *place* of the *Midst* and of the right, and those of the whole *place* of the *Treasury*, each one remains in the *place* of the rank in which he was set from the beginning *until* the All ascends. And each one of them completes his *office* in which he was placed. Concerning the gathering together of the *souls* which have received *mysteries* because of this *office* : all the *souls* which will receive *mysteries* and will pass within the *inheritance* of the light are *sealed*.

Now at this time, Maria, this is the discourse on which thou didst question me with assurance and *certainty*. Now at this time *furthermore*, he who has ears to hear let him hear." * |

---

* Mk. 4.9

---

[1] (7, 8) the place of those of the Midst ... place of those of the right; Schmidt : the place of the Midst ... place of the right.

ⳅ ⲁⲥϣⲱⲡⲉ ϭⲉ ⲛ̄ⲧⲉⲣⲉ ⲓ̅ⲥ̅ ⲟⲩⲱ ⲉϥϫⲱ ⲛ̄ⲛⲉⲓ̈ϣⲁϫⲉ·
ⲁⲥϭⲟⲥ̅ⲥ̅⁺⁺ ⲉⲃⲟⲗ ⲛ̄ϭⲓ ⲙⲁⲣⲓⲁ ⲧⲙⲁⲅⲇⲁⲗⲏⲛⲏ ⲡⲉϫⲁⲥ· ϫⲉ ⲣ̅ⲡ̅ⲁ̅
ⲡⲁⲭⲟⲉⲓⲥ· ⲟⲩⲛ̄-ⲙⲁⲁϫⲉ ⲙ̄ⲙⲁⲣⲙ̄ⲛ̄ⲟⲩⲟⲉⲓⲛ· ⲁⲩⲱ †ⲡⲁ-
ⲣⲁⲗⲁⲙⲃⲁⲛⲉ ⲛ̄ϣⲁϫⲉ ⲛⲓⲙ ⲉⲧⲕϫⲱ ⲙ̄ⲙⲟⲟⲩ· ⲧⲉⲛⲟⲩ ϭⲉ
5 ⲡⲁⲭⲟⲓ̈ⲥ ⲉⲧⲃⲉ ⲡϣⲁϫⲉ ⲉⲛⲧⲁⲕϫⲟⲟϥ ϫⲉ ⲛⲉⲯⲩⲭⲟⲟⲩⲉ
ⲧⲏⲣⲟⲩ ⲙ̄ⲡⲅⲉⲛⲟⲥ ⲛ̄ⲧⲉ ⲧⲙⲛ̄ⲧⲣⲱⲙⲉ ⲛⲁⲓ̈ ⲉⲧⲛⲁϫⲓ ⲛ̄ⲙ̄-
ⲙⲩⲥⲧⲏⲣⲓⲟⲛ ⲙ̄ⲡⲟⲩⲟⲉⲓⲛ ⲥⲉⲛⲁⲣ̄ϣⲟⲣⲡ̄ ⲉϩⲟⲩⲛ ⲉⲧⲉ[ⲕ]-
ⲕⲗⲏⲣⲟⲛⲟⲙⲓⲁ ⲙ̄ⲡⲟⲩⲟⲉⲓⲛ· ϩⲁⲑⲏ ⲛ̄ⲛⲁⲣⲭⲱⲛ ⲧⲏⲣⲟⲩ ⲉⲧ-
ⲛⲁⲙⲉⲧⲁⲛⲟⲓ̈· ⲁⲩⲱ ⲉⲑⲏ ⲛ̄ⲛⲁⲡⲧⲟⲡⲟⲥ ⲧⲏⲣϥ̄ ⲛ̄ⲛⲁⲟⲩⲉⲓ-
10 ⲛⲁⲙ· ⲁⲩⲱ ⲉⲑⲏ ⲙ̄ⲡⲧⲟⲡⲟⲥ ⲧⲏⲣϥ̄ ⲙ̄ⲡⲉⲑⲏⲥⲁⲩⲣⲟⲥ ⲙ̄-
ⲡⲟⲩⲟⲉⲓⲛ· ⲉⲧⲃⲉ ⲡⲉⲓ̈ϣⲁϫⲉ ⲟⲩⲛ ⲡⲁⲭⲟⲉⲓⲥ ⲉⲛⲧⲁⲕϫⲟⲟϥ
ⲉⲣⲟⲛ ⲙ̄ⲡⲓⲟⲩⲟⲉⲓϣ· ϫⲉ ⲛ̄ϣⲟⲣⲡ̄ ⲛⲁⲣ̄ϩⲁⲉ· ⲁⲩⲱ ⲛ̄ϩⲁⲉ
ⲉⲩⲛⲁⲣ̄ϣⲟⲣⲡ̄· ⲉⲧⲉ ⲛ̄ϩⲁⲉⲉⲩ ⲛⲉ ⲡⲅⲉⲛⲟⲥ ⲧⲏⲣϥ̄ ⲛ̄ⲧⲉ ⲛ̄-
ⲣⲱⲙⲉ ⲉⲧⲛⲁⲣ̄ϣⲟⲣⲡ̄ ⲉϩⲟⲩⲛ ⲉⲧⲙⲛ̄ⲧⲉⲣⲟ ⲙ̄ⲡⲟⲩⲟⲉⲓⲛ·
15 ⲛ̄ⲟⲉ⁺ ⲛ̄ⲛⲁⲡⲧⲟⲡⲟⲥ ⲧⲏⲣⲟⲩ ⲛ̄ⲧⲉ ⲡϫⲓⲥⲉ· ⲉⲧⲉ ⲛ̄ⲧⲟⲟⲩ ⲣ̅ⲡ̅ⲁ̅ b
ⲡⲉ ⲛ̄ϣⲟⲣⲡ̄· ⲉⲧⲃⲉ ⲡⲁⲓ̈ ⲟⲩⲛ ⲡⲁⲭⲟⲉⲓⲥ ⲁⲕϫⲟⲟⲥ ⲛⲁⲛ
ϫⲉ ⲡⲉⲧⲉ ⲟⲩⲛ̄-ⲙⲁⲁϫⲉ ⲙ̄ⲙⲟϥ ⲉⲥⲱⲧⲙ̄ ⲙⲁⲣⲉϥⲥⲱⲧⲙ̄ ⲉⲧⲉ
ⲡⲁⲓ̈ ⲡⲉ ϫⲉ ⲛⲉⲕⲟⲩⲱϣ ⲉⲉⲓⲙⲉ ϫⲉ ⲧⲛ̄ⲕⲁⲧⲁⲗⲁⲙⲃⲁⲛⲉ
ⲛ̄ϣⲁϫⲉ ⲛⲓⲙ ⲉⲧⲕϫⲱ ⲙ̄ⲙⲟⲟⲩ· [21] ⲡⲁⲓ̈ ⲟⲩⲛ ⲡⲁⲭⲟⲓ̈ⲥ
20 ⲡⲉ ⲡϣⲁϫⲉ· ⲁⲥϣⲱⲡⲉ ϭⲉ ⲛ̄ⲧⲉⲣⲉⲥⲟⲩⲱ ⲉⲥϫⲱ ⲛ̄ⲛⲉⲓ̈-

---

3 MS ⲙ̄ⲙⲁⲣⲙ̄ⲡⲟⲩⲟⲉⲓⲛ; read ⲙ̄ⲡⲁⲣⲙ̄ⲡⲟⲩⲟⲉⲓⲛ.
7 MS ⲉⲧⲉⲕⲕⲗⲏⲣⲟⲛⲟⲙⲓⲁ; read ⲉⲧⲉⲕⲗⲏⲣⲟⲛⲟⲙⲓⲁ.
8 MS ⲉⲧⲛⲁⲙⲉⲧⲁⲛⲟⲓ̈; better ⲉⲛⲧⲁⲩⲙⲉⲧⲁⲛⲟⲓ̈.
15 MS ⲡⲟⲥ; read ⲉⲑⲏ.
19 omit 21.
20 MS originally ⲛ̄ⲧⲉⲣⲉ ⲓ̅ⲥ̅ ⲟⲩⲱ ⲉϥϫⲱ.

87. Now it happened when Jesus finished saying these words, Maria Magdalene sprang up and said: "My Lord, my man of light has ears and I *receive* all the words which thou dost speak. Now at this time, my Lord, concerning the word which thou didst speak: 'All *souls* of the *race* of mankind who will receive the *mysteries* of the light will be first within the *inheritance* of the light, before all the *archons* which have *repented*, and before those of the whole *place* of the right, and before the whole *place* of the *Treasury* of the Light — concerning this word *now*, my Lord, thou hast once said to us: 'The first will be last and the last will be first' *. That is, the last are the whole *race* of mankind who will be first within the Kingdom of the Light before [1] those of all the *places* of the height, which are themselves first. Because of this *now*, my Lord, thou hast said to us: 'He who has ears to hear, let him hear': ▫ that is, thou didst wish to know whether we have *grasped* every word which thou hast said. This *now* is the word, my Lord."

Now it happened when she finished speaking these |

---

* cf. Mt. 19.30; 20.16; Mk. 10.31; Lk. 13.30

▫ Mk. 4.9

---

[1] (15) before; MS: in the manner of.

ϢⲀϪⲈ Ⲁ ⲠⲤⲰⲦⲎⲢ Ⲣ̄ϢⲠⲎⲢⲈ ⲈⲘⲀϢⲞ ⲈϨⲢⲀⲒ ⲈϪⲚ̄ ⲚⲀⲠⲞ-
ⲪⲀⲤⲒⲤ Ⲛ̄Ⲛ̄ϢⲀϪⲈ ⲈⲦⲈⲤϪⲰ Ⲙ̄ⲘⲞⲞⲨ ⲈⲂⲞⲖ ϪⲈ ⲚⲈⲀⲤⲢ̄-
Π̄ⲚⲀ ⲦⲎⲢⲤ̄ Ⲛ̄ϨⲒⲖⲒⲔⲢⲒⲚⲈⲤ · ⲀϤⲞⲨⲰϨⲘ ⲞⲚ Ⲛ̄ϬⲒ Ⲓ̄Ⲥ̄ ⲠⲈϪⲀϤ
ⲚⲀⲤ ϪⲈ ⲈⲨⲄⲈ ⲦⲈⲠⲚⲈⲨⲘⲀⲦⲒⲔⲎ Ⲛ̄ϨⲒⲖⲒⲔⲢⲒⲚⲈⲤ ⲘⲀⲢⲒⲀ ⲠⲀⲒ
5 ⲠⲈ ⲠⲂⲰⲖ ⲈⲂⲞⲖ Ⲙ̄ⲠϢⲀϪⲈ ·

Ⲍ̅ ⲀⲤϢⲰⲠⲈ ϬⲈ ⲞⲚ Ⲙ̄Ⲛ̄ⲚⲤⲀ ⲚⲈⲒ̈ϢⲀϪⲈ ⲦⲎⲢⲞⲨ ⲀϤⲞⲨⲰϨ
ⲈⲦⲞⲞⲦϤ̄ Ⲛ̄ϬⲒ Ⲓ̄Ⲥ̄ ϨⲘ̄ ⲠϢⲀϪⲈ ⲠⲈϪⲀϤ Ⲛ̄ⲚⲈϤⲘⲀⲐⲎⲦⲎⲤ ·
ϪⲈ* ⲤⲰⲦⲘ̄ ⲦⲀϢⲀϪⲈ Ⲛ̄ⲘⲘⲎⲦⲚ̄ ⲈⲦⲂⲈ ⲠⲈⲞⲞⲨ Ⲛ̄ⲚⲀⲠϪⲒⲤⲈ ^{ⲣⲠⲈ}
Ⲛ̄ⲐⲈ ⲈⲦⲞⲨϢⲞⲞⲠ Ⲙ̄ⲘⲞⲤ ⲔⲀⲦⲀ ⲐⲈ ⲈⲚⲈⲒ̈ϢⲀϪⲈ Ⲛ̄ⲘⲘⲎⲦⲚ̄
10 ϢⲀ ⲠⲞⲞⲨ · ⲦⲈⲚⲞⲨ ϬⲈ ⲞⲨⲚ ⲈⲒ̈ϢⲀⲚϪⲒⲦⲎⲨⲦⲚ̄ ⲈⲠⲦⲞ-
·ⲠⲞⲤ ⲈϤⲀⲈ Ⲙ̄ⲠⲀⲢⲀⲤⲦⲀⲦⲎⲤ ⲠⲀⲒ̈ ⲈⲦⲔⲰⲦⲈ ⲈⲠⲈⲐⲎⲤⲀⲨⲢⲞⲤ
Ⲙ̄ⲠⲞⲨⲞⲈⲒⲚ· ⲀⲨⲰ ⲈⲒ̈ϢⲀⲚϪⲒⲦⲎⲨⲦⲚ̄ ⲈⲠⲦⲞⲠⲞⲤ Ⲙ̄ϤⲀⲈ Ⲙ̄-
ⲠⲀⲢⲀⲤⲦⲀⲦⲎⲤ ⲈⲦⲘ̄ⲘⲀⲨ Ⲛ̄ⲦⲈⲦⲚ̄ⲚⲀⲨ ⲈⲠⲈⲞⲞⲨ ⲈⲦϤϢⲞⲞⲠ
Ⲛ̄ϨⲎⲦϤ̄ · ⲠⲦⲞⲠⲞⲤ Ⲛ̄ⲦⲈⲔⲖⲎⲢⲞⲚⲞⲘⲒⲀ Ⲙ̄ⲠⲞⲨⲞⲈⲒⲚ ⲚⲀϢⲠ
15 Ⲛ̄ⲚⲀϨⲢⲚ̄ⲦⲎⲚⲞⲨ Ⲛ̄ⲦϬⲞⲦ Ⲛ̄ⲞⲨⲠⲞⲖⲒⲤ Ⲙ̄ⲘⲀⲦⲈ Ⲛ̄ⲦⲈ ⲠⲒⲔⲞⲤ-
ⲘⲞⲤ ⲈⲂⲞⲖ Ⲛ̄ⲦⲘ̄Ⲛ̄ⲦⲚⲞϬ ⲈⲦϤϢⲞⲞⲠ Ⲛ̄ϨⲎⲦⲤ̄ Ⲛ̄ϬⲒ ⲪⲀⲈ Ⲙ̄-
ⲠⲀⲢⲀⲤⲦⲀⲦⲎⲤ ⲀⲨⲰ Ⲙ̄Ⲛ̄ ⲠⲚⲞϬ Ⲛ̄ⲞⲨⲞⲈⲒⲚ ⲈⲦϤϢⲞⲞⲠ Ⲛ̄-
ϨⲎⲦϤ̄ · ⲀⲨⲰ Ⲙ̄Ⲛ̄ⲚⲤⲀ ⲚⲀⲒ̈ ϮⲚⲀϢⲀϪⲈ Ⲛ̄ⲘⲘⲎⲦⲚ̄ ⲞⲚ Ⲙ̄-
ⲠⲈⲞⲞⲨ Ⲙ̄ⲠⲠⲀⲢⲀⲤⲦⲀⲦⲎⲤ · ⲈⲦϨⲒⲠⲤⲀϨⲢⲈ Ⲙ̄ⲠⲔⲞⲨⲒ̈* Ⲙ̄ⲠⲀ- ^{ⲣⲠⲈ b}
20 ⲢⲀⲤⲦⲀⲦⲎⲤ · ⲞⲨⲆⲈ Ⲛ̄ϮⲚⲀϢϢⲀϪⲈ Ⲛ̄ⲘⲘⲎⲦⲚ̄ ⲀⲚ ⲈⲚ-
ⲦⲞⲠⲞⲤ Ⲛ̄ⲚⲀⲒ̈ ⲈⲦϨⲒⲠⲤⲀϨⲢⲈ Ⲛ̄ⲘⲠⲀⲢⲀⲤⲦⲀⲦⲎⲤ ⲦⲎⲢⲞⲨ· Ⲙ̄Ⲛ̄-
ⲦⲨⲠⲞⲤ ⲄⲀⲢ Ⲛ̄ϢⲀϪⲈ ⲈⲢⲞⲞⲨ ϨⲘ̄ ⲠⲈⲒ̈ⲔⲞⲤⲘⲞⲤ Ⲙ̄Ⲛ̄-ⲈⲒⲚⲈ
ⲄⲀⲢ ϨⲘ̄ ⲠⲈⲒ̈ⲔⲞⲤⲘⲞⲤ ⲈϤⲈⲒⲚⲈ Ⲙ̄ⲘⲞⲞⲨ · ϪⲈⲔⲀⲤ ⲈⲤⲒⲈⲦⲚ̄-
ⲦⲰⲚϤ ⲈⲢⲞⲞⲨ · ⲞⲨⲆⲈ Ⲙ̄Ⲛ̄-ϬⲞⲦ · ⲞⲨⲆⲈ Ⲙ̄Ⲛ̄-ⲞⲨⲞⲈⲒⲚ

---

11 MS ⲈϤⲀⲤ; read Ⲙ̄ⲪⲀⲤ.
20 MS Ⲛ̄-ϮⲚⲀϢϢⲀϪⲈ; perhaps better Ⲛ̄-ϮⲚⲀϢⲀϪⲈ.

words, the *Saviour* marvelled greatly at the *answers* to the words which she gave, because she had completely become *pure Spirit*. Jesus answered and said to her : "*Excellent*, thou *pure spiritual* one, Maria. This is the interpretation of the discourse."

88. Now it happened, moreover, after all these words Jesus continued with the discourse. He said to his *disciples* : "Hear that I speak with you concerning the glory of those of the height, how they are, *in the way* in which I have spoken to you up till this day. *Now* at this time, when I shall take you to the *place* of the last *helper* (*parastates*) which surrounds the *Treasury* of the Light, and when I shall take you to the *place* of that last *helper* (*parastates*) and you see the glory in which it is, the *place* of the *inheritance* of the light will count to you only as a *city* of the *world* in size, as the result of the greatness in which the last *helper* exists, and of the great light in which it is. And after these things I will speak with you further of the glory of the *helper* which is above the small *helper*. But I will not speak with you of the *places* of those who are above all the *helpers*, *for* there is no *type* in this *world* to describe them, *for* there is no likeness in this *world* which resembles them, so that I can compare them for you; *nor* size; *nor* light | which is similar to them,

ЄϤ⊼ΝΤΟΝⲦ ЄΡΟΟΥ · ϪЄ ЄⲒЄϢⲀϪЄ ЄΡΟΟΥ · ΟΥΜΟΝΟΝ
⳿Ⲙ ΠЄⲒΚΟСΜΟС · ⲀⲗⲗⲀ ⲀΥⲰ ⳿ΜΝΤΟΥ-ЄⲒΝЄ ΟΝ ⳿Ν ΝⲀ-
ΠϪⲒСЄ ⳿ΝⲦⲀⲒΚⲀⲒΟСΥΝΗ · ϪⲒΝ ΠЄΥΤΟΠΟС ЄΠЄСΗⲦ · ЄⲦ-
ΒЄ ΠⲀⲒ 6Є ЄЄⲒЄ ⳿ΜΝ-ΘЄ ⳿ΝϢⲀϪЄ ЄΡΟΟΥ ⳿Μ ΠЄⲒΚΟСΜΟС ·
5 ЄΒΟⲗ ⳿ΜΠΝΟ6 ⳿ΝЄΟΟΥ ⳿ΝΝⲀΠϪⲒСЄ · ⲀΥⲰ ⳿ΜΝ ΤΝΟ6 ⳿Ν6ΟⲦ
⳿ΝⲀⲦ⳿ϢⲒ ЄΡΟС · ЄⲦΒЄ ΠⲀⲒ ΟΥΝ ⳿ΜΝ-ΘЄ ⳿ΝϢⲀϪЄ ЄΡΟϤ
⳿Μ ΠЄⲒΚΟСΜΟС ·

ⲀСϢⲰΠЄ 6Є ⳿ΝⲦЄΡЄ Ⲓ̄С̄ ΟΥⲰ ЄϤϪⲰ ⳿ΝΝЄⲒϢⲀϪЄ Є-
ΝЄϤΜⲀΘΗⲦΗС · ⲀСЄⲒ ЄΘΗ ⳿Ν6Ⲓ ΜⲀΡⲒⲀ ΜⲀΓⲆⲀⲗΗΝΗ ΠЄ-　　ⲣⲡ̄ε̄
10 ϪⲀС ⳿Ν Ⲓ̄С̄ ϪЄ ΠⲀϪΟЄⲒС · ⳿ΜΠⲢ6ⲰΝⲦ ЄΡΟⲒ ЄⲒϢⲒΝЄ ⳿ΜΜΟΚ
ЄΒΟⲗ ϪЄ ⲀⲒЄΝⲰⲬⲗЄⲒ ΝⲀΚ ⳿ΝΟΥΜΗΗϢЄ ⳿ΝСΟΠ · ⲦЄΝΟΥ
6Є ΠⲀϪΟЄⲒС ⳿ΜΠⲢ6ⲰΝⲦ ЄΡΟⲒ ЄⲒϢⲒΝЄ ⳿ΝСⲀ 2ⲰΒ ΝⲒΜ ⳿Ν
ΟΥⲰⲢⳉ̄ ⳿ΜΝ ΟΥⲀСФⲀⲗⲒⲀ ϪЄ ЄΡЄ ΝⲀСΝΗΥ ΚΗΡΥССЄ
⳿ΜΜΟΟΥ 2Μ ΠΓЄΝΟС ⳿ΝⲦЄ ⲦⲘΝⲦΡⲰΜЄ ⳿ΝСЄСⲰⲦ̄ ⳿ΝСЄ-
15 ΜЄⲦⲀΝΟⲒ ⳿ΝСЄΝΟΥ2Μ ЄΝЄΚΡⲒСⲒС ЄⲦΝⲀϢⲦ ⳿ΝⲦЄ ⳿ΝⲀⲢ-
ⲬⲰΝ ⳿ΜΠΟΝΗΡΟС ⳿ΝСЄΒⲰΚ ЄΠϪⲒСЄ ⳿ΝСЄΚⲗΗΡΟΝΟΜⲒ
⳿ΝⲦⲘΝⲦЄΡΟ ⳿ΜΠΟΥΟЄⲒΝ · ЄΒΟⲗ ΠⲀϪΟЄⲒС ϪЄ ΟΥΜΟΝΟΝ
ⲦΝΟ⳿ ⳿ΝϢⲀΝ2ⲦΗϤ 2ⲀΡΟΝ ⳿ΜΜⲒΝ ⳿ΜΜΟΝ · ⲀⲗⲗⲀ ЄΝΟ⳿ ⳿Ν
ϢⲀΝ2ⲦΗϤ 2Ⲁ ΠΓЄΝΟС ⲦΗⲢϤ ⳿ΝⲦЄ ⲦⲘΝⲦΡⲰΜЄ ϪЄ ЄΥЄ-
20 ΝΟΥ2Μ ЄΝЄΚΡⲒСⲒС ⲦΗΡΟΥ ЄⲦΝⲀϢⲦ · ⲦЄΝΟΥ 6Є ΟΥΝ
ΠⲀϪΟЄⲒС ЄⲦΒЄ ΠⲀⲒ ЄΝϢⲒΝЄ ⳿ΝСⲀ 2ⲰΒ ΝⲒΜ 2Ν ΟΥⲰⲢⳉ̄ ·　ⲣⲡ̄ε̄ᵇ
ϪЄ ЄΡЄ ΝⲀСΝΗΥ ΚΗΡΥССЄ ⳿ΜΜΟΟΥ ⳿ΜΠΓЄΝΟС ⲦΗⲢϤ
⳿ΝⲦЄ ⳿ΝΡⲰΜЄ ϪЄ ⳿ΝΝЄΥЄⲒ ЄⲦΟΟⲦΟΥ ⳿ΝΝⲀⲢⲬⲰΝ ЄⲦΝⲀ-
ϢⲦ ⳿ΝⲦЄ ΠΚⲀΚЄ · ⲀΥⲰ ⳿ΝСЄΝΟΥ2Μ ⳿ΝⲦΟΟⲦΟΥ ⳿ΝⲘΠⲀ-
25 ΡⲀⲗΗΜⲦΗС ЄⲦΝⲀϢⲦ ⳿ΝⲦЄ ΠΚⲀΚЄ ЄⲦ2ⲒΒΟⲗ .

16　MS ⳿Ν̄⳿ΜΠΟΝΗΡΟС; read ⳿ΜΠΟΝΗΡΟС.
18　ϣ in ⳿ΝϢⲀΝ2ⲦΗϤ inserted above.
25　ε in ⳿ΝⲦЄ inserted above.

so that I can describe them. *Not only* in this *world, but* they also have no likeness in those of the height of *right-eousness*, from their *place* downwards. Because of this now, there is no means of speaking of them in this *world*, on account of the great glory of those of the height and the great immeasurable magnitude. Because of this *now* there is no means of speaking of it (the glory) in this *world*."

Now it happened when Jesus finished saying these words to his *disciples*, Maria Magdalene came forward. She said to Jesus: "My Lord, be not angry with me that I question thee because I have *troubled* thee many times. Now at this time, my Lord, be not angry with me that I question all things with assurance and *certainty*, because my brothers *preach* them among the *race* of mankind and they hear and *repent*, and are saved from the harsh *judgements* of the *wicked archons*, and they go to the height and *inherit* the Kingdom of the Light. For we, my Lord, are *not only* compassionate among ourselves, *but* we are compassionate to the whole *race* of mankind, so that they may be saved from all harsh *judgments. Now* at this time, my Lord, because of this we question all things with assurance, for my brothers *preach* them to the whole *race* of men, so that they come not into the hands [1] of the harsh *archons* of the darkness, and are saved from the hands of the harsh *paralemptai* of the outer darkness." |

---

[1] (23) come not into the hands; Schmidt: escape from the hands.

ⲁⲥϣⲱⲡⲉ ⲛ̄ⲧⲉⲣⲉ ⲓ̅ⲥ̅ ⲥⲱⲧ̅ⲙ ⲉⲛⲉïϣⲁϫⲉ ⲉⲥϫⲱ ⲙ̄-
ⲙⲟⲟⲩ ⲛ̄ϭⲓ ⲙⲁⲣⲓⲁ· ⲁϥⲟⲩⲱ̅ϩ̅ⲙ ⲛ̄ϭⲓ ⲡⲥⲱⲧⲏⲣ ⲉϥϣⲟⲟⲡ
ϩⲛ ⲟⲩⲛⲟϭ ⲛ̄ⲛⲁ’ ⲉϩⲟⲩⲛ ⲉⲣⲟⲥ· ⲡⲉϫⲁϥ ⲛⲁⲥ ϫⲉ ϣⲓⲛⲉ
ⲛ̄ⲥⲁ ⲡⲉⲧⲉⲟⲩⲉϣϣⲓⲛⲉ ⲛ̄ⲥⲱϥ· ⲁⲩⲱ ⲁⲛⲟⲕ ϯⲛⲁϭⲟⲗⲡ̅ϥ̅
5 ⲛⲉ ⲉⲃⲟⲗ ϩⲛ ⲟⲩⲱⲣ̅ⲭ̅ ⲙ̄ⲛ ⲟⲩⲁⲥⲫⲁⲗⲓⲁ ⲁϫ̅ⲛ̄ ⲡⲁⲣⲁⲃⲟⲗⲏ·
ⲁⲥϣⲱⲡⲉ ϭⲉ ⲛ̄ⲧⲉⲣⲉ ⲙⲁⲣⲓⲁ ⲥⲱⲧ̅ⲙ ⲉⲛⲉïϣⲁϫⲉ ⲉϥϫⲱ
ⲙ̄ⲙⲟⲟⲩ ⲛ̄ϭⲓ ⲡⲥⲱⲧⲏⲣ· ⲁⲥⲣⲁϣⲉ ϩ̅ⲛ ⲟⲩⲛⲟϭ ⲛ̄ⲣⲁϣⲉ·
ⲁⲩⲱ ⲁⲥⲧⲉⲗⲏⲗ ⲉⲙⲁϣⲟ ⲡⲉϫⲁⲥ ⲛ̄ⲓ̅ⲥ̅ ϫⲉ ⲡⲁϫⲟⲉⲓⲥ· ⲉⲉⲓⲉ
ⲡⲙⲉϩⲥⲛⲁⲩ ⲙ̄ⲡⲁⲣⲁⲥⲧⲁⲧⲏⲥ ⲛⲁⲁⲁϥ ⲉⲡϣⲟⲣⲡ ⲙ̄ⲡⲁⲣⲁⲥⲧⲁ-   ⲣⲡ̅ⲍ̅
10 ⲧⲏⲥ ⲛ̄ⲛⲁⲟⲩⲏⲣ ⲛ̄ϭⲟⲧ· ⲁⲩⲱ ϥⲟⲩⲏⲩ ⲙ̄ⲙⲟϥ ⲛ̄ⲛⲁⲟⲩⲏⲣ
ⲛ̄ⲟⲩⲉ· ⲏ̅ ⲙ̄ⲙⲟⲛ ⲛ̄ⲧⲟϥ ϥⲟ’ ⲛ̄ⲟⲩⲟïⲛ ⲛ̄ϩⲟⲩⲟ ⲉⲣⲟϥ ⲛ̄-
ⲛⲁⲟⲩⲏⲣ ⲛ̄ⲕⲱⲃ ⲛ̄ⲥⲟⲡ· ⲁϥⲟⲩⲱ̅ϩ̅ⲙ ⲛ̄ϭⲓ ⲓ̅ⲥ̅ ⲡⲉϫⲁϥ ⲙ̄ⲙⲁ-
ⲣⲓⲁ ϩ̅ⲛ ⲧⲙⲏⲧⲉ ⲛ̄ⲙ̄ⲙⲁⲑⲏⲧⲏⲥ ϫⲉ ϩⲁⲙⲏⲛ ϩⲁⲙⲏⲛ ϯ ·ϫⲱ
ⲙ̄ⲙⲟⲥ ⲛⲏⲧ̅ⲛ· ϫⲉ ⲡⲙⲉϩⲥⲛⲁⲩ ⲙ̄ⲡⲁⲣⲁⲥⲧⲁⲧⲏⲥ ⲟⲩⲏⲩ ⲙ̄-
15 ⲡϣⲟⲣⲡ ⲙ̄ⲡⲁⲣⲁⲥⲧⲁⲧⲏⲥ ϩ̅ⲛ ⲟⲩⲛⲟϭ ⲛ̄ⲟⲩⲉ ⲉⲙ̅ⲛ̄-ϣⲓ ⲉⲣⲟϥ·
ⲉⲡϫⲓⲥⲉ ⲉⲡⲥⲁϩⲣⲉ· ⲁⲩⲱ ⲉⲡ2ⲃⲃⲉ· ⲉⲡⲃⲁⲑⲟⲥ ⲁⲩⲱ ⲉⲧⲉ-
ϣⲓⲏ· ⲙ̄ⲛ ⲧⲟⲩⲗⲁϣⲥⲉ· ⲉϥⲟⲩⲏⲩ ⲅⲁⲣ ⲙ̄ⲙⲟϥ ⲉⲙⲁϣⲟ ϩ̅ⲛ
ⲟⲩⲛⲟϭ ⲛ̄ⲟⲩⲉ ⲉⲙ̅ⲛ̄-ϣⲓ ⲉⲣⲟϥ ϩⲓⲧ̅ⲛ̄ ⲛ̄ⲁⲅⲅⲉⲗⲟⲥ· ⲙ̄ⲛ
ⲛ̄ⲁⲣⲭⲁⲅⲅⲉⲗⲟⲥ ⲁⲩⲱ ϩⲓⲧ̅ⲛ̄ ⲛ̄ⲛⲟⲩⲧⲉ ⲙ̄ⲛ ⲛ̄ⲁ2ⲟⲣⲁⲧⲟⲥ
20 ⲧⲏⲣⲟⲩ· ⲁⲩⲱ ⲛⲁⲁⲁϥ ⲉⲣⲟϥ ⲉⲙⲁϣⲟ ⲉⲙⲁϣⲟ ϩ̅ⲛ ⲟⲩϣⲓ   ⲣⲡ̅ⲍ̅ᵇ
ⲉⲙ̅ⲛ̄-ⲏⲡⲉ ⲉⲣⲟϥ ϩⲓⲧ̅ⲛ̄ ⲛ̄[ⲛ̄]ⲁⲅⲅⲉⲗⲟⲥ· ⲙ̄ⲛ ⲛ̄ⲁⲣⲭⲁⲅⲅⲉⲗⲟⲥ·
ⲁⲩⲱ ϩⲓⲧ̅ⲛ̄ ⲛⲟⲩⲧⲉ ⲙ̄ⲛ ⲛ̄ⲁ2ⲟⲣⲁⲧⲟⲥ ⲧⲏⲣⲟⲩ· ⲁⲩⲱ ϥⲟ’
ⲛ̄ⲟⲩⲟⲉⲓⲛ ⲛ̄ϩⲟⲩⲟ ⲉⲣⲟϥ· ϩ̅ⲛ ⲟⲩϣⲓ ⲉⲙ̅ⲛ̄-ϣⲓ ⲉⲣⲟϥ ⲉⲙⲁϣⲟ ⲉⲙⲁϣⲟ ⲉⲙ̅ⲛ̄-ϣⲓ ⲉⲡⲟⲩⲟⲉⲓⲛ ⲉⲧϥϣⲟⲟⲡ ⲛ̄ϩⲏⲧϥ ⲉⲙ̅ⲛ̄-

---

5   ⲡⲁⲣⲏⲥⲓⲁ , Greek word for ⲱⲣ̅ⲭ̅, inserted in margin.
21 MS ⲛ̄ⲛ̄ⲁⲅⲅⲉⲗⲟⲥ; read ⲛ̄ⲁⲅⲅⲉⲗⲟⲥ.
22 MS ⲛⲟⲩⲧⲉ; read ⲛ̄ⲛⲟⲩⲧⲉ.

It happened when Jesus heard these words which Maria spoke, he, the *Saviour*, answered, having great compassion towards her. He said to her: "Question that which thou dost wish to question, and I will reveal it with assurance and *certainty*, without *parable*."

89. Now it happened when Maria heard these words which the Saviour spoke, she rejoiced with great joy and she was very glad. She said to Jesus: "My Lord, by what magnitude is the second *helper* (*parastates*) greater than the first *helper*, and by what distance is it distant from it, *or rather, how many times more light is it?*"

Jesus answered and said to Maria in the midst of the *disciples*: "*Truly, truly*, I say to you, the second *helper* is distant from the first *helper* by a great distance, for which there is no measure to the height above, and to the *depth* below, and to the length and to the breadth. *For* it is very distant from it by a great distance to which there is no measure by means of [1] the *angels* and the *archangels*, and by means of the gods and all the *invisible ones*. And its magnitude exceeds it by an exceedingly great amount to which there is no measure by means of the *angels* and the *archangels*, and by means of the gods and all the *invisible ones*. And its light exceeds it by an exceedingly great amount to which there is no measure, there being no measure to the light in which it is, and no | measure to it by means of

---

[1] (17, 18) a great distance to which there is no measure by means of; Schmidt: a great immeasurable distance through (see 202.20, 21; 203.1, 7).

ϣι ⲉⲣⲟϥ ϩⲓⲧⲛ̅ ⲛ̅ⲁⲅⲅⲉⲗⲟⲥ ⲙⲛ̅ ⲛ̅ⲁⲣⲭⲁⲅⲅⲉⲗⲟⲥ· ⲁⲩⲱ ϩⲓⲧⲛ̅
ⲛ̅ⲛⲟⲩⲧⲉ· ⲙⲛ̅ ⲛ̅ⲁϩⲟⲣⲁⲧⲟⲥ ⲧⲏⲣⲟⲩ· ⲕⲁⲧⲁ ⲑⲉ ⲉⲛⲧⲁⲓ̈-
ⲟⲩⲱ ⲉⲓ̈ϫⲱ ⲙ̅ⲙⲟⲥ ⲛⲏⲧⲛ̅ ⲛ̅ⲕⲉⲥⲟⲡ· ϩⲟⲙⲟⲓⲱⲥ ⲟⲛ ⲡⲙⲉϩ-
ϣⲟⲙⲛ̅ⲧ ⲙ̅ⲡⲁⲣⲁⲥⲧⲁⲧⲏⲥ ⲙⲛ̅ ⲡⲙⲉϩϥⲧⲟⲟⲩ· ⲙⲛ̅ ⲡⲙⲉϩ-
5 ϯⲟⲩ· ⲉⲩⲛ̅ ⲟⲩⲁ ⲟ' ⲛ̅ⲛⲟϭ ⲉⲟⲩⲁ ⲧⲙ̅ⲡⲥⲟⲡ· ⲁⲩⲱ ϥⲟ'
ⲛ̅ⲟⲩⲟⲉⲓⲛ ⲛ̅ϩⲟⲩⲟ ⲉⲣⲟϥ· ⲁⲩⲱ ϥⲏⲩ ⲙ̅ⲙⲟϥ· ϩⲛ̅ ⲟⲩⲛⲟϭ
ⲛ̅ⲟⲩⲉ ⲉⲙⲛ̅-ϣⲓ ⲉⲣⲟϥ ϩⲓⲧⲛ̅ ⲛ̅ⲁⲅⲅⲉⲗⲟⲥ ⲙⲛ̅ ⲛ̅ⲁⲣⲭⲁⲅⲅⲉ-
ⲗⲟⲥ ⲙⲛ̅ ⲛ̅ⲛⲟⲩⲧⲉ ⲙⲛ̅ ⲛ̅ⲁϩⲟⲣⲁⲧⲟⲥ ⲧⲏⲣⲟⲩ· ⲕⲁⲧⲁ ⲑⲉ
ⲉⲛⲧⲁⲓ̈ⲟⲩⲱ ⲉⲓ̈ϫⲱ ⲙ̅ⲙⲟⲥ ⲛⲏⲧⲛ̅ ⲛ̅ⲕⲉⲥⲟⲡ· ⲁⲩⲱ ⲟⲛ ⲣ̅ⲡ̅ⲏ̅
10 ϯⲛⲁϫⲱ ⲉⲣⲱⲧⲛ̅ ⲙ̅ⲡⲧⲩⲡⲟⲥ ⲙ̅ⲡⲟⲩⲁ ⲡⲟⲩⲁ ϩⲙ̅ ⲡⲉⲩⲥⲱⲣ
ⲉⲃⲟⲗ·

ⲁⲥϣⲱⲡⲉ ϭⲉ ⲛ̅ⲧⲉⲣⲉ ⲓ̅ⲥ̅ ⲟⲩⲱ ⲉϥϫⲱ ⲛ̅ⲛⲉⲓ̈ϣⲁϫⲉ ⲉ-
ⲛⲉϥⲙⲁⲑⲏⲧⲏⲥ· ⲁⲥⲉⲓ ⲟⲛ ⲉⲑⲏ ⲛ̅ϭⲓ ⲙⲁⲣⲓⲁ ⲧⲙⲁⲅⲇⲁⲗⲏⲛⲏ
ⲁⲥⲟⲩⲱϩ ⲉⲧⲟⲟⲧⲥ̅ ⲡⲉϫⲁⲥ ⲛ̅ⲓ̅ⲥ̅ ϫⲉ ⲡⲁϫⲟⲉⲓⲥ· ⲉⲉⲓⲉ ⲛⲉⲣ-
15 ϫⲓ ⲙ̅ⲡⲙⲩⲥⲧⲏⲣⲓⲟⲛ ⲙ̅ⲡⲟⲩⲟⲉⲓⲛ ⲉⲩⲛⲁϣⲱⲡⲉ ϩⲛ̅ ⲁϣ ⲛ̅-
ⲧⲩⲡⲟⲥ ϩⲛ̅ ⲧⲙⲏⲧⲉ ⲙ̅ⲫⲁⲉ ⲙ̅ⲡⲁⲣⲁⲥⲧⲁⲧⲏⲥ· ⲁϥⲟⲩⲱϩⲙ̅
ⲇⲉ ⲛ̅ϭⲓ ⲓ̅ⲥ̅ ⲡⲉϫⲁϥ ⲙ̅ⲙⲁⲣⲓⲁ ϩⲛ̅ ⲧⲙⲏⲧⲉ ⲛ̅ⲙⲙⲁⲑⲏⲧⲏⲥ· ϫⲉ
ⲛⲉⲛⲧⲁⲩϫⲓ ⲛ̅ⲙⲙⲩⲥⲧⲏⲣⲓⲟⲛ ⲛ̅ⲧⲉ ⲡⲟⲩⲟⲉⲓⲛ ⲉⲩϣⲁⲛⲉⲓ'
ⲉⲃⲟⲗ ϩⲙ̅ ⲡⲥⲱⲙⲁ ⲛ̅ⲟⲩⲗⲏ ⲛ̅ⲧⲉ ⲛ̅ⲁⲣⲭⲱⲛ· ⲡⲟⲩⲁ ⲡⲟⲩⲁ
20 ⲕⲁⲧⲁ ⲡⲙⲩⲥⲧⲏⲣⲓⲟⲛ ⲉⲛⲧⲁϥϫⲓⲧϥ̅· ⲉϥⲛⲁϣⲱⲡⲉ ϩⲛ̅ ⲧⲉϥ-
ⲧⲁⲝⲓⲥ· ⲛⲉⲣⲭⲓ-ⲛ̅ⲙⲩⲥⲧⲏⲣⲓⲟⲛ ϩⲱϣϥ ⲉⲧϫⲟⲥⲉ ⲥⲉⲛⲁϭⲱ
ϩⲛ̅ ⲧⲧⲁⲝⲓⲥ ⲉⲧϫⲟⲥⲉ· ⲛⲉⲣⲭⲓ ϩⲱⲟⲩ ⲛ̅ⲙⲙⲩⲥⲧⲏⲣⲓⲟⲛ ⲉⲧ-
ϭⲟϫⲃ̅· ⲥⲉⲛⲁϣⲱⲡⲉ ϩⲛ̅ ⲛ̅ⲧⲁⲝⲓⲥ ⲉⲧϭⲟϫⲃ̅· ϩⲁⲡⲁⲝ ϩⲁ-

---

6 MS ϥⲏⲩ; read ϥⲟⲩⲏⲩ.
19 ⲡ in ⲡⲥⲱⲙⲁ inserted above.
21 MS ⲛ̅ⲙⲩⲥⲧⲏⲣⲓⲟⲛ; read ⲙ̅ⲙⲩⲥⲧⲏⲣⲓⲟⲛ.
22 MS ⲧⲧⲁⲝⲓⲥ; better ⲛ̅ⲧⲁⲝⲓⲥ.

the *angels* and the *archangels*, and by means of the gods
and all the *invisible ones, as* I have already said to you at
another time. *Likewise* also the third, fourth and fifth *helper,*
one is innumerable times greater than the other; and its
light exceeds it and it is distant from it by a great distance,
to which there is no measure by means of the *angels* and
the *archangels* and the gods and all the *invisible ones, as*
I have already said to you at another time. And furthermore
I will say to you the *type* of each one in its distribution."

90. Now it happened when Jesus finished saying these
words to his *disciples*, Maria Magdalene came forward, she
continued and said to Jesus: "My Lord, in what *type* will
those who receive the *mystery* of the light exist in the midst
of the last *helper (parastates)*?"

Jesus *however* answered and said to Maria in the midst
of the *disciples*: "Those who have received the *mysteries*
of the light, when they come forth from the *body* of the
matter of the *archons*, each one will be in his *rank according
to* the *mystery* which he has received. Those who have
received the higher *mysteries* will remain in the higher *ranks*;
on the other hand, those who have received the lower
mysteries will be in the lower *ranks. In a word,* | in the

ΠΑϢⲤ ⲠⲦⲞⲠⲞⲤ Ⲛ̅ⲦⲀ ⲠⲞⲨⲀ ⲠⲞⲨⲀ ⲬⲒ-ⲘⲨⲤⲦⲎⲢⲒⲞⲚ ϢⲀ- Ⲣ̅ⲠⲎ̅^b
ⲢⲞϤ ϤⲚⲀϬⲰ Ⲍ̅Ⲛ ⲦⲈϤⲦⲀⲌⲒⲤ Ⲍ̅ⲢⲀⲓ̈ Ⲍ̅Ⲛ ⲦⲈⲔⲖⲎⲢⲞⲚⲞⲘⲒⲀ Ⲙ̅-
ⲠⲞⲨⲞⲈⲒⲚ· ⲈⲦⲂⲈ ⲠⲀⲓ̈ ϬⲈ Ⲁⲓ̈ⲬⲞⲞⲤ ⲈⲢⲰⲦ̅Ⲛ Ⲙ̅ⲠⲞⲨⲞⲈⲒϢ
ⲬⲈ ⲠⲘⲀ ⲈⲦϤ̅ⲘⲘⲀⲨ Ⲛ̅ϬⲒ ⲠⲈⲦ̅ⲚⲎⲦ· ⲈϤⲚⲀϢⲰⲠⲈ Ⲙ̅ⲘⲀⲨ
5 Ⲛ̅ϬⲒ ⲠⲈⲦⲚⲀⲌⲞ· ⲈⲦⲈ ⲠⲀⲓ̈ ⲠⲈ ⲬⲈ ⲠⲘⲀ Ⲛ̅ⲦⲀ ⲠⲞⲨⲀ ⲠⲞⲨⲀ
ⲬⲒ-ⲘⲨⲤⲦⲎⲢⲒⲞⲚ ϢⲀⲢⲞϤ· ⲈϤⲚⲀϢⲰⲠⲈ Ⲙ̅ⲘⲀⲨ·

Ⲍ ⲀⲤϢⲰⲠⲈ Ⲛ̅ⲦⲈⲢⲈ Ⲓ̅Ⲥ̅ ⲞⲨⲰ ⲈϤⲬⲰ Ⲛ̅ⲚⲈⲒϢⲀⲬⲈ Ⲉ-
ⲚⲈϤⲘⲀⲐⲎⲦⲎⲤ ⲀϤⲈⲒ̇ ⲈⲞⲚ Ⲛ̅ϬⲒ Ⲓ̈ⲰⲌⲀⲚ⟨ⲚⲎⲤ⟩, ⲠⲈⲬⲀϤ Ⲛ̅Ⲓ̅Ⲥ̅
ⲬⲈ ⲠⲀⲬⲞⲈⲒⲤ ⲀⲨⲰ ⲠⲀⲤⲰⲦⲎⲢ· ⲔⲈⲖⲈⲨⲈ ⲌⲰ ⲚⲀⲓ̈ ⲦⲀ-
10 ϢⲀⲬⲈ Ⲙ̅ⲠⲈⲔⲘ̅ⲦⲞ ⲈⲂⲞⲖ· ⲀⲨⲰ Ⲙ̅ⲠⲢ̅ϬⲰⲚⲦ̅ ⲈⲢⲞⲓ̈ Ⲉⲓ̈ϢⲒⲚⲈ
Ⲛ̅ⲤⲀ ⲌⲰⲂ ⲚⲒⲘ Ⲍ̅Ⲛ ⲞⲨⲰⲢⲬ̅· Ⲙ̅Ⲛ ⲞⲨⲀⲤⲪⲀⲖⲒⲀ· ⲈⲂⲞⲖ ⲬⲈ
ⲠⲀⲬⲞⲈⲒⲤ Ⲍ̅Ⲛ ⲞⲨⲈⲢⲎⲦ· ⲀⲔⲈⲢⲎⲦ ⲚⲀⲓ̈ ⲈϬϢⲀⲠ̅ ⲚⲀⲚ ⲈⲂⲞⲖ
ⲈⲦⲂⲈ ⲌⲰⲂ ⲚⲒⲘ Ⲉ†ⲚⲀϢⲚ̅ⲦⲔ ⲈⲢⲞⲞⲨ· ⲦⲈⲚⲞⲨ ϬⲈ ⲠⲀ-
ⲬⲞⲈⲒⲤ Ⲙ̅ⲠⲢ̅ⲌⲈⲠ-ⲖⲀⲀⲨ ⲈⲢⲞⲚ ⲈⲠⲦⲎⲢϤ̅ Ⲍ̅Ⲙ ⲠⲌⲰⲂ ⲈⲦⲚⲚⲀ- Ⲣ̅ⲠⲞ
15 ϢⲚ̅ⲦⲔ ⲈⲢⲞϤ·

Ⲍ ⲀϤⲞⲨⲰϢ̅Ⲙ ⲀⲈ Ⲛ̅ϬⲒ Ⲓ̅Ⲥ̅ Ⲍ̅Ⲛ ⲞⲨⲚⲞϬ Ⲛ̅ⲚⲀ' ⲠⲈⲬⲀϤ Ⲛ̅-
Ⲓ̈ⲰⲌⲀⲚⲚⲎⲤ ⲬⲈ Ⲛ̅ⲦⲞⲔ ⲌⲰⲰⲔ ⲠⲘⲀⲔⲀⲢⲒⲞⲤ Ⲛ̅Ⲓ̈ⲰⲌⲀⲚⲚⲎⲤ
ⲀⲨⲰ ⲠⲘⲈⲢⲒⲦ †ⲔⲈⲖⲈⲨⲈ ⲚⲀⲔ ⲈⲦⲢⲈⲔⲬⲰ Ⲙ̅ⲠϢⲀⲬⲈ ⲈⲦⲈ-
ⲌⲚⲀⲔ ⲀⲨⲰ †ⲚⲀϬⲞⲖⲠ̅Ϥ ⲚⲀⲔ ⲈⲂⲞⲖ Ⲛ̅ⲌⲞ ⲞⲨⲂⲈ ⲌⲞ ⲀⲬⲚ̅
20 ⲠⲀⲢⲀⲂⲞⲖⲎ· ⲀⲨⲰ †ⲚⲀⲬⲰ ⲈⲢⲞⲔ Ⲛ̅ⲌⲰⲂ ⲚⲒⲘ ⲈⲦⲔ̅ⲚⲀ-
ϢⲒⲚⲈ Ⲛ̅ⲤⲰⲞⲨ Ⲍ̅Ⲛ ⲞⲨⲰⲢⲬ̅ Ⲙ̅Ⲛ ⲞⲨⲀⲤⲪⲀⲖⲒⲀ· ⲀϤⲞⲨⲰϢ̅Ⲙ
Ⲛ̅ϬⲒ Ⲓ̈ⲰⲌⲀⲚⲚⲎⲤ ⲠⲈⲬⲀϤ Ⲛ̅Ⲓ̅Ⲥ̅ ⲬⲈ ⲠⲀⲬⲞⲈⲒⲤ· ⲈⲈⲒⲈ ⲠⲦⲞ-
ⲠⲞⲤ ⲈⲚⲦⲀ ⲠⲞⲨⲀ ⲠⲞⲨⲀ ⲬⲒ-ⲘⲨⲤⲦⲎⲢⲒⲞⲚ ϢⲀⲢⲞϤ ⲈϤⲚⲀ-
ϬⲰ Ⲛ̅ⲌⲎⲦϤ̅ ⲀⲨⲰ Ⲙ̅Ⲛ̅Ϥ-ⲈⲌ̅ⲞⲨⲤⲒⲀ Ⲙ̅ⲘⲀⲨ ⲈⲦⲢⲈϤⲂⲰⲔ ⲈⲌ̅Ⲛ-

---

8   MS Ⲓ̈ⲰⲌⲀⲚ; ⲚⲎⲤ on next line omitted.
14   Ⲍ̅Ⲙ dittography.

inheritance of the light each one will remain in the *rank* of the *place* as far as which he received *mysteries*. Concerning this I said to you once : 'The place where your heart is, there will your treasure be' *. That is, the *place* as far as which each one has received *mysteries* is where he will be."

It happened when Jesus finished saying these words to his *disciples*, John came forward, he said to Jesus : "My Lord and my *Saviour*, *command* me also that I speak in thy presence. And be not angry with me that I question thee on all things with assurance and *certainty*. Because, my Lord, with a promise thou hast promised me to reveal to us concerning all things which I shall ask thee. Now at this time, my Lord, do not conceal anything at all from us in the matters on which we will question thee."

But Jesus answered with great compassion, he said to John : "Thou also, thou *blessed* one, John, and thou beloved one, I *command* thee to speak the word which thou dost wish, and I will reveal it to thee, face to face, without *parable*, and I will say to thee everything on which thou dost question me with assurance and *certainty*."

John answered and said to Jesus : "My Lord, will each one remain in the *place* as far as which he has received *mysteries*? And has he no *authority* to go to | other *ranks*

---

*   cf. Mt. 6.21; Lk. 12.34

ⲔⲈⲦⲀⲌⲒⲤ ⲈⲦⲠⲈⲨⲤⲀ2ⲢⲈ · ⲞⲨⲆⲈ ⲘⲚⲦⲨ-ⲈⲌⲞⲨⲤⲒⲀ ⲘⲘⲀⲨ
ⲈⲦⲢⲈⲨⲈⲒ' ⲈⲚⲦⲀⲌⲒⲤ ⲈⲦⲠⲈⲨⲈⲤⲎⲦ · ⲀⲨⲞⲨⲰ2Ⲙ Ⲛ6Ⲓ ⲒⲤ ⲠⲈ-
ⲬⲀⲨ Ⲛ̄ⲒⲰ2ⲀⲚⲚⲎⲤ ⲬⲈ ⲔⲀⲖⲰⲤ ⲘⲈⲚⲦⲞⲒⲅⲈ [ⲬⲈ] ⲦⲈⲦⲚ̄-
ⲰⲒⲚⲈ Ⲛ̄ⲤⲀ 2ⲰⲂ ⲚⲒⲘ 2Ⲛ̄ ⲞⲨⲰⲢⲬ̄ ⲘⲚ̄ ⲞⲨⲀⲤⲪⲀⲖⲒⲀ · * ⲀⲖⲖⲀ ⲢⲠⲞ̄ ᵇ

5 ⲦⲈⲚⲞⲨ 6Ⲉ Ⲓ̈Ⲱ2ⲀⲚⲚⲎⲤ ⲤⲰⲦ̄Ⲙ ⲦⲀⲰⲀⲬⲈ Ⲛ̄ⲘⲘⲀⲔ · ⲞⲨⲞⲚ
ⲚⲒⲘ ⲈⲢⲬⲒ-ⲘⲨⲤⲦⲎⲢⲒⲞⲚ Ⲛ̄ⲦⲈ ⲠⲞⲨⲞⲈⲒⲚ ⲠⲦⲞⲠⲞⲤ ⲈⲚⲦⲀ
ⲠⲞⲨⲀ ⲠⲞⲨⲀ ⲬⲒ-ⲘⲨⲤⲦⲎⲢⲒⲞⲚ ⲰⲀⲢⲞⲨ ⲈⲨⲚⲀ6Ⲱ Ⲛ̄2ⲎⲦ̄Ⲩ ·
ⲀⲨⲰ ⲘⲚ̄ⲦⲀⲨ ⲘⲘⲀⲨ Ⲛ̄ⲦⲈⲌⲞⲨⲤⲒⲀ ⲈⲦⲢⲈⲨⲈⲒ' ⲈⲠⲬⲒⲤⲈ ⲈⲚ-
ⲦⲀⲌⲒⲤ ⲈⲦⲠⲈⲨⲤⲀ2ⲢⲈ · 2ⲰⲤⲦⲈ ⲚⲈⲢⲬⲒ-ⲘⲨⲤⲦⲎⲢⲒⲞⲚ 2Ⲙ̄

10 ⲠⲰⲞⲢ̄Ⲡ Ⲛ̄ⲦⲰⲰ ⲞⲨⲚ̄ⲦⲀⲨ ⲘⲘⲀⲨ Ⲛ̄ⲦⲈⲌⲞⲨⲤⲒⲀ ⲈⲦⲢⲈⲨⲈⲒ'
ⲈⲚⲦⲀⲌⲒⲤ ⲈⲦⲠⲈⲨⲈⲤⲎⲦ · ⲈⲦⲈ Ⲛ̄ⲦⲞⲞⲨ ⲚⲈ Ⲛ̄ⲦⲀⲌⲒⲤ ⲦⲎⲢⲞⲨ
Ⲙ̄ⲠⲘⲈ2ⲰⲞⲘⲚ̄Ⲧ Ⲛ̄ⲬⲰⲢⲎⲘⲀ ⲀⲖⲖⲀ ⲘⲚ̄ⲦⲀⲨ ⲘⲘⲀⲨ Ⲛ̄Ⲧ-
ⲈⲌⲞⲨⲤⲒⲀ ⲈⲦⲢⲈⲨⲈⲒ' ⲈⲠⲬⲒⲤⲈ ⲈⲚⲦⲀⲌⲒⲤ ⲈⲦⲠⲈⲨⲤⲀ2ⲢⲈ · ⲀⲨⲰ
ⲠⲈⲦⲚⲀⲬⲒ Ⲛ̄ⲘⲘⲨⲤⲦⲎⲢⲒⲞⲚ Ⲙ̄ⲠⲒⲰⲞⲢ̄Ⲡ ⲘⲘⲨⲤⲦⲎⲢⲒⲞⲚ ⲈⲦⲈ

15 Ⲛ̄ⲦⲞⲨ ⲠⲈ ⲠⲘⲈ2ⲬⲞⲨⲦⲀⲨⲦⲈ ⲘⲘⲨⲤⲦⲎⲢⲒⲞⲚ ⲈⲂⲞⲖ ⲀⲨⲰ
Ⲛ̄ⲦⲞⲨ ⲠⲈ ⲦⲔⲈⲪⲀⲖⲎ Ⲙ̄ⲠⲱⲞⲢ̄Ⲡ Ⲛ̄ⲬⲰⲢⲎⲘⲀ ⲈⲦ2ⲒⲠⲤⲀⲂⲂⲞⲖ ·
ⲀⲨⲰ ⲞⲨⲚ̄ⲦⲀⲨ Ⲛ̄ⲦⲈⲌⲞⲨⲤⲒⲀ ⲈⲦⲢⲈⲨⲈⲒ' ⲈⲚⲦⲀⲌⲒⲤ ⲦⲎⲢⲞⲨ
ⲈⲦⲠⲈⲨⲂⲞⲖ · ⲀⲖⲖⲀ ⲘⲚ̄ⲦⲀⲨ ⲘⲘⲀⲨ Ⲛ̄ⲦⲈⲌⲞⲨⲤⲒⲀ ⲈⲦⲢⲈⲨⲈⲒ'
ⲈⲚⲦⲞⲠⲞⲤ ⲈⲦⲠⲈⲨⲤⲀ2ⲢⲈ · Ⲏ̇ ⲈⲦⲢⲈⲨⲘⲞⲨⲰ̂Ⲧ ⲘⲘⲞⲞⲨ · ⲀⲨⲰ Ⲣ̄Ⲩ

20 ⲚⲈⲢⲬⲒ-ⲘⲨⲤⲦⲎⲢⲒⲞⲚ 2Ⲛ̄ Ⲛ̄ⲦⲀⲌⲒⲤ Ⲙ̄ⲠⲒⲬⲞⲨⲦⲀⲨⲦⲈ ⲘⲘⲨⲤ-
ⲦⲎⲢⲒⲞⲚ ⲠⲦⲞⲠⲞⲤ Ⲛ̄ⲦⲀ ⲠⲞⲨⲀ ⲠⲞⲨⲀ ⲬⲒ-ⲘⲨⲤⲦⲎⲢⲒⲞⲚ Ⲛ̄-
2ⲎⲦ̄Ⲩ · ⲈⲨⲚⲀⲂⲰⲔ ⲰⲀⲢⲞⲨ · ⲀⲨⲰ ⲨⲚⲀⲰⲰⲠⲈ ⲈⲨⲚ̄ⲦⲀⲨ Ⲙ̄-
ⲘⲀⲨ Ⲛ̄ⲦⲈⲌⲞⲨⲤⲒⲀ ⲈⲦⲢⲈⲨⲘⲞⲨⲰ̂Ⲧ Ⲛ̄Ⲛ̄ⲦⲀⲌⲒⲤ ⲦⲎⲢⲞⲨ ⲘⲚ̄
ⲚⲈⲬⲰⲢⲎⲘⲀ ⲈⲦⲠⲈⲨⲂⲞⲖ · ⲀⲖⲖⲀ ⲘⲚ̄ⲦⲀⲨ ⲘⲘⲀⲨ Ⲛ̄ⲦⲈⲌⲞⲨ-

25 ⲤⲒⲀ ⲈⲦⲢⲈⲨⲂⲰⲔ ⲈⲚⲦⲀⲌⲒⲤ ⲈⲦⲠⲈⲨⲤⲀ2ⲢⲈ Ⲏ̇ ⲈⲦⲢⲈⲨⲘⲞⲨⲰ̂Ⲧ

---

3 omit ⲬⲈ.
9 MS ⲚⲈⲢⲬⲒ ... ⲞⲨⲚ̄ⲦⲀⲨ; better ⲠⲈⲢⲬⲒ ... ⲞⲨⲚ̄ⲦⲀⲨ.

which are above him? *Or* has he no authority to go to the *ranks* which are below him?

91. Jesus answered and said to John : "*In truth* it is *well* that you question [1] all things with assurance and *certainty, but* now John, hear that I speak with thee. Everyone that receives the *mysteries* of the light will remain in the *place* as far as which he has received *mysteries*. And he does not have the *authority* to come to the height to the *ranks* which are above him, *so that* he who receives *mysteries* in the first ordinance has the *authority* to come to the *ranks* below him, which are all the *ranks* of the third *space, but* he does not have the *authority* to come to the height to the *ranks* which are above him. And he who will receive the *mysteries* of the First *Mystery* which is the 24th *mystery* from without and is the *head* of the first *space* on the outside, he has the *authority* to come to all the *ranks* outside him, *but* he has not the *authority* to come to the *places* which are above him, *or* to proceed in [2] them. And of those who received *mysteries* in the *ranks* of the 24 *mysteries*, each one will go as far as the *place* in which he has received *mysteries*, and he will have the *authority* to proceed in all the *ranks* and the *spaces* which are outside him; *but* he has not the *authority* to go to the *ranks* which are above him *or* to proceed | in them. And he who received *mysteries* in the

---

[1] (3) In truth it is well that you question; Schmidt : truly well do you question.
[2] (19) proceed in; Schmidt : traverse (see 205.23, and passages following).

ⲘⲘⲞⲞⲨ ⲀⲨⲰ ⲠⲈⲚⲦⲀϤϪⲒ-ⲘⲨⲤⲦⲎⲢⲒⲞⲚ ϨⲚ Ⲛ̄ⲦⲀⲌⲒⲤ Ⲙ̄ⲠⲒ-
ϢⲞⲢⲠ̄ Ⲙ̄ⲘⲨⲤⲦⲎⲢⲒⲞⲚ ⲈⲦϨ̄Ⲙ ⲠⲘⲈϨϢⲞ̄Ⲙ̄Ⲧ̄ Ⲛ̄ⲬⲰⲢⲎⲘⲀ ⲞⲨⲚ̄-
ⲦⲀϤ Ⲙ̄ⲘⲀⲨ Ⲛ̄ⲦⲈⲌⲞⲨⲤⲒⲀ ⲈⲦⲢⲈϤⲈⲒ· ⲈⲚⲦⲀⲌⲒⲤ ⲦⲎⲢⲞⲨ ⲈⲦ-
ⲠⲈϤⲈⲤⲎⲦ· ⲀⲨⲰ ⲈⲦⲢⲈϤⲘⲞⲨⲰⲦ ⟨Ⲙ̄⟩ⲘⲞⲞⲨ ⲦⲎⲢⲞⲨ· ⲀⲖⲖⲀ
5 Ⲙ̄Ⲛ̄ⲦⲀϤ Ⲛ̄ⲦⲞϤ Ⲙ̄ⲘⲀⲨ Ⲛ̄ⲦⲈⲌⲞⲨⲤⲒⲀ ⲈⲦⲢⲈϤⲂⲰⲔ ⲈⲚⲦⲞⲠⲞⲤ
ⲈⲦⲠⲈϤⲤⲀϨⲢⲈ Ⲏ̄ ⲈⲦⲢⲈϤⲘⲞⲨⲰⲦ ⲘⲘⲞⲞⲨ· ⲀⲨⲰ ⲠⲈⲢⲬⲒ-
ⲘⲨⲤⲦⲎⲢⲒⲞⲚ ϨⲘ ⲠϢⲞⲢⲠ̄ Ⲛ̄ⲦⲢⲒⲠⲚⲈⲨⲘⲀⲦⲞⲤ ⲠⲀⲒ ⲈⲦⲀⲢⲬⲒ
ⲈⲬⲘ ⲠϪⲞⲨⲦⲀϤⲦⲈ Ⲙ̄ⲘⲨⲤⲦⲎⲢⲒⲞⲚ ϨⲒ ⲚⲈⲨⲈⲢⲎⲨ· ⲚⲀⲒ ⲈⲦ-   ⲢϤ b
ⲀⲢⲬⲒ ⲈⲠⲈⲬⲰⲢⲎⲘⲀ Ⲙ̄ⲠⲒϢⲞⲢⲠ̄ Ⲙ̄ⲘⲨⲤⲦⲎⲢⲒⲞⲚ ⲚⲀⲒ Ⲉ|ⲚⲀ-
10 ϪⲰ Ⲙ̄ⲠⲈⲨⲦⲞⲠⲞⲤ ⲈⲢⲰⲦⲚ̄ ϨⲢⲀⲒ ϨⲘ ⲠⲤⲰⲢ ⲈⲂⲞⲖ Ⲙ̄ⲠⲦⲎ-
Ⲣ̄Ϥ· ⲠⲈⲦⲚⲀϪⲒ ⲞⲨⲚ Ⲙ̄ⲠⲘⲨⲤⲦⲎⲢⲒⲞⲚ Ⲙ̄ⲠⲈⲦⲢⲒⲠⲚⲈⲨⲘⲀⲦⲞⲤ
ⲈⲦⲘ̄ⲘⲀⲨ· ⲞⲨⲚ̄ⲦⲀϤ Ⲙ̄ⲘⲀⲨ Ⲛ̄ⲦⲈⲌⲞⲨⲤⲒⲀ ⲈⲦⲢⲈϤⲈⲒ· ⲈⲠⲈⲤ-
ⲤⲎⲦ ⲈⲚⲦⲀⲌⲒⲤ ⲦⲎⲢⲞⲨ ⲈⲦⲠⲈϤⲈⲤⲎⲦ· ⲀⲖⲖⲀ Ⲙ̄Ⲛ̄ⲦⲀϤ Ⲙ̄ⲘⲀⲨ
Ⲛ̄ⲦⲈⲌⲞⲨⲤⲒⲀ ⲈⲦⲢⲈϤⲂⲰⲔ ⲈⲠϪⲒⲤⲈ ⲈⲚⲦⲀⲌⲒⲤ Ⲙ̄ⲠⲈϤⲤⲀϨⲢⲈ·
15 ⲈⲦⲈ Ⲛ̄ⲦⲞⲞⲨ ⲠⲈ Ⲛ̄ⲦⲀⲌⲒⲤ ⲦⲎⲢⲞⲨ Ⲙ̄ⲠⲈⲬⲰⲢⲎⲘⲀ Ⲙ̄ⲠⲒⲀⲦ-
ϢⲀϪⲈ ⲈⲢⲞϤ· ⲀⲨⲰ ⲠⲈⲚⲦⲀϤϪⲒ Ⲙ̄ⲠⲘⲨⲤⲦⲎⲢⲒⲞⲚ Ⲙ̄ⲠⲘⲈϨ-
ⲤⲚⲀⲨ Ⲛ̄ⲦⲢⲒⲠⲚⲈⲨⲘⲀⲦⲞⲤ ⲞⲨⲚ̄ⲦⲀϤ Ⲙ̄ⲘⲀⲨ Ⲛ̄ⲦⲈⲌⲞⲨⲤⲒⲀ
ⲈⲦⲢⲈϤⲈⲒ· ⲈⲚⲦⲀⲌⲒⲤ ⲦⲎⲢⲞⲨ Ⲙ̄ⲠⲒϢⲞⲢⲠ̄ Ⲛ̄ⲦⲢⲒⲠⲚⲈⲨⲘⲀⲦⲞⲤ
ⲀⲨⲰ Ⲛ̄ϤⲘⲞⲨⲰⲦ ⲘⲘⲞⲞⲨ ⲦⲎⲢⲞⲨ Ⲙ̄Ⲛ ⲚⲈⲨⲦⲀⲌⲒⲤ ⲦⲎⲢⲞⲨ
20 ⲈⲦϢⲞⲞⲠ Ⲛ̄ϨⲎⲦⲞⲨ· ⲀⲖⲖⲀ Ⲙ̄Ⲛ̄ⲦⲀϤ Ⲙ̄ⲘⲀⲨ Ⲛ̄ⲦⲈⲌⲞⲨⲤⲒⲀ
ⲈⲦⲢⲈϤⲂⲰⲔ ⲈⲚⲦⲀⲌⲒⲤ Ⲙ̄ⲠϪⲒⲤⲈ ** Ⲙ̄ⲠⲒⲘⲈϨϢⲞⲘⲚⲦ Ⲛ̄ⲦⲢⲒ-   ⲢϤⲀ
ⲠⲚⲈⲨⲘⲀⲦⲞⲤ· ⲀⲨⲰ ⲠⲈⲚⲦⲀϤϪⲒ Ⲙ̄ⲠⲘⲨⲤⲦⲎⲢⲒⲞⲚ Ⲙ̄ⲠⲘⲈϨ-

---

4 MS ⲘⲞⲞⲨ.
5 MS Ⲙ̄ⲘⲀⲨ in margin; Ⲛ̄ⲦⲈⲌⲞⲨⲤⲒⲀ written over erasure.
15 MS ⲠⲈ; read ⲚⲈ.
21 MS Ⲙ̄ⲠϪⲒⲤⲤ; read ⲈⲦⲘ̄ⲠϪⲒⲤⲤ; ⲦⲢⲒ inserted in margin.

ranks of the First *Mystery* which is in the third *space* has the *authority* to come to all the *ranks* which are below him, and to proceed in them all; *but* he has not the *authority* to go to the *places* which are above him, *or* to proceed in them. And he who receives *mysteries* in the first *triple-spirited one* which *rules* over the 24 *mysteries* together — these which *rule* the *space* of the First *Mystery*, whose *place* I will say to you in the distribution of the whole — *now* he who will receive the *mystery* of that *triple-spirited one*, he has the *authority* to come down to all the *ranks* which are below him, *but* he has not the *authority* to go to the height to the *ranks* above him, which are all the *ranks* of the *space* of the Ineffable. And he who has received the *mystery* of the second *triple-spirited one* has the *authority* to come to all the *ranks* of the first *triple-spirited one*, and to proceed in them all and all their *ranks* which are within them; *but* he has not the *authority* to go to the *ranks* of the height of the third *triple-spirited one*. And he who has received the *mystery* of the third | *triple-spirited one* which *rules* the

ϢΟΜΝΤ ΝΤΡΙΠΝΕΥΜΑΤΟС· ΠΑΪ ΕΤΑΡΧΙ ΕΠϢΟΜΝΤ Ν-
ΤΡΙΠΝΕΥΜΑΤΟС· ΜΝ ΠϢΟΜΝΤ ΝΧΩΡΗΜΑ 2Ι ΝΕΥΕΡΗΥ
ΝΤΕ ΠΙϢΟΡΠ ΜΜΥСΤΗΡΙΟΝ · ⟨ΟΥΝΤΑϤ ΜΜΑΥ ΝΤΕΖΟΥ-
СΙΑ ΕΤΡΕϤΒΩΚ ΕΝΤΑΖΙС ΤΗΡΟΥ ΕΤΠΕϤΕСΗΤ⟩ ΑΛΛΑ ΜΝ-
5 ΤΑϤ ΜΜΑΥ ΝΤΕΖΟΥСΙΑ ΕΤΡΕϤΒΩΚ ΕΠΧΙСΕ ΕΝΤΑΖΙС
ΕΤΠΕϤСΑ2ΡΕ ΕΤΕ ΝΤΟΟΥ ΝΕ ΝΤΑΖΙС ΜΠΕΧΩΡΗΜΑ Μ-
ΠΙΑΤϢΑΧΕ ΕΡΟϤ · ΑΥΩ ΠΕΝΤΑϤΧΙ ΜΠΑΥΘΕΝΤΗС Μ-
ΜΥСΤΗΡΙΟΝ ΝΤΕ ΠΙϢΟΡΠ ΜΜΥСΤΗΡΙΟΝ ΝΤΕ ΠΙΑΤϢΑ-
ΧΕ ΕΡΟϤ · ΕΤΕ ΝΤΟϤ ΠΕ ΠΜΝΤСΝΟΟΥС ΜΜΥСΤΗΡΙΟΝ
10 2Ι ΝΕΥΕΡΗΥ ΝΤΕ ΠΙϢΟΡΠ ΜΜΥСΤΗΡΙΟΝ ΝΑΪ ΕΤΑΡΧΙ
ΕΧΝ ΝΕΧΩΡΗΜΑ ΤΗΡΟΥ ΜΠΙϢΟΡΠ ΜΜΥСΤΗΡΙΟΝ· ΠΕΤ-
ΝΑΧΙ ΟΥΝ ΜΠΜΥСΤΗΡΙΟΝ ΕΤΜΜΑΥ· ΟΥΝΤΑϤ ΜΜΑΥ
ΝΤΕΖΟΥСΙΑ ΕΤΡΕϤΜΟΥϢΤ ΝΝΤΑΖΙС ΤΗΡΟΥ ΝΝΕΧΩ-
ΡΗΜΑ ΜΠΙϢΟΜΤ ΝΤΡΙΠΝΕΥΜΑΤΟС ΑΥΩ ΜΝ ΠϢΟΜΝΤ
15 ΝΧΩΡΗΜΑ ΜΠΙϢΟΡΠ ΜΜΥСΤΗΡΙΟΝ· ΑΥΩ ΜΝ ΝΕΥΤΑ- ‖ Ρ̄ϤΑ ᵇ
ΖΙС ΤΗΡΟΥ· ΑΥΩ ΟΥΝΤΑϤ ΜΜΑΥ ΝΤΕΖΟΥСΙΑ ΕΤΡΕϤ-
ΜΟΥϢΤ ΝΝΤΑΖΙС ΤΗΡΟΥ ΝΝΕΚΛΗΡΟΝΟΜΙΑ ΜΠΟΥΟΕΙΝ
ΕΤΡΕϤΜΟΥϢΤ ΜΜΟΟΥ ΧΙΝΒΟΛ Ε2ΟΥΝ· ΑΥΩ ΧΙΝ2ΟΥΝ
ΕΒΟΛ [Ε2ΟΥΝ] ΑΥΩ ΧΙΝ ΤΠΕ ΕΠΕСΗΤ· ΑΥΩ ΧΙΝ ΠΕ-
20 СΗΤ ΕΤΠΕ· ΑΥΩ ΧΙΝ ΠΧΙСΕ ΕΠΒΑΘΟС· ΑΥΩ ΧΙΝ
ΠΒΑΘΟС ΕΠΧΙСΕ· ΑΥΩ ΧΙΝ ΤΕϢΙΗ ΕΤΟΥΑϢСΕ· ΑΥΩ
ΧΙΝ ΤΟΥΑϢСΕ ΕΤΕϢΙΗ· 2ΑΠΑΖ 2ΑΠΛΩС ΟΥΝΤΑϤ Μ-
ΜΑΥ ΝΤΕΖΟΥСΙΑ ΕΜΟΥϢΤ ΝΝΤΟΠΟС ΤΗΡΟΥ ΝΝΕΚΛΗ-

---

1 ΤΡΙ inserted in margin. MS ΕΤΑΡΧΙ; read ΕΤΑΡΧΙ also line 10.
2 Τ in ΠϢΟΜΝΤ inserted above.
3 MS the words ΟΥΝΤΑϤ . . . ΕΤΠΕϤΕСΗΤ omitted.
18 MS originally ΧΙΝ ΒΟΛ Ε2ΟΥΝ; 2ΟΥΝ С inserted in margin; С2ΟΥΝ
   expunged after ΕΒΟΛ.

three *triple-spirited ones* and the three *spaces* of the *First Mystery* together ⟨has the authority to go to all the ranks below him⟩; *but* he does not have the *authority* to go to the height to the *ranks* above him, which are the *ranks* of the *space* of the Ineffable. And he who has received the *authentic mystery* of the First *Mystery* of the Ineffable — which is the twelve *mysteries* of the First *Mystery* together, which *rule* over all the *spaces* of the First *Mystery* — *now* he who will receive that *mystery* has the *authority* to proceed in all the *ranks* of the *spaces* of the three *triple-spirited ones* and the three *spaces* of the First *Mystery*, and all their *ranks*. And he has the *authority* to proceed in all the *ranks* of the *inheritances* of the light, to proceed in them from outside within and from within outside; and from above down and from below up; and from the height to the *depth* and from the *depth* to the height; and from the length to the breadth and from the breath to the length; *in a word* he has the *authority* to proceed in all the *places* of the *inheritances* | of the light, and he has the *authority*

ρονομιλ ⲛ̅ⲧⲉ ⲡⲟⲩⲟⲉⲓⲛ · ⲁⲩⲱ ⲟⲩⲛ̅ⲧⲁϥ ⲙ̅ⲙⲁⲩ ⲛ̅ⲧⲉ-
ⲝⲟⲩⲥⲓⲁ ⲉⲧⲣⲉϥϭⲱ ϩ̅ⲙ ⲡⲧⲟⲡⲟⲥ ⲉⲧⲉϩⲛⲁϥ ϩⲣⲁ⳽ ϩ̅ⲛ ⲧⲉⲕⲗⲏⲣⲟⲛⲟⲙⲓⲁ ⲛ̅ⲧⲙⲛ̅ⲧⲉⲣⲟ ⲙ̅ⲡⲟⲩⲟⲉⲓⲛ · ⲁⲩⲱ ϩⲁⲙⲏⲛ
ϯⲭⲱ ⲙ̅ⲙⲟⲥ ⲉⲣⲱⲧ̅ⲛ ϫⲉ ⲡⲣⲱⲙⲉ ⲉⲧⲙ̅ⲙⲁⲩ ϩ̅ⲙ ⲡⲃⲱⲗ
5 ⲉⲃⲟⲗ ⲙ̅ⲡⲕⲟⲥⲙⲟⲥ · ϥⲛⲁϣⲱⲡⲉ ⲉϥⲟ**ⲛ̅ⲣ̅ⲣⲟ ⲉϩⲣⲁ⳽ ⲉϫ̅ⲛ ⲣ̅ϥ̅ⲃ
ⲛ̅ⲧⲁⲝⲓⲥ ⲧⲏⲣⲟⲩ ⲛ̅ⲧⲉⲕⲗⲏⲣⲟⲛⲟⲙⲓⲁ · ⲁⲩⲱ ⲡⲉⲧⲛⲁϫⲓ ⲙ̅-
ⲡⲙⲩⲥⲧⲏⲣⲓⲟⲛ ⲙ̅ⲡⲓⲁⲧϣⲁϫⲉ ⲉⲣⲟϥ ⲡⲉⲧⲙ̅ⲙⲁⲩ ⲡⲉ ⲉⲧⲉ
ⲁⲛⲟⲕ ⲡⲉ · ⲡⲙⲩⲥⲧⲏⲣⲓⲟⲛ ⲉⲧⲙ̅ⲙⲁⲩ ⲛ̅ⲧⲟϥ ⲡⲉⲧⲥⲟⲟⲩⲛ
ϫⲉ ⲉⲧⲃⲉ ⲟⲩ ⲁ ⲡⲕⲁⲕⲉ ϣⲱⲡⲉ · ⲁⲩⲱ ⲉⲧⲃⲉ ⲟⲩ ⲁϥ-
10 ϣⲱⲡⲉ ⲛ̅ϭⲓ ⲡⲟⲩⲟⲉⲓⲛ · ⲁⲩⲱ ⲡⲙⲩⲥⲧⲏⲣⲓⲟⲛ ⲉⲧⲙ̅ⲙⲁⲩ ·
ⲛ̅ⲧⲟϥ ⲡⲉ ⲉⲧⲥⲟⲟⲩⲛ ϫⲉ ⲉⲧⲃⲉ ⲟⲩ ⲁ ⲡⲕⲁⲕⲉ ⲛ̅ⲛ̅ⲕⲁⲕⲉ
ϣⲱⲡⲉ · ⲁⲩⲱ ⲉⲧⲃⲉ ⲟⲩ ⲁ ⲡⲟⲩⲟⲉⲓⲛ ⲛ̅ⲛⲟⲩⲟⲉⲓⲛ ϣⲱⲡⲉ · ⲁⲩⲱ ⲡⲙⲩⲥⲧⲏⲣⲓⲟⲛ ⲉⲧⲙ̅ⲙⲁⲩ ⲛ̅ⲧⲟϥ ⲡⲉ ⲉⲧⲥⲟⲟⲩⲛ
ϫⲉ ⲉⲧⲃⲉ ⲟⲩ ⲁ ⲛⲉⲭⲗⲟⲥ ϣⲱⲡⲉ · ⲁⲩⲱ ⲉⲧⲃⲉ ⲟⲩ ⲁϥ-
15 ϣⲱⲡⲉ ⲛ̅ϭⲓ ⲡⲉⲑⲏⲥⲁⲩⲣⲟⲥ ⲙ̅ⲡⲟⲩⲟⲉⲓⲛ · ⲁⲩⲱ ⲡⲙⲩⲥⲧⲏⲣⲓⲟⲛ ⲉⲧⲙ̅ⲙⲁⲩ ⲛ̅ⲧⲟϥ ⲡⲉ ⲉⲧⲥⲟⲟⲩⲛ ϫⲉ ⲉⲧⲃⲉ ⲟⲩ ⲁ ⲛⲉⲕⲣⲓⲥⲓⲥ ϣⲱⲡⲉ ⲁⲩⲱ ⲉⲧⲃⲉ ⲟⲩ ⲁϥϣⲱⲡⲉ ⲛ̅ϭⲓ ⲡⲕⲁϩ ⲙ̅-
ⲡⲟⲩⲟⲉⲓⲛ ⲙ̅ⲛ ⲡⲧⲟⲡⲟⲥ ⲛ̅ⲛⲉⲕⲗⲏⲣⲟⲛⲟⲙⲓⲁ ⲙ̅ⲡⲟⲩⲟⲉⲓⲛ ·
ⲁⲩⲱ ⲡⲙⲩⲥⲧⲏⲣⲓⲟⲛ ⲉⲧⲙ̅ⲙⲁⲩ ⲛ̅ⲧⲟϥ ⲡⲉⲧ*ⲥⲟⲟⲩⲛ ϫⲉ ⲉⲧ- ⲣ̅ϥ̅ⲃ ᵇ
20 ⲃⲉ ⲟⲩ ⲁ ⲛ̅ⲕⲟⲗⲁⲥⲓⲥ ⲛ̅ⲛⲣⲉϥⲣ̅ⲛⲟⲃⲉ ϣⲱⲡⲉ · ⲁⲩⲱ ⲉⲧⲃⲉ
ⲟⲩ ⲁⲥϣⲱⲡⲉ ⲛ̅ϭⲓ ⲧⲁⲛⲁⲡⲁⲩⲥⲓⲥ ⲛ̅ⲧⲙⲛ̅ⲧⲉⲣⲟ ⲙ̅ⲡⲟⲩⲟⲉⲓⲛ ·
ⲁⲩⲱ ⲡⲙⲩⲥⲧⲏⲣⲓⲟⲛ ⲉⲧⲙ̅ⲙⲁⲩ ⲛ̅ⲧⲟϥ ⲡⲉⲧⲥⲟⲟⲩⲛ ϫⲉ
ⲉⲧⲃⲉ ⲟⲩ ⲁ ⲛ̅ⲣⲉϥⲣ̅ⲛⲟⲃⲉ ϣⲱⲡⲉ ⲁⲩⲱ ⲉⲧⲃⲉ ⲟⲩ ⲁⲩϣⲱⲡⲉ ⲛ̅ϭⲓ ⲛⲉⲕⲗⲏⲣⲟⲛⲟⲙⲓⲁ ⲙ̅ⲡⲟⲩⲟⲉⲓⲛ · ⲁⲩⲱ ⲡⲙⲩⲥ-
25 ⲧⲏⲣⲓⲟⲛ ⲉⲧⲙ̅ⲙⲁⲩ ⲛ̅ⲧⲟϥ ⲡⲉⲧⲥⲟⲟⲩⲛ ϫⲉ ⲉⲧⲃⲉ ⲟⲩ ⲁⲩϣⲱⲡⲉ ⲛ̅ϭⲓ ⲛ̅ⲁⲥⲉⲃⲏⲥ ⲁⲩⲱ ⲉⲧⲃⲉ ⲟⲩ ⲁⲩϣⲱⲡⲉ ⲛ̅ϭⲓ

to remain in the *place* which pleases him in the *inheritance* of the Kingdom of the Light. And *truly* I say to you : at the dissolution of the *world* that man will rule (be king) over all the *ranks* of the *inheritance*. And he who will receive that *mystery* of the Ineffable — which I am — that *mystery* knows [1] why the darkness came into existence and why the light came into existence. And that *mystery* knows why the darkness of darknesses came into existence and why the light of lights. And that *mystery* knows why the *Chaos(es)* came into existence and why the *Treasury* of the Light. And that *mystery* knows why the *judgments* came into existence, and why the Land of the Light and the *place* of the *inheritances* of the light. And that *mystery* knows why the *punishments* of sinners came into existence, and why the *repose* of the Kingdom of the Light. And that *mystery* knows why sinners came into existence, and why the *inheritances* of the light. And that *mystery* knows why the *impious* came into existence, and why | the *good*. And that *mystery*

---

[1]   (8) knows; lit. is the one that knows (also in parallel passages following).

ⲡⲁⲅⲁⲑⲟⲥ· ⲁⲩⲱ ⲡⲙⲩⲥⲧⲏⲣⲓⲟⲛ ⲉⲧⲙⲙⲁⲩ ⲛⲧⲟϥ ⲡⲉⲧⲥⲟⲟⲩⲛ ϫⲉ ⲉⲧⲃⲉ ⲟⲩ ⲁ ⲛⲉⲕⲣⲓⲥⲓⲥ ⲛⲕⲟⲗⲁⲥⲓⲥ ϣⲱⲡⲉ·
ⲁⲩⲱ ⲉⲧⲃⲉ ⲟⲩ ⲁⲩϣⲱⲡⲉ ⲛϭⲓ ⲛⲉⲡⲣⲟⲃⲟⲗⲟⲟⲩⲉ ⲧⲏⲣⲟⲩ
ⲙⲡⲟⲩⲟⲓ̈ⲛ· ⲁⲩⲱ ⲡⲙⲩⲥⲧⲏⲣⲓⲟⲛ ⲉⲧⲙⲙⲁⲩ ⲛⲧⲟϥ ⲡⲉⲧ-
5 ⲥⲟⲟⲩⲛ ϫⲉ ⲉⲧⲃⲉ ⲟⲩ ⲁ ⲡⲛⲟⲃⲉ ϣⲱⲡⲉ· ⲁⲩⲱ ⲉⲧⲃⲉ
ⲟⲩ ⲁⲩϣⲱⲡⲉ ⲛϭⲓ ⲛⲃⲁⲡⲧⲓⲥⲙⲁ ⲙⲛ ⲙⲙⲩⲥⲧⲏⲣⲓⲟⲛ ⲛⲧⲉ
ⲡⲟⲩⲟⲉⲓⲛ· ⲁⲩⲱ ⲡⲙⲩⲥⲧⲏⲣⲓⲟⲛ ⲉⲧⲙⲙⲁⲩ ⲛⲧⲟϥ ⲡⲉⲧⲥⲟⲟⲩⲛ ϫⲉ ⲉⲧⲃⲉ ⲟⲩ ⲁϥϣⲱⲡⲉ ⲛϭⲓ ⲡⲕⲱϩⲧ ⲛⲧⲉ ⲧⲕⲟ- ⲣϥⲅ
ⲗⲁⲥⲓⲥ· ⲁⲩⲱ ⲉⲧⲃⲉ ⲟⲩ ⲁⲩϣⲱⲡⲉ ⲛϭⲓ ⲛⲉⲥⲫⲣⲁⲅⲓⲥ ⲙ-
10 ⲡⲟⲩⲟⲉⲓⲛ ϫⲉ ⲛⲛⲉ ⲡⲕⲱϩⲧ ⲃⲗⲁⲡⲧⲓ ⲙⲙⲟⲟⲩ· ⲁⲩⲱ ⲡⲙⲩⲥⲧⲏⲣⲓⲟⲛ ⲉⲧⲙⲙⲁⲩ ⲛⲧⲟϥ ⲡⲉⲧⲥⲟⲟⲩⲛ ϫⲉ ⲉⲧⲃⲉ ⲟⲩ ⲁϥϣⲱⲡⲉ ⲛϭⲓ ⲡϭⲱⲛⲧ· ⲁⲩⲱ ⲉⲧⲃⲉ ⲟⲩ ⲁⲥϣⲱⲡⲉ ⲛϭⲓ
†ⲣⲏⲛⲏ· ⲁⲩⲱ ⲡⲙⲩⲥⲧⲏⲣⲓⲟⲛ ⲉⲧⲙⲙⲁⲩ ⲛⲧⲟϥ ⲡⲉⲧⲥⲟⲟⲩⲛ
ϫⲉ ⲉⲧⲃⲉ ⲟⲩ ⲁ ⲡϫⲓⲟⲩⲁ ϣⲱⲡⲉ· ⲁⲩⲱ ⲉⲧⲃⲉ ⲟⲩ ⲁⲩ-
15 ϣⲱⲡⲉ ⲛϭⲓ ⲛϩⲩⲙⲛⲟⲥ ⲙⲡⲟⲩⲟⲉⲓⲛ· ⲁⲩⲱ ⲡⲙⲩⲥⲧⲏⲣⲓⲟⲛ
ⲉⲧⲙⲙⲁⲩ ⲛⲧⲟϥ ⲡⲉⲧⲥⲟⲟⲩⲛ ϫⲉ ⲉⲧⲃⲉ ⲟⲩ ⲁ ⲛⲉⲡⲣⲟⲥ-
ⲉⲩⲭⲟⲟⲩⲉ ⲙⲡⲟⲩⲟⲉⲓⲛ ϣⲱⲡⲉ· ⲁⲩⲱ ⲡⲙⲩⲥⲧⲏⲣⲓⲟⲛ ⲉⲧⲙⲙⲁⲩ ⲛⲧⲟϥ ⲡⲉⲧⲥⲟⲟⲩⲛ ϫⲉ ⲉⲧⲃⲉ ⲟⲩ ⲁ ⲡⲥⲁϩⲟⲩ ϣⲱ-
ⲡⲉ· ⲁⲩⲱ ⲉⲧⲃⲉ ⲟⲩ ⲁϥϣⲱⲡⲉ ⲛϭⲓ ⲡⲉⲥⲙⲟⲩ· ⲁⲩⲱ ⲡⲙⲩⲥ-
20 ⲧⲏⲣⲓⲟⲛ ⲉⲧⲙⲙⲁⲩ ⲛⲧⲟϥ ⲡⲉⲧⲥⲟⲟⲩⲛ ϫⲉ ⲉⲧⲃⲉ ⲟⲩ ⲁ
ⲧⲙⲛⲧⲡⲟⲛⲟⲣⲟⲥ ϣⲱⲡⲉ· ⲁⲩⲱ ⲉⲧⲃⲉ ⲟⲩ ⲁϥϣⲱⲡⲉ ⲛϭⲓ
ⲧⲙⲛⲧⲣⲉϥⲕⲱⲣϣ· ⲁⲩⲱ ⲡⲙⲩⲥⲧⲏⲣⲓⲟⲛ ⲉⲧⲙⲙⲁⲩ ⲛⲧⲟϥ
ⲡⲉⲧⲥⲟⲟⲩⲛ ϫⲉ ⲉⲧⲃⲉ ⲟⲩ ⲁ ⲧⲙⲛⲧⲣⲉϥϩⲱⲧϥ ϣⲱⲡⲉ· ⲣϥⲅ ᵇ
ⲁⲩⲱ ⲉⲧⲃⲉ ⲟⲩ ⲁϥϣⲱⲡⲉ ⲛϭⲓ ⲡⲧⲁⲛϩⲟ ⲛⲛⲉⲯⲩⲭⲟⲟⲩⲉ·
25 ⲁⲩⲱ ⲡⲙⲩⲥⲧⲏⲣⲓⲟⲛ ⲉⲧⲙⲙⲁⲩ ⲛⲧⲟϥ ⲡⲉⲧⲥⲟⲟⲩⲛ ϫⲉ ⲉⲧⲃⲉ ⲟⲩ ⲁⲥϣⲱⲡⲉ ⲛϭⲓ ⲧⲙⲧⲛⲟⲉⲓⲕ· ⲙⲛ ⲧⲡⲟⲣⲛⲓⲁ ⲁⲩⲱ

---

21 MS ⲧⲙⲛⲧⲡⲟⲛⲟⲣⲟⲥ; read ⲧⲙⲛⲧⲡⲟⲛⲏⲣⲟⲥ.

knows why the *punitive judgments* came into existence, and why all the *emanations* of the light. And that *mystery* knows why sin came into existence, and why the *baptisms* and the *mysteries* of the light. And that *mystery* knows why the fire of the *punishment* came into existence, and why the *seals* of the light, so that the fire should not *injure* them. And that *mystery* knows why anger came into existence, and why *peace*. And that *mystery* knows why the oath came into existence, and why the *songs of praise* of the light. And that *mystery* knows why the *prayers* of the light came into existence. And that *mystery* knows why cursing came into existence, and why blessing. And that *mystery* knows why *wickedness* came into existence, and why flattery [1]. And that *mystery* knows why the death-blow came into existence, and why the bringing to life of *souls*. And that *mystery* knows why adultery and *fornication* came into existence, and |

---

[1] (22) flattery ; Schmidt : deception.

ΕΤΒΕ ΟΥ ΑϤϢΩΠΕ Ν̄ϬΙ ΠΤΒΒΟ· ΑΥΩ ΠΜΥⳤΤΗΡΙΟΝ ΕΤ-
Μ̄ΜΑΥ Ν̄ΤΟϤ ΠΕΤⳤΟΟΥΝ ⳉΕ ΕΤΒΕ ΟΥ ΑϤϢΩΠΕ Ν̄ϬΙ
ΤⳤΥΝΟΥⳤΙΑ· ΑΥΩ ΕΤΒΕ ΟΥ ΑⳤϢΩΠΕ Ν̄ϬΙ ΤΕΓΚΡΑ-
ΤΕΙΑ· ΑΥΩ ΠΜΥⳤΤΗΡΙΟΝ ΕΤΜ̄ΜΑΥ Ν̄ΤΟϤ ΠΕΤⳤΟΟΥΝ
5 ⳉΕ ΕΤΒΕ ΟΥ ΑⳤϢΩΠΕ Ν̄ϬΙ ΤΜΝ̄Τⳉ̄Αⳤ̄Ιⳉ̄ΗΤ· ΜΝ̄ ΤΜΝ̄Τ-
ϢΟΥϢΟ· ΑΥΩ ΕΤΒΕ ΟΥ ΑϤϢΩΠΕ Ν̄ϬΙ ΠΕⲐΒΒΙΟ ΜΝ̄
ΤΜΝ̄ΤΡΜΡΑϢ· ΑΥΩ ΠΜΥⳤΤΗΡΙΟΝ ΕΤΜ̄ΜΑΥ Ν̄ΤΟϤ ΠΕΤ-
ⳤΟΟΥΝ ⳉΕ ΕΤΒΕ ΟΥ Α ΠΡΙΜΕ ϢΩΠΕ· ΑΥΩ ΕΤΒΕ ΟΥ
ΑϤϢΩΠΕ Ν̄ϬΙ ΠⳤΩΒΕ· ΑΥΩ ΠΜΥⳤΤΗΡΙΟΝ ΕΤΜ̄ΜΑΥ Ν̄-
10 ΤΟϤ ΠΕΤⳤΟΟΥΝ ⳉΕ ΕΤΒΕ ΟΥ Α ΤΚΑΤΑΛΑΛΙΑ ϢΩΠΕ·
ΑΥΩ ΕΤΒΕ ΟΥ Α ΠϢΑⳉΕ ΕΤΝΑΝΟΥϤ ϢΩΠΕ· ΑΥΩ ρⳅⲁ
ΠΜΥⳤΤΗΡΙΟΝ ΕΤΜ̄ΜΑΥ Ν̄ΤΟϤ ΠΕΤⳤΟΟΥΝ ⳉΕ ΕΤΒΕ ΟΥ
Α ΤΜΝ̄ΤΡΕϤⳉΙⳤΜΗ ϢΩΠΕ· ΑΥΩ ΕΤΒΕ ΟΥ Α ΠΤΜΩϢ
ΜΝ̄ ΠΡΩΜΕ ϢΩΠΕ· ΑΥΩ ΠΜΥⳤΤΗΡΙΟΝ ΕΤΜ̄ΜΑΥ Ν̄ΤΟϤ
15 ΠΕΤⳤΟΟΥΝ ⳉΕ ΕΤΒΕ ΟΥ Α ΠΚΡΜΡΜ ϢΩΠΕ· ΑΥΩ ΕΤ-
ΒΕ ΟΥ ΑⳤϢΩΠΕ Ν̄ϬΙ ΤΜΝ̄ΤΒΑΛϨΗΤ ΜΝ̄ ΠⲐΒΒΙΟ· ΑΥΩ
ΠΜΥⳤΤΗΡΙΟΝ ΕΤΜ̄ΜΑΥ Ν̄ΤΟϤ ΠΕΤⳤΟΟΥΝ ⳉΕ ΕΤΒΕ ΟΥ
ΑⳤϢΩΠΕ Ν̄ϬΙ ΤΜΝ̄ΤΡΕϤΡ̄ΝΟΒΕ· ΑΥΩ ΕΤΒΕ ΟΥ ΑϤ-
ϢΩΠΕ Ν̄ϬΙ ΠΤΒΒΟ· ΑΥΩ ΠΜΥⳤΤΗΡΙΟΝ ΕΤΜ̄ΜΑΥ Ν̄ΤΟϤ
20 ΠΕΤⳤΟΟΥΝ ⳉΕ ΕΤΒΕ ΟΥ ΑⳤϢΩΠΕ Ν̄ϬΙ ΤΜΤⳉΩΩΡΕ·
ΑΥΩ ΕΤΒΕ ΟΥ ΑⳤϢΩΠΕ Ν̄ϬΙ ΤΜΝ̄ΤϬΩΒ· ΑΥΩ ΠΜΥⳤ-
ΤΗΡΙΟΝ ΕΤΜ̄ΜΑΥ Ν̄ΤΟϤ ΠΕΤⳤΟΟΥΝ ⳉΕ ΕΤΒΕ ΟΥ Αⳤ-
ϢΩΠΕ Ν̄ϬΙ ΤΚΙΝΗⳤΙⳤ Μ̄ΠⳤΩΜΑ· ΑΥΩ ΕΤΒΕ ΟΥ Αⳤ-
ϢΩΠΕ Ν̄ϬΙ ΠΕΥΡ̄ϢΑΥ· ΑΥΩ ΠΜΥⳤΤΗΡΙΟΝ ΕΤΜ̄ΜΑΥ
25 Ν̄ΤΟϤ ΠΕΤⳤΟΟΥΝ ⳉΕ ΕΤΒΕ ΟΥ ΑⳤϢΩΠΕ Ν̄ϬΙ ΤΜΝ̄Τ-
ϨΗΚΕ· ΑΥΩ ΕΤΒΕ ΟΥ ΑⳤϢΩΠΕ Ν̄ϬΙ ΤΜΝ̄ΤΡΜΜΑΟ· ΑΥΩ ρⳅⲁ b
ΠΜΥⳤΤΗΡΙΟΝ ΕΤΜ̄ΜΑΥ Ν̄ΤΟϤ ΠΕΤⳤΟΟΥΝ ⳉΕ ΕΤΒΕ ΟΥ

why purity. And that *mystery* knows why *sexual intercourse* came into existence, and why *abstinence*. And that *mystery* knows why pride and boasting came into existence, and why humility and gentleness. And that *mystery* knows why weeping came into existence and why laughter. And that *mystery* knows why *slander* came into existence, and why good report. And that *mystery* knows why obedience came into existence, and why disregard of men. And that *mystery* knows why grumbling came into existence, and why simplicity and humility. And that *mystery* knows why sinfulness came into existence and why purity. And that *mystery* knows why strength came into existence and why weakness. And that *mystery* knows why *movement* [1] of the *body* came into existence, and why their use. And that *Mystery* knows why poverty came into existence and why wealth. And that *mystery* knows why | freedom (?) [2] of the *world* came into

---

[1]   (23) movement; cf. 279.1.
[2]   (211.1) freedom; MS : wealth.

ⲀⲤϢⲰⲠⲈ ⲚϬⲒ ⲦⲘⲚⲦⲢⲘⲘⲀⲞ ⲘⲠⲔⲞⲤⲘⲞⲤ· ⲀⲨⲰ ϪⲈ ⲈⲦⲂⲈ

ⲞⲨ ⲀⲤϢⲰⲠⲈ ⲚϬⲒ ⲦⲘⲚⲦⲤⲀⲨⲞⲚ· ⲀⲨⲰ ⲠⲘⲨⲤⲦⲎⲢⲒⲞⲚ

ⲈⲦⲘⲘⲀⲨ ⲚⲦⲞϤ ⲠⲈⲦⲤⲞⲞⲨⲚ ϪⲈ ⲈⲦⲂⲈ ⲞⲨ ⲀϤϢⲰⲠⲈ ⲚϬⲒ

ⲠⲘⲞⲨ· ⲀⲨⲰ ϪⲈ ⲈⲦⲂⲈ ⲞⲨ ⲀϤϢⲰⲠⲈ ⲚϬⲒ ⲠⲰⲚϨ·

5 Ⲍ ⲀⲤϢⲰⲠⲈ ϬⲈ ⲚⲦⲈⲢⲈ ⲒⲤ ⲞⲨⲰ ⲈϤϪⲰ ⲚⲚⲈⲒϢⲀϪⲈ

ⲈⲚⲈϤⲘⲀⲐⲎⲦⲎⲤ· ⲀⲨⲢⲀϢⲈ ϨⲚ ⲞⲨⲚⲞϬ ⲚⲢⲀϢⲈ· ⲀⲨⲰ ⲀⲨ-

ⲦⲈⲖⲎⲖ ⲈⲨⲤⲰⲦⲘ ⲈⲒⲤ ⲈϤϪⲰ ⲚⲚⲈⲒϢⲀϪⲈ· ⲀϤⲞⲨⲰϨ ⲞⲚ

ⲈⲦⲞⲞⲦϤ ⲚϬⲒ ⲒⲤ ϨⲘ ⲠϢⲀϪⲈ ⲠⲈϪⲀϤ ⲚⲀⲨ ϪⲈ ⲈⲦⲒ ϬⲈ

ⲘⲀⲘⲀⲐⲎⲦⲎⲤ ⲤⲰⲦⲘ ⲦⲈⲚⲞⲨ ⲦⲀϢⲀϪⲈ ⲚⲘⲘⲎⲦⲚ ⲈⲦⲂⲈ

10 ⲠⲤⲞⲞⲨⲚ ⲦⲎⲢϤ ⲘⲠⲘⲨⲤⲦⲎⲢⲒⲞⲚ ⲘⲠⲒⲀⲦϢⲀϪⲈ ⲈⲢⲞϤ· ϪⲈ

ⲠⲘⲨⲤⲦⲎⲢⲒⲞⲚ ⲘⲠⲒⲀⲦϢⲀϪⲈ ⲈⲢⲞϤ ⲈⲦⲘⲘⲀⲨ ⲚⲦⲞϤ ⲠⲈⲦ-

ⲤⲞⲞⲨⲚ ϪⲈ ⲈⲦⲂⲈ ⲞⲨ ⲀⲤϢⲰⲠⲈ ⲚϬⲒ ⲦⲘⲚⲦⲀⲦⲚⲀ'· ⲀⲨⲰ

ϪⲈ ⲈⲦⲂⲈ ⲞⲨ ⲀϤϢⲰⲠⲈ ⲚϬⲒ ⲠⲚⲀ'· ⲀⲨⲰ ⲠⲘⲨⲤⲦⲎⲢⲒⲞⲚ

ⲈⲦⲘⲘⲀⲨ ⲚⲦⲞϤ ⲠⲈⲦⲤⲞⲞⲨⲚ ϪⲈ ⲈⲦⲂⲈ ⲞⲨ ⲀϤϢⲰⲠⲈ ⲚϬⲒ ⲢϤⲈ

15 ⲠⲦⲀⲔⲞ· ⲀⲨⲰ ⲈⲦⲂⲈ ⲞⲨ ⲀϤϢⲰⲠⲈ ⲚϬⲒ ⲠⲒⲀⲈⲒ' ϢⲀ ⲈⲚⲈϨ·

ⲀⲨⲰ ⲠⲘⲨⲤⲦⲎⲢⲒⲞⲚ ⲈⲦⲘⲘⲀⲨ ⲚⲦⲞϤ ⲠⲈⲦⲤⲞⲞⲨⲚ ϪⲈ ⲈⲦ-

ⲂⲈ ⲞⲨ ⲀⲨϢⲰⲠⲈ ⲚϬⲒ ⲚϪⲀⲦϤⲈ· ⲀⲨⲰ ⲈⲦⲂⲈ ⲞⲨ ⲤⲈⲚⲀ-

ⲂⲰⲖ ⲈⲂⲞⲖ· ⲀⲨⲰ ⲠⲘⲨⲤⲦⲎⲢⲒⲞⲚ ⲈⲦⲘⲘⲀⲨ ⲚⲦⲞϤ ⲠⲈⲦ-

ⲤⲞⲞⲨⲚ ϪⲈ ⲈⲦⲂⲈ ⲞⲨ ⲤⲈⲚⲀϢⲰⲠⲈ ⲚϬⲒ ⲚⲈⲐⲎⲢⲒⲞⲚ· ⲀⲨⲰ

20 ⲈⲦⲂⲈ ⲞⲨ ⲤⲈⲚⲀⲂⲰⲖ ⲈⲂⲞⲖ· ⲀⲨⲰ ⲠⲘⲨⲤⲦⲎⲢⲒⲞⲚ ⲈⲦⲘ-

ⲘⲀⲨ ⲚⲦⲞϤ ⲠⲈⲦⲤⲞⲞⲨⲚ ϪⲈ ⲈⲦⲂⲈ ⲞⲨ ⲀⲨϢⲰⲠⲈ ⲚϬⲒ

ⲚⲦⲂⲚⲞⲞⲨⲈ ⲀⲨⲰ ⲈⲦⲂⲈ ⲞⲨ ⲀⲨϢⲰⲠⲈ ⲚϬⲒ ⲚϨⲀⲖⲀⲦⲈ·

ⲀⲨⲰ ⲠⲘⲨⲤⲦⲎⲢⲒⲞⲚ ⲈⲦⲘⲘⲀⲨ ⲚⲦⲞϤ ⲠⲈⲦⲤⲞⲞⲨⲚ ϪⲈ ⲈⲦ-

ⲂⲈ ⲞⲨ ⲀⲨϢⲰⲠⲈ ⲚϬⲒ ⲚⲦⲞⲨ Ⲓ̈Ⲏ· ⲀⲨⲰ ⲈⲦⲂⲈ ⲞⲨ ⲀⲨϢⲰ-

---

1 MS ⲦⲘⲠⲦⲢⲘⲘⲀⲞ; perhaps read ⲦⲘⲠⲦⲢⲘϨⲈ.

9 MS ⲘⲀⲘⲀⲐⲎⲦⲎⲤ; the first ⲘⲀ inserted above; read ⲚⲀⲘⲀⲐⲎⲦⲎⲤ.

21 ⲤⲈ expunged before ⲀⲨϢⲰⲠⲈ, also in next sentence, line 22.

existence, and why slavery. And that *mystery* knows why
death came into existence, and why life."

92.   Now it happened when Jesus finished speaking these
words to his *disciples*, they rejoiced with great joy and they
were glad when they heard Jesus saying these words.

Jesus continued again with the discourse, he said to them :
"Hear now, my *disciples*, *yet* again, that I speak with you
concerning the whole knowledge of the *mystery* of the
Ineffable. Because that *mystery* of the Ineffable knows why
mercilessness came into existence, and why mercy. And
that *mystery* knows why destruction came into existence,
and why the eternal *eternity* [1]. And that *mystery* knows why
reptiles came into existence, and why they will perish. And
that *mystery* knows why *wild beasts* came (lit. will come)
into existence and why they will perish. And that *mystery*
knows why cattle came into existence, and why birds. And
that *mystery* knows why mountains came into existence, and
why | the precious stones within them. And that *mystery*

---

[1]   (15) eternity; see U 226.

ПЕ N̄ϬΙ N̄ѠNЄ ЄТТАЄΙΗΥ ЄТ N̄ 2ΗΤΟΥ · ΑΥѠ ΠΜΥСΤΗ-
ΡΙΟΝ ЄΤΜ̄ΜΑΥ N̄ΤΟϤ ΠЄΤСΟΟΥΝ ΧΕ ЄΤΒЄ ΟΥ ΑСѠ-
ΠЄ N̄ϬΙ ѲΥΛΗ Μ̄ΠΝΟΥΒ · ΑΥѠ ЄΤΒЄ ΟΥ ΑСѠΠЄ N̄ϬΙ
ѲΥΛΗ Μ̄ΠΖΑΤ · ΑΥѠ ΠΜΥСΤΗΡΙΟΝ ЄΤΜ̄ΜΑΥ N̄ΤΟϤ ΠЄТ-   Ρ̄Ϥ̄Є ᵇ
5 СΟΟΥΝ ΧЄ ЄΤΒЄ ΟΥ ΑСѠΠЄ N̄ϬΙ ѲΥΛΗ Μ̄ΠΖΟΜN̄Τ
ΑΥѠ ЄΤΒЄ ΟΥ ΑСѠΠЄ [Μ̄N̄] ѲΥΛΗ Μ̄ΠΒЄΝΙΠЄ · Μ̄N̄
ΠΛΑΪΝΟΝ · ΑΥѠ ΠΜΥСΤΗΡΙΟΝ ЄΤΜ̄ΜΑΥ N̄ΤΟϤ ΠЄ ЄΤ-
СΟΟΥΝ ΧЄ ЄΤΒЄ ΟΥ ΑСѠΠЄ N̄ϬΙ ѲΥΛΗ Μ̄ΠΤΑ2Τ ·
ΑΥѠ ΠΜΥСΤΗΡΙΟΝ ЄΤΜ̄ΜΑΥ N̄ΤΟϤ ΠЄ ЄΤСΟΟΥΝ ΧЄ
10 ЄΤΒЄ ΟΥ ΑСѠΠЄ N̄ϬΙ ѲΥΛΗ Μ̄ΠΑΒΑϬΗЄΙΝ · ΑΥѠ ЄΤ-
ΒЄ ΟΥ ΑСѠΠЄ N̄Τ2ΥΛΗ Μ̄ΠΚΗΡΙΝΟΝ · ΑΥѠ ΠΜΥСΤΗ-
ΡΙΟΝ ЄΤΜ̄ΜΑΥ N̄ΤΟϤ ΠЄ ЄΤСΟΟΥΝ ΧЄ ЄΤΒЄ ΟΥ ΑΥ-
ѠΠЄ N̄ϬΙ N̄ΒΟΤΑΝΗ ЄΤЄ ΝЄN̄Τ2Ϭ ΝЄ · ΑΥѠ ЄΤΒЄ
ΟΥ ΑΥѠΠЄ N̄ϬΙ N̄2ΥΛΗ ΤΗΡΟΥ · ΑΥѠ ΠΜΥСΤΗΡΙΟΝ
15 ЄΤΜ̄ΜΑΥ N̄ΤΟϤ ΠЄ ЄΤСΟΟΥΝ ΧЄ ЄΤΒЄ ΟΥ ΑΥѠΠЄ
N̄ϬΙ Μ̄ΜΟΥЄΙΟΟΥЄ Μ̄ΠΚΑ2 · Μ̄N̄ N̄ΚΑ ΝΙΜ ЄΤN̄2ΗΤΟΥ ·
ΑΥѠ ЄΤΒЄ ΟΥ Α ΠΚЄΚΑ2 ѠΠЄ · ΑΥѠ ΠΜΥСΤΗΡΙΟΝ
ЄΤΜ̄ΜΑΥ N̄ΤΟϤ ΠЄ̈ΤСΟΟΥΝ ΧЄ N̄ΤΑ ΝЄѲΑΛΛΑССΑ ѠѠ-   Ρ̄Ϥ̄Є̄
ΠЄ ЄΤΒЄ ΟΥ Μ̄N̄ Μ̄ΜΟΥЄΙΟΟΥЄ · ΑΥѠ ЄΤΒЄ ΟΥ ΑΥ-
20 ѠΠЄ N̄ϬΙ ΝЄѲΗΡΙΟΝ 2N̄ ΝЄѲΑΛΛΑССΑ · ΑΥѠ ΠΜΥСΤΗ-
ΡΙΟΝ ЄΤΜ̄ΜΑΥ N̄ΤΟϤ ΠЄΤСΟΟΥΝ ΧЄ ЄΤΒЄ ΟΥ ΑС-
ѠΠЄ N̄ϬΙ ѲΥΛΗ Μ̄ΠΚΟСΜΟС · ΑΥѠ ЄΤΒЄ ΟΥ ϤΝΑΒѠΛ
ЄΒΟΛ ЄΠΤΗΡ̄Ϥ ·

ΑϤΟΥѠ2 ΟΝ ЄΤΟΟΤ̄Ϥ N̄ϬΙ ῙС̄ ΠЄΧΑϤ N̄ΝЄϤΜΑѲΗΤΗС
25 ΧЄ ЄΤΙ ϬЄ ΝΑΜΑѲΗΤΗС ΑΥѠ ΝΑѠΒЄЄΡ ΑΥѠ ΝΑ-

---

6   omit Μ̄N̄ before ѲΥΛΗ.
18   the first hand begins again with Ρ̄Ϥ̄Є̄.

knows why the *matter* of gold came into existence, and why the *matter* of silver. And that *mystery* knows why the *matter* of copper came into existence, and why the *matter* of iron and of *stone* (?) [1]. And that *mystery* knows why the *matter* of lead came into existence. And that *mystery* knows why the *matter* of glass came into existence, and why the *matter* of *wax*. And that *mystery* knows why *vegetation*, that is, plants came into existence, and why all *materials*. And that *mystery* knows why the waters of the earth and all things within them came into existence, and why the earth also. And that *mystery* knows why the *sea* and the waters came into existence, and why the *wild beasts* in the *sea*. And that *mystery* knows why the *world-matter* came into existence and why it will perish completely."

93. Jesus continued again, he said to his *disciples* : "*Yet again*, my *disciples* and companions and | brothers, let each

---

[1]   (7) stone; Till : steel also.

ⲥⲛⲏⲩ· ⲙⲁⲣⲉ ⲡⲟⲩⲁ ⲡⲟⲩⲁ ⲛⲏⲫⲉ ⲙ̄ⲡⲉⲡⲛ̄ⲁ̄ ⲉⲧⲛ̄ϩⲏⲧϥ̄ ⲛ̄-
ⲧⲉⲧⲛ̄ϫⲓⲥⲙⲏ ⲁⲩⲱ ⲛ̄ⲧⲉⲧⲛ̄ⲕⲁⲧⲁⲗⲁⲙⲃⲁⲛⲉ ⲛ̄ϣⲁϫⲉ ⲛⲓⲙ
ⲉϯⲛⲁϫⲟⲟⲩ ⲛⲏⲧⲛ̄· ϫⲉ ϫⲓⲛ ⲧⲉⲛⲟⲩ ⲉⲓ̈ⲛⲁϩⲓⲧⲟⲟⲧ ⲉϣⲁϫⲉ ⲛⲙ̄ⲙⲏⲧⲛ̄ ⲉⲧⲃⲉ ⲛ̄ⲥⲟⲟⲩⲛ ⲧⲏⲣⲟⲩ ⲛ̄ⲧⲉ ⲡⲓⲁⲧϣⲁϫⲉ
5 ⲉⲣⲟϥ ϫⲉ ⲡⲙⲩⲥⲧⲏⲣⲓⲟⲛ ⲉⲧⲙ̄ⲙⲁⲩ ⲛ̄ⲧⲟϥ ⲡⲉⲧⲥⲟⲟⲩⲛ ϫⲉ
ⲉⲧⲃⲉ˙ ⲟⲩ ⲁϥϣⲱⲡⲉ ⲛ̄ϭⲓ ⲡⲉⲙⲛⲧ· ⲁⲩⲱ ⲉⲧⲃⲉ ⲟⲩ ⲁϥ- ⲣ̅ϥ̅ⲉ̅ b
ϣⲱⲡⲉ ⲛ̄ϭⲓ ⲡⲉⲓ̈ⲃⲧ̄· ⲁⲩⲱ ⲡⲙⲩⲥⲧⲏⲣⲓⲟⲛ ⲉⲧⲙ̄ⲙⲁⲩ ⲛ̄ⲧⲟϥ
ⲡⲉⲧⲥⲟⲟⲩⲛ ϫⲉ ⲉⲧⲃⲉ ⲟⲩ ⲁϥϣⲱⲡⲉ ⲛ̄ϭⲓ ⲡⲣⲏⲥ· ⲁⲩⲱ
ⲉⲧⲃⲉ ⲟⲩ ⲁϥϣⲱⲡⲉ ⲛ̄ϭⲓ ⲡⲉⲙϩⲓⲧ· ⲉⲧⲓ ϭⲉ ⲟⲛ ⲛⲁⲙⲁⲑⲏ-
10 ⲧⲏⲥ ⲥⲱⲧⲙ̄ ⲁⲩⲱ ⲛ̄ⲧⲉⲧⲛ̄ⲟⲩⲱϩ ⲉⲧⲉⲧⲏⲩⲧⲛ̄ ⲛ̄ⲧⲉⲧⲛ̄ⲛⲏ-
ⲫⲉ ⲛ̄ⲧⲉⲧⲛ̄ⲥⲱⲧⲙ̄ ⲉⲡⲥⲟⲟⲩⲛ ⲧⲏⲣϥ̄ ⲛ̄ⲧⲉ ⲡⲙⲩⲥⲧⲏⲣⲓⲟⲛ
ⲛ̄ⲧⲉ ⲡⲓⲁⲧϣⲁϫⲉ ⲉⲣⲟϥ· ϫⲉ ⲡⲙⲩⲥⲧⲏⲣⲓⲟⲛ ⲉⲧⲙ̄ⲙⲁⲩ ⲛ̄-
ⲧⲟϥ ⲡⲉⲧⲥⲟⲟⲩⲛ ϫⲉ ⲉⲧⲃⲉ ⲟⲩ ⲁⲩϣⲱⲡⲉ ⲛ̄ϭⲓ ⲛ̄ⲇⲁⲓⲙⲟ-
ⲛⲓⲟⲛ· ⲁⲩⲱ ⲉⲧⲃⲉ ⲟⲩ ⲁⲥϣⲱⲡⲉ ⲛ̄ϭⲓ ⲧⲙⲛ̄ⲧⲣⲱⲙⲉ· ⲁⲩⲱ
15 ⲡⲙⲩⲥⲧⲏⲣⲓⲟⲛ ⲉⲧⲙ̄ⲙⲁⲩ ⲛ̄ⲧⲟϥ ⲡⲉⲧⲥⲟⲟⲩⲛ ϫⲉ ⲉⲧⲃⲉ ⲟⲩ
ⲁϥϣⲱⲡⲉ ⲛ̄ϭⲓ ⲡⲕⲁⲩⲙⲁ· ⲁⲩⲱ ⲉⲧⲃⲉ ⲟⲩ ⲁϥϣⲱⲡⲉ ⲛ̄ϭⲓ
ⲡⲁⲏⲣ ⲉⲧⲛⲟⲧⲙ̄· ⲁⲩⲱ ⲡⲙⲩⲥⲧⲏⲣⲓⲟⲛ ⲉⲧⲙ̄ⲙⲁⲩ ⲛ̄ⲧⲟϥ ⲡⲉⲧⲥⲟⲟⲩⲛ ϫⲉ ⲉⲧⲃⲉ ⲟⲩ ⲁⲩϣⲱⲡⲉ ⲛ̄ϭⲓ ⲛ̄ⲥⲓⲟⲩ ⲁⲩⲱ ⲉⲧⲃⲉ ⲣ̅ϥ̅ⲍ̅
ⲟⲩ ⲁⲩϣⲱⲡⲉ ⲛ̄ϭⲓ ⲛ̄ϭⲏⲡⲉ· ⲁⲩⲱ ⲡⲙⲩⲥⲧⲏⲣⲓⲟⲛ ⲉⲧⲙ̄ⲙⲁⲩ
20 ⲛ̄ⲧⲟϥ ⲡⲉⲧⲥⲟⲟⲩⲛ ϫⲉ ⲉⲧⲃⲉ ⲟⲩ ⲁ ⲡⲕⲁϩ ⲣ̄ϣⲁⲕⲉ ⲁⲩⲱ
ⲉⲧⲃⲉ ⲟⲩ ⲁ ⲡⲙⲟⲟⲩ ⲉⲓ̓ ⲉϫⲱϥ· ⲁⲩⲱ ⲡⲙⲩⲥⲧⲏⲣⲓⲟⲛ ⲉⲧ-
ⲙ̄ⲙⲁⲩ ⲛ̄ⲧⲟϥ ⲡⲉⲧⲥⲟⲟⲩⲛ ϫⲉ ⲉⲧⲃⲉ ⲟⲩ ⲡⲕⲁϩ ϣⲟⲟⲩⲉ
ⲁⲩⲱ ⲁ ⲡⲙⲟⲩⲛ̄ϩϣⲟⲩ ⲉⲓ̓ ⲉϫⲱϥ· ⲁⲩⲱ ⲡⲙⲩⲥⲧⲏⲣⲓⲟⲛ
ⲉⲧⲙ̄ⲙⲁⲩ ⲛ̄ⲧⲟϥ ⲡⲉⲧⲥⲟⲟⲩⲛ ϫⲉ ⲉⲧⲃⲉ ⲟⲩ ⲁϥϣⲱⲡⲉ ⲛ̄ϭⲓ
25 ⲡϩⲉⲃⲱⲱⲛ· ⲁⲩⲱ ⲉⲧⲃⲉ ⲟⲩ ⲁϥϣⲱⲡⲉ ⲛ̄ϭⲓ ⲡϩⲉⲛⲟⲩϥⲉ·
ⲁⲩⲱ ⲡⲙⲩⲥⲧⲏⲣⲓⲟⲛ ⲉⲧⲙ̄ⲙⲁⲩ ⲛ̄ⲧⲟϥ ⲡⲉⲧⲥⲟⲟⲩⲛ ϫⲉ ⲉⲧ-

one be *sober* in the *Spirit* that is in him, and may you listen and *grasp* every word which I will say to you, for from now I will begin to speak with you concerning all the knowledges of the Ineffable. That *mystery* knows why the west came into existence, and why the east. And that *mystery* knows why the south came into existence and why the north.

Yet again, my *disciples*, listen and continue to be *sober*, and hear the whole knowledge of the *mystery* of the Ineffable. For that *mystery* knows why *demons* came into existence, and why mankind. And that *mystery* knows why *heat* came into existence, and why sweet *air*. And that *mystery* knows why the stars came into existence, and why the clouds. And that *mystery* knows why the earth dried and why the water came over it. And that *mystery* knows why the earth was dry and why the rain came upon it. And that *mystery* knows why famine came into existence and why plenty. And that *mystery* knows why | frost came

ΒΕ ΟΥ ΑϤϢωΠΕ Ν̄ϬΙ ΠΧΑϤ · ΑΥω ΕΤΒΕ ΟΥ ΑϹϢωΠΕ
Ν̄ϬΙ ϯωΤΕ ΕΤΝΑΝΟΥϹ: ΑΥω ΠΜΥϹΤΗΡΙΟΝ ΕΤΜ̄ΜΑΥ
Ν̄ΤΟϤ ΠΕΤϹΟΟΥΝ ΧΕ ΕΤΒΕ ΟΥ ΑϤϢωΠΕ Ν̄ϬΙ ΠϢΟ-
ΕΙϢ · ΑΥω ΕΤΒΕ ΟΥ ΑϤϢωΠΕ Ν̄ϬΙ ΠΕΚΒΟ ΕΤϨΟΛϬ̄ ·
5 ΑΥω ΠΜΥϹΤΗΡΙΟΝ ΕΤΜ̄ΜΑΥ Ν̄ΤΟϤ ΠΕΤϹΟΟΥΝ ΧΕ ΕΤ-
ΒΕ ΟΥ ΑϹϢωΠΕ Ν̄ϬΙ ΤΕΧΑΛΛΑΖΑ ΑΥω* ΕΤΒΕ ΟΥ ΑϤ- <u>ΡϤΖ</u> ^b
ϢωΠΕ Ν̄ϬΙ ΠΕΧΙωΝ ΕΤΝΟΤΜ̄ · ΑΥω ΠΜΥϹΤΗΡΙΟΝ ΕΤ-
Μ̄ΜΑΥ Ν̄ΤΟϤ ΠΕΤϹΟΟΥΝ ΧΕ ΕΤΒΕ ΟΥ ΑϤϢωΠΕ Ν̄ϬΙ
ΠΤΗΥ Ν̄ΕΜΝ̄Τ · ΑΥω ΕΤΒΕ ΟΥ ΑϤϢωΠΕ Ν̄ϬΙ ΠΤΗΥ Ν̄-
10 ΕΕΙΒΤ̄ · ΑΥω ΠΜΥϹΤΗΡΙΟΝ ΕΤΜ̄ΜΑΥ Ν̄ΤΟϤ ΠΕΤϹΟΟΥΝ
ΧΕ ΕΤΒΕ ΟΥ ΑϤϢωΠΕ Ν̄ϬΙ ΠΚωϨΤ̄ Μ̄ΠΧΙϹΕ ΑΥω ΕΤΒΕ
ΟΥ ΑΥϢωΠΕ Ν̄ϬΙ Ν̄ΚΕΜΟΥΕΙΟΟΥΕ · ΑΥω ΠΜΥϹΤΗΡΙΟΝ
ΕΤΜ̄ΜΑΥ Ν̄ΤΟϤ ΠΕΤϹΟΟΥΝ ΧΕ ΕΤΒΕ ΟΥ ΑϤϢωΠΕ Ν̄ϬΙ
ΠΤΗΥ Ν̄ΕΕΙΒΤ̄ · ΑΥω ΠΜΥϹΤΗΡΙΟΝ ΕΤΜ̄ΜΑΥ Ν̄ΤΟϤ ΠΕΤ-
15 ϹΟΟΥΝ ΧΕ ΕΤΒΕ ΟΥ ΑϤϢωΠΕ Ν̄ϬΙ ΠΤΟΥΡΗϹ ΑΥω
ΕΤΒΕ ΟΥ ΑϤϢωΠΕ Ν̄ϬΙ ΠΤΟΥΜ̄ϨΙΤ · ΑΥω ΠΜΥϹΤΗΡΙΟΝ
ΕΤΜ̄ΜΑΥ Ν̄ΤΟϤ ΠΕΤϹΟΟΥΝ ΧΕ ΕΤΒΕ ΟΥ ΑΥϢωΠΕ
Ν̄ϬΙ Ν̄ϹΙΟΥ Ν̄ΤΠΕ · ΑΥω ΜΝ̄ Ν̄ΑΙϹΚΟϹ Ν̄ΤΕ ΝΕϤωϹΤΗΡ ·
ΑΥω ΕΤΒΕ ΟΥ ΑϤϢωΠΕ Ν̄ϬΙ ΠΕϹ**ΤΕΡΕωΜΑ Μ̄Ν̄ ΝΕϤ-(ΡϤΗ)
20 ΚΑΤΑΠΕΤΑϹΜΑ ΤΗΡΟΥ · ΑΥω ΠΜΥϹΤΗΡΙΟΝ ΕΤΜ̄ΜΑΥ
Ν̄ΤΟϤ ΠΕΤϹΟΟΥΝ ΧΕ ΕΤΒΕ ΟΥ ΑΥϢωΠΕ Ν̄ϬΙ Ν̄ΑΡΧωΝ
Ν̄ΝΕϹΦΕΡΑ · ΑΥω ΕΤΒΕ ΟΥ ΑϹϢωΠΕ Ν̄ϬΙ ΤΕϹΦΕΡΑ Μ̄Ν̄
ΝΕϹΤΥΠΟϹ ΤΗΡΟΥ · ΑΥω ΠΜΥϹΤΗΡΙΟΝ ΕΤΜ̄ΜΑΥ Ν̄ΤΟϤ
ΠΕΤϹΟΟΥΝ ΧΕ ΕΤΒΕ ΟΥ ΑΥϢωΠΕ Ν̄ϬΙ Ν̄ΑΡΧωΝ Ν̄ΤΕ
25 Ν̄ΑΙωΝ · ΑΥω ΕΤΒΕ ΟΥ ΑΥϢωΠΕ Ν̄ϬΙ Ν̄ΑΙωΝ Μ̄Ν̄ ΝΕΥ-
ΚΑΤΑΠΕΤΑϹΜΑ · ΑΥω ΠΜΥϹΤΗΡΙΟΝ ΕΤΜ̄ΜΑΥ Ν̄ΤΟϤ ΠΕΤ-

---

23 MS ΝΕϹΤΥΠΟϹ; read ΝΕϹΤΟΠΟϹ.

into existence, and why beneficial dew. And that *mystery* knows why dust came into existence and why sweet coolness. And that *mystery* knows why *hail* came into existence, and why pleasant *snow*. And that *mystery* knows why the west wind came into existence, and why the east wind. And that *mystery* knows why the fire of the height came into existence, and why the waters. And that *mystery* knows why the east wind came into existence. And that *mystery* knows why the south wind and why the north wind came into existence. And that *mystery* knows why the stars of the sky came into existence, and the *discs* of the *luminaries*, and why the *firmament* with all its *veils*. And that *mystery* knows why the *archons* of the *spheres* came into existence, and why the *sphere* with all its *places* [1]. And that *mystery* knows why the *archons* of the *aeons* came into existence, and why the *aeons* with their *veils*. And that *mystery* | knows why the

---

[1]   (23) places; MS : types.

429

ⲥⲟⲟⲩⲛ ϫⲉ ⲉⲧⲃⲉ ⲟⲩ ⲁⲩϣⲱⲡⲉ ⲛ̅ϭⲓ ⲛ̅ⲁⲣⲭⲱⲛ ⲛ̅ⲧⲉ ⲛ̅-
ⲁⲓⲱⲛ ⲛ̅ⲧⲩⲣⲁⲛⲛⲟⲥ· ⲁⲩⲱ ⲉⲧⲃⲉ ⲟⲩ ⲁⲩϣⲱⲡⲉ ⲛ̅ϭⲓ .ⲛ̅-
ⲁⲣⲭⲱⲛ ⲛ̅ⲧⲁⲩⲙⲉⲧⲁⲛⲟⲓ̈· ⲁⲩⲱ ⲡⲙⲩⲥⲧⲏⲣⲓⲟⲛ ⲉⲧⲙ̅ⲙⲁⲩ
ⲛ̅ⲧⲟϥ ⲡⲉⲧⲥⲟⲟⲩⲛ ϫⲉ ⲉⲧⲃⲉ ⲟⲩ ⲁⲩϣⲱⲡⲉ ⲛ̅ϭⲓ ⲛ̅ⲗⲉⲓ-
5 ⲧⲟⲩⲣⲅⲟⲥ· ⲁⲩⲱ ⲉⲧⲃⲉ ⲟⲩ ⲁⲩϣⲱⲡⲉ ⲛ̅ϭⲓ ⲛ̅ⲇⲉⲕⲁⲛⲟⲥ·
ⲁⲩⲱ ⲡⲙⲩⲥⲧⲏⲣⲓⲟⲛ ⲉⲧⲙ̅ⲙⲁⲩ ⲛ̅ⲧⲟϥ ⲡⲉⲧⲥⲟⲟⲩⲛ ϫⲉ ⲉⲧⲃⲉ* ⲟⲩ ⲁⲩϣⲱⲡⲉ ⲛ̅ϭⲓ ⲛ̅ⲁⲅⲅⲉⲗⲟⲥ· ⲁⲩⲱ ⲉⲧⲃⲉ ⲟⲩ ⲁⲩ-⟨ⲣ̅ⳅⲏᵇ⟩
ϣⲱⲡⲉ ⲛ̅ϭⲓ ⲛ̅ⲁⲣⲭⲁⲅⲅⲉⲗⲟⲥ· ⲁⲩⲱ ⲡⲙⲩⲥⲧⲏⲣⲓⲟⲛ ⲉⲧⲙ̅-
ⲙⲁⲩ ⲛ̅ⲧⲟϥ ⲡⲉⲧⲥⲟⲟⲩⲛ ϫⲉ ⲉⲧⲃⲉ ⲟⲩ ⲁⲩϣⲱⲡⲉ ⲛ̅ϭⲓ ⲛ̅-
10 ϫⲟⲉⲓⲥ· ⲁⲩⲱ ⲉⲧⲃⲉ ⲟⲩ ⲁⲩϣⲱⲡⲉ ⲛ̅ϭⲓ ⲛ̅ⲛⲟⲩⲧⲉ· ⲁⲩⲱ
ⲡⲙⲩⲥⲧⲏⲣⲓⲟⲛ ⲉⲧⲙ̅ⲙⲁⲩ ⲛ̅ⲧⲟϥ ⲡⲉⲧⲥⲟⲟⲩⲛ ϫⲉ ⲉⲧⲃⲉ ⲟⲩ
ϩⲱϥ ⲁ ⲡⲕⲱϩ ϣⲱⲡⲉ ϩ̅ⲙ ⲡϫⲓⲥⲉ· ⲁⲩⲱ ⲉⲧⲃⲉ ⲟⲩ ϩⲱⲥ
ⲁⲥϣⲱⲡⲉ ⲛ̅ϭⲓ ⲧⲙⲛ̅ⲧⲁⲧⲕⲱϩ· ⲁⲩⲱ ⲡⲙⲩⲥⲧⲏⲣⲓⲟⲛ ⲉⲧⲙ̅-
ⲙⲁⲩ ⲛ̅ⲧⲟϥ ⲡⲉⲧⲥⲟⲟⲩⲛ ϫⲉ ⲉⲧⲃⲉ ⲟⲩ ⲁϥϣⲱⲡⲉ ⲛ̅ϭⲓ
15 ⲡⲙⲟⲥⲧⲉ ⲁⲩⲱ ⲉⲧⲃⲉ ⲟⲩ ⲁϥϣⲱⲡⲉ ⲛ̅ϭⲓ ⲡⲙⲉ· ⲁⲩⲱ
ⲡⲙⲩⲥⲧⲏⲣⲓⲟⲛ ⲉⲧⲙ̅ⲙⲁⲩ ⲛ̅ⲧⲟϥ ⲡⲉ ⲉⲧⲥⲟⲟⲩⲛ ϫⲉ ⲉⲧⲃⲉ
ⲟⲩ ⲁ ⲡⲱⲣ̅ϫ̅ ϣⲱⲡⲉ· ⲁⲩⲱ ⲉⲧⲃⲉ ⲟⲩ ⲁϥϣⲱⲡⲉ ⲛ̅ϭⲓ
ⲡϩⲱⲧⲡ̅· ⲁⲩⲱ ⲡⲙⲩⲥⲧⲏⲣⲓⲟⲛ ⲉⲧⲙ̅ⲙⲁⲩ ⲛ̅ⲧⲟϥ ⲡⲉⲧⲥⲟⲟⲩⲛ
ϫⲉ ⲉⲧⲃⲉ ⲟⲩ ⲁ ⲧⲙⲛ̅ⲧⲙⲁⲓ̈ϩⲟⲩⲟ ϣⲱⲡⲉ· ⲁⲩⲱ ⲉⲧⲃⲉ ⲟⲩ
20 ⲁ ⲧⲁⲡⲟⲧⲁⲅⲏ ⲙ̅ⲡⲧⲏⲣϥ̅ ϣⲱⲡⲉ·** ⲁⲩⲱ ⲉⲧⲃⲉ ⲟⲩ ⲁⲥϣⲱⲡⲉ ⲣ̅ⳅⲑ
ⲛ̅ϭⲓ ⲧⲙⲛ̅ⲧⲙⲁⲓ̈ⲭⲣⲏⲙⲁ· ⲁⲩⲱ ⲡⲙⲩⲥⲧⲏⲣⲓⲟⲛ ⲉⲧⲙ̅ⲙⲁⲩ ⲛ̅-
ⲧⲟϥ ⲡⲉⲧⲥⲟⲟⲩⲛ ϫⲉ ⲉⲧⲃⲉ ⲟⲩ ⲁ ⲧⲙⲛ̅ⲧⲙⲁⲓ̈ϩⲏⲧⲥ̅ ϣⲱ-
ⲡⲉ· ⲁⲩⲱ ⲉⲧⲃⲉ ⲟⲩ ⲁϥϣⲱⲡⲉ ⲛ̅ϭⲓ ⲡⲥⲉⲓ· ⲁⲩⲱ ⲡⲙⲩⲥⲧⲏⲣⲓⲟⲛ ⲉⲧⲙ̅ⲙⲁⲩ ⲛ̅ⲧⲟϥ ⲡⲉⲧⲥⲟⲟⲩⲛ ϫⲉ ⲉⲧⲃⲉ ⲟⲩ ⲁⲩ-
25 ϣⲱⲡⲉ ⲛ̅ϭⲓ ⲛ̅ⲥⲩⲛⲍⲩⲅⲟⲥ· ⲁⲩⲱ ⲉⲧⲃⲉ ⲟⲩ ⲁⲩϣⲱⲡⲉ
ⲛ̅ϭⲓ ⲛⲉⲭⲱⲣⲓⲥⲥⲩⲛⲍⲩⲅⲟⲥ· ⲁⲩⲱ ⲡⲙⲩⲥⲧⲏⲣⲓⲟⲛ ⲉⲧⲙ̅ⲙⲁⲩ

17   MS ⲡⲱⲣ̅ϫ̅; read ⲡⲡⲱⲣ̅ϫ̅.

tyrannic archons of the *aeons* [1] came into existence, and why the *archons* which have *repented*. And that *mystery* knows why the *ministers* came into existence, and why the *decans*. And that *mystery* knows why the *angels* came into existence, and why the *archangels*. And that *mystery* knows why the lords came into existence, and why the gods. And that *mystery* knows why envy came into existence in the height, and why lack of envy [2] also. And that *mystery* knows why hatred came into existence, and why love. And that *mystery* knows why disunity came into existence, and why unity. And that *mystery* knows why covetousness came into existence, and why *renunciation* of all things, and why love of *money*. And that *mystery* knows why love of the belly came into existence, and why satiety. And that *mystery* knows why *partners* came into existence, and why the *unpaired ones*. And that *mystery* knows | why godlessness came into exis-

---

[1]   (1) tyrannic archons of the aeons; MS: archons of the tyrannic aeons.
[2]   (13) lack of envy; Schmidt: harmony.

ⲚⲦⲞϤ ⲠⲈⲦⲤⲞⲞⲨⲚ ϪⲈ ⲈⲦⲂⲈ ⲞⲨ ⲀⲤϢⲰⲠⲈ ⲚϬⲒ ⲦⲘⲚⲦ-
ⲀⲦⲚⲞⲨⲦⲈ· ⲀⲨⲰ ⲈⲦⲂⲈ ⲞⲨ ⲀⲤϢⲰⲠⲈ ⲚϬⲒ ⲦⲘⲚⲦⲘⲀÏ-
ⲚⲞⲨⲦⲈ· ⲀⲨⲰ ⲠⲘⲨⲤⲦⲎⲢⲒⲞⲚ ⲈⲦⲘⲘⲀⲨ ⲚⲦⲞϤ ⲠⲈⲦⲤⲞⲞⲨⲚ
ϪⲈ ⲈⲦⲂⲈ ⲞⲨ ⲀⲨϢⲰⲠⲈ ⲚϬⲒ ⲚⲈⳘⲰⲤⲦⲎⲢ· ⲀⲨⲰ ⲈⲦⲂⲈ
5 ⲞⲨ ⲀⲨϢⲰⲠⲈ ⲚϬⲒ ⲚⲈⲤⲠⲒⲚⲐⲎⲢ· ⲀⲨⲰ ⲠⲘⲨⲤⲦⲎⲢⲒⲞⲚ ⲈⲦ-
ⲘⲘⲀⲨ ⲚⲦⲞϤ ⲠⲈⲦⲤⲞⲞⲨⲚ ϪⲈ ⲈⲦⲂⲈ ⲞⲨ ⲀⲨϢⲰⲠⲈ ⲚϬⲒ
ⲚⲈⲦⲢⲒⲀⲆⲨⲚⲀⲘⲒⲤ· ⲀⲨⲰ ⲈⲦⲂⲈ ⲞⲨ ⲀⲨϢⲰⲠⲈ ⲚϬⲒ ⲚⲀⳘⲞ-
ⲢⲀⲦⲞⲤ· ⲀⲨⲰ ⲠⲘⲨⲤⲦⲎⲢⲒⲞⲚ ⲈⲦⲘⲘⲀⲨ ⲚⲦⲞϤ ⲠⲈⲦⲤⲞⲞⲨⲚ
ϪⲈ ⲈⲦⲂⲈ ⲞⲨˣ ⲀⲨϢⲰⲠⲈ ⲚϬⲒ ⲚⲈⲠⲢⲞⲠⲀⲦⲰⲢ· ⲀⲨⲰ ⲈⲦⲂⲈ ⲣ̄ϥ̄ᵇ
10 ⲞⲨ ⲀⲨϢⲰⲠⲈ ⲚϬⲒ Ⲛ̄ⳘⲒⲖⲒⲔⲢⲒⲚⲈⲤ· ⲀⲨⲰ ⲠⲘⲨⲤⲦⲎⲢⲒⲞⲚ ⲈⲦ-
ⲘⲘⲀⲨ ⲚⲦⲞϤ ⲠⲈⲦⲤⲞⲞⲨⲚ ϪⲈ ⲈⲦⲂⲈ ⲞⲨ ⲀϤϢⲰⲠⲈ ⲚϬⲒ
ⲠⲒⲚⲞϬ Ⲛ̄ⲀⲨⲐⲀⲆⲎⲤ· ⲀⲨⲰ ⲈⲦⲂⲈ ⲞⲨ ⲀⲨϢⲰⲠⲈ ⲚϬⲒ ⲚⲈϤ-
ⲠⲒⲤⲦⲞⲤ· ⲀⲨⲰ ⲠⲘⲨⲤⲦⲎⲢⲒⲞⲚ ⲈⲦⲘⲘⲀⲨ ⲚⲦⲞϤ ⲠⲈⲦⲤⲞ-
ⲞⲨⲚ ϪⲈ ⲈⲦⲂⲈ ⲞⲨ ⲀϤϢⲰⲠⲈ ⲚϬⲒ ⲠⲚⲞϬ Ⲛ̄ⲦⲢⲒⲀⲆⲨⲚⲀⲘⲒⲤ·
15 ⲀⲨⲰ ⲈⲦⲂⲈ ⲞⲨ ⲀϤϢⲰⲠⲈ ⲚϬⲒ ⲠⲚⲞϬ Ⲙ̄ⲠⲢⲞⲠⲀⲦⲰⲢ Ⲛ̄Ⲁ-
ⳘⲞⲢⲀⲦⲞⲤ· ⲀⲨⲰ ⲠⲘⲨⲤⲦⲎⲢⲒⲞⲚ ⲈⲦⲘⲘⲀⲨ ⲚⲦⲞϤ ⲠⲈⲦⲤⲞ-
ⲞⲨⲚ ϪⲈ ⲈⲦⲂⲈ ⲞⲨ ⲀϤϢⲰⲠⲈ ⲚϬⲒ ⲠⲘⲀⳘⲘⲚⲦϢⲞⲘⲦⲈ Ⲛ̄-
ⲀⲒⲰⲚ· ⲀⲨⲰ ⲈⲦⲂⲈ ⲞⲨ ⲀϤϢⲰⲠⲈ ⲚϬⲒ ⲠⲦⲞⲠⲞⲤ Ⲛ̄ⲚⲀⲦⲘⲈ-
ⲤⲞⲤ· ⲀⲨⲰ ⲠⲘⲨⲤⲦⲎⲢⲒⲞⲚ ⲈⲦⲘⲘⲀⲨ ⲚⲦⲞϤ ⲠⲈⲦⲤⲞⲞⲨⲚ
20 ϪⲈ ⲈⲦⲂⲈ ⲞⲨ ⲀⲨϢⲰⲠⲈ ⲚϬⲒ Ⲙ̄ⲠⲀⲢⲀⲖⲎⲘⲠⲦⲎⲤ Ⲛ̄ⲦⲘⲈ-
ⲤⲞⲤ· ⲀⲨⲰ ϪⲈ ⲈⲦⲂⲈ ⲞⲨ ⲀⲨϢⲰⲠⲈ ⲚϬⲒ Ⲛ̄ⲠⲀⲢⲐⲈⲚⲞⲤ
Ⲙ̄ⲠⲞⲨⲞⲈⲒⲚ· ⲀⲨⲰ ⲠⲘⲨⲤⲦⲎⲢⲒⲞⲚ ⲈⲦⲘⲘⲀⲨ ⲚⲦⲞϤ ⲠⲈ ⲈⲦ-
ⲤⲞⲞⲨⲚ ϪⲈ ⲈⲦⲂⲈˣˣⲞⲨ ⲀⲨϢⲰⲠⲈ ⲚϬⲒ Ⲛ̄ⲆⲒⲀⲔⲞⲚⲞⲤ Ⲛ̄Ⲧ- [ⲥ]
ⲘⲈⲤⲞⲤ· ⲀⲨⲰ ⲈⲦⲂⲈ ⲞⲨ ⲀⲨϢⲰⲠⲈ ⲚϬⲒ Ⲛ̄ⲀⳘⳘⲈⲖⲞⲤ Ⲛ̄Ⲧ-
25 ⲘⲈⲤⲞⲤ· ⲀⲨⲰ ⲠⲘⲨⲤⲦⲎⲢⲒⲞⲚ ⲈⲦⲘⲘⲀⲨ ⲚⲦⲞϤ ⲠⲈⲦⲤⲞⲞⲨⲚ

---

2 ⲀⲨⲰ . . . ⲦⲘⲚⲦⲘⲀÏⲚⲞⲨⲦⲈ written in margin below by the same hand.

tence, and why the love of God. And that *mystery* knows why the *luminaries* came into existence, and why the *light-sparks*. And that *mystery* knows why the *triple-powered ones* came into existence, and why the *invisible ones*. And that *mystery* knows why the *forefathers* and why the *pure ones* came into existence. And that *mystery* knows why the great Authades came into existence, and why his *faithful ones*. And that *mystery* knows why the great *triple-power* came into existence, and why the great *invisible forefather*. And that *mystery* knows why the thirteenth *aeon* came into existence, and why the *place* of those of the *Midst*. And that *mystery* knows why the *paralemptai* of the *Midst* came into existence, and why the *virgins* of the light. And that *mystery* knows why the *servers* of the *Midst* came into existence, and why the *angels* of the *Midst*. And that *mystery* knows |

ⲭⲉ ⲉⲧⲃⲉ ⲟⲩ ⲁϥϣⲱⲡⲉ ⲛ̄ϭⲓ ⲡⲕⲁϩ ⲙ̄ⲡⲟⲩⲟⲉⲓⲛ · ⲁⲩⲱ
ⲉⲧⲃⲉ ⲟⲩ ⲁϥϣⲱⲡⲉ ⲛ̄ϭⲓ ⲡⲓⲛⲟϭ ⲙ̄ⲡⲁⲣⲁⲗⲏⲙⲡⲧⲏⲥ ⲙ̄ⲡⲟⲩⲟ-
ⲉⲓⲛ · ⲁⲩⲱ ⲡⲙⲩⲥⲧⲏⲣⲓⲟⲛ ⲉⲧⲙ̄ⲙⲁⲩ ⲛ̄ⲧⲟϥ ⲡⲉⲧⲥⲟⲟⲩⲛ ⲭⲉ
ⲉⲧⲃⲉ ⲟⲩ ⲁϥϣⲱⲡⲉ ⲛ̄ϭⲓ ⲛⲉⲫⲩⲗⲁⲝ ⲙ̄ⲡⲧⲟⲡⲟⲥ ⲛ̄ⲛⲁⲟⲩ-
5 ⲛⲁⲙ · ⲁⲩⲱ ⲉⲧⲃⲉ ⲟⲩ ⲁⲩϣⲱⲡⲉ ⲛ̄ϭⲓ ⲛⲉⲡⲣⲟϩⲅⲟⲩⲙⲉⲛⲟⲥ
ⲛ̄ⲛⲁⲓ̈ · ⲁⲩⲱ ⲡⲙⲩⲥⲧⲏⲣⲓⲟⲛ ⲉⲧⲙ̄ⲙⲁⲩ ⲛ̄ⲧⲟϥ ⲡⲉⲧⲥⲟⲟⲩⲛ
ⲭⲉ ⲉⲧⲃⲉ ⲟⲩ ⲁⲥϣⲱⲡⲉ ⲛ̄ϭⲓ ⲧⲡⲩⲗⲏ ⲙ̄ⲡⲱⲛ̄ϩ · ⲁⲩⲱ ⲉⲧⲃⲉ ⲟⲩ ⲁϥϣⲱⲡⲉ ⲛ̄ϭⲓ ⲥⲁⲃⲁⲱⲑ ⲡⲁⲅⲁⲑⲟⲥ · ⲁⲩⲱ ⲡⲙⲩⲥⲧⲏⲣⲓⲟⲛ ⲉⲧⲙ̄ⲙⲁⲩ ⲛ̄ⲧⲟϥ ⲡⲉⲧⲥⲟⲟⲩⲛ ⲭⲉ ⲉⲧⲃⲉ ⲟⲩ
10 ⲁϥϣⲱⲡⲉ ⲛ̄ϭⲓ ⲡⲧⲟⲡⲟⲥ ⲛ̄ⲛⲁⲟⲩⲛⲁⲙ · ⲁⲩⲱ ⲉⲧⲃⲉ ⲟⲩ
ⲁϥϣⲱⲡⲉ ⲛ̄ϭⲓ ⲡⲕⲁϩ ⲙ̄ⲡⲟⲩⲟⲉⲓⲛ ⲉⲧⲉ ⲛ̄ⲧⲟϥ ⲡⲉ ⲡⲉⲑⲏⲥⲁⲩⲣⲟⲥ ⲙ̄ⲡⲟⲩⲟⲉⲓⲛ · ⲁⲩⲱ ⲡⲙⲩⲥⲧⲏⲣ⸰ⲓⲟⲛ ⲉⲧⲙ̄ⲙⲁⲩ ⲛ̄ⲧⲟϥ [ⲥ̄ ᵇ]
ⲡⲉⲧⲥⲟⲟⲩⲛ ⲭⲉ ⲉⲧⲃⲉ ⲟⲩ ⲁⲩϣⲱⲡⲉ ⲛ̄ϭⲓ ⲛⲉⲡⲣⲟⲃⲟⲗⲟⲟⲩⲉ ⲙ̄ⲡⲟⲩⲟⲉⲓⲛ ⲁⲩⲱ ⲉⲧⲃⲉ ⲟⲩ ⲁⲩϣⲱⲡⲉ ⲛ̄ϭⲓ ⲡⲙⲛ̄ⲧ-
15 ⲥⲛⲟⲟⲩⲥ ⲛ̄ⲥⲱⲧⲏⲣ · ⲁⲩⲱ ⲡⲙⲩⲥⲧⲏⲣⲓⲟⲛ ⲉⲧⲙ̄ⲙⲁⲩ ⲛ̄ⲧⲟϥ
ⲡⲉⲧⲥⲟⲟⲩⲛ ⲭⲉ ⲉⲧⲃⲉ ⲟⲩ ⲁⲩϣⲱⲡⲉ ⲛ̄ϭⲓ ⲧϣⲟⲙⲧⲉ ⲙ̄-
ⲡⲩⲗⲏ ⲛ̄ⲧⲉ ⲡⲉⲑⲏⲥⲁⲩⲣⲟⲥ ⲙ̄ⲡⲟⲩⲟⲉⲓⲛ · ⲁⲩⲱ ⲉⲧⲃⲉ ⲟⲩ
ⲁⲩϣⲱⲡⲉ ⲛ̄ϭⲓ ⲡⲉⲯⲓⲥ ⲙ̄ⲫⲩⲗⲁⲝ · ⲁⲩⲱ ⲡⲙⲩⲥⲧⲏⲣⲓⲟⲛ
ⲉⲧⲙ̄ⲙⲁⲩ ⲛ̄ⲧⲟϥ ⲡⲉⲧⲥⲟⲟⲩⲛ ⲭⲉ ⲉⲧⲃⲉ ⲟⲩ ⲁⲩϣⲱⲡⲉ
20 ⲛ̄ϭⲓ ⲛ̄ϩⲁⲧⲣⲉⲉⲩ ⲛ̄ⲥⲱⲧⲏⲣ · ⲁⲩⲱ ⲉⲧⲃⲉ ⲟⲩ ⲁⲩϣⲱⲡⲉ ⲛ̄ϭⲓ
ⲡϣⲟⲙⲛ̄ⲧ ⲛ̄ϩⲁⲙⲏⲛ · ⲁⲩⲱ ⲡⲙⲩⲥⲧⲏⲣⲓⲟⲛ ⲉⲧⲙ̄ⲙⲁⲩ ⲛ̄ⲧⲟϥ
ⲉⲧⲥⲟⲟⲩⲛ ⲭⲉ ⲉⲧⲃⲉ ⲟⲩ ⲁⲩϣⲱⲡⲉ ⲛ̄ϭⲓ ⲡϯⲟⲩ ⲛ̄ϣⲏⲛ
ⲁⲩⲱ ⲉⲧⲃⲉ ⲟⲩ ⲁⲩϣⲱⲡⲉ ⲛ̄ϭⲓ ⲡⲥⲁϣϥ̄ ⲛ̄ϩⲁⲙⲏⲛ · ⲁⲩⲱ
ⲡⲙⲩⲥⲧⲏⲣⲓⲟⲛ ⲉⲧⲙ̄ⲙⲁⲩ ⲛ̄ⲧⲟϥ ⲉⲧⲥⲟⲟⲩⲛ ⲭⲉ ⲉⲧⲃⲉ ⲟⲩ
25 ⲁϥϣⲱⲡⲉ ⲛ̄ϭⲓ ⲡⲕⲉⲣⲁⲥⲙⲟⲥ ⲉⲛϥϣⲟⲟⲡ ⲁⲛ · ⲁⲩⲱ ⲉⲧⲃⲉ ⲥⲁ
ⲟⲩ ⲁϥⲥⲱⲧϥ̄ ⲉⲃⲟⲗ:

---

4   MS ⲁϥϣⲱⲡⲉ; read ⲁⲩϣⲱⲡⲉ.

why the Land of the Light came into existence, and why
the great *paralemptes* of the light. And that *mystery* knows
why the *watchers* of the *place* of those of the right came into
existence, and why the *leaders* of these. And that *mystery*
knows why the *gate* of life came into existence, and why
Sabaoth the *Good*. And that *mystery* knows why the *place*
of those of the right came into existence, and why the Land
of the Light which is the *Treasury* of the Light. And that
mystery knows why the *emanations* of the light came into
existence, and why the twelve *saviours*. And that *mystery*
knows why the three *gates* of the *Treasury* of the Light came
into existence, and why the nine *watchers*. And that *mystery*
knows why the twin *saviours* came into existence, and why
the three *amens*. And that *mystery* knows why the five
trees came into existence, and why the seven *amens*. And
that *mystery* knows why the *mixture* which does not exist
came into existence, and why it was purified." |

ⳅ ⲀϤⲞⲨⲰϨ ⲞⲚ ⲈⲦⲞⲞⲦϤ ⲚϬⲒ ⲒⲤ ⲠⲈⲬⲀϤ ⲚⲚⲈϤⲘⲀⲞⲎⲦⲎⲤ
ⲬⲈ ⲈⲦⲒ ⲚⲀⲘⲀⲐⲎⲦⲎⲤ ⲚⲎⲪⲈ ⲘⲘⲰⲦⲚ ⲀⲨⲰ ⲘⲀⲢⲈ ⲠⲞⲨⲀ
ⲠⲞⲨⲀ ⲘⲘⲰⲦⲚ ⲈⲒⲚⲈ ⲚⲦϬⲞⲘ ⲚⲦⲀⲒⲤⲐⲎⲤⲒⲤ ⲚⲦⲈ ⲠⲞⲨⲞⲈⲒⲚ
ⲈⲐⲎ ⲘⲘⲞϤ. ⲚⲦⲈⲦⲚⲬⲒⲤⲘⲎ ⲈⲂⲞⲖ ϨⲚ ⲞⲨⲰⲢⲬ. ⲬⲒⲚ ⲦⲈ-
5 ⲚⲞⲨ ⲄⲀⲢ ⲈⲒⲚⲀϢⲀⲬⲈ ⲚⲘⲘⲎⲦⲚ ⲈⲠⲦⲞⲠⲞⲤ ⲦⲎⲢϤ ⲚⲦⲀⲖⲎ-
ⲐⲒⲀ ⲚⲦⲈ ⲠⲒⲀⲦϢⲀⲬⲈ ⲈⲢⲞϤ · ⲀⲨⲰ ⲘⲚ ⲐⲈ ⲈⲦϤⲞ ⲘⲘⲞⲤ:

ⳅ ⲀⲤϢⲰⲠⲈ ϬⲈ ⲚⲦⲈⲢⲈ ⲘⲘⲀⲐⲎⲦⲎⲤ ⲤⲰⲦⲘ ⲈⲚⲈⲒϢⲀⲬⲈ
ⲈⲦϤⲬⲰ ⲘⲘⲞⲞⲨ ⲚϬⲒ ⲒⲤ · ⲀⲨⲈⲔⲖⲒⲚⲈ ⲀⲨⲰ ⲀⲨⲔⲀⲦⲞⲞⲦⲞⲨ
ⲈⲂⲞⲖ ⲈⲠⲦⲎⲢϤ · ⲀⲤⲈⲒ ⲈⲐⲎ ⲚϬⲒ ⲘⲀⲢⲒⲀ ⲦⲘⲀⲄⲆⲀⲖⲎⲚⲎ
10 ⲀⲤⲠⲀϨⲦⲤ ⲈⲬⲚ ⲚⲞⲨⲈⲢⲎⲦⲈ ⲚⲒⲤ ⲀⲤⲞⲨⲰϢⲦ ⲈⲢⲞⲞⲨ ·
ⲀⲤⲰϢ ⲈⲂⲞⲖ ⲀⲤⲢⲒⲘⲈ ⲠⲈⲬⲀⲤ ⲬⲈ ⲚⲀ ϨⲀⲢⲞⲒ ⲠⲀⲬⲞⲈⲒⲤ
ⲈⲘⲘⲞⲚ Ⲁ ⲚⲀⲤⲚⲎⲨ ⲤⲰⲦⲘ ⲀⲨⲰ ⲀⲨⲔⲀⲦⲞⲞⲦⲞⲨ ⲈⲂⲞⲖ ⲤⲀᵇ
ϨⲚ ⲚϢⲀⲬⲈ ⲈⲦⲔⲬⲰ ⲘⲘⲞⲞⲨ: ⲦⲈⲚⲞⲨ ϬⲈ ⲠⲀⲬⲞⲈⲒⲤ ⲈⲦ-
ⲂⲈ ⲠⲤⲞⲞⲨⲚ ⲚⲚⲈⲒϢⲀⲬⲈ ⲦⲎⲢⲞⲨ ⲚⲦⲀⲔⲬⲞⲞⲨ ⲈⲨϢⲞⲞⲠ
15 ϨⲢⲀⲒ ϨⲘ ⲠⲘⲨⲤⲦⲎⲢⲒⲞⲚ ⲘⲠⲒⲀⲦϢⲀⲬⲈ ⲈⲢⲞϤ · ⲀⲖⲖⲀ ⲀⲒⲤⲰⲦⲘ
ⲈⲢⲞⲔ ⲈⲔⲬⲰ ⲘⲘⲞⲒ ⲬⲈ ⲬⲒⲚ ⲦⲈⲚⲞⲨ ⲈⲒⲚⲀⲀⲢⲬⲒ ⲚϢⲀⲬⲈ
ⲚⲘⲘⲎⲦⲚ ⲈⲠⲤⲞⲞⲨⲚ ⲦⲎⲢϤ ⲘⲠⲘⲨⲤⲦⲎⲢⲒⲞⲚ ⲘⲠⲒⲀⲦϢⲀⲬⲈ
ⲈⲢⲞϤ · ⲠⲈⲒϢⲀⲬⲈ ⲞⲨⲚ ⲈⲦⲔⲬⲰ ⲘⲘⲞϤ ⲈⲒⲈ ⲘⲠⲀⲦⲔϨⲰⲚ
ⲈϨⲞⲨⲚ ⲈⲬⲰⲔ ⲈⲂⲞⲖ ⲘⲠϢⲀⲬⲈ · ⲈⲦⲂⲈ ⲠⲀⲒ ⲞⲨⲚ ⲚⲀⲤⲚⲎⲨ
20 ⲀⲨⲤⲰⲦⲘ ⲀⲨⲔⲀⲦⲞⲞⲦⲞⲨ ⲈⲂⲞⲖ ⲀⲨⲖⲞ ⲈⲨⲀⲒⲤⲐⲀⲚⲈ ⲬⲈ
ⲈⲔϢⲀⲬⲈ ⲚⲘⲘⲀⲨ ⲚⲀϢ ⲚϨⲈ · ⲈⲦⲂⲈ ⲚϢⲀⲬⲈ ⲈⲦⲔⲬⲰ Ⲙ-
ⲘⲞⲞⲨ ⲚⲀⲨ · ⲦⲈⲚⲞⲨ ϬⲈ ⲠⲀⲬⲞⲈⲒⲤ ⲈϢⲬⲈ ⲈⲢⲈ ⲠⲤⲞⲞⲨⲚ
ⲚⲚⲀⲒ ⲦⲎⲢⲞⲨ ⲈϤϢⲞⲞⲠ ϨⲘ ⲠⲘⲨⲤⲦⲎⲢⲒⲞⲚ ⲈⲦⲘⲘⲀⲨ · ⲈⲒⲈ
ⲚⲒⲘ ⲠⲈ ⲠⲢⲰⲘⲈ ⲈⲦϨⲘ ⲠⲔⲞⲤⲘⲟⲤ ⲈⲦⲈ** ⲞⲨⲚϢϬⲞⲘ Ⲙ- [ⲤⲂ]
25 ⲘⲞϤ ⲈⲚⲞⲒ ⲘⲠⲘⲨⲤⲦⲎⲢⲒⲞⲚ ⲈⲦⲘⲘⲀⲨ ⲘⲚ ⲚⲈϤⲤⲞⲞⲨⲚ ⲦⲎ-

---

2 ⲀⲨⲰ ... ⲘⲘⲰⲦⲚ written in margin below by the same hand.
14 MS ⲈⲨϢⲞⲞⲠ; perhaps better ⲈϤϢⲞⲞⲠ.

94. Jesus continued again and said to his *disciples* : "*Yet* still, my *disciples*, be *sober* and let each one of you bring forward the power of *perception* of the light, that you may listen with assurance [1]. *For* from now I will speak to you of the whole *place* of *truth* of the Ineffable and of the manner in which it is."

Now it happened when the *disciples* heard these words which Jesus said, they *retired* and they despaired completely [2].

Then Maria Magdalene came forward. She prostrated herself at the feet of Jesus, she worshipped at them, she cried out, she wept and said : "Have mercy on me, my Lord, for my brothers have heard and they have despaired because of the words [3] which thou hast said to them. Now at this time, my Lord, concerning the knowledge of all these words which thou hast said to us, that they are in the *mystery* of the Ineffable — *but* I have heard thee ⟨saying to me⟩ [4] : 'From this time I will *begin* to speak with you of the whole knowledge of the *mystery* of the Ineffable' — now this discourse which thou speakest, thou hast not approached the completion of the discourse [5]. *Now* because of this my brothers have heard and despaired, and have ceased to *perceive* in what manner thou dost speak with them. Concerning the words which thou hast said to them, now [6] at this time, my Lord, if the knowledge of all these things is in that *mystery*, what man in the *world* has power to *understand*

---

[1] (4) with assurance; Till : with attention.

[2] (8) they retired and they despaired completely; Till : they became discouraged and they ceased to listen.

[3] (12) they have despaired because of the words; Till : they have ceased to listen to the words (see also 218.20).

[4] (16) I have heard thee ⟨saying to me⟩; Coptic construction grammatically impossible but not emended by Schmidt.

[5] (18) thou hast not approached the completion of the discourse; Till : (or) art thou not yet near to completing the discourse?

[6] (22) with them. Concerning the words which ... to them, now ...; Till : with them about the words which ... to them. Now ...

ΡΟΥ· ΑΥШ ΠΤΥΠΟC ΝΝΕΪϢΑϪΕ ΤΗΡΟΥ ΕΝΤΑΚϪΟΟΥ
ΕΤΒΗΗΤϤ :

ϧ ΑCϢШΠΕ ϬΕ ΝΤΕΡΕ Ι̅C̅ CШΤΜ ΕΝΕΪϢΑϪΕ ΕΤC̅ϪШ
Μ̅ΜΟΟΥ Ν̅ϬΙ ΜΑΡΙΑ ΑϤΕΙΜΕ ϪΕ ΑΥCШΤΜ̅ Ν̅ϬΙ Μ̅ΜΑ-
5 ΘΗΤΗC ΑΥΑΡΧΙ Ν̅ΚΑΤΟΟΤΟΥ ΕΒΟΛ ΑϤϯΤШΚ Ν̅ΗΤ
ΝΑΥ ΠΕϪΑϤ ΝΑΥ ϪΕ Μ̅ΠΡΛΥΠΙ ϬΕ ΝΑΜΑΘΗΤΗC ΕΤΒΕ
ΠΜΥCΤΗΡΙΟΝ Μ̅ΠΙΑΤϢΑϪΕ ΕΡΟϤ· ΕΤΕΤΝ̅ΜΕΕΥΕ ϪΕ
Ν̅ΤΕΤΝ̅ΝΑΝΟΪ Μ̅ΜΟϤ ΑΝ· ϨΑΜΗΝ ϯϪШ Μ̅ΜΟC ΝΗΤΝ̅ ϪΕ
ΠШΤΝ̅ ΠΕ ΠΜΥCΤΗΡΙΟΝ ΕΤΜ̅ΜΑΥ· ΑΥШ ΠΛΟΥΟΝ ΝΙΜ
10 ΠΕ ΕΤΝΑCШΤΜ Ν̅CШΤΝ̅ Ν̅CΕΑΠΟΤΑCCΕ Μ̅ΠΕΪΚΟCΜΟC
ΤΗΡϤ̅ ΜΝ̅ ΘΥΛΗ ΤΗΡC̅ ΕΤΝ̅ϨΗΤϤ· ΑΥШ Ν̅CΕΑΠΟΤΑCCΕ
Μ̅ΜΕΕΥΕ ΝΙΜ Μ̅ΠΟΝΗΡΟΝ ΕΤϢΟΟΠ Ν̅ϨΗΤΟΥ· ΑΥШ
Ν̅CΕΑΠΟΤΑCCΕ Ν̅ΡΡΟΟΥϢ ΤΗΡΟΥ Μ̅ΠΕΪΑΙШΝ·   [C̅Β̅ b]

ϧ ΤΕΝΟΥ ϬΕ ΟΥΝ ϯϪШ Μ̅ΜΟC ΝΗΤΝ̅ ϪΕ ΟΥΟΝ ΝΙΜ
15 ΕΤΝΑΑΠΟΤΑCCΕ Μ̅ΠΚΟCΜΟC ΤΗΡϤ̅ ΜΝ̅ ΝΕΤΝ̅ϨΗΤϤ ΤΗ-
ΡΟΥ· ΑΥШ Ν̅ϤϨΥΠΟΤΑCCΕ Ν̅ΤΜΝ̅ΤΝΟΥΤΕ· ΠΜΥCΤΗ-
ΡΙΟΝ ΕΤΜ̅ΜΑΥ ϤΜΟΤΝ̅ ΝΑϤ Ν̅ϨΟΥΟ ΕΜΜΥCΤΗΡΙΟΝ
ΤΗΡΟΥ Ν̅ΤΜΝ̅ΤΕΡΟ Μ̅ΠΟΥΟΕΙΝ· ΑΥШ ϤΜΑΤϢΟΥ ΕΝΟΪ
Μ̅ΜΟϤ Ν̅ϨΟΥΟ ΕΡΟΟΥ ΤΗΡΟΥ· ΑΥШ ϤΑCΟΟΥΤ Ν̅ϨΟΥΟ
20 ΕΡΟΟΥ ΤΗΡΟΥ· ΠΕΤΝΗΥ ΕϨΟΥΝ ΕΠCΟΟΥΝ Μ̅ΠΜΥCΤΗ-
ΡΙΟΝ ΕΤΜ̅ΜΑΥ· ϢΑϤΑΠΟΤΑCCΕ Μ̅ΠΕΪΚΟCΜΟC ΤΗΡϤ̅ ΜΝ̅
Ν̅ΡΟΟΥϢ ΤΗΡΟΥ ΕΤΝ̅ϨΗΤϤ· ΕΤΒΕ ΠΑΪ ϬΕ ΑΪϪΟΟC Ε-
ΡШΤΝ̅ Μ̅ΠΙΟΥΟΕΙϢ ϪΕ ΟΥΟΝ ΝΙΜ ΕΤϨΑΡΟΟΥϢ ΑΥШ
ΕΤϨΟCΕ ϨΑ ΤΕΥΕΤΠШ· ΑΜΗΪΤΝ̅ ΕΡΑΤ ΤΑϯΜΤΟΝ ΝΗΤΝ̅

---

5 MS ΑΥΑΡΧΙ; read ΑΥΑΡΧΙ.

that *mystery*, with all its knowledges | and the *type* of all these words which thou hast spoken about it?"

95.   Now it happened when Jesus heard these words which Maria said and he knew that the *disciples* had heard and that they had *begun* to despair, he encouraged them and said to them : "Be not now *sorrowful*, my *disciples*, because of the *mystery* of the Ineffable, thinking that you will not *understand* it. *Truly* I say to you, that *mystery* belongs to you and to everyone who will hear you, and *renounce* this whole *world* and all the *matter* within it, and *renounce* every *wicked* thought within themselves, and *renounce* all the cares of this *aeon*. *Now* at this time I say to you, everyone who will *renounce* the whole *world* and everything in it and will *submit* themselves [1] to Godhood, that *mystery* is easier for them than all the *mysteries* of the Kingdom of the Light, and it is more successfully *understood* than them all, and it is lighter than them all. He who comes to know that *mystery* is wont to *renounce* this whole *world* and all the cares within it.

Because of this now I said to you once : 'Everyone who is weary and heavy-laden [2], come to me and I will give you rest. | *For* my burden is light and my yoke is compas-

---

[1]   (16) themselves; lit. himself.
[2]   (24, 25) weary and heavy-laden; lit. oppressed with care and troubled by their burden.

439

ϫⲉ ⲥⲁⲥⲱⲟⲩ ⲅⲁⲣ ⲛ̄ϭⲓ ⲧⲁⲉⲧⲡⲱ**ⲁⲩⲱ ⲟⲩⲣⲙⲣⲁϣ ⲡⲉ ⲥ̄ⲅ̄
ⲡⲁⲛⲁϩⲃⲉϥ· ⲧⲉⲛⲟⲩ ϭⲉ ⲡⲉⲧⲛⲁϫⲓ ⲙ̄ⲡⲙⲩⲥⲧⲏⲣⲓⲟⲛ ⲉⲧⲙ̄-
ⲙⲁⲩ ϣⲁϥⲁⲡⲟⲧⲁⲥⲥⲉ ⲙ̄ⲡⲕⲟⲥⲙⲟⲥ ⲧⲏⲣϥ· ⲁⲩⲱ ⲙ̄ⲛ ⲡⲣⲟⲟⲩϣ ⲛ̄ⲑⲩⲗⲏ ⲧⲏⲣⲥ̄ ⲉⲧⲛ̄ϩⲏⲧϥ̄· ⲉⲧⲃⲉ ⲡⲁ̈ⲓ ϭⲉ ⲟⲩⲛ ⲛⲁ-
5 ⲙⲁⲑⲏⲧⲏⲥ ⲙ̄ⲡⲣ̄ⲗⲩⲡⲉⲓ ⲉⲧⲉⲧⲛ̄ⲙⲉⲉⲩⲉ ϫⲉ ⲡⲙⲩⲥⲧⲏⲣⲓⲟⲛ
ⲉⲧⲙ̄ⲙⲁⲩ ⲛ̄ⲧⲉⲧⲛ̄ⲛⲁⲛⲟ̈ⲓ ⲙ̄ⲙⲟϥ ⲁⲛ· ϩⲁⲙⲏⲛ †ϫⲱ ⲙ̄ⲙⲟⲥ
ⲛⲏⲧⲛ̄ ϫⲉ ⲡⲙⲩⲥⲧⲏⲣⲓⲟⲛ ⲉⲧⲙ̄ⲙⲁⲩ ϥⲙⲁⲧⲱⲟⲩ ⲉⲛⲟ̈ⲓ ⲙ̄-
ⲙⲟϥ ⲛ̄ϩⲟⲩⲟ ⲉⲙⲙⲩⲥⲧⲏⲣⲓⲟⲛ ⲧⲏⲣⲟⲩ· ⲁⲩⲱ ϩⲁⲙⲏⲛ †ϫⲱ
ⲙ̄ⲙⲟⲥ ⲛⲏⲧⲛ̄ ϫⲉ ⲡⲙⲩⲥⲧⲏⲣⲓⲟⲛ ⲉⲧⲙ̄ⲙⲁⲩ ⲡⲱⲧⲛ̄ ⲡⲉ ⲙ̄ⲛ
10 ⲟⲩⲟⲛ ⲛⲓⲙ ⲉⲧⲛⲁⲁⲡⲟⲧⲁⲥⲥⲉ ⲙ̄ⲡⲕⲟⲥⲙⲟⲥ ⲧⲏⲣϥ̄ ⲙ̄ⲛ ⲑⲩⲗⲏ ⲧⲏⲣⲥ̄ ⲉⲧⲛ̄ϩⲏⲧϥ̄· ⲧⲉⲛⲟⲩ ϭⲉ ⲥⲱⲧⲙ̄ ⲛⲁⲙⲁⲑⲏⲧⲏⲥ ⲁⲩⲱ
ⲛⲁϣⲃⲉⲉⲣ ⲁⲩⲱ ⲛⲁⲥⲛⲏⲩ· ⲧⲁⲡⲣⲟⲧⲣⲉⲡⲉ ⲙ̄ⲙⲱⲧⲛ̄ ⲉⲡⲥⲟⲟⲩⲛ ⲙ̄ⲡⲙⲩⲥⲧⲏⲣⲓⲟⲛ ⲙ̄ⲡⲁⲧⲱϣⲁϫⲉ ⲉⲣⲟϥ· ⲛⲁ̈ⲓ ⲉ†ϣⲁϫⲉ
ⲛ̄ⲙⲙⲏⲧⲛ̄* ⲉⲣⲟⲟⲩ ϫⲉ ⲡⲥⲟⲟⲩⲛ ⲅⲁⲣ ⲧⲏⲣϥ̄ †ⲡⲏϩ ⲉϫⲟⲟϥ ⲥ̄ⲅ̄·ᵇ
15 ⲉⲣⲱⲧⲛ̄ ϩⲙ̄ ⲡⲥⲱⲣ ⲉⲃⲟⲗ ⲙ̄ⲡⲧⲏⲣϥ̄· ϫⲉ ⲡⲥⲱⲣ ⲅⲁⲣ ⲉⲃⲟⲗ
ⲙ̄ⲡⲧⲏⲣϥ̄ ⲡⲉ ⲡⲉϥⲥⲟⲟⲩⲛ· ⲁⲗⲗⲁ ⲧⲉⲛⲟⲩ ϭⲉ ⲥⲱⲧⲙ̄ ⲧⲁϣⲁϫⲉ ⲛ̄ⲙⲙⲏⲧⲛ̄ ϩⲛ ⲟⲩⲡⲣⲟⲕⲟⲡⲏ ⲉⲧⲃⲉ ⲡⲥⲟⲟⲩⲛ ⲙ̄ⲡ-
ⲙⲩⲥⲧⲏⲣⲓⲟⲛ ⲉⲧⲙ̄ⲙⲁⲩ ϫⲉ ⲡⲙⲩⲥⲧⲏⲣⲓⲟⲛ ⲉⲧⲙ̄ⲙⲁⲩ ⲛ̄ⲧⲟϥ
ⲡⲉⲧⲥⲟⲟⲩⲛ ϫⲉ ⲉⲧⲃⲉ ⲟⲩ ⲁϥⲥⲕⲩⲗⲗⲉⲓ ⲙ̄ⲙⲟϥ ⲛ̄ϭⲓ ⲡ†ⲟⲩ
20 ⲙ̄ⲡⲁⲣⲁⲥⲧⲁⲧⲏⲥ· ⲁⲩⲱ ⲉⲧⲃⲉ ⲟⲩ ⲁⲩⲡⲣⲟⲉⲗⲑⲉ ⲉⲃⲟⲗ ϩⲛ
ⲛⲓⲁⲡⲁⲧⲱⲣ· ⲁⲩⲱ ⲡⲙⲩⲥⲧⲏⲣⲓⲟⲛ ⲉⲧⲙ̄ⲙⲁⲩ ⲛ̄ⲧⲟϥ ⲡⲉⲧⲥⲟⲟⲩⲛ ϫⲉ ⲉⲧⲃⲉ ⲟⲩ ⲁϥⲥⲕⲩⲗⲗⲉⲓ ⲙ̄ⲙⲟϥ ⲛ̄ϭⲓ ⲡⲛⲟϭ ⲛ̄-
ⲟⲩⲟⲉⲓⲛ ⲛ̄ⲧⲉ ⲛⲓⲟⲩⲟⲉⲓⲛ· ⲁⲩⲱ ⲉⲧⲃⲉ ⲟⲩ ⲁⲩⲡⲣⲟⲉⲗⲑⲉ
ⲉⲃⲟⲗ ϩⲛ ⲛⲓⲁⲡⲁⲧⲱⲣ· ⲁⲩⲱ ⲡⲙⲩⲥⲧⲏⲣⲓⲟⲛ ⲉⲧⲙ̄ⲙⲁⲩ ⲛ̄-
25 ⲧⲟϥ ⲡⲉⲧⲥⲟⲟⲩⲛ ϫⲉ ⲉⲧⲃⲉ ⲟⲩ ⲁϥⲥⲕⲩⲗⲗⲉⲓ ⲙ̄ⲙⲟϥ ⲛ̄ϭⲓ

---

16 MS originally ⲡⲥⲟⲟⲩ'ⲛ; ⲡ crossed out and ⲡⲉϥ inserted above.
23 MS ⲁⲩⲡⲣⲟⲥⲗⲟⲉ; read ⲁϥⲡⲣⲟⲉⲗⲟⲉ.

sionate'*. Now at this time he who will receive that *mystery* is wont to *renounce* the whole *world* and all the *material* cares within it. Because of this *now*, my *disciples*, be not *sorrowful* and think that you will not *understand* that *mystery*. *Truly* I say to you, it is more successfully *understood* than all the *mysteries*. And *truly* I say to you, that *mystery* belongs to you and to all those who will *renounce* the whole *world* and all the *matter* within it. Now at this time, hear, my *disciples* and companions and brothers, that I *urge* you to the knowledge of the *mystery* of the Ineffable. I say these things to you *for* I succeed in saying the whole knowledge to you in the distribution of the All, *for* the distribution of the All is its knowledge. *But* now at this time hear that I speak *progressively* concerning the knowledge of that *mystery* with you. That *mystery* knows why the five *helpers* (*parastatai*) *troubled*[1], and why they *came forth* from the *fatherless ones*. And that *mystery* knows why the great Light of Lights *troubled*, and why it *came forth* from the *fatherless ones*. And that *mystery* knows why the first ordinance *troubled*, |

---

*   cf. Mt. 11.28, 30

---

[1]   (19) troubled; lit. troubled themselves; Schmidt: strained themselves; Till: troubled themselves; see Mk. 5. 35; Lk. 7.6; 8.49 (also 220.22 ff.; 347.5; 349.13).

ⲡϣⲟⲣⲡ̅ ⲛ̅ⲧⲱϣ· ⲁⲩⲱ ⲉⲧⲃⲉ ⲟⲩ ⲁϥⲡⲱⲣ̅ϫ̅ ⲉⲃⲟⲗ ⲉⲥⲁϣ̅ϥ̅
ⲙ̅ⲙⲩⲥⲧⲏⲣⲓⲟⲛ ⲁⲩⲱ ⲉⲧⲃⲉ ⲟⲩ ⲍⲱϣϥ ⲁⲩⲙⲟⲩⲧⲉ ⲉⲣⲟϥ
ϫⲉ ⲡϣⲟⲣⲡ̅ ⲛ̅ⲧⲱϣ· ⲁⲩⲱ ⲉⲧⲃⲉ ⲟⲩ ⲁⲩⲡⲣⲟⲉⲗⲑⲉ ⲉⲃⲟⲗ [ⲥⲁ]
ⲍ̅ⲛ ⲛⲓⲁⲡⲁⲧⲱⲣ· ⲁⲩⲱ ⲡⲙⲩⲥⲧⲏⲣⲓⲟⲛ ⲉⲧⲙ̅ⲙⲁⲩ ⲛ̅ⲧⲟϥ ⲡⲉⲧ-
5 ⲥⲟⲟⲩⲛ ϫⲉ ⲉⲧⲃⲉ ⲟⲩ ⲁϥⲥⲕⲩⲗⲗⲉⲓ ⲙ̅ⲙⲟϥ ⲛ̅ϭⲓ ⲡⲛⲟϭ ⲛ̅-
ⲟⲩⲟⲉⲓⲛ ⲛ̅ⲭⲁⲣⲁⲅⲙⲏ ⲛ̅ⲟⲩⲟⲉⲓⲛ· ⲁⲩⲱ ⲉⲧⲃⲉ ⲟⲩ ⲁⲩⲁⲍⲉⲣⲁⲧⲟⲩ ⲁϫ̅ⲛ̅ ⲡⲣⲟⲃⲟⲗⲏ· ⲁⲩⲱ ⲉⲧⲃⲉ ⲟⲩ ⲁⲩⲡⲣⲟⲉⲗⲑⲉ
ⲉⲃⲟⲗ ⲍ̅ⲛ ⲛⲓⲁⲡⲁⲧⲱⲣ· ⲁⲩⲱ ⲡⲙⲩⲥⲧⲏⲣⲓⲟⲛ ⲉⲧⲙ̅ⲙⲁⲩ ⲛ̅-
ⲧⲟϥ ⲡⲉⲧⲥⲟⲟⲩⲛ ϫⲉ ⲉⲧⲃⲉ ⲟⲩ ⲁϥⲥⲕⲩⲗⲗⲉ ⲙ̅ⲙⲟϥ ⲛ̅ϭⲓ
10 ⲡⲓϣⲟⲣⲡ̅ ⲙ̅ⲙⲩⲥⲧⲏⲣⲓⲟⲛ ⲉⲧⲉ ⲛ̅ⲧⲟϥ ⲡⲉ ⲡⲙⲉⲍϫⲟⲩⲧⲁϥⲧⲉ
ⲙ̅ⲙⲩⲥⲧⲏⲣⲓⲟⲛ ⲉⲃⲟⲗ ⲁⲩⲱ ⲉⲧⲃⲉ ⲟⲩ ⲁϥⲕⲱ ⲍⲣⲁⲓ̈ ⲛ̅ⲍⲏⲧ̅ϥ̅
ⲙ̅ⲡ̅ⲙⲛ̅ⲧⲥⲛⲟⲟⲩⲥ ⲙ̅ⲙⲩⲥⲧⲏⲣⲓⲟⲛ ⲕⲁⲧⲁ ⲧⲏⲡⲉ ⲛ̅ⲧⲁⲣⲓⲑⲙⲏ-
ⲥⲓⲥ ⲛ̅ⲛⲓⲁⲭⲱⲣⲏⲧⲟⲥ ⲛ̅ⲁⲡⲉⲣⲁⲛⲧⲟⲥ· ⲁⲩⲱ ⲉⲧⲃⲉ ⲟⲩ ⲁϥⲡⲣⲟⲉⲗⲑⲉ ⲉⲃⲟⲗ ⲍ̅ⲛ ⲛⲓⲁⲡⲁⲧⲱⲣ· ⲁⲩⲱ ⲡⲙⲩⲥⲧⲏⲣⲓⲟⲛ ⲉⲧ-
15 ⲙ̅ⲙⲁⲩ ⲛ̅ⲧⲟϥ ⲡⲉⲧⲥⲟⲟⲩⲛ ϫⲉ ⲉⲧⲃⲉ ⲟⲩ ⲁⲩⲥⲕⲩⲗⲗⲉⲓ ⲙ̅-
ⲙⲟⲟⲩ ⲛ̅ϭⲓ ⲡ̅ⲙⲛ̅ⲧⲥⲛⲟⲟⲩⲥ ⲛ̅ⲁϭⲓⲛⲏⲧⲟⲥ ⲁⲩⲱ ⲉⲧⲃⲉ ⲟⲩ [ⲥⲁ ᵇ]
ⲣⲱ ⲁⲩⲧⲁⲍⲟⲟⲩ ⲉⲣⲁⲧⲟⲩ ⲙ̅ⲛ ⲛⲉⲩⲧⲁⲝⲓⲥ ⲧⲏⲣⲟⲩ ⲁⲩⲱ
ⲉⲧⲃⲉ ⲟⲩ ⲁⲩⲡⲣⲟⲉⲗⲑⲉ ⲉⲃⲟⲗ ⲍ̅ⲛ ⲛⲓⲁⲡⲁⲧⲱⲣ: ⲁⲩⲱ ⲡⲙⲩⲥⲧⲏⲣⲓⲟⲛ ⲉⲧⲙ̅ⲙⲁⲩ ⲛ̅ⲧⲟϥ ⲡⲉⲧⲥⲟⲟⲩⲛ ϫⲉ ⲉⲧⲃⲉ ⲟⲩ ⲁⲩ-
20 ⲥⲕⲩⲗⲗⲉⲓ ⲙ̅ⲙⲟⲟⲩ ⲛ̅ϭⲓ ⲛⲓⲁⲥⲁⲗⲉⲩⲧⲟⲥ ⲁⲩⲱ ⲉⲧⲃⲉ ⲟⲩ
ⲁⲩⲧⲁⲍⲟⲟⲩ ⲉⲣⲁⲧⲟⲩ ⲉⲩⲡⲟⲣ̅ϫ̅ ⲉⲃⲟⲗ ⲉⲙⲛ̅ⲧⲥⲛⲟⲟⲩⲥ ⲛ̅-
ⲧⲁⲝⲓⲥ ⲁⲩⲱ ⲉⲧⲃⲉ ⲟⲩ ⲁⲩⲡⲣⲟⲉⲗⲑⲉ ⲉⲃⲟⲗ ⲍ̅ⲛ ⲛⲓⲁⲡⲁⲧⲱⲣ
ⲛⲁⲓ̈ ⲉⲧⲏⲡ ⲉⲛⲧⲁⲝⲓⲥ ⲙ̅ⲡⲉⲭⲱⲣⲏⲙⲁ ⲙ̅ⲡⲓⲁⲧϣⲁϫⲉ ⲉⲣⲟϥ:

---

3 MS ⲁⲩⲡⲣⲟⲉⲗⲑⲉ; read ⲁϥⲡⲣⲟⲉⲗⲑⲉ. ⲅ̅ in upper right-hand margin at
end of quire.
6 MS ⲁⲩⲁⲍⲉⲣⲁⲧⲟⲩ; read ⲁϥⲁⲍⲉⲣⲁⲧ̅ϥ̅ .
7 MS ⲁⲩⲡⲣⲟⲉⲗⲑⲉ; read ⲁϥⲡⲣⲟⲉⲗⲟⲉ.

and why it was divided into seven *mysteries*; and moreover why it was called the first ordinance, and why it *came forth* from the *fatherless ones*. And that *mystery* knows why the great light of the *incisions* of light *troubled*, and why it was set up without *emanations*, and why it *came forth* from the *fatherless ones*. And that *mystery* knows why the First *Mystery troubled*, which is the 24th *mystery* from without, and why it laid down [1] within itself the twelve *mysteries according to* the reckoning of the *number* of the *incomprehensible* and the *endless* ones [2], and why it *came forth* from the *fatherless ones*. And that *mystery* knows why the twelve *motionless* ones *troubled*, and why they all stood up with all their *ranks*, and why they *came forth* from the *fatherless ones*. And that *mystery* knows why the *unshakeable ones troubled*, and why they stood up separately in twelve *ranks*, and why they *came forth* from the *fatherless ones*. which belong to the *ranks* of the *space* of the Ineffable. |

---

[1]   (11) laid down; Schmidt: imitated.
[2]   (13) incomprehensible and endless ones; Till: endless incomprehensible ones.

ⲀⲨⲰ ⲠⲘⲨⲤⲦⲎⲢⲒⲟⲚ ⲈⲦⲘⲘⲀⲨ ⲚⲦⲞϤ ⲠⲈⲦⲤⲞⲞⲨⲚ ϪⲈ ⲈⲦ-
ⲂⲈ ⲞⲨ ⲀⲨⲤⲔⲨⲖⲖⲈ ⲘⲘⲞⲞⲨ ⲚϬⲒ ⲚⲒⲀⲈⲚⲚⲞⲎⲦⲞⲤ ⲚⲀⲒ ⲈⲦ-
ⲎⲠ ⲈⲠⲈⲬⲰⲢⲎⲘⲀ ⲤⲚⲀⲨ ⲚⲦⲈ ⲠⲒⲀⲦϢⲀϪⲈ ⲈⲢⲞϤ· ⲀⲨⲰ
ⲈⲦⲂⲈ ⲞⲨ ⲀⲨⲠⲢⲞⲈⲖⲐⲈ ⲈⲂⲞⲖ ϨⲚ ⲚⲒⲀⲠⲀⲦⲰⲢ· ⲀⲨⲰ ⲠⲘⲨⲤ-
5 ⲦⲎⲢⲒⲞⲚ ⲈⲦⲘⲘⲀⲨ ⲚⲦⲞϤ ⲠⲈⲦⲤⲞⲞⲨⲚ ϪⲈ ⲈⲦⲂⲈ ⲞⲨ ⲀⲨ-
ⲤⲔⲨⲖⲖⲒ ⲘⲘⲞⲞⲨ ⲚϬⲒ ⲠⲒⲘⲚⲦⲤⲚⲞⲞⲨⲤ ⲚⲀⲤⲎⲘⲀⲚⲦⲞⲤ·　ⲤⲤ
ⲀⲨⲰ ⲈⲦⲂⲈ ⲞⲨ ⲀⲨⲦⲀϨⲞⲞⲨ ⲈⲢⲀⲦⲞⲨ ⲘⲚⲚⲤⲀ ⲚⲦⲀⲝⲒⲤ ⲦⲎ-
ⲢⲞⲨ ⲚⲚⲒⲀⲘⲨⲚⲀⲚⲦⲞⲤ ⲈⲚⲦⲞⲞⲨ ϨⲰⲰⲞⲨ ϨⲈⲚⲀⲬⲰⲢⲎⲦⲞⲚ
ⲚⲈ ⲚⲀⲠⲈⲢⲀⲚⲦⲞⲤ· ⲀⲨⲰ ⲈⲦⲂⲈ ⲞⲨ ⲢⲰ ⲀⲨⲠⲢⲞⲈⲖⲐⲈ ⲈⲂⲞⲖ
10 ϨⲚ ⲚⲒⲀⲠⲀⲦⲰⲢ· ⲀⲨⲰ ⲠⲘⲨⲤⲦⲎⲢⲒⲞⲚ ⲈⲦⲘⲘⲀⲨ ⲚⲦⲞϤ ⲠⲈⲦ-
ⲤⲞⲞⲨⲚ ϪⲈ ⲈⲦⲂⲈ ⲞⲨ ⲀⲨⲤⲔⲨⲖⲖⲒ ⲘⲘⲞⲞⲨ ⲚϬⲒ ⲚⲒⲀⲘⲨ-
ⲚⲀⲚⲦⲞⲤ ⲚⲀⲒ ⲈⲦⲈ ⲘⲠⲞⲨⲘⲨⲚⲈⲨⲈ ⲘⲘⲞⲞⲨ ⲞⲨⲆⲈ Ⲙ-
ⲠⲞⲨⲚⲦⲞⲨ ⲈⲠⲈⲦⲞⲨⲞⲚϨ ⲈⲂⲞⲖ ⲔⲀⲦⲀ ⲦⲞⲒⲔⲞⲚⲞⲘⲒⲀ ⲘⲠⲒ-
ⲞⲨⲀ ⲚⲞⲨⲰⲦ ⲠⲒⲀⲦϢⲀϪⲈ ⲈⲢⲞϤ· ⲀⲨⲰ ⲈⲦⲂⲈ ⲞⲨ ⲀⲨ-
15 ⲠⲢⲞⲈⲖⲐⲈ ⲈⲂⲞⲖ ϨⲚ ⲚⲒⲀⲠⲀⲦⲰⲢ· ⲀⲨⲰ ⲠⲘⲨⲤⲦⲎⲢⲒⲞⲚ ⲈⲦ-
ⲘⲘⲀⲨ ⲚⲦⲞϤ ⲠⲈⲦⲤⲞⲞⲨⲚ ϪⲈ ⲈⲦⲂⲈ ⲞⲨ ⲀⲨⲤⲔⲨⲖⲖⲒ Ⲙ-
ⲘⲞⲞⲨ ⲚϬⲒ ⲚⲒϨⲨⲠⲈⲢⲂⲀⲐⲞⲤ· ⲀⲨⲰ ⲈⲦⲂⲈ ⲞⲨ ⲀⲨⲤⲞⲢⲞⲨ
ⲈⲂⲞⲖ ⲈⲨⲞ ⲚⲞⲨⲦⲀϨⲒⲤ ⲚⲞⲨⲰⲦ ⲀⲨⲰ ⲈⲦⲂⲈ ⲞⲨ ⲀⲨⲠⲢⲞ-　ⲤⲤ ᵇ
ⲈⲖⲐⲈ ⲈⲂⲞⲖ ϨⲚ ⲚⲒⲀⲠⲀⲦⲰⲢ· ⲀⲨⲰ ⲠⲘⲨⲤⲦⲎⲢⲒⲞⲚ ⲈⲦⲘⲘⲀⲨ
20 ⲚⲦⲞϤ ⲠⲈⲦⲤⲞⲞⲨⲚ ϪⲈ ⲈⲦⲂⲈ ⲞⲨ ⲀⲨⲤⲔⲨⲖⲖⲒ ⲘⲘⲞⲞⲨ Ⲛ-
ϬⲒ ⲠⲘⲚⲦⲤⲚⲞⲞⲨⲤ ⲚⲦⲀϨⲒⲤ ⲚⲚⲒⲀϨⲢⲎⲦⲞⲤ ⲀⲨⲰ ⲈⲦⲂⲈ ⲞⲨ
ⲢⲰ ⲀⲨⲚⲈϨⲞⲨ ⲈⲂⲞⲖ ⲈⲨⲞ ⲚϢⲞⲘⲦⲈ ⲘⲘⲈⲢⲒⲤ· ⲀⲨⲰ ⲈⲦⲂⲈ
ⲞⲨ ⲢⲰ ⲀⲨⲠⲢⲞⲈⲖⲐⲈ ⲈⲂⲞⲖ ϨⲚ ⲚⲒⲀⲠⲀⲦⲰⲢ:
　　ⲀⲨⲰ ⲠⲘⲨⲤⲦⲎⲢⲒⲞⲚ ⲈⲦⲘⲘⲀⲨ ⲚⲦⲞϤ ⲠⲈⲦⲤⲞⲞⲨⲚ ϪⲈ ⲈⲦ-
25 ⲂⲈ ⲞⲨ ⲀⲨⲤⲔⲨⲖⲖⲒ ⲘⲘⲞⲞⲨ ⲚϬⲒ ⲚⲒⲀⲪⲐⲀⲢⲦⲞⲤ ⲦⲎⲢⲞⲨ

6　ⲒⲀ. in upper left-hand margin at beginning of quire.
8　MS ⲚⲚⲒⲀⲘⲨⲠⲀⲚⲦⲞⲤ; read ⲠⲚⲒⲀⲘⲎⲚⲨⲦⲞⲤ; also line 11. MS ϨⲰⲰⲞⲨ;
　　better ϨⲰⲞⲨ.

And that *mystery* knows why the *unthinkable ones*, which belong to the two *spaces*[1] of the Ineffable, *troubled*, and why they *came forth* from the *fatherless ones*. And that *mystery* knows why the twelve *unmarked ones troubled*, and why afterwards all the *ranks* of the *undisclosed ones* stood up, they themselves being *incomprehensible* and *endless*, and why they *came forth* from the *fatherless ones*. And that *mystery* knows why the *undisclosed ones troubled* — these ones which were not *disclosed*, *nor* were they brought to manifestation *according to* the *organisation* of the Only One, the Ineffable — and why they *came forth* from the *fatherless ones*. And that *mystery* knows why the *fathomless* (?) ones *troubled*, and why they were distributed to be one *rank*[2], and why they *came forth* from the *fatherless ones*. And that *mystery* knows why the twelve *ranks* of the *unutterable* ones *troubled*, and why they divided to be three *parts*, and why they *came forth* from the *fatherless ones*.

And that *mystery* knows why all the *imperishable* ones *troubled* | to be twelve *places*, and why they were placed

---

[1]   (3) the two spaces; Schmidt: the second space.

[2]   (18) distributed to be one rank; Schmidt: distributed, being one rank (see 222.22; 223.2, 8).

ЄΥО М̄М̄Ν̄ТСΝΟΟΥС Ν̄ТΟΠΟС· ΑΥШ ЄТΒЄ ΟΥ ΑΥΚΑΑΥ

ЄΥСΗΡ ЄΒΟΛ Ν̄СΑ ΝЄΥЄΡΗΥ ⲒΡΑΪ Ⲋ̄Ν ΟΥΤΑΞ̄ΙС Ν̄ΟΥШТ·

ΑΥШ ЄТΒЄ ΟΥ ΑΥΠΟΡⳜΟΥ ЄΒΟΛ ΑΥΑΑΥ Ν̄ΤΑΞ̄ΙС ΤΑΞ̄ΙС·

ЄΝ̄ΤΟΟΥ ⲋШΟΥ ⲋЄΝΑⳜШΡΗΤΟΝ ΝЄ ΑΥШ ⲋЄΝΑΠЄΡΑΝ-

5 ΤΟΝ ΝЄ· ΑΥШ ЄТΒЄ ΟΥ ΑΥΠΡΟЄΛΘЄ ЄΒΟΛ Ⲋ̄Ν ΝΙΑΠΑ-

ΤШΡ: ΑΥШ ΠΜΥСΤΗΡΙΟΝ ЄΤΜ̄ΜΑΥ Ν̄ΤΟ4 ΠЄΤСΟΟΥΝ [С̄Є]

Ⳝ̄Є ЄΤΒЄ ΟΥ ΑΥСΚΥΛΛΙ М̄ΜΟΟΥ Ν̄ϬΙ ΝΙΑΠЄΡΑΝΤΟΝ

ΑΥШ ЄΤΒЄ ΟΥ ΑΥΤΑⲋΟΟΥ ЄΡΑΤΟΥ ЄΥО М̄М̄Ν̄ТСΝΟΟΥС

Ν̄ⳜШΡΗΜΑ Ν̄ΑΠЄΡΑΝΤΟС ΑΥШ Α4ΚΑΑΥ ЄΥО Ν̄ϢΟΜΤЄ

10 Ν̄ΤΑΞ̄ΙС Ν̄ⳜШΡΗΜΑ ΚΑΤΑ ΤΟΙΚΟΝΟΜΙΑ М̄ΠΙΟΥΛ Ν̄ΟΥШТ

ΠΙΑΤϢΑⳜЄ ЄΡΟ4· ΑΥШ ЄΤΒЄ ΟΥ ΑΥΠΡΟЄΛΘЄ ЄΒΟΛ Ⲋ̄Ν

ΝΙΑΠΑΤШΡ: ΑΥШ ΠΜΥСΤΗΡΙΟΝ ЄΤΜ̄ΜΑΥ Ν̄ΤΟ4 ΠЄΤ-

СΟΟΥΝ Ⳝ̄Є ЄΤΒЄ ΟΥ ΑΥСΚΥΛΛΙ М̄ΜΟΟΥ Ν̄ϬΙ ΠΜΝ̄Τ-

СΝΟΟΥС Ν̄ΑⳜШΡΗΤΟС ΝΑΪ ЄΤΗΠ ЄΝ̄ΤΑΞ̄ΙС М̄ΠΙΟΥΛ Ν̄-

15 ΟΥШТ ΠΙΑΤϢΑⳜЄ ЄΡΟ4 ΑΥШ Ⳝ̄Є ЄΤΒЄ ΟΥ ΡШ ΑΥ-

ΠΡΟЄΛΘЄ ЄΒΟΛ Ⲋ̄Ν ΝΙΑΠΑΤШΡ ϢΑΝΤΟΥΝ̄ΤΟΥ ΡШ ЄΠЄ-

ⳜШΡΗΜΑ Ν̄ΤЄ ΠΙϢΟΡΠ̄ М̄ΜΥСΤΗΡΙΟΝ ЄΤЄ Ν̄ΤΟ4 ΠЄ

ΠΜЄⲋСΝΑΥ Ν̄ⳜШΡΗΜΑ· ΑΥШ ΠΜΥСΤΗΡΙΟΝ ЄΤΜ̄ΜΑΥ Ν̄-

ΤΟ4 ΠЄΤСΟΟΥΝ Ⳝ̄Є ЄΤΒЄ ΟΥ ΑΥСΚΥΛΛΙ М̄ΜΟΟΥ Ν̄ϬΙ

20 ΠΙⳜΟΥΤΑ4ΤЄ Ν̄ΤΒΑ Ν̄ⲋΥΜΝЄΥΤΗС· ΑΥШ ЄΤΒЄ ΟΥ ΡШ [С̄Є͞ᵇ]

ΑΥСΟΡΟΥ ЄΒΟΛ ΠΒΟΛ М̄ΠΚΑΤΑΠЄΤΑСΜΑ М̄ΠΙϢΟΡΠ М̄-

ΜΥСΤΗΡΙΟΝ ЄΤЄ Ν̄ΤΟ4 ΠЄ ΠⲋΑΤΡЄΥ М̄ΜΥСΤΗΡΙΟΝ Ν̄-

ΤЄ ΠΙΟΥΛ Ν̄ΟΥШТ ΠΙΑΤϢΑⳜЄ ЄΡΟ4· ΠΗ ЄΤϬШϢΤ Є-

ⲋΟΥΝ ΑΥШ ΠΗ ЄΤϬШϢΤ ЄΒΟΛ· ΑΥШ ЄΤΒЄ ΟΥ ΡШ ΑΥ-

25 ΠΡΟЄΛΘЄ ЄΒΟΛ Ⲋ̄Ν ΝΙΑΠΑΤШΡ: ΑΥШ ΠΜΥСΤΗΡΙΟΝ ЄΤ-

М̄ΜΑΥ Ν̄ΤΟ4 ΠЄΤСΟΟΥΝ Ⳝ̄Є ЄΤΒЄ ΟΥ ΑΥСΚΥΛΛΙ М̄-

---

9 MS ⲀϤⲔⲀⲀⲨ; read ⲀⲨⲔⲀⲀⲨ.

in one *rank*, distributed one behind another, and why they were divided to make many *ranks*, being moreover incomprehensible and *endless*, and why they *came forth* from the *fatherless ones*. And that *mystery* knows why the *endless ones troubled*, and why they stood up to be twelve *endless spaces* and they were placed to be three *ranks* of *spaces*, according to the *organisation* of the Only One, the Ineffable, and why they *came forth* from the *fatherless ones*. And that *mystery* knows why the twelve *incomprehensible ones*, which belong to the *ranks* of the Only One, the Ineffable, *troubled*, and why they *came forth* from the *fatherless ones* until they were brought to the *space* of the First *Mystery*, which is the second *space*. And that *mystery* knows why the 24 myriad *singers of praise troubled*, and why they were distributed outside the *veil* of the First *Mystery*, which is the twin *mystery* of the Only One, the Ineffable, which looks inwards and which looks outwards, and why they *came forth* from the *fatherless ones*. And that *mystery* knows why | all the *incom-*

ⲘⲞⲞⲨ ⲚϬⲒ ⲚⲀⲬⲰⲢⲎⲦⲞⲤ ⲦⲎⲢⲞⲨ ⲚⲀⲒ ⲚⲦⲀⲒⲞⲨⲰ ⲈⲒⲬⲰ
ⲘⲘⲞⲞⲨ ⲚⲀⲒ ⲈⲦⲤⲚ ⲚⲦⲞⲠⲞⲤ ⲘⲠⲘⲈⲎⲤⲚⲀⲨ ⲚⲬⲰⲢⲎⲘⲀ ⲚⲦⲈ
ⲠⲒⲀⲦϢⲀϪⲈ ⲈⲢⲞϤ ⲈⲦⲈ ⲚⲦⲞϤ ⲠⲈ ⲠⲈⲬⲰⲢⲎⲘⲀ ⲚⲦⲈ ⲠⲒϢⲞ-
ⲢⲠ ⲘⲘⲨⲤⲦⲎⲢⲒⲞⲚ· ⲀⲨⲰ ⲈⲦⲂⲈ ⲞⲨ Ⲁ ⲚⲀⲬⲰⲢⲎⲦⲞⲤ ⲈⲦⲘ-
5 ⲘⲀⲨ ⲘⲚ ⲚⲀⲠⲈⲢⲀⲚⲦⲞⲤ ⲈⲦⲘⲘⲀⲨ ⲀⲨⲠⲢⲞⲈⲖⲐⲈ ⲈⲂⲞⲖ ⲎⲚ
ⲚⲒⲀⲠⲀⲦⲰⲢ· ⲀⲨⲰ ⲠⲒⲘⲨⲤⲦⲎⲢⲒⲞⲚ ⲈⲦⲘⲘⲀⲨ ⲚⲦⲞϤ ⲠⲈⲦ-
ⲤⲞⲞⲨⲚ ϪⲈ ⲈⲦⲂⲈ ⲞⲨ ⲀⲨⲤⲔⲨⲖⲀⲒ ⲘⲘⲞⲞⲨ ⲚϬⲒ ⲠⲬⲞⲨⲦ- ⲤⲌ
ⲀϤⲦⲈ ⲘⲘⲨⲤⲦⲎⲢⲒⲞⲚ ⲘⲠϢⲞⲢⲠ ⲚⲦⲢⲒⲠⲚⲈⲨⲘⲀⲦⲞⲤ ⲀⲨⲰ
ⲈⲦⲂⲈ ⲞⲨ ⲀⲨⲘⲞⲨⲦⲈ ⲈⲢⲞⲞⲨ ϪⲈ ⲠⲬⲞⲨⲦⲀϤⲦⲈ ⲚⲬⲰⲢⲎ-
10 ⲘⲀ ⲘⲠϢⲞⲢⲠ ⲚⲦⲢⲒⲠⲚⲈⲨⲘⲀⲦⲞⲤ· ⲀⲨⲰ ⲈⲦⲂⲈ ⲞⲨ ⲀⲨⲠⲢⲞ-
ⲈⲖⲐⲈ ⲈⲂⲞⲖ ⲎⲘ ⲠⲘⲀⲎⲤⲚⲀⲨ ⲚⲦⲢⲒⲠⲚⲈⲨⲘⲀⲦⲞⲤ· ⲀⲨⲰ
ⲠⲘⲨⲤⲦⲎⲢⲒⲞⲚ ⲈⲦⲘⲘⲀⲨ ⲚⲦⲞϤ ⲠⲈⲦⲤⲞⲞⲨⲚ ϪⲈ ⲈⲦⲂⲈ ⲞⲨ
ⲀⲨⲤⲔⲨⲖⲀⲒ ⲘⲘⲞⲞⲨ ⲚϬⲒ ⲠⲬⲞⲨⲦⲀϤⲦⲈ ⲘⲘⲨⲤⲦⲎⲢⲒⲞⲚ ⲘⲠ-
ⲘⲈⲎⲤⲚⲀⲨ ⲚⲦⲢⲒⲠⲚⲈⲨⲘⲀⲦⲞⲤ· ⲀⲨⲰ ⲈⲦⲂⲈ ⲞⲨ ⲀⲨⲠⲢⲞⲈⲖ-
15 ⲐⲈ ⲈⲂⲞⲖ ⲎⲘ ⲠⲘⲀⲎϢⲞⲘⲚⲦ ⲚⲦⲢⲒⲠⲚⲈⲨⲘⲀⲦⲞⲤ· ⲀⲨⲰ
ⲠⲘⲨⲤⲦⲎⲢⲒⲞⲚ ⲈⲦⲘⲘⲀⲨ ⲚⲦⲞϤ ⲠⲈⲦⲤⲞⲞⲨⲚ ϪⲈ ⲈⲦⲂⲈ ⲞⲨ
ⲀⲨⲤⲔⲨⲖⲀⲒ ⲘⲘⲞⲞⲨ ⲚϬⲒ ⲠⲬⲞⲨⲦⲀϤⲦⲈ ⲘⲘⲨⲤⲦⲎⲢⲒⲞⲚ Ⲙ-
ⲠⲘⲈⲎϢⲞⲘⲚⲦ ⲚⲦⲢⲒⲠⲚⲈⲨⲘⲀⲦⲞⲤ ⲈⲦⲈ ⲚⲦⲞⲞⲨ ⲚⲈ ⲠⲬⲞⲨⲦ-
ⲀϤⲦⲈ ⲚⲬⲰⲢⲎⲘⲀ ⲘⲠⲘⲈⲎϢⲞⲘⲚⲦ ⲚⲦⲢⲒⲠⲚⲈⲨⲘⲀⲦⲞⲤ ⲀⲨⲰ
20 ⲈⲦⲂⲈ ⲞⲨ ⲀⲨⲠⲢⲞⲈⲖⲐⲈ ⲈⲂⲞⲖ ⲎⲚ ⲚⲒⲀⲠⲀⲦⲰⲢ· ⲀⲨⲰ ⲠⲘⲨⲤ- ⲤⲌᵇ
ⲦⲎⲢⲒⲞⲚ ⲈⲦⲘⲘⲀⲨ ⲚⲦⲞϤ ⲠⲈⲦⲤⲞⲞⲨⲚ ϪⲈ ⲈⲦⲂⲈ ⲞⲨ ⲀⲨ-
ⲤⲔⲨⲖⲀⲒ ⲘⲘⲞⲞⲨ ⲚϬⲒ Ⲡ†ⲞⲨ ⲚϢⲎⲚ ⲘⲠϢⲞⲢⲠ ⲚⲦⲢⲒⲠⲚⲈⲨ-
ⲘⲀⲦⲞⲤ· ⲀⲨⲰ ⲈⲦⲂⲈ ⲞⲨ ⲀⲨⲤⲞⲢⲞⲨ ⲈⲂⲞⲖ ⲈⲨⲀⲎⲈⲢⲀⲦⲞⲨ
ⲚⲤⲀ ⲚⲈⲨⲈⲢⲎⲨ ⲀⲨⲰ ⲞⲚ ⲈⲨⲘⲎⲢ ⲈⲎⲞⲨⲚ ⲈⲚⲈⲨⲈⲢⲎⲨ ⲘⲚ
25 ⲚⲈⲨⲦⲀⲜⲒⲤ ⲦⲎⲢⲞⲨ· ⲀⲨⲰ ⲈⲦⲂⲈ ⲞⲨ ⲀⲨⲠⲢⲞⲈⲖⲐⲈ ⲈⲂⲞⲖ

---

19   MS originally ⲘⲠϢⲞⲘⲚⲦ; ⲘⲈⲎ inserted above.

prehensible ones, of which I have just been speaking, *troubled*
— these which are in the *places* of the second *space* of the
Ineffable, which is the *space* of the First *Mystery* — and
why those *incomprehensible* and *endless ones came forth*
from the *fatherless ones*. And that *mystery* knows why the
24 *mysteries* of the first *triple-spirited one troubled*, and why
they were called the 24 *spaces* of the first *triple-spirited one*,
and why they *came forth* from the second *triple-spirited one*.
And that *mystery* knows why the 24 *mysteries* of the second
triple-spirited one troubled, and why they *came forth* from
the third *triple-spirited one*. And that *mystery* knows why the
24 *mysteries* of the third *triple-spirited one* — which are the
spaces of the third *triple-spirited one* — *troubled*, and why
they *came forth* from the *fatherless ones*. And that *mystery* knows why the five trees of the first *triple-spirited one
troubled*, and why they were distributed, standing behind
one another and also bound together with one another and
all their *ranks*, and why they *came forth* from | the *fatherless*

ϨⲚ ⲚⲒⲀⲠⲀⲦⲰⲢ: ⲀⲨⲰ ⲠⲘⲨⲤⲦⲎⲢⲒⲞⲚ ⲈⲦⲘ̄ⲘⲀⲨ Ⲛ̄ⲦⲞϤ ⲠⲈⲦ-
ⲤⲞⲞⲨⲚ ⲬⲈ ⲈⲦⲂⲈ ⲞⲨ ⲀⲨⲤⲔⲨⲖⲀⲒ Ⲙ̄ⲘⲞⲞⲨ Ⲛ̄ϬⲒ Ⲡ†ⲞⲨ
Ⲛ̄ϢⲎⲚ Ⲙ̄ⲠⲘⲀϨⲤⲚⲀⲨ Ⲛ̄ⲦⲢⲒⲠⲚⲈⲨⲘⲀⲦⲞⲤ · ⲀⲨⲰ ⲈⲦⲂⲈ ⲞⲨ
ⲀⲨⲠⲢⲞⲈⲖⲐⲈ ⲈⲂⲞⲖ ϨⲚ̄ ⲚⲒⲀⲠⲀⲦⲰⲢ · ⲀⲨⲰ ⲠⲘⲨⲤⲦⲎⲢⲒⲞⲚ
5 ⲈⲦⲘ̄ⲘⲀⲨ Ⲛ̄ⲦⲞϤ ⲠⲈⲦⲤⲞⲞⲨⲚ ⲬⲈ ⲈⲦⲂⲈ ⲞⲨ ⲀⲨⲤⲔⲨⲖⲀⲒ
Ⲙ̄ⲘⲞⲞⲨ Ⲛ̄ϬⲒ Ⲡ†ⲞⲨ Ⲛ̄ϢⲎⲚ Ⲙ̄ⲠⲘⲀϢⲞⲘⲚ̄Ⲧ Ⲛ̄ⲦⲢⲒⲠⲚⲈⲨⲘⲀ-
ⲦⲞⲤ · ⲀⲨⲰ ⲈⲦⲂⲈ ⲞⲨ ⲀⲨⲠⲢⲞⲈⲖⲐⲈ** ⲈⲂⲞⲖ ϨⲚ̄ ⲚⲒⲀⲠⲀⲦⲰⲢ · [ⲤⲎ]
ⲀⲨⲰ ⲠⲘⲨⲤⲦⲎⲢⲒⲞⲚ ⲈⲦⲘ̄ⲘⲀⲨ Ⲛ̄ⲦⲞϤ ⲠⲈⲦⲤⲞⲞⲨⲚ ⲬⲈ ⲈⲦ-
ⲂⲈ ⲞⲨ ⲀⲨⲤⲔⲨⲖⲀⲒ Ⲙ̄ⲘⲞⲞⲨ Ⲛ̄ϬⲒ ⲚⲈⲠⲢⲞⲀⲬⲰⲢⲎⲦⲞⲤ Ⲙ̄-
10 ⲠϢⲞⲢⲠ̄ Ⲛ̄ⲦⲢⲒⲠⲚⲈⲨⲘⲀⲦⲞⲤ ⲀⲨⲰ ⲈⲦⲂⲈ ⲞⲨ ⲀⲨⲠⲢⲞⲈⲖⲐⲈ
ⲈⲂⲞⲖ ϨⲚ̄ ⲚⲒⲀⲠⲀⲦⲰⲢ · ⲀⲨⲰ ⲠⲘⲨⲤⲦⲎⲢⲒⲞⲚ ⲈⲦⲘ̄ⲘⲀⲨ Ⲛ̄-
ⲦⲞϤ ⲠⲈⲦⲤⲞⲞⲨⲚ ⲬⲈ ⲈⲦⲂⲈ ⲞⲨ ⲀⲨⲤⲔⲨⲖⲀⲒ Ⲙ̄ⲘⲞⲞⲨ Ⲛ̄ϬⲒ
ⲚⲈⲠⲢⲞⲀⲬⲰⲢⲎⲦⲞⲤ Ⲙ̄ⲠⲘⲈϨⲤⲚⲀⲨ Ⲛ̄ⲦⲢⲒⲠⲚⲈⲨⲘⲀⲦⲞⲤ · ⲀⲨⲰ
ⲈⲦⲂⲈ ⲞⲨ ⲀⲨⲠⲢⲞⲈⲖⲐⲈ ⲈⲂⲞⲖ ϨⲚ̄ ⲚⲒⲀⲠⲀⲦⲰⲢ · ⲀⲨⲰ ⲠⲘⲨⲤ-
15 ⲦⲎⲢⲒⲞⲚ ⲈⲦⲘ̄ⲘⲀⲨ Ⲛ̄ⲦⲞϤ ⲠⲈⲦⲤⲞⲞⲨⲚ ⲬⲈ ⲈⲦⲂⲈ ⲞⲨ ⲀⲨ-
ⲤⲔⲨⲖⲀⲒ Ⲙ̄ⲘⲞⲞⲨ Ⲛ̄ϬⲒ ⲚⲈⲠⲢⲞⲀⲬⲰⲢⲎⲦⲞⲤ ⲦⲎⲢⲞⲨ Ⲙ̄ⲠⲘⲈϨ-
ϢⲞⲘⲚ̄Ⲧ Ⲛ̄ⲦⲢⲒⲠⲚⲈⲨⲘⲀⲦⲞⲤ · ⲀⲨⲰ ⲈⲦⲂⲈ ⲞⲨ ⲀⲨⲠⲢⲞⲈⲖⲐⲈ
ⲈⲂⲞⲖ ϨⲚ̄ ⲚⲒⲀⲠⲀⲦⲰⲢ · ⲀⲨⲰ ⲠⲘⲨⲤⲦⲎⲢⲒⲞⲚ ⲈⲦⲘ̄ⲘⲀⲨ Ⲛ̄ⲦⲞϤ
ⲠⲈⲦⲤⲞⲞⲨⲚ ⲬⲈ ⲈⲦⲂⲈ ⲞⲨ ⲀϤⲤⲔⲨⲖⲀⲒ Ⲙ̄ⲘⲞϤ* Ⲛ̄ϬⲒ ⲠϢⲞⲢⲠ̄ [ⲤⲎᵇ]
20 Ⲛ̄ⲦⲢⲒⲠⲚⲈⲨⲘⲀⲦⲞⲤ ⲬⲒⲚ ⲠⲈⲤⲎⲦ ⲚⲀⲒ̈ ⲈⲦⲎⲠ' ⲈⲚⲦⲀⲜⲒⲤ Ⲙ̄ⲠⲒ-
ⲞⲨⲖ Ⲛ̄ⲞⲨⲰⲦ ⲠⲒⲀⲦϢⲀⲬⲈ ⲈⲢⲞϤ · ⲀⲨⲰ ⲈⲦⲂⲈ ⲞⲨ ⲀⲨ-
ⲠⲢⲞⲈⲖⲐⲈ ⲈⲂⲞⲖ ϨⲘ̄ ⲠⲘⲀϨⲤⲚⲀⲨ Ⲛ̄ⲦⲢⲒⲠⲚⲈⲨⲘⲀⲦⲞⲤ · ⲀⲨⲰ
ⲠⲘⲨⲤⲦⲎⲢⲒⲞⲚ ⲈⲦⲘ̄ⲘⲀⲨ Ⲛ̄ⲦⲞϤ ⲠⲈⲦⲤⲞⲞⲨⲚ ⲬⲈ ⲈⲦⲂⲈ ⲞⲨ
ⲀϤⲤⲔⲨⲖⲀⲒ Ⲙ̄ⲘⲞϤ Ⲛ̄ϬⲒ ⲠⲘⲈϨϢⲞⲘⲚ̄Ⲧ Ⲛ̄ⲦⲢⲒⲠⲚⲈⲨⲘⲀⲦⲞⲤ
25 ⲈⲦⲈ Ⲛ̄ⲦⲞϤ ⲠⲈ ⲠϢⲞⲢⲠ̄ Ⲛ̄ⲦⲢⲒⲠⲚⲈⲨⲘⲀⲦⲞⲤ ⲬⲒⲚ ⲠⲬⲒⲤⲈ ·

---

21 MS ⲀⲨⲠⲢⲞⲈⲖⲐⲈ; read ⲀϤⲠⲢⲞⲤⲖⲐⲈ.
22 MS ⲠⲘⲘⲀϨ; the second Ⲙ expunged.

ones. And that *mystery* knows why the five trees of the second *triple-spirited one troubled*, and why they *came forth* from the *fatherless ones.* And that *mystery* knows why the five trees of the third *triple-spirited one troubled*, and why they *came forth* from the *fatherless ones.* And that *mystery* knows why the *proachoretoi* of the first *triple-spirited one troubled*, and why they *came forth* from the *fatherless ones.* And that *mystery* knows why the *proachoretoi* of the second *triple-spirited one troubled*, and why they *came forth* from the *fatherless ones.* And that *mystery* knows why all the *proachoretoi* of the third *triple-spirited one troubled*, and why they *came forth* from the *fatherless ones.* And that *mystery* knows why the first *triple-spirited one* from below, which belongs to the *ranks* [1] of the Only One, the Ineffable, *troubled* and why it *came forth* [2] from the second *triple-spirited one.* And that *mystery* knows why the third *triple-spirited one*, which is the first *triple-spirited one* from above, *troubled*, | and why it *came forth* from the twelfth *pre-triple-*

---

[1] (20) which belongs to the ranks; Schmidt: these (triple-spirited ones) which belong to the ranks.
[2] (22, 23) why it came forth; MS: why they came forth.

ⲀⲨⲰ ⲈⲦⲂⲈ ⲞⲨ ⲀϤⲠⲢⲞⲈⲖⲐⲈ ⲈⲂⲞⲖ ϨⲘ ⲠⲘⲈϨⲘⲚⲦⲤⲚⲞⲞⲨⳄ
ⲘⲠⲢⲞⲦⲢⲒⲠⲚⲈⲨⲘⲀⲦⲞⳄ ⲠⲀⲒ̈ ⲈⲦϨⲘ ⲠϨⲀⲈ ⲚⲦⲞⲠⲞⳄ ⲚⲦⲈ Ⲛ-
ⲀⲠⲀⲦⲰⲢ· ⲀⲨⲰ ⲠⲘⲨⲤⲦⲎⲢⲒⲞⲚ ⲈⲦⲘⲘⲀⲨ ⲚⲦⲞϤ ⲠⲈⲦⲤⲞ-
ⲞⲨⲚ ϪⲈ ⲈⲦⲂⲈ ⲞⲨ ⲀⲨⲤⲰⲢ ⲈⲂⲞⲖ ⲚϬⲒ ⲚⲦⲞⲠⲞⳄ ⲦⲎⲢⲞⲨ
5 ⲈⲦϨⲘ ⲠⲈⲬⲰⲢⲎⲘⲀ ⲘⲠⲒⲀⲦⲰϢⲀϪⲈ ⲈⲢⲞϤ· ⲀⲨⲰ ⲘⲚ ⲚⲈⲦⲚ-
ϨⲎⲦⲞⲨ ⲦⲎⲢⲞⲨ· ⲀⲨⲰ ⲈⲦⲂⲈ ⲞⲨ ⲀⲨⲠⲢⲞⲈⲖⲐⲈ ⲈⲂⲞⲖ ϨⲘ
ⲠϨⲀⲈ ⲘⲘⲈⲖⲞⳄ ⲘⲠⲒⲀⲦⲰϢⲀϪⲈ ⲈⲢⲞϤ: ⲀⲨⲰ ⲠⲘⲨⲤⲦⲎⲢⲒⲞⲚ ⲥ̄ⲑ̄
ⲈⲦⲘⲘⲀⲨ ⲚⲦⲞϤ ⲠⲈⲦⲤⲞⲞⲨⲚ ⲘⲘⲞϤ ⲘⲘⲒⲚ ⲘⲘⲞϤ ϪⲈ ⲈⲦ-
ⲂⲈ ⲞⲨ ⲀϤⲤⲔⲨⲖⲖⲒ ⲘⲘⲞϤ ⲈⲦⲢⲈϤⲠⲢⲞⲈⲖⲐⲈ ⲈⲂⲞⲖ ϨⲘ ⲠⲒ-
10 ⲀⲦⲰϢⲀϪⲈ ⲈⲢⲟϤ ⲈⲦⲈ ⲚⲦⲞϤ ⲠⲈⲦⲀⲢⲬⲒ ⲈϨⲢⲀⲒ̈ ⲈϪⲰⲞⲨ ⲦⲎ-
ⲢⲞⲨ ⲀⲨⲰ ⲚⲦⲞϤ ⲠⲈ ⲚⲦⲀϤⲤⲞⲢⲞⲨ ⲈⲂⲞⲖ ⲦⲎⲢⲞⲨ ⲔⲀⲦⲀ
ⲚⲈⲨⲦⲀⳄⲒⳄ· ⲚⲀⲒ̈ ϬⲈ ⲦⲎⲢⲞⲨ ϮⲚⲀϪⲞⲞⲨ ⲈⲢⲰⲦⲚ ϨⲘ ⲠⲤⲰⲢ
ⲈⲂⲞⲖ ⲘⲠⲦⲎⲢϤ· ϨⲀⲠⲀⳄ ϨⲀⲠⲖⲰⳄ ⲚⲈⲚⲦⲀⲒ̈ϪⲞⲞⲨ ⲈⲢⲰⲦⲚ
ⲦⲎⲢⲞⲨ ⲚⲈⲦⲚⲀϢⲰⲠⲈ ⲘⲚ ⲚⲈⲦⲚⲀⲈⲒ· ⲚⲀⲒ̈ ⲈⲦⲠⲢⲞⲂⲀⲖⲈ
15 ⲀⲨⲰ ⲈⲦⲠⲢⲞⲈⲖⲐⲈ· ⲀⲨⲰ ⲘⲚ ⲚⲈⲦⲚⲂⲞⲖ ϨⲒϪⲰⲞⲨ ⲀⲨⲰ
ⲘⲚ ⲚⲈⲦⲢⲎⲦ ϨⲢⲀⲒ̈ ⲚϨⲎⲦⲞⲨ ⲚⲀⲒ̈ ⲈⲦⲚⲀⲬⲰⲢⲈⲒ ⲈⲠⲘⲀ Ⲙ̄-
ⲠϢⲞⲢⲠ ⲘⲘⲨⲤⲦⲎⲢⲒⲞⲚ· ⲀⲨⲰ ⲘⲚ ⲚⲈⲦϨⲚ ⲠⲈⲬⲰⲢⲎⲘⲀ Ⲙ̄-
ⲠⲒⲀⲦⲰϢⲀϪⲈ ⲈⲢⲞϤ· ⲚⲀⲒ̈ ⲈϮⲚⲀϪⲞⲞⲨ ⲈⲢⲰⲦⲚ ⲈⲂⲞⲖ ϪⲈ
ϮⲚⲀϬⲞⲖⲠⲞⲨ ⲚⲎⲦⲚ ⲈⲂⲞⲖ· ⲀⲨⲰ ϮⲚⲀϪⲞⲞⲨ *ⲈⲢⲰⲦⲚ ⲥ̄ⲑ̄ᵇ
20 ⲔⲀⲦⲀ ⲦⲞⲠⲞⳄ· ⲀⲨⲰ ⲔⲀⲦⲀ ⲦⲀⳄⲒⳄ ⲈϨⲢⲀⲒ̈ ϨⲘ ⲠⲤⲰⲢ ⲈⲂⲞⲖ
ⲘⲠⲦⲎⲢϤ· ⲀⲨⲰ ϮⲚⲀϬⲰⲖⲠ ⲚⲎⲦⲚ ⲈⲂⲞⲖ ⲚⲚⲈⲨⲘⲨⲤⲦⲎⲢⲒⲞⲚ
ⲦⲎⲢⲞⲨ ⲈⲦⲀⲢⲬⲒ ⲈϨⲢⲀⲒ̈ ⲈϪⲰⲞⲨ ⲦⲎⲢⲞⲨ ⲘⲚ ⲚⲈⲨⲠⲢⲞⲦⲢⲒ-
ⲠⲚⲈⲨⲘⲀⲦⲞⳄ ⲘⲚ ⲚⲈⲨϨⲨⲠⲈⲢⲦⲢⲒⲠⲚⲈⲨⲘⲀⲦⲞⳄ· ⲚⲀⲒ̈ ⲈⲦ-
ⲀⲢⲬⲒ ⲈϪⲚ ⲚⲈⲨⲘⲨⲤⲦⲎⲢⲒⲞⲚ ⲘⲚ ⲚⲈⲨⲦⲀⳄⲒⳄ· ⲦⲈⲚⲞⲨ ϬⲈ

---

1 MS originally ⲠⲘⲈϨⳄⲚⲀⲨ; ⳄⲚⲀⲨ expunged.
9 MS ⲘⲘⲒⲚ ⲘⲘⲞϤ expunged after ⲘⲘⲞϤ.
22 MS ⲈⲦⲀⲢⲬⲒ; read ⲈⲦⲀⲢⲬⲒ; also line 24.

spirited one which is in the last *place* of the *fatherless ones.*
And that *mystery* knows why all the *places* in the *space* of
the Ineffable and all within them were distributed, and why
they *came forth* from the last *member* of the Ineffable. And
that *mystery* knows of itself why it *troubled* itself in order to
come forth from the Ineffable, namely from him who *rules*
over them all and has distributed them all *according to* their
ranks.

96. Now all these things I will say to you at the distribution of the All. *In a word* all I have said to you — those
things which will happen and those which will come, which
emanate and which *come forth*, those outside above them
and those which grow within them, which will *occupy* the
place of the First *Mystery*, and those which are in the
space of the Ineffable — these things I will say to you because
I will reveal them to you. And I will say them to you
according to places and *according to ranks* within the distribution of the All. And I will reveal to you all their *mysteries*
which *rule* over them all and their *pre-triple-spirited ones*
and their *hyper-triple-spirited ones* which *rule* over their
mysteries and their *ranks.* |

ⲞⲨⲚ ⲠⲘⲨⲤⲦⲎⲢⲒⲞⲚ ⲘⲠⲒⲀⲦⲰⲀⲬⲈ ⲈⲢⲞϤ · ⲚⲦⲞϤ ⲠⲈⲦⲤⲞ-
ⲞⲨⲚ ⲬⲈ ⲈⲦⲂⲈ ⲞⲨ Ⲁ ⲚⲀⲒ ⲦⲎⲢⲞⲨ ⲰⲰⲠⲈ ⲚⲚⲈⲚⲦⲀⲒ̈ⲬⲞⲞⲨ
ⲌⲚ ⲞⲨⲠⲀⲢ2ⲎⲤⲒⲀ ⲀⲨⲰ ⲚⲦⲀ ⲚⲀⲒ ⲦⲎⲢⲞⲨ ⲰⲰⲠⲈ ⲈⲦⲂⲎⲎⲦϤ ·
ⲀⲨⲰ ⲚⲦⲞϤ ⲠⲈ ⲠⲘⲨⲤⲦⲎⲢⲒⲞⲚ ⲈⲦ2Ⲛ ⲚⲀⲒ ⲦⲎⲢⲞⲨ ⲀⲨⲰ
5 ⲚⲦⲞϤ ⲠⲈ ⲠⲈⲨⲈⲒ' ⲈⲂⲞⲖ ⲦⲎⲢⲞⲨ · ⲀⲨⲰ ⲚⲦⲞϤ ⲠⲈ ⲠⲈⲨⲰⲖ'
Ⲉ2ⲢⲀⲒ̈ ⲦⲎⲢⲞⲨ · ⲀⲨⲰ ⲚⲦⲞϤ ⲠⲈ ⲠⲈⲨⲦⲀ2Ⲟ ⲈⲢⲀⲦϤ ⲦⲎⲢⲞⲨ ·
ⲀⲨⲰ ⲠⲘⲨⲤⲦⲎⲢⲒⲞⲚ ⲘⲠⲒⲀⲦⲰⲀⲬⲈ ⲈⲢⲞϤ ⲚⲦⲞϤ ⲠⲈ ⲠⲘⲨⲤ-
ⲦⲎⲢⲒⲞⲚ ⲈⲦ2Ⲛ ⲚⲀⲒ ⲦⲎⲢⲞⲨ ⲚⲦⲀⲒ̈ⲬⲞⲞⲨ** ⲈⲢⲰⲦⲚ · ⲀⲨⲰ ⲘⲚ [ⲥⲓ]
ⲚⲈ†ⲚⲀⲬⲞⲞⲨ ⲈⲢⲰⲦⲚ 2ⲢⲀⲒ̈ 2Ⲙ ⲠⲤⲰⲢ ⲈⲂⲞⲖ ⲘⲠⲦⲎⲢϤ ·
10 ⲀⲨⲰ ⲚⲦⲞϤ ⲠⲈ ⲠⲘⲨⲤⲦⲎⲢⲒⲞⲚ ⲈⲦ2Ⲛ ⲚⲀⲒ ⲦⲎⲢⲞⲨ · ⲀⲨⲰ
ⲚⲦⲞϤ ⲠⲈ ⲠⲘⲨⲤⲦⲎⲢⲒⲞⲚ ⲚⲞⲨⲰⲦ ⲚⲦⲈ ⲠⲒⲀⲦⲰⲀⲬⲈ ⲈⲢⲞϤ ·
ⲀⲨⲰ ⲠⲤⲞⲞⲨⲚ ⲚⲚⲀⲒ ⲦⲎⲢⲞⲨ ⲚⲦⲀⲒ̈ⲬⲞⲞⲨ ⲈⲢⲰⲦⲚ ⲀⲨⲰ
ⲘⲚ ⲚⲈ†ⲚⲀⲬⲞⲞⲨ ⲈⲢⲰⲦⲚ · ⲘⲚ ⲚⲈⲦⲈ ⲘⲠⲒⲬⲞⲞⲨ ⲈⲢⲰⲦⲚ
ⲚⲀⲒ †ⲚⲀⲬⲞⲞⲨ ⲈⲢⲰⲦⲚ ⲦⲎⲢⲞⲨ 2ⲢⲀⲒ̈ 2Ⲙ ⲠⲤⲰⲢ ⲈⲂⲞⲖ Ⲙ-
15 ⲠⲦⲎⲢϤ ⲘⲚ ⲠⲈⲨⲤⲞⲞⲨⲚ ⲦⲎⲢϤ 2Ⲓ ⲚⲈⲨⲈⲢⲎⲨ ⲬⲈ ⲈⲦⲂⲈ ⲞⲨ
ⲀⲨⲰⲰⲠⲈ · ⲚⲦⲞϤ ⲠⲈ ⲠⲒⲰⲀⲬⲈ ⲚⲞⲨⲰⲦ ⲚⲦⲈ ⲠⲒⲀⲦⲰⲀⲬⲈ
ⲈⲢⲞϤ · ⲀⲨⲰ †ⲚⲀⲬⲰ ⲈⲢⲰⲦⲚ ⲘⲠⲤⲰⲢ ⲈⲂⲞⲖ ⲚⲚⲈⲨⲘⲨⲤ-
ⲦⲎⲢⲒⲞⲚ ⲦⲎⲢⲞⲨ ⲘⲚ ⲚⲦⲨⲠⲞⲤ ⲘⲠⲞⲨⲀ ⲠⲞⲨⲀ ⲘⲘⲞⲞⲨ
ⲘⲚ ⲐⲈ ⲚⲬⲞⲔⲞⲨ ⲈⲂⲞⲖ 2Ⲛ ⲚⲈⲨⲤⲬⲎⲘⲀ ⲦⲎⲢⲞⲨ ⲀⲨⲰ
20 †ⲚⲀⲬⲰ ⲈⲢⲰⲦⲚ ⲘⲠⲘⲨⲤⲦⲎⲢⲒⲞⲚ ⲚⲦⲈ ⲠⲒⲞⲨⲀ ⲚⲞⲨⲰⲦ
ⲘⲠⲒⲀⲦⲰⲀⲬⲈ* ⲈⲢⲞϤ ⲘⲚ ⲚⲈϤⲦⲨⲠⲞⲤ ⲦⲎⲢⲞⲨ ⲘⲚ ⲚⲈϤⲤⲬⲎ- [ⲥⲓ ᵇ]
ⲘⲀ ⲦⲎⲢⲞⲨ ⲀⲨⲰ ⲘⲚ ⲦⲈϤⲞⲒⲔⲞⲚⲞⲘⲒⲀ ⲦⲎⲢⲤ ⲬⲈ ⲈⲦⲂⲈ
ⲞⲨ ⲢⲰ ⲀϤⲠⲢⲞⲈⲖⲐⲈ ⲈⲂⲞⲖ 2Ⲙ Ⲡ2ⲀⲈ ⲘⲘⲈⲖⲞⲤ ⲘⲠⲒⲀⲦⲰⲀ-
ⲬⲈ ⲈⲢⲞϤ ⲈⲂⲞⲖ ⲬⲈ ⲠⲘⲨⲤⲦⲎⲢⲒⲞⲚ ⲈⲦⲘⲘⲀⲨ ⲠⲈ ⲠⲈⲨⲦⲀ2Ⲟ
25 ⲈⲢⲀⲦϤ ⲦⲎⲢⲞⲨ · ⲀⲨⲰ ⲠⲘⲨⲤⲦⲎⲢⲒⲞⲚ ⲚⲦⲈ ⲠⲒⲀⲦⲰⲀⲬⲈ

---

3 MS ⲀⲨⲰ wrongly precedes ⲌⲚ ⲞⲨⲠⲀⲢ2ⲎⲤⲒⲀ.
21 MS ⲘⲠⲒⲀⲦⲰⲀⲬⲈ; read ⲠⲒⲀⲦⲰⲀⲬⲈ.

Now at this time the *mystery* of the Ineffable knows why
all these things of which I have spoken to you *openly* have
happened and by what means they have all happened [1].
And it is the *mystery* within all these things. And it is the
coming forth of them all, and it is the rising up of them
all, and it is the setting up of them all. And the *mystery* of
the Ineffable is the *mystery* which is in all these things which
I have said to you, and those which I will say to you at the
distribution of the All. And it is the *mystery* which is in all
these things; and it is the one *mystery* of the Ineffable, and
the knowledge of all those things which I have said to you,
and those which I will say to you, and those which I have
not said to you; all these I will tell you at the distribution
of the All, and all their knowledge together, why they
happened. It is the one word of the Ineffable. And I will
tell you of the distribution of all their *mysteries*, and the
types of each one of them, and the manner of completion
in all their *patterns* [2]. And I will say to you the *mystery* of
the Only One, the Ineffable, and all its *types*, and all its
patterns, and its whole *organisation*, why it *came forth* from
the last *member* of the Ineffable; because that *mystery* is the
setting up of them all. And the *mystery* of that Ineffable |

---

[1]   (3) by what means they have all happened; Till: for whose sake they have all
     happened.
[2]   (19) patterns; see 31.22, n. 1.

ЕРОЧ ЕТ̄ММАУ ОУШАХЕ ОN N̄ОУШТ ПЕ ПКЕТ ЕЧШООП

2N ТАСПЕ М̄ПIАТШАХЕ ЕРОЧ АУШ N̄ТОЧ ПЕ ТОIКО-

NОМIА М̄ПВШЛ N̄ШАХЕ NIM N̄ТАÏХООУ ЕРШТN̄· АУШ

ПЕТNАХI М̄ПШАХЕ N̄ОУШТ М̄ПМУСТНРIОN ЕТ̄ММАУ

5 ПАÏ Е†NАХООЧ ЕРШТN̄ ТЕNОУ МN̄ NЕЧТУПОС ТНРОУ

МN̄ NЕЧСХНМА ТНРОУ МN̄ ΘЕ N̄ХШК’ ЕВОЛ М̄ПЕЧМУС-

ТНРIОN ЕВОЛ ХЕ N̄ТШТN̄ NЕ N̄ТЕЛIОС М̄ПАNТЕЛIОС

АУШ N̄ТШТN̄ ПЕТNАХШК ЕВОЛ М̄ПСООУN̄** ТНРЧ М̄- СIΛ

ПМУСТНРIОN ЕТ̄ММАУ МN̄ ТЕЧОIКОNОМIА ТНР̄С ХЕ

10 N̄ТШТN̄ ПЕNТАУТАN2ЕТТНУТN̄ ЕМУСТНРIОN NIM:

СШТ̄М 6Е ТЕNОУ ТАХШ ЕРШТN̄ М̄ПМУСТНРIОN ЕТ̄М-

МАУ ЕТЕ ПАÏ ПЕ: ПЕТNАХI 6Е М̄ПШАХЕ N̄ОУШТ М̄-

ПМУСТНРIОN ПАÏ N̄ТАÏХООУ ЕРШТN̄ ЕЧШАNЕI’ ЕВОЛ

2М ПСШМА N̄ОУЛН N̄NАРХШN· N̄СЕЕI N̄6I М̄ПАРАЛНМП-

15 ТНС N̄ЕРINАIОС N̄СЕВОЛЧ ЕВОЛ 2М ПСШМА N̄ОУЛН N̄N-

АРХШN N̄ТЕ М̄ПАРАЛНМПТНС N̄ЕРINАIОС ЕТЕ N̄ТООУ

ПЕ ЕШАУВШЛ ЕВОЛ М̄ΨУХН NIM ЕТNНУ ЕВОЛ 2М ПСШ-

МА· ЕШШПЕ 6Е ЕРШАN N̄ПАРАЛНМПТНС N̄ЕРINАIОС

ЕУШАNВШЛ ЕВОЛ N̄ТЕΨУХН ЕNТАСХI М̄ПЕÏМУСТНРIОN

20 N̄ОУШТ N̄ТЕ ПIАТШАХЕ ЕРОЧ ПАÏ N̄ТАÏОУШ ЕÏХШ М̄-

МОЧ ЕРШТN̄ ТЕNОУ·* АУШ 2N̄ ТЕУNОУ ЕТОУNАВОЛ̄С СIΛᵇ

ЕВОЛ 2М ПСШМА N̄ОУЛН СNАР-ОУNО6 N̄АПОРРОIА N̄-

ОУОЕIN 2РАÏ 2N̄ ТМНТЕ N̄МПАРАЛНМПТНС ЕТ̄ММАУ·

---

9 MS МN̄ ПЕЧ expunged before ХЕ.

16 MS N̄ТЕ; read N̄6I.

18 MS N̄ПАРАЛНМПТНС; read М̄ПАРАЛНМПТНС.

is again one word which also exists in the tongue of the Ineffable, and it is the *organisation* of the release of all the words
which I have said to you. And he who will receive the one
word of that *mystery*, that which I will now say to you, with
all its *types* and all its *patterns* and the manner of completion
of its *mystery* — because you are *perfected* in *all-perfection*
and you will complete all the knowledge of that *mystery*
and all its *organisation*, because to you are all *mysteries*
entrusted — hear now that I say to you that *mystery* which
is this : he who will receive the one word of the *mystery*
which I have told you, when he comes forth from the *material
body* of the archons, the *erinaioi* [1] *paralemptai* come and
release him from the *material body* of the *archons* — the
erinaioi paralemptai are they who release all *souls* which come
forth from the *body*. Now when the *erinaioi paralemptai*
release the *soul* which has received this one *mystery* of the
Ineffable, which I have just said to you, at the hour when
they release it from the *material body* it will become a great
outpouring of light in the midst of those *paralemptai*. | And

---

[1]   (15) erinaioi; c.f. the κῆρες ἐρινύες in Aeschylus *Oresteia* etc.

ⲀⲨⲰ ⲤⲈⲚⲀⲢϨⲞⲦⲈ ⲈⲘⲀϢⲞ ⲚϬⲒ ⟨Ⲙ⟩ⲠⲀⲢⲀⲖⲎⲘⲠⲦⲎⲤ ϨⲚⲦⲰ̄ⲧ
ⲘⲠⲞⲨⲞⲈⲒⲚ ⲚⲦⲈⲮⲨⲬⲎ ⲈⲦⲘⲘⲀⲨ· ⲀⲨⲰ ⲤⲈⲚⲀⲤⲰ̄ϢⲘ̄ ⲚϬⲒ
Ⲙ̄ⲠⲀⲢⲀⲖⲎⲘⲠⲦⲎⲤ ⲚⲤⲈϨⲈ ⲚⲤⲈⲔⲀⲦⲞⲞⲦⲞⲨ ⲈⲂⲞⲖ ⲈⲠⲦⲎⲢϤ̄·
ⲈⲂⲞⲖ ϨⲚ ⲐⲞⲦⲈ Ⲙ̄ⲠⲚⲞϬ ⲚⲞⲨⲞⲈⲒⲚ ⲈⲚⲦⲀⲨⲚⲀⲨ ⲈⲢⲞϤ·
5 ⲀⲨⲰ ⲦⲈⲮⲨⲬⲎ ⲈⲦϪⲒ Ⲙ̄ⲠⲘⲨⲤⲦⲎⲢⲒⲞⲚ Ⲙ̄ⲠⲒⲀⲦϢⲀϪⲈ ⲈⲢⲞϤ
ⲤⲚⲀϨⲰⲖ ⲈⲠϪⲒⲤⲈ ⲈⲤⲞ ⲚⲞⲨⲚⲞϬ ⲚⲀⲠⲞⲢⲢⲞⲒⲀ ⲚⲞⲨⲞⲈⲒⲚ·
ⲀⲨⲰ Ⲛ̄ⲤⲈⲚⲀϢⲦⲀϨⲞⲤ ⲀⲚ Ⲛ̄ϬⲒ Ⲙ̄ⲠⲀⲢⲀⲖⲎⲘⲠⲦⲎⲤ ⲀⲨⲰ Ⲛ̄-
ⲤⲈⲚⲀⲈⲒⲘⲈ ⲀⲚ ϪⲈ ⲀϢ ⲦⲈ ⲦⲈϨⲒⲎ ⲈⲦⲤⲚⲀⲂⲰⲔ Ⲛ̄ϨⲎⲦⲤ ⲈⲂⲞⲖ
ϪⲈ ϢⲀⲤⲢ̄-ⲞⲨⲚⲞϬ Ⲛ̄ϢⲖⲒϬ ⲚⲞⲨⲞⲈⲒⲚ Ⲛ̄ⲤϨⲰⲖ ⲈⲠϪⲒⲤⲈ
10 ⲀⲨⲰ ⲘⲈⲢⲈ ⲖⲀⲀⲨ Ⲛ̄ⲆⲨⲚⲀⲘⲒⲤ ⲈϢϬⲘϬⲞⲘ ⲈⲔⲀⲦⲈⲬⲈ Ⲙ̄- [ⲤⲒⲂ]
ⲘⲞⲤ ⲈⲠⲦⲎⲢϤ̄· ⲞⲨⲆⲈ ⲢⲰ Ⲛ̄ⲚⲈⲨⲈϢϨⲰⲚ ⲈⲢⲞϤ ⲈⲠⲦⲎⲢϤ̄·
ⲀⲖⲖⲀ ϢⲀⲤⲬⲰⲦⲈ Ⲛ̄ⲚⲦⲞⲠⲞⲤ ⲦⲎⲢⲞⲨ Ⲛ̄ⲦⲈ Ⲛ̄ⲀⲢⲬⲰⲚ ⲘⲚ̄
Ⲛ̄ⲦⲞⲠⲞⲤ ⲦⲎⲢⲞⲨ Ⲛ̄ⲚⲈⲠⲢⲞⲂⲞⲖⲞⲞⲨⲈ Ⲙ̄ⲠⲞⲨⲞⲈⲒⲚ ⲀⲨⲰ
ⲘⲈⲤϯ-ⲀⲠⲞⲪⲀⲤⲒⲤ ϨⲚ ⲖⲀⲀⲨ Ⲛ̄ⲦⲞⲠⲞⲤ· ⲞⲨⲆⲈ ⲘⲈⲤϯ-ⲀⲠⲞ-
15 ⲖⲞⲄⲒⲀ· ⲞⲨⲆⲈ ⲘⲈⲤϯ-ⲤⲨⲘⲂⲞⲖⲞⲚ· ⲞⲨⲆⲈ ⲄⲀⲢ Ⲛ̄ⲚⲈϢ
ⲖⲀⲀⲨ Ⲛ̄ϬⲞⲘ Ⲛ̄ⲦⲈ Ⲛ̄ⲀⲢⲬⲰⲚ ⲞⲨⲆⲈ Ⲛ̄ⲚⲈϢ ⲖⲀⲀⲨ Ⲛ̄ϬⲞⲘ
Ⲛ̄ⲦⲈ ⲚⲈⲠⲢⲞⲂⲞⲖⲞⲞⲨⲈ Ⲙ̄ⲠⲞⲨⲞⲈⲒⲚ Ⲛ̄ⲚⲈⲨⲈϢϨⲰⲚ ⲈϨⲞⲨⲚ
ⲈⲦⲈⲮⲨⲬⲎ ⲈⲦⲘⲘⲀⲨ· ⲀⲖⲖⲀ ϢⲀⲢⲈ Ⲛ̄ⲦⲞⲠⲞⲤ ⲦⲎⲢⲞⲨ Ⲛ̄ⲦⲈ
Ⲛ̄ⲀⲢⲬⲰⲚ ⲘⲚ̄ Ⲛ̄ⲦⲞⲠⲞⲤ ⲦⲎⲢⲞⲨ Ⲛ̄ⲦⲈ ⲚⲈⲠⲢⲞⲂⲞⲖⲞⲞⲨⲈ Ⲙ̄-
20 ⲠⲞⲨⲞⲈⲒⲚ· ϢⲀⲢⲈ ⲠⲞⲨⲀ ⲠⲞⲨⲀ ϨⲨⲘⲚⲈⲨⲈ ⲈⲢⲞⲤ ϨⲚ ⲚⲈⲨ-
ⲦⲞⲠⲞⲤ ⲈⲨⲞ Ⲛ̄ϨⲞⲦⲈ ϨⲚ̄ⲦⲰ̄Ϥ Ⲙ̄ⲠⲞⲨⲞⲈⲒⲚ Ⲛ̄ⲦⲀⲠⲞⲢⲢⲞⲒⲀ ⲈⲦ-
ϬⲞⲞⲖⲈ Ⲛ̄ⲦⲈⲮⲨⲬⲎ ⲈⲦⲘⲘⲀⲨ· ϨⲈⲰⲤ ϢⲀⲚⲦⲤⲬⲰⲦⲈ Ⲙ̄- [ⲤⲒⲂᵇ]
ⲘⲞⲞⲨ ⲦⲎⲢⲞⲨ Ⲛ̄ⲤⲂⲰⲔ ⲈⲠⲦⲞⲠⲞⲤ Ⲛ̄ⲦⲈⲔⲖⲎⲢⲞⲚⲞⲘⲒⲀ Ⲛ̄ⲦⲈ
ⲠⲘⲨⲤⲦⲎⲢⲒⲞⲚ Ⲛ̄ⲦⲀⲤϪⲒⲦϤ̄ ⲈⲦⲈ Ⲛ̄ⲦⲞϤ ⲠⲈ ⲠⲘⲨⲤⲦⲎⲢⲒⲞⲚ
25 Ⲙ̄ⲠⲒⲞⲨⲀ ⲚⲞⲨⲰⲦ ⲠⲒⲀⲦϢⲀϪⲈ ⲈⲢⲞϤ· ⲀⲨⲰ Ⲛ̄ⲤϢⲰⲠⲈ ⲈⲤ-

---

1 MS ⲠⲀⲢⲀⲖⲎⲘⲠⲦⲎⲤ; read Ⲙ̄ⲠⲀⲢⲀⲖⲎⲘⲠⲦⲎⲤ.

the *paralemptai* will fear greatly at the light of that *soul*. And the *paralemptai* will be enfeebled and they will fall and desist altogether, because of the fear of the great light which they have seen. And the *soul* which receives the *mystery* of the Ineffable will ascend to the height, being a great *outpouring* of light. And the *paralemptai* will not be able to seize it, and they will not know what is the way in which it will go. For it becomes a great beam of light and flies to the height, and no *power* is able to *restrain* it, *nor* is it able to approach it at all. *But* it penetrates all the *places* of the *archons* and all the *places* of the *emanations* of the light, and it does not give *answer* in any *place*, nor does it give a *defence*[1], *nor* does it give a *secret sign*, *nor* is any power of the *archons*, *nor* any power of the *emanations* of the light able to approach that *soul*. *But* all the *places* of the *archons* and all the places of the *emanations* of the light — each one of them *sings praises* to it in their *places*, as they are in fear of the *outpouring* of light[2] which surrounds that *soul*, *until* it penetrates them all and goes to the *place* of the *inheritance* of the *mystery* which it has received — namely the *mystery* of the Only One, the Ineffable, and it becomes | united within his *members*. *Truly* I say to you that

---

[1] (14) defence; see Kropp (Bibl. 26), III p. 138; see J 116 etc.
[2] (21) the outpouring of light; lit. the light of the outpouring.

ϩⲟⲧⲣ̄ ⲉϩⲟⲩⲛ ⲉⲛⲉϥⲙⲉⲗⲟⲥ· ϩⲁⲙⲏⲛ ϯϫⲱ ⲙ̄ⲙⲟⲥ ⲛⲏⲧⲛ̄
ϫⲉ ⲉⲥⲛⲁϣⲱⲡⲉ ϩⲛ̄ ⲛ̄ⲧⲟⲡⲟⲥ ⲧⲏⲣⲟⲩ ⲙ̄ⲡⲕⲟⲟⲩ ⲛ̄ⲧⲉ ⲟⲩⲣⲱⲙⲉ ⲛⲟⲩϫⲉ ⲛ̄ⲟⲩⲥⲟⲧⲉ· ⲧⲉⲛⲟⲩ ϭⲉ ⲟⲛ ϩⲁⲙⲏⲛ ϯϫⲱ
ⲙ̄ⲙⲟⲥ ⲛⲏⲧⲛ̄ ϫⲉ ⲣⲱⲙⲉ ⲛⲓⲙ ⲉⲧⲛⲁϫⲓ ⲙ̄ⲡⲙⲩⲥⲧⲏⲣⲓⲟⲛ ⲉⲧ-
ⲙ̄ⲙⲁⲩ ⲛ̄ⲧⲉ ⲡⲓⲁⲧϣⲁϫⲉ ⲉⲣⲟϥ· ⲛ̄ϥϫⲟⲕϥ̄ ⲉⲃⲟⲗ ϩⲛ̄ ⲛⲉϥⲧⲩⲡⲟⲥ ⲧⲏⲣⲟⲩ ⲙⲛ̄ ⲛⲉϥⲥⲭⲏⲙⲁ ⲧⲏⲣⲟⲩ· ⲟⲩⲣⲱⲙⲉ ⲡⲉ
ⲉϥϩⲙ̄ ⲡⲕⲟⲥⲙⲟⲥ· ⲁⲗⲗⲁ ϥⲟⲩⲟⲧⲃ̄ ⲉⲛⲁⲅⲅⲉⲗⲟⲥ ⲧⲏⲣⲟⲩ·
ⲁⲩⲱ ϥⲛⲁⲟⲩⲱⲧⲃ̄ ⲛ̄ϩⲟⲩⲟ ⲉⲣⲟⲟⲩ ⲧⲏⲣⲟⲩ· ⲟⲩⲣⲱⲙⲉ ⲡⲉ
ⲉϥϩⲓϫⲙ̄ ⲡⲕⲟⲥⲙⲟⲥ ⲁⲗⲗⲁ ϥⲟⲩⲟⲧⲃ̄ ⲉⲛⲁⲣⲭⲁⲅⲅⲉⲗⲟⲥ ⲧⲏ-
ⲣⲟⲩ· ⲁⲩⲱ ϥⲛⲁⲟⲩⲱⲧⲃ̄ ⲟⲛ ⲛ̄ϩⲟⲩⲟ ⲉⲣⲟⲟⲩ ⲧⲏⲣⲟⲩ·
**ⲟⲩⲣⲱⲙⲉ ⲡⲉ ⲉϥϩⲓϫⲙ̄ ⲡⲕⲟⲥⲙⲟⲥ ⲁⲗⲗⲁ ϥⲟⲩⲟⲧⲃ̄ ⲉⲛⲧⲩ- ⲥⲓⲅ̄
ⲣⲁⲛⲛⲟⲥ ⲧⲏⲣⲟⲩ· ⲁⲩⲱ ϥⲛⲁϫⲓⲥⲉ ⲉⲣⲟⲟⲩ ⲧⲏⲣⲟⲩ· ⲟⲩⲣⲱⲙⲉ ⲡⲉ ⲉϥϩⲓϫⲙ̄ ⲡⲕⲟⲥⲙⲟⲥ ⲁⲗⲗⲁ ϥⲟⲩⲟⲧⲃ̄ ⲉⲛϫⲟⲉⲓⲥ
ⲧⲏⲣⲟⲩ· ⲁⲩⲱ ϥⲛⲁϫⲓⲥⲉ ⲉⲣⲟⲟⲩ ⲧⲏⲣⲟⲩ: ⲟⲩⲣⲱⲙⲉ ⲡⲉ
ⲉϥϩⲓϫⲙ̄ ⲡⲕⲟⲥⲙⲟⲥ ⲁⲗⲗⲁ ϥⲟⲩⲟⲧⲃ̄ ⲉⲛⲛⲟⲩⲧⲉ ⲧⲏⲣⲟⲩ·
ⲁⲩⲱ ϥⲛⲁϫⲓⲥⲉ ⲉⲣⲟⲟⲩ ⲧⲏⲣⲟⲩ· ⲟⲩⲣⲱⲙⲉ ⲡⲉ ⲉϥϩⲓϫⲙ̄
ⲡⲕⲟⲥⲙⲟⲥ ⲁⲗⲗⲁ ϥⲟⲩⲟⲧⲃ̄ ⲉⲛⲉⲫⲱⲥⲧⲏⲣ· ⲧⲏⲣⲟⲩ ⲁⲩⲱ
ϥⲛⲁϫⲓⲥⲉ ⲉⲣⲟⲟⲩ ⲧⲏⲣⲟⲩ· ⲟⲩⲣⲱⲙⲉ ⲡⲉ ⲉϥϩⲓϫⲛ̄ ⲡⲕⲟⲥⲙⲟⲥ ⲁⲗⲗⲁ ϥⲟⲩⲟⲧⲃ̄ ⲉⲛϩⲓⲗⲓⲕⲣⲓⲛⲉⲥ ⲧⲏⲣⲟⲩ ⲁⲩⲱ ϥⲛⲁϫⲓⲥⲉ
ⲉⲣⲟⲟⲩ ⲧⲏⲣⲟⲩ· ⲟⲩⲣⲱⲙⲉ ⲡⲉ ⲉϥϩⲓϫⲙ̄ ⲡⲕⲟⲥⲙⲟⲥ ⲁⲗⲗⲁ
ϥⲟⲩⲟⲧⲃ̄ ⲉⲛⲉⲧⲣⲓⲇⲩⲛⲁⲙⲓⲥ ⲧⲏⲣⲟⲩ· ⲁⲩⲱ ϥⲛⲁϫⲓⲥⲉ ⲉⲣⲟⲟⲩ ⲧⲏⲣⲟⲩ· ⲟⲩⲣⲱⲙⲉ ⲡⲉ ⲉϥϩⲓϫⲙ̄ ⲡⲕⲟⲥⲙⲟⲥ ⲁⲗⲗⲁ ϥⲟⲩ-
ⲟⲧⲃ̄ ⲉⲛⲉⲡⲣⲟⲡⲁⲧⲱⲣ ⲧⲏⲣⲟⲩ ⲁⲩⲱ ϥⲛⲁϫⲓⲥⲉ *ⲉⲣⲟⲟⲩ ⲧⲏ- ⲥⲓⲅ̄ b
ⲣⲟⲩ· ⲟⲩⲣⲱⲙⲉ ⲡⲉ ⲉϥϩⲓϫⲙ̄ ⲡⲕⲟⲥⲙⲟⲥ ⲁⲗⲗⲁ ϥⲟⲩⲟⲧⲃ̄
ⲉⲛⲁϩⲟⲣⲁⲧⲟⲥ ⲧⲏⲣⲟⲩ ⲁⲩⲱ ϥⲛⲁϫⲓⲥⲉ ⲉⲣⲟⲟⲩ ⲧⲏⲣⲟⲩ·
ⲟⲩⲣⲱⲙⲉ ⲡⲉ ⲉϥϩⲓϫⲙ̄ ⲡⲕⲟⲥⲙⲟⲥ ⲁⲗⲗⲁ ϥⲟⲩⲟⲧⲃ̄ ⲉⲡⲛⲟϭ

---

18 MS ⲉϥϩⲓϫⲛ̄; read ⲉϥϩⲓϫⲙ̄.

it will be in all *places* in the length of time [1] in which a man
shoots an arrow. Now at this time, *truly* I say to you that
every man who will receive that *mystery* of the Ineffable and
is completed in all its *types* and all its *patterns*, he is a man in
the *world but* he is superior to all the *angels* and he will be
much superior to them all. He is a man in the *world, but* he is
superior to all the *archangels* and he will be much superior
to them all. He is a man in the *world, but* he is superior to all
the *tyrants* and he will be exalted over them all. He is a man
in the *world, but* he is superior to all the lords and he will
be exalted over them all. He is a man in the *world, but* he
is superior to all the gods and he will be exalted over them
all. He is a man in the *world, but* he is superior to all the
luminaries and he will be exalted over them all. He is a man
in the *world, but* he is superior to all the *pure ones* and
he will be exalted over them all. He is a man in the *world,*
but he is superior to all the *triple powers* and he will be exalted
over them all. He is a man in the *world, but* he is superior to
all the *forefathers* and he will be exalted over them all.
He is a man in the *world,* but he is superior to all the
invisible ones and he will be exalted over them all. He is
a man in the *world, but* he is superior to the great | *invisible*

---

[1] (2) the length of time; Till: the short time.

ⲘⲠⲢⲞⲠⲀⲦⲰⲢ ⲚⲀϨⲞⲢⲀⲦⲞⲤ ⲀⲨⲰ ϤⲚⲀϪⲓⲤⲈ ⲞⲚ ⲈⲢⲞϤ· ⲞⲨ-
ⲢⲰⲘⲈ ⲠⲈ ⲈϤϨⲓⲜⲘ ⲠⲔⲞⲤⲘⲞⲤ ⲀⲖⲖⲀ ϤⲞⲨⲞⲦⳠ ⲈⲚⲀⲦⲘⲈ-
ⲤⲞⲤ ⲦⲎⲢⲞⲨ ⲀⲨⲰ ϤⲚⲀϪⲓⲤⲈ ⲈⲢⲞⲞⲨ ⲦⲎⲢⲞⲨ· ⲞⲨⲢⲰⲘⲈ
ⲠⲈ ⲈϤϨⲓⲜⲘ ⲠⲔⲞⲤⲘⲞⲤ ⲀⲖⲖⲀ ϤⲞⲨⲞⲦⳠ ⲈⲚⲈⲠⲢⲞⲂⲞⲖⲞⲞⲨⲈ
5 ⲚⲦⲈ ⲠⲈⲐⲎⲤⲀⲨⲢⲞⲤ ⲘⲠⲞⲨⲞⲈⲓⲚ ⲀⲨⲰ ϤⲚⲀϪⲓⲤⲈ ⲈⲢⲞⲞⲨ
ⲦⲎⲢⲞⲨ· ⲞⲨⲢⲰⲘⲈ ⲠⲈ ⲈϤϨⲓⲜⲘ ⲠⲔⲞⲤⲘⲞⲤ ⲀⲖⲖⲀ ϤⲞⲨⲞⲦⳠ
ⲈⲠⲔⲈⲢⲀⲤⲘⲞⲤ ⲀⲨⲰ ϤⲚⲀϪⲓⲤⲈ ⲈⲢⲞϤ ⲦⲎⲢϤ· ⲞⲨⲢⲰⲘⲈ ⲠⲈ
ⲈϤϨⲓⲜⲚ ⲠⲔⲞⲤⲘⲞⲤ ⲀⲖⲖⲀ ϤⲞⲨⲞⲦⳠ ⲈⲠⲦⲞⲠⲞⲤ ⲦⲎⲢϤ ⲘⲠⲈ-
ⲐⲎⲤⲀⲨⲢⲞⲤ ⲀⲨⲰ ϤⲚⲀϪⲓⲤⲈ ⲈⲢⲞϤ ⲦⲎⲢϤ· ⲞⲨⲢⲰⲘⲈ ⲠⲈ
10 ⲈϤϨⲓⲜⲚ ⲠⲔⲞⲤⲘⲞⲤ ⲀⲖⲖⲀ ϤⲚⲀⲢⲢⲢⲞ ⲚⲘⲘⲀⲓ ϨⲚ ⲦⲀⲘⲚⲦⲈⲢⲞ·
ⲞⲨⲢⲰⲘⲈ ⲠⲈ ⲈϤϨⲓⲜⲘ ⲠⲔⲞⲤⲘⲞⲤ ⲀⲖⲖⲀ ϤⲞ ⲚⲢⲢⲞ ϨⲘ ⲠⲞⲨ- [ⲤⲓⲀ]
ⲞⲈⲓⲚ· ⲞⲨⲢⲰⲘⲈ ⲠⲈ ⲈϤϨⲓⲜⲘ ⲠⲔⲞⲤⲘⲞⲤ ⲀⲖⲖⲀ ⲚⲞⲨⲈⲂⲞⲖ
ϨⲘ ⲠⲔⲞⲤⲘⲞⲤ ⲀⲚ ⲠⲈ: ⲀⲨⲰ ϨⲀⲘⲎⲚ ϯϪⲰ ⲘⲘⲞⲤ ⲚⲎⲦⲚ
ϪⲈ ⲠⲢⲰⲘⲈ ⲈⲦⲘⲘⲀⲨ ⲠⲈ ⲀⲚⲞⲔ ⲀⲨⲰ ⲀⲚⲞⲔ ⲠⲈ ⲠⲢⲰⲘⲈ
15 ⲈⲦⲘⲘⲀⲨ· ⲀⲨⲰ ϨⲢⲀⲓ ϨⲚ ⲠⲂⲰⲖ ⲈⲂⲞⲖ ⲘⲠⲔⲞⲤⲘⲞⲤ ⲈⲦⲈ
ⲠⲀⲓ ⲠⲈ ⲈⲢϢⲀⲚ ⲠⲦⲎⲢϤ ⲰⲖ ⲈϨⲢⲀⲓ· ⲀⲨⲰ ⲈⲨϢⲀⲚⲰⲖ
ⲈϨⲢⲀⲓ ⲦⲎⲢⲞⲨ ⲚϬⲓ ⲠⲀⲢⲓⲐⲘⲞⲤ ⲚⲚⲈⲯⲨⲬⲞⲞⲨⲈ ⲚⲦⲈⲖⲓⲞⲤ·
ⲀⲨⲰ ⲚⲦⲀϢⲰⲠⲈ ⲈⲓⲞ ⲚⲢⲢⲞ ϨⲚ ⲦⲘⲎⲦⲈ ⲘⲠϨⲀⲈ ⲘⲠⲀⲢⲀⲤ-
ⲦⲀⲦⲎⲤ ⲈⲓⲞ ⲚⲢⲢⲞ ⲈϨⲢⲀⲓ ⲈϪⲚ ⲚⲈⲠⲢⲞⲂⲞⲖⲞⲞⲨⲈ ⲦⲎⲢⲞⲨ
20 ⲘⲠⲞⲨⲞⲈⲓⲚ· ⲀⲨⲰ ⲈⲓⲞ ⲚⲢⲢⲞ ⲈϨⲢⲀⲓ ⲈϪⲘ ⲠⲤⲀϢϤ ⲚϨⲀ-
ⲘⲎⲚ· ⲘⲚ ⲠϤⲞⲨ ⲚϢⲎⲚ· ⲘⲚ ⲠϢⲞⲘⲚⲦ ⲚϨⲀⲘⲎⲚ· ⲘⲚ ⲠⲈ-
ⲯⲓⲤ ⲘϤⲨⲖⲀⳅ· ⲀⲨⲰ ⲈⲓⲞ ⲚⲢⲢⲞ ⲈϪⲘ ⲠⲀⲖⲞⲨ ⲘⲠⲀⲖⲞⲨ·
ⲈⲦⲈ ⲚⲦⲞⲞⲨ ⲚⲈ ⲚϨⲀⲦⲢⲈⲨ ⲚⲤⲰⲦⲎⲢ· ⲀⲨⲰ ⲈⲓⲞ ⲚⲢⲢⲞ [ⲤⲓⲀ ᵇ
ⲈϪⲘ ⲠⲘⲚⲦⲤⲚⲞⲞⲨⲤ ⲚⲤⲰⲦⲎⲢ· ⲘⲚ ⲠⲀⲢⲓⲐⲘⲞⲤ ⲦⲎⲢϤ Ⲛ-

---

1   MS ⲘⲠⲢⲞⲠⲀⲦⲰⲢ inserted in margins.
8   MS ⲈϤϨⲓⲜⲚ; read ⲈϤϨⲓⲜⲘ; also line 10.
15 MS ϨⲚ; read ϨⲘ.

forefather and he will also be exalted above him. He is a man in the *world, but* he is superior to all those of the *Midst* and he will be exalted over them all. He is a man in the *world, but* he is superior to the *emanations* of the *Treasury* of the light and he will be exalted over them all. He is a man in the *world, but* he is superior to the *mixture* and he will be exalted over it all. He is a man in the *world, but* he is superior to the whole *place* of the *Treasury* and he will be exalted over it all. He is a man in the *world, but* he will become ruler (king) with me in my kingdom. He is a man in the *world, but* he is ruler (king) in the light. He is a man in the *world,* but he is not of the *world.* And *truly* I say to you : that man is I and I am that man, and at the dissolution of the *world* — that is, when the All ascends and when the *number* of all the *perfect souls* ascends — I will become [1] ruler (king) in the midst of the last *helper (parastates)*, and ruler (king) over all the *emanations* of the light; and ruler (king) over the seven *amens* and the five trees and the three *amens* and the nine *watchers*; and ruler (king) over the child of the child which are the twin *saviours*; and ruler (king) over the twelve *saviours* and the whole *number* |

---

[1]   (18) I will become; lit. I have become.

ⲛⲉⲯⲩⲭⲟⲟⲩⲉ ⲛ̄ⲧⲉⲗⲓⲟⲥ ⲛⲁⲓ ⲉⲧⲛⲁϫⲓ-ⲙⲩⲥⲧⲏⲣⲓⲟⲛ ⲉ̄ⲙ
ⲡⲟⲩⲟⲉⲓⲛ· ⲁⲩⲱ ⲣⲱⲙⲉ ⲛⲓⲙ ⲉⲧⲛⲁϫⲓ-ⲙⲩⲥⲧⲏⲣⲓⲟⲛ ⲉ̄ⲙ ⲡⲓⲁⲧϣⲁϫⲉ ⲉⲣⲟϥ ⲥⲉⲛⲁϣⲱⲡⲉ ⲛ̄ϣⲃⲣ̄ⲣ̄ⲣⲟ ⲛⲙ̄ⲙⲁⲓ ⲥⲉⲛⲁ-
ⲍⲙⲟⲟⲥ ⲍⲓ ⲟⲩⲛⲁⲙ ⲙ̄ⲙⲟⲓ̈ ⲁⲩⲱ ⲍⲓ ⲍⲃⲟⲩⲣ ⲙ̄ⲙⲟⲓ̈ ⲍⲣⲁⲓ̈ ⲉ̄ⲛ ⲧⲁ-
5 ⲙⲛ̄ⲧⲉⲣⲟ· ⲁⲩⲱ ⲍⲁⲙⲏⲛ ⳁϫⲱ ⲙ̄ⲙⲟⲥ ⲛⲏⲧⲛ̄ ϫⲉ ⲡ̄ⲣⲱⲙⲉ
ⲉⲧⲙ̄ⲙⲁⲩ ⲛ̄ⲧⲟⲟⲩ ⲡⲉ ⲁⲛⲟⲕ’ ⲁⲩⲱ ⲁⲛⲟⲕ ⲡⲉ ⲛ̄ⲧⲟⲟⲩ·
ⲉⲧⲃⲉ ⲡⲁⲓ̈ ϭⲉ ⲁⲓ̈ϫⲟⲟⲥ ⲉⲣⲱⲧⲛ̄ ⲙ̄ⲡⲓⲟⲩⲟⲉⲓϣ ϫⲉ ⲧⲉⲧⲛⲁ-
ⲍⲙⲟⲟⲥ ⲉⲍⲣⲁⲓ̈ ⲉ̄ⲭ̄ⲛ ⲛⲉⲧⲛ̄ⲑⲣⲟⲛⲟⲥ ⲍⲓ ⲟⲩⲛⲁⲙ ⲙ̄ⲙⲟⲓ̈ ⲁⲩⲱ
ⲍⲓ ⲍⲃⲟⲩⲣ ⲙ̄ⲙⲟⲓ̈ ⲍⲣⲁⲓ̈ ⲉ̄ⲛ ⲧⲁⲙⲛ̄ⲧⲉⲣⲟ· ⲁⲩⲱ ⲧⲉⲧⲛⲁⲣ̄ⲣⲟ
10 ⲛ̄ⲙⲙⲁⲓ̈· ⲉⲧⲃⲉ ⲡⲁⲓ̈ ϭⲉ ⲙ̄ⲡⲓⳁⲥⲟ· ⲟⲩⲇⲉ ⲙ̄ⲡⲓϣⲓⲡⲉ ⲉⲓ̈ⲙⲟⲩ-
ⲧⲉ ⲟⲩⲃⲉ-ⲧⲏⲩⲧⲛ̄ ϫⲉ ⲛⲁⲥⲛ̄ⲏⲩ ⲁⲩⲱ ⲛⲁϣⲃⲉⲉⲣ: ⲉⲃⲟⲗ ⲥⲓⲉ
ϫⲉ ⲧⲉⲧⲛⲁϣⲱⲡⲉ ⲛ̄ϣⲃⲣ̄ⲣⲟ ⲛ̄ⲙⲙⲁⲓ̈ ⲍⲣⲁⲓ̈ ⲉ̄ⲛ ⲧⲁⲙⲛ̄ⲧⲉⲣⲟ·
ⲛⲁⲓ̈ ϭⲉ ⲉⲓ̈ϫⲱ ⲙ̄ⲙⲟⲟⲩ ⲉⲣⲱ̄ⲧⲛ ⲉⲓ̈ⲥⲟⲟⲩⲛ ϫⲉ ⳁⲛⲁⳁ
ⲛⲏⲧⲛ̄ ⲙ̄ⲡⲙⲩⲥⲧⲏⲣⲓⲟⲛ ⲙ̄ⲡⲓⲁⲧϣⲁϫⲉ ⲉⲣⲟϥ· ⲉⲧⲉ ⲡⲙⲩⲥ-
15 ⲧⲏⲣⲓⲟⲛ ⲉⲧⲙ̄ⲙⲁⲩ ⲡⲉ ⲁⲛⲟⲕ ⲁⲩⲱ ⲁⲛⲟⲕ ⲡⲉ ⲡⲙⲩⲥⲧⲏⲣⲓⲟⲛ ⲉⲧⲙ̄ⲙⲁⲩ· ⲧⲉⲛⲟⲩ ϭⲉ ⲟⲩⲙⲟⲛⲟⲛ ⲛ̄ⲧⲱ̄ⲧⲛ ⲧⲉⲧⲛⲁⲣ̄-
ⲣⲟ ⲛ̄ⲙⲙⲁⲓ̈· ⲁⲗⲗⲁ ⲣⲱⲙⲉ ⲛⲓⲙ ⲉⲧⲛⲁϫⲓ ⲙ̄ⲡⲙⲩⲥⲧⲏⲣⲓⲟⲛ
ⲙ̄ⲡⲓⲁⲧϣⲁϫⲉ ⲉⲣⲟϥ· ⲥⲉⲛⲁϣⲱⲡⲉ ⲛ̄ϣⲃⲣ̄ⲣⲟ ⲛ̄ⲙⲙⲁⲓ̈ ⲍⲣⲁⲓ̈
ⲉ̄ⲛ ⲧⲁⲙⲛ̄ⲧⲉⲣⲟ· ⲁⲩⲱ ⲁⲛⲟⲕ ⲡⲉ ⲛ̄ⲧⲟⲟⲩ· ⲁⲩⲱ ⲛ̄ⲧⲟⲟⲩ
20 ⲡⲉ ⲁⲛⲟⲕ· ⲁⲗⲗⲁ ⲡⲁⲑⲣⲟⲛⲟⲥ ⲛⲁϣⲱⲡⲉ ⲉϥⲟⲩⲟⲧⲃ̄ ⲉⲣⲟ-
ⲟⲩ· ⲉⲃⲟⲗ ϫⲉ ⲛ̄ⲧⲱⲧⲛ ⲡⲉⲧⲛⲁϣ̄ⲡ̄ϩⲓⲥⲉ ⲉ̄ⲙ ⲡⲕⲟⲥⲙⲟⲥ ⲡⲁⲣⲁ ⲣⲱⲙⲉ ⲛⲓⲙ ⲍⲉⲱⲥ ϣⲁⲛⲧⲉⲧⲛ̄ⲕⲏⲣⲩⲥⲥⲉ ⲛ̄ϣⲁϫⲉ ⲛⲓⲙ
ⲉⳁ ⲛⲁϫⲟⲟⲩ ⲉⲣⲱ̄ⲧⲛ· ⲁⲗⲗⲁ ⲛⲉⲧⲛ̄ⲑⲣⲟⲛⲟⲥ ⲛⲁϣⲱⲡⲉ ⲉⲩ-
ⲗⲟⲭ̄ⲧ ⲉ̄ⲡⲱ̄ⲓ ⲍⲣⲁⲓ̈ ⲉ̄ⲛ ⲧⲁⲙⲛ̄ⲧⲉⲣⲟ· ⲉⲧⲃⲉ ⲡⲁⲓ̈ ⲁⲓ̈ϫ̄ⲟⲟⲥ ⲥⲓⲉ ᵇ
25 ⲉⲣⲱ̄ⲧⲛ ⲙ̄ⲡⲓⲟⲩⲟⲓ̈ϣ ϫⲉ ⲡⲙⲁ ⲉⳁ ⲛⲁϣⲱⲡⲉ ⲙ̄ⲙⲟϥ· ⲥⲉⲛⲁϣⲱⲡⲉ ⲛ̄ⲙⲙⲁⲓ̈ ⲛ̄ϭⲓ ⲡⲁⲕⲉⲙⲛ̄ⲧⲥⲛⲟⲟⲩⲥ ⲛ̄ⲇⲓⲁⲕⲱⲛ· ⲁⲗⲗⲁ

of *perfect souls* which will receive *mysteries* in the light. And all men who will receive *mysteries* in the Ineffable will become fellow-rulers (kings) with me and they will sit on my right and on my left in my kingdom. And *truly* I say to you, those men are I and I am they. Concerning this I said to you once: 'You will sit upon your *thrones* on my right and on my left in my kingdom. And you will become rulers (kings) with me. Because of this, I have not refrained *nor* been ashamed to call you my brothers and companions, because you will become fellow-rulers (kings) with me in my kingdom' *. These things now I say to you, knowing that I will give you the *mystery* of the Ineffable, namely: that *mystery* is I and I am that *mystery*. Now at this time, *not only* will you become rulers (kings) with me, *but* all men who will receive the *mystery* of the Ineffable will become fellow-rulers (kings) with me in my kingdom. And I am they and they are I. *But* my *throne* will be superior to them. *But* because you will receive afflictions in the *world above* all men, *until* you *preach* every word which I will say to you, your *thrones* will be joined to mine in my kingdom. Concerning this I said to you once: 'In the place where I will be, there will also be with me my twelve *servers*' □ [1]. *But* |

---

*   cf. Mt. 19.28; Lk. 22.30
□   cf. Jn. 12.26

---

[1]   (26) see Resch (Bibl. 41) Apocryphon 47, p. 419.

ΜΑΡΙΑ ΤΜΑΓΔΑΛΗΝΗ M̄N ΪѠϨΑΝΝΗС Π̄ΠΑΡΘΕΝΟС СΕΝΑ-
ϢѠΠΕ ΕΥΟΥΟΤB̄ ΕΝΑΜΑΘΗΤΗС ΤΗΡΟΥ· ΑΥѠ ΡѠΜΕ
ΝΙΜ ΕΤΝΑΧΙ-ΜΥСΤΗΡΙΟΝ ϨM̄ ΠΙΑϢΑΧΕ ΕΡΟϤ· СΕΝΑ-
ϢѠΠΕ ϨΙ ϨBΟΥΡ M̄ΜΟΪ ΑΥѠ ϨΙ ΟΥΝΑΜ M̄ΜΟΪ· ΑΥѠ
5 ΑΝΟΚ ΠΕ N̄ΤΟΟΥ ΑΥѠ N̄ΤΟΟΥ ΠΕ ΑΝΟΚ· ΑΥѠ СΕΝΑ-
ϢѠϢ N̄ΜΜΗΤN̄ ϨN ϨѠB ΝΙΜ· ΑΛΛΑ ΠΛΗΝ ΝΕΤN̄ΘΡΟΝΟС
ΝΑϢѠΠΕ ΕΥΟΥΟΤB̄ ΕΠѠΟΥ· ΑΥѠ ΠΑΘΡΟΝΟС ϨѠ
ΑΝΟΚ' ΝΑϢѠΠΕ ΕϤΟΥΟΤB̄ ΕΠѠΤN̄· ΑΥѠ ΡѠΜΕ ΝΙΜ
ΕΤΝΑϨΕ ΕΠΙϢΑΧΕ M̄ΠΙΑϢΑΧΕ ΕΡΟϤ· ϨΑΜΗΝ †ΧѠ M̄-
10 ΜΟС ΕΡѠΤN̄ ΧΕ N̄ΡѠΜΕ ΕΤΝΑСΟΥΝ-ΠϢΑΧΕ ΕΤM̄ΜΑΥ·
СΕΝΑСΟΥN̄-ΠСΟΟΥΝ N̄ΝΕΪϢΑΧΕ ΤΗΡΟΥ· N̄ΤΑΪΧΟΟΥ
ΕΡѠΤN̄· ΝΑΠBΑΘΟС ΑΥѠ M̄N ΝΑΠΧΙСΕ· ΝΑΤΕϢΙΗ M̄N
ΝΑΤΟΥΛѠСΕ· ϨΑΠΑϪ ϨΑΠΛѠС СΕΝΑСΟΥN̄-ΠСΟΟΥΝ N̄- [ϹΙϾ]
ΝΕΪϢΑΧΕ ΤΗΡΟΥ N̄ΤΑΪΧΟΟΥ ΕΡѠΤN̄· ΑΥѠ M̄N ΝΕΤΕ
15 M̄ΠΑ†ΧΟΟΥ ΕΡѠΤN̄· ΝΑΪ †ΝΑΧΟΟΥ ΕΡѠΤN̄ ΚΑΤΑ ΤΟ-
ΠΟС ΑΥѠ ΚΑΤΑ ΤΑϪΙС ϨΡΑΪ ϨM̄ ΠСѠΡ ΕBΟΛ M̄ΠΤΗΡϤ·
ΑΥѠ ϨΑΜΗΝ †ΧѠ M̄ΜΟС ΕΡѠΤN̄ ΧΕ СΕΝΑΕΙΜΕ ΧΕ ΕΡΕ
ΠΚΟСΜΟС ΚΗ ΕϨΡΑΪ N̄ΑϢ M̄ΜΙΝΕ· ΑΥѠ СΕΝΑΕΙΜΕ ΧΕ
ΕΡΕ ΝΑΠΧΙСΕ ΤΗΡΟΥ ΚΗ ΕϨΡΑΪ N̄ΑϢ N̄ΤΥΠΟС· ΑΥѠ СΕ-
20 ΝΑΕΙΜΕ ΧΕ ΕΤBΕ ΟΥ N̄ϨѠB Α ΠΤΗΡϤ ϢѠΠΕ·

ΝΑΪ 6Ε N̄ΤΕΡΕϤΧΟΟΥ N̄6Ι ΠСѠΤΗΡ ΑСϬΟBС ΕBΟΛ N̄6Ι
ΜΑΡΙΑ ΤΜΑΓΔΑΛΗΝΗ ΠΕΧΑС· ΧΕ ΠΑΧΟΕΙС ϤΙ ϨΑΡΟΪ

---

9 MS originally ΕΠΙΑΤѠΧΕ; additional letters inserted in margin.
13 ΠBΛΘΟС expunged before ΤΟΥΛѠСΕ.

Maria Magdalene and John the *Virgin* will be superior to all my *disciples*. And all men who will receive *mysteries* in the Ineffable will be on my left and my right [1]. And I am they and they are I. And they will be equal to you in everything, *except that* your *thrones* will be superior to theirs, and my own *throne* will be superior to yours [2]. And all men who will find the word of the Ineffable, *truly* I say to you: the men who will know that word will know the knowledge of all these words which I have said to you, those of the *depth* and those of the height, those of the length and those of the breadth. *In a word* they will know the knowledge of all these words which I have said to you and those which I have not yet said to you, which I will say to you *according to place* and *according to rank* in the distribution of the All. And *truly* I say to you: they will know in what way the world is established, and they will know in what *type* all those of the height are established, and they will know why the All has come into existence."

97. Now when the *Saviour* had said these things Maria Magdalene sprang up and said: "My Lord, bear with me |

---

[1] (4) on my left and on my right; lit. to left of me and to right of me.

[2] (8, 9) superior to yours. And all men ... Ineffable, truly I say to you; Till: superior to yours and that of all men ... Ineffable. Truly I say to you.

ⲀⲨⲰ ⲘⲠⲢϬⲰⲚⲦ ⲈⲢⲞⲒ ⲈⲒϢⲒⲚⲈ ⲚⲤⲀ ϨⲰⲂ ⲚⲒⲘ ϨⲚ ⲞⲨⲰⲢⲬ
ⲘⲚ ⲞⲨⲀⲤⲪⲀⲖⲒⲀ· ⲦⲈⲚⲞⲨ ϬⲈ ⲠⲀⲬⲞⲈⲒⲤ ⲈⲒⲈ ⲞⲨⲈⲦ ⲠϢⲀ-
ⲬⲈ ⲘⲠⲘⲨⲤⲦⲎⲢⲒⲞⲚ ⲘⲠⲒⲀⲦϢⲀⲬⲈ ⲈⲢⲞϤ ⲀⲨⲰ ⲞⲨⲈⲦ ⲠϢⲀ-
ⲬⲈ ⲘⲠⲤⲞⲞⲨⲚ ⲦⲎⲢϤ· ⲀϤⲞⲨⲰϢⲘ ⲚϬⲒ ⲠⲤⲰⲦⲎⲢ ⲠⲈⲬⲀϤ [ⲤⲒⲈ b]
5 ⲬⲈ ⲈⲢⲈ ⲞⲨⲈⲦ ⲠⲘⲨⲤⲦⲎⲢⲒⲞⲚ ⲘⲠⲒⲀⲦϢⲀⲬⲈ ⲈⲢⲞϤ· ⲀⲨⲰ
ⲞⲨⲈⲦ ⲠϢⲀⲬⲈ ⲘⲠⲤⲞⲞⲨⲚ ⲦⲎⲢϤ· ⲀⲤⲞⲨⲰϢⲘ ⲆⲈ ⲞⲚ ⲚϬⲒ
ⲘⲀⲢⲒⲀ ⲠⲈⲬⲀⲤ ⲘⲠⲤⲰⲦⲎⲢ ⲬⲈ ⲠⲀⲬⲞⲈⲒⲤ ϤⲒ ϨⲀⲢⲞⲒ ⲈⲒϢⲒⲚⲈ
ⲘⲘⲞⲔ ⲀⲨⲰ ⲘⲠⲢϬⲰⲚⲦ ⲈⲢⲞⲒ· ⲦⲈⲚⲞⲨ ϬⲈ ⲠⲀⲬⲞⲈⲒⲤ ⲈⲒ-
ⲘⲎⲦⲒ ⲚⲦⲚⲰⲚϨ ⲚⲦⲚⲤⲞⲨⲚ-ⲠⲤⲞⲞⲨⲚ ⲘⲠϢⲀⲬⲈ ⲦⲎⲢϤ Ⲙ-
10 ⲠⲒⲀⲦϢⲀⲬⲈ ⲈⲢⲞϤ· ⲚⲦⲚⲚⲀⲈϢϬⲘϬⲞⲘ ⲀⲚ ⲈⲔⲖⲎⲢⲞⲚⲞⲘⲒ
ⲚⲦⲘⲚⲦⲈⲢⲞ ⲘⲠⲞⲨⲞⲒⲚ· ⲀϤⲞⲨⲰϢⲘ ⲆⲈ ⲚϬⲒ ⲠⲤⲰⲦⲎⲢ ⲠⲈ-
ⲬⲀϤ ⲘⲘⲀⲢⲒⲀ ⲬⲈ ⲤⲈ· ⲞⲨⲞⲚ ⲄⲀⲢ ⲚⲒⲘ ⲈⲦⲚⲀⲬⲒ ⲘⲠⲘⲨⲤ-
ⲦⲎⲢⲒⲞⲚ ⲚⲦⲘⲚⲦⲈⲢⲞ ⲘⲠⲞⲨⲞⲈⲒⲚ ⲠⲞⲨⲀ ⲠⲞⲨⲀ ⲚⲀⲂⲰⲔ ⲚϤ-
ⲔⲖⲎⲢⲞⲚⲞⲘⲒ ϢⲀ ⲠⲦⲞⲠⲞⲤ ⲚⲦⲀϤϬⲒ-ⲘⲨⲤⲦⲎⲢⲒⲞⲚ ϢⲀⲢⲞϤ·
15 ⲀⲖⲖⲀ ⲚϤⲚⲀⲤⲞⲨⲚ-ⲠⲤⲞⲞⲨⲚ ⲀⲚ ⲘⲠⲦⲎⲢϤ· ⲬⲈ ⲈⲦⲂⲈ ⲞⲨ
Ⲁ ⲚⲀⲒ ⲦⲎⲢⲞⲨ ϢⲰⲠⲈ ⲈⲒⲘⲎⲦⲒ ⲚϤⲤⲞⲨⲚ-ⲠϢⲀⲬⲈ ⲚⲞⲨⲰⲦ
ⲚⲦⲈ ⲠⲒⲀⲦϢⲀⲬⲈ ⲈⲢⲞϤ· ⲈⲦⲈ ⲚⲦⲞϤ ⲠⲈ ⲠⲤⲞⲞⲨⲚ ⲘⲠⲦⲎ-
Ⲣϥ· ⲀⲨⲰ ⲞⲚ ⲪⲀⲚⲈⲢⲰⲤ ⲀⲚⲞⲔ ⲠⲈ ⲠⲤⲞⲞⲨⲚ ⲘⲠⲦⲎⲢϤ· ⲤⲒⲌ
ⲀⲨⲰ ⲞⲚ ⲘⲚϬⲞⲘ ⲚⲤⲞⲨⲚ-ⲠϢⲀⲬⲈ ⲚⲞⲨⲰⲦ ⲚⲦⲈ ⲠⲤⲞ-
20 ⲞⲨⲚ· ⲈⲒⲘⲎⲦⲒ ϬⲈ ⲚϤϪⲒ ⲚϢⲞⲢⲠ ⲘⲠⲘⲨⲤⲦⲎⲢⲒⲞⲚ ⲘⲠⲒⲀⲦ-
ϢⲀⲬⲈ ⲈⲢⲞϤ· ⲀⲖⲖⲀ ⲢⲰⲘⲈ ⲚⲒⲘ ⲈⲦⲚⲀⲬⲒ-ⲘⲨⲤⲦⲎⲢⲒⲞⲚ ϨⲘ
ⲠⲞⲨⲞⲈⲒⲚ ϤⲚⲀⲂⲰⲔ ⲚϬⲒ ⲠⲞⲨⲀ ⲠⲞⲨⲀ ⲚϤⲔⲖⲎⲢⲞⲚⲞⲘⲒ ϢⲀ
ⲠⲦⲞⲠⲞⲤ ⲚⲦⲀϤϪⲒ-ⲘⲨⲤⲦⲎⲢⲒⲞⲚ ϢⲀⲢⲞϤ· ⲈⲦⲂⲈ ⲠⲀⲒ ⲀⲒ-
ⲬⲞⲞⲤ ⲈⲢⲰⲦⲚ ⲘⲠⲒⲞⲨⲞⲈⲒϢ ⲬⲈ ⲠⲈⲦⲠⲒⲤⲦⲈⲨⲈ ⲈⲨⲠⲢⲞ-

and be not angry with me, as I question all things with assurance and *certainty*. Now at this time, my Lord, is the word of the *mystery* of the Ineffable one thing, and the word of the whole knowledge another?"

The *Saviour* answered and said : "Yes, the *mystery* of the Ineffable is one thing and the word of the whole knowledge is another."

But Maria answered again and said to the *Saviour* : "My Lord, bear with me as I question thee and be not angry with me. Now at this time, my Lord, *unless* we live and know the knowledge of the whole word of the Ineffable, will we be unable to *inherit* the Kingdom of the Light?"

The *Saviour however* answered and said to Maria : "Certainly, *for* of everyone who will receive the *mystery* of the Kingdom of the Light, each will go and *inherit* the *place* as far as which he has received *mysteries*. *But* he will not know the knowledge of the All, why all these things came into existence, *unless* he knows the one word of the Ineffable, which is the knowledge of the All, and again *clearly* : I am the knowledge of the All. And furthermore it is not possible to know the one word of knowledge *unless* he first receives the *mystery* [1] of the Ineffable. *But* of all men who will receive mysteries in the light, each one will go and *inherit* the *place* as far as which he has received *mysteries*. Concerning this I once said to you : 'He who *believes* a *prophet* | will receive the reward of a *prophet*, and he who

---

[1] (20) unless he first receives the mystery; Till : unless he receives the First Mystery.

ϥΗΤΗС ϤΝΑΧΙ Μ̄ΠΒΕΚΕ Ν̄ΟΥΠΡΟϤΗΤΗС· ΑΥⲰ ΠΕΤΠΙС-
ΤΕΥΕ ΕΥΔΙΚΑΙΟС ϤΝΑΧΙ Μ̄ΠΒΕΚΕ Ν̄ΟΥΔΙΚΑΙΟС· ΕΤΕ
ΠΑΪ ΠΕ ΧΕ ΠΜΑ Ν̄ΤΑ ΠΟΥΑ ΠΟΥΑ ΧΙ-ΜΥСΤΗΡΙΟΝ ϢΑ-
ΡΟϤ ΕϤΝΑΒⲰΚ ΕΡΟϤ· ΠΕΤΧΙ ΕϤСΟΒΚ̄ ΕϤΝΑΚΛΗΡΟΝΟΜΙ
5 Μ̄ΠΜΥСΤΗΡΙΟΝ ΕΤСΟΒΚ̄· ΑΥⲰ ΠΕΤΝΑΧΙ-ΜΥСΤΗΡΙΟΝ
ΕϤΟΥΟΤΒ̄ ΕϤΝΑΚΛΗΡΟΝΟΜΙ Ν̄ΝΤΟΠΟС ΕΤΧΟСΕ· ΑΥⲰ
ΠΟΥΑ ΠΟΥΑ ΝΑ6Ⲱ 2Μ̄ ΠΕϤΤΟΠΟС 2ΡΑΪ 2Μ̄ ΠΟΥΟΕΙΝ
Ν̄ΤΑΜΝ̄ΤΕΡΟ· ΑΥⲰ ΠΟΥΑ ΠΟΥΑ ΝΑΡ̄-ΤΕϩΟΥСΙΑ ΕΝΤΑ-
ϩΙС ΕΤΠΕϤΕСΗΤ· ΑΛΛΑ Ν̄ϤΝΑΡ̄-ΤΕϩΟΥСΙΑ ΑΝ ΕΒⲰΚ ΕΝ- Ϲ̅Ι̅Ϩ̅ b
10 ΤΑϩΙС ΕΤΠΕϤСΑϩΡΕ· ΑΛΛΑ ΕϤΝΑ6Ⲱ 2Μ̄ ΠΤΟΠΟС Ν̄ΤΕ-
ΚΛΗΡΟΝΟΜΙΑ Μ̄ΠΟΥΟΕΙΝ Ν̄ΤΑΜΝ̄ΤΕΡΟ· ΕϤϢΟΟΠ 2Ν ΟΥ-
ΝΟ6 Ν̄ΟΥΟΪΝ ΕΜΝ̄-ϢΙ ΕΡΟϤ· 2ΙΤΝ̄ Ν̄ΝΟΥΤΕ ΜΝ̄ Ν̄Α2Ο-
ΡΑΤΟС ΤΗΡΟΥ ΑΥⲰ Ν̄ϤϢⲰΠΕ 2Ν ΟΥΝΟ6 Ν̄ΡΑϢΕ ΜΝ̄
ΟΥΝΟ6 Ν̄ΤΕΛΗΛ: ΤΕΝΟΥ 6Ε 2ⲰⲰϤ СⲰΤΜ̄ ΤΑϢΑΧΕ
15 Ν̄ΜΜΗΤΝ̄ ΕΤΒΕ ΠΕΟΟΥ Ν̄ΝΕΤΝΑΧΙ 2ⲰΟΥ Μ̄ΠΜΥСΤΗ-
ΡΙΟΝ Ν̄ΤΕ ΠϢΟΡΠ̄ Μ̄ΜΥСΤΗΡΙΟΝ· ΠΕΤΝΑΧΙ ΟΥΝ Μ̄-
ΠΜΥСΤΗΡΙΟΝ Μ̄ΠϢΟΡΠ̄ Μ̄ΜΥСΤΗΡΙΟΝ ΕΤΜ̄ΜΑΥ· ϤΝΑ-
ϢⲰΠΕ 2Μ̄ ΠΕϤΟΥΟΕΙϢ ΕΤϤΝΗΥ ΕΒΟΛ 2Μ̄ ΠСⲰΜΑ Ν̄ΟΥ-
ΛΗ Ν̄Ν̄ΑΡΧⲰΝ· СΕΝΗΥ Ν̄6Ι Μ̄ΠΑΡΑΛΗΜΠΤⲰΡ Ν̄ΕΡΙΝΑΙΟС
20 Ν̄СΕΕΙΝΕ Ν̄ΤΕΨΥΧΗ Μ̄ΠΡⲰΜΕ ΕΤΜ̄ΜΑΥ ΕΒΟΛ 2Μ̄ ΠСⲰ-
ΜΑ· ΑΥⲰ ΤΕΨΥΧΗ ΕΤΜ̄ΜΑΥ ΝΑΡ̄-ΟΥΝΟ6 Ν̄ϢΛΙ6 Ν̄ΟΥ-
ΟΕΙΝ Ν̄ΤΟΟΤΟΥ Ν̄ΜΠΑΡΑΛΗΜΠΤⲰΡ Ν̄ΕΡΙΝΑΙΟС ΑΥⲰ
Μ̄ΠΑΡΑΛΗΜΠΤΗС ΕΤΜ̄ΜΑΥ ΝΑΡ̄2ΟΤΕ 2ΗΤϤ Μ̄ΠΟΥΟΕΙΝ Ν̄- [Ϲ̅Ι̅Η̅]
ΤΕΨΥΧΗ ΕΤΜ̄ΜΑΥ· ΑΥⲰ ΤΕΨΥΧΗ ΕΤΜ̄ΜΑΥ СΝΑΒⲰΚ
25 ΕΠΧΙСΕ Ν̄СΧⲰΤΕ Ν̄ΝΤΟΠΟС ΤΗΡΟΥ Ν̄ΤΕ Ν̄ΑΡΧⲰΝ· ΜΝ̄
Ν̄ΤΟΠΟС ΤΗΡΟΥ Ν̄ΤΕ ΝΕΠΡΟΒΟΛΟΟΥΕ Μ̄ΠΟΥΟΕΙΝ ΑΥⲰ

---

4 MS ΧΙ ΕϤСΟΒΚ̄; read ΧΙ-ΜΥСΤΗΡΙΟΝ ΕϤСΟΒΚ̄.
8 MS ΕΝΤΑϩΙС; better ⟨ΕΒⲰΚ⟩ ΕΝΤΑϩΙС.

believes a *righteous man* will receive the reward of a *righteous man*' *. That is, each one will go to the *place* as far as which he has received *mysteries*. He who receives a small ⟨*mystery*⟩ [1] will *inherit* what is small. And he who receives a superior *mystery* will *inherit* the elevated *places*. And each one will remain in his *place* in the light of my kingdom. And each one will have *authority* over the *ranks* beneath him. *But* he will not have the *authority* to go to the *ranks* above him. *But* he will remain in the *place* of the *inheritance* of the light of my kingdom, being in a great light to which there is no measure among the gods and all the *invisible ones*, and he will be in great joy and great gladness.

Now at this time moreover, hear that I speak with you concerning the glory of those who will receive the *mystery* of the First *Mystery*. *Now* he who will receive the *mystery* of that *First Mystery*, it will happen at the time when he comes forth from the *body* of *matter* of the *archons*, the *erinaioi paralemptores* come to bring forth the *soul* of that man from the *body*. And that *soul* will become a great beam of light in the hands of the *erinaioi paralemptores*, and those *paralemptai* will be afraid at the light of that *soul*. And that *soul* will go to the height and penetrate all the *places* of the *archons* and all the *places* of the *emanations* of the light. And | it will not give an *answer*, *nor* a *defence*,

---

* cf. Mt. 10.41

---

[1]   (4) a small ⟨mystery⟩; Schmidt : a small one.

ＮＣＮΑϮ-ΑΠΟΦΑСΙС ΑΝ ΟΥΔΕ ΑΠΟΛΟΓΙΑ ΟΥΔΕ СΥΜΒΟ-
ΛΟΝ ２Ｎ ΛΑΑΥ ＮΤΟΠΟС ＮΤΕ ΠΟΥΟΪΝ· ΟΥΔΕ ２Ｎ ΛΑΑΥ
ＮΤΟΠΟС ＮΤΕ ＮΑΡΧΩΝ· ΑΛΛΑ СΝΑΧΩΤΕ ２Ｎ ＮΤΟΠΟС
ΤΗΡΟΥ ΑΥΩ СΝΑΟΥΟΤΒΟΥ ΤΗΡΟΥ· ＮСΒΩΚ ＮСℙℙℙΟ
5 Ε２ΡΑΪ ΕＸＮ ＮΤΟΠΟС ΤΗΡΟΥ ＭΠϢΟℙℙ ＮСΩΤΗΡ· ２Ο-
ΜΟΙΩС ΟΝ ΠΕΤΝΑΧΙ ＭΠΜΕ２СΝΑΥ ＭΜΥСΤΗΡΙΟΝ ＮΤΕ ΠΙ-
ϢΟℙℙ ＭΜΥСΤΗΡΙΟΝ· ＭΝ ΠΜΕ２ϢΟＭＮΤ ＭΝ ΠΜΕ２ϤΤΟΟΥ
２ΕΩС ϢΑΝΤϤΧΙ ＭΠΜΕ２ＭＮΤСΝΟΟΥС ＭΜΥСΤΗΡΙΟΝ ＮΤΕ
ΠΙϢΟℙℙ ＭΜΥСΤΗΡΙΟΝ· ΕϤϢΑΝϢΩΠΕ ２Ｍ ΠΕΟΥΟΪϢ ΕΤ-
10 ΟΥΝΗΥ ΕΒΟΛ ２Ｍ ΠСΩΜΑ ＮΘΥΛΗ ＮΤΕ ＮΑΡΧΩΝ СΕΝΗΥ
ＮϬΙ ＭΠΑΡΑΛΗΜΠΤΩΡ ＮΕΡΙΝΑΙΟС· ＮСΕΕΙΝΕ ＮΤΕΨΥΧΗ ［ＣＩＨᵇ］
ＭΠΡΩΜΕ ΕΤＭΜΑΥ ΕΒΟΛ ２Ｍ ΠСΩΜΑ ＮΘΥΛΗ· ΑΥΩ ΝΕ-
ΨΥΧΟΟΥΕ ΕΤＭΜΑΥ СΕΝΑℙ-ΟΥΝΟϬ ＮϢΛΙϬ ＮΟΥΟΕΙΝ
ＮΤΟΟΤΟΥ ＮＭΠΑΡΑΛΗΜΠΤΩΡ ＮΕΡΙΝΑΙΟС· ΑΥΩ ＭΠΑΡΑ-
15 ΛΗΜΠΤΗС ΕΤＭΜΑΥ СΕΝΑℙ２ΟΤΕ ２ΗΤϤ ＭΠΟΥΟΕΙΝ ＮΤΕ-
ΨΥΧΗ ΕΤＭΜΑΥ· ΑΥΩ СΕΝΑСΩϢＭ ＮСΕ２Ε ΕＸＭ ΠΕΥ２Ο·
ΑΥΩ ΝΕΨΥΧΟΟΥΕ ΕΤＭΜΑΥ СΕΝΑ２ΩΛ ΕΠΧΙСΕ ＮΤΕΥ-
ΝΟΥ· ＮСΕΟΥΩΤＢ ＮＮΤΟΠΟС ΤΗΡΟΥ ＮΤΕ ＮΑΡΧΩΝ·
ΑΥΩ ２Ｎ ＮΤΟΠΟС ΤΗΡΟΥ ＮΤΕ ΝΕΠΡΟΒΟΛΟΟΥΕ ＭΠΟΥ-
20 ΟΕΙΝ· ΑΥΩ ＮСΕΝΑϮ-ΑΠΟΦΑСΙС ΑΝ ΟΥΔΕ ΑΠΟΛΟΓΙΑ
２Ｎ ΛΑΑΥ ＮΤΟΠΟС ΟΥΔΕ СΥΜΒΟΛΟΝ· ΑΛΛΑ ΕСΝΑΧΩΤΕ
２Ｎ ＮΤΟΠΟС ΤΗΡΟΥ· ΑΥΩ ＮСΕΟΥΟΤΒΟΥ ΤΗΡΟΥ Ε-
２ΟΥΝ· ΑΥΩ СΕΝΑℙℙΡΟ Ε２ΡΑΪ ΕＸＮ ＮΤΟΠΟС ΤΗΡΟΥ Ｍ-
ΠＭＮΤСΝΟΟΥС ＮСΩΤΗΡ· ２ΩСΤΕ ΝΕΤΧΙ ＭΠΜΕ²СΝΑΥ ＣＩΘ
25 ＭΜΥСΤΗΡΙΟΝ ＮΤΕ ΠΙϢΟℙℙ ＭΜΥСΤΗΡΙΟΝ СΕΝΑℙℙΡΟ

9　MS ΕΤΟΥΝΗΥ; read ΕΤϤΝΗΥ.
19　MS ２Ｎ ＮΤΟΠΟС; read ＮΤΟΠΟС.
21　MS ΕСΝΑΧΩΤΕ; read СΕΝΑΧΩΤΕ.

nor a *secret sign* in any *place* of the light, *nor* in any *place* of the *archons, but* it will penetrate into all *places* and it will pass through them all, and go and rule over all the *places* of the first *saviour. Likewise* also he who will receive the second *mystery* of the First *Mystery*, with the third and the fourth, *until* he receives the twelfth *mystery* of the First Mystery, when he reaches the time of his coming forth from the *body* of *matter* of the *archons*, the *erinaioi paralemptores* come and bring forth the *soul* of that man from the *body* of *matter.* And those souls will become a great beam of light in the hands of the *erinaioi paralemptores* and those *paralemptai* will be afraid at the light of that *soul* and they will be enfeebled and fall upon their faces. And those *souls* will ascend to the height immediately, and will pass through all the *places* of the *archons* and into all the *places* of the *emanations* of the light. And they will not give *answer or defence* in any *place, nor* a *secret sign, but* they will penetrate into all *places* and pass through them all. And they will rule over all the *places* of the twelve *saviours. So that* those who receive the second *mystery* of the First *Mystery* will rule | over all the *places* of the second *saviour* in the

ⲉϩⲣⲁⲓ ⲉϫⲛ ⲛ̄ⲧⲟⲡⲟⲥ ⲧⲏⲣⲟⲩ ⲙ̄ⲡⲙⲉϩⲥⲛⲁⲩ ⲛ̄ⲥⲱⲧⲏⲣ ϩⲣⲁⲓ
ϩⲛ̄ ⲛⲉⲕⲗⲏⲣⲟⲛⲟⲙⲓⲁ ⲙ̄ⲡⲟⲩⲟⲉⲓⲛ · ϩⲟⲙⲟⲓⲱⲥ ⲟⲛ ⲛⲉⲧϫⲓ
ⲙ̄ⲡⲙⲉϩϣⲟⲙⲛ̄ⲧ ⲙ̄ⲙⲩⲥⲧⲏⲣⲓⲟⲛ ⲛ̄ⲧⲉ ⲡⲓϣⲟⲣⲡ̄ ⲙ̄ⲙⲩⲥⲧⲏⲣⲓⲟⲛ
ⲙⲛ̄ ⲡⲙⲉϩϥⲧⲟⲟⲩ ⲙⲛ̄ ⲡⲙⲉϩ†ⲟⲩ ⲙⲛ̄ ⲡⲙⲉϩⲥⲟⲟⲩ ϩⲉⲱⲥ
5 ϣⲁ ⲡⲙⲉϩⲙⲛ̄ⲧⲥⲛⲟⲟⲩⲥ ⲡⲟⲩⲁ ⲡⲟⲩⲁ ⲛⲁⲣ̄ⲣ̄ⲣⲟ ⲉϩⲣⲁⲓ ⲉϫⲛ̄
ⲛ̄ⲧⲟⲡⲟⲥ ⲧⲏⲣⲟⲩ ⲙ̄ⲡⲥⲱⲧⲏⲣ ⲛ̄ⲧⲁϥϫⲓ ⲙ̄ⲡⲙⲩⲥⲧⲏⲣⲓⲟⲛ ϣⲁⲣⲟϥ · ⲁⲩⲱ ⲡⲉⲧⲛⲁϫⲓ ⲙ̄ⲡⲙⲉϩⲙⲛ̄ⲧⲥⲛⲟⲟⲩⲥ ⲙ̄ⲙⲩⲥⲧⲏⲣⲓⲟⲛ
ϩⲓ ⲛⲉⲩⲉⲣⲏⲩ ⲛ̄ⲧⲉ ⲡⲓϣⲟⲣⲡ̄ ⲙ̄ⲙⲩⲥⲧⲏⲣⲓⲟⲛ ⲉⲧⲉ ⲛ̄ⲧⲟϥ ⲡⲉ
ⲡⲁⲩⲑⲉⲛⲧⲏⲥ ⲙ̄ⲙⲩⲥⲧⲏⲣⲓⲟⲛ · ⲡⲁⲓ ⲉ†ϣⲁϫⲉ ⲛ̄ⲙⲙⲏⲧⲛ̄ ⲉⲧ-
10 ⲃⲏⲏⲧϥ̄ · ⲁⲩⲱ ⲡⲉⲧⲛⲁϫⲓ ⲟⲩⲛ ⲙ̄ⲡⲙ̄ⲛⲧⲥⲛⲟⲟⲩⲥ ⲙ̄ⲙⲩⲥ-
ⲧⲏⲣⲓⲟⲛ ⲉⲧⲙ̄ⲙⲁⲩ ⲛⲁⲓ ⲉⲧⲏⲡ ⲉⲡⲓϣⲟⲣⲡ̄ ⲙ̄ⲙⲩⲥⲧⲏⲣⲓⲟⲛ ·
ⲉϥϣⲁⲛⲉⲓ ⲉⲃⲟⲗ ϩⲙ̄ ⲡⲕⲟⲥⲙⲟⲥ ϥⲛⲁⲭⲱⲧⲉ ⲛ̄ⲛ̄ⲧⲟⲡⲟⲥ ⲧⲏⲣⲟⲩ ⲛ̄ⲧⲉ ⲛ̄ⲁⲣⲭⲱⲛ ⲙⲛ̄ ⲛ̄ⲧⲟⲡⲟⲥ ⲧⲏⲣⲟⲩ ⲛ̄ⲧⲉ ⲡⲟⲩⲟⲉⲓⲛ
ⲉϥⲟ ⲛ̄ⲟⲩⲛⲟϭ ⲛ̄ⲁⲡⲟⲣⲣⲟⲓⲁ ⲛ̄ⲧⲉ ⲡⲟⲩⲟ̈ⲓⲛ · ⲁⲩⲱ ⲟⲛ ϥⲛⲁⲣ̄-   ⳓ⳰ ᵇ
15 ⲣ̄ⲣⲟ ⲉϩⲣⲁⲓ ⲉϫⲛ̄ ⲛ̄ⲧⲟⲡⲟⲥ ⲧⲏⲣⲟⲩ ⲙ̄ⲡⲙ̄ⲛⲧⲥⲛⲟⲟⲩⲥ ⲛ̄ⲥⲱ-
ⲧⲏⲣ · ⲁⲗⲗⲁ ⲛ̄ⲥⲉⲛⲁϣ̄ϣϣ ⲁⲛ ⲙⲛ̄ ⲛⲉⲧϫⲓ ⲙ̄ⲡⲙⲩⲥⲧⲏⲣⲓⲟⲛ
ⲛ̄ⲟⲩⲱⲧ ⲙ̄ⲡⲓⲁⲧϣⲁϫⲉ ⲉⲣⲟϥ · ⲁⲗⲗⲁ ⲡⲉⲧⲛⲁϫⲓ ⲛ̄ⲙⲙⲩⲥⲧⲏ-
ⲣⲓⲟⲛ ⲉⲧⲙ̄ⲙⲁⲩ ϥⲛⲁϭⲱ ϩⲛ̄ ⲛ̄ⲧⲁⲝⲓⲥ ⲉⲧⲙ̄ⲙⲁⲩ ⲉⲃⲟⲗ ϫⲉ
ⲥⲉⲟⲩⲟⲧⲃ̄ · ⲁⲩⲱ ϥⲛⲁϭⲱ ϩⲛ̄ ⲛ̄ⲧⲁⲝⲓⲥ ⲙ̄ⲡⲙ̄ⲛⲧⲥⲛⲟⲟⲩⲥ
20 ⲛ̄ⲥⲱⲧⲏⲣ :

ⲁⲥϣⲱⲡⲉ ⲛ̄ⲧⲉⲣⲉ ⲓ̅ⲥ̅ ⲟⲩⲱ ⲉϥϫⲱ ⲛ̄ⲛⲉⲓ̈ϣⲁϫⲉ ⲉⲛⲉϥⲙⲁⲑⲏⲧⲏⲥ ⲁⲥⲉⲓ̈ ⲉⲑⲏ ⲛ̄ϭⲓ ⲙⲁⲣⲓⲁ ⲧⲙⲁⲅⲇⲁⲗⲏⲛⲏ ⲁⲥ†ⲡⲓ
ⲉⲛⲟⲩⲉⲣⲏⲧⲉ ⲛ̄ⲓ̅ⲥ̅ ⲡⲉϫⲁⲥ ϫⲉ ⲡⲁϫⲟⲉⲓⲥ ϭⲓ ϩⲁⲣⲟⲓ̈ ⲁⲩⲱ
ⲙ̄ⲡⲣ̄ϭⲱⲛⲧ̄ ⲉⲣⲟⲓ̈ ⲉⲓ̈ϣⲓⲛⲉ ⲙ̄ⲙⲟⲕ · ⲁⲗⲗⲁ ⲛⲁ ⲛⲁⲛ ⲡⲁϫⲟⲉⲓⲥ
25 ⲁⲩⲱ ⲛ̄ⲅϭⲱⲗⲡ̄ ⲛⲁⲛ ⲉⲃⲟⲗ ⲛ̄ϩⲱⲃ ⲛⲓⲙ ⲉⲧⲛⲛⲁϣⲓⲛⲉ ⲛ̄-

---

16   MS ⲛ̄ⲥⲉⲛⲁϣ̄ϣϣ; better ⲛ̄ⲥⲉⲛⲁϣϣ.

inheritances of the light. *Likewise* of those who receive the third *mystery* of the First *Mystery* with the fourth, and the fifth and the sixth, *until* the twelfth, each one will rule over all the *places* of the *saviour* as far as whom he has received *mysteries*. And he who will receive the twelfth *mystery* together with the First *Mystery*, this is the *authentic mystery* of which I have spoken to you. And he who will *now* receive that twelfth *mystery* which belongs to the First *Mystery*, when he comes forth from the *world*, he will penetrate all the *places* of the *archons* and all the *places* of the light, being a great *outpouring* of light. And furthermore he will rule over all the *places* of the twelve *saviours*. *But* they will not be equal with those that receive the one *mystery* of the Ineffable. *But* he who will receive that *mystery* will remain in those *ranks* because they are superior, and he will remain in the *ranks* of the twelve saviours."

98. It happened when Jesus finished saying these words to his *disciples*, Maria Magdalene came forward, she kissed the feet of Jesus, she said : "My Lord, bear with me and be not angry with me for questioning thee, *but* have mercy on us, my Lord, and reveal to us all things which we will question. | Now at this time, my Lord, *how* does the First

ⲥⲱⲟⲩ· ⲧⲉⲛⲟⲩ ϭⲉ ⲡⲁⲭⲟⲉⲓⲥ ⲡⲱⲥ ⲡⲓϣⲟⲣⲡ̅ ⲙ̅ⲙⲩⲥⲧⲏ-
ⲣⲓⲟⲛ ⲟⲩⲛⲧⲁϥ ⲙ̅ⲙⲁⲩ ⲙ̅ⲙⲛ̅ⲧⲥⲛⲟⲟⲩⲥ ⲙ̅ⲙⲩⲥⲧⲏⲣⲓⲟⲛ· ⲡⲓⲁⲧϣⲁϫⲉ ⲉⲣⲟϥ ⲟⲩⲙⲩⲥⲧⲏⲣⲓⲟⲛ ⲛ̅ⲟⲩⲱⲧ ⲡⲉⲧⲛ̅ⲧⲁϥ· ⲁϥ-
ⲟⲩⲱϣ︦ⲃ ⲛ̅ϭⲓ ⲓ︦ⲥ︦ ⲡⲉϫⲁϥ ⲛⲁⲥ· ϫⲉ ⲟⲩⲙⲩⲥⲧⲏⲣⲓⲟⲛ ⲛ̅ⲟⲩ-
5 ⲱⲧ ⲙⲉⲛⲧⲟⲓⲅⲉ ⲡⲉⲧⲛ̅ⲧⲁϥ· ⲁⲗⲗⲁ ⲡⲙⲩⲥⲧⲏⲣⲓⲟⲛ ⲉⲧⲙ̅ⲙⲁⲩ [ⲥ︦ⲕ︦]
ϥⲉⲓⲣⲉ ⲛ̅ϣⲟⲙⲛ̅ⲧ ⲙ̅ⲙⲩⲥⲧⲏⲣⲓⲟⲛ ⲉⲡⲓⲙⲩⲥⲧⲏⲣⲓⲟⲛ ⲛ̅ⲟⲩⲱⲧ
ⲡⲉ· ⲁⲗⲗⲁ ⲟⲩⲉⲧ ⲡⲧⲩⲡⲟⲥ ⲙ̅ⲡⲟⲩⲁ ⲡⲟⲩⲁ ⲙ̅ⲙⲟⲟⲩ· ⲁⲩⲱ
ⲟⲛ ϣⲁϥⲣ̅-ϯⲟⲩ ⲙ̅ⲙⲩⲥⲧⲏⲣⲓⲟⲛ ⲉⲩⲁ ⲛ̅ⲟⲩⲱⲧ ⲟⲛ ⲡⲉ· ⲁⲗⲗⲁ
ⲟⲩⲉⲧ ⲡⲧⲩⲡⲟⲥ ⲙ̅ⲡⲟⲩⲁ ⲡⲟⲩⲁ· ⲍⲱⲥⲧⲉ ⲡⲉⲓϯⲟⲩ ⲙ̅ⲙⲩⲥ-
10 ⲧⲏⲣⲓⲟⲛ ⲉⲩϣⲏϣ ⲙⲛ̅ ⲛⲉⲩⲉⲣⲏⲩ ϩⲣⲁⲓ̈ ϩ︦ⲙ︦ ⲡⲙⲩⲥⲧⲏⲣⲓⲟⲛ
ⲛ̅ⲧⲙⲛ̅ⲧⲉⲣⲟ ϩⲣⲁⲓ̈ ϩ︦ⲛ︦ ⲛⲉⲕⲗⲏⲣⲟⲛⲟⲙⲓⲁ ⲙ̅ⲡⲟⲩⲟⲉⲓⲛ· ⲁⲗⲗⲁ
ⲟⲩⲉⲧ ⲡⲧⲩⲡⲟⲥ ⲙ̅ⲡⲟⲩⲁ ⲡⲟⲩⲁ ⲙ̅ⲙⲟⲟⲩ· ⲁⲩⲱ ⲧⲉⲩ-
ⲙⲛ̅ⲧⲉⲣⲟ ⲥⲟⲩⲟⲧ︦ⲃ ⲁⲩⲱ ⲥϫⲟⲥⲉ ⲉⲧⲙⲛ̅ⲧⲉⲣⲟ ⲧⲏⲣⲥ̅ ⲙ̅-
ⲡⲙⲛ̅ⲧⲥⲛⲟⲟⲩⲥ ⲙ̅ⲙⲩⲥⲧⲏⲣⲓⲟⲛ ϩⲓ ⲛⲉⲩⲉⲣⲏⲩ ⲛ̅ⲧⲉ ⲡϣⲟⲣⲡ̅
15 ⲙ̅ⲙⲩⲥⲧⲏⲣⲓⲟⲛ· ⲁⲗⲗⲁ ⲛ̅ⲥⲉϣⲏϣ ⲁⲛ ϩ︦ⲛ︦ ⲧⲙⲛ̅ⲧⲉⲣⲟ ⲙ̅ⲡⲓ-
ϣⲟⲣⲡ̅ ⲙ̅ⲙⲩⲥⲧⲏⲣⲓⲟⲛ ⲛ̅ⲧⲉ ⲡⲓϣⲟⲣⲡ̅ ⲙ̅ⲙⲩⲥⲧⲏⲣⲓⲟⲛ ϩ︦ⲛ︦
ⲧⲙⲛ̅ⲧⲉⲣⲟ ⲙ̅ⲡⲟⲩⲟⲉⲓⲛ· ϩⲟⲙⲟⲓⲱⲥ ⲟⲛ ⲡϣⲟⲙⲛ̅ⲧ ⲙ̅ⲙⲩⲥ-
ⲧⲏⲣⲓⲟⲛ· ⲛ̅ⲥⲉϣⲏϣ ⲁⲛ ϩⲱⲟⲩ ϩⲣⲁⲓ̈ ϩ︦ⲛ︦ ⲧⲙⲛ̅ⲧⲉⲣⲟ ⲉⲧϩ︦ⲙ︦
ⲡⲟⲩⲟⲉⲓⲛ· ⲁⲗⲗⲁ ⲟⲩⲉⲧ ⲡⲧⲩⲡⲟⲥ ⲙ̅ⲡⲟⲩⲁ ⲡⲟⲩⲁ ⲙ̅ⲙⲟⲟⲩ·
20 ⲁⲩⲱ ⲛ̅ⲧⲟⲟⲩ ϩⲱⲟⲩ ⲟⲛ ⲛ̅ⲥⲉϣⲏϣ ⲁⲛ ϩ︦ⲛ︦ ⲧⲙⲛ̅ⲧⲉⲣⲟ ⲙⲛ̅ [ⲥ︦ⲕ︦ ᵇ]
ⲡⲓⲙⲩⲥⲧⲏⲣⲓⲟⲛ ⲛ̅ⲟⲩⲱⲧ ⲛ̅ⲧⲉ ⲡⲓϣⲟⲣⲡ̅ ⲙ̅ⲙⲩⲥⲧⲏⲣⲓⲟⲛ ϩⲣⲁⲓ̈
ϩ︦ⲛ︦ ⲧⲙⲛ̅ⲧⲉⲣⲟ ⲙ̅ⲡⲟⲩⲟⲉⲓⲛ· ⲁⲩⲱ ⲟⲩⲉⲧ ⲡⲧⲩⲡⲟⲥ ⲟⲛ ⲙ̅-
ⲡⲟⲩⲁ ⲡⲟⲩⲁ ⲙ̅ⲙⲟⲟⲩ ⲙ̅ⲡϣⲟⲙⲛ̅ⲧ ⲁⲩⲱ ⲡⲧⲩⲡⲟⲥ ⲙ̅ⲡⲉ-

---

5 ⲓ︦ⲁ︦ in upper right-hand margin at end of quire.
15 MS ⲙ̅ⲡⲓϣⲟⲣⲡ̅; Schmidt : read ⲙ̅ⲛ̅ ⲡⲓϣⲟⲣⲡ̅.
18 MS ⲉⲧϩ︦ⲙ︦ ⲡⲟⲩⲟⲉⲓⲛ; better ⲙ̅ⲡⲟⲩⲟⲉⲓⲛ.

Mystery possess twelve *mysteries* (and) the Ineffable possesses one *mystery*?"

Jesus answered and said to her : "*Certainly* it possesses
one *mystery, but* that *mystery* makes three *mysteries* to be
one *mystery* [1], *but* the *type* of each one of them is different.
And furthermore it makes five *mysteries* to be one also,
but the *type* of each one is different, *so that* these five
mysteries are equal with one another in the *mystery* of the
kingdom in the *inheritances* of the light. *But* the *type* of each
one of them is different. And their kingdom is superior and
more elevated than the whole kingdom of the twelve *mysteries* of the First *Mystery* together, *but* they are not equal
in the kingdom ⟨with the one mystery⟩ [2] of the First *Mystery*
in the Kingdom of the Light.

Likewise also, the three *mysteries* are not equal in the
Kingdom of the Light, *but* the *type* of each of them is
different. And they themselves also are not equal in the
kingdom with the one *mystery* of the First *Mystery* in the
Kingdom of the Light. And furthermore the *type* of each
one of the three and the *type* of the | *pattern* of each one

---

[1]   (6) that mystery makes three mysteries to be one mystery; Schmidt : that
mystery makes three mysteries, although it is the one mystery (see 338.8).
[2]   (15) ⟨with the one mystery⟩; MS of the first mystery; Schmidt emends to :
with the first mystery.

ⲥⲭⲏⲙⲁ ⲙⲡⲟⲩⲁ ⲡⲟⲩⲁ ⲙⲙⲟⲟⲩ ⲥⲉϣⲃⲉⲓⲁⲉⲓⲧ ⲉⲛⲉⲩⲉⲣⲏⲩ·
ⲡϣⲟⲣⲡ ⲙⲉⲛ ⲉⲕϣⲁⲛⲭⲱⲕ ⲉⲃⲟⲗ ⲙⲡⲉϥⲙⲩⲥⲧⲏⲣⲓⲟⲛ ⲉⲓ
ⲛⲉϥⲉⲣⲏⲩ ⲁⲩⲱ ⲛⲅⲁϩⲉⲣⲁⲧⲕ ⲛⲅⲭⲟⲕϥ ⲉⲃⲟⲗ ⲕⲁⲗⲱⲥ ϩⲛ
ⲛⲉϥⲥⲭⲏⲙⲁ ⲧⲏⲣⲟⲩ ϣⲁⲕⲉⲓ ⲉⲃⲟⲗ ϩⲙ ⲡⲉⲕⲥⲱⲙⲁ ⲛⲧⲉⲩ-
5 ⲛⲟⲩ· ⲛⲅⲣ-ⲟⲩⲛⲟϭ ⲛϣⲗⲓϭ ⲛⲟⲩⲟⲉⲓⲛ [ⲛⲁⲡⲟⲣⲣⲟⲓⲁ]· ⲛⲅ-
ⲭⲱⲧⲉ ⲛⲧⲟⲡⲟⲥ ⲛⲓⲙ ⲛⲧⲉ ⲛⲁⲣⲭⲱⲛ ⲙⲛ ⲛⲧⲟⲡⲟⲥ ⲧⲏⲣⲟⲩ
ⲛⲧⲉ ⲡⲟⲩⲟⲉⲓⲛ ⲉⲩⲟ ⲛϩⲟⲧⲉ ⲧⲏⲣⲟⲩ ϩⲏⲧϥ ⲙⲡⲟⲩⲟⲉⲓⲛ
ⲛⲧⲉⲯⲩⲭⲏ ⲉⲧⲙⲙⲁⲩ· ϩⲉⲱⲥ ϣⲁⲛⲧⲥⲃⲱⲕ ⲉⲡⲧⲟⲡⲟⲥ ⲛ-
ⲧⲉⲥⲙⲛⲧⲉⲣⲟ· ⲡⲙⲉϩⲥⲛⲁⲩ ϩⲱⲱϥ ⲙⲙⲩⲥⲧⲏⲣⲓⲟⲛ ⲛⲧⲉ ⲡⲓ-
10 ϣⲟⲣⲡ ⲙⲙⲩⲥⲧⲏⲣⲓⲟⲛ ⲉⲕϣⲁⲛⲭⲱⲕ ⲉⲃⲟⲗ ⲙⲡⲉϥⲙⲩⲥⲧⲏⲣⲓⲟⲛ ⲕⲁⲗⲱⲥ ϩⲛ ⲛⲉϥⲥⲭⲏⲙⲁ ⲧⲏⲣⲟⲩ· ⲡⲣⲱⲙⲉ ϭⲉ ⲉⲧⲛⲁ-
ⲭⲱⲕ** ⲉⲃⲟⲗ ⲙⲡⲉϥⲙⲩⲥⲧⲏⲣⲓⲟⲛ· ⲉϥϣⲁⲛⲭⲱ ⲙⲡⲙⲩⲥⲧⲏ- ⲥⲕⲁ
ⲣⲓⲟⲛ ⲉⲧⲙⲙⲁⲩ ⲉϩⲣⲁⲓ ⲉⲭⲛ ⲧⲁⲡⲉ ⲛⲣⲱⲙⲉ ⲛⲓⲙ ⲉⲧⲛⲏⲩ
ⲉⲃⲟⲗ ϩⲙ ⲡⲥⲱⲙⲁ· ⲁⲩⲱ ⲛϥⲭⲟⲟϥ ⲉϩⲣⲁⲓ ⲉⲡⲉϥⲙⲁⲁⲭⲉ
15 ⲥⲛⲁⲩ ⲉϣⲱⲡⲉ ⲙⲉⲛ ⲡⲣⲱⲙⲉ ⲉⲧⲛⲏⲩ ⲉⲃⲟⲗ ϩⲙ ⲡⲥⲱⲙⲁ
ⲉⲁϥϫⲓ-ⲙⲩⲥⲧⲏⲣⲓⲟⲛ ⲛⲕⲉⲥⲟⲡ· ⲁⲩⲱ ϥⲟ ⲙⲙⲉⲧⲟⲭⲟⲥ ⲉ-
ϩⲟⲩⲛ ⲉⲡϣⲁϫⲉ ⲛⲧⲁⲗⲏⲑⲓⲁ· ϩⲁⲙⲏⲛ †ϫⲱ ⲙⲙⲟⲥ ⲉⲣⲱⲧⲛ
ϫⲉ ⲡⲣⲱⲙⲉ ⲉⲧⲙⲙⲁⲩ ⲉϥϣⲁⲛⲉⲓ' ⲉⲃⲟⲗ ϩⲙ ⲡⲥⲱⲙⲁ ⲛⲟⲩ-
ⲗⲏ· ⲧⲉϥⲯⲩⲭⲏ ⲛⲁⲣ-ⲟⲩⲛⲟϭ ⲛⲁⲡⲟⲣⲣⲟⲓⲁ ⲛⲟⲩⲟⲉⲓⲛ· ⲛⲥ-
20 ⲭⲱⲧⲉ ⲛⲧⲟⲡⲟⲥ ⲛⲓⲙ ϩⲉⲱⲥ ϣⲁⲛⲧⲥⲃⲱⲕ ⲉⲧⲙⲛⲧⲉⲣⲟ ⲙ-
ⲡⲙⲩⲥⲧⲏⲣⲓⲟⲛ ⲉⲧⲙⲙⲁⲩ· ⲉϣⲱⲡⲉ ⲇⲉ ⲛⲧⲟϥ ⲡⲣⲱⲙⲉ ⲉⲧⲙⲙⲁⲩ ⲙⲡϥϫⲓ-ⲙⲩⲥⲧⲏⲣⲓⲟⲛ· ⲁⲩⲱ ⲛϥⲟ ⲙⲙⲉⲧⲟⲭⲟⲥ ⲁⲛ
ⲉⲛϣⲁϫⲉ ⲛⲧⲁⲗⲏⲑⲓⲁ· ϣⲁⲣⲉ ⲡⲉⲧⲭⲱⲕ ⲉⲃⲟⲗ ⲙⲡⲙⲩⲥⲧⲏⲣⲓⲟⲛ ⲉⲧⲙⲙⲁⲩ· ⲉϥϣⲁⲛⲭⲱ ⲙⲡⲙⲩⲥⲧⲏⲣⲓⲟⲛ ⲉⲧⲙⲙⲁⲩ

---

5   omit ⲛⲁⲡⲟⲣⲣⲟⲓⲁ.
12   ⲓⲉ in upper left-hand margin at beginning of quire.

of them is different from the other. The first (mystery of the
First Mystery) *indeed*, if thou completest its *mystery* with
its others and standest and completest it *well* in all its
patterns, thou comest forth from thy *body* immediately, thou
becomest a great beam of light, and dost penetrate all *places*
of the *archons* and all *places* of the light. And they are all
in fear at the light of that *soul until* it goes to the *place*
of its kingdom. The second *mystery* of the First *Mystery*
moreover, if thou completest its *mystery well* in all its
patterns — now the man who will complete its *mystery*,
if he says that *mystery* over the head of any man who comes
forth from the *body* and says it into his two ears, when
indeed the man who comes forth from the *body* has received
mysteries for a second time and he is a *partaker* of the word
of *truth*, *truly* I say to you : that man when he comes forth
from the *body* of *matter*, his *soul* will become a great
outpouring of light. And it will penetrate every *place until*
it goes to the kingdom of that *mystery*. *But* if that man has
not received *mysteries* and he is not a *partaker* of the words
of *truth* — when he who completes that *mystery* says that
mystery | over the head of the man who comes forth from

ⲉϨⲣⲁⲓ ⲉϪⲚ ⲦⲀⲠⲉ ⲘⲠⲢⲰⲘⲉ ⲉⲦⲚⲎⲨ ⲉⲂⲞⲖ ϨⲘ ⲠⲤⲰⲘⲀ·
ⲠⲀⲒ ⲉⲦⲉ ⲘⲠⲈϤϪⲒ-ⲘⲨⲤⲦⲎⲢⲒⲞⲚ ⲚⲦⲉ ⲠⲞⲨⲞⲈⲒⲚ ⲀⲨⲰ ⲉⲚϤ-
*ⲔⲞⲒⲚⲰⲚⲒ ⲀⲚ ⲉⲚϢⲀϪⲈ ⲚⲦⲀⲖⲎⲐⲒⲀ· ϨⲀⲘⲎⲚ ϯϪⲰ ⲘⲘⲞⲤ ⲤⲔⲀ ᵇ
ⲉⲢⲰⲦⲚ ϪⲈ ⲠⲢⲰⲘⲉ ⲉⲦⲘⲘⲀⲨ ⲉϤϢⲀⲚⲈⲒ’ ⲉⲂⲞⲖ ϨⲘ ⲠⲤⲰ-
5 ⲘⲀ· ⲘⲈⲨⲔⲢⲒⲚⲈ ⲘⲘⲞϤ ϨⲚ ⲖⲀⲀⲨ ⲚⲦⲞⲠⲞⲤ ⲚⲦⲉ ⲚⲀⲢⲬⲰⲚ·
ⲞⲨⲆⲈ ⲚⲤⲈⲚⲀϢⲔⲞⲖⲀⲌⲈ ⲘⲘⲞϤ ⲀⲚ ϨⲚ ⲖⲀⲀⲨ ⲚⲦⲞⲠⲞⲤ·
ⲞⲨⲆⲈ ⲘⲠⲔⲰϨⲦ ⲚⲀϪⲰϨ ⲉⲢⲞϤ ⲀⲚ ⲉⲂⲞⲖ ϨⲘ ⲠⲚⲞϬ Ⲙ-
ⲘⲨⲤⲦⲎⲢⲒⲞⲚ ⲚⲦⲉ ⲠⲒⲀⲦϢⲀϪⲈ ⲉⲢⲞϤ ⲉⲦϢⲞⲞⲠ ⲚⲘⲘⲀϤ·
ⲀⲨⲰ ⲤⲈⲚⲀⲤⲠⲞⲨⲆⲀⲌⲈ ϨⲚ ⲞⲨϬⲈⲠⲎ ⲚⲤⲈⲦⲀⲀϤ ⲉⲦⲞⲞⲦⲞⲨ
10 ⲚⲚⲈⲨⲈⲢⲎⲨ ⲚⲤⲈⲢϨⲘⲘⲈ ⲘⲘⲞϤ ⲔⲀⲦⲀ ⲦⲞⲠⲞⲤ ⲀⲨⲰ ⲔⲀⲦⲀ
ⲦⲀⲜⲒⲤ ϨⲈⲰⲤ ϢⲀⲚⲦⲞⲨⲬⲒⲦϤ ⲉⲢⲀⲦⲤ ⲚⲦⲠⲀⲢⲐⲈⲚⲞⲤ Ⲙ-
ⲠⲞⲨⲞⲈⲒⲚ· ⲉⲢⲉ ⲚⲦⲞⲠⲞⲤ ⲦⲎⲢⲞⲨ Ⲟ ⲚϨⲞⲦⲉ ϨⲎⲦϤ Ⲙ-
ⲠⲘⲨⲤⲦⲎⲢⲒⲞⲚ ⲘⲚ ⲠⲘⲀⲈⲒⲚ ⲚⲦⲘⲚⲦⲈⲢⲞ ⲘⲠⲒⲀⲦϢⲀϪⲈ ⲉⲢⲞϤ
ⲠⲀⲒ ⲉⲦϢⲞⲞⲠ ⲚⲘⲘⲀϤ ⲀⲨⲰ ⲉⲨϢⲀⲚϪⲒⲦⲤ ⲉⲢⲀⲦⲤ ⲚⲦⲠⲀⲢ-
15 ⲐⲈⲚⲞⲤ ⲘⲠⲞⲨⲞⲈⲒⲚ· ⲦⲠⲀⲢⲐⲈⲚⲞⲤ ⲘⲠⲞⲨⲞⲈⲒⲚ ⲚⲀⲚⲀⲨ
ⲉⲠⲘⲀⲈⲒⲚ ⲘⲠⲘⲨⲤⲦⲎⲢⲒⲞⲚ ⲚⲦⲘⲚⲦⲈⲢⲞ** ⲘⲠⲒⲀⲦϢⲀϪⲈ ⲉⲢⲞϤ ⟦ⲤⲔⲂ⟧
ⲉϤϢⲞⲞⲠ ⲚⲘⲘⲀϤ· ϢⲀⲤⲢϢⲠⲎⲢⲈ ⲚϬⲒ ⲦⲠⲀⲢⲐⲈⲚⲞⲤ ⲘⲠⲞⲨ-
ⲞⲈⲒⲚ ⲀⲨⲰ ϢⲀⲤⲆⲞⲔⲒⲘⲀⲌⲈ ⲘⲘⲞϤ· ⲀⲖⲖⲀ ⲘⲈⲤⲦⲢⲈⲨϪⲒⲦϤ
ⲉⲠⲞⲨⲞⲈⲒⲚ ϢⲀⲚⲦϤϪⲰⲔ ⲉⲂⲞⲖ ⲚⲦⲠⲞⲖⲒⲦⲒⲀ ⲦⲎⲢⲤ ⲘⲠⲞⲨ-
20 ⲞⲈⲒⲚ ⲚⲦⲉ ⲠⲘⲨⲤⲦⲎⲢⲒⲞⲚ ⲉⲦⲘⲘⲀⲨ ⲉⲦⲉ ⲚⲀⲒ ⲚⲈ ⲚϨⲀⲄⲚⲒⲀ
ⲚⲦⲀⲠⲞⲦⲀⲄⲎ ⲘⲠⲔⲞⲤⲘⲞⲤ· ⲀⲨⲰ ⲘⲚ ⲐⲨⲖⲎ ⲦⲎⲢⲤ ⲉⲦⲚ-
ϨⲎⲦϤ· ϢⲀⲢⲉ ⲦⲠⲀⲢⲐⲈⲚⲞⲤ ⲘⲠⲞⲨⲞⲈⲒⲚ ϢⲀⲤⲤⲪⲢⲀⲄⲒⲌⲈ Ⲙ-
ⲘⲞϤ ϨⲚ ⲞⲨⲤⲪⲢⲀⲄⲒⲤ ⲉⲤⲞⲨⲞⲦⲂ ⲉⲦⲉ ⲦⲀⲒ ⲦⲈ· ⲚⲤⲦⲢⲈⲨ-
ⲚⲞϪϤ ϨⲘ ⲠⲒⲈⲂⲞⲦ ⲠⲒⲈⲂⲞⲦ ⲉⲚⲦⲀϤⲈⲒ ⲉⲂⲞⲖ ϨⲘ ⲠⲤⲰⲘⲀ
25 ⲚⲐⲨⲖⲎ ⲚϨⲎⲦϤ ⲉⲨⲤⲰⲘⲀ ⲉϤⲚⲀⲢ-ⲆⲒⲔⲀⲒⲞⲤ ⲠⲀⲒ ⲉϤⲚⲀϬⲒⲚⲈ
ⲚⲦⲘⲚⲦⲚⲞⲨⲦⲉ ⲚⲦⲀⲖⲎⲐⲒⲀ ⲘⲚ ⲘⲘⲨⲤⲦⲎⲢⲒⲞⲚ ⲉⲦϪⲞⲤⲉ

14　MS ⲉⲨϢⲀⲚϪⲒⲦⲤ; read ⲉⲨϢⲀⲚϪⲒⲦϤ.

the *body*, who has not received *mysteries* of the light and
has not *partaken* of the words of *truth* — *truly* I say to you :
that man when he comes forth from the *body* will not be
judged in any *place* of the *archons*, *nor* will he be *punished*
in any *place*, *nor* will the fire touch him as a result of the
great *mystery* of the Ineffable which is with him. And it will
be *effected with speed* that he be passed by hand from one to
another, and guided *from place to place* and *from rank to
rank*, *until* he be brought before the *Virgin* of the Light.
And all the *places* are in fear at the *mystery* and the sign
of the Kingdom of the Ineffable which is with him. And
when he is brought before the *Virgin* of the Light, the
Virgin of the Light will see the sign of the *mystery* of the
Kingdom of the Ineffable which is with him. The *Virgin*
of the Light will marvel and she will *examine* him, *but* she
will not cause him to be brought to the light until he completes the whole *life course* of the light of that *mystery*,
namely the *purifications* of the *renunciation* of the *world*
with all the *matter* within it. The *Virgin* of the Light *seals*
him with a superior *seal* which is this : in whatever month
he came forth from the *body* she causes him to be cast into
a *body*, that he may become *righteous* and find *true* God-
hood and the elevated *mysteries*, | and *inherit* them and

ⲚϤⲔⲖⲎⲢⲞⲚⲞⲘⲒ ⲘⲘⲞⲞⲨ ⲀⲨⲰ ⲚϤⲔⲖⲎⲢⲞⲚⲞⲘⲒ ⲘⲠⲞⲨⲞⲈⲒⲚ
ⲚϢⲀⲈⲚⲈ2· ⲈⲦⲈ ⲦⲀⲒ ⲦⲈ ⲦⲀϢⲢⲈⲀ ⲘⲠⲘⲈ2ⲤⲚⲀⲨ ⲘⲘⲨⲤ-
ⲦⲎⲢⲒⲞⲚ ⲚⲦⲈ ⲠⲒϢⲞⲢⲠ ⲘⲘⲨⲤⲦⲎⲢⲒⲞⲚ ⲚⲦⲈ ⲠⲒⲀⲦϢⲀϪⲈ
ⲈⲢⲞϤ· ⲠⲘⲈ2ϢⲞⲘⲚⲦ 2ⲰⲰϤ *ⲘⲘⲨⲤⲦⲎⲢⲒⲞⲚ ⲚⲦⲈ ⲠⲒⲀⲦ- [ⲤⲔⲂ ᵇ]
5 ϢⲀϪⲈ ⲈⲢⲞϤ ⲈⲦⲘⲘⲀⲨ· ⲠⲢⲰⲘⲈ ⲘⲈⲚ ⲈⲦⲚⲀϪⲰⲔ ⲈⲂⲞⲖ
ⲘⲠⲘⲨⲤⲦⲎⲢⲒⲞⲚ ⲈⲦⲘⲘⲀⲨ· ⲞⲨⲘⲞⲚⲞⲚ ϪⲈ ⲈϤϢⲀⲚⲈⲒ᾽ ⲈⲂⲞⲖ
2Ⲙ ⲠⲤⲰⲘⲀ ⲈϤⲚⲀⲔⲖⲎⲢⲞⲚⲞⲘⲒ ⲚⲦⲘⲚⲦⲈⲢⲞ ⲘⲠⲘⲨⲤⲦⲎⲢⲒⲞⲚ
ⲀⲖⲖⲀ ⲈϤϢⲀⲚⲦⲀⲘⲒⲞ ⲘⲠⲘⲨⲤⲦⲎⲢⲒⲞⲚ ⲚϤϪⲞⲔϤ ⲈⲂⲞⲖ ⲘⲚ
ⲚⲈϤⲤⲬⲎⲘⲀ ⲦⲎⲢⲞⲨ ⲈⲦⲈ ⲠⲀⲒ ⲠⲈ ϪⲈ ⲈϤϢⲀⲚⲈⲒⲢⲈ ⲘⲠⲘⲨⲤ-
10 ⲦⲎⲢⲒⲞⲚ ⲈⲦⲘⲘⲀⲨ ⲚϤϪⲞⲔϤ ⲈⲂⲞⲖ ⲔⲀⲖⲰⲤ· ⲀⲨⲰ ⲚϤⲞⲚⲞ-
ⲘⲀ2Ⲉ ⲘⲠⲘⲨⲤⲦⲎⲢⲒⲞⲚ ⲈⲦⲘⲘⲀⲨ ⲈϪⲚ ⲞⲨⲢⲰⲘⲈ ⲈϤⲚⲎⲨ Ⲉ-
ⲂⲞⲖ 2Ⲙ ⲠⲤⲰⲘⲀ ⲈⲀϤⲤⲞⲨⲚ-ⲠⲘⲨⲤⲦⲎⲢⲒⲞⲚ ⲈⲦⲘⲘⲀⲨ· ⲠⲀⲒ
ⲈⲀϤϢⲰⲤⲔ Ⲏ ⲘⲘⲞⲚ ⲚⲦⲞϤ ⲘⲠϤϢⲰⲤⲔ· ⲠⲀⲒ ⲈⲦϢⲞⲞⲠ᾽ 2Ⲛ ⲚⲔⲞ-
ⲖⲀⲤⲒⲤ ⲈⲦⲚⲀϢⲦ ⲚⲦⲈ ⲚⲀⲢⲬⲰⲚ· ⲀⲨⲰ ⲘⲚ ⲚⲈⲨⲔⲢⲒⲤⲒⲤ ⲈⲦ-
15 ⲚⲀϢⲦ ⲘⲚ ⲚⲈⲨⲔⲰ2Ⲧ ⲈⲨϢⲞⲂⲈ· 2ⲀⲘⲎⲚ ϯϪⲰ ⲘⲘⲞⲤ ⲚⲎ-
ⲦⲚ ϪⲈ ⲠⲢⲰⲘⲈ ⲈⲚⲦⲀϤⲈⲒ ⲈⲂⲞⲖ 2Ⲙ ⲠⲤⲰⲘⲀ ⲈⲨϢⲀⲚⲞⲚⲞ-
ⲘⲀ2Ⲉ ⲘⲠⲈⲒⲘⲨⲤⲦⲎⲢⲒⲞⲚ ⲈⲦⲂⲎⲎⲦϤ· ⲤⲈⲚⲀⲤⲠⲞⲨⲆⲀ2Ⲉ ⲦⲀ-
ⲬⲨ ⲚⲤⲈⲠⲞⲞⲚⲈϤ ⲈⲂⲞⲖ· ⲚⲤⲈⲦⲀⲀϤ**ⲈⲦⲞⲞⲦⲞⲨ ⲚⲚⲈⲨⲈⲢⲎⲨ ⲤⲔⲄ
2ⲈⲰⲤ ϢⲀⲚⲦⲞⲨϪⲒⲦϤ ⲈⲢⲀⲦⲤ ⲚⲦⲠⲀⲢⲐⲈⲚⲞⲤ ⲘⲠⲞⲨⲞⲈⲒⲚ·
20 ⲀⲨⲰ ⲦⲠⲀⲢⲐⲈⲚⲞⲤ ⲘⲠⲞⲨⲞⲈⲒⲚ ⲚⲀⲤϤⲢⲀⲅⲒ2Ⲉ ⲘⲘⲞϤ 2Ⲛ ⲞⲨ-
ⲤⲪⲢⲀⲅⲒⲤ ⲈⲤⲞⲨⲞⲦⲂ ⲈⲦⲈ ⲦⲀⲒ ⲦⲈ· ⲀⲨⲰ 2Ⲙ ⲠⲒⲈⲂⲞⲦ ⲠⲒⲈⲂⲞⲦ
ⲤⲚⲀⲦⲢⲈⲨⲚⲞϪϤ ⲈⲠⲤⲰⲘⲀ ⲚⲆⲒⲔⲀⲒⲞⲤ ⲠⲀⲒ ⲈⲦⲚⲀ6ⲒⲚⲈ ⲚⲦ-
ⲘⲚⲦⲚⲞⲨⲦⲈ ⲚⲦⲀⲖⲎⲐⲒⲀ ⲘⲚ ⲠⲘⲨⲤⲦⲎⲢⲒⲞⲚ ⲈⲦⲞⲨⲞⲦⲂ ⲚϤ-
ⲔⲖⲎⲢⲞⲚⲞⲘⲒ ⲚⲦⲘⲚⲦⲈⲢⲞ ⲘⲠⲞⲨⲞⲈⲒⲚ· ⲦⲀⲒ 6Ⲉ ⲞⲨⲚ ⲦⲈ
25 ⲦⲀϢⲢⲈⲀ ⲘⲠⲘⲈ2ϢⲞⲘⲚⲦ ⲘⲘⲨⲤⲦⲎⲢⲒⲞⲚ ⲚⲦⲈ ⲠⲒⲀⲦϢⲀϪⲈ
ⲈⲢⲞϤ· ⲦⲈⲚⲞⲨ 6Ⲉ ⲞⲨⲞⲚ ⲚⲒⲘ ⲠⲈⲦⲚⲀϪⲒ ⲈⲂⲞⲖ 2Ⲙ Ⲡ̄ϯⲞⲨ Ⲙ-
ⲘⲨⲤⲦⲎⲢⲒⲞⲚ ⲚⲦⲈ ⲠⲒⲀⲦϢⲀϪⲈ ⲈⲢⲞϤ· ⲠⲀⲒ ⲈϤϢⲀⲚⲈⲒ᾽ ⲈⲂⲞⲖ

inherit the eternal light. This is the ·*gift* of the second *mystery* of the First *Mystery* of the Ineffable.

Moreover the third *mystery* of that Ineffable — the man *indeed* who will complete that *mystery* will *not only inherit* the kingdom of the *mystery* when he comes forth from the *body*, *but* when he accomplishes the *mystery* and completes it with all its *patterns*, that is to say, when he performs that *mystery* and completes it *well*, and he *invokes* that *mystery* over a man who has known that *mystery* as he comes forth from the *body* — whether he has delayed *or* rather whether he has not delayed — who is in the severe *punishments* of the *archons* and in their harsh *judgments* and their various fires [1] — *truly* I say to you : it will be *effected with speed* that the man who has come forth from the *body*, on behalf of whom this *mystery* has been *invoked*, will be removed and be passed *quickly* from one to another *until* he is taken before the *Virgin* of the Light. And the *Virgin* of the Light will *seal* him with a superior *seal* which is this : in whatever month ⟨he came forth⟩ she will cause him to be cast into the *righteous body* which will find *true* Godhood and the superior *mystery*, and *inherit* the Kingdom of the Light. This *now* is the *gift* of the third *mystery* of the Ineffable.

Now at this time everyone who will receive from the five *mysteries* of the Ineffable — when he comes forth | from

---

[1]   (15) various fires; Till : dreadful fires.

ЗМ ПСШМА ΝϤΚΛΗΡΟΝΟΜΙ ϢΑ ΠΤΟΠΟϹ ΜΠΜΥϹΤΗΡΙΟΝ
ΕΤΜΜΑΥ ΑΥШ ΤΜΝΤΕΡΟ ΜΠϮΟΥ ΜΜΥϹΤΗΡΟΝ ΕΤΜΜΑΥ
ϹΟΥΟΤΒ ΕΤΜΝΤΕΡΟ ΜΠΙΜΝΤϹΝΟΟΥϹ ΜΜΥϹΤΗΡΙΟΝ
ΝΤΕ ΠΙϢΟΡΠ ΜΜΥϹΤΗΡΙΟΝ ΑΥШ ϤΟΥΟΤΒ ΕΜΥϹΤΗ-
5 ΡΙΟΝ ΝΙΜ ΕΤΠΕΥΕϹΗΤ· ΑΛΛΑ ΠϮΟΥ ΜΜΥϹΤΗΡΙΟΝ ΕΤ-
ΜΜΑΥ ΝΤΕ ΠΙΑΤϢΑΧΕ ΕΡΟϤ· ϹΕϢΗϢ ΜΝ ΝΕΥΕΡΗΥ C̄Κ̄Γ̄·ᵇ
ЗΡΑΪ ЗΝ ΤΕΥΜΝΤΕΡΟ· ΑΛΛΑ ΝϹΕϢΗϢ ΑΝ ΜΝ ΠϢΟΜΝΤ
ΜΜΥϹΤΗΡΙΟΝ ΝΤΕ ΠΙΑΤϢΑΧΕ ΕΡΟϤ· ΠΕΤΧΙ ЗШШϤ
ΕΒΟΛ ЗΜ ΠϢΟΜΝΤ ΜΜΥϹΤΗΡΙΟΝ ΝΤΕ ΠΙΑΤϢΑΧΕ ΕΡΟϤ·
10 ΕϤϢΑΝΕΙ ΟΝ ΕΒΟΛ ЗΝ ϹШΜΑ ϤΝΑΚΛΗΡΟΝΟΜΙ ϢΑ ΤΜΝΤ-
ΕΡΟ ΜΠΜΥϹΤΗΡΙΟΝ ΕΤΜΜΑΥ· ΑΥШ ΠϢΟΜΝΤ ΜΜΥϹ-
ΤΗΡΙΟΝ ΕΤΜΜΑΥ ϹΕϢΗϢ ΜΝ ΝΕΥΕΡΗΥ ЗΡΑΪ ЗΝ ΤΜΝΤ-
ΕΡΟ· ΑΥШ ϹΕΟΥΟΤΒ ΑΥШ ϹΕΧΟϹΕ ΕΠϮΟΥ ΜΜΥϹΤΗ-
ΡΙΟΝ ΝΤΕ ΠΙΑΤϢΑΧΕ ΕΡΟϤ ЗΡΑΪ ЗΝ ΤΜΝΤΕΡΟ· ΑΛΛΑ
15 ΝϹΕϢΗϢ ΑΝ ΜΝ ΠΜΥϹΤΗΡΙΟΝ ΝΟΥШΤ ΝΤΕ ΠΙΑΤϢΑΧΕ
ΕΡΟϤ· ΠΕΤΧΙ ЗШШϤ ΜΠΜΥϹΤΗΡΙΟΝ ΝΟΥШΤ ΝΤΕ ΠΙ-
ΑΤϢΑΧΕ ΕΡΟϤ· ϤΝΑΚΛΗΡΟΝΟΜΙ ΜΠΤΟΠΟϹ ΝΤΜΝΤΕΡΟ
ΤΗΡϹ ΚΑΤΑ ΘΕ ΝΤΑΪΟΥШ ΕΪΧШ ΕΡШΤΝ ΜΠΕϤϹΟΟΥ
ΤΗΡϤ ΝΚΕϹΟΠ· ΑΥШ ΟΥΟΝ ΝΙΜ ΕΤΝΑΧΙ ΜΠΜΥϹΤΗΡΙΟΝ
20 ΕΤЗΝ ΠΕΧШΡΗΜΑ ΜΠΤΗΡϤ ΜΠΙΑΤϢΑΧΕ ΕΡΟϤ· ΜΝ ΝΚΕ-
ΜΥϹΤΗΡΙΟΝ ΤΗΡΟΥ ΕΤЗΟΛϬ ЗΝ ΜΜΕΛΟϹ ΜΠΙΑΤϢΑΧΕ [C̄Κ̄Λ̄]
ΕΡΟϤ· ΝΑΪ ΕΤΕ ΜΠΑϮϢΑΧΕ ΝΜΜΗΤΝ ΕΤΒΗΗΤΟΥ ΜΝ
ΠΕΥϹШΡ ΕΒΟΛ ΜΝ ΘΕ ΕΤΟΥΑЗΕΡΑΤΟΥ ΜΜΟϹ ΑΥШ ΜΝ
ΠΤΥΠΟϹ ΜΠΟΥΑ ΠΟΥΑ ΝΘΕ ΕΤϤΟ ΜΜΟϹ ΑΥШ ΧΕ ΕΤ-
25 ΒΕ ΟΥ ΑΥΜΟΥΤΕ ΕΡΟϤ ΧΕ ΠΙΑΤϢΑΧΕ ΕΡΟϤ· Η ΕΤΒΕ
ΟΥ ΑϤЗΕΡΑΤϤ ΕϤΠΟΡϢ ΕΒΟΛ ΜΝ ΝΕϤΜΕΛΟϹ ΤΗΡΟΥ·

---

2 ΑΥШ . . . ΕΤΜΜΑΥ written below in margin.
25 ΡΟϤ in margin after ΑΤϢΑΧΕ; Η Ϲ in margin before ΤΒϹ.

the *body* he *inherits* as far as the *place* of that *mystery*. And the kingdom of these five *mysteries* is superior to the kingdom of the twelve *mysteries* of the First *Mystery*, and it is superior to every *mystery* below it. *But* these five *mysteries* of the Ineffable are equal with one another in their kingdom. *But* they are not equal with the three *mysteries* of the Ineffable. Moreover he who receives from the three *mysteries* of the Ineffable when he comes forth from the *body*, he will *inherit* as far as the kingdom of that *mystery*. And these three *mysteries* are equal with one another in the kingdom. And they are superior to, and more elevated than, the five *mysteries* of the Ineffable in the kingdom. *But* they are not equal with the one *mystery* of the Ineffable. Moreover he who receives the one *mystery* of the Ineffable will *inherit* the *place* of the whole kingdom, *as* I have already on another occasion told you of his whole glory.

And everyone who will receive the *mystery* which is in the *space* of the whole of the Ineffable, with all the other *mysteries* which are united in the *members* of the Ineffable — about these I have not yet spoken to you, and about their distribution and the manner of their setting up and the *type* of each one, how it is and why it was called the Ineffable, *or* why it stood spread out with all its *members*, |

ⲀⲨⲰ ⲬⲈ ⲞⲨⲚ ⲞⲨⲎⲢ ⲘⲘⲈⲖⲞⲤ ϢⲞⲞⲠ ϨⲢⲀⲒ ⲚϨⲎⲦϤ ⲘⲚ
ⲚⲈϤⲞⲒⲔⲞⲚⲞⲘⲒⲀ ⲦⲎⲢⲞⲨ ⲚⲀⲒ ⲚⲦⲚⲀⲬⲞⲞⲨ ⲈⲢⲰⲦⲚ ⲀⲚ ⲦⲈ-
ⲚⲞⲨ ⲀⲖⲖⲀ ⲈⲒϢⲀⲚⲚⲞⲨ ⟨ⲈⲬⲰ⟩ ⲈⲢⲰⲦⲚ ⲘⲠⲤⲰⲢ ⲈⲂⲞⲖ ⲘⲠ-
ⲦⲎⲢϤ ⲦⲚⲀⲬⲞⲞⲨ ⲈⲢⲰⲦⲚ ⲦⲎⲢⲞⲨ ⲔⲀⲦⲀ ⲞⲨⲀ ⲞⲨⲀ· ⲬⲈ
5 ⲚⲈϤⲤⲰⲢ ⲄⲀⲢ ⲈⲂⲞⲖ ⲘⲚ ⲦⲈϤϬⲒⲚϢⲀⲬⲈ ⲈⲢⲞϤ ⲚⲐⲈ ⲈⲦϤⲞ
ⲘⲘⲞⲤ ⲘⲚ ⲠϨⲰⲢⲬ ⲚⲚⲈϤⲘⲈⲖⲞⲤ ⲦⲎⲢⲞⲨ ⲈⲨⲎⲠ ⲈⲦⲞⲒⲔⲞ-
ⲚⲞⲘⲒⲀ ⲘⲠⲒⲞⲨⲀ ⲚⲞⲨⲰⲦ ⲠⲚⲞⲨⲦⲈ ⲚⲦⲀⲖⲎⲐⲒⲀ ⲚⲀⲦⲚⲢⲀⲦϤ·
ⲠⲦⲞⲠⲞⲤ ϬⲈ ⲈⲦⲈⲢⲈ ⲠⲞⲨⲀ ⲠⲞⲨⲀ ⲚⲀⲬⲒ-ⲘⲨⲤⲦⲎⲢⲒⲞⲚ ϢⲀ-
ⲢⲞϤ ϨⲢⲀⲒ ϨⲘ ⲠⲈⲬⲰⲢⲎⲘⲀ ⲘⲠⲒⲀⲦϢⲀⲬⲈ ⲈⲢⲞϤ· ϤⲚⲀⲔⲖⲎ-
10 ⲢⲞⲚⲞⲘⲒ ϢⲀ* ⲠⲦⲞⲠⲞⲤ ⲚⲦⲀϤ[ⲀⲢ]ⲬⲒ ϢⲀⲢⲞϤ· ⲀⲨⲰ ⲚⲀ- [ⲤⲔⲀ b]
ⲠⲦⲞⲠⲞⲤ ⲦⲎⲢϤ ⲘⲠⲈⲬⲰⲢⲎⲘⲀ ⲘⲠⲒⲀⲦϢⲀⲬⲈ ⲈⲢⲞϤ· ⲘⲈⲨⲦ-
ⲀⲠⲞⲪⲀⲤⲒⲤ ⲔⲀⲦⲀ ⲦⲞⲠⲞⲤ ⲞⲨⲀⲈ ⲘⲈⲨⲦ-ⲀⲠⲞⲖⲞⲄⲒⲀ ⲞⲨ-
ⲀⲈ ⲘⲈⲨⲦ-ⲤⲨⲘⲂⲞⲖⲞⲚ· ϨⲈⲚⲀⲦⲤⲨⲘⲂⲞⲖⲞⲚ ⲄⲀⲢ ⲚⲈ ⲀⲨⲰ
ⲘⲚⲦⲞⲨ-ⲠⲀⲢⲀⲖⲎⲘⲠⲦⲰⲢ ⲘⲘⲀⲨ· ⲀⲖⲖⲀ ϢⲀⲨⲬⲰⲦⲈ ⲚⲚ-
15 ⲦⲞⲠⲞⲤ ⲦⲎⲢⲞⲨ ϢⲀⲚⲦⲞⲨⲂⲰⲔ ⲈⲠⲦⲞⲠⲞⲤ ⲚⲦⲘⲚⲦⲈⲢⲞ Ⲙ-
ⲠⲘⲨⲤⲦⲎⲢⲒⲞⲚ ⲚⲦⲀⲨⲬⲒⲦϤ· ϨⲞⲘⲞⲒⲰⲤ ⲞⲚ ⲚⲈⲦⲚⲀⲬⲒ-ⲘⲨⲤ-
ⲦⲎⲢⲒⲞⲚ ϨⲘ ⲠⲘⲈϨⲤⲚⲀⲨ ⲚⲬⲰⲢⲎⲘⲀ ⲘⲚⲦⲞⲨ-ⲀⲠⲞⲪⲀⲤⲒⲤ Ⲙ-
ⲘⲀⲨ ⲞⲨⲀⲈ ⲀⲠⲞⲖⲞⲄⲒⲀ ϨⲈⲚⲀⲦⲤⲨⲘⲂⲞⲖⲞⲚ ⲄⲀⲢ ⲚⲈ ϨⲘ
ⲠⲔⲞⲤⲘⲞⲤ ⲈⲦⲘⲘⲀⲨ· ⟨ⲈⲦⲈ⟩ ⲚⲦⲞϤ ⲠⲈ ⲠⲈⲬⲰⲢⲎⲘⲀ ⲘⲠⲒ-
20 ϢⲞⲢⲠ ⲘⲘⲨⲤⲦⲎⲢⲒⲞⲚ ⲚⲦⲈ ⲠⲒϢⲞⲢⲠ ⲘⲘⲨⲤⲦⲎⲢⲒⲞⲚ· ⲀⲨⲰ
ⲚⲀⲠⲘⲈϨϢⲞⲘⲚⲦ ϨⲰⲰϤ ⲚⲬⲰⲢⲎⲘⲀ ⲈⲦϨⲒⲠⲤⲀⲚⲂⲞⲖ' ⲈⲦⲈ
ⲚⲦⲞϤ ⲠⲈ ⲠⲘⲈϨϢⲞⲘⲚⲦ ϨⲰⲰϤ ⲚⲬⲰⲢⲎⲘⲀ ⲬⲒⲚ ⲠⲤⲀⲚ-
ⲂⲞⲖ' ⲞⲨⲚ ⲚⲦⲈ ⲠⲦⲞⲠⲞⲤ ⲠⲦⲞⲠⲞⲤ ϨⲘ ⲠⲈⲬⲰⲢⲎⲘⲀ ⲈⲦ-

---

3 MS ⲈⲬⲰ omitted.
6 MS ⲠϨⲰⲢⲬ; perhaps ⲠϨⲰⲖϬ.
10 MS ⲚⲦⲀϤⲀⲢⲬⲒ.
19 MS ⲈⲦⲈ omitted. MS originally ⲠⲈⲬⲰⲢⲎⲘⲀ ⲘⲠⲒϢⲞⲢⲠ ⲘⲘⲨⲤ-
ⲦⲎⲢⲒⲞⲚ.
23 MS ⲞⲨⲦⲠⲚⲦⲈ; read ⲞⲨⲚ̄ⲦⲈ.

and how many *members* are within it and its whole *organisation*. I will not say these things to you now, *but* when I begin ⟨to tell⟩ you of the distribution of the All I will say them all to you, one *by* one : namely its distribution [1] and its description of how it is, and the harmony [2] of all its *members* which belong to the *organisation* of the Only One, the *true*, inaccessible God. As far as the *place* to which each one will receive *mysteries* in the *space* of the Ineffable, as far as the *place* to which he has received, he will *inherit*. And those of the whole *place* of the *space* of the Ineffable do not give *answer in any place*, *nor* do they give a *defence*, *nor* do they give a *secret sign*, *for* they are without *secret signs* and they have no *paralemptores*, *but* they penetrate all *places* until they go to the *place* of the kingdom of the *mystery* which they have received.

Likewise also, those who will receive *mysteries* in the second *space* have no *answer*, *nor defence*, *for* they are without *secret signs* in that *world* ⟨which⟩ is the *space* of the first *mystery* of the First *Mystery*.

And those of the third *space* which is outside, namely the third *space* from without, every *place* in that *space* has | its

---

[1] (5) distribution; lit. distributions.
[2] (6) harmony; perhaps translation of συμφωνία; see ApJn 50.10; ApJn II 15.27.

ⲘⲘⲀⲨ ⲚⲈϤⲠⲀⲢⲀⲖⲎⲘⲠⲦⲎⲤ** ⲘⲚ ⲚⲈϤⲀⲠⲟⲪⲀⲤⲓⲤ· ⲘⲚ ⲚⲈϤ- ⲤⲔⲈ
ⲀⲠⲟⲖⲟⲅⲓⲀ ⲘⲚ ⲚⲈϤⲤⲨⲘⲂⲟⲖⲟⲚ ⲚⲀⲒ Ⲉ†ⲚⲀⲭⲟⲟⲨ ⲈⲢⲰⲦⲚ
ⲌⲘ ⲠⲈⲞⲨⲞⲈⲓⲱ Ⲉ†ⲚⲀⲭⲱ ⲈⲢⲰⲦⲚ ⲘⲠⲘⲨⲤⲦⲎⲢⲓⲟⲚ ⲈⲦⲘ-
ⲘⲀⲨ· ⲈⲦⲈ ⲠⲀⲒ ⲠⲈ ⲈⲒϢⲀⲚⲞⲨⲱ ⲈⲒⲭⲱ ⲈⲢⲰⲦⲚ ⲘⲠⲤⲰⲢ
5 ⲈⲂⲟⲖ ⲘⲠⲦⲎⲢϤ· ⲠⲖⲎⲚ ⲌⲢⲀⲒ ⲌⲘ ⲠⲂⲰⲖ ⲈⲂⲟⲖ ⲘⲠⲦⲎⲢϤ ⲈⲦⲈ
ⲠⲀⲒ ⲠⲈ ⲈϤϢⲀⲚⲭⲰⲔ' ⲈⲂⲟⲖ Ⲛ̄ϬⲒ ⲠⲀⲢⲒⲐⲘⲟⲤ Ⲛ̄ⲚⲈⲮⲨⲭⲟ-
ⲞⲨⲈ Ⲛ̄ⲦⲈⲖⲓⲟⲤ· ⲀⲨⲱ Ⲛ̄ϤⲭⲰⲔ ⲈⲂⲟⲖ Ⲛ̄ϬⲒ ⲠⲘⲨⲤⲦⲎⲢⲓⲟⲚ
ⲠⲀⲒ Ⲛ̄ⲦⲀ ⲠⲦⲎⲢϤ ϢⲰⲠⲈ ⟨ⲈⲦⲂⲎⲚⲦ̄Ϥ⟩ ⲈⲠⲦⲎⲢϤ †ⲚⲀⲢϢⲞ Ⲛ̄-
ⲢⲟⲘⲠⲈ ⲔⲀⲦⲀ Ⲛ̄ⲢⲞⲘⲠⲈ ⲘⲠⲞⲨⲞⲈⲓⲚ ⲈⲒⲞ Ⲛ̄Ⲣ̄ⲢⲞ ⲈⲌⲢⲀⲒ ⲈⲭⲚ̄
10 ⲚⲈⲠⲢⲟⲂⲟⲖⲟⲞⲨⲈ ⲘⲠⲞⲨⲞⲈⲓⲚ ⲦⲎⲢⲟⲨ ⲘⲚ ⲠⲀⲢⲒⲐⲘⲟⲤ ⲦⲎ-
Ⲣ̄Ϥ Ⲛ̄ⲚⲈⲮⲨⲭⲟⲞⲨⲈ Ⲛ̄ⲦⲈⲖⲓⲟⲤ ⲚⲀⲒ Ⲛ̄ⲦⲀⲨⲭⲒ Ⲛ̄ⲘⲘⲨⲤⲦⲎⲢⲓⲟⲚ
ⲦⲎⲢⲟⲨ·

ⲀⲤϢⲰⲠⲈ Ⲛ̄ⲦⲈⲢⲈ ⲒⲤ ⲞⲨⲱ ⲈϤⲭⲱ Ⲛ̄ⲚⲈⲒϢⲀⲭⲈ ⲈⲚⲈϤ-
ⲘⲀⲐⲎⲦⲎⲤ ⲀⲤⲈⲒ' ⲈⲐⲎ Ⲛ̄ϬⲒ ⲘⲀⲢⲒⲀ ⲦⲘⲀⲅⲆⲀⲖⲎⲚⲎ ⲠⲈⲭⲀⲤ
15 ⲭⲈ ⲠⲀⲭⲞⲈⲓⲤ ⲞⲨⲎⲢ Ⲛ̄ⲢⲟⲘⲠⲈ ⲌⲚ Ⲣ̄ⲢⲞⲘⲠⲈ Ⲛ̄ⲦⲈ ⲠⲔⲟⲤⲘⲟⲤ
ⲠⲈ ⲞⲨⲢⲟⲘⲠⲈ Ⲛ̄ⲦⲈ ⲠⲞⲨⲞⲈⲓⲚ· ⲀϤⲞⲨⲰϢ̄Ⲃ Ⲛ̄ϬⲒ ⲒⲤ ⲠⲈⲭⲀϤ
Ⲙ̄ⲘⲀⲢⲒⲀ ⲭⲈ ⲞⲨⲌⲞⲞⲨ Ⲛ̄ⲦⲈ ⲠⲞⲨⲞⲈⲓⲚ ⲠⲈ ⲘⲎⲦ Ⲛ̄ϢⲈ Ⲛ̄- ⲤⲔⲈ b
ⲢⲟⲘⲠⲈ ⲌⲘ ⲠⲔⲟⲤⲘⲟⲤ· ⲌⲰⲤⲦⲈ ⲘⲀⲂⲦⲀⲤⲈ Ⲛ̄ⲦⲂⲀ Ⲛ̄ⲢⲟⲘⲠⲈ
ⲘⲚ ⲔⲈϬⲈⲤⲦⲂⲀ Ⲛ̄ⲢⲟⲘⲠⲈ Ⲛ̄ⲦⲈ ⲠⲔⲟⲤⲘⲟⲤ ⲠⲈ ⲞⲨⲢⲟⲘⲠⲈ Ⲛ̄-
20 ⲞⲨⲰⲦ Ⲛ̄ⲦⲈ ⲠⲞⲨⲞⲈⲓⲚ· †ⲚⲀⲢⲘⲎⲦ Ⲛ̄ϢⲈ ⲞⲨⲚ Ⲛ̄ⲢⲟⲘⲠⲈ
Ⲛ̄ⲦⲈ ⲠⲞⲨⲞⲈⲓⲚ ⲈⲒⲞ Ⲛ̄Ⲣ̄ⲢⲞ ⲌⲚ ⲦⲘⲎⲦⲈ Ⲙ̄ⲠⲌⲀⲈ ⲠⲀⲢⲀⲤⲦⲀ-
ⲦⲎⲤ· ⲈⲒⲞ Ⲛ̄Ⲣ̄ⲢⲞ ⲌⲢⲀⲒ ⲈⲭⲚ̄ ⲚⲈⲠⲢⲟⲂⲟⲖⲟⲞⲨⲈ ⲦⲎⲢⲟⲨ Ⲙ̄-
ⲠⲞⲨⲞⲈⲓⲚ· ⲀⲨⲱ ⲈⲭⲚ̄ ⲠⲀⲢⲒⲐⲘⲟⲤ ⲦⲎⲢϤ Ⲛ̄ⲚⲈⲮⲨⲭⲟⲞⲨⲈ
Ⲛ̄ⲦⲈⲖⲓⲟⲤ ⲚⲀⲒ ⲈⲚⲦⲀⲨⲭⲒ Ⲛ̄ⲘⲘⲨⲤⲦⲎⲢⲓⲟⲚ Ⲛ̄ⲦⲈ ⲠⲞⲨⲞⲈⲓⲚ·
25 ⲀⲨⲱ Ⲛ̄ⲦⲰⲦⲚ ⲚⲀⲘⲀⲐⲎⲦⲎⲤ ⲘⲚ ⲞⲨⲞⲚ ⲚⲒⲘ ⲈⲦⲚⲀⲭⲒ Ⲙ̄-

---

8   MS ⲈⲦⲂⲎⲚⲦ̄Ϥ omitted.
21 MS ⲠⲀⲢⲀⲤⲦⲀⲦⲎⲤ; read Ⲙ̄ⲠⲀⲢⲀⲤⲦⲀⲦⲎⲤ.

paralemptai and its *answers* and its *defences* and its *secret
signs* which I will tell you at the time when I tell you of that
mystery, which is when I finish speaking with you of the
distribution of the All. *Nevertheless* at the dissolution of the
All, namely when the *number* of *perfect souls* is completed,
and the *mystery*, for the sake of which the All came into
existence, is quite completed, I will spend 1000 years * [1],
according to years of light, as ruler (king) over all the
emanations of the light, and over the whole *number* of
perfect souls which have received all the *mysteries*."

99.   It happened when Jesus finished saying these words
to his *disciples*, Maria Magdalene came forward, she said :
"My Lord, how many years of the *world* is a year of the
light?"

Jesus answered and said to Maria : "A day of light is
1000 years in the world, *so that* 365,000 years of the *world*
are one year of light. I will *now* spend 1000 years of light
as ruler (king) in the midst of the last helpers (*parastatai*)
and as ruler (king) over all the *emanations* of the light,
and over the whole *number* of *perfect souls* which have
received the *mysteries* of the light. And you, my *disciples*
with all those who will receive | the *mystery* of the Ineffable,

---

*   cf. Rev. 20.4

---

[1]   (8, 9) see Resch (Bibl. 41) Apocryphon 94, p. 45.

ⲠⲘⲨⲤⲦⲎⲢⲒⲞⲚ ⲘⲠⲁⲦⲱϪⲀϪⲈ ⲈⲢⲞϤ· ϤⲚⲀϬⲱ ⲚⲘⲘⲀⲓ ⲚⲤⲀ

ⲞⲨⲚⲀⲘ ⲘⲘⲞⲓ ⲀⲨⲱ ⲚⲤⲀ ϨⲂⲞⲨⲢ ⲘⲘⲞⲓ ⲈⲦⲈⲦⲚⲞ ⲚⲢⲢⲞ

ⲚⲘⲘⲀⲓ ϨⲚ ⲦⲀⲘⲚⲦⲈⲢⲞ· ⲀⲨⲱ ⲚⲈⲦϪⲒ ϨⲰⲞⲨ ⲘⲠϢⲞⲘⲚⲦ

ⲘⲘⲨⲤⲦⲎⲢⲒⲞⲚ ⲚⲦⲈ ⲡ†ⲞⲨ ⲘⲘⲨⲤⲦⲎⲢⲒⲞⲚ ⲚⲦⲈ ⲠⲒⲀⲦⲱϪⲀϪⲈ

5 ⲈⲢⲞϤ ⲈⲦⲘⲘⲀⲨ· ⲤⲈⲚⲀⲢϢⲂⲢⲢⲢⲞ ⲚⲘⲘⲎⲦⲚ ϨⲢⲀⲓ ϨⲚ ⲦⲘⲚⲦⲈ-

ⲢⲞ ⲘⲠⲞⲨⲞⲈⲒⲚ· ⲀⲨⲱ ⲚⲤⲈⲚⲀϢⲰϢ ⲚⲘⲘⲎⲦⲚ ⲀⲚ· ⲚⲦⲰ- [Ⲥⲕⲉ

ⲦⲚ ⲘⲚ ⲚⲈⲦϪⲒ ⲘⲠⲘⲨⲤⲦⲎⲢⲒⲞⲚ ⲘⲠⲒⲀⲦⲱϪⲀϪⲈ ⲈⲢⲞϤ ⲈⲨ-

ⲚⲀϬⲱ ϨⲰⲞⲨ ⲘⲚⲚⲤⲰⲦⲚ ⲈⲨⲞ ⲚⲢⲢⲞ· ⲀⲨⲱ ⲚⲈⲦϪⲒ ⲘⲠ-

†ⲞⲨ ⲘⲘⲨⲤⲦⲎⲢⲒⲞⲚ ⲚⲦⲈ ⲠⲒⲀⲦⲱϪⲀϪⲈ ⲈⲢⲞϤ· ⲈⲨⲚⲀϬⲱ

10 ϨⲰⲞⲨ ⲘⲚⲚⲤⲀ ⲠϢⲞⲘⲚⲦ ⲘⲘⲨⲤⲦⲎⲢⲒⲞⲚ ⲈⲨⲞ ϨⲰⲞⲨ ⲚⲢⲢⲞ·

ⲀⲨⲱ ⲞⲚ ⲚⲈⲦϪⲒ ⲘⲠⲘⲈϨⲘⲚⲦⲤⲚⲞⲞⲨⲤ ⲘⲘⲨⲤⲦⲎⲢⲒⲞⲚ ⲚⲦⲈ

ⲠϢⲞⲢⲠ ⲘⲘⲨⲤⲦⲎⲢⲒⲞⲚ ⲈⲨⲚⲀϬⲱ ϨⲰⲞⲨ ⲞⲚ ⲘⲚⲚⲤⲀ ⲡ-

†ⲞⲨ ⲘⲘⲨⲤⲦⲎⲢⲒⲞⲚ ⲚⲦⲈ ⲠⲒⲀⲦⲱϪⲀϪⲈ ⲈⲢⲞϤ· ⲀⲨⲱ ⲈⲨⲞ

ϨⲰⲞⲨ ⲚⲢⲢⲞ ⲕⲀⲦⲀ ⲦⲦⲀⲝⲒⲤ ⲘⲠⲞⲨⲀ ⲠⲞⲨⲀ ⲘⲘⲞⲟⲨ ⲀⲨⲱ

15 ⲚⲈⲦϪⲒ ⲦⲎⲢⲞⲨ ϨⲚ ⲘⲘⲨⲤⲦⲎⲢⲒⲞⲚ ϨⲚ ⲚⲦⲞⲠⲞⲤ ⲦⲎⲢⲞⲨ

ⲘⲠⲈⲬⲰⲢⲎⲘⲀ ⲘⲠⲒⲀⲦⲱϪⲀϪⲈ ⲈⲢⲞϤ· ⲤⲈⲚⲀⲢⲢⲢⲞ ϨⲰⲞⲨ Ⲛ-

ⲤⲈϬⲱ ϨⲰⲞⲨ ⲘⲚⲚⲤⲀ ⲚⲈⲦϪⲒ ϨⲰⲞⲨ ⲘⲠⲘⲨⲤⲦⲎⲢⲒⲞⲚ ⲚⲦⲈ

ⲠϢⲞⲢⲠ ⲘⲘⲨⲤⲦⲎⲢⲒⲞⲚ· ⲈⲨⲤⲎⲢ ⲈⲂⲞⲗ ⲕⲀⲦⲀ ⲠⲈⲞⲞⲨ Ⲙ-

ⲠⲞⲨⲀ ⲠⲞⲨⲀ ⲘⲘⲞⲟⲨ· ϨⲰⲤⲦⲈ ⲚⲈⲦϪⲒ ⲘⲠⲘⲨⲤⲦⲎⲢⲒⲞⲚ

20 ⲈⲦⲞⲨⲞⲦϮ ⲤⲈⲚⲀϬⲱ ϨⲚ ⲚⲦⲞⲠⲞⲤ ⲈⲦⲞⲨⲞⲦϮ· ⲚⲈⲦϪⲒ Ⲛ-

ⲘⲘⲨⲤⲦⲎⲢⲒⲞⲚ ⲈⲦⲤⲞⲂⲕ· ⲤⲈⲚⲀϬⲱ ϨⲚ ⲚⲦⲞⲠⲞⲤ ⲈⲦⲤⲟⲂⲕ [Ⲥⲕⲉ

ⲈⲨⲞ ⲚⲢⲢⲞ [ⲈⲨⲞ ⲚⲢⲢⲞ] ϨⲢⲀⲓ ϨⲘ ⲠⲞⲨⲞⲈⲒⲚ ⲚⲦⲀⲘⲚⲦⲈⲢⲞ:

ⲚⲀⲓ ⲘⲘⲀⲦⲈ ⲚⲈ ⲠⲈⲕⲗⲎⲢⲞⲤ ⲚⲦⲘⲚⲦⲈⲢⲞ ⲚⲦⲈ ⲠⲒϢⲞⲢⲠ Ⲛ-

ⲬⲰⲢⲎⲘⲀ ⲚⲦⲈ ⲠⲒⲀⲦⲱϪⲀϪⲈ ⲈⲢⲞϤ· ⲚⲈⲦϪⲒ ϨⲰⲞϤ ⲚⲘⲘⲨⲤ-

25 ⲦⲎⲢⲒⲞⲚ ⲦⲎⲢⲞⲨ ⲘⲠⲘⲈϨⲤⲚⲀⲨ ⲚⲬⲰⲢⲎⲘⲀ ⲈⲦⲈ ⲚⲦⲞϤ ⲠⲈ

ⲠⲈⲬⲰⲢⲎⲘⲀ ⲚⲦⲈ ⲠⲒϢⲞⲢⲠ ⲘⲘⲨⲤⲦⲎⲢⲒⲞⲚ· ⲤⲈⲚⲀϬⲱ ϨⲰⲞⲨ

---

19   MS ⲘⲠⲘⲨⲤⲦⲎⲢⲒⲞⲚ; read ⲚⲘⲘⲨⲤⲦⲎⲢⲒⲞⲚ.
22   ⲈⲨⲞ ⲚⲢⲢⲞ dittography.

will remain with me on my right and on my left, as rulers
(kings) with me in my kingdom. And those moreover who
receive the three *mysteries* [of the five mysteries] of that
Ineffable will become fellow-rulers (kings) with you in the
Kingdom of the Light. And they will not be equal with you
and with those who receive the *mystery* of the Ineffable;
they will remain as rulers (kings) after you [1]. And those
who receive the five *mysteries* of the Ineffable will also
remain after the three *mysteries* as rulers (kings) likewise.
And furthermore those who receive the twelfth *mystery* of
the First *Mystery* will also remain after the five *mysteries*
of the Ineffable, being rulers (kings) likewise, *according to*
the *rank* of each one of them. And all those who receive
from the *mysteries* in all the *places* of the *space* of the
Ineffable will become rulers (kings) likewise, and also remain
after those who receive the *mystery* of the First *Mystery*.
They are distributed *according to* the glory of each one of
them, *so that* those that receive the superior *mysteries* will
remain in the superior *places*, and those that receive the
inferior *mysteries* will remain in the inferior *places* as rulers
(kings) in the light of my kingdom. These alone are the
portion of the kingdom of the first *space* of the Ineffable.

Those moreover who receive all the *mysteries* of the
second *space*, which is the *space* of the First Mystery, will
likewise remain | in the light of my kingdom, distributed

---

[1] (8) they will remain as rulers (kings) after you; Till: they will remain after
you, although they are kings.

ON ⳘⲣⲀⲓ ⲌⲘ ⲠⲞⲨⲞⲈⲓⲚ ⲚⲦⲀⲘ̅Ⲛ̅ⲦⲈⲢⲞ ⲈⲨⲤⲎⲢ ⲈⲂⲞⲖ ⲔⲀⲦⲀ
ⲠⲈⲞⲞⲨ Ⲙ̅ⲠⲞⲨⲀ ⲠⲞⲨⲀ Ⲙ̅ⲘⲞⲞⲨ· ⲈⲢⲈ ⲠⲞⲨⲀ ⲠⲞⲨⲀ Ⲙ̅-
ⲘⲞⲞⲨ ⲰⲞⲞⲠˈ ⲌⲘ ⲠⲘⲨⲤⲦⲎⲢⲒⲞⲚ Ⲛ̅ⲦⲀϤⲬⲒ ⲰⲀⲢⲞϤ· ⲀⲨⲰ
ⲚⲈⲦⲬⲒ Ⲛ̅ⲘⲘⲨⲤⲦⲎⲢⲒⲞⲚ ⲈⲦⲞⲨⲞⲦ̅Ⲃ̅ ⲤⲈⲚⲀϬⲰ ⳜⲰⲞⲨ ⲌⲚ
5 Ⲛ̅ⲦⲞⲠⲞⲤ ⲈⲦⲬⲞⲤⲈ ⲀⲨⲰ ⲚⲈⲦⲬⲒ Ⲛ̅ⲘⲘⲨⲤⲦⲎⲢⲒⲞⲚ ⲈⲦⲤⲞ-
Ⲃ̅Ⲕ̅· ⲈⲨⲚⲀϬⲰ ⲌⲚ Ⲛ̅ⲦⲞⲠⲞⲤ ⲈⲦⲤⲞⲂ̅Ⲕ̅ ⳘⲣⲀⲓ ⲌⲘ ⲠⲞⲨⲞⲈⲓⲚ
Ⲛ̅ⲦⲀⲘ̅Ⲛ̅ⲦⲈⲢⲞ· ⲠⲀⲓ ⲠⲈ ⲠⲈⲔⲖⲎⲢⲞⲤ Ⲙ̅ⲠⲘⲈⳜ̅ⲤⲚⲀⲨ Ⲛ̅ⲢⲢⲞ Ⲛ̅-
ⲚⲈⲦⲬⲒ Ⲙ̅ⲠⲘⲨⲤⲦⲎⲢⲒⲞⲚ Ⲙ̅ⲠⲘⲈⳜ̅ⲤⲚⲀⲨ Ⲛ̅ⲬⲰⲢⲎⲘⲀ Ⲛ̅ⲦⲈ ⲠⲒ-
ⲰⲞⲢ̅Ⲡ̅ ⲘⲘⲨⲤⲦⲎⲢⲒⲞⲚ: ⲚⲈⲦⲬⲒ ⳜⲰⲞⲨ Ⲛ̅ⲘⲘⲨⲤⲦⲎⲢⲒⲞⲚ Ⲙ̅-
10 ⲠⲘⲈⳜ̅ⲤⲚⲀⲨ Ⲛ̅ⲬⲰⲢⲎⲘⲀ ⲈⲦⲈ Ⲛ̅ⲦⲞϤ ⲠⲈ ⲠⳜⲞⲢ̅Ⲡ̅ Ⲛ̅ⲬⲰⲢⲎⲘⲀ Ⲥ̅Ⲕ̅Ⲍ̅
ⲬⲒⲚ ⲠⲤⲀⲚⲂⲞⲖ· ⲚⲈⲦⲘ̅ⲘⲀⲨ ⳜⲰⲞⲨ ⲞⲚ ⲤⲈⲚⲀϬⲰ Ⲙ̅Ⲛ̅Ⲛ̅ⲤⲀ
ⲠⲘⲈⳜ̅ⲤⲚⲀⲨ Ⲛ̅ⲢⲢⲞ ⲈⲨⲤⲎⲢ ⲈⲂⲞⲖ ⳜⲰⲞⲨ ⲌⲘ ⲠⲞⲨⲞⲈⲓⲚ Ⲛ̅-
ⲦⲀⲘ̅Ⲛ̅ⲦⲈⲢⲞ ⲔⲀⲦⲀ ⲠⲈⲞⲞⲨ Ⲙ̅ⲠⲞⲨⲀ ⲠⲞⲨⲀ Ⲙ̅ⲘⲞⲞⲨ· ⲈⲢⲈ
ⲠⲞⲨⲀ ⲠⲞⲨⲀ ⲚⲀϬⲰ ⲌⲘ ⲠⲦⲞⲠⲞⲤ Ⲛ̅ⲦⲀϤⲬⲒ-ⲘⲨⲤⲦⲎⲢⲒⲞⲚ
15 ⲰⲀⲢⲞϤ ⳜⲰⲤⲦⲈ ⲚⲈⲦⲬⲒ Ⲛ̅ⲘⲘⲨⲤⲦⲎⲢⲒⲞⲚ ⲈⲦⲬⲞⲤⲈ ⲤⲈⲚⲀ-
ϬⲰ ⳜⲰⲞⲨ ⲌⲚ Ⲛ̅ⲦⲞⲠⲞⲤ ⲈⲦⲬⲞⲤⲈ· ⲀⲨⲰ ⲚⲈⲦⲬⲒ Ⲛ̅ⲘⲘⲨⲤ-
ⲦⲎⲢⲒⲞⲚ ⲈⲦⲤⲞⲂ̅Ⲕ̅ˈ ⲤⲈⲚⲀϬⲰ ⳜⲰⲞⲨ ⲌⲚ Ⲛ̅ⲦⲞⲠⲞⲤ ⲈⲦⲤⲞⲂ̅Ⲕ̅·
ⲚⲀⲓ ⲚⲈ ⲠⳜⲞⲘ̅Ⲛ̅Ⲧ̅ Ⲛ̅ⲔⲖⲎⲢⲞⲤ Ⲛ̅ⲦⲈ ⲦⲘ̅ⲚⲦⲈⲢⲞ Ⲙ̅ⲠⲞⲨⲞⳜⲚ·
Ⲛ̅ⲘⲘⲨⲤⲦⲎⲢⲒⲞⲚ Ⲛ̅ⲦⲈ ⲠⲈⳜ̅ⳜⲞⲘ̅Ⲛ̅Ⲧ̅ Ⲛ̅ⲔⲖⲎⲢⲞⲤ Ⲛ̅ⲦⲈ ⲠⲞⲨ-
20 ⲞⲈⲓⲚ ⲤⲈⲞⳜ ⲈⲘⲀⳜⲞ ⲈⲘⲀⳜⲞ ⲦⲈⲦⲚ̅ⲚⲀⳜⲈ ⲈⲢⲞⲞⲨ ⲌⲘ
ⲠⲚⲞϬ ⲤⲚⲀⲨ Ⲛ̅ⲬⲰⲰⲘⲈ Ⲛ̅ⳜⲈⲞⲨ· ⲀⲖⲖⲀ ⳨ⲚⲀ⳨ ⲚⲎⲦⲚ̅ ⲀⲨⲰ
⳨ⲚⲀⲬⲰ ⲈⲢⲰⲦⲚ̅ Ⲛ̅Ⲛ̅ⲚⲞϬ Ⲙ̅ⲘⲨⲤⲦⲎⲢⲒⲞⲚ Ⲙ̅ⲠⲈⲔⲖⲎⲢⲞⲤ ⲠⲈ-
ⲔⲖⲎⲢⲞⲤ· ⲚⲀⲓ ⲈⲦⲞⲨⲞⲦ̅Ⲃ̅ ⲈⲠⲦⲞⲠⲞⲤ ⲠⲦⲞⲠⲞⲤ ⲈⲦⲈ Ⲛ̅ⲦⲞ-
ⲞⲨ ⲠⲈ Ⲛ̅ⲔⲈⲫⲀⲖⲎ ⲔⲀⲦⲀ ⲦⲞⲠⲞⲤ ⲀⲨⲰ ⲔⲀⲦⲀ ⲦⲀ⳽ⲒⲤ· ⲚⲀⲓ Ⲥ̅Ⲕ̅Ⲍ̅ᵇ

---

3 MS ⲌⲘ ⲠⲘⲨⲤⲦⲎⲢⲒⲞⲚ Ⲛ̅ⲦⲀϤⲬⲒ ⲰⲀⲢⲞϤ; better ⲌⲘ ⲠⲦⲞⲠⲞⲤ Ⲛ̅ⲦⲀϤⲬⲒ-
ⲘⲨⲤⲦⲎⲢⲒⲞⲚ ⲰⲀⲢⲞϤ.
19 MS Ⲛ̅ⲘⲘⲨⲤⲦⲎⲢⲒⲞⲚ; read Ⲙ̅ⲘⲨⲤⲦⲎⲢⲒⲞⲚ.

according to the glory of each one of them, each of them being in the *mystery* [1] as far as which he has received. And those moreover who receive the superior *mysteries* will likewise remain in the elevated *places* and those who receive the inferior *mysteries* will remain in the inferior *places* in the light of my kingdom. This is the *portion* of the second ruler (king) for those who receive the *mystery* of the second *space* of the First *Mystery*.

Furthermore those who receive the *mysteries* of the second *space* which is the first *space* from without, they also will remain behind the second ruler (king), distributed in the light of my kingdom, *according to* the glory of each one of them. Each of them will remain in the *place* as far as which he has received *mysteries, so that* those who receive the elevated *mysteries* will remain in the elevated *places* and those who receive the inferior *mysteries* will remain in the inferior *places*.

These are the three *portions* of the Kingdom of the Light. The *mysteries* of these three *portions* of the light are exceedingly numerous. You will find them in the two great Books of Jeu [2]. *But* I will give you and I will say to you the great *mysteries* of every *portion*. Those which are superior to every *place* are the *heads, according to place* and *according to rank*, | which will take the whole *race* of mankind into

---

[1] (3) in the mystery; better : in the place ... mysteries.
[2] (20, 21) Schmidt : [you will find them ... Jeu].

ⲈⲦⲚⲀϪⲒ ⲘⲠⲄⲈⲚⲞⲤ ⲦⲎⲢϤ ⲚⲦⲈ ⲦⲘⲚⲦⲢⲰⲘⲈ ⲈⲂⲞⲨⲚ ⲈⲚ-
ⲦⲞⲠⲞⲤ ⲈⲦϪⲞⲤⲈ ⲔⲀⲦⲀ ⲠⲈⲬⲰⲢⲎⲘⲀ ⲚⲦⲈⲔⲖⲎⲢⲞⲚⲞⲘⲒⲀ
[ⲚⲦⲈ] ⲠⲔⲈⲤⲈⲈⲠⲈ ⲞⲨⲚ ⲘⲘⲨⲤⲦⲎⲢⲒⲞⲚ ⲈⲦⲤⲞⲂⲔ ⲚⲦⲈⲦⲚⲢ-
ⲬⲢⲈⲒⲀ ⲘⲘⲞⲞⲨ ⲀⲚ ⲀⲖⲖⲀ ⲦⲈⲦⲚⲚⲀⳘⲈ ⲈⲢⲞⲞⲨ ⳘⲒ ⲠⲬⲰⲰⲘⲈ
5 ⲤⲚⲀⲨ ⲚⲒⲈⲞⲨ· ⲚⲀⲒ ⲚⲦⲀϤⲤⳘⲀⲒⲤⲞⲨ ⲚϬⲒ ⲈⲚⲰⲬ ⲈⲒϢⲀϪⲈ
ⲚⲘⲘⲀϤ ⲈⲂⲞⲖ ⳘⲘ ⲠϢⲎⲚ ⲘⲠⲤⲞⲞⲨⲚ ⲀⲨⲰ ⲈⲂⲞⲖ ⳘⲘ ⲠϢⲎⲚ
ⲘⲠⲰⲚⳘ ⳘⲢⲀⲒ ⳘⲘ ⲠⲠⲀⲢⲀⲆⲒⲤⲞⲤ ⲚⲀⲆⲀⲘ· ⲦⲈⲚⲞⲨ ϬⲈ ⲞⲨⲚ
ⲈⲒϢⲀⲚⲞⲨⲰ ⲈⲒⲤⲰⲢ ⲚⲎⲦⲚ ⲈⲂⲞⲖ ⲘⲠⲤⲰⲢ ⲈⲂⲞⲖ ⲦⲎⲢϤ·
ϮⲚⲀϮ ⲚⲎⲦⲚ ⲀⲨⲰ ϮⲚⲀϪⲰ ⲈⲢⲰⲦⲚ ⲚⲚⲞϬ ⲘⲘⲨⲤⲦⲎ-
10 ⲢⲒⲞⲚ ⲘⲠϢⲞⲘⲚⲦ ⲚⲔⲖⲎⲢⲞⲤ ⲚⲦⲀⲘⲚⲦⲈⲢⲞ· ⲈⲦⲈ ⲚⲦⲞⲞⲨ
ⲚⲈ ⲚⲔⲈⲪⲀⲖⲎ ⲚⲘⲘⲨⲤⲦⲎⲢⲒⲞⲚ ⲈϮⲚⲀⲦⲀⲀⲨ ⲚⲎⲦⲚ· ⲀⲨⲰ
ⲈϮⲚⲀϪⲞⲞⲨ ⲈⲢⲰⲦⲚ ⳘⲚ ⲚⲈⲨⲤⲬⲎⲘⲀ ⲦⲎⲢⲞⲨ ⳘⲚ ⲚⲈⲨ-
ⲦⲨⲠⲞⲤ ⲦⲎⲢⲞⲨ ⳘⲚ ⲚⲈⲨⲮⲎⲪⲞⲤ· ⳘⲚ ⲚⲈⲤⲪⲢⲀⲄⲒⲤ ⲘⲠⳘⲀⲈ
ⲚⲬⲰⲢⲎⲘⲀ· ⲈⲦⲈ ⲚⲦⲞϤ ⲠⲈ ⲠϢⲞⲢⲠ ⲚⲬⲰⲢⲎⲘⲀ ϪⲒⲚ ⲠⲤⲀ- [ⲤⲔⲎ]
15 ⲚⲂⲞⲖ· ⲀⲨⲰ ϮⲚⲀϪⲰ ⲈⲢⲰⲦⲚ ⲚⲚⲀⲠⲞⲪⲀⲤⲒⲤ ⳘⲚ ⲚⲀⲠⲞ-
ⲖⲞⲄⲒⲀ ⳘⲚ ⲚⲤⲨⲘⲂⲞⲖⲞⲚ ⲘⲠⲈⲬⲰⲢⲎⲘⲀ ⲈⲦⳘⲘⲀⲨ· ⲠⲘⲈⳘ-
ⲤⲚⲀⲨ ⲚⲦⲞϤ ⲚⲬⲰⲢⲎⲘⲀ ⲈⲠⲤⲀⲚⳘⲞⲨⲚ· ⳘⲚⲦⲞⲨ-ⲀⲠⲞⲪⲀ-
ⲤⲒⲤ ⲘⲘⲀⲨ ⲞⲨⲆⲈ ⲀⲠⲞⲖⲞⲄⲒⲀ ⲞⲨⲆⲈ ⲤⲨⲘⲂⲞⲖⲞⲚ· ⲞⲨⲆⲈ
ⲮⲎⲪⲞⲤ ⲞⲨⲆⲈ ⲤⲪⲢⲀⲄⲒⲤ· ⲀⲖⲖⲀ ⳘⲈⲚⲦⲨⲠⲞⲤ ⲘⲘⲀⲦⲈ ⲚⲈ
20 ⳘⲚ ⳘⲈⲚⲤⲬⲎⲘⲀ ⲚⲈⲦⲚⲦⲀⲨ·

    ⲚⲀⲒ ⲦⲎⲢⲞⲨ ⲚⲦⲈⲢⲈϤⲞⲨⲰ ⲈϤϪⲰ ⲘⲘⲞⲞⲨ ⲚϬⲒ ⲠⲤⲰ-
ⲦⲎⲢ ⲈⲚⲈϤⲘⲀⲐⲎⲦⲎⲤ ⲀϤⲈⲒ' ⲈⲐⲎ ⲚϬⲒ ⲀⲚⲆⲢⲈⲀⲤ ⲠⲈϪⲀϤ
ϪⲈ ⲠⲀϪⲞⲈⲒⲤ ⲘⲠⲢϬⲰⲚⲦ ⲈⲢⲞⲒ· ⲀⲖⲖⲀ ϢⲚⳘⲦⲎⲔ ⳘⲀⲢⲞⲒ
ⲀⲨⲰ ⲚⲄϬⲰⲖⳘ ⲚⲀⲒ ⲈⲂⲞⲖ ⲘⲠⲘⲨⲤⲦⲎⲢⲒⲞⲚ ⲘⲠϢⲀϪⲈ ⲈϮ-
25 ⲚⲀϪⲚⲞⲨⲔ ⲈⲢⲞϤ ⲈⲘⲘⲞⲚ ⲀϤϢⲰⲠⲈ ⲈϤⲚⲀϢⲦ ⲚⲚⲀⳘⲢⲀⲒ

---

3 omit ⲚⲦⲈ.
17 MS ⲈⲠⲤⲀⲚⳘⲞⲨⲚ; read ⲈⲦⲠⲤⲀⲚⳘⲞⲨⲚ.

the elevated *places, according to* the *space* of the *inheritance.*
Now you have no *need* for the remainder of the inferior
mysteries, but you will find them in the two Books of Jeu
which Enoch has written as I spoke with him out of the Tree
of Knowledge and out of the Tree of Life in the *paradise*
of Adam. *Now* at this time when I have finished spreading
before you the whole distribution, I will give to you and
I will say to you the great *mysteries* of the three *portions*
of my kingdom. These are the *heads* of the *mysteries* which
I will give you and will say to you in all their *patterns* and
all their *types* and their *ciphers* and the *seals* of the last
space, which is the first *space* from without. And I will say
to you the *answers* and the *defences* and the *secret signs* of
that *space*. On the other hand, the second *space* within
possesses no *answers, or defences, or secret signs, or ciphers,
or seals,* but it possesses only *types* and *patterns.*"

100. When the *Saviour* had finished saying all these things
to his *disciples*, Andrew came forward said : "My Lord,
be not angry with me, *but* have compassion on me and
reveal to me the *mystery* of the discourse on which I will
question thee, for it has become hard for me, and I *understand*
it not." |

ΑΥШ ⲘΠⲒΝΟΪ ⲘⲘΟϤ· ΑϤΟΥШⲈⲘ ⲚϬⲒ ΠСШⲦⲎⲢ ΠⲈΧΑϤ

ΝΑϤ ΧⲈ ϢⲒΝⲈ ⲚСΑ ΠⲈⲦⲔΟΥⲈϢϢⲒΝⲈ ⲚСШϤ· ΑΥШ ⳁ- [ⲤⲔⲎ ᵇ]

ΝΑϬΟⲖΠϤ ΝΑⲔ ⲈΒΟⲖ ⲚⲈⲞ ΟΥΒⲈ ⲈΟ ΑΧⲚ ΠΑⲢΑΒΟⲖⲎ·

ΑϤΟΥШⲈⲘ ΔⲈ ⲚϬⲒ ΑΝΔⲢⲈΑС ΠⲈΧΑϤ ΧⲈ ΠΑΧΟⲈⲒС ⲈΪⲢ-

5 ϢΠⲎⲢⲈ ΑΥШ ⲈΪΘΑΥΜΑΖⲈ ⲈⲘΑϢΟ· ΧⲈ ⲚⲢШⲘⲈ ⲈⲦⲈⲚ

ΠⲔΟСⲘΟС ⲈⲦⲈⲚ ΠСШⲘΑ ⲚⲦⲈΪⲈΥⲖⲎ ΠШС ⲈΥϢΑΝⲈⲒᐟⲈΒΟⲖ

ⲈⲘ ΠⲈΪⲔΟСⲘΟС СⲈΝΑΟΥШⲦⲂ ⲚⲚⲈΪСⲦⲈⲢⲈШⲘΑ ⲘⲚ ΝⲈΪ-

ΑⲢΧШΝ ⲦⲎⲢΟΥ· ⲘⲚ ⲚΧΟⲈⲒС ⲦⲎⲢΟΥ· ⲘⲚ ⲚΝΟΥⲦⲈ ⲦⲎ-

ⲢΟΥ· ⲘⲚ ΝⲈⲒΝΟϬ ⲦⲎⲢΟΥ ⲚΑⲈΟⲢΑⲦΟС ⲘⲚ ΝΑΠⲦΟΠΟС

10 ⲦⲎⲢΟΥ ⲚΝΑⲦⲘⲈСΟС· ΑΥШ ⲘⲚ ΝΑΠⲦΟΠΟС ⲦⲎⲢϤ ⲚΝΑ-

ΟΥΝΑⲘ· ⲘⲚ ⲚΝΟϬ ⲦⲎⲢΟΥ ⲚΝⲈΠⲢΟΒΟⲖΟΟΥⲈ ⲚⲦⲈ ΝΑ-

ΟΥΝΑⲘ· ⲚСⲈⲢΠⲈΥⲈΟΥΝ ⲦⲎⲢΟΥ ⲚСⲈⲔⲖⲎⲢΟΝΟⲘⲒ Ⲛ-

ⲦⲘⲚⲦⲈⲢΟ ⲘΠΟΥΟⲈⲒΝ· ΠⲈΪⲈШΒ ΟΥΝ ΠΑΧΟⲈⲒС ϤⲘΟⲔⲈ

ⲚΝΑⲈⲢΑΪ· ΝΑΪ ϬⲈ ⲚⲦⲈⲢⲈϤΧΟΟΥ ⲚϬⲒ ΑΝΔⲢⲈΑС Α ΠⲈΠΝΑ

15 ⲘΠСШⲢ ⲔⲒⲘ ⲈⲢΑΪ ⲚⲈⲎⲦϤ· ΑϤШϢ ⲈΒΟⲖ ΠⲈΧΑϤ ΧⲈ ⲈⲈШС ⲤⲔⲞ

ϢΑ ⲦΝΑΥ ⲈΪΝΑϤⲒ ⲈΑⲢШⲦⲚ· ⲈⲈШС ϢΑ ⲦΝΑΥ ⲈΪΝΑⲖΝⲈΧⲈ

ⲘⲘШⲦⲚ· ⲈⲒⲦⲈ ΑⲔⲘⲎΝ ΟΝ ⲘΠⲈⲦⲚΝΟΪ ΑΥШ ⲦⲈⲦΝΟ Ⲛ-

ΑⲦСΟΟΥΝ ⲈⲒⲈ ⲚⲦⲈⲦⲚСΟΟΥΝ ΑΝ ⲚⲦШⲦⲚ ΑΥШ ⲚⲦⲈ-

ⲦⲚΝΟΪ ΑΝ ΧⲈ ⲚⲦШⲦⲚ ⲘⲚ ΝΑⲄⲄⲈⲖΟС ⲦⲎⲢΟΥ· ⲘⲚ ΝΑⲢΧ-

20 ΑⲄⲄⲈⲖΟС ⲦⲎⲢΟΥ· ⲘⲚ ⲚΝΟΥⲦⲈ ⲘⲚ ⲚΧΟⲈⲒС· ⲘⲚ Ⲛ-

ΑⲢΧШΝ ⲦⲎⲢΟΥ· ⲘⲚ ⲚΝΟϬ ⲦⲎⲢΟΥ ⲚΑⲈΟⲢΑⲦΟС· ⲘⲚ ΝΑ-

ⲦⲘⲈСΟС ⲦⲎⲢΟΥ· ⲘⲚ ΝΑΠⲦΟΠΟС ⲦⲎⲢϤ ⲚΝΑΟΥΝΑⲘ·

ΑΥШ ⲘⲚ ⲚΝΟϬ ⲦⲎⲢΟΥ ⲚΝⲈΠⲢΟΒΟⲖΟΟΥⲈ ⲚⲦⲈ ΠΟΥ-

---

11 MS ⲚⲦⲈ ⲠⲚΑΟΥΝΑⲘ; better ⲚⲦⲈ ΠΟΥΟⲈⲒΝ.
17 MS ⲈⲒⲦⲈ; read ⲈⲒⲈ.

The Saviour answered and said to him: "Question that which thou dost wish to question, and I will reveal it to thee face to face without *parable*."

Andrew *however* answered and said: "My Lord, I am astonished and I *marvel* greatly *that* when men who are in the *world* and in the *body* of this *matter* come forth this *world*, they will surpass these *firmaments* and all these *archons* and all the lords and all the gods and all these great *invisible ones*, and all those of the *place* of those of the *Midst*, and those of the whole *place* of those of the right, and all the great ones of the *emanations* of the light[1], and enter into them all and *inherit* the Kingdom of the Light. This fact *now*, my Lord, is difficult for me."

Now when Andrew had said these things the *Spirit* of the *Saviour* was moved within him. He cried out and said: "*For* how long shall I bear with you? *For* how long shall I *suffer* you?* Have you *still* not *understood* and are ignorant? □ Do you not know and *understand*[2] that you and all the *angels* and all the *archangels* and the gods and the lords and all the *archons* and all the great *invisible ones* and all those of the *Midst* and those of the whole *place* of those of the right and all the great ones of the *emanations* of the light | and their whole glory, you are all with one

---

*   cf. Mt. 17.17; Mk. 9.19; Lk. 9.41
□   cf. Mt. 15.16, 17

---

[1]   (11) of the light; MS of those of the right.
[2]   (18) do you not know and understand?; Till: you have (thus) never understood and are (still) ignorant.

ΟΕΙΝ· ＭＮ ΠΕ‍ΥΕΟΟΥ ΤΗΡϤ· Ν‍ΤΕΤΝ‍ΖΕΝΕΒΟΛ ΤΗΡΤ‍Ν Ζ‍Ν

ΝΕΤ‍ΝΕΡΗΥ Ζ‍Μ ΠΙΟΥ‍Ω‍Ϣ‍Μ ‍ΝΟΥΩΤ ‍ΜΝ ϯ‍ΖΥΛΗ ‍ΝΟΥΩΤ·

‍ΜΝ ϯΟΥСΙΑ ‍ΝΟΥΩΤ: ΑΥΩ ‍ΝΤΕΤΝ‍ΖΕΝΕΒΟΛ Ζ‍Μ ΠΙΚΕ-

ΡΑСΜΟС ‍ΝΟΥΩΤ ΤΗΡΤ‍Ν· ΑΥΩ ΖΙΤ‍Ν ΤΚΕΛΕΥСΙС ‍ΜΠΙ-

5 Ϣ‍ΟΡ‍Π ‍ΜΜΥСΤΗΡΙΟΝ ΑΥΑΝΑΓΚΑΖΕ ‍ΜΠΚΕΡΑСΜΟС ΖΕΩС

Ϣ‍ΑΝΤΟΥС‍ΩΤϤ ΕΒΟΛ ‍ΝϬΙ ‍ΝΝΟϬ ΤΗΡΟΥ ‍ΝΝΕΠΡΟΒΟΛΟ-　‾СΚΟ b

ΟΥΕ ‍ΝΤΕ ΠΟΥΟΕΙΝ ‍ΜΝ ΠΕΥΕΟΟΥ ΤΗΡϤ· ΑΥΩ Ϣ‍ΑΝ-

ΤΟΥС‍ΩΤϤ ΕΒΟΛ ‍ΜΠΚΕΡΑСΜΟС ΑΥΩ ‍ΝΤΑΥС‍ΩΤϤ ΑΝ

ΕΒΟΛ ΖΙΤΟΟΤΟΥ ‍ΜΜΙΝ ‍ΜΜΟΟΥ· ΑΛΛΑ ‍ΝΤΑΥСΟΤϤΟΥ

10 Ζ‍Ν ΟΥΑΝΑΓΚΗ ΚΑΤΑ ΤΟΙΚΟΝΟΜΙΑ ‍ΜΠΙΟΥΑ ‍ΝΟΥΩΤ’

ΠΙΑΤϢ‍ΑΧΕ ΕΡΟϤ ΑΥΩ ‍ΝΤΟΟΥ ‍ΜΠΟΥ‍Ϣ‍Π‍ΖΙСΕ ΕΠΤΗΡϤ·

ΑΥΩ ‍ΜΠΟΥΜΕΤΑΒΑΛΕ ‍ΜΜΟΟΥ Ζ‍Ν ‍ΝΤΟΠΟС· ΟΥΔΕ ‍Μ-

ΠΟΥСΚΥΛΛΕ ‍ΜΜΟΟΥ ΕΠΤΗΡϤ· ΟΥΔΕ ‍ΜΠΟΥΜΕΤΑΓΓΙΖΕ

‍ΜΜΟΟΥ Ζ‍Ν ΖΕΝС‍ΩΜΑ ΕΥ‍Ϣ‍ΒΕΙΛΕΙΤ· ΟΥΔΕ ‍ΜΠΟΥ‍Ϣ‍ΩΠΕ

15 Ζ‍Ν ΛΑΛΥ ‍ΝΘΛΙΨΙС· ΜΑΛΙСΤΑ ϬΕ ‍ΝΤ‍ΩΤ‍Ν ΕΝΤΕΤ‍Ν-ΠΙ-

СΟΡ‍Μ ‍ΜΠΕΘΗСΑΥΡΟС· ΑΥΩ ‍ΝΤΕΤ‍Ν-ΠСΟΡ‍Μ ‍ΜΠΤΟΠΟС

‍ΝΝΑΟΥΝΑΜ ΑΥΩ ‍ΝΤΕΤ‍Ν-ΠСΟΡ‍Μ ‍ΜΠΤΟΠΟС ‍ΝΝΑΤΜΕ-

СΟС· ΑΥΩ ‍ΝΤΕΤ‍Ν-ΠСΟΡ‍Μ ‍ΝΝΑΖΟΡΑΤΟС ΤΗΡΟΥ ‍ΜΝ ‍Ν-

ΑΡΧΩΝ ΤΗΡΟΥ ΖΑΠΑ‍Ζ ΖΑΠΛ‍ΩС ‍ΝΤΕΤ‍Ν-ΠСΟΡ‍Μ ‍ΝΝΑΪ ΤΗ-　[‾СΛ]

20 ΡΟΥ· ΑΥΩ ΑΤΕΤΝ‍Ϣ‍ΩΠΕ Ζ‍Ν ΖΕΝΝΟϬ ‍ΝΖΙСΕ ‍ΜΝ ΖΕΝΝΟϬ

‍ΝΘΛΙΨΙС ΖΡΑΪ Ζ‍Ν ‍ΜΜΕΤΑΓΓΙСΜΟС Ζ‍Ν ΖΕΝС‍ΩΜΑ ΕΥ‍Ϣ‍Β-

ΕΙΛΕΙΤ ‍ΝΤΕ ΠΚΟСΜΟС· ΑΥΩ ‍ΜΝ‍ΝСΑ ΝΕΪΖΙСΕ ΤΗΡΟΥ

ΕΒΟΛ ΖΙΤΕΤΗΥΤ‍Ν ‍ΜΜΙΝ ‍ΜΜ‍ΩΤ‍Ν· ΑΤΕΤΝΑΓ‍ΩΝΙΖΕ ΑΥΩ

ΑΤΕΤ‍ΝΜΙ‍Ϣ‍Ε· ΕΑΤΕΤΝΑΠΟΤΑССΕ ‍ΜΠΚΟСΜΟС ΤΗΡϤ ‍ΜΝ

25 ΘΥΛΗ ΤΗΡ‍С ΕΤ‍ΝΖΗΤϤ· ΑΥΩ ‍ΜΠΕΤ‍ΝΚΑΤΟΤΤΗΥΤ‍Ν

ΕΒΟΛ ΕΤΕΤ‍Ν‍Ϣ‍ΙΝΕ· ΖΕΩС Ϣ‍ΑΝΤΕΤ‍ΝϬΙΝΕ ‍ΝΜΜΥСΤΗΡΙΟΝ

another out of one dough and one *matter* and one *substance*, and that you are all out of the same *mixture*. And through the *command* of the First *Mystery* the *mixture* was *compelled until* all the great ones of the *emanations* of the light and their whole glory were purified, and until they were purified from the *mixture*. And they have not been purified of themselves, *but* they have been purified from *necessity*, *according to* the *organisation* of the Only One, the Ineffable. And they have not suffered at all, and they have not *changed places*, *nor* have they *troubled* themselves at all, *nor* have they been *transferred* into various *bodies*, *nor* have they been in any *afflictions*. Now you *especially* are the dregs of the *Treasury*, and you are the dregs of the *place* of those of the right, and you are the dregs of the *place* of those of the *Midst*, and you are the dregs of all the *invisible ones* and all the *archons*; *in a word*, you are the dregs of all these. And you have come to be in great sufferings and great *afflictions* from the *transferences* into various *bodies* of the *world*. And after all these sufferings, of yourselves you have *striven* and fought, so that you have *renounced* the whole *world* and all the *matter* in it. And you have not ceased to seek *until* you found all the *mysteries* |

ⲧⲏⲣⲟⲩ ⲛ̄ⲧⲙⲛ̄ⲧⲉⲣⲟ ⲙ̄ⲡⲟⲩⲟⲉⲓⲛ ⲛⲁⲓ̈ ⲛ̄ⲧⲁⲩⲥⲱⲧϥ̄ ⲙ̄ⲙⲱⲧⲛ̄
ⲁⲩⲣ̄ⲧⲏⲩⲧⲛ̄ ⲛ̄ϩⲓⲗⲓⲕⲣⲓⲛⲉⲥ ⲛ̄ⲟⲩⲟⲉⲓⲛ ⲉϥⲥⲟⲧϥ̄ ⲉⲙⲁϣⲟ
ⲁⲩⲱ ⲁⲧⲉⲧⲛ̄ϣⲱⲡⲉ ⲛ̄ⲟⲩⲟⲉⲓⲛ ⲉϥⲥⲟⲧϥ̄ · ⲉⲧⲃⲉ ⲡⲁⲓ̈ ϭⲉ
ⲁⲓ̈ϫⲟⲟⲥ ⲉⲣⲱⲧⲛ̄ ⲙ̄ⲡⲟⲩⲟⲉⲓϣ ϫⲉ ϣⲓⲛⲉ ⲧⲁⲣⲉⲧⲛ̄ϭⲓⲛⲉ ·
5 ⲛ̄ⲧⲁⲓ̈ϫⲱ ⲟⲩⲛ ⲉⲣⲱⲧⲛ̄ ϫⲉ ⲉⲧⲉⲧⲛⲉϣⲓⲛⲉ ⲛ̄ⲥⲁ ⲙ̄ⲙⲩⲥⲧⲏ- [ⲥⲗ ᵇ]
ⲣⲓⲟⲛ ⲙ̄ⲡⲟⲩⲟⲉⲓⲛ ⲛⲁⲓ̈ ⲉϣⲁⲩⲥⲱⲧϥ̄ ⲙ̄ⲡⲥⲱⲙⲁ ⲛ̄ⲑⲩⲗⲏ ·
ⲁⲩⲱ ⲛ̄ⲥⲉⲁⲁϥ ⲛ̄ϩⲓⲗⲓⲕⲣⲓⲛⲉⲥ ⲛ̄ⲟⲩⲟⲓ̈ⲛ ⲉϥⲥⲟⲧϥ̄ ⲉⲙⲁϣⲟ ·
ϩⲁⲙⲏⲛ †ϫⲱ ⲙ̄ⲙⲟⲥ ⲉⲣⲱⲧⲛ̄ ϫⲉ ⲉⲧⲃⲉ ⲡⲅⲉⲛⲟⲥ ⲛ̄ⲧⲉ
ⲧⲙⲛ̄ⲧⲣⲱⲙⲉ ϫⲉ ⲥⲉⲟ ⲛ̄ϩⲩⲗⲓⲕⲟⲛ · ⲛ̄ⲧⲁⲓ̈ⲥⲕⲩⲗⲁⲓ ⲙ̄ⲙⲟⲓ̈
10 ⲁⲓ̈ⲉⲓⲛⲉ ⲛ̄ⲙⲙⲩⲥⲧⲏⲣⲓⲟⲛ ⲧⲏⲣⲟⲩ ⲛⲁⲩ ⲛ̄ⲧⲉ ⲡⲟⲩⲟⲉⲓⲛ ϫⲉ
ⲉⲓ̈ⲉⲥⲱⲧϥ̄ ⲙ̄ⲙⲟⲟⲩ ϫⲉ ⲛ̄ⲧⲟⲟⲩ ⲡⲉ ⲡⲥⲟⲣⲙ̄ ⲛ̄ⲑⲩⲗⲏ ⲧⲏⲣⲥ̄
ⲛ̄ⲧⲉ ⲧⲉⲩϩⲩⲗⲏ · ⲉⲙⲙⲟⲛ ⲉⲛⲉ ⲙⲛ̄-ⲗⲁⲁⲩ ⲙ̄ⲯⲩⲭⲏ ϩⲙ̄ ⲡⲅⲉⲛⲟⲥ ⲧⲏⲣϥ̄ ⲛ̄ⲧⲉ ⲧⲙⲛ̄ⲧⲣⲱⲙⲉ ⲛⲁⲟⲩϫⲁⲓ̈ · ⲁⲩⲱ ⲛ̄ⲛⲉⲩ-
ⲛⲁϣⲕⲗⲏⲣⲟⲛⲟⲙⲓ ⲁⲛ ⲡⲉ ⲛ̄ⲧⲙⲛ̄ⲧⲉⲣⲟ ⲙ̄ⲡⲟⲩⲟⲓ̈ⲛ · ⲛ̄ⲥⲁⲃⲏⲗ
15 ϫⲉ ⲁⲓ̈ⲉⲓⲛⲉ ⲛⲁⲩ ⲛ̄ⲙⲙⲩⲥⲧⲏⲣⲓⲟⲛ ⲛ̄ⲣⲉϥⲥⲱⲧϥ̄ · ⲛⲉⲡⲣⲟⲃⲟⲗⲟⲟⲩⲉ ⲅⲁⲣ ⲙ̄ⲡⲟⲩⲟⲉⲓⲛ ⲛ̄ⲥⲉⲣ̄ⲭⲣⲓⲁ ⲁⲛ ⲙ̄ⲙⲩⲥⲧⲏⲣⲓⲟⲛ ⲥⲉ-
ⲥⲟⲧϥ̄ ⲅⲁⲣ · ⲁⲗⲗⲁ ⲡⲅⲉⲛⲟⲥ ⲛ̄ⲧⲙⲛ̄ⲧⲣⲱⲙⲉ ⲛ̄ⲧⲟⲟⲩ ⲛⲉⲧⲣ̄-
ⲭⲣⲓⲁ ⲙ̄ⲙⲟⲟⲩ ⲉⲃⲟⲗ ϫⲉ ϩⲉⲛⲥⲟⲣⲙ̄ ⲛ̄ϩⲩⲗⲓⲕⲟⲛ ⲧⲏⲣⲟⲩ ⲛⲉ ·
ⲉⲧⲃⲉ ⲡⲁⲓ̈ ϭⲉ ⲁⲓ̈ϫⲟⲟⲥ ⲉⲣⲱⲧⲛ̄ ⲙ̄ⲡⲟⲩⲟⲉⲓϣ ϫⲉ ⲛⲉⲧ- ⲥⲗⲁ
20 ⲙⲟ̄ⲧⲛ ⲛ̄ⲥⲉⲣ̄ⲭⲣⲓⲁ ⲁⲛ ⲙ̄ⲡⲥⲁⲉⲓⲛ ⲁⲗⲗⲁ ⲛⲉⲧϣⲟⲟⲡ ⲕⲁⲕⲱⲥ
ⲛⲉ ⲉⲧⲉ ⲡⲁⲓ̈ ⲡⲉ ϫⲉ ⲛⲁⲡⲟⲩⲟⲉⲓⲛ ⲛ̄ⲥⲉⲣ̄ⲭⲣⲓⲁ ⲁⲛ ⲙ̄ⲙⲩⲥ-
ⲧⲏⲣⲓⲟⲛ ϫⲉ ϩⲉⲛⲟⲩⲟⲉⲓⲛ ⲛ̄ⲧⲟⲟⲩ ⲉⲩⲥⲟⲧϥ̄ ⲛⲉ · ⲁⲗⲗⲁ
ⲡⲅⲉⲛⲟⲥ ⲛ̄ⲧⲙⲛ̄ⲧⲣⲱⲙⲉ ⲛ̄ⲧⲟⲟⲩ ⲛⲉⲧⲣ̄ⲭⲣⲓⲁ ⲙ̄ⲙⲟⲟⲩ ϫⲉ
ϩⲉⲛⲥⲟⲣⲙ̄ ⲛ̄ϩⲩⲗⲓⲕⲟⲛ ⲛⲉ · ⲉⲧⲃⲉ ⲡⲁⲓ̈ ϭⲉ ⲕⲏⲣⲩⲥⲥⲉ ⲙ̄ⲡⲅⲉ-

---

21 MS ⲡⲁⲛⲟⲩⲡⲟⲩⲟⲉⲓⲛ; ⲛⲟⲩ crossed out.

of the Kingdom of the Light which purified you (and) made you to be *pure*, very purified light, and you have become purified light. Concerning this I once said to you: "Seek and ye shall find"*. *Now* I have said to you: "Seek the *mysteries* of the light which purify the *body* of *matter* and make it to be *pure*, very purified light. *Truly* I say to you, concerning the *race* of mankind, because it is *material* I have *troubled* myself, I have brought all the *mysteries* of the light to them, so that I should purify them, because they are the dregs of all the *materials* of their *matter*. Otherwise no *soul* of the whole *race* of mankind would be saved; nor would they be able to *inherit* the Kingdom of the Light unless I had brought to them the *mysteries* of purification. *For* the *emanations* of the light have no *need* of the *mysteries*, *for* they are purified; *but* the *race* of mankind have *need* because they are all *material* dregs. Concerning this I said to you once: "The healthy have no *need* of the physician, *but* they who are *sick*' ▫. That is, those of the light have no *need* of *mysteries* because they are purified lights; *but* the *race* of mankind have *need* of them because they are *material* dregs.

Because of this now, *preach* to the whole *race* | of

* Mt. 7.7; Lk. 11.9

▫ cf. Mt. 9.12; Mk. 2.17; Lk. 5.31

ⲛⲟⲥ ⲛ̄ⲧⲙⲛ̄ⲧⲣⲱⲙⲉ ⲧⲏⲣϥ ϫⲉ ⲙ̄ⲡⲣ̄ⲕⲁⲧⲉⲧⲏⲩⲧⲛ̄ ⲉⲃⲟⲗ
ⲉⲧⲉⲧⲛ̄ϣⲓⲛⲉ ϩ̄ⲙ ⲡⲉϩⲟⲟⲩ ⲙ̄ⲛ ⲧⲉⲩϣⲏ· ϩⲉⲱⲥ ϣⲁⲛⲧⲉ-
ⲧⲛ̄ϩⲉ ⲉⲙⲙⲩⲥⲧⲏⲣⲓⲟⲛ ⲛ̄ⲣⲉϥⲥⲱⲧϥ̄· ⲁⲩⲱ ⲁϫⲓⲥ ⲙ̄ⲡⲅⲉⲛⲟⲥ
ⲛ̄ⲧⲙⲛ̄ⲧⲣⲱⲙⲉ ϫⲉ ⲁⲡⲟⲧⲁⲥⲥⲉ ⲙ̄ⲡⲕⲟⲥⲙⲟⲥ ⲧⲏⲣϥ ⲙ̄ⲛ ⲑⲩ-
5 ⲗⲏ ⲧⲏⲣⲥ̄ ⲉⲧⲛ̄ϩⲏⲧϥ· ⲉⲙⲙⲟⲛ ⲡⲉⲧϫⲓ ⲁⲩⲱ ⲉⲧϯ ϩ̄ⲙ ⲡⲕⲟⲥⲙⲟⲥ ⲁⲩⲱ ⲉⲧⲟⲩⲱⲙ ⲁⲩⲱ ⲉⲧⲥⲱ ϩ̄ⲛ ⲧⲉϥϩⲩⲗⲏ· ⲁⲩⲱ
ⲉⲧⲟⲛⲥ̄ ϩ̄ⲛ ⲛⲉϥⲣⲟⲟⲩϣ ⲧⲏⲣⲟⲩ ⲙ̄ⲛ ⲛⲉϥϩⲟⲙⲓⲗⲓⲁ ⲧⲏⲣⲟⲩ·
ⲉϥⲥⲱⲟⲩϩ ⲛⲁϥ ⲉϩⲟⲩⲛ ⲛ̄ϩⲉⲛⲕⲉϩⲩⲗⲏ ⲉⲣⲁⲧϥ ⲛ̄ⲧⲉϥⲕⲉϩⲩ- ⳽ⲗⲁ ᵇ
ⲗⲏ· ⲉⲃⲟⲗ ϫⲉ ⲡⲉⲓ̈ⲕⲟⲥⲙⲟⲥ ⲧⲏⲣϥ ⲙ̄ⲛ ⲛⲉⲧⲛ̄ϩⲏⲧϥ ⲧⲏⲣϥ·
10 ⲙ̄ⲛ ⲛⲉϥϩⲟⲙⲓⲗⲓⲁ ⲧⲏⲣⲟⲩ ϩⲉⲛⲥⲟⲣⲙ̄ ⲛ̄ϩⲩⲗⲓⲕⲟⲛ ⲛⲉ· ⲁⲩⲱ
ⲥⲉⲛⲁϫⲛⲉ-ⲡⲟⲩⲁ ⲡⲟⲩⲁ ⲉⲣⲟⲟⲩ ⲉⲧⲃⲉ ⲡⲉⲩⲧ̄ⲃⲃⲟ· ⲉⲧⲃⲉ
ⲡⲁⲓ̈ ⲟⲩⲛ ⲁⲓ̈ϫⲟⲟⲥ ⲉⲣⲱⲧⲛ̄ ⲙ̄ⲡⲓⲟⲩⲟⲉⲓϣ ϫⲉ ⲁⲡⲟⲧⲁⲥⲥⲉ
ⲙ̄ⲡⲕⲟⲥⲙⲟⲥ ⲧⲏⲣϥ ⲙ̄ⲛ ⲑⲩⲗⲏ ⲧⲏⲣⲥ̄ ⲉⲧⲛ̄ϩⲏⲧϥ ϫⲉ ⲛ̄ⲛⲉ-
ⲧⲛ̄ⲥⲱⲟⲩϩ ⲛⲏⲧⲛ̄ ⲉϩⲟⲩⲛ ⲛ̄ⲕⲉϩⲩⲗⲏ ⲉⲣⲁⲧⲥ̄ ⲛ̄ⲧⲉⲧⲛ̄ⲕⲉϩⲩ-
15 ⲗⲏ ⲉⲧⲛ̄ϩⲏⲧⲟⲩ· ⲉⲧⲃⲉ ⲡⲁⲓ̈ ⲟⲩⲛ ⲕⲏⲣⲩⲥⲥⲉ ⲙ̄ⲡⲅⲉⲛⲟⲥ ⲧⲏ-
ⲣϥ̄ ⲛ̄ⲧⲉ ⲧⲙⲛ̄ⲧⲣⲱⲙⲉ ϫⲉ ⲁⲡⲟⲧⲁⲥⲥⲉ ⲙ̄ⲡⲕⲟⲥⲙⲟⲥ ⲧⲏⲣϥ
ⲙ̄ⲛ ⲛⲉϥϩⲟⲙⲓⲗⲓⲁ ⲧⲏⲣⲟⲩ ϫⲉ ⲛ̄ⲛⲉⲧⲛ̄ⲥⲱⲟⲩϩ ⲛⲏⲧⲛ̄ ⲉϩⲟⲩⲛ
ⲛ̄ⲕⲉϩⲩⲗⲏ ⲉⲣⲁⲧⲥ̄ ⲛ̄ⲧⲉⲧⲛ̄ⲕⲉϩⲩⲗⲏ ⲉⲧϩⲛ̄ⲧⲏⲛⲟⲩ· ⲁⲩⲱ
ⲁϫⲓⲥ ⲉⲣⲟⲟⲩ ϫⲉ ⲙ̄ⲡⲣ̄ⲕⲁⲧⲉⲧⲏⲩⲧⲛ̄ ⲉⲃⲟⲗ ⲉⲧⲉⲧⲛ̄ϣⲓⲛⲉ
20 ϩ̄ⲙ ⲡⲉϩⲟⲟⲩ ⲙ̄ⲛ ⲧⲉⲩϣⲏ· ⲁⲩⲱ ⲙ̄ⲡⲣ̄ⲁⲛⲁⲕⲧⲉ ⲙ̄ⲙⲱⲧⲛ̄
ϣⲁⲛⲧⲉⲧⲛ̄ϭⲓⲛⲉ ⲛ̄ⲙⲙⲩⲥⲧⲏⲣⲓⲟⲛ ⲛ̄ⲣⲉϥⲥⲱⲧϥ̄· ⲛⲁⲓ̈ ⲉⲧⲛⲁ- [⳽ⲗⲃ]
ⲥⲉⲧⲧⲏⲛⲟⲩ· ⲛ̄ⲥⲉⲣ̄ⲧⲏⲩⲧⲛ̄ ⲛ̄ϩⲓⲗⲓⲕⲣⲓⲛⲉⲥ ⲛ̄ⲟⲩⲟⲉⲓⲛ ⲛ̄ⲧⲉ-

---

1 ⲙⲛ̄ⲧ in ⲧⲙⲛ̄ⲧⲣⲱⲙⲉ inserted in margin.
2 MS originally ⲛ̄ⲧⲉⲧⲛ̄ϭⲓⲛⲉ; ϣ inserted above.
8 MS ⲉⲣⲁⲧϥ̄; read ⲉⲣⲁⲧⲥ̄.
9 MS ⲧⲏⲣϥ̄; better ⲧⲏⲣⲟⲩ.
15 MS ⲉⲧⲛ̄ϩⲏⲧⲟⲩ; read ⲉⲧϩⲛ̄ⲧⲏⲛⲟⲩ.
20 MS ⲁⲛⲁⲕⲧⲉ; read ⲁⲛⲁⲕⲧⲁ.

mankind : do not cease to seek by day and night, *until* you find the *mysteries* of purification. And say to the *race* of mankind : *renounce* the whole *world* and all the *matter* in it. Because he who buys and sells [1] in the *world*, and who eats and drinks of its *matter*, and who lives amongst all its cares and all its *relationships* gathers to himself still further *matter* to his remaining *matter*. Because this whole *world* and all those within it and all its *relationships* are *material* dregs. And each one of them will be questioned concerning his purity. Concerning this *now* I said to you once : '*Renounce* the whole *world* and all the *matter* within it, so that you do not gather for yourselves further *matter* to your remaining *matter* which is within you'. Concerning this *now preach* to the whole *race* of mankind : '*Renounce* the whole *world* and all its *relationships*, lest you gather for yourselves further *matter* to your remaining *matter* which is within you'. And say to them : 'Do not cease from seeking by day and night, and do not *refresh* yourselves until you find the *mysteries* of purification, which will purify you and make you to be *pure* light, so that | you go to the height and *inherit* the light of my kingdom.'

---

[1] (5) buys and sells; lit. receives and gives.

ⲦⲚⲂⲰⲔ' ⲈⲠⲬⲒⲤⲈ ⲚⲦⲈⲦⲚⲔⲖⲎⲢⲞⲚⲞⲘⲒ ⲘⲠⲞⲨⲞⲈⲒⲚ ⲚⲦⲀ-
ⲘⲚⲦⲈⲢⲞ· ⲦⲈⲚⲞⲨ ⳠⲈ ⲚⲦⲞⲔ' ⲞⲚ ⲀⲚⲆⲢⲈⲀⲤ ⲘⲚ ⲚⲈⲔⲤⲚⲎⲨ
ⲦⲎⲢⲞⲨ ⲚⲈⲔϢⲂⲢⲘⲀⲐⲎⲦⲎⲤ· ⲈⲦⲂⲈ ⲚⲈⲦⲚⲀⲠⲞⲦⲀⲅⲎ ⲘⲚ
ⲚⲈⲦⲚⲎⲒⲤⲈ ⲦⲎⲢⲞⲨ ⲚⲦⲀⲦⲈⲦⲚϢⲞⲠⲞⲨ ⲔⲀⲦⲀ ⲦⲞⲠⲞⲤ ⲘⲚ
5 ⲚⲈⲦⲚⲠⲀⲢⲀⲂⲞⲖⲎ ⲔⲀⲦⲀ ⲦⲞⲠⲞⲤ· ⲀⲨⲰ ⲘⲚ ⲚⲈⲦⲚⲘⲈⲦⲀⲅ-
ⲅⲒⲤⲘⲞⲤ ⲎⲚ ⲚⲤⲰⲘⲀ ⲈⲨϢⲂⲈⲒⲀⲈⲒⲦ' ⲀⲨⲰ ⲘⲚ ⲚⲈⲦⲚⲐⲖⲒ̈ⲯⲒⲤ
ⲦⲎⲢⲞⲨ· ⲀⲨⲰ ⲘⲚⲚⲤⲀ ⲚⲀⲒ̈ ⲦⲎⲢⲞⲨ ⲀⲦⲈⲦⲚⲬⲒ ⲚⲘⲘⲨⲤⲦⲎ-
ⲢⲒⲞⲚ ⲚⲢⲈϤⲤⲰⲦϤ· ⲀⲦⲈⲦⲚⲢⲎⲒⲀⲒⲔⲢⲒⲚⲈⲤ ⲚⲞⲨⲞⲈⲒⲚ ⲈϤⲤⲞⲦϤ
ⲈⲘⲀϢⲞ· ⲈⲦⲂⲈ ⲠⲀⲒ̈ ⳠⲈ ⲦⲈⲦⲚⲀⲂⲰⲔ' ⲈⲠⲬⲒⲤⲈ· ⲚⲦⲈⲦⲚⲢ-
10 ⲠϨⲞⲨⲚ ⲚⲚⲦⲞⲠⲞⲤ ⲦⲎⲢⲞⲨ ⲚⲚⲒⲚⲞⳠ ⲦⲎⲢⲞⲨ ⲘⲠⲢⲞⲂⲞⲖⲞ-
ⲞⲨⲈ ⲚⲦⲈ ⲠⲞⲨⲞⲈⲒⲚ· ⲚⲦⲈⲦⲚϢⲰⲠⲈ ⲈⲦⲈⲦⲚⲞ ⲚⲢⲢⲞ ⲎⲚ [ⲤⲖⲂ ᵇ]
ⲦⲘⲚⲦⲈⲢⲞ ⲘⲠⲞⲨⲞⲈⲒⲚ ⲚϢⲀⲈⲚⲈϨ· [ⲦⲀⲒ̈ ⲦⲈ ⲦⲀⲠⲞⲪⲀⲤⲒⲤ
ⲚⲚϢⲀⲬⲈ ⲈⲦⲈⲦⲚϢⲒⲚⲈ ⲚⲤⲰⲞⲨ: ⲦⲈⲚⲞⲨ ⳠⲈ ⲞⲚ ⲀⲚ-
ⲆⲢⲈⲀⲤ ⲀⲒⲦⲒ ⲈⲔϢⲞⲞⲠ' ϨⲚ ⲞⲨⲘⲚⲦⲀⲠⲒⲤⲦⲞⲤ ⲀⲨⲰ ⲘⲚ
15 ⲞⲨⲘⲚⲦⲀⲦⲤⲞⲞⲨⲚ·] ⲀⲖⲖⲀ ⲈⲦⲈⲦⲚϢⲀⲚⲈⲒ' ⲈⲂⲞⲖ ϨⲘ ⲠⲤⲰ-
ⲘⲀ ⲚⲦⲈⲦⲚⲂⲰⲔ' ⲈⲠⲬⲒⲤⲈ ⲚⲦⲈⲦⲚⲠⲰϨ ⲈⲒⲦⲞⲠⲞⲤ ⲚⲚⲀⲢ-
ⲬⲰⲚ· ⲚⲀⲢⲬⲰⲚ ⲦⲎⲢⲞⲨ ⲚⲀⲬⲒϢⲠⲈ ⲚⲚⲀϨⲢⲎⲦⲚ· ⲬⲈ Ⲛ-
ⲦⲈⲦⲚ-ⲠⲤⲞⲢⲘ ⲚⲦⲈⲨϨⲨⲬⲎ· ⲀⲨⲰ ⲀⲦⲈⲦⲚⲢ-ⲞⲨⲞⲈⲒⲚ ⲈϤ-
ⲤⲞⲦϤ ⲚϨⲞⲨⲞ ⲈⲢⲞⲞⲨ ⲦⲎⲢⲞⲨ· ⲀⲨⲰ ⲈⲦⲈⲦⲚϢⲀⲚⲠⲰϨ
20 ⲈⲠⲦⲞⲠⲞⲤ ⲚⲚⲒⲚⲞⳠ ⲚⲀϨⲞⲢⲀⲦⲞⲤ ⲘⲚ ⲠⲦⲞⲠⲞⲤ ⲚⲚⲀⲦⲘⲈ-
ⲤⲞⲤ ⲘⲚ ⲚⲀⲞⲨⲚⲀⲘ ⲘⲚ ⲚⲦⲞⲠⲞⲤ ⲚⲚⲒⲚⲞⳠ ⲦⲎⲢⲞⲨ ⲘⲠⲢⲞ-
ⲂⲞⲖⲎ ⲚⲦⲈ ⲠⲞⲨⲞⲈⲒⲚ· ⲦⲈⲦⲚⲀⲬⲒ-ⲈⲞⲞⲨ ⲚⲚⲀϨⲢⲀⲨ ⲦⲎⲢⲞⲨ
ⲬⲈ ⲚⲦⲰⲦⲚ ⲠⲈ ⲠⲤⲞⲢⲘ ⲚⲦⲈⲨϨⲨⲬⲎ· ⲀⲨⲰ ⲀⲦⲈⲦⲚⲢ-ⲞⲨ-
ⲞⲨⲞⲈⲒⲚ ⲈϤⲤⲞⲦϤ ⲚϨⲞⲨⲞ ⲈⲢⲞⲞⲨ ⲦⲎⲢⲞⲨ· ⲀⲨⲰ ⲚⲦⲞ- ⲤⲖⲅ

---

5   MS ⲠⲈⲦⲦⲠⲀⲢⲀⲂⲞⲖⲎ; read ⲠⲈⲦⲦⲘⲈⲦⲀⲂⲞⲖⲎ; ⲘⲚ ⲚⲈ crossed out before
ⲔⲀⲦⲀ.

12-15   this passage is better transferred to 253.2 ff.

Now at this time, thou Andrew and all thy brothers, thy fellow-*disciples*, because of your *renunciations* and all your sufferings which you have received in *every place*, and your *changes* in *every place*, and your *transferences* into various *bodies*, and all your *afflictions*; and (that) after all these things you have received the *mysteries* of purification, you have become *pure*, very purified light; because of this now, you will go to the height, you will enter into all the *places* of all the great *emanations* of the light, and become rulers (kings) in the eternal Kingdom of the Light [1].

But when you come forth from the *body* and go to the height and reach the *place* of the *archons*, all the *archons* will be put to shame before you, because you are the dregs of their *matter* and you have become more purified light than them all. And when you reach the *place* of the great *invisible* ones, and the *place* of those of the *Midst* and those of the right, and the *places* of all the great *emanations* of the light, you will receive glory before them all because you are the dregs of their *matter*, and you have become more purified light than them all. And all the *places* | will

---

[1] (12-15) This is the answer ... ignorance; this passage interrupts the sequence and is transferred to 253.2.

ΠΟϹ ΤΗΡΟΥ ΝΑ2ΥΜΝΕΥΕ 2ΑΤΕΤΝ2Η 2ΕШϹ ШΑΝΤΕ-
ΤΝΒШΚ ΕΠΤΟΠΟϹ ΝΤΜΝΤΕΡΟ · ⟨ΤΕΝΟΥ 6Ε ΟΝ ΑΝ-
ΔΡΕΑϹ ΔΙΤΙ ΕΚШΟΟΠ 2Ν ΟΥΜΝΤΑΠΙϹΤΟϹ ΑΥШ ΜΝ
ΟΥΑΤϹΟΟΥΝ⟩ ·

5 ΝΑΪ 6Ε ΕϥΧШ ΜΜΟΟΥ Ν6Ι ΠϹШΤΗΡ · ΑϥΕΙΜΕ Ν6Ι
ΔΝΔΡΕΑϹ ΦΑΝΕΡШϹ · ΟΥΜΟΝΟΝ ΝΤΟϥ ΑΛΛΑ ΑΥΕΙΜΕ
ΤΗΡΟΥ Ν6Ι ΜΜΑΘΗΤΗϹ 2Ν ΟΥϹΟΟΥΤΝ ΧΕ ϹΕΝΑ-
ΚΛΗΡΟΝΟΜΙ ΝΤΜΝΤΕΡΟ ΜΠΟΥΟΕΙΝ · ΑΥΠΑ2ΤΟΥ ΤΗ-
ΡΟΥ 2Ι ΝΕΥΕΡΗΥ ΕΧΝ ΝΟΥΕΡΗΤΕ ΝΙϹ · ΑΥШШ Ε-
10 ΒΟΛ ΑΥΡΙΜΕ ΑΥΠΑΡΑΚΑΛΕΙ ΜΠϹШΤΗΡ ΕΥΧШ ΜΜΟϹ ΧΕ
ΠΧΟΕΙϹ ΚШ ΕΒΟΛ ΜΠΝΟΒΕ ΝΤΜΝΤΑΤϹΟΟΥΝ ΜΠΕΝ-
ϹΟΝ: ΑϥΟΥШШΒ Ν6Ι ΠϹШΤΗΡ ΠΕΧΑϥ ΧΕ ┼ΚШ ΕΒΟΛ
ΑΥШ ┼ΝΑΚШ ΕΒΟΛ · ΕΤΒΕ ΠΑΪ 6Ε ΝΤΑϥΤΝΝΟΟΥΤ' Ν6Ι
ΠШΟΡΠ ΜΜΥϹΤΗΡΙΟΝ ΕΤΡΑΚШ ΕΒΟΛ ΝΝΝΟΒΕ ΝΟΥΟΝ
15 ΝΙΜ: ϩ —

   [ϩ — ϩϩ — ϩϩ — ϩϩ — ϩϩ —]

   [ΟΥΜΕΡΟϹ ΝΤΕ ΝΤΕΥΧΟϹ]

   [— ϩϩ — ΜΠϹШΤΗΡ —]

20 . . . .

  . . . .

  . . . .

ΑΥШ ΝΕΤΜΠШΑ ΝΜΜΥϹΤΗΡΙΟΝ ΕΤΚΑΤΟΙΚΙ 2Μ ΠΙΑΤ- ϹΑΓ ᵇ
ШΑΧΕ ΕΡΟϥ · ΕΤΕ ΝΤΟΟΥ ΠΕ ΕΤΕ ΜΠΟΥΠΡΟΕΛΟϹ

2-4 the sentence transferred by Schmidt from 252.13-15; the sense is better if
  the previous line is included as indicated.

17 the title at the foot of column 1 of ϹΑΓ is transferred to the foot of column 2
  of ϹΛΛ.; the text begins again in the middle of a sentence at the top of
  column 2 of ϹΑΓ; the lacuna here is of unknown length.

sing praises before you *until* you go to the *place* of the kingdom. ⟨This is the *answer* to the words which you questioned. Now at this time, Andrew, art thou *still* in *disbelief* and in *ignorance*?⟩"

Now when the Saviour said these things Andrew knew *clearly*, and *not only* he *but* the *disciples* all knew with certainty that they would *inherit* the Kingdom of the Light. They all prostrated themselves together at the feet of Jesus. They cried out, they wept, they *begged* the *Saviour*, saying: "O Lord, forgive the sin of ignorance of our brother."

The *Saviour* answered and said: "I forgive and I will forgive. For this reason has the First *Mystery* sent me, that I should forgive the sins of everyone."

[A *part* of the *Books* of the *Saviour*.] [1]

(Lacuna) [2]

101. And those who are worthy of *mysteries* which *dwell* in the Ineffable which did not *come forth*, | these exist

---

[1] (16) see Introduction p. XIII; the title properly belongs after 255.16.
[2] (19-22) lacuna preceding 253.23.

ⲉⲃⲟⲗ· ⲛⲁⲓ̈ ϣⲟⲟⲡ ϩⲁⲑⲏ ⲙ̅ⲡϣⲟⲣ̅ⲡ̅ ⲙ̅ⲙⲩⲥⲧⲏⲣⲓⲟⲛ· ⲁⲩⲱ ⲕⲁⲧⲁ ⲟⲩⲧⲟⲛⲧ̅ⲛ̅ ⲙ̅ⲛ̅ ⲟⲩϩⲓⲥⲟⲥ ⲛ̅ⲧⲉ ⲡϣⲁϫⲉ ϫⲉ ⲉⲧⲉⲧ̅ⲛ̅ⲛⲟⲓ̈ ⲙ̅ⲙⲟϥ· ϩⲱⲥⲧⲉ ⲛ̅ⲧⲟⲟⲩ ⲛⲉ ⲙ̅ⲙⲉⲗⲟⲥ ⲙ̅ⲡⲓⲁⲧϣⲁϫⲉ ⲉⲣⲟϥ· ⲁⲩⲱ ⲡⲟⲩⲁ ⲡⲟⲩⲁ ⲉϥϣⲟⲟⲡ ⲕⲁⲧⲁ ⲧⲉⲧⲓⲙⲏ ⲙ̅ⲡⲉϥⲉⲟⲟⲩ· ⲧⲁⲡⲉ ⲕⲁⲧⲁ ⲧⲉⲧⲓⲙⲏ ⲛ̅ⲧⲁⲡⲉ· ⲁⲩⲱ ⲡⲃⲁⲗ' ⲕⲁⲧⲁ ⲧⲉⲧⲓⲙⲏ ⲛ̅ⲃ̅ⲃⲁⲗ· ⲁⲩⲱ ⲡⲙⲁⲁϫⲉ ⲕⲁⲧⲁ ⲧⲉⲧⲓⲙⲏ ⲛ̅ⲙ̅ⲙⲁⲁϫⲉ· ⲁⲩⲱ ⲡⲕⲉⲥⲉⲉⲡⲉ ⲛ̅ⲙ̅ⲙⲉⲗⲟⲥ· ϩⲱⲥⲧⲉ ⲉⲣⲉ ⲡϩⲱⲃ ⲟⲩⲱⲛ̅ϩ̅ ⲉⲃⲟⲗ ϫⲉ ⲟⲩⲙⲏⲏϣⲉ ⲙ̅ⲙⲉⲗⲟⲥ ⲡⲉ ⲁⲗⲗⲁ ⲟⲩⲥⲱⲙⲁ ⲛ̅ⲟⲩⲱⲧ ⲡⲉ· ⲡⲁⲓ̈ ⲙⲉⲛ ⲉⲓ̈ϫⲱ ⲙ̅ⲙⲟϥ ϩ̅ⲛ̅ ⲟⲩⲡⲁⲣⲁⲇⲓⲅⲙⲁ ⲙ̅ⲛ̅ ⲟⲩϩⲓⲥⲟⲥ ⲙ̅ⲛ̅ ⲟⲩⲧⲟⲛⲧ̅ⲛ̅· ⲁⲗⲗⲁ ϩ̅ⲛ̅ ⲟⲩⲁⲗⲏⲑⲉⲓⲁ ⲁⲛ ⲙ̅ⲙⲟⲣⲫⲏ· ⲟⲩⲧⲉ ⲛ̅ⲧⲁⲓ̈ⲟⲩⲉⲛ̅ϩ̅-ⲡϣⲁϫⲉ ⲉⲃⲟⲗ ⲁⲛ ϩ̅ⲛ̅ ⲟⲩⲙⲉ ⲁⲗⲗⲁ ⲡⲙⲩⲥⲧⲏⲣⲓⲟⲛ ⲙ̅ⲡⲓⲁⲧϣⲁϫⲉ ⲉⲣⲟϥ· ⲁⲩⲱ ⲙⲉⲗⲟⲥ** ⲛⲓⲙ ⲉⲧ̅ⲛ̅ϩⲏⲧ̅ϥ̅ ⲕⲁⲧⲁ ⲡϣⲁϫⲉ ⲉⲛⲧⲁⲓ̈ⲧⲟⲛⲧ̅ⲛ̅ [ⲥⲗ̅ⲁ̅.] ⲉⲣⲟϥ ⲉⲧⲉ ⲛⲉⲧ̅ⲙ̅ⲙⲁⲩ ⲛⲉⲧⲕⲁⲧⲟⲓⲕⲓ ⲉⲡⲙⲩⲥⲧⲏⲣⲓⲟⲛ ⲙ̅ⲡⲓⲁⲧϣⲁϫⲉ ⲉⲣⲟϥ ⲙ̅ⲛ̅ ⲛⲉⲧⲕⲁⲧⲟⲓⲕⲓ ⲛ̅ϩⲏⲧ̅ϥ̅· ⲁⲩⲱ ⲡⲕⲉϣⲟⲙⲛⲧ ⲛ̅ⲭⲱⲣⲏⲙⲁ ⲉⲧ̅ⲙ̅ⲛ̅ⲛ̅ⲥⲱⲟⲩ ⲕⲁⲧⲁ ⲙ̅ⲙⲩⲥⲧⲏⲣⲓⲟⲛ ⲛⲁⲓ̈ ⲧⲏⲣⲟⲩ ϩ̅ⲛ̅ ⲟⲩⲁⲗⲏⲑⲉⲓⲁ ⲙ̅ⲛ̅ ⲟⲩⲙⲉ· ⲁⲛⲟⲕ ⲡⲉ ⲡⲉⲩⲁϩⲟ ⲧⲏⲣⲟⲩ ⲡⲁⲓ̈ ⲉⲧⲉ ⲙ̅ⲛ̅-ⲕⲉⲁϩⲟ ⲛ̅ⲃ̅ⲗⲗⲁϥ· ⲡⲁⲓ̈ ⲉⲧⲉ ⲙ̅ⲛ̅ⲧ̅ϥ̅-ⲡⲉϥϩⲓⲇⲓⲟⲛ ϩⲓϫ̅ⲙ̅ ⲡⲕⲟⲥⲙⲟⲥ· ⲁⲗⲗⲁ ⲉⲧⲓ ⲟⲩⲛ-ϣⲁϫⲉ ϣⲟⲟⲡ ⲁⲩⲱ ⲟⲩⲛ-ⲙⲩⲥⲧⲏⲣⲓⲟⲛ ⲁⲩⲱ ⲟⲩⲛ-ⲧⲟⲡⲟⲥ· ⲧⲉⲛⲟⲩ ϭⲉ ⲟⲩⲙⲁⲕⲁⲣⲓⲟⲥ ⲡⲉ ⲡⲉⲛⲧⲁϥⲉⲓⲛⲉ ⲛ̅ⲙ̅ⲙⲩⲥⲧⲏⲣⲓⲟⲛ ⲉⲡⲥⲁⲛ̅ⲃⲟⲗ· ⲁⲩⲱ ⲟⲩⲛⲟⲩⲧⲉ ⲡⲉ ⲡⲉⲛⲧⲁϥϭ̅ⲛ̅-ⲛⲉⲓ̈ϣⲁϫⲉ ⲛ̅ⲙ̅ⲙⲩⲥⲧⲏⲣⲓⲟⲛ ⲙ̅ⲡⲙⲉϩⲥⲛⲁⲩ ⲛ̅ⲭⲱⲣⲏⲙⲁ ⲉⲧ̅ⲛ̅ⲧⲙⲏⲧⲉ· ⲁⲩⲱ ⲟⲩⲥ̅ⲱ̅ⲣ̅ ⲡⲉ ⲁⲩⲱ ⲟⲩⲁⲭⲱⲣⲏⲧⲟⲛ ⲡⲉ ⲡⲉⲛⲧⲁϥϭⲓⲛⲉ ⲛ̅ⲛ̅-

9 MS ⲉⲓ̈ϫⲱ; better ⲁⲓ̈ϫⲱ.

17 ϩ̅ⲛ̅ ⲟⲩⲁ expunged before ⲛⲁⲓ̈.

21 MS ⲁϥⲉⲓⲛⲉ; read ⲁϥϭⲓⲛⲉ. MS ⲛ̅ⲙ̅ⲙⲩⲥⲧ. ⲉⲡⲥⲁⲛ̅ⲃⲟⲗ; read ⲛ̅ⲛ̅ϣⲁϫⲉ ⲛ̅ⲙ̅ⲙⲩⲥⲧ. ⟨ⲙ̅ⲡϣⲟⲣ̅ⲡ̅ ⲛ̅ⲭⲱⲣⲏⲙⲁ⟩ ⲉⲡⲥⲁⲛ̅ⲃⲟⲗ

before the First *Mystery*; and *according to* a likeness and an *image* of the word, that you may *understand, so that* they are *members* of the Ineffable and each one exists *according to* the *worth* of his glory. The head *according to* the *worth* of the head; and the eye *according to* the *worth* of eyes; and the ear *according to* the *worth* of ears; and the rest of the *members, so that* the fact is revealed that it is a multitude of *members but* one *body*. This *indeed* I say as a *model* and *image* and likeness, *but* not in a *true form, nor* have I revealed the word truly *but* the *mystery* of the Ineffable. And all the *members* which are within it, *according to* the word with which I have compared it, namely those who *dwell* with the *mystery* of the Ineffable and those who dwell in it, and also the three *spaces* after them *according to* the *mysteries* — to all these in *truth* and verihood, I am their treasure, and excepting me there is no other treasure, and there is not its *like* in the *world. But nevertheless* there are words and *mysteries* and *places. Blessed* now is he who has found [1] the *mysteries* ⟨of the first *space*⟩ without; and he is a god who has found these words of the *mysteries* of the second *space* which is in the *Midst*; and he is a *saviour* and an *incomprehensible one* who has found the | words

---

[1] (21) found; MS : brought (see 254.24). MS : the mysteries; Schmidt : ⟨the words of⟩ the mysteries.

ϢⲀϪⲈ ⲚⲘⲘⲨⲤⲦⲎⲢⲒⲞⲚ [ⲘⲚ ⲚϢⲀϪⲈ] ⲘⲠⲘⲈϨϢⲞⲘⲚⲦ

ⲬⲰⲢⲎⲘⲀ ⲈⲦϨⲒⲠⲤⲀⲚϨⲞⲨⲚ· ⲀⲨⲰ ϤⲞⲨⲞⲦⲂ ⲈⲠⲦⲎⲢϤ· ⲀⲨ

ϤϢⲎⲠ· ⲚⲚⲈⲦϢⲞⲞⲠ· ϨⲘ ⲠⲘⲈϨϢⲞⲘⲚⲦ ⲚⲬⲰⲢⲎⲘⲀ ⲈⲦ

ⲘⲀⲨ· ⲈⲂⲞⲖ ϪⲈ ⲠⲘⲨⲤⲦⲎⲢⲒⲞⲚ ⲈⲦⲞⲨϢⲞⲞⲠ· ⲚϨⲎⲦϤ

5 ⲠⲈⲦⲞⲨⲀϨⲈⲢⲀⲦⲞⲨ ⲚϨⲎⲦϤ ⲀϤϪⲒⲦϤ· ⲈⲦⲂⲈ ⲠⲀⲒ ϬⲈ Ⲁ

ϢⲰϢ ⲞⲨⲂⲎⲨ· ⲠⲈⲚⲦⲀϤϬⲒⲚⲈ ϨⲰⲰϤ ⲚⲚϢⲀϪⲈ ⲚⲘⲘⲨ

ⲦⲎⲢⲒⲞⲚ ⲚⲀⲒ ⲚⲦⲀⲒⲤϨⲀⲒⲤⲞⲨ ⲚⲎⲦⲚ ⲔⲀⲦⲀ ⲞⲨⲦⲞⲚⲦⲚ· Ϫ

ⲚⲦⲞⲞⲨ ⲚⲈ ⲘⲘⲈⲖⲞⲤ ⲘⲠⲒⲀⲦϢⲀϪⲈ ⲈⲢⲞϤ· ϨⲀⲘⲎⲚ †Ϫ

ⲘⲘⲞⲤ ⲚⲎⲦⲚ ϪⲈ ⲠⲈⲚⲦⲀϤϬⲒⲚⲈ ⲚⲚϢⲀϪⲈ ⲚⲘⲘⲨⲤⲦⲎⲢⲒⲞ

10 ⲈⲦⲘⲘⲀⲨ ϨⲚ ⲞⲨⲘⲈ ⲚⲦⲈ ⲠⲚⲞⲨⲦⲈ ϪⲈ ⲠⲢⲰⲘⲈ ⲈⲦⲘⲘⲀ

ⲚⲦⲞϤ ⲠⲈ ⲠϢⲞⲢⲠ ϨⲚ ⲞⲨⲀⲖⲎⲐⲒⲀ· ⲀⲨⲰ ϤϢⲚϢ ⲞⲨⲂⲎ

ϪⲈ ⲈⲦⲂⲈ ⲚϢⲀϪⲈ ⲈⲦⲘⲘⲀⲨ ⲘⲚ ⲘⲘⲨⲤⲦⲎⲢⲒⲞⲚ· [ⲀⲨ

ⲚⲦⲀ ⲠⲦⲎⲢϤ ϨⲰⲰϤ ⲀϨⲈⲢⲀⲦϤ ⲈⲦⲂⲈ ⲠϢⲞⲢⲠ ⲈⲦⲘⲘⲀⲨ· Ⲉ

ⲂⲈ ⲠⲀⲒ ⲠⲈⲚⲦⲀϤϬⲒⲚⲈ ⲚⲚϢⲀϪⲈ ⲚⲘⲘⲨⲤⲦⲎⲢⲒⲞⲚ ⲈⲦⲘⲘⲀ

15 ϤϢⲚϢ ⲘⲚ ⲠϢⲞⲢⲠ· ⲦⲈⲄⲚⲰⲤⲒⲤ ⲄⲀⲢ ⲘⲠⲤⲞⲞⲨⲚ ⲘⲠⲒⲀ

ϢⲀϪⲈ ⲈⲢⲞⲤ ⲚⲦⲀⲒϢⲀϪⲈ ⲚⲚⲘⲎⲦⲚ ⲚϨⲎⲦⲤ ⲘⲠⲞⲞⲨ: ⳾

ⳋ — ⳋ — ⳋ — ⳋ — ⳋ — ⳋ —

⟨ⲞⲨⲘⲈⲢⲞⲤ ⲚⲦⲈ ⲚⲦⲈⲨⲬⲞⲤ⟩

⟨ⲘⲠⲤⲰⲦⲎⲢ⟩

---

1 MS ⲘⲠⲒ ⲠⲒϢⲀϪⲈ better omitted.
3 MS ϤϢⲎⲠ· ⲠⲒⲚⲈⲦϢⲞⲞⲠ; read ϤϢⲚϢ ⲘⲠⲒ ⲠⲈⲦϢⲞⲞⲠ.
7 MS ⲚⲦⲀⲒⲤϨⲀⲒⲤⲞⲨ; Ϩ inserted above.
12 MS ⲀⲨⲰ better omitted.
15 ⲀⲨⲰ expunged before ⲦⲈⲄⲚⲰⲤⲒⲤ.
16 MS ⲈⲢⲞⲤ; read ⲈⲢⲞϤ.

of the *mysteries* ⟨and the words⟩ of the third *space* within.
And he is superior to the All. And he is equal to [1] those
who are in that third *space*. Because he has received the
mystery [2] in which they are and in which they stand, for
this reason he is equal to them. Moreover he who has found
the words of the *mysteries* which I have written [3] to you
as a comparison, that they are *members* of the Ineffable,
truly I say to you, he who has found the words of those
mysteries in God's *truth*, that man is *truly* first, and he is
equal to him (the Ineffable). For because of those words and
mysteries, the All itself [4] stands on account of the First
One. Because of this, he who has found the words of those
mysteries is equal with the First One. *For* the *gnosis* of the
knowledge of the Ineffable is that of which I have spoken
with you today.

⟨A *part* of the *Books* of the *Saviour*⟩ [5]

---

[1] (3) is equal to; MS: is pleasing to.
[2] (4, 5) he has received the mystery; Till: (or) the mystery has received him.
[3] (7) written; Schmidt: described.
[4] (13) the All itself; Till: (or) the All also.
[5] (17) the title is transferred from 253.23.

ⲀϤⲞⲨⲰⲂ ⲞⲚ ⲈⲦⲞⲞⲦϤ Ⲛ̅ϬⲒ ⲒⲤ̅ ⲂⲘ ⲠϢⲀⲬⲈ ⲠⲈⲬⲀϤ Ⲛ̅- ⲤⲀⲈ
ⲚⲈϤⲘⲀⲐⲎⲦⲎⲤ ⲬⲈ ⲈⲒ̈ϢⲀⲚⲂⲰⲔ ⲈⲠⲞⲨⲞⲈⲒⲚ ⲔⲎⲢⲨⲤⲤⲈ Ⲙ̅-
ⲠⲔⲞⲤⲘⲞⲤ ⲦⲎⲢϤ̅ ⲀⲬⲒⲤ ⲈⲢⲞⲞⲨ ⲬⲈ Ⲙ̅Ⲡ̅ⲢⲔⲀⲦⲞⲦⲦⲎⲨⲦ̅Ⲛ
ⲈⲂⲞⲖ Ⲙ̅ⲠⲈⲂⲞⲞⲨ Ⲙ̅Ⲛ ⲦⲈⲨϢⲎ ⲈⲦⲈⲦⲚ̅ϢⲒⲚⲈ ⲀⲨⲰ Ⲙ̅Ⲡ̅Ⲣ-
5 ⲀⲚⲀⲔⲦⲀ Ⲙ̅ⲘⲰⲦ̅Ⲛ ⲂⲈⲰⲤ ϢⲀⲚⲦⲈⲦⲚ̅ϬⲒⲚⲈ Ⲛ̅ⲘⲘⲨⲤⲦⲎⲢⲒⲞⲚ
Ⲛ̅ⲦⲘⲚ̅ⲦⲈⲢⲞ Ⲙ̅ⲠⲞⲨⲞⲈⲒⲚ· ⲚⲀⲒ̈ ⲈⲦⲚⲀⲤⲈⲦϤ̅ⲦⲎⲚⲞⲨ Ⲛ̅ⲤⲈⲢ-
ⲦⲎⲨⲦ̅Ⲛ Ⲛ̅ⲂⲒⲖⲒⲔⲢⲒⲚⲈⲤ Ⲛ̅ⲞⲨⲞⲈⲒⲚ· Ⲛ̅ⲤⲈⲬⲒⲦⲎⲨⲦ̅Ⲛ ⲈⲦⲘⲚ̅Ⲧ-
ⲈⲢⲞ Ⲙ̅ⲠⲞⲨⲞⲒ̈Ⲛ· ⲀⲬⲒⲤ ⲈⲢⲞⲞⲨ ⲬⲈ ⲀⲠⲞⲦⲀⲤⲤⲈ Ⲙ̅ⲠⲔⲞⲤ-
ⲘⲞⲤ ⲦⲎⲢϤ̅· Ⲙ̅Ⲛ ⲐⲨⲖⲎ ⲦⲎⲢⲤ̅ ⲈⲦⲚ̅ⲂⲎⲦϤ̅· ⲀⲨⲰ Ⲙ̅Ⲛ ⲚⲈϤ-
10 ⲢⲞⲞⲨϢ ⲦⲎⲢⲞⲨ· ⲀⲨⲰ Ⲙ̅Ⲛ ⲚⲈϤⲚⲞⲂⲈ ⲦⲎⲢⲞⲨ· ⲂⲀⲠⲀⲜ
ⲂⲀⲠⲖⲰⲤ Ⲙ̅Ⲛ ⲚⲈϤⲂⲞⲘⲒⲖⲒⲀ ⲦⲎⲢⲞⲨ ⲈⲦⲚ̅ⲂⲎⲦϤ̅· ⲬⲈ ⲈⲦⲈⲦⲚ̅-
Ⲙ̅ⲠϢⲀ Ⲛ̅ⲘⲘⲨⲤⲦⲎⲢⲒⲞⲚ Ⲙ̅ⲠⲞⲨⲞⲈⲒⲚ Ⲛ̅ⲦⲈⲦⲚ̅ⲚⲞⲨⲂ̅Ⲙ ⲈⲚⲔⲞ-
ⲖⲀⲤⲒⲤ ⲦⲎⲢⲞⲨ ⲈⲦⲚ̅ Ⲛ̅ⲈⲔⲢⲒⲤⲒⲤ· ⲀⲬⲒⲤ ⲈⲢⲞⲞⲨ ⲬⲈ ⲀⲠⲞ-
ⲦⲀⲤⲤⲈ Ⲙ̅ⲠⲈⲔⲢⲘⲢⲘ· ⲬⲈ ⲈⲦⲈⲦⲚ̅Ⲙ̅ⲠϢⲀ Ⲛ̅ⲘⲘⲨⲤⲦⲎⲢⲒⲞⲚ Ⲙ̅-
15 ⲠⲞⲨⲞⲈⲒⲚ· Ⲛ̅ⲦⲈⲦⲚ̅ⲚⲞⲨⲂ̅Ⲙ ⲈⲠⲔⲰⲂ̅Ⲧ Ⲙ̅ⲠⲒⲂⲞ Ⲛ̅ⲞⲨⲂⲞⲢ· ⲀⲬⲒⲤ ⲤⲀⲈ ᵇ
ⲈⲢⲞⲞⲨ ⲬⲈ ⲀⲠⲞⲦⲀⲤⲤⲈ Ⲛ̅ⲦⲘⲚ̅ⲦⲢⲈϤⲬⲒⲤⲘⲎ ⟨ⲬⲈ ⲈⲦⲈⲦⲚ̅-
Ⲙ̅ⲠϢⲀ Ⲛ̅ⲘⲘⲨⲤⲦⲎⲢⲒⲞⲚ Ⲙ̅ⲠⲞⲨⲞⲈⲒⲚ⟩ Ⲛ̅ⲦⲈⲦⲚ̅ⲚⲞⲨⲂ̅Ⲙ ⲈⲚⲈⲔ-
ⲔⲢⲒⲤⲒⲤ Ⲙ̅ⲠⲒⲂⲞ Ⲛ̅ⲞⲨⲂⲞⲢ· ⲀⲬⲒⲤ ⲈⲢⲞⲞⲨ ⲬⲈ ⲀⲠⲞⲦⲀⲤⲤⲈ Ⲛ̅-
ⲦⲘⲚ̅ⲦⲢⲈϤⲦⲀⲂⲘⲀ· Ⲛ̅ⲦⲈⲦⲚ̅Ⲙ̅ⲠϢⲀ Ⲛ̅ⲘⲘⲨⲤⲦⲎⲢⲒⲞⲚ Ⲙ̅ⲠⲞⲨ-
20 ⲞⲈⲒⲚ· Ⲛ̅ⲦⲈⲦⲚ̅ⲚⲞⲨⲂ̅Ⲙ ⲈⲚⲔⲞⲖⲀⲤⲒⲤ Ⲛ̅ⲀⲢⲒⲎⲖ· ⲀⲬⲒⲤ ⲈⲢⲞⲞⲨ
ⲬⲈ ⲀⲠⲞⲦⲀⲤⲤⲈ Ⲙ̅ⲠⲖⲀ Ⲛ̅ⲚⲞⲨⲬ ⲦⲀⲢⲈⲦⲚ̅Ⲙ̅ⲠϢⲀ Ⲛ̅ⲘⲘⲨⲤ-
ⲦⲎⲢⲒⲞⲚ Ⲙ̅ⲠⲞⲨⲞⲈⲒⲚ Ⲛ̅ⲦⲈⲦⲚ̅ⲚⲞⲨⲂ̅Ⲙ ⲈⲚⲈⲒⲈⲢⲞ Ⲛ̅ⲔⲰⲂ̅Ⲧ Ⲙ̅-

---

3 MS ⲦⲞⲦⲦⲎⲨⲦ̅Ⲛ; read ⲦⲞⲞⲦⲦⲎⲨⲦ̅Ⲛ.
4 ⲀⲨⲰ ... Ⲙ̅ⲘⲰⲦ̅Ⲛ added below in margin.
11 Ⲙ̅Ⲛ better omitted.
16 MS ⲬⲈ . . . Ⲙ̅ⲠⲞⲨⲞⲈⲒⲚ omitted.
21 MS Ⲙ̅ⲠⲖⲀ; read Ⲙ̅ⲠⲖⲀⲤ.

(BOOK III)

102. Jesus continued again with the discourse, he said to his *disciples*: "When I have gone to the light, *preach* to the whole *world*. Say to them : do not cease by day and night from seeking, and do not *refresh* yourselves *until* you find the *mysteries* of the Kingdom of the Light, which will purify you and make you to be *pure* light and will take you to the Kingdom of the Light. Say to them : *renounce* the whole *world* and all the *matter* within it, and all its cares, and all its sins, *in a word*, all its *relationships* which are in it, so that you may be worthy of the *mysteries* of the light, and be saved from all the *punishments* within the *judgments*. Say to them : *renounce* complaining, that you may be worthy of the *mysteries* of the light, and be saved from the fire of the dog-face. Say to them : *renounce* listening (to false-hood), ⟨that you may be worthy of the mysteries of the light⟩ and be saved from the *judgments* of the dog-face. Say to them : *renounce* mischief-making [1], that you may be worthy of the *mysteries* of the light, and be saved from the *punishments* of Ariel [2]. Say to them : *renounce* falsehood, that you may be worthy of the *mysteries* of the light, and be saved from the rivers of fire | of the dog-face. Say to them :

---

[1] (19) mischief-making; Schmidt : ? quarrelsomeness.
[2] (20) Ariel; see Hippol. V.14.6; OnOrgWld 148; Kropp (Bibl. 26) I, R12.

ⲡⲓⲍⲁ ⲛ̄ⲟⲩⲅⲟⲣ· ⲁⲭⲓⲥ ⲉⲣⲟⲟⲩ ϫⲉ ⲁⲡⲟⲧⲁⲥⲥⲉ ⲛ̄ⲛⲓⲙⲛ̄ⲧⲣⲉ
ⲛ̄ⲛⲟⲩϫ ⲛ̄ⲧⲉⲧⲛ̄ⲙⲡϣⲁ ⲛ̄ⲙⲙⲩⲥⲧⲏⲣⲓⲟⲛ ⲙ̄ⲡⲟⲩⲟⲉⲓⲛ ⲧⲁ-
ⲣⲉⲧⲛ̄ⲣⲃⲟⲗ· ⲧⲁⲣⲉⲧⲛ̄ⲛⲟⲩⲅⲙ ⲉⲛⲓⲉⲣⲟ ⲛ̄ⲕⲱⲥⲧ ⲙ̄ⲡⲓⲍⲁ ⲛ̄ⲟⲩ-
ⲅⲟⲣ· ⲁⲭⲓⲥ ⲉⲣⲟⲟⲩ ϫⲉ ⲁⲡⲟⲧⲁⲥⲥⲉ ⲛ̄ⲛⲓⲙⲛ̄ⲧϣⲟⲩϣⲟ ⲙⲛ
5 ⲛⲓⲙⲛ̄ⲧϫⲁⲥⲓϩⲏⲧ ϫⲉ ⲉⲧⲉⲧⲛ̄ⲙⲡϣⲁ ⲛ̄ⲙⲙⲩⲥⲧⲏⲣⲓⲟⲛ ⲙ̄ⲡⲟⲩ-
ⲟⲉⲓⲛ ⲛ̄ⲧⲉⲧⲛ̄ⲛⲟⲩⲅⲙ ⲉⲛⲓϩⲓⲉⲓⲧ ⲛ̄ⲕⲱⲥⲧ ⲛ̄ⲁⲣⲓⲏⲗ· ⲁⲭⲓⲥ
ⲉⲣⲟⲟⲩ ϫⲉ ⲁⲡⲟⲧⲁⲥⲥⲉ ⲛ̄ⲛⲓⲙⲛ̄ⲧⲙⲁⲓ̈ϩⲏⲧϥ̄ ⲛ̄ⲧⲉⲧⲛ̄ⲙⲡϣⲁ [ⲥⲗⲉ]
ⲛ̄ⲙⲙⲩⲥⲧⲏⲣⲓⲟⲛ ⲙ̄ⲡⲟⲩⲟⲉⲓⲛ ⲛ̄ⲧⲉⲧⲛ̄ⲛⲟⲩⲅⲙ ⲉⲛⲉⲕⲣⲓⲥⲓⲥ ⲛ̄-
ⲁⲙⲛ̄ⲧⲉ· ⲁⲭⲓⲥ ⲉⲣⲟⲟⲩ ϫⲉ ⲁⲡⲟⲧⲁⲥⲥⲉ ⲛ̄ⲛⲓⲙⲛ̄ⲧϩⲁϩ ⲛ̄-
10 ϣⲁϫⲉ ⲧⲁⲣⲉⲧⲛ̄ⲙⲡϣⲁ ⲛ̄ⲙⲙⲩⲥⲧⲏⲣⲓⲟⲛ ⲙ̄ⲡⲟⲩⲟⲉⲓⲛ ⲛ̄ⲧⲉ-
ⲧⲛ̄ⲛⲟⲩⲅⲙ ⲉⲛⲕⲱⲥⲧ ⲛ̄ⲁⲙⲛ̄ⲧⲉ· ⲁⲭⲓⲥ ⲉⲣⲟⲟⲩ ϫⲉ ⲁⲡⲟⲧⲁⲥⲥⲉ ⲛ̄ⲛⲓϯⲅⲉ ⲉⲧϩⲟⲟⲩ ⲛ̄ⲧⲉⲧⲛ̄ⲙⲡϣⲁ ⲛ̄ⲙⲙⲩⲥⲧⲏⲣⲓⲟⲛ
ⲙ̄ⲡⲟⲩⲟⲓ̈ⲛ ⲛ̄ⲧⲉⲧⲛ̄ⲛⲟⲩⲅⲙ ⲉⲛⲕⲟⲗⲁⲥⲓⲥ ⲉⲧϩⲛ̄ ⲁⲙⲛ̄ⲧⲉ·
ⲁⲭⲓⲥ ⲉⲣⲟⲟⲩ ϫⲉ ⲁⲡⲟⲧⲁⲥⲥⲉ ⲛ̄ⲛⲓⲙⲛ̄ⲧⲙⲁⲓⲧⲟⲛϩⲟⲩⲟ ϫⲉ
15 ⲉⲧⲉⲧⲛ̄ⲙⲡϣⲁ ⲛ̄ⲙⲙⲩⲥⲧⲏⲣⲓⲟⲛ ⲙ̄ⲡⲟⲩⲟⲉⲓⲛ ⲛ̄ⲧⲉⲧⲛ̄ⲛⲟⲩⲅⲙ
ⲉⲛⲉⲓⲉⲣⲟ ⲛ̄ⲕⲣⲱⲙ ⲛ̄ⲧⲉ ⲡⲓⲍⲁ ⲛ̄ⲟⲩⲅⲟⲣ· ⲁⲭⲓⲥ ⲉⲣⲟⲟⲩ ϫⲉ
ⲁⲡⲟⲧⲁⲥⲥⲉ ⲛ̄ⲛⲓⲙⲛ̄ⲧⲙⲁⲓ̈ⲕⲟⲥⲙⲟⲥ ϫⲉ ⲉⲧⲉⲧⲛ̄ⲙⲡϣⲁ ⲛ̄ⲙ-
ⲙⲩⲥⲧⲏⲣⲓⲟⲛ ⲙ̄ⲡⲟⲩⲟⲉⲓⲛ ⲛ̄ⲧⲉⲧⲛ̄ⲛⲟⲩⲅⲙ ⲉⲛϩⲃⲥⲱ ⲛ̄ⲗⲁⲙ-
ⲭⲁⲧⲡ̄ ϩⲓ ⲕⲱⲥⲧ ⲛ̄ⲧⲉ ⲡⲓⲍⲁ ⲛ̄ⲟⲩⲅⲟⲣ· ⲁⲭⲓⲥ ⲉⲣⲟⲟⲩ ϫⲉ
20 ⲁⲡⲟⲧⲁⲥⲥⲉ ⲛ̄ⲛⲓⲙⲛ̄ⲧⲣⲉϥⲧⲱⲣⲡ̄ ϫⲉ ⲉⲧⲉⲧⲛ̄ⲙⲡϣⲁ ⲛ̄ⲙ-
ⲙⲩⲥⲧⲏⲣⲓⲟⲛ ⲙ̄ⲡⲟⲩⲟⲉⲓⲛ ⲛ̄ⲧⲉⲧⲛ̄ⲛⲟⲩⲅⲙ ⲉⲛⲉⲓⲉⲣⲟ ⲛ̄- [ⲥⲗⲉ b]
ⲕⲣⲱⲙ ⲛ̄ⲧⲉ ⲁⲣⲓⲏⲗ· ⲁⲭⲓⲥ ⲉⲣⲟⲟⲩ ϫⲉ ⲁⲡⲟⲧⲁⲥⲥⲉ ⲛ̄-
ⲛⲓϣⲁϫⲉ ⲉⲑⲟⲟⲩ ϫⲉ ⲉⲧⲉⲧⲛ̄ⲙⲡϣⲁ ⲛ̄ⲙⲙⲩⲥⲧⲏⲣⲓⲟⲛ ⲙ̄-
ⲡⲟⲩⲟⲉⲓⲛ ⲛ̄ⲧⲉⲧⲛ̄ⲛⲟⲩⲅⲙ ⲉⲛⲓⲕⲟⲗⲁⲥⲓⲥ ⲛ̄ⲉⲓⲉⲣⲟ ⲛ̄ⲕⲣⲱⲙ·
25 ⲁⲭⲓⲥ ⲉⲣⲟⲟⲩ ϫⲉ ⲁⲡⲟⲧⲁⲥⲥⲉ ⲛ̄ⲛⲓⲙⲛ̄ⲧⲡⲟⲛⲏⲣⲟⲥ ⲛ̄ⲧⲉⲧⲛ̄-

---

1 MS ⲛⲛⲓⲙⲛⲧⲣⲉ; read ⲛ̄ⲛⲓⲙⲛ̄ⲧⲛ̄ⲛⲟⲩⲧⲣⲉ.
7 ⲓ̅ⲥ̅ in upper right-hand margin at end of quire.
24 MS ⲛ̄ⲉⲓⲉⲣⲟ; read ⲛ̄ⲛⲉⲓⲉⲣⲟ.

nounce false witness ¹ that you may be worthy of the
ysteries of the light, and escape and be saved from the
*v*ers of fire of the dog-face. Say to them : *renounce* pride
*a*d boasting, that you may be worthy of the *mysteries* of
*th*e light, and be saved from the pits of fire of Ariel. Say
to them : *renounce* the love of the belly, that you may be
*o*rthy of the *mysteries* of the light, and be saved from the
*i*dgments of Amente. Say to them : *renounce* talkativeness,
*th*at you may be worthy of the *mysteries* of the light, and
be saved from the fires of Amente. Say to them : *renounce*
*ev*il habits, that you may be worthy of the *mysteries* of the
*lig*ht, and be saved from the *punishments* in Amente. Say
to them : *renounce* covetousness, that you may be worthy of
the *mysteries* of the light, and be saved from the rivers of
*fla*me of the dog-face. Say to them : *renounce* love of the
*wo*rld, that you may be worthy of the *mysteries* of the light,
*an*d be saved from garments of pitch and fire of the dog-
*fac*e. Say to them : *renounce* robbery, that you may be worthy
of the *mysteries* of the light, and be saved from the rivers
of fire of Ariel. Say to them : *renounce* evil speech, that
*yo*u may be worthy of the *mysteries* of the light, and be
*sav*ed from the *punishments* of the rivers of flame. Say to
*the*m : *renounce wickedness,* that you | may be worthy of

---

1) false witness; MS : false witnesses.

Μ̄ΠϢΑ Ν̄Μ̄ΜΥCΤΗΡΙΟΝ Μ̄ΠΟΥΟΕΙΝ Ν̄ΤΕΤΝ̄ΝΟΥϨΜ ΕΝΕ-
ΘΑΛΑCCΑ Ν̄ΚΩϨΤ̄ Ν̄ΑΡΙΗΛ· ΑϪΙC ΕΡΟΟΥ ϪΕ ΑΠΟΤΑCCΕ
Ν̄ΝΙΜΝ̄ΤΑΤΝΑ Ν̄ΤΕΤΝ̄ΜΠϢΑ Ν̄Μ̄ΜΥCΤΗΡΙΟΝ Μ̄ΠΟΥΟΪΝ
Ν̄ΤΕΤΝ̄ΝΟΥϨΜ ΕΝΕΚΡΙCΙC Ν̄ΝΙϨΑ ΝΕΔΡΑΚΩΝ· ΑϪΙC Ε-
⁵ ΡΟΟΥ ϪΕ ΑΠΟΤΑCCΕ Ν̄ΝΙϬΩΝΤ Ν̄ΤΕΤΝ̄ΜΠϢΑ Ν̄Μ̄ΜΥC-
ΤΗΡΙΟΝ Μ̄ΠΟΥΟΕΙΝ Ν̄ΤΕΤΝ̄ΝΟΥϨΜ ΕΝΕΙΕΡΗ Ν̄ΚΡΩΜ Ν̄-
ΝΙϨΑ ΝΕΔΡΑΚΩΝ· ΑϪΙC ΕΡΟΟΥ ϪΕ ΑΠΟΤΑCCΕ Μ̄ΠCΑ-
ϨΟΥ Ν̄ΤΕΤΝ̄ΜΠϢΑ Ν̄Μ̄ΜΥCΤΗΡΙΟΝ Μ̄ΠΟΥΟΕΙΝ Ν̄ΤΕΤΝ̄-
ΝΟΥϨΜ ΕΠΚΩϨΤ̄ Ν̄Ν̄ϨΑΛΑCCΑ Ν̄ΝΙϨΑ ΝΕΔΡΑΚΩΝ· ΑϪΙC
¹⁰ ΕΡΟΟΥ ϪΕ ΑΠΟΤΑCCΕ Μ̄ΠϪΙΟΥΕ Ν̄ΤΕΤΝ̄ΜΠϢΑ *Ν̄Μ-   CΛⲌ
ΜΥCΤΗΡΙΟΝ Μ̄ΠΟΥΟΕΙΝ Ν̄ΤΕΤΝ̄ΝΟΥϨΜ ΕΝϨΑΛΑCCΑ ΕΤ-
ΒΕΕΒΕ Ν̄ΝΙϨΑ ΝΕΔΡΑΚΩΝ· ΑϪΙC ΕΡΟΟΥ ϪΕ ΑΠΟΤΑCCΕ
Ν̄ΝΙϬΩϬΕ Ν̄ΤΕΤΝ̄ΜΠϢΑ Ν̄Μ̄ΜΥCΤΗΡΙΟΝ Μ̄ΠΟΥΟΕΙΝ Ν̄ΤΕ-
ΤΝ̄ΝΟΥϨΜ ΕΪΑΛΤΑΒΑΩΘ· ΑϪΙC ΕΡΟΟΥ ϪΕ ΑΠΟΤΑCCΕ
¹⁵ Ν̄ΤΚΑΤΑΛΑΛΙΑ Ν̄ΤΕΤΝ̄ΜΠϢΑ Ν̄Μ̄ΜΥCΤΗΡΙΟΝ Μ̄ΠΟΥΟΕΙΝ
Ν̄ΤΕΤΝ̄ΝΟΥϨΜ ΕΝΙΕΡϢΟΥ Ν̄ΚΩϨΤ̄ Μ̄ΠΙϨΟ Μ̄ΜΟΥΪ· ΑϪΙC
ΕΡΟΟΥ ϪΕ ΑΠΟΤΑCCΕ Ν̄ΝΙΜΝ̄ΤΡΕϤΜΙϢΕ Μ̄Ν ΝΙϢΟΝΤ
Ν̄ΤΕΤΝ̄ΜΠϢΑ Ν̄Μ̄ΜΥCΤΗΡΙΟΝ Μ̄ΠΟΥΟΕΙΝ Ν̄ΤΕΤΝ̄ΝΟΥϨΜ
ΕΝΕΙΕΡϢΟΥ ΕΤΒ̄ΡΒ̄Ρ Ν̄ΪΑΛΤΑΒΑΩΘ: ΑϪΙC ΕΡΟΟΥ ϪΕ
²⁰ ΑΠΟΤΑCCΕ Ν̄ΝΙΜΝ̄ΤΑΤCΒΩ Ν̄ΤΕΤΝ̄ΜΠϢΑ Ν̄Μ̄ΜΥCΤΗΡΙΟΝ
Μ̄ΠΟΥΟΕΙΝ Ν̄ΤΕΤΝ̄ΝΟΥϨΜ ΕΝΛΙΤΟΥΡΓΟC Ν̄ΤΕ ΪΑΛΤΑ-
ΒΑΩΘ Μ̄Ν Ν̄ΚΩϨΤ̄ Ν̄ΝΕΘΑΛΑCCΑ· ΑϪΙC ΕΡΟΟΥ ϪΕ
ΑΠΟΤΑCCΕ Ν̄ΝΙΜΝ̄ΤΚΑΚΟΥΡΓΟC Ν̄ΤΕΤΝ̄ΜΠϢΑ Ν̄Μ̄ΜΥC-
ΤΗΡΙΟΝ Μ̄ΠΟΥΟΪΝ Ν̄ΤΕΤΝ̄ΝΟΥϨΜ ΕΝΔΑΙΜΟΝΙΟΝ ΤΗ-   CΛⲌ ᵇ
²⁵ ΡΟΥ Ν̄ΤΕ ΪΑΛΤΑΒΑΩΘ Μ̄Ν ΝΕϤΚΟΛΑCΙC ΤΗΡΟΥ· ΑϪΙC

---

6   MS ΕΝΕΙΕΡΗ ; read ΕΝΕΙΕΡΟ.
9   MS Ν̄Ν̄ϨΑΛΑCCΑ ; read Ν̄ΝϾΘΑΛΑCϾΑ ; also line 11.
10   ⲓⲋ̄ in upper left-hand margin at beginning of quire.

the *mysteries* of the light, and be saved from the *seas* of fire of Ariel. Say to them : *renounce* mercilessness, that you may be worthy of the *mysteries* of the light, and be saved from the *judgments* of the *dragon*-faces. Say to them : *renounce* anger, that you may be worthy of the *mysteries* of the light, and be saved from the rivers of flame of the *dragon*-faces. Say to them : *renounce* cursing, that you may be worthy of the *mysteries* of the light, and be saved from the fire of the *seas* of the *dragon*-faces. Say to them : *renounce* theft, that you may be worthy of the *mysteries* of the light, and be saved from the bubbling *seas* of the *dragon*-faces. Say to them : *renounce* violence, that you may be worthy of the *mysteries* of the light, and be saved from Jaldabaoth. Say to them : *renounce slander*, that you may be worthy of the *mysteries* of the light, and be saved from the rivers of fire of the lion-face. Say to them : *renounce* fighting and quarrels, that you may be worthy of the *mysteries* of the light, and be saved from the bubbling rivers of Jaldabaoth. Say to them : *renounce* ignorance, that you may be worthy of the *mysteries* of the light, and be saved from the *ministers* of Jaldabaoth and the *seas* of fire. Say to them : *renounce evil-doing* that you may be worthy of the *mysteries* of the light, and be saved from all the *demons* of Jaldabaoth and all his *punishments*. Say | to them : *renounce frenzy*, that you

ⲈⲢⲞⲞⲨ ϪⲈ ⲀⲠⲞⲦⲀⲤⲤⲈ Ⲛ̄ϯⲀⲠⲞⲚⲞⲒⲀ Ⲛ̄ⲦⲈⲦⲚ̄Ⲙ̄ⲠϢⲀ Ⲛ̄Ⲙ-
ⲘⲨⲤⲦⲎⲢⲒⲞⲚ Ⲙ̄ⲠⲞⲨⲞⲒ̈Ⲛ Ⲛ̄ⲦⲈⲦⲚ̄ⲚⲞⲨⲤⲘ̄ ⲈⲚⲈⲐⲀⲖⲀⲤⲤⲀ Ⲛ̄-
ⲖⲀⲘⲬⲀⲦⲠ̄ Ⲛ̄ⲦⲈ Ⲓ̈ⲀⲖⲦⲀⲂⲀⲰⲐ ⲈⲦⲂ̄ⲢⲂⲢ· ⲀϪⲒⲤ ⲈⲢⲞⲞⲨ ϪⲈ
ⲀⲠⲞⲦⲀⲤⲤⲈ Ⲛ̄ⲚⲒⲘⲚ̄ⲦⲚⲞⲈⲒⲔ’ Ⲛ̄ⲦⲈⲦⲚ̄Ⲙ̄ⲠϢⲀ Ⲛ̄ⲘⲘⲨⲤⲦⲎⲢⲒⲞⲚ
5 Ⲛ̄ⲦⲘⲚ̄ⲦⲈⲢⲞ Ⲙ̄ⲠⲞⲨⲞⲈⲒⲚ Ⲛ̄ⲦⲈⲦⲚ̄ⲚⲞⲨⲤⲘ̄ ⲈⲚⲈⲐⲀⲖⲀⲤⲤⲀ Ⲛ̄-
ⲞⲎⲚ ϨⲒ ⲖⲀⲘⲬⲀⲦⲠ̄ Ⲛ̄ⲦⲈ ⲠⲒϨⲞ Ⲙ̄ⲘⲞⲨⲒ̈· ⲀϪⲒⲤ ⲈⲢⲞⲞⲨ ϪⲈ
ⲀⲠⲞⲦⲀⲤⲤⲈ Ⲛ̄ⲚⲒϨⲰⲦⲂ̄ Ⲛ̄ⲦⲈⲦⲚ̄Ⲙ̄ⲠϢⲀ Ⲛ̄ⲘⲘⲨⲤⲦⲎⲢⲒⲞⲚ Ⲙ̄-
ⲠⲞⲨⲞⲈⲒⲚ Ⲛ̄ⲦⲈⲦⲚ̄ⲚⲞⲨⲤⲘ̄ ⲈⲠⲒⲀⲢⲬⲰⲚ Ⲛ̄ϨⲀ Ⲛ̄ⲘⲤⲀϨ ⲠⲀⲒ̈ ⲈⲦ-
Ϩ̄Ⲙ̄ ⲠϪⲀϤ ⲠⲈ ⲠϢⲞⲢⲠ̄ Ⲛ̄ⲦⲀⲘⲒⲞ· Ϩ̄Ⲙ̄ ⲠⲔⲀⲔⲈ ⲈⲦϨⲒⲂⲞⲖ·
10 ⲀϪⲒⲤ ⲈⲢⲞⲞⲨ ϪⲈ ⲀⲠⲞⲦⲀⲤⲤⲈ Ⲛ̄ⲚⲒⲘⲚ̄ⲦⲀⲦⲚⲀ Ⲙ̄Ⲛ ⲚⲒⲘⲚ̄Ⲧ-
ⲀⲤⲈⲂⲎⲤ Ⲛ̄ⲦⲈⲦⲚ̄Ⲙ̄ⲠϢⲀ Ⲛ̄ⲘⲘⲨⲤⲦⲎⲢⲒⲞⲚ Ⲙ̄ⲠⲞⲨⲞⲈⲒⲚ Ⲛ̄ⲦⲈ-
ⲦⲚ̄ⲚⲞⲨⲤⲘ̄ ⲈⲚⲀⲢⲬⲰⲚ Ⲙ̄ⲠⲔⲀⲔⲈ ⲈⲦϨⲒⲂⲞⲖ: ⲀϪⲒⲤ ⲈⲢⲞⲞⲨ
ϪⲈ ⲀⲠⲞⲦⲀⲤⲤⲈ Ⲛ̄ⲚⲒⲘⲚ̄ⲦⲀⲦⲚⲞⲨⲦⲈ** Ⲛ̄ⲦⲈⲦⲚ̄Ⲙ̄ⲠϢⲀ Ⲛ̄Ⲙ- [ⲤⲖⲎ]
ⲘⲨⲤⲦⲎⲢⲒⲞⲚ Ⲙ̄ⲠⲞⲨⲞⲈⲒⲚ Ⲛ̄ⲦⲈⲦⲚ̄ⲚⲞⲨⲤⲘ̄ ⲈⲠⲢⲒⲘⲈ Ⲙ̄Ⲛ ⲠⲞⲀϨ-
15 Ϭ̄Ϭ Ⲛ̄ⲚⲚⲞⲂϨⲈ· ⲀϪⲒⲤ ⲈⲢⲞⲞⲨ ϪⲈ ⲀⲠⲞⲦⲀⲤⲤⲈ Ⲛ̄ⲚⲈⲪⲀⲢ-
ⲘⲀⲄⲒⲀ Ⲛ̄ⲦⲈⲦⲚ̄Ⲙ̄ⲠϢⲀ Ⲙ̄ⲠⲘⲨⲤⲦⲎⲢⲒⲞⲚ Ⲙ̄ⲠⲞⲨⲞⲈⲒⲚ Ⲛ̄ⲦⲈⲦⲚ̄-
ⲚⲞⲨϨⲘ̄ ⲈⲠⲚⲞϬ Ⲛ̄ϪⲀϤ Ⲙ̄Ⲛ ⲚⲈⲬⲀⲖⲀⲌⲀ Ⲙ̄ⲠⲔⲀⲔⲈ ⲈⲦϨⲒⲂⲞⲖ·
ⲀϪⲒⲤ ⲈⲢⲞⲞⲨ ϪⲈ ⲀⲠⲞⲦⲀⲤⲤⲈ Ⲛ̄ⲚⲒⲘⲚ̄ⲦⲢⲈϤϪⲒⲞⲨⲀ Ⲛ̄ⲦⲈ-
ⲦⲚ̄Ⲙ̄ⲠϢⲀ Ⲛ̄ⲘⲘⲨⲤⲦⲎⲢⲒⲞⲚ Ⲙ̄ⲠⲞⲨⲞⲈⲒⲚ Ⲛ̄ⲦⲈⲦⲚ̄ⲚⲞⲨⲤⲘ̄ Ⲉ-
20 ⲠⲚⲞϬ Ⲛ̄ⲆⲢⲀⲔⲰⲚ Ⲙ̄ⲠⲔⲀⲔⲈ ⲈⲦϨⲒⲂⲞⲖ· ⲀϪⲒⲤ ⲈⲢⲞⲞⲨ ϪⲈ
ⲀⲠⲞⲦⲀⲤⲤⲈ Ⲛ̄ⲚⲈⲤⲂⲰ Ⲙ̄ⲠⲖⲀⲚⲎ Ⲛ̄ⲦⲈⲦⲚ̄Ⲙ̄ⲠϢⲀ Ⲛ̄ⲘⲘⲨⲤⲦⲎ-
ⲢⲒⲞⲚ Ⲙ̄ⲠⲞⲨⲞⲈⲒⲚ Ⲛ̄ⲦⲈⲦⲚ̄ⲚⲞⲨϨⲘ̄ ⲈⲚⲔⲞⲖⲀⲤⲒⲤ ⲦⲎⲢⲞⲨ Ⲙ̄-
ⲠⲚⲞϬ Ⲛ̄ⲆⲢⲀⲔⲰⲚ Ⲙ̄ⲠⲔⲀⲔⲈ ⲈⲦϨⲒⲂⲞⲖ· ⲀϪⲒⲤ ⲈⲚⲈⲦϯⲤⲂⲰ
Ϩ̄Ⲛ ⲚⲈⲤⲂⲰ Ⲙ̄ⲠⲖⲀⲚⲎ Ⲙ̄Ⲛ ⲞⲨⲞⲚ ⲚⲒⲘ ⲈⲦϪⲒⲤⲂⲰ ⲈⲂⲞⲖ ϨⲒ-

---

9   MS Ⲡ̄ⲦⲀⲘⲒⲞ; read Ⲡ̄ⲦⲀⲘⲒⲞⲚ. ⲈⲦ expunged before Ϩ̄Ⲙ̄.
15   MS ⲠⲠⲚⲞⲂϨⲈ; read ⲠⲚⲞⲂϨⲈ.
21   MS originally ⲠⲠⲒⲤⲂⲰ; Ⲓ altered to Ⲉ in later hand; also line 24.

ıy be worthy of the *mysteries* of the light, and be saved
·m the boiling *seas* of pitch of Jaldabaoth. Say to them :
ıounce adultery, that you may be worthy of the *mysteries*
the Kingdom of the Light, and be saved from the *seas*
sulphur and pitch of the lion-face. Say to them : *renounce*
ling, that you may be worthy of the *mysteries* of the light,
1 be saved from the *archon* with a crocodile-face which,
the frost, is the first *chamber* [1] of the outer darkness.
ʋ to them : *renounce* mercilessness and *impiety*, that you
y be worthy of the *mysteries* of the light, and be saved
m the *archons* of the outer darkness. Say to them :
ounce godlessness, that you may be worthy of the
steries of the light, and be saved from the weeping and
ıshing of teeth*. Say to them : *renounce sorceries*, that
ı may be worthy of the *mysteries* of the light, and be saved
m the great frost and the *hail* of the outer darkness. Say
them : *renounce* blasphemy, that you may be worthy of
  mysteries of the light, and be saved from the great
·gon of the outer darkness. Say to them : *renounce*
ɔneous teachings, that you may be worthy of the *mysteries*
the light, and be saved from all the *punishments* of the
at *dragon* of the outer darkness. Say to all those who
ch *erroneous* teachings and all those who learn from
m : | woe to you, for unless you *repent* and give up your

˙. Mt. 8.12; 13.42, 50; 22.13; 24.51; 25.30; Lk. 13.28

·) first chamber; see KephVI p. 30 etc. (also 317.23).

519

ⲦⲞⲞⲦⲞⲨ ⲬⲈ ⲞⲨⲞⲓ ⲚⲎⲦⲚ ⲚⲦⲰⲦⲚ ⲚⲬⲈ ⲈϢⲰⲠⲈ ⲈⲦⲈ-
ⲦⲚⲦⲘⲘⲈⲦⲀⲚⲞⲒ ⲚⲦⲈⲦⲚⲔⲰ ⲚⲤⲰⲦⲚ ⲚⲦⲈⲦⲚⲠⲖⲀⲚⲎ ⲦⲈ- [ⲤⲀⲠ]ᵇ
ⲦⲚⲀⲂⲰⲔ' ⲈⲚⲔⲞⲖⲀⲤⲒⲤ ⲘⲠⲚⲞϬ ⲚⲆⲢⲀⲔⲰⲚ ⲘⲚ ⲠⲔⲀⲔⲈ ⲈⲦ-
�occurred ⲠⲀⲒ ⲈⲦⲚⲀϢⲦ ⲈⲘⲀϢⲞ · ⲀⲨⲰ ⲚⲤⲈⲚⲀⲤⲈⲦⲦⲎⲨⲦⲚ
5 ⲀⲚ ⲈⲠⲔⲞⲤⲘⲞⲤ ⲚϢⲀⲈⲚⲈ�import ⲀⲖⲖⲀ ⲈⲦⲈⲦⲚⲀⲢⲀⲦϢⲰⲠⲈ ϢⲀ-
ⲂⲞⲖ · ⲀⲬⲒⲤ ⲈⲚⲈⲦⲚⲀⲔⲰ ⲚⲤⲰⲞⲨ ⲚⲦⲈⲤⲂⲰ ⲚⲦⲀⲖⲎⲐⲒⲀ
ⲚⲦⲈ ⲠϢⲞⲢⲠ ⲘⲘⲨⲤⲦⲎⲢⲒⲞⲚ ⲬⲈ ⲞⲨⲞⲒ ⲚⲎⲦⲚ ⲚⲦⲰⲦⲚ ⲬⲈ
ⲦⲈⲦⲚⲔⲞⲖⲀⲤⲒⲤ ϨⲞⲞⲨ ⲠⲀⲢⲀ ⲢⲰⲘⲈ ⲚⲒⲘ · ⲈⲦⲈⲦⲚⲀϬⲰ ⲄⲀⲢ
ϨⲘ ⲠⲚⲞϬ ⲚⲬⲀϤ · ⲠⲈⲔⲢⲨⲤⲦⲀⲖⲖⲞⲤ ⲘⲚ ⲦⲈⲬⲀⲖⲀⲌⲀ ϨⲢⲀⲒ
10 ϨⲚ ⲦⲘⲎⲦⲈ ⲘⲠⲈⲆⲢⲀⲔⲰⲚ ⲘⲚ ⲠⲔⲀⲔⲈ ⲈⲦϨⲒⲂⲞⲖ ⲀⲨⲰ Ⲛ-
ⲤⲈⲚⲀⲤⲈⲦⲦⲎⲚⲞⲨ ⲀⲚ ⲈⲠⲔⲞⲤⲘⲞⲤ ⲬⲒⲚ ⲠⲈⲒⲚⲀⲨ ϢⲀⲈⲚⲈϨ ·
ⲀⲖⲖⲀ ⲦⲈⲦⲚⲀⲢϨⲢⲞⲨⲞⲨⲬϤ ⲘⲠⲘⲀ ⲈⲦⲘⲘⲀⲨ · ⲀⲨⲰ ϨⲢⲀⲒ
ϨⲘ ⲠⲂⲰⲖ ⲈⲂⲞⲖ ⲘⲠⲦⲎⲢϤ ⲦⲈⲦⲚⲀⲀⲚϨⲀⲖⲒⲤⲔⲈ ⲚⲦⲈⲦⲚⲢⲀⲦ-
ϢⲰⲠⲈ ϢⲀⲈⲚⲈϨ · ⲀⲬⲒⲤ ϨⲰⲰϤ ⲞⲚ ⲈⲚⲢⲰⲘⲈ ⲚⲦⲈ ⲠⲔⲞⲤ- ⲤⲀⲞ
15 ⲘⲞⲤ ⲬⲈ ϢⲰⲠⲈ ⲚϨⲞⲢⲔϤ ⲚⲦⲈⲦⲚⲬⲒ ⲚⲘⲘⲨⲤⲦⲎⲢⲒⲞⲚ Ⲙ-
ⲠⲞⲨⲞⲈⲒⲚ ⲚⲦⲈⲦⲚⲂⲰⲔ ⲈⲠⲬⲒⲤⲈ ⲚⲦⲘⲚⲦⲈⲢⲞ ⲘⲠⲞⲨⲞⲈⲒⲚ ·
ⲀⲬⲒⲤ ⲈⲢⲞⲞⲨ ⲬⲈ ⲀⲢⲒⲘⲀⲒⲢⲰⲘⲈ ⲚⲦⲈⲦⲚⲘⲠϢⲀ ⲚⲘⲘⲨⲤⲦⲎ-
ⲢⲒⲞⲚ ⲘⲠⲞⲨⲞⲈⲒⲚ ⲚⲦⲈⲦⲚⲂⲰⲔ ⲈⲠⲬⲒⲤⲈ ⲈⲦⲘⲚⲦⲈⲢⲞ ⲘⲠⲞⲨ-
ⲞⲈⲒⲚ · ⲀⲬⲒⲤ ⲈⲢⲞⲞⲨ ⲬⲈ ⲀⲢⲒⲢⲘⲢⲀϢ ⲚⲦⲈⲦⲚⲬⲒ ⲚⲘⲘⲨⲤ-
20 ⲦⲎⲢⲒⲞⲚ ⲘⲠⲞⲨⲞⲈⲒⲚ ⲚⲦⲈⲦⲚⲂⲰⲔ ⲈⲠⲬⲒⲤⲈ ⲈⲦⲘⲚⲦⲈⲢⲞ Ⲙ-
ⲠⲞⲨⲞⲈⲒⲚ · ⲀⲬⲒⲤ ⲈⲢⲞⲞⲨ ⲬⲈ ⲀⲢⲒⲈⲒⲢⲎⲚⲒⲔⲞⲤ ⲚⲦⲈⲦⲚⲬⲒ Ⲛ-
ⲘⲘⲨⲤⲦⲎⲢⲒⲞⲚ ⲘⲠⲞⲨⲞⲈⲒⲚ ⲚⲦⲈⲦⲚⲂⲰⲔ ⲈⲠⲬⲒⲤⲈ ⲈⲦⲘⲚⲦⲈ-
ⲢⲞ ⲘⲠⲞⲨⲞⲈⲒⲚ · ⲀⲬⲒⲤ ⲈⲢⲞⲞⲨ ⲬⲈ ⲀⲢⲒⲚⲀⲎⲦ ⲚⲦⲈⲦⲚⲬⲒ Ⲛ-
ⲘⲘⲨⲤⲦⲎⲢⲒⲞⲚ ⲘⲠⲞⲨⲞⲈⲒⲚ ⲚⲦⲈⲦⲚⲂⲰⲔ ⲈⲠⲬⲒⲤⲈ ⲈⲦⲘⲚⲦⲈ-

---

1   MS ⲚⲬⲈ; read ⲬⲈ. MS originally ⲈⲚϢⲰⲠⲈ; ⲛ expunged.
7   ⲠⲀⲢⲀⲢ expunged before ⲚⲦⲰⲦⲚ.
16 MS ⲚⲦⲘⲚⲦⲈⲢⲞ; read ⲈⲦⲘⲚⲦⲈⲢⲞ.
19 MS originally ⲚⲦⲈⲦⲚϢⲰⲠⲈⲬⲒ; ϢⲰⲠⲈ expunged and crossed out.

error, you will go to the *punishments* of the great *dragon*, and the outer darkness which is very severe, and for eternity you will not be cast into the *world, but* you will become non-existent to the end [1]. Say to those who will abandon the *true* teachings of the First *Mystery* : woe to you, for your *punishment* is severe *beyond* all men [2]. *For* you will remain in the great frost, *ice* and *hail* in the midst of the *dragon* and the outer darkness, and you will not be cast into the *world* from this time henceforth for ever, *but* you will perish [3] in that place. And at the dissolution of the All you will be *consumed* and become non-existent for ever.

Say rather to the men of the *world* : be calm, that you may receive the *mysteries* of the light, and go to the height to the Kingdom of the Light. Say to them : be loving, that you may be worthy of the *mysteries* of the light, and go to the height to the Kingdom of the Light. Say to them : be compassionate, that you may receive the *mysteries* of the light, and go to the height to the Kingdom of the Light. Say to them : be *peaceful*, that you may receive the *mysteries* of the light, and go to the height to the Kingdom of the Light. Say to them : be merciful, that you may receive the *mysteries* of the light, and go to the height to the Kingdom | of the

---

[1]   (5, 6) non-existent to the end; Till : completely non-existent.
[2]   (8) severe beyond all men; Till : more severe than (that) of all (other) men.
[3]   (12) perish; Schmidt : stiffen (cf. 271.23).

ⲣⲟ ⲙ̅ⲡⲟⲩⲟⲉⲓⲛ· ⲁϫⲓⲥ ⲉⲣⲟⲟⲩ ϫⲉ ⲁⲣⲓⲙ̅ⲛ̅ⲧ̅ⲛ̅ⲁ ⲛ̅ⲧⲉⲧ̅ⲛ̅
ⲛ̅ⲙ̅ⲙⲩⲥⲧⲏⲣⲓⲟⲛ ⲙ̅ⲡⲟⲩⲟⲉⲓⲛ ⲛ̅ⲧⲉⲧ̅ⲛ̅ⲃⲱⲕ ⲉⲡϫⲓⲥⲉ ⲉ
ⲙ̅ⲛ̅ⲧⲉⲣⲟ ⲙ̅ⲡⲟⲩⲟⲉⲓⲛ· ⲁϫⲓⲥ ⲉⲣⲟⲟⲩ ϫⲉ *ⲇⲓⲁⲕⲟⲛⲉⲓ ⲉ
ϩⲏⲕⲉ ⲙ̅ⲛ̅ ⲛⲉⲧϣⲱⲛⲉ ⲙ̅ⲛ̅ ⲛⲉⲧϩⲏϫ ⲛ̅ⲧⲉⲧ̅ⲛ̅ϫⲓ ⲛ̅ⲙ̅ⲙⲩⲥⲧ
ⲣⲓⲟⲛ ⲙ̅ⲡⲟⲩⲟⲉⲓⲛ ⲛ̅ⲧⲉⲧ̅ⲛ̅ⲃⲱⲕ ⲉⲡϫⲓⲥⲉ ⲉⲧⲙ̅ⲛ̅ⲧⲉⲣⲟ
ⲡⲟⲩⲟⲉⲓⲛ· ⲁϫⲓⲥ ⲉⲣⲟⲟⲩ ϫⲉ ⲁⲣⲓⲙⲁ̈ⲓⲛⲟⲩⲧⲉ ⲛ̅ⲧⲉⲧ̅ⲛ̅ϫⲓ
ⲙ̅ⲙⲩⲥⲧⲏⲣⲓⲟⲛ ⲙ̅ⲡⲟⲩⲟⲉⲓⲛ ⲛ̅ⲧⲉⲧ̅ⲛ̅ⲃⲱⲕ ⲉⲡϫⲓⲥⲉ ⲉⲧⲙ̅ⲛ̅ⲧ
ⲣⲟ ⲙ̅ⲡⲟⲩⲟⲉⲓⲛ· ⲁϫⲓⲥ ⲉⲣⲟⲟⲩ ϫⲉ ⲁⲣⲓⲇⲓⲕⲁⲓⲟⲥ ⲛ̅ⲧⲉⲧ
ϫⲓ ⲛ̅ⲙ̅ⲙⲩⲥⲧⲏⲣⲓⲟⲛ ⟨ⲙ̅ⲡⲟⲩⲟⲉⲓⲛ⟩ ⲛ̅ⲧⲉⲧ̅ⲛ̅ⲃⲱⲕ ⲉⲡϫⲓⲥⲉ
ⲧⲙ̅ⲛ̅ⲧⲉⲣⲟ ⲙ̅ⲡⲟⲩⲟⲉⲓⲛ· ⲁϫⲓⲥ ⲉⲣⲟⲟⲩ ϫⲉ ⲁⲣⲓⲁⲅⲁⲑⲟⲥ
ⲧⲉⲧ̅ⲛ̅ϫⲓ ⲛ̅ⲙ̅ⲙⲩⲥⲧⲏⲣⲓⲟⲛ ⟨ⲙ̅ⲡⲟⲩⲟⲉⲓⲛ⟩ ⲛ̅ⲧⲉⲧ̅ⲛ̅ⲃⲱⲕ ⲉⲡ:
ⲥⲉ ⲉⲧⲙ̅ⲛ̅ⲧⲉⲣⲟ ⲙ̅ⲡⲟⲩⲟⲉⲓⲛ· ⲁϫⲓⲥ ⲉⲣⲟⲟⲩ ϫⲉ ⲁⲡⲟⲧⲁⲥ
ⲙ̅ⲡⲧⲏⲣϥ̅ ⲛ̅ⲧⲉⲧ̅ⲛ̅ϫⲓ ⲛ̅ⲙ̅ⲙⲩⲥⲧⲏⲣⲓⲟⲛ ⲙ̅ⲡⲟⲩⲟⲉⲓⲛ ⲛ̅ⲧⲉⲧ
ⲃⲱⲕ ⲉⲡϫⲓⲥⲉ ⲉⲧⲙ̅ⲛ̅ⲧⲉⲣⲟ ⲙ̅ⲡⲟⲩⲟⲉⲓⲛ· ⲛⲁ̈ⲓ ⲛⲉ ⲛ̅ϩⲟⲣ
ⲧⲏⲣⲟⲩ ⲛ̅ⲛⲉϩⲓⲟⲟⲩⲉ ⲛ̅ⲛⲉⲧⲙ̅ⲡϣⲁ ⲛ̅ⲙ̅ⲙⲩⲥⲧⲏⲣⲓⲟⲛ ⲙ̅ⲡⲟ
ⲟⲉⲓⲛ· ⲛⲁ̈ⲓ ⲟⲩⲛ ⲛ̅ⲧⲉ̈ⲓⲙⲓⲛⲉ ⲛ̅ⲧⲁⲩⲁⲡⲟⲧⲁⲥⲥⲉ ⲛ̅ⲧ
ⲁⲡⲟⲧⲁⲅⲏ ϯ ⲛⲁⲩ** ⲛ̅ⲙ̅ⲙⲩⲥⲧⲏⲣⲓⲟⲛ ⲙ̅ⲡⲟⲩⲟⲉⲓⲛ ⲁⲩⲱ
ⲡ̅ⲣ̅ϩⲟⲡⲟⲩ ⲉⲣⲟⲟⲩ ⲉⲡⲧⲏⲣϥ̅ ⲕⲁⲛ ⲉϣⲱⲡⲉ ϩⲉⲛⲣⲉ
ⲛⲟⲃⲉ ⲛⲉ ⲁⲩⲱ ⲁⲩϣⲱⲡⲉ ϩ̅ⲛ̅ ⲛⲟⲃⲉ ⲛⲓⲙ ⲙ̅ⲛ̅ ⲁⲛⲟ
ⲛⲓⲙ ⲛ̅ⲧⲁ̈ⲓϫⲟⲟⲩ ⲉⲣⲱⲧ̅ⲛ̅ ⲛ̅ⲧⲉ ⲡⲕⲟⲥⲙⲟⲥ ⲧⲏⲣⲟⲩ ⲛ̅
ⲕⲟⲧⲟⲩ ⲛ̅ⲥⲉⲙⲉⲧⲁⲛⲟⲉ̈ⲓ ⲁⲩⲱ ⲛ̅ⲥⲉϣⲱⲡⲉ ϩ̅ⲛ̅ ⲑⲩⲡⲟⲧ
ⲉ|ϫⲱ ⲙ̅ⲙⲟⲥ ⲛⲏⲧ̅ⲛ̅· ⲧⲉⲛⲟⲩ ϫⲉ ϯ ⲛⲁⲩ ⲛ̅ⲙ̅ⲙⲩⲥⲧⲏⲣ
ⲛ̅ⲧⲙ̅ⲛ̅ⲧⲉⲣⲟ ⲙ̅ⲡⲟⲩⲟⲉⲓⲛ ⲙ̅ⲡ̅ⲣ̅ϩⲟⲡⲟⲩ ⲉⲣⲟⲟⲩ ⲉⲡⲧⲏⲣϥ̅·
ⲃⲉ ⲧⲙ̅ⲛ̅ⲧⲣⲉϥⲣ̅ⲛⲟⲃⲉ ⲅⲁⲣ ⲛ̅ⲧⲁⲛⲉⲓⲛⲉ ⲛ̅ⲙ̅ⲙⲩⲥⲧⲏⲣⲓⲟⲛ
ⲡⲕⲟⲥⲙⲟⲥ· ϫⲉ ⲉ̈ⲓⲉⲕⲱ ⲉⲃⲟⲗ ⲛ̅ⲛⲉⲩⲛⲟⲃⲉ ⲧⲏⲣⲟⲩ
ⲁⲩⲁⲁⲩ ϫⲓⲛ ⲛ̅ϣⲟⲣⲡ· ⲉⲧⲃⲉ ⲡⲁ̈ⲓ ϭⲉ ⲁ̈ⲓϫⲟⲟⲥ ⲉⲣⲱⲧ̅ⲛ̅

9 ⲙ̅ⲡⲟⲩⲟⲉⲓⲛ omitted; also in line 11.
20 ⲧⲏⲣⲟⲩ is unnecessary.
24 MS ⲛ̅ⲧⲁⲛⲉⲓⲛⲉ; read ⲛ̅ⲧⲁ̈ⲓⲉⲓⲛⲉ.
25 ϫ expunged before ⲛ̅ⲧⲁⲩⲁⲁⲩ.

Light. Say to them : be charitable, that you may receive the *mysteries* of the light, and go to the height to the Kingdom of the Light. Say to them : *serve* the poor and the sick and the oppressed, that you may receive the *mysteries* of the light, and go to the height to the Kingdom of the Light. Say to them : be God-loving, that you may receive the *mysteries* of the light, and go to the height to the Kingdom of the Light. Say to them : be *righteous*, that you may receive the *mysteries* ⟨of the light⟩, and go to the height to the Kingdom of the Light. Say to them : be *good*, that you may receive the *mysteries* ⟨of the light⟩, and go to the height to the Kingdom of the Light. Say to them : *renounce* the All, that you may receive the *mysteries* of the light, and go to the height to the Kingdom of the Light.

These are all the *boundaries* of the ways of those who are worthy of the *mysteries* of the light. *Now* to such as have *renounced* with this *renunciation*, give the *mysteries* and do not conceal them from them at all, *even if* they are sinners and have come to be in all sins and all *iniquities* of the *world*, all of which I have told you, so that they may turn round and *repent* and be in *submission*. As I have now said to you : give to them the *mysteries* of the Kingdom of the Light, and do not conceal them from them at all. *For* because of sinfulness I brought the *mysteries* to the *world*, so that I should forgive all their sins which they have committed from the beginning. Concerning this now I once said to you : | 'I have not come to call the *righteous*'*. Now at

---

* cf. Mt. 9.13; Mk. 2.17; Lk. 5.32

ΠΙΟΥΟΕΙϢ ϪΕ Ν̄ΤΑΪΕΙ' ΑΝ ΕΤΑ2Μ̄-Ν̄ΔΙΚΑΙΟС · ΤΕΝΟΥ
6Ε Ν̄ΤΑΪΕΙΝΕ Ν̄ΜΜΥСΤΗΡΙΟΝ ϪΕ ΕΥΕΚϢ ΕΒΟΛ Ν̄Ν̄ΝΟΒΕ
Ν̄ΟΥΟΝ ΝΙΜ ΑΥϢ Ν̄СΕΧΙΤΟΥ ΕΤΜ̄ΝΤΕΡΟ Μ̄ΠΟΥΟΕΙΝ ·
Μ̄ΜΥСΤΗΡΙΟΝ ΓΑΡ Ν̄ΤΟΟΥˑΝΕ ΤΑϢΡΕΑ Μ̄ΠϢΟΡΠ̄ Μ- [CM ᵇ]
5 ΜΥСΤΗΡΙΟΝ · ΕΤΡΕϤΒϢΤΕ ΕΒΟΛ Ν̄Ν̄ΝΟΒΕ ΜΝ̄ Ν̄ΑΝΟΜΙΑ
Ν̄ΡΡΕϤΡ̄ΝΟΒΕ ΤΗΡΟΥ ·

ΑСϢϢΠΕ 6Ε Ν̄ΤΕΡΕ ῙС ΟΥϢ ΕϤϪϢ Ν̄ΝΕΪϢΑϪΕ Ε-
ΝΕϤΜΑΘΗΤΗС · ΑСΕΙ' ΕΘΗ Ν̄6Ι ΜΑΡΙΑ ΠΕΧΑС Μ̄ΠСϢΡ
ϪΕ ΠΑϪΟΕΙС ΕΪΕ ΟΥΝΡϢΜΕ Ν̄ΔΙΚΑΙΟС ΕϤϪΗΚ ΕΒΟΛ 2Ν̄
10 ΤΜΝ̄ΤΔΙΚΑΙΟС ΤΗΡС̄ ΑΥϢ ΠΡϢΜΕ ΕΤΜ̄ΜΑΥ ΕΜΝ̄Τϥ-
ΛΑΑΥ Ν̄ΝΟΒΕ ΕΠΤΗΡϤ · ΠΑΪ Ν̄ΤΕΪΜΙΝΕ СΕΝΑΒΑСΑΝΙΖΕ
Μ̄ΜΟϤ 2Ν̄ Ν̄ΚΟΛΑСΙС ΜΝ̄ ΝΕΚΡΙСΙС Χ̄Ν̄ Μ̄ΜΟΝ · Η̄ Μ̄ΜΟΝ
Ν̄ΤΟϤ ΠΡϢΜΕ ΕΤΜ̄ΜΑΥ СΕΝΑϤΙΤϤ Ε2ΟΥΝ ΕΤΜ̄ΝΤΕΡΟ
Ν̄ΜΠΗΥΕ Χ̄Ν̄ Μ̄ΜΟΝ · ΑϤΟΥϢ2Μ̄ ΔΕ Ν̄6Ι ΠСϢΤΗΡ ΠΕ-
15 ϪΑϤ Μ̄ΜΑΡΙΑ ϪΕ ΟΥΡϢΜΕ Ν̄ΔΙΚΑΙΟС ΠΑΪ ΕϤϪΗΚ ΕΒΟΛ
2Ν̄ ΤΜΝ̄ΤΔΙΚΑΙΟС ΤΗΡС̄ · ΑΥϢ Μ̄ΠϤΡ̄-ΛΑΑΥ Ν̄ΝΟΒΕ ΕΝΕ2 · CMA
ΑΥϢ ΠΑΪ Ν̄ΤΕΪΜΙΝΕ ΕΜΠϤϪΙ-ΛΑΑΥ Μ̄ΜΥСΤΗΡΙΟΝ Ν̄ΤΕ
ΠΟΥΟΕΙΝ ΕΝΕ2 ΕϤϢΑΝϢϢΠΕ Ν̄6Ι ΠΕΥΟΕΙϢ ΕϤΝΗΥ
ΕΒΟΛ 2Μ̄ ΠСϢΜΑ Ν̄ΤΕΥΝΟΥ ϢΑΥΕΙ Ν̄6Ι Μ̄ΠΑΡΑΛΗΜΠΤΗС
20 Μ̄ΠΟΥΑ Μ̄ΠΝΟ6 Ν̄ΤΡΙΔΥΝΑΜΙС · ΝΑΪ ΕΥΝ̄-ΟΥΝΟ6 Ν̄2Η-
ΤΟΥ Ν̄СΕ2ΑΡΠΑΖΕ Ν̄ΤΕѰΥΧΗ Μ̄ΠΡϢΜΕ ΕΤΜ̄ΜΑΥ Ν̄ΤΟ-
ΟΤΟΥ Ν̄ΜΠΑΡΑΛΗΜΠΤΗС Ν̄ΕΡΙΝΑΙΟС · Ν̄СΕΡϢΟΜΝ̄Τ Ν̄-
2ΟΟΥ ΕΥΚϢΤΕ Ν̄ΜΜΑС 2ΡΑΪ 2Ν̄ Ν̄СϢΝΤ̄ ΤΗΡΟΥ Ν̄ΤΕ

---

9   MS ΟΥΝΡϢΜΕ; read ΟΥΡϢΜΕ.
19   MS originally ΠΑΡΑΛΗΜΠΤΗС; Μ̄ inserted above.
20   MS Μ̄ΠΝΟ6; read Π̄ΠΝΟ6.

this time I have brought the *mysteries*, so that the sins of everyone should be forgiven, and that they should be taken to the Kingdom of the Light. *For* the *mysteries* are the *gift* of the First *Mystery* to erase the sins and the *iniquities* of all sinners."

103. Now it happened when Jesus finished saying these words to his *disciples*, Maria came forward. She said to the *Saviour* : "My Lord, will a *righteous* man who is fulfilled in all *righteousness* and that man has committed no sins at all, will such a one as this be *tormented* in the *punishments* and the *judgments* or not? *Or* rather, will that man be brought into the Kingdom of Heaven or not?"

The *Saviour however* answered and said to Maria : "A *righteous* man who is fulfilled in all *righteousness* and has never committed any sins, such a one who has never received any of the *mysteries* of the light, when the time comes that he should go forth from the *body,* in that hour come the *paralemptai* of one of the great *triple powers* — these among which is a great one — and they *snatch* the *soul* [1] of that man from the hands of the *erinaioi paralemptai.* And they spend three days going round with it among all the creations of | the

---

[1] (21) snatch the soul; see J 99; (also 360.3 ff.).

ΠΚΟCΜΟC Μ̄Ν̄ΝCA ΠϢΟΜΝ̄Τ Ν̄2ΟΟΥ· ϢΑΎΧΙΤC ΕΠΕC-
CΗΤ᾽ ΕΠΕΧΛΟC· Ν̄CΕΧΙΤC ΕΒΟΛ 2Ν̄ Ν̄ΚΟΛΑCΙC ΤΗΡΟΥ
Ν̄ΤΕ ΝΕΚΡΙCΙC· Ν̄CΕΤΑΥΟC ΕΝΕΚΡΙCΙC ΤΗΡΟΥ ΑΥϢ ΜΕ-
ΡΕ Ν̄ΚϢ2Τ Ν̄ΝΕΧΛΟC ΜΕΥΕΝϢΧΛΕΙ ΝΑC ΕΜΑΤΕ· ΑΛΛΑ
5 ΕΚΜΕΡΟΥC ϢΑΥΕΝϢΧΛΙ ΝΑC ΠΡΟC ΟΥΚΟΥΪ Ν̄ΟΥΟΕΙϢ· ⲤΜⲀ ᵇ
ΑΥϢ 2Ν̄ ΟΥCΠΟΥΔΗ 2Ν̄ ΟΥ6ΕΠΗ ϢΑΥΝΑ ΝΑC· Ν̄CΕΝ-
ΤC Ε2ΡΑΪ 2Ν̄ ΝΕΧΛΟC Ν̄CΕΧΙΤC ΕΒΟΛ 2Ι ΤΕ2ΙΗ Ν̄ΤΜΗΤΕ
ΕΒΟΛ 2ΙΤΟΟΤΟΥ Ν̄ΝΑΡΧϢΝ ΤΗΡΟΥ ΕΤΜ̄ΜΑΥ ΑΥϢ ΜΕΥ-
ΚΟΛΑΖΕ Μ̄ΜΟC 2Ν̄ ΝΕΥΚΡΙCΙC ΕΤΝΑϢΤ ΑΛΛΑ ϢΑΡΕ
10 ΠΚϢ2Τ Ν̄ΝΕΥΤΟΠΟC ΕΝϢΧΛΕΙ ΝΑC ΕΚΜΕΡΟΥC ΑΥϢ
ΕΥϢΑΝΧΙΤC ΕΠΤΟΠΟC Ν̄ΝΙΑΧΘΑΝΑΒΑC ΠΙΑΤΝΑ· ΜΕΥ-
ΕϢΚΟΛΑΖΕ Μ̄ΜΟC ΜΕΝΤΟΙΓΕ 2Ν̄ ΝΕϤΚΡΙCΙC ΕΘΟΟΥ· ΑΛ-
ΛΑ ϢΑϤΚΑΤΕΧΕ Μ̄ΜΟC Ν̄ΟΥΚΟΥΕΙ Ν̄ΟΥΟΪϢ· ΕΡΕ ΠΚϢ-
2Τ Ν̄ΝΕϤΚΟΛΑCΙC ΕΝϢΧΛΙ ΝΑC ΕΚΜΕΡΟΥC ΑΥϢ ΟΝ 2Ν̄
15 ΟΥ6ΕΠΗ ϢΑΥΝΑ ΝΑC Ν̄CΕΝΤC Ε2ΡΑΪ 2Ν̄ ΝΕΥΤΟΠΟC
ΕΤΜ̄ΜΑΥ· ΑΥϢ ΜΕΥΧΙΤC ΕΒΟΛ 2Ν̄ Ν̄ΑΙϢΝ ΧΕ Ν̄ΝΕ Ν̄- [ⲤⲘⲂ]
ΑΡΧϢΝ Ν̄ΝΑΙϢΝ Ν̄ΝΕΥϤΙΤC Ν̄CΤΕΡΕCΙΜΟΝ ΑΛΛΑ ϢΑΥ-
ΧΙΤC ΕΒΟΛ 2Ι ΤΕ2ΙΗ Μ̄ΠΟΥΟΕΙΠ Μ̄ΠΡΗ Ν̄CΕΧΙΤC ΕΡΑΤC
Ν̄ΤΠΑΡΘΕΝΟC Μ̄ΠΟΥΟΕΙΝ· ϢΑCΔΟΚΙΜΑΖΕ Μ̄ΜΟC Ν̄C2Ε
20 ΕΡΟC ΕCΟΥΟΧ. ΕΝΟΒΕ ΑΥϢ ΜΕCΤΡΕΥΧΙΤC ΕΠΟΥ⟨Ο⟩-
ΕΙΝ ΧΕ ΠΜΑΕΙΝ Ν̄ΤΜΝ̄ΤΕΡΟ Μ̄ΠΜΥCΤΗΡΙΟΝ Ν̄ϤϢΟΟΠ
Ν̄ΜΜΑC ΑΝ· ΑΛΛΑ ϢΑCCϤΡΑΓΙΖΕ Μ̄ΜΟC 2Ν̄ ΟΥCϤΡΑΓΙC

---

8 Π̄ΑΤΝΑ· 2ΟΜΟΙϢC ΟΝ ϢΑΥΧΙΤϤ ΕΒΟΛ 2Ν̄ Ν̄ΚΟΛΑCΙC ΤΗΡΟΥ
    written in lower margin; words perhaps omitted from this line.
11 MS Ν̄ΝΙΑΧΘΑΝΑΒΑC; read Π̄ΙΑΧΘΑΠΑΒΑC. MS ΜΕΥΕϢΚΟΛΑΖΕ; read
    ΜϤΕϢΚΟΛΑΖΕ.
20 MS ΕΠΟΥΕΙΠ; read ΕΠΟΥΟΕΙΝ.
22 MS ϢΑϤCϤΡΑΓΙΖΕ; Ϥ altered to C.

world. After the three days they take it down to the *Chaos* and cast it into all the *punishments* of the *judgments,* and they send it to all the *judgments.* And the fires of the *Chaos(es)* do not *trouble* it greatly, *but* they *trouble* it *in part for* a short time. And *with speed* they quickly have mercy on it, and bring it up from the *Chaos(es),* and take it forth upon the way of the Midst by means of all those *archons* [1]. And they (the archons) do not *punish* it with their harsh *judgments, but* the fire of their *places troubles* it *in part.* And when they take it to the *place* of Jachthanabas [2], the merciless, he is *certainly* not able to *punish* it with his wicked *judgments, but* he *restrains* it for a short time. And the fire of his *punishments troubles* it *in part.* And again quickly they have mercy on it and bring it up from their *places* there. And they do not bring it forth into the *aeons* lest the *archons* of the *aeons* should take it away *by theft, but* they take it forth upon the way of the light of the sun, and bring it to the *Virgin* of the Light. She *examines* it and finds it free from sin. And she does not allow them to take it to the light because it has not the sign of the kingdom of the *mystery. But* she *seals* it with a superior *seal* | and

---

[1]   (8) those archons; MS (perhaps): those merciless archons. And likewise they bring it forth from all the punishments, and they (the archons) ...

[2]   (11) Jachthanabas; see J 141; (also 365.12).

ЄСΟΥΟΤ͞Β Ν͞СΤΡΕΥΝΟΧ͞Ч ЄΠС·ΩΜΑ 2Ν Ν̄ΑΙΩΝ Ν̄ΤΑΙ-
ΚΑΙΟСΥΝΗ ΠΑΪ ЄЧΝΑΡΑΓΛΟΟС Ν̄Ч2Є ЄΜΜΑЄΙΝ Ν̄ΜΜΥСΤΗ-
ΡΙΟΝ Μ̄ΠΟΥΟЄΙΝ Ν̄ЧΚΛΗΡΟΝΟΜΙ Ν̄ΤΜΝ̄ΤЄΡΟ Μ̄ΠΟΥΟЄΙΝ
·ΩΛЄΝЄ2· Є·Ω·ΩΠЄ Ν̄ΤΟЧ ЄЧΡΝΟΒЄ Π̄ΟΥСΟΠ˙ Π̄ СΝΑΥ Π̄
5 ·ΩΟΜΝΤ ΠΑΪ ΟΝ СЄΝΑΤ͞СΤΟЧ ЄΠΚΟСΜΟС ΚΑΤΑ ΠΤΥ-
ΠΟС Ν̄ΝΝΟΒЄ ЄΝΤΑЧΑΑΥ ΝΑΪ ˙Ϯ̄ΝΑΧ·Ω Μ̄ΠЄΥΤΥΠΟС Є-
Ρ·ΩΤΝ ЄΪ·ΩΑΝΟΥ·Ω ЄΪΧ·Ω ЄΡ·ΩΤΝ Μ̄ΠС·ΩΡ ЄΒΟΛ Μ̄ΠΤΗ- [С͞ΜΒ͞ᵇ]
Ρ͞Ч· ΑΛΛΑ 2ΑΜΗΝ 2ΑΜΗΝ ˙Ϯ̄Χ·Ω Μ̄ΜΟС ЄΡ·ΩΤΝ· ΧЄ ΚΑΝ
ΟΥΡ·ΩΜЄ Ν̄ΑΙΚΑΙΟС ЄΜΠ̄ЧΡ-ΛΑΑΥ Ν̄ΝΟΒЄ ЄΠΤΗΡЧ ΜΝ̄-
10 ·Ω6ΟΜ ЄΤΡЄΥΧΙΤЧ ЄΤΜΝ̄ΤЄΡΟ Μ̄ΠΟΥΟЄΙΝ· ЄΒΟΛ ΧЄ
Μ̄ΠΜΑЄΙΝ Ν̄ΤΜΝ̄ΤЄΡΟ Ν̄ΜΜΥСΤΗΡΙΟΝ Ν̄Ч·ΩΟΟΠ Ν̄ΜΜΑЧ
ΑΝ· 2ΑΠΑΧ 2ΑΠΛ·ΩС ΜΝ̄6ΟΜ Ν̄ΧΙ-Ψ̄ΥΧΗ ЄΠΟΥΟЄΙΝ ΑΧΝ̄
Μ̄ΜΥСΤΗΡΙΟΝ Ν̄ΤΜΝ̄ΤЄΡΟ Μ̄ΠΟΥΟЄΙΝ·

ΑС·Ω·ΩΠЄ 6Є Ν̄ΤЄΡЄ Ι͞С ΟΥ·Ω ЄЧΧ·Ω Ν̄ΝЄΙ·ΩΑΧЄ Є-
15 ΝЄЧΜΑΘΗΤΗС ΑЧЄΙ ЄΘΗ Ν̄6Ι Ῑ·ΩΑΝΝΗС ΠЄΧΑЧ ΧЄ ΠΑ-
ΧΟЄΙС ЄΪЄ ·Ω·ΩΠЄ ΟΥΡ·ΩΜЄ Ν̄ΡЄЧΡΝΟΒЄ Μ̄ΠΑΡΑΝΟΜΟС
ЄЧΧΗΚ ЄΒΟΛ Ν̄ΑΝΟΜΙΑ ΝΙΜ· ΑΥ·Ω ΑЧΛΟ Ν̄2ΗΤΟΥ ΤΗ-
ΡΟΥ ЄΤΒЄ ΤΜΝ̄ΤЄΡΟ Ν̄Μ̄ΠΗΥЄ· ΑΥ·Ω ΑЧΑΠΟΤΑССЄ Μ̄-
ΠΚΟСΜΟС ΤΗΡЧ ΜΝ̄ ΘΥΛΗ ΤΗΡС ЄΤΝ̄2ΗΤЧ ΑΥ·Ω Ν̄ΤΝ̄˙
20 ΝΑЧ ΧΙΝ ΤΑΡΧΗ Ν̄ΜΜΥСΤΗΡΙΟΝ Μ̄ΠΟΥΟЄΙΝ ΝΑΪ ЄΤΜ̄ С͞Μ͞Γ
Π·ΩΟΡΠ Ν̄Χ·ΩΡΗΜΑ ΧΙΝ ΠСΑΝΒΟΛ· ΑΥ·Ω ЄЧ·ΩΑΝΧΙ Ν̄-
ΜΜΥСΤΗΡΙΟΝ ΜΝ̄ΝСΑ ΟΥΚΟΥΪ ΟΝ Ν̄ΟΥΟЄΙ·Ω Ν̄ЧΚΟΤЧ
Ν̄ЧΠΑΡΑΒΑ· ΑΥ·Ω ΟΝ ΜΝ̄ΝСΑ ΝΑΪ Ν̄ЧΚΟΤЧ Ν̄ЧΛΟ 2Ν ΝΟ-
ΒЄ ΝΙΜ· ΑΥ·Ω Ν̄ЧΚΟΤЧ Ν̄ЧΑΠΟΤΑССЄ Μ̄ΠΚΟСΜΟС ΤΗΡЧ

---

8 MS originally 2ΑΜΗΝ only.
16 MS ЄΪЄ ·Ω·ΩΠЄ; read ЄΪЄ ЄЧ·ΩΠЄ.

allows them to cast it into the *body* in the *aeons* of *righteousness*. This (man) will become *good* and will find the
sign of the *mysteries* of the light, and will *inherit* the Kingdom
of the Light for ever. If he has committed sin once *or* twice
or thrice he will be cast again into the *world, according to*
the *type* of the sins which he has committed. I will say their
type to you when I finish telling you of the distribution
of the All. *But truly, truly,* I say to you, *even if* a *righteous*
man has committed no sins at all, it is not possible for him
to be taken to the Kingdom of the Light, unless he has the
sign of the kingdom of the *mysteries. In a word* it is impossible
to take *souls* to the light without the *mysteries* of the
Kingdom of the Light."

104. Now it happened when Jesus finished saying these
words to his *disciples*, John came forward and said : "My
Lord, if there is a sinful and *lawless* man who is filled with
all *iniquities*, and he has ceased from them all for the sake
of the Kingdom of Heaven, and he has *renounced* the whole
world and all the *matter* within it. And we give to him from
the *beginning* the *mysteries* of the light which are in the first
space from without. And when he has received the *mysteries*,
after a short time he turns and *transgresses*. And again after
these things, he turns and ceases from all sin. And he turns
and *renounces* the whole *world* | and all *matter* within it,

ⲘⲚ ⲞⲨⲀⲎ ⲦⲎⲢⲤ ⲈⲦⲚ̄ⲌⲎⲦϤ Ⲙ̄Ϥ̄Ⲉ̄Ⲓ ⲞⲚ Ⲛ̄ϤϢⲰⲠⲈ ⲌⲚ ⲞⲨ-

ⲚⲞϬ Ⲙ̄ⲘⲈⲦⲀⲚⲞⲒⲀ· ⲀⲨⲰ Ⲡ̄ⲦⲚⲈⲒⲘⲈ ⲀⲎⲐⲰⲤ Ⲍ̄Ⲛ ⲞⲨⲘⲈ·

ϪⲈ ϤⲞⲨⲈϢ-ⲠⲚⲞⲨⲦⲈ Ⲛ̄ⲦⲚ·†· ⲚⲀϤ Ⲙ̄ⲠⲘⲈⲌⲤⲚⲀⲨ Ⲙ̄ⲘⲨⲤⲦⲎ-

ⲢⲒⲞⲚ Ⲙ̄ⲠϢⲞⲢⲠ̄ Ⲛ̄ⲬⲰⲢⲎⲘⲀ· ⲚⲀⲒ ⲈⲦⲌ̄ⲠⲤⲀⲚ̄ⲂⲞⲖ· ⲌⲞⲘⲞⲒⲰⲤ

5 ⲞⲚ Ⲛ̄ⲞⲨⲰϢⲘ̄ Ⲛ̄ϤⲔⲞⲦϤ Ⲛ̄ϤⲠⲀⲢⲀⲂⲀ· Ⲛ̄ϤϢⲰⲠⲈ ⲞⲚ Ⲍ̄Ⲛ Ⲛ̄-

ⲚⲞⲂⲈ Ⲛ̄ⲦⲈ ⲠⲔⲞⲤⲘⲞⲤ· ⲀⲨⲰ ⲞⲚ ⲘⲚ̄ⲚⲤⲀ ⲚⲀⲒ Ⲛ̄ϤⲔⲞⲦϤ

Ⲛ̄ϤⲀⲞ Ⲍ̄Ⲛ Ⲛ̄ⲚⲞⲂⲈ Ⲛ̄ⲦⲈ ⲠⲔⲞⲤⲘⲞⲤ· ⲀⲨⲰ ⲞⲚ Ⲛ̄ϤⲀⲠⲞⲦⲀⲤⲤⲈ

Ⲙ̄ⲠⲔⲞⲤⲘⲞⲤ ⲦⲎⲢϤ̄ ⲘⲚ ⲞⲨⲀⲎ ⲦⲎⲢⲤ ⲈⲦⲚ̄ⲌⲎⲦϤ· ⲀⲨⲰ ⲞⲚ

Ⲛ̄ϤϢⲰⲠⲈ Ⲍ̄Ⲛ ⲞⲨⲚⲞϬ Ⲙ̄ⲘⲈⲦⲀⲚⲞⲒⲀ· Ⲛ̄ⲦⲚⲈⲒⲘⲈ Ⲍ̄Ⲛ ⲞⲨⲰⲢϪ̄·

10 ⲀⲨⲰ ⲈⲚϤⲌⲨⲠⲞⲔⲢⲒⲚⲈ ⲀⲚ· Ⲛ̄ⲦⲚⲔⲞⲦⲚ̄ Ⲛ̄ⲦⲚ†· ⲚⲀϤ Ⲛ̄Ⲙ- ⲤⲘⲎ^b

ⲘⲨⲤⲦⲎⲢⲒⲞⲚ Ⲛ̄ⲦⲀⲢⲬⲎ ⲚⲀⲒ ⟨ⲈⲦϢⲞⲞⲠ Ⲍ̄Ⲙ ⲠϢⲞⲢⲠ̄ Ⲛ̄ⲬⲰ-

ⲢⲎⲘⲀ ϪⲒⲚ ⲠⲤⲀⲚ̄ⲂⲞⲖ⟩· ⲌⲞⲘⲞⲒⲰⲤ ⲞⲚ Ⲛ̄ϤⲔⲞⲦϤ̄ Ⲛ̄Ϥ̄ⲢⲚⲞⲂⲈ·

ⲀⲨⲰ Ⲛ̄ϤϢⲰⲠⲈ Ⲍ̄Ⲙ ⲠⲒⲦⲨⲠⲞⲤ ⲠⲒⲦⲨⲠⲞⲤ ⲔⲞⲨⲰϢ ⲈⲦⲢⲈⲚ-

ⲔⲰ ⲚⲀϤ ⲈⲂⲞⲖ ⲌⲈⲰⲤ ϢⲀ ⲤⲀϢϤ̄ Ⲛ̄ⲤⲞⲠ ⲀⲨⲰ Ⲛ̄ⲦⲚ†· ⲚⲀϤ

15 Ⲛ̄ⲘⲘⲨⲤⲦⲎⲢⲒⲞⲚ ⲚⲀⲒ ⲈⲦⲌ̄Ⲙ ⲠϢⲞⲢⲠ̄ Ⲛ̄ⲬⲰⲢⲎⲘⲀ ϪⲒⲚ ⲠⲤⲀⲚ-

ⲌⲞⲨⲚ ⲌⲈⲰⲤ ϢⲀ ⲤⲀϢϤ̄ Ⲛ̄ⲤⲞⲠ ϪⲚ ⲘⲘⲞⲚ· ⲀϤⲞⲨⲰϢⲘ̄ ⲞⲚ

Ⲛ̄ϬⲒ ⲠⲤⲰⲦⲎⲢ ⲠⲈϪⲀϤ Ⲛ̄ⲒⲰⲌⲀⲚⲚⲎⲤ ϪⲈ ⲞⲨⲘⲞⲚⲞⲚ ⲔⲰ

ⲚⲀϤ ⲈⲂⲞⲖ ϢⲀ ⲤⲀϢϤ̄ Ⲛ̄ⲤⲞⲠ· ⲀⲖⲖⲀ ⲌⲀⲘⲎⲚ †ϪⲰ Ⲙ̄ⲘⲞⲤ

ⲚⲎⲦⲚ ϪⲈ ⲔⲰ ⲚⲀϤ ⲈⲂⲞⲖ ϢⲀ ⲤⲀϢϤ̄ Ⲛ̄ⲤⲞⲠ Ⲛ̄ⲞⲨⲘⲎⲎϢⲈ

20 Ⲛ̄ⲤⲞⲠ· Ⲛ̄ⲦⲈⲦⲚ̄† ⲚⲀϤ ⲔⲀⲦⲀ ⲤⲞⲠ Ⲛ̄ⲘⲘⲨⲤⲦⲎⲢⲒⲞⲚ ϪⲒⲚ

ⲦⲀⲢⲬⲎ ⲚⲀⲒ ⲈⲦⲌ̄Ⲙ ⲠϢⲞⲢⲠ̄ Ⲛ̄ⲬⲰⲢⲎⲘⲀ ϪⲒⲚ ⲠⲤⲀⲚ̄ⲂⲞⲖ·

ⲀⲢⲎⲨ ⲢⲰ Ⲛ̄ⲦⲈⲦⲚ̄†ⲌⲎⲞⲨ Ⲛ̄ⲦⲈⲨ̈ⲨⲬⲎ Ⲙ̄ⲠⲤⲞⲚ ⲈⲦⲘ̄ⲘⲀⲨ

Ⲛ̄ϤⲔⲀⲎⲢⲞⲚⲞⲘⲒ Ⲛ̄ⲦⲘ̄ⲚⲦⲈⲢⲞ Ⲙ̄ⲠⲞⲨⲞⲈⲒⲚ· ⲈⲦⲂⲈ ⲠⲀⲒ̈ ⲞⲨⲚ

Ⲛ̄ⲦⲈⲢⲈⲦⲚ̄ϪⲚⲞⲨⲒ̈ Ⲙ̄ⲠⲞⲨⲞⲈⲒϢ ⲈⲦⲈⲦⲚ̄ϪⲰ Ⲙ̄ⲘⲞⲤ ϪⲈ ⲈⲢ-

---

11   ⲈⲦϢⲞⲞⲠ . . . ⲠⲤⲀⲚ̄ⲂⲞⲖ omitted after ⲚⲀⲒ̈.

16   MS ⲞⲚ inserted above.

and he comes again and exists in great *repentance*. And we know *truly*, in verihood, that he longs for God, and we give him the second *mystery* of the first *space* which is outside. *Likewise* again he turns and *transgresses* once more, and again he exists in the sins of the *world*. And again after these things he turns and ceases from the sins of the *world*. And again he *renounces* the whole *world* and all the *matter* within it. And again he exists in great *repentance*, and we know with certainty that he is not being *hypocritical*, and we turn and give to him the *mysteries* of the *beginning* ⟨which are in the first *space* from without⟩. *Likewise* again he turns and sins, and he is in *every type* (of sin). Dost thou wish that we forgive him *up to* seven times and that we give him the *mysteries* which are in the first *space* from without [1], *up to* seven times, or not?"

The *Saviour* answered again and said to John : "*Not only* forgive him up to seven times, *but truly* I say to you, forgive him up to seven times, many times over. And give to him *every* time the *mysteries* from the *beginning* which are in the first *space* from without. Perhaps you (will) win the *soul* of that brother, and he (will) *inherit* the Kingdom of the Light. Concerning this *now* you once asked me saying : |

---

[1] (16) from without; MS : from within.

ϢⲀⲚ ⲠⲈⲚⲤⲞⲚ Ⲣ̄ⲚⲞⲂⲈ ⲈⲢⲞⲚ ⲔⲞⲨⲰϢ ⲈⲦⲢⲈⲚⲔⲰ ⲚⲀϤ [ⲤⲘⲀ]
ⲈⲂⲞⲖ ϢⲀ ⲤⲀϢ̄Ϥ Ⲛ̄ⲤⲞⲠ· Ⲁ̈Ⲓ̈ⲞⲨⲰϢ̄Ⲃ Ⲁ̈Ⲓ̈ⲬⲞⲞⲤ ⲚⲎⲦ̄Ⲛ Ⲍ̄Ⲛ
ⲞⲨⲠⲀⲢⲀⲂⲞⲖⲎ ⲈⲒ̈ⲬⲰ Ⲙ̄ⲘⲞⲤ ⲬⲈ ⲞⲨⲘⲞⲚⲞⲚ ϢⲀ ⲤⲀϢ̄Ϥ
Ⲛ̄ⲤⲞⲠ’ ⲀⲖⲖⲀ ϢⲀ ⲤⲀϢ̄Ϥ Ⲛ̄ϢϤⲈ Ⲛ̄ⲤⲞⲠ· ⲦⲈⲚⲞⲨ ϬⲈ ⲔⲰ
5 ⲚⲀϤ ⲈⲂⲞⲖ Ⲛ̄ⲞⲨⲘⲎⲎϢⲈ Ⲛ̄ⲤⲞⲠ Ⲛ̄ⲦⲈⲦⲚ̄† ⲚⲀϤ ⲔⲀⲦⲀ ⲤⲞⲠ
Ⲛ̄ⲘⲘⲨⲤⲦⲎⲢⲒⲞⲚ ⲈⲦⲌ̄ⲒⲠⲤⲀⲚ̄ⲂⲞⲖ· ⲚⲀⲒ̈ ⲈⲦⲌ̄Ⲙ ⲠϢⲞⲢⲠ Ⲛ̄ⲬⲰ-
ⲢⲎⲘⲀ· ⲀⲢⲎⲨ ⲢⲰ Ⲛ̄ⲦⲈⲦⲚ̄†Ⲍ̄ⲎⲨ Ⲛ̄ⲦⲈⲮⲨⲬⲎ Ⲙ̄ⲠⲤⲞⲚ ⲈⲦⲘ̄-
ⲘⲀⲨ Ⲛ̄ϤⲔⲖⲎⲢⲞⲚⲞⲘⲒ Ⲛ̄ⲦⲘⲚ̄ⲦⲈⲢⲞ Ⲙ̄ⲠⲞⲨⲞⲈⲒⲚ· Ⲍ̄ⲀⲘⲎⲚ Ⲍ̄Ⲁ-
ⲘⲎⲚ †ⲬⲰ Ⲙ̄ⲘⲞⲤ ⲚⲎⲦⲚ̄ ⲬⲈ ⲠⲈⲦⲚⲀⲦⲀⲚⲌⲞ Ⲛ̄ⲞⲨⲮⲨⲬⲎ Ⲛ̄-
10 ⲞⲨⲰⲦ· ⲀⲨⲰ Ⲛ̄ϤⲚⲞⲨⲌ̄Ⲙ Ⲙ̄ⲘⲞⲤ ⲬⲰⲢⲒⲤ ⲠⲞⲨⲞ ⲈⲦⲚ̄ⲦⲀϤ
Ⲍ̄Ⲛ ⲦⲘⲚ̄ⲦⲈⲢⲞ Ⲙ̄ⲠⲞⲨⲞⲈⲒⲚ· ϤⲚⲀⲬⲒ Ⲛ̄ⲔⲈⲈⲞⲞⲨ ⲈⲠⲘⲀ Ⲛ̄ⲦⲈ-
ⲮⲨⲬⲎ Ⲛ̄ⲦⲀϤⲚⲞⲨⲌ̄Ⲙ Ⲙ̄ⲘⲞⲤ· Ⲍ̄ⲰⲤⲦⲈ ⲠⲈⲦⲚⲀⲚⲞⲨⲌ̄Ⲙ Ⲛ̄ⲞⲨ-
ⲘⲎⲎϢⲈ Ⲙ̄ⲮⲨⲬⲎ ⲬⲰⲢⲒⲤ ⲠⲈⲞⲞⲨ ⲈⲦⲚ̄ⲦⲀϤ Ⲍ̄Ⲙ ⲠⲈⲞⲞⲨ·
ϤⲚⲀⲬⲒ Ⲛ̄ⲔⲈⲘⲎⲎϢⲈ Ⲛ̄ⲈⲞⲞⲨ ⲈⲠⲘⲀ Ⲛ̄ⲚⲈⲮⲨⲬⲎ Ⲛ̄ⲦⲀϤⲚⲞⲨ- [ⲤⲘⲀ. ᵇ
15 Ⲍ̄Ⲙ Ⲙ̄ⲘⲞⲞⲨ·

　　ⲚⲀⲒ̈ ϬⲈ Ⲛ̄ⲦⲈⲢⲈϤⲬⲞⲞⲨ Ⲛ̄ϬⲒ ⲠⲤⲰⲢ ⲀϤϤⲞϬϤ ⲈⲂⲞⲖ Ⲛ̄ϬⲒ
Ⲓ̈ⲰⲌⲀⲚⲚⲎⲤ ⲠⲈⲬⲀϤ ⲬⲈ ⲠⲀⲬⲞⲈⲒⲤ ϤⲒ Ⲍ̄ⲀⲢⲞⲒ̈ ⲈⲒ̈ϢⲒⲚⲈ Ⲙ̄ⲘⲞⲔ
ⲬⲈ ⲬⲒⲚ ⲦⲈⲚⲞⲨ ⲄⲀⲢ ⲈⲒ̈ⲚⲀⲀⲢⲬⲒ Ⲛ̄ϢⲒⲚⲈ Ⲙ̄ⲘⲞⲔ ⲈⲦⲂⲈ Ⲍ̄ⲰⲂ
ⲚⲒⲘ· ⲈⲦⲂⲈ ⲐⲈ ⲈⲚⲚⲀⲔⲎⲢⲨⲤⲤⲈ Ⲙ̄ⲘⲞⲤ Ⲛ̄ⲦⲘⲚ̄ⲦⲢⲰⲘⲈ· Ⲉ-
20 ϢⲰⲠⲈ ⲞⲨⲚ ⲠⲤⲞⲚ ⲈⲦⲘ̄ⲘⲀⲨ ⲈⲒ̈ϢⲀⲚ† ⲚⲀϤ Ⲛ̄ⲞⲨⲘⲨⲤⲦⲎ-
ⲢⲒⲞⲚ Ⲍ̄Ⲙ ⲠⲘⲨⲤⲦⲎⲢⲒⲞⲚ Ⲛ̄ⲦⲀⲢⲬⲎ ⲚⲀⲒ̈ ⲈⲦϢⲞⲞⲠ Ⲍ̄Ⲙ ⲠϢⲞ-
ⲢⲠ Ⲛ̄ⲬⲰⲢⲎⲘⲀ ⲬⲒⲚ ⲠⲤⲀⲚ̄ⲂⲞⲖ ⲈⲒ̈ϢⲀⲚ† ⲚⲀϤ Ⲛ̄ⲞⲨⲘⲎⲎϢⲈ
Ⲙ̄ⲘⲨⲤⲦⲎⲢⲒⲞⲚ Ⲛ̄ϤⲦⲘⲈⲒⲢⲈ Ⲙ̄ⲠⲈⲘⲠϢⲀ Ⲛ̄ⲦⲘⲚ̄ⲦⲈⲢⲞ Ⲛ̄Ⲙ-

6　ⲈⲦⲌ̄ⲒⲠⲤⲀⲚ̄ⲂⲞⲖ should follow Ⲛ̄ⲬⲰⲢⲎⲘⲀ.
10　MS originally ⲠⲞⲨⲞⲈⲒⲚ; ⲈⲒⲚ expunged; read ⲠⲈⲞⲞⲨ.
13　MS Ⲍ̄Ⲙ ⲠⲈⲞⲞⲨ; read Ⲍ̄Ⲙ ⲠⲞⲨⲞⲈⲒⲚ or Ⲍ̄Ⲛ ⲦⲘⲚ̄ⲦⲈⲢⲞ Ⲙ̄ⲠⲞⲨⲞⲈⲒⲚ.
19　MS originally ⲈⲠⲦⲀⲚⲔⲎⲢ; ⲦⲀ expunged and Ⲁ inserted above.

'If our brother sins against us, dost thou wish that we forgive him up to seven times?' * I answered, I spake to you in a *parable*, saying : '*Not only* up to seven times, *but* up to seventy times seven' ▫. Now at this time forgive him many times and give him *each* time the *mysteries* which are in the first *space* without. Perhaps you (will) win the *soul* of that brother, and he will *inherit* the Kingdom of the Light. *Truly, truly*, I say to you, he who will give life to one *soul* and save it, *apart from* the glory which he has in the Kingdom of the Light, he will receive further glory in return for the *soul* which he has saved. *So that* he who will save a multitude of *souls*, *apart from* the glory which he has in ⟨the Kingdom of⟩ the Light, he will receive much other glory in return for the *souls* which he has saved."

105. Now when the *Saviour* had said these things, John sprang up and said : "My Lord, bear with me that I question thee, *for* from now I will *begin* to question thee concerning everything regarding the manner in which we will *preach* to mankind. *Now* if I give to that brother a *mystery* from the *mysteries* [1] of the *beginning* which are in the first *space* from without, and if I give him many *mysteries* and he does not become worthy of the Kingdom | of Heaven, dost thou

---

*   cf. Mt. 18.21; Lk. 17.4
▫   cf. Mt. 18.22

---

[1]   (21) mysteries; lit. mystery.

ⲠⲎⲨⲈ· ⲔⲞⲨⲰϢ ⲈⲦⲢⲈⲚⲞⲨⲞⲦⲂⲈϤ ⲈϨⲞⲨⲚ ⲈⲘⲘⲨⲤⲦⲎⲢⲒⲞⲚ
Ⲙ̄ⲠⲘⲈϨⲤⲚⲀⲨ Ⲛ̄ⲬⲰⲢⲎⲘⲀ· ⲀⲢⲎⲨ ⲢⲰ Ⲛ̄ⲦⲚ̄ϯϨⲎⲨ Ⲛ̄ⲦⲈⲮⲨⲬⲎ
Ⲙ̄ⲠⲤⲞⲚ ⲈⲦⲘⲘⲀⲨ Ⲛ̄ϤⲔⲞⲦϤ Ⲛ̄ϤⲘⲈⲦⲀⲚⲞⲒ Ⲛ̄ϤⲔⲖⲎⲢⲞⲚⲞⲘⲒ
Ⲛ̄ⲦⲘⲚ̄ⲦⲈⲢⲞ Ⲙ̄ⲠⲞⲨⲞⲈⲒⲚ· ⲔⲞⲨⲰϢ ⲈⲦⲢⲈⲚⲞⲨⲞⲦⲂⲈϤ Ⲉ-
5 ϨⲞⲨⲚ ⲈⲘⲘⲨⲤⲦⲎⲢⲒⲞⲚ Ⲭ̄Ⲛ̄ ⲘⲘⲞⲚ ⲚⲀⲒ̈ ⲈⲦϨⲘ̄ ⲠⲘⲈϨⲤⲚⲀⲨ Ⲥ̄ⲘⲈ̄
Ⲛ̄ⲬⲰⲢⲎⲘⲀ· ⲀϤⲞⲨⲰϢⲘ̄ ⲆⲈ Ⲛ̄ϬⲒ ⲠⲤⲰ̄Ⲣ ⲠⲈⲬⲀϤ Ⲛ̄Ⲓ̈ⲰϨⲀⲚⲚⲎⲤ
ⲬⲈ ⲈϢⲰⲠⲈ ⲞⲨⲤⲞⲚ ⲠⲈ ⲈⲚϤϨⲨⲠⲞⲔⲢⲒⲚⲈ ⲀⲚ· ⲀⲖⲖⲀ ⲈϤ-
ⲞⲨⲈϢ-ⲠⲚⲞⲨⲦⲈ ϨⲚ̄ ⲞⲨⲀⲖⲎⲐⲒⲀ· ⲈⲀⲦⲈⲦⲚ̄ϯ ⲚⲀϤ Ⲛ̄ⲞⲨ-
ⲘⲎⲎϢⲈ Ⲛ̄ⲤⲞⲠ Ⲛ̄ⲘⲘⲨⲤⲦⲎⲢⲒⲞⲚ Ⲛ̄ⲦⲀⲢⲬⲎ· ⲀⲨⲰ ⲠⲀⲒ̈ ⲈⲦⲂⲈ
10 ⲦⲀⲚⲀⲄⲔⲎ Ⲛ̄ⲚⲈⲤⲦⲞⲒⲬⲒⲞⲚ Ⲛ̄ⲐⲒⲘⲀⲢⲘⲈⲚⲎ ⲈⲘⲠϤⲈⲒⲢⲈ Ⲙ̄ⲠⲈⲘ-
ⲠϢⲀ Ⲛ̄ⲘⲘⲨⲤⲦⲎⲢⲒⲞⲚ Ⲛ̄ⲦⲘⲚ̄ⲦⲈⲢⲞ Ⲙ̄ⲠⲞⲨⲞⲒ̈Ⲛ· ⲔⲰ ⲚⲀϤ
ⲈⲂⲞⲖ ⲞⲨⲞⲦⲂⲈϤ ⲈϨⲞⲨⲚ ϯ ⲚⲀϤ Ⲙ̄ⲠϢⲞⲢⲠ̄ Ⲙ̄ⲘⲨⲤⲦⲎⲢⲒⲞⲚ
ⲈⲦϨⲘ̄ ⲠⲘⲈϨⲤⲚⲀⲨ Ⲛ̄ⲬⲰⲢⲎⲘⲀ· ⲀⲢⲎⲨ ⲢⲰ Ⲛ̄ⲦⲈⲦⲚ̄ϯϨⲎⲨ Ⲛ̄ⲦⲈ-
ⲮⲨⲬⲎ Ⲙ̄ⲠⲤⲞⲚ ⲈⲦⲘⲘⲀⲨ· ⲀⲨⲰ ⲈϢⲰⲠⲈ Ⲙ̄ⲠϤⲢ̄-ⲠⲈⲘⲠϢⲀ
15 Ⲛ̄ⲘⲘⲨⲤⲦⲎⲢⲒⲞⲚ Ⲙ̄ⲠⲞⲨⲞⲈⲒⲚ· ⲀⲨⲰ Ⲛ̄ϤⲈⲒⲢⲈ Ⲛ̄ϯⲠⲀⲢⲀⲂⲀⲤⲒⲤ
ⲘⲚ̄ ⲚⲒⲚⲞⲂⲈ ⲚⲒⲚⲞⲂⲈ· ⲀⲨⲰ ⲞⲚ ⲘⲚ̄Ⲛ̄ⲤⲀ ⲚⲀⲒ̈ Ⲛ̄ϤⲔⲞⲦϤ ⲀϤ-
ϢⲰⲠⲈ ϨⲚ̄ ⲞⲨⲚⲞϬ Ⲙ̄ⲘⲈⲦⲀⲚⲞⲒⲀ· ⲀⲨⲰ ⲀϤⲀⲠⲞⲦⲀⲤⲤⲈ Ⲙ̄-
ⲠⲔⲞⲤⲘⲞⲤ ⲦⲎⲢϤ̄ ⲀⲨⲰ ⲀϤⲀⲖⲞ ϨⲚ̄ Ⲛ̄ⲚⲞⲂⲈ ⲦⲎⲢⲞⲨ Ⲛ̄ⲦⲈ
ⲠⲔⲞⲤⲘⲞⲤ Ⲛ̄ⲦⲈⲦⲚⲈⲒⲘⲈ ϨⲚ̄ ⲞⲨⲰⲢⲬ̄ ⲬⲈ Ⲛ̄ⲚⲈϤϨⲨⲠⲞⲔⲢⲒⲚⲈ Ⲥ̄ⲘⲈ̄ᵇ
20 ⲀⲚ· ⲀⲖⲖⲀ ⲈϤⲞⲨⲈϢ-ⲠⲚⲞⲨⲦⲈ ϨⲚ̄ ⲞⲨⲀⲖⲎⲐⲒⲀ· ⲔⲈⲦⲎ-
ⲚⲞⲨ Ⲛ̄ⲞⲨⲰϨⲘ̄ ⲔⲰ ⲚⲀϤ ⲈⲂⲞⲖ’ ⲞⲨⲞⲦⲂⲈϤ ⲈϨⲞⲨⲚ ϯ ⲚⲀϤ
Ⲙ̄ⲠⲘⲈϨⲤⲚⲀⲨ Ⲙ̄ⲘⲨⲤⲦⲎⲢⲒⲞⲚ ϨⲢⲀⲒ̈ ϨⲘ̄ ⲠⲘⲈϨⲤⲚⲀⲨ Ⲛ̄ⲬⲰⲢⲎ-
ⲘⲀ Ⲛ̄ⲦⲈ ⲠϢⲞⲢⲠ̄ Ⲙ̄ⲘⲨⲤⲦⲎⲢⲒⲞⲚ· ⲀⲢⲎⲨ ⲢⲰ Ⲛ̄ⲦⲈⲦⲚ̄ϯϨⲎⲨ
Ⲛ̄ⲦⲈⲮⲨⲬⲎ Ⲙ̄ⲠⲤⲞⲚ ⲈⲦⲘⲘⲀⲨ Ⲛ̄ϤⲔⲖⲎⲢⲞⲚⲞⲘⲒ Ⲛ̄ⲦⲘⲚ̄ⲦⲈⲢⲞ
25 Ⲙ̄ⲠⲞⲨⲞⲈⲒⲚ· ⲀⲨⲰ ⲞⲚ ⲈϢⲰⲠⲈ Ⲙ̄ⲠϤⲈⲒⲢⲈ Ⲙ̄ⲠⲈⲘⲠϢⲀ Ⲛ̄Ⲙ̄-
ⲘⲨⲤⲦⲎⲢⲒⲞⲚ· ⲀⲖⲖⲀ ⲀϤϢⲰⲠⲈ ϨⲚ̄ ϯⲠⲀⲢⲀⲂⲀⲤⲒⲤ ⲘⲚ̄ ⲚⲒⲚⲞ-

---

5   Ⲭ̄Ⲛ̄ Ⲙ̄ⲘⲞⲚ should follow Ⲡ̄ⲬⲰⲢⲎⲘⲀ.

wish that we should let him pass through into the *mysteries*
of the second *space*? Perhaps we (will) win the *soul* of that
brother and he (will) turn and *repent* and *inherit* the Kingdom of the Light. Dost thou wish that we should let him
pass through into the *mysteries* which are in the second
space or not?"

The *Saviour however* answered and said to John : "If he is
a brother who is not *hypocritical, but* longs for God in
truth, if you have given him many times the *mysteries* of the
beginning, and because of the *constraint* of the *elements* [1] of
the *Heimarmene* he has not done what is worthy of the
mysteries of the Kingdom of the Light, forgive him and
pass him within and give him the first *mystery* which is in
the second *space*. Perhaps you (will) win the *soul* of that
brother. And if he does not do what is worthy of the *mysteries*
of the light, and he commits *transgression* and all kinds of
sin, and again after these things he has turned and come
to be in great *repentance*, and he has *renounced* the whole
world, and he has ceased from all sins of the *world* and you
know with certainty that he is not *hypocritical, but* he longs
for God in *truth*, turn yourselves once more, forgive him,
pass him within and give to him the second *mystery* in the
second *space* of the First *Mystery*. Perhaps you (will) win
the *soul* of that brother and he (will) *inherit* the Kingdom
of the Light. And again if he does not do what is worthy
of the *mysteries, but* has come to be in *transgression* and
and all kinds of | sins, and again after these things he has

---

[1]   (10) elements : see Keph. VI. p. 30; Augustine *c. Faust.* II.8; Bousset (Bibl. 10),
pp. 223-37.

535

ⲃⲉ ⲛⲓⲛⲟⲃⲉ· ⲁⲩⲱ ⲟⲛ ⲙⲛ̅ⲛ̅ⲥⲁ ⲛⲁⲓ̈ ⲁ̅ϥⲕⲟⲧ̅ϥ̅ ⲁ̅ϥϣⲱⲡⲉ ϩ̅ⲛ̅

ⲟⲩⲛⲟϭ ⲙ̅ⲙⲉⲧⲁⲛⲟⲓⲁ· ⲁ̅ϥⲁⲡⲟⲧⲁⲥⲥⲉ ⲙ̅ⲡⲕⲟⲥⲙⲟⲥ ⲧⲏⲣ̅ϥ̅

ⲙⲛ ⲑⲩⲗⲏ ⲧⲏⲣ̅ⲥ̅ ⲉⲧⲛ̅ϩⲏⲧ̅ϥ̅ ⲁⲩⲱ ⲁ̅ϥⲗⲟ ϩ̅ⲛ̅ ⲛ̅ⲛⲟⲃⲉ ⲛ̅ⲧⲉ

ⲡⲕⲟⲥⲙⲟⲥ· ⲛ̅ⲧⲉⲧⲛ̅ⲉⲓⲙⲉ ⲁⲗⲏⲑⲱⲥ ϫⲉ ⲛ̅ⲛⲉϥϩⲩⲡⲟⲕⲣⲓⲛⲉ

5 ⲁⲛ ⲁⲗⲗⲁ ⲉϥⲟⲩⲉϣ-ⲡⲛⲟⲩⲧⲉ ⲛ̅ⲧⲙⲉ ⲕⲉⲧⲧⲏⲛⲟⲩ ⲛ̅ⲟⲩⲱϩ̅ⲙ̅

ⲕⲱ ⲛⲁϥ ⲉⲃⲟⲗ ⲁⲩⲱ ⲛ̅ⲧⲉⲧⲛ̅ϫⲓ ⲛ̅ⲧⲟⲟⲧ̅ϥ̅ ⲛ̅ⲧⲉϥⲙⲉⲧⲁⲛⲟⲓⲁ

ⲉⲃⲟⲗ ϫⲉ ⲟⲩϣⲁⲛϩⲧⲏϥ ⲛ̅ⲛⲁⲏⲧ ⲡⲉ ⲡⲓϣⲟⲣ̅ⲡ̅ ⲙ̅ⲙⲩⲥⲧⲏ-

ⲣⲓⲟⲛ· ⲟⲩⲱⲧⲃ ⲟⲛ ⲙ̅ⲡⲣⲱⲙⲉ ⲉⲧⲙ̅ⲙⲁϥ ⲉϩⲟⲩⲛ ⳨ ⲛⲁϥ ⲙ̅- 〔ⲥⲙⲉ〕

ⲡⲓϣⲟⲙ̅ⲛ̅ⲧ̅ ⲙ̅ⲙⲩⲥⲧⲏⲣⲓⲟⲛ ϩⲓ ⲛⲉⲩⲉⲣⲏⲩ ⲉⲧϩⲣⲁⲓ̈ ϩ̅ⲙ̅ ⲡⲙⲉϩ-

10 ⲥⲛⲁⲩ ⲛ̅ⲭⲱⲣⲏⲙⲁ ⲛ̅ⲧⲉ ⲡⲓϣⲟⲣ̅ⲡ̅ ⲙ̅ⲙⲩⲥⲧⲏⲣⲓⲟⲛ· ⲉϣⲱⲡⲉ

ⲉⲣϣⲁⲛ ⲡⲣⲱⲙⲉ ⲉⲧⲙ̅ⲙⲁϥ ⲉϥϣⲁⲛⲡⲁⲣⲁⲃⲁ ⲛ̅ϥϣⲱⲡⲉ ϩ̅ⲛ̅

ⲛⲓⲛⲟⲃⲉ ⲛⲓⲛⲟⲃⲉ· ⲛ̅ⲛⲉⲧⲛ̅ⲕⲱ ⲛⲁϥ ⲉⲃⲟⲗ ϫⲓⲛ ⲡⲉⲓ̈ⲛⲁⲩ·

ⲟⲩⲁⲉ ⲛ̅ⲛⲉⲧⲛ̅ϫⲓ ⲛ̅ⲧⲟⲟⲧ̅ϥ̅ ⲛ̅ⲛⲉϥⲙⲉⲧⲁⲛⲟⲓⲁ· ⲁⲗⲗⲁ ⲙⲁ-

ⲣⲉϥϣⲱⲡⲉ ⲛ̅ϩⲏⲧⲧⲏⲩ̅ⲧ̅ⲛ̅ ϩⲱⲥ ⲥⲕⲁⲛⲁⲗⲟⲥ ⲁⲩⲱ ϩⲱⲥ

15 ⲡⲁⲣⲁⲃⲁⲧⲏⲥ· ϩⲁⲙⲏⲛ ⲅⲁⲣ ⳨ϫⲱ ⲙ̅ⲙⲟⲥ ⲛⲏⲧⲛ̅· ϫⲉ ⲡϣⲟ-

ⲙⲛ̅ⲧ̅ ⲙ̅ⲙⲩⲥⲧⲏⲣⲓⲟⲛ ⲉⲧⲙ̅ⲙⲁϥ ⲥⲉⲛⲁϣⲱⲡⲉ ⲛⲁϥ ⲙ̅ⲙⲛ̅ⲧⲣⲉ

ⲉⲟⲗⲏ ⲛ̅ⲧⲉϥⲙⲉⲧⲁⲛⲟⲓⲁ· ⲁⲩⲱ ⲙⲛ̅ⲧ̅ϥ̅-ⲙⲉⲧⲁⲛⲟⲓⲁ ⲙ̅ⲙⲁⲩ

ϫⲓⲛ ⲡⲉⲓ̈ⲛⲁⲩ· ϩⲁⲙⲏⲛ ⲅⲁⲣ ⳨ϫⲱ ⲙ̅ⲙⲟⲥ ⲉⲣⲱⲧⲛ ϫⲉ

ⲡⲣⲱ⟨ⲙⲉ⟩ ⲉⲧⲙ̅ⲙⲁⲩ ⲙ̅ⲙⲛ̅ⲧⲟⲩⲧⲥⲧⲟ ⲛ̅ⲧⲉϥⲯⲩⲭⲏ ⲉⲡⲕⲟⲥ-

20 ⲙⲟⲥ ⲉⲧϩⲓⲡϫⲓⲥⲉ ϫⲓⲛ ⲡⲉⲓ̈ⲛⲁⲩ· ⲁⲗⲗⲁ ⲉⲥⲛⲁϣⲱⲡⲉ ϩ̅ⲛ̅ ⲙ̅-

ⲙⲁⲛ̅ϣⲱⲡⲉ ⲙ̅ⲡⲉⲇⲣⲁⲕⲱⲛ ⲙ̅ⲡⲕⲁⲕⲉ ⲉⲧϩⲓⲃⲟⲗ· ⲉⲧⲃⲉ ⲛⲉ-

ⲯⲩⲭⲟⲟⲩⲉ ⲅⲁⲣ ⲛ̅ⲛⲉⲓ̈ⲣⲱⲙⲉ ⲛ̅ⲧⲉⲓ̈ⲙⲓⲛⲉ ⲛ̅ⲧⲁⲓ̈ϫⲟⲟⲥ ⲉⲣⲱ- 〔ⲥⲙⲉ〕

ⲧⲛ̅ ⲙ̅ⲡⲓⲟⲩⲟⲉⲓϣ ϩ̅ⲛ̅ ⲟⲩⲡⲁⲣⲁⲃⲟⲗⲏ ⲉⲓ̈ϫⲱ ⲙ̅ⲙⲟⲥ· ϫⲉ ⲉⲣ-

ϣⲁⲛ ⲡⲉⲕⲥⲟⲛ ⲣ̅ⲛⲟⲃⲉ ⲉⲣⲟⲕ· ⲥⲟⲟϩⲉ ⲙ̅ⲙⲟⲕ ⲟⲩⲧⲱⲕ ⲛ̅ⲙ̅-

6　ⲁⲩⲱ . . . ⲉⲃⲟⲗ written in margin below.
19　MS ⲡⲣⲱ; read ⲡⲣⲱⲙⲉ.
20　MS ⲉⲥⲛⲁϣⲱⲡⲉ; read ⲥⲛⲁϣⲱⲡⲉ.
24　MS ⲙ̅ⲙⲟⲕ; read ⲙ̅ⲙⲟϥ.

turned and is in great *repentance*, he has *renounced* the whole
world and all the *matter* within it, and he has ceased from
the sins of the *world* so that you know *truly* that he is not
hypocritical, but he longs for God truly [1], turn yourselves
once more, forgive him and receive from him his *repentance*,
because the First *Mystery* is compassionate and merciful.
Pass that man again within, give him the three *mysteries*
together which are in the second *space* of the First *Mystery*.
If that man *transgresses* and is in all kinds of sins, from
this time do not forgive him *or* receive his *repentance* from
him. *But* let him be among you *as* a *disgrace* and *as* a
transgressor. For truly I say to you, those three *mysteries*
will be witnesses to him of the end of his *repentance* [2], and
from this hour there is no *repentance* for him. *For truly*
I say to you, the *soul* of that man will not be cast back
into [3] the *world* on high from this time, *but* it will be in the
dwellings of the *dragon* of the outer darkness. *For* concerning
the *souls* of men such as these I spoke to you once in a
parable, saying : 'If thy brother sins against thee, reprove
him between | himself and thee alone. If he listens to thee

---

[1] (5) God truly; lit. the God of truth; (also 274.15).
[2] (17) of the end of his repentance; Schmidt : of his last repentance.
[3] (19) will not be cast back into; Till : cannot be brought back to (see 271.19;
275.1).

ⲘⲀϤ ⲘⲘⲒⲚ ⲘⲘⲞⲔ· ⲈϢⲰⲠⲈ ⲈϤϢⲀⲚⲤⲰⲦⲘ ⲚⲤⲰⲔ ⲔⲚⲀϮ-
ⲌⲎⲨ ⲘⲠⲈⲔⲤⲞⲚ· ⲈϢⲰⲠⲈ ⲈϤϢⲀⲚⲦⲘⲤⲰⲦⲘ ⲚⲤⲰⲔ ϪⲒ ⲚⲘ-
ⲘⲀⲔ' ⲚⲔⲈⲞⲨⲀ· ⲈϢⲰⲠⲈ ⲈϤϢⲀⲚⲦⲘⲤⲰⲦⲘ ⲚⲤⲰⲔ ⲘⲚ
ⲠⲔⲈⲞⲨⲀ· ⲀⲚⲒϤ ⲈⲦⲈⲔⲔⲖⲎⲤⲒⲀ· ⲈϢⲰⲠⲈ ⲈϤϢⲀⲚⲦⲘⲤⲰⲦⲘ
5 ⲚⲤⲀ ⲚⲔⲞⲞⲨⲈ· ⲘⲀⲢⲈϤϢⲰⲠⲈ ⲚⲚⲀϨⲢⲎⲦⲚ ϨⲰⲤ ⲠⲀⲢⲀⲂⲀ-
ⲦⲎⲤ ⲀⲨⲰ ϨⲰⲤ ⲤⲔⲀⲚⲆⲀⲖⲞⲚ· [ⲀⲨⲰ] ⲈⲦⲈ ⲠⲀⲒ ⲠⲈ ⲈϢⲰ-
ⲠⲈ ⲈϤϢⲀⲚⲦⲘⲢϢⲀⲨ ϨⲘ ⲠϢⲞⲢⲠ ⲘⲘⲨⲤⲦⲎⲢⲒⲞⲚ ·ϯ· ⲚⲀϤ Ⲙ-
ⲠⲘⲈϨⲤⲚⲀⲨ· ⲀⲨⲰ ⲈϢⲰⲠⲈ ⲈϤⲦⲘⲢϢⲀⲨ ϨⲘ ⲠⲘⲈϨⲤⲚⲀⲨ
·ϯ· ⲚⲀϤ ⲘⲠϢⲞⲘⲚⲦ ϨⲒ ⲚⲈⲨⲈⲢⲎⲨ ⲈⲨⲤⲞⲞⲨϨ ⲈⲦⲈ ⲚⲦⲞⲞⲨ
10 ⲠⲈ ⲦⲈⲔⲔⲖⲎⲤⲒⲀ· ⲀⲨⲰ ⲈϢⲰⲠⲈ ⲈϤϢⲀⲚⲦⲘⲢϢⲀⲨ ϨⲘ ⲠⲘⲈϨ-
ϢⲞⲘⲚⲦ ⲘⲘⲨⲤⲦⲎⲢⲒⲞⲚ ⲘⲀⲢⲈϤϢⲰⲠⲈ ⲚⲚⲀϨⲢⲎⲦⲚ ϨⲰⲤ ⲤⲘⲌ
ⲤⲔⲀⲚⲆⲀⲖⲞⲚ ⲀⲨⲰ ϨⲰⲤ ⲠⲀⲢⲀⲂⲀⲦⲎⲤ· ⲀⲨⲰ ⲠϢⲀϪⲈ Ⲛⲧ-
ⲀⲒϪⲞⲞϤ ⲈⲢⲰⲦⲚ ⲘⲠⲞⲨⲞⲈⲒϢ ϪⲈⲔⲀⲤ ϨⲒⲦⲚ ⲘⲚⲦⲢⲈ ⲤⲚⲀⲨ
ϢⲀ ϢⲞⲘⲚⲦ ⲘⲘⲚⲦⲢⲈ ⲈⲢⲈ ϢⲀϪⲈ ⲚⲒⲘ' ⲀϨⲈⲢⲀⲦϤ· ⲈⲦⲈ
15 ⲠⲀⲒ ⲠⲈ ⲠϢⲞⲘⲚⲦ ⲘⲘⲨⲤⲦⲎⲢⲒⲞⲚ ⲈⲦⲘⲘⲀⲨ ⲤⲈⲚⲀⲢⲘⲚⲦⲢⲈ
ⲈⲦⲈϤϨⲀⲠ ⲘⲘⲈⲦⲀⲚⲞⲒⲀ ⲀⲨⲰ ϨⲀⲘⲎⲚ ·ϯ·ϪⲰ ⲘⲘⲞⲤ ⲈⲢⲰⲦⲚ
ϪⲈ ⲈⲢϢⲀⲚ ⲠⲢⲰⲘⲈ ⲈⲦⲘⲘⲀⲨ ⲈϤϢⲀⲚⲘⲈⲦⲀⲚⲞⲒ· ⲘⲚⲦⲈ-
ⲖⲀⲀⲨ ⲘⲘⲨⲤⲦⲎⲢⲒⲞⲚ ⲔⲰ ⲚⲀϤ ⲈⲂⲞⲖ' ⲚⲚⲈϤⲚⲞⲂⲈ ⲞⲨⲆⲈ
ⲘⲚⲦⲞⲨϪⲒ ⲚⲦⲈϤⲘⲈⲦⲀⲚⲞⲒⲀ ⲚⲦⲞⲞⲦϤ· ⲞⲨⲆⲈ ⲘⲚⲦⲞⲨ-
20 ⲤⲰⲦⲘ ⲈⲢⲞϤ ⲈⲒⲦⲎⲢϤ ϨⲒⲦⲚ ⲖⲀⲀⲨ ⲘⲘⲨⲤⲦⲎⲢⲒⲞⲚ ⲈⲒⲘⲎⲦⲒ
ϨⲒⲦⲚ ⲠϢⲞⲢⲠ ⲘⲘⲨⲤⲦⲎⲢⲒⲞⲚ ⲚⲦⲈ ⲠϢⲞⲢⲠ ⲘⲘⲨⲤⲦⲎⲢⲒⲞⲚ·
ⲘⲚ ⲘⲘⲨⲤⲦⲎⲢⲒⲞⲚ ⲘⲠⲒⲀⲦϢⲀϪⲈ ⲈⲢⲞϤ· ⲚⲀⲒ ⲘⲘⲀⲦⲈ ⲚⲈⲦ-
ⲚⲀϪⲒ ⲚⲦⲘⲈⲦⲀⲚⲞⲒⲀ ⲘⲠⲢⲰⲘⲈ ⲈⲦⲘⲘⲀⲨ ⲚⲦⲞⲞⲦϤ· ⲀⲨⲰ
ⲚⲤⲈⲔⲰ ⲈⲂⲞⲖ ⲚⲚⲈϤⲚⲞⲂⲈ· ⲈⲂⲞⲖ ⲄⲀⲢ ϪⲈ ϨⲈⲚϢⲀⲚϨⲦⲎⲨ

---

6   omit ⲀⲨⲰ.
8   MS ⲘⲠⲒⲘⲈϨⲤⲚⲀⲨ; ϥ added.
10 MS originally ⲚⲦⲈⲔⲔⲖⲎⲤⲒⲀ; ⲡ expunged.
14 MS ⲀϨϨⲈⲢⲀⲦϤ; ϩ expunged.

thou wilt win thy brother. If he does not listen to thee,
take another one with thee. If he does not listen to thee
and the other, bring him to the *congregation*. If he does
not listen to the others, let him be among you *as a transgressor* and *as a disgrace*'*. That is, if he is not suitable in
the first *mystery*, give him the second. And if he is not
suitable in the second, give him the three *mysteries* together,
which are the *congregation*. And if he is not suitable in the
third *mystery*, let him be among you *as a disgrace* and *as
a transgressor*. And the word which I spoke to you once :
'So that by means of two or three witnesses every word
stands' □. That is : those three *mysteries* will bear witness
of his last *repentance*. And *truly* I say to you : if that man
repents, no *mystery* forgives his sins *nor* is his *repentance*
received from him, *nor* is he heard at all by any *mystery*,
except by the first *mystery* of the First *Mystery* and the
mysteries of the Ineffable. It is these alone which receive the
repentance of that man from him, and forgive his sins, | *for*

---

*   cf. Mt. 18.15-17; Lk. 17.3
□   cf. Deut. 19.15; Mt. 18.16

Ⲛ̄ⲚⲀⲎⲦ' ⲚⲈ Ⲙ̄ⲘⲨⲤⲦⲎⲢⲒⲞⲚ ⲈⲦⲘ̄ⲘⲀⲨ Ⲛ̄ⲢⲈϤⲔⲰ ⲈⲂⲞⲖ' Ⲛ̄-
ⲞⲨⲞⲈⲒϢ ⲚⲒⲘ·

ⲚⲀⲒ̈ ϬⲈ Ⲛ̄ⲦⲈⲢⲈϤϪⲞⲞⲨ Ⲛ̄ϬⲒ ⲠⲤⲰ̄Ⲣ ⲀϤⲞⲨⲰϨ ⲞⲚ ⲈⲦⲞⲞⲦϤ ⲤⲘⲌ ᵇ
Ⲛ̄ϬⲒ Ⲓ̈ⲰϨⲀⲚⲚⲎⲤ ⲠⲈϪⲀϤ Ⲙ̄ⲠⲤⲰ̄Ⲣ ϪⲈ ⲠⲀϪⲞⲈⲒⲤ ⲈⲒ̈Ⲉ ϢⲰⲠⲈ
5 ⲞⲨⲤⲞⲚ Ⲛ̄ⲢⲈϤⲢ̄ⲚⲞⲂⲈ ⲈⲘⲀϢⲞ ⲈⲀϤⲀⲠⲞⲦⲀⲤⲤⲈ Ⲙ̄ⲠⲔⲞⲤⲘⲞⲤ
ⲦⲎⲢϤ ⲘⲚ̄ ⲐⲨⲖⲎ ⲦⲎⲢⲤ̄ ⲈⲦⲚ̄ϨⲎⲦϤ· ⲘⲚ̄ ⲚⲈϤⲚⲞⲂⲈ ⲦⲎⲢⲞⲨ
ⲀⲨⲰ ⲘⲚ̄ ⲚⲈϤⲢⲞⲞⲨϢ ⲦⲎⲢⲞⲨ· ⲀⲨⲰ Ⲛ̄ⲦⲚ̄ⲆⲞⲔⲒⲘⲀⲌⲈ Ⲙ̄-
ⲘⲞϤ Ⲛ̄ⲦⲚⲈⲒⲘⲈ ϪⲈ Ⲛ̄ϤϢⲞⲞⲠ' ⲀⲚ ϨⲚ̄ ⲞⲨⲔⲢⲞϤ ⲘⲚ̄ ⲞⲨ-
ϨⲨⲠⲞⲔⲢⲒⲤⲒⲤ ⲀⲖⲖⲀ ⲈϤⲞⲨⲈϢϢⲰⲠⲈ ϨⲚ̄ ⲞⲨⲘⲈ ⲘⲚ̄ ⲞⲨ-
10 ⲀⲖⲎⲐⲒⲀ· Ⲛ̄ⲦⲚⲈⲒⲘⲈ ϪⲈ ⲀϤⲘ̄ⲠϢⲀ Ⲛ̄ⲘⲘⲨⲤⲦⲎⲢⲒⲞⲚ Ⲙ̄ⲠⲘⲈϨ-
ⲤⲚⲀⲨ Ⲛ̄ⲬⲰⲢⲎⲘⲀ· ⲏ̈ ⲠⲘⲈϨϢⲞⲘⲚⲦ· ⲔⲞⲨⲰϢ ϨⲀⲠⲀϨ
ⲈⲦⲢⲈⲚ† ⲚⲀϤ ⲈⲂⲞⲖ ϨⲚ̄ ⲘⲘⲨⲤⲦⲎⲢⲒⲞⲚ Ⲙ̄ⲠⲘⲈϨⲤⲚⲀⲨ Ⲛ̄ⲬⲰ-
ⲢⲎⲘⲀ ⲏ̈ ⲘⲚ̄ ⲠⲘⲀϨϢⲞⲘⲚⲦ ⲈⲘⲠⲀⲦϤϪⲒ-ⲘⲨⲤⲦⲎⲢⲒⲞⲚ ⲈⲠⲦⲎ-
Ⲣϥ Ⲛ̄ⲦⲈ ⲚⲈⲔⲖⲎⲢⲞⲚⲞⲘⲒⲀ Ⲙ̄ⲠⲞⲨⲞⲈⲒⲚ ⲔⲞⲨⲰϢ ⲈⲦⲢⲈⲚ†
15 ⲚⲀϤ ϪⲚ̄ ⲘⲘⲞⲚ· ⲀϤⲞⲨⲰϨⲘ̄ ⲆⲈ Ⲛ̄ϬⲒ ⲠⲤⲰⲦⲎⲢ ⲠⲈϪⲀϤ Ⲛ̄-
Ⲓ̈ⲰϨⲀⲚⲚⲎⲤ ϨⲚ̄ ⲦⲘⲎⲦⲈ Ⲛ̄ⲘⲘⲀⲐⲎⲦⲎⲤ ϪⲈ ⲈⲦⲈⲦⲚ̄ϢⲀⲚⲈⲒⲘⲈ [ⲤⲘⲎ]
ϨⲚ̄ ⲞⲨⲰⲢϪ̄ ϪⲈ Ⲁ ⲠⲢⲰⲘⲈ ⲈⲦⲘ̄ⲘⲀⲨ ⲀϤⲀⲠⲞⲦⲀⲤⲤⲈ Ⲙ̄ⲠⲔⲞⲤ-
ⲘⲞⲤ ⲦⲎⲢϤ ⲘⲚ̄ ⲚⲈϤⲢⲞⲞⲨϢ ⲦⲎⲢⲞⲨ ⲘⲚ̄ ⲚⲈϤϨⲞⲘⲒⲖⲒⲀ ⲦⲎ-
ⲢⲞⲨ ⲘⲚ̄ ⲚⲈϤⲚⲞⲂⲈ ⲦⲎⲢⲞⲨ ⲀⲨⲰ Ⲛ̄ⲦⲈⲦⲚⲈⲒⲘⲈ ϨⲚ̄ ⲞⲨ-
20 ⲀⲖⲎⲐⲒⲀ ϪⲈ ⲈϤϢⲞⲞⲠ ⲀⲚ ϨⲚ̄ ⲞⲨⲔⲢⲞϤ ⲞⲨⲆⲈ Ⲛ̄ⲚⲈϤ-
ϢⲞⲞⲠ' ⲀⲚ ϨⲚ̄ ⲞⲨϨⲨⲠⲞⲔⲢⲒⲤⲒⲤ· ⲞⲨⲆⲈ Ⲛ̄ⲚⲈϤⲞ' Ⲙ̄ⲠⲈⲢⲒⲈⲢ-
ⲄⲞⲤ ⲀⲚ ϪⲈ ⲈϤⲈⲈⲒⲘⲈ ⲈⲚⲈⲦⲘ̄ⲘⲨⲤⲦⲎⲢⲒⲞⲚ ϪⲈ ⲈⲨⲞ Ⲛ̄ⲀϢ

---

3   MS ⲟⲛ inserted above.
9   ⲙⲛ expunged before ⲀⲖⲖⲀ. MS ⲉϤⲟⲩⲉϣⲁⲩϣⲱⲡⲉ; read ⲉϥⲟⲩⲉϣⲡϣⲟⲩⲧⲉ.
10 MS Ⲛ̄Ⲧⲉⲧⲛⲉⲓⲙⲉ; ⲧⲉ expunged.

those *mysteries* are compassionate and merciful, and forgiving at all times."

106.   Now when the *Saviour* had said these things John continued again. He said to the *Saviour* : "My Lord, if a very sinful brother has *renounced* the whole *world* and all the *matter* within it, and all its sins and all its cares, and we *examine* him and know that he is not in cunning or *hypocrisy, but* he longs ⟨for God⟩ [1] in verihood and *truth*, and we know that he has become worthy of the *mysteries* of the second *space or* the third; *in a word*, dost thou wish that we give to him from the *mysteries* of the second *space or* from the *third* before he receives any *mysteries* of the *inheritances* of the light? Dost thou wish that we give to him or not?"

The *Saviour however* answered and said to John in the midst of the *disciples* : "If you know with certainty that that man has *renounced* the *whole world* and all its cares and all its *relationships* and all its sins, and you know in *truth* that he is not in cunning *nor* is he in *hypocrisy*, nor is he *curious* to know about your *mysteries*, in what forms they are, |

---

[1]   (9) he longs ⟨for God⟩ ; MS : he longs to become.

ⲛ̄ⲥⲙⲟⲧ· ⲁⲗⲗⲁ ⲉ·ⲟⲩⲉϣ-ⲡⲛⲟⲩⲧⲉ ⲍ̄ⲛ ⲟⲩⲁⲗⲏⲑⲓⲁ· ⲡⲁⲓ ⲡ-
ⲧⲉⲓ̈ⲙⲓⲛⲉ ⲙ̄ⲡⲣ̄ϩⲟⲡⲟⲩ ⲉⲣⲟϥ· ⲁⲗⲗⲁ ⲧ̄ ⲛⲁϥ ⲉⲃⲟⲗ ⲍ̄ⲛ ⲙ̄-
ⲙⲩⲥⲧⲏⲣⲓⲟⲛ ⲙ̄ⲡⲙⲉϩⲥⲛⲁⲩ ⲛ̄ⲭⲱⲣⲏⲙⲁ ⲙⲛ ⲡⲙⲁϩϣⲟⲙⲛⲧ·
ⲁⲩⲱ ⲛ̄ⲧⲱⲧⲛ ϩⲱⲧⲧⲏ·ⲩ̄ⲧ̄ⲛ ⲛ̄ⲧⲉⲧⲛ̄ⲁⲟⲕⲓⲙⲁⲍⲉ ϫⲉ ⲉ·ϥ̄ⲙ-
5 ⲡϣⲁ ⲛ̄ⲁϣ ⲙ̄ⲙⲩⲥⲧⲏⲣⲓⲟⲛ· ⲁⲩⲱ ⲡⲉⲧϥ̄ⲙⲡϣⲁ ⲙ̄ⲙⲟϥ ⲧⲁⲁϥ
ⲛⲁϥ· ⲁⲩⲱ ⲙ̄ⲡⲣ̄ϩⲱⲡ' ⲉⲣⲟϥ ⲉ·ⲙⲙⲟⲛ ⲉⲧⲉⲧⲛ̄ϣⲁⲛϩⲱⲡ ⲉⲣⲟϥ
ⲧⲉⲧⲛ̄ϭⲏⲡ' ⲉϩⲟⲩⲛ ⲉⲩⲛⲟϭ ⲛ̄ⲕⲣⲓⲙⲁ· ⲉ·ϣⲱⲡⲉ ⲉⲧⲉⲧⲛ̄-   [ⲥⲙⲏ]
ϣⲁⲛ-ⲧ̄ ⲛⲁϥ ⲛ̄ⲟⲩⲥⲟⲡ· ϩ̄ⲙ ⲡⲙⲉϩⲥⲛⲁⲩ ⲛ̄ⲭⲱⲣⲏⲙⲁ ⲏ ϩ̄ⲙ
ⲡⲙⲉϩϣⲟⲙⲛⲧ ⲛ̄ϥⲕⲟⲧϥ ⲟⲛ ⲛ̄ϥⲣ̄ⲛⲟⲃⲉ· ⲉⲧⲉⲧⲛⲉⲟⲩⲱϩ ⲟⲛ
10 ⲉⲧⲟⲧⲧⲏⲩ̄ⲧ̄ⲛ ⲙ̄ⲡⲙⲉϩⲥⲟⲡ ⲥⲛⲁⲩ· ϩⲉⲱⲥ ϣⲁ ⲡⲙⲉϩϣⲟⲙⲛⲧ
ⲛ̄ⲥⲟⲡ· ⲉ·ϣⲱⲡⲉ ⲟⲛ ⲉ·ϥϣⲁⲛⲣ̄ⲛⲟⲃⲉ ⲛ̄ⲛⲉⲧⲛ̄ⲟⲩⲱϩ ⲉⲧⲉ-
ⲧⲏⲩⲧ̄ⲛ ⲉⲧ̄ ⲛⲁϥ· ϫⲉ ⲡϣⲟⲙⲛⲧ ⲙ̄ⲙⲩⲥⲧⲏⲣⲓⲟⲛ ⲉ·ⲧⲙ̄ⲙⲁⲩ
ⲥⲉⲛⲁϣⲱⲡⲉ ⲛⲁϥ ⲙ̄ⲙⲛ̄ⲧⲣⲉ ϩ̄ⲛ ⲧⲉϥϩⲁⲏ ⲙ̄ⲙⲉⲧⲁⲛⲟⲓⲁ· ⲁⲩⲱ
ϩⲁⲙⲏⲛ ⲧ̄ϫⲱ ⲙ̄ⲙⲟⲥ ⲉⲣⲱⲧ̄ⲛ ϫⲉ ⲡⲉⲧⲛⲁ·ⲧ̄-ⲙⲩⲥⲧⲏⲣⲓⲟⲛ
15 ⲙ̄ⲡⲣⲱⲙⲉ ⲉ·ⲧ̄ⲙⲙⲁⲩ ⲛ̄ⲟⲩⲱϩⲙ̄ ϩ̄ⲙ ⲡⲙⲉϩⲭⲱⲣⲏⲙⲁ ⲥⲛⲁⲩ ⲏ
ϩ̄ⲙ ⲡⲙⲉϩϣⲟⲙⲛⲧ ϥϭⲏⲡ' ⲉϩⲟⲩⲛ ⲉⲩⲛⲟϭ ⲛ̄ⲕⲣⲓⲙⲁ· ⲁⲗⲗⲁ
ⲙⲁⲣⲉϥϣⲱⲡⲉ ⲛ̄ⲛⲁϩⲣⲏⲧⲛ̄ ϩⲱⲥ ⲡⲁⲣⲁⲃⲁⲧⲏⲥ ⲁⲩⲱ ϩⲱⲥ
ⲥⲕⲁⲛⲇⲁⲗⲟⲛ· ⲁⲩⲱ ϩⲁⲙⲏⲛ ⲧ̄ϫⲱ ⲙ̄ⲙⲟⲥ ⲉⲣⲱⲧⲛ ϫⲉ
ⲡⲣⲱⲙⲉ ⲉ·ⲧ̄ⲙⲙⲁⲩ ⲙ̄ⲛ̄ⲧⲟⲩⲥⲱⲧⲉ ⲛ̄ⲧⲉϥⲯⲩⲭⲏ ⲉ·ⲡⲕⲟⲥⲙⲟⲥ
20 ϫⲓⲛ ⲡⲉⲓ̈ⲛⲁⲩ· ⲁⲗⲗⲁ ⲡⲉϥⲙⲁⲛ̄ϣⲱⲡⲉ ⲡⲉ ϩ̄ⲛ ⲧⲙⲏⲧⲉ ⲛ̄ⲧ-   [ⲥⲙⲑ]
ⲧⲁⲡⲣⲟ ⲙ̄ⲡⲉⲇⲣⲁⲕⲱⲛ ⲙ̄ⲡⲕⲁⲕⲉ ⲉⲧϩⲓⲃⲟⲗ' ⲡⲙⲁ ⲙ̄ⲡⲣⲓⲙⲉ ⲙⲛ
ⲡⲥⲁϩϭⲉϩ ⲛ̄ⲛⲟⲃϩⲉ· ⲁⲩⲱ ϩ̄ⲙ ⲡⲃⲱⲗ' ⲉⲃⲟⲗ ⲙ̄ⲡⲕⲟⲥⲙⲟⲥ ⲧⲉϥⲯⲩⲭⲏ ⲛⲁⲣ̄ϩⲟⲩⲟⲩ︤ⲭ̄ϥ ⲁⲩⲱ ⲛ̄ⲥⲁⲛϩⲁⲗⲓⲥⲕⲉ ⲉⲡⲭⲁϥ ⲉⲧⲛⲁϣⲧ ⲙ̄ⲛ ⲡⲕⲱϩⲧ ⲉⲧⲛⲁϣⲧ ⲉⲙⲁϣⲟ· ⲁⲩⲱ ⲥⲛⲁⲣ̄ⲁⲧϣⲱ-
25 ⲡⲉ ϣⲁⲉⲛⲉϩ· ⲁⲗⲗⲁ ⲉ·ϣⲱⲡⲉ ⲟⲛ ⲉⲧⲓ ⲉ·ϥϣⲁⲛⲕⲟⲧϥ ⲛ̄ϥ-

---

9   MS ⲟⲛ inserted above.

but that he longs for God in *truth*; do not conceal them from such a one, *but* give to him from the *mysteries* of the second *space* and the third. And do yourselves *examine* of which *mystery* he is worthy, and that of which he is worthy give it to him. And do not conceal from him, lest when you conceal from him you are guilty of a great *judgment*. If you have given to him once from the second *space, or* from the third, and he turns again and sins, continue again to give the second time *until* the third time. If he sins again, do not continue to give to him, so that that third *mystery* may be a witness to him of his last *repentance*. And *truly* I say to you that he who gives *mysteries* to that man again from the second *space or* the third is guilty of a great *judgment*. *But* let him be to you *as* a *transgressor* and *as* a *disgrace*. And truly I say to you, the *soul* of that man is not cast back into the *world* from this hour, *but* his dwelling is in the midst of the jaws of the *dragon* of the outer darkness, the place of weeping and gnashing of teeth*. And at the dissolution of the *world* his *soul* will perish and be *consumed* by the severe frost and the very fierce fire [1], and it will become non-existent for ever. *But* if *yet* again he turns | and *renounces* the whole *world*

---

*   cf. Mt. 8.12 etc.

---

[1]   (24) the severe frost and the very fierce fire; lit. the fierce frost and the very fierce fire.

ⲀⲠⲞⲦⲀⲤⲤⲈ ⲘⲠⲔⲞⲤⲘⲞⲤ ⲦⲎⲢϤ ⲘⲚ ⲚⲈϤⲢⲞⲞⲨⲰ ⲦⲎⲢⲞⲨ
ⲘⲚ ⲚⲈϤⲚⲞⲂⲈ ⲦⲎⲢⲞⲨ· ⲀⲨⲰ ⲚϤϢⲰⲠⲈ ϨⲚ ⲞⲨⲚⲞϬ Ⲙ-
ⲠⲞⲖⲒⲦⲒⲀ ⲘⲚ ⲞⲨⲚⲞϬ ⲘⲘⲈⲦⲀⲚⲞⲒⲀ· ⲘⲚⲦⲈ-ⲖⲀⲀⲨ ⲘⲘⲨⲤ-
ⲦⲎⲢⲒⲞⲚ ϪⲒ ⲚⲦⲞⲞⲦϤ ⲚⲦⲈϤⲘⲈⲦⲀⲚⲞⲒⲀ· ⲞⲨⲦⲈ ⲘⲚⲦⲞⲨ-
5 ⲤⲰⲦⲘ ⲈⲢⲞϤ ⲈⲦⲢⲈⲨⲚⲀ ⲚⲀϤ ⲚⲤⲈϪⲒ ⲚⲦⲞⲞⲦϤ ⲚⲦⲈϤⲘⲈ-
ⲦⲀⲚⲞⲒⲀ ⲚⲤⲈⲔⲰ ⲈⲂⲞⲖ ⲚⲚⲈϤⲚⲞⲂⲈ ⲈⲒⲘⲎⲦⲒ ⲠⲘⲨⲤⲦⲎⲢⲒⲞⲚ
ⲘⲠϢⲞⲢⲠ ⲘⲘⲨⲤⲦⲎⲢⲒⲞⲚ· ⲀⲨⲰ ⲘⲚ ⲠⲘⲨⲤⲦⲎⲢⲒⲞⲚ ⲘⲠⲀ-
ⲦϢⲀϪⲈ ⲈⲢⲞϤ· ⲚⲀⲒ ⲘⲘⲀⲦⲈ ⲚⲈⲦⲚⲀϪⲒ ⲚⲦⲘⲈⲦⲀⲚⲞⲒⲀ Ⲙ-
ⲠⲢⲰⲘⲈ ⲈⲦⲘⲘⲀⲨ ⲚⲦⲞⲞⲦϤ ⲚⲤⲈⲔⲰ ⲈⲂⲞⲖ ⲚⲚⲈϤⲚⲞⲂⲈ· ⲤⲘⲞ ᵇ
10 ⲈⲂⲞⲖ ⲄⲀⲢ ϪⲈ ϨⲈⲚϢⲀⲚϨⲦⲎⲨ ⲚⲚⲀⲎⲦ ⲚⲈ ⲘⲘⲨⲤⲦⲎⲢⲒⲞⲚ
ⲈⲦⲘⲘⲀⲨ· ⲀⲨⲰ ϨⲈⲚⲢⲈϤⲔⲀⲚⲞⲂⲈ ⲈⲂⲞⲖ ⲚⲈ ⲚⲞⲨⲞⲒϢ ⲚⲒⲘ·
ⲚⲀⲒ ⲆⲈ ⲚⲦⲈⲢⲈϤϪⲞⲞⲨ ⲚϬⲒ ⲠⲤⲰⲦⲎⲢ ⲀϤⲞⲨⲰϨ ⲞⲚ Ⲉ-
ⲦⲞⲞⲦϤ ⲚϬⲒ ⲒⲰϨⲀⲚⲚⲎⲤ ⲠⲈϪⲀϤ ϪⲈ ⲠⲀϪⲞⲈⲒⲤ ⲀⲚⲈϪⲈ
ⲘⲘⲞⲒ ⲈⲒϢⲒⲚⲈ ⲘⲘⲞⲔ· ⲀⲨⲰ ⲘⲠⲢϬⲰⲚⲦ ⲈⲢⲞⲒ ⲈⲒϢⲒⲚⲈ ⲄⲀⲢ
15 ⲚⲤⲀ ϨⲰⲂ ⲚⲒⲘ· ϨⲚ ⲞⲨⲰⲢϪ ⲘⲚ ⲞⲨⲀⲤⲪⲀⲖⲒⲀ ⲈⲦⲂⲈ ⲐⲈ
ⲈⲚⲚⲀⲔⲎⲢⲨⲤⲤⲈ ⲘⲘⲞⲤ ⲚⲢⲢⲰⲘⲈ ⲘⲠⲔⲞⲤⲘⲞⲤ· ⲀϤⲞⲨⲰϢⲘ
ⲆⲈ ⲚϬⲒ ⲠⲤⲰⲦⲎⲢ ⲠⲈϪⲀϤ ⲚⲒⲰϨⲀⲚⲚⲎⲤ ϪⲈ ϢⲒⲚⲈ ⲚⲤⲀ
ϨⲰⲂ ⲚⲒⲘ ⲈⲦⲔϢⲒⲚⲈ ⲚⲤⲰⲞⲨ ⲀⲨⲰ ⲀⲚⲞⲔ ·|·ⲚⲀϬⲞⲖⲠⲞⲨ
ⲚⲀⲔ· ⲈⲂⲞⲖ ⲚϨⲞⲨⲞ ⲚϨⲞⲨⲞ ϨⲚ ⲞⲨⲠⲀⲢⲢⲎⲤⲒⲀ ⲀϪⲚ ⲠⲀⲢⲀ-
20 ⲂⲞⲖⲎ· Ⲏ ϨⲚ ⲞⲨⲰⲢϪ· ⲀϤⲞⲨⲰϢⲘ ⲆⲈ ⲚϬⲒ ⲒⲰϨⲀⲚⲚⲎⲤ ⲠⲈ-
ϪⲀϤ ϪⲈ ⲠⲀϪⲞⲈⲒⲤ ⲈⲚϢⲀⲚⲈⲒ ⲈⲚⲔⲎⲢⲨⲤⲤⲈ ⲚⲦⲚⲂⲰⲔ· Ⲉ-
ϨⲢⲀⲒ ⲈⲨⲠⲞⲖⲒⲤ Ⲏ ⲈⲨⲔⲰⲘⲈ· ⲀⲨⲰ ⲚⲤⲈⲈⲒ· ⲈⲂⲞⲖ ϨⲀⲦⲈⲚϨⲎ
ⲚϬⲒ ⲚⲢⲰⲘⲈ ⲚⲦⲠⲞⲖⲒⲤ ⲈⲦⲘⲘⲀⲨ ⲈⲚⲦⲚⲤⲞⲞⲨⲚ ⲀⲚ ϪⲈ ⲞⲨ [ⲤⲠ]
ⲚⲈ· ⲈⲨϢⲞⲞⲠ· ϨⲚ ⲞⲨⲚⲞϬ ⲚⲔⲢⲞϤ ⲘⲚ ⲞⲨⲚⲞϬ ⲚϨⲨⲠⲞ-
25 ⲔⲢⲒⲤⲒⲤ ⲚⲤⲈϢⲞⲠⲚ ⲈⲢⲞⲞⲨ ⲚⲤⲈϪⲒⲦⲚ ⲈϨⲞⲨⲚ ⲈⲠⲈⲨⲎⲒ ⲈⲨ-

5-9   MS script very faded in lower part of column.
19   MS ⲚϨⲞⲨⲞ ⲚϨⲞⲨⲞ; Schmidt : read ⲚϨⲞ ⲘⲚ 20 or ⲚϨⲞ 21 20.
20   ⲟ expunged before ϨⲚ.
20-23 MS last four lines almost erased in column 2.

and all its cares and all its sins, and he is in a great *life course* and great *repentance*, there is no *mystery* to receive his *repentance*, *nor* to hear him to have mercy on him and receive his *repentance* from him and forgive his sins, *except* the *mystery* of the First *Mystery* and the *mystery* of the Ineffable. It is these alone which will receive the *repentance* of that man from him and forgive his sins, *for* those *mysteries* are compassionate and merciful, and they forgive sins at all times."

107.   *But* when the *Saviour* said these things John continued again. He said : "My Lord, *suffer* me questioning thee and be not angry with me, *for* I question everything with assurance and *certainty*, concerning the manner in which we will *preach* to the men of the *world*."
But the *Saviour* answered and said to John : "Question all things about which thou dost question, and I will reveal them to thee more and more [1], *openly* without *parable*, *or* with certainty.

John answered *however* and said : "My Lord, if we come to *preach*, and we go into a *city or* a *village*, and the men of that *city* come forth before us and we do not know who they are; and they are in great cunning and great *hypocrisy*, and they receive us and take us into their houses, | wishing

---

[1]   (19) more and more; Schmidt : face to face.

ΟΥⲰϢ ⲈⲠⲒⲢⲀⲌⲈ Ⲛ̄ⲘⲘΥⲤⲦΗⲢⲒⲞⲚ Ⲛ̄ⲦⲘⲚ̄ⲦⲈⲢⲞ Ⲙ̄ⲠⲞΥⲞⲈⲒⲚ·
ⲀΥⲰ Ⲛ̄ⲤⲈϢⲰⲠⲈ ⲈΥ²ΥⲠⲞⲔⲢⲒⲚⲈ Ⲛ̄ⲘⲘⲀⲚ ²Ⲛ ΘΥⲠⲞⲦⲀⲄΗ·
ⲀΥⲰ Ⲛ̄ⲦⲚⲘⲈⲈΥⲈ ϪⲈ ⲈΥⲞΥⲈϢ-ⲠⲚⲞΥⲦⲈ Ⲛ̄ⲦⲚ̄✝ ⲚⲀΥ Ⲛ̄-
Ⲙ̄ⲘΥⲤⲦΗⲢⲒⲞⲚ Ⲛ̄ⲦⲘⲚ̄ⲦⲈⲢⲞ Ⲙ̄ⲠⲞΥⲞⲈⲒⲚ· ⲀΥⲰ ⲘⲚ̄ⲚⲤⲀ ⲚⲀⲒ̈
⁵ Ⲛ̄ⲦⲚⲈⲒⲘⲈ ϪⲈ Ⲙ̄ⲠⲞΥⲈⲒⲢⲈ Ⲙ̄ⲠⲈⲘⲠϢⲀ Ⲙ̄ⲠⲘΥⲤⲦΗⲢⲒⲞⲚ· ⲀΥⲰ
Ⲛ̄ⲦⲚⲈⲒⲘⲈ ϪⲈ Ⲛ̄ⲦⲀΥ²ΥⲠⲞⲔⲢⲒⲚⲈ Ⲛ̄ⲘⲘⲀⲚ· ⲀΥⲰ Ⲛ̄ⲦⲀΥ-
ϢⲰⲠⲈ Ⲛ̄ⲔⲢⲞϤ ⲈⲢⲞⲚ· ⲀΥⲰ Ⲛ̄ⲔⲈⲘΥⲤⲦΗⲢⲒⲞⲚ ⲀΥⲀⲀΥ Ⲙ̄-
ⲠⲀⲢⲀⲆⲒⲄⲘⲀ ⲔⲀⲦⲀ ⲦⲞⲠⲞⲤ ⲈΥϪⲒⲘⲀⲌⲈ Ⲙ̄ⲘⲞⲚ ⲘⲚ̄ ⲚⲈⲚ-
ⲔⲈⲘΥⲤⲦΗⲢⲒⲞⲚ ⲈⲒ̈Ⲉ ⲞΥ ⲠⲈ ⲠϨⲰⲂ ⲈⲦⲚⲀϢⲰⲠⲈ Ⲛ̄ⲚⲀⲒ̈ Ⲛ̄-
¹⁰ⲦⲈⲒ̈ⲘⲒⲚⲈ· ⲀϤⲞΥⲰϨ²Ⲙ̄ ⲆⲈ Ⲛ̄ϬⲒ ⲠⲤⲰⲦΗⲢ ⲠⲈϪⲀϤ Ⲛ̄Ⲓ̈ⲰϨⲀⲚ- [ⲥⲡ ᵇ]
ⲚΗⲤ· ϪⲈ ⲈⲦⲈⲦⲚ̄ϢⲀⲚⲂⲰⲔ ⲈϨⲢⲀⲒ̈ ⲈΥⲠⲞⲖⲒⲤ Η̄ ⲞΥⲔⲰⲘΗ·
ⲠΗⲒ̈ ⲈⲦⲈⲦⲚⲀⲂⲰⲔ ⲈϨⲞΥⲚ ⲈⲢⲞϤ Ⲛ̄ⲤⲈϢⲈⲠⲦΗΥⲦⲚ̄ ⲈⲢⲞⲞΥ
✝ ⲚⲀΥ Ⲛ̄ⲞΥⲘΥⲤⲦΗⲢⲒⲞⲚ· ⲈϢⲰⲠⲈ ⲈΥⲘⲠϢⲀ ⲈⲒ̈Ⲉ ⲦⲈⲦ-
ⲚⲀ✝ϨΗΥ Ⲛ̄ⲚⲈΥⲯΥⲬⲞⲞΥⲈ Ⲛ̄ⲤⲈⲔⲖΗⲢⲞⲚⲞⲘⲒ Ⲛ̄ⲦⲘⲚ̄ⲦⲈⲢⲞ
¹⁵Ⲙ̄ⲠⲞΥⲞⲈⲒⲚ· ⲀⲖⲖⲀ ⲈϢⲰⲠⲈ ⲈⲚⲤⲈⲘⲠϢⲀ ⲀⲚ ⲀⲖⲖⲀ ⲈΥⲞ
Ⲛ̄ⲔⲢⲞϤ ⲈⲢⲰⲦⲚ̄· ⲀΥⲰ Ⲛ̄ⲤⲈⲢ-Ⲛ̄ⲔⲈⲘΥⲤⲦΗⲢⲒⲞⲚ Ⲙ̄ⲠⲀⲢⲀⲆⲒⲄ-
ⲘⲀ ⲈΥϪⲒⲘⲀⲌⲈ Ⲙ̄ⲘⲰⲦⲚ̄ ⲘⲚ̄ Ⲛ̄ⲔⲈⲘΥⲤⲦΗⲢⲒⲞⲚ ⲈⲒ̈Ⲉ ϢϢ Ⲉ-
ϨⲢⲀⲒ̈ ⲈⲠϢⲞⲢⲠ̄ Ⲙ̄ⲘΥⲤⲦΗⲢⲒⲞⲚ Ⲛ̄ⲦⲈ ⲠϢⲞⲢⲠ̄ Ⲙ̄ⲘΥⲤⲦΗⲢⲒⲞⲚ
ⲠⲀⲒ̈ ⲈϢⲀϤⲚⲀ Ⲛ̄ⲞΥⲞⲚ ⲚⲒⲘ· ⲀϪⲒⲤ ϪⲈ ⲠⲔⲈⲘΥⲤⲦΗⲢⲒⲞⲚ
²⁰Ⲛ̄ⲦⲀⲚⲦⲀⲀϤ Ⲛ̄ⲚⲈⲒ̈ⲯΥⲬⲞⲞΥⲈ Ⲛ̄ⲀⲤⲈⲂΗⲤ ⲀΥⲰ Ⲙ̄ⲠⲀⲢⲀⲚⲞ-
ⲘⲞⲤ ⲈⲘⲠⲞΥⲈⲒⲢⲈ Ⲙ̄ⲠⲈⲘⲠϢⲀ Ⲙ̄ⲠⲈⲔⲘΥⲤⲦΗⲢⲒⲞⲚ· ⲀⲖⲖⲀ
ⲀΥⲀⲀⲚ Ⲙ̄ⲠⲀⲢⲀⲆⲒⲄⲘⲀ· ⲔⲦⲞ Ⲙ̄ⲠⲘΥⲤⲦΗⲢⲒⲞⲚ ⲈⲢⲞⲚ· ⲀΥⲰ
Ⲛ̄ⲄⲀⲀΥ Ⲛ̄ⲀⲖⲖⲞⲦⲢⲒⲞⲤ ⲈⲠⲘΥⲤⲦΗⲢⲒⲞⲚ Ⲛ̄ⲦⲈⲔⲘⲚ̄ⲦⲈⲢⲞ ϢⲀ-

---

5 ΟΥ expunged after ϪⲈ.
8 MS ⲈΥϪⲒⲘⲀⲌⲈ; read ⲈΥⲆⲞⲔⲒⲘⲀⲌⲈ; also in line 17.
17 MS originally Ⲙ̄ⲘⲞⲚⲰⲦⲚ̄; ⲞⲚ expunged.
21 MS originally Ⲙ̄ⲠⲔⲈⲘΥⲤⲦΗⲢⲒⲞⲚ; ⲉ crossed out and ⲉ inserted above, between ⲡ and ⲕ.

to *try* the *mysteries* of the Kingdom of the Light; and if they are *hypocritical* with us in *submission*, and we think that they are longing for God, and we give them the *mysteries* of the Kingdom of the Light; and after these things we know that they do not do what is worthy of the *mystery*, and we know that they have been *hypocritical* with us, and they have been cunning with us; and also that they have made a *mockery* of the *mysteries* in *every place*, as they test us and our *mysteries*: what will become of (men) such as these?"

The *Saviour however* answered and said to John: "When you go into a *city or* a *village*, if you go into a house and they receive you *, give to them a *mystery*. If they are worthy, you will win their *souls* and they will *inherit* the Kingdom of the Light. *But* if they are not worthy, *but* they are being cunning with you, and they are also making a *mockery* of the *mysteries*, testing you and also the *mysteries*, then call upon the first *mystery* of the First *Mystery*, which is merciful to everyone, and say: 'Thou also, O *Mystery* which we have given to these *impious* and lawless *souls* who have not done what is worthy of thy *mystery*[1], *but* they have made a *mockery* of us; return the *mystery* to us, and make them *strangers* to the *mystery* of thy kingdom for | ever.' And

---

*   cf. Mt. 10.11, 12

---

[1]   (21) thy mystery; MS originally: the mystery also.

ⲉⲛⲉϩ· ⲁⲩⲱ ⲛⲟⲩϩⲉ ⲉⲃⲟⲗ ⲙ̄ⲡϣⲟⲉⲓϣ ⲛ̄ⲛⲉⲧⲛ̄ⲟⲩⲉⲣⲏⲧⲉ ⲥⲛ̅ⲁ̅
ⲉⲩⲙ̄ⲛ̄ⲧⲙⲛ̄ⲧⲣⲉ ⲛⲁⲩ ⲉⲧⲉⲧⲛ̄ϫⲱ ⲙ̄ⲙⲟⲥ ⲛⲁⲩ ϫⲉ ⲉⲣⲉ ⲛⲉ-
ⲧⲛ̄ⲯⲩⲭⲟⲟⲩⲉ ⲣ̄ⲟⲉ ⲙ̄ⲡϣⲟⲉⲓϣ ⲙ̄ⲡⲉⲧⲛⲏⲓ̈· ⲁⲩⲱ ϩⲁⲙⲏⲛ
ϯϫⲱ ⲙ̄ⲙⲟⲥ ⲛⲏⲧⲛ̄ ϫⲉ ϩⲛ̄ ⲧⲉⲩⲛⲟⲩ ⲉⲧⲙ̄ⲙⲁⲩ ⲥⲉⲛⲁⲕⲟ-
5 ⲧⲟⲩ ⲉⲣⲱⲧⲛ̄ ⲛ̄ϭⲓ ⲙⲩⲥⲧⲏⲣⲓⲟⲛ ⲛⲓⲙ ⲛ̄ⲧⲁⲧⲉⲧⲛ̄ⲧⲁⲁⲩ ⲛⲁⲩ
ⲁⲩⲱ ⲥⲉⲛⲁϥⲓ ⲛ̄ϩⲏⲧⲟⲩ ⲛ̄ϣⲁϫⲉ ⲛⲓⲙ' ⲙⲛ̄ ⲙⲩⲥⲧⲏⲣⲓⲟⲛ ⲛⲓⲙ
ⲡⲧⲟⲡⲟⲥ ⲛ̄ⲧⲁⲩϫⲓ-ⲥⲭⲏⲙⲁ ϣⲁⲣⲟϥ· ⲉⲧⲃⲉ ⲛ̄ⲣⲱⲙⲉ ⲟⲩⲛ
ⲛ̄ⲧⲉⲓ̈ⲙⲓⲛⲉ ⲛ̄ⲧⲁⲓ̈ϫⲟⲟⲥ ⲉⲣⲱⲧⲛ̄ ϩⲛ̄ ⲟⲩⲡⲁⲣⲁⲃⲟⲗⲏ ⲙ̄ⲡⲓⲟⲩ-
ⲟⲉⲓϣ ⲉⲓ̈ϫⲱ ⲙ̄ⲙⲟⲥ ϫⲉ ⲡⲏⲓ̈ ⲉⲧⲉⲧⲛⲁⲃⲱⲕ ⲉϩⲟⲩⲛ ⲉⲣⲟϥ
10 ⲛ̄ⲥⲉϣⲉⲡⲧⲏⲩⲧⲛ̄ ⲉⲣⲟϥ· ⲁϫⲓⲥ ⲛⲁⲩ ϫⲉ ϯⲣⲏⲛⲏ ⲛⲏⲧⲛ̄·
ⲁⲩⲱ ⲉϣⲱⲡⲉ ⲉⲩⲙ̄ⲡϣⲁ ⲙⲁⲣⲉ ⲧⲉⲧⲛ̄ⲉⲓⲣⲏⲛⲏ ⲉⲓ̈ ⲉϩⲣⲁⲓ̈ ⲉ-
ϫⲱⲟⲩ· ⲁⲩⲱ ⲉϣⲱⲡⲉ ⲉⲛⲥⲉⲙ̄ⲡϣⲁ ⲁⲛ ⲙⲁⲣⲉⲥⲕⲟⲧⲥ̄ ⲉ-
ⲣⲱⲧⲛ̄ ⲛ̄ϭⲓ ⲧⲉⲧⲛ̄ⲉⲓⲣⲏⲛⲏ· ⲉⲧⲉ ⲡⲁⲓ̈ ⲡⲉ ⲉϣⲱⲡⲉ ⲛ̄ⲣⲱⲙⲉ
ⲉⲧⲙ̄ⲙⲁⲩ ⲥⲉⲉⲓⲣⲉ ⲙ̄ⲡⲉⲙⲡϣⲁ ⲛ̄ⲙⲙⲩⲥⲧⲏⲣⲓⲟⲛ· ⲁⲩⲱ ⲉⲩ- ⲥⲛ̅ⲁ̅ ᵇ
15 ⲟⲩⲉϣ-ⲡⲛⲟⲩⲧⲉ ⲛ̄ⲧⲙⲉ ⲉⲓ̈ⲉ ϯ ⲛⲁⲩ ⲛ̄ⲙⲙⲩⲥⲧⲏⲣⲓⲟⲛ ⲛ̄-
ⲧⲙⲛ̄ⲧⲉⲣⲟ ⲙ̄ⲡⲟⲩⲟⲉⲓⲛ· ⲁⲗⲗⲁ ⲉϣⲱⲡⲉ ⲛ̄ⲧⲟϥ ⲉⲩϩⲩⲡⲟ-
ⲕⲣⲓⲛⲉ ⲛ̄ⲙⲙⲏⲧⲛ̄ ⲁⲩⲱ ⲉⲩⲟ ⲛ̄ⲕⲣⲟϥ ⲉⲣⲱⲧⲛ̄ ⲉⲙⲡⲉⲧⲛ̄ⲉⲓⲙⲉ
ⲛ̄ⲧⲉⲧⲛ̄ϯ ⲛⲁⲩ ⲛ̄ⲙⲙⲩⲥⲧⲏⲣⲓⲟⲛ ⲛ̄ⲧⲙⲛ̄ⲧⲉⲣⲟ ⲙ̄ⲡⲟⲩⲟⲉⲓⲛ·
ⲁⲩⲱ ⲟⲛ ⲙⲛ̄ⲛ̄ⲥⲁ ⲛⲁⲓ̈ ⲛ̄ⲥⲉⲣ̄-ⲙ̄ⲙⲩⲥⲧⲏⲣⲓⲟⲛ ⲙ̄ⲡⲁⲣⲁⲇⲓⲅⲙⲁ·
20 ⲁⲩⲱ ⲛ̄ⲥⲉⲣ̄-ⲡⲕⲉⲭⲓⲙⲁⲍⲉ ⲙ̄ⲙⲱⲧⲛ̄ ⲙⲛ̄ ⲛ̄ⲕⲉⲙⲩⲥⲧⲏⲣⲓⲟⲛ·
ⲁⲣⲓⲣⲉ ⲙ̄ⲡⲓϣⲟⲣⲡ̄ ⲙ̄ⲙⲩⲥⲧⲏⲣⲓⲟⲛ ⲛ̄ⲧⲉ ⲡⲓϣⲟⲣⲡ̄ ⲙ̄ⲙⲩⲥⲧⲏ-
ⲣⲓⲟⲛ· ⲁⲩⲱ ϥⲛⲁⲕⲧⲟ ⲉⲣⲱⲧⲛ̄ ⲙ̄ⲙⲩⲥⲧⲏⲣⲓⲟⲛ ⲛⲓⲙ ⲛ̄ⲧⲁⲧⲉ-
ⲧⲛ̄ⲧⲁⲁⲩ ⲛⲁϥ· ⲁⲩⲱ ϥⲛⲁⲁⲁⲩ ⲛ̄ⲁⲗⲗⲟⲧⲣⲓⲟⲥ ⲉⲙⲙⲩⲥⲧⲏⲣⲓⲟⲛ ⲙ̄ⲡⲟⲩⲟⲉⲓⲛ ϣⲁⲉⲛⲉϩ· ⲁⲩⲱ ⲛⲁⲓ̈ ⲛ̄ⲧⲉⲓ̈ⲙⲓⲛⲉ[ⲁⲩⲱ] ⲛ̄-

---

6   MS ⲛⲓⲙ ⲡⲧⲟⲡⲟⲥ; read ⲛⲓⲙ ⲙ̄ⲡⲧⲟⲡⲟⲥ.
20 MS ⲡⲕⲉⲭⲓⲙⲁⲍⲉ; read ⲡⲕⲉⲇⲟⲕⲓⲙⲁⲍⲉ.
23 MS ⲛⲁϥ; read ⲛⲁⲩ.

cast off the dust of your feet * as a witness to them, saying to them : 'May your *souls* become as the dust of your house'. And *truly*, I say to you that in that hour all the *mysteries* which you have given to them will return to you. And all the words and all the *mysteries* of the *place* as far as which they have received *pattern* will be taken from them. *Now* concerning such men, I spoke to you once in a *parable*, saying : 'When you go into a house, and they receive you, say to them : *peace* be with you. And if they are worthy, let your *peace* come upon them. And if they are not worthy, let your *peace* return to you' ◻. That is, if those men do what is worthy of the *mysteries* and long for God truly, give to them the *mysteries* of the Kingdom of the Light. *But* if they are *hypocritical* with you, and cunning towards you without your knowing, and you give to them the *mysteries* of the Kingdom of the Light; and again after these things they make a *mockery* of the *mysteries*, and they make a test of you and also of the *mysteries*, then perform the first *mystery* of the First *Mystery* and it will return to you all the *mysteries* which you have given to them. And it will make them *strangers* to the *mysteries* of the light for ever. And such (men) | will not be cast back [1] into the *world* from this

---

*   cf. Mt. 10.14; Mk. 6.11; Lk. 9.5; 10.11

◻   cf. Mt. 10.12, 13; Mk. 6.10; Lk. 9.4, 5; 10.5, 6

---

[1]   (275.1) cast back; Schmidt : led back.

ⲥⲉⲛⲁⲧ̅ⲥ̅ⲧⲟⲟⲩ ⲁⲛ ⲉⲡⲕⲟⲥⲙⲟⲥ ϫⲓⲛ ⲡⲉⲓ̈ⲛⲁⲩ· ⲁⲗⲗⲁ ϩⲁⲙⲏⲛ ϯϫⲱ ⲙ̅ⲙⲟⲥ ⲉⲣⲱⲧ̅ⲛ̅ ϫⲉ ⲉⲣⲉ ⲡⲉⲩⲙⲁⲛ̅ϣⲱⲡⲉ ϩ̅ⲛ̅ ⲧⲙⲏⲧⲉ ⲛ̅ⲧ̅ⲧⲁⲡⲣⲟ ⲙ̅ⲡⲉⲇⲣⲁⲕⲱⲛ ⲙ̅ⲡⲕⲁⲕⲉ ⲉⲧϩⲓⲃⲟⲗ· ⲉϣⲱⲡⲉ ⲇⲉ ⲉⲧⲓ ϩ̅ⲛ̅ ⲟⲩⲟⲩⲟⲉⲓϣ ⲙ̅ⲙⲉⲧⲁⲛⲟⲓⲁ ⲛ̅ⲥⲉⲁⲡⲟ**ⲧⲁⲥⲥⲉ ⲙ̅ⲡⲕⲟⲥⲙⲟⲥ ⲧⲏⲣϥ̅ ⲙ̅ⲛ ⲑⲩⲗⲏ ⲧⲏⲣⲥ̅ ⲉⲧⲛ̅ϩⲏⲧϥ̅· [ⲥ̅ⲛ̅ⲃ̅] ⲙ̅ⲛ ⲛ̅ⲛⲟⲃⲉ ⲧⲏⲣⲟⲩ ⲛ̅ⲧⲉ ⲡⲕⲟⲥⲙⲟⲥ ⲁⲩⲱ ⲛ̅ⲥⲉϣⲱⲡⲉ ϩ̅ⲛ̅ ⲑⲩⲡⲟⲧⲁⲅⲏ ⲧⲏⲣⲥ̅ ⲛ̅ⲙ̅ⲙⲩⲥⲧⲏⲣⲓⲟⲛ ⲙ̅ⲡⲟⲩⲟⲉⲓⲛ ⲙ̅ⲛ̅ⲧⲉⲗⲁⲁⲩ ⲙ̅ⲙⲩⲥⲧⲏⲣⲓⲟⲛ ⲥⲱⲧ̅ⲙ̅ ⲉⲣⲟⲟⲩ ⲟⲩⲧⲉ ⲙ̅ⲛ̅ⲧⲟⲩⲕⲱ ⲉⲃⲟⲗ ⲛ̅ⲛⲉⲩⲛⲟⲃⲉ· ⲉⲓⲙⲏⲧⲓ ⲙ̅ⲡⲓⲙⲩⲥⲧⲏⲣⲓⲟⲛ ⲛ̅ⲟⲩⲱⲧ ⲛ̅ⲧⲉ ⲡⲓⲁⲧϣⲁϫⲉ ⲉⲣⲟϥ· ⲡⲁⲓ̈ ⲉϣⲁϥⲛⲁ ⲛ̅ⲟⲩⲟⲛ ⲛⲓⲙ ⲁⲩⲱ ⲛ̅ϥⲕⲱ ⲉⲃⲟⲗ ⲛ̅ⲛ̅ⲛⲟⲃⲉ ⲛ̅ⲟⲩⲟⲛ ⲛⲓⲙ:

ⲁⲥϣⲱⲡⲉ ⲛ̅ⲧⲉⲣⲉ ⲓ̅ⲥ̅ ⲟⲩⲱ ⲉϥϫⲱ ⲛ̅ⲛⲉⲓ̈ϣⲁϫⲉ ⲉⲛⲉϥⲙⲁⲑⲏⲧⲏⲥ· ⲁⲥⲟⲩⲱϣ̅ⲧ̅ ⲛ̅ϭⲓ ⲙⲁⲣⲓⲁ ⲉⲛⲟⲩⲉⲣⲏⲧⲉ ⲛ̅ⲓ̅ⲥ̅ ⲁⲥϯⲡⲓ ⲉⲣⲟⲟⲩ· ⲡⲉϫⲁⲥ ⲛ̅ϭⲓ ⲙⲁⲣⲓⲁ ϫⲉ ⲡⲁϫⲟⲉⲓⲥ ⲁⲛⲉⲭⲉ ⲙ̅ⲙⲟⲓ̈ ⲉⲓ̈ϣⲓⲛⲉ ⲙ̅ⲙⲟⲕ ⲁⲩⲱ ⲙ̅ⲡⲣ̅ϭⲱⲛ̅ⲧ ⲉⲣⲟⲓ̈· ⲁϥⲟⲩⲱϩ̅ⲙ̅ ⲛ̅ϭⲓ ⲡⲥⲱⲧⲏⲣ ⲡⲉϫⲁϥ ⲙ̅ⲙⲁⲣⲓⲁ ϫⲉ ϣⲓⲛⲉ ⲛ̅ⲥⲁ ⲡⲉⲧⲉⲣⲉⲟⲩⲉϣϣⲓⲛⲉ ⲛ̅ⲥⲱϥ· ⲁⲩⲱ ⲁⲛⲟⲕ ϯⲛⲁϭⲟⲗⲡϥ̅ | ⲛⲉ ⲉⲃⲟⲗ ϩ̅ⲛ̅ ⲟⲩⲡⲁⲣⲣⲏⲥⲓⲁ· ⲁⲥⲟⲩⲱϩ̅ⲙ̅ ⲇⲉ ⲛ̅ϭⲓ ⲙⲁⲣⲓϩⲁⲙ ⲡⲉϫⲁⲥ ϫⲉ ⲡⲁϫⲟⲉⲓⲥ *ⲉⲓ̈ⲉ ϣⲱⲡⲉ ⲟⲩⲥⲟⲛ ⲛ̅ⲁⲅⲁⲑⲟⲥ ⲁⲩⲱ ⲉⲛⲁⲛⲟⲩϥ· [ⲥ̅ⲛ̅ⲃ̅ b] ⲉⲁⲛⲡⲗⲏⲣⲟⲩ ⲙ̅ⲙⲟϥ ϩ̅ⲛ̅ ⲙ̅ⲙⲩⲥⲧⲏⲣⲓⲟⲛ ⲧⲏⲣⲟⲩ ⲙ̅ⲡⲟⲩⲟⲉⲓⲛ· ⲁⲩⲱ ⲡⲥⲟⲛ ⲉⲧⲙ̅ⲙⲁⲩ ⲉⲟⲩⲛ̅ⲧⲁϥ ⲙ̅ⲙⲁⲩ ⲛ̅ⲟⲩⲥⲟⲛ ⲏ̅ ⲟⲩⲥⲩⲅⲅⲉⲛⲏⲥ· ϩⲁⲡⲁⲝ ϩⲁⲡⲗⲱⲥ ⲉⲟⲩⲛ̅ⲧⲁϥ ⲙ̅ⲙⲁⲩ ⲛ̅ⲟⲩⲣⲱⲙⲉ ⲉⲡⲧⲏⲣϥ̅· ⲁⲩⲱ ⲡⲁⲓ̈ ⲉⲩⲣⲉϥⲣ̅ⲛⲟⲃⲉ ⲡⲉ ⲁⲩⲱ ⲉⲩⲁⲥⲉⲃⲏⲥ ⲡⲉ· ⲏ̅ ⲙ̅ⲙⲟⲛ ⲛ̅ⲧⲟϥ ⲉⲛⲟⲩⲣⲉϥⲣ̅ⲛⲟⲃⲉ ⲁⲛ ⲡⲉ ⲁⲩⲱ ⲡⲁⲓ̈ ⲛ̅ⲧⲉⲓ̈ⲙⲓⲛⲉ ⲁϥⲉⲓ' ⲉⲃⲟⲗ ϩ̅ⲛ̅ ⲥⲱⲙⲁ· ⲁⲩⲱ ⲉⲣⲉ ⲡϩⲏⲧ ⲙ̅ⲡⲥⲟⲛ

---

9 MS ⲙ̅ⲡⲓⲙⲩⲥⲧⲏⲣⲓⲟⲛ; read ⲡⲓⲙⲩⲥⲧⲏⲣⲓⲟⲛ.
19 ⲓ̅ⲋ̅ in upper right-hand margin at end of quire.

time. *But truly* I say to you : their dwelling-place is in the midst of the jaws of the *dragon* of the outer darkness. *But even if, in a time of repentance*, they *renounce* the whole *world* and all the *matter* within it and all the sins of the *world*, and are in complete *submission* to the *mysteries*[1] of the light, no *mystery* can hear them *or* forgive their sins, *except* the one *mystery* of the Ineffable which is merciful to everyone and forgives the sins of everyone."

108.   It happened when Jesus finished saying these words to his *disciples*, Maria worshipped at the feet of Jesus and kissed them. Maria said : "My Lord, *suffer* me to question thee and be not angry with me.'

The *Saviour* answered and said to Maria : "Question what thou dost wish to question, and I will reveal it *openly*."

Maria answered *however* and said : "My Lord, if there is a *good* and excellent brother whom we have *filled* with all the *mysteries* of the light; and that brother has a brother *or* a *relative, in a word*, he actually has a man and this one is a sinner and *impious, or* even[2] if he is not a sinner, and such a one has gone forth from the *body*; and the heart of the |

---

[1]   (6, 7) are in complete submission to the mysteries; Till : come completely into dependence on the mysteries.
[2]   (24) or even; Till : but.

ⲚⲀⲄⲀⲐⲞⲤ ⲈϤⲘⲞⲔϩ ⲀⲨⲰ ⲈϤⲖⲨⲠⲒ ϩⲀⲢⲞϤ ϪⲈ ϤϢⲞⲞⲠ ϩⲢⲀⲒ

ϨⲚ ϨⲈⲚⲔⲢⲒⲤⲒⲤ ⲘⲚ ϨⲈⲚⲔⲞⲖⲀⲤⲒⲤ · ⲦⲈⲚⲞⲨ ϬⲈ ⲠⲀϪⲞⲈⲒⲤ

ⲞⲨ ⲠⲈⲦⲚⲚⲀⲀⲀϤ ϢⲀⲚⲦⲞⲨⲠⲞⲞⲚⲈϤ ⲈⲂⲞⲖ ϨⲚ ⲚⲔⲞⲖⲀⲤⲒⲤ

ⲘⲚ ⲚⲈⲔⲢⲒⲤⲒⲤ ⲈⲦⲚⲀϢ̄Ⲧ · ⲀϤⲞⲨⲰϩⲘ ⲀⲈ Ⲛ̄ϬⲒ ⲠⲤⲰⲦⲎⲢ ⲠⲈ-

5 ϪⲀϤ Ⲙ̄ⲘⲀⲢⲒⲀ ϪⲈ ⲈⲦⲂⲈ ⲠⲈⲒϢⲀϪⲈ ⲞⲨⲚ ⲀⲒ̈ϪⲞⲞϤ ⲈⲢⲰⲦⲚ̄

Ⲛ̄ⲔⲈⲤⲞⲠ' ⲀⲖⲖⲀ ⲤⲰⲦ̄Ⲙ ⲞⲨⲚ ⲦⲀϪⲞⲞϤ Ⲛ̄ⲞⲨⲰϩⲘ ϪⲈ ⲈⲦⲈ-

Ⲧ̄ⲚⲈϢⲰⲠⲈ ⲈⲦⲈⲦⲚⲈϪⲎⲔ ⲈⲂⲞⲖ Ⲙ̄ⲘⲨⲤⲦⲎⲢⲒⲞⲚ ⲚⲒⲘ ϪⲈ ⲤⲚⲄ̄

ⲈⲨⲈⲘⲞⲨⲦⲈ ⲞⲨⲂⲈ ⲦⲎⲨⲦ̄Ⲛ ϪⲈ ⲚⲈⲦϪⲎⲔ' ⲈⲂⲞⲖ Ⲙ̄ⲠⲖⲎ-

ⲢⲰⲘⲀ ⲚⲒⲘ · ⲦⲈⲚⲞⲨ ϬⲈ ⲢⲰⲘⲈ ⲚⲒⲘ Ⲛ̄ⲢⲈϤⲢ̄ⲚⲞⲂⲈ Ⲏ̄ ⲘⲘⲞⲚ

10 Ⲛ̄ⲦⲞϤ ⲈϨⲈⲚⲢⲈϤⲢ̄ⲚⲞⲂⲈ ⲀⲚ ⲚⲈ · ⲞⲨⲘⲞⲚⲞⲚ ϪⲈ ⲈⲦⲈⲦⲚ̄-

ϢⲀⲚⲞⲨⲰϢ ⲈⲦⲢⲈⲨϢⲰⲠ ⲈⲢⲞⲞⲨ ϨⲚ ⲚⲈⲔⲢⲒⲤⲒⲤ ⲘⲚ Ⲛ̄ⲔⲞ-

ⲖⲀⲤⲒⲤ ⲈⲦⲚⲀϢ̄Ⲧ ⲀⲖⲖⲀ ⲈⲦⲢⲈⲨⲠⲞⲞⲚⲞⲨ ⲈⲨⲤⲰⲘⲀ Ⲛ̄ⲀⲒ-

ⲔⲀⲒⲞⲤ ⲠⲀⲒ̈ ⲈⲦϤⲚⲀϨⲈ ⲈⲘⲘⲨⲤⲦⲎⲢⲒⲞⲚ Ⲛ̄ⲦⲘⲚ̄ⲦⲚⲞⲨⲦⲈ Ⲛ̄Ϥ-

ⲂⲰⲔ ⲈⲠϪⲒⲤⲈ Ⲛ̄ϤⲔⲖⲎⲢⲞⲚⲞⲘⲒ Ⲛ̄ⲦⲘⲚ̄ⲦⲈⲢⲞ Ⲙ̄ⲠⲞⲨⲞⲈⲒⲚ ·

15 ⲀⲢⲒⲢⲈ Ⲙ̄ⲠⲘⲈϨϢⲞⲘⲚⲦ Ⲙ̄ⲘⲨⲤⲦⲎⲢⲒⲞⲚ ⲚⲦⲈ ⲠⲒⲀⲦϢⲀϪⲈ Ⲉ-
ⲓ
ⲢⲞϤ ⲀⲨⲰ Ⲛ̄ⲦⲈⲦⲚ̄ϪⲞⲞⲤ ϪⲈ ϤⲒ Ⲛ̄ⲦⲈⲮⲨⲬⲎ Ⲛ̄ⲚⲒⲘ Ⲛ̄ⲢⲰⲘⲈ

ⲠⲀⲒ̈ ⲈⲦⲚⲘⲈⲈⲨⲈ ⲈⲢⲞϤ ϨⲘ ⲠⲈⲚϨⲎⲦ ϤⲒⲦϤ ϨⲚ ⲔⲞⲖⲀⲤⲒⲤ ⲚⲒⲘ

Ⲛ̄ⲦⲈ Ⲛ̄ⲀⲢⲬⲰⲚ · ⲀⲨⲰ ⲤⲠⲞⲨⲀⲀⲌⲈ ϨⲚ ⲞⲨϬⲈⲠⲎ Ⲛ̄ⲦⲈⲦⲚ̄-

ϪⲒⲦⲤ ⲈⲢⲀⲦⲤ Ⲛ̄ⲦⲠⲀⲢⲐⲈⲚⲞⲤ Ⲙ̄ⲠⲞⲨⲞⲈⲒⲚ · ⲀⲨⲰ ϨⲢⲀⲒ̈ ϨⲘ

20 ⲠⲈⲒ̈ⲈⲂⲞⲦ ⲠⲈⲒ̈ⲈⲂⲞⲦ Ⲛ̄ⲦⲈ ⲦⲠⲀⲢⲐⲈⲚⲞⲤ Ⲙ̄ⲠⲞⲨⲞⲈⲒⲚ ⲤⲪⲢⲀ-

ⲄⲒⲌⲈ Ⲙ̄ⲘⲞϤ ϨⲚ ⲞⲨⲤⲪⲢⲀⲄⲒⲤ ⲈⲤⲞⲨⲞⲦⲂ̄ · ⲀⲨⲰ ϨⲢⲀⲒ̈ ϨⲘ ⲠⲈⲒ̈- ⲤⲚⲄ̄ b

ⲈⲂⲞⲦ ⲠⲈⲒ̈ⲈⲂⲞⲦ ⲘⲀⲢⲈ ⲦⲠⲀⲢⲐⲈⲚⲞⲤ Ⲙ̄ⲠⲞⲨⲞⲈⲒⲚ ⲚⲞϪϤ

ⲈⲨⲤⲰⲘⲀ ⲈϤⲚⲀⲢ̄ⲀⲒⲔⲀⲒⲞⲤ Ⲛ̄ϤⲢ̄ⲀⲄⲀⲐⲞⲤ Ⲛ̄ϤⲂⲰⲔ' ⲈⲠϪⲒⲤⲈ

Ⲛ̄ϤⲔⲖⲎⲢⲞⲚⲞⲘⲒ Ⲛ̄ⲦⲘⲚ̄ⲦⲈⲢⲞ Ⲙ̄ⲠⲞⲨⲞⲈⲒⲚ · ⲚⲀⲒ̈ ⲀⲈ ⲈⲦⲈⲦⲚ̄-

25 ϢⲀⲚϪⲞⲞⲨ ϨⲀⲘⲎⲚ ✝ϪⲰ Ⲙ̄ⲘⲞⲤ ⲈⲢⲰⲦⲚ̄ · ϪⲈ ϢⲀⲨⲤⲠⲞⲨ-

ⲀⲀⲌⲈ Ⲛ̄ϬⲒ ⲚⲈⲦϨⲨⲠⲞⲨⲢⲄⲒ ⲦⲎⲢⲞⲨ ϨⲚ Ⲛ̄ⲦⲀϨⲒⲤ ⲦⲎⲢⲞⲨ Ⲛ̄-

---

1 MS ⲈϨⲀⲢⲞϤ; Ⲉ expunged.

7 ⲓⲍ̄ in upper left-hand margin at beginning of quire.

16 MS Ⲛ̄ⲦⲢⲰⲘⲈ; Ⲧ expunged. ⲤⲚⲄ̄ lower part of column faded in places.

good brother is troubled and *sorrowful* about him, that he is in *judgments* and *punishments*; now at this time, my Lord, what shall we do until he is returned from the *punishments* and the severe judgments?"

The *Saviour* answered *however* and said to Maria : "I have spoken to you concerning these words at another time, *but now* hear that I say it once more, so that you may become completed in all *mysteries*, so that you may be called : those who are completed in every *pleroma*. Now at this time all men, sinners *or* even if they are not sinners, *not only* if you want that they should be taken from the *judgments* and the severe *punishments*, *but* that they should be returned to a *righteous body* which will find the *mysteries* of Godhood and go to the height and *inherit* the Kingdom of the Light, then perform the third *mystery* of the Ineffable, and say : 'Take the *soul* of such and such a man, of whom we are thinking in our hearts, out of all the *punishments* of the *archons*. And *hasten* with speed to take it before the *Virgin* of the light. And every month let the *Virgin* of the Light *seal* him with a superior *seal*. And every month may the *Virgin* of the Light cast him into a *body* which will become *righteous* and *good*, and go to the height and *inherit* the Kingdom of the Light.' *But* when you have said these things, *truly* I say to you that all those who *serve* in all the *ranks* of | the *judgments* of the *archons hasten* and they hand

ΝΕΚΡΙⲤΙⲤ Ⲛ̄ΤΕ Ⲛ̄ΑΡΧⲰΝ Ⲛ̄ⲤⲈϮ Ⲛ̄ΤΕΨΥΧΗ ΕΤⲘ̄ΜΑΥ Ⲉ-
ΤΟΟΤΟΥ Ⲛ̄ΝΕΥΕΡΗΥ ϨⲈⲰⲤ ϢΑΝΤΟΥϪΙΤⲤ̄ ΕΡΑΤⲤ̄ Ⲛ̄-
ΤΠΑΡΘΕΝΟⲤ Ⲙ̄ΠΟΥΟΕΙΝ· ΑΥⲰ ϢΑΡΕ ΤΠΑΡΘΕΝΟⲤ Ⲙ̄-
ΠΟΥΟΕΙΝ ϢΑⲤⲤⳘΡΑΓΙⲌΕ Ⲙ̄ΜΟⲤ ϨⲚ̄ Ⲙ̄ΜΑΪ̈Ν Ⲛ̄ΤΜⲚ̄ΤΕΡΟ
5 Ⲙ̄ΠΙΑΤϢΑϪΕ ΕΡΟϤ· ΑΥⲰ ϢΑⲤΤΑΑⲤ Ⲛ̄ΝΕⲤΠΑΡΑΛΗΜΤⲰΡ·
ΑΥⲰ ϢΑΡΕ Ⲙ̄ΠΑΡΑΛΗⲘΠΤΗⲤ ΝΟϪⲤ̄ ΕΥⲤⲰΜΑ ΕϤΝΑΡ̄ΔΙ-
ΚΑΙΟⲤ ΑΥⲰ ΕϤΝΑϨΕ ΕⲘΜΥⲤΤΗΡΙΟΝ Ⲙ̄ΠΟΥΟΕΙΝ Ⲛ̄ϤⲢ̄-
ΑΓΑΘΟⲤ Ⲛ̄ϤΒⲰΚ ΕΠϪΙⲤⲈ Ⲛ̄ϤΚΛΗΡΟΝΟΜΙ Ⲛ̄ΤΜⲚ̄ΤΕΡΟ Ⲙ̄- [ⲤⲨⲆ.]
ΠΟΥΟΕΙΝ· ΕΙⲤ ΠΑΪ̈ ΠΕ ΕΤΕΤⲚ̄ϪΝΟΥ Ⲙ̄ΜΟΪ̈ ΕΡΟϤ·
10 ΑⲤΟΥⲰ ϢⲂ̄ Ⲛ̄ϬΙ ΜΑΡΙΑ ΠΕϪΑⲤ ϪΕ ΤΕΝΟΥ ϬⲈ ΠΑϪΟ-
ΕΙⲤ ΕΪ̈Ε Ⲙ̄ΠΚⲘ̄-ΜΥⲤΤΗΡΙΟΝ Ⲛ̄ΤΟϤ ΕΠΚΟⲤΜΟⲤ ϪΕΚΑⲤ ΕⲚ-
ΝΕ ΠΡⲰΜΕ ΜΟΥ ϨΙΤⲘ̄ ΠΜΟΥ ΕΤΗΠ' ΕΡΟϤ ϨΙΤⲚ̄ Ⲛ̄ΑΡΧⲰΝ
Ⲛ̄ΘΙΜΑΡΜΕΝΗ· ϪΕ ΕϢⲰΠΕ ΕⲤΗΠ' ΕΥΑ ΕΤΡΕϤΜΟΥ ϨΙΤⲚ̄
ΤⲤΗϤΕ· Η̄ ΕΤΡΕϤΜΟΥ ϨΙΤⲚ̄ ⲘΜΟΥΕΙΟΟΥΕ Η̄ ϨⲚ̄ ϨΕΝΒΑ-
15 ⲤΑΝΟⲤ ΜⲚ̄ ϨΕΝΒΑⲤΑΝΙⲤΜΟⲤ ΜⲚ̄ ϨΕΝϨΥΒΡΙⲤΙⲤ ΕΤϨⲚ̄ Ⲛ̄-
ΝΟΜΟⲤ Η̄ ϨΙΤⲚ̄ ΚΕΜΟΥ ΕϤϨΟΟΥ· ΕΪ̈Ε Ⲙ̄ΠΚⲘ̄-ΜΥⲤΤΗΡΙΟΝ
ΕΠΚΟⲤΜΟⲤ ϪΕΚΑⲤ ΕⲚΝΕ ΠΡⲰΜΕ ΜΟΥ Ⲛ̄ϨΗΤΟΥ ϨΙΤⲚ̄ Ⲛ̄-
ΑΡΧⲰΝ Ⲛ̄ΘΙΜΑΡΜΕΝΗ· ΑΛΛΑ ϪΕΚΑⲤ ΕϤΕΜΟΥ ϨⲚ̄ ΟΥΜΟΥ
Ⲛ̄ϢⲠⲚ̄ϢⲰⲠ· ϪΕΚΑⲤ ΕⲚΝΕϤϢ̄Π-ΛΑΑΥ Ⲛ̄ϨΙⲤⲈ ϨΙΤⲚ̄ ΝΕΪ̈-
20 ΜΟΥ Ⲛ̄ΤΕΪ̈ΜΙΝΕ· ΕΒΟΛ ΓΑΡ ϪΕ ΑΝΟΝ Ⲛ̄ϨΟΥΟ ΝΑϢΕ ΝΕΤ-
ΠΗΤ' Ⲛ̄ⲤⲰΝ ΕΤΒΗΗΤⲔ̄· ΑΥⲰ ΝΑϢΕ ΝΕΤΔΙⲰΚΕ Ⲛ̄ⲤⲰΝ [ⲤⲨⲆ.]
ΕΤΒΕ ΠΕΚΡΑΝ· ϪΕΚΑⲤ ΕΥϢΑΝΒΑⲤΑΝΙⲌΕ Ⲙ̄ΜΟΝ ΕΝΕΧⲰ
Ⲙ̄ΠΜΥⲤΤΗΡΙΟΝ Ⲛ̄ΤΝΕΙ ΕΒΟΛ ϨⲚ̄ ⲤⲰΜΑ Ⲛ̄ΤΕΥΝΟΥ ΕⲘ-
ΠⲚ̄ϢⲠ-ΛΑΑΥ Ⲛ̄ϨΙⲤⲈ· ΑϤΟΥⲰϢⲘ̄ Ⲛ̄ϬΙ ΠⲤⲰΡ ΠΕϪΑϤ Ⲛ̄ΝΕϤ-
25 ΜΑΘΗΤΗⲤ ΤΗΡΟΥ ϪΕ ΕΤΒΕ ΠΕΪ̈ϢΑϪΕ ΕΤΕΤⲚ̄ϢΙΝΕ
Ⲙ̄ΜΟΪ̈ ΕΡΟϤ ΑΪ̈ΧΟΟϤ ΝΗΤⲚ̄ Ⲛ̄ΚΕⲤΟΠ· ΑΛΛΑ ⲤⲰΤⲘ̄ ΟΝ
ΤΑΧΟΟⲤ ΕΡⲰΤⲚ̄ Ⲛ̄ΚΕⲤΟΠ· ΟΥΜΟΝΟΝ Ⲛ̄ΤⲰΤⲚ̄ ΑΛΛΑ
ΡⲰΜΕ ΝΙⲘ' ΕΤΝΑΧⲰΚ ΕΒΟΛ Ⲙ̄ΠϢΟΡⲠ̄ Ⲙ̄ΜΥⲤΤΗΡΙΟΝ

that *soul* to one another *until* they cast it before the *Virgin* of the Light. And the *Virgin* of the Light *seals* it with the sign of the Kingdom of the Ineffable. And she gives it to her *paralemptores*, and the *paralemptai* cast it into a *body* which will become *righteous* and find the *mysteries* of the light and become *good*, and go to the height and *inherit* the Kingdom of the Light. Behold this is what you ask me."

109.   Maria answered and said : "Now at this time, my Lord, hast thou not brought *mysteries* into the *world* so that a man should not die through the death which is allotted to him by the *archons* of the *Heimarmene*, whether it be alloted to one that he should die by the sword, *or* that he should die by water, *or* in *torments* and *tortures* and *ill-treatment* in the *laws*, *or* by another bad death? Hast thou not brought *mysteries* into the world so that with them a man should not die through the *archons* of the *Heimarmene*, *but* that he should die by a sudden death so that he should not suffer any afflictions through deaths of this kind? *For* they are very many which persecute us for thy sake. And they are many which *persecute* us for the sake of thy name, so that when they *torment* us we may say the *mystery*, and go forth from the *body* immediately without receiving any afflictions."

The *Saviour* answered and said to all his *disciples* : "Concerning these words on which you question me, I have spoken to you at another time *but* hear again that I tell you once more. *Not only* you but every man who will complete the first *mystery* | of the First *Mystery* of the Ineffable, he *now* who ⲛ̄ⲧⲉ ⲡⲓϣⲟⲣ̄ⲡ̄ ⲙ̄ⲙⲩⲥⲧⲏⲣⲓⲟⲛ ⲛ̄ⲧⲉ ⲡⲓⲁ̄ⲧ̄ϣⲁϫⲉ ⲉⲣⲟϥ· ⲡⲉⲧⲛⲁⲉⲓⲣⲉ ⲟⲩⲛ ⲙ̄ⲡⲙⲩⲥⲧⲏⲣⲓⲟⲛ ⲉⲧⲙ̄ⲙⲁⲩ· ⲛ̄ϥ̄ϫⲟⲕϥ ⲉⲃⲟⲗ ϩⲛ̄ ⲛⲉϥⲥⲭⲏⲙⲁ ⲙⲛ̄ ⲛⲉϥⲧⲩⲡⲟⲥ ⲧⲏⲣⲟⲩ ⲙⲛ̄ ⲛⲉϥϭⲓⲛⲁϩⲉⲣⲁⲧⲟⲩ ⲉϥⲉⲓⲣⲉ ⲙⲉⲛ ⲙ̄ⲙⲟϥ ⲛ̄ϥ̄ⲛⲏⲩ ⲁⲛ ⲉⲃⲟⲗ ϩⲛ̄ ⲥⲱⲙⲁ· ⲁⲗⲗⲁ ⲙ̄ⲛ̄ⲛ̄ⲥⲁ ⲧⲣⲉϥϫⲱⲕ' ⲉⲃⲟⲗ ⲙ̄ⲡⲙⲩⲥⲧⲏⲣⲓⲟⲛ ⲉⲧⲙ̄ⲙⲁⲩ ⲙⲛ̄ ⲛⲉϥⲥⲭⲏⲙⲁ ⲙⲛ̄ ⲛⲉϥⲧⲩⲡⲟⲥ ⲧⲏⲣⲟⲩ· ⲙ̄ⲛ̄ⲛ̄ⲥⲱⲥ ϭⲉ ⲛⲁⲩ ⲛⲓⲙ' ⲉⲧϥ̄ⲛⲁⲟⲛⲟⲙⲁⲍⲉ ⲙ̄ⲡⲙⲩⲥⲧⲏⲣⲓⲟⲛ ⲉⲧⲙ̄ⲙⲁⲩ ** ϥⲛⲁⲛⲟⲩϩ̄ⲙ̄ ⲉⲛⲏ ⲧⲏⲣⲟⲩ ⲥ̄ⲛ̄ⲉ̄ ⲉⲧⲏⲡ' ⲉⲣⲟϥ ϩⲓⲧⲛ̄ ⲛ̄ⲁⲣⲭⲱⲛ ⲛ̄ⲑⲓⲙⲁⲣⲙⲉⲛⲏ· ⲁⲩⲱ ⲛ̄ⲧⲉⲩⲛⲟⲩ ⲉⲧⲙ̄ⲙⲁⲩ ϥⲛⲏⲩ ⲉⲃⲟⲗ ϩⲙ̄ ⲡⲥⲱⲙⲁ ⲛ̄ⲑⲩⲗⲏ ⲛ̄ⲛ̄ⲁⲣⲭⲱⲛ ⲁⲩⲱ ⲧⲉϥⲯⲩⲭⲏ ⲛⲁⲣ̄-ⲟⲩⲛⲟϭ ⲛ̄ⲁⲡⲟⲣⲣⲟⲓⲁ ⲛ̄ⲟⲩⲟⲉⲓⲛ ⲛ̄ⲥ̄ϩⲱⲗ ⲉⲡϫⲓⲥⲉ ⲁⲩⲱ ⲛ̄ⲥ̄ϫⲱⲧⲉ ⲛ̄ⲧⲟⲡⲟⲥ ⲛⲓⲙ ⲛ̄ⲧⲉ ⲛ̄ⲁⲣⲭⲱⲛ ⲙⲛ̄ ⲧⲟⲡⲟⲥ ⲛⲓⲙ' ⲛ̄ⲧⲉ ⲡⲟⲩⲟⲉⲓⲛ ϩⲉⲱⲥ ϣⲁⲛ̄ⲧ̄ⲥ̄ⲃⲱⲕ ⲉⲡⲧⲟⲡⲟⲥ ⲛ̄ⲧⲉⲥⲙ̄ⲛ̄ⲧ̄ⲉ̄ⲣ̄ⲟ· ⲟⲩⲧⲉ ⲙⲉⲥϯⲁⲡⲟⲫⲁⲥⲓⲥ ⲟⲩⲧⲉ ⲁⲡⲟⲗⲟⲅⲓⲁ ϩⲛ̄ ⲗⲁⲁⲩ ⲛ̄ⲧⲟⲡⲟⲥ· ⲟⲩⲁⲧⲥⲩⲙⲃⲟⲗⲟⲛ ⲅⲁⲣ ⲧⲉ·

ⲛⲁⲓ̈ ϭⲉ ⲛ̄ⲧⲉⲣⲉϥϫⲟⲟⲩ ⲛ̄ϭⲓ ⲓ̄ⲥ̄ ⲁⲥⲟⲩⲱϩ ⲉⲧⲟⲟⲧⲥ̄ ⲛ̄ϭⲓ ⲙⲁⲣⲓⲁ ⲁⲥⲡⲁϩⲧⲥ̄ ⲉϫⲛ̄ ⲛ̄ⲟⲩⲉⲣⲏⲧⲉ ⲛ̄ⲓ̄ⲥ̄ ⲁⲥϯⲡⲓ ⲉⲣⲟⲟⲩ ⲡⲉϫⲁⲥ ϫⲉ ⲡⲁϫⲟⲉⲓⲥ ⲉⲧⲓ ϯⲛⲁϣⲓⲛⲉ ⲙ̄ⲙⲟⲕ ϭⲱⲗ̄ⲡ̄ ⲛⲁⲛ ⲉⲃⲟⲗ' ⲁⲩⲱ ⲙ̄ⲡⲣ̄ϩⲱⲡ' ⲉⲣⲟⲛ· ⲁϥⲟⲩⲱϩ̄ⲙ̄ ⲛ̄ϭⲓ ⲓ̄ⲥ̄ ⲡⲉϫⲁϥ ⲙ̄ⲙⲁⲣⲓⲁ ϫⲉ ϣⲓⲛⲉ ⲛ̄ⲥⲁ ⲡⲉⲧⲉⲧⲛ̄ϣⲓⲛⲉ ⲛ̄ⲥⲱϥ·* ⲁⲩⲱ ⲁⲛⲟⲕ ⲥ̄ⲛ̄ⲉ̄ b ϯⲛⲁϭⲱⲗ̄ⲡ̄ ⲛⲏⲧⲛ̄ ⲉⲃⲟⲗ ϩⲛ̄ ⲟⲩⲡⲁⲣⲣⲏⲥⲓⲁ ⲁϫⲛ̄ ⲡⲁⲣⲁⲃⲟⲗⲏ· ⲁⲥⲟⲩⲱϩ̄ⲙ̄ ⲛ̄ϭⲓ ⲙⲁⲣⲓⲁ ⲡⲉϫⲁⲥ ϫⲉ ⲡⲁϫⲟⲉⲓⲥ ⲉⲓ̈ⲉ ⲙ̄ⲡⲕⲙ̄ⲙⲩⲥⲧⲏⲣⲓⲟⲛ ⲉⲡⲕⲟⲥⲙⲟⲥ ⲉⲧⲃⲉ ⲧⲙ̄ⲛ̄ⲧ̄ϩⲏⲕⲉ ⲙⲛ̄ ⲧⲙ̄ⲛ̄ⲧ̄ⲣ̄ⲙ̄ⲙⲁⲟ· ⲁⲩⲱ ⲉⲧⲃⲉ ⲧⲙ̄ⲛ̄ⲧ̄ϭⲱⲃ ⲙⲛ̄ ⲧⲙ̄ⲛ̄ⲧ̄ϫⲱⲱⲣⲉ· ⲁⲩⲱ

1 ⲛ̄ⲧⲉ ⲡⲓϣⲟⲣ̄ⲡ̄ . . . ⲙ̄ⲡⲙⲩⲥⲧⲏⲣⲓⲟⲛ written below in margin.
25 MS ⲙⲛ̄ ⲙ ; ⲙ expunged.

will perform that *mystery* and complete it in its *patterns* and all its *types* and its stations, when *indeed* he performs it he does not come forth from the *body*, *but* after he has completed that *mystery* with its *patterns* and all its *types*. Now thereafter, every time he will *invoke* that *mystery* he will be saved from all those things which are allotted to him by the *archons* of the *Heimarmene*. And in that hour he will come forth from the *body* of *matter* of the *archons*, and his *soul* will become a great *outpouring* of light and will fly to the height, and penetrate all the *places* of the *archons* and all the *places* of the light, *until* it goes to the *place* of its kingdom. *Neither* does it give *answers nor defences* in any *place*, for it is without *secret sign*."

110. Now when Jesus said these things Maria continued again, she prostrated herself at the feet of Jesus, she kissed them and said : "My Lord, *yet still* I will question thee. Reveal to us and do not conceal from us." Jesus answered and said to Maria : "Question that which you question, and I will reveal to you *openly* without *parable*."

Maria answered and said : "My Lord, hast thou not brought *mysteries* to the *world* concerning poverty and riches [1], and concerning weakness and strength, and | con-

---

[1] (24) poverty and riches etc.; lit. the poverty and the riches etc.

ⲈⲦⲂⲈ Ⲛ̄ⲤⲒⲚⲎⲤⲒⲤ ⲘⲚ̄ Ⲛ̄ⲤⲰⲘⲀ ⲈⲦⲞⲨⲞⲬ· ⲌⲀⲠⲀⳄ ⲌⲀⲠⲖⲰⲤ
ⲈⲦⲂⲈ ⲚⲀⲒ̈ Ⲛ̄ⲦⲈⲒ̈ⲘⲒⲚⲈ ⲦⲎⲢⲞⲨ ⲬⲈⲔⲀⲤ ⲈⲚⲰ̄ⲀⲚⲂⲰⲔ ⲈⳞⲢⲀⲒ̈
ⳞⲚ Ⲛ̄ⲦⲞⲠⲞⲤ Ⲛ̄ⲦⲈⲬⲰⲢⲀ· ⲀⲨⲰ Ⲛ̄ⲤⲈⲦⲘⲠⲒⲤⲦⲈⲨⲈ ⲈⲢⲞⲚ
ⲀⲨⲰ Ⲛ̄ⲤⲈⲦⲘⲤⲰⲦⲘ Ⲛ̄ⲤⲀ ⲚⲈⲚⲰ̄ⲀⲬⲈ· Ⲛ̄ⲦⲚⲈⲒⲢⲈ Ⲛ̄ⲞⲨⲘⲨⲤ-
5 ⲦⲎⲢⲒⲞⲚ Ⲛ̄ⲦⲈⲒ̈ⲘⲒⲚⲈ ⳞⲚ Ⲛ̄ⲦⲞⲠⲞⲤ ⲈⲦⲘ̄ⲘⲀⲨ· ⲬⲈⲔⲀⲤ ⲈⲨⲈ-
ⲈⲒⲘⲈ ⲀⲖⲎⲐⲰⲤ ⳞⲚ ⲞⲨⲘⲈ ⲬⲈ ⲈⲚⲔⲎⲢⲨⲤⲤⲈ Ⲛ̄Ⲛ̄Ⲱ̄ⲀⲬⲈ ⟨Ⲙ̄-
ⲠⲚⲞⲨⲦⲈ⟩ Ⲙ̄ⲠⲦⲎⲢϤ· ⲀϤⲞⲨⲰⳞⲘ Ⲛ̄ϬⲒ ⲠⲤⲰⲢ ⲠⲈⲬⲀϤ Ⲙ̄ⲘⲀ-
ⲢⲒⲀ ⳞⲚ ⲦⲘⲎⲦⲈ Ⲛ̄ⲘⲘⲀⲐⲎⲦⲎⲤ ⲬⲈ ⲈⲦⲂⲈ ⲠⲈⲒ̈ⲘⲨⲤⲦⲎⲢⲒⲞⲚ
ⲈⲦⲈⲦⲚ̄Ⲱ̄ⲒⲚⲈ Ⲙ̄ⲘⲞⲒ̈ ⲈⲢⲞϤ ⲀⲒ̈ⲦⲀⲀϤ ⲚⲎⲦⲚ̄ Ⲛ̄ⲔⲈⲤⲞⲠ ⲀⲖⲖⲀ   [ⲤⲚⲈ̄]
10 ϯⲚⲀⲞⲨⲰⳞⲘ ⲞⲚ Ⲛ̄ⲦⲀⲬⲰ ⲈⲢⲰⲦⲚ̄ Ⲙ̄ⲠⲰ̄ⲀⲬⲈ· ⲦⲈⲚⲞⲨ ϬⲈ
ⲞⲨⲚ ⲘⲀⲢⲒⲀ ⲞⲨⲘⲞⲚⲞⲚ Ⲛ̄ⲦⲰⲦⲚ̄ ⲀⲖⲖⲀ ⲢⲰⲘⲈ ⲚⲒⲘ’ ⲈⲦⲚⲀ-
ⲬⲰⲔ ⲈⲂⲞⲖ Ⲙ̄ⲠⲘⲨⲤⲦⲎⲢⲒⲞⲚ Ⲙ̄ⲠⲦⲞⲨⲚⲈⲤ-ⲢⲈϤⲘⲞⲞⲨⲦ· ⲠⲀⲒ̈
Ⲱ̄ⲀϤⲐⲈⲢⲀⲠⲈⲨⲈ Ⲛ̄Ⲛ̄ⲀⲒⲘⲞⲚⲒⲞⲚ ⲘⲚ̄ ⲘⲞⲔ̄Ⲥ ⲚⲒⲘ· ⲘⲚ̄ Ⲱ̄Ⲱ-
ⲚⲈ ⲚⲒⲘ· ⲀⲨⲰ ⲘⲚ̄ Ⲛ̄Ⲃ̄ⲀⲖⲈⲈⲨ· ⲀⲨⲰ ⲘⲚ̄ Ⲛ̄ϬⲀⲖⲈⲈⲨ ⲘⲚ̄ Ⲛ̄-
15 ϬⲀⲚⳞ· ⲘⲚ̄ Ⲛ̄ⲈⲘⲠⲞ· ⲘⲚ̄ Ⲛ̄ⲔⲰϤⲞⲤ· ⲠⲀⲒ̈ Ⲛ̄ⲦⲀⲒ̈ⲦⲀⲀϤ ⲚⲎ-
ⲦⲚ̄ Ⲙ̄ⲠⲒⲞⲨⲞⲈⲒ̄Ⲱ· ⲠⲈⲦⲚⲀϤⲒ ⲈⲞⲨⲘⲨⲤⲦⲎⲢⲒⲞⲚ Ⲛ̄ϤⲬⲞⲔϤ
ⲈⲂⲞⲖ· ⲘⲚ̄ⲚⲤⲰⲤ ϬⲈ ⲈϤⲰ̄ⲀⲚⲀⲒⲦⲒ Ⲛ̄ⳞⲰⲂ ⲚⲒⲘ· ⲘⲚ̄Ⲧ̄ⳞⲎⲔⲈ ⳞⲒ
ⲘⲚ̄Ⲧ̄Ⲣ̄ⲘⲘⲀⲞ· ⲘⲚ̄Ⲧ̄ϬⲰⲂ ⳞⲒ ⲘⲚ̄ⲦⲬⲰⲰⲢⲈ· ⲤⲒⲚⲰⲤⲒⲤ ⳞⲒ ⲤⲰ-
ⲘⲀ ⲈϤⲞⲨⲞⲬ· ⲘⲚ̄ ⲐⲈⲢⲀⲠⲒⲀ ⲚⲒⲘ’ Ⲛ̄ⲦⲈ ⲠⲤⲰⲘⲀ· ⲀⲨⲰ ⲘⲚ̄
20 ⲠⲦⲞⲨⲚⲈⲤ-ⲢⲈϤⲘⲞⲞⲨⲦ· ⲀⲨⲰ ⲈⲐⲈⲢⲀⲠⲈⲨⲈ Ⲛ̄Ⲛ̄ϬⲀⲖⲈ ⲘⲚ̄
Ⲛ̄ⲂⲀⲖⲈⲈⲨ ⲘⲚ̄ Ⲛ̄ⲔⲰϤⲞⲤ ⲘⲚ̄ Ⲛ̄ⲈⲘⲠⲞ· ⲘⲚ̄ Ⲱ̄ⲰⲚⲈ ⲚⲒⲘ ⲘⲚ̄
ⲘⲞⲔ̄Ⲥ ⲚⲒⲘ· ⲌⲀⲠⲀⳄ ⲌⲀⲠⲖⲰⲤ ⲠⲈⲦⲚⲀⲬⲰⲔ ⲈⲂⲞⲖ Ⲙ̄ⲠⲘⲨⲤ-
ⲦⲎⲢⲒⲞⲚ ⲈⲦⲘ̄ⲘⲀⲨ Ⲛ̄ϤⲀⲒ̈ⲦⲒ Ⲛ̄ⳞⲰⲂ ⲚⲒⲘ’ ⲈⲚⲦⲀⲒ̈ⲬⲞⲞⲨ ⲤⲈⲚⲀ-
Ⲱ̄ⲰⲠⲈ ⲚⲀϤ ⳞⲚ ⲞⲨⲤⲠⲞⲨⲆⲎ·   [ⲤⲚⳞ̄]

---

1   MS Ⲛ̄ⲤⲒⲚⲎⲤⲒⲤ; but line 18 ⲤⲒⲚⲰⲤⲒⲤ; perhaps read ⲔⲒⲚⲎⲤⲒⲤ; cf. 210.23.
7   Ⲙ̄ⲠⲚⲞⲨⲦⲈ omitted.
13   MS ⲠⲀⲒ̈ Ⲱ̄ⲀϤⲐⲈⲢⲀⲠⲈⲨⲈ; read ⲠⲀⲒ̈ ⲈⲰ̄ⲀϤⲐⲈⲢⲀⲠⲈⲨⲈ.
16   MS ⲠⲈⲦⲚⲀϤⲒ ⲈⲞⲨⲘⲨⲤⲦⲎⲢⲒⲞⲚ; read ⲠⲈⲦⲚⲀϤⲒ Ⲛ̄ⲞⲨⲘⲨⲤⲦⲎⲢⲒⲞⲚ.

cerning *plagues*[1] and sound *bodies, in a word,* all things of this kind? So that when we go to *places* of the *country,* and they do not *believe* us and they do not listen to our words, and we perform a *mystery* of this kind in those *places,* then they know *truly* and verily that we are *preaching* the words ⟨of the God⟩ of All."

The *Saviour* answered and said to Maria in the midst of the *disciples*: "Concerning this *mystery* upon which you question me, I gave it to you once, *but* I will repeat again and say the word to you. *Now* at this time, Maria, *not only* you *but* all men who will complete the *mystery* of the raising of the dead: this *cures demons* and all pains and all sicknesses and the blind and the lame and the maimed and the dumb and the *deaf,* this I have given to you once. He who will take a *mystery* and complete it, if now afterwards he *asks* for anything: poverty and riches, weakness and strength, *plague* or sound *body,* and all *cures* of the *body,* and the raising of the dead, and *curing* of the lame and the blind and the *deaf* and the dumb and all sicknesses and pains, *in a word,* he who completes that *mystery* and *asks* for any thing which I have said, it will happen to him *with speed."* |

---

[1]   (1, 18) plague(s); Till: movement(s) (see 210.23).

ⲚⲀⲒ ϬⲈ ⲚⲦⲈⲢⲈϤϪⲞⲞⲨ ⲚϬⲒ ⲠⲤⲰⲦⲎⲢ· ⲀⲨⲈⲒ' ⲈⲐⲎ ⲚϬⲒ
ⲘⲘⲀⲐⲎⲦⲎⲤ ⲀⲨⲰϢ ⲈⲂⲞⲗ ⲦⲎⲢⲞⲨ ϨⲒ ⲚⲈⲨⲈⲢⲎⲨ ⲈⲨϪⲰ
ⲘⲘⲞⲤ ϪⲈ ⲠⲤⲰⲦⲎⲢ ⲀⲔⲀⲂⲦⲚ ⲈⲘⲀϢⲞ ⲈⲘⲀϢⲞ ⲈⲂⲞⲗ ⲚⲘ-
ⲘⲚⲦⲚⲞϬ ⲈⲦⲔϪⲰ ⲘⲘⲞⲞⲨ ⲚⲀⲚ ⲀⲨⲰ ϪⲈ ⲀⲔϤⲒ ⲚⲚⲈⲚ-
5 ⲮⲨⲬⲎ ⲀⲨⲰ ⲀⲨⲢϨⲞⲒ ⲚⲈⲒ' ⲈⲂⲞⲗ ⲚϨⲎⲦⲚ ⲈϨⲞⲨⲚ ⲈⲢⲞⲔ·
ⲈⲂⲞⲗ ⲄⲀⲢ ϪⲈ ϨⲈⲚⲈⲂⲞⲗ ⲚϨⲎⲦⲔ ⲚⲈ· ⲦⲈⲚⲞⲨ ϬⲈ ⲈⲦⲂⲈ
ⲚⲈⲒⲘⲚⲦⲚⲞϬ ⲀⲨⲗⲒⲂⲈ ⲚϬⲒ ⲚⲈⲚⲮⲨⲬⲞⲞⲨⲈ ⲚⲀⲒ ⲈⲦⲔϪⲰ Ⲙ-
ⲘⲞⲞⲨ ⲈⲢⲞⲚ· ⲀⲨⲰ ⲀⲨⲐⲗⲒⲂⲈ ⲈⲘⲀϢⲞ ⲈⲘⲀϢⲞ ⲈⲨⲞⲨⲰϢ
ⲈⲈⲒ' ⲈⲂⲞⲗ ⲚϨⲎⲦⲚ ⲈⲠϪⲒⲤⲈ ⲈⲠⲦⲞⲠⲞⲤ ⲈⲦⲈⲔⲘⲚⲦⲈⲢⲞ· ⲚⲀⲒ
10 ϬⲈ ⲚⲦⲈⲢⲞⲨϪⲞⲞⲨ ⲚϬⲒ ⲘⲘⲀⲐⲎⲦⲎⲤ ⲀϤⲞⲨⲰϨ ⲞⲚ ⲈⲦⲞ-
ⲞⲦϤ ⲚϬⲒ ⲠⲤⲰⲦⲎⲢ ⲠⲈϪⲀϤ ⲚⲚⲈϤⲘⲀⲐⲎⲦⲎⲤ· ϪⲈ ⲈⲦⲈⲦⲚ-
ϢⲀⲚⲂⲰⲔ' ⲈϨⲈⲚⲠⲞⲗⲒⲤ Ⲏ ϨⲈⲚⲘⲚⲦⲈⲢⲞ Ⲏ ϨⲈⲚⲬⲰⲢⲀ· ⲔⲎ-
ⲢⲨⲤⲤⲈ ⲚⲀⲨ ⲚϢⲞⲢⲠ ⲈⲦⲈⲦⲚϪⲰ ⲘⲘⲞⲤ ϪⲈ ϢⲒⲚⲈ ⲚⲚⲀⲨ
ⲚⲒⲘ· ⲀⲨⲰ**ⲘⲠⲢⲔⲀⲦⲈⲦⲎⲨⲦⲚ ⲈⲂⲞⲗ· ϨⲈⲰⲤ ϢⲀⲚⲦⲈⲦⲚ-   ⲤⲚⲌ
15 ϬⲒⲚⲈ ⲚⲘⲘⲨⲤⲦⲎⲢⲒⲞⲚ ⲘⲠⲞⲨⲞⲈⲒⲚ· ⲚⲀⲒ ⲈⲦⲚⲀϪⲒⲦⲎⲨⲦⲚ
ⲈϨⲞⲨⲚ ⲈⲦⲘⲚⲦⲈⲢⲞ ⲘⲠⲞⲨⲞⲈⲒⲚ· ⲀϪⲒⲤ ⲈⲢⲞⲞⲨ ϪⲈ ϨⲢ-
ⲦⲎⲨⲦⲚ ⲈⲢⲰⲦⲚ ⲈⲚⲈⲤⲂⲰ ⲘⲠⲗⲀⲚⲎ ⲈⲘⲘⲞⲚ ⲞⲨⲚ ⲞⲨⲘⲎ-
 ⲎϢⲈ ⲚⲎⲨ ϨⲘ ⲠⲀⲢⲀⲚ ⲈⲨϪⲰ ⲘⲘⲞⲤ ϪⲈ ⲀⲚⲞⲔ ⲠⲈ ⲈⲚ-
ⲀⲚⲞⲔ' ⲀⲚ ⲠⲈ· ⲀⲨⲰ ⲤⲈⲚⲀⲠⲗⲀⲚⲀ ⲚⲞⲨⲘⲎⲎϢⲈ· ⲦⲈⲚⲞⲨ
20 ϬⲈ ⲢⲰⲘⲈ ⲚⲒⲘ ⲈⲦⲚⲎⲨ ⲈⲢⲀⲦⲦⲎⲨⲦⲚ ⲚⲤⲈⲠⲒⲤⲦⲈⲨⲈ ⲈⲢⲰ-
ⲦⲚ ⲀⲨⲰ ⲚⲤⲈⲤⲰⲦⲘ ⲚⲤⲀ ⲚⲈⲦⲚϢⲀϪⲈ· ⲀⲨⲰ ⲚⲤⲈⲈⲒⲢⲈ
ⲘⲠⲈⲘⲠϢⲀ ⲚⲘⲘⲨⲤⲦⲎⲢⲒⲞⲚ ⲘⲠⲞⲨⲞⲈⲒⲚ· ⲈⲒⲈ ϯ ⲚⲀⲨ ⲚⲘ-
ⲘⲨⲤⲦⲎⲢⲒⲞⲚ ⲘⲠⲞⲨⲞⲈⲒⲚ ⲀⲨⲰ ⲘⲠⲢϨⲞⲠⲞⲨ ⲈⲢⲞⲞⲨ· ⲀⲨⲰ
ⲠⲈⲦⲘⲠϢⲀ ⲚⲘⲘⲨⲤⲦⲎⲢⲒⲞⲚ ⲈⲦϪⲞⲤⲈ ⲦⲀⲀⲨ ⲚⲀϤ· ⲀⲨⲰ
25 ⲠⲈⲦⲘⲠϢⲀ ⲚⲘⲘⲨⲤⲦⲎⲢⲒⲞⲚ ⲈⲦⲤⲞⲂⲔ ⲦⲀⲀⲨ ⲚⲀϤ· ⲀⲨⲰ

---

9 MS ⲚⲦⲈⲔⲘⲚⲦⲈⲢⲞ.
17 MS originally ⲈⲚⲒⲤⲂⲰ; Ⲓ altered to Ⲉ in later hand.

Now when the *Saviour* said these things, the *disciples* came forward, they all cried out together, saying : "O *Saviour*, thou hast maddened us exceedingly with the great things which thou hast said to us, and because thou didst take away our *souls* and they strove to come forth from us towards thee, *for* they are from thee [1]. Now at this time because of these great things which thou hast said to us, our *souls* have been maddened, and they were *afflicted* exceedingly, wishing to come forth from us to the height to the *place* of thy kingdom."

111.   Now when the *disciples* said these things the *Saviour* continued again, he said to his *disciples* : "When you go to *cities or* kingdoms *or countries, preach* to them first, saying : seek at all times and do not cease *until* you find the *mysteries* of the light, which will take you into the Kingdom of the Light. Say to them : beware of *erroneous* teachings, for many will come in my name, saying : I am he, although it is not I, and will lead many into *error* [*]. Now at this time to all men who come before you and *believe* in you and hear your words and do what is worthy of the *mysteries* of the light, give to them the *mysteries* of the light and do not conceal them from them. And to him that is worthy of the *mysteries* which are superior, give them to him. And to him that is worthy of the *mysteries* which are inferior, give them to him and |

---

[*]   Mt. 24.4, 5

---

[1]   (6) they are from thee; Schmidt : we are from thee.

ⲘⲠⲢϨⲈⲠ-ⲖⲀⲀⲨ ⲈⲖⲀⲀⲨ· ⲠⲘⲨⲤⲦⲎⲢⲒⲞⲚ ⲚⲦⲞϤ ⲘⲠⲦⲞⲨⲚⲈⲤ-
ⲢⲈϤⲘⲞⲞⲨⲦ' ⲀⲨⲰ ⲈⲐⲈⲢⲀⲠⲈⲨⲈ ⲚⲚϢⲰⲚⲈ ⲘⲠⲢⲦⲀⲀϤ Ⲛ-
ⲖⲀⲀⲨ ⲞⲨⲆⲈ ⲘⲠⲢϮⲤⲂⲰ ⲚϨⲎⲦϤ ϪⲈ ⲠⲘⲨⲤⲦⲎⲢⲒⲞⲚ ⲈⲦⲘ-
ⲘⲀⲨ ⲠⲀⲚⲀⲢⲬⲰⲚ ⲠⲈ· ⲚⲦⲞϤ ⲘⲚ ⲚⲈϤⲞⲚⲞⲘⲀⲤⲒⲀ ⲦⲎⲢⲞⲨ·
5 ⲈⲦⲂⲈ ⲠⲀⲒ ⲞⲨⲚ *ⲘⲠⲢⲦⲀⲀϤ ⲚⲖⲀⲀⲨ ⲞⲨⲆⲈ ⲘⲠⲢϮⲤⲂⲰ Ⲛ-
ϨⲎⲦϤ· ϨⲈⲰⲤ ϢⲀⲚⲦⲈⲦⲚⲦⲀⲬⲢⲞ ⲚⲦⲠⲒⲤⲦⲒⲤ ϨⲘ ⲠⲔⲞⲤⲘⲞⲤ
ⲦⲎⲢϤ· ϪⲈⲔⲀⲤ ⲈⲦⲈⲦⲚϢⲀⲚⲂⲰⲔ' ⲈϨⲢⲀⲒ ⲈϨⲈⲚⲠⲞⲖⲒⲤ· Ⲏ
ϨⲈⲚⲬⲰⲢⲀ ⲀⲨⲰ ⲚⲤⲈⲦⲘϢⲈⲠⲦⲎⲨⲦⲚ ⲈⲢⲞⲞⲨ ⲀⲨⲰ ⲚⲤⲈ-
ⲦⲘⲠⲒⲤⲦⲈⲨⲈ ⲈⲢⲰⲦⲚ ⲚⲤⲈⲦⲘⲤⲰⲦⲘ ⲚⲤⲀ ⲚⲈⲦⲚϢⲀϪⲈ· Ⲛ-
10 ⲦⲈⲦⲚⲦⲞⲨⲚⲈⲤ-ϨⲈⲚⲢⲈϤⲘⲞⲞⲨⲦ ϨⲚ ⲚⲦⲞⲠⲞⲤ ⲈⲦⲘⲘⲀⲨ·
ⲀⲨⲰ ⲚⲦⲈⲦⲚⲐⲈⲢⲀⲠⲈⲨⲈ ⲚⲚϬⲀⲖⲈⲈⲨ ⲘⲚ ⲚⲂⲀⲖⲈⲈⲨ ⲘⲚ
ⲚϢⲰⲚⲈ ⲈⲦϢⲂⲈⲒⲀⲈⲒⲦ ϨⲚ ⲚⲦⲞⲠⲞⲤ ⲈⲦⲘⲘⲀⲨ· ⲀⲨⲰ ⲈⲂⲞⲖ
ϨⲒⲦⲚ ⲚⲀⲒ ⲦⲎⲢⲞⲨ ⲚⲦⲈⲒⲘⲒⲚⲈ· ⲤⲈⲚⲀⲠⲒⲤⲦⲈⲨⲈ ⲈⲢⲰⲦⲚ ϪⲈ
ⲈⲦⲈⲦⲚⲔⲎⲢⲨⲤⲤⲈ ⲘⲠⲚⲞⲨⲦⲈ ⲘⲠⲦⲎⲢϤ· ⲀⲨⲰ ⲚⲤⲈⲠⲒⲤⲦⲈⲨⲈ
15 ⲈϢⲀϪⲈ ⲚⲒⲘ' ⲚⲦⲈⲦⲎⲨⲦⲚ· ⲈⲦⲂⲈ ⲠⲀⲒ ϬⲈ ⲞⲨⲚ ⲚⲦⲀⲒϮ
ⲚⲎⲦⲚ ⲘⲠⲘⲨⲤⲦⲎⲢⲒⲞⲚ ⲈⲦⲘⲘⲀⲨ· ϨⲈⲰⲤ ϢⲀⲚⲦⲈⲦⲚⲦⲀⲬⲢⲞ
ⲚⲦⲠⲒⲤⲦⲒⲤ ϨⲘ ⲠⲔⲞⲤⲘⲞⲤ ⲦⲎⲢϤ·

　　　ⲚⲀⲒ ϬⲈ ⲚⲦⲈⲢⲈϤϪⲞⲞⲨ ⲚϬⲒ ⲠⲤⲰⲢ ⲀϤⲞⲨⲰϨ ⲞⲚ ⲈⲦⲞⲞⲦϤ
ϨⲘ ⲠϢⲀϪⲈ ⲠⲈϪⲀϤ ⲘⲘⲀⲢⲒⲀ ϪⲈ ⲦⲈⲚⲞⲨ ϬⲈ ⲞⲨⲚ ⲤⲰⲦⲘ
20 ⲘⲀⲢⲒⲀ· ⲈⲦⲂⲈ **ⲠϢⲀϪⲈ ⲈⲚⲦⲀϢⲚⲦ ⲈⲢⲞϤ ϪⲈ ⲚⲒⲘ ⲠⲈⲦⲀⲚⲀⲄ-
ⲔⲀⲌⲈ ⲘⲠⲢⲰⲘⲈ ϨⲈⲰⲤ ϢⲀⲚⲦϤⲢⲚⲞⲂⲈ· ⲦⲈⲚⲞⲨ ϬⲈ ⟨ⲤⲰⲦⲘ
ϪⲈ⟩ ϢⲀⲨⲘⲒⲤⲈ ⲘⲠϢⲎⲢⲈ ϢⲎⲘ' ⲈⲢⲈ ⲦϬⲞⲘ ⲤⲞⲂⲔ ⲚϨⲎⲦϤ·
ⲀⲨⲰ ⲈⲤⲤⲞⲂⲔ ⲚϨⲎⲦϤ ⲚϬⲒ ⲦⲈⲮⲨⲬⲎ· ⲀⲨⲰ ⲈϤⲤⲞⲂⲔ ⲚϨⲎⲦϤ
ⲚϬⲒ ⲠⲔⲈⲀⲚⲦⲒⲘⲒⲘⲞⲚ ⲘⲠⲚⲀ ϨⲀⲠⲀϨ ϨⲀⲠⲖⲰⲤ ⲈⲨⲤⲞⲂⲔ Ⲙ-

12　MS ⲈⲦϢⲂⲒⲀⲈⲒⲦ; Ⲉ inserted over ⲓ.
18　MS originally ⲀϤⲞⲨⲰϨⲘ; Ⲙ expunged.
21　ⲤⲰⲦⲘ ϪⲈ omitted.

do not conceal anything from anyone. Do not give the *mystery* of the raising of the dead and *healing* of the sick to anyone *nor* teach in it, for that *mystery* is of the *archons*, it and all its *invocations*. For this reason *now* do not give it to anyone *nor* teach in it *until* you confirm the *faith* in the whole *world*. So that when you go into *cities or countries*, and they do not receive you and they do not *believe* you and they do not listen to your words, then raise the dead in those *places*, and *cure* the lame and the blind and the various sicknesses in those *places*. And by means of all such things as these they will *believe* you, that you are *preaching* the God of All, and will *believe* all words of yours. *Now* for this reason I have given you that *mystery until* you confirm the *faith* in the whole *world*."

Now when the *Saviour* had said these things he continued again with the discourse. He said to Maria : "*Now* at this time hear, Maria, concerning the word about which you questioned me : 'Who *compels* men *until* they commit sin?'

Now at this time ⟨hear⟩ : when the child is born, the power in him is small, and the *soul* in him is small, and the *spirit counterpart* also is small in him. *In a word,* | the three

ΠϢΟΜ̄Ν̄Τ 21 ΝΕΥΕΡΗΥ· ΕΜΝ̄ΛΛΛΥ Μ̄ΜΟΟΥ ΛΙⲤΟⲀΝΕ
ΕⲀⲀⲀⲨ Ν̄ϨⲰⲂ' ΕΙΤΕ ΠΕΤΝⲀΝΟΥϤ ΕΙΤΕ ΠΕΘΟΟΥ· ΕΒΟⲀ
Μ̄ΠΕϨΡΟϢ Ν̄ΤⲂϢϪΕ ΕΤϨΟΡϢ ΕΜⲀϢΟ· ⲀΥⲰ ΟΝ ΕϤⲤΟⲂⲔ̄
Ν̄ϬΙ ΠΚΕⲤⲰΜⲀ ⲀΥⲰ ϢⲀΡΕ ΠϢΗΡΕ ϢΗΜ' ΟΥⲰΜ ΕΒΟⲀ ϨΝ̄
5 ΝΕΤΡΥϕΟΟΥΕ Μ̄ΠΚΟⲤΜΟⲤ Ν̄ΤΕ Ν̄ⲀΡⲬⲰΝ· ⲀΥⲰ ϢⲀΡΕ
ΤϬΟΜ ⲤⲰⲔ' ΝⲀⲤ ΕΒΟⲀ' Μ̄ΠΜΕΡΟⲤ Ν̄ΤϬΟΜ' ΕΤϨΝ̄ ΝΕΤΡΥ-
ϕΟΟΥΕ· ⲀΥⲰ ϢⲀΡΕ ΤΕⲮΥⲬΗ ⲤⲰⲔ' ΝⲀⲤ ΕΒΟⲀ Μ̄ΠΜΕ-
ΡΟⲤ Ν̄ΤΕⲮΥⲬΗ ΕΤϨΝ̄ ΝΕΤΡΥϕΟΟΥΕ· ⲀΥⲰ ϢⲀΡΕ ΠⲀΝ-
ΤΙΜΙΜΟΝ Μ̄ΠΝ̄Ᾱ ⲤⲰⲔ' ΝⲀϤ ΕΒΟⲀ Μ̄ΠΜΕΡΟⲤ Ν̄ΤⲔⲀⲔΙⲀ
10 ΕΤϨΝ̄* ΝΕΤΡΥϕΟΟΥΕ ΜΝ̄ ΝΕϤΕΠΙΘΥΜΙⲀ· ⲀΥⲰ ϢⲀΡΕ [ⲤΠΗ b
ΠⲤⲰΜⲀ ϨⲰⲰϤ ⲤⲰⲔ ΝⲀϤ Ν̄ΟΥⲀΗ ΕΝ̄ⲤⲀΙⲤΟⲀΝΕ ⲀΝ ΕΤϨΝ̄
ΝΕΤΡΥϕΟΟΥΕ· ΤΜΟΙΡⲀ Ν̄ΤΟϤ ΜΕⲤϪΙ ΕΒΟⲀ ϨΝ̄ ΝΕΤΡΥ-
ϕΟΟΥΕ· ΕΒΟⲀ ϪΕ Ν̄ⲤΤΗϨ ⲀΝ ΕϨΟΥΝ Ν̄ΜΜⲀΥ· ⲀⲀⲀⲀ
ΤϬΟΤ ΕϢⲀⲤΕΙ' ΕΠΚΟⲤΜΟⲤ Ν̄ϨΗΤⲤ̄ ϢⲀⲤⲂⲰⲔ' ΟΝ Ν̄ϨΗΤⲤ̄
15 ⲀΥⲰ ⲔⲀΤⲀ ⲔΟΥΪ ⲔΟΥΪ ϢⲀΡΕ ΤϬΟΜ ΜΝ̄ ΤΕⲮΥⲬΗ ΜΝ̄
ΠⲀΝΤΙΜΙΜΟΝ Μ̄ΠΝ̄Ᾱ ϢⲀΥⲢΝΟϬ· ⲀΥⲰ ϢⲀΡΕ ΠΟΥⲀ·ΠΟΥⲀ
Μ̄ΜΟΟΥ ϢⲀϤⲀΙⲤΟⲀΝΕ ⲔⲀΤⲀ ΤΕϤϕΥⲤΙⲤ· ΤϬΟΜ ΜΕΝ
ϢⲀⲤⲀΙⲤΟⲀΝΕ ΕϢΙΝΕ Ν̄ⲤⲀ ΠΟΥΟΕΙΝ Μ̄ΠⲬΙⲤΕ· ΤΕⲮΥⲬΗ
ϨⲰⲰⲤ ϢⲀⲤⲀΙⲤΟⲀΝΕ ΕϢΙΝΕ Ν̄ⲤⲀ ΠΤΟΠΟⲤ Ν̄ΤⲀΙⲔⲀΙΟ-
20 ⲤΥΝΗ ΠⲀΪ ΕΤΤΗϨ· ΕΤΕ Ν̄ΤΟϤ ΠΕ ΠΤΟΠΟⲤ Ν̄ΤⲤΥⲄⲔΡⲀ-
ⲤΙⲤ· ΠⲀΝΤΙΜΙΜΟΝ ϨⲰⲰϤ Μ̄ΠΝ̄Ᾱ ϢⲀϤϢΙΝΕ Ν̄ⲤⲀ ⲔⲀⲔΙⲀ
ΤΗΡΟΥ ΜΝ̄ Ν̄ΕΠΙΘΥΜΙⲀ ΜΝ̄ ΝΟΒΕ ΝΙΜ· ΠⲤⲰΜⲀ ϨⲰⲰϤ
ΜΕϤⲀΙⲤΟⲀΝΕ ΕⲀⲀⲀⲨ ΕΙΜΗΤΙ Ν̄ϤΤⲀⲀΕ-ϬΟΜ ΕΒΟⲀ ϨΝ̄ ΤϨΥ-
ⲀΗ·** ⲀΥⲰ Ν̄ΤΕΥΝΟΥ ϢⲀΥⲀΙⲤΟⲀΝΕ Μ̄ΠϢΟΜ̄Ν̄Τ ΠΟΥⲀ Ⲥ̄ⲚⲐ
25 ΠΟΥⲀ ⲔⲀΤⲀ ΤΕϤϕΥⲤΙⲤ· ⲀΥⲰ ϢⲀΡΕ ⟨Μ̄ΠⲀΡⲀⲀΗΜΠΤΗⲤ⟩

---

15 MS originally Ν̄ΤΕⲮΥⲬΗ; Μ inserted above before Ν̄.
25 supply Μ̄ΠⲀΡⲀⲀΗΜΠΤΗⲤ before Ν̄ΕΡΙΠⲀΙΟⲤ.

together are small. None of them *feels* anything *either* good
or bad, because of the weight of forgetfulness [1] which is
very heavy. And again he is small in his *body*, and the child
eats from the *foods* [2] of the *world* of the *archons*, and the
power draws to itself from the *part* of the power which is in
the *foods*. And the *soul* draws to itself from the *part* of the
soul which is in the *foods*. And the *spirit counterpart* draws
to itself from the *part* of the *evil* which is in the *foods*, and
also his (the child's) *desires* [3]. And on the other hand the *body*
draws to itself from the *insensate matter* which is in the
foods. *Destiny*, however, is not taken from the *foods*, because
it is not mixed with them. *But* the form which comes to the
world with it also goes with it. And little *by* little the power
and the *soul* and the *spirit counterpart* become greater. And
each one of them *perceives according to* his *nature*. The power
perceives in order to seek the light of the height. The *soul*,
on the other hand, *perceives* in order to seek the *place* of
righteousness which is mixed, which is the *place* of the
mixing. The *spirit counterpart* however seeks all *evil* and
the *desires* and all sins. The *body* does not itself *perceive*
anything *unless* it receives power from the *matter*. And
straightway each one of the three *perceives* according to its
nature. And the | *erinaioi* ⟨*paralemptai*⟩ instruct the

---

[1] (3) forgetfulness; Till: inability to perceive.
[2] (5-13) foods; perhaps delicacies; see Epiph. 26.9.
[3] (10) his (the child's) desires; Till: its (the part's) desires; Schmidt: its (the
spirit's) desires.

ⲚⲈⲢⲓⲚⲀⲒⲞⲤ ⲌⲰⲞⲨ ⲰⲀⲨⲦⲀⲨⲞ ⲚⲚⲀⲒⲦⲞⲨⲢⲄⲞⲤ ⲚⲤⲈⲀⲕⲟ-
ⲗⲞⲨⲐⲒ ⲚⲀⲨ· ⲚⲤⲈⲢⲘⲚⲦⲢⲈ ⲚⲚⲞⲂⲈ ⲚⲒⲘ ⲈⲦⲞⲨⲈⲒⲢⲈ Ⲙ̄-
ⲘⲞⲞⲨ· ⲈⲦⲂⲈ ⲐⲈ ⲈⲦⲞⲨⲚⲀⲕⲞⲗⲀⲌⲈ Ⲙ̄ⲘⲞⲞⲨ ⲌⲚ̄ ⲚⲈⲔⲢⲒ-
ⲤⲒⲤ· ⲀⲨⲰ Ⲙ̄Ⲛ̄ⲚⲤⲀ ⲚⲀⲒ̈ ⲞⲚ ⲰⲀⲢⲈ ⲠⲀⲚⲦⲒⲘⲒⲘⲞⲚ Ⲙ̄ⲠⲚ̄Ⲁ·
5 ⲰⲀϤⲈⲠⲒⲚⲞⲒ̈ ⲀⲨⲰ Ⲛ̄ϤⲀⲒⲤⲐⲀⲚⲈ Ⲛ̄ⲚⲚⲞⲂⲈ ⲦⲎⲢⲞⲨ· ⲘⲚ̄ ⲘⲠⲈ-
ⲐⲞⲞⲨ ⲈⲚⲦⲀⲨⲌⲞⲚⲞⲨ ⲈⲦⲞⲞⲦϤ̄ ⲈⲦⲈⲮⲨⲬⲎ Ⲛ̄ϬⲒ Ⲛ̄ⲀⲢⲬⲰⲚ
Ⲛ̄ⲦⲚⲞϬ Ⲛ̄ⲌⲒⲘⲀⲢⲘⲈⲚⲎ· ⲀⲨⲰ Ⲛ̄ϤⲀⲀⲨ Ⲛ̄ⲦⲈⲮⲨⲬⲎ· ⲀⲨⲰ
ⲰⲀⲢⲈ ⲦϬⲞⲘ ⲈⲦⲌⲒⲌⲞⲨⲚ ⲰⲀⲤⲔⲒⲘ’ ⲈⲦⲈⲮⲨⲬⲎ· ⲈⲦⲢⲈⲤ-
ⲰⲒⲚⲈ Ⲛ̄ⲤⲀ ⲠⲦⲞⲠⲞⲤ Ⲙ̄ⲠⲞⲨⲞⲈⲒⲚ· ⲀⲨⲰ Ⲙ̄Ⲛ̄ ⲦⲘⲚ̄ⲦⲚⲞⲨⲦⲈ
10 ⲦⲎⲢⲤ̄· ⲀⲨⲰ ⲰⲀⲢⲈ ⲠⲀⲚⲦⲒⲘⲒⲘⲞⲚ Ⲙ̄ⲠⲚ̄Ⲁ ⲰⲀϤⲢⲒⲔⲈ Ⲛ̄ⲦⲈ-
ⲮⲨⲬⲎ ⲀⲨⲰ ⲰⲀϤⲀⲚⲀⲄⲔⲀⲌⲈ Ⲙ̄ⲘⲞⲤ Ⲛ̄ϤⲦⲢⲈⲤⲈⲒⲢⲈ Ⲛ̄ⲚⲈϤⲀ-
ⲚⲞⲘⲒⲀ ⲦⲎⲢⲞⲨ· ⲀⲨⲰ Ⲙ̄Ⲛ̄ ⲚⲈϤⲠⲀⲐⲞⲤ ⲦⲎⲢⲞⲨ· Ⲙ̄Ⲛ̄ ⲚⲈϤ-
ⲚⲞⲂⲈ ⲦⲎⲢⲞⲨ ⲈⲤⲘⲎⲚ ⲈⲂⲞⲗ’ ⲀⲨⲰ ⲰⲀϤϬⲰ ⲈϤⲦⲞ [ⲚⲞⲨ]- ⲥⲡⲑ ᵇ
ⲈⲦⲈⲮⲨⲬⲎ· ⲀⲨⲰ ⲈϤⲞ Ⲛ̄ⲬⲀⲬⲈ ⲈⲢⲞⲤ· ⲈϤⲦⲢⲈⲤⲈⲒⲢⲈ Ⲛ̄-
15 ⲚⲈⲒ̈ⲠⲈⲐⲞⲞⲨ ⲦⲎⲢⲞⲨ ⲘⲚ̄ ⲚⲈⲒ̈ⲚⲞⲂⲈ ⲦⲎⲢⲞⲨ· ⲀⲨⲰ ⲰⲀϤ-
ⲦⲰⲂⲤ̄ Ⲛ̄ⲚⲀⲈⲒⲦⲞⲨⲢⲄⲞⲤ Ⲛ̄ⲈⲢⲒⲚⲀⲒⲞⲤ ⲬⲈ ⲈⲨⲈⲢⲘⲚⲦⲢⲈ ⲈⲢⲞⲤ
ⲌⲚ̄ ⲚⲞⲂⲈ ⲚⲒⲘ ⲈϤⲚⲀⲦⲢⲈⲤⲈⲒⲢⲈ Ⲙ̄ⲘⲞⲞⲨ· ⲈⲦⲒ ⲞⲚ ⲈⲤⲈⲒ’
ⲈⲤⲚⲀⲘ̄ⲦⲞⲚ Ⲙ̄ⲘⲞⲤ ⲌⲚ̄ ⲦⲈⲨⲰⲎ ⟨Ⲏ̄⟩ Ⲍ̄Ⲙ ⲠⲈⲌⲞⲞⲨ. ⲰⲀϤⲔⲒⲘ’
ⲈⲢⲞⲤ ⲌⲚ̄ ⲌⲈⲚⲢⲀⲤⲞⲨ· Ⲏ̄ ⲌⲚ̄ ⲌⲈⲚⲈⲠⲒⲐⲨⲘⲒⲀ Ⲛ̄ⲦⲈ ⲠⲔⲞⲤⲘⲞⲤ·
20 ⲀⲨⲰ ⲰⲀϤⲦⲢⲈⲤⲈⲠⲒⲐⲨⲘⲒ ⲈⲌⲰⲂ ⲚⲒⲘ’ Ⲛ̄ⲦⲈ ⲠⲔⲞⲤⲘⲞⲤ ⲌⲀ-
ⲠⲀⲝ ⲌⲀⲠⲀⲰⲤ ⲰⲀϤⲌⲞⲔⲚ̄Ⲥ̄ ⲈⲚⲈⲌⲂⲎⲨⲈ ⲦⲎⲢⲞⲨ Ⲛ̄ⲦⲀⲨⲌⲞⲚⲞⲨ
ⲈⲦⲞⲞⲦϤ̄ Ⲛ̄ϬⲒ Ⲛ̄ⲀⲢⲬⲰⲚ· ⲀⲨⲰ ⲰⲀϤⲰⲰⲠⲈ Ⲛ̄ⲬⲀⲬⲈ ⲘⲚ̄
ⲦⲈⲮⲨⲬⲎ ⲈϤⲦⲢⲈⲤⲈⲒⲢⲈ Ⲙ̄ⲠⲈⲦⲈⲚ̄ⲌⲚⲀⲤ ⲀⲚ· ⲦⲈⲚⲞⲨ ϬⲈ

---

6 MS originally ⲈⲦⲞⲞⲦϤ̄ Ⲛ̄ϬⲒ ⲦⲈⲮⲨⲬⲎ Ⲛ̄ⲠⲀⲢⲬⲰⲚ; later altered to
ⲈⲦⲞⲞⲦϤ̄ ⲈⲦⲈⲮⲨⲬⲎ Ⲛ̄ϬⲒ Ⲛ̄ⲀⲢⲬⲰⲚ.
13 MS ⲈϤⲦⲞ Ⲛ̄ⲞⲨⲈⲦⲈⲮⲨⲬⲎ; read ⲈϤⲦⲞ ⲈⲦⲈⲮⲨⲬⲎ.
18 Ⲏ̄ omitted.

ministers to *accompany* them, and they bear witness to all sins which are committed, because of the manner in which they will *punish* them in the *judgments*. And after these things again the *spirit counterpart observes* and *perceives* all the sins and the wickedness which the *archons* of the great *Heimarmene* have commanded for the *soul*, and it (the spirit counterpart) makes them for the *soul*. And the power within moves the *soul* to seek after the *place* of the light and the whole Godhood. And the *spirit counterpart* inclines the *soul* and *compels* it to commit all its *iniquities*, with all its *passions* and all its sins continually. And it remains allotted to the *soul*, and it is hostile to it and causes it to commit all these wicked things and all these sins. And the *erinaioi ministers* seal it, because they are witnesses of it in all sins which it will cause it to commit. *Yet* further, when it comes to rest at night ⟨*or*⟩ by day, it moves it with dreams *or* with *desires* of the *world*, and it causes it to *desire* everything of the *world*. *In a word*, it incites it to all things which the *archons* have commanded for it. And it becomes hostile to the *soul*, causing it to do what it does not wish. *Now* at this time, | Maria, this

ΟΥΝ ΜΑΡΙΑ ΕΪΕ ΠΑΪ ΠΕ ΠΧΑΧΕ Ν̄ΤΕΨΥΧΗ· ΑΥΩ ΠΑΪ
ΠΕΤΑΝΑΓΚΑΖΕ Μ̄ΜΟC 2ΕΩC ϢΑΝΤC̄Ρ̄-ΝΟΒΕ ΝΙΜ· ΤΕΝΟΥ
6Ε ΟΥΝ ΕϤϢΑΝϢΩΠΕ Ν̄ϤΧΩΚ' ΕΒΟΛ Ν̄6Ι ΠΕΟΥΟΕΙϢ
Μ̄ΠΡΩΜΕ ΕΤΜ̄ΜΑΥ· Ν̄ϢΟΡΠ̄ ΜΕΝ ϢΑCΕΙ' ΕΒΟΛ Ν̄6Ι
5 ΤΜΟΙΡΑ Ν̄CΑΓΕ Μ̄ΠΡΩΜΕ Ε2ΟΥΝ ΕΠΜΟΥ 2ΙΤΝ̄ Ν̄ΑΡΧΩΝ [C̄ξ]
ΜΝ ΝΕΥΜ̄ΡΡΕ· ΝΑΪ Ν̄ΤΑΥΜΟΡΟΥ Ν̄2ΗΤΟΥ 2ΙΤΝ̄ ΘΙΜΑΡ-
ΜΕΝΗ· ΑΥΩ Μ̄Ν̄Ν̄CΩC ϢΑΥΕΙ' Ν̄6Ι Μ̄ΠΑΡΑΛΗΜΠΤΩΡ
Ν̄ΕΡΙΝΑΙΟC· Ν̄CΕΕΙΝΕ Ν̄ΤΕΨΥΧΗ ΕΤΜ̄ΜΑΥ ΕΒΟΛ 2Ν̄
CΩΜΑ· ΑΥΩ Μ̄Ν̄Ν̄CΩC ϢΑΡΕ Μ̄ΠΑΛΑΛΗΜΠΤΩΡ Ν̄ΕΡΙ-
10 ΝΑΙΟC ϢΑΥΡ̄-ϢΟΜΝ̄Τ Ν̄2ΟΟΥ ΕΥΚΩΤΕ ΜΝ ΤΕΨΥΧΗ
ΕΤΜ̄ΜΑΥ 2ΡΑΪ 2Ν̄ Ν̄ΤΟΠΟC ΤΗΡΟΥ· ΕΥΤΑΥΟ Μ̄ΜΟC
ΕΝΑΙΩΝ ΤΗΡΟΥ Ν̄ΤΕ Ν̄ΚΟCΜΟC· ΕΥΟΥΗ2 Ν̄CΑ ΤΕΨΥ-
ΧΗ ΕΤΜ̄ΜΑΥ Ν̄6Ι ΠΑΝΤΙΜΙΜΟΝ Μ̄ΠΝ̄Α ΜΝ ΤΜΟΙΡΑ ΑΥΩ
ϢΑΡΕ Τ6ΟΜ ΑΝΑΧΩΡΙ ΕΡΑΤC̄ Ν̄ΤΠΑΡΘΕΝΟC Μ̄ΠΟΥΟΕΙΝ·
15 ΑΥΩ Μ̄Ν̄Ν̄CΑ ΠϢΟΜΝ̄Τ Ν̄2ΟΟΥ ϢΑΡΕ Μ̄ΠΑΡΑΛΗΜΠΤΩΡ
Ν̄ΕΡΙΝΑΙΟC ϢΑΥΕΙΝΕ Ν̄ΤΕΨΥΧΗ ΕΤΜ̄ΜΑΥ [ΕΠΕCΗΤ] ΕΠΕC-
ΗΤ ΕΑΜΝ̄ΤΕ Ν̄ΤΕ ΠΕΧΛΑΟC ΑΥΩ ΕΥϢΑΝΕΙΝΕ Μ̄ΜΟC
ΕΠΕCΗΤ' ΕΠΕΧΛΑΟC· ϢΑΥΤΑΑC ΕΤΟΟΤΟΥ Ν̄ΝΕΤΚΟ-
ΛΑΖΕ· ΑΥΩ ϢΑΡΕ Μ̄ΠΑΡΑΛΗΜΠΤΗC ΑΝΑΧΩΡΙ ΕΝΕΥΤΟ- [C̄ξ b]
20 ΠΟC ΚΑΤΑ ΤΟΙΚΟΝΟΜΙΑ Ν̄ΝΕ2ΒΗΥΕ Ν̄ΝΑΡΧΩΝ ΕΤΒΕ
Τ6ΙΝΕΙ' ΕΒΟΛ Ν̄ΝΕΨΥΧΟΟΥΕ· ΑΥΩ ϢΑΡΕ ΠΑΝΤΙΜΙΜΟΝ
Μ̄ΠΝ̄Α ϢΑϤϢΩΠΕ Μ̄ΠΑΡΑΛΗΜΠΤΗC Ν̄ΤΕΨΥΧΗ ΕϤΤΟ
ΕΡΟC ΕϤCΟΟ2Ε Μ̄ΜΟC ΚΑΤΑ ΤΚΟΛΑCΙC ΕΤΒΕ Ν̄ΝΟΒΕ
Ν̄ΤΑϤΤΡΕCΕΙΡΕ Μ̄ΜΟΟΥ· ΑΥΩ ϢΑϤϢΩΠΕ 2Ν ΟΥΝΟ6
25 Μ̄ΜΝ̄ΤΧΑΧΕ Ε2ΟΥΝ ΕΤΕΨΥΧΗ· ΑΥΩ ΕΡϢΑΝ ΤΕΨΥΧΗ

---

4 Ν̄ϢΟΡΠ̄ expunged after ΕΒΟΛ.
9 MS Μ̄ΠΑΛΑΛΗΜΠΤΩΡ; read Μ̄ΠΑΡΑΛΗΜΠΤΩΡ.
16 MS ΕΠΕCΗΤ dittography.

is the enemy of the *soul*, and it is this which *compels* it *until* it commits all sins. *Now* at this time when the time of that man is completed, first comes the *destiny* and *guides* the man towards death by means of the *archons* and their bonds, with which they are bound by the *Heimarmene*. And afterwards the *erinaioi paralemptores* come and bring that *soul* forth from the *body*. And then the *erinaioi paralemptores* spend three days going round with that *soul* in all the *places*, and sending it to all the *aeons* of the *world*. And the *spirit counterpart* and the *destiny* follow that *soul*, and the power *withdraws* to the *Virgin* of the Light. And after three days the *erinaioi paralemptores* lead that *soul* down to Amente of the *Chaos*, and when they have brought it down to the *Chaos* they hand it over to those who *punish*. And the *paralemptai withdraw* to their *places according to* the *organisation* of the works of the *archons* in relation to the coming forth of the *souls*. And the *spirit counterpart* becomes *paralemptes* of the *soul*, as it is allotted to it to reprove it by *every punishment* on account of the sins which it has caused it to commit. And it has great hostility towards the *soul*. And when the *soul* | completes the *punishments* in the

ⲭⲱⲕ ⲉⲃⲟⲗ ϩⲛ̄ ⲛ̄ⲕⲟⲗⲁⲥⲓⲥ ϩⲛ̄ ⲛⲉⲭⲗⲟⲥ ⲕⲁⲧⲁ ⲛ̄ⲛⲟⲃⲉ ⲛ̄ⲧ-
ⲁⲥⲉⲓⲣⲉ ⲙ̄ⲙⲟⲟⲩ· ϣⲁⲣⲉ ⲡⲁⲛⲧⲓⲙⲓⲙⲟⲛ ⟨ⲙ̄ⲡ̄ⲛ̄ⲁ̄⟩ ⲛ̄ⲧⲥ ⲉϩⲣⲁⲓ̈ ϩⲛ̄
ⲛⲉⲭⲗⲟⲥ ⲉϥⲧⲟ ⲉⲣⲟⲥ ⲉϥⲥⲟⲟϩⲉ ⲙ̄ⲙⲟⲥ ⲕⲁⲧⲁ ⲧⲟⲡⲟⲥ ⲉⲧⲃⲉ
ⲛ̄ⲛⲟⲃⲉ ⲛ̄ⲧⲁⲥⲁⲁⲩ· ⲁⲩⲱ ϣⲁϥⲛ̄ⲧⲥ ⲉⲃⲟⲗ ϩⲓ ⲧⲉϩⲓⲏ ⲛ̄ⲛⲁⲣ-
5 ⲭⲱⲛ ⲛ̄ⲧⲙⲏⲧⲉ· ⲁⲩⲱ ⲉϥϣⲁⲛⲡⲱϩ ⲉⲣⲟⲟⲩ· ϣⲁⲩϣ̄ⲛ̄ⲧⲥ
ⲉⲙⲙⲩⲥⲧⲏⲣⲓⲟⲛ ⲛ̄ⲧⲙⲟⲓⲣⲁ· ⲁⲩⲱ ⲉⲥϣⲁⲛⲧⲙ̄ϩⲉ ⲉⲣⲟⲟⲩ
ϣⲁⲩϣⲓⲛⲉ ⲛ̄ⲧⲉⲩⲙⲟⲓⲣⲁ· ⲁⲩⲱ ϣⲁⲣⲉ ⲛ̄ⲁⲣⲭⲱⲛ ⲉⲧⲙ̄ⲙⲁⲩ
ϣⲁⲩⲕⲟⲗⲁⲍⲉ ⲛ̄ⲧⲉⲯⲩ̈ⲭ̈ⲏ ⲉⲧⲙ̄ⲙⲁⲩ ⲕⲁⲧⲁ ⲛ̄ⲛⲟⲃⲉ ⲉⲧ- ⲥ̅ⲝ̅ⲁ̅
ⲥ̄ⲙ̄ⲡϣⲁ ⲙ̄ⲙⲟⲟⲩ· ⲛⲁⲓ̈ ϯⲛⲁⲭⲱ ⲉⲣⲱⲧⲛ̄ ⲙ̄ⲡⲧⲩⲡⲟⲥ ⲛ̄ⲛⲉⲩ-
10 ⲕⲟⲗⲁⲥⲓⲥ ϩⲣⲁⲓ̈ ϩⲙ̄ ⲡϣⲱⲣ ⲉⲃⲟⲗ ⲙ̄ⲡⲧⲏⲣϥ· ⲉⲥϣⲁⲛϣⲱⲡⲉ
ϭⲉ ⲟⲩⲛ ⲉϥϣⲁⲛⲭⲱⲕ' ⲉⲃⲟⲗ ⲛ̄ϭⲓ ⲡⲉⲩⲟⲉⲓϣ ⲛ̄ⲛⲕⲟⲗⲁⲥⲓⲥ
ⲛ̄ⲧⲉⲯⲩⲭⲏ ⲉⲧⲙ̄ⲙⲁⲩ ϩⲣⲁⲓ̈ ϩⲛ̄ ⲛⲉⲕⲣⲓⲥⲓⲥ ⲛ̄ⲛⲁⲣⲭⲱⲛ ⲛ̄ⲧⲙⲏ-
ⲧⲉ· ϣⲁⲣⲉ ⲡⲁⲛⲧⲓⲙⲓⲙⲟⲛ ⲙ̄ⲡ̄ⲛ̄ⲁ̄ ϣⲁϥⲉⲓⲛⲉ ⲛ̄ⲧⲉⲯⲩ̄ⲭⲏ
ⲉϩⲣⲁⲓ̈ ϩⲛ̄ ⲛ̄ⲧⲟ̇ⲡⲟⲥ ⲧⲏⲣⲟⲩ ⲛ̄ⲛⲁⲣⲭⲱⲛ ⲛ̄ⲧⲙⲏⲧⲉ· ϣⲁϥ-
15 ⲭⲓⲧⲥ ⲉϩⲣⲁⲓ̈ ⲙ̄ⲡⲉⲙⲧⲟ ⲉⲃⲟⲗ ⲙ̄ⲡⲟⲩⲟⲉⲓⲛ ⲙ̄ⲡⲣⲏ· ⲕⲁⲧⲁ
ⲧⲕⲉⲗⲉⲩⲥⲓⲥ ⲙ̄ⲡϣⲟⲣⲡ̄ ⲛ̄ⲣⲱⲙⲉ ⲓ̄ⲉ̄ⲟⲩ· ⲁⲩⲱ ϣⲁϥⲭⲓⲧⲥ
ⲉⲣⲁⲧⲥ ⲛ̄ⲧⲉⲕⲣⲓⲧⲏⲥ ⲧⲡⲁⲣⲑⲉⲛⲟⲥ ⲙ̄ⲡⲟⲩⲟⲉⲓⲛ· ϣⲁⲥⲇⲟⲕⲓⲙⲁⲍⲉ ⲛ̄ⲧⲉⲯⲩⲭⲏ ⲉⲧⲙ̄ⲙⲁⲩ ⲛ̄ⲥϩⲉ ⲉⲣⲟⲥ ⲉⲩⲯⲩⲭⲏ ⲛ̄ⲣⲉϥⲣ̄-
ⲛⲟⲃⲉ ⲧⲉ· ⲁⲩⲱ ϣⲁⲥⲛⲟⲩϫⲉ ⲛ̄ⲧⲉⲥϭⲟⲙ ⲛ̄ⲟⲩⲟⲉⲓⲛ ⲉϩⲟⲩⲛ
20 ⲉⲣⲟⲥ ⲉⲧⲃⲉ ⲡⲉⲥⲧⲁϩⲟ ⲉⲣⲁⲧϥ̄· ⲙ̄ⲛ ⲡⲥⲱⲙⲁ· ⲙ̄ⲛ ⲧⲕⲟⲓⲛⲱ-
ⲛⲓⲁ ⲛ̄ⲧⲁⲓⲥⲑⲏⲥⲓⲥ· ⲛⲁⲓ̈ ⲉϯⲛⲁⲭⲱ ⲙ̄ⲡⲉⲩⲧⲩⲡⲟⲥ ⲉⲣⲱⲧⲛ̄
ϩⲙ̄ ⲡϣⲱⲣ ⲉⲃⲟⲗ ⲙ̄ⲡⲧⲏⲣϥ·*ⲁⲩⲱ ϣⲁⲣⲉ ⲧⲡⲁⲣⲑⲉⲛⲟⲥ ⲙ̄- ⲥ̅ⲝ̅ⲁ̅ b
ⲡⲟⲩⲟⲉⲓⲛ ϣⲁⲥⲥⲫⲣⲁⲅⲓⲍⲉ ⲛ̄ⲧⲉⲯⲩⲭⲏ ⲉⲧⲙ̄ⲙⲁⲩ· ⲛ̄ⲥⲧⲁⲗⲟ
ⲉⲩⲁ ⲛ̄ⲛⲉⲥⲡⲁⲣⲁⲗⲏⲙⲧⲏⲥ· ⲛ̄ⲥⲧⲣⲉⲩⲛⲟϫ̄ϥ ⲉⲩⲥⲱⲙⲁ ⲉϥ-

---

1   MS ϩⲛ̄ ⲛ̄ⲕⲟⲗⲁⲥⲓⲥ; better ⲛ̄ⲛ̄ⲕⲟⲗⲁⲥⲓⲥ.
2   supply ⲙ̄ⲡ̄ⲛ̄ⲁ̄.
5   MS ⲉϥϣⲁⲛⲡⲱϩ; read ⲉⲥϣⲁⲛⲡⲱϩ.
17, 18   MS originally ϣⲁϥⲇⲟⲕⲓⲙⲁⲍⲉ and ⲛ̄ϥϩⲉ; ϥ altered to ⲥ.
24   MS originally ⲛⲉⲥⲡⲁⲣⲁⲗⲏⲙⲧⲏⲥ; ⲛ̄ inserted above.

Chaos(es), *according to* the sins which it has committed, the ⟨*spirit*⟩ *counterpart* brings it up from the *Chaos(es)*, as it is allotted to it to reprove it in *every place* on account of the sins which it has committed. And it brings it forth upon the path of the *archons* of the Midst. And when it reaches them they question it upon the *mysteries* of the *destiny*, and when it does not find them, they (the archons) seek their *destiny*. And those *archons* punish that *soul according to* the sins of which it is worthy — I will tell you the *type* of their *punishments* in the distribution of the All. *Now* when it happens that the time of the *punishments* of that *soul* in the *judgments* of the *archons* of the *Midst* is completed, the *spirit counterpart* brings the *soul* out of all the *places* of the *archons* of the *Midst*. It takes it into the presence of the light of the sun, *according to* the *command* of the First Man, Jeu. And it brings it before the *judge*, the *Virgin* of the Light. She *examines* that *soul* and finds that it is a sinful *soul*, and she casts into it her light-power for the sake of its setting up with the *body*, and with the *communion* of *perception* whose *type* I will tell you in the distribution of the All. And the *Virgin* of the Light *seals* that *soul* and gives it to one of her *paralemptai*, and causes them to cast it into a *body* | which

ⲘⲠⲰⲀ ⲚⲚⲚⲞⲂⲈ ⲚⲦⲀⲤⲀⲀⲨ· ⲀⲨⲰ ϨⲀⲘⲎⲚ ϯϪⲰ ⲘⲘⲞⳠ
ⲈⲢⲰⲦⲚ ϪⲈ ⲚⲚⲈⳠⲔⲰ ⲚⲦⲈⲮⲨⲬⲎ ⲈⲦⲘⲘⲀⲨ ⲈⲂⲞⲖ ϨⲚ Ⲙ-
ⲘⲈⲦⲀⲂⲞⲖⲎ ⲘⲠⳠⲰⲘⲀ· ⲈⲘⲠⳠϯ ⲘⲠⲈⳠϨⲀⲈ ⲚⲔⲨⲔⲖⲞⳠ ⲔⲀⲦⲀ
ⲚⲈⲦⳠⲘⲠⲰⲀ ⲘⲘⲞⲞⲨ· ⲚⲀⲒ ⳠⲈ ⲦⲎⲢⲞⲨ ϯⲚⲀϪⲰ ⲘⲠⲈⲨ-
5 ⲦⲨⲠⲞⳠ ⲈⲢⲰⲦⲚ ⲘⲚ ⲠⲦⲨⲠⲞⳠ ⲚⲚⳠⲰⲘⲀ Ⲉ⳰ⲀⲨⲚⲞⲬⲞⲨ
ⲈⲢⲞⲞⲨ· ⲔⲀⲦⲀ ⲚⲚⲞⲂⲈ ⲚⲦⲈⲮⲨⲬⲎ ⲦⲈⲮⲨⲬⲎ ⲚⲀⲒ ϯⲚⲀ-
ϪⲞⲞⲨ ⲈⲢⲰⲦⲚ ⲦⲎⲢⲞⲨ ⲈⳠⲀⲚⲞⲨⲰ ⲈⳠⲬⲰ ⲈⲢⲰⲦⲚ Ⲙ-
ⲠⳠⲰⲢ ⲈⲂⲞⲖ ⲘⲠⲦⲎⲢⳠ·

ⲀⳠⲞⲨⲰϨ ⲞⲚ ⲈⲦⲞⲞⲦⳠ ⲚⳠⲒ ⲒⳠ ϨⲘ ⲠⲰⲀϪⲈ ⲠⲈϪⲀⳠ ϪⲈ
10 Ⲉ⳰ⲰⲠⲈ ϨⲰⲰⳠ ⲞⲨⲮⲨⲬⲎ ⲦⲈ ⲈⲘⲈⳠⳠⲰⲦⲘ ⲚⳠⲀ ⲠⲀⲚⲦⲒⲘⲒ-
ⲘⲞⲚ ⲘⲠⲚⲀ ϨⲢⲀⲒ ϨⲚ ⲚⲈⳠϨⲂⲎⲨⲈ ⲦⲎⲢⲞⲨ· ⲀⲨⲰ ⲦⲀⲒ ⲀⳠⲢ-
ⲀⲄⲀⲐⲞⳠ ⲀⳠⲬⲒ ⲚⲘⲘⲨⲤⲦⲎⲢⲒⲞⲚ ⲘⲠⲞⲨⲞⲈⲒⲚ ⲚⲀⲒ ⲈⲦϨⲘ
ⲠⲘⲈϨⳠⲚⲀⲨ ⲚⲬⲰⲢⲎⲘⲀ· Ⲏ ⲚⲦⲞⳠ ⲚⲀⲒ** ⲈⲦϨⲘ ⲠⲘⲈϨ⳰ⲞⲘⲚⲦ [ⳠϪⲂ]
ⲚⲬⲰⲢⲎⲘⲀ ⲚⲀⲒ ⲈⲦϨⲒⲠⳠⲀⲚϨⲞⲨⲚ· Ⲉ⳰ⲀⲚϪⲰⲔ ⲈⲂⲞⲖ ⲚⳠⲒ
15 ⲠⲈⲞⲨⲞⲈⲒ⳰ ⟨ⲘⲠⲈⲒ' ⲈⲂⲞⲖ⟩ ⲚⲦⲈⲮⲨⲬⲎ ⲈⲦⲘⲘⲀⲨ ⲈⲂⲞⲖ ϨⲘ
ⲠⳠⲰⲘⲀ· ⲀⲨⲰ ⳰ⲀⲢⲈ ⲠⲀⲚⲦⲒⲘⲒⲘⲞⲚ ⲘⲠⲚⲀ ⳰ⲀⳠⲞⲨⲀϨⳠ
ⲚⳠⲀ ⲦⲈⲮⲨⲬⲎ ⲈⲦⲘⲘⲀⲨ ⲚⲦⲞⳠ ⲘⲚ ⲦⲘⲞⲒⲢⲀ ⳰ⲀⳠⲞⲨⲀϨⳠ
ⲚⳠⲰⳠ ϨⲚ ⲦⲈϨⲒⲎ ⲈⲦⳠⲚⲀⲂⲰⲔ ⲘⲘⲞⳠ ⲈⲠϪⲒⳠⲈ· ⲀⲨⲰ ⲈⲘ-
ⲠⲀⲦⳠⲞⲨⲈ ⲈⲠϪⲒⳠⲈ ⳰ⲀⳠϪⲰ ⲘⲠⲘⲨⲤⲦⲎⲢⲒⲞⲚ ⲘⲠⲂⲰⲖ
20 ⲈⲂⲞⲖ ⲚⲚⲈⳠⲪⲢⲀⲄⲒⳠ· ⲘⲚ ⲘⲘⲢⲢⲈ ⲦⲎⲢⲞⲨ ⲘⲠⲀⲚⲦⲒⲘⲒⲘⲞⲚ
ⲘⲠⲚⲀ· ⲚⲀⲒ ⲚⲦⲀ ⲚⲀⲢⲬⲰⲚ ⲘⲞⲢⳠ ⲚϨⲎⲦⲞⲨ ⲈϨⲞⲨⲚ ⲈⲦⲈ-
ⲮⲨⲬⲎ ⲀⲨⲰ ⲈⲨ⳰ⲀⲚϪⲞⲞⲨ ⳰ⲀⲨⲂⲰⲖ ⲈⲂⲞⲖ ⲚⳠⲒ ⲘⲘⲢⲢⲈ
ⲘⲠⲀⲚⲦⲒⲘⲒⲘⲞⲚ ⲘⲠⲚⲀ· ⲚⳠⲖⲞ ⲈⳠⲚⲎⲨ ⲈϨⲞⲨⲚ ⲈⲦⲈⲮⲨⲬⲎ
ⲈⲦⲘⲘⲀⲨ· ⲀⲨⲰ ⳰ⲀⳠⲔⲰ ⲈⲂⲞⲖ ⲚⲦⲈⲮⲨⲬⲎ ⲔⲀⲦⲀ ⲚⲈⲚ-
25 ⲦⲞⲖⲞⲞⲨⲈ ⲚⲦⲀⲨϨⲞⲚⲞⲨ ⲈⲦⲞⲞⲦⳠ ⲚⳠⲒ ⲚⲀⲢⲬⲰⲚ ⲚⲦⲚⲞⳠ
ⲚϨⲒⲘⲀⲢⲘⲈⲚⲎ· ⲈⲨϪⲰ ⲘⲘⲞⳠ ⲚⲀⳠ ϪⲈ ⲘⲠⲢⲔⲰ ⲈⲂⲞⲖ

_____

15   MS ⲘⲠⲈⲒ' ⲈⲂⲞⲖ omitted.

is worthy of the sins which it has committed. And *truly*
I say to you that she does not release that *soul* from the
changes of the *body* before it has done its last *cycle, according
to* its worthiness. Now I will tell you the *type* of all these
things and the *type* of the *bodies* into which every *soul* is cast,
according to the sins (which it has committed). All these
things I will tell you when I shall have finished telling you
of the distribution of the All."

112.   Jesus continued again with the discourse and said :
"Moreover if there is a *soul* which has not listened to the
spirit counterpart in all his works, and becomes *good* and
receives the *mysteries* of the light which are in the second
space, or those which are in the third *space* which are within,
when the time ⟨of the coming forth⟩ of that *soul* from the
body is completed, the *spirit counterpart* follows after that
soul. It, with the *destiny*, follows after it on the path on
which it is to go to the height. And before it is far from the
height [1] it (the soul) says the *mystery* of the releasing of
the *seals* and all the bonds of the *spirit counterpart*, with
which the *archons* bound it (the spirit counterpart) to the
soul. And when they are said, the bonds of the *spirit counterpart* are released, it ceases to come into that *soul*, and it
releases the *soul according to* the *injunctions* which the *archons*
of the great *Heimarmene* have enjoined, saying to it : 'Release
not | this *soul* unless it says to thee the *mystery* of the

---

[1]   (19) it is far from the height; Schmidt : it withdraws upwards; see Crum 470b.

ⲛ̄ⲧⲉⲓ̈ⲯⲩⲭⲏ· ⲉⲓⲙⲏⲧⲓ ⲛ̄ⲥⲭⲱ ⲉⲣⲟⲕ ⲙ̄ⲡⲙⲩⲥⲧⲏⲣⲓⲟⲛ ⲙ̄ⲡⲃⲱⲗ
ⲛ̄ⲥⲫⲣⲁⲅⲓⲥ ⲛⲓⲙ ⲛⲁⲓ̈ ⲛ̄ⲧⲁⲛⲙⲟⲣⲕ̄ ⲛ̄ϩⲏⲧⲟⲩ ⲉϩⲟⲩⲛ ⲉⲧⲉ- [ⲥ̅ⲝⲃ ᵇ]
ⲯⲩⲭⲏ· ⲉⲥϣⲁⲛϣⲱⲡⲉ ⲟⲩⲛ ϭⲉ ⲉⲣϣⲁⲛ ⲧⲉⲯⲩⲭⲏ ⲉⲥ-
ϣⲁⲛⲭⲱ ⲙ̄ⲡⲙⲩⲥⲧⲏⲣⲓⲟⲛ ⲙ̄ⲡⲃⲱⲗ ⲉⲃⲟⲗ ⲛ̄ⲛⲉⲥⲫⲣⲁⲅⲓⲥ· ⲙ̄ⲛ
5 ⲙ̄ⲙⲣⲣⲉ ⲧⲏⲣⲟⲩ ⲙ̄ⲡⲁⲛⲧⲓⲙⲓⲙⲟⲛ ⲙ̄ⲡ̄ⲛ̄ⲁ· ⲛ̄ϥⲗⲟ ⲉϥⲛⲏⲩ ⲉ-
ϩⲟⲩⲛ ⲉⲧⲉⲯⲩⲭⲏ ⲛ̄ϥⲗⲟ ⲉϥⲙⲏⲣ ⲉϩⲟⲩⲛ ⲉⲣⲟⲥ· ⲁⲩⲱ ϩ̄ⲛ
ⲧⲉⲩⲛⲟⲩ ⲉⲧⲙ̄ⲙⲁⲩ ϣⲁϥⲭⲱ ⲛ̄ⲟⲩⲙⲩⲥⲧⲏⲣⲓⲟⲛ ⲛ̄ϥⲕⲱ
ⲉⲃⲟⲗ ⲛ̄ⲧⲙⲟⲓⲣⲁ ⲉⲡⲥⲥⲧⲟⲡⲟⲥ ⲉⲣⲁⲧⲟⲩ ⲛ̄ⲛⲁⲣⲭⲱⲛ ⲉⲧϩⲓ
ⲧⲉϩⲓⲏ ⲛ̄ⲧⲙⲏⲧⲉ· ⲁⲩⲱ ϣⲁⲥⲭⲱ ⲙ̄ⲡⲙⲩⲥⲧⲏⲣⲓⲟⲛ ⲛ̄ⲥⲁⲡⲟⲗⲩ
10 ⲙ̄ⲡⲁⲛⲧⲓⲙⲓⲙⲟⲛ ⲙ̄ⲡ̄ⲛ̄ⲁ· ⲉⲣⲁⲧⲟⲩ ⲛ̄ⲛⲁⲣⲭⲱⲛ ⲛ̄ⲑⲓⲙⲁⲣⲙⲉⲛⲏ
ⲉⲡⲧⲟⲡⲟⲥ ⲛ̄ⲧⲁⲩⲙⲟⲣϥ̄ ⲉⲣⲟⲥ ⲛ̄ϩⲏⲧϥ̄· ⲁⲩⲱ ϩ̄ⲛ ⲧⲉⲩⲛⲟⲩ
ⲉⲧⲙ̄ⲙⲁⲩ ϣⲁⲥⲣ̄-ⲟⲩⲛⲟϭ ⲛ̄ⲁⲡⲟⲣⲣⲟⲓⲁ ⲛ̄ⲟⲩⲟⲉⲓⲛ· ⲉⲥⲟ ⲛ̄-
ⲟⲩⲟⲉⲓⲛ ⲉⲙⲁϣⲟ ⲉⲙⲁϣⲟ· ⲁⲩⲱ ϣⲁⲣⲉ ⲙ̄ⲡⲁⲣⲁⲗⲏⲙⲡⲧⲱⲣ
ⲛ̄ⲉⲣⲓⲛⲁⲓⲟⲥ· ⲛⲁⲓ̈ ⲛ̄ⲧⲁⲩⲛ̄ⲧⲥ ⲉⲃⲟⲗ ϩ̄ⲙ ⲡⲥⲱⲙⲁ· ϣⲁⲩⲣ̄-
15 ϩⲟⲧⲉ ϩⲏⲧϥ̄ ⲙ̄ⲡⲟⲩⲟⲉⲓⲛ ⲛ̄ⲧⲉⲯⲩⲭⲏ ⲉⲧⲙ̄ⲙⲁⲩ ⲛ̄ⲥⲉϩⲉ ⲉϩⲣⲁⲓ̈
ⲉⲝ̄ⲙ ⲡⲉⲩϩⲟ· ⲁⲩⲱ ϩ̄ⲛ ⲧⲉⲩⲛⲟⲩ ⲉⲧⲙ̄ⲙⲁⲩ ϣⲁⲣⲉ ⲧⲉⲯⲩⲭⲏ ⲉⲧⲙ̄ⲙⲁⲩ ϣⲁⲥⲣ̄-ⲟⲩⲛⲟϭ ⲛ̄ⲁⲡⲟⲣⲣⲟⲓⲁ ⲛ̄ⲟⲩⲟⲉⲓⲛ·
ⲁⲩⲱ ϣⲁⲥⲣ̄-ⲧⲛ̄ϩ ⲛ̄ⲟⲩⲟⲉⲓⲛ ⲧⲏⲣⲥ̄· ⲁⲩⲱ ⲛ̄ⲥⲭⲱⲧⲉ ⲛ̄ⲧⲟ- ⲥ̅ⲝⲅ
ⲡⲟⲥ ⲛⲓⲙ ⲛ̄ⲧⲉ ⲛ̄ⲁⲣⲭⲱⲛ· ⲙ̄ⲛ ⲛ̄ⲧⲁⲝⲓⲥ ⲧⲏⲣⲟⲩ ⲛ̄ⲧⲉ ⲡⲟⲩ-
20 ⲟⲉⲓⲛ· ϩⲉⲱⲥ ϣⲁⲛⲧⲥⲃⲱⲕ' ⲉⲡⲧⲟⲡⲟⲥ ⲛ̄ⲧⲉⲥⲙ̄ⲛ̄ⲧⲉⲣⲟ ⲛ̄ⲧ-
ⲁⲥⲭⲓ-ⲙⲩⲥⲧⲏⲣⲓⲟⲛ ϣⲁⲣⲟϥ· ⲉϣⲱⲡⲉ ϩⲱⲱϥ ⲟⲩⲯⲩⲭⲏ ⲧⲉ
ⲉⲁⲥⲭⲓ-ⲙⲩⲥⲧⲏⲣⲓⲟⲛ ϩ̄ⲙ ⲡϣⲟⲣⲡ̄ ⲛ̄ⲭⲱⲣⲏⲙⲁ ⲉⲧϩⲓⲡⲥⲁⲛ̄ⲃⲟⲗ·
ⲁⲩⲱ ⲙⲛ̄ⲛ̄ⲥⲁ ⲧⲣⲉⲥⲭⲓ ⲛ̄ⲙ̄ⲙⲩⲥⲧⲏⲣⲓⲟⲛ ⲛ̄ⲥⲭⲟⲕⲟⲩ ⲉⲃⲟⲗ·
ⲁⲩⲱ ⲛ̄ⲥⲕⲟⲧⲥ̄ ⲛ̄ⲥⲣ̄ⲛⲟⲃⲉ ⲛ̄ⲟⲩⲱϩ̄ⲙ ⲙ̄ⲛ̄ⲛ̄ⲥⲁ ⲡⲭⲱⲕ ⲉⲃⲟⲗ
25 ⲛ̄ⲙⲙⲩⲥⲧⲏⲣⲓⲟⲛ· ⲁⲩⲱ ⲟⲛ ⲉϥϣⲁⲛⲭⲱⲕ ⲉⲃⲟⲗ ⲛ̄ϭⲓ ⲡⲉ-

---

7 MS ϣⲁϥⲭⲱ . . . ⲛ̄ϥⲕⲱ; read ϣⲁⲥⲭⲱ . . . ⲛ̄ⲥⲕⲱ.
24 MS ⲛ̄ⲥⲕⲟⲧⲥ̄; ⲧⲙ wrongly inserted above in later hand.

releasing of every *seal* with which we have bound thee to the *soul*. *Now* when it happens that the *soul* says the *mystery* of the releasing of its *seals* and all the bonds of the *spirit counterpart*, it (the spirit) ceases entering into the *soul* and ceases being bound to it. And at that time it (the soul) says a *mystery* and releases the *destiny* to its *place* in the presence of the *archons* which are on the way of the Midst. And it says the *mystery* and *releases* the *spirit counterpart* in the presence of the *archons* of the *Heimarmene* to the *place* in which it was bound to it. And at that time it (the soul) becomes a great *outpouring* of light, being of exceeding light. And the *erinaioi paralemptores* which have brought it forth from the *body* are afraid at the light of that *soul*, and they fall upon their faces. And at that time that soul becomes a great *outpouring* of light and becomes entirely winged with light, and penetrates every *place* of the *archons* and all their *ranks* of light, *until* it goes to the *place* of its kingdom, as far as which it has received *mysteries*. Moreover if a *soul* has received *mysteries* in the first *space* without, and after it has received the *mysteries* and completed them, it turns and sins again after the completion of the *mysteries*; and when the | time of the coming forth of that *soul* is completed,

ⲞⲨⲞⲈⲒⲰ ⲘⲠⲒ ⲈⲂⲞⲗ ⲚⲦⲈⲮⲨⲬⲎ ⲈⲦⲘⲘⲀⲨ · ϢⲀⲨⲈⲒ' ⲚϬⲒ
ⲘⲠⲀⲢⲀⲗⲎⲘⲠⲦⲎⲤ ⲚⲈⲢⲒⲚⲀⲒⲞⲤ ⲚⲤⲈⲈⲒⲚⲈ ⲚⲦⲈⲮⲨⲬⲎ ⲈⲦⲘ̄-
ⲘⲀⲨ ⲈⲂⲟⲗ ϨⲚ ⲤⲰⲘⲀ · ⲀⲨⲰ ϢⲀⲢⲈ ⲦⲘⲞⲒⲢⲀ ⲘⲚ ⲠⲀⲚⲦⲒ-
ⲘⲒⲘⲞⲚ ⲘⲠⲚⲀ̄ · ϢⲀⲨⲞⲨⲀϨⲞⲨ ⲚⲤⲀ ⲦⲈⲮⲨⲬⲎ ⲈⲦⲘⲘⲀⲨ
5 ⲈⲂⲟⲗ ϪⲈ ⲠⲀⲚⲦⲒⲘⲒⲘⲞⲚ ⲘⲠⲚⲀ̄ ⲈϤⲘⲎⲢ ⲈϨⲞⲨⲚ ⲈⲢⲞϤ ϨⲚ
ⲚⲈⲤⲪⲢⲀⲄⲒⲤ ⲘⲚ Ⲙ̄ⲘⲢⲢⲈ Ⲛ̄ⲚⲀⲢⲬⲰⲚ ϢⲀϤϤⲀⲔⲞⲗⲞⲨⲐⲒ ⲚⲤⲀ
ⲦⲈⲮⲨⲬⲎ ⲈⲦⲘ̄ⲘⲀⲨ ⲈⲤⲘⲞⲞϢⲈ ϨⲒ ⲚⲈϨⲒⲞⲞⲨⲈ ⲘⲠⲀⲚⲦⲒ-
ⲘⲒⲘⲞⲚ ⲘⲠⲚⲀ̄ · ϢⲀⲤϪⲰ ⲘⲠⲘⲨⲤⲦⲎⲢⲒⲞⲚ ⲘⲠⲂⲰⲗ ⲈⲂⲟⲗ [ⲤϬ̄ⲅ] b
Ⲛ̄ⲘⲘⲢⲢⲈ ⲦⲎⲢⲞⲨ ⲘⲚ ⲚⲈⲤⲪⲢⲀⲄⲒⲤ ⲦⲎⲢⲞⲨ ⲚⲦⲀ Ⲛ̄ⲀⲢⲬⲰⲚ
10 ⲘⲞⲨⲢ ⲘⲠⲀⲚⲦⲒⲘⲒⲘⲞⲚ ⲘⲠⲚⲀ̄ ⲚϨⲎⲦⲞⲨ ⲈϨⲞⲨⲚ ⲈⲦⲈⲮⲨⲬⲎ ·
ⲀⲨⲰ ⲈⲢϢⲀⲚ ⲦⲈⲮⲨⲬⲎ ϪⲰ ⲘⲠⲘⲨⲤⲦⲎⲢⲒⲞⲚ ⲘⲠⲂⲰⲗ ⲈⲂⲟⲗ
Ⲛ̄ⲚⲈⲤⲪⲢⲀⲄⲒⲤ · ⲚⲦⲈⲨⲚⲞⲨ ϢⲀⲨⲂⲰⲗ ⲈⲂⲟⲗ ⲚϬⲒ Ⲙ̄ⲘⲢⲢⲈ Ⲛ̄-
ⲚⲈⲤⲪⲢⲀⲄⲒⲤ ⲚⲀⲒ ⲈⲦⲘⲎⲢ ϨⲘ ⲠⲀⲚⲦⲒⲘⲒⲘⲞⲚ ⲘⲠⲚⲀ̄ ⲈϨⲞⲨⲚ
ⲈⲦⲈⲮⲨⲬⲎ · ⲀⲨⲰ ⲈⲢϢⲀⲚ ⲦⲈⲮⲨⲬⲎ ⲈⲤϢⲀⲚϪⲰ ⲘⲠⲘⲨⲤ-
15 ⲦⲎⲢⲒⲞⲚ ⲘⲠⲂⲰⲗ ⲈⲂⲟⲗ Ⲛ̄ⲚⲈⲤⲪⲢⲀⲄⲒⲤ · ⲀⲨⲰ ⲚⲦⲈⲨⲚⲞⲨ
ϢⲀϤⲂⲰⲗ ⲈⲂⲟⲗ ⲚϬⲒ ⲠⲀⲚⲦⲒⲘⲒⲘⲞⲚ ⲘⲠⲚⲀ̄ · ⲀⲨⲰ ϢⲀϤⲗⲟ
ⲈϤⲦⲟ ⲈⲦⲈⲮⲨⲬⲎ · ⲀⲨⲰ ⲚⲦⲈⲨⲚⲞⲨ ⲈⲦⲘ̄ⲘⲀⲨ ϢⲀⲤϪⲰ
Ⲛ̄ⲞⲨⲘⲨⲤⲦⲎⲢⲒⲞⲚ ⲚϬⲒ ⲦⲈⲮⲨⲬⲎ Ⲛ̄ⲤⲔⲀⲦⲈⲬⲈ ⲘⲠⲀⲚⲦⲒⲘⲒ-
ⲘⲞⲚ ⲘⲠⲚⲀ̄ ⲘⲚ ⲦⲘⲞⲒⲢⲀ · Ⲛ̄ⲤⲔⲀⲀⲨ ⲈⲨⲞⲨⲎϨ Ⲛ̄ⲤⲰⲤ · ⲀⲗⲗⲀ
20 ⲈⲘⲚ ⲞⲨⲞⲚ Ⲙ̄ⲘⲞⲞⲨ Ⲟ ⲚⲦⲈⲨⲈϨⲞⲨⲤⲒⲀ · ⲀⲗⲗⲀ ⲚⲦⲞⲤ ⲈⲤⲟ
ⲚⲦⲈⲨⲈϨⲞⲨⲤⲒⲀ · ⲀⲨⲰ ⲚⲦⲈⲨⲚⲞⲨ ⲈⲦⲘ̄ⲘⲀⲨ ϢⲀⲢⲈ ⲘⲠⲀ-
ⲢⲀⲗⲎⲘⲠⲦⲰⲢ ⲚⲦⲈⲮⲨⲬⲎ ⲈⲦⲘ̄ⲘⲀⲨ ⲘⲚ Ⲙ̄ⲘⲨⲤⲦⲎⲢⲒⲞⲚ ⲚⲦ-
ⲀⲤϪⲒⲦⲞⲨ ϢⲀⲨⲈⲒ ⲚⲤⲈϨⲀⲢⲠⲀⲌⲈ ⲚⲦⲈⲮⲨⲬⲎ ⲈⲦⲘ̄ⲘⲀⲨ ⲚⲦⲞⲞ-
ⲞⲦⲞⲨ** ⲚⲘⲠⲀⲢⲀⲗⲎⲘⲠⲦⲎⲤ ⲚⲈⲢⲒⲚⲀⲒⲞⲤ · ⲀⲨⲰ ϢⲀⲢⲈ Ⲙ̄ⲠⲀ- [ⲤϬ̄ⲇ]
25 ⲢⲀⲗⲎⲘⲠⲦⲎⲤ ϢⲀⲨⲀⲚⲀⲬⲰⲢⲒ ⲈⲚⲈϨⲂⲎⲨⲈ Ⲛ̄ⲚⲀⲢⲬⲰⲚ ⲠⲢⲞⲤ

---

5 MS ⲈⲢⲟϤ; read ⲈⲢⲞⲤ.
7 MS Ⲙ̄ⲠⲀⲚⲦⲒⲘⲒⲘⲞⲚ Ⲙ̄ⲠⲚⲀ̄; read ⲘⲚ ⲠⲀⲚⲦⲒⲘⲒⲘⲞⲚ Ⲙ̄ⲠⲚⲀ̄.

the *erinaioi paralemptai* come and bring forth that *soul*
from the *body*. And the *destiny* and the *spirit counterpart*
follow that *soul*, because the *spirit counterpart* is bound to
it with the *seals* and the bonds of the *archons*, and it
accompanies that *soul* as it proceeds upon the paths of the
spirit counterpart[1]. It (the soul) says the *mystery* of the
releasing of all the bonds and all the *seals*, with which the
archons bound the *spirit counterpart* to that *soul*. And when
the *soul* says the *mystery* of the releasing of the *seals*,
immediately the bonds of the *seals* which bind the *spirit
counterpart*[2] to the *soul* are released. And when the *soul*
says the *mystery* of the releasing of the *seals*, immediately
the *spirit counterpart* is released, and it ceases to be allotted
to the *soul*[3]. And immediately the *soul* says a *mystery*,
it *restrains* the *spirit counterpart* and the *destiny* and leaves
them following after[4] it. *But* none of them have *authority*,
but it has *authority* over them[5]. And at that time the
paralemptores of that *soul*, with the *mysteries* which it has
received, come and *snatch* that soul from the hands of the
erinaioi paralemptai, and the *paralemptai withdraw* to the
works of the *archons for the purpose of* | the *organisation* of

---

[1]   (7) paths of the spirit counterpart; Schmidt: paths with the ...
[2]   (13) which bind the spirit counterpart; Schmidt: which are bound in the ...
[3]   (14-17) And when the soul ... allotted to the soul; Till: delete as erroneous
      repetition of the preceding passage.
[4]   (19) leaves them following after it; Till: allows them to follow it; Schmidt:
      dismisses those that follow it.
[5]   (20, 21) none of them have authority ... over them; Schmidt: no one of them
      is in its (lit. their) power, but it (the soul) is in their power; Till: neither of
      them determine what happens to them, only the soul (does so).

ΤΟΙΚΟΝΟΜΙΑ Μ̄ΠΙΝΕ ΕΒΟΛ' Ν̄ΝΕΨΥΧΟΟΥΕ · ΑΥΩ ϢΑΡΕ

Μ̄ΠΑΡΑΛΗΜΠΤΗС 2ΩϢϤ Ν̄ΤΕΨΥΧΗ ΕΤΜ̄ΜΑΥ · ΝΑΪ ΕΤΗΠ

ΕΠΟΥΟΕΙΝ ϢΑΥΡ̄-ΤΝ2 Ν̄ΟΥΟΕΙΝ ΕΤΕΨΥΧΗ ΕΤΜ̄ΜΑΥ ·

ΑΥΩ Ν̄СΕΡ̄-ΕΝΑΥΜΑ Ν̄ΟΥΟΕΙΝ ΕΡΟС · ΑΥΩ ΜΕΥΧΙΤС

5 ΕΒΟΛ 2Ν̄ ΝΕΧΛΟС ΧΕ ΟΥΚ ΕΞΕСΤΙ ΕΧΙ-ΨΥΧΗ ΕΑϤΧΙ-

ΜΥСΤΗΡΙΟΝ ΕΒΟΛ 2Ν̄ ΝΕΧΛΟС · ΑΛΛΑ ΕϢΑΥΧΙΤС ΕΒΟΛ

2Ι ΤΕ2ΙΗ Ν̄ΝΑΡΧΩΝ Ν̄ΤΜΗΤΕ · ΑΥΩ ΕСϢΑΝΠΩ2 ΕΝΑΡ-

ΧΩΝ Ν̄ΤΜΗΤΕ · ϢΑΥΕΙ' ΕΒΟΛ 2ΗΤС Ν̄ΤΕΨΥΧΗ Ν̄6Ι Ν̄-

ΑΡΧΩΝ ΕΤΜ̄ΜΑΥ ΕΥϢΟΟΠ 2Ν̄ ΟΥΝΟ6 Ν̄2ΟΤΕ ΜΝ̄ ΟΥ-

10 ΚΩ2Τ ΕϤΝΑϢΤ · ΜΝ̄ 2ΕΝ2Ο ΕΥϢΟΒΕ · 2ΑΠΑΞ 2ΑΠΛΩС

ΕΥϢΟΟΠ 2Ν̄ ΟΥΝΟ6 Ν̄2ΟΤΕ ΕΜΝ̄-ϢΙ ΕΡΟС · ΑΥΩ Ν̄ΤΕΥ-

ΝΟΥ ΕΤΜ̄ΜΑΥ ϢΑΡΕ ΤΕΨΥΧΗ ϢΑСΧΩ Μ̄ΠΜΥСΤΗΡΙΟΝ

Ν̄ΤΕΥΑΠΟΛΟΓΙΑ · ΑΥΩ ϢΑΥΡ2ΟΤΕ ΕΜΑϢΟ Ν̄СΕ2Ε ΕΧΜ̄

ΠΕΥ2Ο · ΕΥΟ Ν̄2ΟΤΕ *2ΗΤϤ Μ̄ΠΜΥСΤΗΡΙΟΝ Ν̄ΤΑСΧΟΟϤ · [С2Λ

15 ΑΥΩ ΜΝ̄ ΤΕΥΑΠΟΛΟΓΙΑ · ΑΥΩ ϢΑΡΕ ΤΕΨΥΧΗ ΕΤΜ̄ΜΑΥ

ϢΑСΑΠΟΛΥ ΝΑΥ Ν̄ΤΕΥΜΟΙΡΑ · ΕСΧΩ Μ̄ΜΟС ΝΑΥ ΧΕ ΧΙ

ΝΗΤΝ̄ Ν̄ΤΕΤΝ̄ΜΟΙΡΑ · Ν̄ϯΝΗΥ ΑΝ ΕΝΕΤΝ̄ΤΟΠΟС ΧΙΝ Μ̄-

ΠΕΪΝΑΥ · ΑΪΡ̄-ΑΛΛΟΤΡΙΟС ΕΡΩΤΝ ϢΑΕΝΕ2 · ΕΪΝΑΒΩΚ Ε-

ΠΤΟΠΟС Ν̄ΤΑΚΛΗΡΟΝΟΜΙΑ · ΝΑΪ ΔΕ ΕСϢΑΝΟΥΩ ΕСΧΩ

20 Μ̄ΜΟΟΥ Ν̄6Ι ΤΕΨΥΧΗ · ϢΑΡΕ Μ̄ΠΑΡΑΛΗΜΠΤΗС Μ̄ΠΟΥΟ-

ΕΙΝ ϢΑΥ2ΩΛ' Ν̄ΜΜΑС ΕΠΧΙСΕ · ΑΥΩ ϢΑΥΧΙΤС ΕΒΟΛ

2Ν̄ Ν̄ΑΙΩΝ Ν̄ΘΙΜΑΡΜΕΝΗ · ΕСϯ Ν̄ΤΑΠΟΛΟΓΙΑ Μ̄ΠΤΟΠΟС

⟨ΠΤΟΠΟС⟩ ΝΑϤ · ΜΝ̄ ΝΕϤСΦΡΑΓΙС · ΝΑΪ ϯΝΑΧΟΟΥ ΕΡΩ-

ΤΝ 2Μ ΠСΩΡ ΕΒΟΛ Ν̄ΜΜΥСΤΗΡΙΟΝ · ΑΥΩ ϢΑСϯ Ν̄ΝΑΡ-

25 ΧΩΝ Μ̄ΠΑΝΤΙΜΙΜΟΝ Μ̄ΠΝΛ · ΑΥΩ ϢΑСΧΩ ΕΡΟΟΥ Μ̄-

---

5 MS ΕΑϤΧΙ; read ΕΑСΧΙ.
23 MS ΠΤΟΠΟС omitted.

the coming forth of *souls*. Moreover the *paralemptai* of that *soul* which belong to the light become wings of light for that *soul*. And they become a *garment* of light for it. And they do not lead it to the *Chaos(es)*, because it is *not permitted* to lead a *soul* which has received *mysteries* to the *Chaos(es)*, *but* they lead it upon the path of the *archons* of the Midst. And when it reaches the *archons* of the *Midst*, those *archons* come forth against the soul in great fearfulness, with fierce fire and changing faces [1]. *In a word*, they are of great fearfulness to which there is no measure. And at that time the *soul* says the *mystery* of their *defences*. And they are greatly afraid and fall upon their faces in fear at the *mystery* which it has said, and at their *defences*. And that *soul dismisses* their *destiny* to them, saying: receive back your *destiny*; I do not come to your *places* from this time; I have become a *stranger* to you for ever and I shall go to the *place* of my *inheritance*. When the *soul* finishes saying these things, the *paralemptai* of the light fly up with it to the height, and they take it forth from the *aeons* of the *Heimarmene*, and it gives the *defence* of ⟨every⟩ *place* to it and its *seals* which I will tell you at the distribution of the *mysteries*. And it gives the *spirit counterpart* to the *archons* and it says to them | the *mystery* of the bonds with which

---

[1]   (10) changing faces; Till: dreadful faces.

ΠΜΥСΤΗΡΙΟΝ N̄M̄M̄P̄Ρ̄Ε N̄ΤΑΥΜΟΡϤ N̄Ζ̄ΗΤΟΥ ΕΖΟΥΝ

ΕΡΟϤ· ΑΥⲰ ϢΑСΧΟΟС ΝΑΥ ΧΕ M̄ΜΗΕΙΤ̄Ν ΠΕΤ̄ΝΑΝΤΙ-

ΜΙΜΟΝ M̄Π̄Ν̄Α· N̄†ΝΗΥ ΑΝ ΕΠΕΤ̄ΝΤΟΠΟС ΧΙΝ M̄ΠΕΪΝΑΥ·

ΑΪΡ-ΑΛΛΟΤΡΙΟС ΕΡⲰΤ̄Ν N̄ϢΑΕΝΕΖ· ΑΥⲰ ϢΑС† N̄ΤΕ-

5 СϤΡΑΓΙС M̄ΠΟΥΑ^{**}ΠΟΥΑ ΝΑϤ· M̄Ν ΤΕϤΑΠΟΛΟΓΙΑ· ΝΑΪ <u>СΖΕ</u>

ΔΕ ΕСϢΑΝΟΥⲰ ΕСΧⲰ M̄ΜΟΟΥ N̄ϬΙ ΤΕΨΥΧΗ· ϢΑΡΕ

M̄ΠΑΡΑΛΗΜΠΤΗС M̄ΠΟΥΟΕΙΝ ϢΑΥΖⲰΛ N̄ΜΜΑС ΕΠΧΙСΕ·

ΑΥⲰ ϢΑΥΧΙΤС ΕΒΟΛ ΖΝ N̄ΑΙⲰΝ N̄ΘΙΜΑΡΜΕΝΗ· ΑΥⲰ

ϢΑΥΧΙΤС ΕΖΡΑΪ ΖΝ N̄ΑΙⲰΝ ΤΗΡΟΥ· ΕС† N̄ΤΑΠΟΛΟΓΙΑ

10 M̄ΠΤΟΠΟС ΠΤΟΠΟС ΝΑϤ· M̄Ν ΤΑΠΟΛΟΓΙΑ N̄ΝΤΟΠΟС

ΤΗΡΟΥ· M̄Ν ΝΕСϤΡΑΓΙС M̄Ν N̄ΤΥΡΑΝΝΟС M̄Π̄Ρ̄ΡΟ ΠΑΔΑ-

ΜΑС· ΑΥⲰ ϢΑС†-ΤΑΠΟΛΟΓΙΑ N̄ΝΑΡΧⲰΝ ΤΗΡΟΥ N̄Ν-

ΤΟΠΟС ΤΗΡΟΥ N̄ΤΕΖΒΟΥΡ· ΝΑΪ ΕΤΝΑΧⲰ ΕΡⲰΤ̄Ν N̄-

ΝΕΥΑΠΟΛΟΓΙΑ ΤΗΡΟΥ M̄Ν ΝΕΥСϤΡΑΓΙС· M̄ΠΕΥΟΕΙϢ

15 ΕΤΝΑΧⲰ ΕΡⲰΤ̄Ν M̄ΠСⲰΡ ΕΒΟΛ N̄ΜΜΥСΤΗΡΙΟΝ· ΑΥⲰ

ΟΝ ϢΑΡΕ M̄ΠΑΡΑΛΗΜΠΤΗС ΕΤM̄ΜΑΥ ϢΑΥΧΙ N̄ΤΕΨΥΧΗ

ΕΤM̄ΜΑΥ ΕΡΑΤС N̄ΤΠΑΡΘΕΝΟС M̄ΠΟΥΟΕΙΝ· ΑΥⲰ ΟΝ

ϢΑΡΕ ΤΕΨΥΧΗ ΕΤM̄ΜΑΥ ϢΑС† N̄ΤΠΑΡΘΕΝΟС M̄ΠΟΥ-

ΟΕΙΝ N̄ΝΕСϤΡΑΓΙС· M̄Ν ΠΕΟΟΥ N̄Ν̄Ζ̄ΥΜΝΟС· ΑΥⲰ ϢΑ-

20 ΡΕ[*] ΤΠΑΡΘΕΝΟС M̄ΠΟΥΟΕΙΝ· ΑΥⲰ M̄Ν ΤΚΕСΑϢϤΕ M̄- <u>СΖΕ</u>^b

ΠΑΡΘΕΝΟС M̄ΠΟΥΟΪΝ ϢΑΥΔΟϬΙΜΑΖΕ ΤΗΡΟΥ N̄ΤΕΨΥ-

ΧΗ ΕΤM̄ΜΑΥ N̄СΕϬΙΝΕ ΤΗΡΟΥ N̄ΝΕΥΜΑΕΙΝ N̄Ζ̄ΗΤС· M̄Ν

ΝΕΥСϤΡΑΓΙС· M̄Ν ΝΕΥΒΑΠΤΙСΜΑ· M̄Ν ΠΕΥΧΡΙСΜΑ· ΑΥⲰ

ϢΑΡΕ ΤΠΑΡΘΕΝΟС M̄ΠΟΥΟΕΙΝ ϢΑССϤΡΑΓΙΖΕ N̄ΤΕΨΥΧΗ

---

2   MS ΕΡΟϤ; read ΕΡΟС.

11   MS M̄Ν N̄ΤΥΡΑΝΝΟС; read N̄Ν̄ΤΥΡ.

it (the *spirit counterpart*) was bound to it. And it says to
them : take your *spirit counterpart*; I do not come to your
places from this time; I have become a *stranger* to you for
ever. And it gives the *seal* of each one to it, and its *defence*.
But when the *soul* has finished saying these things, the
paralemptai of the light fly with it to the height and take it
forth from the *aeons* of the *Heimarmene*. And they take
it out among all the *aeons*, and it gives the *defence* of every
place to it, and the *defence* of all the *places* [1], and the *seals*
of the *tyrants* [2] of the ruler (king) Adamas. And it gives
the *defence* of all the *archons* [3] of all the *places* of the left,
all of whose *defences* and *seals* I will tell you at the time
when I shall tell you of the distribution of the *mysteries*.
And furthermore those *paralemptai* take that *soul* to the
presence of the *Virgin* of the Light. And that *soul* gives
the *Virgin* of the Light the *seals* and the glory of the *songs
of praise*. And the *Virgin* of the Light and the seven other
virgins of the light all *examine* that *soul*, and they all find
their signs within it, and their *seals* and their *baptisms* and
their *inunction*. And the *Virgin* of the Light *seals* that *soul*. |

---

[1]   (10) the defence of all the places; Schmidt : the defence to all the places.
[2]   (11) of the tyrants; Schmidt : to the tyrants; MS : and the tyrants.
[3]   (12) of all the archons; Schmidt : to all the archons.

ⲉⲧⲙⲙⲁⲩ· ⲁⲩⲱ ⲙ̄ⲡⲁⲣⲁⲗⲏⲙⲡⲧⲏⲥ ⲙ̄ⲡⲟⲩⲟⲉⲓⲛ ϣⲁⲩⲃⲁⲡⲧⲓⲍⲉ ⲛ̄ⲧⲉⲯⲩⲭⲏ ⲉⲧⲙⲙⲁⲩ ⲛ̄ⲥⲉϯ ⲛⲁⲥ ⲙ̄ⲡⲉⲭⲣⲓⲥⲙⲁ ⲙ̄ⲡⲛ̄ⲓ-
ⲕⲟⲛ. ⲁⲩⲱ ϣⲁⲣⲉ ⲧⲟⲩⲉⲓ· ⲧⲟⲩⲉⲓ· ⲛ̄ⲙⲡⲁⲣⲑⲉⲛⲟⲥ ⲙ̄ⲡⲟⲩ-
ⲟⲉⲓⲛ· ϣⲁⲩⲥⲫⲣⲁⲅⲓⲍⲉ ⲙ̄ⲙⲟⲥ ⲍ̄ⲛ ⲛⲉⲩⲥⲫⲣⲁⲅⲓⲥ· ⲁⲩⲱ ⲟⲛ
5 ϣⲁⲣⲉ ⲙ̄ⲡⲁⲣⲁⲗⲏⲙⲡⲧⲏⲥ ⲙ̄ⲡⲟⲩⲟⲉⲓⲛ ϣⲁⲩⲧⲁⲁⲥ ⲉⲧⲟⲟⲧϥ̄
ⲛ̄ⲡⲛⲟϭ ⲥⲁⲃⲁⲱⲑ ⲡⲁⲅⲁⲑⲟⲥ ⲡⲁⲓ̈ ⲉⲧϩⲓⲣ̄ⲛ ⲧⲡⲩⲗⲏ ⲙ̄ⲡⲱⲛ̄ϩ
ϩ̄ⲙ ⲡⲧⲟⲡⲟⲥ ⲛ̄ⲛⲁⲟⲩⲛⲁⲙ· ⲡⲁⲓ̈ ⲉϣⲁⲩⲙⲟⲩⲧⲉ ⲉⲣⲟϥ ϫⲉ
ⲡⲉⲓⲱⲧ· ⲁⲩⲱ ϣⲁⲣⲉ ⲧⲉⲯⲩⲭⲏ ⲉⲧⲙⲙⲁⲩ ϣⲁⲥϯ ⲛⲁϥ ⲙ̄-
ⲡⲉⲟⲟⲩ ⲛ̄ⲛⲉϥϩⲩⲙⲛⲟⲥ ⲙ̄ⲛ ⲛⲉϥⲥⲫⲣⲁⲅⲓⲥ ⲙ̄ⲛ ⲛⲉϥⲁⲡⲟⲗⲟ-
10 ⲅⲓⲁ· ⲁⲩⲱ* ϣⲁⲣⲉ ⲥⲁⲃⲁⲱⲑ ⲡⲛⲟϭ ⲛ̄ⲁⲅⲁⲑⲟⲥ ϣⲁϥⲥⲫⲣⲁ- [ⲥ̄ⲝ̄ⲉ̄]
ⲅⲓⲍⲉ ⲙ̄ⲙⲟⲥ ϩ̄ⲛ ⲛⲉϥⲥⲫⲣⲁⲅⲓⲥ· ⲁⲩⲱ ϣⲁⲣⲉ ⲧⲉⲯⲩⲭⲏ ϣⲁⲥϯ
ⲛ̄ⲧⲉⲥⲉⲡⲓⲥⲧⲏⲙⲏ ⲙ̄ⲛ ⲡⲉⲟⲟⲩ ⲛ̄ⲛ̄ϩⲩⲙⲛⲟⲥ· ⲙ̄ⲛ ⲛⲉⲥⲫⲣⲁⲅⲓⲥ ⲙ̄ⲡⲧⲟⲡⲟⲥ ⲧⲏⲣϥ̄ ⲛ̄ⲛⲁⲟⲩⲛⲁⲙ· ϣⲁⲩⲥⲫⲣⲁⲅⲓⲍⲉ ⲙ̄ⲙⲟⲥ
ⲧⲏⲣⲟⲩ ϩ̄ⲛ ⲛⲉⲩⲥⲫⲣⲁⲅⲓⲥ ⲁⲩⲱ ϣⲁⲣⲉ ⲙⲉⲗⲭⲓⲥⲉⲇⲉⲕ ⲡⲛⲟϭ
15 ⲙ̄ⲡⲁⲣⲁⲗⲏⲙⲡⲧⲏⲥ ⲙ̄ⲡⲟⲩⲟⲉⲓⲛ ⲡⲁⲓ̈ ⲉⲧϩ̄ⲛ ⲡⲧⲟⲡⲟⲥ ⲛ̄ⲛⲁ-
ⲟⲩⲛⲁⲙ· ⲁⲩⲱ ϣⲁϥⲥⲫⲣⲁⲅⲓⲍⲉ ⲛ̄ⲧⲉⲯⲩⲭⲏ ⲉⲧⲙ̄ⲙⲁⲩ ⲁⲩⲱ
ϣⲁⲣⲉ ⲙ̄ⲡⲁⲣⲁⲗⲏⲙⲡⲧⲱⲣ ⲙ̄ⲙⲉⲗⲭⲓⲥⲉⲇⲉⲕ· ϣⲁⲩⲥⲫⲣⲁⲅⲓⲍⲉ
ⲛ̄ⲧⲉⲯⲩⲭⲏ ⲉⲧⲙ̄ⲙⲁⲩ· ⲁⲩⲱ ⲛ̄ϥⲭⲓⲧⲥ ⲉⲡⲉⲑⲏⲥⲁⲩⲣⲟⲥ ⲙ̄-
ⲡⲟⲩⲟⲉⲓⲛ· ⲁⲩⲱ ϣⲁⲥϯ ⲙ̄ⲡⲉⲟⲟⲩ ⲙ̄ⲛ ⲧⲉⲧⲓⲙⲏ ⲙ̄ⲛ ⲡⲧⲁⲓ̈ⲟ
20 ⲛ̄ⲛ̄ϩⲩⲙⲛⲟⲥ· ⲙ̄ⲛ ⲛⲉⲥⲫⲣⲁⲅⲓⲥ ⲧⲏⲣⲟⲩ ⲛ̄ⲛ̄ⲧⲟⲡⲟⲥ ⲧⲏⲣⲟⲩ
ⲙ̄ⲡⲟⲩⲟⲉⲓⲛ ⲁⲩⲱ ϣⲁⲣⲉ ⲛⲁⲡⲧⲟⲡⲟⲥ ⲧⲏⲣⲟⲩ ⲙ̄ⲡⲉⲑⲏⲥⲁⲩ-
ⲣⲟⲥ ⲙ̄ⲡⲟⲩⲟⲉⲓⲛ ϣⲁⲩⲥⲫⲣⲁⲅⲓⲍⲉ ⲙ̄ⲙⲟⲥ ϩ̄ⲛ ⲛⲉⲩⲥⲫⲣⲁⲅⲓⲥ·
ⲁⲩⲱ ϣⲁⲥⲃⲱⲕ ⲉⲡⲧⲟⲡⲟⲥ ⲛ̄ⲧⲉⲕⲗⲏⲣⲟⲛⲟⲙⲓⲁ·** [ⲥ̄ⲝ̄ⲉ̄ b·]

---

15 MS ⲉⲧϩ̄ⲛ; read ⲉⲧϩ̄ⲙ.
18 MS ⲛ̄ϥⲭⲓⲧⲥ; read ⲛ̄ⲥⲉⲭⲓⲧⲥ.

And the *paralemptai* of the light *baptise* that *soul* and give
it the *spiritual inunction*. And each one of the *virgins* of the
light *seals* it with their *seals*. And also the *paralemptai* of
the light give it into the hands of the Great Sabaoth, the
Good, who is above the *gate* of life in the *place* of the right,
who is called the Father. And that *soul* gives him the glory
of his *songs of praise* and his *seals* and his *defences*. And
Sabaoth the Great and *Good seals* it with his *seals*. And the
soul gives its *knowledge* and the glory of the *songs of praise*
and the *seals* of the whole *place* [1] of those of the right. They
all *seal* it with their *seals*, and Melchisedek, the great
paralemptes of the light, who is in the *place* of those of the
right, *seals* that *soul*. And the *paralemptores* of Melchisedek
seal that *soul* and they take it to the *Treasury* of the Light;
and it gives glory and *honour* and the eulogy of *songs of*
praise, and all the *seals* of all the *places* of the light. And
all those of the *place* of the *Treasury* of the Light *seal* it
with their *seals*, and it goes to the *place* of the *inheritance*." |

---

[1]   (13) of the whole place; Schmidt : to the whole place.

ⲚⲀⲒ ⲤⲈ Ⲛ̄ⲦⲈⲢⲈ ⲠⲤⲰⲢ ⲬⲞⲞⲨ ⲈⲚⲈⲨⲘⲀⲐⲎⲦⲎⲤ ⲠⲈⲬⲀⲨ
ⲚⲀⲨ ⲬⲈ ⲦⲈⲦⲚ̄ⲚⲞⲒ ⲬⲈ ⲈⲒ̈ⲰⲀⲬⲈ Ⲛ̄ⲘⲘⲎⲦⲚ̄ ⲚⲀⲰ Ⲛ̄ⲤⲈ·
ⲀⲤⲰⲞⲤⳲ ⲞⲚ ⲈⲂⲞⲖ’ Ⲛ̄ⲘⲒ ⲘⲀⲢⲒⲀ ⲠⲈⲬⲀⲤ ⲬⲈ ⲤⲈ ⲠⲀⲬⲞⲈⲒⲤ
†ⲚⲞⲒ ⲬⲈ ⲈⲔⲰⲀⲬⲈ Ⲛ̄ⲘⲘⲀⲒ ⲚⲀⲰ Ⲛ̄ⲤⲈ· ⲀⲨⲰ †ⲚⲀⲔⲀⲦⲀ-
5 ⲖⲀⲘⲂⲀⲚⲈ Ⲙ̄ⲘⲞⲞⲨ ⲦⲎⲢⲞⲨ· ⲦⲈⲚⲞⲨ ⲤⲈ ⲈⲦⲂⲈ ⲚⲈⲒ̈ⲰⲀⲬⲈ
ⲈⲦⲔ̄ⲬⲰ Ⲙ̄ⲘⲞⲞⲨ· Ⲁ ⲠⲀⲚⲞⲨⲤ Ⲣ̄-ⲨⲦⲞⲞⲨ Ⲛ̄ⲚⲞⲎⲘⲀ ⳢⲢⲀⲒ̈
Ⲛ̄ⳢⲎⲦ· ⲀⲨⲰ Ⲁ ⲠⲀⲢⲘ̄Ⲛ̄ⲞⲨⲞⲈⲒⲚ ⲀⲨⲀⲄⲈ ⲀⲨⲰ ⲀⲨⲦⲈⲖⲎⲖ
ⲀⲨⲂⲢⲂⲢ ⳢⲢⲀⲒ̈ Ⲛ̄ⳢⲎⲦ’ ⲈⲨⲞⲨⲰⲰ ⲈⲒ’ ⲈⲂⲞⲖ Ⲛ̄ⳢⲎⲦ· ⲀⲨⲰ
Ⲛ̄ⲨⲂⲰⲔ ⲈⳢⲞⲨⲚ ⲈⳢⲎⲦⲔ̄· ⲦⲈⲚⲞⲨ ⲤⲈ ⲞⲨⲚ ⲠⲀⲬⲞⲈⲒⲤ ⲤⲰⲦⲘ̄
10 ⲦⲀⲬⲰ ⲈⲢⲞⲔ Ⲙ̄ⲠⲈⲨⲦⲞⲞⲨ Ⲛ̄ⲚⲞⲎⲘⲀ Ⲛ̄ⲦⲀⲨⲰⲰⲠⲈ ⳢⲢⲀⲒ̈
Ⲛ̄ⳢⲎⲦ· ⲠⲰⲞⲢⲠ̄ ⲘⲈⲚ Ⲛ̄ⲚⲞⲎⲘⲀ Ⲛ̄ⲦⲀⲨⲰⲰⲠⲈ ⳢⲢⲀⲒ̈ Ⲛ̄ⳢⲎⲦ
ⲈⲦⲂⲈ ⲠⲰⲀⲬⲈ Ⲛ̄ⲦⲀⲔⲬⲞⲞⲨ ⲬⲈ ⲦⲈⲚⲞⲨ ⲤⲈ ⲰⲀⲢⲈ ⲦⲈ-
ⲮⲨⲬⲎ ⲰⲀⲤ† Ⲛ̄ⲦⲀⲠⲞⲖⲞⲄⲒⲀ ⲘⲚ̄ ⲦⲈⲤⲪⲢⲀⲄⲒⲤ Ⲛ̄ⲚⲀⲢⲬⲰⲚ
ⲦⲎⲢⲞⲨ ⲈⲦⳢ̄Ⲛ̄ Ⲛ̄ⲦⲞⲠⲞⲤ Ⲙ̄ⲠⲢ̄ⲢⲞ ⲠⲀⲆⲀⲘⲀⲤ· ⲀⲨⲰ ⲰⲀⲤ†
15 Ⲛ̄ⲦⲀⲠⲞⲖⲞⲄⲒⲀ** ⲘⲚ̄ ⲦⲈⲦⲒⲘⲎ ⲘⲚ̄ ⲠⲈⲞⲞⲨ Ⲛ̄ⲚⲈⲨⲤⲪⲢⲀⲄⲒⲤ Ⲥ̄Ⳅ̄Ⳅ̄
ⲦⲎⲢⲞⲨ· ⲘⲚ̄ Ⲛ̄ⳢⲨⲘⲚⲞⲤ Ⲛ̄Ⲛ̄ⲦⲞⲠⲞⲤ Ⲙ̄ⲠⲞⲨⲞⲈⲒⲚ ⲈⲦⲂⲈ ⲠⲈⲒ̈-
ⲰⲀⲬⲈ ⲞⲨⲚ Ⲛ̄ⲦⲀⲔⲬⲞⲞⲨ ⲈⲢⲞⲚ Ⲙ̄ⲠⲒⲞⲨⲞⲒ̈Ⲱ· Ⲛ̄ⲦⲈⲢⲞⲨⲈⲒⲚⲈ
ⲚⲀⲔ Ⲛ̄†ⲤⲀⲦⲈⲈⲢⲈ ⲀⲔⲚⲀⲨ ⲈⲢⲞⲤ ⲈⲤⲞ Ⲛ̄ⳢⲀⲦ ⳱Ⳡ ⳢⲞⲘⲚ̄Ⲧ·
Ⲛ̄ⲦⲀⲔⲰⲒⲚⲈ ⲬⲈ ⲦⲀⲚⲒⲘ ⲦⲈ ⲦⲈⲒ̈Ⳅ̄ⲒⲔⲰⲚ ⲠⲈⲬⲀⲨ ⲬⲈ ⲦⲀⲠⲢ̄ⲢⲞ
20 ⲦⲈ· Ⲛ̄ⲦⲈⲢⲈⲔⲚⲀⲨ ⲆⲈ ⲈⲢⲞⲤ ⲬⲈ ⲤⲦⲎⳢ Ⲛ̄ⳢⲀⲦ ⳱Ⳡ ⳢⲞⲘⲚ̄Ⲧ·
ⲠⲈⲬⲀⲔ ⲬⲈ † Ⲛ̄ⲦⲞ ⲞⲨⲚ Ⲛ̄ⲦⲀⲠⲢ̄ⲢⲞ Ⲙ̄ⲠⲢ̄ⲢⲞ· ⲀⲨⲰ ⲦⲀ-
ⲠⲚⲞⲨⲦⲈ Ⲙ̄ⲠⲚⲞⲨⲦⲈ· ⲈⲦⲈ ⲠⲀⲒ̈ ⲠⲈ ⲬⲈ ⲈⲢⲰⲀⲚ ⲦⲈⲮⲨⲬⲎ
ⲬⲒ-ⲘⲨⲤⲦⲎⲢⲒⲞⲚ ⲰⲀⲤ† Ⲛ̄ⲦⲀⲠⲞⲖⲞⲄⲒⲀ Ⲛ̄Ⲛ̄ⲀⲢⲬⲰⲚ ⲦⲎⲢⲞⲨ·
ⲘⲚ̄ ⲠⲦⲞⲠⲞⲤ Ⲙ̄ⲠⲢ̄ⲢⲞ ⲠⲀⲆⲀⲘⲀⲤ· ⲀⲨⲰ ⲰⲀⲤ† Ⲛ̄ⲦⲈⲮⲨⲬⲎ

---

24 MS ⲘⲚ̄ ⲠⲦⲞⲠⲞⲤ ; perhaps better Ⲙ̄ⲠⲦⲞⲠⲞⲤ. MS Ⲛ̄ⲦⲈⲮⲨⲬⲎ; read
Ⲛ̄Ⲓ ⲦⲈⲮⲨⲬⲎ.

113. Now when the *Saviour* had said these things to his *disciples* he said to them : "Do you *understand* in what manner I am speaking with you?"

Maria sprang up again and said : "Yes my Lord, I *understand* in what manner thou speakest, and I will *grasp* all of them (the words). Now at this time, concerning these words which thou hast spoken, my *understanding* (*mind*) has produced four *thoughts* within me. And my man of light [1] has *guided* (me), and has rejoiced and has welled up within me, wishing to come forth from me, and to go towards thee. *Now* at this time, my Lord, hear and I will say to thee the four *thoughts* which have come into existence within me. The first *thought* which has come into being within me, concerning the word which thou hast spoken : 'Now at this time the *soul* gives the *defence* and the *seal* to all the *archons* which are in the *places* of the ruler (king) Adamas. And it gives the *defence* and the *honour* and the glory of all their *seals* and the *songs of praise* to the *places* of the light.' Concerning these words *now* thou hast said to us once when a *stater* [2] was brought to thee, and thou didst see that it was of silver and copper, thou didst question : 'Whose is this *image*?' They said : 'That of the king'. *But* when thou sawest that it was mixed, of silver and copper, thou didst say : 'Give *therefore* what is of the king to the king, and what is of God, to God' *. That is to say, when the *soul* receives *mysteries*, it gives the *defence* to all the *archons* of the *place* of the ruler (king) Adamas [3]. And the *soul* gives | the *honour* and the glory to all those of the

---

*   cf. Mt. 22.19-21; Mk. 12.15-17; Lk. 20.24, 25

---

[1]   (7) man of light; see U 239.
[2]   (18) stater; Schmidt : denarius; see Crum 366a.
[3]   (23, 24) all the archons of the place of ... Adamas; MS : all the archons and the place of ... Adamas (see 292.14).

ⲚⲦⲦⲒⲘⲎ ⲘⲚ ⲠⲈⲞⲞⲨ ⲚⲚⲀⲠⲦⲞⲠⲞⲤ ⲦⲎⲢⲞⲨ ⲘⲠⲞⲨⲞⲈⲒⲚ·
ⲀⲨⲰ ⲠϢⲀϪⲈ ϪⲈ ⲀⲤⲦⲀⲀⲦⲈ ⲚⲦⲈⲢⲈⲔⲚⲀⲨ ⲈⲢⲞⲤ ⲈⲤⲞ
Ⲛ̄ⲌⲀⲦ’ ⲌⲒ ⲌⲞⲘ̄ⲚⲦ· ⲚⲦⲞϤ ⲠⲈ ⲠⲦⲨⲠⲞⲤ ⲚⲦⲀⲒ̈ ⲈⲢⲈ ⲦϬⲞⲘ
Ⲙ̄ⲠⲞⲨⲞⲈⲒⲚ Ⲛ̄ⲌⲎⲦ̄Ϥ ⲈⲦⲈ ⲚⲦⲞϤ ⲠⲈ Ⲡ̄ⲌⲀⲦ*ⲈⲦⲤⲞⲦⲠ̄· ⲀⲨⲰ ⲤⲌⲌ̄ᵇ

5 ⲈϤⲚ̄ⲌⲎⲦ̄Ⲥ Ⲛ̄ϬⲒ ⲠⲀⲚⲦⲒⲘⲒⲘⲞⲚ Ⲙ̄ⲠⲚ̄Ⲁ· ⲈⲦⲈ ⲚⲦⲞϤ ⲠⲈ Ⲡ̄ⲌⲞⲘⲚⲦ
Ⲛ̄ⲌⲨⲖⲒⲔⲞⲚ· ⲈⲒ̈Ⲉ ⲠⲀⲒ̈ ⲠⲀϪⲞⲈⲒⲤ ⲠⲈ ⲠϢⲞⲢⲠ̄ Ⲛ̄ⲚⲞⲎⲘⲀ· ⲠⲘⲈⲌ-
ⲤⲚⲀⲨ ⲌⲰⲰϤ Ⲛ̄ⲚⲞⲎⲘⲀ ⲚⲦⲀⲔⲞⲨⲰ ⲈⲔϪⲰ Ⲙ̄ⲘⲞϤ ⲚⲀⲚ
ⲦⲈⲚⲞⲨ ⲈⲦⲂⲈ ⲦⲈⲮⲨⲬⲎ ⲈⲢϪⲒ-ⲘⲨⲤⲦⲎⲢⲒⲞⲚ· ϪⲈ ⲈⲤϢⲀⲚⲈⲒ’
ⲈⲠⲦⲞⲠⲞⲤ Ⲛ̄ⲚⲀⲢⲬⲰⲚ Ⲛ̄ⲦⲈⲌⲒⲎ Ⲛ̄ⲦⲘⲎⲦⲈ· ⲀⲨⲰ ϢⲀⲨⲈⲒ’

10 ⲈⲂⲞⲖ ⲌⲀⲦⲈⲨⲌⲎ Ⲍ̄Ⲛ ⲞⲨⲚⲞϬ Ⲛ̄ⲌⲞⲦⲈ ⲈⲘⲀϢⲞ ⲈⲘⲀϢⲞ·
ⲀⲨⲰ ϢⲀⲢⲈ ⲦⲈⲮⲨⲬⲎ ϢⲀⲤⲦ̄ Ⲙ̄ⲠⲘⲨⲤⲦⲎⲢⲒⲞⲚ Ⲛ̄ⲐⲞⲦⲈ
ⲚⲀϤ· ⲀⲨⲰ ϢⲀⲤⲢ̄ⲌⲞⲦⲈ ⲌⲀⲦⲈⲤⲌⲎ· ⲀⲨⲰ ϢⲀⲤⲦ̄ Ⲛ̄ⲦⲘⲞⲒⲢⲀ
ⲈⲠⲈⲤⲦⲞⲠⲞⲤ· ⲀⲨⲰ ϢⲀⲤⲦ̄ Ⲙ̄ⲠⲀⲚⲦⲒⲘⲒⲘⲞⲚ Ⲙ̄ⲠⲚ̄Ⲁ ⲈⲠⲈϤ-
ⲦⲞⲠⲞⲤ· ⲀⲨⲰ ϢⲀⲤⲦ̄ Ⲛ̄ⲦⲀⲠⲞⲖⲞⲄⲒⲀ ⲘⲚ ⲚⲈⲤⲪⲢⲀⲄⲒⲤ Ⲙ̄-

15 ⲠⲞⲨⲀ ⲠⲞⲨⲀ Ⲛ̄ⲚⲀⲢⲬⲰⲚ ⲈⲦⲌⲒ ⲚⲈⲌⲒⲞⲞⲨⲈ ⟨Ⲛ̄ⲦⲘⲎⲦⲈ⟩· ⲀⲨⲰ
ϢⲀⲤⲦ̄ Ⲛ̄ⲦⲦⲒⲘⲎ ⲘⲚ ⲠⲈⲞⲞⲨ ⲘⲚ ⲠⲦⲀⲈⲒⲞ Ⲛ̄ⲚⲈⲤⲪⲢⲀⲄⲒⲤ·
ⲘⲚ Ⲛ̄ⲌⲨⲘⲚⲞⲤ Ⲛ̄ⲚⲀⲠⲦⲞⲠⲞⲤ ⲦⲎⲢⲞⲨ Ⲙ̄ⲠⲞⲨⲞⲈⲒⲚ· ⲈⲦⲂⲈ
ⲠⲈⲒ̈ϢⲀϪⲈ ⲠⲀϪⲞⲈⲒⲤ**ⲈⲚⲦⲀⲔϪⲞⲞϤ ⲌⲒⲦ̄Ⲛ ⲦⲦⲀⲠⲢⲞ Ⲙ̄ⲠⲀⲨ- [ⲤⲌⲎ]
ⲖⲞⲤ ⲠⲈⲚⲤⲞⲚ Ⲙ̄ⲠⲒⲞⲨⲞⲈⲒϢ ϪⲈ ⲘⲀ-ⲠⲦⲈⲖⲞⲤ Ⲙ̄ⲠⲀⲠⲦⲈⲖⲞⲤ·

20 ⲀⲨⲰ ⲘⲀ-ⲐⲞⲦⲈ Ⲙ̄ⲠⲀⲐⲞⲦⲈ· ⲘⲀ-ⲠⲈⲪⲞⲢⲞⲤ Ⲙ̄ⲠⲀⲠⲈⲪⲞⲢⲞⲤ·
ⲀⲨⲰ ⲘⲀ-ⲦⲈⲦⲒⲘⲎ Ⲙ̄ⲠⲀⲦⲦⲒⲘⲎ· ⲀⲨⲰ ⲘⲀ-ⲠⲦⲀⲈⲒⲞ Ⲙ̄ⲠⲀ-

---

4 MS Ⲛ̄ⲌⲎⲦ̄Ϥ; read Ⲛ̄ⲌⲎⲦ̄Ⲥ.
10 MS ⲌⲀⲦⲈⲨⲌⲎ; read ⲌⲀⲦⲈⲤⲌⲎ.
12 MS ϢⲀⲤⲢ̄ⲌⲞⲦⲈ; read ϢⲀⲨⲢ̄ⲌⲞⲦⲈ.
15 MS Ⲛ̄ⲦⲘⲎⲦⲈ omitted.
18 Ⲓ̄Ⲍ̄ in upper right-hand margin at end of quire.
21 MS ⲦⲈⲦⲒⲘⲎ; read Ⲧ̄ⲦⲒⲘⲎ.

place of the light. And the word : 'It shone when thou didst
see that it was of silver and copper' : that is the *type* of
this, that the power of light within it (the soul) is the silver
which is purified, the *spirit counterpart* within it is the
material copper. This, my Lord, is the first *thought*.

The second *thought*, moreover, thou hast now just finished
saying to us concerning the *soul* which receives *mysteries* :
'When it comes to the *place* of the *archons* of the path of the
Midst, they come forth before it in exceeding fearfulness.
And the *soul* gives the *mystery* of fear to ⟨them⟩ [1], and they
fear before it. And it gives the *destiny* to its *place*, and it
gives the *spirit counterpart* to its *place*. And it gives the
defence and the *seals* of each one to the *archons* which are
upon the paths ⟨of the Midst⟩. And it gives the *honour* and
the glory and the eulogy of the *seals* and the *songs of praise*
to all those of the *place* of the light.' Concerning this
word my Lord, thou hast once spoken through the mouth
of Paul, our brother, saying : 'Give *tribute* to whom *tribute*
is due, fear to whom fear, give *custom* to whom *custom* is
due, give *honour* to whom *honour* is due, and give eulogy |

---

[1]   (12) to ⟨them⟩ ; MS : to him.

ΠΤΑΪΟ· ΑΥѠ ⲘⲠⲢΚΑ-ΛΑΑΥ ⲈⲢѠⲦⲚ ⲚⲦⲚ ΛΑΑΥ· ⲈⲦⲈ
ΠΑΪ ΠΑΧΟⲈΙⲤ ϪⲈ ⲦⲈΨΥΧΗ ⲈⲢΧΙ-ⲘΥⲤⲦΗⲢΙΟⲚ· ϢΑⲤ†
ⲚⲦΑΠΟΛΟΓΙΑ ⲚⲚⲦⲞⲠⲞⲤ ⲦΗⲢΟΥ· ⲈⲦⲈ ΠΑΪ ΠΑΧΟⲈΙⲤ ΠⲈ
ΠⲘⲈ2ⲤⲚΑΥ ⲚⲚⲞΗⲘΑ· ΠⲘⲈ2ϢⲞⲘⲚⲦ 2ѠѠϤ ⲚⲚⲞΗⲘΑ·
5 ⲈⲦⲂⲈ ΠϢΑΧⲈ ⲚⲦΑΚΧⲞⲞϤ ⲈⲢⲞⲚ ⲘΠΙⲞΥⲞⲈΙϢ ϪⲈ ΠΑⲚⲦⲒ-
ⲘΙⲘⲞⲚ ⲘⲠⲚⲀ ϢΑϤϢѠΠⲈ ⲚΧΑΧⲈ ⲈⲦⲈΨΥΧΗ ⲈϤⲦⲢⲈⲤ-
ⲈΙⲢⲈ ⲚⲚⲞⲂⲈ ⲚⲒⲘ 2Ι ΠΑΘⲞⲤ ⲚⲒⲘ· ΑΥѠ ϢΑϤⲤⲞⲞ2Ⲉ ⲘⲘⲞⲤ
2Ⲛ ⲚΚⲞΛΑⲤΙⲤ ⲈⲦⲂⲈ ⲚⲚⲞⲂⲈ ⲦΗⲢⲞΥ ⲚⲦΑϤⲦⲢⲈⲤΑΑΥ· 2Α-
ΠΑϪ 2ΑΠΛѠⲤ ϢΑϤⲢΧΑΧⲈ ⲈⲦⲈΨΥΧΗ ⲘⲘΙⲚⲈ ⲚⲒⲘ· ⲈⲦⲂⲈ
10 ΠⲈΪϢΑΧⲈ ⲞΥⲚ ⲚⲦΑΚΧⲞⲞϤ ⲈⲢⲞⲚ ⲘΠΙⲞΥⲞⲈΙϢ· ϪⲈ
ⲚΧΙΧⲈⲈΥ ⲘΠⲢѠⲘⲈ ⲚⲈ ⲚⲈϤⲢⲘⲚΗΪ· ⲈⲦⲈ ⲚⲢⲘⲚΗΪ ⲚⲦⲈ- [ⲤϪΗ ᵇ]
ΨΥΧΗ ΠⲈ ΠΑⲚⲦΙⲘΙⲘⲞⲚ ⲘⲠⲚⲀ ⲘⲚ ⲦⲘⲞΙⲢΑ· ⲚΑΪ ⲈⲦⲞ
ⲚΧΑΧⲈ ⲈⲦⲈΨΥΧΗ ⲚⲞΥⲞⲈΙϢ ⲚⲒⲘ· ⲈΥⲦⲢⲈⲤⲈΙⲢⲈ ⲚⲚⲞⲂⲈ
ⲚⲒⲘ ⲘⲚ ⲀⲚⲞⲘΙΑ ⲚⲒⲘ· ⲈΙⲤ ΠΑΪ ΠΑΧⲞⲈΙⲤ ΠⲈ ΠⲘⲈ2ϢⲞⲘⲚⲦ
15 ⲚⲚⲞΗⲘΑ· ΠⲘⲈ2ϤⲦⲞⲞΥ 2ѠѠϤ ⲚⲚⲞΗⲘΑ ⲈⲦⲂⲈ ΠϢΑΧⲈ
ⲚⲦΑΚΧⲞⲞϤ· ϪⲈ ⲈϢѠΠⲈ ⲈⲢϢΑⲚ ⲦⲈΨΥΧΗ ⲈΙ' ⲈⲂⲞΛ 2Ⲙ
ΠⲤѠⲘΑ ⲚⲤⲘⲞⲞϢⲈ 2Ⲛ ⲦⲈ2ΙΗ ⲘⲚ ΠΑⲚⲦΙⲘΙⲘⲞⲚ ⲘⲠⲚⲀ·
ΑΥѠ ⲈⲤϢΑⲚⲦⲘ2Ⲉ ⲈΠⲘΥⲤⲦΗⲢΙⲞⲚ ⲘⲠⲂѠΛ ⲈⲂⲞΛ ⲚⲘⲘⲢⲢⲈ
ⲦΗⲢⲞΥ ⲘⲚ ⲚⲈⲤϤⲢΑΓΙⲤ· ⲚΑΪ ⲈⲦⲘΗⲢ 2Ⲙ ΠΑⲚⲦΙⲘΙⲘⲞⲚ Ⲙ-
20 ⲠⲚⲀ ⲚϤΛⲞ ⲈϤⲦⲞ ⲈⲢⲞⲤ· ⲈϢѠΠⲈ ⲞΥⲚ ⲈϤϢΑⲚⲦⲘ2Ⲉ
ⲈⲢⲞϤ ϢΑⲢⲈ ΠΑⲚⲦΙⲘΙⲘⲞⲚ ⲘⲠⲚⲀ· ϢΑϤΧΙ ⲚⲦⲈΨΥΧΗ
ⲈⲢΑⲦⲤ ⲚⲦΠΑⲢΘⲈⲚⲞⲤ ⲘΠⲞΥⲞⲈΙⲚ ⲦⲈΚⲢΙⲦΗⲤ· ΑΥѠ ϢΑⲢⲈ
ⲦⲈΚⲢΙⲦΗⲤ ⲦΠΑⲢΘⲈⲚⲞⲤ ⲘΠⲞΥⲞⲈΙⲚ· ϢΑⲤΔⲞΚΙⲘΑⳌⲈ Ⲛ-
ⲦⲈΨΥΧΗ ⲚⲤ2Ⲉ ⲈⲢⲞⲤ ⲈΑⲤⲢⲚⲞⲂⲈ· ΑΥѠ ⲈⲘⲠⲤΚⲈ2Ⲉ ⲈⲘ-

---

20 MS ⲈϤϢΑⲚⲦⲘ2Ⲉ; read ⲈⲤϢΑⲚⲦⲘ2Ⲉ.

to whom eulogy is due; and do not owe anything to another' * ¹. That is, my Lord, the *soul* which receives ² *mysteries* gives the *defence* to all *places*. This, my Lord, is the
second *thought*.

The third *thought*, moreover, concerning the word which
thou hast once said to us : 'The *spirit counterpart* is hostile
to the *soul*, causing it to do all sins and all *passions*. And it
reproves it in the *punishments* for all the sins which it has
committed. In a word, it becomes hostile to the *soul* in every
way.' *Now* concerning this word thou hast once said to us :
'The enemies of a man are they of his household' ᵒ; that
is, they of the household of the *soul* are the *spirit counterpart* and the *destiny*, which are hostile to the *soul* at all times,
causing it to commit all sins and all *iniquities*. Behold, this,
my Lord, is the third *thought*.

The fourth *thought* moreover, concerning the word which
thou hast spoken : 'If the *soul* comes forth from the *body*
and proceeds upon the way with the *spirit counterpart*, and
it has not found the *mystery* of the releasing of all the bonds
and the *seals* which bind to the *spirit counterpart*, so that
it ceases to be allotted to it (the soul); *now* if it does not
find it, the *spirit counterpart* takes the *soul* to the presence
of the *Virgin* of the Light, the *judge*. And the *judge*, the
Virgin of the Light, *examines* the *soul* and finds that it has
sinned, and she also does not find | *mysteries* of the light with

---

*   cf. Rom. 13.7, 8
ᵒ   cf. Mt. 10.36

---

¹   (1) do not owe anything to another; Till : do not allow a debt to exist with
    anyone.
²   (2) the soul which receives; Till : the soul which has received.

ΜΥϹΤΗΡΙΟΝ ⲘⲠΟΥΟΕΙΝ ⲚⲘⲘⲀϹ· ⲀΥⲰ ϢⲀϹΤⲀ̈ⲀϹ ⲚΟΥⲀ ⲥⲍⲑ
ⲚⲚΕϹⲠⲀⲢⲀⲖΗⲘⲠΤΗϹ· ⲀΥⲰ ϢⲀⲢΕ ⲠΕϹⲠⲀⲢⲀⲖΗⲘⲠΤΗϹ
ϢⲀϥⲚ̄ΤϹ Ⲛ̄ϥⲚΟⲬ̄Ϲ ΕⲠϹⲰⲘⲀ ⲀΥⲰ ⲘΕϹΕⲒ ΕⲂΟⲖ ⲌⲚ̄ Ⲙ̄
ⲘΕΤⲀⲂΟⲖΗ ⲘⲚ̄ ⲠϹⲰⲘⲀ ΕⲘⲠϹ† ⲘⲠⲌⲀΕ Ⲛ̄ⲔΥⲔⲖΟϹ· ΕΤⲂΕ
5 ⲠΕⲒϢⲀⲬΕ ΟΥⲚ ⲠⲀⲬΟΕΙϹ Ⲛ̄ΤⲀⲔⲬΟΟϥ ΕⲢΟⲚ ⲘⲠΙΟΥ
ΟΕΙϢ ⲬΕ ϢⲰⲠΕ ΕⲔⲂΗⲖ ΕⲂΟⲖ ⲘⲚ̄ ⲠΕⲔⲬⲀⲬΕ ΕⲠⲌΟϹΟⲚ
ΕⲔⳆΙ ΤΕⳆΙΗ Ⲛ̄ⲘⲘⲀϥ· ⲘΗⲠⲰϹ Ⲛ̄ΤΕ ⲠΕⲔⲬⲀⲬΕ Ⲛ̄ϥΤⲀⲀⲔ
ⲘⲠΕⲔⲢΙΤΗϹ· ⲀΥⲰ Ⲛ̄ΤΕ ⲠΕⲔⲢΙΤΗϹ Ⲛ̄ϥΤⲀⲀⲔ ⲘⲠⳆΥⲠΗⲢΕ
ΤΗϹ· Ⲛ̄ΤΕ ⲠⳆΥⲠΗⲢΕΤΗϹ ΝΟⲬ̄Ⲕ ΕⲠΕϢΤΕⲔΟ· ⲀΥⲰ Ⲛ̄
10 ⲚΕⲔΕⲒ ΕⲂΟⲖ ⲌⲘ̄ ⲠⲘⲀ ΕΤⲘⲘⲀΥ ΕⲘⲠⲔ† ⲘⲠⲌⲀΕ Ⲛ̄ⲖΥⲠ
ΤΟⲚ· ΕΤⲂΕ ⲠⲀ̈Ι ⲠΕ ⲠϢⲀⲬΕ ⲪⲀⲚΕⲢⲰϹ ⲬΕ ΨΥⲬΗ ⲚΙⲘ
ΕΤⲚΗΥ ΕⲂΟⲖ ⲌⲚ̄ ϹⲰⲘⲀ· ⲚϹⲘΟΟϢΕ ⳆΙ ΤΕⳆΙΗ ⲘⲚ̄ ⲠⲀⲚΤΙ
ⲘΙⲘΟⲚ ⲘⲠⲚ̄Ⲁ̄· ⲀΥⲰ Ⲛ̄ϹΤⲘ̄ⳆΕ ΕⲠⲘΥϹΤΗⲢΙΟⲚ ⲘⲠⲂⲰⲖ
ΕⲂΟⲖ Ⲛ̄ⲚΕϹⲪⲢⲀⳄΙϹ ΤΗⲢΟΥ ⲘⲚ̄ ⲘⲘⲢⲢΕ ΤΗⲢΟΥ· ⲚϹⲂⲰⲖ
15 ΕⲂΟⲖ ⲘⲠⲀⲚΤΙⲘΙⲘΟⲚ ⲘⲠⲚ̄Ⲁ̄ ΕϥⲘΗⲢ ΕⳆΟΥⲚ ΕⲢΟϹ· ΕⲒΕ
ΤΕΨΥⲬΗ ΕΤⲘⲘⲀΥ ⲘⲠϹⲬⲒ-ⲘΥϹΤΗⲢΙΟⲚ ⳆⲘ ΠΟΥΟΕΙⲚ· ⲥⲍⲑ ᵇ
ΕⲘⲠϹⳆΕ ΕⲘⲘΥϹΤΗⲢΙΟⲚ ⲘⲠⲂⲰⲖ ΕⲂΟⲖ ⲘⲠⲀⲚΤΙⲘΙⲘΟⲚ
ⲘⲠⲚ̄Ⲁ̄ ΕϥⲘΗⲢ ΕⳆΟΥⲚ ΕⲢΟϹ· ΕϹΤⲘ̄ⳆΕ ΟΥⲚ ΕⲢΟϥ· ϢⲀⲢΕ
ⲠⲀⲚΤΙⲘΙⲘΟⲚ ⲘⲠⲚ̄Ⲁ̄ ϢⲀϥⳄΙ Ⲛ̄ΤΕΨΥⲬΗ ΕΤⲘⲘⲀΥ ΕⲢⲀΤϹ
20 Ⲛ̄ΤⲠⲀⲢⲐΕⲚΟϹ ⲘⲠΟΥΟΕΙⲚ· ⲀΥⲰ ϢⲀⲢΕ ΤⲠⲀⲢⲐΕⲚΟϹ Ⲙ̄
ⲠΟΥΟ̈ΙⲚ ⲀΥⲰ ΤΕⲔⲢΙΤΗϹ ΕΤⲘⲘⲀΥ· ϢⲀϹ† Ⲛ̄ΤΕΨΥⲬΗ
ΕΤⲘⲘⲀΥ ΕΤΟΟΤϥ ⲚΟΥⲀ ⲚⲚΕϹⲠⲀⲢⲀⲖΗⲘⲠΤΗϹ· ⲀΥⲰ
ϢⲀⲢΕ ⲠΕϹⲠⲀⲢⲀⲖΗⲘⲠΤΗϹ ϢⲀϥⲚΟⲬ̄Ϲ ΕΤΕϹⲪⲀΙⲢⲀ Ⲛ̄ⲀΙⲰⲚ

---

1 ⲒⲎ̄ in upper left-hand margin at beginning of quire.
4 MS ⲘⲚ̄ ⲠϹⲰⲘⲀ; read ⲘⲠϹⲰⲘⲀ.
6 MS originally ΕϢⲰⲠΕ; Ε erased.
23 MS Ⲛ̄ⲀΙⲰⲚ; read Ⲛ̄Ⲛ̄ⲀΙⲰⲚ.

it, she gives it to one of her *paralemptai*. And her *paralemptes*
brings it and casts it into a *body*, and it does not come
forth from the *changes* of the *body*[1] before it has done the
last *cycle*.' *Now* concerning this word, my Lord, thou hast
once said to us : 'Agree with thine enemy *whilst* thou art
upon the way with him, *lest* thy enemy hand thee to the
judge, and the *judge* hand thee to the *officer*, and the *officer*
cast thee into the prison, and thou dost not come forth
from that place before thou hast given the last *farthing*' *.
Concerning this, the word is *clear* : every *soul* which comes
forth from the *body*, and proceeds upon the way with the
spirit counterpart and does not find the *mystery* of the
releasing of all the *seals* and all the bonds, so that it releases
itself from the *spirit counterpart* which is bound to it,
that *soul* which has not received *mysteries* in the light and
has not found the *mysteries* of the releasing of[2] the *spirit
counterpart* which is bound in it, *now* if it does not find it,
the *spirit counterpart* takes that *soul* to the presence of the
Virgin of the Light. And that *Virgin* of the Light and *judge*
gives that *soul* into the hands of one of her *paralemptai*,
and her *paralemptes* casts it into the *sphere* of the aeons, |

---

* cf. Mt. 5.25, 26

---

[1] (4) of the body; MS : and the body.
[2] (17) releasing of; Schmidt : releasing from.

ΑΥΩ ΜΕСΕΙ' ΕΒΟΛ 2Ν ΜΜΕΤΑΒΟΛΗ ΜΠСΩΜΑ· ΕΜΠС†
ΜΠ2ΛΕ ΝΚΥΚΛΟС ΕΤΗΠ' ΕΡΟС· ΠΑΪ ΟΥΝ ΠΑΧΟΕΙС ΠΕ
ΠΜΕ24ΤΟΟΥ ΝΝΟΗΜΑ:

ΑСΩΩΠΕ 6Ε ΝΤΕΡΕ ΙС СΩΤΜ ΕΝΕΪΩΑΧΕ ΕСΧΩ Μ-
5 ΜΟΟΥ Ν6Ι ΜΑΡΙΑ· ΠΕΧΑ4 ΧΕ ΕΥΓΕ ΤΠΑΝΜΑΚΑΡΙΟС
ΜΑΡΙΑ ΤΕΠΠΝΙΚΗ· ΝΑΪ ΝΕ ΝΒΩΛ ΕΒΟΛ ΝΝΩΑΧΕ ΝΤΑΪ-
ΧΟΟΥ· ΑСΟΥΩ2Μ Ν6Ι ΜΑΡΙΑ ΠΕΧΑС ΧΕ ΠΑΧΟΕΙС·
ΑΙΤΙ †ΩΙΝΙ ΜΜΟΚ ΕΒΟΛ ΓΑΡ ΧΕ ΧΙΝ ΤΕΝΟΥ ΕΪΝΑ2Ι- [co]
ΤΟΟΤ Ε4ΝΤΚ Ε2ΩΒ ΝΙΜ 2Ν ΟΥΩΡΧ· ΕΤΒΕ ΠΑΪ ΟΥΝ
10 ΠΑΧΟΕΙС ΑΡΙ2ΑΡΩ2ΗΤ ΝΜΜΑΝ ΝΓ6ΩΛΠ ΝΑΝ ΕΒΟΛ Ν-
2ΩΒ ΝΙΜ' ΕΤΝΝΑΩΝΤΚ ΕΡΟΟΥ· ΕΤΒΕ ΘΕ 2ΩΩ4 ΕΡΕ
ΝΑСΝΗΥ ΝΑΚΗΡΥССΕ ΜΠΓΕΝΟС ΝΤΜΝΤΡΩΜΕ ΤΗΡ4· ΝΑΪ
ΔΕ ΝΤΕΡΕСΧΟΟΥ ΜΠСΩΡ· Α4ΟΥΩ2Μ 2ΩΩ4 Ν6Ι ΠСΩ-
ΤΗΡ ΠΕΧΑ4 ΝΑС Ε4ΩΟΟΠ 2Ν ΟΥΝΟ6 ΝΝΑ' Ε2ΟΥΝ
15 ΕΡΟС· ΧΕ 2ΑΜΗΝ 2ΑΜΗΝ †ΧΩ ΜΜΟС ΝΗΤΝ ΧΕ ΟΥ-
ΜΟΝΟΝ †ΝΑ6ΩΛΠ ΝΗΤΝ ΕΒΟΛ Ν2ΩΒ ΝΙΜ ΕΤΕΤΝΑΩΙΝΕ
ΝСΩΟΥ· ΑΛΛΑ ΧΙΝ ΤΕΝΟΥ ΟΝ †ΝΑ6ΩΛΠ ΝΗΤΝ ΕΒΟΛ
Ν2ΕΝΚΟΟΥΕ ΝΑΪ ΕΤΕ ΜΠΕΤΝΝΟΪ ΜΜΟΟΥ Ε4ΩΙΝΕ Ν-
СΩΟΥ· ΝΑΪ ΕΤΕ ΜΠΟΥΑΛΕ ΕΧΜ Π2ΗΤ ΝΡΡΩΜΕ· ΝΑΪ
20 ΕΤΕ ΝСΕСΟΟΥΝ ΜΜΟΟΥ ΑΝ Ν6Ι ΝΚΕΝΟΥΤΕ ΤΗΡΟΥ
ΕΤ2Ν ΝΡΩΜΕ· ΤΕΝΟΥ 6Ε ΟΥΝ ΝΤΟ ΜΑΡΙΑ ΩΙΝΕ ΝСΑ
ΠΕΤΕΡΕΩΙΝΕ ΝСΩ4 ΑΥΩ ΑΝΟΚ †ΝΑ6ΟΛΠ4 ΝΕ ΕΒΟΛ [co b]
Ν2Ο ΜΝ 2Ο ΑΧΝ ΠΑΡΑΒΟΛΗ· ΑСΟΥΩ2Μ ΔΕ Ν6Ι ΜΑΡΙΑ
ΠΕΧΑС ΧΕ ΠΑΧΟΕΙС ΕΪΕ ΕΩΑΡΕ ΝΒΑΠΤΙСΜΑ ΚΑΝΟΒΕ
25 ΕΒΟΛ ΝΑΩ ΝΤΥΠΟС· ΑΪСΩΤΜ ΕΡΟΚ ΕΚΧΩ ΜΜΟС·

---

8   MS †ΩΙΝΙ; read †ΩΙΝΕ.

and it does not come forth from the *changes* of the *body* until it has done the last *cycle* allotted to it. *Now* this, my Lord, is the fourth *thought*."

114.   Now it happened when Jesus heard these words which Maria spoke, he said: "*Excellent*, thou *all-blessed* Maria, thou *spiritual one*. This is the interpretation of the words which I have said."

Maria answered and said: "My Lord, *yet* (further) I question thee, *for* from this time I will proceed to question thee on all things with assurance. Because of this *now*, my Lord, be compassionate to us and reveal to us all things about which we will question thee, for the sake of the manner in which my brothers will *preach* to the whole *race* of mankind."

But when she had said these things to the Saviour, the *Saviour* himself answered and said to her with great mercy towards her: "*Truly, truly*, I say to you, *not only* will I reveal all things to you about which you question, *but* from this time I will also reveal to you other things about which you did not *understand*, to question them, which have not arisen in the hearts of men *, which all the gods which are among men also do not know. *Now* at this time thou, Maria, question what thou dost question, and I will reveal it to thee face to face without *parable*.

115.   Maria *however* answered and said: "My Lord, in what *type* do *baptisms* forgive sins? I have heard thee saying: |

---

*   cf. 1 Cor. 2.9

ϫⲉ ϣⲁⲣⲉ ⲛ̄ⲗⲓⲧⲟⲩⲣⲅⲟⲥ ⲛ̄ⲉⲣⲓⲛⲁⲓⲟⲥ ϣⲁⲩⲁⲕⲟⲗⲟⲩⲑⲉⲓ
ⲛ̄ⲥⲁ ⲧⲉⲯⲩⲭⲏ ⲉⲩⲟ ⲙ̄ⲙⲛ̄ⲧⲣⲉ ⲉⲣⲟⲥ ⲛ̄ⲛⲟⲃⲉ ⲛⲓⲙ ⲉⲧⲥ̄ⲉⲓⲣⲉ
ⲙ̄ⲙⲟⲟⲩ ϫⲉⲕⲁⲥ ⲉⲩⲉⲥⲟⲟϩⲉ ⲙ̄ⲙⲟⲥ ϩⲛ̄ ⲛⲉⲕⲣⲓⲥⲓⲥ· ⲧⲉⲛⲟⲩ ϭⲉ ⲟⲩⲛ ⲡⲁϫⲟⲉⲓⲥ· ϣⲁⲣⲉ ⲙ̄ⲙⲩⲥⲧⲏⲣⲓⲟⲛ ⲛ̄ⲛⲃⲁⲡ-
5 ⲧⲓⲥⲙⲁ· ϣⲁⲩϥⲱⲧⲉ ⲉⲃⲟⲗ ⲛ̄ⲛⲟⲃⲉ ⲉⲧⲛ̄ⲧⲟⲟⲧⲟⲩ ⲛ̄ⲛ̄-
ⲗⲓⲧⲟⲩⲣⲅⲟⲥ ⲛ̄ⲉⲣⲓⲛⲁⲓⲟⲥ· ϫⲉ ⲛ̄ⲧⲟⲟⲩ ⲙⲉⲛ ϣⲁⲩⲣⲡⲉⲩ-
ⲱⲃϣ̄· ⲧⲉⲛⲟⲩ ϭⲉ ⲟⲩⲛ ⲡⲁϫⲟⲉⲓⲥ ϫⲱ ⲉⲣⲟⲛ ⲙ̄ⲡⲧⲩⲡⲟⲥ
ⲉϣⲁⲩⲕⲁⲛⲟⲃⲉ ⲉⲃⲟⲗ· ⲁⲗⲗⲁ ⲧⲛ̄ⲟⲩⲱϣ ⲉⲉⲓⲙⲉ ⲉⲣⲟⲟⲩ
ϩⲛ̄ ⲟⲩⲱⲣⲭ̄· ⲁϥⲟⲩⲱϣ̄ⲃ ⲇⲉ ⲛ̄ϭⲓ ⲡⲥⲱⲧⲏⲣ ⲡⲉϫⲁϥ ⲙ̄-
10 ⲙⲁⲣⲓⲁ ϫⲉ ⲕⲁⲗⲱⲥ ⲙⲉⲛ ⲁϫⲟⲟⲥ· ⲛ̄ⲗⲓⲧⲟⲩⲣⲅⲟⲥ ⲙⲉⲛⲧⲟⲓⲅⲉ ⲛ̄ⲧⲟⲟⲩ ⲛⲉ ⲉϣⲁⲩⲣⲙⲛ̄ⲧⲣⲉ ⲛ̄ⲛⲟⲃⲉ ⲛⲓⲙ· ⲁⲗⲗⲁ
ϣⲁⲩϭⲱ ⲟⲛ ϩⲛ̄ ⲛⲉⲕⲣⲓⲥⲓⲥ ⲉⲩⲁⲙⲁϩⲧⲉ ⲛ̄ⲛⲉⲯⲩⲭⲟⲟⲩⲉ· ⲥ̄ⲟⲗ
ⲉⲩⲥⲟⲟϩⲉ ⲛ̄ⲛⲉⲯⲩⲭⲟⲟⲩⲉ ⲧⲏⲣⲟⲩ ⲛ̄ⲣⲣⲉϥⲣ̄ⲛⲟⲃⲉ· ⲛⲁⲓ̈
ⲉⲧⲉ ⲙ̄ⲡⲟⲩϫⲓ-ⲙⲩⲥⲧⲏⲣⲓⲟⲛ· ⲁⲩⲱ ϣⲁⲩⲕⲁⲧⲉⲭⲉ ⲙ̄ⲙⲟⲟⲩ
15 ϩⲛ̄ ⲛⲉⲭⲁⲟⲥ ⲉⲩⲕⲟⲗⲁⲍⲉ ⲙ̄ⲙⲟⲟⲩ· ⲁⲩⲱ ⲙⲉⲣⲉ ⟨ⲛ̄ⲗⲓⲧⲟⲩⲣ-
ⲅⲟⲥ⟩ ⲛ̄ⲉⲣⲓⲛⲁⲓⲟⲥ ⲉⲧⲙ̄ⲙⲁⲩ ⲙⲉⲩϭⲙϭⲟⲙ’ ⲉⲥⲛ̄-ⲛⲉⲭⲁⲟⲥ
ⲉⲃⲟⲗ ⲉⲧⲣⲉⲩⲉⲓ’ ⲉⲛⲧⲁⲝⲓⲥ ⲉⲧϩⲓⲡⲥⲁϩⲣⲉ ⲛ̄ⲛⲉⲭⲁⲟⲥ ⲛ̄ⲥⲉ-
ⲥⲟⲟϩⲉ ⲛ̄ⲛⲉⲯⲩⲭⲟⲟⲩⲉ ⲉⲧⲛⲏⲩ ⲉⲃⲟⲗ ϩⲛ̄ ⲛ̄ⲧⲟⲡⲟⲥ ⲉⲧ-
ⲙ̄ⲙⲁⲩ· ⲧⲉⲛⲟⲩ ϭⲉ ⲛⲉⲯⲩⲭⲟⲟⲩⲉ ⲉⲣⲭⲓ-ⲙⲩⲥⲧⲏⲣⲓⲟⲛ
20 ⲟⲩⲕ ⲉⲝⲉⲥⲧⲓ ⲉⲧⲣⲉⲩⲃⲓⲁⲍⲉ ⲙ̄ⲙⲟⲟⲩ ⲛ̄ⲥⲉϫⲓⲧⲟⲩ ⲉⲃⲟⲗ
ϩⲛ̄ ⲛⲉⲭⲁⲟⲥ· ϫⲉ ⲉⲩⲉⲥⲟⲟϩⲉ ⲙ̄ⲙⲟⲟⲩ ⲛ̄ϭⲓ ⲛ̄ⲗⲉⲓⲧⲟⲩⲣ-
ⲅⲟⲥ ⲛ̄ⲉⲣⲓⲛⲁⲓⲟⲥ· ⲁⲗⲗⲁ ϣⲁⲣⲉ ⲛ̄ⲗⲓⲧⲟⲩⲣⲅⲟⲥ ⲛ̄ⲉⲣⲓⲛⲁⲓⲟⲥ
ϣⲁⲩⲥⲟⲟϩⲉ ⲛ̄ⲛⲉⲯⲩⲭⲟⲟⲩⲉ ⲛ̄ⲣⲣⲉϥⲣ̄ⲛⲟⲃⲉ· ⲛ̄ⲥⲉⲁⲙⲁϩⲧⲉ
ⲛ̄ⲛⲁⲓ̈ ⲉⲧⲉ ⲙ̄ⲡⲟⲩϫⲓ-ⲙⲩⲥⲧⲏⲣⲓⲟⲛ ⲛⲁⲓ̈ ⲉϣⲁⲩⲛ̄ⲧⲟⲩ ⲉⲃⲟⲗ

14　MS originally ⲁⲩⲕⲁⲧⲉⲭⲉ; ϣ inserted above.
15　MS ⲛ̄ⲗⲓⲧⲟⲩⲣⲅⲟⲥ omitted.

'The *erinaioi ministers accompany* the *soul*, and they are witnesses to it of all the sins which it commits, so that they may reprove it in the *judgments*'. *Now* at this time, my Lord, do the *mysteries* of the *baptisms* wipe out the sins which are in the hands of the *erinaioi ministers*, so that they forget them? *Now* at this time, my Lord, tell us the *type* how they forgive, *but* we wish to know it with assurance."

The *Saviour* answered *however*, he said to Maria : "*Well* hast thou spoken. The *ministers certainly* are those who witness to all sins. *But* they remain in the *judgments* as they seize the *souls* and reprove all the *souls* of sinners, who have not received *mysteries*. And they *restrain* them in the *Chaos(es)*, *punishing* them. And those *erinaioi* (ministers) are not able to pass out from the *Chaos(es)* to come to the *ranks* which are above the *Chaos(es)*, and to reprove the *souls* which come forth from those *places*. Now at this time it is *not permitted* that the *souls* which have received *mysteries* should *suffer violence*, and be taken into the *Chaos(es)*, so that the *erinaioi ministers* reprove them. *But* the *erinaioi ministers* reprove the *souls* of sinners, and they detain those who have not received *mysteries*, who are brought forth from | the *Chaos(es)*. But the *souls* which have received

ⲎⲚ ⲚⲈⲬⲀⲞⲤ· ⲚⲈⲮⲨⲬⲞⲞⲨⲈ ⲚⲦⲞⲞⲨ ⲈⲢⲬⲒ-ⲘⲨⲤⲦⲎⲢⲒⲞⲚ
ⲘⲚⲦⲞⲨ-ⲌⲰⲂ ⲈⲤⲞⲞⲌⲈ ⲘⲘⲞⲞⲨ ⲬⲈ ⲘⲈⲨⲈⲒ' ⲈⲂⲞⲖ ⲌⲚ
ⲚⲈⲨⲦⲞⲠⲞⲤ ⲀⲨⲰ ⲞⲚ ⲈⲨⲰⲀⲚⲈⲒ' ⲘⲈⲨⲈⲰϬⲘϬⲞⲘ ⲈⲀⲌⲈ- ⲤⲞⲖ ᵇ
ⲢⲀⲦⲞⲨ ⲈⲢⲞⲞⲨ· ⲠⲖⲎⲚ ⲢⲰ ⲘⲈⲨⲈⲰⲬⲒⲦⲞⲨ ⲈⲂⲞⲖ ⲌⲚ ⲚⲈ-
5 ⲬⲀⲞⲤ ⲈⲦⲘⲘⲀⲨ· ⲤⲰⲦⲘ ⲞⲚ ⲦⲀⲬⲰ ⲈⲢⲰⲦⲚ ⲘⲠⲰⲀⲬⲈ
ⲌⲚ ⲞⲨⲀⲖⲎⲐⲒⲀ ⲬⲈ ⲈⲰⲀⲢⲈ ⲠⲘⲨⲤⲦⲎⲢⲒⲞⲚ ⲘⲠⲂⲀⲠⲦⲒⲤⲘⲀ
ⲔⲀⲚⲞⲂⲈ ⲈⲂⲞⲖ ⲚⲀⲰ ⲚⲦⲨⲠⲞⲤ· ⲦⲈⲚⲞⲨ ϬⲈ ⲞⲨⲚ ⲈⲢ-
ⲰⲀⲚ ⲚⲈⲮⲨⲬⲞⲞⲨⲈ ⲢⲚⲞⲂⲈ ⲈⲦⲒ ⲈⲨⲌⲒⲬⲘ ⲠⲔⲞⲤⲘⲞⲤ·
ⲰⲀⲨⲈⲒ' ⲘⲈⲚⲦⲞⲒⲄⲈ ⲚϬⲒ ⲚⲖⲒⲦⲞⲨⲢⲄⲞⲤ ⲚⲈⲢⲒⲚⲀⲒⲞⲤ· ⲚⲤⲈⲢ-
10 ⲘⲚⲦⲢⲈ ⲚⲚⲞⲂⲈ ⲚⲒⲘ' ⲈⲦⲈⲢⲈ ⲦⲈⲮⲨⲬⲎ ⲈⲒⲢⲈ ⲘⲘⲞⲞⲨ· ⲬⲈ
ⲘⲎⲠⲰⲤ ⲢⲰ ⲚⲤⲈⲈⲒ' ⲈⲂⲞⲖ ⲌⲚ ⲚⲦⲞⲠⲞⲤ ⲚⲦⲈ ⲚⲈⲬⲀⲞⲤ·
ⲬⲈⲔⲀⲤ ⲈⲨⲈⲤⲞⲞⲌⲈ ⲘⲘⲞⲤ ⲌⲚ ⲚⲈⲔⲢⲒⲤⲒⲤ ⲚⲀⲒ ⲈⲦⲠⲂⲞⲖ
ⲚⲚⲈⲬⲀⲞⲤ ⲬⲈⲔⲀⲤ ⲈⲨⲈⲤⲞⲞⲌⲈ ⲘⲘⲞⲤ· ⲀⲨⲰ ⲰⲀⲢⲈ
ⲠⲀⲚⲦⲒⲘⲒⲘⲞⲚ ⲘⲠⲚⲀ ⲰⲀϤⲢⲘⲚⲦⲢⲈ ⲚⲚⲞⲂⲈ ⲚⲒⲘ' ⲈⲦⲤⲚⲀⲀⲀⲨ
15 ⲚϬⲒ ⲦⲈⲮⲨⲬⲎ ⲬⲈⲔⲀⲤ ⲌⲰⲰⲤ ⲈϤⲈⲤⲞⲞⲌⲈ ⲘⲘⲞⲤ ⲌⲚ ⲚⲈ-
ⲔⲢⲒⲤⲒⲤ ⲚⲀⲒ ⲈⲦⲠⲂⲞⲖ ⲚⲚⲈⲬⲀⲞⲤ· ⲞⲨⲘⲞⲚⲞⲚ ⲬⲈ ϤⲢⲘⲚⲦⲢⲈ
ⲘⲘⲞⲞⲨ· ⲀⲖⲖⲀ ⲚⲞⲂⲈ ⲚⲒⲘ ⲚⲦⲈ ⲚⲈⲮⲨⲬⲞⲞⲨⲈ ⲰⲀϤⲤⲪⲢⲀ-
ⲄⲒⲌⲈ ⲚⲚⲚⲞⲂⲈ ⲚϤⲦⲞϬⲞⲨ ⲈⲌⲞⲨⲚ ⲈⲦⲈⲮⲨⲬⲎ· ⲬⲈⲔⲀⲤ [ⲤⲞⲂ]
ⲈⲢⲈ ⲚⲀⲢⲬⲰⲚ ⲦⲎⲢⲞⲨ ⲚⲢⲢⲈϤⲢⲚⲞⲂⲈ ⲚⲚⲈⲔⲢⲒⲤⲒⲤ ⲈⲨⲈ-
20 ⲤⲞⲨⲰⲚⲤ ⲬⲈ ⲞⲨⲮⲨⲬⲎ ⲚⲢⲈϤⲢⲚⲞⲂⲈ ⲦⲈ· ⲀⲨⲰ ⲬⲈ
ⲈⲨⲈⲈⲒⲘⲈ ⲈⲦⲎⲠⲈ ⲚⲚⲚⲞⲂⲈ ⲚⲦⲀⲤⲀⲀⲨ ⲈⲂⲞⲖ ⲌⲚ ⲚⲈⲤⲪⲢⲀ-
ⲄⲒⲤ ⲚⲦⲀϤⲦⲞϬⲞⲨ ⲈⲢⲞⲤ ⲚϬⲒ ⲠⲀⲚⲦⲒⲘⲒⲘⲞⲚ ⲘⲠⲚⲀ ⲬⲈⲔⲀⲤ
ⲈⲨⲈⲔⲞⲖⲀⲌⲈ ⲘⲘⲞⲤ ⲔⲀⲦⲀ ⲦⲎⲠⲈ ⲚⲚⲚⲞⲂⲈ ⲚⲦⲀⲤⲀⲀⲨ·
ⲦⲀⲒ ⲦⲈ ⲐⲈ ⲈⲰⲀⲨⲀⲀⲤ ⲘⲮⲨⲬⲎ ⲚⲒⲘ ⲚⲢⲈϤⲢⲚⲞⲂⲈ· ⲦⲈ-
25 ⲚⲞⲨ ϬⲈ ⲠⲈⲦⲚⲀⲬⲒ ⲚⲘⲘⲨⲤⲦⲎⲢⲒⲞⲚ ⲚⲚⲂⲀⲠⲦⲒⲤⲘⲀ ⲰⲀⲢⲈ

---

13 ⲬⲈⲔⲀⲤ ⲈⲨⲈⲤⲞⲞⲌⲈ ⲘⲘⲞⲤ better omitted.
15 MS ⲌⲰⲰⲤ ; read ⲌⲰⲰϤ.
19 MS ⲚⲢⲢⲈϤⲢⲚⲞⲂⲈ ⲚⲚⲈⲔⲢⲒⲤⲒⲤ; read ⲚⲚⲈⲔⲢⲒⲤⲒⲤ ⲚⲢⲢⲈϤⲢⲚⲞⲂⲈ.

mysteries, they cannot reprove because they do not come forth from their *places*. And also when they come, they are not able to stand against them, and *furthermore* they are not able to take them into those *Chaos(es)*.

Hear, moreover, and I will say the word to you in *truth* in which *type* the *mystery* of the *baptism* forgives sins. *Now* at this time, when the *souls* commit sin while they are *still* in the *world*, the *erinaioi ministers* are *certain* to come and they bear witness to all the sins which the *soul* commits, *lest* they come forth from the *places* of the *Chaos*, so that they reprove it in the *judgments* which are outside the *Chaos*[1]. And the *spirit counterpart* bears witness to all the sins which the *soul* commits, so that it also reproves it in the *judgments* which are outside the *Chaos(es)*. *Not only* does it witness to them, *but* — all the sins of the *souls* — it *seals* the sins and fixes them within the *soul*, so that all the *archons* of the *judgments* of sinners recognise that it is a sinful *soul*, and so that they know the number of the sins which it has committed, by means of the *seals* which the *spirit counterpart* has fixed to it, so that they should *punish* it *according to* the number of the sins which it has committed. Thus is it done to all sinful *souls*.

Now at this time, he who will receive the *mysteries* of the *baptisms*, | the *mysteries*[2] of those things are a great

---

[1]   (13) dittography omitted; MS : reprove it in the ... chaos so that they reprove it.
[2]   (299.1) mysteries; Schmidt : mystery.

ⲘⲘⲨⲤⲦⲎⲢⲒⲞⲚ ⲚⲚⲈⲦⲘⲘⲀⲨ ϢⲀϤϢⲰⲠⲈ ⲚⲞⲨⲚⲞϬ ⲚⲔⲰϨⲦ
ⲈϤⲚⲀϢⲦ ⲈⲘⲀⲦⲈ ⲚⲤⲀⲂⲈ ⲚϤⲢⲈⲔϨ-ⲚⲚⲞⲂⲈ· ⲀⲨⲰ ϢⲀⲨⲂⲰⲔ
ⲈϨⲞⲨⲚ ⲈⲦⲈⲨⲮⲨⲬⲎ ϨⲚ ⲞⲨⲠⲈⲐⲎⲠ' ⲚϤⲞⲨⲰⲘ ⲈϨⲞⲨⲚ ⲚⲤⲀ
ⲚⲚⲞⲂⲈ ⲦⲎⲢⲞⲨ· ⲚⲀⲒ ⲚⲦⲀϤⲦⲞϬⲞⲨ ⲈϨⲞⲨⲚ ⲈⲢⲞⲤ ⲚϬⲒ
5 ⲠⲀⲚⲦⲒⲘⲒⲘⲞⲚ ⲘⲠⲚⲀ· ⲀⲨⲰ ⲈϤϢⲀⲚⲞⲨⲰ ⲈϤⲔⲀⲐⲀⲢⲒⳕⲈ Ⲛ-
ⲚⲚⲞⲂⲈ ⲦⲎⲢⲞⲨ ⲚⲀⲒ ⲚⲦⲀϤⲦⲞϬⲞⲨ ⲈⲢⲞⲤ ⲚϬⲒ ⲠⲀⲚⲦⲒⲘⲒⲘⲞⲚ
ⲘⲠⲚⲀ ϢⲀⲨⲂⲰⲔ ⲞⲚ ⲈϨⲞⲨⲚ ⲈⲠⲤⲰⲘⲀ ϨⲚ ⲞⲨⲠⲈⲐⲎⲠ' [ⲤⲞⲂ ᵇ]
ⲚϤⲀⲒⲰⲔⲈ ⲚⲤⲀ ⲚⲀⲒⲰⲔⲎⲦⲤ ⲦⲎⲢⲞⲨ ϨⲚ ⲞⲨⲠⲈⲐⲎⲠ' ⲚϤ-
ⲠⲞⲢϪⲞⲨ ⲈⲠⲤⲀ ⲘⲠⲘⲈⲢⲞⲤ ⲘⲠⲤⲰⲘⲀ· ϢⲀϤⲀⲒⲰⲔⲈ ⲄⲀⲢ
10 ⲚⲤⲀ ⲠⲀⲚⲦⲒⲘⲒⲘⲞⲚ ⲘⲠⲚⲀ ⲘⲚ ⲦⲘⲞⲒⲢⲀ· ⲚϤⲠⲞⲢϪⲞⲨ ⲚⲤⲀ-
ⲂⲞⲖ ⲚⲦϬⲞⲘ ⲘⲚ ⲦⲈⲮⲨⲬⲎ ⲚϤⲔⲀⲀⲨ ϨⲒⲠⲤⲀ ⲘⲠⲤⲰⲘⲀ·
ϨⲰⲤⲦⲈ ⲠⲀⲚⲦⲒⲘⲒⲘⲞⲚ ⲘⲠⲚⲀ ⲘⲚ ⲦⲘⲞⲒⲢⲀ ⲘⲚ ⲠⲤⲰⲘⲀ·
ϢⲀϤⲠⲞⲢϪⲞⲨ ⲈⲨⲘⲈⲢⲞⲤ· ⲦⲈⲮⲨⲬⲎ ϨⲰⲰϤ ⲘⲚ ⲦϬⲞⲘ
ϢⲀϤⲠⲞⲢϪⲞⲨ ⲈⲔⲈⲘⲈⲢⲞⲤ· ⲠⲘⲨⲤⲦⲎⲢⲒⲞⲚ ϨⲰⲰϤ ⲘⲠⲂⲀⲠ-
15 ⲦⲒⲤⲘⲀ ϢⲀϤϬⲰ ϨⲚ ⲦⲈⲨⲘⲎⲦⲈ ⲘⲠⲈⲤⲚⲀⲨ· ⲚϤϬⲰ ⲈϤ-
ⲠⲰⲢϪ ⲘⲘⲞⲞⲨ ⲈⲚⲈⲨⲈⲢⲎⲨ· ϪⲈⲔⲀⲤ ⲈϤⲈⲦⲂⲂⲞⲞⲨ ⲚϤ-
ⲔⲀⲐⲀⲢⲒⳕⲈ ⲘⲘⲞⲞⲨ ϪⲈ ⲚⲚⲈⲨϪⲰϨⲘ ⲈⲂⲞⲖ ϨⲚ ⲐⲨⲖⲎ·
ⲦⲈⲚⲞⲨ ϬⲈ ⲞⲨⲚ ⲘⲀⲢⲒⲀ ⲦⲀⲒ ⲦⲈ ⲐⲈ ⲈϢⲀⲢⲈ ⲘⲘⲨⲤⲦⲎ-
ⲢⲒⲞⲚ ⲚⲚⲂⲀⲠⲦⲒⲤⲘⲀ ⲔⲀⲚⲞⲂⲈ ⲈⲂⲞⲖ· ⲀⲨⲰ ⲘⲚ ⲀⲚⲞⲘⲒⲀ
20 ⲚⲒⲘ·

ⲚⲀⲒ ϬⲈ ⲚⲦⲈⲢⲈϤϪⲞⲞⲨ ⲚϬⲒ ⲠⲤⲰⲦⲎⲢ ⲠⲈϪⲀϤ ⲚⲚⲈϤⲘⲀ-
ⲐⲎⲦⲎⲤ· ϪⲈ ⲦⲈⲦⲚⲚⲞⲒ ϪⲈ ⲈⲒϢⲀϪⲈ ⲚⲘⲘⲎⲦⲚ ⲚⲀϢ ⲚϨⲈ·
ⲀⲤϬⲞϬⲤ ⲈⲂⲞⲖ ⲚϬⲒ ⲘⲀⲢⲒⲀ ⲠⲈϪⲀⲤ** ϪⲈ ⲤⲈ ⲠⲀϪⲞⲈⲒⲤ ϨⲚ [ⲤⲞⲄ]
ⲞⲨⲘⲈ †ⲀⲔⲢⲒⲂⲀⳕⲈ ⲚⲤⲀ ϢⲀϪⲈ ⲚⲒⲘ' ⲈⲦⲔϪⲰ ⲘⲘⲞⲞⲨ·
25 ⲈⲦⲂⲈ ⲠϢⲀϪⲈ ⲞⲨⲚ ⲘⲠⲔⲰ ⲈⲂⲞⲖ ⲚⲚⲚⲞⲂⲈ ⲚⲦⲀⲔϪⲞⲞϤ
ⲈⲢⲞⲚ ⲘⲠⲒⲞⲨⲞⲈⲒϢ ϨⲚ ⲞⲨⲠⲀⲢⲀⲂⲞⲖⲎ ⲈⲔϪⲰ ⲘⲘⲞⲤ ϪⲈ
ⲚⲦⲀⲒⲈⲒ' ⲈⲚⲞⲨϪⲈ ⲚⲞⲨⲔⲰϨⲦ ⲈϨⲢⲀⲒ ⲈϪⲘ ⲠⲔⲀϨ· ⲀⲨⲰ

---

1 MS ⲘⲘⲨⲤⲦⲎⲢⲒⲞⲚ ... ϢⲀϤϢⲰⲠⲈ; read ⲘⲘⲨⲤⲦⲎⲢⲒⲞⲚ ... ϢⲀⲨ·ϢⲰⲠⲈ.

and wise fire which is very powerful and burns sins. And
it goes [1] secretly into the *soul* and consumes all the sins
which the *spirit counterpart* has fixed within it. And when
it has finished *purifying* all the sins which the *spirit counterpart* fixed in it, it goes also into the *body* secretly and it
pursues all the *persecutors* secretly. And it separates them
to the side of the *part* of the *body*. *For* it pursues the
spirit counterpart and the *destiny* and separates them out
of the power and the *soul*, and places them upon the side of
the *body*, *so that* it separates the *spirit counterpart* and the
destiny and the *body* to one *part*. The *soul*, on the other
hand, and the power, it separates to another *part*. The
mystery of the *baptism* remains in the midst of the two
and continues to separate them from one another, so that it
makes them pure, and *purifies* them so that they are not
defiled with *matter. Now* at this time, Maria, this is the
manner in which the *mysteries* of the *baptisms* forgive
sins and all *iniquities*."

116. Now when the *Saviour* had said these things, he
said to his *disciples*: "Do you *understand* in what manner
I am speaking with you?"

Maria sprang up and said: "Yes, my Lord, in truth
I *understand thoroughly* every word which thou dost speak.
Now concerning the discourse on the forgiveness of sins,
thou didst speak to us once in a *parable*, saying: 'I have
come to cast fire upon the earth'*; and | also: 'What will

---

* cf. Lk. 12.49

---

[1] (2, 7) it goes; lit. they go.

ON OY ΠΕ†ΟΥΑϣϥ Ν̄ⲤⲀ ΤΡΕϥΜΟΥ2· ⲀΥⲰ ON ⲀⲔΠΟΡⲭ̄
ⲈⲂⲞⲖ ⲪⲀΝΕΡⲰⲤ ⲈⲔⲬⲰ Μ̄ΜⲞⲤ ⲬⲈ ⲞΥΝ̄ΤⲀⲒ̈ ⲞΥⲂⲀΠΤⲒⲤ-
ΜⲀ Μ̄ΜⲀΥ ⲈⲂⲀΠΤⲒⲌⲈ Ν̄2ΗΤϥ· ⲀΥⲰ Ν̄Ⲁϣ Ν̄2Ε †ΝⲀⲖⲀΝⲈⲬⲈ
ϣⲀΝΤϥⲬⲰⲔ' ⲈⲂⲞⲖ· ⲈΤⲈΤⲚ̄ΜⲈⲈΥⲈ ⲬⲈ Ν̄ΤⲀⲒ̈ⲈⲒ' ⲈΝⲞΥⲬⲈ
5 Ν̄ⲞΥⲈⲒΡΗΝΗ ⲈⲬΜ̄ ΠⲔⲀ2· Μ̄ΜⲞΝ· ⲀⲖⲖⲀ ⲞΥΠⲰΡⲭ̄ ΠⲈ
Ν̄ΤⲀⲒ̈ⲈⲒ' ⲈΝⲞΥⲬⲈ Μ̄ΜⲞϥ· ⲬⲒΝ ΤⲈΝⲞΥ ΓⲀΡ ⲞΥΝ-†ⲞΥ
ΝⲀϣⲰΠⲈ 2Ν̄ ⲞΥΗⲒ̈ Ν̄ⲞΥⲰΤ· ⲞΥΝ-ϣⲞΜΝ̄Τ ΝⲀΠⲰϣ
ⲈⲬΝ̄ ⲤΝⲀΥ· ⲀΥⲰ ⲤΝⲀΥ ⲈⲬΝ̄ ϣⲞΜΝ̄Τ· ΠⲀⲒ̈ ΠⲀⲬⲞⲈⲒⲤ
ΠⲈ ΠϣⲀⲬⲈ Ν̄ΤⲀⲔⲬⲞⲞϥ ⲪⲀΝⲈΡⲰⲤ· ΠϣⲀⲬⲈ ΜⲈΝ Ν̄Τ-
10 ⲀⲔⲬⲞⲞϥ ⲬⲈ Ν̄ΤⲀⲒ̈ⲈⲒ' ⲈΝⲞΥⲬⲈ Ν̄ⲞΥⲔⲰ2Τ ⲈⲬΜ̄ ΠⲔⲀ2·
ⲀΥⲰ ⲞΥ ΠⲈ†ⲞΥⲀϣϥ Ν̄ⲤⲀ ΤΡⲈϥΜⲞΥ2· ⲈΤⲈ ΠⲀⲒ̈ ⟨ΠⲈ⟩ ⲥ̄ⲟⲣ ᵇ
ΠⲀⲬⲞⲈⲒⲤ ⲬⲈ ⲀⲔⲈⲒΝⲈ Ν̄ΜΜΥⲤΤΗΡⲒⲞΝ Ν̄ΤⲈ Ν̄ⲂⲀΠΤⲒⲤΜⲀ
ⲈΠⲔⲞⲤΜⲞⲤ· ⲀΥⲰ ⲞΥ ΠⲈΤⲈ2ΝⲀⲔ' Ν̄ⲤⲀ ΤΡⲈϥⲞΥⲰΜ'
Ⲉ2ⲞΥΝ Ν̄ⲤⲀ Ν̄ΝⲞⲂⲈ ΤΗΡⲞΥ Ν̄ΤⲈΨΥⲬΗ Ν̄ϥⲔⲀⲐⲀΡⲒⲌⲈ
15 Μ̄ΜⲞⲞΥ· ⲀΥⲰ ON ΜΝ̄Ν̄ⲤⲰⲤ ⲀⲔΠⲞΡⲭ̄ϥ ⲈⲂⲞⲖ ⲪⲀΝⲈΡⲰⲤ
ⲈⲔⲬⲰ Μ̄ΜⲞⲤ· ⲬⲈ ⲞΥΝΤⲀⲒ̈ ⲞΥⲂⲀΠΤⲒⲤΜⲀ Μ̄ΜⲀΥ ⲈⲂⲀΠ-
ΤⲒⲌⲈ Ν̄2ΗΤϥ· ⲀΥⲰ Ν̄Ⲁϣ Ν̄2Ε †ΝⲀⲖⲀΝⲈⲬⲈ 2ⲈⲰⲤ ϣⲀΝΤϥ-
ⲬⲰⲔ' ⲈⲂⲞⲖ· ⲈΤⲈ ΠⲀⲒ̈ ΠⲈ ⲬⲈ Ν̄ΓΝⲀϬⲰ ⲀΝ 2Μ̄ ΠⲔⲞⲤΜⲞⲤ
2ⲈⲰⲤ ϣⲀΝΤⲈ Ν̄ⲂⲀΠΤⲒⲤΜⲀ ⲬⲰⲔ' Ν̄ⲤⲈⲔⲀⲐⲀΡⲒⲌⲈ Ν̄ΝⲈ-
20 ΨΥⲬⲞⲞΥⲈ Ν̄ΤⲈⲖⲒⲞⲤ· ⲀΥⲰ ON ΠϣⲀⲬⲈ Ν̄ΤⲀⲔⲬⲞⲞϥ
ⲈΡⲞΝ Μ̄ΠⲒⲞΥⲞⲈⲒϣ ⲬⲈ ⲈΤⲈΤⲚ̄ΜⲈⲈΥⲈ ⲬⲈ Ν̄ΤⲀⲒ̈ⲈⲒ' Ⲉ-
ΝⲞΥⲬⲈ Ν̄ⲞΥⲈⲒΡΗΝΗ ⲈⲬΜ̄ ΠⲔⲀ2· Μ̄ΜⲞΝ· ⲀⲖⲖⲀ ⲞΥΠⲰΡⲭ̄

---

1 MS ⲀⲔΠⲞⲣⲭ̄; read ⲀⲔΠⲞⲣⲭ̄ϥ.
11 MS ΠⲈ omitted.

I except that it burns?' * ¹ And also thou hast *clearly* distin-
guished, saying : 'I have a *baptism* to be *baptised* with, and
how will I *suffer* until it be fulfilled? Do you think that
I have come to cast *peace* upon the earth? No, *but* division
have I come to cast. *For* from this time five will be in one
house, three will be divided against two and two against
three' ᵙ ². This, my Lord, is the word which thou hast said
clearly. Moreover, the word which thou didst say : 'I have
come to cast fire upon the earth and what will I except
that it burns?' ° is this, my Lord : thou hast brought into
the *world* the *mysteries* of *baptism,* and what pleases thee
except that it (the baptism) ³ consumes all the sins of the
soul and *purifies* them? And also after this thou hast distin-
guished *clearly,* saying : 'I have a *baptism* to be *baptised*
with and how will I *suffer* until it be fulfilled?' ᵅ; that is :
thou will not remain in the *world until* the *baptisms* are
completed and the *perfect souls* are *purified.* And furthermore the word which thou didst say to us once : 'Do you
think that I have come to cast *peace* upon the earth? No, *but* |

---

*   cf. Lk. 12.49
ᵙ   cf. Lk. 12.50-52
°   cf. Lk. 12.49
ᵅ   cf. Lk. 12.50

---

¹   (1, 11) except that it burns; Schmidt : that it burns.
²   (6-8) cf. GTh 84.
³   (13) except that it (the baptism) consumes; Schmidt : except that they consume;
Till : is that they consume.

ⲡⲉ ⲛ̄ⲧⲁⲓⲉⲓˋ ⲉⲛⲟⲩϫⲉ ⲙ̄ⲙⲟϥ· ϫⲉ ϫⲓⲛ ⲧⲉⲛⲟⲩ ⲅⲁⲣ ⲟⲩⲛ-
ϯⲟⲩ ⲛⲁϣⲱⲡⲉ ϩⲛ̄ ⲟⲩⲏⲓ̈ ⲛ̄ⲟⲩⲱⲧ· ⲟⲩⲛ-ϣⲟⲙⲛ̄ⲧ ⲛⲁⲡⲱϣ ⲉϫⲛ̄ ⲥⲛⲁⲩ· ⲁⲩⲱ ⲥⲛⲁⲩ ⲉϫⲛ̄ ϣⲟⲙⲛ̄ⲧ· ⲉⲧⲉ ⲡⲁⲓ̈
ⲡⲉ ⲡⲙⲩⲥⲧⲏⲣⲓⲟⲛ ⲛ̄ⲛⲃⲁⲡⲧⲓⲥⲙⲁ**ⲛ̄ⲧⲁⲕⲛ̄ⲧϥ ⲉⲡⲕⲟⲥⲙⲟⲥ· [ⲥⲟⲗ]

5 ⲉⲁϥⲣ̄-ⲟⲩⲡⲱⲣ︤ϫ︥ ϩⲣⲁⲓ̈ ϩⲛ̄ ⲛ̄ⲥⲱⲙⲁ ⲛ̄ⲧⲉ ⲡⲕⲟⲥⲙⲟⲥ ⲉⲃⲟⲗ
ϫⲉ ⲡⲁⲛⲧⲓⲙⲓⲙⲟⲛ ⲙ̄ⲡⲛ︤ⲁ︥ ⲙⲛ̄ ⲡⲥⲱⲙⲁ ⲙⲛ̄ ⲧⲙⲟⲓⲣⲁ· ⲁϥ-
ⲡⲟⲣϫⲟⲩ ⲉⲩⲙⲉⲣⲟⲥ· ⲧⲉⲯⲩⲭⲏ ϩⲱⲱⲥ ⲙⲛ̄ ⲧϭⲟⲙˋ ⲁϥ-
ⲡⲟⲣϫⲟⲩ ⲉⲕⲉⲙⲉⲣⲟⲥ· ⲉⲧⲉ ⲡⲁⲓ̈ ⲡⲉ ϫⲉ ⲟⲩⲛ-ϣⲟⲙⲛ̄ⲧ
ⲛⲁⲡⲱϣ ⲉϫⲛ̄ ⲥⲛⲁⲩ ⲁⲩⲱ ⲥⲛⲁⲩ ⲉϫⲛ̄ ϣⲱⲙⲛ̄ⲧ·

10 ⲛⲁⲓ̈ ⲇⲉ ⲛ̄ⲧⲉⲣⲉⲥϫⲟⲟⲩ ⲛ̄ϭⲓ ⲙⲁⲣⲓⲁ ⲡⲉϫⲁϥ ⲛ̄ϭⲓ ⲡⲥⲱⲧⲏⲣ ϫⲉ ⲉⲩⲅⲉ ⲧⲉⲡⲛ̄ⲛⲓⲕⲏ ⲛ̄ϩⲓⲗⲓⲕⲣⲓⲛⲉⲥ ⲛ̄ⲟⲩⲟⲉⲓⲛ ⲙⲁⲣⲓⲁ
ⲡⲁⲓ̈ ⲡⲉ ⲡⲃⲱⲗ ⲉⲃⲟⲗ ⲙ̄ⲡϣⲁϫⲉ: ⲁⲥⲟⲩⲱϩⲙ ⲟⲛ ⲛ̄ϭⲓ ⲙⲁⲣⲓⲁ ⲡⲉϫⲁⲥ ϫⲉ ⲡⲁϫⲟⲉⲓⲥ ⲉⲧⲓ ⲟⲛ ⲉⲓ̈ⲛⲁⲟⲩⲱϩ ⲉⲧⲟⲟⲧˋ
ⲉϣⲓⲛⲉ ⲙ̄ⲙⲟⲕ· ⲧⲉⲛⲟⲩ ϭⲉ ⲡⲁϫⲟⲉⲓⲥ ⲁⲛⲉⲭⲉ ⲙ̄ⲙⲟⲓ̈ ⲉⲓ̈-

15 ϣⲓⲛⲉ ⲙ̄ⲙⲟⲕ· ⲉⲓⲥϩⲏⲏⲧⲉ ⲙⲉⲛ ϩⲛ̄ ⲟⲩⲡⲁⲣⲣⲏⲥⲓⲁ ⲁⲛⲉⲓⲙⲉ
ⲉⲡⲧⲩⲡⲟⲥ ⲉϣⲁⲣⲉ ⲛ̄ⲃⲁⲡⲧⲓⲥⲙⲁ ⲕⲁⲛⲟⲃⲉ ⲉⲃⲟⲗ· ⲧⲉⲛⲟⲩ
ϩⲱⲱϥ ⲡⲙⲩⲥⲧⲏⲣⲓⲟⲛ ⲙ̄ⲡⲉⲓ̈ϣⲟⲙⲛ̄ⲧ ⲛ̄ⲭⲱⲣⲏⲙⲁ· ⲙⲛ̄ ⲙ̄ⲙⲩⲥ-
ⲧⲏⲣⲓⲟⲛ ⲙ̄ⲡⲉⲓ̈ϣⲟⲣⲡ ⲙ̄ⲙⲩⲥⲧⲏⲣⲓⲟⲛ· ⲙⲛ̄ ⲙ̄ⲙⲩⲥⲧⲏⲣⲓⲟⲛ ⲙ̄ⲡⲓ-
ⲁⲧϣⲁϫⲉ ⲉⲣⲟϥ· ⲉϣⲁⲩⲕⲁⲛⲟⲃⲉ ⲉⲃⲟⲗ ⲛ̄ⲁϣ ⲛ̄ⲧⲩⲡⲟⲥ· [ⲥⲟⲗ]ᵇ

20 ⲉϣⲁⲩⲕⲱ ⲉⲃⲟⲗ ⲙ̄ⲡⲧⲩⲡⲟⲥ ⲛ̄ⲛⲃⲁⲡⲧⲓⲥⲙⲁ ϫⲛ̄ ⲙ̄ⲙⲟⲛ·
ⲁϥⲟⲩⲱϣⲃ ⲟⲛ ⲛ̄ϭⲓ ⲡⲥⲱⲧⲏⲣ ⲡⲉϫⲁϥ ϫⲉ ⲙ̄ⲙⲟⲛ· ⲁⲗⲗⲁ
ⲙ̄ⲙⲩⲥⲧⲏⲣⲓⲟⲛ ⲧⲏⲣⲟⲩ ⲙ̄ⲡϣⲟⲙⲛ̄ⲧ ⲛ̄ⲭⲱⲣⲏⲙⲁ ⲉϣⲁⲩⲕⲱ
ⲉⲃⲟⲗ ϩⲛ̄ ⲧⲉⲯⲩⲭⲏ· ⲁⲩⲱ ⲛ̄ⲧⲟⲡⲟⲥ ⲧⲏⲣⲟⲩ ⲛ̄ⲧⲉ ⲛ̄ⲁⲣ-

---

17 MS ⲡⲙⲩⲥⲧⲏⲣⲓⲟⲛ; read ⲙ̄ⲙⲩⲥⲧⲏⲣⲓⲟⲛ.
22 MS ⲙ̄ⲡϣⲟⲙ︤ⲡⲧ︥ probably originally ⲙ̄ⲡϣⲟⲣⲡ; ⲣⲡ erased, and altered
by later hand to ⲙⲛ̄ⲧ.
23 MS ϩⲛ̄ ⲧⲉⲯⲩⲭⲏ ⲁⲩⲱ ⲛ̄ⲧⲟⲡⲟⲥ ⲧⲏⲣⲟⲩ; read ⲛ̄ⲧⲉⲯⲩⲭⲏ ϩⲛ̄ ⲛ̄ⲧⲟⲡⲟⲥ
ⲧⲏⲣⲟⲩ.

division have I come to cast. *For* from this time five will be in one house, three will be divided against two and two against three' *. This is the *mystery* of the *baptisms* which thou hast brought [1] into the *world*, and it has made a separation in the *bodies* of the *world*, because it has separated the *spirit counterpart* and the *body* and the *destiny* into one *part*. The *soul* on the other hand and the power, it has separated into another *part*. That is, there will be three divided against two and two against three." □

When Maria had said these things, *however*, the *Saviour* said to her : "*Excellent*, thou *spiritual* one of *pure* light, Maria. This is the interpretation of the discourse".

117. Maria answered again and said : "My Lord, *yet* again will I continue to question thee. Now at this time, my Lord, *suffer* me that I question thee. Behold, we have recognised *openly* the *type* in which the *baptisms* forgive sins. Now also the *mysteries* [2] of these three *spaces* and the *mysteries* of this First *Mystery* and the *mysteries* of the Ineffable : in what *type* do they forgive sins? Do they forgive in the *type* of the *baptisms* or not?"

The *Saviour* answered again and said : "No, *but* all the *mysteries* of the three *spaces* forgive the *soul* in all the *places* of the *archons* | for all the sins which the *soul* has

---

* cf. Lk. 12.51, 52

□ cf. Lk. 12.52

---

[1] (3, 4) this is the mystery ... which thou hast brought; Schmidt : thou hast brought the mystery ...

[2] (17) mysteries; MS : mystery.

ⲭⲱⲛ ⲛ̅ⲛ̅ⲛⲟⲃⲉ ⲧⲏⲣⲟⲩ ⲛ̅ⲧⲁⲥⲁⲁⲩ ⲛ̅ϭⲓ ⲧⲉⲯⲩⲭⲏ ϫⲓⲛ
ⲛ̅ϣⲟⲣⲡ̅ ϣⲁⲩⲕⲁⲁⲩ ⲛⲁⲥ ⲉⲃⲟⲗ· ⲁⲩⲱ ⲟⲛ ϣⲁⲩⲕⲱ ⲉⲃⲟⲗ
ⲛ̅ⲛ̅ⲛⲟⲃⲉ ⲉⲧⲥ̅ⲛⲁⲁⲁⲩ ⲙ̅ⲛ̅ⲛ̅ⲥⲁ ⲛⲁⲓ̈· ϩⲉⲱⲥ ϣⲁ ⲡⲉⲟⲩⲟⲉⲓϣ ⲉⲧⲉⲣⲉ ⲡⲟⲩⲁ ⲡⲟⲩⲁ ⲛ̅ⲙ̅ⲙⲩⲥⲧⲏⲣⲓⲟⲛ ⲛⲁⲁⲙⲁϩⲧⲉ
5 ϣⲁⲣⲟϥ· ⲛⲁⲓ̈ †ⲛⲁⲭⲱ ⲉⲣⲱⲧⲛ̅ ⲙ̅ⲡⲉⲩⲟⲉⲓϣ ⲉⲣⲉ ⲡⲟⲩⲁ
ⲡⲟⲩⲁ ⲛ̅ⲙ̅ⲙⲩⲥⲧⲏⲣⲓⲟⲛ ⲛⲁⲁⲙⲁϩⲧⲉ ϣⲁⲣⲟϥ· ϩⲣⲁⲓ̈ ϩⲙ̅
ⲡⲥⲱⲣ ⲉⲃⲟⲗ ⲙ̅ⲡⲧⲏⲣϥ̅· ⲁⲩⲱ ⲟⲛ ⲡⲙⲩⲥⲧⲏⲣⲓⲟⲛ ⲙ̅ⲡⲓ-
ϣⲟⲣⲡ̅ ⲙ̅ⲙⲩⲥⲧⲏⲣⲓⲟⲛ· ⲙ̅ⲛ̅ ⲙ̅ⲙⲩⲥⲧⲏⲣⲓⲟⲛ ⲙ̅ⲡⲓⲁⲧϣⲁϫⲉ
ⲉⲣⲟϥ ⲉϣⲁⲩⲕⲱ ⲉⲃⲟⲗ ⲛ̅ⲧⲉⲯⲩⲭⲏ ϩⲛ̅ ⲛ̅ⲧⲟⲡⲟⲥ ⲧⲏⲣⲟⲩ
10 ⲛ̅ⲧⲉ ⲛⲁⲣⲭⲱⲛ· ⲛⲟⲃⲉ ⲛⲓⲙ' ⲙ̅ⲛ̅ ⲁⲛⲟⲙⲓⲁ ⲛⲓⲙ' ⲛ̅ⲧⲁⲥⲁⲁⲩ
ⲛ̅ϭⲓ ⲧⲉⲯⲩⲭⲏ· ⲁⲩⲱ ⲟⲛ ϫⲉ ϣⲁⲩⲕⲁⲁⲩ ⲧⲏⲣⲟⲩ ⲛⲁⲥ
ⲉⲃⲟⲗ·** ⲁⲗⲗⲁ ⲙⲉⲩⲉⲡ-ⲛⲟⲃⲉ ⲉⲣⲟⲥ ϫⲓⲛ ⲡⲉⲓ̈ⲛⲁⲩ ϩⲉⲱⲥ ⲥ̅ⲟⲉ
ϣⲁⲉⲛⲉϩ ⲛ̅ⲉⲛⲉϩ· ⲉⲧⲃⲉ ⲧⲇⲱⲣⲉⲁ ⲙ̅ⲡⲛⲟϭ ⲙ̅ⲙⲩⲥⲧⲏⲣⲓⲟⲛ
ⲉⲧⲙ̅ⲙⲁⲩ· ⲙ̅ⲛ̅ ⲡⲉⲩⲉⲟⲟⲩ ⲉⲧⲛⲁϣⲱϥ ⲉⲙⲁϣⲟ ⲉⲙⲁϣⲟ·
15 ⲛⲁⲓ̈ ϭⲉ ⲛ̅ⲧⲉⲣⲉϥϫⲟⲟⲩ ⲛ̅ϭⲓ ⲡⲥⲱⲧⲏⲣ ⲡⲉϫⲁϥ ⲛ̅ⲛⲉϥ-
ⲙⲁⲑⲏⲧⲏⲥ ϫⲉ ⲧⲉⲧⲛ̅ⲛⲟⲓ̈ ϫⲉ ⲉⲓ̈ϣⲁϫⲉ ⲛ̅ⲙ̅ⲙⲏⲧⲛ̅ ⲛ̅ⲁϣ
ⲛ̅ϩⲉ· ⲁⲥⲟⲩⲱϣⲃ̅ ⲟⲛ ⲛ̅ϭⲓ ⲙⲁⲣⲓⲁ ⲡⲉϫⲁⲥ ϫⲉ ⲥⲉ ⲡⲁⲭⲟ-
ⲉⲓⲥ· ⲁⲓ̈ⲟⲩⲱ ⲉⲓ̈ϩⲁⲣⲡⲁⲍⲉ ⲛ̅ϣⲁϫⲉ ⲛⲓⲙ' ⲉⲧⲕ̅ϫⲱ ⲙ̅ⲙⲟⲟⲩ·
ⲧⲉⲛⲟⲩ ϭⲉ ⲟⲩⲛ ⲡⲁⲭⲟⲉⲓⲥ ⲉⲧⲃⲉ ⲡϣⲁϫⲉ ⲉⲧⲕ̅ϫⲱ ⲙ̅-
20 ⲙⲟϥ ϫⲉ ϣⲁⲣⲉ ⲙ̅ⲙⲩⲥⲧⲏⲣⲓⲟⲛ ⲧⲏⲣⲟⲩ ⲙ̅ⲡϣⲟⲙⲛⲧ ⲛ̅ⲭⲱ-
ⲣⲏⲙⲁ ϣⲁⲩⲕⲁⲛⲟⲃⲉ ⲉⲃⲟⲗ· ⲁⲩⲱ ⲛ̅ⲥⲉϩⲱⲃⲥ̅ ⲉⲃⲟⲗ' ⲉϫⲛ̅
ⲛⲉⲩⲁⲛⲟⲙⲓⲁ· ⲛ̅ⲧⲁϥⲡⲣⲟⲫⲏⲧⲉⲩⲉ ⲟⲩⲛ ⲙ̅ⲡⲓⲟⲩⲟⲉⲓϣ ϩⲁ
ⲡⲉⲓ̈ϣⲁϫⲉ ⲛ̅ϭⲓ ⲇⲁⲅⲉⲓⲇ' ⲡⲉⲡⲣⲟⲫⲏⲧⲏⲥ· ⲉϥϫⲱ ⲙ̅ⲙⲟⲥ·
ϫⲉ ⲛⲁⲓ̈ⲁⲧⲟⲩ ⲛ̅ⲛⲉⲛⲧⲁⲩⲕⲱ ⲉⲃⲟⲗ ⲛ̅ⲛⲉⲩⲛⲟⲃⲉ· ⲙ̅ⲛ̅
25 ⲛⲉⲛⲧⲁⲩϩⲱⲃⲥ̅ ⲉⲃⲟⲗ' ⲉϫⲛ̅ ⲛⲉⲩⲁⲛⲟⲙⲓⲁ· ⲛ̅ⲧⲁϥⲡⲣⲟⲫⲏ-

---

11   MS ⲁⲩⲱ ⲟⲛ; read ⲁⲩⲱ ⟨ⲟⲩⲙⲟⲛ⟩ⲟⲛ.

committed from the beginning. They forgive it for them, and also they forgive the sins which it will commit afterwards *up to* the time as far as which each one of the *mysteries* will be powerful. The time, as far as which each one of the *mysteries* will be powerful, I will say to you at the distribution of the All. And again, the *mystery* of the First *Mystery* and the *mysteries* of the Ineffable forgive the *soul* in all the *places* of the *archons* for all the sins and all the *iniquities* which the *soul* has committed. And (not only) do they forgive it for them all, *but* they do not reckon sin to it from this time *until* eternity, because of the *gift* of that great *mystery* and its exceedingly great glories [1]."

118. Now when the *Saviour* had said these things, he said to his *disciples*: "Do you *understand* the manner in which I speak to you?"

Maria answered again and said: "Yes, my Lord, I have already *grasped* every word which thou sayest. *Now* at this time, my Lord, concerning the word which thou didst speak: 'All the *mysteries* of the three *spaces* forgive sins and cover over their (the soul's) *iniquities*'; *now* about this word David the *prophet prophesied* once, saying: 'Blessed are they whose sins are forgiven, and those whose *iniquities* are covered' *. [*Now* he has *prophesied* | once upon this word].

---

* Ps. 31.1

---

[1] (14) its ... glories; lit. their glory.

ΤΕΥΕ *ΟΥΝ ᲖᲐ ΠΕΪϢᲐΧΕ ‾ΜΠΙΟΥΟΕΙϢ· ᲐΥϢ ΠϢᲐΧΕ ‾ϹΟΕ ᵇ

‾ΝΤᲐΚΧΟΟᲘ ΧΕ ΠΜΥϹΤΗΡΙΟΝ ‾ΝΤΕ ΠΙϢΟΡΠ ‾ΜΜΥϹΤΗ-

ΡΙΟΝ ‾ΜΝ ΠΜΥϹΤΗΡΙΟΝ ‾ΜΠΙᲐΤϢᲐΧΕ ΕΡΟᲘ ΧΕ ΡϢΜΕ

ΝΙΜ' ΕΤΝᲐΧΙ ‾ΝΜΜΥϹΤΗΡΙΟΝ ΕΤ‾ΜΜᲐΥ· ΟΥΜΟΝΟΝ ΧΕ

5　ϢᲐΥΚϢ ΕΒΟᲚ ‾ΝΝΟΒΕ ‾ΝΤᲐΥᲐᲐΥ ΧΙΝ ‾ΝϢΟΡΠ· ᲐᲚᲚᲐ

ΜΕΥ‾Ρ-ΠΚΕϢΠ' ΡϢ ΕΡΟΟΥ ΧΙΝ ‾ΜΠΕΪΝᲐΥ ϢᲐΕΝΕᲖ· ΕΤΒΕ

ΠΕΪϢᲐΧΕ ΟΝ ‾ΝΤᲐᲘΠΡΟΦΗΤΕΥΕ ᲖᲐΡΟᲘ ‾ΜΠΙΟΥΟΕΙϢ

‾ΝᲜΙ ᲚᲐΥΕΙᲐ' ΕᲘΧϢ ‾ΜΜΟϹ ΧΕ ΝᲐΪᲐΤΟΥ ‾ΝΝΕΤΕ ‾Μ-

ΠΧΟΕΙϹ ΠΝΟΥΤΕ ΝᲐΕΠ-ΝΟΒΕ ΕΡΟΟΥ ᲐΝ· ΕΤΕ ΠᲐΪ ΠΕ

10　‾ΝϹΕΝᲐΕΠ-ΝΟΒΕ ΕΡΟᲘ ᲐΝ ΧΙΝ ΠΕΪΝᲐΥ· ‾ΝΕΡΧΙ ‾ΝΜΜΥϹ-

ΤΗΡΙΟΝ ‾ΜΠΙϢΟΡΠ ‾ΜΜΥϹΤΗΡΙΟΝ ‾ΜΝ ‾ΝΕΡΧΙ ‾ΝΜΜΥϹΤΗ-

ΡΙΟΝ ‾ΜΠΙᲐΤϢᲐΧΕ ΕΡΟᲘ· ΠΕΧᲐᲘ ΧΕ ΕΥΓΕ ΤΕΠΝΙΚΗ

‾ΝᲖΙᲚΙΚΡΙΝΕϹ ‾ΝΟΥΟΕΙΝ ΜᲐΡΙᲐ ΠᲐΪ ΠΕ ΠΒϢᲚ ΕΒΟᲚ ‾Μ-

ΠϢᲐΧΕ· ᲐϹΟΥϢᲖ ΟΝ ΕΤΟΟ‾ΤϹ ‾ΝᲜΙ ΜᲐΡΙᲐ ΠΕΧᲐϹ ΧΕ

15　ΠᲐΧΟΕΙϹ· ΕΪΕ ΕΡϢᲐΝ ΠΡϢΜΕ ΧΙ-ΜΥϹΤΗΡΙΟΝ ᲖΝ ‾Μ-

ΜΥϹΤΗΡΙΟΝ ‾ΜΠΙϢΟΡΠ ‾ΜΜΥϹΤΗΡΙΟΝ ** ᲐΥϢ ΟΝ ‾ΝᲘΚΟΤᲘ　‾[ϹΟΕ

‾ΝᲘΡΝΟΒΕ ‾ΝᲘΠᲐΡᲐΒᲐ· ᲐΥϢ ΟΝ ‾ΜΝ‾ΝϹᲐ ΝᲐΪ ‾ΝᲘΚΟΤᲘ

‾ΝᲘΜΕΤᲐΝΟΪ ᲐΥϢ ‾ΝᲘΠΡΟϹΕΥΧΕ ᲖΜ ΠΕᲘΜΥϹΤΗΡΙΟΝ

ΠΕᲘΜΥϹΤΗΡΙΟΝ ϹΕΝᲐΚϢ ΝᲐᲘ ΕΒΟᲚ ‾ΧΝ ΜΜΟΝ· ᲐᲘΟΥ-

20　ϢᲖΜ ‾ΝᲜΙ ΠϹϢΤΗΡ ΠΕΧᲐᲘ ‾ΜΜᲐΡΙᲐ ΧΕ ᲖᲐΜΗΝ ᲖᲐΜΗΝ

†ΧϢ ‾ΜΜΟϹ ΝΗ‾ΤΝ ΧΕ ΟΥΟΝ ΝΙΜ ΕΤΝᲐΧΙ ‾ΝΜΜΥϹΤΗ-

ΡΙΟΝ ‾ΜΠΙϢΟΡΠ ‾ΜΜΥϹΤΗΡΙΟΝ· ᲐΥϢ ΟΝ ‾ΝᲘΚΟΤᲘ ‾ΝᲘ-

ΠᲐΡᲐΒᲐ ‾ΜΜ‾ΝΤϹΝΟΟΥϹ ‾ΝϹΟΠ ᲐΥϢ ΟΝ ‾ΝᲘΜΕΤᲐΝΟΪ ‾ΙΒ

‾ΝϹΟΠ ΕᲘΠΡΟϹΕΥΧΕ ᲖΜ ΠΜΥϹΤΗΡΙΟΝ ‾ΜΠΙϢΟΡΠ ‾ΜΜΥϹ-

10　MS ΕΡΟᲘ; read ΕΡΟΟΥ.

17　MS ‾ΝᲘΡΠΟΒΕ; Ი inserted above.

23　ᲐΥϢ ΟΝ . . . ‾ΝϹΟΠ written below in margin.

And the word which thou didst speak : 'The *mystery* of the First *Mystery* and the *mystery* of the Ineffable, all men who will receive those *mysteries*, *not only* do they forgive the sins which they have committed from the beginning, *but* they also do not reckon them to them from this time for ever' : concerning this word David once *prophesied* about it, saying : 'Blessed are they to whom the Lord God does not reckon sin' *; that is, from this time sins will not be reckoned to those who receive the *mysteries* of the First *Mystery* and who receive the *mysteries* of the Ineffable."

He said : "*Excellent*, thou *spiritual* one of *pure* light, Maria. This is the interpretation of the discourse."

Maria continued again and said : "My Lord, if the man receives *mysteries* from the *mysteries* of the First *Mystery* and he turns again and sins and *transgresses*, and again after this he turns and *repents*, and he *prays* in each of his *mysteries*, will he be forgiven or not?"

The *Saviour* answered and said to Maria : "*Truly, truly,* I say to you, everyone who will receive the *mysteries* of the First *Mystery*, and turns again and *transgresses* twelve times, and again he *repents* twelve times and he prays in the *mystery* of the First *Mystery*, | he will be forgiven.

---

* Ps. 31.2

ⲦⲎⲢⲒⲞⲚ ⲤⲈⲚⲀⲔⲰ ⲚⲀϤ ⲈⲂⲞⲖ· ⲀⲨⲰ ⲞⲚ Ⲛ̄ⲤⲈⲠⲀⲢⲀⲂⲀ
Ⲙ̄Ⲛ̄ⲤⲀ ⲠⲘⲚ̄ⲦⲤⲚⲞⲞⲨⲤ Ⲛ̄ⲤⲞⲠ Ⲛ̄ϤⲔⲞⲦϤ Ⲛ̄ϤⲠⲀⲢⲀⲂⲀ Ⲛ̄-
ⲤⲈⲚⲀⲔⲰ ⲚⲀϤ ⲈⲂⲞⲖ ⲀⲚ ϢⲀⲈⲚⲈⲊ· ⲈⲦⲢⲈϤⲔⲞⲦϤ ⲈⲠⲈϤ-
ⲘⲨⲤⲦⲎⲢⲒⲞⲚ ⲠⲈϤⲘⲨⲤⲦⲎⲢⲒⲞⲚ· ⲀⲨⲰ ⲠⲀⲒ̈ Ⲙ̄Ⲛ̄Ⲧϥ-ⲘⲈⲦⲀ-
5 ⲚⲞⲒⲀ Ⲙ̄ⲘⲀⲨ· ⲈⲒⲘⲎⲦⲒ Ⲛ̄Ϥ ϪⲒ Ⲛ̄ⲘⲘⲨⲤⲦⲎⲢⲒⲞⲚ Ⲙ̄ⲠⲒⲀⲦϢⲀϪⲈ
ⲈⲢⲞϤ· ⲠⲀⲒ̈ ⲈϢⲀϤⲚⲀ Ⲛ̄ⲞⲨⲞⲈⲒϢ ⲚⲒⲘ· ⲀⲨⲰ ⲞⲚ Ⲛ̄ϤⲔⲰ
ⲈⲂⲞⲖ Ⲛ̄ⲞⲨⲞⲈⲒϢ ⲚⲒⲘ·

ⲀⲤⲞⲨⲰϨ ⲞⲚ ⲈⲦⲞⲞⲦⲤ̄ Ⲛ̄ϬⲒ ⲘⲀⲢⲒⲀ ⲠⲈϪⲀⲤ· ϪⲈ ⲠⲀ-
ϪⲞⲈⲒⲤ ⲈϢⲰⲠⲈ ⲆⲈ Ⲛ̄ⲦⲞϤ Ⲛ̄ⲈⲢϪⲒ Ⲛ̄ⲘⲘⲨⲤⲦⲎⲢⲒⲞⲚ Ⲙ̄ⲠⲒ-
10 ϢⲞⲢⲠ̄ Ⲙ̄ⲘⲨⲤⲦⲎⲢⲒⲞⲚ· ⲀⲨⲰ Ⲛ̄ⲤⲈⲔⲞⲦⲞⲨ Ⲛ̄ⲤⲈⲠⲀⲢⲀⲂⲀ
ⲀⲨⲰ Ⲛ̄ⲤⲈⲈⲒ' ⲈⲂⲞⲖ *Ϩ̄Ⲛ ⲤⲰⲘⲀ ⲈⲘⲠⲞⲨⲘⲈⲦⲀⲚⲞⲒ̈· ⲤⲈⲚⲀ- [Ⲥⲟⲉ ᵇ
ⲔⲖⲎⲢⲞⲚⲞⲘⲒ Ⲛ̄ⲦⲘⲚ̄ⲦⲢ̄ⲢⲞ Ϫ̄Ⲛ Ⲙ̄ⲘⲞⲚ· ϪⲈ ⲀⲨϪⲒ ⲢⲰ Ⲛ̄-
ⲦⲀⲰⲢⲈⲀ Ⲙ̄ⲠⲒϢⲞⲢⲠ̄ Ⲙ̄ⲘⲨⲤⲦⲎⲢⲒⲞⲚ· ⲀϤⲞⲨⲰϨⲘ̄ Ⲛ̄ϬⲒ ⲠⲤⲰ-
ⲦⲎⲢ ⲠⲈϪⲀϤ Ⲙ̄ⲘⲀⲢⲒⲀ· ϪⲈ ϨⲀⲘⲎⲚ ϨⲀⲘⲎⲚ †ϪⲰ Ⲙ̄ⲘⲞⲤ
15 ⲚⲎⲦⲚ̄ ϪⲈ ⲢⲰⲘⲈ ⲚⲒⲘ' ⲈⲢϪⲒ-ⲘⲨⲤⲦⲎⲢⲒⲞⲚ Ϩ̄Ⲙ ⲠϢⲞⲢⲠ̄ Ⲙ̄-
ⲘⲨⲤⲦⲎⲢⲒⲞⲚ ⲈⲀϤⲠⲀⲢⲀⲂⲀ Ⲙ̄ⲠϢⲞⲢⲠ̄ Ⲛ̄ⲤⲞⲠ Ⲙ̄Ⲛ ⲠⲘⲈϨⲤⲚⲀⲨ
Ⲙ̄Ⲛ ⲠⲘⲈϨϢⲞⲘⲚ̄Ⲧ ⲀⲨⲰ ⲠⲀⲒ̈ Ⲛ̄ϤⲈⲒ' ⲈⲂⲞⲖ Ϩ̄Ⲛ ⲤⲰⲘⲀ ⲈⲘ-
ⲠϤⲘⲈⲦⲀⲚⲞⲒ̈· ⲦⲈϤⲔⲢⲒⲤⲒⲤ ⲞⲨⲞⲦⲂ̄ Ⲛ̄ϨⲞⲨⲞ ⲠⲀⲢⲀ ⲔⲢⲒⲤⲒⲤ
ⲚⲒⲘ· ⲠⲈϤⲘⲀⲚ̄ϢⲰⲠⲈ ⲄⲀⲢ ⲠⲈ Ϩ̄Ⲛ ⲦⲘⲎⲦⲈ Ⲛ̄ⲦⲦⲀⲠⲢⲞ Ⲙ̄-
20 ⲠⲈⲆⲢⲀⲔⲰⲚ Ⲙ̄ⲠⲔⲀⲔⲈ ⲈⲦϨⲒⲂⲞⲖ· ⲀⲨⲰ Ⲛ̄ϨⲀⲈ Ⲛ̄ⲚⲀⲒ̈ ⲦⲎⲢⲞⲨ
ϤⲚⲀⲢ̄-ϨⲢⲞⲨⲞⲨϪⲨ̄ϥ Ϩ̄Ⲛ Ⲛ̄ⲔⲞⲖⲀⲤⲒⲤ· ⲀⲨⲰ Ⲛ̄ϤⲀⲚϨⲀⲖⲒⲤⲔⲈ
Ⲛ̄ϢⲀⲈⲚⲈϨ· ϪⲈ ⲀϤϪⲒ Ϩ̄Ⲛ ⲦⲀⲰⲢⲈⲀ Ⲙ̄ⲠⲒϢⲞⲢⲠ̄ Ⲙ̄ⲘⲨⲤⲦⲎ-
ⲢⲒⲞⲚ Ⲙ̄ⲠϤϬⲰ Ⲛ̄ϨⲎⲦⲤ̄·

ⲀⲤⲞⲨⲰϨⲘ̄ Ⲛ̄ϬⲒ ⲘⲀⲢⲒⲀ ⲠⲈϪⲀⲤ ϪⲈ ⲠⲀϪⲞⲈⲒⲤ ⲈⲒ̈Ⲉ ⲢⲰⲘⲈ
25 ⲚⲒⲘ' ⲈⲦⲚⲀϪⲒ-ⲘⲨⲤⲦⲎⲢⲒⲞⲚ Ⲙ̄ⲠⲘⲨⲤⲦⲎⲢⲒⲞⲚ Ⲙ̄ⲠⲒⲀⲦϢⲀϪⲈ
ⲈⲢⲞϤ· ⲀⲨⲰ ⲀⲨⲠⲀⲢⲀⲂⲀ ⲀⲨⲖⲞ Ϩ̄Ⲛ ⲦⲈⲨⲠⲒⲤⲦⲒⲤ· ⲀⲨⲰ ⲞⲚ

---

1 MS Ⲛ̄ⲤⲈⲠⲀⲢⲀⲂⲀ; read Ⲛ̄ϤⲠⲀⲢⲀⲂⲀ.
24 MS originally ⲀϤⲞⲨⲰϨⲘ̄; ϥ crossed out and ⲥ inserted above.

And if he *transgresses* again after the twelfth time and turns
and *transgresses*, he will not be forgiven for ever that he
should turn to each of his *mysteries*. And this (man) has
no *repentance*, *except* he receive the *mysteries* of the Ineffable
who is merciful at all times and forgives at [1] all times."

119. Maria continued again and said : "My Lord, *but*
if those who receive the mysteries of the First *Mystery*
turn and *transgress* and come forth from the *body* before
repenting, will they *inherit* the kingdom or not? Because
they have indeed received the *gift* of the First *Mystery*."

The *Saviour* answered, he said to Maria : "*Truly, truly,*
I say to you, every man who receives *mysteries* in the First
Mystery and has *transgressed* the first time, and the second,
and the third, if he comes forth from the *body* before
repenting, his *judgment* exceeds *beyond* all *judgments*. *For*
his dwelling-place is in the midst of the jaws of the *dragon*
of the outer darkness. And at the end of all these things,
he will perish in the *punishments*, and he will be *consumed*
for ever, because he has received from the *gift* of the First
Mystery and he has not remained in it."

Maria answered and said : "My Lord, all men who will
receive *mysteries* of the *mystery* of the Ineffable, and have
transgressed, and have ceased in their *faith*, and again |

---

[1] (6) who is merciful ... and forgives; Schmidt : which are merciful ... and
forgive.

ⲙⲛⲛⲥⲁ ⲛⲁⲓ ⲁⲓⲧⲓ ⲉⲩⲟⲛⲍ̅ ⲁⲩⲕⲟⲧⲟⲩ ⲁⲩⲙⲉⲧⲁⲛⲟⲓ ⲥⲉ-
ⲛⲁⲕⲱ ⲛⲁⲩ ⲉⲃⲟⲗ ⲛ̅ⲁⲟⲩⲏⲣ ⲛ̅ⲥⲟⲡ · ⲁ ϥⲟⲩ ⲱ ⲍ̅ⲙ ⲛ̅ϭⲓ ⲡⲥⲱⲣ   ⲥ̅ⲟ̅ⲍ̅
ⲡⲉⲭⲁ ϥ ⲙ̅ⲙⲁⲣⲓⲁ · ⲭⲉ ⲍⲁⲙⲏⲛ ⲍⲁⲙⲏⲛ ϯ ⲭ ⲱ ⲙ̅ⲙⲟⲥ ⲛⲏⲧⲛ
ⲭⲉ ⲣⲱⲙⲉ ⲛⲓⲙ · ⲉⲧⲛⲁ ⲭ ⲓ ⲛ̅ⲙⲙⲩⲥⲧⲏⲣⲓⲟⲛ ⲙ̅ⲡⲓⲁⲧ ⲱ ⲁ ⲭⲉ
5 ⲉⲣⲟ ϥ · ⲟⲩⲙⲟⲛⲟⲛ ⲉ ϥ ⲱ ⲁⲛⲡⲁⲣⲁⲃⲁ ⲛ̅ⲟⲩⲥⲟⲡ · ⲁⲩ ⲱ ⲟⲛ
ⲛ̅ ϥ ⲕⲟⲧ ϥ ⲛ̅ ϥ ⲙⲉⲧⲁⲛⲟⲓ ⲥⲉⲛⲁⲕ ⲱ ⲛⲁ ϥ ⲉⲃⲟⲗ · ⲁⲗⲗⲁ ⲉ ϥ -
ⲱ ⲁⲛⲡⲁⲣⲁⲃⲁ ⲛ̅ⲟⲩⲟⲓ ⲱ ⲛⲓⲙ · ⲁⲩ ⲱ ⲟⲛ ⲉⲧⲓ ⲉ ϥ ⲟⲛ ⲍ̅ ⲛ̅ ϥ -
ⲕⲟⲧ ϥ ⲛ̅ ϥ ⲙⲉⲧⲁⲛⲟⲓ ⲡⲁⲓ ⲉⲛ ϥ ⲱⲟⲟⲡ ⲁⲛ ⲍ̅ⲛ ⲟⲩⲍⲩⲡⲟⲕⲣⲓ-
ⲥⲓⲥ · ⲁⲩ ⲱ ⲟⲛ ⲛ̅ ϥ ⲕⲟⲧ ϥ ⲛ̅ ϥ ⲙⲉⲧⲁⲛⲟⲓ · ⲁⲩ ⲱ ⲛ̅ ϥ ⲡⲣⲟⲥⲉⲩ ⲭ ⲉ
10 ⲍ̅ⲛ ⲛⲉ ϥ ⲙⲩⲥⲧⲏⲣⲓⲟⲛ ⲛⲉ ϥ ⲙⲩⲥⲧⲏⲣⲓⲟⲛ · ⲥⲉⲛⲁⲕ ⲱ ⲛⲁ ϥ ⲉⲃⲟⲗ
ⲛ̅ⲟⲩⲟⲉⲓ ⲱ ⲛⲓⲙ · ⲉⲃⲟⲗ ⲭⲉ ⲁ ϥ ⲭ ⲓ ⲉⲃⲟⲗ ⲍ̅ⲛ ⲧⲁ ⲱ ⲣⲉⲁ ⲛ̅ⲙ-
ⲙⲩⲥⲧⲏⲣⲓⲟⲛ ⲙ̅ⲡⲓⲁⲧ ⲱ ⲁ ⲭⲉ ⲉⲣⲟ ϥ · ⲁⲩ ⲱ ⲟⲛ ⲉⲃⲟⲗ ⲭⲉ
ⲍⲉⲛⲛⲁⲏⲧ ⲛⲉ ⲙ̅ⲙⲩⲥⲧⲏⲣⲓⲟⲛ ⲉⲧⲙ̅ⲙⲁⲩ · ⲁⲩ ⲱ ⲍⲉⲛⲣⲉ ϥ ⲕ ⲱ
ⲉⲃⲟⲗ ⲛⲉ ⲛ̅ⲟⲩⲟⲉⲓ ⲱ ⲛⲓⲙ ·
15 ⲁⲥⲟⲩ ⲱ ⲍ̅ⲙ ⲟⲛ ⲛ̅ϭⲓ ⲙⲁⲣⲓⲁ ⲡⲉⲭⲁⲥ ⲛ̅ ⲓ̅ⲥ̅ ⲭⲉ ⲡⲁ ⲭ ⲟⲉⲓⲥ ·
ⲉⲓⲉ ⲛⲉⲣ ⲭ ⲓ ⲛ̅ⲙⲙⲩⲥⲧⲏⲣⲓⲟⲛ ⲙ̅ⲡⲓⲁⲧ ⲱ ⲁ ⲭⲉ ⲉⲣⲟ ϥ · ⲁⲩ ⲱ
ⲟⲛ ⲁⲩⲕⲟⲧⲟⲩ ⲁⲩⲡⲁⲣⲁⲃⲁ ⲁⲩⲗⲟ ⲍ̅ⲛ ⲧⲉⲩⲡⲓⲥⲧⲓⲥ · ⲁⲩ ⲱ
ⲟⲛ ⲁⲩⲉⲓ ⲉⲃⲟⲗ ⲍ̅ⲙ ⲡⲥ ⲱ ⲙⲁ ⲉⲙⲡⲟⲩⲙⲉⲧⲁⲛⲟⲓ · ⲟⲩ ⲟⲛ ⲥ̅ⲟ̅ⲍ̅ ᵇ
ⲡⲉⲧⲛⲁ ⲱ ⲱⲡⲉ ⲛ̅ⲛⲁⲓ ⲛ̅ⲧⲉⲓⲙⲓⲛⲉ · ⲁ ϥ ⲟⲩ ⲱ ⲍ̅ⲙ ⲇⲉ ⲛ̅ϭⲓ ⲡⲥ ⲱ -
20 ⲧⲏⲣ ⲡⲉⲭⲁ ϥ ⲙ̅ⲙⲁⲣⲓⲁ · ⲭⲉ ⲍⲁⲙⲏⲛ ⲍⲁⲙⲏⲛ ϯ ⲭ ⲱ ⲙ̅ⲙⲟⲥ
ⲛⲏⲧ̅ⲛ · ⲭⲉ ⲣⲱⲙⲉ ⲛⲓⲙ · ⲉⲧⲛⲁ ⲭ ⲓ ⲍ̅ⲛ ⲙ̅ⲙⲩⲥⲧⲏⲣⲓⲟⲛ ⲙ̅ⲡⲓ-
ⲁⲧ ⲱ ⲁ ⲭⲉ ⲉⲣⲟ ϥ · ⲍⲉⲛⲙⲁⲕⲁⲣⲓⲟⲥ ⲛⲉ ⲙⲉⲛⲧⲟⲓⲅⲉ ⲛⲉ ⲯ ⲩ-
ⲭ ⲟⲟⲩⲉ ⲉⲧⲛⲁ ⲭ ⲓ ⲍ̅ⲛ ⲙ̅ⲙⲩⲥⲧⲏⲣⲓⲟⲛ ⲉⲧⲙ̅ⲙⲁⲩ · ⲁⲗⲗⲁ ⲉⲩ-
ⲱ ⲁⲛⲕⲟⲧⲟⲩ ⲛ̅ⲥⲉⲡⲁⲣⲁⲃⲁ ⲁⲩ ⲱ ⲛ̅ⲥⲉⲉⲓ ⲉⲃⲟⲗ ⲍ̅ⲛ ⲥ ⲱ ⲙⲁ
25 ⲉⲙⲡⲟⲩⲙⲉⲧⲁⲛⲟⲓ · ⲛ̅ⲣⲱⲙⲉ ⲉⲧⲙ̅ⲙⲁⲩ ⲧⲉⲩⲕⲣⲓⲥⲓⲥ ⲍⲟⲟⲩ
ⲉⲍⲟⲩⲉ ⲕⲣⲓⲥⲓⲥ ⲛⲓⲙ · ⲁⲩ ⲱ ⲟⲩⲛⲟϭ ⲧⲉ ⲉⲙⲁ ⲱ ⲟ ⲉⲙⲁ ⲱ ⲟ ·
ⲕⲁⲛ ⲉ ⲱ ⲱⲡⲉ ⲛⲉ ⲯ ⲩ ⲭ ⲟⲟⲩⲉ ⲉⲧⲙ̅ⲙⲁⲩ ⲉⲍⲉⲛⲃ̅ⲣⲣⲉ ⲛⲉ ·

---

27   MS ⲉⲍⲉⲛⲃ̅ⲣⲣⲉ; read ⲍⲉⲛⲃ̅ⲣⲣⲉ.

after these things, while they are *still* living, have turned and have *repented*, how many times will they be forgiven?"

The *Saviour* answered and said to Maria : "*Truly, truly,* I say to you, every man who will receive the *mysteries* of the *Ineffable, not only* if he *transgresses* once and again turns and *repents* will he be forgiven, *but* every time if he *transgresses* and while he is *still* living he turns again and *repents*, and this is not in *hypocrisy*. And if he turns and *repents* and *prays* in each of his *mysteries* he will be forgiven every time, because he has received from the *gift* of the *mysteries* of the Ineffable, and also because those *mysteries* are merciful and forgiving at all times."

Maria answered and said to Jesus : "My Lord, those who receive the *mysteries* of the Ineffable, and have turned again and *transgressed* and ceased in their *faith*, and furthermore have come forth from the *body* before they *repented*, what will happen to such as these?"

The *Saviour however* answered and said to Maria : "*Truly, truly*, I say to you, all men who will receive from the *mysteries* of the Ineffable, the *souls* which will receive from those *mysteries* are *certainly blessed. But* if they turn and *transgress* and come forth from the *body* before *repenting*, the *judgment* of those men is much worse than all *judgments,* and it is exceedingly severe. *Even if* those *souls* are new, | and it is

611

ⲀⲨⲰ ⲈⲠⲈⲨϢⲞⲢⲠ̄ Ⲛ̄ⲤⲞⲠ ⲠⲈ Ⲛ̄ⲈⲒˀ ⲈⲠⲔⲞⲤⲘⲞⲤ· Ⲛ̄ⲤⲈⲚⲀ-
ⲔⲞⲦⲞⲨ ⲀⲚ ⲈⲘⲘⲈⲦⲀⲂⲞⲖⲎ Ⲙ̄ⲠⲔⲞⲤⲘⲞⲤ Ⲛ̄ⲦⲈ Ⲛ̄ⲤⲰⲘⲀ
ⲬⲒⲚ ⲠⲈⲒ̈ⲚⲀⲨ ⲀⲨⲰ ⲘⲈⲨⲈϢⲢ̄-ⲖⲀⲀⲨ Ⲛ̄Ⲁ̄ⲰⲂ· ⲀⲖⲖⲀ ⲈϢⲀⲨ-
ⲚⲞⲬⲞⲨ ⲈⲠⲤⲀⲚ̄ⲂⲞⲖ· ⲈⲠⲔⲀⲔⲈ ⲈⲦⲀ̄ⲒⲂⲞⲖˀ ⲀⲨⲰ Ⲛ̄ⲤⲈⲀⲚⲀ̄-
5 ⲖⲒⲤⲔⲈ Ⲛ̄ⲤⲈⲢ̄ⲀⲦϢⲰⲠⲈ ϢⲀⲈⲚⲈⲀ̄·

ⲚⲀⲒ̈ ⲆⲈ Ⲛ̄ⲦⲈⲢⲈϤⲬⲞⲞⲨ Ⲛ̄ϬⲒ ⲠⲤⲰ̈ⲦⲎⲢ ⲠⲈⲬⲀϤ Ⲛ̄ⲚⲈϤ- [ⲤⲞⲎ]
ⲘⲀⲐⲎⲦⲎⲤ ⲬⲈ ⲦⲈⲦⲚ̄ⲚⲞⲒ̈ ⲬⲈ ⲈⲒ̈ϢⲀⲬⲈ Ⲛ̄ⲘⲘⲎⲦⲚ̄ ⲚⲀϢ
Ⲛ̄Ⲁ̄Ⲉ· ⲀⲤⲞⲨⲰⲀ̄Ⲙ̄ Ⲛ̄ϬⲒ ⲘⲀⲢⲒⲀ ⲠⲈⲬⲀⲤ ⲬⲈ ⲤⲈ ⲠⲀⲬⲞⲈⲒⲤ
ⲀⲒ̈Ⲁ̄ⲢⲠⲀⲌⲈ Ⲛ̄Ⲛ̄ϢⲀⲬⲈ Ⲛ̄ⲦⲀⲔⲬⲞⲞⲨ· ⲦⲈⲚⲞⲨ ϬⲈ ⲠⲀⲬⲞⲈⲒⲤ
10 ⲠⲀⲒ̈ ⲠⲈ ⲠϢⲀⲬⲈ Ⲛ̄ⲦⲀⲔⲬⲞⲞϤ ⲬⲈ ⲚⲈⲦⲚⲀⲬⲒ Ⲛ̄ⲘⲘⲨⲤⲦⲎ-
ⲢⲒⲞⲚ Ⲙ̄ⲠⲒⲀⲦϢⲀⲬⲈ ⲈⲢⲞϤ· Ⲁ̄ⲈⲚⲘⲀⲔⲀⲢⲒⲞⲤ ⲘⲈⲚⲦⲞⲒⲄⲈ ⲚⲈ
ⲚⲈⲮⲨⲬⲞⲞⲨⲈ ⲈⲦⲘ̄ⲘⲀⲨ· ⲀⲖⲖⲀ ⲈⲨϢⲀⲚⲔⲞⲦⲞⲨ Ⲛ̄ⲤⲈⲠⲀ-
ⲢⲀⲂⲀ Ⲛ̄ⲤⲈⲖⲞ Ⲛ̄ⲦⲈⲨⲠⲒⲤⲦⲒⲤ· ⲀⲨⲰ Ⲛ̄ⲤⲈⲈⲒˀ ⲈⲂⲞⲖ Ⲁ̄Ⲛ ⲤⲰⲘⲀ
ⲈⲘⲠⲞⲨⲘⲈⲦⲀⲚⲞⲒ̈· ⲘⲈⲨⲢ̄ϢⲀⲨ ϬⲈ ⲬⲒⲚ ⲠⲈⲒ̈ⲚⲀⲨ ⲈⲔⲞⲦⲞⲨ
15 ⲈⲘⲘⲈⲦⲀⲂⲞⲖⲎ Ⲙ̄ⲠⲤⲰⲘⲀ· ⲞⲨⲆⲈ ⲖⲀⲀⲨ Ⲛ̄Ⲁ̄ⲰⲂ· ⲀⲖⲖⲀ
ϢⲀⲨⲚⲞⲬⲞⲨ ⲈⲠⲤⲀ̄ⲂⲂⲞⲖˀ ⲈⲠⲔⲀⲔⲈ ⲈⲦⲀ̄ⲒⲂⲞⲖ· ⲤⲈⲚⲀⲀⲚⲀ̄-
ⲖⲒⲤⲔⲈ Ⲙ̄ⲘⲞⲞⲨ Ⲁ̄Ⲙ̄ ⲠⲘⲀ ⲈⲦⲘ̄ⲘⲀⲨ· ⲀⲨⲰ ⲤⲈⲚⲀⲢ̄ⲀⲦϢⲰⲠⲈ
ϢⲀⲈⲚⲈⲀ̄· ⲈⲦⲂⲈ ⲠϢⲀⲬⲈ Ⲛ̄ⲦⲀⲔⲬⲞⲞϤ ⲈⲢⲞⲚ Ⲙ̄ⲠⲒⲞⲨⲞⲈⲒϢ
ⲈⲔⲬⲰ Ⲙ̄ⲘⲞⲤ· ⲬⲈ ⲚⲀⲚⲞⲨ ⲠⲈⲀ̄ⲘⲞⲨ· ⲈⲢϢⲀⲚ ⲠⲈⲀ̄ⲘⲞⲨ
20 ⲂⲀⲀⲂⲈ ⲈⲨⲚⲀⲘⲞⲖⲀ̄Ϥ Ⲁ̄Ⲛ ⲞⲨˑ ⲘⲈϤⲢ̄ϢⲀⲨ ⲈⲦⲔⲞⲠⲢⲒⲀ· ⲞⲨⲆⲈ [ⲤⲞⲎ ᵇ]
ⲈⲠⲔⲀⲀ̄· ⲀⲖⲖⲀ ⲈϢⲀⲨⲚⲞⲬ̄Ϥ ⲈⲂⲞⲖ· ⲈⲦⲈ ⲠⲀⲒ̈ ⲠⲈ ⲬⲈ ⲞⲨ-
ⲘⲀⲔⲀⲢⲒⲞⲤ ⲠⲈ ⲮⲨⲬⲎ ⲚⲒⲘˀ ⲈⲦⲚⲀⲬⲒ Ⲁ̄Ⲛ Ⲙ̄ⲘⲨⲤⲦⲎⲢⲒⲞⲚ

---

1   MS originally ⲈⲠⲈⲔⲞⲚⲞⲘⲞⲤ; ⲚⲞ expunged, and Ⲥ inserted above.
2   MS originally ⲈⲘⲈⲦⲀⲂⲞⲖⲎ Ⲙ̄ⲠⲔⲞⲤⲘⲞⲤ ⲤⲰⲘⲀ; Ⲙ in ⲈⲘⲈⲦⲀⲂⲞⲖⲎ inserted above
      and Ⲛ̄ⲦⲈ Ⲛ̄ in margins before ⲤⲰⲘⲀ.
15 MS ⲞⲨⲆⲈ ⲖⲀⲀⲨ; read ⲞⲨⲆⲈ ⲈⲖⲀⲀⲨ.
18 MS ⲠϢⲀⲬⲈ; read ⲠⲈⲒϢⲀⲬⲈ.

their first time of coming to the *world*, from this time they will not return to the *changes* of the *world* of the *body*. And they are not able to do anything, *but* they are cast outside to the outer darkness, and are *consumed* and become non-existent for ever."

120.   When the *Saviour* had said these things, *however*, he said to his *disciples* : "Do you *understand* in what manner I am speaking with you?"

Maria answered and said : "Yes, my Lord, I have *grasped* the words which thou hast spoken. Now at this time, my Lord, this is the word which thou hast spoken : 'Those who will receive the *mysteries* of the Ineffable, those *souls* are *certainly blessed. But* if they turn and *transgress* and cease in their *faith*, and they come forth from the *body* before *repenting*, it is not possible now from this time to return to the *changes* of the *body*, *nor* anything *except* to be cast outside to the outer darkness. They will be *consumed* in that *place*, and they will become non-existent for ever'. Concerning (this) word thou hast once said to us : 'Salt is good; if the salt becomes insipid, with what will it be salted? It is no use for the *dung nor* for the earth, *but* it is cast out' *. That is, *blessed* is every *soul* that will receive from the *mysteries* | of the Ineffable. *But* if they once *transgress*,

---

* cf. Mt. 5.13; Mk. 9.50; Lk. 14.34, 35

ⲘⲠⲒⲀⲦⲰⲀϪⲈ ⲈⲢⲞϤ· ⲀⲖⲖⲀ ⲈⲨϢⲀⲚⲠⲀⲢⲀⲂⲀ ⲚⲞⲨⲤⲞⲠ·
ⲘⲈⲨⲢϢⲀⲨ ⲚⲔⲞⲦⲞⲨ ⲈⲠⲤⲰⲘⲀ ϪⲒⲚ ⲠⲈⲒⲚⲀⲨ· ⲞⲨⲆⲈ
ⲈⲖⲀⲀⲨ ⲚϨⲰⲂ· ⲀⲖⲖⲀ ⲈϢⲀⲨⲚⲞⲬⲞⲨ ⲈⲠⲔⲀⲔⲈ ⲈⲦϨⲒⲂⲞⲖ·
ⲚⲤⲈⲀⲚϨⲀⲖⲒⲤⲔⲈ ⲘⲘⲞⲞⲨ ⲘⲠⲘⲀ ⲈⲦⲘⲘⲀⲨ· ⲚⲀⲒ ⲆⲈ Ⲛ-
5 ⲦⲈⲢⲈⲤϪⲞⲞⲨ ⲚⲠⲤⲰⲦⲏⲢ· ⲠⲈϪⲀϤ ϪⲈ ⲈⲨⲄⲈ ⲦⲈⲠⲚⲒⲔⲎ
ⲚϨⲒⲀⲒⲔⲢⲒⲚⲈⲤ ⲘⲀⲢⲒⲀ· ⲠⲀⲒ ⲠⲈ ⲠⲂⲰⲖ ⲈⲂⲞⲖ ⲘⲠϢⲀϪⲈ·

ⲀⲤⲞⲨⲰϨ ⲞⲚ ⲈⲦⲞⲞⲦⲤ ⲚϬⲒ ⲘⲀⲢⲒⲀ ⲠⲈϪⲀⲤ ϪⲈ ⲠⲀⲬⲞⲒⲤ·
ⲈⲒⲈ ⲢⲰⲘⲈ ⲚⲒⲘ· ⲚⲦⲀⲨϪⲒ ⲚⲘⲘⲨⲤⲦⲎⲢⲒⲞⲚ ⲘⲠⲒϢⲞⲢⲠ Ⲙ-
ⲘⲨⲤⲦⲎⲢⲒⲞⲚ· ⲘⲚ ⲘⲘⲨⲤⲦⲎⲢⲒⲞⲚ ⲘⲠⲒⲀⲦϢⲀϪⲈ ⲈⲢⲞϤ· ⲚⲀⲒ
10 ⲈⲦⲈ ⲘⲠⲞⲨⲠⲀⲢⲀⲂⲀ· ⲀⲖⲖⲀ ⲈⲢⲈ ⲦⲈⲨⲠⲒⲤⲦⲒⲤ ϨⲚ ⲘⲘⲨⲤⲦⲎ-
ⲢⲒⲞⲚ ϨⲚ ⲞⲨⲤⲞⲞⲨⲦⲚ ⲀϪⲚ ϨⲨⲠⲞⲔⲢⲒⲤⲒⲤ· ⲚⲀⲒ ϬⲈ ⲈⲂⲞⲖ
ϨⲒⲦⲚ ⲦⲀⲚⲀⲄⲔⲎ ⲚⲐⲒⲘⲀⲢⲘⲈⲚⲎ· ⲀⲨⲰ ⲞⲚ ⲀⲨⲢⲚⲞⲂⲈ· ⲀⲨⲰ
ⲞⲚ ⲀⲨⲔⲞⲦⲞⲨ ⲀⲨⲘⲈⲦⲀⲚⲞⲒ· ⲀⲨⲰ ⲞⲚ ⲀⲨⲠⲢⲞⲤⲈⲨⲬⲈ Ⲥ̄Ⲟ̄Ⲑ̄
ϨⲚ ⲚⲈⲨⲘⲨⲤⲦⲎⲢⲒⲞⲚ ⲚⲈⲨⲘⲨⲤⲦⲎⲢⲒⲞⲚ· ⲤⲈⲚⲀⲔⲰ ⲚⲀⲨ
15 ⲈⲂⲞⲖ ⲚⲀⲞⲨⲎⲢ ⲚⲤⲞⲠ· ⲀϤⲞⲨⲰϨⲘ ⲆⲈ ⲚϬⲒ ⲠⲤⲰⲦⲎⲢ ⲠⲈ-
ϪⲀϤ ⲘⲘⲀⲢⲒⲀ ϨⲚ ⲦⲘⲎⲦⲈ ⲚⲚⲈϤⲘⲀⲐⲎⲦⲎⲤ ϪⲈ ϨⲀⲘⲎⲚ
ϨⲀⲘⲎⲚ ϮϪⲰ ⲘⲘⲞⲤ ⲈⲢⲰⲦⲚ ϪⲈ ⲢⲰⲘⲈ ⲚⲒⲘ· ⲈⲦⲚⲀϪⲒ
ⲚⲘⲘⲨⲤⲦⲎⲢⲒⲞⲚ ⲘⲠⲒⲀⲦϢⲀϪⲈ ⲈⲢⲞϤ· ⲀⲨⲰ ⲞⲚ ⲘⲚ ⲘⲘⲨⲤ-
ⲦⲎⲢⲒⲞⲚ ⲘⲠⲒϢⲞⲢⲠ ⲘⲘⲨⲤⲦⲎⲢⲒⲞⲚ· ⲚⲀⲒ ϨⲒⲦⲚ ⲦⲀⲚⲀⲄⲔⲎ
20 ⲚⲐⲒⲘⲀⲢⲘⲈⲚⲎ ⲤⲈⲢⲚⲞⲂⲈ ⲚⲤⲞⲠ ⲚⲒⲘ· ⲀⲨⲰ ⲈⲦⲒ ⲈⲨⲞⲚϨ
ⲚⲤⲈⲔⲞⲦⲞⲨ ⲚⲤⲈⲘⲈⲦⲀⲚⲞⲒ· ⲀⲨⲰ ⲞⲚ ⲚⲤⲈϬⲰ ϨⲚ ⲚⲈⲨ-
ⲘⲨⲤⲦⲎⲢⲒⲞⲚ ⲚⲈⲨⲘⲨⲤⲦⲎⲢⲒⲞⲚ· ⲤⲈⲚⲀⲔⲰ ⲚⲀⲨ ⲈⲂⲞⲖ Ⲛ-
ⲞⲨⲞⲈⲒϢ ⲚⲒⲘ· ϪⲈ ⲘⲘⲨⲤⲦⲎⲢⲒⲞⲚ ⲈⲦⲘⲘⲀⲨ ϨⲈⲚⲚⲀⲎⲦ·
ⲚⲈ· ϨⲈⲚⲢⲈϤⲔⲰ ⲈⲂⲞⲖ· ⲚⲈ ⲚⲞⲨⲞⲈⲒϢ ⲚⲒⲘ· ⲈⲦⲂⲈ ⲠⲀⲒ
25 ⲞⲨⲚ ⲀⲒϪⲞⲞⲤ ⲈⲢⲰⲦⲚ ⲘⲠⲒⲞⲨⲞⲈⲒϢ· ϪⲈ ⲘⲘⲨⲤⲦⲎⲢⲒⲞⲚ
ⲈⲦⲘⲘⲀⲨ· ⲞⲨⲘⲞⲚⲞⲚ ϪⲈ ⲤⲈⲚⲀⲔⲰ ⲚⲀⲨ ⲈⲂⲞⲖ ⲚⲚⲈⲨ-

---

5 MS originally ⲚⲦⲈⲢⲈϤϪⲞⲞⲨ ⲚϬⲒ ⲠⲤⲰⲦⲎⲢ; ϥ altered to ⲥ, and ϬⲒ
crossed out; read ⲚⲦⲈⲢⲈⲤϪⲞⲞⲨ ⲘⲠⲤⲰⲦⲎⲢ.

they are not fit to return to the *body* from this time, *or* for anything *but* they are cast to the outer darkness, and are *consumed* in that place."

But when she had said these things to the *Saviour*, he said : "*Excellent*, thou *spiritual* and *pure* Maria. This is the interpretation of the word."

Maria continued again and said : "My Lord, all men who have received the *mysteries* of the First Mystery, and the *mysteries* of the Ineffable, who have not *transgressed but* whose *faith* in the *mysteries* was firm, without *hypocrisy*; and now through the *constraint* of the *Heimarmene* these have sinned again, and again they have turned and have *repented*, and again they have *prayed* in each of their *mysteries* : how many times will they be forgiven?"

The *Saviour however* answered and said to Maria in the midst of his *disciples* : "*Truly*, *truly*, I say to you, all men who will receive the *mysteries* of the Ineffable with the *mysteries* of the First *Mystery*, who sin every time through the *constraint* of the *Heimarmene*, and while they are *still* living turn and *repent* and also continue in each of their *mysteries*, they will be forgiven every time, because those *mysteries* are merciful and forgiving at all times. *Now* because of this I said to you once : 'Those *mysteries* will *not only* forgive their | sins which they have committed from the

ⲚⲞⲂⲈ ⲚⲦⲀⲨⲀⲀⲨ ϪⲒⲚ ⲚϢⲞⲢⲠ· ⲀⲨⲰ ⲘⲈⲨⲞⲠⲞⲨ ⲈⲢⲞϤ
ϪⲒⲚ ⲠⲈⲨⲚⲀⲨ· ⲚⲈⲚⲦⲀⲒϪⲞⲞⲨ ⲈⲢⲰⲦⲚ ϪⲈ ϢⲀⲨϪⲒ-ⲘⲈⲦⲀ-
ⲚⲞⲒⲀ ⲚⲞⲨⲞⲒϢ *ⲚⲒⲘ· ⲀⲨⲰ ⲤⲈⲚⲀⲔⲰ ⲈⲂⲞⲖ ⲞⲚ ⲚⲚⲚⲞⲂⲈ ⲤⲞⲞᵇ
ⲈϢⲀⲨⲀⲀⲨ ⲚⲞⲨⲰϨⲘ· ⲈϢⲰⲠⲈ ⲚⲦⲞϤ ⲚⲈⲢϪⲒ-ⲘⲨⲤⲦⲎⲢⲒⲞⲚ
5 ϨⲘ ⲠⲘⲨⲤⲦⲎⲢⲒⲞⲚ ⲘⲠⲒⲀⲦϢⲀϪⲈ ⲈⲢⲞϤ· ⲘⲚ ⲘⲘⲨⲤⲦⲎⲢⲒⲞⲚ
ⲘⲠⲒϢⲞⲢⲠ ⲘⲘⲨⲤⲦⲎⲢⲒⲞⲚ: ⲀⲨⲰ ⲚⲤⲈⲔⲞⲦⲞⲨ ⲚⲤⲈⲢⲚⲞⲂⲈ·
ⲀⲨⲰ ⲚⲤⲈⲈⲒ ⲈⲂⲞⲖ ϨⲚ ⲤⲰⲘⲀ ⲈⲘⲠⲞⲨⲘⲈⲦⲀⲚⲞⲒ· ⲈⲨⲚⲀ-
ϢⲰⲠⲈ ϨⲰⲞⲨ ⲞⲚ ⲚⲐⲈ ⲚⲚⲎ ⲈⲚⲦⲀⲨⲠⲀⲢⲀⲂⲀ ⲘⲠⲞⲨ-
ⲘⲈⲦⲀⲚⲞⲒ· ⲠⲈⲨⲘⲀⲚϢⲰⲠⲈ ϨⲰⲞⲨ ⲞⲚ ⲠⲈ ⲦⲘⲎⲦⲈ ⲚⲦ-
10 ⲦⲀⲠⲢⲞ ⲘⲠⲈⲆⲢⲀⲔⲰⲚ ⲘⲠⲔⲀⲔⲈ ⲈⲦϨⲒⲂⲞⲖ· ⲀⲨⲰ ⲤⲈⲚⲀ-
ⲀⲚϨⲀⲖⲒⲤⲔⲈ ⲘⲘⲞⲞⲨ ⲚⲤⲈⲢⲀⲦϢⲰⲠⲈ ϢⲀⲈⲚⲈϨ· ⲈⲦⲂⲈ ⲠⲀⲒ
†ϪⲰ ⲘⲘⲞⲤ ⲚⲎⲦⲚ ϪⲈ ⲢⲰⲘⲈ ⲚⲒⲘ ⲈⲦⲚⲀϪⲒ ⲚⲘⲘⲨⲤⲦⲎ-
ⲢⲒⲞⲚ· ⲈⲚⲈⲨⲤⲞⲞⲨⲚ ⲘⲠⲈⲞⲨⲞⲈⲒϢ ⲈⲦⲞⲨⲚⲎⲨ ⲈⲂⲞⲖ ϨⲘ
ⲠⲤⲰⲘⲀ ⲚϨⲎⲦϤ· ⲚⲈⲨⲚⲀⲢϨⲘⲘⲈ ⲘⲘⲞⲞⲨ ⲠⲈ ⲚⲤⲈⲦⲘⲢ-
15 ⲚⲞⲂⲈ· ϪⲈ ⲈⲨⲈⲔⲖⲎⲢⲞⲚⲞⲘⲒ ⲚⲦⲘⲚⲦⲈⲢⲞ ⲘⲠⲞⲨⲞⲈⲒⲚ ϢⲀ-
ⲈⲚⲈϨ·

ⲚⲀⲒ ϬⲈ ⲚⲦⲈⲢⲈϤϪⲞⲞⲨ ⲚϬⲒ ⲠⲤⲰⲦⲎⲢ ⲈⲚⲈϤⲘⲀⲐⲎⲦⲎⲤ
ⲠⲈϪⲀϤ ⲚⲀⲨ· ϪⲈ ⲦⲈⲦⲚⲚⲞⲒ ϬⲈ ϪⲈ ⲈⲒϢⲀϪⲈ ⲚⲘⲘⲎⲦⲚ [ⲤⲠ]
ⲚⲀϢ ⲚϨⲈ· ⲀⲤⲞⲨⲰϨⲘ ⲚϬⲒ ⲘⲀⲢⲒⲀ ⲠⲈϪⲀⲤ ϪⲈ ⲤⲈ ⲠⲀ-
20 ϪⲞⲈⲒⲤ· ϨⲚ ⲞⲨⲀⲔⲢⲒⲂⲒⲀ ⲀⲒⲀⲔⲢⲒⲂⲀⲤⲈ ⲚⲤⲀ ϢⲀϪⲈ ⲚⲒⲘ ⲈⲦⲔ-
ϪⲰ ⲘⲘⲞⲞⲨ· ⲈⲦⲂⲈ ⲠⲈⲒϢⲀϪⲈ ⲞⲨⲚ ⲚⲦⲀⲔϪⲞⲞϤ ⲈⲢⲞⲚ
ⲘⲠⲒⲞⲨⲞⲈⲒϢ ϪⲈ ⲈⲚⲈϤⲤⲞⲞⲨⲚ ⲚϬⲒ ⲠϪⲞⲈⲒⲤ ⲘⲠⲎⲒ ϪⲈ
ⲈⲢⲈ ⲠⲢⲈϤϪⲒⲞⲨⲈ ⲚⲎⲨ ⲚⲀϢ ⲚⲚⲀⲨ ϨⲚ ⲦⲈⲨϢⲎ ⲈϬⲰⲦϨ
ⲈⲠⲎⲒ· ⲚⲈϤⲚⲀⲢⲞⲈⲒⲤ ⲞⲚ ⲚⲈ ⲚϤⲦⲘⲔⲀ-ⲢⲰⲘⲈ ⲈϬⲰⲦϨ ⲈⲠⲈϤ-
25 ⲎⲒ· ⲚⲀⲒ ϬⲈ ⲚⲦⲈⲢⲈⲤϪⲞⲞⲨ ⲚϬⲒ ⲘⲀⲢⲒⲀ· ⲠⲈϪⲀϤ ⲚϬⲒ ⲠⲤⲰ-
ⲦⲎⲢ· ϪⲈ ⲈⲨⲄⲈ ⲦⲈⲠⲚⲒⲔⲎ ⲘⲀⲢⲒⲀ ⲠⲀⲒ ⲠⲈ ⲠϢⲀϪⲈ· ⲀϤⲞⲨⲰϨ

---

1 MS ⲀⲨⲰ; read ⲀⲖⲖⲀ. MS ⲈⲢⲞϤ; read ⲈⲢⲞⲞⲨ.

beginning, but they are not reckoned to them from this time'. About these I have said to you : 'They receive *repentance* at all times and they will also forgive the sins which have been committed afresh.' If, on the other hand, they receive *mysteries* from the *mystery* of the Ineffable and the *mysteries* of the First *Mystery*, and they turn and commit sin and come forth from the *body* without *repenting*, they will themselves be like those who have *transgressed* and have not *repented.* Their dwelling-place is also in the midst of the jaws of the *dragon* of outer darkness, and they will be *consumed* and become non-existent for ever. Because of this I say to you : all men who receive *mysteries*, if they knew their time of coming forth from the *body*, would direct themselves so that they do not sin, so that they may *inherit* the Kingdom of the Light for ever."

121. Now when the *Saviour* had said these things to his *disciples*, he said to them : "Do you now *understand* in what manner I am speaking with you?"

Maria answered and said : "Yes, my Lord, with *accuracy* I have *understood thoroughly* [1] all the discourses which thou hast spoken. *Now* concerning this word, thou hast said [2] to us once : 'If the lord of the house had known at what time in the night the thief would come, to ransack [3] the house, he would have watched and not allowed anyone [4] to ransack his house' *"

Now when Maria had said these things, the *Saviour* said : "*Excellent*, thou *spiritual one*, Maria. This is the word." |

---

*   cf. Mt. 24.43; Lk. 12.39

---

[1]   (20) understood thoroughly; Schmidt : traced thoroughly; Till : thoroughly inquired into.

[2]   (21) this word, thou hast said; lit. this word which thou hast said; (also 314.3).

[3]   (23, 24) to ransack; Till : to break into.

[4]   (24) anyone; Schmidt : the man.

ON ЄⲦⲞⲞⲦϤ ⲚϬⲒ ⲠⲤⲰⲢ ⲠЄⲬⲀϤ ⲚⲚЄϤⲘⲀⲐⲎⲦⲎⲤ ⲬЄ ⲦЄ-
ⲚⲞⲨ ϬЄ ⲔⲎⲢⲨⲤⲤЄ ⲚⲢⲰⲘЄ ⲚⲒⲘ ЄⲦⲚⲀⲬⲒ-ⲘⲨⲤⲦⲎⲢⲒⲞⲚ ⳨Ⲙ
ⲠⲞⲨⲞⲒ̈Ⲛ· Ⲁ⳪ⲒⲤ ⲚⲀⲨ ЄⲦЄⲦⲚⲬⲰ ⲘⲘⲞⲤ ⲬЄ ⳨ⲢⲦⲎⲚⲞⲨ
ЄⲢⲰⲦⲚ ⲘⲠⲢⲢⲚⲞⲂЄ· ⲘⲎⲠⲞⲦЄ ⲚⲦЄⲦⲚⲚⲞⲨⲬЄ ⲚⲞⲨ⳨ⲞⲞⲨ
5 ⲚⲤⲀ ⲞⲨ⳨ⲞⲞⲨ· ⲀⲨⲰ ⲚⲦЄⲦⲚЄⲒ̈ ЄⲂⲞⳊ ⳨Ⲛ ⲤⲰⲘⲀ ЄⲘⲠЄ-
ⲦⲚⲘЄⲦⲀⲚⲞⲒ̈ ⲚⲦЄⲦⲚⲢⲀⳊⳊⲞⲦⲢⲒⲞⲤ ЄⲦⲘⲚⲦЄⲢⲞ ⲘⲠⲞⲨⲞЄⲒⲚ
ⲱⲀⲈⲚЄ⳨·

ⲚⲀⲒ̈ ⲚⲦЄⲢЄϤϪⲞⲞⲨ ⲚϬⲒ ⲠⲤⲰⲢ· ⲀⲤⲞⲨⲰ⳨Ⲙ ⲚϬⲒ ⲘⲀⲢⲒⲀ [ⲥⲡᵇ]
ⲠЄⲬⲀⲤ ϪЄ ⲠⲀⲬⲞЄⲒⲤ· ⲚⲀⲱЄ ⲦⲘⲚⲦⲚⲀⲎⲦ ⲚⲚЄⲒ̈ⲘⲨⲤⲦⲎ-
10 ⲢⲒⲞⲚ ЄⲦⲔⲀⲚⲞⲂЄ ЄⲂⲞⳊ ⲚⲞⲨⲞЄⲒⲱ ⲚⲒⲘ· ⲀϤⲞⲨⲰ⳨Ⲙ ⲚϬⲒ
ⲠⲤⲰⲢ ⲠЄⲬⲀϤ ⲘⲘⲀⲢⲒⲀ ⳨Ⲛ ⲦⲘⲎⲦЄ ⲚⲘⲘⲀⲐⲎⲦⲎⲤ· ⲬЄ
ЄⲱϪЄ ⲞⲨⲢⲢⲞ ⲘⲠⲞⲞⲨ ЄⲨⲢⲰⲘЄ ⲠЄ ⲚⲦЄ ⲠⲔⲞⲤⲘⲞⲤ·
Ϥ⳨ ⲚⲞⲨⲆⲰⲢЄⲀ ⲚⲢⲢⲰⲘЄ ⲚⲦЄϤ⳨Є· ⲀⲨⲰ ⲚϤⲔⲰ ЄⲂⲞⳊ
ⲞⲚ ⲚⲚⲪⲞⲚЄⲨⲤ ⲘⲚ ⲚⲢЄϤⲚⲔⲞⲦⲔ ⲘⲚ ⳨ⲞⲞⲨⲦ· ⲘⲚ ⲠⲔЄ-
15 ⲤЄЄⲠЄ ⲚⲚⲞⲂЄ ЄⲦ⳨ⲞⲢⲱ ЄⲘⲀϢⲞ ⲚⲀⲒ̈ ЄⲨⲘⲠϢⲀ ⲘⲠⲘⲞⲨ·
ЄⲱϢЄ ⲆЄ ЄⲢⲞϤ ЄⲨⲢⲰⲘЄ ⲠЄ ⲚⲦЄ ⲠⲔⲞⲤⲘⲞⲤ ЄⳊϤЄⲒⲢЄ
ⲘⲠⲀⲒ̈· ⲘⲀⳊⲒⲤⲦⲀ ϬЄ ⲠⲒⲀⲦⲱⲀϪЄ ЄⲢⲞϤ ⲘⲚ ⲠⲒϢⲞⲢⲠ Ⲙ-
ⲘⲨⲤⲦⲎⲢⲒⲞⲚ· ⲚⲀⲒ̈ ЄⲦⲞ ⲚⲬⲞⲒⲤ Є⳨ⲢⲀⲒ̈ Є⳨Ⲙ ⲠⲦⲎⲢϤ· ЄⲨⲚ-
ⲦⲀⲨ ⲘⲘⲀⲨ ⲚⲦЄ⳨ⲞⲨⲤⲒⲀ ⳨Ⲛ ⳨ⲰⲂ ⲚⲒⲘ· ЄⲢ-ⲠЄⲦЄ⳨-ⲚⲀⲨ·
20 ЄⲦⲢЄⲨⲔⲰ ЄⲂⲞⳊ ⲚⲞⲨⲞⲚ ⲚⲒⲘ ЄⲢⲬⲒ-ⲘⲨⲤⲦⲎⲢⲒⲞⲚ· Ⲏ Ⲙ-
ⲘⲞⲚ ⲚⲦⲞϤ ЄϢⲰⲠЄ ⲞⲨⲢⲢⲞ ⲘⲠⲞⲞⲨ ⲚϤ⳨ ⲚⲞⲨЄⲚⲆⲨⲘⲀ
ⲚⲢⲢⲞ ⳨Ⲓ ⲞⲨⲘⲀⲦⲞⲒ̈ ⲚϤⲬⲞⲞⲨϤ Є⳨ЄⲚⲔЄⲦⲞⲠⲞⲤ ⲚϤЄⲒⲢЄ
Ⲛ⳨ЄⲚ⳨ⲰⲦⲂ· ⲘⲚ ⳨ЄⲚⲚⲞⲂЄ ЄⲨ⳨ⲞⲢⲱ ЄⲨⲘⲠϢⲀ ⲘⲠⲘⲞⲨ ⲥⲡⲀ
ⲀⲨⲰ ⲘЄⲨⲞⲠⲞⲨ ЄⲢⲞϤ· ⲀⲨⲰ ⲘЄⲨЄϢⲢ-ⳊⳊⲀⲨ ⲘⲠЄⲐⲞⲞⲨ
25 ⲚⲀϤ· ϪЄ ⲠЄⲚⲆⲨⲘⲀ ⲘⲠⲢⲢⲞ ⲦⲞ ⳨ⲒⲱⲱϤ· ⲘⲀⳊⲒⲤⲦⲀ ϬЄ ⲚЄⲦ-
ⲪⲞⲢⲒ ⲚⲘⲘⲨⲤⲦⲎⲢⲒⲞⲚ ⲚⲚЄⲚⲆⲨⲘⲀ ⲘⲠⲒⲀⲦⲱⲀϪЄ ЄⲢⲞϤ·
ⲘⲚ ⲚⲀⲠϢⲞⲢⲠ ⲘⲘⲨⲤⲦⲎⲢⲒⲞⲚ· ⲚⲀⲒ̈ ЄⲦⲞ ⲚⲬⲞЄⲒⲤ ЄⲚⲀ-

The *Saviour* continued again and said to his *disciples*:
"Now at this time *preach* to all men who will receive
mysteries in the light. Say to them: 'Take heed that you do
not sin, *lest* you spend day after day [1] and come forth from
the *body* without having *repented*, and become *strangers* to
the Kingdom of the Light for ever'."

When the *Saviour* had said these things, Maria answered
and said: "My Lord, great is the compassion of these
mysteries which forgive sin at all times."

The *Saviour* answered and said to Maria in the midst of
the *disciples*: "If today a king, who is a man of the *world*,
gives a *gift* to men of his kind, and he forgives *murderers*
and pederasts and the other very serious sins which are
worthy of death, if it is fitting to him who is a man of the
world to have done this, *especially* now do the Ineffable
and the First *Mystery* who are the rulers over the All have
the *authority* in all things to do what pleases them, so that
they forgive everyone who receives [2] *mysteries*. *Or* if, on the
other hand, a king today puts a royal *garment* upon a soldier
and sends him to other *places*, and he commits murders
and serious sins which are worthy of death, they are not
reckoned to him and it is not possible to do any harm to
him because he is clothed with the royal *garment*. Much
more so now are those who *wear* the *garments* of the
mysteries [3] of the Ineffable and those of the First *Mystery*,
who are rulers over | all those of the height and all those
of the *depth*."

---

[1] (4, 5) spend day after day; Schmidt: add evil to evil (see 315.1).
[2] (20) receives; Till: has received; Schmidt: will receive.
[3] (26) the garments of the mysteries; lit. the mysteries of the garments.

ⲡⲭⲓⲥⲉ ⲧⲏⲣⲟⲩ· ⲙⲛ ⲛⲁⲡⲃⲁⲑⲟⲥ ⲧⲏⲣⲟⲩ· ⲙⲛⲛⲥⲁ ⲛⲁⲓ ⲁ
ⲓ̅ⲥ̅ ⲛⲁⲩ ⲉⲩⲥϩⲓⲙⲉ ⲉⲁⲥⲉⲓ' ⲉⲙⲉⲧⲁⲛⲟⲓ· ⲁϥⲃⲁⲡⲧⲓⲍⲉ ⲙⲙⲟⲥ
ⲛϣⲟⲙⲛⲧ ⲛⲥⲟⲡ ⲁⲩⲱ ⲛⲉⲙⲡⲥⲉⲓⲣⲉ ⲙⲡⲉⲙⲡϣⲁ ⲛⲛⲃⲁⲡⲧⲓⲥ-
ⲙⲁ· ⲁⲩⲱ ⲁ ⲡⲥⲱⲧⲏⲣ ⲟⲩⲱϣ ⲉⲡⲓⲣⲁⲍⲉ ⲙⲡⲉⲧⲣⲟⲥ ⲉⲛⲁⲩ
5 ⲭⲉ ⲉⲛⲉⲁϥϣⲱⲡⲉ ⲛⲛⲁⲏⲧ· ⲁⲩⲱ ⲛⲣⲉϥⲕⲱ ⲉⲃⲟⲗ ⲕⲁⲧⲁ
ⲑⲉ ⲉⲛⲧⲁϥϩⲱⲛ ⲉⲧⲟⲟⲧⲟⲩ ⲙⲙⲟⲥ· ⲡⲉⲭⲁϥ ⲉϩⲟⲩⲛ ⲉϩⲙ
ⲡⲉⲧⲣⲟⲥ ⲭⲉ ⲉⲓⲥ ϣⲟⲙⲛⲧ ⲛⲥⲟⲡ' ⲁⲓ̈ⲃⲁⲡⲧⲓⲍⲉ ⲛⲧⲉⲓ̈ⲯⲩⲭⲏ·
ⲁⲩⲱ ϩⲙ ⲡⲉⲓ̈ϣⲟⲙⲛⲧ ⲛⲥⲟⲡ' ⲙⲡⲥⲉⲓⲣⲉ ⲙⲡⲉⲙⲡϣⲁ ⲛⲙⲙⲩⲥⲧⲏⲣⲓⲟⲛ ⲙⲡⲟⲩⲟⲉⲓⲛ· ⲉⲧⲃⲉ ⲟⲩ ϭⲉ *ⲥⲟⲩⲱⲥϥ ⲙⲡⲕⲉⲥⲱ- ⲥⲡⲁ ᵇ
10 ⲙⲁ· ⲧⲉⲛⲟⲩ ϭⲉ ⲟⲩⲛ ⲡⲉⲧⲣⲟⲥ ⲁⲣⲓⲣⲉ ⲙⲡⲙⲩⲥⲧⲏⲣⲓⲟⲛ ⲙ-
ⲡⲟⲩⲟⲉⲓⲛ ⲡⲁⲓ ⲉϣⲁϥϣⲱⲧ' ⲉⲃⲟⲗ ⲛⲛⲉⲯⲩⲭⲏ ϩⲛ ⲛⲉⲕⲗⲏⲣⲟⲛⲟⲙⲓⲁ ⲙⲡⲟⲩⲟⲉⲓⲛ· ⲁⲣⲓⲣⲉ ⲙⲡⲙⲩⲥⲧⲏⲣⲓⲟⲛ ⲉⲧⲙⲙⲁⲩ ⲛϥϣⲱⲧ' ⲉⲃⲟⲗ ⲛⲧⲉⲯⲩⲭⲏ ⲛⲧⲉⲓ̈ⲥϩⲓⲙⲉ ϩⲛ ⲛⲉⲕⲗⲏⲣⲟⲛⲟⲙⲓⲁ ⲙⲡⲟⲩⲟⲉⲓⲛ· ⲛⲁⲓ ϭⲉ ⲛⲧⲉⲣⲉϥⲭⲟⲟⲩ ⲛϭⲓ ⲡⲥⲱ-
15 ⲧⲏⲣ ⲁϥⲡⲓⲣⲁⲍⲉ ⟨ⲙⲡⲉⲧⲣⲟⲥ⟩ ⲉⲛⲁⲩ ⲭⲉ ⲉⲛⲉⲁϥϣⲱⲡⲉ ⲛ-
ⲛⲁⲏⲧ' ⲛⲣⲉϥⲕⲱ ⲉⲃⲟⲗ· ⲛⲁⲓ ϭⲉ ⲛⲧⲉⲣⲉϥⲭⲟⲟⲩ ⲛϭⲓ ⲡⲥⲱⲧⲏⲣ ⲡⲉⲭⲁϥ ⲛϭⲓ ⲡⲉⲧⲣⲟⲥ ⲭⲉ ⲡⲁⲭⲟⲉⲓⲥ ⲕⲁⲁⲥ ⲙⲡⲉⲓ̈-
ⲕⲉⲥⲟⲡ· ⲛⲧⲛϯ ⲛⲁⲥ ⲛⲙⲙⲩⲥⲧⲏⲣⲓⲟⲛ ⲉⲧⲭⲟⲥⲉ· ⲁⲩⲱ
ⲉⲥϣⲁⲛⲣⲱϣⲁⲩ ⲁⲕⲕⲁⲁⲥ ⲁⲥⲕⲗⲏⲣⲟⲛⲟⲙⲓ ⲛⲧⲙⲛⲧⲉⲣⲟ ⲙⲡⲟⲩ-
20 ⲟⲉⲓⲛ· ⲉϣⲱⲡⲉ ⲇⲉ ⲉⲥϣⲁⲛⲧⲙⲣⲱϣⲁⲩ ⲁⲕϣⲁⲁⲧⲥ ⲉⲃⲟⲗ'
ϩⲛ ⲧⲙⲛⲧⲉⲣⲟ ⲙⲡⲟⲩⲟⲉⲓⲛ· ⲛⲁⲓ ϭⲉ ⲛⲧⲉⲣⲉϥⲭⲟⲟⲩ ⲛϭⲓ ⲡⲉⲧⲣⲟⲥ ⲁϥⲉⲓⲙⲉ ⲛϭⲓ ⲡⲥⲱⲧⲏⲣ ⲭⲉ ⲁ ⲡⲉⲧⲣⲟⲥ ϣⲱⲡⲉ ⲛ-
ⲛⲁⲏⲧ ⲛⲧⲉϥϩⲉ ⲁⲩⲱ ⲛⲣⲉϥⲕⲱ ⲉⲃⲟⲗ·

   ⲛⲁⲓ ϭⲉ ⲧⲏⲣⲟⲩ ⲛⲧⲉⲣⲟⲩϣⲱⲡⲉ ⲡⲉⲭⲁϥ ⲛϭⲓ ⲡⲥⲱ̅ⲧⲏⲣ **[ⲥⲡⲃ]
25 ⲛⲛⲉϥⲙⲁⲑⲏⲧⲏⲥ· ⲭⲉ ⲁⲧⲉⲧⲛⲛⲟⲓ ⲛⲛⲉⲓ̈ϣⲁⲭⲉ ⲧⲏⲣⲟⲩ ⲙⲛ

---

15 MS ⲙⲡⲉⲧⲣⲟⲥ omitted.
19 MS ⲁⲕⲕⲁⲁⲥ ⲁⲥⲕⲁⲏⲣⲟⲛⲟⲙⲓ; read ⲁⲕⲕⲁⲁⲥ ⲉⲥⲕⲗⲏⲣⲟⲛⲟⲙⲓ.
24 MS ⲡⲉⲭⲁⲩ ; ⲩ crossed out, and ϥ inserted above.

122. After these things Jesus saw a woman who had come to *repent*. He had *baptised* her three times and she had not done what was worthy of the *baptisms*. And the *Saviour* wished to *try* Peter to see whether he was merciful and forgiving *as* he had commanded them. He addressed Peter: "Behold, I have *baptised* this *soul* three times, and at this third time [1] it has not done what is worthy of the *mysteries* of the light. Why does it make the *body* also idle? *Now* at this time, Peter, perform the *mystery* of the light which cuts off *souls* from the *inheritance* of the light. Perform that *mystery* and cut off the *soul* of this woman from the *inheritance* of the light."

Now when the *Saviour* said these things he *tried* (Peter) to see whether he was merciful and forgiving.

Now when the *Saviour* had said these things, Peter said: "My Lord, leave her again this time, so that we give her the higher *mysteries*. And if she is suitable thou hast allowed her to *inherit* the Kingdom of the Light. *But* if she is not suitable thou hast cut her off from the Kingdom of the Light."

Now when Peter had said these things, the *Saviour* knew that Peter was merciful like himself, and forgiving.

Now when all these things had happened, the *Saviour* said to his *disciples*: Have you *understood* all these words and | the *type* of this woman?"

---

[1] (8) at this third time; lit. at these three times.

ⲡⲧⲩⲡⲟⲥ ⲛ̄ⲧⲉⲓ̈ⲥϩⲓⲙⲉ· ⲁⲥⲟⲩⲱϣⲙ̄ ⲛ̄ϭⲓ ⲙⲁⲣⲓⲁ ⲡⲉⲭⲁⲥ ϫⲉ
ⲡⲁⲭⲟⲉⲓⲥ ⲁⲓ̈ⲛⲟⲓ̈ ⲛ̄ⲙⲙⲩⲥⲧⲏⲣⲓⲟⲛ ⲛ̄ⲛϣⲁϫⲉ ⲛ̄ⲧⲁⲩϣⲱⲡⲉ
ⲛ̄ⲧⲉⲓ̈ⲥϩⲓⲙⲉ· ⲉⲧⲃⲉ ⲛ̄ϣⲁϫⲉ ⲟⲩⲛ ⲛ̄ⲧⲁⲩϣⲱⲡⲉ ⲙ̄ⲙⲟⲥ·
ⲛ̄ⲧⲁⲕϫⲟⲟⲥ ⲉⲣⲟⲛ ⲙ̄ⲡⲓⲟⲩⲟⲉⲓϣ ϩⲛ̄ ⲟⲩⲡⲁⲣⲁⲃⲟⲗⲏ ⲉⲕϫⲱ
5 ⲙ̄ⲙⲟⲥ· ϫⲉ ⲛⲉⲟⲩⲛⲧⲉ-ⲟⲩⲣⲱⲙⲉ ⲟⲩⲃⲱ ⲛ̄ⲕⲛ̄ⲧⲉ ϩⲙ̄
ⲡⲉϥⲙⲁ ⲛ̄ⲉⲗⲟⲟⲗⲉ· ⲁϥⲉⲓ ⲇⲉ ⲉϥϣⲓⲛⲉ ⲛ̄ⲥⲁ ⲡⲉϥⲕⲁⲣⲡⲟⲥ
ⲁⲩⲱ ⲙ̄ⲡϥ̄ϩⲉ ⲉⲟⲩⲟⲛ ϩⲓⲱⲱⲥ· ⲡⲉϫⲁϥ ⲛ̄ⲛⲁϩⲣⲙ̄ ⲡⲉϭⲙⲉ
ϫⲉ ⲉⲓⲥ ϣⲟⲙⲧⲉ ⲛ̄ⲣⲟⲙⲡⲉ ϯⲛⲏⲩ ϯϣⲓⲛⲉ ⲛ̄ⲥⲁ ⲕⲁⲣⲡⲟⲥ
ϩⲛ̄ ⲧⲉⲓ̈ⲃⲱ ⲛ̄ⲕⲛ̄ⲧⲉ· ⲁⲩⲱ ⲛ̄ϯϩⲏⲩ ⲁⲛ ⲉⲟⲩⲟⲛ ⲛ̄ϩⲏⲧⲥ̄·
10 ϣⲁⲁⲧⲥ̄ ϭⲉ ⲉⲧⲃⲉ ⲟⲩ ⲥⲟⲩⲱⲥϥ̄ ⲙ̄ⲡⲕⲉⲕⲁϩ· ⲛ̄ⲧⲟϥ ⲇⲉ
ⲁϥⲟⲩⲱϣⲃ̄ ⲡⲉϫⲁϥ ⲛⲁϥ ϫⲉ ⲡⲁⲭⲟⲉⲓⲥ ⲁⲗⲟⲕ ϩⲁⲣⲟⲥ ⲛ̄-
ⲧⲉⲓ̈ⲕⲉⲣⲟⲙⲡⲉ ϣⲁⲛϯϭⲣⲏ ⲙ̄ⲡⲉⲥⲕⲱⲧⲉ ⲧⲁϯ-ⲙⲉϩⲣⲟ ⲛⲁⲥ·
ⲉϣⲱⲡⲉ ⲇⲉ ⲉⲥϣⲁⲛⲧⲁⲩⲟ ⲉⲃⲟⲗ ⲛ̄ⲕⲉⲣⲟⲙⲡⲉ ⲁⲕⲕⲁⲁⲥ·
ⲉϣⲱⲡⲉ ⲇⲉ ⲉⲕⲧⲙ̄ϩⲉ ⲉⲟⲩⲟⲛ ⲁⲕϣⲁⲁⲧⲥ̄· ⲉⲓⲥ* ⲡⲁⲓ̈ ⲡⲁ- [ⲥ̄ⲡ̄ⲃ ᵇ]
15 ⲭⲟⲉⲓⲥ ⲡⲉ ⲡⲃⲱⲗ ⲉⲃⲟⲗ ⲙ̄ⲡϣⲁϫⲉ· ⲁϥⲟⲩⲱϣⲙ̄ ⲛ̄ϭⲓ ⲡⲥⲱⲧⲏⲣ ⲡⲉϫⲁϥ ⲙ̄ⲙⲁⲣⲓⲁ ϫⲉ ⲉⲩⲅⲉ ⲧⲉⲡⲛⲓⲕⲏ ⲡⲁⲓ̈ ⲡⲉ ⲡϣⲁϫⲉ·
     ⲁⲥⲟⲩⲱϩ ⲟⲛ ⲉⲧⲟⲟⲧⲥ̄ ⲛ̄ϭⲓ ⲙⲁⲣⲓⲁ ⲡⲉϫⲁⲥ ⲙ̄ⲡⲥⲱⲧⲏⲣ
ϫⲉ ⲡⲁⲭⲟⲉⲓⲥ ⲉⲓⲉ ⲟⲩⲣⲱⲙⲉ ⲉⲁϥϫⲓ-ⲙⲩⲥⲧⲏⲣⲓⲟⲛ· ⲁⲩⲱ
ⲙ̄ⲡϥ̄ⲉⲓⲣⲉ ⲙ̄ⲡⲉⲙⲡϣⲁ ⲛ̄ⲙⲙⲩⲥⲧⲏⲣⲓⲟⲛ· ⲁⲗⲗⲁ ⲁϥⲕⲟⲧϥ̄ ⲁϥⲣ̄-
20 ⲛⲟⲃⲉ· ⲙⲛ̄ⲛ̄ⲥⲁ ⲛⲁⲓ̈ ⲟⲛ ⲁϥⲙⲉⲧⲁⲛⲟⲓ̈ ⲁⲩⲱ ⲁϥϣⲱⲡⲉ ϩⲛ̄
ⲟⲩⲛⲟϭ ⲙ̄ⲙⲉⲧⲁⲛⲟⲓⲁ· ⲉϩⲉⲥⲧⲓ ⲟⲛ ⲛⲁⲥⲛⲏⲩ ⲉⲟⲩⲁϩⲙⲉϥ
ⲉⲡⲙⲩⲥⲧⲏⲣⲓⲟⲛ ⲛ̄ⲧⲁϥϫⲓⲧϥ̄· ⲏ̄ ⲙⲙⲟⲛ ⲛ̄ⲧⲟϥ ⲉϯ ⲛⲁϥ ⲛ̄-
ⲟⲩⲙⲩⲥⲧⲏⲣⲓⲟⲛ ϩⲛ̄ ⲙ̄ⲙⲩⲥⲧⲏⲣⲓⲟⲛ ⲉⲧⲡⲉϥⲉⲥⲏⲧ· ⲉϩⲉⲥⲧⲓ
ⲟⲩⲛ ϫⲛ̄ ⲙ̄ⲙⲟⲛ· ⲁϥⲟⲩⲱϣⲙ̄ ⲇⲉ ⲛ̄ϭⲓ ⲡⲥⲱⲧⲏⲣ ⲡⲉϫⲁϥ
25 ⲙ̄ⲙⲁⲣⲓⲁ ϫⲉ ϩⲁⲙⲏⲛ ϩⲁⲙⲏⲛ ϯϫⲱ ⲙ̄ⲙⲟⲥ ⲛⲏⲧⲛ̄ ϫⲉ ⲟⲩⲇⲉ

---

21   MS ⲟⲛ ⲛⲁⲥⲛⲏⲩ; better ⲟⲩⲛ ⲛ̄ⲛⲁⲥⲛⲏⲩ.

Maria answered and said : "My Lord, I have *understood* the *mysteries* of the things spoken which have happened to this woman. Now concerning the things spoken which have happened to her, thou hast spoken to us once in a *parable*, saying : 'There was a man who had a fig-tree in his vineyard. He came to seek its *fruit but* he could not find one upon it. He said to the gardener : behold, I have come for three years seeking *fruit* on this fig-tree and I do not find one upon it. Cut it down now. Why does it make the ground idle? *But* he answered and said to him : my lord, withhold from it for another year until I dig around it and give it dung. If *however* it bears (in) another year, thou hast left it, *but* if thou dost not find anything thou hast cut it down' *. Behold, this my Lord, is the interpretation of the things spoken."

The *Saviour* answered and said to Maria : "*Excellent*, thou *spiritual one*, this is the word."

123. Maria continued again, she said to the *Saviour* : "My Lord, if a man who has received *mysteries* has not done what is worthy of the *mysteries*, but has turned and has sinned, and after these things he has *repented* and has been in great *repentance*, is it *permitted* to my brothers to give him once again the *mystery* which he has received *or*, on the other hand, to give him a *mystery* among the lower *mysteries*? *Now* is it *permitted* or not?

The *Saviour however* answered and said to Maria : "*Truly, truly*, I say to you, *neither* | the *mystery* which he has

---

* cf. Lk. 13.6-9

ΠΜΥⲤΤΗΡΙΟΝ ⲚΤΑϤ϶ΙΤϤ· ΟΥⲆⲈ ΠⲈΤ϶ΑΠⲈϤⲈⲤΗΤ ΜⲈΥ-

ⲤⲰΤΜ ⲈΡΟϤ ⲈⲔⲰ ⲈΒΟⲖ ⲚⲚⲈϤⲚΟΒⲈ· ΑⲖⲖΑ ΜΜΥⲤΤΗ-

ΡΙΟΝ ⲈΤ϶ΟⲤⲈ ⲈⲚⲈⲚΤΑϤϪΙΤΟΥ· ⲚΤΟΟΥ ΠⲈ ⲈϢΑΥ-

ⲤⲰΤΜ ⲈΡΟϤ ΑΥⲰ ⲚⲤⲈⲔⲰ ⲈΒΟⲖ ⲚⲚⲈϤⲚΟΒⲈ· ΤⲈⲚΟΥ

5 ϬⲈ ΟΥⲚ ΜΑΡΙΑ**ΜΑΡⲈ ΝΟΥⲤⲚΗΥ † ⲚΑϤ ΜΠΜΥⲤΤΗΡΙΟΝ ⲤⲠⲄ

ⲈΤ϶ΟⲤⲈ ⲈΠⲈⲚΤΑϤϪΙΤϤ· ΑΥⲰ ⲤⲈⲚΑϪΙ ⲚΤⲈϤΜⲈΤΑⲚΟΙΑ

ⲚΤΟΟΤϤ ΑΥⲰ ⲚⲤⲈⲔⲰ ⲈΒΟⲖ ⲚⲚⲈϤⲚΟΒⲈ· ΠΗ ΜⲈⲚ ϪⲈ

ΑϤϪΙΤϤ ⲚⲔⲈⲤΟΠ' ΑΥⲰ ⲚⲔΟΟΥⲈ ϪⲈ ΑϤΟΥΟΤΒΟΥ

ⲈΤΠⲈ· ΠΑΪ ΜⲈⲚ ΜⲈϤⲤⲰΤΜ ⲈΡΟϤ ⲈⲔⲰ ⲈΒΟⲖ ⲚⲚⲈϤⲚΟΒⲈ·

10 ΑⲖⲖΑ ΠΜΥⲤΤΗΡΙΟΝ ⲈΤ϶ΟⲤⲈ ⲈΠⲈⲚΤΑϤϪΙΤϤ ⲚΤΟϤ ΠⲈ

ⲈϢΑϤⲔⲰ ⲈΒΟⲖ ⲚⲚⲈϤⲚΟΒⲈ· ΑⲖⲖΑ ⲈϢⲰΠⲈ ⲚΤΟϤ ⲈΑϤϪΙ-

ϢΟΜⲚΤ ΜΜΥⲤΤΗΡΙΟΝ ϨΜ ΠⲈϪⲰΡΗΜΑ ⲤⲚΑΥ· Η ϨΜ

ΠΜⲈϨϢΟΜⲚΤ ⲈϨΟΥⲚ· ΑΥⲰ ΠΑΪ ΑϤⲔΟΤϤ ΑϤΠΑΡΑΒΑ·

ΜⲈΡⲈ ⲖΑΑΥ ΜΜΥⲤΤΗΡΙΟΝ ⲤⲰΤΜ ⲈΡΟϤ ⲈΤΡⲈΥ†ΤΟΟΤϤ

15 ϨⲚ ΤⲈϤΜⲈΤΑⲚΟΙΑ· ΟΥⲆⲈ ⲚⲈΤϪΟⲤⲈ· ΟΥⲆⲈ ⲚⲈΤ϶ΑΠⲈ-

ⲤΗΤ ΜΜΟϤ· ⲈΙΜΗΤΙ ΠΜΥⲤΤΗΡΙΟΝ ΜΠΙϢΟΡΠ ΜΜΥⲤΤΗ-

ΡΙΟΝ· ΜⲚ ΜΜΥⲤΤΗΡΙΟΝ ΜΠΙΑΤϢΑϪⲈ ⲈΡΟϤ· ⲚΤΟΟΥ ΠⲈ

ⲈϢΑΥⲤⲰΤΜ ⲈΡΟϤ ⲚⲤⲈϪΙ ⲚΤΟΟΤϤ ⲚΤⲈϤΜⲈΤΑⲚΟΙΑ·

ΑⲤΟΥⲰϨΜ ⲚϬΙ ΜΑΡΙΑ ΠⲈϪΑⲤ ϪⲈ ΠΑϪΟⲈΙⲤ· ⲈΪⲈ ΟΥ-

20 ΡⲰΜⲈ ⲈΑϤϪΙ-ΜΥⲤΤΗΡΙΟΝ ϢΑ ⲤⲚΑΥ Η ϢΑ ϢΟΜⲚΤ ϨΡΑΪ

ϨΜ *ΠΜⲈϨϪⲰΡΗΜΑ ⲤⲚΑΥ Η ΠΜⲈϨϢΟΜⲚΤ ⲚϪⲰΡΗΜΑ· ⲤⲠⲄ b

ΑΥⲰ ΠΑΪ ΜΠϤΠΑΡΑΒΑ· ΑⲖⲖΑ ⲈΤΙ ⲈϤϢΟΟΠ' ϨⲚ ΤⲈϤΠΙⲤΤΙⲤ

---

17 MS the words ΜΠΙ ΜΜΥⲤΤΗΡΙΟΝ ΜΠΙϢΟΡΠ ΜΜΥⲤΤΗΡΙΟΝ expunged
after ΜΜΥⲤΤΗΡΙΟΝ.

22 MS ⲚϤΠΑΡΑΒΑ; Π inserted above in later hand, giving ⲚΠϤΠΑΡΑΒΑ =
ΜΠϤΠΑΡΑΒΑ. MS originally ΟΥΠΙⲤΤΙⲤ; ΟΥ crossed out, and ΤⲈϤ inserted
above.

received, *nor* that which is below it [1], listen to him to forgive his sins, but the *mysteries* which are above those he has received, it is they which listen to him and forgive his sins. *Now* at this time, Maria, let thy brothers give to him the *mystery* which is higher than that which he has received, and they will receive his *repentance* from him and forgive his sins — this (mystery) *indeed* because he received it once again, and the others because he passed them over, these do not listen [2] to him to forgive his sins — *but* the *mystery* which is higher than that which he has received is the one which forgives his sins. *But* on the other hand, if he has received three *mysteries* in the second *space or* in the third (space), and has turned and *transgressed*, no *mysteries* listen to him to help him in his *repentance*; neither those above *nor* those below him, *except* the *mystery* of the First *Mystery* and the *mystery* of the Ineffable, it is they which listen to him and receive his *repentance* from him."

Maria answered and said : "My Lord, what of a man who has received *mysteries* as far as two *or* three in the second *or* third *space*, and has not transgressed, *but* is still in his *faith* | with certainty and without *hypocrisy*?" [3]

---

[1] (1) that which is below it; Schmidt : the lower one.

[2] (9) these do not listen; lit. this does not listen.

[3] (313.1) Schmidt (emended Coptic text) : ⟨is it permitted to him to receive mysteries in the space which pleases him or not?⟩

ⲞⲨⲤⲞⲞⲨⲦⲚ ⲀⲨⲰ ⲀⲬⲚ ϨⲨⲠⲞⲔⲢⲒⲤⲒⲤ· *** ⲀϤⲞⲨⲰϢⲂ
ⲆⲈ ⲚϬⲒ ⲠⲤⲰⲦⲎⲢ ⲠⲈⲬⲀϤ ⲘⲘⲀⲢⲒⲀ· ϪⲈ ⲢⲰⲘⲈ ⲚⲒⲘ ⲚⲦ-
ⲀϤϪⲒ-ⲘⲨⲤⲦⲎⲢⲒⲞⲚ ϨⲘ ⲠⲘⲈϨⲤⲚⲀⲨ ⲚⲬⲰⲢⲎⲘⲀ· ⲀⲨⲰ ϨⲘ
ⲠⲘⲈϨϢⲞⲘⲚⲦ· ⲀⲨⲰ ⲞⲚ ⲘⲠϤⲠⲀⲢⲀⲂⲀ· ⲀⲖⲖⲀ ⲈⲦⲒ ⲈϤ-
5 ϢⲞⲞⲠ' ϨⲚ ⲦⲈϤⲠⲒⲤⲦⲒⲤ ⲀⲬⲚ ϨⲨⲠⲞⲔⲢⲒⲤⲒⲤ· ⲈⲜⲈⲤⲦⲒ ⲚⲚⲀⲒ
ⲚⲦⲈⲒⲘⲒⲚⲈ ⲈϪⲒ-ⲘⲨⲤⲦⲎⲢⲒⲞⲚ ϨⲘ ⲠⲈⲬⲰⲢⲎⲘⲀ ⲈⲦⲈϨⲚⲀϤ·
ϪⲒⲚ ⲚϢⲞⲢⲠ' ϨⲈⲰⲤ ϢⲀ ϨⲀⲈ ⲈⲂⲞⲖ ϪⲈ ⲘⲠⲞⲨⲠⲀⲢⲀⲂⲀ:
     ⲀⲤⲞⲨⲰϨ ⲞⲚ ⲈⲦⲞⲞⲦⲤ ⲚϬⲒ ⲘⲀⲢⲒⲀ ⲠⲈϪⲀⲤ ϪⲈ ⲠⲀ-
ϪⲞⲈⲒⲤ· ⲈⲒⲈ ⲞⲨⲢⲰⲘⲈ ⲈⲀϤⲤⲞⲨⲚ-ⲦⲘⲚⲦⲚⲞⲨⲦⲈ ⲀⲨⲰ ⲀϤϪⲒ
10 ϨⲚ ⲘⲘⲨⲤⲦⲎⲢⲒⲞⲚ ⲘⲠⲞⲨⲞⲈⲒⲚ· ⲀⲨⲰ ⲀϤⲔⲞⲦϤ ⲀϤⲠⲀⲢⲀⲂⲀ
ⲀϤⲀⲚⲞⲘⲒ ⲘⲠϤⲔⲞⲦϤ ⲈⲘⲈⲦⲀⲚⲞⲒ̈· ⲀⲨⲰ ⲞⲨⲢⲰⲘⲈ ϨⲰⲰϤ
ⲈⲘⲠϤϨⲈ ⲈⲦⲘⲚⲦⲚⲞⲨⲦⲈ ⲞⲨⲆⲈ ⲘⲠϤⲤⲞⲨⲰⲚⲤ· ⲀⲨⲰ
ⲠⲢⲰⲘⲈ ⲈⲦⲘⲘⲀⲨ ⲈⲨⲢⲈϤⲢⲚⲞⲂⲈ ⲠⲈ· ⲀⲨⲰ ⲞⲚ ⲞⲨⲀⲤⲈ- [ⲤⲠⲀ
ⲂⲎⲤ ⲠⲈ· ⲀⲨⲰ ⲀⲨⲈⲒ' ⲈⲂⲞⲖ ϨⲚ ⲤⲰⲘⲀ ⲘⲠⲈⲤⲚⲀⲨ· ⲚⲒⲘ
15 ⲘⲘⲞⲞⲨ ⲠⲈⲦⲚⲀϪⲒ-ϨⲒⲤⲈ ⲚϨⲞⲨⲞ ϨⲚ ⲚⲈⲔⲢⲒⲤⲒⲤ. ⲀϤⲞⲨⲰϨⲘ
ⲞⲚ ⲚϬⲒ ⲠⲤⲰⲦⲎⲢ ⲠⲈϪⲀϤ ⲘⲘⲀⲢⲒⲀ ϪⲈ ϨⲀⲘⲎⲚ ϨⲀⲘⲎⲚ
ϮϪⲰ ⲘⲘⲞⲤ ⲈⲢⲞ ϪⲈ ⲠⲢⲰⲘⲈ ⲚⲦⲀϤⲤⲞⲨⲚ-ⲦⲘⲚⲦⲚⲞⲨⲦⲈ·
ⲠⲀⲒ̈ ⲚⲦⲀϤϪⲒ ⲚⲘⲘⲨⲤⲦⲎⲢⲒⲞⲚ ⲘⲠⲞⲨⲞⲒ̈Ⲛ· ⲀⲨⲰ ⲀϤⲢⲚⲞⲂⲈ
ⲈⲘⲠϤⲔⲞⲦϤ ⲈⲘⲈⲦⲀⲚⲞⲒ̈· ϤⲚⲀϪⲒ-ϨⲒⲤⲈ ϨⲚ ⲚⲔⲞⲖⲀⲤⲒⲤ ⲚⲦⲈ
20 ⲚⲈⲔⲢⲒⲤⲒⲤ ϨⲚ ϨⲈⲚⲚⲞϬ ⲚϨⲒⲤⲈ ⲘⲚ ϨⲈⲚⲔⲢⲒⲤⲒⲤ ⲚⲞⲨⲘⲎⲎϢⲈ
ⲚⲔⲰⲂ ⲚⲤⲞⲠ' ⲈⲘⲀϢⲞ ⲈⲘⲀϢⲞ ⲠⲀⲢⲀ ⲠⲢⲰⲘⲈ ⲚⲀⲤⲈⲂⲎⲤ
ⲀⲨⲰ ⲘⲠⲀⲢⲀⲚⲞⲘⲞⲤ ⲠⲀⲒ̈ ⲈⲦⲈ ⲘⲠϤⲤⲞⲨⲚ-ⲦⲘⲚⲦⲚⲞⲨⲦⲈ·
ⲦⲈⲚⲞⲨ ϬⲈ ⲠⲈⲦⲈ ⲞⲨⲚ-ⲘⲀⲀϪⲈ ⲘⲘⲞϤ ⲈⲤⲰⲦⲘ ⲘⲀⲢⲈϤ-
ⲤⲰⲦⲘ· ⲚⲀⲒ̈ ϬⲈ ⲚⲦⲈⲢⲈϤϪⲞⲞⲨ ⲚϬⲒ ⲠⲤⲰⲦⲎⲢ· ⲀⲤϬⲞϬⲤ

---

1   the next sentence omitted; probably ⲈⲜⲈⲤⲦⲒ ⲞⲨⲚ ⲚⲀϤ ⲈϪⲒ-ⲘⲨⲤⲦⲎⲢⲒⲞⲚ
ϨⲘ ⲠⲈⲬⲰⲢⲎⲘⲀ ⲈⲦⲈϨⲚⲀϤ ⲬⲚ ⲘⲘⲞⲚ.

13   ⲒⲎ in upper right-hand margin at end of quire.

15   ϨⲒⲤⲈ inserted in margin.

The *Saviour* answered *however* and said to Maria : "Every man who has received *mysteries* in the second *space* and in the third, and has not *transgressed, but still* is in his *faith* without *hypocrisy*, it is *permitted* to those of this kind to receive *mysteries* in the *space* which pleases him, from the first *as far as* the last, because they have not *transgressed*."

124. Maria continued again and said : "My Lord, what of a man who has known Godhood and has received from the *mysteries* of the light, and has turned and *transgressed* and committed *iniquity* and has not turned to *repent*, and a man, on the other hand, who has not found Godhood *nor* known it, and that man is a sinner and he is also *impious*; and they both come forth from the *body*, which of them will receive the greater suffering in the *judgments*?"

The *Saviour* answered again and said to Maria : "*Truly, truly*, I say to thee : the man who has known Godhood and has received the *mysteries* of the light, and has sinned and has not turned to *repent*, he will receive sufferings in the *punishments* of the *judgments* with very many times greater sufferings and *judgments than* the *impious* and *lawless* man who has not known Godhood. Now at this time, he who has ears to hear, let him hear." *

Now when the *Saviour* had said these things, | Maria

---

* Mk. 4.9

ⲉⲃⲟⲗ ⲛ̄ϭⲓ ⲙⲁⲣⲓⲁ ⲡⲉϫⲁⲥ ϫⲉ ⲡⲁϫⲟⲉⲓⲥ· ⲟⲩⲛ-ⲙⲁⲁϫⲉ
ⲙ̄ⲡⲁⲣ̄ⲙ̄ⲛ̄ⲟⲩⲟⲉⲓⲛ ⲁⲩⲱ ⲁⲓ̈ⲛⲟⲓ̈ ⲙ̄ⲡϣⲁϫⲉ ⲧⲏⲣ̄ϥ ⲛ̄ⲧⲁⲕ-
ϫⲟⲟϥ· ⲉⲧⲃⲉ ⲡⲉⲓ̈ϣⲁϫⲉ ⲟⲩⲛ ⲛ̄ⲧⲁⲕϫⲟⲟϥ ⲉⲣⲟⲛ ⲙ̄ⲡⲓ-
ⲟⲩⲟⲉⲓϣ ϩⲛ̄ ⲟⲩⲡⲁⲣⲁⲃⲟⲗⲏ ϫⲉ *ⲡϩⲙ̄ϩⲁⲗ ⲛ̄ⲧⲁϥⲉⲓⲙⲉ ⲉ- [ⲥ̄ⲡ̄ⲁ̄ b]
ⲡⲟⲩⲱϣ ⲙ̄ⲡⲉϥϫⲟⲉⲓⲥ ⲁⲩⲱ ⲙ̄ⲡϥ̄ⲥⲟⲃⲧⲉ ⲟⲩⲇⲉ ⲙ̄ⲡϥ̄ⲉⲓⲣⲉ
ⲙ̄ⲡⲟⲩⲱϣ ⲙ̄ⲡⲉϥϫⲟⲉⲓⲥ ϥⲛⲁϫⲓ ⲛ̄ϩⲉⲛⲛⲟϭ ⲛ̄ⲥⲛϣⲉ· ⲡⲉⲧⲉ
ⲙ̄ⲡϥ̄ⲉⲓⲙⲉ ⲇⲉ· ⲁⲩⲱ ⲙ̄ⲡϥ̄ⲉⲓⲣⲉ ϥⲛⲁⲣ̄ⲙ̄ⲡϣⲁ ⲛ̄ϩⲉⲛⲕⲟⲩⲓ̈· ϫⲉ
ⲟⲩⲟⲛ ⲛⲓⲙ' ⲉⲛⲧⲁⲩⲧⲁⲛϩⲟⲩⲧ̄ϥ̄ ⲉϩⲟⲩⲟ ⲥⲉⲛⲁϣⲓⲛⲉ ⲛ̄ⲥⲁ
ϩⲟⲩⲟ ⲉⲃⲟⲗ ϩⲓⲧⲟⲟⲧ̄ϥ̄· ⲁⲩⲱ ⲡⲉⲛⲧⲁⲩϭⲁⲗⲉ-ϩⲁϩ ⲉⲣⲟϥ·
ⲥⲉⲛⲁϣⲁⲧ̄ϥ̄ ⲛ̄ϩⲁϩ· ⲉⲧⲉ ⲡⲁⲓ̈ ⲡⲉ ⲡⲁϫⲟⲉⲓⲥ ⲡⲉⲣⲥⲟⲩⲛ̄-
ⲧⲙ̄ⲛ̄ⲧ̄ⲛⲟⲩⲧⲉ· ⲁⲩⲱ ⲁϥϭⲓⲛⲉ ⲛ̄ⲙ̄ⲙⲩⲥⲧⲏⲣⲓⲟⲛ ⲙ̄ⲡⲟⲩⲟⲉⲓⲛ
ⲁϥⲡⲁⲣⲁⲃⲁ· ⲥⲉⲛⲁⲕⲟⲗⲁⲍⲉ ⲙ̄ⲙⲟϥ ϩⲛ̄ ⲟⲩⲛⲟϭ ⲛ̄ⲕⲣⲓⲥⲓⲥ ⲛ̄-
ϩⲟⲩⲟ ⲉⲡⲉⲧⲉⲙ̄ⲡϥ̄ⲥⲟⲩⲛ̄-ⲧⲙ̄ⲛ̄ⲧ̄ⲛⲟⲩⲧⲉ· ⲡⲁⲓ̈ ⲡⲁϫⲟⲉⲓⲥ ⲡⲉ
ⲡⲃⲱⲗ ⲉⲃⲟⲗ ⲙ̄ⲡϣⲁϫⲉ·

ⲁⲥⲟⲩⲱϩ ⲟⲛ ⲉⲧⲟⲟⲧ̄ⲥ̄ ⲛ̄ϭⲓ ⲙⲁⲣⲓⲁ ⲡⲉϫⲁⲥ ⲙ̄ⲡⲥⲱⲧⲏⲣ
ϫⲉ ⲡⲁϫⲟⲓ̈ⲥ ⲉϣϫⲉ ⲉⲣⲉ ⲧⲡⲓⲥⲧⲓⲥ ⲙ̄ⲛ̄ ⲙ̄ⲙⲩⲥⲧⲏⲣⲓⲟⲛ ⲛⲏⲩ
ⲛ̄ⲟⲩⲱⲛ̄ϩ̄ ⲉⲃⲟⲗ· ⲧⲉⲛⲟⲩ ϭⲉ ⲟⲩⲛ ⲉⲣϣⲁⲛ ϩⲉⲛⲯⲩⲭⲏ
ⲉⲩϣⲁⲛⲉⲓ' ⲉⲡⲕⲟⲥⲙⲟⲥ ⲛ̄ⲟⲩⲙⲏⲏϣⲉ ⲛ̄ⲕⲩⲕⲗⲟⲥ ⲁⲩⲱ ⲛ̄-
ⲥⲉⲁⲙⲉⲗⲓ ⲛ̄ⲥⲉ**ⲧⲙ̄ϫⲓ-ⲙⲩⲥⲧⲏⲣⲓⲟⲛ ⲉⲩⲕⲱ ⲛ̄ϩⲧⲏⲩ ϫⲉ ⲉⲩ- ⲥ̄ⲡ̄ⲉ̄
ϣⲁⲛⲉⲓ' ⲉⲡⲕⲟⲥⲙⲟⲥ ⲛ̄ⲕⲉⲕⲩⲕⲗⲟⲥ ⲥⲉⲛⲁϫⲓⲧⲟⲩ· ⲉⲓ̈ⲉ ⲟⲩⲕ-
ⲟⲩⲛ ⲛ̄ⲥⲉϩⲏϣ | ⲁⲛ ⲥⲉⲡⲏϩ ⲉϫⲓ ⲛ̄ⲙ̄ⲙⲩⲥⲧⲏⲣⲓⲟⲛ· ⲁϥⲟⲩ-
ⲱϣ̄ⲃ̄ ⲛ̄ϭⲓ ⲡⲥⲱⲧⲏⲣ ⲡⲉϫⲁϥ ⲛ̄ⲛⲉϥⲙⲁⲑⲏⲧⲏⲥ· ϫⲉ ⲕⲏⲣⲩⲥⲥⲉ ⲙ̄ⲡⲕⲟⲥⲙⲟⲥ ⲧⲏⲣ̄ϥ̄ ⲉⲧⲉⲧ̄ⲛ̄ϫⲱ ⲙ̄ⲙⲟⲥ ⲛ̄ⲣ̄ⲣⲱⲙⲉ ϫⲉ
ⲙⲓϣⲉ ⲉⲣⲱⲧ̄ⲛ̄ ⲛ̄ⲧⲉⲧ̄ⲛ̄ϫⲓ ⲛ̄ⲙ̄ⲙⲩⲥⲧⲏⲣⲓⲟⲛ ⲙ̄ⲡⲟⲩⲟⲉⲓⲛ ϩ̄ⲙ̄
ⲡⲉⲓ̈ⲟⲩⲟⲉⲓϣ ⲉⲧϩⲏϫ' ⲛ̄ⲧⲉⲧ̄ⲛ̄ⲃⲱⲕ' ⲉϩⲟⲩⲛ ⲉⲧⲙ̄ⲛ̄ⲧ̄ⲉⲣⲟ

19 ⲓ̄ⲑ̄ in upper left-hand margin at beginning of quire.
21 MS ⲁⲛⲥⲉⲡⲏϩ : read ⲁⲛ ⲛ̄ⲥⲉⲡⲏϩ.

sprang up and said : "My Lord, my man of light has ears, and I have *understood* the whole discourse which thou hast spoken. Concerning this word *now*, thou hast once spoken to us in a *parable* thus : 'The servant who knew the will of his lord and did not make ready, *nor* did he do the will of his lord, he will receive great blows. *But* he who did not know and did nothing, he will be worthy of small (blows). For from everyone to whom much has been entrusted, much shall be sought from him, and from those to whom much has been assigned, much shall be required' *. That is, my Lord, he who knows Godhood and has found the *mysteries* of the light and has *transgressed* will be *punished* with a greater *judgment* than he who does not know Godhood. This, my Lord, is the interpretation of the word."

125. Maria continued again and said to the *Saviour* : "My Lord, if the *faith* and the *mysteries* have come to be revealed, *now* at this time when *souls* come into the *world* in many *cycles* and they *neglect* to receive *mysteries*, being confident that when they come into the *world* to other *cycles* they will receive them, are they *not therefore* in danger that they do not attain to receiving the *mysteries*?"

The *Saviour* answered and said to his disciples : "*Preach* to the whole *world* and say to men : strive that you receive the *mysteries* of the light in this restricted time, so that you go into the Kingdom | of the Light. Do not spend

---

* cf. Lk. 12.47-48

ⲘⲠⲞⲨⲞⲈⲒⲚ· ⲘⲠⲢⲚⲞⲨⲬⲈ ⲚⲞⲨⲌⲞⲞⲨ ⲈⲌⲞⲨⲚ ⲈⲨⲌⲞⲞⲨ· Ⲏ
ⲞⲨⲔⲨⲔⲖⲞⲤ ⲈⲌⲞⲨⲚ ⲈⲨⲔⲨⲔⲖⲞⲤ· ⲚⲦⲈⲦⲚⲔⲀⲌⲦⲎⲦⲚ ⲬⲈ
ⲦⲈⲦⲚⲠⲎⲌ ⲈⲬⲒ ⲚⲘⲘⲨⲤⲦⲎⲢⲒⲞⲚ ⲈⲚϢⲀⲚⲈⲒ' ⲈⲠⲔⲞⲤⲘⲞⲤ Ⲛ-
ⲔⲈⲔⲨⲔⲖⲞⲤ· ⲀⲨⲰ ⲚⲀⲒ ⲚⲤⲈⲤⲞⲞⲨⲚ ⲀⲚ ⲬⲈ ⲈϤⲚⲀϢⲰⲠⲈ
5 ⲦⲚⲀⲨ ⲚϬⲒ ⲠⲀⲢⲒⲐⲘⲞⲤ ⲚⲚⲈⳘⲨⲬⲞⲞⲨⲈ ⲚⲚⲦⲈⲖⲒⲞⲤ· ⲬⲈ
ⲈϤϢⲀⲚϢⲰⲠⲈ ⲄⲀⲢ ⲚϬⲒ ⲠⲀⲢⲒⲐⲘⲞⲤ ⲚⲚⲈⳘⲨⲬⲞⲞⲨⲈ ⲚⲦⲈ-
ⲖⲒⲞⲤ· †ⲚⲀϢⲦⲀⲘ' ϬⲈ ⲈⲘⲠⲨⲖⲎ ⲘⲠⲞⲨⲞⲈⲒⲚ· ⲀⲨⲰ ⲘⲚ-
ⲖⲀⲀⲨ ⲚⲀⲂⲰⲔ' ⲈⲌⲞⲨⲚ ⲬⲒⲚ ⲠⲈⲒⲚⲀⲨ· ⲞⲨⲆⲈ ⲘⲚ-ⲖⲀⲀⲨ
ⲚⲎⲨ ⲈⲂⲞⲖ ⲘⲚⲚⲤⲰⲤ*ⲈⲂⲞⲖ ⲬⲈ ⲀϤⲬⲰⲔ' ⲈⲂⲞⲖ ⲚϬⲒ ⲠⲀ- ⲥⲡⲉ ᵇ
10 ⲢⲒⲐⲘⲞⲤ ⲚⲚⲈⳘⲨⲬⲞⲞⲨⲈ ⲚⲦⲈⲖⲒⲞⲤ· ⲀⲨⲰ ⲀϤⲬⲰⲔ ⲈⲂⲞⲖ
ⲚϬⲒ ⲠⲘⲨⲤⲦⲎⲢⲒⲞⲚ ⲘⲠϢⲞⲢⲠ ⲘⲘⲨⲤⲦⲎⲢⲒⲞⲚ· ⲠⲀⲒ ⲚⲦⲀ
ⲠⲦⲎⲢϤ ϢⲰⲠⲈ ⲈⲦⲂⲎⲎⲦϤ· ⲈⲦⲈ ⲀⲚⲞⲔ ⲠⲈ ⲠⲘⲨⲤⲦⲎⲢⲒⲞⲚ
ⲈⲦⲘⲘⲀⲨ· ⲀⲨⲰ ⲬⲒⲚ ⲠⲈⲒⲚⲀⲨ· ⲘⲚ-ⲖⲀⲀⲨ ⲚⲀⲂⲰⲔ' ⲈⲠⲞⲨ-
ⲞⲈⲒⲚ· ⲀⲨⲰ ⲘⲚ-ⲖⲀⲀⲨ ⲚⲀϢⲈⲒ' ⲈⲂⲞⲖ ⲬⲈ ⲌⲢⲀⲒ ⲌⲘ ⲠⲬⲰⲔ'
15 ⲈⲂⲞⲖ ⲘⲠⲈⲞⲨⲞⲈⲒϢ ⲘⲠⲀⲢⲒⲐⲘⲞⲤ ⲚⲚⲈⳘⲨⲬⲞⲞⲨⲈ ⲚⲦⲈ-
ⲖⲒⲞⲤ ⲌⲀⲐⲎ ⲈⲘⲠⲀ†ⲔⲰ ⲈⲂⲞⲖ ⲘⲠⲔⲰⲌⲦ ⲈⲠⲔⲞⲤⲘⲞⲤ·
ⲈⲦⲢⲈϤⲤⲰⲦϤ (Ⲛ)ⲚⲀⲒⲰⲚ ⲘⲚ ⲚⲔⲀⲦⲀⲠⲈⲦⲀⲤⲘⲀ· ⲘⲚ ⲚⲈⲤⲦⲈ-
ⲢⲈⲰⲘⲀ ⲘⲚ ⲠⲔⲀⲌ ⲦⲎⲢϤ ⲘⲚ ⲚⲔⲈⲌⲨⲖⲎ ⲦⲎⲢⲞⲨ ⲈⲦⲌⲒⲬⲰϤ·
ⲀⲒⲦⲒ ⲞⲚ ⲈⲨϢⲞⲞⲠ' ⲚϬⲒ ⲦⲘⲚⲦⲢⲰⲘⲈ· ⲌⲢⲀⲒ ⲞⲨⲚ ⲌⲘ ⲠⲈⲨ-
20 ⲞⲈⲒϢ ⲈⲦⲘⲘⲀⲨ ⲤⲚⲀⲢⲌⲞⲨⲈ-ⲞⲨⲰⲚⲌ ⲈⲂⲞⲖ ⲚϬⲒ ⲦⲠⲒⲤⲦⲒⲤ
ⲘⲚ ⲘⲘⲨⲤⲦⲎⲢⲒⲞⲚ ⲌⲚ ⲚⲈⲌⲞⲞⲨ ⲈⲦⲘⲘⲀⲨ· ⲀⲨⲰ ⲞⲨⲚ-ⲌⲀⲌ
ⲚⳘⲨⲬⲎ ⲚⲎⲨ ⲌⲒⲦⲚ ⲚⲔⲨⲔⲖⲞⲤ ⲚⲦⲈ ⲘⲘⲈⲦⲀⲂⲞⲖⲎ ⲚⲦⲈ
ⲠⲤⲰⲘⲀ· ⲀⲨⲰ ⲈⲨⲚⲎⲨ ⲈⲠⲔⲞⲤⲘⲞⲤ ⲈⲨⲚ-ⲌⲞⲒⲚⲈ ⲚⲌⲎⲦⲞⲨ
ⲌⲘ ⲠⲈⲒⲞⲨⲞⲒϢ**ⲦⲈⲚⲞⲨ ⲈⲀⲨⲤⲰⲦⲘ ⲈⲢⲞⲒ ⲈⲒ†ⲤⲂⲰ ⲌⲘ [ⲥⲡⲉ

---

3 MS ⲈⲚϢⲀⲚⲈⲒ'; read ⲈⲦⲈⲦⲚϢⲀⲚⲈⲒ'.
5 MS ⲚⲚⲦⲈⲖⲒⲞⲤ; read ⲚⲦⲈⲖⲒⲞⲤ.
17 a letter erased before ⲚⲀⲒⲰⲚ; read ⲚⲚⲀⲒⲰⲚ.
19 MS ⲈⲨϢⲞⲞⲠ; better ⲈⲤϢⲞⲞⲠ.
24 the letter Ⲁ erased before ⲦⲈⲚⲞⲨ.

day upon day *or cycle* upon *cycle*, being confident that you
will attain to receiving the *mysteries* when you come [1] into
the *world* in another *cycle*. And these do not know when
the time of the *number* of the *perfect souls* will come about,
for when the *number* of the *perfect souls* exists I will shut
the *gates* of the light. And no one will go within from
this hour. *Nor* will anyone come forth afterwards, because
the *number* of the *perfect souls* is completed, and the
mystery of the First *Mystery* is completed, for the sake of
which the All came into existence : that is, I am that
Mystery. And from that hour no one will go into the light,
and no one will come forth. For at the completion of the
time of the *number* of the *perfect* souls, before I lay fire
to the *world* in order to purify the *aeons* and the *veils*
and the *firmaments* and the whole earth and all the *matter*
which is upon it, mankind is *still* in existence. *Now* in that
time, in those days the *faith* and the *mysteries* will be the
more revealed. And many *souls* will come by means of the
cycles of the *changes* of the *body*. And as they come into
the *world*, some of them at that time who have heard me
teaching about | the completion of the *number* of the *perfect*

---

[1]   (3) when you come; MS : when we come.

ⲡⲭⲱⲕ ⲉⲃⲟⲗ ⲙ̄ⲡⲁⲣⲓⲑⲙⲟⲥ ⲛ̄ⲧⲉⲗⲓⲟⲥ ⲛ̄ⲛⲉⲯⲩⲭⲟⲟⲩⲉ ⲥⲉⲛⲁϩⲉ ⲉⲙⲙⲩⲥⲧⲏⲣⲓⲟⲛ ⲙ̄ⲡⲟⲩⲟⲉⲓⲛ ⲁⲩⲱ ⲛ̄ⲥⲉϫⲓⲧⲟⲩ· ⲁⲩⲱ
ⲥⲉⲛⲏⲩ ⲉϩⲣⲁⲓ̈ ⲉⲣⲛ̄ ⲙ̄ⲡⲩⲗⲏ ⲙ̄ⲡⲟⲩⲟⲉⲓⲛ· ⲛ̄ⲥⲉϩⲉ ⲉⲣⲟϥ
ⲉⲁϥϫⲱⲕ ⲉⲃⲟⲗ ⲛ̄ϭⲓ ⲡⲁⲣⲓⲑⲙⲟⲥ ⲛ̄ⲛⲉⲯⲩⲭⲟⲟⲩⲉ ⲛ̄ⲧⲉⲗⲓⲟⲥ·
5 ⲉⲧⲉ ⲛ̄ⲧⲟϥ ⲡⲉ ⲡⲭⲱⲕ ⲉⲃⲟⲗ ⲙ̄ⲡϣⲟⲣⲡ̄ ⲙ̄ⲙⲩⲥⲧⲏⲣⲓⲟⲛ·
ⲁⲩⲱ ⲛ̄ⲧⲟϥ ⲡⲉ ⲡⲥⲟⲟⲩⲛ ⲙ̄ⲡⲧⲏⲣϥ· ⲁⲩⲱ ⲥⲉⲛⲁϩⲉ ⲉⲣⲟⲥ
ⲉⲁⲓ̈ϣⲧⲁⲙ' ⲉⲣⲛ̄ ⲙ̄ⲡⲩⲗⲏ ⲙ̄ⲡⲟⲩⲟⲉⲓⲛ· ⲁⲩⲱ ⲙ̄ⲛ̄ϭⲟⲙ' ⲉⲧⲣⲉ
ⲗⲁⲁⲩ ⲉⲓ' ⲉϩⲟⲩⲛ· ⲏ̄ ⲉⲧⲣⲉ ⲗⲁⲁⲩ ⲉⲓ' ⲉⲃⲟⲗ ϫⲓⲛ ⲡⲉⲓ̈ⲛⲁⲩ·
ⲛⲉⲯⲩⲭⲟⲟⲩⲉ ⲟⲩⲛ ⲉⲧⲙ̄ⲙⲁⲩ ⲥⲉⲛⲁⲧⲱϩⲙ̄ ⲉϩⲟⲩⲛ ⲉⲙ-
10 ⲡⲩⲗⲏ ⲙ̄ⲡⲟⲩⲟⲉⲓⲛ· ⲉⲩⲭⲱ ⲙ̄ⲙⲟⲥ ϫⲉ ⲡϫⲟⲉⲓⲥ ⲁⲟⲩⲱⲛ
ⲛⲁⲛ· ϯⲛⲁⲟⲩⲱϣⲃ̄ ⲧⲁϫⲟⲟⲥ ⲛⲁⲩ ϫⲉ ⲛ̄ϯⲥⲟⲟⲩⲛ ⲙ̄-
ⲙⲱⲧⲛ̄ ⲁⲛ ϫⲉ ⲛ̄ⲧⲉⲧⲛ̄ ϩⲉⲛⲉⲃⲟⲗ ⲧⲱⲛ· ⲁⲩⲱ ⲥⲉⲛⲁϫⲟⲟⲥ
ⲛⲁⲓ̈ ϫⲉ ⲁⲛϫⲓ ⲉⲃⲟⲗ ϩⲛ̄ ⲛⲉⲕⲙⲩⲥⲧⲏⲣⲓⲟⲛ ⲁⲩⲱ ⲁⲛϫⲱⲕ'
ⲉⲃⲟⲗ ⲛ̄ⲧⲉⲕⲥⲃⲱ ⲧⲏⲣⲥ̄ ⲁⲩⲱ ⲁⲕϯ*ⲥⲃⲱ ⲛⲁⲛ ϩⲛ̄ ⲛⲉⲡⲗⲁ- ⟦ⲥⲡⲉ ᵇ⟧
15 ⲧⲉⲓⲁ· ⲁⲩⲱ ϯⲛⲁⲟⲩⲱϣⲃ̄ ⲧⲁϫⲟⲟⲥ ⲛⲁⲩ ϫⲉ ⲛ̄ϯⲥⲟⲟⲩⲛ
ⲁⲛ ⲙ̄ⲙⲱⲧⲛ̄ ϫⲉ ⲛ̄ⲧⲉⲧⲛ̄ ⲛⲓⲙ· ⲛⲉⲧⲣ̄ϩⲱⲃ ⲉⲧⲁⲛⲟⲙⲓⲁ· ⲙⲛ̄
ⲙ̄ⲡⲉⲑⲟⲟⲩ ϩⲉⲱⲥ ϣⲁ ⲧⲉⲛⲟⲩ· ⲉⲧⲃⲉ ⲡⲁⲓ̈ ⲃⲱⲕ ⲉⲡⲕⲁⲕⲉ
ⲉⲧϩⲓⲃⲟⲗ· ⲁⲩⲱ ϩⲛ̄ ⲧⲉⲩⲛⲟⲩ ⲉⲧⲙ̄ⲙⲁⲩ ⲥⲉⲛⲁⲃⲱⲕ' ⲉⲡⲕⲁⲕⲉ ⲉⲧϩⲓⲃⲟⲗ· ⲡⲙⲁ ⲉⲧϥ̄ⲙⲙⲁⲩ ⲛ̄ϭⲓ ⲡⲣⲓⲙⲉ ⲙⲛ̄ ⲡϭⲁϩϭⲉϩ ⲛ̄-
20 ⲛⲟⲃϩⲉ· ⲉⲧⲃⲉ ⲡⲁⲓ̈ ϭⲉ ⲟⲩⲛ ⲕⲏⲣⲩⲥⲥⲉ ⲙ̄ⲡⲕⲟⲥⲙⲟⲥ ⲧⲏⲣϥ·
ⲁϫⲓⲥ ⲉⲣⲟⲟⲩ ϫⲉ ⲙⲓϣⲉ ⲉⲣⲱⲧⲛ̄ ⲁⲡⲟⲧⲁⲥⲥⲉ ⲙ̄ⲡⲕⲟⲥⲙⲟⲥ
ⲧⲏⲣϥ̄ ⲙⲛ̄ ⲑⲩⲗⲏ ⲧⲏⲣⲥ̄ ⲉⲧⲛ̄ϩⲏⲧϥ̄· ⲛ̄ⲧⲉⲧⲛ̄ϫⲓ ⲛ̄ⲙ̄ⲙⲩⲥⲧⲏⲣⲓⲟⲛ
ⲙ̄ⲡⲟⲩⲟⲉⲓⲛ· ⲉⲙⲡⲁⲧϥ̄ϫⲱⲕ ⲉⲃⲟⲗ ⲛ̄ϭⲓ ⲡⲁⲣⲓⲑⲙⲟⲥ ⲛ̄ⲛⲉ-
ⲯⲩⲭⲟⲟⲩⲉ ⲛ̄ⲧⲉⲗⲓⲟⲥ· ϫⲉⲕⲁⲥ ⲉⲛⲛⲉⲩⲕⲁⲧⲏⲛⲟⲩ ϩⲓⲣⲛ̄ ⲡⲣⲟ

---

1   MS ⲙ̄ⲡⲁⲣⲓⲑⲙⲟⲥ ⲛ̄ⲧⲉⲗⲓⲟⲥ ⲛ̄ⲛⲉⲯⲩⲭⲟⲟⲩⲉ; read ⲙ̄ⲡⲁⲣⲓⲑⲙⲟⲥ ⲛ̄ⲛⲉⲯⲩ-
    ⲭⲟⲟⲩⲉ ⲛ̄ⲧⲉⲗⲓⲟⲥ.

souls will find the *mysteries* of the light, and they will receive them, and they will come to the *gates* of the light, and they will find that the *number* of the *perfect souls* is completed, which is the completion of the First *Mystery* and that is the knowledge of the All. And they will find that I have shut the *gates* of the light, and it is not possible for anyone to enter within *or* for anyone to come forth from this time. *Now* those *souls* will knock, at the *gates* of the light, saying : 'O Lord, open to us.' I will answer and say to them : 'I do not know you, whence you are.' And they will say to me : 'We have received from thy *mysteries*, and we have completed thy whole teaching, and thou hast taught us upon the *streets*.' And I will answer and say to them : 'I do not know you, who you are, you who do deeds of *iniquity* and evil *up till* now*. Because of this go to the outer darkness.' And in that hour they will go to the outer darkness, that place where is weeping and gnashing of teeth □. Because of this *now*, *preach* to the whole *world*. Say to them : strive that you *renounce* the whole *world* and all the *matter* in it, that you may receive the *mysteries* of the light, before the *number* of the *perfect souls* is completed, that you may not be left before the door | of the *gate* of the light, and be taken

Mt 7, 22 f.

---

*   cf. Mt. 7.22, 23; 25.11, 12
□   cf. Mt. 8.12; 22.13; Lk. 13.24-28

ⲛ̅ⲧⲡⲩⲗⲏ ⲙ̅ⲡⲟⲩⲟⲉⲓⲛ· ⲁⲩⲱ ⲛ̅ⲥⲉⲭⲓⲧⲏⲩⲧ̅ⲛ̅ ⲉⲡⲕⲁⲕⲉ ⲉⲧ-
ϩⲓⲃⲟⲗ· ⲧⲉⲛⲟⲩ ϭⲉ ⲟⲩⲛ ⲡⲉⲧⲉ ⲟⲩⲛ-ⲙⲁⲁⲭⲉ ⲙ̅ⲙⲟϥ ⲉⲥⲱ̅-
ⲧ̅ⲙ ⲙⲁⲣⲉϥⲥⲱⲧ̅ⲙ·

ⲛⲁⲓ̈ ϭⲉ ⲛ̅ⲧⲉⲣⲉϥϫⲟⲟⲩ ⲛ̅ϭⲓ ⲡⲥⲱⲧⲏⲣ· ⲁⲥϭⲟⲃⲥ̅ ⲟⲛ

5 ⲉⲃⲟⲗ ⲛ̅ϭⲓ ⲙⲁⲣⲓⲁ ⲡⲉⲭⲁⲥ ϫⲉ ⲡⲁϫⲟⲉⲓⲥ ⲟⲩⲙⲟⲛⲟⲛ ϫⲉ ⲥ̅ⲡⲍ̅
ⲟⲩⲛ-ⲙⲁⲁⲭⲉ ⲙ̅ⲡⲁⲣⲙ̅ⲛⲟⲩⲟⲉⲓⲛ· ⲁⲗⲗⲁ ⲁⲥⲥⲱⲧ̅ⲙ ⲛ̅ϭⲓ ⲧⲁⲯⲩⲭⲏ ⲁⲩⲱ ⲁⲥⲛⲟⲓ̈ ⲛ̅ϣⲁⲭⲉ ⲛⲓⲙ· ⲉⲧ̅ⲕ̅ϫⲱ ⲙ̅ⲙⲟⲟⲩ· ⲧⲉⲛⲟⲩ ϭⲉ ⲟⲩⲛ ⲡⲁϫⲟⲉⲓⲥ ⲉⲧⲃⲉ ⲛ̅ϣⲁⲭⲉ ⲛ̅ⲧⲁⲕϫⲟⲟⲩ
ϫⲉ ⲕⲏⲣⲩⲥⲥⲉ ⲛ̅ⲣ̅ⲣⲱⲙⲉ ⲛ̅ⲧⲉ ⲡⲕⲟⲥⲙⲟⲥ ⲁϫⲓⲥ ⲉⲣⲟⲟⲩ

10 ϫⲉ ⲙⲓϣⲉ ⲉⲣⲱⲧ̅ⲛ̅ ϫⲓ ⲛ̅ⲙⲙⲩⲥⲧⲏⲣⲓⲟⲛ ⲙ̅ⲡⲟⲩⲟⲉⲓⲛ ϩ̅ⲙ
ⲡⲉⲓ̈ⲟⲩⲟⲉⲓϣ ⲉⲧϩⲏⲭ’ ϫⲉ ⲉⲧⲉⲧ̅ⲛⲉⲕⲗⲏⲣⲟⲛⲟⲙⲓ ⲛ̅ⲧⲙ̅ⲛ̅ⲧⲉⲣⲟ
ⲙ̅ⲡⲟⲩⲟⲉⲓⲛ·

ⲁⲥⲟⲩⲱϩ ⲟⲛ ⲉⲧⲟⲟⲧ̅ⲥ̅ ⲛ̅ϭⲓ ⲙⲁⲣⲓⲁ ⲡⲉⲭⲁⲥ ⲛ̅ⲓ̅ⲥ̅ ϫⲉ
ⲡⲁϫⲟⲉⲓⲥ ⲉⲓ̈ⲉ ⲉⲣⲉ ⲡⲕⲁⲕⲉ ⲉⲧϩⲓⲃⲟⲗ’ ⲟ ⲛ̅ⲁϣ ⲛ̅ⲧⲩⲡⲟⲥ·

15 ⲏ̅ ⲙ̅ⲙⲟⲛ ⲛ̅ⲧⲟϥ ⲟⲩⲛ ⲟⲩⲏⲣ ⲙ̅ⲙⲁ ⲛ̅ⲕⲟⲗⲁⲥⲓⲥ ⲛ̅ϩⲏⲧϥ·
ⲁϥⲟⲩⲱϣ̅ⲙ ⲇⲉ ⲛ̅ϭⲓ ⲓ̅ⲥ̅ ⲡⲉⲭⲁϥ ⲙ̅ⲙⲁⲣⲓⲁ· ϫⲉ ⲡⲕⲁⲕⲉ ⲉⲧϩⲓⲃⲟⲗ ⲟⲩⲛⲟϭ ⲛ̅ⲇⲣⲁⲕⲱⲛ ⲡⲉ ⲉⲣⲉ ⲡⲉϥⲥⲁⲧ’ ⲛ̅ϩⲟⲩⲛ ⲛ̅-
ⲣⲱϥ ⲉϥⲙ̅ⲡⲃⲟⲗ ⲙ̅ⲡⲕⲟⲥⲙⲟⲥ ⲧⲏⲣϥ ⲁⲩⲱ ⲉϥⲕⲱⲧⲉ ⲉⲡⲕⲟⲥⲙⲟⲥ ⲧⲏⲣϥ ⲉⲣⲉ ⲟⲩⲙⲏⲛϣⲉ ⲛ̅ⲧⲟⲡⲟⲥ ⲛ̅ⲕⲣⲓⲥⲓⲥ ⲛ̅ϩⲟⲩⲛ

20 ⲛ̅ϩⲏⲧϥ ⲉϥⲟ ⲙ̅ⲙⲛ̅ⲧⲥⲛⲟⲟⲩⲥ ⲛ̅ⲧⲁⲙⲓⲟⲛ ⲛ̅ⲕⲟⲗⲁⲥⲓⲥ ⲉⲩ- ⲥ̅ⲡⲍ̅ᵇ
ⲛⲁϣ̅ⲧ· ⲉⲣⲉ ⲟⲩⲁⲣⲭⲱⲛ ϩ̅ⲙ ⲡⲧⲁⲙⲓⲟⲛ ⲡⲧⲁⲙⲓⲟⲛ ⲉⲣⲉ ⲡϩⲟ
ⲛ̅ⲛⲁⲣⲭⲱⲛ ϣⲟⲃⲉ ⲉⲛⲉⲩⲉⲣⲏⲩ· ⲡϣⲟⲣ̅ⲡ ⲇⲉ ⲛ̅ⲁⲣⲭⲱⲛ ⲉⲧϣⲟⲟⲡ’ ϩ̅ⲙ ⲡϣⲟⲣⲡ ⲛ̅ⲧⲁⲙⲓⲟⲛ ⲟⲩϩⲟ ⲛ̅ⲙⲥⲁϩ ⲡⲉ ⲉⲣⲉ
ⲡⲉϥⲥⲁⲧ’ ⲛ̅ϩⲟⲩⲛ ⲛ̅ⲣⲱϥ ⲉⲣⲉ ϫⲁϥ ⲛⲓⲙ ⲛⲏⲩ ⲉⲃⲟⲗ ϩ̅ⲛ

25 ⲧⲧⲁⲡⲣⲟ ⲙ̅ⲡⲉⲇⲣⲁⲕⲱⲛ ⲙ̅ⲛ ϣⲟⲉⲓϣ ⲛⲓⲙ· ⲙ̅ⲛ ⲁⲣⲟϣ

---

25 MS originally ⲛ̅ⲟϣⲟⲉⲓϣ; ⲛⲟ expunged, and ⲙ̅ⲛ inserted in margin.

to the outer darkness. *Now* at this time, he who has ears to hear let him hear." *

Now when the *Saviour* had said these things, Maria sprang up again and said : "My Lord, *not only* does my man of light have ears, *but* my *soul* has heard and has *understood* every word which thou sayest. *Now* at this time, my Lord, concerning the words which thou hast spoken : '*Preach* to the men of the *world*, say to them : strive to receive the *mysteries* of the light in this restricted time, so that you may *inherit* the Kingdom of the Light'." (lacuna) [1]

126. Maria continued again, she said to Jesus : "My Lord, of what *type* is the outer darkness, *or* rather, how many *places* of *punishment* are there in it?"

Jesus *however* answered and said to Maria : "The outer darkness is a great *dragon* whose tail is in its mouth, and it is outside the *whole* world, and it surrounds the whole *world*. And there is a great number of *places* of *judgment* within it, and it has twelve *chambers* of severe *punishments*, and an *archon* is in every *chamber* and the faces of the *archons* are different from one another. The first *archon* *moreover* which is in the first *chamber* has a crocodile-face and his tail is in his mouth, and all freezing comes out of the mouth of the *dragon*, and all dust | and all cold and all

---

*   Mk. 4.9

---

[1]   (12) the interpretation of the preceding paragraph in the light of Mt. 7.22, 23 and Lk. 13.24-28 is lacking.

ΝΙΜ· ΜΝ ϢⲰΝΕ ΝΙΜ ΕΤϢⲀⲂⲂΙⲀⲈΙΤ· ΠⲀϊ ⲈϢⲀⲨΜΟⲨΤⲈ
ⲈΠⲈϤⲀⲨⲐⲈΝΤΙΚΟΝ ⲚⲢⲀΝ 2Μ ΠⲈϤΤΟΠΟⲤ ϪⲈ ⲈΝϪⲐ̄ΟΝΙΝ·
ⲀⲨⲰ ΠⲀⲢⲬⲰΝ ⲈΤϢΟΟΠ 2Μ ΠΜⲈ2ⲤΝⲀⲨ ⲚΤⲀΜΙΟΝ ΟⲨ2Ο
Ⲛ̄ⲈΜΟⲨ ΠⲈ ΠⲈϤⲀⲨⲐⲈΝΤΙΚΟΝ Ⲛ̄2Ο· ΠⲀϊ ⲈϢⲀⲨΜΟⲨΤⲈ
5 ⲈⲢΟϤ 2Μ ΠⲈⲨΤΟΠΟⲤ ϪⲈ ⲬⲀⲢⲀⲬⲀⲢ· ⲀⲨⲰ ΠⲀⲢⲬⲰΝ ⲈΤ-
ϢΟΟΠ 2Μ ΠΜⲈ2ϢΟΜΝΤ ⲚΤⲀΜΙΟΝ ΟⲨ2Ο Ⲛ̄ΟⲨ2ΟⲢ ΠⲈ
ΠⲈϤⲀⲨⲐⲈΝΤΗⲤ Ⲛ̄2Ο ΠⲀϊ ⲈϢⲀⲨΜΟⲨΤⲈ ⲈⲢΟϤ 2Μ ΠⲈⲨ-
ΤΟΠΟⲤ ϪⲈ ⲀⲢⲬⲀⲢⲰⲬ·** ⲀⲨⲰ ΠⲀⲢⲬⲰΝ ⲈΤϢΟΟΠ 2Μ [ⲤⲠⲎ]
ΠΜⲈ2ϤΤΟΟⲨ ⲚΤⲀΜΙΟΝ ΟⲨ2Ο Ⲛ̄2ΟϤ ΠⲈ ΠⲈϤⲀⲨⲐⲈΝΤΗⲤ
10 Ⲛ̄2Ο· ΠⲀϊ ⲈϢⲀⲨΜΟⲨΤⲈ ⲈⲢΟϤ 2Μ ΠⲈⲨΤΟΠΟⲤ ϪⲈ ⲀⲬⲢⲰ-
ⲬⲀⲢ· ⲀⲨⲰ ΠⲀⲢⲬⲰΝ ⲈΤϢΟΟΠ 2Μ ΠΜⲈ2†ΟⲨ ⲚΤⲀΜΙΟΝ
ΟⲨ2Ο Ⲙ̄ΜⲀⲤⲈ Ⲛ̄ΚⲀΜⲈ ΠⲈ ΠⲈϤⲀⲨⲐⲈΝΤΙΚΟΝ Ⲛ̄2Ο· ΠⲀϊ
ⲈϢⲀⲨΜΟⲨΤⲈ ⲈⲢΟϤ 2Μ ΠⲈⲨΤΟΠΟⲤ ϪⲈ ΜⲀⲢⲬΟⲨⲢ·
ⲀⲨⲰ ΠⲀⲢⲬⲰΝ ⲈΤϢΟΟΠ 2Μ ΠΜⲈ2ⲤΟΟⲨ ⲚΤⲀΜΙΟΝ·
15 ΟⲨ2Ο Ⲛ̄ⲢΙⲢⲚ̄ΤΟΟⲨ ΠⲈ ΠⲈϤ2Ο Ⲛ̄ⲀⲨⲐⲈΝΤΗⲤ· ΠⲀϊ Ⲉ-
ϢⲀⲨΜΟⲨΤⲈ ⲈⲢΟϤ 2Μ ΠⲈⲨΤΟΠΟⲤ ϪⲈ ⲖⲀΜⲬⲀΜⲰⲢ·
ⲀⲨⲰ ΠⲀⲢⲬⲰΝ Ⲙ̄ΠΜⲈ2ⲤⲀϢϤ ⲚΤⲀΜΙΟΝ· ΟⲨ2Ο Ⲛ̄ⲀⲢϤ̄ ΠⲈ
ΠⲈϤⲀⲨⲐⲈΝΤΗⲤ Ⲛ̄2Ο· ΠⲀϊ ⲈϢⲀⲨΜΟⲨΤⲈ ⲈⲢΟϤ 2Μ ΠⲈϤ-
ⲀⲨⲐⲈΝΤΙΚΟΝ ⲚⲢⲀΝ 2Μ ΠⲈⲨΤΟΠΟⲤ ϪⲈ ⲖΟⲨⲬⲀⲢ· ⲀⲨⲰ
20 ΠⲀⲢⲬⲰΝ Ⲙ̄ΠΜⲈ2ϢΜΟⲨΝ ⲚΤⲀΜΙΟΝ· ΟⲨ2Ο Ⲛ̄ΝΟⲨⲢⲈ ΠⲈ
ΠⲈϤⲀⲨⲐⲈΝΤΗⲤ Ⲛ̄2Ο· ΠⲀϊ ⲈϢⲀⲨΜΟⲨΤⲈ ⲈΠⲈϤⲢⲀΝ 2Μ
ΠⲈⲨΤΟΠΟⲤ ϪⲈ ⲖⲀⲢⲀⲰⲬ· ⲀⲨⲰ ΠⲀⲢⲬⲰΝ Ⲙ̄ΠΜⲈ2ⲮΙΤ
ⲚΤⲀΜΙΟΝ ΟⲨ2Ο Ⲛ̄ⲤΙΤ ΠⲈ ΠⲈϤ2Ο Ⲛ̄ⲀⲨⲐⲈΝΤΗⲤ· ΠⲀϊ [ⲤⲠⲎ]ᵇ
ⲈϢⲀⲨΜΟⲨΤⲈ ⲈΠⲈϤⲢⲀΝ 2Μ ΠⲈⲨΤΟΠΟⲤ ϪⲈ ⲀⲢⲬⲈⲰⲬ·
25 ⲀⲨⲰ ΠΜⲈ2ΜΗΤ' ⲚΤⲀΜΙΟΝ ΟⲨⲚ̄-ΟⲨΜΗΗϢⲈ Ⲛ̄ⲀⲢⲬⲰΝ Ⲛ̄-
2ΗΤϤ̄ ⲈⲢⲈ ⲤⲀϢϤⲈ Ⲛ̄ⲀΠⲈ Ⲛ̄ⲀⲢⲀΚⲰΝ Ⲙ̄ΠΟⲨⲀ ΠΟⲨⲀ
Ⲙ̄ΜΟΟⲨ 2ⲢⲀϊ 2Μ ΠⲈⲨ2Ο Ⲛ̄ⲀⲨⲐⲈΝΤΗⲤ· ⲀⲨⲰ ΠⲈΤ2Ι-
ϪⲰΟⲨ ΤΗⲢΟⲨ ϢⲀⲨΜΟⲨΤⲈ ⲈΠⲈϤⲢⲀΝ 2Μ ΠⲈⲨΤΟΠΟⲤ

the various diseases; this one is called by his *authentic* name in his *place* : Enchthonin [1]. And the *archon* which is in the second *chamber*, a cat-face is his *authentic* face; this one is called in their *place* [2] : Charachar. And the *archon* which is in the third *chamber*, a dog-face is his *authentic* face; this one is called in their *place* : Archaroch. And the *archon* which is in the fourth *chamber*, a serpent-face is his *authentic* face; this one is called in their *place* : Achrochar. And the *archon* which is in the fifth *chamber*, a black bull-face is his *authentic* face; this one is called in their *place* : Marchur. And the *archon* which is in the sixth *chamber*, a mountain pig-face is his *authentic* face; this one is called in their *place* : Lamchamor. And the *archon* which is in the seventh *chamber*, a *bear*-face is his *authentic* face; this one is called by his *authentic* name in their *place* : Luchar. And the *archon* of the eighth *chamber*, a vulture-face is his *authentic* face; this one is called by his name in their *place* : Laraoch. And the *archon* of the ninth *chamber*, a basilisk-face is his *authentic* face; this one is called by his name in their *place* : Archeoch. And the tenth *chamber* : there is a great number of *archons* within it, each one having seven *dragon* heads with their *authentic* face. And the one over them all is called by his name in their *place* : | Zarmaroch. And the eleventh *chamber* :

---

[1] (2) Enchthonin; on magical names, see Kropp (Bibl. 26), III p. 117 ff; (also 357.13-17).

[2] (5) their place; Schmidt : his place (passim to 319.10).

ϫⲉ ⲌⲀⲢⲘⲀⲢⲰⲬ· ⲀⲨⲰ ⲠⲘⲈϨⲘⲚ̄ⲦⲞⲨⲈ Ⲛ̄ⲦⲀⲘⲒⲞⲚ ⲞⲨⲚ-
ⲞⲨⲘⲎⲎϢⲈ Ⲛ̄ⲀⲢⲬⲰⲚ Ⲙ̄ⲠⲘⲀ ⲈⲦⲘ̄ⲘⲀⲨ ⲈⲢⲈ ⲤⲀϢϤⲈ Ⲛ̄ⲀⲠⲈ
Ⲛ̄ϨⲀ Ⲛ̄ⲈⲘⲞⲨ· Ⲙ̄ⲠⲞⲨⲀ ⲠⲞⲨⲀ Ⲙ̄ⲘⲞⲞⲨ ϨⲘ ⲠⲈⲨϨⲞ Ⲛ̄ⲀⲨ-
ⲐⲈⲚⲦⲎⲤ· ⲀⲨⲰ ⲠⲚⲞϬ ⲈⲦϨⲒϪⲰⲞⲨ ϢⲀⲨⲘⲞⲨⲦⲈ ⲈⲢⲞϤ
5 ϨⲘ ⲠⲈⲨⲦⲞⲠⲞⲤ ϪⲈ Ⲣ̄ⲰⲬⲀⲢ· ⲀⲨⲰ ⲠⲘⲈϨⲘⲚ̄ⲦⲤⲚⲞⲞⲨⲤ
Ⲛ̄ⲦⲀⲘⲒⲞⲚ ⲞⲨⲚ-ⲞⲨⲘⲎⲎϢⲈ Ⲛ̄ⲀⲢⲬⲰⲚ Ⲛ̄ϨⲎⲦϤ̄ ⲈⲚⲀϢⲰⲞⲨ
ⲈⲘⲀⲦⲈ· ⲈⲢⲈ ⲤⲀϢϤⲈ Ⲛ̄ⲀⲠⲈ Ⲛ̄ϨⲀ Ⲛ̄ⲞⲨϨⲞⲢ Ⲙ̄ⲠⲞⲨⲀ ⲠⲞⲨⲀ
Ⲙ̄ⲘⲞⲞⲨ ϨⲢⲀⲒ̈ ϨⲘ ⲠⲈⲨϨⲞ Ⲛ̄ⲀⲨⲐⲈⲚⲦⲎⲤ· ⲀⲨⲰ ⲠⲚⲞϬ ⲈⲦ-
ϨⲒϪⲰⲞⲨ ⲈϢⲀⲨⲘⲞⲨⲦⲈ ⲈⲢⲞϤ ϨⲘ ⲠⲈⲨⲦⲞⲠⲞⲤ ϪⲈ Ⲭ̄ⲢⲎ- ⲥⲡⲑ
10 Ⲙ̄ⲀⲰⲢ· ⲚⲈⲒ̈ⲀⲢⲬⲰⲚ ϬⲈ Ⲙ̄ⲠⲈⲒ̈ⲘⲚ̄ⲦⲤⲚⲞⲞⲨⲤ Ⲛ̄ⲦⲀⲘⲒⲞⲚ ⲈⲨ-
Ⲛ̄ϨⲞⲨⲚ Ⲛ̄ϨⲎⲦϤ̄ Ⲙ̄ⲠⲈⲆⲢⲀⲔⲰⲚ Ⲙ̄ⲠⲔⲀⲔⲈ ⲈⲦϨⲒⲂⲞⲖ· ⲀⲨⲰ
ⲞⲨⲚ̄ⲦⲈ-ⲠⲞⲨⲀ ⲠⲞⲨⲀ Ⲙ̄ⲘⲞⲞⲨ ⲞⲨⲢⲀⲚ ⲔⲀⲦⲀ ⲞⲨⲚⲞⲨ·
ⲀⲨⲰ ϢⲀⲢⲈ ⲠⲞⲨⲀ ⲠⲞⲨⲀ Ⲙ̄ⲘⲞⲞⲨ ϢⲒⲂⲈ Ⲙ̄ⲠⲈϤϨⲞ ⲔⲀⲦⲀ
ⲞⲨⲚⲞⲨ· ⲀⲨⲰ ⲞⲚ ⲠⲈⲒ̈ⲘⲚ̄ⲦⲤⲚⲞⲞⲨⲤ Ⲛ̄ⲦⲀⲘⲒⲞⲚ ⲞⲨⲚ̄ⲦⲈ-
15 ⲠⲞⲨⲀ ⲠⲞⲨⲀ Ⲙ̄ⲘⲞⲞⲨ ⲞⲨⲢⲞ ⲈϤⲞⲨⲎⲚ ⲈⲠϪⲒⲤⲈ· ϨⲰⲤⲦⲈ
ⲠⲈⲆⲢⲀⲔⲰⲚ Ⲙ̄ⲠⲔⲀⲔⲈ ⲈⲦϨⲒⲂⲞⲖ’ ϤⲞ Ⲙ̄ⲘⲚ̄ⲦⲤⲚⲞⲞⲨⲤ Ⲛ̄ⲦⲀ-
ⲘⲒⲞⲚ Ⲛ̄ⲔⲀⲔⲈ· ⲈⲨⲚ̄-ⲞⲨⲢⲞ Ⲙ̄ⲠⲦⲀⲘⲒⲞⲚ ⲠⲦⲀⲘⲒⲞⲚ ⲈϤⲞⲨⲎⲚ
ⲈⲠϪⲒⲤⲈ· ⲀⲨⲰ ⲞⲨⲚ̄-ⲞⲨⲀⲄⲄⲈⲖⲞⲤ Ⲛ̄ⲦⲈ ⲠϪⲒⲤⲈ ⲈϤⲢⲞⲈⲒⲤ
ⲈⲠⲞⲨⲀ ⲠⲞⲨⲀ Ⲛ̄Ⲛ̄ⲢⲞ Ⲛ̄Ⲛ̄ⲦⲀⲘⲒⲞⲚ· ⲚⲀⲒ̈ Ⲛ̄ⲦⲀ Ⲓ̈ⲈⲞⲨ ⲠϢⲞⲢⲠ̄
20 Ⲛ̄ⲢⲰⲘⲈ ⲠⲈⲠⲒⲤⲔⲞⲠⲞⲤ Ⲛ̄ⲦⲈ ⲠⲞⲨⲞⲈⲒⲚ ⲠⲈⲠⲢⲈⲤⲂⲨⲦⲎⲤ Ⲙ̄-
ⲠϢⲞⲢⲠ̄ Ⲛ̄ⲦⲰϢ Ⲛ̄ⲦⲞϤ ⲠⲈ Ⲛ̄ⲦⲀϤⲔⲀⲀⲨ ⲈⲨⲢⲞⲈⲒⲤ ⲈⲠⲈⲆⲢⲀ-
ⲔⲰⲚ ϪⲈ Ⲛ̄ⲚⲈϤϤⲀⲦⲀⲔⲦⲒ ⲘⲚ̄ Ⲛ̄ⲀⲢⲬⲰⲚ ⲦⲎⲢⲞⲨ Ⲛ̄ⲚⲈϤⲦⲀ-
ⲘⲒⲞⲚ ⲈⲦⲚ̄ϨⲎⲦϤ̄· ⲥⲡⲑ b

ⲚⲀⲒ̈ ϬⲈ Ⲛ̄ⲦⲈⲢⲈϤϪⲞⲞⲨ Ⲛ̄ϬⲒ ⲠⲤⲰⲦⲎⲢ· ⲀⲤⲞⲨⲰϨⲘ̄ Ⲛ̄ϬⲒ
25 ⲘⲀⲢⲒⲀ ⲦⲘⲀⲄⲆⲀⲖⲎⲚⲎ ⲠⲈϪⲀⲤ· ϪⲈ ⲠⲀϪⲞⲈⲒⲤ ⲈⲒ̈Ⲉ ⲞⲨⲔ-
ⲞⲨⲚ ⲚⲈⲮⲨⲬⲞⲞⲨⲈ ⲈϢⲀⲨϪⲒⲦⲞⲨ ⲈⲠⲦⲞⲠⲞⲤ ⲈⲦⲘ̄ⲘⲀⲨ
ϢⲀⲨϪⲒⲦⲞⲨ ⲈⲂⲞⲖ ϨⲒⲦⲚ̄ ⲠⲈⲒ̈ⲘⲚ̄ⲦⲤⲚⲞⲞⲨⲤ Ⲛ̄ⲢⲞ Ⲛ̄Ⲛ̄ⲦⲀⲘⲒⲞⲚ

there is a great number of *archons* in that place, each one
of them having seven cat heads [1] with their *authentic* face.
And the great one over them is called in their *place* : Rochar.
And the twelfth *chamber* : there is a very great number of
archons in it, each one of them having seven dog heads with
their *authentic* face. And the great one over them is called
in their *place* : Chremaor.

Now these *archons* of these twelve *chambers* are inside the
dragon of the outer darkness. And each of them has a name
according to the hour. And each one of them changes his
face *according to* the hour. And furthermore, to each of
these twelve *chambers*, there is a door opening to the height,
so that the *dragon* of the outer darkness has twelve *chambers* [2]
of darkness, and there is a door to every *chamber* opening
to the height. And there is an *angel* of the height watching
at each of the doors of the *chambers*, whom Jeu, the First
Man, the *Overseer* of the Light, the *Messenger* of the First
Ordinance, has placed to keep watch over the *dragon*, so
that it does not *rebel*, together with all the *archons* of its
chambers which are within it.

127. When the *Saviour* had said these things, Maria
Magdalene answered and said : My Lord, are *not therefore*
the *souls* which are taken to that *place* taken through these
twelve doors of the *chambers*, | each one *according to* the
judgment of which he is worthy?"

---

[1] (3, 7) cat heads; lit. cat-faced heads; dog heads; lit. dog-faced heads.
[2] (16) has twelve chambers; Till : consists of twelve chambers.

ΠΟΥΑ ΠΟΥΑ ΚΑΤΑ ΤΕΚΡΙCΙC ΕΤ϶ΜΠϢΑ Μ̄ΜΟC: Α϶ΟΥ-
ΩϨΜ Ν̄ϬΙ ΠCΩΤΗΡ ΠΕΧΑ϶ Μ̄ΜΑΡΙΑ ΧΕ ΜΕΥΧΙ-ΛΑΑΥ Μ̄-
Ψ̄ΥΧΗ ΕϨΟΥΝ ΕΠΕΔΡΑΚΩΝ ΕΒΟΛ Ϩ̄Ν ΝΕΪΡΟ· ΑΛΛΑ ΤΕ-
Ψ̄ΥΧΗ Ν̄ΝΡΕϤΧΙΟΥΑ ΑΥΩ ΝΕΤϢΟΟΠ Ϩ̄Ν ΟΥCΒΩ Μ̄ΠΛΑ-
5 ΝΗ· Μ̄Ν ΟΥΟΝ ΝΙΜ ΕΤ†CΒΩ Ϩ̄Ν ΝΕΠΛΑΝΗ· ΑΥΩ Μ̄Ν
Ν̄ΡΕϤΝ̄ΚΟΤΚ̄ Μ̄Ν ϨΟΟΥΤ· ΑΥΩ Μ̄Ν ΤΑΝΙΡΩΜΕ ΕΤCΟΟϤ·
ΑΥΩ Μ̄Ν Ν̄ΑCΕΒΗC· Μ̄Ν ΡΩΜΕ ΝΙΜ' Ν̄ΑΤΝΟΥΤΕ· ΑΥΩ
ΝΕϤΟΝΕΥC· Μ̄Ν Ν̄ΝΟΕΙΚ· ΑΥΩ Μ̄Ν ΝΕϤΑΡΜΑΚΟC· ΝΕ-
Ψ̄ΥΧΟΟΥΕ ΟΥΝ ΤΗΡΟΥ Ν̄ΤΕΪΜΙΝΕ ΕΥϢΑΝΤΜ̄ΜΕΤΑΝΟΪ
10 ΕΤΙ ΕΥΟΝϨ̄· ΑΛΛΑ Ν̄CΕϬΩ Ϩ̄Μ ΠΕΥΝΟΒΕ ΕϤΜΗΝ· Μ̄Ν
Ν̄ΚΕΨ̄ΥΧΟΟΥΕ ΤΗΡΟΥ· ΝΑΪ ΕΝΤΑΥϢΩΧΠ̄ Ν̄ΒΟΛ ΤΑΪ [Ϭϥ]
ΕΤΕ Ν̄ΤΟΟΥ ΠΕ Ν̄ΤΑΥΧΙ Ν̄ΤΕΥΗΠ̄C Ν̄ΚΥΚΛΟC ΕΤΗΠ
ΕΡΟΟΥ Ϩ̄Ν ΤΕCϤΕΡΑ ΕΜΠΟΥΜΕΤΑΝΟΪ· ΑΛΛΑ ϨΡΑΪ Ϩ̄Μ
ΠΕΥϨΑΕ Ν̄ΚΥΚΛΟC CΕΝΑΧΙ Ν̄ΝΕΨ̄ΥΧΟΟΥΕ ΕΤΜ̄ΜΑΥ·
15 Ν̄ΤΟΟΥ Μ̄Ν ΝΕΨ̄ΥΧΟΟΥΕ ΤΗΡΟΥ Ν̄ΤΑΪΟΥΩ ΕΪΧΩ Μ̄-
ΜΟΟΥ· CΕΝΑΧΙΤΟΥ ΕΒΟΛ Ϩ̄Ν ΤΤΑΠΡΟ Μ̄ΠCΑΤ Μ̄ΠΕΔΡΑ-
ΚΩΝ ΕϨΟΥΝ ΕΝΤΑΜΙΟΝ Μ̄ΠΚΑΚΕ ΕΤϨΙΒΟΛ· ΑΥΩ ΕΥ-
ϢΑΝΟΥΩ ΕΥΧΙ Ν̄ΝΕΨ̄ΥΧΟΟΥΕ ΕϨΟΥΝ ΕΠΚΑΚΕ ΕΤϨΙ-
ΒΟΛ Ϩ̄Ν ΤΤΑΠΡΟ Μ̄ΠΕϤCΑΤ· ϢΑϤΚΩΤΕ ΟΝ Μ̄ΠΕϤCΑΤ'
20 ΕϨΟΥΝ ΕΡΩϤ Μ̄ΜΙΝ Μ̄ΜΟϤ Ν̄ϤϢΤΑΜ' ΕΡΩΟΥ· ΤΑΪ ΤΕ
ΘΕ ΕΤΟΥΝΑΧΙ Ν̄ΝΕΨ̄ΥΧΟΟΥΕ ΕϨΟΥΝ ΕΠΚΑΚΕ ΕΤϨΙΒΟΛ·
ΑΥΩ ΟΥΝΤΕ-ΠΕΔΡΑΚΩΝ Μ̄ΠΚΑΚΕ ΕΤϨΙΒΟΛ' ΟΥΝ̄ΤΑϤ
Μ̄ΜΑΥ Μ̄ΜΝ̄ΤCΝΟΟΥC Ν̄ΡΑΝ Ν̄ΑΥΘΕΝΤΗC ΝΑΪ ΕΤϨΡΑΪ
Ϩ̄Ν ΝΕϤΡΩΟΥ· ΟΥΡΑΝ ΚΑΤΑ ΠΟΥΑ ΠΟΥΑ Ν̄ΝΡΩΟΥ Ν̄-
25 Ν̄ΤΑΜΙΟΝ· ΑΥΩ ΠΕΪΜΝ̄ΤCΝΟΟΥC Ν̄ΡΑΝ CΕϢΒΒΙΑΕΙΤ' [Ϭϥ b]
ΕΝΕΥΕΡΗΥ· ΑΛΛΑ ΕΥϨΡΑΪ Ϩ̄Ν ΝΕΥΕΡΗΥ Μ̄ΠΜΝ̄ΤCΝΟΟΥC·
ϨΩCΤΕ ΠΕΤΝΑΧΩ Ν̄ΟΥΑ Ν̄ΝΡΑΝ ΕϤΧΩ Ν̄ΝΡΑΝ ΤΗΡΟΥ·

***

10 MS ΕϤΜΗΝ; read ΕΥΜΗΝ.

The *Saviour* answered and said to Maria : "No *souls* are taken into the *dragon* through these doors, *except* the *soul* of the slanderers and those who are in *erroneous* teaching, and all those who teach *errors*, and the pederasts, and those (souls) of men who are defiled and the *impious* and all godless men, and the *murderers* and adulterers and *poisoners*. *Now* all *souls* of this kind if they do not *repent* while they are *still* living, *but* continue to remain in their sins, with all the other *souls* who have remained outside — namely those who have received their number of *cycles* which are allotted to them in the *sphere*, without having *repented* — [*but*] in their last *cycle* those *souls* will be taken, together with all the *souls* of which I have just spoken. They will be taken through the mouth of the tail of the *dragon* into the *chamber* of the outer darkness. And when the *souls* finish being taken into the outer darkness in the mouth of its tail, it returns its tail into its own mouth and encloses them. This is the manner in which the *souls* are taken into the outer darkness. And the *dragon* of the outer darkness has twelve *authentic* names which are in its doors, a name *according to* each of the doors of the *chambers*. And these twelve names are different from one another, *but* the twelve are within one another, *so that* he who says one of the names says all the names. | Now these things I will say to you in

ⲚⲀⲒ ϬⲈ ⲦⲚⲀⲬⲞⲞⲨ ⲈⲢⲰⲦⲚ ϨⲘ ⲠⲤⲰⲢ ⲈⲂⲞⲖ ⲦⲎⲢϤ· ⲦⲀⲒ
ϬⲈ ⲦⲈ ⲐⲈ ⲈⲦϤϢⲞⲞⲠ ⲘⲘⲞⲤ ⲚϬⲒ ⲠⲔⲀⲔⲈ ⲈⲦϨⲒⲂⲞⲖ· ⲈⲦⲈ
ⲚⲦⲞϤ ⲠⲈ ⲠⲈⲆⲢⲀⲔⲰⲚ·

ⲚⲀⲒ ϬⲈ ⲚⲦⲈⲢⲈϤⲬⲞⲞⲨ ⲚϬⲒ ⲠⲤⲰⲢ ⲀⲤⲞⲨⲰϨⲘ ⲚϬⲒ ⲘⲀⲢⲒⲀ
5 ⲠⲈⲬⲀⲤ ⲘⲠⲤⲰⲦⲎⲢ ⲬⲈ ⲠⲀⲬⲞⲈⲒⲤ ⲈⲒⲈ ⲚⲔⲞⲖⲀⲤⲒⲤ ⲘⲠⲈ-
ⲆⲢⲀⲔⲰⲚ ⲈⲦⲘⲘⲀⲨ ⲚⲀϢⲦ ⲈⲘⲀⲦⲈ ⲠⲀⲢⲀ ⲚⲔⲞⲖⲀⲤⲒⲤ ⲚⲚⲈⲔ-
ⲔⲢⲒⲤⲒⲤ ⲦⲎⲢⲞⲨ· ⲀϤⲞⲨⲰϨⲘ ⲚϬⲒ ⲠⲤⲰⲢ ⲠⲈⲬⲀϤ ⲘⲘⲀⲢⲒⲀ
ⲬⲈ ⲞⲨⲘⲞⲚⲞⲚ ⲬⲈ ⲤⲈⲘⲞⲔϨ ⲠⲀⲢⲀ ⲚⲔⲞⲖⲀⲤⲒⲤ ⲦⲎⲢⲞⲨ
ⲚⲚⲈⲔⲢⲒⲤⲒⲤ· ⲀⲖⲖⲀ ⲯⲨⲬⲎ ⲚⲒⲘ' ⲈⲦⲞⲨⲚⲀⲬⲒⲦⲞⲨ ⲈⲠⲦⲞⲠⲞⲤ
10 ⲈⲦⲘⲘⲀⲨ ⲤⲈⲚⲀⲢ-ϨⲢⲞⲨⲞⲨⲬϤ ϨⲘ ⲠⲬⲀϤ ⲈⲦⲚⲀϢⲦ· ⲀⲨⲰ
ⲘⲚ ⲚⲈⲬⲀⲖⲀⲌⲀ· ⲀⲨⲰ ⲘⲚ ⲠⲔⲰϨⲦ ⲈⲦⲚⲀϢⲦ ⲈⲘⲀϢⲞ·
ⲚⲀⲒ ⲈⲦϢⲞⲞⲠ ϨⲘ ⲠⲦⲞⲠⲞⲤ ⲈⲦⲘⲘⲀⲨ· ⲀⲖⲖⲀ ϨⲘ ⲠⲔⲈⲂⲰⲖ ⲤϤⲀ
ⲈⲂⲞⲖ' ⲘⲠⲔⲞⲤⲘⲞⲤ· ⲈⲦⲈ ⲠⲀⲒ ⲠⲈ ϨⲘ ⲠⲰⲖ' ⲈϨⲢⲀⲒ ⲘⲠⲦⲎⲢϤ
ⲚⲈⲯⲨⲬⲞⲞⲨⲈ ⲈⲦⲘⲘⲀⲨ ⲤⲈⲚⲀⲀⲚϨⲀⲖⲒⲤⲔⲈ ϨⲒⲦⲘ ⲠⲬⲀϤ
15 ⲈⲦⲚⲀϢⲦ· ⲀⲨⲰ ⲘⲚ ⲠⲔⲰϨⲦ ⲈⲦⲚⲀϢⲦ ⲈⲘⲀϢⲞ· ⲀⲨⲰ
ⲤⲈⲚⲀⲢⲀⲦϢⲰⲠⲈ ϢⲀⲈⲚⲈϨ·

ⲀⲤⲞⲨⲰϨⲘ ⲚϬⲒ ⲘⲀⲢⲒⲀ ⲠⲈⲬⲀⲤ· ⲬⲈ ⲈⲒⲈ ⲞⲨⲞⲒ ⲚⲚⲈ-
ⲯⲨⲬⲞⲞⲨⲈ ⲚⲢⲢⲈϤⲢⲚⲞⲂⲈ· ⲦⲈⲚⲞⲨ ϬⲈ ⲞⲨⲚ ⲠⲀⲬⲞⲈⲒⲤ
ⲠⲔⲰϨⲦ ⲈⲦϨⲘ ⲠⲦⲞⲠⲞⲤ ⲚⲦⲈ ⲦⲘⲚⲦⲢⲰⲘⲈ ϤⲬⲎϤ· ⲬⲈ
20 ⲠⲔⲰϨⲦ ⲈⲦϨⲚ ⲀⲘⲚⲦⲈ ⲬⲎϤ· ⲀϤⲞⲨⲰϨⲘ ⲚϬⲒ ⲠⲤⲰⲦⲎⲢ
ⲠⲈⲬⲀϤ ⲘⲘⲀⲢⲒⲀ· ⲬⲈ ϨⲀⲘⲎⲚ ⲦⲬⲰ ⲘⲘⲞⲤ ⲈⲢⲞ ⲬⲈ
ϤⲬⲎϤ ⲚϬⲒ ⲠⲔⲰϨⲦ ⲈⲦϨⲚ ⲀⲘⲚⲦⲈ ⲚϨⲞⲨⲞ ⲈⲠⲔⲰϨⲦ ⲈⲦϨⲚ
ⲦⲘⲚⲦⲢⲰⲘⲈ ⲘⲯⲒⲤ ⲚⲔⲰⲂ ⲚⲤⲞⲠ· ⲀⲨⲰ ⲠⲔⲰϨⲦ ⲈⲦϨⲚ
ⲚⲔⲞⲖⲀⲤⲒⲤ ⲘⲠⲚⲞϬ ⲚⲬⲀⲞⲤ· ϤⲚⲀϢⲦ ⲚϨⲞⲨⲞ ⲈⲠⲈⲦϨⲚ
25 ⲀⲘⲚⲦⲈ ⲚⲯⲒⲤ ⲚⲔⲰⲂ ⲚⲤⲞⲠ· ⲀⲨⲰ ⲠⲔⲰϨⲦ ⲈⲦϨⲚ ⲚⲈ-
ⲔⲢⲒⲤⲒⲤ ⲚⲚⲀⲢⲬⲰⲚ ⲈⲦϨⲒ ⲦⲈϨⲒⲎ ⲚⲦⲘⲎⲦⲈ· ϤⲚⲀϢⲦ ⲚϨⲞⲨⲞ ⲤϤⲀ

---

1 MS ⲦⲎⲢϤ; read ⲘⲠⲦⲎⲢϤ.
25 MS ⲚⲯⲒⲤ; read ⲘⲯⲒⲤ.

the distribution of the All. This now is the manner in which the outer darkness, which is the *dragon*, exists."

Now when the *Saviour* had said these things, Maria answered and said to the *Saviour*: "My Lord, are the *punishments* of that *dragon* much more severe *than* the *punishments* of all the judgments?"

The *Saviour* answered and said to Maria: "*Not only* are they painful *beyond* all the *punishments* of the *judgments*, *but* every *soul* which will be taken to that *place* will perish in the severe frost and the *hail* and the very fierce fire which are in that *place*. *But* also at the dissolution of the *world*, namely at the ascension of the All, those *souls* will be *consumed* by the severe frost and the very fierce fire, and they will become non-existent for ever."

Maria answered and said: "Woe to the *souls* of the sinners. Now at this time, my Lord, is the fire which is in the *place* of mankind hotter, or is the fire which is in Amente hotter?"

The *Saviour* answered and said to Maria: "*Truly*, I say to you, the fire which is in Amente is nine times hotter than the fire which is among mankind. And the fire which is in the *punishments* of the great *Chaos* is nine times fiercer than that which is in Amente. And the fire which is in the *judgments* of the *archons* which are upon the path of the Midst is nine times fiercer than | the fire of the *punishments*

ЄΠΚШ2T Ν̄ΝΚΟΛΑϹΙϹ ЄT2Μ ΠΝΟ6 Ν̄ΧΛΟϹ Μ̄ΨΙϹ Ν̄ΚШΒ
Ν̄ϹΟΠ· ΑΥШ Π̄ΚШ2T ЄT2Μ ΠЄΔΡΑΚШΝ Μ̄ΠΚΑΚЄ ЄT2Ι-
ΒΟΛ Μ̄Ν ΝЄΚΡΙϹΙϹ THΡΟΥ ЄTΝ̄2HTϤ· ϹЄΝΑϢT Ν̄2ΟΥΟ
ЄΠΚШ2T ЄT2Ν̄ Ν̄ΚΟΛΑϹΙϹ THΡΟΥ ЄT2Ν̄ ΝЄΚΡΙϹΙϹ Ν̄Ν̄-
5 ΑΡΧШΝ· ΝΑΪ ЄT2Ι TЄ2ΙΗ Ν̄TΜΗTЄ ϤΝΑϢT Ν̄2ΟΥΟ ЄΡΟΟΥ
Ν̄ϢϤЄ Ν̄ΚШΒ Ν̄ϹΟΠ·

ΝΑΪ ΔЄ Ν̄TЄΡЄϤΧΟΟΥ Ν̄6Ι ΠϹШTHΡ ЄΜΑΡΙΑ ΑϹ2ΙΟΥЄ
Є2ΟΥΝ 2Ν TЄϹΜЄϹTΝ̄2HT· ΑϹШϢ ЄΒΟΛ ΑϹΡΙΜЄ Ν̄TΟϹ
Μ̄Ν Μ̄ΜΑΘΗTHϹ THΡΟΥ 2Ι ΟΥϹΟΠ· ΠЄΧΑϹ ΧЄ ΟΥΟЇ
10 Ν̄ΡΡЄϤΡΝΟΒЄ ΧЄ ΝΑϢЄ ΝЄΥΚΡΙϹΙϹ ЄΜΑϢΟ· ΑϹЄΙ ЄΘΗ
Ν̄6Ι ΜΑΡΙ2ΑΜ ΑϹΠΑ2T̄Ϲ̄ ЄΧ̄Ν̄ ΝΟΥЄΡΗTЄ Ν̄Ϲ ΑϹΟΥШϢT
ЄΡΟΟΥ· ΠЄΧΑϹ ΧЄ ΠΑΧΟЄΙϹ ΑΝЄΧЄ Μ̄ΜΟЇ ЄЇϢΙΝЄ
Μ̄ΜΟΚ· ΑΥШ Μ̄ΠΡ6ШΝ̄T ЄΡΟЇ ΧЄ ϮЄΝШΧΛЄΙ ΝΑΚ Ν̄2Α2
Ν̄ϹΟΠ· ΧЄ ΧΙΝ TЄΝΟΥ ΓΑΡ ЄЇΝΑΑΡΧΙ Ν̄ϢΙΝЄ Μ̄ΜΟΚ· [ϹϤΒ]
15 ЄTΒЄ 2ШΒ ΝΙΜ 2Ν ΟΥШΡΧ̄· ΑϤΟΥШ2Μ̄ Ν̄6Ι ΠϹШTHΡ
ΠЄΧΑϤ Μ̄ΜΑΡΙΑ ΧЄ ϢΙΝЄ Ν̄ϹΑ 2ШΒ ΝΙΜ ЄTЄΡЄΟΥЄϢ-
ϢΙΝЄ Ν̄ϹШΟΥ· ΑΥШ ΑΝΟΚ ϮΝΑ6ΟΛΠΟΥ ΝЄ ЄΒΟΛ 2Ν
ΟΥΠΑΡΡΗϹΙΑ ΑΧ̄Ν̄ ΠΑΡΑΒΟΛΗ· ΑϹΟΥШ2Μ̄ Ν̄6Ι ΜΑΡΙΑ
ΠЄΧΑϹ ΧЄ ΠΑΧΟЄΙϹ ЄЇЄ ΟΥΡШΜЄ Ν̄ΑΓΑΘΟϹ ЄΑϤΧШΚ
20 ЄΒΟΛ Μ̄ΜΥϹTHΡΙΟΝ ΝΙΜ· ЄΟΥΝTΑϤ Μ̄ΜΑΥ Ν̄ΟΥϹΥΓΓЄ-
ΝΗϹ 2ΑΠΑΞ 2ΑΠΛШϹ ЄΟΥΝTΑϤ Μ̄ΜΑΥ Ν̄ΟΥΡШΜЄ· ΑΥШ
ΠΡШΜЄ ЄTΜ̄ΜΑΥ ЄΥΑϹЄΒHϹ ΠЄ ЄΑϤЄΙΡЄ Ν̄ΝΟΒЄ ΝΙΜ
ЄΥΜ̄ΠϢΑ Μ̄ΠΚΑΚЄ ЄT2ΙΒΟΛ· ΑΥШ Μ̄ΠϤΜЄTΑΝΟЇ· Η̄
Μ̄ΜΟΝ ЄΑϤΧШΚ ЄΒΟΛ Ν̄TЄϤΗΠϹ Ν̄ΚΥΚΛΟϹ 2Ν Μ̄ΜЄTΑ-
25 ΒΟΛΗ Μ̄ΠϹШΜΑ· ΑΥШ ЄΜΠϤΡϢΑΥ ΛΑΑΥ Ν̄6Ι ΠΡШΜЄ
ЄTΜ̄ΜΑΥ· ЄΑϤЄΙ ЄΒΟΛ 2Ν ϹШΜΑ· ΑΥШ ΑΝЄΙΜЄ ЄΡΟϤ

which are in the great *Chaos*. And the fire which is in the *dragon* of the outer darkness and all the *judgments* which are in it is seventy times fiercer than the fire which is in all the *punishments* in the *judgments* of the *archons* which are upon the path of the Midst."

128. When *however* the *Saviour* had said these things to Maria, she beat her breast, she cried out, and she and all the *disciples* wept at once. She said: "Woe to the sinners, for their *judgments* are very numerous."

Mariam came forward, she prostrated herself at the feet of Jesus, she kissed them, she said: "My Lord, *suffer* me that I question thee, and be not angry with me that I *trouble* thee many times, *for* from this time I will *begin* to question thee concerning all things with assurance."

The *Saviour* answered and said to Maria: "Question everything which thou dost wish to question, and I will reveal them *openly* without *parable*."

Maria answered and said: "My Lord, if a *good* man has fulfilled all the *mysteries*, and he has a *relative, in a word,* he has a man and that man is an *impious one* who has committed all the sins which are worthy[1] of the outer darkness; and he has not *repented*; *or* he has completed his number of *cycles* in the *changes* of the *body*, and that man has done nothing profitable[2] and has come forth from the *body*; and we have known of him | *certainly* that he has

---

[1] (23) which are worthy; Schmidt: and who is worthy.

[2] (25) has done nothing profitable; Till: was altogether useless.

ⲁⲥⲫⲁⲗⲱⲥ ϫⲉ ⲁϥⲣⲛⲟⲃⲉ ⲉϥⲙⲡϣⲁ ⲙ̄ⲡⲕⲁⲕⲉ ⲉⲧϩⲓⲃⲟⲗ`
ⲉⲓⲉ ⲟⲩ ⲡⲉⲧⲛ̄ⲛⲁⲁⲁϥ ϣⲁⲛⲧ̄ⲛⲛⲟⲩϩ̈ⲙ ⲙ̄ⲙⲟϥ ⲉⲛⲕⲟⲗⲁⲥⲓⲥ [ⲥ̄ϥ̄ⲃ ᵇ]
ⲙ̄ⲡⲉⲇⲣⲁⲕⲱⲛ ⲙ̄ⲡⲕⲁⲕⲉ ⲉⲧϩⲓⲃⲟⲗ ⲁⲩⲱ ⲛ̄ⲥⲉⲡⲟⲟⲛⲉϥ ⲉⲩⲥⲱⲙⲁ ⲛ̄ⲇⲓⲕⲁⲓⲟⲥ ⲉϥⲛⲁϩⲉ ⲉⲙⲙⲩⲥⲧⲏⲣⲓⲟⲛ ⲛ̄ⲧⲙⲛ̄ⲧⲉⲣⲟ
5 ⲙ̄ⲡⲟⲩⲟⲉⲓⲛ· ⲁⲩⲱ ⲛ̄ϥⲣⲁⲅⲁⲑⲟⲥ ⲛ̄ϥⲃⲱⲕ` ⲉⲡϫⲓⲥⲉ· ⲛ̄ϥ-
ⲕⲗⲏⲣⲟⲛⲟⲙⲓ ⲛ̄ⲧⲙⲛ̄ⲧⲉⲣⲟ ⲙ̄ⲡⲟⲩⲟⲉⲓⲛ· ⲁϥⲟⲩⲱϩⲙ ⲛ̄ϭⲓ
ⲡⲥⲱⲧⲏⲣ ⲡⲉϫⲁϥ ⲙ̄ⲙⲁⲣⲓⲁ ϫⲉ ⲉϣⲱⲡⲉ ⲟⲩⲣⲉϥⲣ̄ⲛⲟⲃⲉ ⲡⲉ
ⲉϥⲙⲡϣⲁ ⲙ̄ⲡⲕⲁⲕⲉ ⲉⲧϩⲓⲃⲟⲗ· ⲏ̄ ⲙ̄ⲙⲟⲛ ⲛ̄ⲧⲟϥ ⲁϥⲣⲛⲟⲃⲉ
ⲕⲁⲧⲁ ⲛ̄ⲕⲟⲗⲁⲥⲓⲥ ⲙ̄ⲡⲕⲉⲥⲉⲉⲡⲉ ⲛ̄ⲕⲟⲗⲁⲥⲓⲥ· ⲁⲩⲱ ⲡⲁⲓ̈
10 ⲙ̄ⲡϥ̄ⲙⲉⲧⲁⲛⲟⲓ̈· ⲏ̄ ⲙ̄ⲙⲟⲛ ⲛ̄ⲧⲟϥ ⲟⲩⲣⲱⲙⲉ ⲛ̄ⲣⲉϥⲣ̄ⲛⲟⲃⲉ
ⲉⲁϥϫⲱⲕ ⲉⲃⲟⲗ` ϩⲛ̄ ⲧⲉϥⲏⲡⲥ ⲛ̄ⲕⲩⲕⲗⲟⲥ ϩⲛ̄ ⲙ̄ⲙⲉⲧⲁⲃⲟⲗⲏ
ⲙ̄ⲡⲥⲱⲙⲁ· ⲁⲩⲱ ⲡⲁⲓ̈ ⲙ̄ⲡϥ̄ⲙⲉⲧⲁⲛⲟⲓ̈· ⲉⲣϣⲁⲛ ⲛ̄ⲣⲱⲙⲉ
ⲟⲩⲛ ⲉⲧⲙ̄ⲙⲁⲩ ⲛⲁⲓ̈ ⲉⲛⲧⲁⲓ̈ϫⲟⲟⲩ ⲉⲩϣⲁⲛⲉⲓ` ⲉⲃⲟⲗ ϩⲙ̄
ⲡⲥⲱⲙⲁ ⲛ̄ⲥⲉϫⲓⲧⲟⲩ` ⲉⲡⲕⲁⲕⲉ ⲉⲧϩⲓⲃⲟⲗ· ⲧⲉⲛⲟⲩ ϭⲉ
15 ⲉϣⲱⲡⲉ ⲧⲉⲧⲛⲟⲩⲱϣ ⲉⲡⲟⲟⲛⲟⲩ ⲉⲃⲟⲗ ϩⲛ̄ ⲛ̄ⲕⲟⲗⲁⲥⲓⲥ
ⲙ̄ⲡⲕⲁⲕⲉ ⲉⲧϩⲓⲃⲟⲗ` ⲙ̄ⲛ̄ ⲕⲣⲓⲥⲓⲥ ⲛⲓⲙ· ⲁⲩⲱ ⲛ̄ⲥⲉⲡⲟⲟⲛ̈ⲟⲩ ⲥ̄ϥ̄ⲅ̄
ⲉⲩⲥⲱⲙⲁ ⲛ̄ⲇⲓⲕⲁⲓⲟⲥ ⲡⲁⲓ̈ ⲉϥⲛⲁϩⲉ ⲉⲙⲙⲩⲥⲧⲏⲣⲓⲟⲛ ⲙ̄-
ⲡⲟⲩⲟⲉⲓⲛ ⲛ̄ϥⲃⲱⲕ ⲉⲡϫⲓⲥⲉ ⲛ̄ϥⲕⲗⲏⲣⲟⲛⲟⲙⲓ ⲛ̄ⲧⲙⲛ̄ⲧⲉⲣⲟ
ⲙ̄ⲡⲟⲩⲟⲉⲓⲛ· ⲁⲣⲓⲣⲉ ⲙ̄ⲡⲓⲙⲩⲥⲧⲏⲣⲓⲟⲛ ⲛ̄ⲟⲩⲱⲧ` ⲛ̄ⲧⲉ ⲡⲓ-
20 ⲁⲧϣⲁϫⲉ ⲉⲣⲟϥ ⲡⲁⲓ̈ ⲉϣⲁϥⲕⲁⲛⲟⲃⲉ ⲉⲃⲟⲗ ⲛ̄ⲟⲩⲟⲉⲓϣ
ⲛⲓⲙ` ⲁⲩⲱ ⲉⲧⲉⲧⲛ̄ϣⲁⲛⲟⲩⲱ ⲉⲧⲉⲧⲛ̄ⲉⲓⲣⲉ ⲙ̄ⲡⲙⲩⲥⲧⲏⲣⲓⲟⲛ·
ⲁϫⲓⲥ ϫⲉ ⲧⲉⲯⲩⲭⲏ ⲛ̄ⲛⲓⲙ ⲛ̄ⲣⲱⲙⲉ ⲧⲁⲓ̈ ⲉϯⲙⲉⲉⲩⲉ ⲉⲣⲟⲥ
ϩⲙ̄ ⲡⲁϩⲏⲧ· ⲉϣⲱⲡⲉ ⲉⲥⲛ̄ ⲡⲧⲟⲡⲟⲥ ⲛ̄ⲛ̄ⲕⲟⲗⲁⲥⲓⲥ ⲛ̄ⲛ̄-
ⲧⲁⲙⲓⲟⲛ ⲙ̄ⲡⲕⲁⲕⲉ ⲉⲧϩⲓⲃⲟⲗ` ⲏ̄ ⲙ̄ⲙⲟⲛ ⲛ̄ⲧⲟϥ ⲉϣⲱⲡⲉ
25 ⲉⲥⲛ̄ ⲡⲕⲉⲥⲉⲉⲡⲉ ⲛ̄ⲛ̄ⲕⲟⲗⲁⲥⲓⲥ ⲛ̄ⲧⲉ ⲛ̄ⲧⲁⲙⲓⲟⲛ ⲙ̄ⲡⲕⲁⲕⲉ
ⲉⲧϩⲓⲃⲟⲗ` ⲙ̄ⲛ̄ ⲡⲕⲉⲥⲉⲉⲡⲉ ⲛ̄ⲛ̄ⲕⲟⲗⲁⲥⲓⲥ ⲛ̄ⲛⲉⲇⲣⲁⲕⲱⲛ ⲉⲩⲉ-

---

11   MS ϩⲛ̄ ⲧⲉϥⲏⲡⲥ; better ⲛ̄ⲧⲉϥⲏⲡⲥ.

sinned and is worthy of the outer darkness; what should
we do to him so that we save him from the *punishments*
of the *dragon* of the outer darkness, so that he is returned
to a *righteous body* which will find the *mysteries* of the Kingdom of the Light, and become *good* and go to the height,
and *inherit* the Kingdom of the Light?"

The *Saviour* answered and said to Maria : "If he is a sinner
worthy of the outer darkness; *or* if he has sinned *according
to* the *punishments* of the rest of the *punishments*, and he has
not *repented*; *or* if a sinful man has completed his number
of *cycles* in the *changes* of the *body* and has not *repented*
— *now* when these men of whom I have spoken come forth
from the *body* and have been taken to the outer darkness,
now at this time, if you want to return them from the
punishments of the outer darkness and all the *judgments*,
and return them to a *righteous body* which will find the
mysteries of the light, and go to the height and *inherit*
the Kingdom of the Light — perform the one *mystery* of
the Ineffable which forgives sins at all times. And when
you have finished performing the *mystery*, say : 'The *soul*
of such and such a man on whom I think in my heart, when
it comes to the *place* of the *punishments* of the *chambers*
of the outer darkness; *or* when it is in the rest of the
punishments of the *chambers* of the outer darkness and the
rest of the *punishments* of the *dragon* : | may it be returned

647

ΠΟΟΝΟΥ ΕΒΟΛ' Ν̄2ΗΤΟΥ ΤΗΡΟΥ· ΑΥω ΕϣωΠΕ ΕС-
ϣΑΝΧωΚ' ΕΒΟΛ Ν̄ΤΕСΗΠ Ν̄ΚΥΚΛΟС 2Ν̄ Μ̄ΜΕΤΑΒΟΛΗ·
ΕΥΕΧΙΤС ΕΡΑΤС̄ Ν̄ΤΠΑΡΘΕΝΟС Μ̄ΠΟΥΟΕΙΝ· ΑΥω Ν̄ΤΕ
ΤΠΑΡΘΕΝΟС Μ̄ΠΟΥΟΕΙΝ СΦΡΑΓΙΖΕ Μ̄ΜΟΥ 2Ν̄ ΤΕСΦΡΑ-
5 ΓΙС Ν̄ΤΕ ΠΙΑΤϣΑΧΕ ΕΡΟΥ· ΑΥω Ν̄СΝΟΧ̄С̄ 2Μ̄ ΠΕΪΕΒΟΤ' ‾С̄Μ̄Γ̄·ᵇ
ΠΕΪΕΒΟΤ ΕΥСωΜΑ Ν̄ΔΙΚΑΙΟС ΠΑΪ ΕΤΝΑ2Ε ΕΜΜΥСΤΗ-
ΡΙΟΝ Μ̄ΠΟΥΟΕΙΝ Ν̄2ΗΤΥ ΑΥω Ν̄СΡΑΓΑΘΟС Ν̄СΒωΚ' Ε-
ΠΧΙСΕ Ν̄СΚΛΗΡΟΝΟΜΙ Ν̄ΤΜΝ̄ΤΕΡΟ Μ̄ΠΟΥΟΕΙΝ· ΑΥω
ΟΝ ΕϣωΠΕ ΑСΧωΚ ΕΒΟΛ Ν̄ΝΚΥΚΛΟС Ν̄ΜΜΕΤΑΒΟΛΗ
10 ΕΥΕΧΙ Ν̄ΤΕΨΥΧΗ ΕΤΜ̄ΜΑΥ ΕΡΑΤ̄С̄ Ν̄ΤСΑϣϥΕ Μ̄ΠΑΡΘΕ-
ΝΟС Μ̄ΠΟΥΟΕΙΝ· ΝΑΪ ΕΤ2ΙΧΜ̄ ΠΒΑΠΤΙСΜΑ· Ν̄СΕΚΛΑΥ
2ΙΧ̄Ν̄ ΤΕΨΥΧΗ ΕΤΜ̄ΜΑΥ· Ν̄СΕСΦΡΑΓΙΖΕ Μ̄ΜΟС 2Μ̄ ΠΜΑΪΝ
Ν̄ΤΜΝ̄ΤΕΡΟ Μ̄ΠΙΑΤϣΑΧΕ ΕΡΟΥ Ν̄СΕΧΙΤΥ 2Α2ΤΝ̄ Ν̄ΤΑ2ΙС
Μ̄ΠΟΥΟΕΙΝ· ΝΑΪ ΕΤΕΤΝ̄ΝΑΧΟΟΥ ΕΤΕΤΝ̄ϣΑΝΧωΚ ΕΒΟΛ
15 Μ̄ΠΜΥСΤΗΡΙΟΝ· 2ΑΜΗΝ †Χω Μ̄ΜΟС ΝΗΤΝ̄ ΧΕ ΤΕΨΥΧΗ
ΕΤΕΤΝ̄ΝΑΕΥΧΕ ΕΧωС· ΕϣωΠΕ ΜΕΝ ΕС2Μ̄ ΠΕΔΡΑΚωΝ
Μ̄ΠΚΑΚΕ ΕΤ2ΙΒΟΛ· ϥΝΑΝΟΥ2Ε Μ̄ΠΕϥСΑΤ' ΕΒΟΛ 2Ν̄ Ρωϥ·
ΑΥω Ν̄ϥΚΑΒΟΛ Ν̄ΤΕΨΥΧΗ ΕΤΜ̄ΜΑΥ· ΑΥω ΟΝ ΕϣωΠΕ
ΕС2Ν̄** ΤΟΠΟС ΝΙΜ' Ν̄ΤΕ ΝΕΚΡΙСΙС Ν̄ΤΕ Ν̄ΑΡΧωΝ· 2ΑΜΗΝ [С̄Ϥ̄Δ̄]
20 †Χω Μ̄ΜΟС ΕΡωΤΝ̄ ΧΕ СΕΝΑ2ΑΡΠΑΖΕ Μ̄ΜΟС 2Ν̄ ΟΥ-
СΠΟΥΔΗ Ν̄6Ι Μ̄ΠΑΡΑΛΗΜΠΤΗС Μ̄ΜΕΛΧΙСΕΔΕΚ ΕΙΤΕ Εϥ-
ϣΑΝΚΑΒΟΛ Μ̄ΜΟС Ν̄6Ι ΠΕΔΡΑΚωΝ· Η̄ Μ̄ΜΟΝ Ν̄ΤΟϥ
ΕС2Ν̄ ΝΕΚΡΙСΙС Ν̄ΤΕ Ν̄ΑΡΧωΝ· 2ΑΠΑϪ 2ΑΠΛωС СΕΝΑ2ΑΡ-
ΠΑΖΕ Μ̄ΜΟС Ν̄6Ι Μ̄ΠΑΡΑΛΗΜΠΤωΡ Μ̄ΜΕΛΧΙСΕΔΕΚ' 2Ν̄

2　MS ν̄ΤΕСΗΠ; read ν̄ΤΕСΗΠС̄.
4　MS Μ̄ΜΟϥ; read Μ̄ΜΟС.
13　MS Ν̄СΕΧΙΤϥ̄; read Ν̄СΕΧΙΤС̄.

from them all. And when it finishes its number of *cycles* in the *changes*, may it be taken to the presence of the *Virgin* of the Light; and may the *Virgin* of the Light *seal* it with the *seal* of the Ineffable, and cast it in that very month into a *righteous body* which will find [1] the *mysteries* of the light in it, and become *good*, and go to the height and *inherit* the Kingdom of the Light. And furthermore, when it has completed the *cycles* of the *changes*, may that *soul* be taken to the presence of the seven *virgins* of the light which are in charge of (lit. over) the *baptism*. And may they place it (the baptism) upon that *soul*, and *seal* it with the sign of the Kingdom of the Ineffable, and may they take it to the *ranks* of the light.' These things you will say when you have completed the *mystery. Truly*, I say to you : the *soul* for which you shall *pray*, if *indeed* it is in the *dragon* of the outer darkness, it will withdraw its tail out of its mouth, and release [2] that *soul*. And furthermore, if it is in any *place* of the *judgments* of the *archons*, *truly* I say to you, the *paralemptai* of Melchisedek will *speedily snatch* it up, *whether* the *dragon* has released it, *or* whether it is in the *judgments* of the *archons*. *In a word*, the *paralemptores* of Melchisedek will *snatch* it |

---

[1]   (6) which will find; Till : ⟨and the soul⟩ will find.
[2]   (18) release; Till : cast out, spew out.

ⲦⲞⲠⲞⲤ ⲚⲒⲘ ⲈⲦⲤⲚ̄ϨⲎⲦⲞⲨ· ⲀⲨⲰ ⲤⲈⲚⲀⲬⲒⲦⲤ̄ ⲈⲠⲦⲞⲠⲞⲤ
Ⲛ̄ⲦⲘⲈⲤⲞⲤ ⲈⲢⲀⲦⲤ̄ Ⲛ̄ⲦⲠⲀⲢⲐⲈⲚⲞⲤ Ⲙ̄ⲠⲞⲨⲞⲈⲒⲚ ⲀⲨⲰ ϢⲀⲢⲈ
ⲦⲠⲀⲢⲐⲈⲚⲞⲤ Ⲙ̄ⲠⲞⲨⲞⲈⲒⲚ ϢⲀⲤⲆⲞϬⲒⲘⲀⲌⲈ Ⲙ̄ⲘⲞⲤ Ⲛ̄ⲤⲚⲀⲨ
ⲈⲠⲘⲀⲒ̈Ⲛ Ⲛ̄ⲦⲘⲚ̄ⲦⲈⲢⲞ Ⲙ̄ⲠⲒⲀⲦϢⲀⲬⲈ ⲈⲢⲞϤ ⲈϤϢⲞⲞⲠ ϨⲚ
5 ⲦⲈ✝ⲨⲬⲎ ⲈⲦⲘ̄ⲘⲀⲨ· ⲀⲨⲰ ⲈϢⲰⲠⲈ Ⲙ̄ⲠⲀⲦⲤ̄ⲬⲰⲔ ⲈⲂⲞⲖ
Ⲛ̄ⲦⲈⲤϨⲠⲤ̄ Ⲛ̄ⲔⲨⲔⲖⲞⲤ ϨⲚ ⲦϬⲒⲚϢⲒⲂⲈ Ⲛ̄ⲦⲈ✝ⲨⲬⲎ Ⲏ̄ ϨⲚ
ⲠⲤⲰⲘⲀ· ϢⲀⲢⲈ ⲦⲠⲀⲢⲐⲈⲚⲞⲤ Ⲙ̄ⲠⲞⲨⲞⲈⲒⲚ ϢⲀⲤⲤⲪⲢⲀⲅⲒⲌⲈ
Ⲙ̄ⲘⲞⲤ ϨⲚ ⲞⲨⲤⲪⲢⲀⲅⲒⲤ ⲈⲤⲞⲨⲞⲦⲂ̄· ⲀⲨⲰ Ⲛ̄ⲤⲤⲠⲞⲨⲆⲀⲌⲈ [ⲤϤⲆ ᵇ]
Ⲛ̄ⲤⲦⲢⲈⲨⲚⲞⲬⲤ̄ ϨⲘ ⲠⲈⲒ̈ⲈⲂⲞⲦ’ ⲠⲈⲒ̈ⲈⲂⲞⲦ ⲈⲨⲤⲰⲘⲀ Ⲛ̄ⲆⲒ-
10 ⲔⲀⲒⲞⲤ ⲠⲀⲒ̈ ⲈϤⲚⲀϨⲈ ⲈⲘⲘⲨⲤⲦⲎⲢⲒⲞⲚ Ⲙ̄ⲠⲞⲨⲞⲈⲒⲚ· ⲀⲨⲰ
ⲈϤⲚⲀⲢ̄ⲀⲅⲀⲐⲞⲤ Ⲛ̄ϤⲂⲰⲔ’ ⲈⲠϪⲒⲤⲈ ⲈⲦⲘⲚ̄ⲦⲈⲢⲞ Ⲙ̄ⲠⲞⲨⲞⲈⲒⲚ·
ⲀⲨⲰ ⲈϢⲰⲠⲈ ⲦⲈ✝ⲨⲬⲎ ⲈⲦⲘ̄ⲘⲀⲨ ⲀⲤϪⲒ Ⲛ̄ⲦⲈⲤϨⲠⲤ̄ Ⲛ̄-
ⲔⲨⲔⲖⲞⲤ· ϢⲀⲢⲈ ⲦⲠⲀⲢⲐⲈⲚⲞⲤ Ⲙ̄ⲠⲞⲨⲞⲈⲒⲚ ϢⲀⲤⲆⲞϬⲒ-
ⲘⲀⲌⲈ Ⲙ̄ⲘⲞⲤ ⲘⲈⲤⲔⲀⲀⲨ ⲈⲔⲞⲖⲀⲌⲈ Ⲙ̄ⲘⲞⲤ ⲈⲂⲞⲖ ϪⲈ ⲀⲤϪⲒ
15 Ⲛ̄ⲦⲈⲤϨⲠⲤ̄ Ⲛ̄ⲔⲨⲔⲖⲞⲤ· ⲀⲖⲖⲀ ϢⲀⲤⲦⲀⲀⲤ ⲈⲦⲞⲞⲦⲞⲨ Ⲛ̄-
ⲦⲤⲀϢϤⲈ Ⲙ̄ⲠⲀⲢⲐⲈⲚⲞⲤ Ⲙ̄ⲠⲞⲨⲞⲈⲒⲚ· ⲀⲨⲰ ϢⲀⲢⲈ ⲦⲤⲀϢϤⲈ
Ⲙ̄ⲠⲀⲢⲐⲈⲚⲞⲤ Ⲙ̄ⲠⲞⲨⲞⲈⲒⲚ ϢⲀⲨⲆⲞϬⲒⲘⲀⲌⲈ Ⲛ̄ⲦⲈ✝ⲨⲬⲎ
ⲈⲦⲘ̄ⲘⲀⲨ ⲀⲨⲰ ϢⲀⲨⲂⲀⲠⲦⲒⲌⲈ Ⲙ̄ⲘⲞⲤ ϨⲚ ⲚⲈⲨⲂⲀⲠⲦⲒⲤⲘⲀ·
ⲀⲨⲰ Ⲛ̄ⲤⲈ✝ ⲚⲀⲤ Ⲙ̄ⲠⲈⲬⲢⲒⲤⲘⲀ Ⲙ̄ⲠⲚ̄ⲚⲒⲔⲞⲚ Ⲛ̄ⲤⲈⲬⲒⲦⲤ̄ ⲈⲠⲈ-
20 ⲐⲎⲤⲀⲨⲢⲞⲤ Ⲙ̄ⲠⲞⲨⲞⲈⲒⲚ Ⲛ̄ⲤⲈⲔⲀⲀⲤ ϨⲚ ⲐⲀⲎ Ⲛ̄ⲦⲀⲝⲒⲤ Ⲙ̄-
ⲠⲞⲨⲞⲈⲒⲚ ϨⲈⲰⲤ ϢⲀ ⲠⲰⲖ ⲈϨⲢⲀⲒ̈ Ⲛ̄ⲚⲈ✝ⲨⲬⲞⲞⲨⲈ ⲦⲎⲢⲞⲨ
Ⲛ̄ⲦⲈⲖⲒⲞⲤ· ⲀⲨⲰ ⲈⲨϢⲀⲚⲤⲞⲂⲦⲈ ⲈⲤⲰⲔ Ⲛ̄Ⲛ̄ⲔⲀⲦⲀⲠⲈⲦⲀⲤ- ⲤϤⲈ
ⲘⲀ Ⲙ̄ⲠⲦⲞⲠⲞⲤ Ⲛ̄ⲚⲀⲞⲨⲚⲀⲘ’ ϢⲀⲨⲤⲰⲦϤ Ⲛ̄ⲦⲈ✝ⲨⲬⲎ ⲈⲦⲘ̄-
ⲘⲀⲨ Ⲛ̄ⲞⲨⲰϨⲘ̄· ⲀⲨⲰ Ⲛ̄ⲤⲈⲔⲀⲐⲀⲢⲒⲌⲈ Ⲙ̄ⲘⲞⲤ Ⲛ̄ⲤⲈⲔⲀⲀⲤ
25 ϨⲚ Ⲛ̄ⲦⲀⲝⲒⲤ Ⲙ̄ⲠϢⲞⲢⲠ̄ Ⲛ̄ⲤⲰⲦⲎⲢ ⲠⲀⲒ̈ ⲈⲦϨⲘ̄ ⲠⲈⲐⲎⲤⲀⲨⲢⲞⲤ
Ⲙ̄ⲠⲞⲨⲞⲈⲒⲚ·

---

6 MS ϨⲚ ⲠⲤⲰⲘⲀ; better ϨⲚ ⲦϬⲒⲚϢⲒⲂⲈ Ⲙ̄ⲠⲤⲰⲘⲀ.
17 MS Ⲙ̄ⲘⲞⲤ expunged before Ⲛ̄ⲦⲈ✝ⲨⲬⲎ.

from all the *places* in which it is. And they will take it to the *place* of the *Midst* to the presence of the *Virgin* of the Light. And the *Virgin* of the Light *examines* it and she sees the sign of the Kingdom of the Ineffable which is in that *soul*. And if it has not yet completed its number of *cycles* in the changes of the *soul or* in ⟨the changes of⟩ the *body*, the *Virgin* of the Light *seals* it with an excellent *seal* and *hastens* to cause it to be cast in that very month into a *righteous body* which will find the *mysteries* of the light. And it will become *good*, and go to the height to the Kingdom of the Light. And if that *soul* has received its number of *cycles*, then the *Virgin* of the Light will *examine* it, and she does not allow it to be *punished* because it has received its number of *cycles*, *but* she gives it into the hands of the seven *virgins* of the light. And the seven *virgins* of the light *examine* that *soul* and *baptise* it with their *baptisms*, and give it the *spiritual inunction*, and take it to the *Treasury* of the Light. and place it in the last *rank* of the light until the ascension of all the *perfect souls*. And when they prepare to draw the *veils* of the *place* of those of the right, they cleanse that *soul* once more and *purify* it, and place it in the *ranks* of the first *saviour* who is in the *Treasury* of the Light." |

ⲀⲤϢⲰⲠⲈ ϬⲈ ⲚⲦⲈⲢⲈ ⲠⲤⲰⲦⲎⲢ ⲞⲨⲰ ⲈϤⲬⲰ ⲚⲚⲈⲒ̈ϢⲀⲬⲈ
ⲈⲚⲈϤⲘⲀⲐⲎⲦⲎⲤ · ⲀⲤⲞⲨⲰϨⲘ̄ ⲚϬⲒ ⲘⲀⲢⲒϨⲀⲘ ⲠⲈⲬⲀⲤ ⲚⲒⲤ̄ ⲬⲈ
ⲠⲀⲬⲞⲈⲒⲤ ⲀⲒ̈ⲤⲰⲦⲘ̄ ⲈⲢⲞⲔ ⲈⲔⲬⲰ Ⲙ̄ⲘⲞⲤ ⲬⲈ ⲠⲈⲦⲚⲀⲬⲒ
ϨⲚ Ⲙ̄ⲘⲨⲤⲦⲎⲢⲒⲞⲚ Ⲙ̄ⲠⲀⲦ ϢⲀ ϪⲈ ⲈⲢⲞϤ · Ⲏ̄ ⲠⲈⲦⲚⲀⲬⲒ ϨⲚ
5 Ⲙ̄ⲘⲨⲤⲦⲎⲢⲒⲞⲚ Ⲙ̄ⲠⲒϢⲞⲢⲠ̄ Ⲙ̄ⲘⲨⲤⲦⲎⲢⲒⲞⲚ · ϢⲀⲨⲢ̄-ϨⲈⲚϢⲖⲒϬ
Ⲛ̄ⲞⲨⲞⲈⲒⲚ Ⲙ̄Ⲛ ϨⲈⲚⲀⲠⲞⲢⲢⲞⲒⲀ Ⲛ̄ⲞⲨⲞⲈⲒⲚ Ⲛ̄ⲤⲈⲬⲰⲦⲈ Ⲛ̄ⲦⲞ-
ⲠⲞⲤ ⲚⲒⲘ· ϨⲈⲰⲤ ϢⲀⲚⲦⲞⲨⲂⲰⲔ ⲈⲠⲦⲞⲠⲞⲤ Ⲛ̄ⲦⲈⲨⲔⲖⲎⲢⲞ-
ⲚⲞⲘⲒⲀ· ⲀϤⲞⲨⲰϨⲘ̄ Ⲛ̄ϬⲒ ⲠⲤⲰⲦⲎⲢ ⲠⲈⲬⲀϤ Ⲙ̄ⲘⲀⲢⲒⲀ ϪⲈ
ⲈⲨϢⲀⲚⲬⲒ Ⲙ̄ⲠⲘⲨⲤⲦⲎⲢⲒⲞⲚ ⲈⲦⲒ ⲈⲨⲞⲚϨ· ⲀⲨⲰ ⲈⲨϢⲀⲚⲈⲒ̈
10 ⲈⲂⲞⲖ ϨⲚ ⲤⲰⲘⲀ ϢⲀⲨⲢ̄-ϨⲈⲚϢⲖⲒϬ Ⲛ̄ⲞⲨⲞⲈⲒⲚ Ⲙ̄Ⲛ ϨⲈⲚ-
ⲀⲠⲞⲢⲢⲞⲒⲀ Ⲛ̄ⲞⲨⲞⲈⲒⲚ Ⲛ̄ⲤⲈⲬⲰⲦⲈ Ⲛ̄ⲦⲞⲠⲞⲤ ⲚⲒⲘ· ϨⲈⲰⲤ Ⲥ̅Ⲏ̅Ⲥ̅ ᵇ
ϢⲀⲚⲦⲞⲨⲂⲰⲔ ⲈⲠⲦⲞⲠⲞⲤ Ⲛ̄ⲦⲈⲨⲔⲖⲎⲢⲞⲚⲞⲘⲒⲀ· ⲀⲖⲖⲀ Ⲉ-
ϢⲰⲠⲈ ⲈϨⲈⲚⲢⲈϤⲢ̄ⲚⲞⲂⲈ Ⲛ̄ⲦⲞϤ ⲚⲈ ⲈⲀⲨⲈⲒ̈ ⲈⲂⲞⲖ Ϩ̄Ⲙ ⲠⲤⲰ-
ⲘⲀ ⲈⲘⲠⲞⲨⲘⲈⲦⲀⲚⲞⲒ̈· ⲀⲨⲰ Ⲛ̄ⲦⲈⲦⲚ̄ⲈⲒⲢⲈ ϨⲀⲢⲞⲞⲨ Ⲙ̄ⲠⲘⲨⲤ-
15 ⲦⲎⲢⲒⲞⲚ Ⲙ̄ⲠⲒⲀⲦ ϢⲀ ϪⲈ ⲈⲢⲞϤ ⲬⲈ ⲈⲨⲈⲠⲞⲞⲚⲞⲨ ⲈⲂⲞⲖ
ϨⲚ Ⲛ̄ⲔⲞⲖⲀⲤⲒⲤ ⲚⲒⲘ Ⲛ̄ⲤⲈⲚⲞⲬⲞⲨ ⲈⲨⲤⲰⲘⲀ Ⲛ̄ⲆⲒⲔⲀⲒⲞⲤ ⲠⲀⲒ̈
ⲈϤⲚⲀⲢⲀⲄⲀⲐⲞⲤ Ⲛ̄ϤⲔⲖⲎⲢⲞⲚⲞⲘⲈⲒ Ⲛ̄ⲦⲘⲚ̄ⲦⲈⲢⲞ Ⲙ̄ⲠⲞⲨⲞⲈⲒⲚ·
Ⲏ̄ Ⲙ̄ⲘⲞⲚ Ⲛ̄ⲦⲞϤ Ⲛ̄ⲤⲈⲬⲒⲦϤ ⲈⲐⲀ̄Ⲏ Ⲛ̄ⲦⲀⲜ̄ⲒⲤ Ⲙ̄ⲠⲞⲨⲞⲈⲒⲚ·
ⲘⲈⲨⲈϢϬⲘ̄ϬⲞⲘ ⲈⲬⲰⲦⲈ Ⲛ̄Ⲛ̄ⲦⲞⲠⲞⲤ ⲬⲈ Ⲛ̄ⲦⲞⲞⲨ ⲀⲚ
20 ⲈⲦⲈⲒⲢⲈ Ⲙ̄ⲠⲘⲨⲤⲦⲎⲢⲒⲞⲚ· ⲀⲖⲖⲀ ϢⲀⲢⲈ Ⲙ̄ⲠⲀⲢⲀⲖⲎⲘⲠⲦⲎⲤ
Ⲙ̄ⲘⲈⲖⲬⲒⲤⲈⲆⲈⲔ· ϢⲀⲨⲈⲒ̈ Ⲛ̄ⲤⲰⲞⲨ Ⲛ̄ⲤⲈⲬⲒⲦⲞⲨ ⲈⲢⲀⲦⲤ̄ Ⲛ̄-
ⲦⲠⲀⲢⲐⲈⲚⲞⲤ Ⲙ̄ⲠⲞⲨⲞⲈⲒⲚ· ⲀⲨⲰ ⲞⲨⲘⲎⲎϢⲈ Ⲛ̄ⲤⲞⲠ· ϢⲀⲢⲈ
Ⲛ̄ⲖⲒⲦⲞⲨⲢⲄⲞⲤ Ⲛ̄ⲚⲈⲔⲢⲒⲦⲎⲤ Ⲛ̄ⲚⲀⲢⲬⲰⲚ ϢⲀⲨⲤⲠⲞⲨⲆⲀⲌⲈ
Ⲛ̄ⲤⲈⲬⲒ Ⲛ̄ⲚⲈⲮⲨⲬⲞⲞⲨⲈ ⲈⲦⲘ̄ⲘⲀⲨ Ⲛ̄ⲤⲈⲦⲀⲖⲨ ⲈⲦⲞⲞⲦⲞⲨ
25 Ⲛ̄ⲚⲈⲨⲈⲢⲎⲨ ϨⲈⲰⲤ ϢⲀⲚⲦⲞⲨⲬⲒⲦⲤ̄ ⲈⲢⲀⲦⲤ̄ Ⲛ̄ⲦⲠⲀⲢⲐⲈⲚⲞⲤ [Ⲥ̅Ⲏ̅Ⲋ̅]
Ⲙ̄ⲠⲞⲨⲞⲈⲒⲚ·

---

23 MS Ⲛ̄ⲚⲈⲔⲢⲒⲦⲎⲤ; better Ⲛ̄ⲚⲈⲔⲢⲒⲤⲒⲤ.

129. Now it happened when the *Saviour* finished saying these words to his *disciples*, Mariam answered and said to Jesus : "My Lord, I have heard thee say : he who will receive from the *mystery* of the Ineffable, *or* he who will receive from the *mystery* of the First *Mystery*, they will become beams of light and *outpourings* of light, and will penetrate every *place until* they go to the *place* of their *inheritance*."

The *Saviour* answered and said to Maria : "If they receive the *mystery* while they are still alive, when they come forth from the *body* they become beams of light and *outpourings* of light, and they penetrate every *place until* they go to the *place* of their *inheritance*. *But* if they are sinners, on the other hand, and they come forth from the *body* and have not *repented*, and you perform for them the *mystery* of the Ineffable, so that they should be returned from all the *punishments* and cast into a *righteous body* which will become *good* and *inherit* the Kingdom of the Light, *or* else that they should be brought to the last *rank* of the light : they are not able to penetrate the *places* because it is not they who perform the *mystery*. *But* the *paralemptai* of Melchisedek come after them and take them to the presence of the *Virgin* of the Light. And the *ministers* of the *judgments* [1] of the *archons hasten* many times to take those *souls*, and they hand them to one another *until* they take them to the presence of the *Virgin* of the Light." |

---

[1]   (23) judgments; MS : judges.

ⲁⲥⲟⲩⲱϩ ⲟⲛ ⲉⲧⲟⲟⲧ̅ⲥ̅ ⲛ̅ϭⲓ ⲙⲁⲣⲓⲁ ⲡⲉϫⲁⲥ ⲙ̅ⲡⲥⲱⲧⲏⲣ ϫⲉ ⲡⲁϫⲟⲉⲓⲥ ⲉ̈ⲓ̈ⲉ ⲟⲩⲣⲱⲙⲉ ⲉⲁϥϫⲓ ⲛ̅ⲙ̅ⲙⲩⲥⲧⲏⲣⲓⲟⲛ ⲙ̅ⲡⲟⲩⲟⲉⲓⲛ ⲛⲁ̈ⲓ ⲉⲧϩ̅ⲙ̅ ⲡϣⲟⲣ̅ⲡ̅ ⲛ̅ϫⲱⲣⲏⲙⲁ ⲉⲧⲙ̅ⲡⲥⲁⲛ̅ⲃⲟⲗ· ⲁⲩⲱ ⲛ̅ⲧⲉⲣⲉϥϫⲱⲕ ⲉⲃⲟⲗ ⲛ̅ϭⲓ ⲡⲉⲟⲩⲟⲉⲓϣ ⲛ̅ⲙ̅ⲙⲩⲥⲧⲏⲣⲓⲟⲛ ⲉⲧⲟⲩⲁⲙⲁϩⲧⲉ ϣⲁⲣⲟⲟⲩ· ⲁⲩⲱ ⲡⲣⲱⲙⲉ ⲉⲧⲙ̅ⲙⲁⲩ ⲛ̅ϥⲟⲩⲱϩ ⲉⲧⲟⲟⲧ̅ϥ̅ ⲛ̅ⲟⲩⲱϩ̅ⲙ̅ ⲉϫⲓ-ⲙⲩⲥⲧⲏⲣⲓⲟⲛ ϩ̅ⲛ̅ ⲙ̅ⲙⲩⲥⲧⲏⲣⲓⲟⲛ ⲉⲧϩⲓⲡⲥⲁⲛϩⲟⲩⲛ ⲛ̅ⲙ̅ⲙⲩⲥⲧⲏⲣⲓⲟⲛ ⲉⲛⲧⲁϥⲟⲩⲱ ⲉϥϫⲓ ⲙ̅ⲙⲟⲟⲩ ⲁⲩⲱ ⲟⲛ ⲁϥⲣ̅-ⲡⲕⲉⲁⲙⲉⲗⲓ ⲛ̅ϭⲓ ⲡⲣⲱⲙⲉ ⲉⲧⲙ̅ⲙⲁⲩ· ⲉⲙⲡ̅ϥ̅ⲡⲣⲟⲥⲉⲩⲭⲉ ϩ̅ⲛ̅ ⲧⲉⲡⲣⲟⲥⲉⲩⲭⲏ ⲉϣⲁⲥϥⲓ ⲛ̅ⲧⲕⲁⲕⲓⲁ ⲛ̅ⲛⲉⲧⲣⲩⲫⲟⲟⲩⲉ ⲉⲧϥ̅ⲟⲩⲱⲙ ⲙ̅ⲙⲟⲟⲩ ⲙ̅ⲛ̅ ⲛⲉⲧϥ̅ⲥⲱ ⲙ̅ⲙⲟⲟⲩ· ⲁⲩⲱ ⲉⲃⲟⲗ ϩⲓⲧ̅ⲛ̅ ⲧⲕⲁⲕⲓⲁ ⲛ̅ⲛⲉⲧⲣⲩⲫⲟⲟⲩⲉ ⲁⲩⲙⲟⲣ̅ϥ̅ ⲉϩⲟⲩⲛ ⲉⲡⲁⲝⲱⲛ ⲛ̅ⲑⲓⲙⲁⲣⲙⲉⲛⲏ ⲛ̅ⲛ̅ⲁⲣⲭⲱⲛ· ⲁⲩⲱ ϩⲓⲧ̅ⲛ̅ ⲧⲁⲛⲁⲅⲕⲏ ⲛ̅ⲛⲉⲥⲧⲟⲓⲭⲓⲟⲛ ⲁϥⲣ̅ⲛⲟⲃⲉ ⲛ̅ⲟⲩⲱϩ̅ⲙ̅· ⲙ̅ⲛ̅ⲛ̅ⲥⲁ ⲡϫⲱⲕ *ⲉⲃⲟⲗ ⲙ̅ⲡⲉⲩⲟⲉⲓϣ ⲉⲣⲉ ⲡⲙⲩⲥⲧⲏⲣⲓⲟⲛ ⲁⲙⲁϩⲧⲉ [ⲥϥⲉ] ϣⲁⲣⲟϥ· ϫⲉ ⲁϥⲁⲙⲉⲗⲓ ⲙ̅ⲡ̅ϥ̅ⲡⲣⲟⲥⲉⲩⲭⲉ ϩ̅ⲛ̅ ⲧⲉⲡⲣⲟⲥⲉⲩⲭⲏ· ⲧⲁ̈ⲓ ⲉϣⲁⲥϥⲓ ⲛ̅ⲧⲕⲁⲕⲓⲁ ⲛ̅ⲛⲉⲯⲩⲭⲟⲟⲩⲉ ⲁⲩⲱ ⲉⲥⲕⲁⲑⲁⲣⲓⲍⲉ ⲙ̅ⲙⲟⲟⲩ· ⲁⲩⲱ ⲡⲣⲱⲙⲉ ⲉⲧⲙ̅ⲙⲁⲩ ⲁϥⲉⲓ' ⲉⲃⲟⲗ ϩ̅ⲛ̅ ⲥⲱⲙⲁ ⲉⲙⲡⲁⲧ̅ϥ̅ⲙⲉⲧⲁⲛⲟⲓ̈ ⲛ̅ⲟⲩⲱϩ̅ⲙ̅ ⲛ̅ϥϫⲓ-ⲙⲩⲥⲧⲏⲣⲓⲟⲛ ⲛ̅ⲟⲩⲱϩ̅ⲙ̅ ϩ̅ⲛ̅ ⲙ̅ⲙⲩⲥⲧⲏⲣⲓⲟⲛ ⲛⲁ̈ⲓ ⲉⲧϩⲓϩⲟⲩⲛ ⲛ̅ⲙ̅ⲙⲩⲥⲧⲏⲣⲓⲟⲛ ⲛ̅ⲧⲁϥⲟⲩⲱ ⲉϥϫⲓ ⲙ̅ⲙⲟⲟⲩ· ⲛⲁ̈ⲓ ⲉϣⲁⲩϫⲓ ⲛ̅ⲟⲩⲱϩ̅ⲙ̅ ⲛ̅ⲧⲙⲉⲧⲁⲛⲟⲓⲁ ⲛ̅ⲥⲉⲕⲱ ⲉⲃⲟⲗ ⲛ̅ⲛ̅ⲛⲟⲃⲉ· ⲁⲩⲱ ⲛ̅ⲧⲉⲣⲉϥⲉⲓ' ⲉⲃⲟⲗ ϩ̅ⲛ̅ ⲥⲱⲙⲁ ⲁⲛⲉⲓⲙⲉ ϩ̅ⲛ̅ ⲟⲩⲱⲣ̅ϫ̅ ϫⲉ ⲁⲩϥⲓⲧ̅ϥ̅ ⲉϩⲟⲩⲛ ⲉⲧⲙⲏⲧⲉ ⲙ̅ⲡⲉⲇⲣⲁⲕⲱⲛ ⲙ̅ⲡⲕⲁⲕⲉ ⲉⲧϩⲓⲃⲟⲗ· ⲉⲃⲟⲗ ⲛ̅ⲛ̅ⲛⲟⲃⲉ ⲉⲛⲧⲁϥⲁⲁⲩ· ⲁⲩⲱ ⲡⲣⲱⲙⲉ ⲉⲧⲙ̅ⲙⲁⲩ ⲙ̅ⲛ̅ⲧ̅ϥ̅-ⲃⲟⲏⲑⲟⲥ ϩⲓϫ̅ⲙ̅ ⲡⲕⲟⲥⲙⲟⲥ ⲟⲩⲇⲉ ϣⲁⲛϩⲧⲏϥ ⲉⲧⲣⲉϥⲉⲓⲣⲉ ⲙ̅ⲡⲙⲩⲥⲧⲏⲣⲓⲟⲛ ⲙ̅ⲡⲓⲁⲧϣⲁϫⲉ ⲉⲣⲟϥ· ϩⲉⲱⲥ ϣⲁⲛⲧⲟⲩⲡⲟⲟⲛⲉϥ

---

5 MS ϣⲁⲣⲟⲟⲩ; read ϣⲁⲣⲟϥ.

130. Maria continued again, she said to the *Saviour*:
"My Lord, if a man has received the *mysteries* of the light
which are in the first *space* without, and when the time
of the *mysteries*, to which they extend [1], is completed; and
that man continues once more to receive *mysteries* in the
mysteries which are within the *mysteries* which he has already
received; and furthermore that man has become *neglectful*,
so that he has not *prayed* in the *prayer* which takes away the
evil of the *foods* which he eats and drinks; and through the
evil of the *foods* he has been bound to the *axis* of the *Heimarmene* of the *archons*; and through the *constraint* of the *elements* he has sinned once more after the completion of the
time to which the *mystery* extends, because he has been
neglectful and has not *prayed* in the *prayer* which takes away
the *evil* of the *souls* and *purifies* them; and that man has come
forth from the *body* before he has *repented* once more, and
has received *mysteries* once more in the *mysteries* which are
within the *mysteries* which he has already received, these
which receive *repentance* and forgive sins once more; and
when he comes forth from the *body* we have known with
certainty that he was taken into the midst of the *dragon*
of the outer darkness, because of the sins which he has
committed; and that man has no *helper* in the *world, nor*
compassionate one, who would perform the *mystery* of the
Ineffable, *until* he is returned | from the midst of the *dragon*

---

[1]   (5) the time of the mysteries to which they extend; MS : the time of the mysteries
which extend to them (see 327.14, 15).

ЄΒΟΛ Ν̄ΤΜΗΤΕ Μ̄ΠΕΔΡΑΚШΝ Μ̄ΠΚΑΚΕ ΕΤ2ΙΒΟΛ· Ν̄СЄ-
ΧΙΤ̄Ч Є2ΟΥΝ ΕΤΜ̄Ν̄ΤΕΡΟ Μ̄ΠΟΥΟΪΝ· ΤΕΝΟΥ 6Є ΟΥΝ
ΠΑΧΟΪС**ЄΪЄ ΟΥ ΠЄΤЧΝΑΑΑЧ ШΑΝΤЧΝΟΥ2Μ ΕΝΚΟΛΑСΙС C̄Ч2
Μ̄ΠΕΔΡΑΚШΝ Μ̄ΠΚΑΚΕ ΕΤ2ΙΒΟΛ· Μ̄ΠШΡ ΠΧΟЄΙС Μ̄ΠΡ-
5 ΚΑΑЧ Ν̄СШΚ' ЄΒΟΛ ΧΕ ΑЧШΠ2ΙСЄ 2ΡΑΪ 2Ν̄ Ν̄ΔΙШΓΜΟС·
ΑΥШ 2ΡΑΪ 2Ν̄ ΤΜΝ̄ΤΝΟΥΤΕ ΤΗΡ̄С ΕΤЧШΟΟΠ Ν̄2ΗΤ̄С·
ΤΕΝΟΥ 6Є ΟΥΝ ΠСШΤΗΡ ΝΑ ΝΑΪ· ΜΗΠШС Ν̄ΤΕ ΟΥΑ
Ν̄ΝΕΝСΥΓΓΕΝΗС ШШΠΕ 2Μ ΠЄΪΤΥΠΟС Ν̄ΤΕΪΜΙΝΕ· ΑΥШ
ΝΑ Ν̄ΝΕΨΥΧΟΟΥΕ ΤΗΡΟΥ ΕΤΝΑШШΠΕ 2Μ ΠЄΪΤΥΠΟС·
10 ΧΕ Ν̄ΤΟΚ ΠΕ ΠШΟШ̄Τ ΕΤΑΟΥШΝ ΕΡΜ̄ΠΤΗΡ̄Ч· ΑΥШ
ΕΤШΤΑΜ ΕΡΜ̄ΠΤΗΡ̄Ч· ΑΥШ ΠΕΚΜΥСΤΗΡΙΟΝ ΠΕΤΑΜΑ2ΤΕ
Μ̄ΜΟΟΥ ΤΗΡΟΥ· ΑΪΟ ΠΧΟЄΙС ΝΑ' Ν̄ΝΕΨΥΧΟΟΥΕ Ν̄ΤΕΪ-
ΜΙΝΕ· ΧΕ ΑΥΟΝΟΜΑΖΕ ΡШ Ν̄ΝΕΚΜΥСΤΗΡΙΟΝ Ν̄ΟΥ2ΟΟΥ
Ν̄ΟΥШΤ· ΑΥШ ΑΥΠΙСΤΕΥΕ ΕΡΟΟΥ 2Ν̄ ΟΥΜΕ· ΑΥШ
15 ΧΕ ΝΕΥШΟΟΠ' ΑΝ 2Ν̄ ΟΥ2ΥΠΟΚΡΙСΙС· ΑΪΟ ΠΧΟЄΙС
† ΝΑΥ Ν̄ΟΥΔШΡΕΑ 2ΡΑΪ 2Ν̄ ΤΕΚΜ̄Ν̄ΤΑΓΑΘΟС· ΑΥШ
† ΝΑΥ Ν̄ΟΥΜΟΤΝΕС 2Ν̄ *ΤΕΚΜ̄Ν̄ΤΝΑΗΤ·   C̄Ч2 ᵇ

ΝΑΪ 6Є Ν̄ΤΕΡΕСΧΟΟΥ Ν̄6Ι ΜΑΡΙΑ ΑЧΜΑΚΑΡΙΖΕ Μ̄ΜΟС
Ν̄6Ι ΠСШΤΗΡ ΕΜΑШΟ ΕΜΑШΟ· ЄΒΟΛ Ν̄Ν̄ШΑΧΕ ΕΤ̄СΧШ
20 Μ̄ΜΟΟΥ· ΑΥШ ΑЧШШΠΕ 2Ν̄ ΟΥΝΟ6 Ν̄ΝΑ Ν̄6Ι ΠСШΤΗΡ·
ΠΕΧΑЧ Μ̄ΜΑΡΙΑ ΧΕ ΡШΜΕ ΝΙΜ' ΕΤΝΑШШΠΕ 2Μ ΠЄΪ-
ΤΥΠΟС ΕΝΤΑΧΟΟЧ· ΑΙΤΙ ΕΥΟΝ̄2 † ΝΑΥ Μ̄ΠΜΥСΤΗ-
ΡΙΟΝ Ν̄ΟΥΑ· Μ̄ΠΜΝ̄ΤСΝΟΟΥС Ν̄ΡΑΝ· Ν̄ΤΕ Ν̄ΤΑΜΙΟΝ
Μ̄ΠΕΔΡΑΚШΝ Μ̄ΠΚΑΚΕ ΕΤ2ΙΒΟΛ' ΝΑΪ Ε†ΝΑΤΑΑΥ ΝΗΤ̄Ν
25 ЄΪШΑΝΟΥШ ЄΪСШΡ ЄΒΟΛ ΝΗΤ̄Ν Μ̄ΠΤΗΡ̄Ч ΧΙΝ 2ΟΥΝ
ЄΒΟΛ ΑΥШ ΧΙΝ ΒΟΛ' Є2ΟΥΝ· ΑΥШ ΡШΜΕ ΝΙΜ ΕΤΝΑ2Ε

---

10 MS ΕΤΑΟΥШΝ; read ΕΤΟΥШΝ.

of the outer darkness and taken into the Kingdom of the
Light : *now* at this time, my Lord, what will become of him [1]
until he is saved from the *punishments* of the *dragon* of the
outer darkness? By no means, O Lord, abandon him, because
he has endured suffering in the *persecutions* and in all the
godliness in which he was. *Now* at this time, O *Saviour*,
have mercy upon me, *lest* one of our *relatives* should be
of such a *type* as this. And have mercy on all the *souls*
which will be of this *type*. For thou art the key which opens
the door of the All, and which closes the door of the All [2].*
And it is thy *mystery* which controls them all. Now, O Lord,
have mercy upon the *souls* of this kind, for they have *invoked*
thy *mysteries* for a single day, and they have truly *believed*
in them, and they were not in *hypocrisy*. Now, O Lord,
give to them a *gift* in thy *goodness*, and give them rest in
thy mercy."

When Maria had said these things, the *Saviour blessed* her
very greatly on account of the words which she had spoken.
And the *Saviour*, with great mercy [3], said to Maria : "All
men who will be of this *type* of which thou hast spoken,
while they are *still* living, give to them the *mystery* of one
of the twelve names of the *chambers* of the *dragon* of the
outer darkness, which I shall give you when I have finished
setting forth to you the All, from within out, and from
without in. And all men who will find | the *mystery* of one

---

* cf. Rev. 3.7

---

[1] (3) what will become of him?; Till : what must he do?.
[2] (10) see Resch (Bibl. 41), Apocryphon 58, p. 431.
[3] (20) with great mercy; lit. was in a great mercy.

ⲉⲡⲙⲩⲥⲧⲏⲣⲓⲟⲛ ⲛ̅ⲟⲩⲁ ⲙ̅ⲡⲙⲛ̅ⲧⲥⲛⲟⲟⲩⲥ ⲛ̅ⲣⲁⲛ ⲛ̅ⲧⲉ ⲡⲉⲇⲣⲁⲕⲱⲛ ⲉⲧⲙ̅ⲙⲁⲩ ⲙ̅ⲡⲕⲁⲕⲉ ⲉⲧϩⲓⲃⲟⲗˋ ⲁⲩⲱ ⲣⲱⲙⲉ ⲛⲓⲙ
ⲕⲁⲛ ⲉϩⲉⲛⲣⲉϥⲣ̅ⲛⲟⲃⲉ ⲛⲉ ⲉⲙⲁϣⲟ · ⲁⲩⲱ ⲉⲁⲩϫⲓ ⲛ̅ⲙⲙⲩⲥ-
ⲧⲏⲣⲓⲟⲛ ⲙ̅ⲡⲟⲩⲟⲉⲓⲛ ⲛ̅ϣⲟⲣⲡ̅ ⲙⲛ̅ⲛ̅ⲥⲱⲥ ⲁⲩⲡⲁⲣⲁⲃⲁ · ⲏ̅
5 ⲙ̅ⲙⲟⲛ ⲛ̅ⲧⲟϥ ⲙ̅ⲡⲟⲩⲣ̅-ⲗⲁⲁⲩ ⲙ̅ⲡⲙⲩⲥⲧⲏⲣⲓⲟⲛ ⲉⲡⲧⲏⲣϥ̅ · ⲛⲁⲓ̈
ⲉⲩϣⲁⲛⲭⲱⲕ ⲉⲃⲟⲗ ⲛ̅ⲛⲉⲩⲕⲩⲕⲗⲟⲥ ϩⲛ̅ ⲙⲙⲉⲧⲁⲃⲟⲗⲏ ⲁⲩⲱ [ⲥⲩⲏ]
ⲛⲁⲓ̈ ⲛ̅ⲧⲉⲓ̈ⲙⲓⲛⲉ ⲉⲩϣⲁⲛⲉⲓˋ ⲉⲃⲟⲗ ϩⲛ̅ ⲥⲱⲙⲁ ⲉⲙⲡⲟⲩⲙⲉⲧⲁ-
ⲛⲟⲓ̈ ⲛ̅ⲟⲩⲱϩⲙ̅ · ⲁⲩⲱ ⲛ̅ⲥⲉⲭⲓⲧⲟⲩ ⲛ̅ⲕⲟⲗⲁⲥⲓⲥ ⲉⲧϩⲛ̅ⲧⲙⲏⲧⲉ
ⲙ̅ⲡⲉⲇⲣⲁⲕⲱⲛ ⲙ̅ⲡⲕⲁⲕⲉ ⲉⲧϩⲓⲃⲟⲗ · ⲁⲩⲱ ⲛ̅ⲥⲉϣⲱϫⲡ̅ ϩⲛ̅
10 ⲛ̅ⲕⲩⲕⲗⲟⲥ ⲛ̅ⲥⲉϣⲱϫⲡ̅ ϩⲛ̅ ⲛ̅ⲕⲟⲗⲁⲥⲓⲥ ϩⲛ̅ ⲧⲙⲏⲧⲉ ⲙ̅ⲡⲉ-
ⲇⲣⲁⲕⲱⲛ ⲁⲩⲱ ⲛⲁⲓ̈ ⲉⲩⲥⲟⲟⲩⲛ ⲙ̅ⲡⲙⲩⲥⲧⲏⲣⲓⲟⲛ ⲛ̅ⲟⲩⲁ
ⲙ̅ⲡⲙⲛ̅ⲧⲥⲛⲟⲟⲩⲥ ⲛ̅ⲣⲁⲛ ⲛ̅ⲧⲉ ⲛ̅ⲁⲅⲅⲉⲗⲟⲥ ⲉⲩⲟⲛϩ̅ ⲉⲩϣⲟⲟⲡ
ϩⲙ̅ ⲡⲕⲟⲥⲙⲟⲥ · ⲁⲩⲱ ⲛ̅ⲥⲉⲭⲱ ⲛ̅ⲟⲩⲁ ⲛ̅ⲛⲉⲩⲣⲁⲛ ⲉⲩ-
ⲛ̅ϩⲟⲩⲛ ϩⲛ̅ ⲧⲙⲏⲧⲉ ⲛ̅ⲛ̅ⲕⲟⲗⲁⲥⲓⲥ ⲙ̅ⲡⲉⲇⲣⲁⲕⲱⲛ ⲁⲩⲱ ⲡⲛⲁⲩ
15 ⲉⲧⲟⲩⲛⲁⲭⲟⲟϥ ϣⲁϥⲥⲁⲗⲉⲩⲉ ⲛ̅ϭⲓ ⲡⲉⲇⲣⲁⲕⲱⲛ ⲧⲏⲣϥ̅ ⲁⲩⲱ
ϣⲁϥϣⲧⲟⲣⲧⲣ̅ ⲉⲙⲁϣⲟ ⲉⲙⲁϣⲟ · ⲁⲩⲱ ⲡⲧⲁⲙⲓⲟⲛ ⲉⲧⲟⲩ-
ⲛ̅ϩⲏⲧϥ̅ ⲛ̅ϭⲓ ⲛⲉⲯⲩⲭⲟⲟⲩⲉ ⲛ̅ⲣ̅ⲣⲱⲙⲉ ⲉⲧⲙ̅ⲙⲁⲩ · ϣⲁⲣⲉ ⲡⲉϥ-
ⲣⲟ ⲟⲩⲱⲛ ⲛ̅ⲥⲁ ⲧⲡⲉ · ⲁⲩⲱ ϣⲁⲣⲉ ⲡⲁⲣⲭⲱⲛ ⲙ̅ⲡⲧⲁⲙⲓⲟⲛ
ⲉⲧⲟⲩϣⲟⲟⲡ ⲛ̅ϩⲏⲧϥ̅ ⲛ̅ϭⲓ ⲛ̅ⲣⲱⲙⲉ ⲉⲧⲙ̅ⲙⲁⲩ · ⲁⲩⲱ ϣⲁϥ-
20 ⲛⲟⲩϫⲉ ⲛ̅ⲛⲉⲯⲩⲭⲟⲟⲩⲉ ⲛ̅ⲣ̅ⲣⲱⲙⲉ ⲉⲧⲙ̅ⲙⲁⲩ ⲉⲃⲟⲗ ϩⲛ̅ [ⲥⲩⲏ ᵇ]
ⲧⲙⲏⲧⲉ ⲙ̅ⲡⲉⲇⲣⲁⲕⲱⲛ ⲙ̅ⲡⲕⲁⲕⲉ ⲉⲧϩⲓⲃⲟⲗ · ϫⲉ ⲁⲩϩⲉ ⲉⲡⲙⲩⲥⲧⲏⲣⲓⲟⲛ ⲙ̅ⲡⲣⲁⲛ ⲙ̅ⲡⲉⲇⲣⲁⲕⲱⲛ · ⲁⲩⲱ ⲉⲣϣⲁⲛ ⲡⲁⲣⲭⲱⲛ ⲛⲟⲩϫⲉ ⲉⲃⲟⲗ ⲛ̅ⲛⲉⲯⲩⲭⲟⲟⲩⲉ · ϣⲁⲣⲉ ⲛ̅ⲁⲅⲅⲉⲗⲟⲥ
ⲛ̅ⲓ̈ⲉⲟⲩ ⲡϣⲟⲣⲡ̅ ⲛ̅ⲣⲱⲙⲉ · ⲛⲁⲓ̈ ⲉⲧⲣⲟⲉⲓⲥ ⲉⲛⲧⲁⲙⲓⲟⲛ ⲙ̅ⲡⲙⲁ
25 ⲉⲧⲙ̅ⲙⲁⲩ · ϣⲁϥⲥⲡⲟⲩⲇⲁⲍⲉ ⲛ̅ⲧⲉⲩⲛⲟⲩ ⲛ̅ϥϩⲁⲣⲡⲁⲍⲉ ⲛ̅ⲧⲉ-
ⲯⲩⲭⲏ ⲉⲧⲙ̅ⲙⲁⲩ ϣⲁⲛⲧϥ̅ϫⲓⲧⲥ̅ ⲉⲣⲁⲧϥ̅ ⲛ̅ⲓ̈ⲉⲟⲩ ⲡϣⲟⲣⲡ̅

---

14 ⲁⲩⲱ ⲡⲛⲁⲩ ... ⲡⲉⲇⲣⲁⲕⲱⲛ written below in margin.

of the twelve names of that *dragon* of the outer darkness; and all men, *even if* they are great sinners and they have received the *mysteries* of the light first and afterwards have *transgressed*; *or* on the other hand, they have not performed any *mystery* at all: these men, when they have completed their *cycles* in the *changes*, and when such as these have come forth from the *body* without *repenting* once more, and they are taken to the *punishments* which are in the midst of the *dragon* of the outer darkness, and they are left in the *cycles*, and they are left in the *punishments* in the midst of the *dragon*; and if these have known the *mystery* of one of the twelve names of the *angels* while they were alive and in the *world*, and they say one of their names while they are inside in the midst of the *punishments* of the *dragon*: at the time when they shall say it, the whole *dragon* will be *shaken* and will be exceedingly agitated. And the door of the *chamber* in which are the *souls* of those men opens upwards. And the *archon* of the *chamber* in which are those men casts the *souls* of those men forth from the midst of the *dragon* of the outer darkness, because they have found the *mystery* of the name of the *dragon*. And when the *archon* casts forth the *souls*, the *angels* of Jeu, the First Man, who watch over the *chambers* of that place, *hasten* immediately and *snatch* that *soul*, so that they take [1] it to the presence of Jeu, the First | Man, the *Messenger*

---

[1] (23-26) the angels ... hasten ... and snatch ... so that they take; MS: he hastens ... and snatches ... so that he takes.

ⲚⲢⲰⲘⲈ ⲠⲈⲠⲢⲈⲤⲂⲈⲨⲦⲎⲤ ⲘⲠϢⲞⲢⲠ ⲚⲦⲰϢ· ⲀⲨⲰ ϢⲀⲢⲈ
ⲒⲈⲞⲨ ⲠϢⲞⲢⲠ ⲚⲢⲰⲘⲈ ϢⲀϤⲚⲀⲨ ⲈⲚⲈⲮⲨⲬⲞⲞⲨⲈ ⲚϤⲆⲞⲄⲒ-
ⲘⲀⲌⲈ ⲘⲘⲞⲞⲨ· ϢⲀϤϪⲈ ⲈⲢⲞⲞⲨ ⲈⲀⲨϪⲰⲔ' ⲈⲂⲞⲖ ⲚⲚⲈⲨ-
ⲔⲨⲔⲖⲞⲤ· ⲀⲨⲰ ⲞⲨⲔ ⲈⲌⲈⲤⲦⲒ ⲈⲦⲢⲈⲨⲚⲦⲞⲨ ⲈⲠⲔⲞⲤⲘⲞⲤ
5 ⲚⲞⲨⲰϨⲘ· ϪⲈ ⲮⲨⲬⲎ ⲚⲒⲘ ⲈⲦⲞⲨⲚⲀⲚⲞⲬⲞⲨ ⲈⲠⲔⲀⲔⲈ
ⲈⲦϨⲒⲂⲞⲖ· ⲞⲨⲔ ⲈⲌⲈⲤⲦⲒ ⲈⲚⲦⲞⲨ ⲈⲠⲔⲞⲤⲘⲞⲤ ⲚⲞⲨⲰϨⲘ·
ϢⲀⲨⲔⲀⲀⲨ ⲚⲦⲞⲞⲦⲞⲨ ⲚϬⲒ ⲘⲠⲀⲢⲀⲖⲎⲘⲠⲦⲎⲤ ⲚⲒⲈⲞⲨ
ⲈϢⲰⲠⲈ ⲈⲘⲠⲞⲨϪⲰⲔ ⲈⲂⲞⲖ ⲚⲦⲈⲨⲎⲠⲤ ⲚⲔⲨⲔⲖⲞⲤ ϨⲚ ⸎ ⲤⲨⲞ
ⲘⲘⲈⲦⲀⲂⲞⲖⲎ ⲘⲠⲤⲰⲘⲀ· ⲀⲨⲰ ϢⲀⲚⲦⲞⲨⲈⲒⲢⲈ ⲘⲠⲘⲨⲤⲦⲎ-
10 ⲢⲒⲞⲚ ⲘⲠⲒⲀⲦϢⲀϪⲈ ⲈⲢⲞϤ ϨⲀⲢⲞⲞⲨ· ϢⲀⲚⲦⲞⲨⲔⲞⲦⲞⲨ ⲈⲨ-
ⲤⲰⲘⲀ ⲚⲀⲄⲀⲐⲞⲤ· ⲠⲀⲒ ⲈϤⲚⲀϨⲈ ⲈⲘⲘⲨⲤⲦⲎⲢⲒⲞⲚ ⲘⲠⲞⲨⲞ-
ⲈⲒⲚ ⲚϤⲔⲖⲎⲢⲞⲚⲞⲘⲒ ⲚⲦⲘⲚⲦⲈⲢⲞ ⲘⲠⲞⲨⲞⲈⲒⲚ· ⲈϢⲰⲠⲈ ⲆⲈ
ⲈϤϢⲀⲚⲆⲞⲄⲒⲘⲀⲌⲈ ⲘⲘⲞⲞⲨ ⲚϬⲒ ⲒⲈⲞⲨ ⲚϤϨⲈ ⲈⲢⲞⲞⲨ Ⲉ-
ⲀⲨϪⲰⲔ ⲈⲂⲞⲖ ⲚⲚⲈⲨⲔⲨⲔⲖⲞⲤ· ⲀⲨⲰ ⲞⲨⲔ ⲈⲌⲈⲤⲦⲒ ⲚⲀⲨ
15 ⲈⲔⲞⲦⲞⲨ ⲈⲠⲔⲞⲤⲘⲞⲤ ⲚⲞⲨⲰϨⲘ· ⲀⲨⲰ ⲠⲔⲈⲘⲀⲒⲚ ⲘⲠⲒ-
ⲀⲦϢⲀϪⲈ ⲈⲢⲞϤ ⲚϤϢⲞⲞⲠ ⲚⲘⲘⲀⲨ ⲀⲚ· ⲀⲨⲰ ϢⲀϤⲚⲀ
ⲚⲀⲨ ⲚϬⲒ ⲒⲈⲞⲨ· ϢⲀϤϪⲒⲦⲞⲨ ⲈⲢⲀⲦⲞⲨ ⲚⲦⲤⲀϢϤⲈ ⲘⲠⲀⲢ-
ⲐⲈⲚⲞⲤ ⲘⲠⲞⲨⲞⲒⲚ ϢⲀⲨⲂⲀⲠⲦⲒⲌⲈ ⲘⲘⲞϤ ϨⲢⲀⲒ ϨⲚ ⲚⲈⲨ-
ⲂⲀⲠⲦⲒⲤⲘⲀ· ⲀⲖⲖⲀ ⲘⲈⲨϮ ⲚⲀⲨ ⲘⲠⲈⲬⲢⲒⲤⲘⲀ ⲘⲠⲚⲒⲔⲞⲚ·
20 ⲀⲨⲰ ϢⲀⲨϪⲒⲦⲞⲨ ⲈⲠⲈⲐⲎⲤⲀⲨⲢⲞⲤ ⲘⲠⲞⲨⲞⲈⲒⲚ· ⲀⲖⲖⲀ
ⲘⲈⲨⲔⲀⲀⲨ ϨⲚ ⲚⲦⲀⲌⲒⲤ ⲚⲦⲈⲔⲖⲎⲢⲞⲚⲞⲘⲒⲀ· ⲈⲂⲞⲖ ϪⲈ ⲘⲚ-
ⲘⲀⲒⲚ ⲞⲨⲆⲈ ⲘⲚ-ⲤⲪⲢⲀⲄⲒⲤ ⲚⲦⲈ ⲠⲒⲀⲦϢⲀϪⲈ ⲈⲢⲞϤ ⲚⲘ- ⸎ ⲤⲨⲞ ᵇ
ⲘⲀⲨ· ⲀⲖⲖⲀ ϢⲀⲨⲚⲞⲨϨⲘ ⲈⲔⲞⲖⲀⲤⲒⲤ ⲚⲒⲘ· ⲀⲖⲖⲀ ϢⲀⲨ-
ⲔⲀⲀⲨ ϨⲘ ⲠⲞⲨⲞⲈⲒⲚ ⲘⲠⲈⲐⲎⲤⲀⲨⲢⲞⲤ ⲚⲤⲀ ⲞⲨⲤⲀ ⲞⲨⲀ-
25 ⲀⲦⲞⲨ ϨⲈⲰⲤ ϢⲀ ⲠⲰϨ' ⲈϨⲢⲀⲒ ⲘⲠⲦⲎⲢϤ ⲀⲨⲰ ϨⲘ ⲠⲈⲞⲨⲞ-
ⲈⲒϢ ⲈⲦⲞⲨⲚⲀⲤⲰϢ' ⲚⲚⲔⲀⲦⲀⲠⲈⲦⲀⲤⲘⲀ ⲘⲠⲈⲐⲎⲤⲀⲨⲢⲞⲤ

---

18   MS ⲘⲘⲞϤ; read ⲘⲘⲞⲞⲨ.

of the First Ordinance. And Jeu, the First Man, sees the
souls and he *examines* them. He finds that they have completed their *cycles*, and it is *not permitted* to bring them
once more into the *world*, because it is *not permitted* to
bring into the *world* once more any *soul* which is cast [1] into
the outer darkness. If they have not completed their number
of *cycles* in the *changes* of the *body*, the *paralemptai* of Jeu
keep them with them until they have performed the *mystery*
of the Ineffable for them, and they return them to a *good
body* which will find the *mysteries* of the light, and *inherit*
the Kingdom of the Light. *But* if Jeu *examines* them, and
he finds that they have completed their *cycles*, and it is
not permitted for them to return to the *world* once more,
and also the sign of the Ineffable is not with them : Jeu has
mercy upon them, and he takes them to the presence of
the seven *virgins* of the light. They *baptise* them with their
baptisms, *but* they do not give to them the *spiritual inunction*,
and they take them to the *Treasury* of the Light. *But* they
do not place them in the *ranks* of the *inheritance*, because
there is no sign *or seal* of the Ineffable with them. *But* they
save ⟨them⟩ [2] from all *punishments*. *And* they place them
in the light of the *Treasury* on one side apart, *until* the
ascension of the All, and until the time when the *veil* of
the *Treasury* of the Light will be drawn. | Those *souls* are

---

[1]   (5) any soul which is cast; lit. any souls which will be cast.
[2]   (23) they save ⟨them⟩; Till : they are saved.

ⲘⲠⲞⲨⲞⲈⲓⲚ· ϢⲀⲨⲤⲰⲦϤ ⲚⲚⲈⲮⲨⲬⲞⲞⲨⲈ ⲈⲦⲘⲘⲀⲨ Ⲛ-
ⲞⲨⲰ̅Ꙅ̅Ⲙ ⲚⲤⲈⲔⲀⲐⲀⲢⲒⲌⲈ Ⲙ̅ⲘⲞⲞⲨ ⲈⲘⲀϢⲞ ⲈⲘⲀϢⲞ· ⲀⲨⲰ
Ⲛ̅ⲤⲈϯ-ⲘⲨⲤⲦⲎⲢⲒⲞⲚ ⲚⲀⲨ Ⲛ̅ⲞⲨⲰ̅Ꙅ̅Ⲙ ⲚⲤⲈⲔⲀⲀⲨ Ꙅ̅Ⲛ ⲐⲀⲎ
Ⲛ̅ⲦⲀ̅Ⲝ̅ⲒⲤ ⲈⲦꙄ̅Ⲙ ⲠⲈⲐⲎⲤⲀⲨⲢⲞⲤ· ⲀⲨⲰ Ⲛ̅ⲤⲈⲚⲞⲨ�Ꙅ̅Ⲙ Ⲛ̅ϬⲒ ⲚⲈ-
5 ⲮⲨⲬⲞⲞⲨⲈ ⲈⲦⲘ̅ⲘⲀⲨ ⲈⲚⲔⲞⲗⲀⲤⲒⲤ ⲦⲎⲢⲞⲨ Ⲛ̅ⲦⲈ ⲚⲈⲔⲢⲒⲤⲒⲤ·
ⲚⲀⲒ̈ ⲆⲈ Ⲛ̅ⲦⲈⲢⲈϤϪⲞⲞⲨ Ⲛ̅ϬⲒ ⲠⲤⲰⲦⲎⲢ ⲠⲈϪⲀϤ Ⲛ̅ⲚⲈϤⲘⲀ-
ⲐⲎⲦⲎⲤ ϪⲈ ⲀⲦⲈⲦⲚ̅ⲚⲞⲒ̈ ϪⲈ ⲈⲒ̈ϢⲀϪⲈ Ⲛ̅ⲘⲘⲎⲦⲚ̅ Ⲛ̅ⲀϢ Ⲛ̅Ꙅ̅Ⲉ:
ⲀⲤⲞⲨⲰ̅Ꙅ̅Ⲙ ⲞⲚ Ⲛ̅ϬⲒ ⲘⲀⲢⲒⲀ ⲠⲈϪⲀⲤ ϪⲈ ⲠⲀϪⲞⲈⲒⲤ ⲠⲀⲒ̈ ⲠⲈ
ⲠϢⲀϪⲈ Ⲛ̅ⲦⲀⲔϪⲞⲞϤ ⲈⲢⲞⲚ Ⲙ̅ⲠⲒⲞⲨⲞⲈⲒϢ Ꙅ̅Ⲛ ⲞⲨⲠⲀ̅Ⲣ̅ⲀⲂⲞⲗⲎ [Ⲧ̅]
10 ⲈⲔϪⲰ Ⲙ̅ⲘⲞⲤ ϪⲈ ⲔⲰ ⲚⲎⲦⲚ̅ Ⲛ̅ⲞⲨϢⲂⲎⲢ ⲈⲂⲞⲗ Ꙅ̅Ⲙ ⲠⲀⲘⲰ-
ⲚⲀⲤ Ⲛ̅ⲦⲈ ⲦⲀⲆⲒⲔⲒⲀ ϪⲈⲔⲀⲤ ⲈⲦⲈⲦⲚ̅ϢⲀⲚϢⲰ̅Ⲝ̅Ⲡ ⲈϤⲈⲬⲒ-
ⲦⲎⲨⲦⲚ̅ ⲈꙀⲞⲨⲚ ⲈⲚⲈⲤⲔⲎⲚⲎ ϢⲀⲈⲚⲈꙀ· ⲚⲒⲘ ⲞⲨⲚ ϬⲈ ⲠⲈ
ⲠⲀⲘⲰⲚⲀⲤ Ⲛ̅ⲦⲈ ⲦⲀⲆⲒⲔⲒⲀ· ⲈⲒⲘⲎⲦⲒ ⲠⲈⲆⲢⲀⲔⲰⲚ Ⲙ̅ⲠⲔⲀⲔⲈ
ⲈⲦꙀⲒⲂⲞⲗ· ⲈⲦⲈ ⲠⲀⲒ̈ ⲠⲈ ⲠϢⲀϪⲈ ϪⲈ ⲠⲈⲦⲚⲀⲚⲞⲒ̈ Ⲙ̅ⲠⲘⲨⲤ-
15 ⲦⲎⲢⲒⲞⲚ Ⲙ̅ⲠⲞⲨⲀ Ⲛ̅Ⲛ̅ⲢⲀⲚ Ⲙ̅ⲠⲈⲆⲢⲀⲔⲰⲚ Ⲙ̅ⲠⲔⲀⲔⲈ ⲈⲦꙀⲒⲂⲞⲗ
ⲈϤϢⲀⲚϢⲰ̅Ⲝ̅Ⲡ Ꙅ̅Ⲙ ⲠⲔⲀⲔⲈ ⲈⲦꙀⲒⲂⲞⲗ· Ⲏ̅ ⲈϤϢⲀⲚϪⲰⲔ ⲈⲂⲞⲗ
Ꙅ̅Ⲛ Ⲛ̅ⲔⲨⲔⲗⲞⲤ Ⲛ̅Ⲙ̅ⲘⲈⲦⲀⲂⲞⲗ ⲀⲨⲰ Ⲛ̅ϤϪⲰ Ⲙ̅ⲠⲢⲀⲚ Ⲙ̅ⲠⲈ-
ⲆⲢⲀⲔⲰⲚ· ϤⲚⲀⲚⲞⲨꙀ̅Ⲙ Ⲛ̅ϤⲈⲒ̈ ⲈꙀⲢⲀⲒ̈ Ꙅ̅Ⲙ ⲠⲔⲀⲔⲈ· ⲀⲨⲰ
Ⲛ̅ⲤⲈⲬⲒⲦϤ ⲈⲠⲞⲨⲞⲈⲒⲚ Ⲙ̅ⲠⲈⲐⲎⲤⲀⲨⲢⲞⲤ· ⲠⲀⲒ̈ ⲠⲈ ⲠϢⲀϪⲈ
20 ⲠⲀϪⲞⲈⲒⲤ· ⲀϤⲞⲨⲰꙀ̅Ⲙ ⲞⲚ Ⲛ̅ϬⲒ ⲠⲤⲰⲢ ⲠⲈϪⲀϤ Ⲙ̅ⲘⲀⲢⲒⲀ
ϪⲈ ⲈⲨⲄⲈ ⲦⲈ̅Ⲡ̅Ⲛ̅ⲒⲔⲎ Ⲛ̅ꙀⲒⲗⲒⲔⲢⲒⲚⲈⲤ· ⲠⲀⲒ̈ ⲠⲈ ⲠⲂⲰⲗ ⲈⲂⲞⲗ
Ⲙ̅ⲠϢⲀϪⲈ·

ⲀⲤⲞⲨⲰꙀ ⲞⲚ ⲈⲦⲞⲞⲦⲤ̅ Ⲛ̅ϬⲒ ⲘⲀⲢⲒⲀ ⲠⲈϪⲀⲤ ϪⲈ ⲠⲀϪⲞⲈⲒⲤ
ϢⲀⲢⲈ ⲠⲈⲆⲢⲀⲔⲰⲚ *Ⲙ̅ⲠⲔⲀⲔⲈ ⲈⲦꙀⲒⲂⲞⲗ· ϢⲀϤⲈⲒ̈ ⲈꙀⲞⲨⲚ [Ⲧ̅ᵇ]

3　MS originally Ⲙ̅ⲠⲘⲨⲤⲦⲎⲢⲒⲞⲚ; ⲘⲠ erased.
9　Ⲓ̅Ⲟ̅ in upper right-hand margin at end of quire.
10　MS ⲠⲀⲘⲰⲚⲀⲤ; read ⲠⲘⲀⲘⲰⲚⲀⲤ; also line 13.

then once more cleansed and very much *purified*, and they
are given *mysteries* once more, and they are placed [1] in the
last *rank* which is in the *Treasury*. And those *souls* are saved
from all the *punishments* of the *judgments*."

When *however* the *Saviour* had said these things, he said
to his *disciples*: "Have you *understood* in what manner
I was speaking to you?"

Maria answered again and said: "My Lord, this is the
word which thou hast spoken to us once in a *parable*, saying:
'Make to yourselves a friend from the *mammon* of *unright-
eousness*, so that when you remain behind he takes you into
the eternal *habitations*' * [2]. *Now* who is the *mammon* of *un-
righteousness*, *except* the *dragon* of the outer darkness? This
is the word: he who will *understand* the *mystery* of one of
the names of the *dragon* of the outer darkness, if he remains
behind in the outer darkness *or* if he completes the *cycles* [3]
of the *changes* and he says the name of the *dragon*, he will
be saved, and will come forth from the darkness, and will
be taken to the light of the *Treasury*. This is the word,
my Lord."

The *Saviour* answered again and said to Maria: "*Excellent*,
thou *spiritual* and *pure* one. This is the interpretation of
the word."

131. Maria continued again and said: "My Lord, does
the *dragon* of the outer darkness come into | this *world*,
or does he not come?"

---

* cf. Lk. 16.9

---

[1] (1-3) those souls are ... cleansed and ... purified and given mysteries ...
and placed; Schmidt: they cleanse those souls and ... purify them and give
them mysteries ... and ... place them.
[2] (12) into the eternal habitations; lit. into the tents for ever.
[3] (16, 17) if he completes the cycles; Till: if he is completed in the cycles.

ЄΠЄÏКОСМОС ХЄ МЄЧЄІ· ΑЧОУѠ2М ΝϬІ ΠСѠТΗР ΠЄ-
ХΑЧ ММΑРΙΑ ХЄ 2ОТΑΝ ЄРЄ ΠОУОЄΙΝ МΠРΗ ΝВОΛ·
ѠΑЧ2ѠВС МΠКΑКЄ МΠЄДРΑКѠΝ· ЄѠѠΠЄ ДЄ ЄРѠΑΝ
ΠРΗ Р-ΠЄСΗТ МΠКОСМОС· ѠΑРЄ ΠКΑКЄ МΠЄДРΑКѠΝ
5 ϬѠ ΝΛΙКТЧ МΠРΗ· ΑУѠ ѠΑРЄ ΠΝΙЧ МΠКΑКЄ ЄΙ· Є2ОУΝ
ЄΠКОСМОС МΠЄСМОТ· ΝОУКΑΠΝОС 2Ν ТЄУѠΗ· ЄТЄ
ΠΑÏ ΠЄ ЄРѠΑΝ ΠРΗ СѠК· ЄРОЧ ΝΝЄЧΑКТΙΝ· МΝѠϬОМ
ГΑР МΠКОСМОС ЄТѠОУΝ 2Α ΠКΑКЄ МΠЄДРΑКѠΝ 2Ν
ТЄЧΑΛΗΘΙΑ ММОРФΗ· ЄММОΝ ѠΑЧВѠΛ ЄВОΛ ΝЧТΑКО
10 2Ι ОУСОΠ·

　　ΝΑÏ ΝТЄРЄЧХООУ ΝϬІ ΠСѠТΗР· ΑСОУѠ2 ОΝ Є-
ТООТС ΝϬІ МΑРΙΑ ΠЄХΑС МΠСѠТΗР ХЄ ΠΑХОЄΙС
ЄТΙ ✝ѠΙΝЄ ММОК ΑУѠ МΠР2ѠΠ ЄРОÏ· ТЄΝОУ ϬЄ ΠΑ-
ХОЄΙС ЄÏЄ ΝΙМ ΠЄТΑΝΑГКΑZЄ МΠРѠМЄ 2ЄѠС ѠΑΝТЧР-
15 ΝОВЄ· ΑЧОУѠ2М ΝϬІ ΠСѠТΗР ΠЄХΑЧ ММΑРΙΑ ХЄ Ν-　ТΑ
ΑРХѠΝ ΝΘΙМΑРМЄΝΗ ΝТООУ ΝЄТΑΝΑГКΑZЄ МΠРѠМЄ
2ЄѠС ѠΑΝТЧРΝОВЄ· ΑСОУѠ2М ΝϬІ МΑРΙΑ ΠЄХΑС М-
ΠСѠТΗР ХЄ ΠΑХОЄΙС· МΗТΙ РѠ ѠΑРЄ ΝΑРХѠΝ ѠΑУЄΙ·
ЄΠЄСΝТ· ЄΠКОСМОС ΝСЄΑΝΑГКΑZЄ МΠРѠМЄ 2ЄѠС
20 ѠΑΝТЧРΝОВЄ· ΑЧОУѠ2М ΝϬІ ΠСѠТΗР ΠЄХΑЧ ⟨М⟩МΑРΙΑ
ХЄ ЄѠΑУЄΙ· ΑΝ ΝТЄÏ2Є ЄΠЄСΝТ· ЄΠКОСМОС· ΑΛΛΑ
ЄѠΑРЄ ΝΑРХѠΝ ΝΘΙМΑРМЄΝΗ· ЄРѠΑΝ ОУѰУХΗ Ν-
ΑРХΑΙОΝ ЄΙ· ЄСΝΗУ ЄΠЄСΝТ ЄВОΛ 2ΙТООТОУ ѠΑРЄ
ΝΑРХѠΝ ΝТΝОϬ Ν2ΙМΑРМЄΝΗ ЄТММΑУ ΠΑÏ ЄТ2Ν Ν-

15　К̄ in upper left left-hand margin at beginning of quire.
20　MS мΑРΙΑ; read ммΑРΙΑ.
24　MS ΠΑÏ; read ΝΑÏ.

The *Saviour* answered and said to Maria : "*When* the light of the sun is outside (the world) it covers the darkness of the *dragon*. *But* when the sun is beneath the *world*, the darkness of the *dragon* remains as a *veil* of the sun. And the breath of the darkness enters into the *world* in the form of *smoke* at night, that is, when the sun draws to itself its *rays*. *For* the *world* is not able to bear the darkness of the *dragon* in its *true form*, else it would be dissolved and perish at the same time."

When the *Saviour* had said these things, Maria continued again, she said to the *Saviour* : "My Lord, I *still* question thee and do not conceal from me. Now at this time, my Lord, who *compels* a man *until* he sins?"

The *Saviour* answered and said to Maria : "The *archons* of the *Heimarmene* are the ones who *compel* a man *until* he sins."

Maria answered and said to the *Saviour* : "My Lord, do *perhaps* the *archons* come down to the *world* and *compel* a man *until* he sins?"

The *Saviour* answered and said to Maria : "They do not come in this manner down to the *world, but* the *archons* of the *Heimarmene* — when an *ancient soul* is about to come down by means of them — the *archons* of that great *Heimarmene* who are in the | *places* of the *head* of the *aeons*, which

ΤΟΠΟС ⲚΤΚΕΦΑΛΗ ⲚΤΕ ⲚΑΙⲰⲚ ΕΤΕ ΠΤΟΠΟС ΕΤⲘⲘΑΥ
ⲚΤΟϤ ΠΕ ΕϢΑΥΜΟΥΤΕ ΕΡΟϤ ϪΕ ΠΤΟΠΟС ⲚΤⲘⲚΤΕΡΟ
ⲘΠΑΔΑΜΑС· ΑΥⲰ ΠΤΟΠΟС ΕΤⲘⲘΑΥ ⲚΤΟϤ ΠΕ ΕΤ-
ⲘΠΕΜΤΟ ΕΒΟΛ ⲚΤΠΑΡΘΕΝΟС ⲘΠΟΥΟΪⲚ· ϢΑΡΕ ⲚΑΡΧⲰⲚ
5 ⲘΠΤΟΠΟС ⲚΤΚΕΦΑΛΗ ΕΤⲘⲘΑΥ ϢΑϤϯ ⲚΤΕѰΥΧΗ Ⲛ- ⲦⲀᵇ
ΑΡΧΑΙΟⲚ ⲚΟΥΑΠΟΤ ⲚΒϢΕ ΕΒΟΛ ⳞⲘ ΠΕСΠΕΡΜΑ ⲚΤΚΑ-
ΚΙΑ ΕϤΜΕⳞ ΕΒΟΛ ⳞⲚ ΕΠΙΘΥΜΙΑ ⲚΙⲘ' ΕΤϢΟΒΕ· ΑΥⲰ ⲘⲚ
ⲂϢΕ ⲚΙⲘ· ΑΥⲰ ⳞⲚ ΤΕΥΝΟΥ ΕΤΕΡΕ ΤΕѰΥΧΗ ΕΤⲘⲘΑΥ
ΝΑСⲰ ⳞⲘ ΠΑΠΟΤ· ϢΑСⲢΠⲰΒϢ ⲚΤΟΠΟС ⲚΙⲘ' ⲚΤΑСΒⲰΚ
10 ΕΡΟΟΥ· ⲘⲚ ⲚΚΟΛΑСΙС ΤΗΡΟΥ ⲚΤΑСϢΕ ⲚⳞΗΤΟΥ· ΑΥⲰ
ϢΑΡΕ ΠΑΠΟΤ ⲘΜΟΥⲚ̄ΒϢΕ ΕΤⲘⲘΑΥ ϢΑϤϢⲰΠΕ Ⲛ-
СⲰΜΑ ΠΒΟΛ ⲚΤΕѰΥΧΗ· ΑΥⲰ ϢΑϤϢⲰΠΕ ΕϤΕΙΝΕ Ⲛ-
ΤΕѰΥΧΗ ⳞⲚ СΜΟΤ ⲚΙⲘ' ΑΥⲰ ΕϤⳞΟΜΟΙⲰСΕ ΕΡΟС ΕΤΕ
ΠΑΪ ΠΕ ΕϢΑΥΜΟΥΤΕ ΕΡΟϤ ϪΕ ΠΑⲚΤΙΜΙΜΟⲚ ⲘⲠⲚ̄Ⲁ·
15 ΕϢⲰΠΕ ⳞⲰⲰϤ ΟΥѰΥΧΗ ⲚΒⲢⲢΕ ΤΕ ϢΑΥϤΙ ΕΒΟΛ ⳞⲚ
ΤϤⲰΤΕ ⲚΤΕ ⲚΑΡΧⲰⲚ· ΑΥⲰ ΕΒΟΛ ⳞⲚ ⲘΜΟΥΕΙΟΟΥΕ
ⲚΤΕ ΝΕΥΒΑΛ· Ⲏ̄ ⲘΜΟⲚ ⲚΤΟϤ ΕΒΟΛ ⳞⲘ ΠⲚΙϤΕ ⲚΤΕ
ΤΕΥΤΑΠΡΟ ⳞΑΠΑⳞ ⳞΑΠΛⲰС ΕϢⲰΠΕ ΟΥΕΒΟΛ ⳞⲚ ⲂⲂⲢⲢΕ ⲦⲂ̄
ⲘѰΥΧΗ· Ⲏ̄ ΟΥΕΒΟΛ ⳞⲚ ΝΕѰΥΧΟΟΥΕ ⲚΤΕΪΜΙⲚΕ ΤΕ
20 ΕϢⲰΠΕ ΟΥΕΒΟΛ ⳞⲚ ΤϤⲰΤΕ ΤΕ· ϢΑΡΕ Π̄ϮΟΥ ⲚΝΟ6
ⲚΑΡΧⲰⲚ ⲚΤΝΟ6 ⲚⳞΙΜΑΡΜΕΝΗ· ϢΑΥϤΙ ⲚΤϤⲰΤΕ ⲚⲚ-
ΑΡΧⲰⲚ ΤΗΡΟΥ ⲚΤΕ ΝΕΥΑΙⲰⲚ ⲚСΕΟΥΟϢΜΟΥ ⲘⲚ
ΝΕΥΕΡΗΥ ⳞΙ ΟΥСΟΠ ⲚСΕΠⲰϢ ⲘΜΟϤ ⲚСΕΛΛϤ ⲘѰΥΧΗ·
Ⲏ̄ ⲘΜΟⲚ ⲚΤΟϤ ΕϢⲰΠΕ ΟΥСΟⲢⲘ ΤΕ ⲚΤΕ ΠСⲰΤϤ Ⲙ-
25 ΠΟΥΟΕΙⲚ ϢΑΡΕ ΜΕΛΧΙСΕΔΕΚ' ϤΙΤϤ̄ ⲚΤΕ ⲚΑΡΧⲰⲚ ϢΑΡΕ

---

5 MS ϢΑϤϯ; read ϢΑΥϯ.
15 MS ΤΕ ϢΑΥϤΙ; read ΤΕ ΕϢΑΥϤΙ.

is that *place* which is called the *place* of the kingdom of
Adamas and that *place* which is in the presence of the *Virgin*
of the Light, the *archons* of that *place* of the *head* give to the
ancient soul a cup of forgetfulness from the *seed* of *evil*,
filled with all the various *desires* and with all forgetfulness.
And immediately when that *soul* will drink from the cup,
it forgets all the *places* to which it has gone, and all the
punishments into which it has gone. And that cup of water
of forgetfulness becomes a *body* outside the *soul,* and it
becomes like to the *soul* in every form, and it *resembles* it
and this is what is called the *spirit counterpart.* If, on the
other hand, it is a new *soul* (which) they take [1] from the
sweat of the *archons,* and from the tears of their eyes, *or*
else from the breath of their mouths — *in a word,* if it is
one from among new *souls or* one from *souls* of this kind,
if it is from the sweat — then the five great *archons* of the
great *Heimarmene* take the sweat of all the *archons* of their
aeons, and they knead ⟨it⟩ [2] together with one another and
they divide it and make a *soul* of it; *or* else, if it is dregs of
what is purified of the light, Melchisedek takes it [3] from the
archons. | The five great *archons* of the great *Heimarmene*

---

[1] (15) they take; lit. they are wont to take.
[2] (22) ⟨it⟩; lit. them (also 334.8, 12, 15).
[3] (25) it; i.e. the dregs; cf. 334.11.

ⲡ̄ϯⲟⲩ ⲛ̄ⲛⲟϭ ⲛ̄ⲁⲣⲭⲱⲛ ⲛ̄ⲧⲉ ⲧⲛⲟϭ ⲛ̄ϩⲓⲙⲁⲣⲙⲉⲛⲏ ϣⲁⲩ-
ⲟⲩⲱϣⲙ ⲙ̄ⲡⲥⲟⲣⲙ ϩⲓ ⲛⲉϥⲉⲣⲏⲩ ⲛ̄ⲥⲉⲙⲉⲣⲓⲍⲉ ⲙ̄ⲙⲟϥ ⲛ̄-
ⲥⲉⲁⲁϥ ⲙ̄ⲯⲩⲭⲏ ⲯⲩⲭⲏ· ϫⲉⲕⲁⲥ ⲉⲣⲉ ⲡⲟⲩⲁ ⲡⲟⲩⲁ ⲛ̄ⲛ̄-
ⲁⲣⲭⲱⲛ ⲛ̄ⲧⲉ ⲛ̄ⲁⲓⲱⲛ ⲉⲣⲉ ⲡⲟⲩⲁ ⲡⲟⲩⲁ ⲙ̄ⲙⲟⲟⲩ ⲕⲱ
5 ⲙ̄ⲡⲉϥⲙⲉⲣⲟⲥ ϩⲛ̄ ⲧⲉⲯⲩⲭⲏ· ⲉⲧⲃⲉ ⲡⲁⲓ̈ ⲟⲩⲛ ⲉⲩⲟⲩⲱϣⲙ
ⲙ̄ⲙⲟⲟⲩ ϩⲓ ⲛⲉⲩⲉⲣⲏⲩ· ϫⲉ ⲉⲩⲉϫⲓ ⲧⲏⲣⲟⲩ ⲉⲃⲟⲗ ϩⲛ̄ ⲧⲉ-
ⲯⲩⲭⲏ· ⲁⲩⲱ* ϣⲁⲣⲉ ⲡ̄ϯⲟⲩ ⲛ̄ⲛⲟϭ ⲛ̄ⲁⲣⲭⲱⲛ ⲉⲩϣⲁⲛ- [ⲧⲃ ᵇ]
ⲙⲉⲣⲓⲍⲉ ⲙ̄ⲙⲟⲟⲩ ⲛ̄ⲥⲉⲁⲁⲩ ⲙ̄ⲯⲩⲭⲏ ⲉⲩⲉⲓⲛⲉ ⲙ̄ⲙⲟⲟⲩ ⲉⲃⲟⲗ
ϩⲛ̄ ⲧϥⲱⲧⲉ ⲛ̄ⲛⲁⲣⲭⲱⲛ· ⲉϣⲱⲡⲉ ⲇⲉ ⲟⲩⲉⲃⲟⲗ ϩⲙ̄ ⲡⲥⲟⲣⲙ
10 ⲡⲉ ⲙ̄ⲡⲥⲱⲧϥ ⲙ̄ⲡⲟⲩⲟⲉⲓⲛ· ϣⲁⲣⲉ ⲙⲉⲗⲭⲓⲥⲉⲭⲉⲕ' ⲡⲛⲟϭ
ⲙ̄ⲡⲁⲣⲁⲗⲏⲙⲡⲧⲏⲥ ⲙ̄ⲡⲟⲩⲟⲉⲓⲛ ϥⲓⲧⲥ̄ ⲛ̄ⲧⲉ ⲛ̄ⲁⲣⲭⲱⲛ ⲏ̈ ⲙ̄ⲙⲟⲛ
ⲛ̄ⲧⲟϥ ⲉϣⲱⲡⲉ ϩⲉⲛⲉⲃⲟⲗ ⲛⲉ ϩⲛ̄ ⲙ̄ⲙⲟⲩⲉⲓⲟⲟⲩⲉ ⲛ̄ⲧⲉ ⲛⲉⲩ-
ⲃⲁⲗ· ⲏ̈ ⲉⲃⲟⲗ ϩⲙ̄ ⲡⲛⲓϥⲉ ⲛ̄ⲧⲉⲩⲧⲁⲡⲣⲟ ϩⲁⲡⲁϩ ϩⲁⲡⲗⲱⲥ
ⲉⲃⲟⲗ ϩⲛ̄ ⲛⲉⲯⲩⲭⲟⲟⲩⲉ ⲛ̄ⲧⲉⲓ̈ⲙⲓⲛⲉ· ⲉⲣϣⲁⲛ ⲡ̄ϯⲟⲩ ⲛ̄-
15 ⲁⲣⲭⲱⲛ ⲉⲩϣⲁⲛⲙⲉⲣⲓⲍⲉ ⲙ̄ⲙⲟⲟⲩ ⲛ̄ⲥⲉⲁⲁⲩ ⲙ̄ⲯⲩⲭⲏ ⲯⲩⲭⲏ·
ⲏ̈ ⲙ̄ⲙⲟⲛ ⲛ̄ⲧⲟϥ ⲟⲩⲯⲩⲭⲏ ⲛ̄ⲁⲣⲭⲁⲓⲟⲛ ⲧⲉ ϣⲁⲣⲉ ⲡⲁⲣⲭⲱⲛ
ϩⲱⲱϥ ⲡⲁⲓ̈ ⲉⲧϣⲟⲟⲡ ϩⲛ̄ ⲛ̄ⲕⲉⲫⲁⲗⲏ ⲛ̄ⲧⲉ ⲛ̄ⲁⲓⲱⲛ· ϣⲁϥ-
ⲟⲩⲱϣⲙ ⲙ̄ⲡⲁⲡⲟⲧ ⲛ̄ⲧⲃϣⲉ ⲛ̄ⲧⲉ ⲡⲉⲥⲡⲉⲣⲙⲁ ⲛ̄ⲧⲕⲁⲕⲓⲁ·
ϣⲁϥⲟⲩⲟϣⲙⲉϥ ⲙⲛ̄ ⲧⲟⲩⲉⲓ' ⲧⲟⲩⲉⲓ' ⲛ̄ⲛⲉⲯⲩⲭⲟⲟⲩⲉ ⲛ̄-
20 ⲃⲃⲣⲉ ϩⲙ̄ ⲡⲉⲩⲟ̈ⲉⲓϣ ⲉⲧϥϣⲟⲟⲡ' ϩⲙ̄ ⲡⲧⲟⲡⲟⲥ ⲛ̄ⲧⲕⲉⲫⲁⲗⲏ· ⲧ̄ⲅ̄
ⲁⲩⲱ ϣⲁⲣⲉ ⲡⲁⲡⲟⲧ' ⲛ̄ⲧⲃϣⲉ ⲉⲧⲙ̄ⲙⲁⲩ· ϣⲁϥϣⲱⲡⲉ ⲛ̄-
ⲁⲛⲧⲓⲙⲓⲙⲟⲛ ⲙ̄ⲡⲛ̄ⲁ ⲛ̄ⲧⲉⲯⲩⲭⲏ ⲉⲧⲙ̄ⲙⲁⲩ· ⲁⲩⲱ ϣⲁϥϭⲱ
ⲡⲃⲟⲗ ⲛ̄ⲧⲉⲯⲩⲭⲏ ⲉϥⲟ ⲛ̄ⲉⲛⲇⲩⲙⲁ ⲉⲣⲟⲥ· ⲉϥⲉⲓⲛⲉ ⲙ̄ⲙⲟⲥ
ⲙ̄ⲙⲓⲛⲉ ⲛⲓⲙ ⲉϥⲟ ⲛ̄ⲕⲟⲉⲓ̈ϩ ⲛ̄ⲉⲛⲇⲩⲙⲁ ⲡⲉⲥⲃⲟⲗ· ⲁⲩⲱ ϣⲁⲣⲉ
25 ⲡ̄ϯⲟⲩ ⲛ̄ⲛⲟϭ ⲛ̄ⲁⲣⲭⲱⲛ ⲛ̄ⲧⲛⲟϭ ⲛ̄ϩⲓⲙⲁⲣⲙⲉⲛⲏ ⲛ̄ⲧⲉ ⲛ̄ⲁⲓⲱⲛ·
ⲁⲩⲱ ⲙⲛ̄ ⲡⲁⲣⲭⲱⲛ ⲙ̄ⲡⲇⲓⲥⲕⲟⲥ ⲙ̄ⲡⲣⲏ· ⲙⲛ̄ ⲡⲁⲣⲭⲱⲛ ⲙ̄-

---

2 ⲛⲉϥⲉⲣⲏⲩ; better ⲛⲉⲩⲉⲣⲏⲩ.

knead the dregs together, they *divide* it and they make various *souls* from it [1], so that each one of the *archons* of the *aeons*, each one of them places his *part* in the *soul*. Because of this *now*, they knead [2] ⟨it⟩ [3] together, so that they all take (part in) [4] the *soul*. And the five great *archons*, when they *divide* ⟨it⟩ and make ⟨it⟩ into a *soul*, they bring ⟨it⟩ from the sweat of the *archons*.

But if it (the soul) is from the dregs of what is purified of the light, Melchisedek, the great *paralemptes* of the light, takes it (the dregs) from the *archons*, *or* else, if ⟨it⟩ is from the tears of their eyes *or* from the breath of their mouth, *in a word* from *souls* of this kind, when the five *archons* *divide* ⟨it⟩ and make various *souls*; *or* on the other hand, if it is an *ancient soul*, the *archon* himself who is in the *heads* of the *aeons* mixes the cup of forgetfulness of the *seed* of *evil* [5], and he kneads it with each one of the new *souls* at the time when he is in the *place* of the *head*. And that cup of forgetfulness becomes a *spirit counterpart* for that *soul*. And it remains outside the *soul* as a *garment* for it, resembling it in every way as a sheathing *garment* outside it. And the five great *archons* of the great *Heimarmene* of the *aeons* and the *archon* of the *disc* of the sun and the *archon* of |

---

[1]   (3) make various souls from it; Schmidt: make it into various souls; Till: make every single soul from it.
[2]   (5, 19) knead; Schmidt: mix.
[3]   (6, 8) ⟨it⟩; lit. them.
[4]   (6) take (part in); lit. take from.
[5]   (18) of the seed of evil; Schmidt: with the seed of evil.

ⲡⲇⲓⲥⲕⲟⲥ ⲙ̄ⲡⲟⲟ2· ϣⲁⲩⲛⲓϥⲉ ⲉ2ⲟⲩⲛ ⲉⲧⲙⲏⲧⲉ ⲛ̄ⲧⲉⲯⲩⲭⲏ
ⲉⲧⲙ̄ⲙⲁⲩ· ⲁⲩⲱ ⲛ̄ϥⲉⲓ· ⲉⲃⲟⲗ ⲛ̄2ⲏⲧⲥ̄ ⲛ̄ϭⲓ ⲟⲩⲙⲉⲣⲟⲥ ⲉⲃⲟⲗ
2ⲛ̄ ⲧⲁϭⲟⲙ ⲡⲁⲓ̈ ⲛ̄ⲧⲁ ⲡ2ⲁⲉ ⲙ̄ⲡⲁⲣⲁⲥⲧⲁⲧⲏⲥ ⲛⲟⲭⲥ̄ ⲉ2ⲟⲩⲛ
ⲉⲡⲕⲉⲣⲁⲥⲙⲟⲥ· ⲁⲩⲱ ϣⲁⲣⲉ ⲡⲙⲉⲣⲟⲥ ⲛ̄ϭⲟⲙ ⲉⲧⲙ̄ⲙⲁⲩ
5 ϣⲁϥϭⲱ 2ⲓ2ⲟⲩⲛ ⲛ̄ⲧⲉⲯⲩⲭⲏ ⲉϥⲃⲏⲗ· ⲉⲃⲟⲗ· ⲉϥϣⲟⲟⲡ· 2ⲓⲭⲛ̄
ⲧⲉϥⲉⲝⲟⲩⲥⲓⲁ ⲙ̄ⲙⲓⲛ ⲙ̄ⲙⲟϥ· ⲡⲣⲟⲥ ⲧⲟⲓⲕⲟⲛⲟⲙⲓⲁ ⲉⲛⲧⲁⲩ-   ⲧ̄ⲅ b
ⲕⲁⲁϥ ⲛ̄2ⲏⲧⲥ̄ ⲉⲧⲣⲉϥϯ-ⲁⲓⲥⲑⲏⲥⲓⲥ ⲛ̄ⲧⲉⲯⲩⲭⲏ· ⲭⲉⲕⲁⲥ ⲉⲥⲉ-
ϣⲓⲛⲉ ⲛ̄ⲥⲁ ⲛⲉ2ⲃⲏⲩⲉ ⲙ̄ⲡⲟⲩⲟⲉⲓⲛ ⲙ̄ⲡⲭⲓⲥⲉ ⲛ̄ⲟⲩⲟⲉⲓϣ ⲛⲓⲙ·
ⲁⲩⲱ ϣⲁⲣⲉ ⲧϭⲟⲙ ⲉⲧⲙ̄ⲙⲁⲩ ϣⲁⲥ2ⲟⲙⲟⲓⲱⲥⲉ ⲉⲧⲙⲓⲛⲉ ⲛ̄-
10 ⲧⲉⲯⲩⲭⲏ 2ⲛ̄ ⲥⲙⲟⲧ ⲛⲓⲙ· ⲁⲩⲱ ⲉⲥⲉⲓⲛⲉ ⲙ̄ⲙⲟⲥ· ⲙⲉⲥⲉϣⲣ̄-
ⲡⲃⲟⲗ ⲛ̄ⲧⲉⲯⲩⲭⲏ· ⲁⲗⲗⲁ ϣⲁⲥϭⲱ ⲡⲉⲥ2ⲟⲩⲛ· ⲕⲁⲧⲁ ⲑⲉ
ⲉⲛⲧⲁⲓ̈2ⲱⲛ ⲛⲁⲥ ⲭⲓⲛ ⲛ̄ϣⲟⲣⲡ ⲉⲓ̈ⲛⲁⲛⲟⲭⲥ̄ ⲉ2ⲟⲩⲛ ⲉⲡϣⲟⲣⲡ
ⲛ̄ⲧⲱϣ ⲛ̄ⲧⲁⲓ̈2ⲱⲛ ⲛⲁⲥ ⲉⲧⲣⲉⲥϭⲱ ⲡⲃⲟⲗ ⲛ̄ⲛⲉⲯⲩⲭⲟⲟⲩⲉ·
ⲡⲣⲟⲥ ⲧⲟⲓⲕⲟⲛⲟⲙⲓⲁ ⲙ̄ⲡϣⲟⲣⲡ ⲙ̄ⲙⲩⲥⲧⲏⲣⲓⲟⲛ· 2ⲱⲥⲧⲉ
15 ⲛⲉⲓ̈ϣⲁⲭⲉ ⲧⲏⲣⲟⲩ ϯⲛⲁⲭⲟⲟⲩ ⲉⲣⲱⲧⲛ̄ 2ⲙ̄ ⲡⲥⲱⲣ ⲉⲃⲟⲗ·
⟨ⲙ̄ⲡⲧⲏⲣϥ⟩ ⲉⲧⲃⲉ ⲧϭⲟⲙ· ⲁⲩⲱ ⲉⲧⲃⲉ ⲧⲕⲉⲯⲩⲭⲏ ⲭⲉ ⲉⲩⲣ̄-
2ⲱⲃ ⲉⲣⲟⲟⲩ ⲛ̄ⲁϣ ⲛ̄ⲧⲩⲡⲟⲥ· ⲏ̈ ⲛⲓⲙ ⲛ̄ⲧⲟϥ ⲛ̄ⲁⲣⲭⲱⲛ ⲡⲉⲧ-
ⲣ̄2ⲱⲃ ⲉⲣⲟⲥ· ⲏ̈ ⲟⲩ ⲧⲉ ⲧⲙⲓⲛⲉ ⲧⲙⲓⲛⲉ ⲛ̄ⲧⲉⲯⲩⲭⲏ· 2ⲱⲥⲧⲉ
ϯⲛⲁⲭⲟⲟⲩ ⲉⲣⲱⲧⲛ̄ 2ⲙ̄ ⲡⲥⲱⲣ ⲉⲃⲟⲗ ⲙ̄ⲡⲧⲏⲣϥ· ⲭⲉ ⲟⲩⲛ̄-
20 ⲟⲩⲏⲣ ⲣ̄2ⲱⲃ ⲉⲧⲉⲯⲩⲭⲏ· ⲁⲩⲱ ϯⲛⲁⲭⲱ ⲉⲣⲱⲧⲛ̄ ⲙ̄ⲡⲣⲁⲛ
ⲛ̄ⲛⲉⲧⲣ̄2ⲱⲃ ⲧⲏⲣⲟⲩ ⲉⲧⲉⲯⲩⲭⲏ· ⲁⲩⲱ ϯⲛⲁⲭⲱ ⲉⲣⲱⲧⲛ̄   [ⲧ̄ⲇ]
ⲙ̄ⲡⲧⲩⲡⲟⲥ ⲛ̄ⲧⲁⲩⲧⲁⲙⲓⲟ ⲙ̄ⲡⲁⲛⲧⲓⲙⲓⲙⲟⲛ ⲙ̄ⲡⲛ̄ⲁ ⲙⲛ̄ ⲧⲕⲉ-
ⲙⲟⲓⲣⲁ· ⲁⲩⲱ ϯⲛⲁⲭⲱ ⲉⲣⲱⲧⲛ̄ ⲙ̄ⲡⲣⲁⲛ ⲛ̄ⲧⲉⲯⲩⲭⲏ ⲉⲙ-
ⲡⲁⲧⲥ̄ⲥⲱⲧϥ̄ ⲉⲃⲟⲗ· ⲁⲩⲱ ⲡⲉⲥⲣⲁⲛ ⲟⲛ ⲉⲩϣⲁⲛⲥⲟⲧϥ̄
25 ⲛ̄ⲥⲣ̄2ⲓⲗⲓⲕⲣⲓⲛⲉⲥ· ⲁⲩⲱ ϯⲛⲁⲭⲱ ⲉⲣⲱⲧⲛ̄ ⲙ̄ⲡⲣⲁⲛ ⲙ̄ⲡⲁⲛⲧⲓ-

---

2 MS ⲛ̄2ⲏⲧⲥ̄; read ⲛ̄2ⲏⲧⲟⲩ.
16 MS ⲙ̄ⲡⲧⲏⲣϥ̄ omitted.
24 MS originally ⲉⲩϣⲁⲛⲥⲟⲧϥ̄; ⲥ added.

the *disc* of the moon breathe into the midst of that *soul*.
And a *part* of my power, which the last *helper* cast into the
mixture, comes forth from them [1]. And that *part* of the power
remains within the *soul*, released and existing upon its own
authority for the sake of the *organisation* in which it was
placed to give *perception* to the *soul*, so that it should seek
after the things of the light of the height at all times. And
that power *resembles* the form of the *soul* in every way, and
it is like to it. It is not able to exist outside the *soul, but*
it remains within it *according to* the manner in which I commanded it from the beginning. When I was about to cast it
into the first ordinance, I commanded it to remain outside
the *souls for the sake of* the *organisation* of the First *Mystery*.
Therefore I will speak all these words to you at the distribution ⟨ of the All⟩ concerning the power and also concerning the *soul*, in which *type* it is acted upon; *or* rather,
which are the *archons* which act upon it; *or* what is each
different form of the *soul. Therefore* I will speak to you
at the distribution of the All of how many act upon the
soul. And I will say to you the name of all those which
act upon the *soul*. And I will say to you the *type* in which
the *spirit counterpart* and the *destiny* were made. And I will
say to you the name of the *soul* before it is purified, and
its name also after it is cleansed and made *pure*. And I will say
to you the name of the | *spirit counterpart*. And I will say

---

[1] (2) from them; MS : from it.

ⲘⲒⲘⲞⲚ ⲘⲠⲚⲀ· ⲀⲨⲰ ϯⲚⲀⲬⲰ ⲈⲢⲰⲦⲚ ⲘⲠⲢⲀⲚ ⲚⲦⲘⲞⲒⲢⲀ·
ⲀⲨⲰ ϯⲚⲀⲬⲰ ⲈⲢⲰⲦⲚ ⲘⲠⲢⲀⲚ ⲚⲘⲘⲢⲢⲈ ⲦⲎⲢⲞⲨ· ⲚⲀⲒ Ⲉ-
ϢⲀⲢⲈ ⲚⲀⲢⲬⲰⲚ ⲘⲞⲨⲢ ⲘⲠⲀⲚⲦⲒⲘⲒⲘⲞⲚ ⲘⲠⲚⲀ ⲚϨⲎⲦⲞⲨ
ⲈϨⲞⲨⲚ ⲈⲦⲈⲮⲨⲬⲎ· ⲀⲨⲰ ϯⲚⲀⲬⲰ ⲈⲢⲰⲦⲚ ⲘⲠⲢⲀⲚ ⲚⲚ-
5 ⲀⲤⲔⲀⲚⲞⲤ ⲦⲎⲢⲞⲨ ⲚⲀⲒ ⲈϢⲀⲨⲢϨⲰⲂ ⲈⲦⲈⲮⲨⲬⲎ ϨⲢⲀⲒ ϨⲚ
ⲚⲤⲰⲘⲀ ⲚⲦⲈⲮⲨⲬⲎ ϨⲚ ⲠⲔⲞⲤⲘⲞⲤ ⲀⲨⲰ ϯⲚⲀⲬⲰ ⲈⲢⲰⲦⲚ
ⲬⲈ ⲈⲨⲢϨⲰⲂ ⲈⲚⲈⲮⲨⲬⲞⲞⲨⲈ ⲚⲀϢ ⲚϨⲈ· ⲀⲨⲰ ϯⲚⲀⲬⲰ
ⲈⲢⲰⲦⲚ ⲘⲠⲦⲨⲠⲞⲤ ⲚⲦⲞⲨⲈⲒ ⲦⲞⲨⲈⲒ ⲚⲚⲈⲮⲨⲬⲎ· ⲀⲨⲰ
ϯⲚⲀⲬⲰ ⲈⲢⲰⲦⲚ ⲘⲠⲦⲨⲠⲞⲤ ⲚⲚⲈⲮⲨⲬⲞⲞⲨⲈ ⲚⲢⲢⲰⲘⲈ ⲘⲚ [ⲦⲀᵇ]
10 ⲚⲀⲚϨⲀⲀⲀⲦⲈ· ⲘⲚ ⲚⲀⲚⲈⲐⲎⲢⲒⲞⲚ· ⲘⲚ ⲚⲬⲀⲦϤⲈ· ⲀⲨⲰ
ϯⲚⲀⲬⲰ ⲈⲢⲰⲦⲚ ⲘⲠⲦⲨⲠⲞⲤ ⲚⲚⲈⲮⲨⲬⲞⲞⲨⲈ ⲦⲎⲢⲞⲨ ⲘⲚ
ⲚⲀⲚⲀⲢⲬⲰⲚ ⲦⲎⲢⲞⲨ ⲈⲦⲦⲀⲨⲞ ⲘⲘⲞⲞⲨ ⲈⲠⲔⲞⲤⲘⲞⲤ ⲬⲈ
ⲈⲦⲈⲦⲚϢⲰⲠⲈ ⲈⲦⲈⲦⲚⲬⲎⲔ ⲈⲂⲞⲀ' ϨⲚ ⲤⲞⲞⲨⲚ ⲚⲒⲘ· ⲚⲀⲒ
ⲦⲎⲢⲞⲨ ϯⲚⲀⲬⲞⲞⲨ ⲈⲢⲰⲦⲚ ϨⲢⲀⲒ ϨⲘ ⲠⲤⲰⲢ ⲈⲂⲞⲀ ⲘⲠⲦⲎⲢϤ·
15 ⲀⲨⲰ ⲘⲚⲚⲤⲀ ⲚⲀⲒ ⲦⲎⲢⲞⲨ ϯⲚⲀⲬⲰ ⲈⲢⲰⲦⲚ ⲬⲈ ⲈⲦⲂⲈ ⲞⲨ
ϨⲰϢϤ Ⲁ ⲚⲀⲒ ⲦⲎⲢⲞⲨ ϢⲰⲠⲈ· ⲤⲰⲦⲘ ⲞⲨⲚ ⲚⲦⲀϢⲀⲬⲈ
ⲚⲘⲘⲎⲦⲚ ⲈⲦⲂⲈ ⲦⲈⲮⲨⲬⲎ ⲔⲀⲦⲀ ⲐⲈ ⲈⲚⲦⲀⲒⲬⲞⲞⲤ ⲬⲈ Ⲉ-
ϢⲀⲢⲈ ⲠϯⲞⲨ ⲚⲚⲞϬ ⲚⲀⲢⲬⲰⲚ ⲚⲦⲚⲞϬ ⲚϨⲒⲘⲀⲢⲘⲈⲚⲎ ⲚⲦⲈ
ⲚⲀⲒⲰⲚ· ⲀⲨⲰ ⲘⲚ ⲚⲀⲢⲬⲰⲚ ⲘⲠⲀⲒⲤⲔⲞⲤ ⲘⲠⲢⲎ· ⲘⲚ ⲚⲀⲢ-
20 ⲬⲰⲚ ⲘⲠⲀⲒⲤⲔⲞⲤ ⲘⲠⲞⲞϨ· ϢⲀⲨⲚⲒϤⲈ ⲈϨⲞⲨⲚ ⲈϨⲚ ⲦⲈ-
ⲮⲨⲬⲎ ⲈⲦⲘⲘⲀⲨ· ⲀⲨⲰ ⲚϤⲈⲒ ⲈⲂⲞⲀ ⲚϨⲎⲦⲞⲨ ⲚϬⲒ ⲞⲨ- ⲦⲈ
ⲘⲈⲢⲞⲤ ⲈⲂⲞⲀ ϨⲚ ⲦⲀϬⲞⲘ ⲔⲀⲦⲀ ⲐⲈ ⲚⲦⲀⲒⲞⲨⲰ ⲈⲒⲬⲰ
ⲘⲘⲞⲤ ⲈⲢⲰⲦⲚ· ⲀⲨⲰ ϢⲀⲢⲈ ⲠⲘⲈⲢⲞⲤ ⲚⲦϬⲞⲘ ⲈⲦⲘⲘⲀⲨ
ϢⲀϤϬⲰ ϨⲒϨⲞⲨⲚ ⲚⲦⲈⲮⲨⲬⲎ ⲬⲈ ⲈⲤⲈϢⲀϨⲈⲢⲀⲦⲤ ⲚϬⲒ ⲦⲈ-

---

6 MS ⲈⲦϨⲚ; ⲈⲦ expunged; read ϨⲘ.
12 MS ⲈⲦⲦⲀⲨⲞ; Schmidt : read ⲈⲦⲀⲨⲞ.
22 MS originally ⲞⲨⲘⲈⲢⲞⲤ ⲚϨⲚ; ⲈⲂⲞⲀ added in margin, and Ⲛ crossed out.

to you the name of the *destiny*. And I will say to you the
name of all the bonds with which the *archons* bind the
spirit counterpart within the *soul*. And I will say to you the
name of all the *decans* which act upon the *soul* in the *bodies*
of the *soul* in the *world*, and I will say to you in what manner
the *souls* are acted upon. And I will say to you the *type*
of each one of the *souls*. And I will say to you the *type* of the
souls of men, and those of birds, and those of *beasts*, and
(those of) *reptiles*. And I will say to you the *type* of all the
souls and all those of the *archons* that send them [1] into the
world, so that you will be completed in all knowledge. All
these things I will say to you in the distribution of the All.
And after all these things I will say to you for what reason
all these things have happened.

Hear *now* and I will speak to you concerning the *soul*:
as I have said, the five great *archons* of the great *Heimarmene*
of the *aeons*, and the *archons* of the *disc* of the sun, and
the *archons* of the *disc* of the moon breathe into that *soul*.
And there comes forth from them a *part* of my power, *as*
I have already said to you. And that *part* of the power
remains within the *soul*, so that the *soul* is able to stand. |

---

[1] (12) those of the archons that send them; Schmidt's emendation of the Coptic
is doubtful.

ⲯⲩⲭⲏ· ⲁⲩⲱ ϣⲁⲩⲕⲱ | ⲙ̄ⲡⲁⲛⲧⲓⲙⲓⲙⲟⲛ ⲙ̄ⲡⲛ̄ⲁ̄ ⲡⲃⲟⲗ ⲛ̄ⲧⲉⲯⲩⲭⲏ ⲉϥⲣⲟⲉⲓⲥ ⲉⲣⲟⲥ ⲁⲩⲱ ⲉϥⲧⲟ ⲉⲣⲟⲥ· ⲁⲩⲱ ϣⲁⲣⲉ ⲛ̄ⲁⲣⲭⲱⲛ ⲙⲟⲣ̄ϥ ⲉϩⲟⲩⲛ ⲉⲧⲉⲯⲩⲭⲏ ϩⲣⲁï ϩⲛ̄ ⲛⲉⲩⲥⲫⲣⲁⲅⲓⲥ ⲙⲛ̄ ⲛⲉⲩⲙ̄ⲣ̄ⲣⲉ· ⲁⲩⲱ ϣⲁⲩⲥⲫⲣⲁⲅⲓⲍⲉ ⲙ̄ⲙⲟϥ ⲉϩⲟⲩⲛ ⲉⲣⲟⲥ ϫⲉ ⲉϥⲉⲁⲛⲁⲅⲕⲁⲍⲉ ⲙ̄ⲙⲟⲥ ⲛ̄ⲟⲩⲟⲉⲓϣ ⲛⲓⲙ ϫⲉ ⲉϥⲉⲉⲓⲣⲉ ⲛ̄ⲛⲉⲩⲡⲁⲑⲟⲥ ⲙⲛ̄ ⲛⲉⲩⲁⲛⲟⲙⲓⲁ ⲧⲏⲣⲟⲩ ⲉⲧⲙⲏⲛ ⲉⲃⲟⲗ ϫⲉⲕⲁⲥ ⲉⲥⲉⲣ̄ϩⲙ̄ϩⲁⲗ ⲛⲁⲩ ⲛ̄ⲟⲩⲟⲉⲓϣ ⲛⲓⲙ· ⲁⲩⲱ ⲛ̄ⲥⲉϭⲱ ϩⲁ ⲧⲉⲩϩⲩⲡⲟⲧⲁⲅⲏ ⲛ̄ⲟⲩⲟⲉⲓϣ ⲛⲓⲙ ϩⲣⲁï ϩⲛ̄ ⲙ̄ⲙⲉⲧⲁⲃⲟⲗⲏ ⲛ̄ⲧⲉ ⲡⲥⲱⲙⲁ· ⲁⲩⲱ ϣⲁⲩⲥⲫⲣⲁⲅⲓⲍⲉ ⲙ̄ⲙⲟϥ ⲉϩⲟⲩⲛ ⲉⲣⲟⲥ ⲉⲧⲣⲉⲥϣⲱⲡⲉ ϩⲛ̄ ⲛⲟⲃⲉ ⲛⲓⲙ· ⲙⲛ̄ ⲉⲡⲓⲑⲩⲙⲓⲁ ⲛⲓⲙ ⲛ̄ⲧⲉ ⲡⲕⲟⲥⲙⲟⲥ· ⲉⲧⲃⲉ ⲡⲁï ⲟⲩⲛ ⲛ̄ⲧⲉ*ïⲙⲓⲛⲉ ⲛ̄ⲧⲁïⲉⲓⲛⲉ ⲛ̄ⲙ̄ⲙⲩⲥⲧⲏⲣⲓⲟⲛ ⲉⲡⲕⲟⲥⲙⲟⲥ ⲛⲁï ⲉϣⲁⲩⲃⲱⲗ ⲉⲃⲟⲗʼ ⲛ̄ⲙ̄ⲙ̄ⲣ̄ⲣⲉ ⲧⲏⲣⲟⲩ ⲙ̄ⲡⲁⲛⲧⲓⲙⲓⲙⲟⲛ ⲙ̄ⲡⲛ̄ⲁ̄· ⲁⲩⲱ ⲙⲛ̄ ⲛⲉⲥⲫⲣⲁⲅⲓⲥ ⲧⲏⲣⲟⲩ ⲛⲁï ⲉⲧⲙⲏⲣ ⲉϩⲟⲩⲛ ⲉⲧⲉⲯⲩⲭⲏ ⲛⲁï ⲉϣⲁⲩⲉⲓⲣⲉ ⲛ̄ⲧⲉⲯⲩⲭⲏ ⲛ̄ⲉⲗⲉⲩⲑⲉⲣⲟⲥ· ⲁⲩⲱ ϣⲁⲩⲥⲱⲧⲉ ⲙ̄ⲙⲟⲥ ⲛ̄ⲧⲟⲟⲧⲟⲩ ⲛ̄ⲛⲉⲥⲉⲓⲟⲧⲉ ⲛ̄ⲁⲣⲭⲱⲛ· ⲁⲩⲱ ϣⲁⲩⲁⲁⲥ ⲛ̄ϩⲓⲗⲓⲕⲣⲓⲛⲉⲥ ⲛ̄ⲟⲩⲟⲉⲓⲛ· ⲛ̄ⲥⲉϫⲓⲧ̄ⲥ̄ ⲉϩⲣⲁï ⲉⲧⲙ̄ⲛ̄ⲧ̄ⲉⲣⲟ ⲙ̄ⲡⲉⲥⲉⲓⲱⲧʼ ⲡⲓϣⲟⲣ̄ⲡ̄ ⲛ̄ⲉⲓʼ· ⲡⲓϣⲟⲣ̄ⲡ̄ ⲙ̄ⲙⲩⲥⲧⲏⲣⲓⲟⲛ ϣⲁⲉⲛⲉϩ· ⲉⲧⲃⲉ ⲡⲁï ϭⲉ ⲟⲩⲛ ⲁïϫⲟⲟⲥ ⲉⲣⲱⲧⲛ̄ ⲙ̄ⲡⲓⲟⲩⲟïϣ ϫⲉ ⲡⲉⲧⲉ ⲛ̄ϥⲛⲁⲕⲁ-ⲉⲓⲱⲧʼ ⲁⲛ ϩⲓ ⲙⲁⲁⲩ ⲛ̄ⲥⲱϥ ⲛ̄ϥⲉⲓʼ ⲛ̄ϥⲟⲩⲁϩϥ̄ ⲛ̄ⲥⲱï ⲡⲁï ⲛ̄ϥⲙ̄ⲡϣⲁ ⲙ̄ⲙⲟï ⲁⲛ· ⲛ̄ⲧⲁïϫⲟⲟⲥ ⲟⲩⲛ ⲙ̄ⲡⲉⲩⲟⲉⲓϣ ⲉⲧⲙ̄ⲙⲁⲩ ϫⲉ ⲉⲧⲉⲧⲛ̄ⲉⲕⲱ ⲛ̄ⲥⲱⲧⲛ̄ ⲛ̄ⲛⲉⲧⲛ̄ⲉⲓⲟⲧⲉ ⲛ̄ⲁⲣⲭⲱⲛ· ⲧⲁⲣ̄ⲧⲏⲩⲧⲛ̄ ⲛ̄ϣⲏⲣⲉ ⲙ̄ⲡⲓϣⲟⲣ̄ⲡ̄ ⲙ̄ⲙⲩⲥⲧⲏⲣⲓⲟⲛ ⲛ̄ϣⲁⲉⲛⲉϩ· [ⲧⲉ b]

5 MS ⲉϥⲉⲉⲓⲣⲉ; read ⲉⲥⲉⲉⲓⲣⲉ.
6 MS ⲉⲧⲙⲏⲛ; read ⲉⲩⲙⲏⲛ.
7 MS ⲛ̄ⲥⲉϭⲱ; read ⲛ̄ⲥ̄ϭⲱ.

And they place the *spirit counterpart* outside the *soul* to watch over it, and it is allotted to it. And the *archons* bind it to the *soul* with their *seals* and their bonds. And they *seal* it to it, so that it *compels* it at all times to enact their *passions* and all their *iniquities* continually [1], so that it serves them at all times, and it remains in *submission* to them at all times in the *changes* of the *body*. And they *seal* it (the spirit counterpart) to it (the soul), so that it is in all sins and all *desires* of the *world*. For this reason *now* I have brought into the *world* in this manner the *mysteries* which release all the bonds of the *spirit counterpart* and all the *seals* which are bound to the *soul* — these which make the *soul free* and save it from the hands of its fathers, the *archons*. And they make it *pure* light, and they take it forth to the kingdom of its father, the first to appear, the First *Mystery*, for ever. *Now* concerning this I have said to you once: 'He who does not leave father and mother and come and follow me is not worthy of me' *. *Now* I said at that time: 'You should leave your fathers, the *archons*, so that I make you sons of the First *Mystery* for ever'." |

---

*   cf. Mt. 10.37; Lk. 14.26

---

[1]   (6) to enact their passions and all their iniquities continually; lit. to enact all their continual passions and iniquities.

ⲚⲀⲒ ⲆⲈ ⲚⲦⲈⲢⲈϤϪⲞⲞⲨ ⲚϬⲒ ⲠⲤⲰⲦⲎⲢ ⲀⲤϬⲞⲦⲤ ⲈⲂⲞⲖ

ⲚϬⲒ ⲤⲀⲖⲰⲘⲎ ⲠⲈϪⲀⲤ ϪⲈ ⲠⲀϪⲞⲈⲒⲤ ⲈϢϪⲈ ⲚⲈⲚⲈⲒⲞⲦⲈ

ⲚⲈ ⲚⲀⲢⲬⲰⲚ ⲈⲒⲈ ⲠⲰⲤ ⲤⲎ2 2Ⲙ ⲠⲚⲞⲘⲞⲤ ⲘⲘⲰⲨⲤⲎⲤ ϪⲈ [ⲧⲉ̅]

ⲠⲈⲦⲚⲀⲔⲰ ⲚⲤⲰϤ ⲘⲠⲈϤⲈⲒⲰⲦ ⲘⲚ ⲦⲈϤⲘⲀⲀⲨ 2Ⲛ ⲞⲨⲘⲞⲨ

5 ⲘⲀⲢⲈϤⲘⲞⲨ· ⲈⲒⲈ ⲞⲨⲔⲞⲨⲚ ⲚⲦⲀ ⲠⲚⲞⲘⲞⲤ ϢⲀϪⲈ ⲀⲚ 2Ⲁ-

ⲢⲞϤ· ⲚⲀⲒ ⲆⲈ ⲚⲦⲈⲢⲈⲤϪⲞⲞⲨ ⲚϬⲒ ⲤⲀⲖⲰⲘⲎ· Ⲁ ⲦϬⲞⲘ Ⲙ-

ⲠⲞⲨⲞⲈⲒⲚ ⲈⲦ2Ⲛ ⲘⲀⲢⲒⲀ ⲦⲘⲀⲄⲆⲀⲖⲎⲚⲎ· ⲀⲤⲂⲢⲂⲢ 2ⲢⲀⲒ Ⲛ-

2ⲎⲦⲤ ⲠⲈϪⲀⲤ ⲘⲠⲤⲰⲦⲎⲢ ϪⲈ ⲠⲀϪⲞⲈⲒⲤ ⲔⲈⲖⲈⲨⲈ ⲚⲀⲒ ⲦⲀ-

ϢⲀϪⲈ ⲘⲚ ⲦⲀⲤⲰⲚⲈ ⲤⲀⲖⲰⲘⲎ ⲦⲀⲬⲰ ⲈⲢⲞⲤ ⲘⲠⲂⲰⲖ ⲈⲂⲞⲖ

10 ⲘⲠϢⲀϪⲈ ⲚⲦⲀⲤϪⲞⲞϤ· ⲀⲤϢⲰⲠⲈ ϬⲈ ⲚⲦⲈⲢⲈ ⲠⲤⲰⲦⲎⲢ

ⲤⲰⲦⲘ ⲈⲚⲈⲒϢⲀϪⲈ ⲈⲤϪⲰ ⲘⲘⲞⲞⲨ ⲚϬⲒ ⲘⲀⲢⲒⲀ· ⲀϤⲘⲀⲔⲀ-

ⲢⲒⲌⲈ ⲘⲘⲞⲤ ⲈⲘⲀϢⲞ ⲈⲘⲀϢⲞ· ⲀϤⲞⲨⲰ2Ⲙ ⲚϬⲒ ⲠⲤⲰⲦⲎⲢ

ⲠⲈϪⲀϤ ⲘⲘⲀⲢⲒⲀ ϪⲈ †ⲔⲈⲖⲈⲨⲈ ⲚⲈ ⲘⲀⲢⲒⲀ ⲈⲦⲢⲈϪⲰ Ⲙ-

ⲠⲂⲰⲖ ⲈⲂⲞⲖ ⲘⲠϢⲀϪⲈ ⲚⲦⲀⲤϪⲞⲞϤ ⲚϬⲒ ⲤⲀⲖⲰⲘⲎ· ⲚⲀⲒ

15 ⲆⲈ ⲚⲦⲈⲢⲈϤϪⲞⲞⲨ ⲚϬⲒ ⲠⲤⲰⲦⲎⲢ· Ⲁ ⲘⲀⲢⲒⲀ ϤϬⲞⲦⲤ Ⲉ2ⲞⲨⲚ

2Ⲛ ⲤⲀⲖⲰⲘⲎ ⲀⲤⲀⲤⲠⲀⲌⲈ ⲘⲘⲞⲤ ⲠⲈϪⲀⲤ ϪⲈ ⲦⲀⲤⲰⲚⲈ ⲤⲀ-

ⲖⲰⲘⲎ· ⲈⲦⲂⲈ ⲠϢⲀϪⲈ* ⲚⲦⲀϪⲞⲞϤ ϪⲈ ϤⲤⲎ2 2Ⲙ ⲠⲚⲞⲘⲞⲤ [ⲧⲉ̅ᵇ]

ⲘⲘⲰⲨⲤⲎⲤ ϪⲈ ⲠⲈⲦⲚⲀⲔⲰ ⲚⲤⲰϤ ⲘⲠⲈϤⲈⲒⲰⲦ ⲘⲚ ⲦⲈϤ-

ⲘⲀⲀⲨ 2Ⲛ ⲞⲨⲘⲞⲨ ⲘⲀⲢⲈϤⲘⲞⲨ· ⲦⲈⲚⲞⲨ ϬⲈ ⲞⲨⲚ ⲦⲀ-

20 ⲤⲰⲚⲈ ⲤⲀⲖⲰⲘⲎ· ⲚⲦⲀ ⲠⲚⲞⲘⲞⲤ ⲀⲚ ϪⲈ-ⲠⲀⲒ ⲈⲦⲂⲈ ⲦⲈ-

ⲮⲨⲬⲎ ⲞⲨⲦⲈ ⲈⲦⲂⲈ ⲠⲤⲰⲘⲀ ⲞⲨⲦⲈ ⲈⲦⲂⲈ ⲠⲀⲚⲦⲒⲘⲒⲘⲞⲚ

ⲘⲠ̅Ⲛ̅Ⲁ̅· ϪⲈ ⲚⲀⲒ ⲄⲀⲢ ⲦⲎⲢⲞⲨ ⲚϢⲎⲢⲈ ⲚⲈ ⲚⲦⲈ ⲚⲀⲢⲬⲰⲚ·

ⲀⲨⲰ 2ⲈⲚⲈⲂⲞⲖ Ⲛ2ⲎⲦⲞⲨ ⲚⲈ· ⲀⲖⲖⲀ ⲚⲦⲀ ⲠⲚⲞⲘⲞⲤ ϪⲈ-

ⲠⲀⲒ ⲈⲦⲂⲈ ⲦϬⲞⲘ ⲚⲦⲀⲤⲈⲒ' ⲈⲂⲞⲖ 2Ⲙ ⲠⲤⲰⲦⲎⲢ ⲦⲀⲒ ⲈⲦⲞ

---

3   MS ⲤⲎ2; read ϤⲤⲎ2.

132. When *however* the *Saviour* had said these things, Salome sprang up. She said : "My Lord, if our fathers are the *archons*, *how* is it that it is written in the *Law* of Moses : 'He who shall leave his father and his mother shall die the death?' Did the Law *not therefore* speak of it?"

But when Salome had said these things, the power of light within Maria Magdalene welled up. She said to the *Saviour* : "My Lord, *command* me, that I speak with my sister Salome, so that I tell her the interpretation of the word of which she has spoken."

Now it happened when the *Saviour* heard these words which Maria said, he *blessed* her exceedingly. The *Saviour* answered and said to Maria : "I *command* thee, Maria, to say the interpretation of the word which Salome has spoken."

But when the *Saviour* had said these things, Maria sprang towards Salome, she *embraced* her and said : "My sister Salome, concerning the word which thou hast spoken, it is written in the *Law* of Moses : 'He who shall leave his father and his mother shall die the death'*. *Now* at this time, my sister Salome, the *Law* has not said this concerning the *soul*, *nor* concerning the *body*, *nor* concerning the *spirit counterpart*, *for* all these are sons of the *archons* and come from them, *but* the *Law* has said this concerning the power which came forth from the *Saviour*, which is | the man of

---

* cf. Ex. 21.17; Mt. 15.4; Mk. 7.10

ⲚⲢⲘⲚⲞⲨⲞⲈⲓⲚ ⲠⲈⲚⲎⲞⲨⲚ ⲘⲠⲞⲞⲨ · ⲚⲦⲀ ⲠⲚⲞⲘⲞⲤ ⲞⲚ

ⲬⲞⲞⲤ ⲬⲈ ⲞⲨⲞⲚ ⲚⲓⲘ ⲈⲦⲚⲀⲤⲰ ⲠⲂⲞⲖ ⲘⲠⲤⲰⲦⲎⲢ ⲘⲚ

ⲚⲈⳘⲘⲨⲤⲦⲎⲢⲒⲞⲚ ⲚⲈⳘⲈⲒⲞⲦⲈ ⲦⲎⲢⲞⲨ · ⲞⲨⲘⲞⲚⲞⲚ ⲬⲈ ⲎⲚ

ⲞⲨⲘⲞⲨ ⳘⲚⲀⲘⲞⲨ · ⲀⲖⲖⲀ ⲎⲚ ⲞⲨⲦⲀⲔⲞ ⳘⲚⲀⲦⲀⲔⲞ · ⲚⲀⲒ

5 ⳜⲈ ⲚⲦⲈⲢⲈⲤⲬⲞⲞⲨ ⲚⳜⲒ ⲘⲀⲢⲒⲀ · Ⲁ ⲤⲀⲖⲰⲘⲎ ⳘⲞⳜⲤ ⲈⲎⲞⲨⲚ

ⲎⲚ ⲘⲀⲢⲒⲀ ⲀⲤⲀⲤⲠⲀⲌⲈ ⲘⲘⲞⲤ ⲚⲞⲨⲰⲎⲘ · ⲠⲈⳜⲀⲤ ⲚⳜⲒ ⲤⲀ-

ⲖⲰⲘⲎ ⳜⲈ ⲞⲨⲚ-ⳜⲞⲘ ⳯ⲘⲠⲤⲰⲦⲎⲢ ⲚⳘⲀⲀⲦ ⲚⲚⲞⲈⲢⲞⲤ Ⲛ- ⲦⲌ

ⲦⲞⲨⲎⲈ ⲎⲰⲰⲦⲈ · ⲀⲤⳘⲰⲠⲈ ⲚⲦⲈⲢⲈ ⲠⲤⲰⲦⲎⲢ ⲤⲰⲦⲘ ⲈⲚ-

ⳘⲀⳜⲈ ⲘⲘⲀⲢⲒⲀ ⲀⳘⲘⲀⲔⲀⲢⲒⲌⲈ ⲘⲘⲞⲤ ⲈⲘⲀⳘⲞ ⲈⲘⲀⳘⲞ ·

10 ⲀⳘⲞⲨⲰⲎⲘ ⲞⲚ ⲚⳜⲒ ⲠⲤⲰⲦⲎⲢ ⲠⲈⳜⲀⳘ ⲘⲘⲀⲢⲒⲀ ⲎⲚ ⲦⲘⲎⲦⲈ

ⲘⲘⲀⲐⲎⲦⲎⲤ · ⳜⲈ ⲤⲰⲦⲘ ⳜⲈ ⲘⲀⲢⲒⲀ ⳜⲈ ⲚⲒⲘ ⲠⲈⲦⲀⲚⲀⲄⲔⲀ-

ⲌⲈ ⲘⲠⲢⲰⲘⲈ ⲎⲈⲰⲤ ⳘⲀⲚⲦⳘⲢⲚⲞⲂⲈ · ⲦⲈⲚⲞⲨ ⳜⲈ ⳘⲀⲢⲈ Ⲛ-

ⲀⲢⳜⲰⲚ ⳘⲀⲨⲤⳘⲢⲀⲄⲒⲌⲈ ⲘⲠⲀⲚⲦⲒⲘⲒⲘⲞⲚ ⲘⲠⲚⲀ ⲈⲎⲞⲨⲚ ⲈⲦⲈ-

ⲯⲨⲬⲎ ⳜⲈ ⲚⲚⲈⳘⲤⲀⲖⲈⲨⲈ ⲘⲘⲞⲤ ⲚⲚⲀⲨ ⲚⲒⲘ’ ⲈⳘⲦⲢⲈⲤⲈⲒⲢⲈ

15 ⲚⲚⲞⲂⲈ ⲚⲒⲘ ⲘⲚ ⲀⲚⲞⲘⲒⲀ ⲚⲒⲘ · ⲀⲨⲰ ⲞⲚ ⳘⲀⲨⲎⲰⲚ Ⲉ-

ⲦⲞⲞⲦⳘ ⲘⲠⲀⲚⲦⲒⲘⲒⲘⲞⲚ ⲘⲠⲚⲀ ⲈⲨⳜⲰ ⲘⲘⲞⲤ ⲚⲀⳘ · ⳜⲈ

ⲈⲢⳘⲀⲚ ⲦⲈⲯⲨⲬⲎ ⲞⲚ ⲈⲒ’ ⲈⲂⲞⲖ ⲎⲚ ⲤⲰⲘⲀ · ⲘⲠⲢⲤⲀⲖⲈⲨⲈ

ⲘⲘⲞⲤ ⲈⲔⲦⲞ ⲈⲢⲞⲤ ⲈⲔⲤⲞⲞⲎⲈ ⲘⲘⲞⲤ ⲎⲚ ⲚⲦⲞⲠⲞⲤ ⲦⲎⲢⲞⲨ

ⲚⲦⲈ ⲚⲈⲔⲢⲒⲤⲒⲤ ⲔⲀⲦⲀ ⲦⲞⲠⲞⲤ · ⲈⲦⲂⲈ ⲚⲚⲞⲂⲈ ⲦⲎⲢⲞⲨ ⲚⲦ-

20 ⲀⲔⲦⲢⲈⲤⲈⲒⲢⲈ ⲘⲘⲞⲞⲨ ⳜⲈⲔⲀⲤ ⲈⲨⲈⲔⲞⲖⲀⲌⲈ ⲘⲘⲞⲤ ⲎⲚ Ⲛ-

ⲦⲞⲠⲞⲤ ⲦⲎⲢⲞⲨ ⲚⲦⲈ ⲚⲈⲔⲢⲒⲤⲒⲤ · ⳜⲈ ⲚⲚⲈⲤⳘⳜⳘⳘⳚⳘⳘ ⲦⲌ ᵇ

ⲈⲂⲰⲔ’ ⲈⲠⳜⲒⲤⲈ ⲈⲠⲞⲨⲞⲒⲚ ⳜⲈ ⲈⲤⲈⲦⲢⲈⲨⲔⲞⲦⲤ ⲈⲎⲞⲨⲚ ⲈⲘ-

ⲘⲈⲦⲀⲂⲞⲖⲎ ⲚⲦⲈ ⲠⲤⲰⲘⲀ · ⲎⲀⲠⲀⳎ ⲎⲀⲠⲖⲰⲤ ⳘⲀⲨⲎⲰⲚ ⲚⲦⲈ

ⲠⲀⲚⲦⲒⲘⲒⲘⲞⲚ ⲘⲠⲚⲀ ⳜⲈ ⲘⲠⲢⲤⲀⲖⲈⲨⲈ ⲘⲘⲞⲤ ⲈⲠⲦⲎⲢⳘ ⲎⲚ

25 ⲀⲖⲀⲨ ⲚⲚⲀⲨ · ⲈⲒⲘⲎⲦⲒ ⲚⲤⳜⲒ-ⲘⲨⲤⲦⲎⲢⲒⲞⲚ ⲚⲤⲂⲰⲖ ⲈⲂⲞⲖ’

ⲚⲚⲈⲤⳘⲢⲀⲄⲒⲤ ⲦⲎⲢⲞⲨ ⲘⲚ ⲘⲘⲢⲢⲈ ⲦⲎⲢⲞⲨ ⲚⲦⲀⲚⲘⲞⲢⲔ

---

7 MS originally ⳜⲚⳘⲀⲀⲦ; Ⳝ expunged.
23 MS ⲚⲦⲈ ⲠⲀⲚⲦⲒⲘⲒⲘⲞⲚ ⲘⲠⲚⲀ; read ⲈⲦⲞⲞⲦⳘ ⲘⲠⲀⲚⲦⲒⲘⲒⲘⲞⲚ ⲘⲠⲚⲀ.

light within us today. The *Law* has thus said : 'Everyone who will remain outside (in relation to) the *Saviour* and his *mysteries*, all his fathers [1], *not only* will he die the death, *but* he will be destroyed with destruction'* "

Now when Maria had said these things, Salome sprang towards Maria, she *embraced* her once more. Salome said : 'The *Saviour* has power to make me *understanding* like thyself."

It happened when the *Saviour* heard the words of Maria, he *blessed* her exceedingly. The *Saviour* answered again and said to Maria in the midst of the *disciples* : "Hear now, Maria, who it is that *compels* a man *until* he sins. Now at this time the *archons seal* the *spirit counterpart* to the *soul*, so that it may not *shake* it at all times, causing it (the soul) to commit all sins and all *iniquities*. And furthermore they command the *spirit counterpart*, saying to it : 'When the *soul* comes forth from the *body*, do not *shake* it, as thou art allotted to it in all *places* of the *judgments*, to reprove it in every *place* in respect of all the sins which thou hast caused it to commit, so that it is *punished* in all *places* of the *judgments*, so that it should not be able to go to the height to the light, and is made to return [2] into the *changes* of the *body*.' *In a word* they command the *spirit counterpart* : 'Do not shake it at all at any time, *unless* it has not said [3] the *mysteries*, and it has not released all the *seals* and all the bonds with which we have bound thee | to it. And if it

---

* cf. Ex. 21.17

---

[1] (3) his mysteries, all his fathers; lit. all his mysteries, his fathers.
[2] (22) is made to return; Schmidt : and to return.
[3] (25) said; lit. received; (also 340.1).

ⲚϨⲎⲦⲞⲨ ⲈϨⲞⲨⲚ ⲈⲢⲞⲤ· ⲀⲨⲰ ⲈⲤϢⲀⲚⲬⲒ ⲚⲘⲘⲨⲤⲦⲎⲢⲒⲞⲚ
ⲚⲤⲂⲰⲗ ⲈⲂⲟⲗ ⲚⲚⲈⲤⲪⲢⲀⲄⲒⲤ ⲦⲎⲢⲞⲨ ⲘⲚ ⲘⲘⲢⲢⲈ ⲦⲎⲢⲞⲨ ⲘⲚ
ⲦⲀⲠⲞⲗⲞⲄⲒⲀ ⲘⲠⲦⲞⲠⲞⲤ ⲀⲨⲰ ⲈⲤϢⲀⲚⲂⲰⲔ ⲔⲀⲀⲤ ⲈⲂⲟⲗ
ⲈⲈⲒ· ⲈⲀⲤⲰⲠ' ⲈⲚⲀⲠⲞⲨⲞⲈⲒⲚ ⲘⲠⲬⲒⲤⲈ· ⲀⲨⲰ ⲀⲤⲢⲀⲗⲗⲟ-
5 ⲦⲢⲒⲞⲤ ⲈⲢⲟⲚ ⲀⲨⲰ ⲈⲢⲟⲔ· ⲀⲨⲰ ⲚⲄⲚⲀϢⲀⲘⲀϨⲦⲈ ⲘⲘⲞⲤ
ⲀⲚ ⲬⲒⲚ ⲠⲈⲒⲚⲀⲨ· ⲈϢⲰⲠⲈ ⲚⲦⲞϤ ⲈⲤϢⲀⲚⲦⲘⲬⲰ ⲚⲘⲘⲨⲤ-
ⲦⲎⲢⲒⲞⲚ ⲘⲠⲂⲰⲗ ⲈⲂⲟⲗ ⲚⲚⲈⲔⲘⲢⲢⲈ ⲘⲚ ⲚⲈⲔⲤⲪⲢⲀⲄⲒⲤ ⲘⲚ
ⲚⲀⲠⲞⲗⲞⲄⲒⲀ ⲘⲠⲦⲞⲠⲞⲤ ⲀⲘⲀϨⲦⲈ ⲘⲘⲞⲤ ⲘⲠⲢⲔⲀⲀⲤ ⲈⲂⲟⲗ'
ⲈⲔⲈⲤⲞⲞϨⲈ** ⲘⲘⲞⲤ ϨⲚ ⲚⲔⲞⲗⲀⲤⲒⲤ ⲘⲚ ⲚⲦⲞⲠⲞⲤ ⲦⲎⲢⲞⲨ [ⲦⲎ]
10 ⲚⲦⲈ ⲚⲈⲔⲢⲒⲤⲒⲤ· ⲈⲦⲂⲈ ⲚⲞⲂⲈ ⲚⲒⲘ' ⲚⲦⲀⲔⲦⲢⲈⲤⲈⲒⲢⲈ ⲘⲘⲞⲞⲨ·
ⲀⲨⲰ ⲘⲚⲚⲤⲀ ⲚⲀⲒ ⲬⲒⲦⲞⲨ ⲈⲢⲀⲦⲤ ⲚⲦⲠⲀⲢⲐⲈⲚⲞⲤ ⲘⲠⲞⲨ-
ⲞⲈⲒⲚ ⲦⲀⲒ ⲈϢⲀⲤⲦⲚⲚⲞⲞⲨⲤⲞⲨ ⲈⲠⲔⲨⲔⲗⲟⲤ ⲚⲔⲈⲤⲞⲠ' ⲚⲀⲒ
ⲚⲈ ⲈϢⲀⲢⲈ ⲚⲀⲢⲬⲰⲚ ⲚⲦⲚⲞϬ ⲚϨⲒⲘⲀⲢⲘⲈⲚⲎ ⲚⲦⲈ ⲚⲀⲒⲰⲚ
ⲈϢⲀⲨⲦⲀⲀⲨ ⲈⲦⲟⲟⲦϤ ⲘⲠⲀⲚⲦⲒⲘⲒⲘⲞⲚ ⲘⲠⲚⲀ ⲀⲨⲰ ϢⲀⲢⲈ
15 ⲚⲀⲢⲬⲰⲚ ϢⲀⲨⲘⲞⲨⲦⲈ ⲈⲚⲗⲒⲦⲞⲨⲢⲄⲞⲤ ⲚⲦⲈ ⲚⲈⲨⲀⲒⲰⲚ
ⲈⲨⲘⲈϨ ⲦⲬⲈ· ⲈϢⲀⲨϮ ⲚⲀⲨ ⲚⲦⲈⲯⲨⲬⲎ ⲘⲠⲀⲚⲦⲒⲘⲒⲘⲞⲚ
ⲘⲠⲚⲀ ⲈⲨⲘⲎⲢ ⲈϨⲞⲨⲚ ⲈⲚⲈⲨⲈⲢⲎⲨ· ⲈⲢⲈ ⲠⲀⲚⲦⲒⲘⲒⲘⲞⲚ
ⲘⲠⲚⲀ ⲠⲂⲟⲗ ⲚⲦⲈⲯⲨⲬⲎ ⲈⲢⲈ ⲠⲘⲒⲄⲘⲀ ⲚⲦϬⲞⲘ ⲪⲞⲨⲚ
ⲚⲦⲈⲯⲨⲬⲎ ⲈϤⲠⲈⲨϨⲞⲨⲚ ⲘⲠⲈⲤⲚⲀⲨ· ⲬⲈⲔⲀⲀⲤ ⲈⲨⲈϢϬⲘ-
20 ϬⲞⲘ ⲚⲀϨⲈⲢⲀⲦⲞⲨ· ⲈⲂⲟⲗ ⲬⲈ ⲦϬⲞⲘ ⲚⲦⲞⲤ ⲈϢⲀⲤⲦⲀϨⲞⲞⲨ
ⲈⲢⲀⲦⲞⲨ ⲘⲠⲈⲤⲚⲀⲨ· ⲀⲨⲰ ϢⲀⲢⲈ ⲚⲀⲢⲬⲰⲚ ϢⲀⲨϨⲰⲚ Ⲉ-
ⲦⲞⲟⲦⲞⲨ ⲚⲚⲗⲒⲦⲞⲨⲢⲄⲞⲤ ⲈⲨⲬⲰ ⲘⲘⲞⲤ ⲚⲀⲨ ⲬⲈ ⲠⲀⲒ
ⲠⲈ ⲠⲦⲨⲠⲞⲤ ⲈⲦⲈⲦⲚⲀⲔⲀⲀϤ ϨⲘ ⲠⲤⲰⲘⲀ ⲚⲐⲨⲗⲎ ⲚⲦⲈ [ⲦⲎ ᵇ]
ⲠⲔⲞⲤⲘⲞⲤ· ⲈϢⲀⲨⲬⲞⲞⲤ ⲘⲈⲚ ⲚⲀⲨ ⲬⲈ ⲔⲰ ⲘⲠⲘⲒⲄⲘⲀ
25 ⲚⲦϬⲞⲘ' ⲪⲞⲨⲚ ⲚⲦⲈⲯⲨⲬⲎ ϨⲒϨⲞⲨⲚ ⲘⲘⲞⲞⲨ ⲦⲎⲢⲞⲨ· ⲬⲈ

---

1 MS ⲈⲤϢⲀⲚⲬⲒ; read ⲈⲤϢⲀⲚⲬⲰ.
15 MS ⲚⲀⲒⲰⲚ; ⲈⲨ inserted above.
16 MS ⲘⲠⲀⲚⲦⲒⲘⲒⲘⲞⲚ; read ⲘⲚ ⲠⲀⲚⲦⲒⲘⲒⲘⲞⲚ.

says the *mysteries* and releases all the *seals*, and all the
bonds, and the *defence* of the *place*, and as it goes, allow it to
come, as it belongs to those of the light of the height, and it
has become a *stranger* to us and to thee. And thou wilt not
be able to seize it from this time. On the other hand, if it
has not said the *mysteries* of the releasing of thy bonds
and thy *seals*, and the *defences* of the *place*, seize it and do
not allow it to go forth. Do thou reprove it in the *punish-*
ments and all the *places* of the *judgments* in respect of all
the sins which thou hast caused it to commit. And after
these things, take them (the souls) to the presence of the
Virgin of the Light who sends them once more into the
cycle.' The *archons* of the great *Heimarmene* of the *aeons*
hand these (souls) over to the *spirit counterpart*, and the
archons call the *ministers* of their *aeons* which number 365 [1],
and give to them the *soul* and the *spirit counterpart* which
are bound to one another, so that the *spirit counterpart*
is outside the *soul*, and the *mixture* of the power is inside
the *soul* as the innermost of the two. Thus they are able
to stand because the power is that which maintains them
both upright. And the *archons* command the *ministers*, saying
to them : 'This is the *type* which you will place in the *body*
of *matter* of the *world*.' They say to them *moreover* : 'Place
the *mixture* of the power within the *soul* inside of them
all, so that | they may be able to stand, for this is their

---

[1] (16) 365 ministers; see U 243; (also 342.14).

ЄΥЄϢϬ̄ΜϬΟΜ' ЄΛϨЄΡΑΤΟΥ · ϪЄ Ν̄ΤΟC ΠЄ ΠЄΥΤΑϨΟ
ЄΡΑΤΟΥ · ΑΥⲱ Μ̄Ν̄Ν̄CΑ ΤЄΨΥΧΗ ΚⲰ Μ̄ΠΑΝΤΙΜΙΜΟΝ
Μ̄ΠΝ̄Α ΤΑΪ ΤЄ ΘЄ ЄϢΑΥϨⲰΝ ЄΤΟΟΤΟΥ Ν̄ΝЄΥΛΙΤΟΥΡ-
ΓΟC Μ̄ΜΟC · ϪЄ ЄΥЄΚΑΑΥ ϨΡΑΪ Ϩ̄Ν Ν̄CⲰΜΑ Μ̄ΠΑΝΤΙ-
5 ΤΥΠΟC · ΑΥⲱ Μ̄Ν̄Ν̄CΑ ΠЄΪCΜΟΤ ϢΑΡЄ Ν̄ΛΙΤΟΥΡΓΟC
Ν̄ΝΑΡΧⲰΝ ϢΑΥЄΙΝЄ Ν̄ΤϬΟΜ ΜΝ̄ ΤЄΨΥΧΗ ΜΝ̄ ΠΑΝΤΙ-
ΜΙΜΟΝ Μ̄ΠΝ̄Α ϢΑΥΝ̄ΤΟΥ Μ̄ΠϢΟΜΝ̄Τ ЄΠЄCΗΤ ЄΠΚΟC-
ΜΟC ΑΥⲱ ϢΑΥΠⲰϮ ⟨Μ̄ΜΟΟΥ⟩ ЄΠΚΟCΜΟC Ν̄ΝΑΡΧⲰΝ
Ν̄ΤΜΗΤЄ ϢΑΡЄ Ν̄ΑΡΧⲰΝ ϨⲰⲰϤ Ν̄ΤΜΗΤЄ ϢΑΥΜΟΥⲱ̄Τ
10 Μ̄ΠΑΝΤΙΜΙΜΟΝ Μ̄ΠΝ̄Α ΜΝ̄ ΤΚЄΜΟΙΡΑ ϨⲰⲰϤ ЄΠЄϤΡΑΝ
ΠЄ ΤΜΟΙΡΑ ϢΑϤϬΑΓЄ Μ̄ΠΡⲰΜЄ ϢΑΝΤϤΤΡЄΥϨⲰΤⲂ̄ Μ̄ΜΟϤ
Ϩ̄Μ ΠΜΟΥ ЄΤϤΗΠ' ЄΡΟϤ ·** ΤΑΪ ЄΝΤΑΥΜΟΡC̄ ЄϨΟΥΝ ЄΤЄ- Τⲱ̄
ΨΥΧΗ Ν̄Ϭ̄Ι Ν̄ΑΡΧⲰΝ Ν̄ΤΝΟϬ Ν̄ϨΙΜΑΡΜЄΝΗ ΑΥⲱ ϢΑΡЄ
Ν̄ΛΙΤΟΥΡΓΟC Ν̄ΤЄCϤЄΡΑ ϢΑΥΜΟΥΡ Ν̄ΤЄΨΥΧΗ ΜΝ̄
15 ΤϬΟΜ ΜΝ̄ ΠΑΝΤΙΜΙΜΟΝ Μ̄ΠΝ̄Α ΑΥⲱ ΜΝ̄ ΤΜΟΙΡΑ ϢΑΥ-
ΠΟϢΟΥ ΤΗΡΟΥ Ν̄CЄΛΑΥ Μ̄ΜЄΡΟC CΝΑΥ Ν̄CЄΚⲰΤЄ
Ν̄CΑ ΠΡⲰΜЄ ΜΝ̄ ΤΚЄCϨΙΜЄ Ϩ̄Μ ΠΚΟCΜΟC ΝΑΪ ЄΝΤΑΥϮ-
ΜΑЄΙΝ ΝΑΥ ϪЄ ЄΝΑΧΟΟΥCΟΥ ЄϨΟΥΝ ЄΡΟΟΥ ΑΥⲱ
ϢΑΥϮ-ΟΥΜЄΡΟC Μ̄ΠϨΟΟΥΤ' ΑΥⲱ ΟΥΜЄΡΟC Ν̄ΤЄCϨΙΜЄ
20 ϨΡΑΪ Ϩ̄Ν ΟΥΤΡΟΦΗ Ν̄ΤЄ ΠΚΟCΜΟC Η̈ ϨΡΑΪ Ϩ̄Ν ΟΥΝΙϤЄ
Ν̄ΤЄ ΠΑΗΡ' Η̈ Ϩ̄Ν ΟΥΜΟΟΥ Η̈ Ϩ̄Ν ΟΥЄΙΔΟC ЄϢΑΥCΟΟϤ ·
ΝΑΪ ΤΗΡΟΥ ϮΝΑΧΟΟΥ ЄΡⲰΤΝ̄ ΜΝ̄ ΤΜΙΝЄ Ν̄ΤЄΨΥΧΗ
ΤЄΨΥΧΗ · ΜΝ̄ ΠΤΥΠΟC ЄΤЄϢΑΥΒⲰΚ' ЄϨΟΥΝ ЄΝCⲰΜΑ
ЄΙΤЄ ΡⲰΜЄ ЄΙΤЄ ϨΑΛΗΤ' ЄΙΤЄ Ν̄ΤⲂ̄ΝΟΟΥЄ ЄΙΤЄ ΘΗΡΙΟΝ

---

2   MS several letters erased before ΨΥΧΗ; ЄΤЄ written over erasure.
8   MS Μ̄ΜΟΟΥ omitted.
18 MS ЄΝΑΧΟΟΥCΟΥ; read CЄΝΑΧΟΟΥCΟΥ.
24 MS Ν̄ΤⲂ̄ΝΟΟΥЄ; read ΤⲂ̄ΝΟΟΥЄ.

establishment, and place the *spirit counterpart* behind the *soul.*' This is the manner in which they command their *ministers*, that they should place them [1] in the *bodies* of the *anti-type*. And after this form, the *ministers* of the *archons* bring the power and the *soul* and the *spirit counterpart*. They bring the three of them down to the *world*, and they pour ⟨them⟩ upon the *world* of the *archons* of the Midst. The *archons* of the Midst, on the other hand, examine the *spirit counterpart* and also the *destiny* named *moira* (which) *guides* the man [2] until it causes him to die by the death appointed for him. This (destiny) the *archons* of the great *Heimarmene* have bound to the *soul*. And the *ministers* of the *sphere* bind the *soul* and the power and the *spirit counterpart* and the *destiny*, they divide them all and they make them into two *parts*. And they seek for the man and also the woman in the *world* to whom signs have been given that they should be sent into them. And they give a *part* to the man and a *part* to the woman in a *foodstuff* of the *world*, *or* in a breath of the *air*, *or* in water, *or* in a *kind* which they drink. All these things I will say to you, with the kind of each *soul* and the *type*; how they go into the *bodies*, *whether* of men, *whether* of birds, *whether* of cattle, *whether* of *wild beasts*, |

---

[1] (4) place them; Schmidt: place it; MS: place them (the mixture of the power and the spirit counterpart).

[2] (10, 11) grammatically, the subject of the sentence is the spirit counterpart (m), and not destiny (f).

ⲉⲓⲧⲉ ϫⲁⲧϥⲉ· ⲉⲓⲧⲉ ⲉⲓⲇⲟⲥ ⲛⲓⲙ’ ⲉⲧϩ̅ⲙ̅ ⲡⲕⲟⲥⲙⲟⲥ ϯⲛⲁϫⲱ ⲉⲣⲱⲧ̅ⲛ̅ ⲙ̅ⲡⲉⲩⲧⲩⲡⲟⲥ ϫⲉ ⲉϣⲁⲩⲃⲱⲕ ⲛ̅ⲁϣ ⲛ̅ⲧⲩⲡⲟⲥ ⲉ- ⲧⲟ b ϩⲟⲩⲛ ⲉⲛⲣⲱⲙⲉ ϯⲛⲁϫⲟⲟⲩ ⲉⲣⲱⲧ̅ⲛ̅ ϩ̅ⲙ̅ ⲡⲥⲱⲣ ⲉⲃⲟⲗ ⲙ̅ⲡⲧⲏⲣϥ̅· ⲧⲉⲛⲟⲩ ϭⲉ ⲉⲣϣⲁⲛ ⲛ̅ⲗⲓⲧⲟⲩⲣⲅⲟⲥ ⲛ̅ⲛ̅ⲁⲣⲭⲱⲛ ⲉⲩϣⲁⲛⲛⲟⲩϫⲉ ⲙ̅ⲡⲙⲉⲣⲟⲥ ⲉϩⲟⲩⲛ ⲉⲧⲉⲥϩⲓⲙⲉ· ⲁⲩⲱ ⲡⲕⲉⲙⲉⲣⲟⲥ ⲉϩⲟⲩⲛ ⲉⲡϩⲟⲟⲩⲧ ⲙ̅ⲡⲉⲥⲙⲟⲧ ⲛ̅ⲧⲁϊϫⲟⲟϥ ⲉⲣⲱⲧ̅ⲛ̅· ⲕⲁⲛ ⲉϣⲱⲡⲉ ⲥⲉⲟⲩⲏⲩ ⲛ̅ⲛⲉⲩⲉⲣⲏⲩ ϩ̅ⲛ̅ ⲟⲩⲟⲩⲉ ⲉⲛⲁϣⲱϥ ϣⲁⲣⲉ ⲛ̅ⲗⲓⲧⲟⲩⲣⲅⲟⲥ ⲁⲛⲁⲅⲕⲁⲍⲉ ⲙ̅ⲙⲟⲟⲩ ϩ̅ⲛ̅ ⲟⲩⲡⲉⲑⲏⲡ ⲛ̅ⲥⲉⲥⲩⲙⲫⲱⲛⲓ ⲙ̅ⲛ̅ ⲛⲉⲩⲉⲣⲏⲩ ϩ̅ⲛ̅ ⲟⲩⲥⲩⲙⲫⲱⲛⲓⲁ ⲛ̅ⲧⲉ ⲡⲕⲟⲥⲙⲟⲥ· ⲁⲩⲱ ϣⲁⲣⲉ ⲡⲁⲛⲧⲓⲙⲓⲙⲟⲛ ⲙ̅ⲡⲛ̅ⲁ̅ ⲉⲧϩ̅ⲙ̅ ⲡϩⲟⲟⲩⲧ ϣⲁϥⲉⲓ’ ⲉⲡⲙⲉⲣⲟⲥ ⲉⲧϭⲁⲗⲏⲩⲧ’ ⲉⲡⲕⲟⲥⲙⲟⲥ ϩ̅ⲛ̅ ⲑⲩⲗⲏ ⲙ̅ⲡⲉϥⲥⲱⲙⲁ ϣⲁϥϥⲓⲧ̅ⲥ̅ ⲛ̅ϥⲛⲟϫ̅ⲥ̅ ⲉϩⲣⲁϊ ⲉⲧⲙⲏⲧⲣⲁ ⲛ̅ⲧⲉⲥϩⲓⲙⲉ ⟨ⲉⲩⲙⲉⲣⲟⲥ⟩ ⲉϥϭⲁⲗⲏⲩⲧ’ ⲉⲡⲉⲥⲡⲉⲣⲙⲁ ⲛ̅ⲧⲕⲁⲕⲓⲁ ⲁⲩⲱ ϩ̅ⲛ̅ ⲧⲉⲩⲛⲟⲩ ⲉⲧⲙ̅ⲙⲁⲩ ϣⲁⲣⲉ ⲡϣⲟⲙ̅ⲛ̅ⲧ̅ ⲛ̅ϣⲉⲥⲉⲧⲏ ⲛ̅ⲗⲓⲧⲟⲩⲣⲅⲟⲥ ⲛ̅ⲧⲉ ⲛ̅ⲁⲣⲭⲱⲛ ϣⲁⲩⲃⲱⲕ ⲉϩⲣⲁϊ ⲉϩⲏⲧ̅ⲥ̅ ⲛ̅ⲥⲉ- [ⲧⲓ] ϭⲟϊⲗⲉ ⲉⲣⲟⲥ· ϣⲁⲣⲉ ⲛ̅ⲗⲓⲧⲟⲩⲣⲅⲟⲥ ⲙ̅ⲡⲙⲉⲣⲟⲥ ⲥⲛⲁⲩ ⲛ̅ⲛⲉⲩⲉⲣⲏⲩ· ⲁⲩⲱ ⲟⲛ ϣⲁⲣⲉ ⲛ̅ⲗⲓⲧⲟⲩⲣⲅⲟⲥ ⲕⲁⲧⲉⲭⲉ ⲙ̅ⲡⲉⲥⲛⲟϥ ⲛ̅ⲧⲣⲟⲫⲏ ⲛⲓⲙ ⲛ̅ⲧⲉ ⲧⲉⲥϩⲓⲙⲉ ⲉⲧⲥ̅ⲛⲁⲟⲩⲟⲙⲟⲩ ⲙ̅ⲛ̅ ⲛⲉⲧⲥ̅ⲛⲁⲥⲟⲟⲩ ϣⲁⲩⲕⲁⲧⲉⲭⲉ ⲙ̅ⲙⲟⲟⲩ ϩⲣⲁϊ ⲛ̅ϩⲏⲧ̅ⲥ̅ ⲛ̅ⲧⲉⲥϩⲓⲙⲉ ϩⲉⲱⲥ ϣⲁ ϩⲙⲉ ⲛ̅ϩⲟⲟⲩ· ⲁⲩⲱ ⲙ̅ⲛ̅ⲛ̅ⲥⲁ ⲡⲉϩⲙⲉ ⲛ̅ϩⲟⲟⲩ· ϣⲁⲩⲟⲩⲱϣ̅ⲙ̅ ⲙ̅ⲡⲉⲥⲛⲟϥ ⲛ̅ⲧϭⲟⲙ ⲛ̅ⲛⲉⲧⲣⲟⲫⲟⲟⲩⲉ ϣⲁⲩⲟⲩⲟϣⲙⲉϥ ⲕⲁⲗⲱⲥ ϩⲣⲁϊ ϩ̅ⲛ̅ ⲧⲙⲏⲧⲣⲁ ⲛ̅ⲧⲉⲥϩⲓⲙⲉ ⲙ̅ⲛ̅ⲛ̅ⲥⲁ ⲡⲉϩⲙⲉ ⲛ̅ϩⲟⲟⲩ· ϣⲁⲩⲣ̅-ⲕⲉⲙⲁⲁⲃ ⲛ̅ϩⲟⲟⲩ ⲉⲩⲕⲱⲧ ⲛ̅ⲛⲉϥⲙⲉⲗⲟⲥ ϩ̅ⲛ̅ ⲑⲓⲕⲱⲛ ⲙ̅ⲡⲥⲱⲙⲁ ⲙ̅ⲡⲣⲱⲙⲉ ϣⲁⲣⲉ ⲡⲟⲩⲁ ⲡⲟⲩⲁ ϣⲁϥⲕⲱⲧ ⲛ̅ⲟⲩⲙⲉⲗⲟⲥ· ⲛⲁϊ ⲉϯⲛⲁϫⲱ ⲉⲣⲱⲧ̅ⲛ̅ ⲛ̅-

12 MS ϣⲁϥϥⲓⲧ̅ⲥ̅ ⲛ̅ϥⲛⲟϫ̅ⲥ̅ ; Schmidt: read ϣⲁϥϥⲓⲧ̅ϥ̅ ⲛ̅ϥⲛⲟϫ̅ϥ̅.
13 MS ⲉⲩⲙⲉⲣⲟⲥ omitted.
25 MS originally ϣⲁϥⲕⲱ; ⲧ inserted above.

whether of reptiles, *whether* any *kind* which is in the world. I will tell you their *type*, in which *type* they go into men. I will say them to you in the distribution of the All. Now at this time when the *ministers* of the *archons* cast the *part* into the woman and the other *part* into the man, in the form which I have said to you, *even if* they are far from one another at a great distance, the *ministers compel* them secretly so that they *accord* with one another in an *accord* of the *world*. And the *spirit counterpart* which is in the man comes to the *part* which is assigned to the *world* in the *matter* of his *body*. It takes it (the matter) and casts it into the *womb* of the woman ⟨to a *part*⟩ which is assigned to the *seed* of *evil*. And at that moment the 365 *ministers* of the *archons* go into her womb and they dwell in it. The *ministers* ⟨unite⟩ the two *parts* together. And further the *ministers restrain* the blood of all *food* of the woman — what she will eat and what she will drink — they *restrain* them within the womb of the woman for *up to* 40 days. And after 40 days they knead the blood of the power of the *foods*, they knead it *well* in the *womb* of the woman. After 40 days they take another 30 days to build his *members* in the *image* of the *body* of the man. Each one of them builds a *member*; these I will say to you | — the *decans*

ⲡ̄ⲁⲉⲕⲁⲛⲟⲥ ⲉⲧⲟⲩⲛⲁⲕⲟⲧϥ· †ⲛⲁⲭⲟⲟⲩ ⲉⲣⲱⲧⲛ̄ ⲍ̄ⲙ ⲡⲥⲱⲣ
ⲉⲃⲟⲗ ⲙ̄ⲡⲧⲏⲣϥ· ⲉⲥϣⲁⲛϣⲱⲡⲉ ⲟⲩⲛ ⲙ̄ⲛ̄ⲛ̄ⲥⲁ ⲛⲁⲓ̈ ⲉⲣϣⲁⲛ
ⲛ̄ⲗⲓⲧⲟⲩⲣⲅⲟⲥ ϫⲱⲕ ⲉⲃⲟⲗ ⲙ̄ⲡⲥⲱⲙⲁ ⲧⲏⲣϥ̄ ⲙ̄ⲛ ⲛⲉϥⲙⲉⲗⲟⲥ
ⲧⲏⲣⲟⲩ ⲍ̄ⲣⲁⲓ̈ ⲍ̄ⲛ ϣϥⲉ ⲛ̄ⲍ̄ⲟⲟⲩ· ⲁⲩⲱ ⲙ̄ⲛ̄ⲛ̄ⲥⲁ ⲛⲁⲓ̈ ϣⲁⲣⲉ [ⲡ̄ᵇ]
5 ⲛ̄ⲗⲓⲧⲟⲩⲣⲅⲟⲥ ϣⲁⲩⲕⲁⲗⲉ ⲉⲍⲟⲩⲛ ⲉⲡⲥⲱⲙⲁ ⲉⲛⲧⲁⲩⲕⲟⲧϥ̄·
ⲛ̄ϣⲟⲣⲡ ⲙⲉⲛ ϣⲁⲩⲕⲁⲗⲉ ⲙ̄ⲡⲁⲛⲧⲓⲙⲓⲙⲟⲛ ⲙ̄ⲡ̄ⲛ̄ⲁ ⲙ̄ⲛ̄ⲛ̄ⲥⲱⲥ
ϣⲁⲩⲕⲁⲗⲉ ⲛ̄ⲧⲉⲯⲩⲭⲏ ⲡⲉⲩⲍⲟⲩⲛ ⲁⲩⲱ ⲙ̄ⲛ̄ⲛ̄ⲥⲱⲥ ϣⲁⲩ-
ⲕⲁⲗⲓ ⲙ̄ⲡⲙⲓⲅⲙⲁ ⲛ̄ⲧϭⲟⲙ ⲉⲍⲟⲩⲛ ⲉⲧⲉⲯⲩⲭⲏ ⲁⲩⲱ ⲧⲙⲟⲓⲣⲁ
ϣⲁⲩⲕⲁⲗⲥ ⲡⲉⲩⲃⲟⲗ ⲧⲏⲣⲟⲩ· ⲉⲛ̄ⲥⲧⲏⲍ ⲉⲍⲟⲩⲛ ⲛ̄ⲙⲙⲁⲩ
10 ⲁⲛ ⲉⲥⲁⲕⲟⲗⲟⲩⲑⲓ ⲛⲁⲩ ⲉⲥⲟⲩⲏⲍ ⲛ̄ⲥⲱⲟⲩ ⲁⲩⲱ ⲙ̄ⲛ̄ⲛ̄ⲥⲁ
ⲛⲁⲓ̈ ϣⲁⲣⲉ ⲛ̄ⲗⲓⲧⲟⲩⲣⲅⲟⲥ ϣⲁⲩⲥⲫⲣⲁⲅⲓⲍⲉ ⲙ̄ⲙⲟⲟⲩ ⲉⲍⲟⲩⲛ
ⲉⲛⲉⲩⲉⲣⲏⲩ ⲍ̄ⲛ ⲛ̄ⲥⲫⲣⲁⲅⲓⲥ ⲧⲏⲣⲟⲩ ⲛ̄ⲧⲁⲩⲧⲁⲁⲩ ⲛⲁⲩ ⲛ̄ϭⲓ
ⲛ̄ⲁⲣⲭⲱⲛ ⲁⲩⲱ ϣⲁⲩⲥⲫⲣⲁⲅⲓⲍⲉ ⲡⲉⲍⲟⲟⲩ ⲛ̄ⲧⲁⲩⲟⲩⲱⲍ
ⲛ̄ⲍⲏⲧ̄ⲥ ⲛ̄ⲧⲉⲥⲍⲓⲙⲉ ϣⲁⲩⲥⲫⲣⲁⲅⲓⲍⲉ ⲙ̄ⲙⲟϥ ⲉⲍⲟⲩⲛ ⲉⲧϭⲓϫ
15 ⲛ̄ⲍⲃⲟⲩⲣ ⲛ̄ⲧⲉ ⲡⲉⲡⲗⲁⲥⲙⲁ· ⲁⲩⲱ ϣⲁⲩⲥⲫⲣⲁⲅⲓⲍⲉ ⲙ̄ⲡⲉ-
ⲍⲟⲟⲩ ⲉⲛⲧⲁⲩϫⲉⲕ-ⲡⲥⲱⲙⲁ ⲉⲃⲟⲗʼ ⲉⲧϭⲓϫ ⲛ̄ⲟⲩⲛⲁⲙ· ⲁⲩⲱ
ϣⲁⲩⲥⲫⲣⲁⲅⲓⲍⲉ ⲙ̄ⲡⲉⲍⲟⲟⲩ ⲉⲛⲧⲁ ⲛ̄ⲁⲣⲭⲱⲛ ⲧⲁⲁⲩ ⲉⲧⲟⲟⲧⲟⲩ ⲉⲧⲙⲏⲧⲉ ⲙⲡⲉⲕⲣⲁⲛⲓⲟⲛ ⲙ̄ⲡⲥⲱⲙⲁ ⲙ̄ⲡⲉⲡⲗⲁⲥⲙⲁ· ⲁⲩⲱ
ϣⲁⲩⲥⲫⲣⲁⲅⲓⲍⲉ ⲙ̄ⲡⲉⲍⲟⲟⲩ ⲉⲛⲧⲁ ⲧⲉⲯⲩⲭⲏ ⲉⲓʼ ⲉⲃⲟⲗ ⲍ̄ⲛ ⲧⲓⲁ
20 ⲛ̄ⲁⲣⲭⲱⲛ ⲉϣⲁⲩⲥⲫⲣⲁⲅⲓⲍⲉ ⲙ̄ⲙⲟϥ ⲉⲡⲉⲕⲣⲁⲛⲓⲟⲛ ⲙ̄ⲡⲉⲡⲗⲁⲥ-
ⲙⲁ· ⲁⲩⲱ ϣⲁⲩⲥⲫⲣⲁⲅⲓⲍⲉ ⲙ̄ⲡⲉⲍⲟⲟⲩ ⲉⲛⲧⲁⲩⲟⲩⲉϣⲙ-ⲙ̄
ⲙⲉⲗⲟⲥ ⲁⲩⲱ ⲁⲩⲡⲟⲣϫ̄ϥ ⲉⲃⲟⲗ ⲉⲩⲯⲩⲭⲏ· ϣⲁⲩⲥⲫⲣⲁⲅⲓⲍⲉ

---

3 MS originally ⲙ̄ⲡⲓ ⲡⲥⲱⲙⲁ; ⲛ expunged.
7 MS originally ⲛ̄ⲧⲉⲩⲯⲩⲭⲏ; ⲩ erased. MS ⲙⲡⲉⲩⲍⲟⲩⲛ; ⲙ expunged.
9 MS originally ϣⲁⲩⲕⲁⲁⲩ; ⲥ written over ⲩ.
10 two letters erased before ⲉⲥⲁⲕⲟⲗⲟⲩⲑⲓ.
11 ⲉⲍⲟⲩⲛ ⲉⲛⲉⲩⲉⲣⲏⲩ ... ϣⲁⲩⲥⲫⲣⲁⲅⲓⲍⲉ added below in margin.
13 MS ⲡⲉⲍⲟⲟⲩ; read ⲙ̄ⲡⲉⲍⲟⲟⲩ.
20 MS ⲉϣⲁⲩⲥⲫⲣⲁⲅⲓⲍⲉ; read ϣⲁⲩⲥⲫⲣⲁⲅⲓⲍⲉ; perhaps add ⲛ̄ⲍⲃⲟⲩⲣ after
    ⲉⲡⲉⲕⲣⲁⲛⲓⲟⲛ.

which are to build it, I will say them to you in the distribution
of the All. *Now* when after these things the *ministers* complete
the whole *body* with all its *members* in 70 days, after these
things the *ministers call* within the *body* which they have
built. *Thus* first they *call* the *spirit counterpart*. Afterwards
they *call* the *soul* within them, and afterwards they *call* the
mixture of the power in the *soul*, and they place the *destiny*
outside them all, so that it is not mixed with them, as it
accompanies them and follows after them. And after these
things the *ministers seal* them to each other with all the
seals which the *archons* have given them. And they *seal*
the day on which they came to dwell in the womb of the
woman. They *seal* it in the left hand of the *figure*. And they
seal the day on which they completed the *body* on the
right hand. And they *seal* the day on which the *archons*
gave them up to them in the middle of the *skull* of the
body of the *figure*. And they *seal* the day on which the
soul came forth from the *archons*, they *seal* it on ⟨the left
of⟩ the *skull* of the *figure*. And they *seal* the day on which
they kneaded the *limbs* and they divided it to be a *soul*,
they *seal* | it on the right of the *skull* of the *figure*. And the

ⲙ̅ⲙⲟϥ ⲍ̅ⲙ ⲡⲉⲕⲣⲁⲛⲓⲟⲛ ⲛ̅ⲟⲩⲛⲁⲙ ⲙ̅ⲡⲉⲡⲗⲁⲥⲙⲁ· ⲁⲩⲱ ⲡⲉⲍⲟⲟⲩ ⲛ̅ⲧⲁⲩⲙⲟⲩⲣ ⲙ̅ⲡⲁⲛⲧⲓⲙⲓⲙⲟⲛ ⲙ̅ⲡ̅ⲛ̅ⲁ̅ ⲉⲣⲟⲥ ϣⲁⲩⲥⲫⲣⲁⲅⲓⲍⲉ ⲙ̅ⲙⲟϥ ⲉⲡⲁⲍⲟⲩ ⲛ̅ⲭⲱϥ ⲙ̅ⲡⲉⲡⲗⲁⲥⲙⲁ ⲁⲩⲱ ⲡⲉⲍⲟⲟⲩ ⲛ̅ⲧⲁⲩⲛⲓϥⲉ ⲛ̅ⲧϭⲟⲙ ⲉⲍⲟⲩⲛ ⲉⲡⲥⲱⲙⲁ ⲛ̅ϭⲓ ⲛ̅ⲁⲣⲭⲱⲛ
5 ϣⲁⲩⲥⲫⲣⲁⲅⲓⲍⲉ ⲙ̅ⲙⲟϥ ⲉⲡⲁⲅⲕⲉⲫⲁⲗⲟⲛ ⲉⲧⲍ̅ⲛ̅ ⲧⲙⲏⲧⲉ ⲛ̅-
ⲭⲱϥ ⲙ̅ⲡⲉⲡⲗⲁⲥⲙⲁ· ⲁⲩⲱ ⲟⲛ ⲉⲡⲍⲏⲧ ⲙ̅ⲡⲉⲡⲗⲁⲥⲙⲁ ⲁⲩⲱ
ⲟⲛ ⲧⲏⲡ̅ⲥ̅ ⲛ̅ⲣⲟⲙⲡⲉ ⲉⲧⲥ̅ⲛⲁⲗⲁⲩ ⲛ̅ϭⲓ ⲧⲉⲯⲩⲭⲏ ⲍ̅ⲙ ⲡⲥⲱ-
ⲙⲁ· ϣⲁⲩⲥⲫⲣⲁⲅⲓⲍⲉ ⲙ̅ⲙⲟϥ ⲉⲧⲧⲉⲍⲛⲉ ⲧⲁⲓ ⲉⲧⲍ̅ⲛ̅ ⲡⲉⲡⲗⲁⲥ-
ⲙⲁ· ⲍⲱⲥⲧⲉ ⲛⲉⲓⲥⲫⲣⲁⲅⲓⲥ ⲧⲏⲣⲟⲩ ϣⲁⲩⲥⲫⲣⲁⲅⲓⲍⲉ ⲙ̅ⲙⲟⲟⲩ
10 ⲉⲡⲉⲡⲗⲁⲥⲙⲁ· ⲛⲉⲓⲥⲫⲣⲁⲅⲓⲥ ⲧⲏⲣⲟⲩ ϯⲛⲁⲭⲱ ⲙ̅ⲡⲉⲩⲣⲁⲛ ⲧ̅ⲓ̅ⲁ̅ᵇ
ⲉⲣⲱⲧ̅ⲛ̅ ⲙ̅ⲡⲥⲱⲣ ⲉⲃⲟⲗ ⲙ̅ⲡⲧⲏⲣϥ ⲁⲩⲱ ⲙ̅ⲛ̅ⲛ̅ⲥⲁ ⲡⲥⲱⲣ ⲉⲃⲟⲗ
ϯⲛⲁⲭⲱ ⲉⲣⲱⲧ̅ⲛ̅ ⲙ̅ⲡⲧⲏⲣϥ ϫⲉ ⲉⲧⲃⲉ ⲟⲩ ⲛ̅ⲍⲱⲃ ⲁ ⲛⲁⲓ ⲧⲏⲣⲟⲩ ϣⲱⲡⲉ· ⲁⲩⲱ ⲉϣⲱⲡⲉ ⲧⲉⲧⲛ̅ⲟⲩⲉϣⲛⲟⲓ̈ ⲁⲛⲟⲕ ⲡⲉ
ⲡⲙⲩⲥⲧⲏⲣⲓⲟⲛ ⲉⲧⲙ̅ⲙⲁⲩ· ⲧⲉⲛⲟⲩ ϭⲉ ⲟⲩⲛ ϣⲁⲣⲉ ⲛ̅ⲗⲓⲧⲟⲩⲣ-
15 ⲅⲟⲥ ϣⲁⲩϫⲱⲕ ⲉⲃⲟⲗ ⲙ̅ⲡⲣⲱⲙⲉ ⲧⲏⲣϥ ⲁⲩⲱ ⲛⲉⲓⲥⲫⲣⲁⲅⲓⲥ
ⲧⲏⲣⲟⲩ ⲛ̅ⲧⲁⲩⲥⲫⲣⲁⲅⲓⲍⲉ ⲙ̅ⲡⲥⲱⲙⲁ ⲛ̅ⲍⲏⲧⲟⲩ ϣⲁⲣⲉ ⲛ̅ⲗⲓ-
ⲧⲟⲩⲣⲅⲟⲥ ϣⲁⲩⲙ̅-ⲫⲓ̈ⲁⲗⲓⲟⲛ ⲧⲏⲣϥ ⲛ̅ⲥⲉⲭⲓⲧⲟⲩ ⲛ̅ⲛⲁⲣⲭⲱⲛ
ⲧⲏⲣⲟⲩ ⲛ̅ⲉⲣⲓⲛⲁⲓⲟⲥ ⲛⲁⲓ ⲉⲧⲍⲓϫⲛ̅ ⲛ̅ⲕⲟⲗⲁⲥⲓⲥ ⲧⲏⲣⲟⲩ ⲛ̅ⲧⲉ
ⲛⲉⲕⲣⲓⲥⲓⲥ ⲁⲩⲱ ⲛⲁⲓ ⲉϣⲁⲩⲧⲁⲗⲩ ⲛ̅ⲛⲉⲩⲡⲁⲣⲁⲗⲏⲙⲡⲧⲏⲥ ⲛ̅-
20 ⲥⲉⲉⲓⲛⲉ ⲛ̅ⲛⲉⲩⲯⲩⲭⲟⲟⲩⲉ ⲉⲃⲟⲗ ⲍ̅ⲛ ⲥⲱⲙⲁ ⲛⲁⲓ ⲉϣⲁⲩϯ
ⲛⲁⲩ ⲙ̅ⲫⲓ̈ⲁⲗⲓⲟⲛ ⲛ̅ⲛⲉⲥⲫⲣⲁⲅⲓⲥ ϫⲉⲕⲁⲥ ⲉⲩⲉⲉⲓⲙⲉ ⲉⲡⲉⲟⲩ-
ⲟⲉⲓϣ ⲉⲧⲟⲩⲛⲁⲉⲓⲛⲉ ⲛ̅ⲛⲉⲯⲩⲭⲟⲟⲩⲉ ⲉⲃⲟⲗ ⲍ̅ⲛ ⲛ̅ⲥⲱⲙⲁ
[ⲁⲩⲱ ϫⲉⲕⲁⲥ ⲉⲩⲛⲁⲉⲓⲙⲉ ⲉⲡⲉⲟⲩⲟⲉⲓ⟨ϣ⟩ ⲉⲧⲟⲩ⟩ⲛⲁⲉⲓⲛⲉ [ⲧ̅ⲓ̅ⲃ̅]
ⲛ̅ⲛⲉⲯⲩⲭⲟⲟⲩⲉ ⲉⲃⲟⲗ ⲍ̅ⲛ ⲥⲱⲙⲁ] ⲁⲩⲱ ϫⲉⲕⲁⲥ ⲉⲩⲛⲁⲉⲓⲙⲉ

---

1 MS ⲙ̅ⲡⲉⲡⲗⲁ expunged before ⲛ̅ⲟⲩⲛⲁⲙ.
11 ⲙ̅ⲡⲧⲏⲣϥ should be added after ⲡⲥⲱⲣ ⲉⲃⲟⲗ at end of line.
13 MS ⲧⲉⲧⲛ̅ⲟⲩⲉϣⲛⲟⲓ̈; read ⲧⲉⲧⲛ̅ⲡⲉϣⲛⲟⲓ̈.
23 omit as dittography ⲁⲩⲱ ϫⲉⲕⲁⲥ ... ⲉⲃⲟⲗ ⲍ̅ⲛ ⲥⲱⲙⲁ.

day on which they bound the *spirit counterpart* to it (the soul), they *seal* to the back of the head of the *figure*. And the day on which the *archons* breathed the power into the *body*, they *seal* to the *brain* which is in the middle of the head of the figure, and also to the heart of the *figure*. And furthermore the number of years which the *soul* is to spend in the *body*, they *seal* to the forehead which is on the *figure*. *Thus* do they *seal* all these *seals* to the *figure*. I will say to you the names of all these *seals* in the distribution of the All. And after the distribution of the All, I will say to you for what reason all these things have happened. And if you are able to *understand*[1] : I am that *mystery. Now* at this time the *ministers* complete the whole man, and the *ministers* bring the whole *identity* of all these *seals* with which they have *sealed* the *body*, and they take them (the seals) to all the *erinaioi archons* which are over all the *punishments* of the *judgments*. And these give them to their *paralemptai*, so that they bring forth their *souls* from the *bodies*. These give to them the *identity* of the *seals*, so that they should know the time when they should bring forth the *souls* from the *bodies* [and so that they should know the time when ⟨they⟩ should bring forth the *souls* from the *bodies*], and so that they should know | the time when they

---

[1] (13) are able to understand; MS : want to understand.

ⲉⲡⲉⲩⲟⲉⲓϢ ⲉⲧⲟⲩⲛⲁⲙⲓⲥⲉ ⲙ̄ⲡⲥⲱⲙⲁ ⲛ̄ϨⲎⲧϤ Ϫⲉⲕⲁⲥ ⲉⲩⲉ-
ⲧ̄ⲛ̄ⲛⲟⲟⲩ ⲛ̄ⲛⲉⲩⲗⲓⲧⲟⲩⲣⲅⲟⲥ ⲛ̄ⲥⲉⲁϨⲉⲣⲁⲧⲟⲩ ⲛ̄ⲥⲉⲁⲕⲟ-
ⲗⲟⲩⲑⲓ ⲛ̄ⲥⲁ ⲧⲉⲯⲩⲭⲎ ⲛ̄ⲥⲉⲣ̄ⲙⲛ̄ⲧⲣⲉ ⲛ̄ⲛⲟⲃⲉ ⲛⲓⲙ ⲉⲧⲥ̄ⲛⲁ-
ⲁⲁⲩ ⲛ̄ⲧⲟⲟⲩ ⲙⲛ̄ ⲡⲁⲛⲧⲓⲙⲓⲙⲟⲛ ⲙ̄ⲡ̄ⲛ̄ⲁ̄ ⲉⲧⲃⲉ ⲑⲉ ⲉⲧ-
5 ⲟⲩⲛⲁⲕⲟⲗⲁⲍⲉ ⲙ̄ⲙⲟⲥ Ϩ̄ⲛ ⲧⲉⲕⲣⲓⲥⲓⲥ ⲁⲩⲱ ⲉⲣϢⲁⲛ ⲛ̄ⲗⲓ-
ⲧⲟⲩⲣⲅⲟⲥ ⲉⲩϢⲁⲛ†ⲙ̄ⲫⲓⲁⲓⲟⲛ ⲛ̄ⲛⲉⲥⲫⲣⲁⲅⲓⲥ ⲛ̄ⲛ̄ⲁⲣⲭⲱⲛ
ⲛ̄ⲉⲣⲓⲛⲁⲓⲟⲥ Ϣⲁⲩⲁⲛⲁⲭⲱⲣⲓ ⲉⲧⲟⲓⲕⲟⲛⲟⲙⲓⲁ ⲛ̄ⲛⲉⲩϨⲃⲎⲩⲉ
ⲉⲧⲧⲎϢ ⲛⲁⲩ Ϩⲓⲧ̄ⲛ ⲛ̄ⲁⲣⲭⲱⲛ ⲛ̄ⲧⲛⲟϬ ⲛ̄ϨⲓⲙⲁⲣⲙⲉⲛⲎ ⲁⲩⲱ
ⲉⲩϢⲁⲛⲭⲱⲕ' ⲉⲃⲟⲗ ⲛ̄Ϭⲓ ⲧⲎⲡⲥ ⲛ̄ⲉⲃⲟⲧ ⲙ̄ⲡⲉⲭⲡⲟ ⲙ̄ⲡϢⲎⲣⲉ
10 ϢⲎⲙ Ϣⲁⲩⲙⲓⲥⲉ ⲙ̄ⲡϢⲎⲣⲉ ϢⲎⲙ ⲉⲥⲥⲟⲃⲕ̄ ⲛ̄ϨⲎⲧϤ ⲛ̄Ϭⲓ
ⲡⲙⲓⲅⲙⲁ ⲛ̄ⲧϬⲟⲙ ⲁⲩⲱ ⲉⲥⲥⲟⲃⲕ̄ ⲛ̄ϨⲎⲧϤ ⲛ̄Ϭⲓ ⲧⲉⲯⲩⲭⲎ
ⲁⲩⲱ ⲉϤⲧⲥ̄ⲃⲕⲎⲩ ⲛ̄ϨⲎⲧϤ̄ ⲛ̄Ϭⲓ ⲡⲁⲛⲧⲓⲙⲓⲙⲟⲛ ⲙ̄⟨ⲡ̄ⲛ̄ⲁ̄⟩ ⲧⲙⲟⲓⲣⲁ
ⲛ̄ⲧⲟϤ˙ⲉⲩⲛⲟϬ ⲧⲉ ⲉⲛⲥ̄ⲧⲎϨ ⲁⲛ ⲉϨⲟⲩⲛ ⲉⲡⲥⲱⲙⲁ ⲛ̄ⲧⲉⲩ- [ⲧⲓⲃᵇ]
ⲟⲓⲕⲟⲛⲟⲙⲓⲁ ⲁⲗⲗⲁ ⲉⲥⲁⲕⲟⲗⲟⲩⲑⲉⲓ ⲛ̄ⲥⲁ ⲧⲉⲯⲩⲭⲎ ⲙⲛ̄
15 ⲡⲥⲱⲙⲁ ⲙⲛ̄ ⲡⲁⲛⲧⲓⲙⲓⲙⲟⲛ ⲙ̄ⲡ̄ⲛ̄ⲁ̄ Ϩⲉⲱⲥ Ϣⲁ ⲡⲉⲩⲟⲉⲓϢ
ⲉⲧⲉⲣⲉ ⲧⲉⲯⲩⲭⲎ ⲛⲎⲩ ⲉⲃⲟⲗ Ϩ̄ⲙ ⲡⲥⲱⲙⲁ ⲛ̄ϨⲎⲧϤ ⲉⲧⲃⲉ
ⲡⲧⲩⲡⲟⲥ ⲙ̄ⲡⲙⲟⲩ ⲉⲧⲥ̄ⲛⲁϨⲟⲧⲃⲉϤ ⲛ̄ϨⲎⲧϤ̄ ⲕⲁⲧⲁ ⲡⲉⲧⲎⲡ
ⲉⲣⲟϤ Ϩⲓⲧ̄ⲛ ⲛ̄ⲁⲣⲭⲱⲛ ⲛ̄ⲧⲛⲟϬ ⲛ̄ϨⲓⲙⲁⲣⲙⲉⲛⲎ ⲉⲓⲧⲉ ⲉϤⲛⲁⲙⲟⲩ
Ϩⲓⲧ̄ⲛ ⲟⲩⲑⲎⲣⲓⲟⲛ Ϣⲁⲣⲉ ⲧⲙⲟⲓⲣⲁ ⲁⲅⲉ ⲙ̄ⲡⲉⲑⲎⲣⲓⲟⲛ ⲉϨⲟⲩⲛ
20 ⲉⲣⲟϤ ϢⲁⲛⲧϤϨⲱⲧⲃ ⲙ̄ⲙⲟϤ· �destroyed̄ ⲉϤⲛⲁⲙⲟⲩ Ϩⲓⲧ̄ⲛ ⲟⲩϪⲁⲧϤⲉ
Ꞩ ⲉϤⲛⲁϨⲉ ⲉⲩϨⲓⲉⲓⲧ Ϩ̄ⲛ ⲟⲩⲧⲟⲡ Ꞩ ⲉϤⲛⲁϢϬⲧ ⲙ̄ⲙⲟϤ
ⲙ̄ⲙⲓⲛ ⲙ̄ⲙⲟϤ Ꞩ ⲛ̄ⲧⲟϤ ⲉϤⲛⲁⲙⲟⲩ Ϩ̄ⲛ ⲟⲩⲙⲟⲟⲩ Ꞩ Ϩⲓⲧ̄ⲛ
ⲛⲁⲓ ⲛ̄ⲧⲉ⟨ⲓ⟩ⲙⲓⲛⲉ Ꞩ ⲛ̄ⲧⲟϤ Ϩⲓⲧ̄ⲛ ⲕⲉⲙⲟⲩ ⲉϤⲥⲟⲟⲩ ⲉⲛⲁⲓ Ꞩ
ⲉⲛⲁⲛⲟⲩϤ Ϩⲁⲡⲁⲝ Ϩⲁⲡⲗⲱⲥ ⲧⲙⲟⲓⲣⲁ ⲧⲉ ⲉϢⲁⲥⲁⲛⲁⲅⲕⲁⲍⲉ

---

9 MS ⲉⲩϢⲁⲛϪⲱⲕ; better ⲉⲥϢⲁⲛϪⲱⲕ.
10 MS ⲉⲥⲥⲟⲃⲕ̄; read ⲉϤⲥⲟⲃⲕ̄.
12 MS damaged; read ⲙ̄⟨ⲡ̄ⲛ̄ⲁ̄⟩.
21 Ϩⲓⲉⲓⲧ added in margin.

should give birth to the *body*. (This is) in order that they should send their *ministers*, that they should stand and that they with the *spirit counterpart* should *accompany* the *soul*, and that they should bear witness to all the sins which it has committed, in relation to the manner in which it will be *punished* in the *judgment*. When the *ministers* give the *identity* of the *seals* to the *erinaioi archons*, they *withdraw* to the *organisation* of their affairs which is appointed for them by the *archons* of the great *Heimarmene*. And when the number of months for the birth of the child is completed, the child is born. The *mixture* of the power within him is small; and the *soul* within him is small; and the *spirit counterpart* within him is small; the *destiny*, on the other hand, is large. It (the destiny) is not mixed within the *body* of their *organisation* [1], *but* it *accompanies* the *soul* and the *body* and the *spirit counterpart until* the time when the *soul* comes forth from the *body*, for the sake of the *type* of the death by which he is to die, *according to* what is appointed to him by the *archons* of the great *Heimarmene*. *In a word*, the *destiny* is what *compels* his death to him; *whether* he is to die through a *wild beast*, (and) the *destiny guides* the *wild beast* to him until it kills him; *or* ⟨*whether*⟩ he is to die through a snake [2] *or* to fall into a pit by misfortune, *or* to hang himself, *or* to die in water, *or* through something of this kind, *or* through other deaths which are worse than these, *or* better. | This

---

[1]   (13, 14) of their organisation; Till : (meaning) to guide them (the various parts).
[2]   (20) snake; lit. reptile.

ⲘⲠⲈϤⲘⲞⲨ ⲈⲌⲞⲨⲚ ⲈⲢⲞϤ ⲠⲀⲒ ⲠⲈ ⲠⲌⲰⲂ ⲚⲦⲘⲞⲒⲢⲀ ⲀⲨⲰ

ⲘⲚⲦ⳥-ⲔⲈⲌⲰⲂ ⲚⲤⲀ ⲠⲀⲒ ⲀⲨⲰ ϢⲀⲢⲈ ⲦⲘⲞⲒⲢⲀ ⲀⲔⲞⲖⲞⲨ-

ⲐⲈⲒ ⲚⲤⲀ ⲠⲢⲰⲘⲈ ⲈⲦⲘⲘⲀⲨ** ϢⲀ ⲠⲈⲌⲞⲞⲨ ⲘⲠⲈϤⲘⲞⲨ·   T̄Ī̄Ē̄

ⲀⲤⲞⲨⲰ̄Ⲍ̄Ⲙ̄ Ⲛ̄ϬⲒ ⲘⲀⲢⲒⲀ ⲠⲈⲬⲀⲤ ⲬⲈ ⲈⲒⲈ ⲢⲰⲘⲈ ⲚⲒⲘ ⲈⲦ-

5 ⲌⲒⲬⲘ̄ ⲠⲔⲞⲤⲘⲞⲤ ⲈⲒⲈ ⲌⲰⲂ ⲚⲒⲘ ⲈⲦⲎⲠ' ⲈⲢⲞⲞⲨ ⲌⲒⲦⲚ ⲐⲒ-

ⲘⲀⲢⲘⲈⲚⲎ ⲈⲒⲦⲈ ⲀⲄⲀⲐⲞⲚ ⲈⲒⲦⲈ ⲠⲈⲐⲞⲞⲨ ⲈⲒⲦⲈ ⲚⲞⲂⲈ ⲈⲒⲦⲈ

ⲘⲞⲨ ⲈⲒⲦⲈ ⲰⲚ̄Ⲍ̄ ⲌⲀⲠⲀ̄Ⲝ̄ ⲌⲀⲠⲀⲰⲤ ⲌⲰⲂ ⲚⲒⲘ' ⲈⲦⲎⲠ ⲈⲢⲞⲞⲨ

ⲌⲒⲦⲚ Ⲛ̄ⲀⲢⲬⲰⲚ Ⲛ̄ⲐⲒⲘⲀⲢⲘⲈⲚⲎ ⲤⲈⲚⲀⲬⲠⲒⲂⲰⲔ Ⲛ̄ⲌⲎⲦⲞⲨ·

ⲀϤⲞⲨⲰ̄Ϣ̄Ⲃ̄ Ⲛ̄ϬⲒ ⲠⲤⲰⲦⲎⲢ ⲠⲈⲬⲀϤ Ⲙ̄ⲘⲀⲢⲒⲌⲀⲘⲘⲎ ⲬⲈ ⲌⲀ-

10 ⲘⲎⲚ ϮⲬⲰ Ⲙ̄ⲘⲞⲤ ⲈⲢⲰⲦⲚ̄ ⲬⲈ ⲌⲰⲂ ⲚⲒⲘ ⲈⲦⲎⲠ' ⲈⲠⲞⲨⲀ

ⲠⲞⲨⲀ ⲌⲒⲦⲚ ⲐⲒⲘⲀⲢⲘⲈⲚⲎ ⲈⲒⲦⲈ ⲀⲄⲀⲐⲞⲚ ⲚⲒⲘ ⲈⲒⲦⲈ ⲚⲞⲂⲈ

ⲚⲒⲘ ⲌⲀⲠⲀ̄Ⲝ̄ ⲌⲀⲠⲀⲰⲤ ⲌⲰⲂ ⲚⲒⲘ ⲈⲦⲎⲠ ⲈⲢⲞⲞⲨ ϢⲀⲨⲂⲰⲔ

Ⲛ̄ⲌⲎⲦⲞⲨ ⲈⲦⲂⲈ ⲠⲀⲒ ϬⲈ Ⲛ̄ⲦⲀⲒⲈⲒⲚⲈ Ⲙ̄ⲠϢⲞ̄Ϣ̄Ⲧ̄· Ⲛ̄ⲘⲘⲨⲤⲦⲎ-

ⲢⲒⲞⲚ Ⲛ̄ⲦⲘⲚ̄ⲦⲈⲢⲞ Ⲛ̄ⲘⲠⲎⲨⲈ Ⲏ̄ Ⲙ̄ⲘⲞⲚ ⲚⲈⲘⲚ̄-ⲀⲖⲀⲨ Ⲛ̄ⲤⲀⲢ̄Ⲝ̄

15 ⲚⲀⲞⲨⲬⲀⲒ ⲠⲈ ⲌⲒⲬⲘ̄ ⲠⲔⲞⲤⲘⲞⲤ ⲬⲈ ⲀⲬⲚ̄ ⲘⲨⲤⲦⲎⲢⲒⲞⲚ ⲄⲀⲢ

ⲘⲚ̄-ⲀⲖⲀⲨ ⲚⲀⲂⲰⲔ' ⲈⲦⲘⲚ̄ⲦⲈⲢⲞ Ⲙ̄ⲠⲞⲨⲞⲈⲒⲚ ⲈⲒⲦⲈ ⲆⲒⲔⲀⲒⲞⲤ

ⲈⲒⲦⲈ ⲢⲈϤⲢ̄ⲚⲞⲂⲈ· ⲈⲦⲂⲈ ⲠⲀⲒ ⲞⲨⲚ Ⲛ̄ⲦⲈⲒⲘⲒⲚⲈ Ⲛ̄ⲦⲀⲒⲈⲒⲚⲈ

Ⲛ̄ⲚϢⲞ̄Ϣ̄Ⲧ̄ Ⲛ̄ⲘⲘⲨⲤⲦⲎⲢⲒⲞⲚ* ⲈⲠⲔⲞⲤⲘⲞⲤ ⲬⲈ ⲈⲒⲈⲂⲰⲖ ⲈⲂⲞⲖ   T̄Ī̄Ē̄ b

Ⲙ̄ⲢⲢⲈϤⲢ̄ⲚⲞⲂⲈ ⲚⲀⲒ ⲈⲦⲚⲀⲠⲒⲤⲦⲈⲨⲈ ⲈⲢⲞⲒ ⲀⲨⲰ ⲈⲦⲚⲀⲤⲰⲦⲘ̄

20 ⲚⲤⲰⲒ ⲬⲈⲔⲀⲤ ⲈⲒⲈⲂⲞⲖⲞⲨ ⲈⲂⲞⲖ ⲌⲢⲀⲒ Ⲍ̄Ⲛ̄ Ⲙ̄ⲘⲢⲢⲈ ⲘⲚ̄ ⲚⲈ-

ⲤⲪⲢⲀⲄⲒⲤ Ⲛ̄ⲚⲀⲒⲰⲚ Ⲛ̄ⲦⲈ Ⲛ̄ⲀⲢⲬⲰⲚ Ⲛ̄ⲦⲀⲘⲞⲢⲞⲨ ⲈⲌⲞⲨⲚ

ⲈⲚⲈⲤⲪⲢⲀⲄⲒⲤ ⲘⲚ̄ ⲚⲈⲚⲆⲨⲘⲀ ⲘⲚ̄ Ⲛ̄ⲦⲀⲜⲒⲤ Ⲙ̄ⲠⲞⲨⲞⲈⲒⲚ ⲬⲈ-

ⲔⲀⲤ ⲠⲈϮⲚⲀⲂⲞⲖϤ ⲈⲂⲞⲖ ⲌⲒⲬⲘ̄ ⲠⲔⲞⲤⲘⲞⲤ Ⲍ̄Ⲛ̄ Ⲙ̄ⲘⲢⲢⲈ ⲘⲚ̄

ⲚⲈⲤⲪⲢⲀⲄⲒⲤ Ⲛ̄ⲚⲀⲒⲰⲚ Ⲛ̄ⲦⲈ Ⲛ̄ⲀⲢⲬⲰⲚ ⲈⲨⲈⲂⲞⲖϤ ⲈⲂⲞⲖ ⲌⲢⲀⲒ

---

11 MS ⲤⲈⲚⲈⲒⲦⲈ; ⲤⲈⲚ expunged.

13 MS originally Ⲙ̄ⲠϢⲞⲘ̄Ⲛ̄Ⲧ̄; ⲘⲚ expunged and Ϣ added.

21 Ⲛ̄ⲚⲀⲒⲰⲚ . . . ⲈⲚⲈⲤⲪⲢⲀⲄⲒⲤ written in margin above; it was first intended
to write the sentence below, and Ⲛ̄ⲚⲀⲒ appears in lower margin.

is the work of the *destiny*, and it has no other work apart
from this. And the *destiny accompanies* that man until the
day of his death."

133. Maria answered and said : "For all men who are
in the *world*, must all things which are appointed for them
through the *Heimarmene*, *whether good or* evil, *or* sin, *or*
death, *or* life, *in a word* must all things which are appointed
for them through the *archons* of the *Heimarmene* come to
them?"

The *Saviour* replied and said to Mariam : "*Truly*, I say
to you : all things which are appointed to each one through
the *Heimarmene*, *whether* all *good*, *whether* all sin, *in a word*,
everything which is appointed for them will come to them.
Now because of this I have brought the key of the *mysteries*
of the Kingdom of Heaven, *or* else no *flesh* would be saved
in the *world*. *For* without *mysteries* no one will go to the
Kingdom of the Light, *either righteous* or sinners. *Now*
because of this I have thus brought the keys of the *mysteries*
to the *world*, so that I may release the sinners who will
believe in me, and will obey me so that I may release them
from the bonds and the *seals* of the *aeons* of the *archons*,
that I may bind them to the *seals* and the *garments* and the
ranks of the light. Thus he whom I will release in the
world from the bonds and the *seals* of the *aeons* of the
archons will be released | in the height from the bonds and

ⲍⲘ ⲠⲬⲓⲤⲈ ⲚⲘⲘⲢⲢⲈ ⲘⲚ ⲚⲈⲤⲪⲢⲀⲄⲓⲤ ⲚⲦⲈ ⲚⲀⲓⲰⲚ ⲚⲚⲀⲢ-
ⲬⲰⲚ ⲀⲨⲰ ⲠⲈ⳨ⲚⲀⲘⲞⲢ⳨ ⲍⲓⲬⲘ ⲠⲔⲞⲤⲘⲞⲤ ⲈⲍⲞⲨⲚ ⲈⲚⲈⲤ-
ⲤⲪⲢⲀⲄⲓⲤ ⲘⲠ ⲠⲈⲚⲀⲨⲘⲀ ⲘⲚ ⲚⲦⲀⲌⲓⲤ ⲘⲠⲞⲨⲞⲈⲓⲚ ⲚⲤⲈ-
ⲘⲞⲢ⳨ ⲍⲘ ⲠⲔⲀⲍ ⲘⲠⲞⲨⲞⲈⲓⲚ ⲈⲌⲞⲨⲚ ⲈⲚⲦⲀⲌⲓⲤ ⲚⲚⲈⲔⲖⲎⲢⲞ-
5 ⲚⲞⲘⲓⲀ ⲘⲠⲞⲨⲞⲈⲓⲚ· ⲈⲦⲂⲈ ⲚⲢⲈ⳨ⲢⲚⲞⲂⲈ ⲞⲨⲚ ⲚⲦⲀⲓⲤⲔⲨⲖⲖⲓ
ⲘⲘⲞⲓ ⲘⲠⲈⲓⲤⲞⲠ ⲀⲓⲈⲓⲚⲈ ⲘⲘⲨⲤⲦⲎⲢⲓⲞⲚ ⲚⲀⲨ ⲬⲈ ⲈⲓⲈⲂⲞ-
ⲖⲞⲨ ⲈⲂⲞⲖ ⲚⲦⲞⲞⲦⲞⲨ ⲚⲚⲀⲓⲰⲚ ⲚⲦⲈ ⲚⲀⲢⲬⲰⲚ ⲚⲦⲀⲘⲞ-
ⲢⲞⲨ ⲈⲌⲞⲨⲚ ⲈⲚⲈⲔⲖⲎⲢⲞⲚⲞⲘⲓⲀ ⲘⲠⲞⲨⲞⲈⲓⲚ ⲞⲨⲘⲞⲚⲞⲚ
ⲚⲢⲈ⳨ⲢⲚⲞⲂⲈ ⲀⲖⲖⲀ ⲚⲔⲀⲓⲆⲓⲔⲀⲓⲞⲤ ⲬⲈ ⲈⲓⲈϯ ⲚⲀⲨ ⲚⲘ-
10 ⲘⲨⲤⲦⲎⲢⲓⲞⲚ ⲚⲤⲈⲬⲓⲦⲞⲨ ⲈⲠⲞⲨⲞⲈⲓⲚ ⲬⲈ Ⲁ⳪Ⲛ ⲘⲨⲤⲦⲎ- [ⲦⲓⲀ]
ⲢⲓⲞⲚ ⲄⲀⲢ ⲘⲚⲰϭⲞⲘ ⲈⲬⲓⲦⲞⲨ ⲈⲠⲞⲨⲞⲈⲓⲚ ⲈⲦⲂⲈ ⲠⲀⲓ ⲞⲨⲚ
ⲘⲠⲓⲍⲞⲠⲤ ⲀⲖⲖⲀ ⲀⲓⲰϢ ⲈⲂⲞⲖ ⲪⲀⲚⲈⲢⲰⲤ ⲀⲨⲰ ⲚⲦⲀⲓⲠⲰⲢ⳨
ⲈⲂⲞⲖ ⲀⲚ ⲚⲢⲢⲈ⳨ⲢⲚⲞⲂⲈ ⲀⲖⲖⲀ ⲚⲦⲀⲓⲰϢⲞⲨ ⲈⲂⲞⲖ ⲀⲨⲰ
ⲀⲓⲬⲞⲞⲤ ⲈⲢⲰⲘⲈ ⲚⲓⲘ ⲚⲢⲈ⳨ⲢⲚⲞⲂⲈ ⲘⲚ ⲚⲆⲓⲔⲀⲓⲞⲤ ⲈⲓⲬⲰ
15 ⲘⲘⲞⲤ ⲬⲈ ϢⲓⲚⲈ ⲦⲀⲢⲈⲦⲚϭⲓⲚⲈ ⲦⲰⲍⲘ ⲦⲀⲢⲞⲨⲞⲨⲰⲚ
ⲚⲎⲦⲚ ⲬⲈ ⲞⲨⲞⲚ ⲄⲀⲢ ⲚⲓⲘ ⲈⲦϢⲓⲚⲈ ⲍⲚ ⲞⲨⲀⲖⲎⲐⲓⲀ ⳨ⲚⲀ-
ϭⲓⲚⲈ ⲀⲨⲰ ⲠⲈⲦⲦⲰⲍⲘ ⲤⲈⲚⲀⲞⲨⲰⲚ ⲚⲀ⳨ ⲚⲦⲀⲓⲬⲞⲞⲤ ⲄⲀⲢ
ⲈⲢⲰⲘⲈ ⲚⲓⲘ ⲬⲈ ⲈⲨⲈϢⲓⲚⲈ ⲚⲤⲀ ⲘⲘⲨⲤⲦⲎⲢⲓⲞⲚ ⲚⲦⲘⲚⲦⲈⲢⲞ
ⲘⲠⲞⲨⲞⲈⲓⲚ ⲚⲀⲓ ⲈⲦⲚⲀⲦⲂⲂⲞ ⲘⲘⲞⲞⲨ ⲚⲤⲈⲀⲀⲨ ⲚⲍⲓⲖⲓⲔⲢⲓ-
20 ⲚⲈⲤ ⲚⲤⲈⲬⲓⲦⲞⲨ ⲈⲠⲞⲨⲞⲈⲓⲚ· ⲈⲦⲂⲈ ⲠⲀⲓ ϭⲈ Ⲁ ⲒⲰⲍⲀⲚⲚⲎⲤ
ⲠⲂⲀⲠⲦⲓⲤⲦⲎⲤ Ⲁ⳨ⲠⲢⲞⲪⲎⲦⲈⲨⲈ ⲍⲀⲢⲞⲓ Ⲉ⳨ⲬⲰ ⲘⲘⲞⲤ· ⲬⲈ
ⲀⲚⲞⲔ ⲘⲈⲚ ⲀⲓⲂⲀⲠⲦⲓⲌⲈ ⲘⲘⲰⲦⲚ ⲍⲚ ⲞⲨⲘⲞⲞⲨ ⲈⲨⲘⲈⲦⲀ-

---

1 MS ⲚⲘⲘⲢⲢⲈ; read ⲍⲚ ⲘⲘⲢⲢⲈ.
9 MS ⲚⲔⲀⲓⲆⲓⲔⲀⲓⲞⲤ; read ⲚⲔⲈⲆⲓⲔⲀⲓⲞⲤ.
13 MS ⲚⲦⲀⲓϢⲞⲨ; read ⲚⲦⲀⲓⲰϢ.

the *seals* of the *aeons* of the *archons*. And he whom I will
bind in the *world* within the *seals* and the *garments* and the
ranks of the light will be bound in the Land of Light within
the *ranks* of the *inheritances* of the light. *Now* for the sake
of sinners I have *troubled* myself at this time, I have brought
the *mysteries* to them, so that I may release them from the
aeons of the *archons*, and bind them within the *inheritances*
of the light. *Not only* sinners, *but* the *righteous* ones, so that
I may give to them the *mysteries* that they be taken to the
light, *for* without *mysteries* it is not possible to be taken to
the light. *Now* because of this I have not hidden it, *but*
I have proclaimed *clearly*. And I have not separated sinners,
but I have proclaimed and I have spoken to all men, the
sinners and the *righteous*, saying : 'Seek and ye shall find,
knock and it shall be opened to you. *For* everyone who seeks
in *truth* will find, and to him that knocks it will be opened' *.
For I have said to all men that they should seek the *mysteries*
of the Kingdom of the Light which will cleanse them and
make them *pure* and take them to the light. Now because
of this, John the *Baptist prophesied* about me, saying : 'I have
indeed baptised you with water unto *repentance* | for the

---

*   cf. Mt. 7.7, 8; Lk. 11.9, 10

ΝΟΙΑ ЄΠΚШ ЄΒΟΛ Ν̄ΝЄΤ̄ΝΝΟΒЄ ΠЄΤΝΗΥ Μ̄Ν̄Ν̄ΣШΪ ΨΟΥ- [Τ͞Ι͞Λ^b]
ΟΤΒ ЄΡΟΪ· ΠΑΪ ЄΤЄΡЄ ΠЄΨΑ Ζ̄Ν ΤЄΨ6ΙΧ ЄΨΝΑΤ͞ΒΒΟ
Μ̄ΠЄΨΧΝΟΟΥ· ΠΤШΖ ΜЄΝ Ν̄ΨΡΟΚΖΨ Ζ̄Ν ΟΥΚШΖΤ ЄΜЄΨ-
ШϢΜ· ΠЄΨΣΟΥΟ ΔЄ Ν̄ΨΣΥΝΑΓЄ Μ̄ΜΟΨ ЄΖΟΥΝ Є-
5　ΤЄΨΑΠΟΘΗΚΗ· Ν̄ΤΑ Τ6ΟΜ' ЄΤΖ̄Ν ΪШΖΑΝΝΗΣ ΠΡΟΦΗ-
ΤЄΥЄ ΖΑΡΟΪ ЄΣΣΟΟΥΝ ΧЄ †ΝΑЄΙΝЄ Ν̄ΜΜΥΣΤΗΡΙΟΝ Є-
ΠΚΟΣΜΟΣ Ν̄ΤΑΚΑΘΑΡΙΖЄ Ν̄ΝΝΟΒЄ Ν̄ΡΡЄΨΡΝΟΒЄ ΝΑΪ ЄΤ-
ΝΑΠΙΣΤЄΥЄ ЄΡΟΪ Ν̄ΣЄΣШΤΜ̄ ⟨Ν̄⟩ΣШΪ Ν̄ΤΑΛΑΥ Ν̄ΖΙΛΙΚΡΙ-
ΝЄΣ Ν̄ΟΥΟЄΙΝ Ν̄ΤΑΧΙΤΟΥ ЄΠΟΥΟЄΙΝ·

10　ΝΑΪ 6Є Ν̄ΤЄΡЄΨΧΟΟΥ Ν̄6Ι Ι͞Σ ΑΣΟΥШϢ͞Β Ν̄6Ι ΜΑΡΙΑ
ΠЄΧΑΣ ΧЄ ΠΑΧΟЄΙΣ ЄΪЄ ЄΡϢΑΝ Ν̄ΡШΜЄ ΒШΚ ΧЄ ЄΥ-
ϢΙΝЄ Ν̄ΣЄЄΙ' ЄΧ̄Ν ΖЄΝΣΒШ Μ̄ΠΛΑΝΗ ЄΥΝΑЄΙΜЄ ЄΤШΝ
ΧЄ ЄΥΗΠ' ЄΡΟΚ Χ̄Ν ΜΜΟΝ· ΑΨΟΥШϢ͞Β Ν̄6Ι ΠΣШΤΗΡ
ΠЄΧΑΨ Μ̄ΜΑΡΙΑ ΧЄ ΑΪΧΟΟΣ ЄΡШΤ̄Ν Μ̄ΠΙΟΥΟЄΙϢ ΧЄ
15　ϢШΠЄ Ν̄ΘЄ Ν̄ΝΙΣΑΒЄ Ν̄ΤΡΑΠЄΖЄΙΤΗΣ ΧЄ ΠЄΤ̄ΝΑΝΟΥΨ Τ͞Ι͞Σ
ΧΙΤ̄Ψ ΠЄΘΟΟΥ ΝΟΧ̄Ψ ЄΒΟΛ· ΤЄΝΟΥ 6Є ΑΧΙΣ Ν̄ΡШΜЄ
ΝΙΜ ЄΤΝΑϢΙΝЄ Ζ̄Ν ΤΜ̄ΝΤΝΟΥΤЄ ΧЄ ЄΡϢΑΝ ΟΥΤΗΥ
Ν̄ΜΖΙΤ' ЄΙ' ЄΒΟΛ ϢΑΤЄΤ̄ΝЄΙΜЄ ΧЄ ΟΥΚΒΟ ΠЄΤΝΑϢШ-
ΠЄ· ЄΡϢΑΝ ΟΥΤΟΥΡΗΣ ЄΙ' ЄΒΟΛ ϢΑΤЄΤ̄ΝЄΙΜЄ ΧЄ ΟΥ-
20　ΚΑΥΜΑ Μ̄Ν ΟΥΖΜΟΜ ΠЄΤΝΑϢШΠЄ· ΤЄΝΟΥ 6Є ΑΧΙΣ
ЄΡΟΟΥ ΧЄ ЄϢΧЄ ΑΤЄΤ̄ΝΣΟΥΝ̄-ΦΟ Ν̄ΤΠЄ Μ̄Ν ΠΚΑΖ
ЄΒΟΛ Ζ̄Ν Ν̄ΤΗΥ· ЄΡϢΑΝ ΖΟΪΝЄ 6Є ΤЄΝΟΥ ЄΙ' ЄΡΑΤ-
ΤΗΥΤ̄Ν Ν̄ΣЄΚΗΡΥΣΣЄ ΝΗΤ̄Ν Ν̄ΟΥΜ̄ΝΤΝΟΥΤЄ Ν̄ΤЄΤ̄Ν-

4　MS ΧΝ ΠЄΨΣΟΥΟ; ΧΝ expunged.
8　MS damaged.
18　ΚΒΟ ... ϢΑΤЄΤ̄ΝЄΙΜЄ ΧЄ ΟΥ written in upper margin.
22　MS ΝΖΟΙΝЄ; Ν expunged.

forgiveness of your sins. He who comes after me surpasses me, whose winnowing fan is in his hand. He will purify his threshing floor. The chaff *indeed* he will burn in an unquenchable fire. *But* his wheat he will *gather* in his *barn'**. The power which was in John *prophesied* about me, knowing that I would bring the *mysteries* to the *world*, and would *purify* the sins of the sinners who would *believe* in me and obey me, and would make them to be *pure* light, and take them to the light."

134. Now when Jesus had said these things, Maria answered and said : "My Lord, when men go and seek, and they come upon the teachings of *error*, whence will they know whether they belong to thee or not?"

The *Saviour* answered and said to Maria : "I have said to you once : 'Become like the wise *money-changers*, take what is good, cast away what is evil' [1]. Now at this time say to all men who will seek Godhood : 'When a north wind comes, you know that cold will come to pass. When a south wind comes, you know that *heat* and burning will come to pass' □. Now at this time say to them : 'If you know the face of the heaven and the earth by means of the wind, if some now at this time come to you and they *preach* Godhood to you, you | know with certainty their words have been in

---

*   cf. Mt. 3.11, 12; Lk. 3.16, 17
□   cf. Mt. 16.3

---

[1]   (15) agraphon; see Resch (Bibl. 41) Logion 43, pp. 116-117.

ЄΙΜЄ 2Ν ΟΥШΡΧ̄ ΧЄ Α ΝЄΥШΑΧЄ СΥМФШΝЄΙ ΑΥШ

ΑΥ2ΟΡΜΑΖЄ Є2Ν ΝЄΤΝШΑΧЄ ΤΗΡΟΥ ΝΑΪ ЄΝΤΑΪΧΟΟΥ

ЄΡШΤ̄Ν 2ΙΤ̄Ν ΜΑΡΤΥΡΙΑ СΝΤЄ ШΑ ШΟΜΤЄ· ΑΥШ Є-

ΑΥСΥМФШΝЄΙ 2М ΠΤΑ2Ο ЄΡΑΤ̄Ч М̄ΠΑΗΡ М̄Ν М̄ΠΗΥЄ М̄Ν

5 Ν̄ΚΥΚΛΟС М̄Ν Ν̄ΑСΤΗΡ М̄Ν М̄ФШСΤΗΡ М̄Ν ΠΚΑ2 ΤΗΡ̄Ч

М̄Ν ΝЄΤΝ̄2ΗΤ̄Ч ΤΗΡΟΥ М̄Ν Ν̄ΚЄΜΟΥЄΙΟΟΥЄ ΤΗΡΟΥ М̄Ν

ΝЄΤΝ̄2ΗΤΟΥ ΤΗΡΟΥ· ΑΧΙС ЄΡΟΟΥ ΧЄ ΝЄΤΝΗΥ *ШΑ- Τ̄ῙЄ b

ΡШΤΝ Ν̄ΤЄ ΝЄΥШΑΧЄ 2ΟΡΜΑΖЄ ΑΥШ Ν̄СЄСΥМФШΝΙ

Є2М ΠСΟΟΥΝ ΤΗΡ̄Ч ΝЄΝΤΑΪΧΟΟΥ ЄΡШΤ̄Ν ЄΪЄΧΙΤΟΥ

10 ЄΥΗΠ ЄΡΟΝ· ΝΑΪ ΝЄ ЄΤЄΤΝΑΧΟΟΥ ЄΝΡШМЄ ЄΤЄΤΝ-

ΚΗΡΥССЄ ΝΑΥ ΧЄΚΑС ЄΥΝΑ2ΟΡΟΥ ЄΡΟΟΥ ЄΝЄСΒШ М̄-

ΠΛΑΝΗ· ΤЄΝΟΥ 6Є ΟΥΝ ЄΤΒЄ Ν̄ΡЄЧΡΝΟΒЄ Ν̄ΤΑΪСΚΥΛΛ

М̄ΜΟΪ ΑΪЄΙ' ЄΠΚΟСΜΟС ΧЄ ЄΪЄΝΟΥ2М̄ М̄ΜΟΟΥ ЄΒΟΛ ΧЄ

Ν̄ΑΙΚΑΙΟС Ν̄ΤΟΟΥ ΝΑΪ ЄΤЄ М̄ΠΟΥΡ̄-ΛΑΑΥ М̄ΠЄΘΟΟΥ

15 ЄΝЄ2 ΑΥШ ΝΑΪ ЄΤЄ М̄ΠΟΥΡ̄ΝΟΒЄ ЄΠΤΗΡ̄Ч· 2ΑΠ̄С ЄΡΟΟΥ

ΠЄ ЄΤΡЄΥ2Є ЄМ̄МΥСΤΗΡΙΟΝ ΝΑΪ ЄΤ2Ι Ν̄ΧШШМЄ Ν̄ΪЄΟΥ

ΝΑΪ Ν̄ΤΑΪΤΡЄ ЄΝШΧ' С2ΑΪСΟΥ 2ΡΑΪ 2М̄ ΠΠΑΡΑΔΙСΟС

ЄΪШΑΧЄ Ν̄М̄МΑЧ ЄΒΟΛ 2М̄ ΠШΗΝ М̄ΠСΟΟΥΝ ΑΥШ ЄΒΟΛ

2М̄ ΠШΗΝ М̄ΠШΝ2̄· ΑΥШ ΑΪΤΡЄЧΚΑΑΥ 2Ν ΤΠЄΤΡΑ Ν̄Α-

20 ΡΑΡΑΛ ΑΥШ ΑΪΚШ Ν̄ΚΑΛΑΠΑΤΑΥΡШΘ' ΠΑΡΧШΝ ЄΤ2ΙΧ̄Ν [Τ̄ῙЧ̄]

6ΜΜΟΥΤ ΠΑΪ ЄΤЄΡЄ ΤΟΥЄΡΗΤЄ** Ν̄ΪЄΟΥ 2ΙΧШЧ ΑΥШ

Ν̄ΤΟЧ ЄΤΚШΤЄ ЄΝΑΙШΝ ΤΗΡΟΥ· М̄Ν Ν̄2ΙΜΑΡΜЄΝΗ·

ΠΑΡΧШΝ ЄΤМ̄МΑΥ ΑΪΚΑΛЧ ЄЧΡΟЄΙС ЄΝΧШШМЄ Ν̄ΪЄΟΥ

ЄΤΒЄ ΠΚΑΤΑΚΛΥСΜΟС· ΑΥШ ΧЄ Ν̄ΝЄ ΛΑΑΥ Ν̄ΑΡΧШΝ

---

3 MS ΜΜΑΡΤΥΡΙΑ; Μ expunged.

14 MS originally Π̄ΑΪΤΟΟΥ; ΑΪ expunged.

21 Κ̄ in upper right-hand margin at end of quire.

accord, and have *fitted* with all your words, which I have said to you through two or three witnesses *, and they have been in *accord* with the establishment of the *air* and the heaven and the *cycles* and the *stars* and the *luminaries* and the whole earth and all things within it, and also all the waters and all things within them;' say to them : 'Those who come to you, and whose words *fit* and are in *accord* with the whole knowledge which I have said to you, I will accept as belonging to us.' This is what you will say to men when you *preach* to them, so that they may guard themselves from the teachings of *error*. *Now* at this time, for the sake of sinners, I have *troubled* myself. I have come to the *world* that I might save them. Because even for the *righteous* themselves who have never done evil, and have not committed sins at all, it is necessary that they should find the *mysteries* which are in the Books of Jeu, which I caused Enoch to write in *Paradise* when I spoke with him from the Tree of Knowledge and from the Tree of Life. And I caused him to place them in the *rock* of Ararad □, and I placed the *archon* Kalapatauroth, which is over Gemmut ¹, upon whose head ² are the feet of Jeu, and who goes round all the *aeons* and the *Heimarmene*, I placed that *archon* to watch over the Books of Jeu because of the *Flood*, so that none of the *archons* | should *envy* them and destroy them — these which

---

*   cf. Deut. 19.15; Mt. 18.16; 2 Cor. 13.1; 1 Tim. 5.19; Heb. 10.28
□   cf. Gen. 8.4

---

¹   (21) Gemmut; Schmidt/Till : seven stars, probably the Pleiades; see Crum 821a; ParaShem 47.
²   (21) upon whose head; Till : (or) upon whom.

ⲫⲑⲟⲛⲓ ⲉⲣⲟⲟⲩ ⲛ̄ⲥⲉⲧⲁⲕⲟⲟⲩ ⲛⲁⲓ̈ ⲉⲧ̄ⲛⲁⲧⲁⲁⲩ ⲛⲏⲧⲛ̄ ⲉⲓ̈-
ⲱⲁⲛⲟⲩⲱ ⲉⲓ̈ϫⲱ ⲉⲣⲱⲧⲛ̄ ⲙ̄ⲡⲥⲱⲣ ⲉⲃⲟⲗ ⲙ̄ⲡⲧⲏⲣϥ·

ⲛⲁⲓ̈ ϭⲉ ⲛ̄ⲧⲉⲣⲉϥϫⲟⲟⲩ ⲛ̄ϭⲓ ⲡⲥⲱⲧⲏⲣ ⲁⲥⲟⲩⲱϣⲃ ⲛ̄ϭⲓ
ⲙⲁⲣⲓⲁ ⲡⲉϫⲁⲥ ϫⲉ ⲡⲁϫⲟⲉⲓⲥ· ⲉⲓⲉ ⲛⲓⲙ ϭⲉ ϩⲱⲱϥ ⲡⲉ
5 ⲡⲣⲱⲙⲉ ⲉⲧϩⲓϫⲛ̄ ⲡⲕⲟⲥⲙⲟⲥ ⲉⲧⲉ ⲙ̄ⲡϥ̄ⲣⲛⲟⲃⲉ ⲉⲡⲧⲏⲣϥ ⲡⲁⲓ̈
ⲉϥⲟⲩⲟϫ ⲉⲁⲛⲟⲙⲓⲁ· ⲉϥϣⲁⲛⲟⲩⲭⲁⲓ̈ ⲅⲁⲣ ⲉⲟⲩⲁ ⲛ̄ϥⲛⲁϣ-
ⲟⲩⲭⲁⲓ̈ ⲁⲛ ⲉⲕⲉⲟⲩⲁ ϫⲉⲕⲁⲥ ⲉϥⲉϩ ⲉⲙ̄ⲙⲩⲥⲧⲏⲣⲓⲟⲛ ⲉⲧϩⲓ
ⲛ̄ϫⲱⲱⲙⲉ ⲛ̄ⲓ̈ⲉⲟⲩ· ϯϫⲱ ⲙ̄ⲙⲟⲥ ⲅⲁⲣ ϫⲉ ⲙⲛ-ⲣⲱⲙⲉ ϩⲓϫⲛ̄
ⲡⲕⲟⲥⲙⲟⲥ ⲉϥⲛⲁϣⲟⲩⲭⲁⲓ̈ ⲉⲛⲟⲃⲉ ⲉϥϣⲁⲛⲟⲩⲭⲁⲓ̈ ⲅⲁⲣ ⲉ-
10 ⲟⲩⲁ ⲛ̄ϥⲛⲁϣⲟⲩⲭⲁⲓ̈ ⲁⲛ ⲉⲕⲉⲟⲩⲁ· ⲁϥⲟⲩⲱϩⲙ̄ ⲛ̄ϭⲓ ⲡⲥⲱⲧⲏⲣ ⲡⲉϫⲁϥ ⲙ̄ⲙⲁⲣⲓⲁ· ϫⲉ ϯϫⲱ ⲙ̄ⲙⲟⲥ ⲛⲏⲧⲛ̄ ϫⲉ ⲥⲉⲛⲁϩⲉ   [ⲧⲓⲉ ᵇ]
ⲉⲟⲩⲁ ϩⲛ̄ ϣⲟ· ⲥⲛⲁⲩ ϩⲛ̄ ⲟⲩⲧⲃⲁ· ⲉⲧⲃⲉ ⲡϫⲱⲕ ⲉⲃⲟⲗ
ⲙ̄ⲡⲙⲩⲥⲧⲏⲣⲓⲟⲛ ⲙ̄ⲡϣⲟⲣⲡ̄ ⲙ̄ⲙⲩⲥⲧⲏⲣⲓⲟⲛ· ⲛⲁⲓ̈ ϯⲛⲁϫⲱ
ⲉⲣⲱⲧⲛ̄ ⲉⲓ̈ϣⲁⲛⲟⲩⲱ ⲉⲓ̈ⲥⲱⲣ ⲉⲃⲟⲗ ⲛⲏⲧⲛ̄ ⲙ̄ⲡⲧⲏⲣϥ· ⲉⲧⲃⲉ
15 ⲡⲁⲓ̈ ϭⲉ ⲁⲓ̈ⲥⲕⲩⲗⲗⲉⲓ ⲙ̄ⲙⲟⲓ̈ ⲁⲓ̈ⲉⲓⲛⲉ ⲛ̄ⲙⲙⲩⲥⲧⲏⲣⲓⲟⲛ ⲉⲡⲕⲟⲥⲙⲟⲥ ϫⲉ ⲥⲉϣⲟⲟⲡ ⲧⲏⲣⲟⲩ ϩⲁ ⲡⲛⲟⲃⲉ· ⲁⲩⲱ ⲥⲉϣⲁⲁⲧ
ⲧⲏⲣⲟⲩ ⲛ̄ⲧⲁⲱⲣⲉⲁ ⲛ̄ⲙⲙⲩⲥⲧⲏⲣⲓⲟⲛ· ⲁⲥⲟⲩⲱϩⲙ̄ ⲛ̄ϭⲓ ⲙⲁⲣⲓⲁ
ⲡⲉϫⲁⲥ ⲙ̄ⲡⲥⲱⲧⲏⲣ ϫⲉ ⲡⲁϫⲟⲓ̈ⲥ ϩⲁⲑⲏ ⲉⲙⲡⲁⲧⲕⲉⲓ̓ ⲉⲡⲧⲟⲡⲟⲥ ⲛ̄ⲛⲁⲣⲭⲱⲛ· ⲁⲩⲱ ϩⲁⲑⲏ ⲉⲙⲡⲁⲧⲕⲉⲓ̓ ⲉϩⲣⲁⲓ̈ ⲉⲡⲕⲟⲥⲙⲟⲥ
20 ⲙ̄ⲡⲉ-ⲗⲁⲁⲩ ⲙ̄ⲯⲩⲭⲏ ⲃⲱⲕ̓ ⲉⲡⲟⲩⲟⲓ̈ⲛ· ⲁϥⲟⲩⲱϣⲃ ⲛ̄ϭⲓ
ⲡⲥⲱⲧⲏⲣ ⲡⲉϫⲁϥ ⲙ̄ⲙⲁⲣⲓⲁ ϫⲉ ϩⲁⲙⲏⲛ ϩⲁⲙⲏⲛ ϯϫⲱ ⲙ̄ⲙⲟⲥ
ⲉⲣⲱⲧⲛ̄ ϫⲉ ϩⲁⲑⲏ ⲉⲙⲡⲁϯⲉⲓ̓ ⲉⲡⲕⲟⲥⲙⲟⲥ· ⲙ̄ⲡⲉ-ⲗⲁⲁⲩ ⲙ̄-
ⲯⲩⲭⲏ ⲃⲱⲕ ⲉϩⲟⲩⲛ ⲉⲡⲟⲩⲟⲉⲓⲛ· ⲁⲩⲱ ⲧⲉⲛⲟⲩ ϭⲉ ⲛ̄ⲧⲉ-
ⲣⲓⲉⲓ̓ ⲁⲓ̈ⲟⲩⲱⲛ ⲉ̄ⲙⲡⲩⲗⲏ ⲙ̄ⲡⲟⲩⲟⲉⲓⲛ· ⲁⲩⲱ ⲁⲓ̈ⲟⲩⲱⲛ ⲛ̄ⲛⲉ-
25 ϩⲓⲟⲟⲩⲉ ⲉⲧϫⲓ ⲉϩⲟⲩⲛ ⲉⲡⲟⲩⲟⲉⲓⲛ· ⲁⲩⲱ ⲧⲉⲛⲟⲩ ϭⲉ
ⲡⲉⲧⲛⲁⲉⲓⲣⲉ ⲙ̄ⲡⲉⲙⲡϣⲁ ⲛ̄ⲙⲙⲩⲥⲧⲏⲣⲓⲟⲛ ⲙⲁⲣⲉϥϫⲓ ⲛ̄ⲙ- ⲧⲓⲍ

---

24 MS ⲉ̄ⲙⲡⲩⲗⲏ; read ⲛ̄ⲙⲡⲩⲗⲏ.
26 ⲕ̄ⲁ in upper left-hand margin at beginning of quire.

I shall give to you when I have finished speaking to you of the distribution of the All."

Now when the *Saviour* had said these things, Maria answered and said: "My Lord, who then now is the man in the *world* who has not sinned at all, who is safe from *iniquity*? *For* if he is safe from one he will not be able to be safe from another, so that he finds the *mysteries* which are in the Books of Jeu. *For* I say that no man in the *world* will be saved from sin, *for* if he is saved from one he will not be saved from another."

The *Saviour* answered and said to Maria: "I say to you, there will be found one in a thousand*, two in ten thousand[1], for the sake of the completion of the *mystery* of the First *Mystery*. These I will say to you when I have finished setting out to you the All. Because of this now I have *troubled* myself, I have brought the *mysteries* to the *world* because all (men) are under sin. And they all lack the *gift* of the *mysteries*."

135. Maria answered and said to the Saviour: "My Lord, before thou didst come to the *place* of the *archons*, and before thou didst come into the *world*, did no *soul* go to the light?"

The *Saviour* answered and said to Maria: "Truly, *truly*, I say to you, before I came to the *world* no *soul* went into the light. And now at this time as I have come I have opened the *gates* of the light. And I have opened the ways which lead into the light. And now at this time, he who will do what is worthy of the *mysteries*, let him receive the *mysteries* | and go to the light."

---

* cf. Eccles. 7.8

---

[1] (12) agraphon; see Iren. I.24.6; Epiph. 24.5; GTh 86.1-3.

ⲘⲨⲤⲦⲎⲢⲒⲞⲚ ⲚϤⲂⲰⲔ ⲈⲠⲞⲨⲞⲈⲒⲚ: ⲀⲤⲞⲨⲰϨ ⲞⲚ ⲈⲦⲞⲞⲦⲤ
ⲚϬⲒ ⲘⲀⲢⲒⲀ ⲠⲈⲬⲀⲤ ϪⲈ ⲠⲀⲬⲞⲈⲒⲤ· ⲀⲖⲖⲀ ⲀⲒⲤⲰⲦⲘ ϪⲈ Ⲁ
ⲚⲈⲠⲢⲞⲫⲎⲦⲎⲤ ⲂⲰⲔ' ⲈⲠⲞⲨⲞⲈⲒⲚ· ⲀϤⲞⲨⲰϨ ⲞⲚ ⲈⲦⲞⲞⲦϤ
ⲚϬⲒ ⲠⲤⲰⲦⲎⲢ ⲠⲈϪⲀϤ ⲘⲘⲀⲢⲒⲀ ϪⲈ ϨⲀⲘⲎⲚ ϨⲀⲘⲎⲚ ϯϪⲰ
5 ⲘⲘⲞⲤ ⲚⲈ ϪⲈ ⲘⲠⲈ-ⲖⲀⲀⲨ ⲘⲠⲢⲞⲫⲎⲦⲎⲤ ⲂⲰⲔ ⲈⲠⲞⲨⲞⲈⲒⲚ·
ⲀⲖⲖⲀ ⲚⲦⲀ ⲚⲀⲢⲬⲰⲚ ⲚⲦⲈ ⲚⲀⲒⲰⲚ ⲚⲦⲀⲨϢⲀϪⲈ ⲚⲘⲘⲀⲨ
ⲈⲂⲞⲖ ϨⲚ ⲚⲀⲒⲰⲚ ⲀⲨϯ ⲚⲀⲨ ⲘⲠⲘⲨⲤⲦⲎⲢⲒⲞⲚ ⲚⲦⲈ ⲚⲀⲒⲰⲚ
ⲀⲨⲰ ⲚⲦⲈⲢⲒⲈⲒ' ⲈⲠⲦⲞⲠⲞⲤ ⲚⲚⲀⲒⲰⲚ· ϨⲎⲖⲒⲀⲤ ⲀⲒⲔⲞⲦϤ ⲀⲒⲦⲚ-
ⲚⲞⲞⲨϤ ⲈⲠⲤⲰⲘⲀ ⲚⲒⲰϨⲀⲚⲚⲎⲤ ⲠⲂⲀⲠⲦⲒⲤⲦⲎⲤ· ⲠⲔⲈⲤⲈⲈⲠⲈ
10 ⲆⲈ ⲀⲒⲔⲞⲦⲞⲨ ⲈϨⲈⲚⲤⲰⲘⲀ ⲚⲆⲒⲔⲀⲒⲞⲤ ⲚⲀⲒ ⲈⲦⲚⲀϨⲈ ⲈⲘ-
ⲘⲨⲤⲦⲎⲢⲒⲞⲚ ⲘⲠⲞⲨⲞⲈⲒⲚ ⲚⲤⲈⲂⲰⲔ' ⲈⲠϪⲒⲤⲈ ⲚⲤⲈⲔⲖⲎⲢⲞ-
ⲚⲞⲘⲒ ⲚⲦⲘⲚⲦⲈⲢⲞ ⲘⲠⲞⲨⲞⲈⲒⲚ· ⲀⲂⲢⲀϨⲀⲘ ⲚⲦⲞϤ ⲘⲚ ⲒⲤⲀⲀⲔ
ⲘⲚ ⲒⲀⲔⲰⲂ ⲀⲒⲔⲰ ⲚⲀⲨ ⲈⲂⲞⲖ ⲚⲚⲈⲨⲚⲞⲂⲈ ⲦⲎⲢⲞⲨ ⲘⲚ
ⲚⲈⲨⲀⲚⲞⲘⲒⲀ· ⲀⲨⲰ ⲀⲒϯ ⲚⲀⲨ ⲚⲘⲘⲨⲤⲦⲎⲢⲒⲞⲚ ⲘⲠⲞⲨⲞⲈⲒⲚ
15 ϨⲢⲀⲒ ϨⲚ ⲚⲀⲒⲰⲚ· ⲀⲨⲰ ⲀⲒⲔⲀⲀⲨ ϨⲘ ⲠⲦⲞⲠⲞⲤ ⲚⲒⲀⲂⲢⲀϢⲐ ⲦⲒⲌ ᵇ
ⲘⲚ ⲚⲀⲢⲬⲰⲚ ⲦⲎⲢⲞⲨ ⲚⲦⲀⲨⲘⲈⲦⲀⲚⲞⲒ· ⲀⲨⲰ ⲈⲒⲂⲰⲔ' Ⲉ-
ⲠϪⲒⲤⲈ ⲦⲀⲈⲒ' ⲈⲒⲚⲀⲂⲰⲔ' ⲈⲠⲞⲨⲞⲈⲒⲚ ϯⲚⲀϤⲒ ⲚⲚⲈⲨⲮⲨⲬⲎ
ⲚⲘⲘⲀⲒ ⲈⲠⲞⲨⲞⲈⲒⲚ· ⲀⲖⲖⲀ ϨⲀⲘⲎⲚ ϯϪⲰ ⲘⲘⲞⲤ ⲚⲈ ⲘⲀⲢⲒⲀ
ϪⲈ ⲚϤⲚⲀⲂⲰⲔ' ⲀⲚ ⲈⲠⲞⲨⲞⲈⲒⲚ ⲈⲘⲠⲒϤⲒ ⲚⲦⲞⲨⲮⲨⲬⲎ ⲚⲦⲞ
20 ⲘⲚ ⲦⲀⲚⲞⲨⲤⲚⲎⲨ ⲦⲎⲢⲞⲨ ⲈⲠⲞⲨⲞⲈⲒⲚ· ⲠⲔⲈⲤⲈⲈⲠⲈ ⲆⲈ
ⲘⲠⲀⲦⲢⲒⲀⲢⲬⲎⲤ ⲘⲚ ⲚⲆⲒⲔⲀⲒⲞⲤ ϪⲒⲚ ⲘⲠⲈⲞⲨⲞⲈⲒϢ ⲚⲀⲆⲀⲘ
ϨⲈⲰⲤ ϢⲀ ⲦⲈⲚⲞⲨ ⲚⲈⲦϨⲚ ⲚⲀⲒⲰⲚ ⲘⲚ ⟨ⲚⲦⲀⲌⲒⲤ⟩ ⲦⲎⲢⲞⲨ
ⲚⲦⲈ ⲚⲀⲢⲬⲰⲚ· ⲚⲦⲈⲢⲒⲈⲒ'ⲈⲠⲦⲞⲠⲞⲤ ⲚⲀⲒⲰⲚ ⲀⲒⲦⲢⲈⲨⲔⲞⲦⲞⲨ
ⲈϨⲈⲚⲤⲰⲘⲀ ⲦⲎⲢⲞⲨ ⲈⲨⲚⲀⲢⲆⲒⲔⲀⲒⲞⲤ ⲚϬⲒ ⲦⲠⲀⲢⲐⲈⲚⲞⲤ Ⲙ-

---

19 MS ⲚϤⲚⲀⲂⲰⲔ; read ⲚⲤⲈⲚⲀⲂⲰⲔ.
22 MS indistinct.
23 MS indistinct; read ⲀⲒⲦⲢⲈⲨⲔⲞⲦⲞⲨ.
24 MS ⲦⲚϬⲒ; Ⲧ expunged.

Maria continued again and said : "*But*, my Lord, I have heard that the *prophets* went to the light."

The *Saviour* continued again and said to Maria : "*Truly, truly*, I say to thee, no *prophet* went to the light. *But* the *archons* of the *aeons* have spoken with them out of the *aeons*, they given to them the *mystery* of the *aeons*. And when I came to the *place* of the *aeons*, I returned Elias, I sent him to the *body* of John the *Baptist. But* the rest I have returned to *righteous bodies* which will find the *mysteries* of the light, and go to the height and *inherit* the Kingdom of the Light. On the other hand, I forgave Abraham, and Isaac, and Jacob, all their sins and their *iniquities*, and I gave to them the *mysteries* of the light in the *aeons*, and I put them in the *place* of Jabraoth and all the *archons* who have *repented.* And when I go to the height and I am about to go to the light, I will carry their *souls* with me to the light. *But truly* I say to thee, Maria, that they will not go[1] to the light before I carry thy *soul* and those of all thy brothers to the light. *But* the rest of the *patriarchs* and the *righteous ones*, from the time of Adam *until* the present, which are in the *aeons* and all (the *ranks*) of the *archons*, when I came to the *place* of the *aeons*, I caused them all, (through) the *Virgin* of the Light, to return to bodies which will become *righteous* |

---

[1] (19) they will not go; MS : he will not go.

ΠΟΥΟΕΙΝ ΝΑϊ ΕΤΝΑϨΕ Ε‾ΜΜΥΣΤΗΡΙΟΝ ΤΗΡΟΥ· Μ‾ΠΟΥ-
ΟΕΙΝ Ν‾ΣΕΒΩΚ ΕϨΟΥΝ Ν‾ΣΕΚΛΗΡΟΝΟΜΙ Ν‾ΤΜ‾Ν‾ΤΕΡΟ Μ‾-
ΠΟΥΟΕΙΝ· ΑΣΟΥΩϨΜ‾ Ν‾ϬΙ ΜΑΡΙΑ ΠΕΧΑΣ ΧΕ ΑΝ ϨΕΝ-
ΜΑΚΑΡΙΟΣ ΑΝΟΝ ΠΑΡΑ ΡΩΜΕ ΝΙΜ Ν‾ΝΕϊΜ‾Ν‾ΤΝΟϬ ΕΝΤ-
5 ΑΚϬΟΛΠΟΥ ΝΑΝ ΕΒΟΛ· ΑϤΟΥΩϨΜ‾ Ν‾ϬΙ ΠΣΩΤΗΡ ΠΕΧΑϤ
Μ‾ΜΑΡΙΑ ΜΝ‾ Μ‾ΜΑΘΗΤΗΣ ΤΗΡΟΥ ΧΕ ΕΤΙ †ΝΑϬΩΛΠ' ᵀᴵᴴ
ΝΗΤ‾Ν ΕΒΟΛ Ν‾ΜΜ‾ΝΤΝΟϬ ΤΗΡΟΥ Ν‾ΤΕ ΠΧΙΣΕ ΧΙΝ ΠΣΑ-
ΝϨΟΥΝ Ν‾ΤΕ ΝΙΣΑΝϨΟΥΝ ϨΕΩΣ ϢΑ ΠΣΑΝΒΟΛ Ν‾ΤΕ ΝΙ-
ΣΑ‾ΝΒΟΛ ΧΕ ΕΤΕΤΝΕϢΩΠΕ ΕΤΕΤ‾ΝΧΗΚ ΕΒΟΛ Ϩ‾Ν ΣΟ-
10 ΟΥΝ ΝΙΜ' ΑΥΩ ΜΝ‾ ΠΛΗΡΩΜΑ ΝΙΜ' ΜΝ‾ ΠΧΙΣΕ Ν‾ΝΧΙΣΕ·
ΜΝ‾ Ν‾ΒΑΘΟΣ Ν‾ΝΒΑΘΟΣ· ΑΣΟΥΩϨ ΟΝ ΕΤΟΟΤ‾Σ Ν‾ϬΙ ΜΑΡΙΑ
ΠΕΧΑΣ Μ‾ΠΣΩΤΗΡ ΧΕ ΠΑΧΟΕΙΣ ΕΙΣϨΗΤΕ ΑΝΕΙΜΕ Ϩ‾Ν
ΟΥΠΑΡΡΗΣΙΑ Ϩ‾Ν ΟΥΩΡΧ‾ ΦΑΝΕΡΩΣ ΧΕ ΑΚΕΙΝΕ Ν‾Ν-
ϢΟϢΤ Ν‾ΜΜΥΣΤΗΡΙΟΝ Ν‾ΤΜ‾Ν‾ΤΕΡΟ Μ‾ΠΟΥΟΕΙΝ ΝΑϊ Ε-
15 ϢΑΥΚΩ ΕΒΟΛ Ν‾ΝΝΟΒΕ Ν‾ΝΕΨΥΧΟΟΥΕ Ν‾ΣΕΚΑΘΑΡΙΖΕ
Μ‾ΜΟΟΥ Ν‾ΣΕΛΑΥ Ν‾ϨΙΛΙΚΡΙΝΕΣ Ν‾ΟΥΟΕΙΝ Ν‾ΣΕΧΙΤΟΥ
ΕΠΟΥΟΕΙΝ:　⳥—⳥—⳥—

　　　Ϳ　⳥—⳥—⳥⳥⳥—⳥⳥⳥—⳥⳥⳥—⳥⳥
　　　—⳥—⳥—⳥—⳥—⳥—⳥—⳥—⳥
20　　⳥　ΟΥΜΕΡΟΣ Ν‾ΝΤΕΥΧΟΣ Μ‾ΠΣΩΤΗΡ　⳥
　　　—⳥—⳥—⳥—,⳥—⳥—⳥—⳥—⳥

4　MS Ν‾ΝΕϊΜ‾Ν‾ΤΝΟϬ ; read ΕΤΒΕ ΝΕϊΜ‾Ν‾ΤΝΟϬ.

17　the subtitle is written in the first column of page ᵀᴵᴴ ; 4 lines remain at the foot of this column ; the text begins again in column 2.

and find all the *mysteries* of the light, and enter in and *inherit* the Kingdom of the Light."

Maria answered and said: "*Blessed* are we *above* all men for these great things which thou hast revealed to us."

The *Saviour* answered, he said to Maria and all the *disciples*: "I will *yet* reveal to you all the great things of the height, from the innermost of the inner *as far as* the outermost of the outer, so that you may be completed in all knowledge and all *pleromas*, and in the height of the heights, and the *depth* of the *depths*."

Maria continued and said to the *Saviour*: "My Lord, behold we have known *openly* with certainty and *clarity* that thou hast brought the keys of the *mysteries* of the Kingdom of the Light, which forgive sins to the *souls* and *purify* them, and make them to be *pure* light and take them to the light."

A *Part* of the *Books* of the *Saviour*.

ⲀⲤϢⲰⲠⲈ ϬⲈ ⲚⲦⲈⲢⲞⲨⲤ-ⲢⲞⲨ ⲘⲠⲈⲚⲬⲞⲈⲒⲤ ⲒⲤ Ⲁ4ⲦⲰⲞⲨⲚ [ⲦⲎ ᵇ]
ⲈⲂⲞⲖ ⲌⲚ ⲚⲈⲦⲘⲞⲞⲨⲦ ⲘⲠⲈ4ⲘⲈⲌϢⲞⲘⲚⲦ Ⲛ2ⲞⲞⲨ· ⲀⲨⲤⲰ-
ⲞⲨ2 ⲈⲢⲞ4 Ⲛ6Ⲓ ⲚⲈ4ⲘⲀⲐⲎⲦⲎⲤ ⲀⲨⲦⲰⲂⲌ ⲘⲘⲞ4 ⲈⲨⲬⲰ
ⲘⲘⲞⲤ· ⲬⲈ ⲠⲈⲚⲬⲞⲈⲒⲤ ϢⲚ2ⲦⲎⲔ 2ⲀⲢⲞⲚ ⲬⲈ ⲀⲚⲔⲀ-ⲈⲒⲰⲦ·
5 2Ⲓ ⲘⲀⲀⲨ ⲚⲤⲰⲚ ⲘⲚ ⲠⲔⲞⲤⲘⲞⲤ ⲦⲎⲢ4 ⲀⲚⲞⲨⲀ2Ⲛ ⲚⲤⲰⲔ:
ⲦⲞⲦⲈ ⲒⲤ Ⲁ4Ⲁ2ⲈⲢⲀⲦ4 ⲘⲚ ⲚⲈ4ⲘⲀⲐⲎⲦⲎⲤ 2ⲒⲬⲚ ⲠⲘⲞⲞⲨ
ⲘⲠⲰⲔⲈⲀⲚⲞⲤ Ⲁ4ⲈⲠⲒⲔⲀⲖⲈⲒ ⲚⲦⲈⲒⲠⲢⲞⲤⲈⲨⲬⲎ Ⲉ4ⲬⲰ ⲘⲘⲞⲤ
ⲬⲈ ⲤⲰⲦⲘ ⲈⲢⲞⲒ ⲠⲀⲈⲒⲰⲦ' ⲠⲈⲒⲰⲦ ⲘⲘⲚⲦⲈⲒⲰⲦ ⲚⲒⲘ ⲠⲀ-
ⲠⲈⲢⲀⲚⲦⲞⲚ ⲘⲠⲞⲨⲞⲈⲒⲚ· ⲀⲈⲒⲞⲨⲰ· ⲒⲀⲰ· ⲀⲰⲒ· ⲰⲒⲀ·
10 ⲮⲒⲚⲰⲐⲈⲢ· ⲐⲈⲢⲚⲰⲮ· ⲚⲰⲮⲒⲦⲈⲢ· ⲌⲀⲄⲞⲨⲢⲎ· ⲠⲀⲄⲞⲨⲢⲎ·
ⲚⲈⲐⲘⲞⲘⲀϢⲐ· ⲚⲈⲮⲒⲞⲘⲀϢⲐ· ⲘⲀⲢⲀⲬⲀⲬⲐⲀ· ⲐⲰⲂⲀⲢⲢⲀ-
ⲂⲀⲨ· ⲐⲀⲢⲚⲀⲬⲀⲬⲀⲚ· ⲌⲞⲢⲞⲔⲞⲐⲞⲢⲀ· ⲒⲈⲞⲨ· ⲤⲀⲂⲀⲰⲐ:
ⲚⲀⲒ ⲀⲈ Ⲉ4ⲬⲰ ⲘⲘⲞⲞⲨ Ⲛ6Ⲓ ⲒⲤ ⲚⲈⲢⲈ ⲐⲰⲘⲀⲤ ⲘⲚ ⲀⲚ-
ⲀⲢⲈⲀⲤ ⲘⲚ ⲒⲀⲔⲰⲂⲞⲤ ⲘⲚ ⲤⲒⲘⲰⲚ ⲠⲔⲀⲚⲀⲚⲒⲦⲎⲤ ⲚⲈⲨ2Ⲓ
15 ⲠⲈⲘⲚⲦ ⲠⲈ ⲈⲢⲈ 2ⲢⲀⲨ ⲔⲎⲦ' ⲈⲠⲈⲒⲂⲦ ̈ⲪⲒⲖⲒⲠⲠⲞⲤ ⲀⲈ ⲘⲚ ⲦⲒⲐ
ⲂⲀⲢⲐⲞⲖⲞⲘⲀⲒⲞⲤ ⲚⲈⲨ2Ⲓ ⲠⲢⲎⲤ ⲠⲈ ⲈⲨⲔⲎⲦ Ⲉ2ⲎⲦ· ⲠⲔⲈ-
ϢⲰⲬⲠ ⲀⲈ ⲘⲘⲀⲐⲎⲦⲎⲤ ⲘⲚ ⲘⲘⲀⲐⲎⲦⲢⲒⲀ ⲚⲤ2ⲒⲘⲈ ⲚⲈⲨ-
Ⲁ2ⲈⲢⲀⲦⲞⲨ ⲠⲈ 2ⲒⲠⲀ2ⲞⲨ ⲚⲒⲤ· ⲒⲤ ⲀⲈ ⲚⲈ4Ⲁ2ⲈⲢⲀⲦ4 ⲠⲈ
2ⲒⲬⲘ ⲠⲈⲐⲨⲤⲒⲀⲤⲦⲎⲢⲒⲞⲚ· ⲀⲨⲰ Ⲁ4ϢϢ ⲈⲂⲞⲖ Ⲛ6Ⲓ ⲒⲤ Ⲉ4-
20 ⲔⲰⲦⲈ ⲘⲘⲞ4 ⲈⲠⲈ4ⲦⲈⲨ-ⲖⲀⲔ2 ⲚⲦⲈ ⲠⲔⲞⲤⲘⲞⲤ ⲘⲚ ⲚⲈ4-
ⲘⲀⲐⲎⲦⲎⲤ ⲈⲨ6ⲞⲞⲖⲈ ⲦⲎⲢⲞⲨ Ⲛ2ⲈⲚ2ⲂⲞⲤ ⲚⲚⲈⲒⲀⲀⲨ· Ⲉ4-
ⲬⲰ ⲘⲘⲞⲤ ⲬⲈ ⲒⲀⲰ· ⲒⲀⲰ· ⲒⲀⲰ· ⲦⲀⲒ ⲦⲈ ⲦⲈ42ⲈⲢⲘⲎⲚⲈⲒⲀ·
ⲒⲰⲦⲀ· ⲬⲈ Ⲁ ⲠⲦⲎⲢ4 ⲈⲒ' ⲈⲂⲞⲖ· ⲀⲖⲪⲀ ⲬⲈ ⲤⲈⲚⲀⲔⲦⲞⲞⲨ
Ⲉ2ⲞⲨⲚ· Ⲱ'Ⲱ' ⲬⲈ 4ⲚⲀϢⲰⲠⲈ Ⲛ6Ⲓ ⲠⲬⲰⲔ ⲚⲚⲬⲰⲔ ⲦⲎ-
25 ⲢⲞⲨ· ⲚⲀⲒ ⲀⲈ ⲚⲦⲈⲢⲈ4ⲬⲞⲞⲨ Ⲛ6Ⲓ ⲒⲤ ⲠⲈⲬⲀ4· ⲬⲈ ⲒⲀⲪⲐⲀ·

---

22 ïⲁⲱ inserted above.

(BOOK IV)

136. Now it happened when they *crucified* our Lord Jesus, he rose from the dead on the third day *. His *disciples* gathered to him, they entreated him, saying: "Our Lord, have compassion on us, for we have left father and mother and the whole *world* behind us, and we have followed thee ▫."

Then Jesus stood with his *disciples* beside the water of the *ocean* and *pronounced* this *prayer*, saying: "Hear me, my Father, thou father of all fatherhoods, thou *infinite* Light: αεηιουω. ϊαω. αωϊ. ωϊα. ψινωθερ. θερνωψ. νωψιτερ. ζαγουρη. παγουρη. νεθμομαωθ. νεψιομαωθ. μαραχαχθα. θωβαρραβαυ. θαρναχαχαν. ζοροχοθορα. ϊεου. σαβαωθ."

As Jesus was saying these things *however*, Thomas, Andrew, James and Simon the Canaanite ° were in the west, with their faces turned to the east. *But* Philip and Bartholomew were in the south, (with their faces) turned to the north. The rest of the *disciples* and women *disciples however* were standing behind Jesus. *But* Jesus was standing before the *altar*.

And Jesus cried out as he turned to the four corners of the *world* with his *disciples*, and they were all robed in linen garments, and he said: "ϊαω. ϊαω. ϊαω. This is its *interpretation*: iota, because the All came forth; alpha, because it will return again; omega, because the completion of all completions will happen [1].

When *however* Jesus had said these things, he said: "ϊαφθα. | ϊαφθα. μουναηρ. μουναηρ. ερμανουηρ. ερμα-

---

* cf. 1 Cor. 15.4
▫ cf. Mt. 10.37; 19.27, 29; Mk. 10.28, 29; Lk. 14.26; 18.28, 29
° cf. Mt. 10.4; Mk. 3.18

---

[1] (22) ιαω; see J 124; Burkitt (Bibl. 13b).

ⲓ̈ⲁⲫⲑⲁ· ⲙⲟⲩⲛⲁⲏⲣ· ⲙⲟⲩⲛⲁⲏⲣ· ⲉⲣⲙⲁⲛⲟⲩⲏⲣ· ⲉⲣⲙⲁⲛ-
ⲟⲩⲏⲣ· ⲉⲧⲉ ⲡⲁⲓ̈ ⲡⲉ ⲡⲉⲓⲱⲧ' ⲙ̅ⲙ̅ⲛ̅ⲧⲉⲓⲱⲧ' ⲛⲓⲙ ⲛ̅ⲧⲉ ⲛⲓ-
ⲁⲡⲉⲣⲁⲛⲧⲟⲛ· ⲉⲕⲉⲥⲱⲧ̅ⲙ̅ ⲉⲣⲟⲓ̈ ⲉⲧⲃⲉ ⲛⲁⲙⲁⲑⲏⲧⲏⲥ ⲉⲛⲧ-
ⲁⲓ̅ⲛ̅ⲧⲟⲩ ⲙ̅ⲡⲉⲕⲙ̅ⲧⲟ ⲉⲃⲟⲗ ϫⲉ ⲉⲩⲉⲡⲓⲥⲧⲉⲩⲉ ⲉϣⲁϫⲉ ⲛⲓⲙ
5 ⲛ̅ⲧⲉ ⲧⲉⲕⲁⲗⲏⲑⲓⲁ· ⲁⲩⲱ ⲛ̅ⲅⲉⲓⲣⲉ ⲛ̅ϩⲱⲃ ⲛⲓⲙ ⲉⲧ̅ⲛⲁϣⲱ ⲉ-
ϩⲣⲁⲓ̈ ⲟⲩⲃⲏⲕ ⲉⲧⲃⲏⲏⲧⲟⲩ· ϫⲉ ϯⲥⲟⲟⲩⲛ ⲙ̅ⲡⲣⲁⲛ ⲙ̅ⲡⲉⲓⲱⲧ'
ⲙ̅ⲡⲉⲑⲏⲥⲁⲩⲣⲟⲥ ⲙ̅ⲡⲟⲩⲟⲉⲓⲛ· ⲡⲁⲗⲓⲛ ⲟⲛ ⲁϥϣⲱ ⲉⲃⲟⲗ
ⲛ̅ϭⲓ ⲓ̅ⲥ̅ ⲉⲧⲉ ⲁⲃⲉⲣⲁⲛⲉⲛⲑⲱⲣ ⲡⲉ ⲉϥϫⲱ ⲙ̅ⲡⲣⲁⲛ ⲙ̅ⲡⲉⲓⲱⲧ'
ⲙ̅ⲡⲉⲑⲏⲥⲁⲩⲣⲟⲥ ⲙ̅ⲡⲟⲩⲟⲓⲛ· ⲁⲩⲱ ⲡⲉϫⲁϥ· ϫⲉ ⲙⲁⲣⲉ ⲙ̅-
10 ⲙⲩⲥⲧⲏⲣⲓⲟⲛ ⲧⲏⲣⲟⲩ ⲛ̅ⲛⲁⲣⲭⲱⲛ ⲙ̅ⲛ̅ ⲛⲉϩⲟⲩⲥⲓⲁ ⲙ̅ⲛ̅ ⲛⲁⲅⲅⲉⲗⲟⲥ ⲙ̅ⲛ̅ ⲛ̅ⲁⲣⲭⲁⲅⲅⲉⲗⲟⲥ ⲙ̅ⲛ̅ ϭⲟⲙ ⲛⲓⲙ ⲙ̅ⲛ̅ ϩⲱⲃ ⲛⲓⲙ
ⲛ̅ⲧⲉ ⲡⲁϩⲟⲣⲁⲧⲟⲥ ⲛ̅ⲛⲟⲩⲧⲉ ⲁⲅⲣⲁⲙⲙⲁⲭⲁⲙⲁⲣⲉⲓ· ⲙ̅ⲛ̅ ⲧⲃⲁⲣⲃⲏⲗⲱ ⲧⲉⲃⲇⲉⲗⲗⲁ· ⲙⲁⲣⲟⲩϩ̅ⲛⲧⲟⲩ ⲡⲥⲁ ⲟⲩⲥⲁ ⲛ̅ⲥⲉⲡⲟⲣ-
ϫⲟⲩ ⲉⲃⲟⲗ' ⲛ̅ⲟⲩⲛⲁⲙ· ⲛ̅ⲧⲉⲩⲛⲟⲩ ⲇⲉ ⲉⲧⲙ̅ⲙⲁⲩ ⲁ ⲙ̅ⲡⲏⲩⲉ
15 ⲧⲏⲣⲟⲩ ⲉⲓ' ⲉⲡⲉⲙ̅ⲛⲧ ⲙ̅ⲛ̅ ⲛ̅ⲁⲓⲱⲛ ⲧⲏⲣⲟⲩ ⲙ̅ⲛ̅ ⲧⲉⲥⲫⲉⲣⲁ
ⲙ̅ⲛ̅ ⲛⲉⲩⲁⲣⲭⲱⲛ ⲙ̅ⲛ̅ ⲛⲉⲩⲇⲩⲛⲁⲙⲓⲥ ⲧⲏⲣⲟⲩ ⲁⲩⲡⲱⲧ ⲧⲏⲣⲟⲩ ⲉⲡⲉⲙ̅ⲛⲧ ⲉϩⲃⲟⲩⲣ ⲙ̅ⲡⲁⲓⲥⲕⲟⲥ ⲙ̅ⲡⲣⲏ ⲙ̅ⲛ̅ ⲡⲁⲓⲥⲕⲟⲥ
ⲙ̅ⲡⲟⲟϩ· ⲛⲉⲣⲉ ⲡⲁⲓⲥⲕⲟⲥ ⲇⲉ ⲙ̅ⲡⲣⲏ ⲛⲉϥⲟ ⲛⲟⲩⲛⲟϭ ⲛ̅-
ⲁⲣⲁⲕⲱⲛ ⲉⲣⲉ ⲡⲉϥⲥⲁⲧ ⲛ̅ϩⲟⲩⲛ ⲛ̅ⲣⲱϥ ⲉϥⲁⲗⲉ ⲉ̅ⲥⲁϣϥⲉ [ⲧ̅ⲕ̅]
20 ⲛ̅ⲇⲩⲛⲁⲙⲓⲥ ⲛ̅ⲧⲉϩⲃⲟⲩⲣ· ⲉⲩⲥⲱⲕ ϩⲁⲣⲟϥ ⲛ̅ϭⲓ ϥⲧⲟ ⲛ̅ⲇⲩ-
ⲛⲁⲙⲓⲥ ⲉⲩⲟ ⲙ̅ⲡⲉⲓⲛⲉ ⲛ̅ϩⲉⲛϩⲧⲟ ⲛ̅ⲟⲩⲱⲃ̅ϣ· ⲛⲉⲣⲉ ⲧⲃⲁⲥⲓⲥ
ⲇⲉ ⲙ̅ⲡⲟⲟϩ ⲛⲉⲥⲟ ⲙ̅ⲡⲧⲩⲡⲟⲥ ⲛ̅ⲟⲩϫⲟⲓ̈ ⲉⲣⲉ ⲟⲩⲁⲣⲁⲕⲱⲛ
ⲛ̅ϩⲟⲟⲩⲧ ⲙ̅ⲛ̅ ⲟⲩⲁⲣⲁⲕⲱⲛ ⲛ̅ⲥϩⲓⲙⲉ ⲉⲩⲟ ⲛ̅ϩⲓⲉ ⲉⲣⲟϥ· ⲉⲣⲉ
ⲙⲁⲥⲉ ⲥⲛⲁⲩ ⲛ̅ⲟⲩⲱⲃ̅ϣ ⲥⲱⲕ ϩⲁⲣⲟϥ· ⲉⲣⲉ ⲡⲉⲓⲛⲉ ⲛ̅ⲟⲩ-

8　MS ⲁⲃⲉⲣⲁⲛⲉⲛⲑⲱⲣ; ⲣ expunged. MS originally ⲙ̅ⲙⲟⲥ ⲡⲣⲁⲛ; ⲙⲟⲥ
expunged.
12　MS originally ⲁⲭⲣⲁ . . .; ⲭ expunged and ⲅ written above.
21　MS originally ⲉⲣⲉ; ⲛ inserted above.

νουηρ. which is: O Father of all fatherhoods of the *infinite ones*, hear me for the sake of my *disciples* whom I have brought into thy presence that they may *believe* every word of thy *truth*. And do thou perform everything about which I shall cry out to thee, because I know the name of the Father of the *Treasury* of the Light."

Then Jesus, who is Aberamentho [1], cried out *again*, saying the name of the Father of the *Treasury* of the Light, and he said : "May all the *mysteries* of the *archons* and the *powers* (exousiai) and the *angels* and the *archangels*, and all powers and all things of the *Invisible* God Agrammachamarei [2] and the Barbelo, the *leech*, approach one side and divide themselves to the right."

In that moment *however* all the heavens came to the west, with all the *aeons* and the *sphere* and their *archons* and all their *powers*. They all ran to the west to the left [3] of the *disc* of the sun and the *disc* of the moon. *But* the *disc* of the sun was a great *dragon* whose tail was in its mouth, and it carried seven *powers* [4] of the left. And four *powers* having the likeness of white horses drew it. *But* the *base* of the moon was of the *type* of a boat, and a male *dragon* and a female *dragon* steered it, while two white bulls drew it. And the likeness of a | child was at the back of

---

[1] (8) Aberamentho; see Burkitt (Bibl. 13b).
[2] (12) Agrammachamarei; see Kropp (Bibl. 26) III, p. 123; Scholem (Bibl. 50).
[3] (15) ran to the west to the left; see J 104.
[4] (19) carried seven powers; lit. mounted seven powers.

ϢΗΡΕ ϢΗΜ' ϨΙΠΑϨΟΥ ⲘΠΟΟϨ ΕϤϨⲢⲘⲘΕ ⲚⲚΕⲆⲢΑⲔⲰⲚ
ΕΥΤⲰⲢⲠ ⲘΠΟΥΟΕΙⲚ ⲚⲚΑⲢⲬⲰⲚ ⲚΤΟΟΤΟΥ ΕⲢΕ ΟΥϨΟ
ⲚΑΜΟΥ ⲚϨΙΘΗ ⲘΜΟϤ· ΑΥⲰ ΠⲔΟⲤΜΟⲤ ΤΗⲢϤ ⲘⲚ ⲚΤΟΥ-
ΕΙΗ ⲘⲚ ⲚΕΘΑⲖΑⲤⲤΑ ΑΥΠⲰΤ ΤΗⲢΟΥ ΕΠΕⲘⲚΤ ΕΤΕϨⲂΟΥⲢ·
5 ΑΥⲰ Ⲓ̅Ⲥ̅ ⲘⲚ ⲚΕϤΜΑΘΗΤΗⲤ ΑΥϬⲰ ⲚΤΜΗΤΕ ⲚΟΥΤΟΠΟⲤ
ⲚΑΕⲢΙⲚΟⲚ ϨⲚ ⲚΕϨΙΟΟΥΕ ⲚΤΕϨΙΗ ⲚΤΜΗΤΕ ΤΑⲒ ΕΤϨΑ-
ΠΕⲤⲚΤ ⲚΤΕⲤⳜΕⲢΑ· ΑΥⲰ ΑΥΕⲒ' ΕΤΕϨΟΥⲒ̈ΤΕ ⲚΤΑⳄΙⲤ
ⲚΤΕϨΙΗ ΕΤϨⲚ ΤΜΗΤΕ· Ⲓ̅Ⲥ̅ ⲆΕ ΑϤϨΕⲢΑΤϤ ϨⲚ ΠΑΗⲢ ⲘΠΕⲤ-
ΤΟΠΟⲤ ⲘⲚ ⲚΕϤΜΑΘΗΤΗⲤ· ΠΕⲬΕ ⲘⲘΑΘΗΤΗⲤ ⲚⲒ̅Ⲥ̅ ⲚΑϤ
10 ⲬΕ ΟΥ ΠΕ ΠΕⲒ̈ΤΟΠΟⲤ ΕΤⲚⲚϨΗΤϤ· ΠΕⲬΕ Ⲓ̅Ⲥ̅ ⲬΕ ⲚΑⲒ̈ ⲚΕ   [Ⲧ̅Ⲕ̅ᵇ]
ⲚΤΟΠΟⲤ ⲚΤΕϨΙΗ ⲚΤΜΗΤΕ· ΑⲤϢⲰΠΕ ΓΑⲢ ⲚΤΕⲢΟΥΑΤΑⲔ-
ΤΙ ⲚϬΙ ⲚΑⲢⲬⲰⲚ ⲘΠΑⲆΑΜΑⲤ ΑΥΜΟΥⲚ ΕⲂΟⲖ' ΕΥⲢϨⲰⲂ
ΕΤⲤΥⲚΟΥⲤΙΑ ΕΥⲬΠΕ-ΑⲢⲬⲰⲚ ϨΙ ΑⲢⲬΑΓΓΕⲖΟⲤ ϨΙ ΑΓΓΕ-
ⲖΟⲤ ϨΙ ⲖΕΙΤΟΥⲢΓΟⲤ ϨΙ ⲆΕⲔΑⲚΟⲤ. ΑϤΕⲒ' ΕⲂΟⲖ Ϩ̅Ⲛ̅ ΟΥⲚΑΜ
15 ⲚϬΙ ΙΕΟΥ ΠΕΙⲰΤ ⲘΠΑΕΙⲰΤ'· ΑϤΜΟΥⲢ ⲘΜΟΟΥ ϨⲚ ΟΥ-
ϨΙΜΑⲢΜΕⲚΗ ⲚⲤⳜΑΙⲢΑ· ΟΥⲚ-ⲘⲚΤⲤⲚΟΟΥⲤ ΓΑⲢ ⲚΑΙⲰⲚ
ϢΟΟΠ ΕⲢΕ ⲤΑⲂΑⲰΘ ΠΑⲆΑΜΑⲤ ΑⲢⲬΙ ΕⳄⲚ ⲤΟΟΥ ΑΥⲰ
ΕⲢΕ Ⲓ̈ΑⲂⲢΑⲰΘ' ΠΕϤⲤΟⲚ ΑⲢⲬΙ ΕⳄⲚ ⲔΕⲤΟΟΥ· ΤΟΤΕ ϬΕ
Ⲓ̈ΑⲂⲢΑⲰΘ' ΑϤΠΙⲤΤΕΥΕ ΕⲘΜΥⲤΤΗⲢΙΟⲚ ⲘΠΟΥΟⲒ̈Ⲛ ⲘⲚ ⲚΕϤ-
20 ΑⲢⲬⲰⲚ· ΑΥⲰ ΑϤⲢϨⲰⲂ ϨⲚ ⲘⲘΥⲤΤΗⲢΙΟⲚ ⲘΠΟΥΟΕΙⲚ ΑϤ-
ⲔⲰ ⲚⲤⲰϤ ⲘΠΜΥⲤΤΗⲢΙΟⲚ ⲚΤⲤΥⲚΟΥⲤΙΑ· ⲤΑⲂΑⲰΘ ⲆΕ
ⲚΤΟϤ ΠΑⲆΑΜΑⲤ ΑϤϬⲰ ΕϤⲢϨⲰⲂ ϨⲚ ΤⲤΥⲚΟΥⲤΙΑ ⲘⲚ ⲚΕϤ-
ΑⲢⲬⲰⲚ· ΑΥⲰ ⲚΤΕⲢΕϤⲚΑΥ ⲚϬΙ ΙΕΟΥ ΠΕΙⲰΤ ⲘΠΑΕΙⲰΤ
ⲬΕ ΑϤΠΙⲤΤΕΥΕ ⲚϬΙ Ⲓ̈ΑⲂⲢΑⲰΘ' ΑϤϤΙΤϤ ⲘⲚ ⲚΑⲢⲬⲰⲚ ΤΗ-
25 ⲢΟΥ ΕⲚΤΑΥΠⲒⲤΤΕΥΕ ⲚⲘΜΑϤ· ΑϤϢⲰΠ ΕⲢΟϤ ϨⲚ ΤΕ-   Ⲧ̅Ⲕ̅Α̅
ⲤⳜΑΙⲢΑ ΑϤⲬΙΤϤ ΕΥΑΗⲢ ΕϤⲤΟΤϤ ⲘΠΕⲘΤΟ ΕⲂΟⲖ Ⲙ-

---

8 ⲚΤΕϨΙΗ added in margin.

the moon, and guided the *dragons* as they stole the light
of the *archons* from them, while a cat-face was in front
of it [1]. And the whole *world* and the mountains and the
seas all fled to the left to the west. And Jesus with his
disciples remained in the Midst in an *airy place* on the
paths of the way of the Midst which is below the *sphere*.
And they came to the first *rank* of the way of the Midst.
But Jesus stood in the *air* of its (the way of the Midst) *place*
with his *disciples*.

The disciples of Jesus said to him : "What is this *place*
in which we are?" Jesus said : "These are the places of the
way of the Midst. *For* it happened, when the *archons* of
the Adamas *rebelled*, and they continued to be concerned
with *sexual intercourse*, begetting *archons* and *archangels*
and *angels* and *ministers* and *decans*, then Jeu, the Father
of my Father, came from the right. He bound them in
a *Heimarmene-sphere*. *For* there were twelve *aeons*; Sabaoth,
the Adamas, *ruled* over six, and Jabraoth, his brother, *ruled*
over the other six. Now *then* Jabraoth *believed* in the *mys-*
teries of the light with his *archons*. And he practised the
mysteries of the light and he abandoned the *mystery* of *sexual*
intercourse. But Sabaoth, the Adamas, with his *archons*,
continued to practise *sexual intercourse*. And when Jeu, the
Father of my Father, saw that Jabraoth *believed*, he carried
him with all the *archons* which had *believed* with him, he
received him to himself in the *sphere*, he took him to a
purified *air* in the presence of | the light of the sun, between

---

[1] (1-3) at the back of the moon ... in front of it; Till : behind the moon ...;
Schmidt : in the stern ... in the bows.

ΠΟΥΟΕΙΝ Μ̄ΠΡΗ ΟΥΤΩΟΥ Ν̄Ν̄ΤΟΠΟС Ν̄ΝΑΤΜΕСΟС ΑΥΩ
ΟΥΤΩΟΥ Ν̄Ν̄ΤΟΠΟС Ν̄ΠΑ2ΟΡΑΤΟС Ν̄ΝΟΥΤΕ · ΑЧΚΑΑЧ
Μ̄ΜΑΥ Μ̄Ν̄ ΝΑΡΧΩΝ ΕΝΤΑΥΠΙСΤΕΥΕ ΕΡΟЧ · ΑΥΩ ΑЧ&#X1;Ι
Ν̄СΑΒΑΩΘ ΠΑΔΑΜΑС Μ̄Ν̄ ΝΕЧΑΡΧΩΝ ΝΑΪ ΕΤΕ Μ̄ΠΟΥΡ̄-
5 2ΩΒ 2Ν̄ Μ̄ΜΥСΤΗΡΙΟΝ Μ̄ΠΟΥΟΕΙΝ ΑΛΛΑ ΕΑΥΜΟΥΝ ΕΒΟΛ
ΕΥΡ̄2ΩΒ 2Ν̄ Μ̄ΜΥСΤΗΡΙΟΝ Ν̄ΤСΥΝΟΥСΙΑ ΑЧΜΟΡΟΥ Ε-
2ΟΥΝ ΕΤΕСΦΑΙΡΑ · ΑЧΜΟΥΡ Μ̄ΜΝ̄ΤΩΜΗΝ Ν̄ΩΕ Ν̄ΑΡΧΩΝ
2Μ̄ ΠΑΙΩΝ ΠΑΙΩΝ · ΑЧΚΩ Ν̄ΩΜΤΩΕ СΕ 2ΙΧΩΟΥ · ΑЧΚΩ
Ν̄ΚΕ&#X2;ΟΥ Ν̄ΝΟ6 ΝΑΡΧΩΝ ΕΥΑΡΧΙ ΕΧ̄Ν̄ ΠΩΜΤΩΕ СΕ ·
10 ΑΥΩ ΕΧ̄Ν̄ ΝΑΡΧΩΝ ΤΗΡΟΥ ΕΤΜΗΡ · ΝΑΪ ΝΕΤΕΩΑΥ-
ΜΟΥΤΕ ΕΡΟΟΥ 2Μ̄ ΠΚΟСΜΟС ΤΗΡЧ Ν̄ΤΜΝ̄ΤΡΩΜΕ Ν̄ΝΕΪ-
ΡΑΝ · ΠΕ2ΟΥΕΙΤ᾽ ΕΩΑΥΜΟΥΤΕ ΕΡΟЧ ΧΕ ΚΡΟΝΟС ·
ΠΜΕ2СΝΑΥ ΧΕ ΑΡΗС · ΠΜΕ2ΩΟΜΝ̄Τ ΧΕ 2ΕΡΜΗС · ΠΜΕ2-
ЧΤΟΟΥ ΧΕ ΤΑΦΡΟΔΙΤΗ · ΠΜΕ2&#X2;ΟΥ᾽ ΧΕ ΠΖΕΥС ·   Τ̄Κ̄Α ᵇ
15 ΑЧΟΥΩ2 ΟΝ ΕΤΟΟΤЧ Ν̄6Ι ῙС̄ ΠΕΧΑЧ · ΧΕ СΩΤΜ ΟΝ
ΤΑΧΩ ΕΡΩΤΝ̄ Μ̄ΠΕΥΜΥСΤΗΡΙΟΝ · ΑСΩΩΠΕ 6Ε Ν̄ΤΕΡΕЧ-
ΜΟΡΟΥ 2Ι ΝΑΪ Ν̄6Ι ῙΕΟΥ ΑЧСΩΚ Ν̄ΟΥΔΥΝΑΜΙС ΕΒΟΛ
2Μ̄ ΠΝΟ6 Ν̄Α2ΟΡΑΤΟС ΑЧΜΟΡС 2Μ̄ ΠΑΪ ΕΤΕΩΑΥΜΟΥΤΕ
ΕΡΟЧ ΧΕ ΚΡΟΝΟС · ΑΥΩ ΟΝ ΑЧСΩΚ᾽ Ν̄ΚΕ6ΟΜ ΕΒΟΛ
20 2Ν̄ ῙΨ̄ΑΝΤΑ ΧΟΥΪΝ ΧΑΪΝ ΧΟΥΧΕΩΧ · ΕΟΥΑ ΠΕ 2Ι ΠΩΟ-
Μ̄Ν̄Τ Ν̄ΤΡΙΔΥΝΑΜΙС Ν̄ΝΟΥΤΕ · ΑЧΜΟΡС̄ 2Ν̄ ΑΡΗС · ΑΥΩ
ΑЧСΩΚ Ν̄ΟΥΔΥΝΑΜΙС ΕΒΟΛ 2Ν̄ ΧΑΪΝΧΩΩΧ · ΕΥΟΥΑ
ΟΝ ΠΕ 2Ι ΠΙΩΟΜΝ̄Τ Ν̄ΤΡΙΔΥΝΑΜΙС Ν̄ΝΟΥΤΕ ΑЧΜΟΡС̄
2Μ̄ ΦΕΡΜΗС · ΠΑΛΙΝ ΟΝ ΑЧСΩΚ᾽ Ν̄ΟΥΔΥΝΑΜΙС ΕΒΟΛ
25 2Ν̄ ΤΠΙСΤΙС ΤСΟΦΙΑ ΤΩΕΕΡΕ Ν̄ΤΒΑΡΒΗΛΟС ΑЧΜΟΥΡ Μ̄-
ΜΟС 2Ν̄ ΑΦΡΟΔΙΤΗ · ΑΥΩ ΟΝ ΑЧ&#X1;2ΤΗЧ ΧΕ СΕΡ̄ΧΡΙΑ

---

2   MS Ν̄ΠΑ2ΟΡΑΤΟС; read Μ̄ΠΑ2ΟΡΑΤΟС.
8   MS originally СΕΤΗ; ΤΗ expunged.

the *places* of those of the *Midst* and between the *places* of the *Invisible* God. He placed him there with the *archons* which had *believed* in him. And he carried Sabaoth, the Adamas, with his *archons* which did not practise the *mysteries* of the light *but* continued to practise the *mysteries* of *sexual intercourse*. He bound them within the *sphere*. He bound 1800 *archons* in every *aeon*. He placed 360 over them. He placed five other great *archons* to *rule* over the 360 and over all the *archons* which are bound, which are called in the whole *world* of mankind by these names. The first is called Cronos, the second Ares, the third Hermes, the fourth Aphrodite, the fifth Zeus."

137.   Jesus continued again and said : "Hear now that I tell you of their *mysteries*. Now it happened, when Jeu had bound them thus, he drew a *power* out of the great *invisible one* and bound it to that one which is called Cronos. And he drew another power out of ϊψανταχουνχαϊνχουχεωχ, which is one of the three *triple-powered* gods, and bound it to Ares. And he drew a *power* out of χαινχωωωχ [1], which is also one of the three *triple-powered* gods, and bound it to Hermes. Then *again* he drew a *power* out of the Pistis Sophia, the daughter of the Barbelo, and bound it to Aphrodite. And furthermore he noticed that they *needed* | a rudder in

---

[1]   (22) χαινχωωωχ = Bainchooch; see Kropp (Bibl. 26) III, p. 124; IMG-E p. 78 etc. (also 382.1).

ⲚⲞⲨϨⲒⲈ ⲈⲦⲢⲈϤⲢϨⲘⲘⲈ ⲘⲠⲔⲞⲤⲘⲞⲤ ⲘⲚ ⲚⲀⲒⲰⲚ ⲚⲦⲈⲤⲪⲈⲢⲀ
ⲬⲈ ⲚⲚⲈⲨⲦⲀⲔⲞϤ ϨⲚ ⲦⲈⲨⲠⲞⲚⲎⲢⲒⲀ· ⲀϤⲂⲰⲔ' ⲈϨⲢⲀⲒ ⲈⲦⲘⲈ-
ⲤⲞⲤ ⲀϤⲤⲰⲔ ⲚⲞⲨⲆⲨⲚⲀⲘⲒⲤ ⲈⲂⲞⲖ ϨⲘ·· ⲠⲔⲞⲨⲒ ⲚⲤⲀⲂⲀⲰⲐ [ⲦⲔⲂ]
ⲠⲀⲄⲀⲐⲞⲤ ⲠⲀⲦⲘⲈⲤⲞⲤ ⲀϤⲘⲞⲢⲤ ϨⲚ ⲌⲈⲨⲤ ⲈⲂⲞⲖ ⲬⲈ ⲞⲨ-
5 ⲀⲄⲀⲐⲞⲤ ⲠⲈ· ⲈⲦⲢⲈϤⲢϨⲘⲘⲈ ⲘⲘⲞⲞⲨ ϨⲚ ⲦⲈϤⲘⲚⲦⲀⲄⲀⲐⲞⲤ·
ⲀⲨⲰ ⲀϤⲔⲰ ⲚⲦϬⲒⲚⲔⲰⲦⲈ ⲚⲦⲈϤⲦⲀⳜⲒⲤ ϨⲒ ⲚⲀⲒ ⲈⲦⲢⲈϤⲢ-ⲘⲚⲦ-
ϢⲞⲘⲦⲈ ⲚⲈⲂⲞⲦ ϨⲘ ⲠⲀⲒⲰⲚ ⲠⲀⲒⲰⲚ ⲈϤⲤⲦⲎⲢⲒⳜⲈ ⲬⲈⲔⲀⲀⲤ
ⲀⲢⲬⲰⲚ ⲚⲒⲘ' ⲈⲦϤⲚⲎⲨ ⲈⲬⲰⲞⲨ ⲈϤⲈⲂⲰⲖ ⲈⲂⲞⲖ ⲚⲦⲔⲀⲔⲒⲀ
ⲚⲦⲈⲨⲠⲞⲚⲎⲢⲒⲀ· ⲀⲨⲰ ⲀϤϮ ⲚⲀϤ ⲚⲀⲒⲰⲚ ⲤⲚⲀⲨ ⲘⲘⲀⲚ-
10 ϢⲰⲠⲈ ⲈⲨⲘⲠⲈⲘⲦⲞ ⲈⲂⲞⲖ ⲚⲚⲀϤⲈⲢⲘⲎⲤ· ⲀⲒⲬⲰ ⲈⲢⲰⲦⲚ
ⲘⲠϢⲞⲢⲠ ⲚⲤⲞⲠ' ⲚⲚⲢⲀⲚ ⲘⲠⲈⲒϮⲞⲨ ⲚⲚⲞϬ ⲚⲀⲢⲬⲰⲚ ⲚⲀⲒ
ⲈⲦⲈϢⲀⲢⲈ ⲚⲢⲰⲘⲈ ⲘⲠⲔⲞⲤⲘⲞⲤ ⲘⲞⲨⲦⲈ ⲈⲢⲞⲞⲨ ⲚϨⲎⲦⲞⲨ·
ⲤⲰⲦⲘ ⲞⲚ ⲦⲈⲚⲞⲨ ⲦⲀⲬⲰ ⲈⲢⲰⲦⲚ ⲚⲚⲈⲨⲔⲈⲢⲀⲚ ⲚⲀⲪⲐⲀⲢ-
ⲦⲞⲤ ⲈⲦⲈ ⲚⲀⲒ ⲚⲈ· ⲰⲢⲒⲘⲞⲨⲐ' ⲈⲢⲚ ⲔⲢⲞⲚⲞⲤ· ⲘⲞⲨⲚⲒⲬⲞⲨ-
15 ⲚⲀⲪⲰⲢ ⲈⲢⲚ ⲀⲢⲎⲤ· ⲦⲀⲢⲠⲈⲦⲀⲚⲞⲨⲪ ⲈⲢⲚ ⲪⲈⲢⲘⲎⲤ· ⲬⲰⲤⲒ
ⲈⲢⲚ ⲦⲀⲪⲢⲞⲆⲒⲦⲎ· ⲬⲰⲚⲂⲀⲖ ⲈⲢⲚ ⲌⲈⲨⲤ· ⲈⲦⲈ ⲚⲀⲒ ⲚⲈⲨ-
ⲢⲀⲚ ⲚⲀϤⲐⲀⲢⲦⲞⲤ:

ⲚⲦⲈⲢⲞⲨⲤⲰⲦⲘ ⲆⲈ ⲈⲚⲀⲒ ⲚϬⲒ ⲘⲘⲀⲐⲎⲦⲎⲤ ⲀⲨⲠⲀϨⲦⲞⲨ [ⲦⲔⲂᵇ]
ⲀⲨⲞⲨⲰϢⲦ ⲚⲒⲤ ⲠⲈⲬⲀⲨ· ⲬⲈ ⲚⲀⲒⲀⲦⲚ ⲀⲚⲞⲚ ⲠⲀⲢⲀ ⲢⲰⲘⲈ
20 ⲚⲒⲘ ⲬⲈ ⲀⲔϬⲰⲖⲠ ⲚⲀⲚ ⲈⲂⲞⲖ ⲚⲚⲈⲒⲚⲞϬ ⲚϢⲠⲎⲢⲈ· ⲀⲨ-
ⲞⲨⲰϨ ⲞⲚ ⲈⲦⲞⲞⲦⲞⲨ ⲀⲨⲦⲰⲂϨ ⲘⲘⲞϤ ⲈⲨⲬⲰ ⲘⲘⲞⲤ·
ⲬⲈ ⲦⲚⲦⲰⲂϨ ⲘⲘⲞⲔ ϬⲰⲖⲠ ⲚⲀⲚ ⲈⲂⲞⲖ ⲬⲈ ϨⲈⲚⲞⲨ ϨⲰⲰϤ
ⲚⲈ ⲚⲈⲒϨⲒⲞⲞⲨⲈ· ⲀⲨⲰ ⲀⲤϨⲚⲦⲤ ⲈϨⲞⲨⲚ ⲈⲢⲞϤ ⲚϬⲒ ⲘⲀⲢⲒ-
ϨⲀⲘ' ⲀⲤⲠⲀϨⲦⲤ ⲀⲤⲞⲨⲰϢⲦ ⲈⲚⲈϤⲞⲨⲈⲢⲎⲦⲈ ⲀⲨⲰ ⲀⲤϮⲠⲒ
25 ⲈⲚⲈϤϬⲒⲬ· ⲠⲈⲬⲀⲤ ⲬⲈ ϨⲀⲒⲞ ⲠⲀⲬⲞⲈⲒⲤ ϬⲰⲖⲠ ⲚⲀⲚ ⲈⲂⲞⲖ

---

14 MS originally ⲈⲚⲀⲒ; ⲦⲈ inserted above.
15 MS originally ⲈⲢⲘⲎⲤ; ⲫ inserted above.
21 MS originally ⲀⲨⲦⲰϨⲂ.

order to guide the *world* with the *aeons* of the *sphere* so
that it (the world) might not be destroyed by their wickedness. He went into the *Midst*, he drew a *power* out of the
Little Sabaoth, the *Good*, he of the *Midst*, he bound it to
Zeus because he is *good*, so that he should guide them
with his *goodness*. And he established the circuit of his
rank thus : that he should spend thirteen months in every
aeon, *firmly fixed*, so that he should release all the *archons*
over which he comes from the *evil* of their *wickedness*. And
he gave to him two *aeons* as dwellings in the neighbourhood
(lit. presence) of those of Hermes. I have told you for the
first time the names of these five great *archons*, by which
the men of the *world* call them. Hear again now that I tell
you their *imperishable* names [1] also, which are these : Orimuth corresponds to Cronos; Munichunaphor corresponds
to Ares; Tarpetanuph corresponds to Hermes; Chosi corresponds to Aphrodite; Chonbal corresponds to Zeus [2]; these
are their *imperishable* names."

138. *But* when the *disciples* heard these things, they
prostrated themselves, they worshipped Jesus and said :
"Blessed are we *beyond* all men, for thou hast revealed to
us these great marvels." They continued, they entreated
him, saying : "We beg thee, reveal to us, what are these
ways?" And Mariam approached him, she prostrated herself,
she worshipped at his feet and she kissed his hands. She
said : "Now my Lord, reveal to us | what is the *use* of the

---

[1] (13) on magical names, see note on 318.2.
[2] (14, 15) on planetary names and gnostic aeons, see Kropp (Bibl. 26) III,
pp. 26-39; Origen *c.Cels.* VI 22.

ϪЄ ΟΥ ΤЄ ΤЄΧΡΙΑ ⲚⲚЄ2ΙΟΟΥЄ ⲚΤΜΗΤЄ · ΑⲚⲤΩΤⲘ ΓΑΡ

ЄΡΟΚ ϪЄ ЄΥΚΗ 2ΙϪⲚ 2ЄⲚⲚΟϬ Ⲛ̄ΚΟⲖΑⲤΙⲤ · ΟΥ ϬЄ ΤЄ

ΘЄ ΠЄⲚϪΟЄΙⲤ ЄΤⲚⲚΑЄϪΙⲖ Ⲏ̄ ЄΤⲚⲚΑΡΒΟⲖ ЄΡΟΟΥ Ⲏ̄

ЄϢΑΥΑΜΑ2ΤЄ Ⲛ̄ⲚЄΨΥΧΟΟΥЄ ⲚΑϢ Ⲛ̄2Є · Ⲏ̄ ϢΑΥΡΟΥΗΡ

5 ⲚΟΥΟЄΙϢ 2Ⲛ ⲚЄΥΚΟⲖΑⲤΙⲤ · Ϣ̄Ⲛ2ΤΗΚ 2ΑΡΟⲚ ΠЄⲚϪΟЄΙⲤ

ΠЄⲚⲤΩΤΗΡ ϪЄ Ⲛ̄ⲚЄΥϤΙ Ⲛ̄ⲚЄⲚΨΥΧΟΟΥЄ Ⲛ̄ϬΙ Ⲙ̄ΠΑΡΑ-

ⲖΗΜΠΤΗⲤ Ⲛ̄ⲚЄΚΡΙⲤΙⲤ Ⲛ̄ⲚЄ2ΙΟΟΥЄ Ⲛ̄ΤΜΗΤЄ · ΑΥΩ ϪЄ

Ⲛ̄ⲚЄΥΚΡΙⲚЄ Ⲙ̄ΜΟⲚ 2Ⲛ ⲚЄΥΚΟⲖΑⲤΙⲤ ЄΘΟΟΥ · ΤΑΡⲚ̄ΚⲖΗ-   ‾ΤΚΓ

ΡΟⲚΟΜΙ 2ΩΩⲚ Ⲙ̄ΠΟΥΟЄΙⲚ Ⲙ̄ΠЄΚЄΙΩΤ' ϪЄ Ⲛ̄ⲚЄⲚϢΩΠЄ

10 ЄⲚΟ Ⲛ̄ЄΒΙΗⲚ ЄⲚϢΑΑΤ ⲤΑΒΟⲖ Ⲙ̄ΜΟΚ · ⲚΑΪ ϬЄ ЄⲤϪΩ

Ⲙ̄ΜΟΟΥ Ⲛ̄ϬΙ ΜΑΡΙ2ΑΜ ЄⲤΡΙΜЄ · ΑϤΟΥΩϢΒ Ⲛ̄ϬΙ Ι̅Ⲥ̅ 2Ⲛ

ΟΥⲚΟϬ Ⲙ̄ΜⲚ̄ΤϢΑⲚ2ΤΗϤ ΠЄϪΑϤ ⲚΑΥ · ϪЄ ΑⲖΗΘΩⲤ

ⲚΑⲤⲚΗΥ ΑΥΩ ⲚΑΜЄΡΑΤЄ ⲚΑΪ ЄⲚΤΑΥΚΑ-ЄΙΩΤ' 2Ι ΜΑΑΥ

Ⲛ̄ⲤΩΟΥ ЄΤΒЄ ΠΑΡΑⲚ · ϪЄ †ⲚΑ† ⲚΗΤⲚ̄ Ⲙ̄ΜΥⲤΤΗΡΙΟⲚ

15 ⲚΙⲘ' ⲘⲚ̄ ⲤΟΟΥⲚ ⲚΙⲘ · †ⲚΑ† ⲚΗΤⲚ̄ Ⲙ̄ΠΜΥⲤΤΗΡΙΟⲚ Ⲙ̄-

Π̄ⲘⲚ̄ΤⲤⲚΟΟΥⲤ Ⲛ̄ΑΙΩⲚ Ⲛ̄ⲚΑΡΧΩⲚ ⲘⲚ̄ ⲚЄΥⲤϤΡΑΓΙⲤ ⲘⲚ̄

ⲚЄΥΨΗϤΟⲤ ⲘⲚ̄ ΘЄ Ⲛ̄ЄΠΙΚΑⲖЄΙ Ⲙ̄ΜΟΟΥ ЄΒΩΚ ЄⲚЄΥ-

ΤΟΠΟⲤ · ΑΥΩ ΟⲚ †ⲚΑ† ⲚΗΤⲚ̄ Ⲙ̄ΠΜΥⲤΤΗΡΙΟⲚ Ⲙ̄ΠΜЄ2-

ⲘⲚ̄ΤϢΟΜΤЄ Ⲛ̄ΑΙΩⲚ ⲘⲚ̄ ΘЄ Ⲛ̄ЄΠΙΚΑⲖЄΙ ЄΒΩΚ' ЄⲚЄΥ-

20 ΤΟΠΟⲤ · ΑΥΩ †ⲚΑ† ⲚΗΤⲚ̄ ⲚⲚЄΥΨΗϤΟⲤ ⲘⲚ̄ ⲚЄΥⲤϤΡΑ-

ΓΙⲤ · ΑΥΩ †ⲚΑ† ⲚΗΤⲚ̄ Ⲙ̄ΠΜΥⲤΤΗΡΙΟⲚ Ⲙ̄ΠΒΑΠΤΙⲤΜΑ Ⲛ̄-

ⲚΑΤΜЄⲤΟⲤ ⲘⲚ̄ ΘЄ Ⲛ̄ЄΠΙΚΑⲖЄΙ ЄΒΩΚ ЄⲚЄΥΤΟΠΟⲤ ΑΥΩ

ⲚЄΥΨΗϤΟⲤ ⲘⲚ̄ ⲚЄΥⲤϤΡΑΓΙⲤ †ⲚΑΤΑΜΩΤⲚ ЄΡΟΟΥ ·   ‾ΤΚΓ‾ᵇ

ΑΥΩ †ⲚΑ† ⲚΗΤⲚ̄ Ⲙ̄ΠΒΑΠΤΙⲤΜΑ Ⲛ̄ⲚΑΤΟΥⲚΑⲘ' ΠЄⲚΤΟ-

25 ΠΟⲤ · ⲘⲚ̄ ⲚЄϤΨΗϤΟⲤ ⲘⲚ̄ ⲚЄϤⲤϤΡΑΓΙⲤ ΑΥΩ ⲘⲚ̄ ΘЄ Ⲛ̄ЄΠΙ-

ways of the *Midst*? *For* we have heard from thee that they
are set over great *punishments*. Now my Lord, how shall
we *escape or* be released from them, *or* how are the *souls*
seized, *or* how long do they spend in their punishments?
Have compassion on us, our Lord, our *Saviour*, lest the
paralemptai of the *judgments* of the ways of the Midst carry
off our *souls*, and lest they *judge* us in their evil *punishments*,
so that we ourselves may *inherit* the light of thy Father,
so that we shall not be wretched and separated from thee."

Now as Mariam said these things, weeping, Jesus answered
with great compassion. He said to them : "*Truly*, my brothers
and my beloved ones, who have left father and mother for
the sake of my name *, I will give to you all *mysteries* and
all knowledge. I will give to you the *mystery* of the twelve
aeons of the *archons*, and their *seals* and their *ciphers*, and
the manner of *calling upon* them in order to go to their
places. And furthermore I will give to you the *mystery* of
the thirteenth *aeon* and the manner of *calling upon* (them)
in order to go to their places; and I will give to you their
ciphers and their *seals*. And I will give to you the *mystery*
of the *baptism* of those of the *Midst*, and the manner of
calling upon (them) in order to go to their *places*; and I will
tell you their *ciphers* and their *seals*. And I will give to you
the baptism of those of the right, our *place*, with its *ciphers*
and its *seals*, and the manner of | *calling upon* (them) in

---

* cf. Mt. 19.29; Mk. 10.29

ⲔⲀⲖⲈⲒ ⲈⲂⲰⲔ ⲈⲘⲀⲨ· ⲀⲨⲰ ϮⲚⲀϮ ⲚⲎⲦⲚ ⲘⲠⲚⲟⳠ ⲘⲘⲨⲤⲦⲎ-
ⲢⲒⲞⲚ ⲚⲦⲈ ⲠⲈⲐⲎⲤⲀⲨⲢⲞⲤ ⲘⲠⲞⲨⲞⲈⲒⲚ· ⲀⲨⲰ ⲘⲚ ⲐⲈ Ⲛ-
ⲈⲠⲒⲔⲀⲖⲈⲒ ⲈⲂⲰⲔ' ⲈⲘⲀⲨ · ϮⲚⲀϮ ⲚⲎⲦⲚ ⲘⲘⲨⲤⲦⲎⲢⲒⲞⲚ ⲚⲒⲘ
ⲘⲚ ⲤⲞⲞⲨⲚ ⲚⲒⲘ ⲬⲈ ⲈⲨⲈⲘⲞⲨⲦⲈ ⲈⲢⲰⲦⲚ ⲬⲈ ⲚϢⲎⲢⲈ Ⲙ-
5 ⲠⲈⲠⲖⲎⲢⲰⲘⲀ ⲈⲦⲬⲎⲔ' ⲈⲂⲞⲖ ⲚⲤⲞⲞⲨⲚ ⲚⲒⲘ ⳌⲒ ⲘⲨⲤⲦⲎⲢⲒⲞⲚ
ⲚⲒⲘ· ⲚⲦⲈⲦⲚ ⳌⲈⲚⲘⲀⲔⲀⲢⲒⲞⲤ ⲚⲦⲰⲦⲚ ⲠⲀⲢⲀ ⲢⲰⲘⲈ ⲚⲒⲘ
ⲈⲦⳌⲒⲬⲘ ⲠⲔⲀⳌ ⲬⲈ Ⲁ ⲚϢⲎⲢⲈ ⲘⲠⲞⲨⲞⲈⲒⲚ ⲈⲒ' ⳌⲘ ⲠⲈⲦⲚ-
ⲞⲨⲞⲈⲒϢ·

Ⲁ϶ⲞⲨⲰⳌ ⲞⲚ ⲈⲦⲞⲞⲦϤ ⳌⲘ ⲠϢⲀⲬⲈ ⲚⳠⲒ ⲒⲤ ⲠⲈⲬⲀϤ·
10 ⲬⲈ ⲀⲤϢⲰⲠⲈ ⳠⲈ ⲘⲚⲚⲤⲀ ⲚⲀⲒ Ⲁ϶ⲈⲒ ⲚⳠⲒ ⲠⲈⲒⲰⲦ ⲘⲠⲀⲈⲒⲰⲦ
ⲈⲦⲈ ⲠⲀⲒ ⲠⲈ ⲒⲈⲞⲨ· Ⲁ϶϶Ⲓ ⲚⲔⲈϢⲞⲘⲚⲦ ⲚϢⲈ ⲘⲚ ⲤⲈ Ⲛ-
ⲀⲢⲬⲰⲚ ⳌⲚ ⲚⲀⲢⲬⲰⲚ ⲞⲚ ⲘⲠⲀⲖⲀⲘⲀⲤ· ⲚⲀⲒ ⲈⲦⲈ ⲘⲠⲞⲨ-
ⲠⲒⲤⲦⲈⲨⲈ ⲈⲠⲘⲨⲤⲦⲎⲢⲒⲞⲚ ⲘⲠⲞⲨⲞⲈⲒⲚ Ⲁ϶ⲘⲞⲢⲞⲨ ⳌⲚ ⲚⲈⲒ-
ⲦⲞⲠⲞⲤ ⲚⲀⲈⲢⲒⲞⲚ ⲈⲦⲚⳌⲎⲦⲞⲨ ⲦⲈⲚⲞⲨ ⳌⲀⲢⲞⲤ ⲚⲦⲈⲤⳘⲀⲒⲢⲀ· [ⲦⲔⲆ]
15 Ⲁ϶ⲔⲀⲐⲒⲤⲦⲀ ⲚⲔⲈϮⲞⲨ ⲚⲚⲟⳠ ⲚⲀⲢⲬⲰⲚ ⲈⲬⲰⲞⲨ ⲈⲦⲈ ⲚⲀⲒ
ⲚⲈ ⲚⲈⲦϢⲞⲞⲠ' ⳌⲒ ⲦⲈⳌⲒⲎ ⲚⲦⲘⲎⲦⲈ ⲠⲈⳌⲞⲨⲈⲒⲦ' ⲚⲀⲢⲬⲰⲚ
ⲚⲦⲈⳌⲒⲎ ⲚⲦⲘⲎⲦⲈ ⲈϢⲀⲨⲘⲞⲨⲦⲈ ⲈⲢⲞϤ ⲬⲈ ⲦⲠⲀⲢⲀⲠⲖⲎⳠ·
ⲞⲨⲀⲢⲬⲰⲚ ⲈϤⲞ ⲘⲘⲞⲢⳘⲎ ⲚⲤⳌⲒⲘⲈ ⲠⲈ· ⲈⲢⲈ ⲠⲈϤϤⲰ ⲤⲰϢⲈ
ⲈⲠⲈⲤⲎⲦ' ⲈⲬⲚ ⲚⲈϤⲞⲨⲈⲢⲎⲦⲈ· ⲈⲢⲈ ⲬⲞⲨⲦⲎ ⲚⲀⲢⲬⲒⲆⲀⲒ-
20 ⲘⲞⲚⲒⲞⲚ ⳌⲀⲢⲀⲦⲤ ⲚⲦⲈⲤⲈⳌⲞⲨⲤⲒⲀ ⲈⲨⲀⲢⲬⲒ ⲈⲬⲚ ⲔⲈⲘⲚⲎϢⲈ
ⲚⲆⲀⲒⲘⲞⲚⲒⲞⲚ· ⲀⲨⲰ ⲚⲈⲒⲆⲀⲒⲘⲞⲚⲒⲞⲚ ⲈⲦⲘⲘⲀⲨ ⲚⲦⲞⲞⲨ
ⲚⲈ ⲈϢⲀⲨⲂⲰⲔ' ⲈⳌⲞⲨⲚ ⲈⲚⲢⲰⲘⲈ ⲚⲤⲈⲦⲢⲈⲨⳠⲰⲚⲦ ⲚⲤⲈ-
ⲤⳌⲞⲨ ⲀⲨⲰ ⲚⲤⲈⲔⲀⲦⲀⲖⲀⲖⲒ· ⲀⲨⲰ ⲚⲦⲞⲞⲨ ⲚⲈ ⲈϢⲀⲨϤⲒ
ⲚⲚⲈⲨⲯⲨⲬⲞⲞⲨⲈ ⲚⲤⲦⲈⲢⲈⲤⲒⲘⲞⲚ ⲚⲤⲈⲬⲞⲞⲨ ⲈⲂⲞⲖ ⳌⲒⲦⲘ
25 ⲠⲈⲨⲔⲢⲰⲘ' ⲚⲔⲀⲔⲈ ⲘⲚ ⲚⲈⲨⲔⲞⲖⲀⲤⲒⲤ ⲘⲠⲞⲚⲎⲢⲞⲚ· ⲠⲈⲬⲀⲤ
ⲚⳠⲒ ⲘⲀⲢⲒⳌⲀⲘ' ⲬⲈ Ⲛ϶ⲚⲀⲈⲄⲔⲀⳠⲈⲒ ⲀⲚ ⲈⲒϢⲒⲚⲈ ⲘⲘⲞⲔ ⲘⲠⲢ-

---

16 ⲠⲈⳌⲞⲨⲈⲒⲦ ... ⲚⲦⲘⲎⲦⲈ inserted in margin above.

order to go there. And I will give to you the great *mystery* of the *Treasury* of the Light, and the manner of *calling upon* (them) in order to go there. I will give to you all *mysteries* and all knowledge, so that you may be called: 'Sons of the *pleroma*, complete in all knowledge and all *mysteries*'. You are *blessed beyond* all men upon the earth, for the Sons of the Light have come in your time."

139. Jesus continued again with the discourse, he said: "Now it happened after these things the Father of my Father, who is Jeu, came. He carried off another 360 *archons* among the *archons* of the Adamas which did not *believe* in the *mystery* of the light. He bound them in these *airy places* in which we are now, beneath the *sphere*. He *set* another five great *archons* over them, namely these which are upon the way of the Midst. The first *archon* of the way of the Midst is called Paraplex[1], an *archon* having a woman's *form*, whose hair reaches down to her feet. Under her *authority* are 25 *archdemons* which *rule* over another multitude of *demons*. And it is these *demons* which go into men and incite them to anger and cursing and *slander*, and it is they who carry off the *souls* by *theft*, and send them through their dark smoke[2] and their *wicked punishments*."

Mariam said: "I will not *tire* of asking thee. Be not |

---

[1]   (17) Paraplex; see J 140.
[2]   (25) smoke; Schmidt: smoke; lit. fire (the Coptic is translated as "smoke" in this and parallel passages when qualified by the adjective "dark").

ΝΟΥϬϹ ΕΡΟΪ ΕΪϢΙΝΕ ΝϹΑ ϨⲰΒ ΝΙΜ· ΠΕΧΕ ΙⲤ ΧΕ ϢΙΝΕ

ΝϹΑ * ΠΕΤΕϨΝΕ· ΠΕΧΑϹ Ν̄ϬΙ ΜΑΡΙϨΑΜ ΧΕ ΠΑΧΟΕΙϹ [ΤΚΑ]ᵇ

ΤΟΥΝΟΥΕΙΑΤ̄Ν ΕΒΟΛ' ΧΕ ΕϢΑΥϤΙ Ν̄ΝΕΨΥΧΟΟΥΕ Ν̄-

ϹΤΕΡΕϹΙΜΟΝ Ν̄ΑϢ Ν̄ϨΕ ΧΕ ΕΡΕ ΝΑϹΝΗΥ ϨⲰΟΥ ΝΟΪ

5 Μ̄ΜΟΟΥ· ΠΕΧΕ ΙⲤ ΕΤΕ ΑΒΕΡΑΝΕΝΘⲰ ΠΕ· ΧΕ ΕΠΕΙΔΗ

ΠΕΙⲰΤ Μ̄ΠΑΕΙⲰΤ· ΕΤΕ ΠΑΪ ΠΕ ῙΕΟΥ Ν̄ΤΟϤ ΠΕ ΠΕ-

ΠΡΟΝΟΗΤΟϹ Ν̄ΝΑΡΧⲰΝ ΤΗΡΟΥ ΜΝ̄ Ν̄ΝΟΥΤΕ ΜΝ̄ Ν̄-

ΔΥΝΑΜΙϹ ΝΑΪ ΕΝΤΑΥϢⲰΠΕ ϨΝ̄ ΘΥΛΗ Μ̄ΠΟΥΟΕΙΝ Μ̄ΠΕ-

ΘΗϹΑΥΡΟϹ· ΑΥⲰ ΖΟΡΟΚΟΘΟΡΑ ΜΕΛΧΙϹΕΔΕΚ· Ν̄ΤΟϤ

10 ϨⲰⲰϤ ΠΕ ΠΕΠΡΕϹΒΕΥΤΗϹ Ν̄ΝΟΥΟΕΙΝ ΤΗΡΟΥ ΕΤΟΥ-

ϹⲰΤϤ̄ Μ̄ΜΟΟΥ ϨΝ̄ ΝΑΡΧⲰΝ· ΕϤΧΙ Μ̄ΜΟΟΥ ΕϨΟΥΝ ΕΠΕ-

ΘΗϹΑΥΡΟϹ Μ̄ΠΟΥΟΕΙΝ· ΠΕΪϹΝΑΥ Μ̄ΜΑΤΕ ΝΕ Ν̄ΝΟϬ

Ν̄ΟΥΟΕΙΝ· ΕΤΕΥΤΑϨΙϹ ΤΕ ΤΑΪ ΕΤΡΕΥΕΙ' ΕΠΕϹΗΤ ΕΝ-

ΑΡΧⲰΝ Ν̄ϹΕϹⲰΤϤ̄ Ν̄ϨΗΤΟΥ· ΑΥⲰ Ν̄ΤΕ ΖΟΡΟΚΟΘΟΡΑ

15 ΜΕΛΧΙϹΕΔΕΚ Νϥϥ̄Ι Μ̄ΠϹⲰΤϤ̄ Ν̄ΝΟΥΟΕΙΝ ΕΝΤΑΥϹΟΤϤΟΥ

ϨΝ̄ ΝΑΡΧⲰΝ Νϥ̄ΧΙΤΟΥ ΕΠΕΘΗϹΑΥΡΟϹ Μ̄ΠΟΥΟΕΙΝ· ΕϹ- ΤΚϬ

ϢΑΝϢⲰΠΕ Ν̄ϬΙ ΤΕΨΗϤΟϹ ΑΥⲰ ΜΝ̄ ΠΕΟΥΟΕΙϢ Ν̄ΤΕΥ-

ΤΑϨΙϹ ΕΤΡΕΥΕΙ' ΕϨΡΑΪ ΕΝΑΡΧⲰΝ Ν̄ϹΕϨΕΧϨⲰΧΟΥ Ν̄-

ϹΕΘΛΙΒΕ Μ̄ΜΟΟΥ ΕΥϤΙ-ϹⲰΤϤ̄ ϨΝ̄ ΝΑΡΧⲰΝ· ϨΝ̄ ΤΕΥΝΟΥ

20 ΔΕ ΕΤΟΥΝΑΚΑΑΥ ΕΒΟΛ ϨΜ̄ ΠϨΟΧϨ̄Χ̄ Μ̄ΠΕΘΛΙΒΕ Ν̄ϹΕ-

ΑΝΑΧⲰΡΙ ΕϨΡΑΪ ΕΝΤΟΠΟϹ Μ̄ΠΕΘΗϹΑΥΡΟϹ Μ̄ΠΟΥΟΕΙΝ

ϢΑϹϢⲰΠΕ ΕΥϢΑΝΠⲰϨ ΕΝΤΟΠΟϹ Ν̄ΤΜΕϹΟϹ ϢΑΡΕ.

ΖΟΡΟΚΟΘΟΡΑ ΜΕΛΧΙϹΕΔΕΚ ϢΑϥϤ̄Ι Ν̄ΝΟΥΟΕΙΝ Νϥ̄ΧΙ-

---

2 Ν̄ϬΙ added in margin. MS originally Μ̄ΜΑΡΙϨΑΜ; Μ̄ expunged.

5 MS originally ΑΒΕΡΑΝΘⲰ; ΝΕ inserted above.

20 MS Μ̄ΠΕΘΛΙΒΕ; read ΜΝ̄ ΠΕΘΛΙΒΕ.

angry with me for questioning everything." Jesus said:
"Question what thou dost wish." Mariam said: "My Lord,
reveal to us in what manner the *souls* are carried off by
theft, so that my brothers also understand."

Jesus, who is Aberamentho, said: "*Since* the Father of
my Father, who is Jeu, is the *provider* of all the *archons*
and the gods and the *powers* which have come into existence
in the *matter* of the light of the *Treasury*, and Zorokothora [1] Melchisedek is the *messenger* of all the lights which
are purified in the *archons*, as he takes them into the
Treasury of the Light, then these two alone are the great
lights. Their *rank* is this, that they come down to the
archons and they (the lights) are purified in them. And
Zorokothora Melchisedek takes what is purified of the lights
which have been purified in the *archons*, and takes them
to the *Treasury* of the Light. When the *cipher* and the time
of their *rank* comes and causes them to come down to the
archons [2], they oppress them and *afflict* them, taking away
what is purified from the *archons*. *But* at the time that they
cease from [3] oppression and *affliction* [4], they *withdraw* to the
places of the *Treasury* of the Light. It happens when they
reach the *places* of the *Midst*, Zorokothora Melchisedek
bears the lights and takes | them into the *gate* of those of

---

[1]   (9) Zorokothora: see Kropp (Bibl. 26) III, p. 127; J 110; (cf. 353.12).
[2]   (16, 17) when the cipher ... archons; Schmidt takes this passage as con-
      tinuous with the preceding one.
[3]   (20) they cease from; Till: they set them free from.
[4]   (20) oppression and affliction; MS: oppression of affliction.

ⲦⲞⲨ ⲈϨⲢⲀⲒ ⲌⲚ ⲦⲠⲨⲖⲎ ⲚⲚⲀⲦⲘⲈⲤⲞⲤ ⲚϤϪⲒⲦⲞⲨ ⲈⲠⲈⲐⲎ-
ⲤⲀⲨⲢⲞⲤ ⲘⲠⲞⲨⲞⲈⲒⲚ · ⲀⲨⲰ ϢⲀⲢⲈ ⲒⲈⲞⲨ ϨⲰϢϤ ⲀⲚⲀⲬⲰⲢⲒ
ⲘⲘⲞϤ ⲈⲚⲦⲞⲠⲞⲤ ⲚⲚⲀⲦⲞⲨⲚⲀⲘ · ϢⲀ ⲠⲈⲞⲨⲞⲒϢ ⲞⲚ ⲚⲦⲈ-
ⲮⲎⲪⲞⲤ ⲈⲦⲢⲈⲨⲈⲒ' ⲈⲂⲞⲖ · ϢⲀⲢⲈ ⲚⲀⲢⲬⲰⲚ ϬⲈ ⲀⲦⲀⲕⲦⲒ
5 ϨⲒⲦⲚ ⲠϬⲰⲚⲦ ⲚⲦⲈⲨⲠⲞⲚⲎⲢⲒⲀ ⲌⲚ ⲦⲈⲨⲚⲞⲨ ⲈⲨⲘⲞⲞϢⲈ
ⲈϨⲢⲀⲒ ⲘⲚ ⲚⲞⲨⲞⲈⲒⲚ ⲈⲂⲞⲖ ϪⲈ ⲚⲤⲈϨⲀϨ ⲦⲎⲨ ⲀⲚ ⲘⲠⲚⲀⲨ
ⲈⲦⲘⲘⲀⲨ · ⲀⲨⲰ ϢⲀⲨϤⲒ ⲚⲚⲈⲮⲨⲬⲞⲞⲨⲈ ⲈⲦⲞⲨⲚⲀⲈϢ-
ⲦⲞⲢⲠⲞⲨ ⲚⲤⲦⲈⲢⲈⲤⲒⲘⲞⲚ ⲚⲤⲈⲀⲚϨⲀⲖⲒⲤⲔⲈ ⲘⲘⲞⲞⲨ ϨⲒⲦⲚ ⲦⲔⲤ[b]
ⲠⲈⲨⲔⲢⲰⲘ ⲚⲔⲀⲔⲈ ⲘⲚ ⲠⲈⲨⲔⲰϨⲦ ⲘⲠⲞⲚⲎⲢⲞⲚ · ⲦⲞⲦⲈ ϬⲈ
10 ⲚⲈⲮⲨⲬⲞⲞⲨⲈ ⲚⲢⲢⲈϤϬⲰⲚⲦ ⲘⲚ ⲚⲢⲈϤⲤⲀϨⲞⲨ ⲘⲚ ⲚⲢⲈϤ-
ⲔⲀⲦⲀⲖⲀⲖⲒ · ϢⲀⲤϤⲒⲦⲞⲨ ⲚϬⲒ ⲦⲈⲒⲈϪⲞⲨⲤⲒⲀ ϪⲈ ⲦⲠⲀⲢⲀⲠⲖⲎϪ
ⲘⲚ ⲚⲀⲀⲒⲘⲞⲚⲒⲞⲚ ⲈⲦϨⲀⲢⲀⲦⲤ ⲚⲤϪⲞⲞⲨ ⲈⲂⲞⲖ ϨⲒⲦⲘ ⲠⲈ-
ⲔⲢⲰⲘ ⲚⲔⲀⲔⲈ ⲀⲨⲰ ⲚⲤⲦⲀⲔⲞⲞⲨ ϨⲒⲦⲘ ⲠⲈⲤⲔⲰϨⲦ ⲘⲠⲞ-
ⲚⲎⲢⲞⲚ · ⲚⲤⲈⲀⲢⲬⲒ ⲚⲰϪⲚ ⲀⲨⲰ ⲈⲂⲰⲖ ⲈⲂⲞⲖ · ϢⲀⲨⲢ-ϢⲈ
15 ⲘⲀⲂϢⲞⲘⲦⲈ ⲚⲢⲞⲘⲠⲈ ⲘⲚ ⲮⲒⲤ ⲚⲈⲂⲞⲦ' ϨⲚ ⲚⲔⲞⲖⲀⲤⲒⲤ Ⲛ-
ⲚⲈⲤⲦⲞⲠⲞⲤ ⲈⲤⲂⲀⲤⲀⲚⲒⲌⲈ ⲘⲘⲞⲞⲨ ϨⲘ ⲠⲔⲰϨⲦ ⲚⲦⲈⲤⲠⲞ-
ⲚⲎⲢⲒⲀ · ϢⲀⲤϢⲰⲠⲈ ϬⲈ ⲘⲚⲚⲤⲀ ⲚⲈⲒⲞⲨⲞⲈⲒϢ ⲦⲎⲢⲞⲨ ⲈⲢ-
ϢⲀⲚ ⲦⲈⲤⲪⲀⲒⲢⲀ ⲔⲰⲦⲈ ⲚⲦⲈ ⲠⲔⲞⲨⲒ ⲚⲤⲀⲂⲀⲰⲐ' ⲠⲌⲈⲨⲤ·
ⲚϤⲈⲒ' ⲈⲠⲈϨⲞⲨⲈⲒⲦ' ⲚⲚⲀⲒⲰⲚ ⲚⲦⲈⲤⲪⲀⲒⲢⲀ ⲠⲀⲒ ⲈⲦⲈϢⲀⲨ-
20 ⲘⲞⲨⲦⲈ ⲈⲢⲞϤ ϨⲘ ⲠⲔⲞⲤⲘⲞⲤ ϪⲈ ⲠⲈⲔⲢⲒⲞⲤ ⲚⲦⲈ ⲦⲂⲞⲨ-
ⲂⲀⲤⲦⲒ ⲈⲦⲈ ⲦⲀⲪⲢⲞⲆⲒⲦⲎ ⲦⲈ** ⲈⲤϢⲀⲚⲈⲒ' ⲈⲠⲘⲈϨⲤⲀϢϤ Ⲛ- [ⲦⲔⲈ
ⲞⲒⲔⲞⲤ ⲚⲦⲈⲤⲪⲈⲢⲀ ⲈⲦⲈ ⲠⲌⲨⲅⲞⲤ ⲠⲈ ϢⲀⲨⲤⲰⲔ ⲚⲚⲔⲀⲦⲀ-
ⲠⲈⲦⲀⲤⲘⲀ ⲈⲦⲞⲨⲦⲰⲞⲨ ⲚⲚⲀϨⲂⲞⲨⲢ ⲘⲚ ⲚⲀⲞⲨⲚⲀⲘ · ⲀⲨⲰ
ϢⲀϤϬⲰϢⲦ ⲈⲂⲞⲖ ϨⲘ ⲠϪⲒⲤⲈ ϨⲚ ⲚⲀⲞⲨⲚⲀⲘ ⲚϬⲒ ⲠⲚⲞϬ
25 ⲚⲤⲀⲂⲀⲰⲐ' ⲠⲀⲅⲀⲐⲞⲤ ⲚⲦⲈ ⲠⲔⲞⲤⲘⲞⲤ ⲦⲎⲢϤ ⲘⲚ ⲦⲈⲤⲪⲀⲒⲢⲀ
ⲦⲎⲢⲤ ⟨ϢⲦⲞⲢⲦⲢ⟩ ϨⲀⲐⲎ ⲈⲘⲠⲀⲦϤϬⲰϢⲦ · ⲚϤϬⲰϢⲦ ⲈⲠⲈ-

---

26 ϢⲦⲞⲢⲦⲢ or ⲔⲒⲘ omitted.

the *Midst*, and takes them to the *Treasury* of the Light; and Jeu also *withdraws* himself to the *places* of those of the right, until the time of the *cipher* that they should go forth again [1]. Now the *archons rebel* through the anger of their *wickedness*, going forth immediately with the lights because they (Jeu and Melchisedek) are not present at that time. And they carry the *souls* which they are able to snatch up by *theft*, and they *consume* them through their dark smoke and their *wicked* fire. *Then* this *power* (*exousia*) Paraplex, with the *demons* which are under her, takes the *souls* of the hot-tempered, the cursers and the *slanderers*, and sends them through the dark smoke, and destroys them through her *wicked* fire, so that they *begin* to perish and be dissolved. They (the souls) spend 133 years and 9 months in the *punishments* of her *places*, while she (Paraplex) *torments* them in the fire of her *wickedness*. Now it happens after all these times, when the *sphere* turns and the Little Sabaoth, Zeus, comes to the first *aeon* of the *sphere*, which in the *world* is called the *Ram* (Aries), Bubastis which is Aphrodite comes to the seventh *house* of the *sphere* which is the *Balance* (Libra), then the *veils* are drawn aside which are between those of the left and those of the right. And the Great Sabaoth, the *Good*, looks forth from the height upon those of the right. And the whole *world* and the whole *sphere* ⟨are in agitation⟩ before he looks. He looks | down

---

[1] (3, 4) those of the right, until ... again. Now the archons rebel; Schmidt: those of the right. Until ... again, the archons rebel.

ⲤⲎⲦ ⲈⲬⲚ ⲚⲦⲞⲠⲞⲤ ⲚⲦⲠⲀⲢⲀⲠⲖⲎⲌ· ⲚⲦⲈ ⲚⲈⲤⲦⲞⲠⲞⲤ ⲂⲰⲖ
ⲈⲂⲞⲖ· ⲚⲤⲈⲦⲀⲔⲞ· ⲀⲨⲰ ⲚⲈⲮⲨⲬⲞⲞⲨⲈ ⲦⲎⲢⲞⲨ ⲈⲦⲎⲚ
ⲚⲈⲤⲔⲞⲖⲀⲤⲓⲤ ϢⲀⲨϤⲓⲦⲞⲨ ⲚⲤⲈⲦⲤⲦⲞⲞⲨ ⲈⲦⲈⲤⳘⲀⲓⲢⲀ Ⲛ-
ⲔⲈⲤⲞⲠ· ⲈⲂⲞⲖ ϪⲈ ⲀⲨⲦⲀⲔⲞ ⲎⲚ ⲚⲔⲞⲖⲀⲤⲓⲤ ⲚⲦⲠⲀⲢⲀⲠⲖⲎⲌ·
5 ⲀϤⲞⲨⲰⲎ ⲞⲚ ⲈⲦⲞⲞⲦϤ ⲎⲘ ⲠϢⲀϪⲈ ⲠⲈϪⲀϤ· ϪⲈ ⲦⲘⲈⲎ-
ⲤⲚⲦⲈ ⲚⲦⲀⳢⲓⲤ ⲈϢⲀⲨⲘⲞⲨⲦⲈ ⲈⲢⲞⲤ ϪⲈ ⲀⲢⲓⲞⲨⲐ· ⲦⲈⲤⲞ-
ⲞϢⲈ· ⲈⲨⲀⲢⲬⲰⲚ ⲚⲤⲎⲓⲘⲈ ⲦⲈ ⲈⲤⲔⲎⲘ· ⲦⲎⲢⲤ ⲈⲢⲈ ⲔⲈ-
ⲘⲚⲦⲀϤⲦⲈ ⲚⲆⲀⲓⲘⲞⲚⲓⲞⲚ ⲎⲀⲢⲀⲦⲤ ⲈⲨⲀⲢⲬⲓ ⲈⲬⲚ ⲔⲈⲘⲚⲎϢⲈ
ⲚⲆⲀⲓⲘⲰⲚ· ⲀⲨⲰ ⲚⲈⲓⲆⲀⲓⲘⲞⲚⲓⲞⲚ ⲈⲦⲘⲘⲀⲨ ⲈⲦⲎⲀⲢⲀⲦⲤ [ⲦⲔⲈ ᵇ]
10 ⲚⲀⲢⲓⲞⲨⲐ· ⲦⲈⲤⲞⲞϢⲈ ⲚⲦⲞⲞⲨ ⲚⲈ ⲈϢⲀⲨⲂⲰⲔ· ⲈⲞⲨⲚ
ⲈⲚⲢⲰⲘⲈ ⲚⲢⲈϤⲦⲀⳘⲘⲀ ϢⲀⲚⲦⲞⲨⲚⲈⲎⲤⲈ ⲚⲚⲓⲠⲞⲖⲈⲘⲞⲤ ⲚⲦⲈ
ⲎⲈⲚⲎⲰⲦⲂ ϢⲰⲠⲈ ⲚⲤⲈϮ ⲚϢⲞⲦ· ⲘⲠⲈⲨⲎⲎⲦ Ⲉ1 ⳘⲰⲚⲦ ⲈⲦⲢⲈ
ⲎⲈⲚⲎⲰⲦⲂ ϢⲰⲠⲈ· ⲀⲨⲰ ⲚⲈⲮⲨⲬⲞⲞⲨⲈ ⲈⲦⲤⲚⲀϤⲓⲦⲞⲨ Ⲛ-
ⲤⲦⲈⲢⲈⲤⲓⲘⲞⲚ Ⲛ6ⲓ ⲦⲈⲓⲈⳢⲞⲨⲤⲓⲀ ϢⲀⲨⲢ-ϢⲈ ⲘⲚ ⲘⲚⲦ-
15 ϢⲞⲘⲦⲈ ⲚⲢⲞⲘⲠⲈ ⲎⲚ ⲚⲈⲤⲦⲞⲠⲞⲤ ⲈⲤⲂⲀⲤⲀⲚⲓⳎⲈ ⲘⲘⲞⲞⲨ
ⲎⲓⲦⲘ ⲠⲈⲤⲔⲢⲰⲘ ⲚⲔⲀⲔⲈ· ⲘⲚ ⲠⲈⲤⲔⲰⲎⲦ ⲘⲠⲞⲚⲎⲢⲞⲚ ⲚⲤⲈ-
ⲎⲰⲚ ⲈⲞⲨⲚ ⲈⲠⲦⲀⲔⲞ· ⲀⲨⲰ ⲘⲚⲚⲤⲀ ⲚⲀⲓ ⲈⲢϢⲀⲚ ⲦⲈ-
ⲤⳘⲀⲓⲢⲀ ⲔⲰⲦⲈ ⲚϤⲈⲓ Ⲛ6ⲓ ⲠⲔⲞⲨⲓ ⲚⲤⲀⲂⲀⲰⲐ· ⲠⲀⲄⲀⲐⲞⲤ
ⲠⲀⲓ ⲈⲦⲈϢⲀⲨⲘⲞⲨⲦⲈ ⲈⲢⲞϤ ⲎⲘ ⲠⲔⲞⲤⲘⲞⲤ ϪⲈ ⳎⲈⲨⲤ·
20 ⲈϤϢⲀⲚⲈⲓ· ⲈⲠⲘⲈⲎϤⲦⲞⲞⲨ ⲚⲀⲓⲰⲚ ⲚⲦⲈ ⲦⲈⲤⳘⲀⲓⲢⲀ ⲈⲦⲈ
ⲠⲔⲀⲢⲔⲓⲚⲞⲤ ⲠⲈ ⲀⲨⲰ ⲚⲤⲈⲓ· Ⲛ6ⲓ ⲦⲂⲞⲨⲂⲀⲤⲦⲓ ⲦⲀⲓ ⲈⲦⲈ-
ϢⲀⲨⲘⲞⲨⲦⲈ ⲈⲢⲞⲤ ⲎⲘ ⲠⲔⲞⲤⲘⲞⲤ ϪⲈ ⲦⲀⳘⲢⲞⲆⲓⲦⲎ ⲚⲤⲈⲓ
ⲈⲠⲘⲈⲎⲘⲎⲦ ⲚⲀⲓⲰⲚ ⲚⲦⲈ ⲦⲈⲤⳘⲀⲓⲢⲀ ⲠⲀⲓ ⲈϢⲀⲨⲘⲞⲨⲦⲈ ⲦⲔⳍ
ⲈⲢⲞϤ ϪⲈ ⲠⲀⲓⲄⲞⲔⲈⲢⲞⲤ· ⲦⲞⲦⲈ ϢⲀⲨⲤⲰⲔ· ⲚⲚⲔⲀⲦⲀⲠⲈ-
25 ⲦⲀⲤⲘⲀ ⲈⲦⲞⲨⲦϢⲞⲨ ⲚⲚⲈⲎⲂⲞⲨⲢ ⲘⲚ ⲚⲀⲞⲨⲚⲀⲘ· Ⲛϥ-

---

21 MS originally ⲚϤⲈⲓ; ϥ crossed out, and Ⲥ inserted above.
24 MS originally ⲀⲓⲄⲞⲔⲈⲢⲞⲤ; Ⲡ inserted above.
25 MS ⲚⲚⲈⲎⲂⲞⲨⲢ; read ⲚⲚⲀⲎⲂⲞⲨⲢ.

upon the *places* of the Paraplex, so that her *places* are dissolved and destroyed. And all the *souls* which are in her *punishments* are taken and once more returned again to the *sphere* because they were perishing[1] in the *punishments* of the Paraplex."

140. He continued further with the discourse and said : "The second *rank* is called Ariuth, the Ethiopian Woman, which is a female *archon*, completely black, under which are 14 other *demons* which *rule* over a multitude of other *demons*. And those *demons* which stand under Ariuth, the Ethiopian Woman, are those which go into quarrelsome men until they cause *fights*, and murders happen, and they harden their hearts in anger[2], so that murders happen. And the *souls* which this *power* (*exousia*) carries off by *theft* spend 113 years in her *places*, while she *torments* them through her dark smoke and her *wicked* fire, and they approach destruction. And after these things when the *sphere* turns and the Little Sabaoth, the *Good*, who is called Zeus in the *world*, comes, when he comes to the fourth *aeon* of the *sphere*, that is, the *Crab* (Cancer), and Bubastis who is called Aphrodite in the *world* comes to the tenth *aeon* of the *sphere* which is called the *Goat* (Capricorn), then the *veils* which are between those of the left and those of the right are drawn aside. | And Jeu looks forth upon

---

[1]   (4) they were perishing; lit. they perished (perfect); (cf. also 363.6; 364.6; 365.8; 366.11).

[2]   (12) they harden their hearts in anger; lit. they give hardness and anger to their hearts.

ϬⲱϢⲧ ⲉⲃⲟⲗ ϩⲓ ⲟⲩⲛⲁⲙ̕ ⲛ̅ϭⲓ ⲓⲉⲟⲩ ⲛ̅ⲧⲉ ⲡⲕⲟⲥⲙⲟⲥ ⲧⲏⲣϥ̅
Ϣⲧⲟⲣⲧⲣ̅ ⲁⲩⲱ ⲛ̅ϥⲕⲓⲙ̕ ⲙ̅ⲛ ⲛ̅ⲁⲓⲱⲛ ⲧⲏⲣⲟⲩ ⲛ̅ⲧⲉⲥⲫⲉⲣⲁ
ⲛ̅ϥϬⲱϢⲧ ⲉϫⲛ̅ ⲙ̅ⲙⲁⲛ̅Ϣⲱⲡⲉ ⲛ̅ⲁⲣⲓⲟⲩⲑ ⲧⲉϬⲟⲟϢⲉ ⲁⲩⲱ
ⲛ̅ⲧⲉ ⲛⲉⲥⲧⲟⲡⲟⲥ ⲃⲱⲗ ⲉⲃⲟⲗ̕ ⲛ̅ⲥⲉⲧⲁⲕⲟ ⲛ̅ⲥⲉϥⲓ ⲛ̅ⲛⲉⲯⲩ-
⁵ ⲭⲟⲟⲩⲉ ⲧⲏⲣⲟⲩ ⲉⲧϩⲛ̅ ⲛⲉⲥⲕⲟⲗⲁⲥⲓⲥ ⲛ̅ⲥⲉⲧⲥⲧⲟⲟⲩ ⲉⲧⲉⲥⲫⲁⲓⲣⲁ ⲛ̅ⲕⲉⲥⲟⲡ̕ ⲉⲃⲟⲗ ϫⲉ ⲁⲩⲧⲁⲕⲟ ϩⲓⲧⲙ̅ ⲡⲉⲥⲕⲣⲱⲙ
ⲛ̅ⲕⲁⲕⲉ ⲙ̅ⲛ ⲡⲉⲥⲕⲱϩⲧ̅ ⲙ̅ⲡⲟⲛⲏⲣⲟⲛ·

ⲁ̅ϥⲟⲩⲱϩ ⲟⲛ ⲉⲧⲟⲟⲧϥ̅ ⲡⲉϫⲁϥ· ϫⲉ ⲧⲙⲉϩϢⲟⲙⲧⲉ ⲛ̅-
ⲧⲁ̅ⲝⲓⲥ ⲉϢⲁⲩⲙⲟⲩⲧⲉ ⲉⲣⲟⲥ ϫⲉ ⲑⲉⲕⲁⲧⲏ ⲡⲓϢⲟⲙⲛ̅ⲧ ⲛ̅ϩⲟ·
¹⁰ ⲟⲩⲛ-ⲕⲉϩⲟⲩⲧⲥⲁϢϥⲉ ⲇⲉ ⲛ̅ⲇⲁⲓⲙⲟⲛⲓⲟⲛ ϩⲁ ⲧⲉⲥⲉ̅ⲝⲟⲩ-
ⲥⲓⲁ ⲉⲛ̅ⲧⲟⲟⲩ ⲛⲉ ⲉϢⲁⲩⲃⲱⲕ̕ ⲉϩⲟⲩⲛ ⲉⲛⲣⲱⲙⲉ ⲛ̅ⲥⲉⲧⲣⲉⲩ-
ⲱⲣ̅ⲕ̅ ⲛ̅ⲛⲟⲩϫ ⲁⲩⲱ ⲛ̅ⲥⲉϫⲓϬⲟⲗ· ⲁⲩⲱ ⲛ̅ⲥⲉⲙⲉⲣⲉ-ⲡⲉⲧⲉ   ⲧⲕ̅ⲍ̅ᵇ
ⲙ̅ⲡϢⲟⲩ ⲁⲛ ⲡⲉ· ⲛⲉⲯⲩⲭⲟⲟⲩⲉ ϭⲉ ⲉⲧⲥⲛⲁϥⲓⲧⲟⲟⲩ ⲛ̅-
ⲥⲧⲉⲣⲉⲥⲓⲙⲟⲛ ⲛ̅ϭⲓ ⲑⲉⲕⲁⲧⲏ Ϣⲁⲥⲧⲁⲁⲩ ⲉⲧⲟⲟⲧⲟⲩ ⲛ̅ⲛⲉⲥ-
¹⁵ ⲇⲁⲓⲙⲟⲛⲓⲟⲛ ⲉⲧϩⲁⲣⲁⲧⲥ̅ ⲛ̅ⲥⲉⲃⲁⲥⲁⲛⲓⲍⲉ ⲙ̅ⲙⲟⲟⲩ ϩⲓⲧⲛ̅ ⲡⲉⲥⲕⲣⲱⲙ ⲛ̅ⲕⲁⲕⲉ ⲙ̅ⲛ ⲡⲉⲥⲕⲱϩⲧ̅ ⲙ̅ⲡⲟⲛⲏⲣⲟⲛ ⲉⲩⲑⲗⲓⲃⲉ ⲙ̅-
ⲙⲟⲟⲩ ⲉⲙⲁⲧⲉ ϩⲓⲧⲛ̅ ⲛ̅ⲇⲁⲓⲙⲟⲛⲓⲟⲛ· ⲁⲩⲱ Ϣⲁⲩⲣ̅-Ϣⲉ ⲙ̅ⲛ
† ⲛ̅ⲣⲟⲙⲡⲉ ⲙ̅ⲛ ⲥⲟⲟⲩ ⲛ̅ⲉⲃⲟⲧ ⲉⲩⲕⲟⲗⲁⲍⲉ ⲙ̅ⲙⲟⲟⲩ ϩⲛ̅
ⲛⲉⲥⲕⲟⲗⲁⲥⲓⲥ ⲉⲑⲟⲟⲩ· Ϣⲁⲩⲁⲣⲭⲓ ⲇⲉ ⲛ̅ⲱϫⲛ̅ ⲁⲩⲱ ⲉ-
²⁰ ⲧⲁⲕⲟ· ⲁⲩⲱ ⲙ̅ⲛ̅ⲛⲥⲁ ⲛⲁⲓ ⲉⲣϢⲁⲛ ⲧⲉⲥⲫⲁⲓⲣⲁ ⲕⲱⲧⲉ ⲛ̅ϥⲉⲓ̕
ⲛ̅ϭⲓ ⲡⲕⲟⲩⲉⲓ ⲛ̅ⲥⲁⲃⲁⲱⲑ̕ ⲡⲁⲅⲁⲑⲟⲥ ⲡⲁⲧⲙⲉⲥⲟⲥ ⲡⲁⲓ̈ ⲉ-
Ϣⲁⲩⲙⲟⲩⲧⲉ ⲉⲣⲟϥ ϩⲙ̅ ⲡⲕⲟⲥⲙⲟⲥ ϫⲉ ⲍⲉⲩⲥ· ⲛ̅ϥⲉⲓ̕ ⲉⲡⲙⲉϩ-
Ϣⲙⲟⲩⲛ ⲛ̅ⲁⲓⲱⲛ ⲛ̅ⲧⲉ ⲧⲉⲥⲫⲁⲓⲣⲁ ⲡⲁⲓ̈ ⲉϢⲁⲩⲙⲟⲩⲧⲉ ⲉⲣⲟϥ
ϫⲉ ⲡⲉⲥⲕⲟⲣⲡⲓⲟⲥ ⲁⲩⲱ ⲛ̅ⲥⲉⲓ̕ ⲛ̅ϭⲓ ⲧⲃⲟⲩⲃⲁⲥⲧⲓ ⲧⲁⲓ̈ ⲉ-
²⁵ Ϣⲁⲩⲙⲟⲩⲧⲉ ⲉⲣⲟⲥ ϫⲉ ⲧⲁⲫⲣⲟⲇⲓⲧⲏ ⲛ̅ⲥⲉⲓ̕ ⲉⲡⲙⲉϩⲥⲛⲁⲩ
ⲛ̅ⲁⲓⲱⲛ ⲛ̅ⲧⲉ ⲧⲉⲥⲫⲉⲣⲁ ⲡⲁⲓ̈ ⲉϢⲁⲩⲙⲟⲩⲧⲉ ⲉⲣⲟϥ** ϫⲉ [ⲧⲕ̅ⲏ̅]
ⲡⲧⲁⲩⲣⲟⲥ· Ϣⲁⲩⲥⲱⲕ ⲛ̅ⲛ̅ⲕⲁⲧⲁⲡⲉⲧⲁⲥⲙⲁ ⲉⲧⲟⲩⲧϢⲟⲩ
ⲛ̅ⲛⲁϩⲃⲟⲩⲣ ⲙ̅ⲛ ⲛⲁⲟⲩⲛⲁⲙ ⲛ̅ϥϬⲱϢⲧ ⲉⲃⲟⲗ ϩⲙ̅ ⲡϫⲓⲥⲉ

the right. And the whole *world* is in agitation, and it moves
with all the *aeons* of the *sphere*. And he (Jeu) looks upon the
dwelling-places of Ariuth, the Ethiopian Woman, and her
places are dissolved and destroyed. And all the *souls* which
are in her *punishments* are carried off and returned again
once more to the *sphere*, because they were perishing through
the dark smoke and the *wicked* fire."

He continued again and said : "The third *rank* is called
Hekate, the Three-faced [1]. *But* another 27 *demons* are under
her *authority*, and it is they which go into men and cause
them to swear false oaths and to lie and to desire what is
not theirs. Now the *souls* which Hekate carries off *by theft*,
she gives to her *demons* which are under her, and they
torment them with her dark smoke and her *wicked* fire, and
they (the souls) are greatly *afflicted* by the *demons*. And
they spend 105 years and six months being *punished* in her
wicked *punishments*. *But* they *begin* to perish and to be
destroyed. And after these things, when the *sphere* turns,
the Little Sabaoth, the *Good*, he of the *Midst*, who is called
Zeus in the *world*, comes, and he comes to the eighth *aeon*
of the *sphere* which is called the *Scorpion* (Scorpio); and
Bubastis, who is called Aphrodite, comes, and she comes
to the second *aeon* of the *sphere* which is called the *Bull*
(Taurus), then the *veils* which are between those of the
left and those of the right are drawn aside. And Zorokothora
Melchisedek looks forth from the height, | and the *world*

---

[1]   (19) Hekate; as triple, see IMG-E p. 189 ff.; also Hippol. IV.4.8; Dieterich
(Bibl. 15) p. 77, n. 3; Kropp (Bibl. 26) III, p. 149.

ⲚϬⲒ ⲠⲌⲞⲢⲞⲔⲞⲐⲞⲢⲀ ⲘⲈⲀⲬⲒⲤⲈⲀⲈⲔ' ⲚⲦⲈ ⲠⲔⲞⲤⲘⲞⲤ ⲔⲒⲘ

ⲘⲚ ⲚⲦⲞⲨⲈⲒⲎ ⲀⲨⲱ ⲚⲦⲈ ⲚⲀⲢⲬⲰⲚ ⲱⲦⲞⲢⲦⲢ̅ Ⲛ̅ϤϬⲰϢⲦ

ⲈⲬⲚ̅ ⲚⲦⲞⲠⲞⲤ ⲦⲎⲢⲞⲨ ⲚⲐⲈⲔⲀⲦⲎ ⲚⲦⲈ ⲚⲈⲤⲦⲞⲠⲞⲤ ⲂⲰⲀ

ⲈⲂⲞⲀ Ⲛ̅ⲤⲈⲦⲀⲔⲞ · ⲀⲨⲱ Ⲛ̅ⲤⲈϤⲒ Ⲛ̅ⲚⲈⲯⲨⲬⲞⲞⲨⲈ ⲦⲎⲢⲞⲨ

5 ⲈⲦⲌ̅Ⲛ̅ ⲚⲈⲤⲔⲞⲀⲀⲤⲒⲤ Ⲛ̅ⲤⲈⲦⲤⲦⲞⲞⲨ ⲈⲦⲈⲤⲪⲀⲒⲢⲀ Ⲛ̅ⲔⲈⲤⲞⲠ'

ⲈⲂⲞⲀ ⲬⲈ ⲀⲨⲰⲬⲚ̅ Ⲍ̅Ⲙ ⲠⲔⲰϨⲦ̅ Ⲛ̅ⲚⲈⲤⲔⲞⲀⲀⲤⲒⲤ ·

ⲀϤⲞⲨⲰⲌ ⲞⲚ ⲈⲦⲞⲞⲦϤ ⲠⲈⲬⲀϤ ⲬⲈ ⲦⲘⲈⲌⲦⲞ Ⲛ̅ⲦⲀⲈⲒⲤ

ⲈⲱⲀⲨⲘⲞⲨⲦⲈ ⲈⲢⲞϤ ⲬⲈ Ⲡ̅ⲠⲀⲢⲌⲈⲀⲢⲰⲚ ⲠⲦⲨⲪⲰⲚ ⲈⲨ-

ⲀⲢⲬⲰⲚ Ⲛ̅ⲬⲰⲰⲢⲈ ⲠⲈ ⲈⲨⲱⲞⲞⲠ Ⲍ̅Ⲁ ⲦⲈϤⲈⲌⲞⲨⲤⲒⲀ Ⲛ̅ϬⲒ

10 ⲘⲀⲂⲤⲚⲞⲞⲨⲤ Ⲛ̅ⲀⲀⲒⲘⲞⲚⲒⲞⲚ ⲈⲚⲦⲞⲞⲨ ⲚⲈ ⲈⲱⲀⲨⲂⲰⲔ Ⲉ-

ⲌⲞⲨⲚ ⲈⲚⲢⲰⲘⲈ Ⲛ̅ⲤⲈⲦⲢⲈⲨⲈⲠⲒⲐⲨⲘⲒ ⲀⲨⲱ Ⲛ̅ⲤⲈⲠⲞⲢⲚⲈⲨⲈ

Ⲛ̅ⲤⲈⲢ̅ⲚⲞⲈⲒⲔ Ⲛ̅ⲤⲈⲱⲰⲠⲈ ⲈⲨⲈⲒⲢⲈ* Ⲛ̅ⲦⲤⲨⲚⲞⲨⲤⲒⲀ ⲈⲨⲘⲎⲚ [ⲦⲔ̅Ⲏ ᵇ]

ⲈⲂⲞⲀ · ⲚⲈⲯⲨⲬⲞⲞⲨⲈ ϬⲈ ⲈⲦϤⲚⲀϤⲒⲦⲞⲨ Ⲛ̅ⲤⲦⲈⲢⲈⲤⲒⲘⲞⲚ

Ⲛ̅ϬⲒ ⲠⲈⲒ̈ⲀⲢⲬⲰⲚ ⲱⲀⲨⲢ̅-ⲱⲈⲘⲀⲂⲱⲘⲎⲚⲈ Ⲛ̅ⲢⲞⲘⲠⲈ Ⲍ̅Ⲛ ⲚⲈϤ-

15 ⲦⲞⲠⲞⲤ ⲈⲨⲂⲀⲤⲀⲚⲒⲌⲈ Ⲙ̅ⲘⲞⲞⲨ Ⲛ̅ϬⲒ ⲚⲈϤⲀⲀⲒⲘⲞⲚⲒⲞⲚ ϨⲒⲦⲘ̅

ⲠⲈϤⲔⲢⲰⲘ' Ⲛ̅ⲔⲀⲔⲈ ⲘⲚ̅ ⲠⲈϤⲔⲰϨⲦ̅ Ⲙ̅ⲠⲞⲚⲎⲢⲞⲚ Ⲛ̅ⲤⲈⲀⲢⲬⲒ

ⲈⲀⲚϨⲀⲀⲒⲤⲔⲈ ⲀⲨⲱ ⲈⲦⲀⲔⲞ · ⲱⲀⲤⲱⲰⲠⲈ ϬⲈ ⲈⲢϢⲀⲚ ⲦⲈ-

ⲤⲪⲀⲒⲢⲀ ⲔⲰⲦⲈ Ⲛ̅ϤⲈⲒ' Ⲛ̅ϬⲒ ⲠⲔⲞⲨⲈⲒ Ⲛ̅ⲤⲀⲂⲀⲰⲐ ⲠⲀⲄⲀⲐⲞⲤ

ⲠⲀⲦⲘⲈⲤⲞⲤ ⲠⲀⲒ̈ ⲈⲱⲀⲨⲘⲞⲨⲦⲈ ⲈⲢⲞϤ ⲬⲈ ⲌⲈⲨⲤ · ⲈϤϢⲀⲚ-

20 ⲈⲒ' ⲈⲠⲘⲈⲌⲯⲒⲤ Ⲛ̅ⲀⲒⲰⲚ Ⲛ̅ⲦⲈⲤⲪⲀⲒⲢⲀ · ⲠⲀⲒ̈ ⲈⲱⲀⲨⲘⲞⲨⲦⲈ

ⲈⲢⲞϤ ⲬⲈ ⲠⲀⲞⲌⲞⲦⲎⲤ · ⲀⲨⲱ Ⲛ̅ⲦⲈ ⲦⲂⲞⲨⲂⲀⲤⲦⲒ ⲦⲈⲒ̈ Ⲉ-

ⲱⲀⲨⲘⲞⲨⲦⲈ ⲈⲢⲞⲤ Ⲍ̅Ⲙ ⲠⲔⲞⲤⲘⲞⲤ ⲬⲈ ⲦⲀⲪⲢⲞⲀⲒⲦⲎ Ⲛ̅ⲤⲈⲒ'

ⲈⲠⲘⲈⲌⲱⲞⲘⲚ̅Ⲧ Ⲛ̅ⲀⲒⲰⲚ Ⲛ̅ⲦⲈⲤⲪⲈⲢⲀ ⲠⲀⲒ̈ ⲈⲱⲀⲨⲘⲞⲨⲦⲈ

---

5 MS originally Ⲛ̅ⲔⲞⲀⲀⲤⲒⲤ; ⲈⲤ inserted above.
7 MS originally ⲦⲘⲈⲌⲱⲞⲘⲦⲈ; ⲱⲞⲘⲦⲈ expunged.
8 MS ⲈⲢⲞϤ; read ⲈⲢⲞⲤ.

with the mountains moves, and the *archons* are in agitation.
And he looks upon all the *places* of Hekate, and her *places*
are dissolved and destroyed. And all the *souls* which are
in her *punishments* are carried off and returned once more
to the *sphere*, because they were perishing in the fire of
her *punishments*."

He continued again and said : "The fourth *rank* is called
the *Assessor* (Parhedron)[1] Typhon[2], a powerful *archon*,
under the authority of whom are 32 *demons*. It is they
which go into men and cause them to *desire*, and to *fornicate*,
and commit adultery, and to practise *sexual intercourse*
continually. Now the *souls* which this *archon* will carry off
by theft spend 138 years in his *places*, while his *demons*
torment them through his dark smoke and his *wicked* fire,
so that they *begin* to be *consumed* and to be destroyed.
Now it happens when the *sphere* turns, the Little Sabaoth,
the *Good*, he of the *Midst* who is called Zeus, comes. And
when he comes to the ninth *aeon* of the *sphere*, which is
called the *Archer* (Sagittarius), and when Bubastis, who is
called Aphrodite in the *world*, comes to the third *aeon* of
the *sphere* which is called | the *Twins* (Gemini), then the

---

[1]   (8) assessor (πάρεδρον); perhaps : familiar; see Iren. I.23.4.
[2]   (8) Typhon; see J 141.

ЄⲢⲞϤ ⲬЄ ⲠⲀⲓⲆⲨⲘⲞⲤ· ϢⲀⲨⲤⲰⲔ ⲚⲚⲔⲀⲦⲀⲠЄⲦⲀⲤⲘⲀ ЄⲦ-
ⲞⲨⲦⲰⲞⲨ ⲚⲚⲀⲖⲂⲞⲨⲢ ⲘⲚ ⲚⲀⲞⲨⲚⲀⲘ’ ⲚϤϬⲰϢⲦ ЄⲂⲞⲖ ** ⲚϬⲓ ⲦⲔⲐ
ⲌⲀⲢⲀⲌⲀⲌ· ⲠⲀⲓ ЄⲦЄϢⲀⲢЄ ⲚⲀⲢⲭⲰⲚ ⲘⲞⲨⲦЄ ЄⲢⲞϤ ϨⲘ ⲠⲢⲀⲚ
ⲚⲞⲨⲀⲢⲭⲰⲚ ⲚⲬⲰⲰⲢЄ ⲚⲦЄ ⲚЄⲨⲦⲞⲠⲞⲤ ⲬЄ ⲘⲀⲤⲔЄⲖⲖⲓ·
5 ⲀⲨⲰ ⲚϤϬⲰϢⲦ ЄⲬⲚ ⲘⲘⲀⲚϢⲰⲠЄ ⲘⲠⲠⲀⲢϨЄⲆⲢⲰⲚ ⲠⲦⲨ-
ⲫⲰⲚ ⲚⲦЄ ⲚЄϤⲦⲞⲠⲞⲤ ⲂⲰⲖ ЄⲂⲞⲖ ⲚⲤЄⲦⲀⲔⲞ· ⲚⲤЄϤⲓ Ⲛ-
ⲚЄⲨⲮⲨⲭⲞⲞⲨЄ ⲦⲎⲢⲞⲨ ЄⲦϨⲚ ⲚЄϤⲔⲞⲖⲀⲤⲓⲤ ⲚⲤЄⲦⲤⲦⲞⲞⲨ
ЄⲦЄⲤⲫⲀⲓⲢⲀ ⲚⲔЄⲤⲞⲠ· ЄⲂⲞⲖ ⲬЄ ⲀⲨⲤⲂⲞⲔ’ ϨⲓⲦⲘ ⲠЄϤⲔⲢⲰⲘ
ⲚⲔⲀⲔЄ ⲀⲨⲰ ϨⲓⲦⲘ ⲠЄϤⲔⲰϨⲦ ⲘⲠⲞⲚⲎⲢⲞⲚ·

10 ⲠⲀⲖⲓⲚ ⲞⲚ ⲀϤⲞⲨⲰϨ ЄⲦⲞⲞⲦϤ ϨⲘ ⲠϢⲀⲬЄ ⲠЄⲬⲀϤ Ⲛ-
ⲚЄϤⲘⲀⲐⲎⲦⲎⲤ ⲬЄ ⲦⲘЄϨ† ⲚⲦⲀⲝⲓⲤ ЄϢⲀⲨⲘⲞⲨⲦЄ ЄⲠЄⲨ-
ⲀⲢⲭⲰⲚ ⲬЄ ⲒⲀⲭⲐⲀⲚⲀⲂⲀⲤ· ЄⲨⲀⲢⲭⲰⲚ ⲚⲬⲰⲰⲢЄ ⲠЄ· ЄⲨ-
ϨⲀⲢⲀⲦϤ ⲚϬⲓ ϨЄⲚⲔЄⲘⲎⲎϢЄ ⲚⲆⲀⲓⲘⲞⲚⲓⲞⲚ· ⲚⲦⲞⲞⲨ ⲚЄ
ЄϢⲀⲨⲂⲰⲔ’ ЄϨⲞⲨⲚ ЄⲚⲢⲰⲘЄ ⲚⲤЄⲦⲢЄⲨϢⲰⲠЄ ⲚⲢЄϤⲬⲓϨⲞ
15 ЄⲨⲖⲆⲓⲔЄⲓ ⲚⲚⲆⲓⲔⲀⲓⲞⲤ ⲀⲨⲰ ЄⲨⲬⲓ ⲘⲠϨⲞ ⲚⲢⲢЄϤⲢⲚⲞⲂЄ
ЄⲨⲬⲓ-ⲆⲰⲢⲞⲚ ЄⲬⲘ * ϤⲀⲠ ⲘⲘЄ ЄⲨⲦⲀⲔⲞ ⲘⲘⲞϤ ЄⲨⲰⲂϢ ⲦⲔⲐ ᵇ
ⲘⲘⲞⲞⲨ ЄⲚϨⲎⲔЄ ⲘⲚ ⲚЄⲦϢⲀⲀⲦ’ ЄⲨⲦⲀϢⲞ ⲚⲦⲂϢЄ ϨⲚ
ⲦЄⲨⲮⲨⲭⲎ ⲘⲚ ⲠⲢⲞⲞⲨϢ ЄⲦЄ ⲘⲚ-ϨⲎⲨ ⲚϨⲎⲦϤ ⲬЄ Ⲛ-
ⲚЄⲨⲢⲠⲘЄЄⲨЄ ⲘⲠЄⲨⲰⲚϨ ⲬЄⲔⲀⲤ ЄⲨϢⲀⲚЄⲓ’ ЄⲂⲞⲖ ϨⲚ
20 ⲤⲰⲘⲀ ЄⲨЄϬⲓⲦⲞⲨ ⲚⲤⲦЄⲢЄⲤⲓⲘⲞⲚ· ⲚЄⲨⲮⲨⲭⲞⲞⲨЄ ϬЄ ЄⲦ-
ϤⲚⲀϤⲓⲦⲞⲨ ⲚⲤⲦЄⲢЄⲤⲓⲘⲞⲚ ⲚϬⲓ ⲠЄⲒⲀⲢⲭⲰⲚ ϢⲀⲨϢⲰⲠЄ
ϨⲚ ⲚЄϤⲔⲞⲖⲀⲤⲓⲤ ⲚϢЄⲦⲀⲒⲞⲨ ⲚⲢⲞⲘⲠЄ ⲘⲚ ϢⲘⲞⲨⲚ Ⲛ-
ЄⲂⲞⲦ’ ⲚϤⲀⲚϨⲀⲖⲓⲤⲔЄ ⲘⲘⲞⲞⲨ ϨⲓⲦⲘ ⲠЄϤⲔⲢⲰⲘ ⲚⲔⲀⲔЄ ⲘⲚ
ⲠЄϤⲔⲰϨⲦ ⲘⲠⲞⲚⲎⲢⲞⲚ ЄⲨⲐⲖⲓⲂЄ ⲘⲘⲞⲞⲨ ЄⲘⲀⲦЄ ϨⲓⲦⲘ
25 ⲠϢⲀϨ ⲘⲠЄϤⲔⲰϨⲦ· ⲀⲨⲰ ЄⲢϢⲀⲚ ⲦЄⲤⲫⲀⲓⲢⲀ ⲔⲰⲦЄ ⲚϤЄⲓ’

8　MS originally ⲠЄⲤⲔⲢⲰⲘ; Ⲥ crossed out, and Ϥ inserted above.
11　MS originally ЄⲢⲞⲤ ⲠЄⲨⲀⲢⲭⲰⲚ; ⲢⲞⲤ expunged; read ЄⲠЄⲤⲀⲢⲭⲰⲚ.

veils which are between those of the left and those of the right are drawn aside. And Zarazaz looks forth, whom the *archons* call by the name of a powerful *archon* of their *places*, Maskelli[1]. And he looks upon the dwelling-places of the *Assessor* (Parhedron) Typhon, so that his *places* are dissolved and are destroyed. And all the *souls* which are in his *punishments* are carried off and returned to the *sphere* once more, because they were being diminished through his dark smoke and through his *wicked* fire."

He continued *again* with the discourse and said to his *disciples* : "The *archon* of the fifth *rank* is called[2] Jachthanabas, a powerful *archon*, under whom stand a multitude of *demons*. It is they which go into men and cause them to be partial, *wronging* the *righteous* and showing favour to sinners by receiving *gifts* to suppress a true judgment, forgetting the poor and needy, while they (the demons) increase forgetfulness in their *souls* and concern for things of no value, so that they take no thought for their lives[3] until, when they come forth from the *body*, they are carried off *by theft*. Now the *souls* which this *archon* will carry off *by theft* are in his *punishments* for 150 years and eight months. And he *consumes* them through his dark smoke and his *wicked* fire, and they are *afflicted* greatly through the flame of his fire. And when the *sphere* turns, | the Little

---

[1]   (3, 4) Zarazaz = Maskelli; on Maskelli, see Kropp (Bibl. 26) III, p. 127.
[2]   (11, 12) the archon of the fifth rank is called ...; lit. the fifth rank, its archon is wont to be called ....
[3]   (18, 19) souls ..... lives; lit. soul ... life.

ⲛ̄ϭⲓ ⲡⲕⲟⲩⲓ̈ ⲛ̄ⲥⲁⲃⲁⲱⲑ ⲡⲁⲅⲁⲑⲟⲥ ⲡⲁⲓ̈ ⲉϣⲁⲩⲙⲟⲩⲧⲉ ⲉⲣⲟϥ

ϩⲙ̄ ⲡⲕⲟⲥⲙⲟⲥ ϫⲉ ⲍⲉⲩⲥ ⲛ̄ϥⲉⲓ ⲉⲡⲙⲉϩⲙ̄ⲛ̄ⲧⲟⲩⲉ ⲛ̄ⲁⲓⲱⲛ

ⲛ̄ⲧⲉ ⲧⲉⲥⲫⲉⲣⲁ· ⲡⲁⲓ̈ ⲉϣⲁⲩⲙⲟⲩⲧⲉ ⲉⲣⲟϥ ϫⲉ ⲡϩⲩⲁⲣⲏ-

ⲭⲟⲟⲥ· ⲁⲩⲱ ⲛ̄ⲥⲉⲓ ⲛ̄ϭⲓ ⲧⲃⲟⲩⲃⲁⲥⲧⲓ ⲉⲡⲙⲉϩϯⲟⲩ ⲛ̄ⲁⲓⲱⲛ

5 ⲛ̄ⲧⲉⲥⲫⲉⲣⲁ ⲡⲁⲓ̈ ⲉϣⲁⲩⲙⲟⲩⲧⲉ ⲉⲣⲟϥ ϫⲉ ⲡⲗⲉⲱⲛ ⲉϣⲁⲩ- [ⲧⲁ]

ⲥⲱⲕ ⲛ̄ⲛ̄ⲕⲁⲧⲁⲡⲉⲧⲁⲥⲙⲁ ⲉⲧⲟⲩⲧⲱⲟⲩ ⲛ̄ⲛⲁϩⲃⲟⲩⲣ ⲙ̄ⲛ ⲛⲁ-

ⲟⲩⲛⲁⲙ ⲛ̄ϥϭⲱϣⲧ ⲉⲃⲟⲗ ϩⲙ̄ ⲡϫⲓⲥⲉ ⲛ̄ϭⲓ ⲡⲛⲟϭ ⲛ̄ⲓ̈ⲁⲱ

ⲡⲁⲅⲁⲑⲟⲥ ⲡⲁⲧⲙⲉⲥⲟⲥ ⲉϩⲣⲁⲓ̈ ⲉϫⲛ̄ ⲛ̄ⲧⲟⲡⲟⲥ ⲛ̄ⲓ̈ⲁⲭⲑⲁⲛⲁ-

ⲃⲁⲥ ⲉⲧⲉ ⲛⲉϥⲧⲟⲡⲟⲥ ⲃⲱⲗ ⲉⲃⲟⲗ ⲛ̄ⲥⲉⲧⲁⲕⲟ ⲁⲩⲱ ⲛ̄ⲥⲉϥⲓ

10 ⲛ̄ⲛⲉⲯⲩⲭⲟⲟⲩⲉ ⲧⲏⲣⲟⲩ ⲉⲧϩ̄ⲛ ⲛⲉϥⲕⲟⲗⲁⲥⲓⲥ ⲛ̄ⲥⲉⲧ̄ⲥⲧⲟⲟⲩ

ⲉⲧⲉⲥⲫⲁⲓⲣⲁ ⲛ̄ⲟⲩⲱϩⲙ̄· ⲉⲃⲟⲗ ϫⲉ ⲁⲩⲧⲁⲕⲟ ϩⲓⲧⲛ̄ ⲛⲉϥⲕⲟ-

ⲗⲁⲥⲓⲥ· ⲛⲁⲓ̈ ϭⲉ ⲛⲉ ⲛⲉⲡⲣⲁϩⲓⲥ ⲛ̄ⲛⲉϩⲓⲟⲟⲩⲉ ⲛ̄ⲧⲙⲏⲧⲉ ⲉⲛⲧ-

ⲁⲧⲉⲧⲛ̄ϣⲛ̄ⲧ ⲉⲣⲟⲟⲩ:

ⲛ̄ⲧⲉⲣⲟⲩⲥⲱⲧⲙ̄ ⲇⲉ ⲉⲛⲁⲓ̈ ⲛ̄ϭⲓ ⲙ̄ⲙⲁⲑⲏⲧⲏⲥ ⲁⲩⲡⲁϩⲧⲟⲩ

15 ⲁⲩⲟⲩⲱϣⲧ ⲛⲁϥ ⲉⲩϫⲱ ⲙ̄ⲙⲟⲥ ϫⲉ ⲃⲟⲏⲑⲉⲓ ⲉⲣⲟⲛ ⲡⲉⲛ-

ϫⲟⲉⲓⲥ ⲛ̄ⲅϣ̄ⲛϩ̄ⲧⲏⲕ ϩⲁⲣⲟⲛ ϫⲉ ⲉⲛⲉⲟⲩϫⲁⲓ̈ ⲉⲛⲉⲓ̈ⲕⲟⲗⲁⲥⲓⲥ

ⲉⲑⲟⲟⲩ ⲉⲧⲥ̄ⲃⲧⲱⲧ ⲛ̄ⲛⲣⲉϥⲣ̄ⲛⲟⲃⲉ· ⲟⲩⲟⲓ̈ ⲛⲁⲩ ⲟⲩⲟⲓ̈ ⲛⲁⲩ

ⲛ̄ϣⲏⲣⲉ ⲛ̄ⲣⲣⲱⲙⲉ ϫⲉ ⲉⲩⲟ ⲛ̄ⲑⲉ ⲛ̄ϩⲉⲛⲃ̄ⲗⲗⲉⲉⲩ ϭⲟⲙϭⲙ̄ [ⲧⲁ ᵇ]

ϩⲙ̄ ⲡⲕⲁⲕⲉ ⲉⲛⲥⲉⲛⲁⲩ ⲉⲃⲟⲗ ⲁⲛ· ϣⲛ̄ϩ̄ⲧⲏⲕ ϩⲁⲣⲟⲛ ⲡϫⲟⲉⲓⲥ

20 ϩⲛ̄ ⲧⲉⲓ̈ⲛⲟϭ ⲙ̄ⲙⲛ̄ⲧⲃⲁⲗⲉ ⲉⲧⲛ̄ϣⲟⲟⲡ ϩⲣⲁⲓ̈ ⲛ̄ϩⲏⲧⲥ̄· ⲁⲩⲱ

ⲛ̄ⲅϣ̄ⲛϩ̄ⲧⲏⲕ ϩⲁ ⲡⲅⲉⲛⲟⲥ ⲧⲏⲣϥ̄ ⲛ̄ⲧⲙⲛ̄ⲧⲣⲱⲙⲉ ϫⲉ ⲁⲩϭⲱⲣϭ̄

ⲉⲛⲉⲩⲯⲩⲭⲟⲟⲩⲉ ⲛ̄ⲑⲉ ⲛ̄ⲛⲓⲙⲟⲩⲓ̈ ⲉⲩⲡⲁϩⲥ̄ ⲉⲩⲥⲟⲃⲧⲉ ⲙ̄ⲙⲟⲥ

ⲛ̄ⲧⲣⲟⲫⲏ ⲛ̄ⲛⲉⲩⲕⲟⲗⲁⲥⲓⲥ ϩⲓⲧⲛ̄ ⲧⲃⲱϣⲉ ⲙ̄ⲛ ⲧⲙⲛ̄ⲧⲁⲧⲥⲟⲟⲩⲛ

ⲉⲧⲛ̄ϩⲏⲧⲟⲩ· ϣⲛ̄ϩ̄ⲧⲏⲕ ϭⲉ ϩⲁⲣⲟⲛ· ⲡⲉⲛϫⲟⲉⲓⲥ ⲡⲉⲛⲥⲱⲣ

---

5 MS ⲡⲁⲓ̈ ⲉϣⲁⲩⲥⲱⲕ; ⲡⲁⲓ̈ crossed out and expunged; read ϣⲁⲩⲥⲱⲕ.

8 ⲡⲁⲓ̈ expunged before ⲉϩⲣⲁⲓ̈.

9 MS ⲉⲧⲉ; read ⲛ̄ⲧⲉ.

12 ϩⲓⲟⲟⲩⲉ expunged before ⲡⲣⲁϩⲓⲥ.

20 MS originally ⲉⲧϣⲟⲟⲡ; ⲛ̄ inserted above.

Sabaoth, the *Good*, who is called Zeus in this *world*, comes, and he comes to the eleventh *aeon* of the *sphere* which is called the *Water Carrier*[1] (Aquarius), and when Bubastis comes to the fifth *aeon* of the *sphere* which is called the *Lion* (Leo), then the *veils* which are between those of the left and those of the right are drawn aside. And the great Jao, the *Good*, he of the *Midst*, looks forth upon the *places* of Jachthanabas, so that his *places*[2] are dissolved and destroyed. And all the *souls* which are in his *punishments* are carried off and returned to the *sphere* once more, because they were being destroyed through his *punishments*. These are the *actions* of the ways of the Midst about which you have asked."

141. When *however* the *disciples* had heard these things, they prostrated themselves, they worshipped him, saying: "*Help* us, our Lord, and have compassion upon us, so that we may be saved from these evil *punishments* which are prepared for sinners. Woe to them, woe to them, the sons of men, for they are like blind men, groping in the darkness, and they do not see. Have compassion upon us, O Lord, in this great blindness in which we are. And be compassionate to the whole *race* of mankind, for they (the archons) pursue their *souls* like lions after prey, and prepare it (the prey) as *food* for their *punishments*, through the forgetfulness and the ignorance which is in them. Have compassion upon us, our Lord, our *Saviour*, | have mercy upon us and save us in this great distress."

---

[1] (3, 4) water carrier; lit. water pourer.
[2] (9) so that his places; lit. whose places.

ⲚⲄⲚⲀ ⲤⲀⲢⲞⲚ ⲚⲄⲚⲀⲤⲘⲚ ⲤⲘ ⲠⲈⲒ̈ⲚⲞⲤ Ⲛ̅ⲈⲂⲀ· ⲠⲈⲬⲈ Ⲓ̅Ⲥ̅ Ⲛ̅-
ⲚⲈϤⲘⲀⲐⲎⲦⲎⲤ ⲬⲈ ⲦⲰⲔ' Ⲛ̅ϨⲎⲦ Ⲙ̅ⲠⲢ̅ⲢϨⲞⲦⲈ ⲬⲈ Ⲛ̅ⲦⲈⲦⲚ̅
ϨⲈⲚⲘⲀⲔⲀⲢⲒⲞⲤ· ⲬⲈ ϯⲚⲀⲢⲦⲎⲨⲦⲚ̅ Ⲛ̅ⲬⲞⲈⲒⲤ ⲈⲬ̅Ⲛ̅ ⲚⲀⲒ̈
ⲦⲎⲢⲞⲨ ⲀⲨⲰ ϯⲚⲀⲦⲢⲈⲨϨⲨⲠⲞⲦⲀⲤⲤⲈ ⲚⲎⲦⲚ̅ ⲦⲎⲢⲞⲨ· ⲀⲢⲒ-
5 ⲠⲘⲈⲈⲨⲈ ⲬⲈ Ⲁ̈Ⲓ̈ⲞⲨⲰ ⲈⲒ̈ⲬⲰ Ⲙ̅ⲘⲞⲤ ⲚⲎⲦⲚ̅ ϨⲀⲐⲎ ⲈⲘⲠⲀ-
ⲦⲞⲨⲤ-ⲢⲞⲨ Ⲙ̅ⲘⲞⲒ̈ ⲬⲈ ϯⲚⲀϯ ⲚⲎⲦⲚ̅ Ⲛ̅ⲚⳘⲞϢⲦ Ⲛ̅ⲦⲘⲚ̅ⲦⲈⲢⲞ
Ⲛ̅ⲘⲠⲎⲨⲈ· ⲦⲈⲚⲞⲨ ⲞⲚ ϯⲬⲰ Ⲙ̅ⲘⲞⲤ ⲚⲎⲦⲚ̅ ⲬⲈ ϯⲚⲀⲦⲀⲀⲨ   ⲦⲀⲀ
ⲚⲎⲦⲚ̅ :

ⲚⲀⲒ̈ ⲞⲈ Ⲛ̅ⲦⲈⲢⲈϤⲬⲞⲞⲨ Ⲛ̅ⲞⲒ Ⲓ̅Ⲥ̅ ⲀϤϨⲨⲘⲚⲈⲨⲈ ϨⲘ̅ ⲠⲚⲞⲞ
10 Ⲛ̅ⲢⲀⲚ ⲀⲨϨⲰⲠ Ⲛ̅ⲞⲒ Ⲛ̅ⲦⲞⲠⲞⲤ Ⲛ̅ⲦⲈϨⲒⲎ Ⲛ̅ⲦⲘⲎⲦⲈ· ⲀⲨⲰ Ⲁ
Ⲓ̅Ⲥ̅ ⲘⲚ̅ ⲚⲈϤⲘⲀⲐⲎⲦⲎⲤ ⲀⲨⲞⲰ ϨⲒⲬ̅Ⲛ̅ ⲞⲨⲀⲎⲢ Ⲛ̅ⲞⲨⲞⲒ̈Ⲛ Ⲉ-
ⲚⲀϢⲰϤ ⲈⲘⲀⲦⲈ· ⲠⲈⲬⲈ Ⲓ̅Ⲥ̅ Ⲛ̅ⲚⲈϤⲘⲀⲐⲎⲦⲎⲤ ⲬⲈ ϨⲰⲚ
ⲈϨⲞⲨⲚ ⲈⲢⲞⲒ̈ ⲀⲨⲰ ⲀⲨϨⲰⲚ ⲈϨⲞⲨⲚ ⲈⲢⲞϤ· ⲀϤⲔⲞⲦϤ ⲈⲠⲈ-
ϤⲦⲈⲨ-ⲖⲀⲔϨ Ⲛ̅ⲦⲈ ⲠⲔⲞⲤⲘⲞⲤ ⲀϤⲬⲰ Ⲙ̅ⲠⲚⲞⲞ Ⲛ̅ⲢⲀⲚ ⲈϨⲢⲀⲒ̈
15 ⲈⲬ̅Ⲛ̅ ⲦⲈⲨⲀⲠⲈ ⲀϤⲤⲘⲞⲨ ⲈⲢⲞⲞⲨ ⲀϤⲚⲒϤⲈ ⲈϨⲞⲨⲚ Ⲉ̅Ⲛ̅ⲚⲈⲨ-
ⲂⲀⲖ· ⲠⲈⲬⲈ Ⲓ̅Ⲥ̅ ⲚⲀⲨ ⲬⲈ ⲞⲰϢⲦ ⲈϨⲢⲀⲒ̈ ⲀⲚⲀⲨ ⲬⲈ ⲈⲦⲈⲦⲚ̅-
ⲚⲀⲨ ⲈⲞⲨ· ⲀⲨⲰ ⲀⲨϤⲒ Ⲛ̅ⲚⲈⲨⲂⲀⲖ ⲈϨⲢⲀⲒ̈ ⲀⲨⲚⲀⲨ ⲈⲨⲚⲞⲞ
Ⲛ̅ⲞⲨⲞⲈⲒⲚ ⲈⲚⲀϢⲰϤ ⲈⲘⲀⲦⲈ ⲈⲚⲚⲈϢ-Ⲣ̅Ⲙ̅Ⲛ̅ⲔⲀϨ ϢⲀⲬⲈ
ⲈⲢⲞϤ· ⲠⲈⲬⲀϤ ⲞⲚ ⲚⲀⲨ Ⲛ̅ⲞⲨⲰϨⲘ̅ ⲬⲈ ⲞⲰϢⲦ ⲈⲂⲞⲖ ϨⲘ̅
20 ⲠⲞⲨⲞⲈⲒⲚ ⲀⲚⲀⲨ ⲬⲈ ⲈⲦⲈⲦⲚ̅ⲚⲀⲨ ⲈⲞⲨ· ⲠⲈⲬⲀⲨ ⲬⲈ ⲈⲚ-
ⲚⲀⲨ ⲈⲞⲨⲔⲰϨⲦ ⲘⲚ̅ ⲞⲨⲘⲞⲞⲨ ⲘⲚ̅ ⲞⲨⲎⲢⲠ ⲘⲚ̅ ⲞⲨⲤⲚⲞϤ·
ⲠⲈⲬⲈ Ⲓ̅Ⲥ̅ ⲈⲦⲈ ⲀⲂⲈⲢⲀⲘⲈⲚⲐⲰ ⲠⲈ ⲈϨⲞⲨⲚ ⲈϨ̅Ⲛ̅ ⲚⲈϤⲘⲀⲐⲎ-   ⲦⲀⲀ ᵇ
ⲦⲎⲤ ⲬⲈ ϨⲀⲘⲎⲚ ϯⲬⲰ Ⲙ̅ⲘⲞⲤ ⲚⲎⲦⲚ̅ ⲬⲈ Ⲙ̅ⲠⲒ̅Ⲛ̅-ⲖⲀⲀⲨ Ⲉ-
ⲠⲔⲞⲤⲘⲞⲤ ⲈⲒ̈ⲚⲎⲨ Ⲛ̅ⲤⲀ ⲠⲈⲒ̈ⲔⲰϨⲦ ⲘⲚ̅ ⲠⲈⲒ̈ⲘⲞⲞⲨ ⲘⲚ̅ ⲠⲈⲒ̈-

---

11   MS originally ⲞⲨϨⲀⲎⲢ; Ϩ expunged.
15   MS originally ⲈϨⲢⲀⲨ Ⲛ̅ⲚⲈⲨⲂⲀⲖ; ϨⲢⲀⲨ expunged.
23   ⲉ expunged before ϨⲀⲘⲎⲚ.

Jesus said to his disciples: "Have courage and do not fear, for you are *blessed*. For I will make you rulers over all these things, and I will cause all things to be *submitted* to you. Remember that I already said to you before I was *crucified*: 'I will give you the keys of the Kingdom of Heaven'*. Now again I say to you: "I will give them to you'."

When Jesus had said these things he *sang praise* to the great name. The *places* of the way of the Midst were concealed, and Jesus with his *disciples* remained upon an *air* of very strong light.

Jesus said to his *disciples*: "Approach me." And they approached him. He turned to the four corners of the *world*. He said the great name over their heads, he blessed them, he breathed into their eyes □. Jesus said to them: "Look up, see what you see." And they raised their eyes, they saw a great, very strong light, of which no man on earth could speak.

He said to them again once more: "Look away from the light and see what you see." They said: "We see fire and water and wine and blood."

Jesus, who is Aberamentho, said to his *disciples*: "*Truly, I say to you, when I came I brought nothing to the world* except this fire and this water and this | wine and this blood.

---

* cf. Mt. 16.19
□ cf. Joh. 20.22

ΗΡΠ ΜΝ ΠΕῙCΝΟϥ· ⲀῙⲘ-ΠΜΟΟⲨ ΜΝ ΠΚⲰⲌⲦ ⲌΜ ΠΤΟΠΟC
ΜΠΟⲨΟῙΝ Ν̄ⲦΕ ΝΙΟⲨΟΕῙΝ Μ̄ΠΕⲐΗCⲀⲨΡΟC Μ̄ΠΟⲨΟΕΙΝ·
ⲀῙΝ̄-ΠΗΡΠ ΜΝ ΠΕCΝΟϥ ⲌΜ ΠΤΟΠΟC Ν̄ⲦΒⲀΡΒΗⲖΟC· ⲀⲨⲰ
Μ̄ΝΝCⲀ ΟⲨϢΗΜ Ν̄ΟⲨΟΕΙϢ Ⲁ ΠⲀΕΙⲰⲦ Τ̄ΝΝΟΟⲨ ΝⲀῙ
5 Μ̄ΠΕΠΝⲀ ΕΤΟⲨⲀⲀΒ Μ̄ΠΤⲨΠΟC Ν̄ΟⲨϬΡΟΟΜΠΕ· ΠΚⲰⲌⲦ
ⲆΕ ΜΝ ΠΜΟΟⲨ ΜΝ ΠΗΡΠ ⲀⲨϢⲰΠΕ ΕⲨΚⲀⲐⲀΡΙⲌΕ Ν̄Ν-
ΝΟΒΕ ΤΗΡΟⲨ Μ̄ΠΚΟCΜΟC· ΠΕCΝΟϥ ⲌⲰⲰϥ ⲀϥϢⲰΠΕ
ΝⲀῙ Μ̄ΜⲀΕΙΝ ΕΤΒΕ ΠCⲰΜⲀ Ν̄ΤΜΝ̄ΤΡⲰΜΕ· ΠⲀῙ ΕΝΤ-
ⲀῙϪΙΤϥ ⲌΜ ΠΤΟΠΟC Ν̄ΤΒⲀΡΒΗⲖΟC ⳁΝΟϬ Ν̄ⲆⲨΝⲀΜΙC
10 Ν̄ⲦΕ ΠⲀⲌΟΡⲀΤΟC Ν̄ΝΟⲨⲦΕ· ΠΕΠΝⲀ ⲌⲰⲰϥ ΕϥCⲰΚ ⲌΗ-
ΤΟⲨ Μ̄ⲮⲨⲬΗ ΝΙΜ ΕϥϪΙ Μ̄ΜΟΟⲨ ΕΠΤΟΠΟC Μ̄ΠΟⲨΟῙΝ· [ⲦⲀΒ]
ΕΤΒΕ ΠⲀῙ ⲀῙϪΟΟC ΝΗΤΝ̄ ϪΕ Ν̄ⲦⲀΙΕΙ′ ΕΝΟⲨϪΕ Ν̄ΟⲨ-
ΚⲰⲌⲦ ΕⲬΜ ΠΚⲀⲌ· ΕⲦΕ ΠⲀῙ ΠΕ ϪΕ Ν̄ⲦⲀΙΕΙ′ ΕΚⲀⲐⲀΡΙⲌΕ
Ν̄ΝΝΟΒΕ Μ̄ΠΚΟCΜΟC ΤΗΡϥ ⲌΝ ΟⲨΚⲰⲌⲦ· ⲀⲨⲰ ΕΤΒΕ
15 ΠⲀῙ ⲀῙϪΟΟC Ν̄ΤCⲀΜⲀΡΙΤΗC ϪΕ ΕΝΕΡΕCΟΟⲨΝ ΠΕ Ν̄-
ⲦⲀⲰΡΕⲀ Μ̄ΠΝΟⲨⲦΕ ⲀⲨⲰ ϪΕ ΝΙΜ ΠΕⲦϪⲰ Μ̄ΜΟC ΝΕ
ϪΕ ⲀⲨΕΙC Ν̄ⲦⲀCⲰ· ΝΕΡⲀⲖⲀΙⲦΙ Μ̄ΜΟϥ ΠΕ Ν̄ϥⳁ ΝΕ Ν̄ΟⲨ-
ΜΟΟⲨ ΕϥΟΝⲌ Ν̄ϥϢⲰΠΕ ΝΕ Ν̄ΟⲨΠΗΓΗ ⟨Μ̄ΜΟΟⲨ⟩ Ν̄ⲌΗΤΕ
ΕϥϤϬΕ ΕⲌΟⲨΝ ΕⲨⲰΝ̄Ⲍ Ν̄ϢⲀΕΝΕⲌ· ⲀⲨⲰ ΟΝ ΕΤΒΕ ΠⲀῙ
20 ⲀῙϪΙ Ν̄ΟⲨⲀΠΟⲦ′ Ν̄ΗΡΠ ⲀῙCΜΟⲨ ΕΡΟϥ ⲀῙⲦⲀⲀϥ ΝΗΤΝ̄ ϪΕ
ΠⲀῙ ΠΕ ΠΕCΝΟϥ Ν̄ⲦⲆΙⲀⲐΗΚΗ ΕΤΟⲨΝⲀΠΟΝϥ ΕΒΟⲖ ⲌⲀ-

---

2 ⲌΜΠⲦΟ expunged before Μ̄ΠΕⲐΗCⲀⲨΡΟC.
11 Ⲕ̄Ⲁ in upper right-hand margin at end of quire.
17 MS ΝΕΡⲀⲖⲀΙⲦΙ; read ΝΕΡΕⲀΙⲦΙ.
18 Μ̄ΜΟΟⲨ omitted.

I have brought the water and the fire from the *place* of the lights of the *Treasury* of the Light. I have brought the wine and the blood from the *place* of the Barbelo. And after a little time my Father sent to me the Holy *Spirit* in the *type* of a dove *. *But* the fire, the water and the wine have come into existence to *purify* all the sins of the *world*. On the other hand, the blood was for me a sign concerning the *body* of mankind, which I received in the *place* of the Barbelo, the great *power* of the *Invisible* God [1]. Furthermore the *Spirit* draws all *souls* together and takes them to the *place* of the light. Because of this, I have said to you: 'I have come to cast fire upon the earth' ▫. That is, I have come to *purify* the sins of the whole *world* with fire. And because of this I said to the Samaritan woman: 'If thou hadst known the *gift* of God, and who it is who says to thee: give me to drink, thou wouldst have *asked* him and he would have given thee living water and it would have been a *source* ⟨of water⟩ in thee springing up to eternal life' ○. And also because of this I took a cup of wine, I blessed it, I gave it to you, saying: 'This is the blood of the *covenant* which will be shed | for you for the forgiveness

---

* cf. Mt. 3.16; Lk. 3.22; Joh. 1.32
▫ cf. Lk. 12.49
○ cf. Joh. 4.10, 14

---

[1] (10) Invisible God; see J 39.

ⲣⲱⲧⲛ̅ ⲉⲡⲕⲱ ⲉⲃⲟⲗ ⲛ̅ⲛⲉⲧⲛ̅ⲛⲟⲃⲉ· ⲁⲩⲱ ⲟⲛ ⲉⲧⲃⲉ ⲡⲁⲓ̈
ⲁⲩⲭⲟ ⲛ̅ⲧⲗⲟⲅⲭⲏ ⲉϩⲟⲩⲛ ⲉⲡⲁⲥⲡⲓⲣ· ⲁϥⲉⲓ̓ ⲉⲃⲟⲗ ⲛ̅ϭⲓ ⲟⲩⲙⲟⲟⲩ ⲙ̅ⲛ ⲟⲩⲥⲛⲟϥ· ⲛⲁⲓ̈ ⲇⲉ ⲛⲉ ⲙ̅ⲙⲩⲥⲧⲏⲣⲓⲟⲛ ⲙ̅ⲡⲟⲩⲟ-
ⲉⲓⲛ ⲉϣⲁⲩⲕⲁ-ⲛⲟⲃⲉ ⲉⲃⲟⲗ ⲉⲧⲉ ⲛ̅ⲧⲟⲟⲩ ⲛⲉ ⲛ̅ⲟⲛⲟⲙⲁⲥⲓⲁ
5 ⲙ̅ⲛ ⲛ̅ⲣⲁⲛ ⲙ̅ⲡⲟⲩⲟⲉⲓⲛ·   [ⲧⲁⲃ]ᵇ

ⲁⲥϣⲱⲡⲉ ϭⲉ ⲙ̅ⲛ̅ⲛ̅ⲥⲁ ⲛⲁⲓ̈ ⲁϥⲕⲉⲗⲉⲩⲉ ⲛ̅ϭⲓ ⲓ̅ⲥ̅ ϫⲉ ⲙⲁⲣⲉ
ⲛ̅ⲇⲩⲛⲁⲙⲓⲥ ⲧⲏⲣⲟⲩ ⲛ̅ⲧⲉϩⲃⲟⲩⲣ ⲉⲓ̓ ⲉⲛⲉⲩⲧⲟⲡⲟⲥ· ⲁⲩⲱ
ⲁ ⲓ̅ⲥ̅ ⲙ̅ⲛ ⲛⲉϥⲙⲁⲑⲏⲧⲏⲥ ϭⲱ ϩⲓϫⲙ̅ ⲡⲧⲟⲟⲩ ⲛ̅ⲧⲅⲁⲗⲓⲗⲁⲓⲁ·
ⲁⲩⲟⲩⲱϩ ⲟⲛ ⲉⲧⲟⲟⲧⲟⲩ ⲛ̅ϭⲓ ⲙ̅ⲙⲁⲑⲏⲧⲏⲥ ⲁⲩⲧⲱⲃ̅ϩ ⲙ̅ⲙⲟϥ
10 ϫⲉ ϣⲁ ⲧⲛⲁⲩ ϭⲉ ⲙ̅ⲡⲕ̅ⲧⲣⲉⲩⲕⲱ ⲉⲃⲟⲗ ⲛ̅ⲛⲉⲛⲛⲟⲃⲉ ⲉⲛⲧ-
ⲁⲛⲁⲁⲩ ⲙ̅ⲛ ⲛⲉⲛⲁⲛⲟⲙⲓⲁ· ⲁⲩⲱ ⲛ̅ⲅ̅ⲧⲣⲉⲛⲙ̅ⲡϣⲁ ⲛ̅ⲧⲙⲛ̅ⲧⲉⲣⲟ
ⲙ̅ⲡⲉⲕⲉⲓⲱⲧ̓ ⲓ̅ⲥ̅ ⲇⲉ ⲡⲉϫⲁϥ ⲛⲁⲩ ϫⲉ ϩⲁⲙⲏⲛ ϯϫⲱ ⲙ̅ⲙⲟⲥ
ⲛⲏⲧⲛ̅ ϫⲉ ⲟⲩⲙⲟⲛⲟⲛ ϯⲛⲁⲕⲁⲑⲁⲣⲓⲍⲉ ⲛ̅ⲛⲉⲧⲛ̅ⲛⲟⲃⲉ· ⲁⲗⲗⲁ
ϯⲛⲁⲧⲣⲉⲧⲛ̅ⲙ̅ⲡϣⲁ ⲟⲛ ⲛ̅ⲧⲙⲛ̅ⲧⲉⲣⲟ ⲙ̅ⲡⲁⲉⲓⲱⲧ̓ ⲁⲩⲱ ϯⲛⲁϯ
15 ⲛⲏⲧⲛ̅ ⲙ̅ⲡⲙⲩⲥⲧⲏⲣⲓⲟⲛ ⲙ̅ⲡⲕⲁ-ⲛⲟⲃⲉ ⲉⲃⲟⲗ ϩⲓϫⲙ̅ ⲡⲕⲁϩ· ϫⲉⲕⲁⲥ ⲡⲉⲧⲉⲧⲛⲁⲕⲱ ⲛⲁϥ ⲉⲃⲟⲗ ϩⲓϫⲙ̅ ⲡⲕⲁϩ ⲉⲩⲉⲕⲱ ⲛⲁϥ
ⲉⲃⲟⲗ ϩⲛ̅ ⲙ̅ⲡⲏⲩⲉ ⲁⲩⲱ ⲡⲉⲧⲉⲧⲛⲁⲙⲟⲣϥ̅ ϩⲓϫⲙ̅ ⲡⲕⲁϩ ϥⲛⲁϣⲱⲡⲉ ⲉϥⲙⲏⲣ ϩⲛ̅ ⲙ̅ⲡⲏⲩⲉ· ϯⲛⲁϯ ⲛⲏⲧⲛ̅ ⲙ̅ⲡⲙⲩⲥⲧⲏⲣⲓⲟⲛ
ⲛ̅ⲧⲙⲛ̅ⲧⲉⲣⲟ ⲛ̅ⲙ̅ⲡⲏⲩⲉ ϫⲉⲕⲁⲁⲥ ⲛ̅ⲧⲱⲧⲛ̅ ϩⲱⲧ̈ⲧⲏⲩⲧⲛ̅ ⲉ- ⲧⲁⲅ̄
20 ⲧⲉⲧⲛⲉⲁⲁⲩ ⲛ̅ⲣ̅ⲣⲱⲙⲉ· ⲓ̅ⲥ̅ ⲇⲉ ⲡⲉϫⲁϥ ⲛⲁⲩ ϫⲉ ⲁⲛⲓⲛⲉ
ⲛⲁⲓ̈ ⲛ̅ⲟⲩⲕⲱϩⲧ̅ ⲙ̅ⲛ ϩⲉⲛϣϩⲉ ⲛ̅ⲉⲗⲟⲟⲗⲉ· ⲁⲩⲛ̅ⲧⲟⲩ ⲛⲁϥ
ⲁϥⲧⲁⲗⲟ ⲉϩⲣⲁⲓ̈ ⲛ̅ⲧⲉⲡⲣⲟⲥⲫⲟⲣⲁ ⲁϥⲕⲱ ⲛ̅ⲁⲅⲅⲓⲟⲛ ⲥⲛⲁⲩ
ⲛ̅ⲏⲣⲡ̅ ⲟⲩⲁ ϩⲓ ⲟⲩⲛⲁⲙ̓ ⲁⲩⲱ ⲡⲕⲉⲟⲩⲁ ϩⲓ ϩⲃⲟⲩⲣ ⲛ̅ⲧⲉ-
ⲡⲣⲟⲥⲫⲟⲣⲁ· ⲁϥⲕⲱ ⲛ̅ⲧⲉⲡⲣⲟⲥⲫⲟⲣⲁ ϩⲓⲑⲏ ⲙ̅ⲙⲟⲟⲩ· ⲁϥⲕⲱ

---

4 MS originally ⲛⲟⲙⲁⲥⲓⲁ; ⲟⲛ inserted above.
19 ⲕⲃ̄ in upper left-hand margin at beginning of quire.

of your sins' *. And also because of this the *spear* was thrust
into my side and there came forth water and blood °. These
moreover are the *mysteries* of the light which forgive sins,
which are the *invocations* and the names of the light."

Now it happened after these things, Jesus *commanded*:
"Let all the *powers* of the left go to their *places*." And
Jesus with his *disciples* remained upon the mountain of
Galilee °. The *disciples* continued again, they entreated him:
"For how long now hast thou not caused the sins which
we have committed and our *iniquities* to be forgiven, and
made us worthy of the Kingdom of thy Father?"

But Jesus said to them: "*Truly* I say to you, *not only* will
I *purify* your sins, *but* I will also make you worthy of the
Kingdom of my Father. And I will give to you the *mystery*
of forgiveness upon earth, so that he whom you will forgive
upon earth will be forgiven in heaven, and he whom you will
bind upon earth will be bound in heaven ^ 1. I will give
to you the *mystery* of the Kingdom of Heaven so that
you yourselves 2 perform them (the mysteries) for men."

142. Jesus *moreover* said to them: "Bring me fire and
vine branches 3." They brought them to him. He lifted
up the *offering*, he placed two *pitchers* of wine, one on the
right and the other on the left of the *offering*. He placed the
offering in front of them. He placed | a cup of water in front

---

*   cf. Mt. 26.27, 28
□   cf. Joh. 19.34
°   cf. Mt. 28.16
^   cf. Mt. 16.19; 18.18; Joh. 20.23

---

1   (17, 18) heaven; lit. the heavens.
2   (19) you yourselves; Till: (or) you also.
3   (21) vine branches; lit. vine wood; see J 106.

ⲚⲞⲨⲀⲠⲞⲦ ⲘⲘⲞⲞⲨ ϨⲀⲦⲘ ⲠⲈϨⲚⲀⲀⲨ ⲚⲎⲢⲠ ⲈⲦϨⲒ ⲞⲨⲚⲀⲘ·

ⲀⲨⲰ ⲀϤⲔⲰ ⲚⲞⲨⲀⲠⲞⲦ ⲚⲎⲢⲠ ϨⲀⲦⲘ ⲠⲈϨⲚⲀⲀⲨ ⲚⲎⲢⲠ

ⲈⲦϨⲒ ϨⲂⲞⲨⲢ ⲀⲨⲰ ⲀϤⲔⲰ ⲚϨⲈⲚⲞⲒⲔ ⲔⲀⲦⲀ ⲦⲎⲠⲈ ⲚⲘ-

ⲘⲀⲐⲎⲦⲎⲤ ϨⲚ ⲦⲘⲎⲦⲈ ⲚⲚⲀⲠⲞⲦ· ⲀϤⲔⲰ ⲚⲞⲨⲀⲠⲞⲦ Ⲙ-

5 ⲘⲞⲞⲨ ϨⲒⲠⲀϨⲞⲨ ⲚⲚⲞⲈⲒⲔ· ⲀϤⲀϨⲈⲢⲀⲦϤ ⲚϬⲒ ⲒⲤ ϨⲒⲐⲎ ⲚⲦⲈ-

ⲠⲢⲞⲤⲪⲞⲢⲀ ⲀϤⲔⲰ ⲚⲘⲘⲀⲐⲎⲦⲎⲤ ϨⲒⲠⲀϨⲞⲨ ⲘⲘⲞϤ ⲈⲨ-

ϬⲞⲞⲖⲈ ⲦⲎⲢⲞⲨ ⲚϨⲈⲚϨⲂⲞⲤ ⲚⲚϬⲒⲀⲀⲨ· ⲈⲢⲈ ⲦⲈ·ⲨⲎⲪⲞⲤ

ⲘⲠⲢⲀⲚ ⲘⲠⲈⲒⲰⲦ ⲘⲠⲈⲐⲎⲤⲀⲨⲢⲞⲤ ⲘⲠⲞⲨⲞⲈⲒⲚ ϨⲚ ⲚⲈⲨϬⲒⲬ·

ⲀϤⲰϢ ⲈⲂⲞⲖ ⲚⲦⲈⲒϨⲈ ⲈϤϪⲰ ⲘⲘⲞⲤ ϪⲈ ⲤⲰⲦⲘ ⲈⲢⲞⲒ

10 ⲠⲀⲈⲒⲰⲦ· ⲠⲈⲒⲰⲦ ⲘⲘⲚⲦⲈⲒⲰⲦ ⲚⲒⲘ ⲠⲀⲠⲈⲢⲀⲚⲦⲞⲚ ⲚⲞⲨⲞ- ‾ⲦⲀⲄ b

ⲈⲒⲚ· ⲒⲀⲰ· ⲒⲞⲨⲰ· ⲒⲀⲰ· ⲀⲰⲒ· ⲰⲒⲀ ·ⲨⲒⲚⲰⲐⲈⲢ· ⲐⲈⲢⲰ·ⲨⲒⲚ·

Ⲱ·ⲨⲒⲐⲈⲢ· ⲚⲈϤⲐⲞⲞⲘⲀⲰⲐ· ⲚⲈⲪⲒⲞⲘⲀⲰⲐ· ⲘⲀⲢⲀⲬⲀⲬⲞⲀ·

ⲘⲀⲢⲘⲀⲢⲀⲬⲐⲀ· ⲒⲎⲀⲚⲀ ⲘⲈⲚⲀⲘⲀⲚ· ⲀⲘⲀⲚⲎ ⲦⲞⲨ ⲞⲨⲢⲀ-

ⲚⲞⲨ· ⲒⳓⲢⲀⲒ ϨⲀⲘⲎⲚ ϨⲀⲘⲎⲚ· ⲤⲞⲨⲂⲀⲒⲂⲀⲒ· ⲀⲠⲠⲀⲀⲠ· ϨⲀ-

15 ⲘⲎⲚ· ϨⲀⲘⲎⲚ· ⲀⲈⲢⲀⲀⲢⲀⲒ ϨⲀ ⲠⲀϨⲞⲨ ϨⲀⲘⲎⲚ ϨⲀⲘⲎⲚ·

ⲤⲀⲢⲤⲀⲢⲤⲀⲢⲦⲞⲨ ϨⲀⲘⲎⲚ ϨⲀⲘⲎⲚ· ⲔⲞⲨⲔⲒⲀⲘⲒⲚ ⲘⲒⲀⲒ· ϨⲀ-

ⲘⲎⲚ ϨⲀⲘⲎⲚ· ⲒⲀⲒ· ⲒⲀⲒ· ⲦⲞⲨⲀⲠ ϨⲀⲘⲎⲚ ϨⲀⲘⲎⲚ ϨⲀⲘⲎⲚ·

ⲘⲀⲒⲚ ⲘⲀⲢⲒ· ⲘⲀⲢⲒⲎ· ⲘⲀⲢⲈⲒ· ϨⲀⲘⲎⲚ ϨⲀⲘⲎⲚ ϨⲀⲘⲎⲚ· ⲤⲰⲦⲘ

ⲈⲢⲞⲒ ⲠⲀⲈⲒⲰⲦ ⲠⲈⲒⲰⲦ ⲚⲘⲘⲚⲦⲈⲒⲰⲦ ⲚⲒⲘ· ϮⲈⲠⲒⲔⲀⲖⲈⲒ

20 ⲘⲘⲰⲦⲚ ϨⲰⲦⲦⲎⲨⲦⲚ ⲚⲢⲈϤⲔⲀ-ⲚⲞⲂⲈ ⲈⲂⲞⲖ ⲚⲢⲈϤⲔⲀⲐⲀⲢⲒⳌⲈ

ⲚⲚⲀⲚⲞⲘⲒⲀ· ⲔⲰ ⲈⲂⲞⲖ ⲚⲚⲚⲞⲂⲈ ⲚⲚⲈⲨⲨⲬⲎ ⲚⲚⲈⲒⲘⲀⲐⲎ-

ⲦⲎⲤ ⲈⲚⲦⲀⲨⲞⲨⲀϨⲞⲨ ⲚⲤⲰⲒ ⲀⲨⲰ ⲚⲦⲈⲦⲚⲔⲀⲐⲀⲢⲒⳌⲈ Ⲛ-

ⲚⲈⲨⲀⲚⲞⲘⲒⲀ· ⲚⲦⲈⲦⲚⲦⲢⲈⲨⲘⲠϢⲀ ⲚⲰⲠ· ⲈϨⲞⲨⲚ ⲈⲦⲘⲚⲦⲈ-

ⲢⲞ ⲘⲠⲀ·ⲈⲒⲰⲦ· ⲠⲈⲒⲰⲦ ⲘⲠⲈⲐⲎⲤⲀⲨⲢⲞⲤ ⲘⲠⲞⲨⲞⲈⲒⲚ ϪⲈ [ⲦⲀⲖ]

25 ⲀⲨⲞⲨⲀϨⲞⲨ ⲚⲤⲰⲒ ⲀⲨⲰ ⲀⲨϨⲀⲢⲈϨ ⲈⲚⲀⲈⲚⲦⲞⲖⲎ· ⲦⲈⲚⲞⲨ

ϬⲈ ⲠⲀⲈⲒⲰⲦ ⲠⲈⲒⲰⲦ ⲘⲘⲚⲦⲈⲒⲰⲦ ⲚⲒⲘ· ⲘⲀⲢⲈⲨⲈⲒ ⲚϬⲒ Ⲛ-

---

5 MS ⲚⲚⲚⲞⲈⲒⲔ; third Ⲛ expunged.

19 MS ⲚⲘⲘⲚⲦⲈⲒⲰⲦ; read ⲘⲘⲚⲦⲈⲒⲰⲦ.

of the pitcher of wine which was on the right. And he placed a cup of wine in front of the pitcher of wine which was on the left. And he placed loaves *according to* the number of the *disciples* in the midst of the cups. He placed a cup of water behind the loaves. Jesus stood before the *offering*. He placed his *disciples* behind him, all robed in linen garments, while the *cipher* of the name of the Father of the *Treasury* of the Light was in their hands. He cried out thus, saying : "Hear me, my Father, thou father of all fatherhoods, thou *infinite* Light ϊαω, ϊουω. ϊαω. αωϊ. ωϊα. ψινωθερ. θερωψιν. ωψιθερ. νεφθομαωθ. νεφιομαωθ. μαρα-χαχθα. μαρμαραχθα. ιηανα. μεναμαν. αμανηϊ. *of heaven* ϊσραϊ *Amen, amen* σουβαϊβαϊ. αππααπ. *Amen, amen.* δε-ρααραϊ behind them, *Amen, amen.* σαρσαρσαρτου. *Amen, amen.* κουκιαμιν μιαϊ. *Amen, amen.* ϊαϊ. ϊαϊ. τουαπ. *Amen, amen, amen.* μαϊν μαρι. μαριη. μαρει. *Amen, amen, amen.* Hear me, my Father, thou Father of all Fatherhoods. I *call upon* you also, you forgivers of sins, you *purifiers* of *iniquities*. Forgive the sins of the *souls* of these *disciples* which have followed me and *purify* their *iniquities*. Make them worthy to be numbered within the Kingdom of my Father, the Father of the *Treasury* of the Light, because they have followed me and they have kept my *injunctions*. Now at this time, my Father, thou Father of all Fatherhoods, may the forgivers of sins come, | whose names are these :

ⲢⲈϤⲔⲀ-ⲚⲞⲂⲈ ⲈⲂⲞⲖ· ⲈⲦⲈ ⲚⲈⲨⲢⲀⲚ ⲚⲈ ⲚⲀⲒ· ϬⲒϤⲒⲢⲈϤⲚⲒ-
ⲬⲒⲈⲨ· ⲌⲈⲚⲈⲒ· ⲂⲈⲢⲒⲘⲞⲨ· ⲤⲞⲬⲀⲂⲢⲒⲬⲎⲢ· ⲈⲨⲐⲀⲢⲒ· ⲚⲀⲚⲀⲒ
ⲀⲒⲈⲒⲤⲂⲀⲀⲘⲎⲢⲒⲬ· ⲘⲈⲨⲚⲒⲠⲞⲤ· ⲬⲒⲢⲒⲈ· ⲈⲚⲦⲀⲒⲢ· ⲘⲞⲨⲐⲒⲞⲨⲢ·
ⲤⲘⲞⲨⲢ· ⲠⲈⲨⲬⲎⲢ· ⲞⲞⲨⲤⲬⲞⲨⲤ· ⲘⲒⲚⲒⲞⲚⲞⲢ· ⲒⲤⲞⲬⲞⲂⲞⲢ-
5 ⲞⲀ· ⲤⲰⲦⲘ ⲈⲢⲞⲒ ⲈⲒⲈⲠⲒⲔⲀⲖⲈⲒ ⲘⲘⲰⲦⲚ ⲔⲰ ⲈⲂⲞⲖ ⲚⲚ-
ⲚⲞⲂⲈ ⲚⲚⲈⲒⲮⲨⲬⲞⲞⲨⲈ· ⲀⲨⲰ ϤⲰⲦⲈ ⲈⲂⲞⲖ ⲚⲚⲈⲨⲀⲚⲞⲘⲒⲀ·
ⲘⲀⲢⲞⲨⲘⲠⲰⲀ ⲚⲰⲠ ⲈⲀⲞⲨⲚ ⲈⲦⲘⲚⲦⲈⲢⲞ ⲘⲠⲀⲈⲒⲰⲦ ⲠⲈⲒⲰⲦ
ⲘⲠⲈⲐⲎⲤⲀⲨⲢⲞⲤ ⲘⲠⲞⲨⲞⲈⲒⲚ· ⲬⲈ ⲀⲚⲞⲔ ϮⲤⲞⲞⲨⲚ Ⲛ-
ⲚⲈⲔⲚⲞϬ ⲚⲆⲨⲚⲀⲘⲒⲤ ⲀⲨⲰ ϮⲈⲠⲒⲔⲀⲖ ⲘⲘⲞⲞⲨ· ⲀⲨⲎⲢ·
10 ⲂⲈⲂⲢⲰ· ⲀⲐⲢⲞⲚⲒ· ⲎⲞⲨϤⲈϤ· ⲎⲰⲚⲈ· ⲤⲞⲨϤⲈⲚ· ⲔⲚⲒⲦⲞⲨ-
ⲤⲞⲬⲢⲈⲰϤ· ⲘⲀⲨⲰⲚⲂⲒ· ⲘⲚⲈⲨⲰⲢ· ⲤⲞⲨⲰⲚⲒ· ⲬⲰⲬⲈ-
ⲦⲈⲰϤ· ⲬⲰⲬⲈ·* ⲈⲦⲈⲰϤ· ⲘⲈⲘⲰⲬ· ⲀⲚⲎⲘϤ· ⲔⲰ ⲈⲂⲞⲖ [ⲦⲀⲖ ᵇ
ⲚⲚⲚⲞⲂⲈ ⲚⲚⲈⲒⲮⲨⲬⲞⲞⲨⲈ ϤⲰⲦⲈ ⲈⲂⲞⲖ ⲚⲚⲈⲨⲀⲚⲞⲘⲒⲀ
ⲚⲈⲚⲦⲀⲨⲀⲀⲨ ⲈⲨⲤⲞⲞⲨⲚ ⲀⲨⲰ ⲚⲈⲚⲦⲀⲨⲀⲀⲨ ⲈⲚⲤⲈⲤⲞⲞⲨⲚ
15 ⲀⲚ· ⲚⲈⲚⲦⲀⲨⲀⲀⲨ ⲀⲚ ⲞⲨⲠⲞⲢⲚⲈⲒⲀ ⲘⲚ ⲞⲨⲘⲚⲦⲚⲞⲈⲒⲔ'
ⲀⲈⲰⲤ ⲰⲀⲀⲞⲨⲚ ⲈⲠⲞⲞⲨ ⲚⲀⲞⲞⲨ ⲔⲀⲀⲨ ⲚⲀⲨ ⲈⲂⲞⲖ· ⲀⲨⲰ
ⲚⲄⲦⲢⲈⲨⲘⲠⲰⲀ ⲚⲰⲠ' ⲈⲀⲞⲨⲚ ⲈⲦⲘⲚⲦⲈⲢⲞ ⲘⲠⲀⲈⲒⲰⲦ
ⲚⲤⲈⲘⲠⲰⲀ ⲚⲬⲒ ⲈⲂⲞⲖ ⲀⲚ ⲦⲈⲒⲠⲢⲞⲤϤⲞⲢⲀ ⲠⲀⲈⲒⲰⲦ' ⲈⲦ-
ⲞⲨⲀⲀⲂ· ⲈⲰⲰⲠⲈ ϬⲈ ⲠⲀⲈⲒⲰⲦ ⲀⲔⲤⲰⲦⲘ ⲈⲢⲞⲒ ⲀⲨⲰ ⲀⲔⲔⲰ
20 ⲈⲂⲞⲖ ⲚⲚⲚⲞⲂⲈ ⲚⲚⲈⲒⲮⲨⲬⲎ ⲀⲨⲰ ⲀⲔϤⲰⲦⲈ ⲈⲂⲞⲖ ⲚⲚⲈⲨ-
ⲀⲚⲞⲘⲒⲀ· ⲀⲨⲰ ⲀⲔⲦⲢⲈⲨⲘⲠⲰⲀ ⲚⲰⲠ' ⲈⲀⲞⲨⲚ ⲈⲦⲈⲔⲘⲚⲦⲈ-
ⲢⲞ· ⲈⲔⲈϮ ⲚⲀⲒ ⲚⲞⲨⲘⲀⲒⲚ ⲀⲚ ⲦⲈⲒⲠⲢⲞⲤϤⲞⲢⲀ· ⲀⲨⲰ ⲀϤ-
ⲰⲰⲠⲈ ⲚϬⲒ ⲠⲘⲀⲒⲚ ⲚⲦⲀ ⲒⲤ ⲬⲞⲞϤ· ⲠⲈⲬⲈ ⲒⲤ ⲈⲀⲞⲨⲚ
ⲈⲀⲚ ⲚⲈϤⲘⲀⲐⲎⲦⲎⲤ· ⲬⲈ ⲢⲀⲰⲈ ⲚⲦⲈⲦⲚⲦⲈⲖⲎⲖ ⲬⲈ ⲀⲨⲔⲰ
25 ⲈⲂⲞⲖ ⲚⲚⲈⲦⲚⲚⲞⲂⲈ ⲀⲨⲰ ⲀⲨϤⲰⲦⲈ ⲈⲂⲞⲖ ⲚⲚⲈⲦⲚⲀⲚⲞⲘⲒⲀ· ⲦⲀⲈ

---

19 ⲠⲀⲒ expunged before ⲈⲰⲰⲠⲈ.

σιφιρεψνιχιευ. ζενει. βεριμου. σοχαβριχηρ. ευθαρι. νanaϊ. διεισβαλμηριχ. μευνιπος. χιριε. ενταϊρ. μουθιουρ. σμουρ. πευχηρ. οουσχους. μινιονορ. ϊσοχοβορθα. Hear me as I *call upon* you. Forgive the sins of these *souls* and wipe out their *iniquities*. May they be worthy to be numbered within the Kingdom of my Father, the Father of the Treasury of the Light. For I know thy great *powers* and I *call upon* them: αυηρ. βεβρω. αθρονι. η ουρεφ. η ωνε. σουφεν. κνιτουσοχρεωφ. μαυωνβι. μνευωρ. σουωνι. χωχετεωφ. χωχε. ετεωφ. μεμωχ. ανημφ. Forgive the sins of these *souls*; wipe out their *iniquities* which they have committed knowingly and unknowingly. Forgive them these which they have committed in *fornication* and adultery *until* the present day. And make them worthy to be numbered within the Kingdom of my Father, and worthy to partake of this *offering*, my holy Father. Now my Father, if thou hast heard me, and thou hast forgiven the sins of these *souls* and thou hast wiped out their *iniquities*, and thou hast made them worthy to be numbered within thy Kingdom, do thou give me a sign in this *offering*." And the sign of which Jesus spoke happened.

Jesus said to his *disciples*: "Rejoice and be glad, because your sins are forgiven, and your *iniquities* are wiped out, |

ΑΥΩ ΑΤΕΤΝΩΠ' ΕϨΟΥΝ ΕΤΜΝΤΕΡΟ ΜΠΑΪΩΤ· ΝΑΪ ΔΕ
ΝΤΕΡΕϤΧΟΟΥ Α ΜΜΑΘΗΤΗC ΡΑϢΕ ϨΝ ΟΥΝΟϬ ΝΡΑϢΕ·
ΠΕΧΕ ΙC ΝΑΥ ΧΕ ΤΑΪ ΤΕ ΘΕ ΑΥΩ ΠΑΪ ΠΕ ΠΜΥCΤΗ-
ΡΙΟΝ ΕΤΕΤΝΑΑΑϤ ΝΡΡΩΜΕ ΕΤΝΑΠΙCΤΕΥΕ ΕΡΩΤΝ ΕΜΝ-
5 ΚΡΟϤ ΝϨΗΤΟΥ ΑΥΩ ΕΥCΩΤΜ ΝCΑ-ΤΗΥΤΝ ϨΝ ϢΑΧΕ
ΝΙΜ' ΕΤΝΑΝΟΥϤ· ΑΥΩ ΝΕΥΝΟΒΕ ΜΝ ΝΕΥΑΝΟΜΙΑ CΕ-
ΝΑϤΟΤΟΥ ΕΒΟΛ ϢΑ ΠΕϨΟΟΥ ΕΝΤΑΤΕΤΝΕΙΡΕ ΝΑΥ Μ-
ΠΕΪΜΥCΤΗΡΙΟΝ· ΑΛΛΑ ϨΩΠ' ΜΠΕΪΜΥCΤΗΡΙΟΝ ΜΠΡΤΑΑϤ
ΝΡΩΜΕ ΝΙΜ· ΕΙΜΗΤΙ ΠΕΤΝΑΕΙΡΕ ΝϨΩΒ ΝΙΜ' ΕΝΤΑΪΧΟΟΥ
10 ΝΗΤΝ ϨΝ ΝΑΕΝΤΟΛΗ· ΠΑΪ ΟΥΝ ΠΕ ΠΜΥCΤΗΡΙΟΝ ΝΤΑ-
ΛΗΘΕΙΑ ΜΠΒΑΠΤΙCΜΑ ΝΝΕΤΟΥΝΑΚΩ ΕΒΟΛ ΝΝΕΥΝΟΒΕ
ΑΥΩ ΝΕΤΟΥΝΑϨΩΒC ΕΒΟΛ ΕΧΝ ΝΕΥΑΝΟΜΙΑ· ΠΑΪ ΠΕ
ΠΒΑΠΤΙCΜΑ ΝΤϢΟΡΠ ΜΠΡΟCΦΟΡΑ ΕΤΧΙΜΟΕΙΤ ΕϨΟΥΝ Ε-
ΠΤΟΠΟC ΝΤΑΛΗΘΙΑ· ΑΥΩ ΕϨΟΥΝ*ΕΠΤΟΠΟC ΜΠΟΥΟΕΙΝ· ΤΛΕ ᵇ
15 ΜΝΝCΑ ΝΑΪ ΟΝ ΠΕΧΑΥ ΝΑϤ ΝϬΙ ΝΕϤΜΑΘΗΤΗC ΧΕ
ϨΡΑΒΒΕΙ ϬΩΛΠ ΝΑΝ ΕΒΟΛ ΜΠΜΥCΤΗΡΙΟΝ ΜΠΟΥΟΕΙΝ
ΝΤΕ ΠΕΚΕΙΩΤ ΕΠΕΙΔΗ ΑΝCΩΤΜ ΕΡΟΚ ΕΚΧΩ ΜΜΟC
ΧΕ ΟΥΝ-ΚΕΒΑΠΤΙCΜΑ ΝΚΡΩΜ· ΑΥΩ ΟΥΝ-ΚΕΒΑΠΤΙCΜΑ
ΜΠΝΑ ΕϤΟΥΑΑΒ ΝΤΕ ΠΟΥΟΕΙΝ· ΑΥΩ ΟΥΝ-ΟΥΤΩϨC
20 ΜΠΝΑΤΙΚΟΝ ΝΑΪ ΕϢΑΥΧΙ ΝΝΕΨΥΧΟΟΥΕ ΕΠΕΘΗCΑΥ-
ΡΟC ΜΠΟΥΟΕΙΝ· ΧΩ ϬΕ ΕΡΟΝ ΜΠΕΥΜΥCΤΗΡΙΟΝ ΤΑΡΝ-
ΚΛΗΡΟΝΟΜΙ ϨΩΩΝ ΝΤΜΝΤΕΡΟ ΜΠΕΚΕΙΩΤ· ΠΕΧΕ ΙC
ΝΑΥ ΧΕ ΝΕΪΜΥCΤΗΡΙΟΝ ΕΤΕΤΝϢΙΝΕ ΝCΩΟΥ· ΜΝ-
ΜΥCΤΗΡΙΟΝ ΕϤΟΥΟΤΒ ΕΡΟΟΥ· ΕϤΝΑΧΙ ΝΤΕΤΝΨΥΧΗ
25 ΕΠΟΥΟΕΙΝ ΝΤΕ ΝΙΟΥΟΕΙΝ ΕΝΤΟΠΟC ΝΤΑΛΗΘΕΙΑ ΜΝ
ΤΜΝΤΑΓΑΘΟC ΜΠΤΟΠΟC ΝΠΕΤΟΥΑΑΒ ΝΤΕ ΝΕΤΟΥΑΑΒ

---

26 MS ΜΠΤΟΠΟC; read ΕΠΤΟΠΟC. MS ΝΠΕΤΟΥΑΑΒ; read ΜΠΕΤΟΥΑΑΒ.

and you are numbered within the Kingdom of my Father."
But when he had said these things, the *disciples* rejoiced with
great joy.

Jesus said to them : "This is the manner and this is the
mystery which you shall perform for men who will *believe*
in you, without guile in them, and who obey you with all
good words. And their sins and their *iniquities* will be wiped
out until the day on which you have performed this *mystery*
for them. *But* hide this *mystery*, and do not give it to any
man, *except* him who will do everything which I have said
to you in my *injunctions*. This *now* is the *true mystery* of the
baptism for those whose sins will be forgiven, and whose
iniquities will be covered over. This is the *baptism* of the
first *offering* which leads the way into the *place* of the
truth [1] and into the *place* of the light."

143.   After these things his *disciples* said to him : "Rabbi,
reveal to us the *mystery* of the light of thy Father, *since*
we have heard thee saying : 'There is one *baptism* of fire,
and there is another *baptism* of the Holy *Spirit* of the light,
and there is a *spiritual* inunction [2]; these take the *souls* to the
Treasury of the Light'. Say to us now their *mystery*, so that
we also *inherit* the kingdom of thy Father."

Jesus said to them : "There is no *mystery* which is superior
to these *mysteries* about which you question, which will take
your *souls* to the Light of Lights, to the *places* of *truth* and
goodness; to the *place* of the Holy of all Holies; | to the

---

[1]   (14) place of the truth; Schmidt : true place (see note on 122.10).

[2]   (18 ff.) 3 baptisms; see J 102.

ⲧⲏⲣⲟⲩ· ⲉⲡⲧⲟⲡⲟⲥ ⲉⲧⲉ ⲙ̅ⲛ̅-ⲥ̅ϩⲓⲙⲉ ⲛ̅ϩⲏⲧ̅ϥ̅· ⲟⲩⲇⲉ ⲙ̅ⲛ̅-
ϩⲟⲟⲩⲧ· ⲟⲩⲇⲉ ⲙ̅ⲛ̅-ⲙⲟⲣⲫⲏ ϩ̅ⲙ̅ ⲡⲧⲟⲡⲟⲥ ⲉⲧⲙ̅ⲙⲁⲩ ⲁⲗⲗⲁ [ⲧⲗⲉ̅]
ⲟⲩⲟⲩⲟⲉⲓⲛ ⲡⲉ ⲉϥⲙⲏⲛ ⲉⲃⲟⲗ' ⲛ̅ⲁⲧϣⲁϫⲉ ⲉⲣⲟϥ· ⲙ̅ⲛ̅
ⲡⲉⲧⲟⲩⲟⲧ̅ⲃ̅ ϭⲉ ⲉⲛⲉⲓ̈ⲙⲩⲥⲧⲏⲣⲓⲟⲛ ⲉⲧⲉⲧ̅ⲛ̅ϣⲓⲛⲉ ⲛ̅ⲥⲱⲟⲩ
5 ⲉⲓⲙⲏⲧⲓ ⲉⲡⲙⲩⲥⲧⲏⲣⲓⲟⲛ ⲛ̅ⲧⲥⲁϣϥⲉ ⲙ̅ⲫⲱⲛⲏ ⲙ̅ⲛ̅ ⲧⲉⲩϩⲙⲉ-
ⲯⲓⲧⲉ ⲛ̅ⲁⲩⲛⲁⲙⲓⲥ ⲁⲩⲱ ⲛⲉⲩⲯⲏⲫⲟⲥ ⲁⲩⲱ ⲙ̅ⲛ̅ ⲡⲣⲁⲛ ⲉⲧ-
ⲟⲩⲟⲧ̅ⲃ̅ ⲉⲣⲟⲟⲩ ⲧⲏⲣⲟⲩ· ⲡⲣⲁⲛ ⲉⲧⲉⲣⲉ ⲣⲁⲛ ⲛⲓⲙ ϣⲟⲟⲡ
ϩⲣⲁⲓ̈ ⲛ̅ϩⲏⲧ̅ϥ̅· ϩⲓ ⲟⲩⲟⲉⲓⲛ ⲛⲓⲙ' ϩⲓ ⲁⲩⲛⲁⲙⲓⲥ ⲛⲓⲙ· ⲡⲉⲧⲥⲟⲟⲩⲛ ϭⲉ ⲙ̅ⲡⲣⲁⲛ ⲉⲧⲙ̅ⲙⲁⲩ ⲉϥϣⲁⲛⲉⲓ' ⲉⲃⲟⲗ ϩ̅ⲙ̅ ⲡⲥⲱⲙⲁ
10 ⲛ̅ⲟⲩⲗⲏ ⲛ̅ⲛⲉϣ-ⲁⲗⲁⲩ ⲛ̅ⲕⲣⲱⲙ ⲟⲩⲇⲉ ⲗⲁⲗⲁⲩ ⲛ̅ⲕⲁⲕⲉ ⲟⲩⲇⲉ
ⲉⲝⲟⲩⲥⲓⲁ ⲟⲩⲇⲉ ⲁⲣⲭⲱⲛ ⲛ̅ⲧⲉ ⲧⲉⲥⲫⲁⲓⲣⲁ ⲛ̅ϩⲓⲙⲁⲣⲙⲉⲛⲏ
ⲟⲩⲇⲉ ⲁⲅⲅⲉⲗⲟⲥ ⲟⲩⲇⲉ ⲁⲣⲭⲁⲅⲅⲉⲗⲟⲥ ⲟⲩⲇⲉ ⲇⲩⲛⲁ-
ⲙⲓⲥ ⲛ̅ⲛⲉⲩⲉϣⲕⲁⲧⲉⲭⲉ ⲛ̅ⲧⲉⲯⲩⲭⲏ ⲉⲧⲥⲟⲟⲩⲛ ⲙ̅ⲡⲣⲁⲛ ⲉⲧ-
ⲙ̅ⲙⲁⲩ· ⲁⲗⲗⲁ ⲉϥϣⲁⲛⲉⲓ' ⲉⲃⲟⲗ ϩ̅ⲙ̅ ⲡⲕⲟⲥⲙⲟⲥ ⲛ̅ϥⲭⲱ ⲙ̅-
15 ⲡⲣⲁⲛ ⲉⲧⲙ̅ⲙⲁⲩ ⲉⲡⲕⲱϩ̅ⲧ̅ ϣⲁϥϣⲱⲙ· ⲁⲩⲱ ϣⲁⲣⲉ ⲡⲕⲁⲕⲉ
ⲁⲛⲁⲭⲱⲣⲉⲓ· ⲁⲩⲱ ⲉϥϣⲁⲛⲭⲟⲟϥ ⲉⲛⲇⲁⲓⲙⲟⲛⲓⲟⲛ ⲙ̅ⲛ̅ ⲙ̅-
ⲡⲁⲣⲁⲗⲏⲙⲡⲧⲏⲥ ⲙ̅ⲡⲕⲁⲕⲉ ⲉⲧϩⲓⲃⲟⲗ· ⲙ̅ⲛ̅ ⲛⲉⲩⲁⲣⲭⲱⲛ ⲙ̅ⲛ̅ [ⲧⲗⲉ̅ᵇ]
ⲛⲉⲩⲉⲝⲟⲩⲥⲓⲁ ⲙ̅ⲛ̅ ⲛⲉⲩⲇⲩⲛⲁⲙⲓⲥ ⲥⲉⲛⲁⲧⲁⲕⲟ ⲧⲏⲣⲟⲩ ⲛ̅ⲧⲉ
ⲡⲉⲩϣⲁϩ ⲙⲟⲩϩ· ⲛ̅ⲥⲉⲱϣ ⲉⲃⲟⲗ ϫⲉ ⲕⲟⲩⲁⲁⲃ· ⲕⲟⲩⲁⲁⲃ
20 ⲡⲉⲧⲟⲩⲁⲁⲃ ⲛ̅ⲧⲉ ⲛⲉⲧⲟⲩⲁⲁⲃ ⲧⲏⲣⲟⲩ· ⲁⲩⲱ ⲉⲩϣⲁⲛⲭⲱ
ⲙ̅ⲡⲣⲁⲛ ⲉⲧⲙ̅ⲙⲁⲩ ⲉⲙⲡⲁⲣⲁⲗⲏⲙⲡⲧⲏⲥ ⲛ̅ⲧⲉ ⲛⲉⲕⲣⲓⲥⲓⲥ
ⲉⲑⲟⲟⲩ ⲙ̅ⲛ̅ ⲛⲉⲩⲉⲝⲟⲩⲥⲓⲁ ⲙ̅ⲛ̅ ⲛⲉⲩϭⲟⲙ ⲧⲏⲣⲟⲩ ⲁⲩⲱ
ⲧⲕⲉⲃⲁⲣⲃⲏⲗⲱ ⲙ̅ⲛ̅ ⲡⲁϩⲟⲣⲁⲧⲟⲥ ⲛ̅ⲛⲟⲩⲧⲉ ⲙ̅ⲛ̅ ⲡϣⲟⲙ̅ⲛⲧ̅
ⲛ̅ⲛⲟⲩⲧⲉ ⲛ̅ⲧⲣⲓⲇⲩⲛⲁⲙⲓⲥ· ⲛ̅ⲧⲉⲩⲛⲟⲩ ⲉⲧⲟⲩⲛⲁⲭⲱ ⲙ̅ⲡⲉⲓ̈
25 ⲣⲁⲛ ϩ̅ⲛ̅ ⲛ̅ⲧⲟⲡⲟⲥ ⲉⲧⲙ̅ⲙⲁⲩ ⲥⲉⲛⲁϩⲉ ⲧⲏⲣⲟⲩ ⲉϫ̅ⲛ̅ ⲛⲉⲩⲉⲣⲏⲩ ⲛ̅ⲥⲉⲃⲱⲗ ⲉⲃⲟⲗ ⲛ̅ⲥⲉⲧⲁⲕⲟ ⲛ̅ⲥⲉⲱϣ ⲉⲃⲟⲗ ϫⲉ ⲡⲟⲩ-

---

5   MS ⲉⲡⲙⲩⲥⲧⲏⲣⲓⲟⲛ; read ⲡⲙⲩⲥⲧⲏⲣⲓⲟⲛ.
26   MS originally ⲛ̅ⲥⲉⲱϣ; ϣ expunged; ⲃ and ⲗ inserted above.

place in which there is neither woman *nor* man; *nor* are there *forms* in that *place*, *but* a perpetual ineffable light. Now there is nothing superior to these *mysteries* about which you question, *except* the *mystery* of the seven *voices* and their 49 *powers* and their *ciphers*, and the name which is superior to them all, the name within which are all names, and all lights and all *powers*. Now he who knows that name, when he comes forth from the *body* of *matter*, neither fire *nor* darkness, *nor power (exousia) nor archon* of the *Heimarmene-sphere*, *nor angel nor archangel nor power* can *restrain* the *soul* which knows that name. *But* when he (the man) comes forth from the *world* and says that name to the fire, it is extinguished; and the darkness *withdraws*. And when he says it to the *demons* and the *paralemptai* of the outer darkness, with their *archons* and their *powers (exousiai)* and their *powers (dunameis)*, they will all be destroyed, and their flame will burn, and they will cry out : 'Holy, holy art thou, thou holiest among all holy ones'. And when that name is said to the *paralemptai* of the wicked *judgments* and their *powers (exousiai)*, and all their powers and the Barbelo also, and the *invisible* god and the three *triple-powered* gods, immediately when that name is said in those *places*, they will all fall upon one another and be dissolved and destroyed. And they will cry out : | 'O Light of all

ΟΕΙΝ Ν̄ΤΕ ΟΥΟΕΙΝ ΝΙΜ ΕΤϢΟΟΠ' Ζ̄Ν ΝΙΑΠΕΡΑΝΤΟΝ Ν̄-
ΟΥΟΕΙΝ ΑΡΙΠΕΝΜΕΕΥΕ ΖⲰⲰΝ Ν̄ΓϹⲰΤϤ̄ Μ̄ΜΟΝ·

    Ν̄ΤΕΡΕϤΟΥⲰ ΔΕ ΕϤΧⲰ Ν̄ΝΕΪϢΑΧΕ Ν̄ϬΙ ῙϹ ΑΥⲰϢ
ΕΒΟΛ ΤΗΡΟΥ Ν̄ϬΙ ΝΕϤΜΑΘΗΤΗϹ ΑΥΡΙΜΕ Ζ̄Ν ΟΥΝΟϬ
⁵ Ν̄ΖΡΟΟΥ ΕΥΧⲰ Μ̄ΜΟϹ ΧΕ ✳ ✳ ✳ ✳ ✳ ✳ ✳ ✳ ✳ ✳ ✳ ✳ ✳ ✳
⟨ΜΝ̄ΝϹΑ ΝΑΪ Ν̄ϹΕΧΙΤϹ ΕΒΟΛ Ζ̄Ν ΝΕΙΕΡⲰΟΥ Ν̄ΚΡⲰΜ ΜΝ̄
ΖΕΝΘΑΛΑϹϹΑ Ν̄ΚⲰ⁺ΖΤ Ν̄ϹΕΤΙΜⲰΡΕΙ Μ̄ΜΟϹ Ν̄ΖΗΤΟΥ Ν̄- ᵀᴹᴱ
ΚΕϹΟΟΥ Ν̄ΕΒΟΤ ΜΝ̄ ϢΜΟΥΝ Ν̄ΖΟΟΥ· ΜΝ̄ΝϹΑ ΝΑΪ Ν̄ϹΕ-
ΧΙΤϹ ΕΖΡΑΪ ΖΙ ΤΕΖΙΗ Ν̄ΤΜΗΤΕ Ν̄ΤΕ ΠΟΥΑ ΠΟΥΑ Ν̄ΝΑΡΧⲰΝ
¹⁰ Ν̄ΤΕΖΙΗ Ν̄ΤΜΗΤΕ ΚΟΛΑΖΕ Μ̄ΜΟϹ Ζ̄Ν ΝΕϤΚΟΛΑϹΙϹ Ν̄ΚΕ-
ϹΟΟΥ Ν̄ΕΒΟΤ ΜΝ̄ ϢΜΟΥΝ Ν̄ΖΟΟΥ· ΜΝ̄ΝϹΑ ΝΑΪ Ν̄ϹΕ-
ΧΙΤϹ Ν̄ΤΠΑΡΘΕΝΟϹ Μ̄ΠΟΥΟΕΙΝ ΤΑΪ ΕϢΑϹΚΡΙΝΕ Ν̄ΝΙ-
ΑΓΑΘΟϹ ΜΝ̄ ΝΙΠΟΝΗΡΟϹ Ν̄ϹΚΡΙΝΕ Μ̄ΜΟϹ· ΑΥⲰ ΕΡϢΑΝ
ΤΕϹΦΑΙΡΑ ΚⲰΤΕ ϢΑϹΤΑΛΥ ΕΤΟΟΤΟΥ Ν̄ΝΕϹΠΑΡΑΛΗΜΠ-
¹⁵ΤΗϹ Ν̄ϹΕΝΟΧϹ ΕΝΑΙⲰΝ Ν̄ΤΕϹΦΑΙΡΑ· ΑΥⲰ ϢΑΡΕ Ν̄-
ΛΙΤΟΥΡΓΟϹ Ν̄ΤΕϹΦΑΙΡΑ ΧΙΤϹ ΕΒΟΛ' ΕΥΜΟΟΥ ΕϤΖΑ-
ΠΕϹΗΤ Ν̄ΤΕϹΦΑΙΡΑ Ν̄ϤΡ-ΟΥΚⲰΖΤ ΕϤΒΡΒΡ Ν̄ϤΟΥⲰΜ' Ε-
ΖΟΥΝ Ν̄ϹⲰϹ ϢΑΝΤϤ̄ΚΑΘΑΡΙΖΕ Μ̄ΜΟϹ ΤΟΝⲰ· ΑΥⲰ
ϢΑϤΕΙ' Ν̄ϬΙ ΪΑΛΟΥΖΑΜ Π̄ΠΑΡΑΛΗΜΠΤΗϹ Ν̄ϹΑΒΑⲰΘ' ΠΑ-
²⁰ΔΑΜΑϹ ΠΑΪ ΕϢΑϤϯ Μ̄ΠΑΠΟΤ' Ν̄ΤΒϢΕ Ν̄ΝΕΨΥΧΟΟΥΕ
Ν̄ϤΕΙΝΕ Ν̄ΟΥ⋅ΑΠΟΤ' ΕϤΜΕΖ ΕΒΟΛ Ζ̄Μ ΠΜΟΟΥ Ν̄ΤΒϢΕ ᵀᴹᴱ ᵇ
Ν̄ϤΤΑΛΥ Ν̄ΤΕΨΥΧΗ Ν̄ϹϹΟΟϤ Ν̄ϹΡΠⲰΒϢ Μ̄ΜΑ ΝΙΜ' ΜΝ̄
ΤΟΠΟϹ ΝΙΜ' ΕΝΤΑϹΒⲰΚ ΕΡΟΟΥ· Ν̄ϹΕΝΟΧϹ ΕΖΡΑΪ ΕΥ-
ϹⲰΜΑ ΕϤΝΑΡ-ΠΕϤΟΥΟΕΙϢ ΕϢΑϤ̄ΜΚΑΖ ΕΠΕϤΖΗΤ' ΕϤΜΗΝ
²⁵ΕΒΟΛ· ΤΑΪ ΤΕ ΤΚΟΛΑϹΙϹ Μ̄ΠΡⲰΜΕ Ν̄ΡΕϤϹΑΖΟΥ·

---

5   lacuna of 4 leaves = 8 pages (ΤΛΖ - ΤΜΔ).
24   MS originally ϹϤΝΑϢΑϤΜ̄ΚΑΖ; ϤΝΑ expunged.

Lights who art in the *infinite* lights, remember us and save us'."

But when Jesus had finished saying these words, all his *disciples* cried out. They wept with loud voices, saying ...

Lacuna of 8 pages (4 leaves)

144. ⟨After these things it is taken through rivers of fire and seas of fire⟩ and it (the soul) is *punished* in them for another six months and eight days. After these things it is taken upon the way of the Midst, so that each one of the *archons* of the way of the Midst *punishes* it with his *punishment* for another six months and eight days. After these things it is taken to the *Virgin* of the Light who *judges* the *good* and the *wicked*, and she *judges* it. And when the *sphere* turns, she gives it into the hands of her *paralemptai*, and they cast it into the *aeons* of the *sphere*. And the *ministers* of the *sphere* take it forth to a water which is below the *sphere* which becomes a boiling fire that consumes[1] it until it *purifies* it completely. And there comes Jalouham[2], the *paralemptes* of Sabaoth, the Adamas, he who gives the cup of forgetfulness to the *souls*, and he brings a cup full of the water of forgetfulness and he gives it to the *soul*, and it drinks it and forgets every place and all *places* to which it has gone. And it is cast into[3] a *body* in which it will spend its time[4] continuing to be troubled in heart. This is the *punishment* of the man who curses." |

---

[1]   (17) consumes; Till: eats into (also 376.3; 378.15; 379.15; 382.20, 21).

[2]   (19) Jalouham; perhaps Elohim; see Bousset (Bibl. 9) p. 10; (cf. also 333.6ff.).

[3]   (23) cast into; Till: stuck into.

[4]   (23) it will spend its time; lit. he will spend his time; (also 376.8).

ⲁⲥⲟⲩⲱϩ ⲟⲛ ⲉⲧⲟⲟⲧⲥ̄ ⲛ̄ϭⲓ ⲙⲁⲣⲓϩⲁⲙ ⲡⲉⲭⲁⲥ ϫⲉ ⲡⲁⲭⲟⲉⲓⲥ ⲉⲓ̈ⲉ ⲡⲣⲱⲙⲉ ⲛ̄ⲣⲉϥⲕⲁⲧⲁⲗⲁⲗⲓ ⲉϥⲙⲏⲛ ⲉⲃⲟⲗ ⲉϥϣⲁⲛⲉⲓ̈
ⲉⲃⲟⲗ ϩⲛ̄ ⲥⲱⲙⲁ ⲉϥⲛⲁⲃⲱⲕ ⲉⲧⲱⲛ ⲏ̄ ⲟⲩ ⲧⲉ ⲧⲉϥⲕⲟⲗⲁ-
ⲥⲓⲥ· ⲡⲉϫⲉ ⲓ̄ⲥ̄ ϫⲉ ⲟⲩⲣⲱⲙⲉ ⲛ̄ⲣⲉϥⲕⲁⲧⲁⲗⲁⲗⲓ ⲉϥⲙⲏⲛ
5 ⲉⲃⲟⲗ ⲉϥϣⲁⲛϫⲱⲕ ⲉⲃⲟⲗ ⲛ̄ϭⲓ ⲡⲉϥⲟⲩⲟⲉⲓϣ ϩⲓⲧⲛ̄ ⲧⲉⲥⲫⲁⲓⲣⲁ ⲉⲧⲣⲉϥⲉⲓ̈ ⲉⲃⲟⲗ ϩⲛ̄ ⲥⲱⲙⲁ ϣⲁⲩⲉⲓ̈ ⲛ̄ⲥⲱϥ ⲛ̄ϭⲓ
ⲁⲃⲓⲟⲩⲧ· ⲙⲛ̄ ⲭⲁⲣⲙⲱⲛ ⲙ̄ⲡⲁⲣⲁⲗⲏⲙⲡⲧⲏⲥ ⲛ̄ⲁⲣⲓⲏⲗ ⲛ̄ⲥⲉⲉⲓⲛⲉ
ⲛ̄ⲧⲉϥⲯⲩⲭⲏ ⲉⲃⲟⲗ ϩⲛ̄ ⲥⲱⲙⲁ ⲛ̄ⲥⲉⲣ̄-ϣⲟⲙⲛ̄ⲧ ⲛ̄ϩⲟⲟⲩ ⲉⲩϯ-
ⲟⲩⲟⲓ̈ ⲛ̄ⲙⲙⲁⲥ ⲉⲩⲧⲥⲁⲃⲟ ⲙ̄ⲙⲟⲥ ⲉⲛⲥⲱⲛⲧ ⲙ̄ⲡⲕⲟⲥⲙⲟⲥ·
10 ⲙⲛ̄ⲛ̄ⲥⲁ ⲛⲁⲓ̈ ⲛ̄ⲥⲉϫⲓⲧⲥ̄ ⲉⲡⲉⲥⲏⲧ ⲉⲁⲙⲛ̄ⲧⲉ ⲉⲣⲁⲧϥ̄ ⲛ̄ⲁⲣⲓⲏⲗ· [ⲧⲙⲉ
ⲛ̄ϥⲕⲟⲗⲁⲍⲉ ⲙ̄ⲙⲟⲥ ϩⲛ̄ ⲛⲉϥⲕⲟⲗⲁⲥⲓⲥ ⲙ̄ⲙⲛ̄ⲧⲟⲩⲉ ⲛ̄ⲉⲃⲟⲧ
ⲙⲛ̄ ⲭⲟⲩⲧⲟⲩⲉ ⲛ̄ϩⲟⲟⲩ ⲙⲛ̄ⲛ̄ⲥⲱⲥ ⲛ̄ⲥⲉϫⲓⲧⲥ̄ ⲉⲡⲉⲭⲗⲁⲟⲥ
ⲉⲣⲁⲧϥ̄ ⲛ̄ⲓ̈ⲁⲗⲇⲁⲃⲁⲱⲑ ⲙⲛ̄ ⲡⲉϥⲥⲙⲉⲯⲓⲧ ⲛ̄ⲇⲁⲓⲙⲟⲛⲓⲟⲛ ⲛ̄ⲧⲉ
ⲡⲟⲩⲁ ⲡⲟⲩⲁ ⲛ̄ⲛⲉϥⲇⲁⲓⲙⲟⲛⲓⲟⲛ ⲃⲱⲕ ⲉⲃⲟⲗ ϩⲓϫⲱⲥ ⲛ̄ⲕⲉ-
15 ⲙⲛ̄ⲧⲟⲩⲉ ⲛ̄ⲉⲃⲟⲧ ⲙⲛ̄ ⲕⲉⲭⲟⲩⲧⲟⲩⲉ ⲛ̄ϩⲟⲟⲩ ⲉⲩⲫⲣⲁⲅⲉⲗ-
ⲗⲟⲩ ⲙ̄ⲙⲟⲥ ϩⲓⲧⲛ̄ ϩⲉⲛⲙⲁⲥⲧⲓⲅⲝ ⲛ̄ⲕⲣⲱⲙ· ⲙⲛ̄ⲛ̄ⲥⲁ ⲛⲁⲓ̈ ⲛ̄ⲥⲉ-
ϫⲓⲧⲥ̄ ⲉⲃⲟⲗ ϩⲛ̄ ⲛⲉⲓⲉⲣⲱⲟⲩ ⲛ̄ⲕⲣⲱⲙ· ⲙⲛ̄ ϩⲉⲛⲑⲁⲗⲁⲥⲥⲁ ⲛ̄-
ⲕⲱϩⲧ ⲉⲩⲃⲣ̄ⲃⲣ̄ ⲛ̄ⲥⲉⲧⲓⲙⲱⲣⲉⲓ ⲙ̄ⲙⲟⲥ ⲛ̄ϩⲏⲧⲟⲩ ⲛ̄ⲕⲉⲙⲛ̄ⲧⲟⲩⲉ
ⲛ̄ⲉⲃⲟⲧ ⲙⲛ̄ ⲭⲟⲩⲧⲟⲩⲉ ⲛ̄ϩⲟⲟⲩ· ⲁⲩⲱ ⲙⲛ̄ⲛ̄ⲥⲁ ⲛⲁⲓ̈ ϣⲁⲩ-
20 ϥⲓⲧⲥ̄ ⲉϩⲣⲁⲓ̈ ϩⲓ ⲧⲉϩⲓⲏ ⲛ̄ⲧⲙⲏⲧⲉ ⲛ̄ⲧⲉ ⲡⲟⲩⲁ ⲡⲟⲩⲁ ⲛ̄ⲛⲁⲣⲭⲱⲛ
ϩⲛ̄ ⲧⲉϩⲓⲏ ⲛ̄ⲧⲙⲏⲧⲉ ⲕⲟⲗⲁⲍⲉ ⲙ̄ⲙⲟⲥ ϩⲛ̄ ⲛⲉϥⲕⲟⲗⲁⲥⲓⲥ ⲛ̄-
ⲕⲉⲙⲛ̄ⲧⲟⲩⲉ ⲛ̄ⲉⲃⲟⲧ ⲙⲛ̄ ⲭⲟⲩⲧⲟⲩⲉ ⲛ̄ϩⲟⲟⲩ· ⲙⲛ̄ⲛ̄ⲥⲁ ⲛⲁⲓ̈ [ⲧⲙⲉ
ϣⲁⲩϥⲓⲧⲥ̄ ⲛ̄ⲧⲡⲁⲣⲑⲉⲛⲟⲥ ⲙ̄ⲡⲟⲩⲟⲉⲓⲛ ⲧⲁⲓ̈ ⲉϣⲁⲥⲕⲣⲓⲛⲉ
ⲛ̄ⲛ̄ⲇⲓⲕⲁⲓⲟⲥ ⲙⲛ̄ ⲛ̄ⲣⲉϥⲣ̄ⲛⲟⲃⲉ ⲛ̄ⲥⲕⲣⲓⲛⲉ ⲙ̄ⲙⲟⲥ· ⲁⲩⲱ ⲉⲣ-
25 ϣⲁⲛ ⲧⲉⲥⲫⲁⲓⲣⲁ ⲕⲱⲧⲉ ⲙ̄ⲙⲟⲥ ϣⲁⲥⲧⲁⲁⲥ ⲉⲧⲟⲟⲧⲟⲩ ⲛ̄-
ⲛⲉⲥⲡⲁⲣⲁⲗⲏⲙⲡⲧⲏⲥ ⲛ̄ⲥⲉⲛⲟϫⲥ̄ ⲉⲃⲟⲗ ⲉⲛⲁⲓⲱⲛ ⲛ̄ⲧⲉⲥⲫⲁⲓⲣⲁ·

Mariam continued again and said: "My Lord, the man who continuously *slanders*, when he comes forth from the *body*, where will he go, *or* what is his *punishment?*"

Jesus said: "A man who *slanders* continuously, when his time through the *sphere* is completed, so that he comes forth from the *body*, Abiut [1] and Charmon [2], the *paralemptai* of Ariel, come for him, and they bring forth his *soul* from the *body* and they spend three days proceeding with it, teaching it of the creation of the *world*. After these things they take it down to Amente to the presence of Ariel. And he *punishes* it in his *punishments* for eleven months and 21 days. Afterwards they take it to the *Chaos* to the presence of Jaldabaoth with his 49 demons, and each one of his *demons* attacks it for another eleven months and 21 days as they *flagellate* it with fiery *scourges*. After these things they take it forth into the rivers of fire and boiling *seas* of fire, and in them they *take revenge* on it for another eleven months and 21 days. And after these things they carry it out upon the way of the *Midst*, and each one of the *archons* in the way of the Midst *punishes* it in his *punishments* for another eleven months and 21 days. After these things they carry it to the *Virgin* of the Light who *judges* the *righteous* and the sinners, and she *judges* it. And when the *sphere* turns, she gives it into the hands of her *paralemptai*, and they cast it into the *aeons* of the *sphere*. | And the

---

[1] (7) Abiut; see Kropp (Bibl. 26) I, M4.
[2] (7) Charmon; perhaps Egyptian Chnoumis; see IMG-E p. 54 ff.

ⲁⲩⲱ ⲛ̄ⲧⲉ ⲗⲓⲧⲟⲩⲣⲅⲟⲥ ⲛ̄ⲧⲉⲥⲫⲁⲓⲣⲁ ϫⲓⲧⲥ̄ ⲉⲃⲟⲗ' ⲉⲩⲙⲟⲟⲩ ⲉϥϩⲁⲡⲉⲥⲏⲧ ⲛ̄ⲧⲉⲥⲫⲁⲓⲣⲁ ⲛ̄ϥⲣ̄-ⲟⲩⲕⲣⲱⲙ' ⲉϥⲃⲣ̄ⲃⲣ̄
ⲛ̄ϥⲟⲩⲱⲙ ⲉϩⲟⲩⲛ ⲛ̄ⲥⲱⲥ ϣⲁⲛⲧ̄ϥⲕⲁⲑⲁⲣⲓⲍⲉ ⲙ̄ⲙⲟⲥ ⲧⲟⲛⲱ·
ⲁⲩⲱ ϣⲁϥⲉⲓⲛⲉ ⲙ̄ⲡⲁⲡⲟⲧ' ⲛ̄ⲧⲃ̄ϣⲉ ⲛ̄ϭⲓ ⲓ̈ⲁⲗⲟⲩϩⲁⲙ ⲡ̄ⲡⲁⲣⲁ-
5 ⲗⲏⲙⲡⲧⲏⲥ ⲛ̄ⲥⲁⲃⲁⲱⲑ' ⲡⲁⲁⲅⲁⲥ ⲛ̄ϥⲧⲁⲁϥ ⲛ̄ⲧⲉⲯⲩⲭⲏ ⲛ̄ⲥ-
ⲥⲟⲟϥ ⲛ̄ⲥⲣ̄ⲡⲱⲃϣ̄ ⲙ̄ⲙⲁ ⲛⲓⲙ' ⲙ̄ⲛ ϩⲱⲃ ⲛⲓⲙ' ⲙ̄ⲛ ⲧⲟⲡⲟⲥ
ⲛⲓⲙ' ⲉⲛⲧⲁⲥⲃⲱⲕ ⲉⲣⲟⲟⲩ· ⲛ̄ⲥⲉⲧⲁⲁⲥ ⲉϩⲣⲁⲓ̈ ⲉⲩⲥⲱⲙⲁ
ⲉϥⲛⲁⲣ̄-ⲡⲉϥⲟⲩⲟⲉⲓϣ ⲉϥϩⲉϫϩⲱϫ· ⲧⲁⲓ̈ ⲧⲉ ⲧⲉⲕⲣⲓⲥⲓⲥ ⲙ̄-
ⲡⲣⲱⲙⲉ ⲛ̄ⲣⲉϥⲕⲁⲧⲁⲁⲁⲓ·

10 ⲡⲉϫⲁⲥ ⲛ̄ϭⲓ ⲙⲁⲣⲓϩⲁⲙ' ϫⲉ ⲟⲩⲟⲓ̈ ⲟⲩⲟⲓ̈ ⲛ̄ⲣⲣⲉϥⲣ̄ⲛⲟⲃⲉ·
ⲁⲥⲟⲩⲱϣⲃ̄ ϩⲱⲱⲥ ⲛ̄ϭⲓ ⲥⲁⲗⲱⲙⲏ ⲡⲉϫⲁⲥ ϫⲉ ⲡⲁϫⲟⲉⲓⲥ ⲧ̅ⲙ̅
ⲓ̅ⲥ̅ ⲟⲩⲣⲱⲙⲉ ⲛ̄ⲣⲉϥϩⲱⲧⲃ̄ ⲉⲙⲡ̄ϥⲣ̄ⲛⲟⲃⲉ ⲉⲛⲉϩ ⲛ̄ⲥⲁ ϩⲱⲧⲃ̄
ⲉϥϣⲁⲛⲉⲓ' ⲉⲃⲟⲗ ϩⲛ̄ ⲥⲱⲙⲁ ⲟⲩ ⲧⲉ ⲧⲉϥⲕⲟⲗⲁⲥⲓⲥ· ⲁϥⲟⲩ-
ⲱϣⲃ̄ ⲛ̄ϭⲓ ⲓ̅ⲥ̅ ⲡⲉϫⲁϥ ϫⲉ ⲟⲩⲣⲱⲙⲉ ⲛ̄ⲣⲉϥϩⲱⲧⲃ̄ ⲉⲙⲡ̄ϥⲣ̄-
15 ⲛⲟⲃⲉ ⲉⲛⲉϩ ⲛ̄ⲥⲁ ϩⲱⲧⲃ̄ ⲉⲣϣⲁⲛ ⲡⲉϥⲟⲩⲟⲉⲓϣ ϫⲱⲕ ⲉⲃⲟⲗ'
ϩⲓⲧⲛ̄ ⲧⲉⲥⲫⲁⲓⲣⲁ ⲉⲧⲣⲉϥⲉⲓ' ⲉⲃⲟⲗ ϩⲛ̄ ⲥⲱⲙⲁ ϣⲁⲩⲉⲓ' ⲛ̄ϭⲓ
ⲙ̄ⲡⲁⲣⲁⲗⲏⲙⲡⲧⲏⲥ ⲛ̄ⲓ̈ⲁⲗⲇⲁⲃⲁⲱⲑ ⲛ̄ⲥⲉⲉⲓⲛⲉ ⲛ̄ⲧⲉϥⲯⲩⲭⲏ
ⲉⲃⲟⲗ ϩⲛ̄ ⲥⲱⲙⲁ ⲛ̄ⲥⲉⲙⲟⲣⲥ̄ ϩⲛ̄ ⲛⲉⲥⲟⲩⲉⲣⲏⲧⲉ ⲛ̄ⲥⲁ ⲟⲩⲛⲟϭ ⲛ̄ⲇⲁⲓⲙⲱⲛ ⲛ̄ϩⲁⲛ ⲛ̄ϩⲧⲟ ⲛ̄ϥⲣ̄-ϣⲟⲙⲛ̄ⲧ ⲛ̄ϩⲟⲟⲩ ⲉϥ-
20 ⲕⲱⲧⲉ ⲛ̄ⲙⲙⲁⲥ ϩⲙ̄ ⲡⲕⲟⲥⲙⲟⲥ· ⲙ̄ⲛ̄ⲛⲥⲁ ⲛⲁⲓ̈ ϣⲁⲩϫⲓⲧⲥ̄
ⲉⲃⲟⲗ ⲉⲙⲙⲁ ⲙ̄ⲡ̄ϫⲁϥ ⲙ̄ⲛ ⲡⲉϫⲓⲱⲛ ⲛ̄ⲥⲉⲧⲓⲙⲱⲣⲉⲓ ⲙ̄ⲙⲟⲥ
ⲙ̄ⲙⲁⲩ ⲛ̄ϣⲟⲙⲧⲉ ⲛ̄ⲣⲟⲙⲡⲉ ⲙ̄ⲛ ⲥⲟⲟⲩ ⲛ̄ⲉⲃⲟⲧ· ⲙ̄ⲛ̄ⲛⲥⲁ
ⲛⲁⲓ̈ ⲛ̄ⲥⲉϫⲓⲧⲥ̄ ⲉϩⲣⲁⲓ̈ ⲉⲡⲉϫⲁⲟⲥ ⲉⲣⲁⲧϥ̄ ⲛ̄ⲓ̈ⲁⲗⲇⲁⲃⲁⲱⲑ'
ⲙ̄ⲛ ⲡⲉϥⲙⲉϩⲯⲓⲧ ⲛ̄ⲇⲁⲓⲙⲟⲛⲓⲟⲛ ⲛ̄ⲥⲉⲙⲁⲥⲧⲓⲅⲟⲩ ⲙ̄ⲙⲟⲥ ⲛ̄ϭⲓ ⲧ̅ⲙ̅ᵇ

---

1 MS ⲗⲓⲧⲟⲩⲣⲅⲟⲥ; read ⲛ̄ⲗⲓⲧⲟⲩⲣⲅⲟⲥ.
12 ⲓ̅ⲥ̅ inserted above.
19 MS ⲛ̄ϩⲁⲛ̄ⲛ̄ϩⲧⲟ; read ⲛ̄ϩⲁⲗ ⲛ̄ϩⲧⲟ.

ministers of the *sphere* take it forth to a water which is below the *sphere*, which becomes a boiling fire that consumes it until it *purifies* it completely. And Jalouham, the *paralemptes* of Sabaoth, the Adamas, brings the cup of forgetfulness and gives it to the *soul*, and it drinks it and forgets every place and everything, and all *places* to which it has gone. And it is given to a *body* in which it will spend its time being oppressed. This is the *judgment* of the man who *slanders*."

145.   Mariam said : "Woe, woe to sinners."

Salome answered and said : "My Lord Jesus, a murderer who has never sinned, except for murder, what is his *punishment* when he comes forth from the *body*?"

Jesus answered and said : "A murderer who has never sinned except for murder, when his time is completed through the *sphere* that he should come forth from the *body*, the *paralemptai* of Jaldabaoth come and bring his *soul* forth from the *body* and bind it by its feet behind a great horse-faced *demon*, which spends three days going round with it in the *world*. After these things they take it forth to the places of frost and *snow* [1], and they *take revenge* on it there for three years and six months. After these things it is taken down to the *Chaos* to the presence of Jaldabaoth and his 49 *demons*, and each of his *demons scourges* it | for another

---

[1]   (21) frost and snow; lit. the frost and the snow; (also 380.6).

ⲛⲉϥⲇⲁⲓⲙⲟⲛⲓⲟⲛ ⲛ̄ⲕⲉϣⲟⲙⲧⲉ ⲛ̄ⲣⲟⲙⲡⲉ [ⲉⲡⲟⲩⲁ] ⲙⲛ̄
ⲥⲟⲟⲩ ⲛ̄ⲉⲃⲟⲧ· ⲙⲛ̄ⲛⲥⲁ ⲛⲁⲓ̈ ϣⲁⲩⲭⲓⲧⲥ ⲉⲡⲉⲭⲁⲟⲥ ⲉⲣⲁⲧⲥ̄
ⲛ̄ⲧⲡⲉⲣⲥⲉⲫⲟⲛⲏ ⲛ̄ⲥⲉⲧⲓⲙⲱⲣⲉⲓ ⲙ̄ⲙⲟⲥ ϩⲛ̄ ⲛⲉⲥⲕⲟⲗⲁⲥⲓⲥ
ⲛ̄ⲕⲉϣⲟⲙⲧⲉ ⲛ̄ⲣⲟⲙⲡⲉ ⲙⲛ̄ ⲥⲟⲟⲩ ⲛ̄ⲉⲃⲟⲧ· ⲙⲛ̄ⲛⲥⲁ ⲛⲁⲓ̈
5 ϣⲁⲩϭⲓⲧⲥ̄ ⲉϩⲣⲁⲓ̈ ϩⲓ ⲧⲉϩⲓⲏ ⲛ̄ⲧⲙⲏⲧⲉ ⲛ̄ⲧⲉ ⲡⲟⲩⲁ ⲡⲟⲩⲁ
ⲛ̄ⲛⲁⲣⲭⲱⲛ ⲛ̄ⲧⲉϩⲓⲏ ⲛ̄ⲧⲙⲏⲧⲉ ⲧⲓⲙⲱⲣⲉⲓ ⲙ̄ⲙⲟⲥ ϩⲛ̄ ⲛ̄ⲕⲟⲗⲁ-
ⲥⲓⲥ ⲛ̄ⲛⲉϥⲧⲟⲡⲟⲥ ⲛ̄ⲕⲉϣⲟⲙⲧⲉ ⲛ̄ⲣⲟⲙⲡⲉ ⲙⲛ̄ ⲥⲟⲟⲩ ⲛ̄-
ⲉⲃⲟⲧ· ⲙⲛ̄ⲛⲥⲁ ⲛⲁⲓ̈ ⲛ̄ⲥⲉⲭⲓⲧⲥ ⲛ̄ⲧⲡⲁⲣⲑⲉⲛⲟⲥ ⲙ̄ⲡⲟⲩⲟⲉⲓⲛ
ⲧⲁⲓ̈ ⲉϣⲁⲥⲕⲣⲓⲛⲉ ⲛ̄ⲛ̄ⲇⲓⲕⲁⲓⲟⲥ ⲙⲛ̄ ⲛ̄ⲣⲉϥⲣ̄ⲛⲟⲃⲉ ⲛ̄ⲥⲕⲣⲓⲛⲉ
10 ⲙ̄ⲙⲟⲥ· ⲁⲩⲱ ⲉⲣϣⲁⲛ ⲧⲉⲥⲫⲁⲓⲣⲁ ⲕⲱⲧⲉ ϣⲁⲥⲕⲉⲗⲉⲩⲉ
ⲛ̄ⲥⲉⲛⲟϫⲥ̄ ⲉⲡⲕⲁⲕⲉ ⲉⲧϩⲓⲃⲟⲗ· ϣⲁ ⲡⲉⲩⲟⲓ̈ϣ ⲉⲧⲟⲩⲛⲁϥⲓ
ⲙ̄ⲡⲕⲁⲕⲉ ⲛ̄ⲧⲙⲏⲧⲉ ϣⲁⲥⲱϫⲛ̄ ⲛ̄ⲥⲃⲱⲗ ⲉⲃⲟⲗ ⲧⲁⲓ̈ ⲧⲉ ⲧⲕⲟⲗⲁⲥⲓⲥ ⲙ̄ⲡⲣⲱⲙⲉ ⲛ̄ⲣⲉϥϩⲱⲧⲃ·

ⲡⲉⲭⲁϥ ⲛ̄ϭⲓ ⲡⲉⲧⲣⲟⲥ ϫⲉ ⲡⲁϫⲟⲓ̈ⲥ ⲙⲁⲣⲉ ⲛⲉϩⲓⲟⲙⲉ ϩⲱ
15 ⲉⲣⲟⲟⲩ ⲉⲩϣⲓⲛⲉ ⲧⲁⲣⲛ̄ϣⲓⲛⲉ ϩⲱⲱⲛ· ⲡⲉⲭⲉ ⲓ̄ⲥ̄ ⲙ̄ⲙⲁⲣⲓϩⲁⲙ̄
ⲙⲛ̄ ⲛⲉϩⲓⲟⲙⲉ ϫⲉ ⲕⲁ-ⲡⲙⲁ ⲛ̄ⲛⲉⲧⲛ̄ⲥⲛⲏⲩ ⲛ̄ϩⲟⲟⲩⲧ ⲛ̄ⲥⲉ-
ϣⲓⲛⲉ ϩⲱⲟⲩ· ⲁϥⲟⲩⲱϣ̄ⲃ ⲛ̄ϭⲓ ⲡⲉⲧⲣⲟⲥ ⲡⲉⲭⲁϥ ϫⲉ ⲡⲁϫⲟⲉⲓⲥ ⲉⲓ̈ⲉ ⲟⲩⲣⲱⲙⲉ ⲛ̄ⲥⲟⲟⲛⲉ ⲛ̄ⲣⲉϥϫⲓⲟⲩⲉ ⲉⲡⲉϥⲛⲟⲃⲉ
ⲡⲉ ⲡⲁⲓ̈ ⲉϥⲙⲏⲛ ⲉⲃⲟⲗ· ⲉϥϣⲁⲛⲉⲓ· ⲉⲃⲟⲗ ϩⲛ̄ ⲥⲱⲙⲁ ⲟⲩ ⲧⲉ
20 ⲧⲉϥⲕⲟⲗⲁⲥⲓⲥ· ⲡⲉⲭⲉ ⲓ̄ⲥ̄ ϫⲉ ⲡⲁⲓ̈ ⲛ̄ⲧⲉⲓ̈ⲙⲓⲛⲉ ⲉⲣϣⲁⲛ ⲡⲉϥⲟⲩⲟⲉⲓϣ ϫⲱⲕ· ⲉⲃⲟⲗ ϩⲓⲧⲛ̄ ⲧⲉⲥⲫⲁⲓⲣⲁ ϣⲁⲩⲉⲓ· ⲛ̄ⲥⲱϥ
ⲛ̄ϭⲓ ⲙ̄ⲡⲁⲣⲁⲗⲏⲙⲡⲧⲏⲥ ⲛ̄ⲁⲇⲱⲛⲓⲥ· ⲛ̄ⲥⲉⲛ̄-ⲧⲉϥⲯⲩⲭⲏ ⲉⲃⲟⲗ
ϩⲛ̄ ⲥⲱⲙⲁ ⲛ̄ⲥⲉⲣ̄-ϣⲟⲙⲛ̄ⲧ ⲛ̄ϩⲟⲟⲩ ⲉⲩⲕⲱⲧⲉ ⲛ̄ⲙⲙⲁⲥ ⲉⲩⲧⲥⲁⲃⲟ ⲙ̄ⲙⲟⲥ ⲉⲛⲥⲱⲛⲧ ⲙ̄ⲡⲕⲟⲥⲙⲟⲥ ⲙⲛ̄ⲛⲥⲁ ⲛⲁⲓ̈ ϣⲁⲩ-
25 ϫⲓⲧⲥ̄ ⲉⲡⲉⲥⲏⲧ ⲉⲁⲙⲛ̄ⲧⲉ ⲉⲣⲁⲧϥ ⲛ̄ⲁⲣⲓⲏⲗ· ⲛ̄ϥⲧⲓⲙⲱⲣⲉⲓ ⲙ̄ⲙⲟⲥ

---

1 MS ⲉⲡⲟⲩⲁ; Schmidt: should be omitted.
14 ⲕ̄ⲃ̄ in upper right-hand margin at end of quire.

three years [1] and six months. Then they take it to the *Chaos* to the presence of Persephone, and they *take revenge* on it with her *punishments* for another three years and six months. Then they take it forth upon the way of the Midst, and each of the *archons* of the way of the Midst *takes revenge* on it in the *punishments* of his *places* for another three years and six months. After these things they bring it to the *Virgin* of the Light who *judges* the *righteous* and the sinners, and she *judges* it. And when the *sphere* turns, she *commands* that it be cast to the outer darkness, until the time when the darkness of the Midst will be lifted and it is destroyed and dissolved. This is the *punishment* of the murderer."

146. Peter said: "My Lord, let the women cease to question, that we also may question."

Jesus said to Mariam and the women: "Give way to the men, your brothers [2], that they may question also."

Peter answered and said: "My Lord, a robber and thief whose sin has continued to be this, when he comes forth from the *body*, what is his *punishment*?"

Jesus said: "When the time of such a one is completed through the *sphere*, the *paralemptai* of Adonis [3] come for him, and they bring his *soul* forth from the *body*, and they spend three days going round with it, teaching it of the creation of the *world*. After these things they take it down to Amente to the presence of Ariel, and he *takes revenge* on it | in his *punishments* for three months and eight days

---

[1] (1) each of his demons ... three years; MS: "each of" follows "years"; Schmidt deletes "each of".

[2] (16) give way to the men, your brothers; lit. leave place to your male brothers.

[3] (22) Adonis; see ApJn 40, 42.

ϩⲛ ⲛⲉϥⲕⲟⲗⲁⲥⲓⲥ ⲛϣⲟⲙⲛⲧ ⲛⲉⲃⲟⲧ' ⲙⲛ ϣⲙⲟⲩⲛ ⲛϩⲟⲟⲩ ⲙⲛ ⲟⲩⲛⲟⲩ ⲥⲛⲧⲉ· ⲙⲛⲛⲥⲁ ⲛⲁï ⲛⲥⲉϫⲓⲧⲥ ⲉⲡⲉⲭⲁⲟⲥ ⲉ- [ΤΜΗ b] ⲣⲁⲧϥ ⲛïⲁⲗⲇⲁⲃⲁⲱⲑ' ⲙⲛ ⲡⲉϥϩⲙⲉⲯⲓⲧ' ⲛⲇⲁⲓⲙⲟⲛⲓⲟⲛ ⲛⲧⲉ ⲡⲟⲩⲁ ⲡⲟⲩⲁ ⲛⲛⲉϥⲇⲁⲓⲙⲟⲛⲓⲟⲛ ⲧⲓⲙⲱⲣⲉⲓ ⲙⲙⲟⲥ ⲛⲕⲉϣⲟⲙⲛⲧ ⲛⲉⲃⲟⲧ' ⲙⲛ ϣⲙⲟⲩⲛ ⲛϩⲟⲟⲩ ⲙⲛ ⲟⲩⲛⲟⲩ ⲥⲛⲧⲉ· ⲙⲛⲛⲥⲁ ⲛⲁï ϣⲁⲩϫⲓⲧⲥ ⲉϩⲣⲁï ϩⲓ ⲧⲉϩⲓⲏ ⲛⲧⲙⲏⲧⲉ ⲛⲧⲉ ⲡⲟⲩⲁ ⲡⲟⲩⲁ ⲛⲛⲁⲣⲭⲱⲛ ⲛⲧⲉϩⲓⲏ ⲛⲧⲙⲏⲧⲉ ⲧⲓⲙⲱⲣⲉⲓ ⲙⲙⲟⲥ ϩⲓⲧⲙ ⲡⲉϥⲕⲣⲱⲙ' ⲛⲕⲁⲕⲉ ⲙⲛ ⲡⲉϥⲕⲱϩⲧ ⲙⲡⲟⲛⲏⲣⲟⲛ ⲛⲕⲉϣⲟⲙⲛⲧ ⲛⲉⲃⲟⲧ ⲙⲛ ϣⲙⲟⲩⲛ ⲛϩⲟⲟⲩ ⲙⲛ ⲟⲩⲛⲟⲩ ⲥⲛⲧⲉ· ⲙⲛⲛⲥⲁ ⲛⲁï ϣⲁⲩϫⲓⲧⲥ ⲉϩⲣⲁï ⲉⲧⲡⲁⲣⲑⲉⲛⲟⲥ ⲙⲡⲟⲩⲟⲉⲓⲛ ⲧⲁï ⲉϣⲁⲥⲕⲣⲓⲛⲉ ⲛⲛⲇⲓⲕⲁⲓⲟⲥ ⲙⲛ ⲛⲣⲉϥⲣⲛⲟⲃⲉ ⲛⲥⲕⲣⲓⲛⲉ ⲙⲙⲟⲥ ⲁⲩⲱ ⲉⲣϣⲁⲛ ⲧⲉⲥⲫⲁⲓⲣⲁ ⲕⲱⲧⲉ ϣⲁⲥⲧⲁⲁⲥ ⲛⲛⲉⲥⲡⲁⲣⲁⲗⲏⲙⲡⲧⲏⲥ ⲛⲥⲉⲛⲟϫⲥ ⲉⲛⲁⲓⲱⲛ ⲛⲧⲉⲥⲫⲁⲓⲣⲁ ⲛⲥⲉϫⲓⲧⲥ ⲉⲃⲟⲗ ⲉⲩⲙⲟⲟⲩ ⲉϥϩⲁⲡⲉⲥⲏⲧ ⲛⲧⲉⲥⲫⲁⲓⲣⲁ ⲛϥⲣ-ⲟⲩⲕⲣⲱⲙ [ΤΜΟ] ⲉϥⲃⲣⲃⲣ ⲛϥⲟⲩⲱⲙ ⲉϩⲟⲩⲛ ⲛⲥⲱⲥ ϣⲁⲛⲧⲥⲕⲁⲑⲁⲣⲓⲍⲉ ⲙⲙⲟⲥ ⲧⲟⲛⲱ· ⲙⲛⲛⲥⲁ ⲛⲁï ϣⲁϥⲉⲓ ⲛϭⲓ ïⲁⲗⲟⲩϩⲁⲙ' ⲡⲡⲁⲣⲁⲗⲏⲙⲡⲧⲏⲥ ⲛⲥⲁⲃⲁⲱⲑ' ⲡⲁⲇⲁⲙⲁⲥ ⲛϥⲉⲓⲛⲉ ⲙⲡⲁⲡⲟⲧ ⲛⲧⲃϣⲉ ⲛϥⲧⲁⲁϥ ⲛⲧⲉⲯⲩⲭⲏ ⲛⲥⲥⲟⲟϥ ⲛⲥⲣⲡⲱⲃϣ ⲛϩⲱⲃ ⲛⲓⲙ ⲙⲛ ⲧⲟⲡⲟⲥ ⲛⲓⲙ' ⲉⲛⲧⲁⲥⲃⲱⲕ ⲉⲣⲟⲟⲩ ⲛⲥⲉⲛⲟϫⲥ ⲉⲩⲥⲱⲙⲁ ⲛϭⲁⲗⲉ ⲁⲩⲱ ⲛϭⲁⲛⲁϩ ⲁⲩⲱ ⲛⲃⲗⲗⲉ· ⲧⲁï ⲧⲉ ⲧⲕⲟⲗⲁⲥⲓⲥ ⲙⲡⲣⲱⲙⲉ ⲛⲣⲉϥϫⲓⲟⲩⲉ:

ⲁϥⲟⲩⲱϣⲃ ⲛϭⲓ ⲁⲛⲇⲣⲉⲁⲥ ⲡⲉϫⲁϥ· ϫⲉ ⲟⲩⲣⲱⲙⲉ ⲛϫⲁⲥⲓϩⲏⲧ ⲛⲣⲉϥⲥⲱϣ ⲉϥϣⲁⲛⲉⲓ' ⲉⲃⲟⲗ ϩⲛ ⲥⲱⲙⲁ ⲉⲩⲛⲁⲣⲟⲩ ⲛⲁϥ· ⲡⲉϫⲉ ⲓⲥ ϫⲉ ⲡⲁï ⲛⲧⲉïⲙⲓⲛⲉ ⲉⲣϣⲁⲛ ⲡⲉϥⲟⲩⲟⲉⲓϣ ϫⲱⲕ ⲉⲃⲟⲗ ϩⲓⲧⲛ ⲧⲉⲥⲫⲁⲓⲣⲁ ϣⲁⲩⲉⲓ' ⲛⲥⲱϥ ⲛϭⲓ ⲙⲡⲁⲣⲁⲗⲏⲙⲡⲧⲏⲥ ⲛⲁⲣⲓⲏⲗ ⲛⲥⲉϫⲓ ⲛⲧⲉϥⲯⲩⲭⲏ ⟨ⲉⲃⲟⲗ ϩⲛ ⲥⲱⲙⲁ⟩

---

14 ⲕⲅ in upper left-hand margin at beginning of quire.
26 ⲉⲃⲟⲗ ϩⲛ ⲥⲱⲙⲁ omitted.

and two hours. After these things they take it to the *Chaos* to the presence of Jaldabaoth and his 49 *demons*. And each of his *demons takes revenge* on it for another three months and eight days and two hours. After these things they take it upon the way of the Midst, and each one of the *archons* of the way of the Midst *takes revenge* on it by means of his dark smoke and his *wicked* fire for another three months and eight days and two hours. After these things they take it forth to the *Virgin* of the Light who *judges* the *righteous* and the sinners, and she *judges* it. And when the *sphere* turns, she gives it to her *paralemptai* and they cast it to the *aeons* of the *sphere*. And they (the ministers of the sphere) take it to a water which is below the *sphere*. And it becomes a boiling fire which consumes it until it *purifies* it completely. After these things Jalouham, the *paralemptes* of Sabaoth the Adamas, comes and he brings the cup of forgetfulness. And he gives it to the *soul*, and it drinks it and forgets everything and all *places* to which it has gone. And they cast it into a lame, crooked and blind *body*. This is the *punishment* of the thief."

Andrew answered and said: "A proud, scornful man, when he comes forth from the *body*, what will happen to him?"

Jesus said: "When the time of such a one is completed through the *sphere*, the *paralemptai* of Ariel come for him, and they take his *soul* ⟨forth from the body⟩, | and they

ⲠⲤⲈⲢ-ϢⲞⲘⲚⲦ ⲚⲌⲞⲞⲨ ⲈⲨⲦⲞⲨⲞⲒ̈ ⟨Ⲛ̄ⲘⲘⲀⲤ⟩ ⲌⲘ̄ ⲠⲔⲞⲤⲘⲞⲤ
ⲈⲨⲦⲤⲀⲂⲞ Ⲙ̄ⲘⲞⲤ ⲈⲚⲤⲰⲚⲦ Ⲙ̄ⲠⲔⲞⲤⲘⲞⲤ· ⲘⲚ̄ⲚⲤⲀ ⲚⲀⲒ̈ ⲦⲘⲞ̄ᵇ
ϢⲀⲨϪ̄ⲒⲦⲤ̄ ⲈⲠⲈⲤⲎⲦ ⲈⲀⲘⲚ̄ⲦⲈ ⲈⲢⲀⲦϤ Ⲛ̄ⲀⲢⲒⲎⲖ’ Ⲛ̄ϤⲦⲒⲘⲰⲢⲒ
Ⲙ̄ⲘⲞⲤ ⲌⲚ ⲚⲈϤⲔⲞⲖⲀⲤⲒⲤ Ⲛ̄ϪⲞⲨⲰⲦ’ Ⲛ̄ⲈⲂⲞⲦ ⲘⲚ̄ⲚⲤⲀ ⲚⲀⲒ̈
⁵ ϢⲀⲨϪ̄ⲒⲦⲤ̄ ⲈⲠⲈⲬⲖⲞⲤ ⲈⲢⲀⲦϤ Ⲙ̄ⲀⲖⲖⲀⲂⲀⲰⲐ’ ⲘⲚ ⲠⲈϤⲌⲘⲈ-
ⲮⲒⲦ Ⲛ̄ⲀⲖⲒⲘⲞⲚⲒⲞⲚ ⲀⲨⲰ Ⲛ̄ϤⲦⲒⲘⲰⲢⲒ Ⲙ̄ⲘⲞⲤ ⲘⲚ ⲚⲈϤⲀⲖⲒ-
ⲘⲞⲚⲒⲞⲚ ⲔⲀⲦⲀ ⲞⲨⲀ ⲞⲨⲀ ⲚⲔⲈϪⲞⲨⲰⲦ’ Ⲛ̄ⲈⲂⲞⲦ· ⲘⲚ̄ⲚⲤⲀ
ⲚⲀⲒ̈ ϢⲀⲨϤⲒⲦⲤ ⲈⲌⲢⲀⲒ̈ ⲌⲒ ⲦⲈⲌⲒⲎ Ⲛ̄ⲦⲘⲎⲦⲈ Ⲛ̄ⲦⲈ ⲠⲞⲨⲀ ⲠⲞⲨⲀ
Ⲛ̄ⲚⲀⲢⲬⲰⲚ Ⲛ̄ⲦⲈⲌⲒⲎ Ⲛ̄ⲦⲘⲒⲦⲈ Ⲛ̄ϤⲔⲞⲖⲀⲌⲈ Ⲙ̄ⲘⲞⲤ Ⲛ̄ⲔⲈ-
¹⁰ ϪⲞⲨⲰⲦ’ Ⲛ̄ⲈⲂⲞⲦ· ⲀⲨⲰ ⲘⲚ̄ⲚⲤⲀ ⲚⲀⲒ̈ ϢⲀⲨϪ̄ⲒⲦⲤ̄ Ⲛ̄ⲦⲠⲀⲢ-
ⲐⲈⲚⲞⲤ Ⲙ̄ⲠⲞⲨⲞⲈⲒⲚ Ⲛ̄ⲤⲔⲢⲒⲚⲈ Ⲙ̄ⲘⲞⲤ ⲀⲨⲰ ⲈⲢϢⲀⲚ ⲦⲈ-
ⲤⲪⲀⲒⲢⲀ ⲔⲰⲦⲈ ϢⲀⲤⲦⲀⲀⲤ Ⲛ̄ⲘⲈⲤⲠⲀⲢⲀⲖⲎⲘⲠⲦⲎⲤ Ⲛ̄ⲤⲈ-
ⲚⲞⲬ̄Ⲥ ⲈⲚⲀⲒⲰⲚ Ⲛ̄ⲦⲈⲤⲪⲀⲒⲢⲀ· ⲀⲨⲰ ϢⲀⲢⲈ Ⲛ̄ⲖⲒⲦⲞⲨⲢⲄⲞⲤ
Ⲛ̄ⲦⲈⲤⲪⲀⲒⲢⲀ Ϫ̄ⲒⲦⲤ̄ ⲈⲂⲞⲖ ⲈⲨⲘⲞⲞⲨ ⲈϤϢⲀⲠⲈⲤⲎⲦ Ⲛ̄ⲦⲈ-
¹⁵ ⲤⲪⲀⲒⲢⲀ Ⲛ̄ϤⲢ-ⲞⲨⲔⲢⲰⲘ ⲈϤ̄ⲂⲢ̄ⲂⲢ̄ Ⲛ̄ⲞⲨⲰⲘ’ ⲈⲌⲞⲨⲚ Ⲛ̄ⲤⲰⲤ [ⲦⲠ]
ϢⲀⲚⲦϤⲔⲀⲐⲀⲢⲒⲌⲈ Ⲙ̄ⲘⲞⲤ· ⲀⲨⲰ ϢⲀϤⲈⲒ’ Ⲛ̄ϬⲒ Ⲓ̈ⲀⲖⲞⲨⲌⲀⲘ
ⲠⲠⲀⲢⲀⲖⲎⲘⲠⲦⲎⲤ Ⲛ̄ⲤⲀⲂⲀⲰⲐ’ ⲠⲀⲀⲀⲘⲀⲤ Ⲛ̄ϤⲈⲒⲚⲈ Ⲙ̄ⲠⲀⲠⲞⲦ
Ⲙ̄ⲘⲞⲨⲚ̄ⲂϢⲈ Ⲛ̄ϤⲦⲀⲀϤ Ⲛ̄ⲦⲈⲮⲨⲬⲎ Ⲛ̄ⲤⲤⲞⲞϤ Ⲛ̄ⲤⲢ̄ⲠⲰ̄Ⲃ̄Ϣ
Ⲛ̄ⲌⲰⲂ ⲚⲒⲘ ⲘⲚ ⲦⲞⲠⲞⲤ ⲚⲒⲘ’ ⲈⲚⲦⲀⲤⲂⲰⲔ ⲈⲢⲞⲞⲨ ⲀⲨⲰ
²⁰ Ⲛ̄ⲤⲈⲚⲞⲬ̄Ⲥ ⲈⲌⲢⲀⲒ̈ ⲈⲨⲤⲰⲘⲀ Ⲛ̄ⲔⲰ⟨ⲪⲞ⟩Ⲥ ⲈⲚⲈϬⲰϤ· Ⲛ̄ⲦⲈ
ⲞⲨⲞⲚ ⲚⲒⲘ ϬⲰ ⲈⲨⲤⲰϢ Ⲙ̄ⲘⲞϤ ⲦⲀⲒ̈ ⲦⲈ ⲦⲔⲞⲖⲀⲤⲒⲤ Ⲙ̄-
ⲠⲢⲰⲘⲈ Ⲛ̄ϪⲀⲤⲒⲌⲎⲦ Ⲛ̄ⲢⲈϤⲤⲰϢ:

ⲠⲈϪⲀϤ Ⲛ̄ϬⲒ ⲐⲰⲘⲀⲤ ϪⲈ ⲞⲨⲢⲰⲘⲈ Ⲛ̄ⲢⲈϤϪⲈ-ⲞⲨⲀ ⲈϤ-
ⲘⲎⲚ ⲈⲂⲞⲖ’ ⲞⲨ ⲦⲈ ⲦⲈϤⲔⲞⲖⲀⲤⲒⲤ· ⲠⲈϪⲈ Ⲓ̄Ⲥ̄ ϪⲈ ⲠⲀⲒ̈ Ⲛ̄-

---

1 supply Ⲛ̄ⲘⲘⲀⲤ.
20 MS indistinct; Ⲛ̄ⲔⲰ . . . Ⲥ.

spend three days proceeding ⟨with it⟩ in the *world*, teaching
it of the creation of the *world*. After these things they take
it down to Amente to the presence of Ariel. And he *takes
revenge* on it in his *punishments* for 20 months. After these
things they take it to the *Chaos* to the presence of Jaldabaoth
and his 49 *demons*, and he *takes revenge* on it with his
demons, one *by* (*according to*) one for another 20 months.
After these things they take it forth upon the way of the
Midst. And each one of the *archons* of the way of the
Midst *punishes* it for another 20 months. And after these
things they take it to the *Virgin* of the Light and she *judges*
it. And when the *sphere* turns, she gives it to her *paralemptai*
and they cast it into the *aeons* of the *sphere*. And the
ministers of the *sphere* take it forth to a water which is
below the *sphere* which becomes a boiling fire which consumes it until it *purifies* it. And Jalouham, the *paralemptes*
of Sabaoth, the Adamas, comes and he brings the cup of
water of forgetfulness. And he gives it to the *soul*, and it
drinks it and forgets everything and all *places* to which
it has gone. And they cast it into a *lame* [1] and ugly *body*,
so that everyone continually despises it. This is the *punishment* of the proud and scornful man."

Thomas said : "A continual blasphemer, what is his
punishment?

Jesus said : | "When the time of such a one is completed

---

[1]   (20) lame : perhaps deaf (κωφός).

ⲦⲈⲒⲘⲒⲚⲈ ⲈⲢϢⲀⲚ ⲠⲈϤⲞⲨⲞⲈⲒϢ ϪⲰⲔ ⲈⲂⲞⲖ ϨⲒⲦⲚ ⲦⲈ-
ⲤⲪⲀⲒⲢⲀ ϢⲀⲨⲈⲒ' ⲚⲤⲰϤ ⲚϬⲒ ⲘⲠⲀⲢⲀⲖⲎⲘⲠⲦⲎⲤ ⲚⲒⲀⲖⲖⲀ-
ⲂⲀⲰⲐ' ⲚⲤⲈⲘⲞⲢϤ ⲚⲤⲀ ⲠⲈϤⲖⲀⲤ ⲚⲤⲀ ⲞⲨⲚⲞϬ ⲚⲀⲒⲘⲰⲚ
ⲚϨⲀ ⲚϨⲦⲞ ⲚⲤⲈⲢ-ϢⲞⲘⲚⲦ ⲚϨⲞⲞⲨ ⲈⲨϮⲞⲨⲞⲒ ⲚⲘⲘⲀϤ
5 ϨⲘ ⲠⲔⲞⲤⲘⲞⲤ ⲚⲤⲈⲦⲒⲘⲰⲢⲈⲒ ⲘⲘⲞϤ· ⲘⲚⲚⲤⲀ ⲚⲀⲒ ϢⲀⲨ-
ϪⲒⲦϤ ⲈⲂⲞⲖ ⲈⲠⲘⲀ ⲘⲠϪⲀϤ ⲘⲚ ⲠⲈϤⲒⲰⲚ ⲚⲤⲈⲦⲒⲘⲰⲢⲈⲒ [ⲧⲏ ᵇ]
ⲘⲘⲞϤ ⲘⲘⲀⲨ ⲘⲘⲚⲦⲞⲨⲈ ⲚⲢⲞⲘⲠⲈ· ⲘⲚⲚⲤⲀ ⲚⲀⲒ ϢⲀⲨ-
ϪⲒⲦϤ ⲈⲠⲈⲤⲎⲦ ⲈⲠⲈⲬⲖⲞⲤ ⲈⲢⲀⲦϤ ⲚⲒⲀⲖⲖⲀⲂⲀⲰⲐ ⲘⲚ
ⲠⲈϤϨⲘⲈϤⲒⲦ ⲚⲀⲒⲘⲞⲚⲒⲞⲚ ⲚⲦⲈ ⲠⲞⲨⲀ ⲠⲞⲨⲀ ⲚⲚⲈϤⲀⲒ-
10 ⲘⲞⲚⲒⲞⲚ ⲦⲒⲘⲰⲢⲈⲒ ⲘⲘⲞϤ ⲚⲔⲈⲘⲚⲦⲞⲨⲈ ⲚⲢⲞⲘⲠⲈ ⲘⲚⲚⲤⲀ
ⲚⲀⲒ ϢⲀⲨϪⲒⲦϤ ⲈⲂⲞⲖ ⲈⲠⲔⲀⲔⲈ ⲈⲦϨⲒⲂⲞⲖ' ϢⲀ ⲠⲈϨⲞⲞⲨ
ⲈⲦⲞⲨⲚⲀⲔⲢⲒⲚⲈ ⲘⲠⲚⲞϬ ⲚⲀⲢⲬⲰⲚ ⲚϨⲀ ⲚⲀⲢⲀⲔⲰⲚ ⲈⲦ-
ⲔⲰⲦⲈ ⲈⲠⲔⲀⲔⲈ ⲀⲨⲰ ϢⲀⲢⲈ ⲦⲈⲮⲨⲬⲎ ⲈⲦⲘⲘⲀⲨ ϢⲀⲤⲢ-
ϨⲢⲞⲨⲞⲨϪⲈϤ ⲚⲤⲀⲚϨⲀⲖⲒⲤⲔⲈ ⲚⲤⲂⲰⲖ ⲈⲂⲞⲖ· ⲦⲀⲒ ⲦⲈ ⲦⲈ-
15 ⲔⲢⲒⲤⲒⲤ ⲘⲠⲢⲰⲘⲈ ⲚⲢⲈϤϪⲈ-ⲞⲨⲀ·

ⲠⲈϪⲀϤ ⲚϬⲒ ⲂⲀⲢⲐⲞⲖⲞⲘⲀⲒⲞⲤ ϪⲈ ⲞⲨⲢⲰⲘⲈ ⲚⲢⲈϤⲚⲔⲞⲦⲔ
ⲘⲚ ϨⲞⲞⲨⲦ ⲞⲨ ⲦⲈ ⲦⲈϤⲦⲒⲘⲰⲢⲒⲀ· ⲠⲈϪⲀϤ ⲚϬⲒ Ⲓ̄Ⲥ̄ ϪⲈ
ⲠⲢⲰⲘⲈ ⲚⲢⲈϤⲚⲔⲞⲦⲔ ⲘⲚ ϨⲞⲞⲨⲦ ⲘⲚ ⲠⲢⲰⲘⲈ ⲈⲦⲞⲨⲚ̄-
ⲔⲞⲦⲔ ⲚⲘⲘⲀϤ ⲠⲈⲒϢⲒ ⲚⲞⲨⲰⲦ ⲠⲈ ⲚⲐⲈ Ⲙ̄ⲠⲢⲰⲘⲈ ⲚⲢⲈϤϪⲈ- ⲧⲏⲁ
20 ⲞⲨⲀ· ⲈⲢϢⲀⲚ ⲠⲈⲞⲨⲞⲈⲒϢ ϬⲈ ϪⲰⲔ ⲈⲂⲞⲖ ϨⲒⲦⲚ ⲦⲈ-
ⲤⲪⲀⲒⲢⲀ ϢⲀⲨⲈⲒ' ⲚⲤⲀ ⲦⲈⲨⲮⲨⲬⲎ ⲚϬⲒ ⲘⲠⲀⲢⲀⲖⲎⲘⲠⲦⲎⲤ
ⲚⲒⲀⲖⲖⲀⲂⲀⲰⲐ' ⲚϤⲦⲒⲘⲰⲢⲈⲒ ⲘⲘⲞⲞⲨ ⲘⲚ ⲠⲈϤϨⲘⲈϤⲒⲦ Ⲛ-
ⲀⲒⲘⲞⲚⲒⲞⲚ ⲚⲘⲚⲦⲞⲨⲈ ⲚⲢⲞⲘⲠⲈ· ⲘⲚⲚⲤⲀ ⲚⲀⲒ ϢⲀⲨϤⲒ-
ⲦⲞⲨ ⲈⲂⲞⲖ ⲈϨⲈⲚⲈⲒⲈⲢϢⲞⲨ ⲚⲔⲢⲰⲘ' ⲘⲚ ϨⲈⲚⲐⲀⲖⲀⲤⲤⲀ Ⲛ-
25 ⲀⲘⲢⲎϨⲈ ⲈⲨⲂⲢⲂⲢ ⲈⲨⲘⲈϨ ⲚⲀⲒⲘⲰⲚ ⲚϨⲀ ⲚⲢⲒⲢ ⲚⲦⲞⲞⲨ

---

20   MS ⲠⲈⲞⲨⲞⲤⲒϢ; better ⲠⲈϤⲞⲨⲞⲈⲒϢ.
23   originally ⲚϨⲘⲈ; ϨⲘⲈ expunged; ⲘⲚⲦⲞⲨⲈ in margin.

through the *sphere*, the *paralemptai* of Jaldabaoth come for
him, and they bind him by his tongue behind a great horse-
faced *demon*, and they spend three days proceeding with
him in the *world* and *taking revenge* on him. After these
things they take him forth to the place of frost and *snow*,
and they *take revenge* on him there for eleven years. After
these things they take him down to the *Chaos* to the presence
of Jaldabaoth and his 49 *demons*, and each one of his
demons takes revenge on him for another eleven years. After
these things they take him forth to the outer darkness until
the day when the great *dragon*-faced *archon* which surrounds
the darkness will be *judged*, and that *soul* perishes and is
consumed and dissolves. This is the *judgment* of the blasphemer."

147. Bartholomew said: "A pederast, what is the *vengeance* on him?"

Jesus said: "The measure of the pederast and of the man
with whom he sleeps is the same as that of the blasphemer.
When now the time is completed through the *sphere*, the
paralemptai of Jaldabaoth come for their *souls*, and with his
49 *demons* he *takes revenge* on them for eleven years. After
these things they take them forth to rivers of fire and *seas*
of boiling bitumen, which are full of pig [1]-faced *demons* |

---

[1]   (25) lit. mountain-pig.

ϢⲀⲨⲞⲨⲰⲘ ⲈϨⲞⲨⲚ ⲚⲤⲰⲞⲨ ⲚⲤⲈⲬⲒⲘⲤⲈ ⲘⲘⲞⲞⲨ ϨⲚ
ⲚⲈⲒⲈⲢϢⲞⲨ ⲚⲔⲢⲰⲘ ⲚⲔⲈⲘⲚⲦⲞⲨⲈ ⲚⲢⲞⲘⲠⲈ ⲘⲚⲚⲤⲀ ⲚⲀⲒ
ϢⲀⲨϬⲒⲦⲞⲨ ⲈⲂⲞⲖ ⲈⲠⲔⲀⲔⲈ ⲈⲦϨⲒⲂⲞⲖ' ϢⲀ ⲠⲈϨⲞⲞⲨ ⲘⲪⲀⲠ
ⲈⲦⲞⲨⲚⲀⲔⲢⲒⲚⲈ ⲘⲠⲚⲞϬ ⲚⲔⲀⲔⲈ ⲈϢⲀⲨⲂⲰⲖ' ⲈⲂⲞⲖ ⲚⲤⲈ-
5 ⲦⲀⲔⲞ ·

ⲠⲈⲬⲀϤ ⲚϬⲒ ⲐⲰⲘⲀⲤ ⲬⲈ ⲀⲚⲤⲰⲦⲘ ⲬⲈ ⲞⲨⲚ-ϨⲞⲒ̈ⲚⲈ
ϨⲒⲬⲘ ⲠⲔⲀϨ ⲈϢⲀⲨϤⲒ ⲘⲠⲈⲤⲠⲈⲢⲘⲀ ⲚⲚϨⲞⲞⲨⲦ ⲘⲚ ⲦⲈ-
ϢⲢⲰ ⲚⲦⲈⲤϨⲒⲘⲈ ⲚⲤⲈⲦⲀⲀⲨ ⲈⲨⲀⲢϢⲒⲚ ⲚⲤⲈⲞⲨⲞⲘϤ ⲈⲨⲬⲰ   ⎯‾ⲦⲠⲀ ᵇ
ⲘⲘⲞⲤ ⲬⲈ ⲈⲚⲠⲒⲤⲦⲈⲨⲈ ⲈⲚⲤⲀⲨ ⲘⲚ Ⲓ̈ⲀⲔⲰⲂ· ⲀⲢⲀ ϨⲎ ⲞⲨ
10 ϨⲰⲂ' ⲈϢϢⲈ ⲠⲈ ⲬⲚ ⲘⲘⲞⲚ· Ⲁ ⲒⲤ ⲆⲈ ϬⲰⲚⲦ ⲈⲠⲔⲞⲤⲘⲞⲤ
ⲘⲠⲚⲀⲨ ⲈⲦⲘⲘⲀⲨ· ⲀⲨⲰ ⲠⲈⲬⲀϤ ⲚⲐⲰⲘⲀⲤ ⲬⲈ ϨⲀⲘⲎⲚ
ϯⲬⲰ ⲘⲘⲞⲤ ⲬⲈ ⲚⲞⲂⲈ ⲚⲒⲘ' ϨⲒ ⲀⲚⲞⲘⲒⲀ ⲚⲒⲘ ⲠⲈⲒ̈ⲚⲞⲂⲈ
ⲞⲨⲞⲦⲂ ⲈⲢⲞⲞⲨ· ⲚⲀⲒ̈ ⲚⲦⲈⲒ̈ⲘⲒⲚⲈ ⲈⲨⲚⲀⲬⲒⲦⲞⲨ ⲚⲤⲀ ⲦⲞⲞ-
ⲦⲞⲨ ⲈⲠⲔⲀⲔⲈ ⲈⲦϨⲒⲂⲞⲖ' ⲞⲨⲆⲈ ⲚⲚⲈⲨⲦⲤⲦⲞⲞⲨ ⲈⲦⲈ-
15 ⲤⲪⲀⲒⲢⲀ ⲚⲞⲨⲰϨⲘ· ⲀⲖⲖⲀ ⲈⲨⲚⲀⲀⲚϨⲀⲖⲒⲤⲔⲈ ⲘⲘⲞⲨ ⲚⲤⲈ-
ⲦⲀⲔⲞⲞⲨ ϨⲘ ⲠⲔⲀⲔⲈ ⲈⲦϨⲒⲂⲞⲖ' ⲠⲘⲀ ⲈⲦⲈ ⲘⲚ-ⲚⲀ ⲚϨⲎⲦϤ
ⲞⲨⲆⲈ ⲘⲚ-ⲞⲨⲞⲈⲒⲚ· ⲀⲖⲖⲀ ⲠⲢⲒⲘⲈ ⲠⲈ ⲘⲚ ⲠϬⲀϨϬⲈ ⲚⲚ-
ⲞⲂϨⲈ ⲠⲈ· ⲀⲨⲰ ⲮⲨⲬⲎ ⲚⲒⲘ' ⲈⲦⲞⲨⲚⲀⲬⲒⲦⲞⲨ ⲈⲠⲔⲀⲔⲈ
ⲈⲦϨⲒⲂⲞⲖ· ⲘⲈⲨⲦⲤⲦⲞⲞⲨ ⲚⲞⲨⲰϨⲘ ⲀⲖⲖⲀ ϢⲀⲨⲦⲀⲔⲞ ⲚⲤⲈ-
20 ⲂⲰⲖ ⲈⲂⲞⲖ :

ⲀϤⲞⲨⲰϢⲂ ⲚϬⲒ Ⲓ̈ⲰϨⲀⲚⲚⲎⲤ ⲬⲈ ⲈⲒ̈Ⲉ ⲞⲨⲢⲰⲘⲈ ⲈⲘⲠϤⲢ- [ⲦⲚⲂ]
ⲚⲞⲂⲈ ⲀⲖⲖⲀ ⲈϤⲢ-ⲀⲄⲀⲐⲞⲚ ⲈϤⲘⲎⲚ ⲈⲂⲞⲖ' ⲈⲘⲠϤϨⲈ ⲆⲈ
ⲈⲚⲈⲔⲘⲨⲤⲦⲎⲢⲒⲞⲚ ⲈⲦⲢⲈϤⲞⲨⲰⲦⲂ ⲚⲚⲀⲢⲬⲰⲚ ⲈϤϢⲀⲚⲈⲒ'
ⲈⲂⲞⲖ ϨⲚ ⲤⲰⲘⲀ ⲈⲨⲚⲀⲢ-ⲞⲨ ⲚⲀϤ: ⲠⲈⲬⲈ ⲒⲤ ⲬⲈ ⲠⲢⲰⲘⲈ
25 ⲚⲦⲈⲒ̈ⲘⲒⲚⲈ ⲈⲢϢⲀⲚ ⲠⲈϤⲞⲨⲞⲈⲒϢ ⲬⲰⲔ ⲈⲂⲞⲖ ϨⲒⲦⲚ ⲦⲈ-
ⲤⲪⲀⲒⲢⲀ ϢⲀⲨⲈⲒ' ⲚⲤⲀ ⲦⲈϤⲮⲨⲬⲎ ⲚϬⲒ ⲘⲠⲀⲢⲀⲖⲎⲘⲠⲦⲎⲤ

which devour them and immerse them in the rivers of fire
for another eleven years. After these things they carry them
forth to the outer darkness until the day of judgment when
the great darkness will be *judged*, when they will dissolve
and be destroyed."

Thomas said; "We have heard that there are some upon
the earth who take male *sperm* and female menstrual blood
and make a dish of lentils and eat it, saying: 'We *believe* in
Esau and Jacob'[1]. Is this *then* a seemly thing or not?"

Jesus *however* was angry with the *world* at that time. And
he said to Thomas: "*Truly* I say that this sin surpasses every
sin and every *iniquity*. (Men) of this kind will be taken
immediately to the outer darkness, and will *not* be returned
again into the *sphere*. *But* they will be *consumed* and perish
in the outer darkness, the *place* in which there is no pity,
nor is there light. *But* there is weeping and gnashing of
teeth*. And every *soul* which is taken to the outer darkness
is not returned again, *but* is destroyed and dissolves."

John answered: "A man who has not committed sin, *but*
has continually done *good*, *but* he has not found thy *mysteries*
in order to pass the *archons*: when he comes forth from
the *body*, what will be done with him?"

Jesus said: "When the time of such a man is completed
through the *sphere*, the *paralemptai* of | Bainchoooch, who

---

* cf. Mt. 8.12 etc.

---

[1] (9) compare J 100; on libertine gnostics, see Epiph. 26.4, 5.

ⲛ̄ⲃⲁⲓ̈ⲛ̄ⲭⲱⲱⲱⲭ' ⲉⲟⲩⲁ ⲡⲉ ϩⲓ ⲡⲓϣⲟⲙⲛⲧ ⲛ̄ⲛⲟⲩⲧⲉ ⲛ̄ⲧⲣⲓⲇⲩⲛⲁⲙⲓⲥ ⲛ̄ⲥⲉϫⲓ ⲛ̄ⲧⲉϥⲯⲩⲭⲏ ϩⲛ̄ ⲟⲩⲣⲁϣⲉ ⲙⲛ̄ ⲟⲩⲧⲉⲗⲏⲗ ⲛ̄ⲥⲉⲣ̄-ϣⲟⲙⲛⲧ ⲛ̄ϩⲟⲟⲩ ⲉⲩⲕⲱⲧⲉ ⲛ̄ⲙⲙⲁⲥ ⲉⲩⲧⲥⲁⲃⲟ ⲙ̄ⲙⲟⲥ ⲉⲛⲥⲱⲛⲧ ⲙ̄ⲡⲕⲟⲥⲙⲟⲥ ϩⲛ̄ ⲟⲩⲣⲁϣⲉ ⲙⲛ̄ ⲟⲩⲧⲉⲗⲏⲗ' ⲙⲛ̄ⲛ̄ⲥⲁ ⲛⲁⲓ̈ ϣⲁⲩϫⲓⲧⲥ ⲉⲡⲉⲥⲏⲧ ⲉⲁⲙⲛ̄ⲧⲉ ⲛ̄ⲥⲉⲧⲥⲁⲃⲟⲥ ⲉⲛⲕⲟⲗⲁⲥⲧⲏⲣⲓⲟⲛ ⲉⲧϩⲛ̄ ⲁⲙⲛ̄ⲧⲉ· ⲛ̄ⲛⲉⲩⲛⲁⲧⲓⲙⲱⲣⲉⲓ ⲇⲉ ⲙ̄ⲙⲟⲥ ⲁⲛ ⲛ̄ϩⲏⲧⲟⲩ ⲁⲗⲗⲁ ⲉⲩⲛⲁⲧⲥⲁⲃⲟⲥ ⲙ̄ⲙⲁⲧⲉ ⲉⲣⲟⲟⲩ· ⲁⲩⲱ ⲡⲉⲗⲁϩⲱⲃ' ⲙ̄ⲡϣⲁϩ ⲛ̄ⲛ̄ⲕⲟⲗⲁⲥⲓⲥ |* ϣⲁϥϣⲱⲡⲉ ⲉϥⲧⲁϩⲟ ⲙ̄ⲙⲟⲥ [ⲧⲡⲃ b] ⲙ̄ⲙⲁⲧⲉ ⲛ̄ⲟⲩϣⲏⲙ ⲙⲛ̄ⲛ̄ⲥⲁ ⲛⲁⲓ̈ ⲛ̄ⲥⲉϥⲓⲧⲥ ⲉϩⲣⲁⲓ̈ ϩⲓ ⲧⲉϩⲓⲏ ⲛ̄ⲧⲙⲏⲧⲉ ⲛ̄ⲥⲉⲧⲥⲁⲃⲟⲥ ⲉⲛⲕⲟⲗⲁⲥⲓⲥ ⲛ̄ⲛⲉϩⲓⲟⲟⲩⲉ ⲛ̄ⲧⲙⲏⲧⲉ ⲉⲣⲉ ⲡⲉⲗⲁϩⲱⲃ ⲙ̄ⲡϣⲁϩ ⲧⲁϩⲟ ⲙ̄ⲙⲟⲥ ⲛ̄ⲟⲩϣⲏⲙ· ⲙⲛ̄ⲛ̄ⲥⲁ ⲛⲁⲓ̈ ⲛ̄ⲥⲉϫⲓⲧⲥ ⲛ̄ⲧⲡⲁⲣⲑⲉⲛⲟⲥ ⲙ̄ⲡⲟⲩⲟⲉⲓⲛ ⲛ̄ⲥⲕⲣⲓⲛⲉ ⲙ̄ⲙⲟⲥ ⲛ̄ⲥⲕⲁⲁⲥ ϩⲁⲧⲛ̄ ⲡⲕⲟⲩⲓ̈ ⲛ̄ⲥⲁⲃⲁⲱⲑ ⲡⲁⲅⲁⲑⲟⲥ ⲡⲁⲧⲙⲉⲥⲟⲥ ϣⲁⲛⲧⲉ ⲧⲉⲥⲫⲁⲓⲣⲁ ⲕⲱⲧⲉ ⲛ̄ⲧⲉ ⲍⲉⲩⲥ ⲙⲛ̄ ⲧⲁⲫⲣⲟⲇⲓⲧⲏ ⲛ̄ⲥⲉⲉⲓ' ⲙ̄ⲡⲉⲙⲧⲟ ⲉⲃⲟⲗ ⲛ̄ⲧⲡⲁⲣⲑⲉⲛⲟⲥ ⲙ̄ⲡⲟⲩⲟⲉⲓⲛ· ⲛ̄ⲧⲉ ⲕⲣⲟⲛⲟⲥ ⲙⲛ̄ ⲁⲣⲏⲥ ⲉⲓ' ⲛ̄ⲥⲁ ⲡⲁϩⲟⲩ ⲙ̄ⲙⲟⲥ· ⲧⲟⲧⲉ ϣⲁⲥϥⲓ ⲛ̄ⲧⲉⲯⲩⲭⲏ ⲛ̄ⲇⲓⲕⲁⲓⲟⲥ ⲉⲧⲙ̄ⲙⲁⲩ ⲛ̄ⲥⲉⲧⲁⲁⲥ ⲉⲧⲟⲟⲧⲟⲩ ⲛ̄ⲛⲉⲥⲡⲁⲣⲁⲗⲏⲙⲡⲧⲏⲥ ⲛ̄ⲥⲉⲛⲟⲭⲥ ⲉⲛⲁⲓⲱⲛ ⲛ̄ⲧⲉⲥⲫⲁⲓⲣⲁ ⲁⲩⲱ ⲛ̄ⲧⲉ ⲛ̄ⲗⲓⲧⲟⲩⲣⲅⲟⲥ ⲛ̄ⲧⲉⲥⲫⲁⲓⲣⲁ ⲛ̄ⲥⲉϫⲓⲧⲥ ⲉⲃⲟⲗ' ⲉⲩⲙⲟⲟⲩ ⲉϥϩⲁⲡⲉⲥⲏⲧ ⲛ̄ⲧⲉⲥⲫⲁⲓⲣⲁ ⲛ̄ϥⲣ̄-ⲟⲩⲕⲣⲱⲙ ** ⲉϥⲃⲣ̄ⲃⲣ̄ ⲛ̄ϥⲟⲩⲱⲙ ⲧⲡⲅ ⲉϩⲟⲩⲛ ⲛ̄ⲥⲱⲥ ϣⲁⲛⲧϥⲕⲁⲑⲁⲣⲓⲍⲉ ⲙ̄ⲙⲟⲥ ⲧⲟⲛⲱ· ⲁⲩⲱ ϣⲁϥⲉⲓ' ⲛ̄ϭⲓ ⲓ̈ⲁⲗⲟⲩϩⲁⲙ' ⲡⲡⲁⲣⲁⲗⲏⲙⲡⲧⲏⲥ ⲛ̄ⲥⲁⲃⲁⲱⲑ ⲡⲁⲇⲁⲙⲁⲥ· ⲡⲁⲓ̈ ⲉϣⲁϥϯ ⲙ̄ⲡⲁⲡⲟⲧ' ⲛ̄ⲧⲃ̄ϣⲉ ⲛ̄ⲛⲉⲯⲩⲭⲟⲟⲩⲉ· ⲁⲩⲱ ϣⲁϥⲉⲓⲛⲉ ⲙ̄ⲡⲙⲟⲩⲛ̄ⲃϣⲉ ⲛ̄ϥⲧⲁⲁϥ ⲛ̄ⲧⲉⲯⲩⲭⲏ

1 MS ϩⲓ; read ϩⲛ̄.
6 MS ⲛ̄ⲛⲉⲩⲛⲁⲧⲓⲙⲱⲣⲉⲓ; read ⲛ̄ⲉⲩⲛⲁⲧⲓⲙ.
17 MS ⲛ̄ⲥⲉⲧⲁⲁⲥ; read ⲛ̄ⲥⲧⲁⲁⲥ.
24 MS originally ⲙ̄ⲡⲟⲩ; ⲙ inserted above. MS originally ⲛ̄ⲛⲉⲧⲉⲯⲩⲭⲏ; ⲛⲉ expunged.

is one of the three *triple-powered* gods, come for his *soul*; and they take his *soul* with joy and gladness. And they spend three days going round with it, teaching it of the creation of the *world* with joy and gladness. After these things they take it down to Amente, and teach it of the *places of correction* in Amente. *But* they will not *take revenge* on it in them. *But* they will only teach it of them, and the smoke of the flame of the *punishments* only reaches it a little. After these things they take it forth upon the way of the Midst, and teach it of the *punishments* of the ways of the Midst, and the smoke of the flame reaches it a little. After these things they take it to the *Virgin* of the Light, and she *judges* it and places it in the presence of the Little Sabaoth, the *Good*, he of the *Midst*, until the *sphere* turns, and Zeus and Aphrodite come into the presence of [1] the *Virgin* of the Light, and Cronos and Ares come behind her. *Then* she carries that *righteous soul* and gives it [2] into the hands of her *paralemptai*, and they cast it into the *aeons* of the *sphere*. And the *ministers* of the *sphere* take it forth to a water which is below the *sphere*, and it becomes [3] a boiling fire and consumes it until it *purifies* it completely. And Jalouham, the *paralemptes* of Sabaoth, the Adamas, comes. It is he who gives the cup of forgetfulness to *souls*. And he brings the water of forgetfulness and gives it to the *soul*, | and

---

[1] (15) into the presence of; Till: before; (also 383.26; 384.20).
[2] (17) and gives it; MS: and it is given.
[3] (20) it becomes; Schmidt: there arises.

⟨ N̄CCOOϤ⟩ N̄CP̄ΠⲰBϢ N̄2ⲰB NIM' M̄N TOΠOC NIM' ENT-
ACBⲰK EPOOY· M̄N̄N̄CⲰC ϢAϤEI' N̄ճI OYΠAPAΛHMΠTHC
N̄TE ΠKOYEI N̄CABAⲰΘ' ΠAΓAΘOC ΠATMECOC ϢAϤEINE
2ⲰⲰϤ N̄OYAΠOT' EϤME2 N̄NOHMA 2I M̄N̄TCABE AYⲰ
5 EPE TNHⲯIC N̄2HTϤ· N̄ϤTAAϤ N̄TEⲯYXH N̄CENŌX̄C EY-
CⲰMA EN̄CN̄AϢ-N̄KOT̄K̄ AN OYAE EN̄CN̄AϢ-ⲰBϢ AN
ETBE ΠIAΠOT N̄TE TNHⲯIC ENTAYTAAϤ NAC AΛΛA
EϤNAϢⲰΠE EϤXⲰⲰKE M̄ΠEC2HT EϤMHN EBOΛ' ECϢINE
N̄CA M̄MYCTHPION M̄ΠOYOEIN ϢAN̄TC̄2E EP⟨O⟩OY 2IT̄M̄ ⲦⲨⲅᵇ
10 ΠTⲰϢ N̄TΠAPΘENOC M̄ΠOYOEIN N̄CKΛHPONOMI M̄-
ΠOYOEIN N̄ϢAEN62·

ΠEXE MAPI2AM' XE EIE OYPⲰME EAϤP̄-NOBE NIM' 2I
ANOMIA NIM EMΠᵖϤ2E M̄MYCTHPION M̄ΠOYOEIN EϤNAXI
N̄TEYKOΛACIC THPOY N̄OYCOΠ N̄OYⲰT· ΠEXE Ⲓ̄C̄ XE
15 CE ϤNAXITOY· EϢⲰΠE ON ENTAϤP̄-ϢOMN̄T N̄NOBE
EϤNAXI N̄TKOΛACIC N̄ϢOMN̄T·

ΠEXE ⲒⲰ2ANNHC XE EIE OYPⲰME EAϤP̄-NOBE NIM
2I ANOMIA NIM' EϤAE AE AϤ2E EM̄MYCTHPION M̄ΠOYO-
EIN OYN̄-ճOM M̄MOϤ ETPEϤOYXAI̅· ΠEXE Ⲓ̄C̄ XE ΠAI
20 N̄TEIMINE ENTAϤP̄-NOBE NIM 2I ANOMIA NIM' N̄Ϥ2E EM̄-
MYCTHPION M̄ΠOYOEIN N̄ϤAAY N̄ϤXOKOY EBOΛ' N̄Ϥ-
TMKA-TOOTϤ EBOΛ' OYAE N̄ϤTMP̄NOBE EϤNAKΛHPO-
NOMI M̄ΠEΘHCAYPOC M̄ΠOYOEIN· ΠEXE Ⲓ̄C̄ N̄NEϤMAΘH-
THC XE EϢⲰΠE EPϢAN TĒC⟨ⲫ⟩AIPA KⲰTE N̄TE KPO- [ⲦⲨⲇ]
25 NOC M̄N APHC EI' N̄CA ΠA2OY N̄TΠAPΘENOC M̄ΠOYO-
EIN AYⲰ N̄TE ZEYC M̄N TAⲪPOΔITH EI' M̄ΠEMTO EBOΛ

---

1 MS N̄CCOOϤ omitted.

⟨it drinks it⟩ and forgets everything and every *place* to which it has gone. Afterwards a *paralemptes* of the Little Sabaoth, the *Good*, he of the *Midst*, also brings a cup which is filled with *understanding* and wisdom, and there is *soberness* in it. And he gives it to the *soul*, and it is cast into a *body* which is not able [1] to sleep *nor* is it able to forget, because of the cup of *soberness* which was given to it. *But* it will be a goad to its heart continually, to seek [2] for the *mysteries* of the light until it finds them, through the ordinance of the *Virgin* of the Light, and *inherits* the eternal light."

148. Mariam said: "A man who has committed every sin and every *iniquity*, and has not found the *mysteries* of the light, will he receive the *punishment* for them all at once?"

Jesus said: "Yes, he will receive it. If he has committed three sins he will receive the *punishment* for three."

John said: "A man who has committed every sin and every *iniquity*, *but* at last has found the *mysteries* of the light: is it possible for him to be saved?"

Jesus said: "Such a one who has committed every sin and every *iniquity*, and finds the *mysteries* of the light, and performs them and completes them, and does not cease from them *nor* does he commit sin: he will *inherit* the *Treasury* of the Light."

Jesus said to his *disciples*: "If when the *sphere* turns, Cronos and Ares come behind the *Virgin* of the Light, and Zeus and Aphrodite come into the presence | of the *Virgin* and

---

[1] (6) a body which is not able; Till: a body in which it is not able.
[2] (8) a goad ... to seek; Schmidt: a whip ... to ask.

ⲛ̄ⲧⲡⲁⲣⲑⲉⲛⲟⲥ ⲉⲩϩ̄ⲛ̄ ⲛⲉⲩⲁⲓⲱⲛ ⲙ̄ⲙⲓⲛ ⲙ̄ⲙⲟⲟⲩ ϣⲁⲩⲥⲱⲕ'
ⲛ̄ⲛ̄ⲕⲁⲧⲁⲕⲉⲧⲁⲡⲉⲧⲁⲥⲙⲁ ⲛ̄ⲧⲡⲁⲣⲑⲉⲛⲟⲥ ϣⲁⲥϣⲱⲡⲉ ⲉⲥ-
ⲣⲟⲟⲩⲧ ⲙ̄ⲡⲛⲁⲩ ⲉⲧⲙ̄ⲙⲁⲩ ⲉⲥⲛⲁⲩ ⲉⲡⲉⲓ̈ⲥⲓⲟⲩ ⲥⲛⲁⲩ ⲡ̄-
ⲟⲩⲟⲉⲓⲛ ⲙ̄ⲡⲉⲥⲙ̄ⲧⲟ ⲉⲃⲟⲗ ⲁⲩⲱ ⲯⲩⲭⲏ ⲛⲓⲙ ⲉⲧⲥⲛⲁ-
5 ⲛⲟⲭⲟⲩ ⲉⲡⲕⲩⲕⲗⲟⲥ ⲛ̄ⲛⲁⲓⲱⲛ ⲛ̄ⲧⲉⲥⲫⲁⲓⲣⲁ ⲙ̄ⲡⲛⲁⲩ ⲉⲧ-
ⲙ̄ⲙⲁⲩ ⲉⲧⲣⲉⲩⲉⲓ' ⲉⲃⲟⲗ ⲉⲡⲕⲟⲥⲙⲟⲥ ϣⲁⲩϣⲱⲡⲉ ⲛ̄ⲇⲓ-
ⲕⲁⲓⲟⲥ ⲛ̄ⲁⲅⲁⲑⲟⲥ ⲁⲩⲱ ϣⲁⲩϩⲉ ⲉⲙ̄ⲙⲩⲥⲧⲏⲣⲓⲟⲛ ⲙ̄ⲡⲟⲩⲟ-
ⲉⲓⲛ ⲙ̄ⲡⲉⲓ̈ⲥⲟⲡ ϣⲁⲥⲧⲛ̄ⲛⲟⲟⲩⲥⲟⲩ ⲛ̄ⲕⲉⲥⲟⲡ' ⲛ̄ⲥⲉϩⲉ ⲉⲙ̄-
ⲙⲩⲥⲧⲏⲣⲓⲟⲛ ⲙ̄ⲡⲟⲩⲟⲉⲓⲛ· ⲉϣⲱⲡⲉ ϩⲱⲱϥ ⲉⲣϣⲁⲛ ⲁⲣⲏⲥ
10 ⲙ̄ⲛ ⲕⲣⲟⲛⲟⲥ ⲉⲓ' ⲙ̄ⲡⲉⲙ̄ⲧⲟ ⲉⲃⲟⲗ ⲛ̄ⲧⲡⲁⲣⲑⲉⲛⲟⲥ ⲉⲣⲉ ⲍⲉⲩⲥ
ⲙ̄ⲛ ⲧⲁⲫⲣⲟⲇⲓⲧⲏ ϩⲓ ⲡⲁϩⲟⲩ ⲙ̄ⲙⲟⲥ ⲉⲛ̄ⲥⲛⲁⲩ ⲉⲣⲟⲟⲩ ⲁⲛ·
ⲯⲩⲭⲏ ⲛⲓⲙ ⲉⲧⲥ̄ⲛⲁⲛⲟⲭⲟⲩ ⲉⲛⲥⲱⲛ̄ⲧ ⲛ̄ⲧⲉⲥⲫⲉⲣⲁ ⲙ̄ⲡⲛⲁⲩ [ⲧⲡⲁ]ᵇ
ⲉⲧⲙ̄ⲙⲁⲩ ϣⲁⲩϣⲱⲡⲉ ⲙ̄ⲡⲟⲛⲏⲣⲟⲥ ⲁⲩⲱ ⲛ̄ⲣⲉϥϭⲱⲛ̄ⲧ ⲁⲩⲱ
ⲙⲉⲩϩⲉ ⲉⲙ̄ⲙⲩⲥⲧⲏⲣⲓⲟⲛ ⲙ̄ⲡⲟⲩⲟⲉⲓⲛ:
15 ⲛⲁⲓ̈ ϭⲉ ⲉⲣⲉ ⲓ̄ⲥ̄ ϫⲱ ⲙ̄ⲙⲟⲟⲩ ⲛ̄ⲛⲉϥⲙⲁⲑⲟⲧⲏⲥ ϩⲛ̄ ⲧⲙⲏⲧⲉ
ⲛ̄ⲁⲙⲛ̄ⲧⲉ· ⲁⲩⲱϣ ⲉⲃⲟⲗ ⲁⲩⲣⲓⲙⲉ ⲛ̄ϭⲓ ⲙ̄ⲙⲁⲑⲟⲧⲏⲥ· ϫⲉ
ⲟⲩⲟⲓ̈ ⲟⲩⲟⲓ̈ ⲛ̄ⲣⲣⲱⲙⲉ ⲛ̄ⲣⲉϥⲣ̄ⲛⲟⲃⲉ ⲛⲁⲓ̈ ⲉⲣⲉ ⲧⲁⲙⲉⲗⲓⲁ
ⲛ̄ⲕⲟⲧⲕ̄ ⲉⲃⲟⲗ ϩⲓϫⲱⲟⲩ ⲙ̄ⲛ ⲧⲃ̄ϣⲉ ⲛ̄ⲛⲁⲣⲭⲱⲛ ϣⲁⲛⲧⲟⲩⲉⲓ'
ⲉⲃⲟⲗ ϩⲛ̄ ⲥⲱⲙⲁ· ⲛ̄ⲥⲉϫⲓⲧⲟⲩ ⲉⲛⲉⲓ̈ⲕⲟⲗⲁⲥⲓⲥ· ⲛⲁ ⲛⲁⲛ·
20 ⲛⲁ ⲛⲁⲛ· ⲡϣⲏⲣⲉ ⲙ̄ⲡⲉⲧⲟⲩⲁⲁⲃ' ⲛ̄ⲅ̄ϣ̄ⲛ̄ϩ̄ⲧⲏⲕ ϩⲁⲣⲟⲛ ϫⲉ
ⲉⲛⲉⲟⲩϫⲁⲓ̈ ⲉⲛⲉⲓ̈ⲕⲟⲗⲁⲥⲓⲥ ⲙ̄ⲛ ⲛⲉⲓ̈ⲕⲣⲓⲥⲓⲥ ⲉⲩⲥ̄ⲃⲧⲱⲧ ⲛ̄ⲣ̄-
ⲣⲉϥⲣ̄ⲛⲟⲃⲉ· ⲉⲙⲙⲟⲛ ⲁⲛⲣ̄ⲛⲟⲃⲉ ϩⲱⲱⲛ ⲡⲉⲛϫⲟⲉⲓⲥ ⲁⲩⲱ
ⲡⲉⲛⲟⲩⲟⲉⲓⲛ:

ⲋ̄ —ⲝ̄ⲋ̄— ⲝ̄ⲋ̄— ⲝ̄ⲋ̄— ⲝ̄ⲋ̄— ⲝ̄ⲋ̄— ⲝ̄ⲋ̄— ⲝ̄ⲋ̄— ⲋ̄

---

2 MS ⲛ̄ⲛ̄ⲕⲁⲧⲁⲕⲉⲧⲁⲡⲉⲧⲁⲥⲙⲁ; read ⲛ̄ⲛ̄ⲕⲁⲧⲁⲡⲉⲧⲁⲥⲙⲁ.
23 the main text ends here, leaving about 6 lines uninscribed at the foot of
column 2.

they are in their own *aeons*, the *veils* of the *Virgin* are
drawn aside. And she is glad in that hour as she sees
these two stars of light in her presence. And all *souls* which
she will cast into the *cycle* of the *aeons* of the *sphere* at that
hour, so that they come forth in the *world*, become [1] *righteous* and *good*, and they find the *mysteries* of the light at
this time; she sends them again to find the *mysteries* of
the light. If on the other hand Ares and Cronos come into
the presence of the *Virgin*, while Zeus and Aphrodite are
behind her, so that she does not see them, all *souls* which
she will cast into the creation of the *sphere* in that hour
become *wicked* and ill-tempered, and do not [2] find the *mysteries* of the light."

Now when Jesus had said these things to his *disciples* in
the midst of Amente, the *disciples* cried out and wept : "Woe,
woe to the sinful men upon whom rests the *negligence* and
the forgetfulness of the *archons*, until they come forth from
the *body* and are cast into these *punishments*. Have mercy
on us, have mercy on us, thou Son of the Holy One, and have
compassion on us, so that we are saved from these *punishments* and these *judgments* which are prepared for sinners,
since we also have sinned, our Lord and our Light."

---

[1]   (6) become; lit. are wont to become; (also 384.13).
[2]   (14) do not; lit. are not wont to.

ⲡⲆⲓⲕⲀⲓⲟⲥ. ⲀⲨⲈⲓ' ⲈⲂⲞⲖ ϢⲞⲘⲦ ϢⲞⲘⲦ· ⲈⲠⲈϤⲦⲞⲞⲨ
ⲚⲔⲖⲓⲘⲀ ⲚⲦⲠⲈ ⲀⲨⲦⲀϢⲈⲞⲓϢ ⲘⲠⲈⲨⲀⲄⲄⲈⲖⲓⲞⲚ ⲚⲦⲘⲚⲦⲈⲢⲞ
ϨⲘ ⲠⲔⲞⲤⲘⲞⲤ ⲦⲎⲢϤ ⲈⲢⲈ ⲠⲈⲬⲤ ⲈⲚⲈⲢⲄⲈⲓ ⲚⲘⲘⲀⲨ ϨⲘ
ⲠϢⲀⲬⲈ ⲘⲠⲦⲀⲬⲢⲞ ⲘⲚ ⲘⲘⲀⲈⲓⲚ ⲈⲦⲞⲨⲎϨ ⲚⲤⲰⲞⲨ ⲘⲚ
5 ⲚⲈϢⲠⲎⲢⲈ· ⲀⲨⲰ ⲚⲦⲈⲓϨⲈ ⲀⲨⲤⲞⲨⲚ-ⲦⲘⲚⲦⲈⲢⲞ ⲘⲠⲚⲞⲨⲦⲈ
ϨⲘ ⲠⲔⲀϨ ⲦⲎⲢϤ ⲀⲨⲰ ϨⲘ ⲠⲔⲞⲤⲘⲞⲤ ⲦⲎⲢϤ ⲘⲠⲓⲤⲢⲀⲎⲖ·
ⲈⲨⲘⲚⲦⲘⲚⲦⲢⲈ ⲚⲚϨⲈⲐⲚⲞⲤ ⲦⲎⲢⲞⲨ ⲚⲀⲓ ⲈⲦϢⲞⲞⲠ ϪⲓⲚ
ⲘⲘⲀ ⲚϢⲀ· ϢⲀ ⲘⲘⲀ ⲚϨⲰⲦⲠ.

10 ̅ϡ ϥ ϥ ϥ ϥ ϥ ϥ ϥ ϥ ϥ
   ϡ ϥ ϥ ϥ ϥ ϥ ϥ ϥ ϥ ϥ

   ·   ·   ·   ·   ·   ·   ·   ·   ·

   ·   ·   ·   ·   ·   ·   ·   ·   ·

   ̅ϡ ϥ ϥ ϥ ϥ ϥ ϥ ϥ ϥ ϥ
   ϡ ϥ ϥ ϥ ϥ ϥ ϥ ϥ ϥ ϥ

---

1 a text by a later hand is written in the first column of the recto of the last
   unpaginated leaf.
11 two lines, each of about 12 letters, are erased; they probably contained the
   title of this text.

... the *righteous*. They came forth three by three to the four *regions* [1] of the heavens. They preached the *Gospel* of the Kingdom in the whole *world* while the Christ *worked* with them through the word of confirmation and the signs which followed them and the marvels. And in this way the Kingdom of God was known upon the whole earth and in the whole *world* of Israel, as a witness to all *peoples* which exist from the places of the East to the places of the West [2].

---

[1] (2) four regions; see J 91; (cf. also 367.14).
[2] (8) East ... West; lit. places of rising ... places of setting.

BIBLIOGRAPHY

1. Althaner, B. Patrology. Translated by H. C. Graef; Freiburg : Herder, 5th ed. 1958; Edinburgh-London : Nelson, 1960.
2. Amélineau, E. La Pistis Sophia : ouvrage gnostique de Valentin, traduit du Copte en français avec une introduction. Paris, 1895.
3. Andresen, C. "Pistis Sophia," Lexikon der Alten Welt (Zürich : Artemis, 1965), 2334.
4. Anonymous. "Pistis Sophia," The Oxford Dictionary of the Christian Church (ed. F. L. Cross and E. A. Livingstone : Oxford University Press, 2nd ed. 1974), 1093-94.
5. Anonymous. "Pistis Sophia," The Westminster Dictionary of Church History (ed. J. C. Brauer : Philadelphia : Westminster, 1971), 661.
6. Anonymous. "Gnosticism," The New Encyclopaedia Britannica (15th ed.; Chicago : Encyclopaedia Britannica, 1974), Micropaedia 4, 587-88.
7. Baur, F. C. Die christliche Gnosis oder die christliche Religionsphilosophie in ihrer geschichtlichen Entwicklung. Darmstadt : Wissenschaftliche Buchgesellschaft, 1967 (reprint of the 1835 edition).
8. Böhlig, A. Mysterion und Wahrheit : Gesammelte Beiträge zur spätantiken Religionsgeschichte (AGSJU VI.) Leiden : E. J. Brill, 1968.
9. Bousset, W. "Gnosticism." The Encyclopaedia Britannica (11th ed.; Cambridge : University Press, 1910-11), 12, 152-54.
10. Bousset, W. Hauptprobleme der Gnosis. Göttingen : Vandenhoeck & Ruprecht, 1907. Reprinted 1973.
11. Bozzone, A. M. "Pistis Sophia," Dizionario Ecclesiastico 3 (ed. A. Mercati; A. Pelzer; A. M. Bozzone; Torino : Unione Tipografico-Editrice Torinese, 1958), 235.
12. Brandon, S. G. F. "Pistis Sophia," A Dictionary of Comparative Religion (ed. S. F. G. Brandon; London : Weidenfeld and Nicolson/New York : Charles Scribner's Sons, 1970), 504.
13. Burkitt, F. C. "Pistis Sophia," JThS a) 23 (London 1921/22) 271-280; b) 26 (1923/24) 391-99; c) 27 (1925/26) 148-57.
14. Carmignac, J. "Le genre littéraire du 'péshèr' dans la Pistis Sophia," RQ 4 (1963/64), 497-522.
15. Dieterich, A. Abraxas. Studien zur Religionsgeschichte des spätern Altertums. Leipzig : B.G. Teubner 1891.
16. Dulaurier, E. "Notice sur le manuscrit copte-thébain intitulé : La Fidèle Sagesse (tpistis sophia) et sur la publication projetée du texte et de la traduction française de ce manuscrit," JA 4ᵉ sér., 9 (Paris 1847) 534-548.
17. Enslin, M. S. "Pistis Sophia," The Interpreter's Dictionary of the Bible 3 (ed. G. A. Buttrick; New York and Nashville : Abingdon, 1962), 820.

BIBLIOGRAPHY

18. Faye, E. de. Gnostiques et gnosticisme. Ch. 3 : "Écrits gnostiques en langue copte," (Paris 1913) 247-311. 2nd ed. 1925.

19. Harnack, A. von. "Über das gnostische Buch Pistis Sophia". TU 7/2. Leipzig 1891.

20. Harnack, A. von. "Die Pistis Sophia und die im Papyrus Brucianus saec. V. vel VI. enthaltenen gnostischen Schriften." Die Chronologie der altchristlichen Literatur 2/2 (Leipzig 1904) 193-95.

21. Harris, J. R. The Odes and Psalms of Solomon now first published from the Syriac version. Cambridge 1909. 2nd ed. 1912. Re-edited by Harris, J. R. and Mingana, A. Manchester : Text 1916; Translation and Notes 1920.

22. Horner, G. Pistis Sophia. Literally translated from the Coptic. With an Introduction by G. F. Legge. London : SPCK, 1924.

23. Jonas, H. Gnosis und spätantiker Geist; Teil I : Die mythologische Gnosis mit einer Einleitung zur Geschichte und Methodologie der Forschung. Göttingen : Vandenhoeck & Ruprecht, 1934; reprinted 1954, 1964.

24. Kragerud, A. Die Hymnen der Pistis Sophia. Oslo : Universitetsforlagets Trykningssentral, 1967.

25. Koestlin, K. R. "Das gnostische System des Buches Pistis Sophia". Theologisches Jahrbuch 13 (hrsg. von Baur und Zeller, Bielefeld-Leipzig 1854) 1-104, 137-96.

26. Kropp, A. M. Ausgewählte koptische Zaubertexte. 3 Bde. Brussels : Édition de la fondation Égyptologique Reine Élisabeth, 1930-31.

27. G.-Larraya, J. A. "Pistis Sofia," Enciclopedia della Biblia 5 (Barcelona : Ediciones Garriga, 1963), 1125; = "Pistis Sofia," Enciclopedia della Biblia 5 (Torino : Elle Di Ci/Torino-Leumann, 1971), 788-89.

28. Legge, F. Forerunners and Rivals of Christianity from 330 BC to 330 AD. New Hyde Park, New York : University Books, 1964 (originally published by Cambridge University Press, 1915).

29. Leisegang, H. Die Gnosis. (Kröners Taschenausgabe 32) Stuttgart : Alfred Kröner, 4th ed. 1955.

30. Leisegang, H. "Pistis Sophia," Paulys Real-Encyclopädie der classischen Altertumswissenschaft 20 : 2 (hrsg. G. Wissowa et al; Waldsee : Alfred Druckenmüller, 1950), 1813-21.

31. Ludin Jansen, H. "Bibelske tekster i Pistis Sophia," DTT 21 (1958), 210-18.

32. Ludin Jansen, H. "Er Sofia-teksten en mysterieliturgi?" NTT 68 (1967), 91-93 (NTA 13. 740).

33. Ludin Jansen, H. "Gnostic Interpretation in Pistis Sophia," Proceedings of the IXth International Congress for the History of Religions, Tokyo and Kyoto 1958 (Tokyo : Maruzen, 1960), 106-11.

34. Mead, G. R. S. Pistis Sophia; A Gnostic Miscellany. Englished, with an Introduction and Annotated Bibliography. London : J. M. Watkins, 1896; 2nd ed. 1921; reprinted : University Books, 1974.

35. Moffatt, J. "Pistis Sophia," HRE 10 (Edinburgh : T. and T. Clark, 1917) 45-48.

36. Norman, J. G. G. "Pistis Sophia," The New International Dictionary of the Christian Church (ed. J. D. Douglas; Grand Rapids : Zondervan/Exeter; Paternoster 1974) 783.

37. Odeberg, H. 3 Enoch or the Hebrew Book of Enoch. Cambridge : University Press, 1928. Part I, pp. 188-92; Appendix II.

38. Peterson, E. "Pistis Sophia," Enciclopedia Cattolica 9 (Città del Vaticano : Ente per l'Enciclopedia Cattolica e per il Libro Cattolico, 1952), 1974.

39. Quispel, G. "Pistis Sophia," Christelijke Encyclopedie 5 (ed. F. W. Grosheide en G. P. van Itterzon; Kampen; J. H. Kok, 1960), 461.

40. Quispel, G. "Pistis Sophia," RGG 5 (hrsg. K. Galling : Tübingen : J. C. B. Mohr/Paul Siebeck, 1961), 368-88.

41. Resch, A. "Agrapha. Aussercanonische Evangelienfragmente," TU 5/4 (Leipzig 1882).

42. Schmid, J. "Pistis Sophia," Lexikon für Theologie und Kirche 8 (hrsg. J. Höfer und K. Rahner; Freiburg : Herder, 1963), 524.

43. Schmidt, C. Koptisch-gnostische Schriften, Bd. 1 : Die Pistis Sophia. Die beiden Bücher des Jeû. Unbekanntes altgnostisches Werk. (Die griechischen christlichen Schriftsteller der ersten drei Jahrhunderte 13), Leipzig 1905.

44. Schmidt, C. Koptisch-gnostische Schriften; Bd. 1 : Die Pistis Sophia. Die beiden Bücher des Jeû. Unbekanntes altgnostisches Werk. 2 Aufl. bearbeitet ... von W. Till. Berlin : Akademie-Verlag, 1954; 3 Aufl. 1959; Reprinted 1962.

45. Schmidt, C. "Bemerkungen zum Dialekt der Pistis Sophia," ZAS (Leipzig 1905) 139-41.

46. Schmidt, C. Pistis Sophia. Coptica 2, Kopenhagen : Gyldendalske Boghandel-Nordisk Forlag, 1925.

47. Schmidt, C. Pistis Sophia. Ein gnostisches Originalwerk des 3. Jahrhunderts aus dem Koptischen übersetzt. Leipzig, 1925.

48. Schmidt, C. "Die Urschrift der Pistis Sophia." ZNW 24 (Giessen 1925) 218-40.

49. Schmidt, E. H. Die Gnosis. Grundlagen der Weltanschauung einer edleren Kultur. 2 Bde. Leipzig : E. Diederichs, 1903-07. Reprinted Aalen, Verlag Schilling, 1968.

50. Scholem, G. Jewish Gnosticism, Merkabah Mysticism and Talmudic Tradition. New York : The Jewish Theological Seminary of America, 1960, pp. 94-100 : Appendix B.

51. Schwartze, M. G. Pistis Sophia : opus gnosticum Valentino adiudicatum e codice manuscripto coptico Londinensi descriptum. Latine vertit M. G. Schwartze. Edidit J. H. Petermann. Berlin, 1851 bzw. 1853.

52. Theron, D. J. "Paul's Concept of ἀλήθεια: A comparative study with special reference to the Septuagint, Philo, the Hermetic literature, and Pistis Sophia." Dissertation, Princeton Theological Seminary, DDAU 17 (1949/50), 7.

53. Unnik, W. C. van "Die 'Zahl der vollkommenen Seelen' in der Pistis Sophia," Festschrift für Otto Michel zum 60. Geburtstag (AGSJU, V; hrsg. O. Betz; M. Hengel; und P. Schmidt; Leiden/Köln : E. J. Brill, 1963), 467-77.

BIBLIOGRAPHY

54. Widengren, G. "Die Hymnen der Pistis Sophia und die gnostische Schrift-auslegung," Liber Amicorum : Studies in honour of C. J. Bleeker (Supplements to Numen, XVII; Leiden : E. J. Brill, 1969), 269-81.
55. Worrell, W. H. "The Odes of Solomon and the Pistis Sophia." JThS 13 (London 1912) 29-46.

KEY TO WORDS OF GREEK ORIGIN

Believe, to πιστεύειν 47, 56, 57, 75, 79, 80, 81, 85, 92, 93 etc.

Beneficent χρηστός 54, 82, 103, 152, 155, 181, 183

Beyond παρά 4 etc.; *Compared with*; *Than* 31 etc.; *Above* 11 etc.

Bless, to μακαρίζειν 56, 83, 117, 328, 338, 339

Blessed μακάριος 4, 15, 26, 28, 33, 40, 56, 60, 62, 71, 77, 112, 117, 120, 132, 134, 136 etc.

Body σῶμα 11, 12, 13, 28, 35, 36, 63, 69, 117, 122, 125, 128, 130, 131, 133, 135, 158, 160 etc.

Book τεῦχος (253), 255, 352

Book τόμος 127

Boundary ὅριον 17; ὅρος 17, 261

Brain ἐγκέφαλος 344

Branch κλάδος 117

Bull (Taurus) ταῦρος 363

But ἀλλά 3 etc.; *Except* 320

But δέ 1 etc.; also *However*

Call, to καλεῖν 343

Call upon, to ἐπικαλεῖν 25, 27, 29, 31, 353, 358, 370, 371; *Pronounce, to* 353

Certainly ἀσφαλῶς 323

Certainly see *In truth*

Certainty ἀσφάλεια 184, 185, 190, 191, 198, 201, 202, 204, 205, 234, 272

Chamber ταμεῖον 259, 317, 318, 319, 320, 323, 328, 329

Change, to μεταβάλλειν 249

Change μεταβολή 252, 286, 295, 296, 306, 315, 322, 323, 324, 331 etc.

Chaos χάος 44, 46, 47, 49, 50, 57, 61, 63, 64, 68 etc.

Cipher ψῆφος 36, 247, 358, 370, 373

City πόλις 52, 56, 182, 200, 272, 273, 280

Clarity, with see *Clearly*

Clearly φανερῶς 150, 183, 234, 253, 295, 300, 347; *Clarity, with* 352

Coal ἄνθραξ 100

Come forth, to προέρχεσθαι (προελ-

θεῖν) 3, 17, 195, 220, 221, 222, 223, 224, 225, 226, 227, 253

Command, to κελεύειν 15, 26, 65, 66, 77, 116, 117, 120, 123, 127, 136

Command κέλευσις 10, 11, 12, 13, 17, 19, 20, 25, 30, 37, 38, 48, 68, 78, 84, 98, 99, 112 etc.

Communion κοινωνία 285

Compared with see *Beyond*

Compel, to ἀναγκάζειν 71, 92, 114, 249, 281, 283, 284, 332, 337, 339, 342, 345

Comprehend, to see *Occupy, to*

Concur, to see *Meet, to*

Confess, to ὁμολογεῖν 74

Confused, to be ἀπορεῖν 121

Congregation ἐκκλησία 96, 269

Constraint see *Necessity*

Consume, to ἀναλίσκεσθαι 39, 260, 271, 304, 306, 307, 308, 321, 361, 364, 365, 380, 381

Contemplate, to θεωρεῖν 40

Counterpart ἀντίμιμον 63, 281, 282, 283, 284, 285, 286, 287, 288, 289, 293, 294, 298 etc.

Country χώρα 181, 279, 280, 281

Course δρόμος 32, 34, 38, 39

Covenant διαθήκη 83, 368

Crab (Cancer) καρκίνος 362

Creditor δανειστής 108

Crucify, to σταυροῦν 353, 367; also *Crucifixion* 10

Cure, to θεραπεύειν 279, 281

Cure θεραπεία 279

Curious περίεργος 270

Custom φόρος 293

Cycle κύκλος 34, 35, 36, 37, 39, 286, 295, 296, 314, 315, 320 etc.

Danger κίνδυνος 11, 98

Dare, to τολμᾶν 130, 169

Deaf κωφός 279; 379

Deal with, to χρῆσθαι 49

Decan δεκανός 2, 14, 31, 63, 77, 215, 336, 343, 355

For γάρ 4 etc.
Forefather προπάτωρ 19, 23, 24, 40, 43, 186, 216, 230, 231
Form μορφή 116, 137, 186, 187, 196, 254, 332, 359, 373
Fornicate, to πορνεύειν 364
Fornication πορνεία 209, 371
Free ἐλεύθερος 73, 337
Frenzy ἀπονοία 259
Fruit καρπός 103, 117, 311
Furthermore λοιπόν 198
Furthermore see *Again*

Garment ἔνδυμα 9, 10, 15, 16, 17, 18, 19, 21, 24, 37, 40, 41, 42, 106, 129, 171, 289 etc.
Gate πύλη 18, 20, 21, 22, 23, 45, 48, 51, 54, 169
Gather, to συνάγειν 348
Generation γενεά 56, 83, 108
Gift δωρεά 241, 262, 302, 304, 305, 309, 328, 350, 368
Gift δῶρον 365
Girdle ζώνη 106, 109
Glad, to be see *Rejoice, to*
Gnosis γνῶσις 16, 77, 255
Goat (Capricorn) αἰγόκερως 362
Good ἀγαθός 12, 14, 28, 79, 80, 94, 123, 124, 125, 127, 128, 129 etc.
Good thing ἀγαθόν 82, 102, 165, 182
Gospel εὐαγγέλιον 385
Grace χάρις 151, 152
Grasp, to καταλαμβάνειν 199, 213, 292
Grass χόρτος 66, 67
Grave τάφος 73, 74, 158, 160
Guide, to ἄγειν 284, 292, 341, 345

Habitation σκηνή 331
Hail χάλαζα 214, 259, 260, 321
Hasten, to see *Speed, to effect with*
Hastener σπουδαστής 34
Head κεφαλή 1, 4, 205, 246, 247, 333, 334
Heat καῦμα 213, 348
Heaven οὐρανός 370

Hegumen ἡγούμενος 196
Heimarmene εἱμαρμένη 19, 22, 23, 25, 26, 27, 28, 29, 30, 32, 33, 34, 35 etc.
Help, to βοηθεῖν 47, 56, 62, 69, 70, 84, 85, 87, 95, 98, 99, 104, 107, 110, 118, 129, 137 etc.
Help βοήθεια 47, 59, 62, 93, 142, 144, 175
Helper βοηθός 59, 62, 73, 103, 163, 327
Helper παραστάτης 2, 3, 14, 18, 195, 196, 200, 202, 203 etc.
Honour τιμή 291, 292, 293; also *Worth* 254
Hope, to ἐλπίζειν 76, 83, 167
Hope ἐλπίς 59, 114, 115, 143, 147
House οἶκος 2, 21, 22, 23, 361
How πῶς 21, 40, 42, 238, 248, 338
How see *According to*
However see *But*
Hyper-triple-spirited ὑπερτριπνεύματος 226
Hypocrisy ὑπόκρισις 270, 272, 305, 307, 313, 328
Hypocritical, to be ὑποκρίνεσθαι 265, 267, 268, 273, 274

Ice κρύσταλλος 260
Identity see *Peculiar*
Ill-treatment ὕβρισις 277
Image ἴσος 254
Image εἰκών 63, 292, 342
Immortal ἀθάνατος 126
Impact ὁρμή 140
Imperishable ἄφθαρτος 222, 357
Impious ἀσεβής 50, 59, 89, 208, 273, 275, 313, 320, 322
In general ἁπλῶς 3
In part ἐκ μέρους 263
In truth μέντοιγε 191, 205; also *Certainly* 238, 263, 297, 298, 305, 306
Incision(s) χαραγμή (χαραγμαί) 2, 3, 18, 221
Incomprehensible ἀχώρητος 171, 221, 222, 223, 224, 254; see *Pre-incomprehensible*

Permitted, it is ἔξεστι 289, 297, 311, 313, 330

Persecute, to διώκειν 45, 46, 50, 53, 55, 109, 277; *Pursue, to* 299

Persecution διωγμός 11, 328

Persecutor διωκητής 299

Phantom φάντασμα 121

Pitcher ἀγγεῖον 369

Place τόπος 1 etc.

Place of correction κολαστήριον 382

Plague σίνησις(σίνωσις) 279

Pledge παραθήκη 117, 118

Pleroma πλήρωμα 4, 9, 16, 28, 56, 60, 77, 190, 276, 352, 359

Pneumatic see *Spiritual*

Poisoner φαρμακός 320

Portion κλῆρος 51, 245, 246, 247; *Lots* κλῆροι 89

Power δύναμις 4, 16, 45, 46, 98, 99, 137, 138, 229, 354, 356, 357, 360, 368, 369, 373

Powers ἐξουσίαι 2, 20, 23, 40, 77, 354, 361, 362, 373

Pray, to εὐχεσθαι 324

Pray, to προσεύχεσθαι 303, 305, 307, 327

Prayer προσευχή 209, 327, 353

Preach, to κηρύσσειν 122, 123, 124, 125, 128, 201, 232, 251, 256, 266 etc.

Pre-triple-spirited προτριπνεύματος 226

Prevent, to κωλύειν 120, 149, 151, 152, 162

Proachoretos προαχώρητος 225

Progressively προκοπή 220

Pronounce, to see *Call upon, to*

Prophesy, to προφητεύειν 28, 52, 58, 62, 66, 72, 73, 76, 78, 81, 88, 94, 100, 102, 107, 111, 114, 117, 119, 120, 121 etc.

Prophet προφήτης 12, 13, 27, 28, 52, 58, 81, 181, 234, 302, 351

Proverb see *Parable*

Provider προνόητος 360

Psalm ψαλμός 52, 58, 62, 66, 73, 76, 78, 81, 88, 94, 100, 102, 111 etc.

Punish, to see *Avenge, to*

Punish, to κολάζειν 240, 263, 283, 284, 285, 297, 298, 314, 325, 339 etc.

Punishment κόλασις 208, 209, 241, 256, 257, 258, 259, 260, 262 etc.

Pure εἰλικρινής 115, 116, 195, 200, 216, 230, 250

Purification ἀγνεία 240

Purify, to καθαρίζειν 299, 300, 325, 327, 331, 348, 352, 368, 369, 370, 374, 376, 378, 379, 382

Pursue, to see *Persecute, to*

Put on, to see *Wear, to*

Quickly ταχύ 241

Race γένος 10, 27, 65, 122, 123, 124, 162, 179, 180, 184, 195, 199, 201 etc.

Rage(s) see *Wrath*

Ram (Aries) κριός 361

Rank(s) τάξις (τάξεις) 2, 3 etc.

Rather see *Nevertheless*

Ray ἀκτίς 5, 7, 332

Reality see *Truth*

Rebel, to ἀτακτεῖν 26, 38, 319, 355, 361

Receive, to παραλαμβάνειν 199

Reckoning (Number) ἀρίθμησις 196, 197, 221

Refresh, to ἀνακτᾶσθαι 251, 256

Region κλίμα 385

Rejoice, to εὐφραίνεσθαι 55, 96, 163; *Glad, to be* 88

Relationship(s) ὁμιλία 251, 256, 270

Relative συγγενής 275, 322, 328

Release, to ἀπολύειν 287; also *Dismiss, to* 289

Renounce, to ἀποτάσσεσθαι 219, 220, 249, 251, 256, 258, 259, 261, 264, 265

Renunciation ἀποταγή 215, 240, 252, 261

Repent, to μετανοεῖν 51, 52, 98, 197, 198, 199, 201, 215, 260, 261, 267 etc.

Repentance μετάνοια 47, 52, 56, 58, 60, 61, 62 etc.

Repose ἀνάπαυσις 208

Resemble, to ὁμοιοῦν 333, 335

Restrain, to κατέχειν 37, 141, 147, 170, 172, 173, 229, 263, 288, 297, 342

GREEK WORDS

διάψαλμα 74, 103, 174
δίδυμος (δίδυμοι) 365
δίκαιος 55, 89, 103, 123, 124, 128, 235, 240, 241, 261, 262, 276, 277, 323, 324 etc.
δικαιοσύνη 51, 55, 59, 74, 82, 88, 94, 97, 101, 102, 106, 119, 120, 121, 122 etc.
δίσκος 214, 334, 335, 336, 354
διωγμός 11, 328
διώκειν 45, 46, 50, 53, 55, 109, 277, 299
διωκητής 299
δοκιμάζειν 240, 263, 270, 271, 285, 290, 294, 325, 330
δράκων 137, 138, 141, 143, 148, 149, 258, 259, 260, 268, 271, 275, 304
δρόμος 32, 34, 38, 39
δύναμις 4, 16, 45, 46, 98, 99, 137, 138, 229, 354, 356, 357, 360, 368, 369, 373
δυνατός 102
δωρεά 241, 262, 302, 304, 305, 309, 328, 350, 368
δῶρον 365

ἐγκακεῖν 359
ἐγκέφαλος 344
ἐγκράτεια 210
ἔθνος 67, 385
εἶδος 186, 187, 341, 342
εἰκών 63, 292, 342
εἰλικρινής 115, 116, 195, 200, 216, 230, 250
εἱμαρμένη 19, 22, 23, 25, 26, 27, 28, 29, 30, 32, 33, 34, 35 etc.
εἰμήτι 98, 99, 185, 234, 269, 272, 275 etc.
εἰρήνη 97, 101, 119, 120, 121, 122, 123, 124, 125, 127, 128, 209, 274
εἰρηνικός 96, 101, 260
εἴτε ... εἴτε 282, 324, 341, 345, 346
ἐκκλησία 96, 269
ἐκκλίνειν 218
ἐκ μέρους 263
ἐλάχιστος 20
ἐλεύθερος 73, 337
ἐλπίζειν 76, 83, 167

ἐλπίς 59, 114, 115, 143, 147
ἔνδυμα 9, 10, 15, 16, 17, 18, 19, 21, 24, 37, 40, 41, 42, 106, 129, 171, 289 etc.
ἐνέργεια 158, 160
ἐνεργεῖν 25, 385
ἐνοχλεῖν 96, 201, 263, 322
ἐντολή 286, 370, 372
ἐξαιρεῖσθαι 358
ἔξεστι 289, 297, 311, 313, 330
ἐξουσία 9, 15, 32, 155, 157, 169, 170, 205, 206, 207, 208, 235, 288, 309 etc.
ἐξουσίαι 2, 20, 23, 40, 77, 354, 361, 362, 373
ἐπειδή 4, 17, 30, 31, 43, 85, 98, 172, 360, 372
ἐπιθυμεῖν 43, 45, 178, 283, 364
ἐπιθυμία 282, 283, 333, 337
ἐπικαλεῖν 25, 27, 29, 31, 353, 358, 370, 371
ἐπινοεῖν 283
ἐπισκοπή 108
ἐπίσκοπος 25, 34, 195, 319
ἐπιστήμη 291
ἐριναῖος 228, 235, 236, 262, 283, 284, 287, 288, 297, 298, 344, 345
ἑρμηνεία 126, 353
ἔτι 15, 20, 84, 187 etc.
εὐαγγέλιον 385
εὐφραίνεσθαι 55, 88, 96; εὐφραίνειν 163
εὔχεσθαι 324
ἕως 10, 60, 178, 190 etc.

ζυγός 361
ζώνη 106, 109

ἤ 3, 5, 6, 8, 22, 30 etc.
ἡγούμενος 196

θάλασσα 53, 55, 181, 212, 258, 355, 375, 380
θαυμάζειν 248
θεραπεία 279
θεραπεύειν 279, 281
θεωρεῖν 40

θηρίον 35, 77, 211, 212, 336, 341, 345
θησαυρός 2 etc.
θλίβειν 36, 54, 63, 64, 66, 70, 74, 89, 95, 101, 137, 150, 154, 164, 179, 180 etc.
θλῖψις 64, 70, 81, 83, 118, 119, 143, 179, 180, 249, 252
θρονός 90, 126, 232, 233
θυρεός 95
θυσιαστήριον 353

ἴδιος (ἴδιον) 63, 254, 344, 345
ἴσος 254

καθαρίζειν 299, 300, 325, 327, 331, 348, 352, 368, 369, 370, 374, 376, 378, 379, 382
καθιστάνει 108, 359
καὶ γάρ 82
καιρός 67, 168
κακία 102, 282, 327, 333, 334, 342, 357
κακοῦργος 258
κακῶς 115, 250
καλεῖν 343
καλῶς 29, 34, 60, 62, 83, 89, 97, 101, 112, 115, 117, 123, 125, 155, 161, 163 etc.
κἄν 261, 264, 305, 329, 342
καπνός 66, 332
καρκίνος 362
καρπός 103, 117, 311
κατά 3 etc.
κατακλυσμός 349
καταλαλιά 210, 258
καταλαλεῖν 359, 361, 375, 376
καταλαμβάνειν 199, 213, 292
καταπέτασμα 1, 23, 41, 42, 43, 45, 186, 194, 195, 214, 223 etc.
κατέχειν 37, 141, 147, 170, 172, 173, 229, 263, 288, 297, 342
κατοικεῖν 253, 254
καῦμα 213, 348
κελεύειν 15, 26, 65, 66, 77, 116, 117, 120, 123, 127, 136
κέλευσις 10, 11, 12, 13, 17, 19, 20, 25,

30, 37, 38, 48, 68, 78, 84, 98, 99, 112 etc.
κεραννύναι 67
κερασμός 14, 77, 78, 217, 231, 249, 335
κεφαλή 1, 4, 205, 246, 247, 333, 334
κήρινον 212
κηρύσσειν 122, 123, 124, 125, 128, 201, 232, 250, etc.
κίνδυνος 11, 98
κίνησις 210
κλάδος 117
κληρονομεῖν 52, 56, 80, 82, 120, 122, 123, 124, 234, 235 etc.
κληρονομία 33, 80, 90, 189, 191, 192, 193, 194 etc.
κληρονόμος 124
κλῆρος 51, 89, 245, 246, 247
κλίμα 385
κοινωνεῖν 240
κοινωνία 285
κολάζειν 240, 263, 283, 284, 285, 297, 298, 314, 325, 339 etc.
κόλασις 208, 209, 241, 256, 257, 258, 259, 260, 262, 263 etc.
κολαστήριον 382
κοπρία 306
κόσμησις 24, 188
κόσμος 6, 7, 8, 11, 12 etc.
κρανίον 343, 344
κρῖμα 271
κρίνειν 90, 97, 240, 358, 374, 377, 378, 379, 380, 381, 382
κριός 361
κρίσις 201, 208, 209, 241, 256, 257, 258, 262 etc.
κριτής 177, 285, 294, 295, 326
κρύσταλλος 260
κύκλος 34, 35, 36, 37, 39, 286, 295, 296, 314, 315, 320 etc.
κωλύειν 120, 149, 151, 152, 162
κώμη 272, 273
κωφός 279, (379)

λάϊνον 212
λαός 67, 96

προσεύχεσθαι 303, 305, 307, 327
προσευχή 209, 327, 353
προσφορά 369, 370, 371, 372
προτρέπειν 120, 220
προτριπνεύματος 226
προφητεύειν 28, 52, 58, 62, 66, 72, 73, 76, 78, 81, 88, 94, 100, 102, 107 etc.
προφήτης 12, 13, 27, 28, 52, 58, 81, 125, 181, 234, 235, 302, 351
πύλη 18, 20, 21, 22, 23, 45, 48, 51, 54, 169
πῶς 21, 40, 42, 238, 248, 338

σαλεύειν 87, 107, 329, 339
σάρξ 39, 66, 110, 346
σιγή 6
σίνησις (σίνωσις)? 279
σκανδαλιζεῖν 50
σκάνδαλον 54, 268, 269, 271
σκεπάζειν 151, 153
σκεῦος 89, 177
σκηνή 331
σκορπίος 363
σκύλλειν 220, 221, 222, 223, 224, 225, 249, 250, 347, 349, 350
σκώπτειν 48, 107
σοφία 159
σπέρμα 56, 82, 142, 156, 157, 159, 333, 334, 342, 381
σπινθήρ 23, 40, 216
σπουδάζειν 240, 241, 276, 325, 326, 329
σπουδαστής 34
σπουδή 263, 279, 324
στατήρ 292
σταυροῦν 10, 353, 367
στερέωμα 19, 20, 21, 214, 248, 315
στερησίμως 263, 359, 360, 361, 362, 363, 364, 365
στηρίζειν 357
στοιχεῖον 267, 327
συγγενής 275, 322, 328
σύγκρασις 282
συγχωρεῖν 65, 66
σύζυγος 43, 45, 49, 64, 70, 87, 92, 215
σύμβολον 229, 236, 243, 244, 247, 278

συμφωνεῖν 342, 349
συμφωνία 342
συνάγειν 348
συναγωγή 78
συνουσία 210, 355, 356, 364
συντέλεια 191, 196
σφαῖρα 2, 12, 19 etc.
σφραγίζειν 168, 197, 198, 240, 241, 263, 276, 277, 285 etc.
σφραγίς 34, 197, 209, 240, 241, 247, 263, 276, 286, 287 etc.
σχῆμα 31, 35, 38, 227, 228, 230, 239, 241, 247 etc.
σῶμα 11, 12, 13, 28, 35, 36, 63, 69, 117, 122, 125, 128, 131 etc.
σωτήρ 4, 7, 26, 29, 32, 33, 57, 60, 61, 66, 82, 85, 86 etc.
σωτῆρες 2, 3, 11, 14, 18, 90, 191, 194 etc. J 119

ταλαιπωρία 54, 74, 167
ταμεῖον 259, 317, 318, 319, 320, 323, 328, 329
τάξις (τάξεις) 2, 3 etc.
τάφος 73, 74, 158, 160
ταῦρος 363
ταχύ 241
τέλειος 33, 37, 39, 77, 90, 126, 196, 197, 228, 231, 232 etc.
τέλος 293
τεῦχος (253), 255, 352
τέχνη 130, 132
τιμή 254, 291, 292, 293
τιμωρεῖν 374, 375, 376, 377, 378, 379, 380, 382
τιμωρία 380
τολμᾶν 130, 169
τόμος 127
τοξότης 364
τόπος 1 etc.
τότε 5, 8, 26, 38 etc.
τράπεζα 54, 90
τραπεζίτης 348
τύραννος 23, 25, 37, 40, 41, 77, 78, 138, 139, 144, 146, 168, 215, 230, 290

SELECTED WORDS OF COPTIC ORIGIN

Tree; fig – 311; olive – 103; the five trees 3, 18, 191, 194, 197, 217, 231

Triangle 30, 31, 38

Truth 30, 31, 82 etc.

Twelfth aeon 145, 146, 178; twelve aeons 23, 24, 41, 46, 110, 138, 146, 169, 171, 172, 186, 187, 188, 355

Twin (saviours) 3, 18, 194, 197, 217, 231

Vengeance 50

Vine; – branch 369; – yard 121, 311

Voice(s) 126; also 6, 47, 63, 66

Vulture; – face 318

Wall(s) 133

Way(s) 12, 13, 79, 82, 143 etc.

Water(s) 12, 52, 54, 213, 367, 369, 370; – of forgetfulness 333, 379, 382

West 181, 213, 353; – wind 214, 348

Wilderness (Desert) 66, 100, 182

Wind 95, 132, 135 etc.; north –, south –, east –, west – 214

Wine 54, 367, 368, 369, 370

Wing(s) 142, 144; – of light 287, 289

Witness(es) 72, 82, 95, 257, 385

Woman (Women) 28, 58 etc.

Wonder(s) 74, 178, 179, 180, 181

Year(s) 1, 89, 244, 311

Youth 59, 74, 82, 165, 191

Zeal; see Envy

PROPER NAMES

David : the prophet ⲆⲀⲨⲈⲒⲆ (ⲆⲀⲨⲒⲆ) 52, 58, 62, 66, 73, 76, 78, 81, 88, 100, 102, 107, 111, 119, 120, 124, 125, 127, 142, 144, 146, 148, 151, 163, 165, 167, 174, 177, 181, 183, 302

Egypt : ⲕⲏⲙⲥ 27, 28
Elias : the prophet ⲀⲎⲗⲓⲀⲥ 12, 13, 351
Elisabeth : the mother of John the Baptist ⲈⲗⲓⲤⲀⲃⲈⲦ 12, 124
Enchthonin : crocodile-faced 1st archon in the 1st chamber of the darkness Ⲉⲛⲭⲑⲟⲛⲓⲛ 318
Enoch : author of the two Books of Jeu Ⲉⲛⲱⲭ 247, 349
Esau : ⲏⲤⲀⲨ 381
Ethiopian woman : see Ariuth

Gabriel : ⲅⲀⲃⲣⲓⲏⲗ 12, 13, 129, 133, 134, 139, 141, 148
Galilee ⲅⲀⲗⲓⲗⲀⲓⲀ 369
Gemmut : seven stars, probably the Pleiades ⲋⲙⲙⲟⲨⲦ 349

Hecate : the three-faced, 3rd rank of the Way of the Midst ⲀⲈⲕⲀⲦⲏ 363, 364
Hermes : 3rd of the 5 great archons of the sphere ⲀⲈⲣⲙⲏⲤ 356, 357

Isaac : ⲓⲤⲀⲁⲕ 351
Isaiah : ⲏⲤⲀⲓⲀⲥ 27, 28
Israel : ⲓⲤⲣⲁⲏⲗ, ⲓⲏⲗ, ⲓⲤⲗ 53, 83, 385

Jabraoth : the brother of Adamas and ruler over 6 aeons ⲒⲀⲃⲣⲀⲱⲑ 128, 351, 355
Jachthanabas : ⲒⲀⲭⲑⲀⲛⲁⲃⲀⲥ 5th rank of the Way of the Midst 263, 365, 366
Jacob : ⲒⲀⲕⲱⲃ 351, 381
Jaldabaoth : lion-faced archon in the Chaos ⲒⲀⲗⲇⲀⲃⲀⲱⲑ (ⲒⲀⲗⲦⲀⲃⲀⲱⲑ) 46, 258, 259, 375, 376, 378, 379, 380
Jaluham : paralemptes of Adamas ⲒⲀⲗⲟⲨϨⲀⲙ 374, 376, 378, 379, 382
James : the disciple ⲒⲀⲕⲕⲱⲃⲟⲥ 94, 97, 142, 149, 174, 175, 353
Jao : the Great, the Good, of the Midst ⲒⲀⲱ 196, (353), 366
Jao : the Little, the Good, of the Midst ⲒⲀⲱ 12
Jesus : ⲒⲤ = ⲒⲏⲤⲟⲨⲤ pass.
Jeu : ⲒⲈⲟⲨ the First Man 285, 319, 329, 330; the overseer of the light 25, 31, 34, 194, 195, 319; the angel of light 91, 94; the Father of Jesus' Father (353), 355, 359, 360, 363
John : the Baptist ⲒⲱϨⲀⲛⲛⲏⲥ 12, 13, 123, 124, 125, 347, 348, 351
John : the disciple ⲒⲱϨⲀⲛⲛⲏⲥ 65, 66, 68, 127, 129, 205, 233, 264, 265, 266, 267, 270, 272, 273, 381, 383
Joseph : the father of Jesus ⲒⲱⲤⲏϥ 121

Kalapatauroth : the archon over Gemmut ⲔⲀⲗⲀⲡⲀⲦⲀⲨⲣⲱⲑ 349

Lamchamor : mountain pig-faced archon in the 6th chamber of the outer darkness ⲗⲀⲙⲭⲀⲙⲱⲣ 318

799

Marchur: black bull-faced archon in the 5th chamber of the outer darkness
ⲘⲀⲢⲬⲞⲨⲢ 318

Maria Magdalene: ⲘⲀⲢⲒⲀⲘ (ⲘⲀⲢⲒⲀ) ⲘⲀⲄⲀⲀⲀⲎⲚⲎ 26, 28, 29, 33, 34, 43, 52,
56, etc.

Maria: mother of Jesus ⲘⲀⲢⲒⲀ 13, 116, 117, 120, 123, 124, 125

Martha: ⲘⲀⲢⲐⲀ 61, 62, 111, 112, 163, 164, 176, 177

Matthew: ⲘⲀⲐⲐⲀⲒⲞⲤ, ⲘⲀⲞⲀⲒⲞⲤ 71, 72, 88, 90, 157, 161

Melchisedek: ⲘⲈⲀⲬⲒⲤⲈⲀⲈⲔ ⲘⲈⲀⲬⲒⲤⲈⲀⲤⲔ 34, 35, 36, 194, 195, 291, 324, 326,
333, 334 see also Zorokothora

Michael: ⲘⲒⲬⲀⲎⲀ 129, 133, 134, 139, 141, 148

Moses: ⲘⲰⲨ̈ⲤⲎⲤ 72, 338

Munichunaphor: imperishable name of Ares ⲘⲞⲨⲚⲒⲬⲞⲨⲚⲀ ⲫⲰⲢ 357

Olives, Mount of: ⲠⲦⲞⲞⲨ ⲙ̅ⲡ̅ϫⲞⲈⲒⲦ, 9, 15, 171, 173

Orimuth: imperishable name of Cronos ⲰⲢⲒⲘⲞⲨⲐ 357

Paraplex: female archon of the Way of the Midst ⲠⲀⲢⲀⲠⲀⲎⲝ 359, 361, 362

Parhedron: see Typhon

Paul: ⲠⲀⲨⲀⲞⲤ 293

Persephone: in the Chaos ⲠⲈⲢⲤⲈ ⲫⲞⲚⲎ 377

Peter: ⲠⲈⲦⲢⲞⲤ   58, 60, 100, 101, 132, 136, 162, 310, 377

Philip: ⲫⲒⲀⲒⲠⲠⲞⲤ 32, 71, 72, 73, 75, 181, 184, 353

Pistis Sophia: ⲠⲒⲤⲦⲒⲤ ⲤⲞ ⲫⲒⲀ 42 etc.; see also Sophia

Rochar: cat-faced archon with 7 heads in the 11th chamber of the darkness ⲢⲰⲬⲀⲢ
319

Sabaoth, Adamas: see Adamas

Sabaoth: the Great, the Good, in the place of those of the right ⲤⲀⲂⲀⲰⲐ
14, 28, 123-129, 194, 195, 361

Sabaoth: the Little, the Good ⲤⲀⲂⲀⲰⲐ 128, 357, 382, 383

Sabaoth: called Zeus ⲤⲀⲂⲀⲰⲐ ⲠⲌⲈⲨⲤ 361, 363, 364, 366

Salome: ⲤⲀⲀⲰⲘⲎ 102, 103, 114, 115, 338, 339, 376

Samaritan woman ⲦⲤⲀⲘⲀⲢⲒⲦⲎⲤ 368

Simon: the Canaanite ⲤⲒⲘⲰⲚ ⲠⲔⲀⲚⲀⲚⲒⲦⲎⲤ 353

Solomon ⲤⲞⲀⲞⲘⲰⲚ 114, 117, 132, 133, 136, 151, 152, 154, 157, 158, 159

Sophia: ⲤⲞ ⲫⲒⲀ 45, 46, 104, 112, 131, 144, 147, 148, 178, 181, 183 etc.

Tarpetanuph: imperishable name of Hermes ⲦⲀⲢⲠⲈⲦⲀⲚⲞⲨ ⲫ 357

Thomas: ⲐⲰⲘⲀⲤ 71, 72, 81, 83, 150, 151, 155, 353, 379, 381

Typhon: the Assessor, 4th rank of the Way of the Midst ⲦⲨ ⲫ ⲱⲚ 364, 365

Zarazaz: = Maskelli, in the place of the Midst ⲌⲀⲢⲀⲌⲀⲌ 365

Zarmaroch : archon with 7 dragon-heads, in the 10th chamber of the darkness
ⲌⲀⲢⲘⲀⲢⲰⲬ 319

Zeus : 5th of the great archons of the sphere ⲌⲈⲨⲤ 356, 357, 382, 383, 384
see also Sabaoth

Zorokothora : ⲌⲞⲢⲞⲔⲞⲐⲞⲢⲀ 353; — Melchisedek ⲌⲞⲢⲞⲔⲞⲐⲞⲢⲀ ⲘⲈⲖⲬⲒⲤⲈ-
ⲆⲈⲔ 360, 363

REFERENCES

OLD TESTAMENT

Gen.		84.11	119, 120, 121, 122, 124,
8.4	349		125, 127, 128
Ex.		87	73, 74
21.17	338, 339	90	142, 143
Deut.		90.1	144
19.15	72, 269, 349	90.2	144
Ps. (LXX)		90.3	144
7.1-6	174	90.4	144, 145
7.11-16	177	90.5	145
24	82, 83	90.6	145, 146
29.1-3	163	90.7	146
29.10, 11	163	90.8	147
30.1-18	88, 89	90.9	147, 148
31.1, 2	303	90.10-14	148
34	94-97	101.1-21	66, 67
39.1-3	167	102.1-5	165
50.1-4	111, 112	106.1-21	181-183
51	102, 103	108.1-27	107-110
68	52-56	119	100, 101
69	62	129	76, 77
70.1-13	59, 60	Eccles.	
81.1	78	7.28	350
84.10	119, 121, 122, 123, 124,	Is.	
	125, 127, 128	19.3, 12	27, 28

NEW TESTAMENT

Mt.		5.25, 26	295
3.11	12	6.21	204
3.11, 12	348	7.7	250
3.13	123, 125	7.7, 8	184, 347
3.16	1, 121, 129, 368	7.22, 23	316
5.3-7	62	8.12	259, 271, 316, 381
5.12	8, 10, 11, 15	9.12	250
5.13	306	9.13	262

REFERENCES

GNOSTIC LITERATURE

REFERENCES

46	42	II, 4 Hypostasis of the Archons	
50	243	143	14, 46
66	12	II, 5 On the Origin of the World	
71-75	63	148	46, 256
72	19	151	14
Sophia of Jesus Christ		III, 2 Gospel of the Egyptians	
90	26	42	13
Nag Hammadi Codices		43	3
II, 1 Apocryphon of John		50	3
15	243	58	14
21, 26	63	64	3, 12
II, 2 Gospel of Thomas		IV, 2 Gospel of the Egyptians	
84	3, 26, 300	52	3, 13
86	350	62	3
90	102	VII, 1 Paraphrase of Shem	
II, 3 Gospel of Philip		8	9
59, 63	26	47	349

HERMETIC LITERATURE

Corpus Hermeticum		Stobaeus Excerpta	
I 9	19	VI	2
		VIII 2-4	31, 227

MANICHAEAN LITERATURE

Kephalaia			
VI	3, 259	XIX	3